Taxation of Business Entities

2026 Edition

GREGORY A. CARNES, Ph.D., CPA
Raburn Eminent Scholar of Accounting
University of North Alabama
Florence, Alabama

SUZANNE YOUNGBERG, MST, CPA
Northern Illinois University
DeKalb, Illinois

WILEY

Group VP: Amanda Miller
Editorial Director: Justin Vaughan
Editor: Jennifer Manias
Marketing Manager: Molly Firlotte
Senior Managing Editor: Judy Howarth

Development Editor: Edward Dodd
Content Refinement Specialist: Rajeev Kumar
Cover Design: Jon Boylan
Cover Photo: ©DenisKoltovskyi/Shutterstock

Published by John Wiley & Sons, Inc., Hoboken, New Jersey.

Published simultaneously in Canada.

Library of Congress Cataloging-in-Publication Data has been applied for.

Print ISBN: 978-1-119-74418-4
Epub ISBN: 978-1-119-93087-7
Epdf ISBN: 978-1-119-93086-0

The inside back cover will contain printing identification and country of origin if omitted from this page. In addition, if the ISBN on the cover differs from the ISBN on this page, the one on the cover is correct.

Cover image(s): ©DenisKoltovskyi/Shutterstock

Cover design: Wiley
SKY10125127_082825

DEDICATIONS

To my wife, Jan, and my children and grandchildren—I am very grateful for their support and love. And to my dad, Charles Carnes, who introduced me to the world of accounting, and who along with my mom provided a great example for me to follow.

—Gregory Carnes

To my insanely patient and understanding husband, Mark, my children, Stefanie, Eric, and Jamie, who help me remember what it's like to be the student, and my grandbabies, Maverick, Cayton, and Autumn, for providing me laughter and love when I need it most.

—Suzanne Youngberg

Brief Contents

Learning the Big Picture of Tax to Be a Valued Tax Professional

Dear Students,

So, you have decided to become an accountant. Have you ever heard someone say "You don't look like an accountant? You're not boring!" Some people's impressions of accountants, and in particular tax accountants, are not favorable. They think we wear pocket protectors, a green visor, and work in a basement crunching numbers to complete tax returns by a deadline. Even Benjamin Franklin stated that "... in this world, nothing is certain except death and taxes." Yikes! Why would I want to work in a field where the perception is so negative and measured on the same level as death?

Thankfully, this perception is inaccurate. Tax professionals are actually very personable, creative, and helpful! Tax professionals are advocates for their clients, and, as such, work with them to develop and execute appropriate tax planning strategies. Most everyone must file an individual tax return. Business owners certainly want to structure their transactions in a tax-efficient manner that maximizes their after-tax income. Therefore, a tax professional is respected and trusted by their clients, which makes for a rewarding career.

How can we change the impression that taxation is boring, or too complex to learn? By providing you with a foundation built on the principles of taxation, you will see that there is logic and organization to the tax law, which makes learning the tax law less complex than you may have feared. We help you understand the "big picture" and the **Why** behind the tax laws, which will make you a better problem-solver. We accomplish this by doing the following:

- We demonstrate a logical, step-by-step problem-solving approach for many tax transactions.
- Reading comprehension assessment and practice opportunities are presented immediately following each learning point, because students comprehend best by applying what they just read.
- We bring the *real world* to the classroom by providing chapter content and end-of-chapter problems that focus on tax planning skills, analytical skills, communication skills, and the ability to identify and address ethical dilemmas.
- We provide professional video content for each chapter to supplement what professors do in the classroom.

Many of you will be looking forward to taking the CPA Exam. This text will prepare you for the new CPA Evolution Exam, which began in 2024. We will help you develop the skills needed to be successful when solving CPA Exam problems that test higher-level skills, as we provide many task-based simulations for you to work, similar to the ones you will encounter on the exam.

Taxation is challenging, but very rewarding, so dive in! If you enjoy problem solving, critical thinking, attention to detail, communicating with people, and adding direct value to others, a career in tax is perfect for you!

What Are Our Stories?

GREGORY CARNES My love for education and learning began very early in life. I attended an excellent college prep school, Baylor, in Chattanooga, TN, which is where I discovered how to be curious and creative, and to push myself intellectually. My father majored in accounting in college, and worked in public accounting and industry his entire career. So, I first learned about accounting careers from him, and I decided I would give it a try at college. I had great accounting instructors at Lipscomb University, especially Dr. Axel Swang and Professor Charles Frasier. I worked at Charles Frasier's accounting firm during my senior year, which is when I decided that the tax route was best for me, and I would leave the audits to others. After graduation, I decided to specialize in taxation and began the Master of Science in Accounting with Tax Emphasis program at the University of Memphis. I received a very good foundation in the tax law, especially from Dr. Rodger Bolling, who would later be my colleague at Northern Illinois University.

After working at Ernst & Whinney (now Ernst & Young) in Nashville, TN, I decided to pursue a career as a professor and enrolled in the Ph.D. in Accounting program at Georgia State University. Upon graduating in 1991, my first teaching position was at Louisiana State University where I made many lifelong friends, some of whom are also my coauthors on research publications. After three years at LSU, I took a position at Northern Illinois University, which was a nationally ranked accounting school with a graduate tax program. While I had to endure 12 long winters while at NIU, this was a great opportunity for me professionally, and it is where I met my coauthor, Suzanne Youngberg. I later became Department Chair of Accountancy at NIU, and this also gave me the opportunity for national leadership roles, such as serving as President of the Accounting Program Leadership Group and on the board of the Federation of Schools of Accountancy. I left NIU in 2005 to become Dean of the College of Business at Lipscomb University, my alma mater. In 2007, I accepted the position of Raburn Eminent Scholar of Accounting at the University of North Alabama, and I served as Dean of the Sanders College of Business and Technology at UNA from 2013 to 2024. While at UNA, I have served as Chair of the Shoals Chamber of Commerce Board of Directors, Chair of the Board of the Shoals Business Incubator, and President of the Rotary International chapter in Florence, AL.

My other professional interests also relate to taxation. I have authored the tax material for CPA review courses for more than 20 years; delivered tax training for national accounting firms and approximately 25 accounting state societies; and published approximately 30 articles in leading academic and professional journals.

There is no doubt that what I enjoy the most professionally is teaching tax to accounting students and helping them find great jobs to begin their careers. My goal is that this book will help students become more curious and creative, and help them learn to challenge themselves intellectually. Writing this book has been a great adventure, and it would have never been finished if not for the support of my wife, Jan, my family, and my professional colleagues at UNA. I hope it helps you become a better problem solver and thinker as you begin your professional career.

SUZANNE YOUNGBERG Being raised by hardworking parents who worked in corporate accounting, I was introduced to the field at an early age. After taking three high school accounting courses and being known as the penny-pincher of the family, I pursued my Bachelor of Science in Accountancy at Northern Illinois University. I was not a straight A student in college and worked very hard to earn my grades from outstanding professors who set a high bar. This early introduction to working hard to achieve my goals has carried through to all areas of my life. After working in taxation for a medium-sized public accounting firm in Chicago, passing the CPA Exam, and earning my Master of Science in Taxation from DePaul University, I was given the opportunity to teach one tax class at North Central College in Naperville, IL. I fell in love with teaching and have never looked back. Instructing students, understanding their difficulties in mastering the material, and celebrating their achievements were all extremely satisfying to me. When NIU asked me back to teach tax at my alma mater, I was thrilled!

While teaching, I have maintained my own tax practice specializing in individual tax and small businesses. Most of the examples and stories I share in class have come from my clients and their experiences. Keeping one foot in tax practice while the other in teaching has greatly benefitted me. Bringing "real-world" projects to class helps the students relate to the material and remember it longer.

My NIU colleagues, Dr. Kate Mantzke and Dr. Brad Cripe, took me under their wing and introduced me to writing a professional article. Their instruction and patience were invaluable to me as I learned the ropes of writing. While at NIU, I have earned seven Department of Accountancy Instructor of the Year awards. It means a lot to me to be recognized by the students I treasure.

All of this could not have happened without the loving support and encouragement of my family. My husband is also a tax geek like myself and has contributed in significant ways as he understands the demands of working in tax. I enjoy spending time with my family, playing pickleball, and hiking in my free time. Included in my bucket list is to hike every national park in the United States!

What Makes Our Approach to Learning Tax Distinctive?

Learning the tax law can be challenging for students. This book provides an innovative approach that includes the features described below, so that students will not only know the law, but also "the big picture" and the **Why** behind it. Our approach also provides ample opportunities for students to practice their skills, enabling them to solve real-world problems and develop solutions for taxpayers.

Step-by-Step Problem Solving and Practice

Step-by-step problem-solving visuals in the text and step-by-step worked-out Examples are integrated into many of the discussions in the text.

We provide a clear, step-by-step format for problem-solving, with related flowcharts to help students understand the decision-making process.

ILLUSTRATION 4.2 Determining the Taxation of Dividends

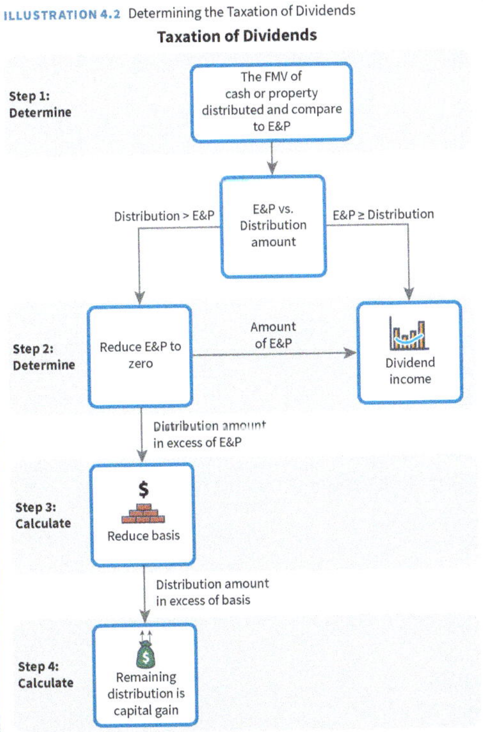

Evaluating the Tax Consequences for Shareholders of Dividend Distributions

Having received a dividend, the taxpayer must determine the tax consequences of the distribution. There are four steps in determining if dividend income should be taxed at ordinary income rates or long-term capital gain rates. Illustration 4.2 provides a flow chart showing these steps.

Step 1. **Determine: The fair market value of the cash and property distributed to the shareholder.**

Step 2. **Determine: To what extent the dividend distribution comes from the corporation's earnings and profits.** You treat the distribution as dividend income to the extent of the corporation's earnings and profits. The dividend is taxed as ordinary income unless it is a qualified dividend, in which case it is taxed as long-term capital gain.

Example feature boxes present exercises with solutions that provide students with an understanding of discussions in the textbook.

EXAMPLE 4.1.4
Dividends: Earnings & Profits and Basis

Juan purchases 1,000 shares of stock in UTK, Inc., a domestic corporation, in Year 3 for $12,000. In January, Year 5, the corporation distributes $20,000 in cash to him. Juan's share of the corporation's earnings and profits at the end of Year 5 is $6,000. He still owns the stock at the end of Year 5. What are the tax effects of the $20,000 distribution?

SOLUTION

To determine the tax effects of Juan's dividend distribution, we follow the steps outlined in Illustration 4.2:

Step 1. First, we determine the fair market value of the distribution. In this case, the value is $20,000.

Step 2. Next, we determine to what extent the dividend income comes from UTK's earnings and profits. Juan's dividend income, to the extent of the corporation's earnings and profits, is $6,000. It is a qualified dividend because Juan has met the 61-day holding period requirement and the stock is from a domestic corporation.

Step 3. Next, we calculate the portion of the dividend distribution (if any) that exceeds UTK's earnings and profits and use it to reduce the basis in the stock. Here, the remaining $14,000 of the dividend distribution reduces Juan's basis in the stock from $12,000 to zero.

Step 4. Finally, we calculate the portion of the dividend distribution (if any) that remains after the stock basis is reduced to zero. After Juan reduces his stock basis to zero, there is still $2,000 remaining from the distribution. Juan treats this remainder ($2,000) as a long-term capital gain because Juan has owned the stock for more than one year.

PRACTICE PROBLEM 4.1.1
Tax Consequences of a Dividend Distribution

Darshanna owns 100% of Utica, Inc., a domestic corporation, which she purchased 11 months ago on January 31 for $1,000. Utica, Inc. pays a cash dividend on December 31 to Darshanna of $3,750 when Utica's earnings and profits (E&P) were $1,800. What is the tax effect to Darshanna from the receipt of the cash dividend?

SOLUTION

To determine the tax effects of Darshanna's dividend distribution, we follow the Steps outlined in Illustration 4.2:

Step 1: The fair market value of the distribution is $3,750.

Step 2: This is treated as dividend income to the extent of the corporation's earnings and profits, which is $1,800. It is a qualified dividend because the 61-day holding period requirement is met and the dividend is from a domestic corporation.

Step 3: The remaining $1,950 of the distribution reduces the basis of the stock, but not below zero. Darshanna's basis is $1,000, and it is reduced to zero.

Step 4: The remainder of the distribution, $950, is treated as short-term capital gain because Darshanna has owned the stock for less than one year.

Practice Problems with solutions provide further opportunities for students to apply their understanding. These are presented immediately after each learning point, because students comprehend best by applying what they just read.

Concept Check questions are provided at the end of each learning point so students can be sure they understood the reading.

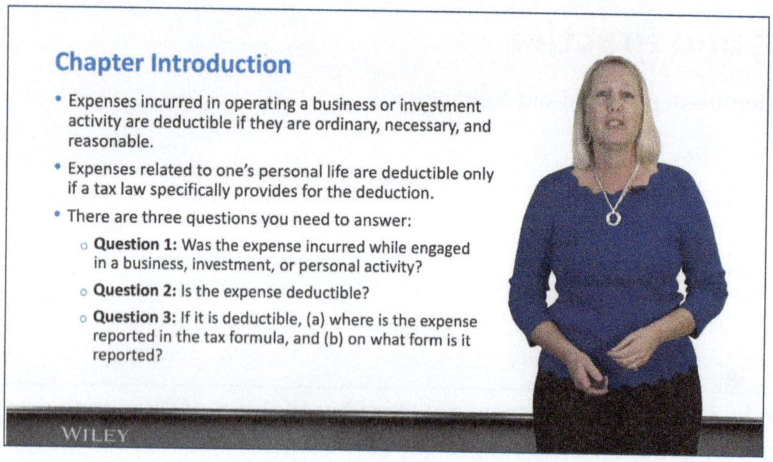

We provide ***author-led video content for each learning objective*** in the chapter. These videos introduce the most important learning points for the chapter material and review a few end-of-chapter problems, allowing professors to use more class time to solve problems and answer questions.

On the ***student companion site***, each chapter contains practice questions students can work through to further apply their understanding of tax concepts.

Solution Walkthrough videos show students how to solve a similar problem.

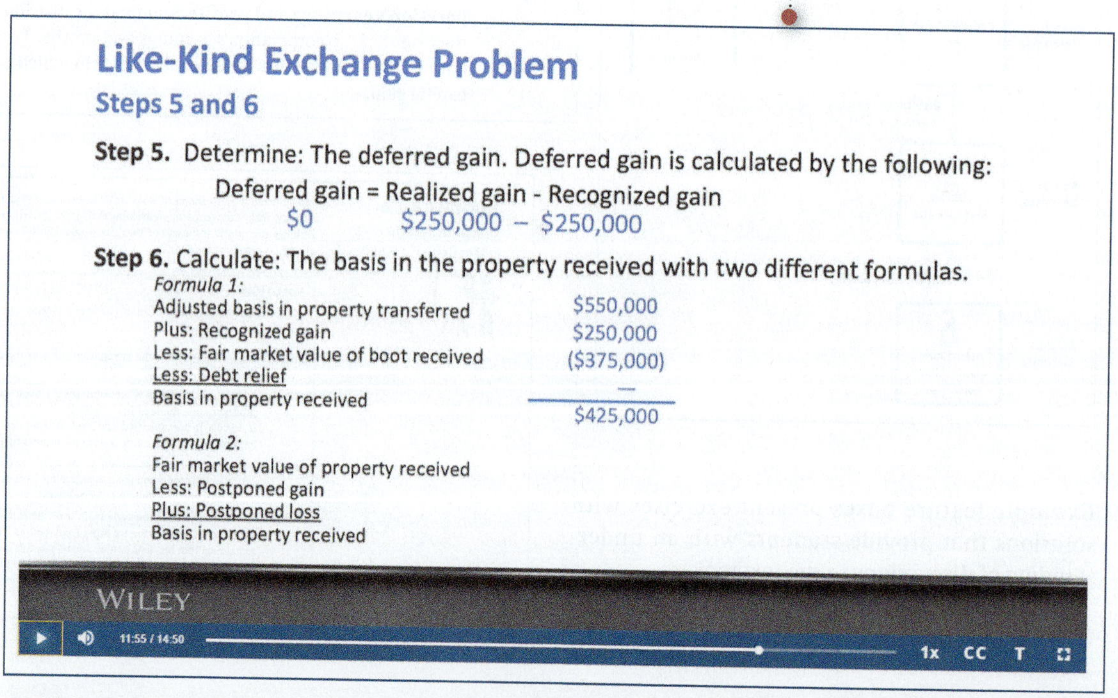

The Big Picture

Integrated throughout chapter discussions, we present the "big picture," not just tax rules. Many students memorize the tax rules but never understand the "big picture" behind the reasons the laws exist. As a result, they are not prepared to recognize tax issues, solve problems for their clients, or develop tax planning solutions. We present both the "big picture" and the tax laws so students can develop critical thinking and problem-solving skills.

We explain the "why" behind tax laws to help students see the "big picture."

Why **Why does the 12-month rule exist for prepaid expenses?** If the 12-month rule did not exist, cash-basis taxpayers could reduce their income by prepaying large expenses near the end of the tax year. Presume that a sole proprietorship knew in December of the current tax year that it was going to be in the 37% tax bracket because of some large sales this year. Next year, it expects to be in the 24% tax bracket. So, if it accelerates expenses into the current year, it will save $37 in taxes for every $100 of deductions, whereas next year it would save only $24 of taxes for the same payment.

Such a situation raises an interesting question: Should you advise the business to prepay expenses this year? Yes, you should, but within certain limits. It must ensure that the benefit the business receives from the prepayment will not extend beyond 12 months from when benefits begin, and in no case should it extend beyond the end of the following tax year. In that case, it can deduct the prepayment! But if it gets greedy and prepays expenses for which the benefit will continue past 12 months, then none of the prepayment may be deductible in the current year. The intent of Congress with the 12-month rule is to make sure that taxpayers will not get a deduction in the current year for prepaying expenses that are not due for more than one year in the future.

1. **Business,[2] investment, or personal activity** Every transaction engaged in by a taxpayer will be either a business activity, an investment activity, or a personal activity. This classification determines the tax effects of the transaction.
2. **Asset classification** Every asset can be classified as:
   a. either an ordinary asset, a Section 1231 asset, or a capital asset; *and*
   b. either personalty or realty.
3. **Basis recovery** You can recover the basis in an asset only one time, by expensing the cost, depreciating the cost, and/or recovering the cost when you sell the asset. Basis in an asset can never be less than zero.

We provide a logical foundation for the tax law. By first explaining the fundamental principles of income taxation in Chapter 1, we then present the tax rules as an application of the logical foundation, which helps the students to better remember the rules.

Each chapter begins with a roadmap that shows the Learning Objectives that students will need to understand within the chapter, the chapter Topics, and a list of Practice Opportunities, all organized in one place.

LEARNING OBJECTIVES	TOPICS	PRACTICE OPPORTUNITIES
1 Determine the tax consequences of shareholder distributions taxed as dividends.	**4.1 Distributions Taxed as Dividends** • Dividend Rules for Shareholders • Qualified Dividend Income • Evaluating the Tax Consequences for Shareholders of Dividend Distributions • Stock Dividends • Constructive Dividends	• Example 4.1.1 Form 1099-DIV • Example 4.1.2 Dividend Record Date • Example 4.1.3 Qualified Dividend Income • Example 4.1.4 Dividends: Earnings & Profits and Basis • Example 4.1.5 Nontaxable Common Stock Dividend • Example 4.1.6 Preferred Stock Dividend • Example 4.1.7 Constructive Dividends • Practice Problem 4.1.1 Tax Consequences of a Dividend Distribution • Practice Problem 4.1.2 Stock Dividends and Basis

Advanced Topic—Drilling Down

Redemption Used to Pay Estate Taxes

A redemption of stock to pay estate taxes can qualify as a sale or exchange of stock if *both* of the following requirements are met:[35]

- The value of the stock of the redeeming corporation included in the shareholder's gross estate must exceed 35% of the value of the gross estate after reduction for expenses, indebtedness, and losses related to the estate.
- The amount treated as a sale or exchange of stock cannot exceed the sum of the estate and inheritance taxes (including any interest) imposed on the estate, plus the amount of funeral and administration expenses allowed as deductions for the estate.

We clearly delineate fundamental content from advanced content. For an introductory tax course, the fundamental content will be sufficient material for most professors and students. The advanced content can be easily excluded, if desired.

Potential Pitfalls examine areas of the tax law that can be confusing.

Potential Pitfall

When computing the stock ownership percentage after the sale of stock, don't forget to reduce the total number of shares outstanding in the denominator by the number of shares sold back to the corporation. This is a common mistake that you want to avoid.

Tax Return Guidance

If a shareholder deducts a loss from the S corporation, the shareholder must report their stock basis and debt basis (defined below) on Form 7203, S Corporation Shareholder Stock and Debt Basis Limitations, including any limitations on the ability to use deductions or credits on the shareholder's tax return. Form 7203 must also be completed if the shareholder sells shares in the S corporation.

Tax Return Guidance boxes explain how to report tax items on tax returns and provide samples of relevant tax forms.

Tax Planning Tips are incorporated into the chapter text, so students know that understanding these are vital to being a tax professional.

Tax Planning Tip

The tax rate for both the *accumulated earnings tax* and the *personal holding company tax* is 20%. A corporation would never pay both taxes, because a personal holding company is not subject to the accumulated earnings tax. Because these excise taxes are in addition to the federal income tax, the total tax rate for a corporation who pays one of these is 41% (21% for federal income tax and 20% for excise tax). Both excise taxes are easy to avoid, so it is important for corporations to plan properly so they can avoid these additional tax burdens.

Tax Forms: Planning and Reporting

With in-class activities and end-of-chapter problems assignable by the instructor, students can walk through completing different types of tax forms to apply key concepts from each chapter.

Chapter 4—Corporate Taxation: Distributions, Redemptions, and Liquidations

In-Class Activity

Greg is the sole shareholder of Red Rock Corporation. Greg receives a cash distribution of $50,000 on December 31. Red Rock Corporation has current E&P of $15,000 and accumulated E&P of $25,000. Greg's basis in Red Rock is $35,000. What are the tax consequences from the distribution to Greg?

Tax Compliance and Reporting Problem

Compliance

1. **(LO1, 2, 3) Form 1120 and Schedule C** Axel Corporation (FEIN: 36-1234567) is a regular C corporation with a calendar year-end. In the current year, Axel reported the following information on its income statement.

Gross revenue	$1,750,000
Municipal interest income	$ 1,250
Dividend income from Dart Corp.	$ 3,300
Long-term capital gain	$ 12,000
Cost of goods sold	$ 330,000
Advertising	$ 14,000
Wages paid	$ 238,000
Depreciation	$ 76,000
Charitable contributions	$ 120,000
Utilities	$ 22,000
Office expense	$ 4,900
Insurance expense	$ 19,000
Entertainment expense	$ 4,000

Axel owned 5% of Dart Corporation. Axel Corporation's address is 100 State Street, Chicago, IL 60606. The corporation paid $200,000 in federal estimated payments. Complete Form 1120 pages 1 and 2.

Many Types of End-of-Chapter Problems

We provide many different types of end-of-chapter problems that include a range of complexity levels and types of skill development.

- Discussion Questions
- Multiple Choice Questions
- Brief Exercises
- Application Problems
- Tax Planning Problems
- Communication Problems
- Ethics and Professional Responsibility Problems
- Tax Compliance Problems
- Research Problems
- Excel Problems

Excel problems for each chapter provide students an opportunity to practice Excel skills in the context of solving tax problems.

Excel Problem

Technology

1. (LO3) **Dividends Received Deduction** Cherry, Inc. would like to know their dividend received deduction (DRD) in each of the following cases. Assume all dividends received were from a domestic corporation.

Case	Ownership in dividend-paying corporation	Dividends received	Cherry's net income before DRD
1	12%	$10,000	$15,000
2	25%	$10,000	$ 9,000
3	32%	$10,000	$ 6,000

Create an Excel spreadsheet to develop your solution.

We also reference in the chapter text which end-of-chapter problems apply to the material presented in each section. An example of the problems assigned to the material related to the qualified dividend income appears here.

Qualified Dividend Income

In this section, we take a closer look at qualified dividends. The major advantage of qualified dividends for individuals is that they are taxed at the same rates as long-term capital gains (LTCG) for individuals. The LTCG rate is 0% if the individual is in lower tax brackets, such as the 10% bracket. For higher tax brackets, such as the 37% bracket, the LTCG rate is 15% or 20%.[3]

Related exercises: Discussion Questions 2 and 3
Application Problem 1

Connecting to the Profession

Professional Skills Make the Difference

Special emphasis is placed on preparing students to be critical thinkers and excellent communicators to better prepare them for their professional careers. We provide Application cases at the end of each chapter that focus on communications, ethics and professional responsibilities, and tax compliance.

CPA Exam Preparation: Task-Based Simulation

1. (LO3) **Calculating the Dividends Received Deduction** Sunshine Inc., a calendar-year corporation, has been profitable in recent years. In 20XX, Sunshine has gross income from sales operations of $125,000 and expenses from operations of $65,000. Sunshine has made investments in four other corporations and has received dividend income from each. Sunshine's ownership percentage of each corporation is as follows:

GetFit, Inc.	5%
Yellow Inc.	19%
Sol, Inc.	5%
Orange, Inc.	10%

Please refer to the Exhibits tab to access the following resources:

- Form 1099—DIV GetFit, Inc.
- Form 1099—DIV Yellow, Inc.
- Form 1099—DIV Sol, Inc.
- Form 1099—DIV Orange, Inc.

For each item in column A, calculate the requested information and enter it in the associated cell in column B.

Go to Wiley's book companion site to complete the Task-Based Simulation.

To prepare students for working with realistic tax planning and compliance scenarios, we include actual source documents for students to use when completing tax returns and task-based simulations. Many chapters include a ***Task-Based Simulation*** similar to the ones on the CPA Exam. We also include ***Tax Planning Problems*** in the end-of-chapter content in each chapter, and a ***Comprehensive Tax Return Problem*** at the end of Chapters 5, 7, and 10.

Spotlight on the Law integrates tax law with hot topics that are important for the profession. Students can relate to the topics chosen because they are interesting and part of everyday life.

Spotlight on the Law

Which Is Better—Qualified Stock Redemption or Dividend? It Depends!

Horn Corporation (HC) is a calendar-year, accrual-basis C corporation. Dom Ram, who is in a 32% tax bracket for ordinary income and 15% bracket for LTCG, purchased his 40% ownership in HC ten years ago for $40,000. In the current year, HC redeems all of Ram's shares for $100,000 while HC has earnings and profits of $500,000. If this transaction is a qualified stock redemption, Ram will have a long-term capital gain of $60,000 ($100,000 − $40,000), and he will pay tax of $9,000 ($60,000 × 15%). If the transaction does not qualify as a stock redemption, then Ram will pay tax of $15,000 ($100,000 × 15%) on his dividend income.

What if Ram is a corporation and not an individual? Because of the dividends received deduction (DRD) for corporations, Ram would prefer the transaction be a dividend. If it is a qualified stock redemption, then Ram will have a long-term capital gain of $60,000 ($100,000 − $40,000), and it will pay tax of $12,600 ($60,000 × 21%). On the other hand, if the transaction does not qualify as a stock redemption, then Ram will have a dividends received deduction (see Chapter 3, LO3, Corporate Taxable Income) on the dividend income received. Ram's DRD will be $65,000 ($100,000 × 65%), so only $35,000 of the dividend payment will be taxed. Therefore, Ram will pay tax of $7,350 ($35,000 × 21%) on its dividend income.

As you can see, shareholders may want different outcomes depending on their entity type. Individual shareholders favor a qualified stock redemption to receive the preferential rate on their long-term capital gain and the ability to use their basis to offset the payment received. Corporate shareholders favor a dividend treatment, because it can use the dividends received deduction.

Featured Professionals Show Possible Career Paths

This section features a tax professional who works in public accounting or industry. Students can learn from the professional's stories and experiences. Advice is also provided to guide the student regarding other skills needed to become a successful tax accountant.

Featured Professional: Kay L. Hegarty, CPA

Kay has worked as a tax specialist for 35 years as a former partner at RSM US LLP. She is currently a Professor of Practice at the University of Iowa, teaching tax law to accounting majors.

From Classroom to Career Tax professionals must have technical competence in their understanding of the law. In my experience, the most difficult part of being a tax practitioner is competence in understanding how to deal with people, whether it be the client or coworkers. In today's complex world, one person cannot complete work alone; teamwork is essential. The most talented tax specialist is nothing if she cannot explain the issues and their resolution to the client who has hired her to be member of their team. The true test of success is the satisfaction of the client, not the tax professional.

Professional Skills Before providing answers to the client, a tax professional must first listen to identify the issues, whether they be matters of fact, law, or emotion. The best tax advice is worthless if the client disagrees with the facts or cannot process application of the law because their emotions or biases cloud their perceptions or judgment.

Future Tax Landscape In my lifetime, the most profound change to the profession will be the impact of artificial intelligence. AI must be embraced, or the tax professional will be left behind. AI should be viewed as a powerful tool to be used by the professional but it will not replace human judgment.

Chapter opening stories provide real-world applications of tax policy and situations.

Fundamentals of Corporate Taxation

Gorodenkoff/Adobe Stock

Before studying this chapter, you should know or, if necessary, review:

1.1 Basics of Business Entity Taxation

1.2 Fundamentals of Property Transactions

Chapter Introduction

VIDEO CONTENT

Olivia and Aiden are professors of data analytics at A&M University. They have been consulting with a few businesses for the last two years to assist them in creating problem-solving processes for their research and development work. They see significant opportunity to leave the university and do this work full-time. They are considering creating a corporation so that they can have the liability protection that is afforded corporate shareholders. They each plan to invest $400,000 in the business. They will also contribute technology, equipment, and certain intellectual property to the corporation. They have come to you seeking advice on the tax consequences of forming a corporation.

In this chapter, you will learn the tax rules for corporate formations, as well as the basic rules for computing taxable income for a corporation. We also present the most common rules for accounting methods and periods for a corporation, as well as two penalty taxes that a corporation may have to pay if it inappropriately accumulates income. We are not implying that a corporation would be the best business entity choice for Aiden and Olivia, but we do want you to see how the corporate tax laws could impact them.

An Interactive, Multimedia Learning Experience

This 2026 edition of *Taxation of Business Entities* includes an enhanced eBook that engages students with a variety of video and interactive content designed to complement and enrich the reading experience. Every new copy of the paperback textbook includes access to the eBook, and the video and interactive content is signposted throughout.

VIDEO CONTENT — Each learning objective includes author-led video content that introduces the most important learning points for the chapter material and reviews a few end-of-chapter problems, allowing professors to use more class time to solve problems and answer questions.

DOWNLOAD DOCUMENTS & TEMPLATES — Appearing throughout the enhanced eBook, downloadable tax forms facilitate study and help familiarize students with federal tax documents.

INTERACTIVE SELF SCORING QUIZZES — Each learning objective includes a self-scoring ***Concept Check Quiz*** to help students prepare for higher stakes assessments and exams.

The eBook also contains hyperlinks at key areas in each chapter that link instructional content to practice. These hyperlinks make it easy for students to apply their learning with multiple types of assessment.

With ***Wiley Reader***, students learn wherever they are, at home or on the go. Listen with text-to-speech. Download your Wiley books for offline access. Notes, highlights, and bookmarks sync with the web experience, and with personalization settings, you can make Wiley Reader your own.

You'll find several additional resources online at the ***student companion site***, www.wiley.com/go/carnes/businessentities26stu, including:

- ***Practice Quizzes***
- ***Task Based Simulations***
- ***In-Class Activities***
- ***Comprehensive Tax Return Problems***
- ***Lecture PowerPoints***

One final note: At the time of this writing, a tax bill is under consideration in the U.S. Congress. If a bill passes that includes provisions retroactive to 2025, we will provide an addendum to this text covering any relevant tax law changes as soon as possible.

Preparing for the CPA Exam

Tax Content

Becoming a CPA will be one of the greatest accomplishments of your professional career. CPAs are trusted business advisors, and those who have this distinction are respected not just by the accounting profession, but by the entire business community. Our goal in writing this book is to help you have a successful career, and one of the first steps is to pass the CPA Exam. The federal income tax laws are currently tested in the Regulation section of the CPA Exam. This book provides the understanding of the individual income tax law that you need for Regulation. Regulation also tests the income tax laws for business entities which we cover in *Taxation of Business Entities*.

In 2024, the structure of the CPA Exam underwent a significant change, known as *CPA Evolution*. There are now three *Core* parts of the exam, which every candidate must pass:

- Core—Financial Accounting and Reporting (FAR)
- Core—Auditing and Attestation (AUD)
- Core—Taxation and Regulation (REG)

There are also three *Discipline* areas, and each candidate must pass one of these areas:

- Business Analysis and Reporting (BAR)
- Information Systems and Controls (ISC)
- Tax Compliance and Planning (TCP)

Fundamentals of Taxation—Individuals and Business Entities focuses on the fundamentals of taxation as it relates to individuals and business entities. *Fundamentals of Taxation* provides a comprehensive foundation to pass Taxation and Regulation (REG). *Taxation of Business Entities* focuses on the taxation of business entities in a more comprehensive manner and also includes specialized topics such as:

- Taxes on the Financial Statements
- Income Taxation of Estates and Trusts
- Gift and Estate Taxation
- Taxation of Multinational Transactions
- State and Local Taxation

If you decide to focus on Tax Compliance and Planning (TCP) for your Discipline area on the CPA Exam, you will need to know the topics in *Taxation of Business Entities*.

Task-Based Simulations

Your score on task-based simulations (TBSs) makes up 50% of your score on the CPA Exam. TBSs are problems that test higher-level problem skills and usually take 5–20 minutes to solve. Some TBSs also include source documents that you must analyze to find the information for the problem, such as financial statements, K-1s, invoices, and contracts. To help you prepare for the CPA Exam, many chapters have at least one gradable TBS for you to work (see example below).

CPA Exam Preparation: Task-Based Simulation

1. (LO4) **S Corporation Distributions** Stefanie, Jamie, and Lydia own Classic Brides, a calendar-year S corporation, in Chicago, IL. Stefanie and Jamie each own 30% and Lydia owns 40%. Classic Brides is a boutique bridal shop servicing brides, bridesmaids, and mothers of the bride and groom since Year 1. Classic Brides has always been an S corporation. Classic Brides has book income of $52,800 for Year 3. See the book income calculation in the Exhibits tab. Lydia's beginning stock basis is $10,000. Lydia also made a loan to Classic Brides o $5,000. Classic Brides's beginning accumulated adjustments account (AAA) is $30,000.

Go to Wiley's book companion site to complete the Task-Based Simulation.

For Instructors

To ensure our instructors are prepared to most effectively teach these resources, you'll find several additional resources online at www.wiley.com/go/carnes/businessentities26, including: ***In-Class Activities with Solutions, Comprehensive Tax Return Problems with Solutions, AICPA Mapping,*** and a ***Computerized Test Bank for End-of-Chapter Assessments***. You will also be able to access the following:

Solutions Manual

For each chapter, the ***Solutions Manual*** provides robust solutions for the end-of-chapter questions along with additional question information.

Test Bank

Test bank questions are also provided for each chapter, containing a variety of multiple choice questions, exercises, and written responses to assess students' performances. A ***Computerized Test Bank*** allows for creation of exams exportable in various formats for print or use within your university LMS.

Instructor Lesson Plans

Instructor Lesson Plans for each chapter can help you plan your classes and assignments with chapter overviews, suggested assignments, and engagement ideas.

Lesson Plan:

	Tax Core Review	Tax Discipline (TCP)
Prework Assignment	• Watch Content Review Video (LO3 through DRD and LO4 and LO6 through general business credit) • Read LO3 through DRD prior to class • Read LO4 prior to class • Read LO6 through general business credit prior to class • Complete DQ 5-12,17,18,19,22,23 • Complete MC 6,7,8,9,10,11,12,13,14,18,19,22	• Watch Content Review Video • Read all sections prior to class • Complete DQ 1,2,4,6,10,17,20,22 • Complete MC 2,4,6,10,11,12,15,19
In Class	• Review LO3 and AP 10,11,15,17 • Review LO4 and AP 20,21 • Review LO6 and AP 36,37	• Review LO1 and AP 1, 4, 6 • Review LO2 and AP 9 • Review LO3 and AP 11, 14, 17, 18 • Review LO4 and AP 20, 21, 23, 25, 31 • Review LO5 and AP 34, 35 • Review LO6 and AP 36, 37 • Complete in class activity
Suggested Homework	• BE 5,6,7,8,9,10,11,13,14 • AP 10,11,15,17,20,21,36,37 • TPP 2	• BE: 2,4,8,10,16 • AP:2,3,5,7,9,10,13,16,18,19,24,26,30,34,36 • TPP: 1,2
Professional Development Skills	• In Review and Practice, read Communication Application (LO3) and Ethics and Professional Responsibility Application (LO4) • Ethics Problem (LO3)	• In Review and Practice, read Communication Application (LO3) and Ethics and Professional Responsibility Application (LO4) • Communication Problem (LO1) • Ethics Problem (LO3) • Research Problem (LO5)

Lecture PowerPoints

Lecture PowerPoints for each chapter provide a content overview that instructors can use for lessons and students can review for exams.

Acknowledgments

The development and writing of this book have been a team effort. We have benefitted tremendously from the superb individuals with whom we have had the privilege to work. Special thanks to Ed Dodd, Development Editor for both of our tax textbooks, who has almost become a family member over the last five years. Ed is the consummate professional who has added tremendous value to our books. And thanks to Jennifer Manias, Editor; and Judy Howarth, Senior Managing Editor for keeping all the moving parts of the project in sync so we could focus on writing.

We also want to express our appreciation to Victoria Pisto, our original Editor; Veronica Schram, Senior Manager; Molly Firlotte, Marketing Manager; and Rajeev Kumar, Senior Project Manager, Lumina; Radhika Madhiseelan, Permissions Specialist; Jeff Johnson, Senior Customer Solutions Integration Manager; Amy Kopperude, Lumina; Amity Watts, Lumina; Jennifer Apt, Lumina; Nicole Repasky, Senior Course Production Operations Specialist, and Jon Boylan, Creative Product Design. Each of these individuals contributed to this successful project, and we are grateful for their excellent work.

Special gratitude to Kay Hegarty, retired partner from RSM and Professor of Practice at the University of Iowa. Kay completed the original draft of Chapter 10, Taxes on the Financial Statements, and also reviewed many chapters for us. We want to thank Ying Chen for her assistance with accuracy reviewing and Mark Youngberg for his development of the Excel problems.

We also thank John Ward at Trailhead Video for his work on the videos for this book, Julia Camp at Providence College for her work on Lecture PowerPoints, and Kristen Whiteley (Park University) and Charmaine Alexander (University of Massachusetts Global) for their work on the Test Bank.

Please send us your comments and suggestions as you use our materials. We welcome your feedback.

GREGORY A. CARNES
gacarnes@una.edu
Muscle Shoals, Alabama

SUZANNE YOUNGBERG
youngberg@niu.edu
Saint Charles, Illinois

Taxation of Business Entities has benefitted greatly from the input of focus group participants, manuscript reviewers, those who have sent comments by letter or e-mail, ancillary authors, and proofers. We greatly appreciate the constructive suggestions and innovative ideas of reviewers and the creativity and accuracy of the ancillary authors and checkers, both those listed here and many others who wished to remain anonymous. Both *Taxation of Business Entities* and *Fundamentals of Taxation—Individuals and Business Entities* were carefully checked by a team of accuracy reviewers; we thank them as well.

Reviewers

Zhuoli Axelton, *University of Wisconsin–Green Bay*
Jake Brock, *University of the Cumberlands*
Ian Burt, *Niagra University*
Julia Camp, *Providence College*
Holly Chase, *Alfred State College of Technology*
Linda Christiansen, *Indiana University*
M. Catherine Cleaveland, *Kennesaw State University*
Emma Cole, *University of Montevallo*
Laurie Conklin, *Western Governors University*
Quintin Davis, *Baltimore City Community College*
James Doering, *Arkansas State University*
Keith Donnelly, *State University of New York Brockport*
Felicia Farrar, *Alabama A&M University*
Richard Green, *Texas A&M University–San Antonio*
Geoffrey Gurka, *Colorado Mesa University*
Kay L. Hegarty, *University of Iowa*
Helen Hurwitz, *Saint Louis University*
Harvey Hutchinson, *University of Virginia*
Paul Johnson, *Mississippi Gulf Coast Community College*
Jim Jurinski, *University of Portland*
Joe Krupka, *Florida State University*
James Lewis, *Binghampton University State University of New York*
Ji Li, *Californian State University, Bakersfield*
Francine J. Lipman, *University of Nevada, Las Vegas*
Gary Liu, *Montana State University*
Elizabeth Lyon, *California State University, Sacramento*
Richard Malamud, *California State University, Dominguez Hills*
Cathryn Meegan, *Jacksonville University*
William J. Moser, *University of Michigan*
Ken Orbach, *Florida Atlantic University*
Danny A. Pannese, *Sacred Heart University*
Dave Repp, *Strayer University*
Eduardo Rivas, *Quinsigamond Community College*
Kristen Rosacker, *Minnesota State University, Mankato*
Rhoda M. Sautner, *University of Mary*
Jason W. Stanfield, *Ball State University*
Kenn Tacchino, *Widener University*
Jun Yang Tan, *University of Portland*
Nicole Wald, *Minot State University*
Stephanie Walton, *Louisiana State University*
Kristen Whiteley, *Park University*
Marvin J. Williams, *University of Houston–Downtown*
Courtney Yazzie, *Clemson University*

Table of Contents

12 Gift and Estate Taxes 12-1

13 Taxation of Multinational Transactions 13-1

14 State and Local Taxation 14-1

CHAPTER 1

Basics of Business Entity Taxation

Hayssen, Shutterstock

Chapter Introduction

VIDEO CONTENT

In this text, we focus on the income taxation of business entities. We present this material in five parts, as follows:

I. Introduction to Business Entities
II. Taxation of Corporations
III. Taxation of Flow-Through Entities
IV. Choice of Business Entity
V. Special Topics

- Chapter 9: Choice of Business Entity
- Chapter 10: Taxes on the Financial Statements
- Chapter 11: Overview of Income Taxation of Trusts and Estates
- Chapter 12: Gift and Estate Taxes
- Chapter 13: Taxation of Multinational Transactions
- Chapter 14: State and Local Taxation
- Chapter 15: Taxation of Exempt Entities
- Chapter 16: Tax Research and Professional Issues

One of the most exciting times in the lives of many individuals is when they decide to launch a new business. This decision comes with many opportunities, but also with risks and challenges. New business owners will quickly learn that managing taxes efficiently is a must for the business to be successful. The owners may be familiar with the individual income tax laws, but they quickly realize that they know little about the taxation of business entities, or about how to transfer a mature business to future generations. These new business owners would benefit from the knowledge in this text, because our focus is on applying the tax laws to business entities.

The income tax rules for business entities are similar to the income tax rules for individuals in the context of income, deductions, and property transactions. This is an advanced tax course that assumes you have already completed a fundamentals-level tax course. However, during our many years of teaching taxation of business entities, we have found that there is some content from your previous tax course that is useful to review to make sure you are prepared for the rest of this book. Therefore, in the latter sections of this chapter, we review the principles of income, deductions, and property transactions that are critical to your understanding of the material presented for business entities. We begin by providing the foundational principles for income taxation, and then discuss the business lifecycle and the compliance responsibilities for all tax professionals.

The eight *Foundational Principles for Income Taxation* are as follows:

Foundational Principles for Income Taxation[1]

Comprehensive Principles

1. **Business,[2] investment, or personal activity** Every transaction engaged in by a taxpayer will be either a business activity, an investment activity, or a personal activity. This classification determines the tax effects of the transaction.
2. **Asset classification** Every asset can be classified as:
   a. either an ordinary asset, a Section 1231 asset, or a capital asset; *and*
   b. either personalty or realty.
3. **Basis recovery** You can recover the basis in an asset only one time, by expensing the cost, depreciating the cost, and/or recovering the cost when you sell the asset. Basis in an asset can never be less than zero.

Income Principle

4. **Income recognition** Income will be taxable if the taxpayer's wealth has increased, the taxpayer has realized this increase in wealth, and the law does not provide a specific exclusion for this type of income. Every time you recognize income, you need to increase your basis in an asset equal to the amount of recognized income.

Deduction Principle

5. **Deductible expenditures** Expenses incurred in operating a business or investment activity are deductible if they are ordinary, necessary, and reasonable. Expenses related to one's personal life are deductible only if a tax law specifically provides for the deduction.

Property Transactions Principles

6. **Property transactions—Gain or loss** You must compute a realized gain or loss every time there is a sale or disposition of property. The gain or loss may be either recognized and included in taxable income, deferred, or excluded. A taxpayer must recognize all realized gains and losses unless a tax law provides otherwise.

[1]A deeper discussion of these principles can be found in *Fundamentals of Taxation—Individuals and Business Entities: A Practical Approach.*

[2]When listing types of activities, "business" refers to activities that can also be referred to as "trade or business" in the tax law.

7. **Property transactions—Basis** For fully taxable transactions, the basis in the asset received is always the property's fair market value. The basis of the asset received is the same as the basis in the asset transferred to the extent that the taxpayer defers the realized gain or loss.
8. **Property transactions—Holding period** For a fully taxable transaction, the holding period of property received never includes the holding period of the property transferred. For a tax-deferred transaction, the holding period of property received always includes the holding period of the property transferred.

Related exercise: Brief Exercise 1

LEARNING OBJECTIVES	TOPICS	PRACTICE OPPORTUNITIES

1 Understand how income tax rules apply to various business entities.	**1.1 Basics of Business Entity Taxation**
	• Business Lifecycle
	  • Formation of a Business
	  • Business Operations
	  • Operating Distributions to Owners
	  • Liquidating Distributions or Sale of Business
	• Legal Forms of Business
	• Tax Classifications for Businesses
		• Practice Problem 1.1.1 Formation of a Business
		• Practice Problem 1.1.2 Distributions

2 Understand the compliance requirements for business entities.	**1.2 Tax Compliance for Business Entities**
	• Filing Requirements
	  • Tax Return Due Dates and Tax Forms
	  • Statute of Limitations
	• Taxpayer Penalties
	  • Failure to File
	  • Underpayment of Estimated Tax
	  • Failure to Pay Penalty
	  • Accuracy Penalties
		• Example 1.2.1 Statute of Limitations
		• Example 1.2.2 Failure to File Penalty
		• Example 1.2.3 Late-Filing Penalty for Partnership
		• Example 1.2.4 Underpayment Penalty
		• Example 1.2.5 Failure to Pay Penalty and Interest
		• Example 1.2.6 Reasonable Cause
		• Example 1.2.7 Negligence
		• Example 1.2.8 Fraud
		• Practice Problem 1.2.1 Determining the Statute of Limitations Period
		• Practice Problem 1.2.2 Determining Penalties Due—C Corporation
		• Practice Problem 1.2.3 Determining Penalties Due—S Corporation

LEARNING OBJECTIVES	TOPICS	PRACTICE OPPORTUNITIES

3 Understand the fundamental rules for property transactions that apply to the taxation of business entities.	**1.3 Review of Fundamentals of Property Transactions**
	• Gains and Losses from Sales and Dispositions
	  • Amount Realized
	  • Adjusted Basis
	  • Realized Gain or Loss
	  • Recognized Gains and Losses
	  • Deferred Gains and Losses
	  • Related-Party Losses
	• Classification of Assets
	  • Definition of Ordinary Assets, Capital Assets, and Section 1231 Assets
	• Spotlight on the Law—Classification of an Asset
	  • Realty vs. Personalty
	  • Holding Period
		• Example 1.3.1 Adjusted Basis
		• Example 1.3.2 Sale of an Asset
		• Example 1.3.3 Tax-Deferred Transaction
		• Example 1.3.4 Related-Party Loss
		• Example 1.3.5 Right of Offset
		• Example 1.3.6 Qualified Appraisal
		• Example 1.3.7 Copyrights
		• Example 1.3.8 Classification of Assets
		• Example 1.3.9 Personalty vs. Realty
		• Practice Problem 1.3.1 Classification of Assets
		• Practice Problem 1.3.2 Adjusted Basis Computation
		• Practice Problem 1.3.3 Computing Recognized Gain
		• Practice Problem 1.3.4 Sale of Assets between Related Parties

4 Determine the tax consequences of disposing of Section 1231 assets.	**1.4 Review of Section 1231 Assets**
	• Netting Section 1231 Gains and Losses
	• Depreciation Recapture Rules
	  • Section 1245 Recapture
	  • Section 1250 Recapture
	  • Reporting Sales of Business Assets: Form 4797
	  • Dispositions That Do *Not* Trigger Depreciation Recapture
		• Example 1.4.1 Netting Section 1231 Gains and Losses
		• Example 1.4.2 Net Section 1231 Gains
		• Example 1.4.3 Lookback Rule
		• Example 1.4.4 Section 1245 Recapture, All Gain Is Ordinary
		• Example 1.4.5 Section 1245 Recapture and Section 1231 Gain
		• Example 1.4.6 Section 1245 Asset Sold at a Loss
		• Example 1.4.7 Section 197 Intangibles
		• Example 1.4.8 Sale of a Building—Straight-Line Depreciation
		• Example 1.4.9 Sale of a Building—Accelerated Depreciation
		• Example 1.4.10 Sale of a Building—Corporations
		• Practice Problem 1.4.1 Determining Net Section 1231 Gains and Losses
		• Practice Problem 1.4.2 Applying the Lookback Rule
		• Practice Problem 1.4.3 Sale of Tangible Business-Use Asset
		• Practice Problem 1.4.4 Sale of Realty by a Partnership
		• Practice Problem 1.4.5 Sale of Realty by a Corporation

LEARNING OBJECTIVES	TOPICS	PRACTICE OPPORTUNITIES

5 Compute the qualified business income deduction.	**1.5 Review of Qualified Business Income Deduction**
	• Qualified Business Income
	• Rental Real Estate
	• Determining the Qualified Business Income Deduction (Steps 1–5)
	• Determining the Qualified Business Income Deduction (Steps 6–7)
	• Determining the Qualified Business Income Deduction (Step 8)
	• Advanced Topics—Drilling Down
	  • QBI Losses
	  • Phase-In of QBI Limitations
		• Example 1.5.1 QBI Deduction for Case 1 Scenarios
		• Example 1.5.2 QBI Deduction for Case 3 Scenarios
		• Example 1.5.3 Qualified Property
		• Example 1.5.4 Wage/Property Limitation for Case 1 Scenario
		• Example 1.5.5 Wage/Property Limitation for Case 3 Scenario
		• Example 1.5.6 Overall QBI Limitation—Scenario #1
		• Example 1.5.7 Overall QBI Limitation—Scenario #2
		• Example 1.5.8 Overall QBI Limitation
		• Example 1.5.9 QBI Deduction for Column 2 Scenario with Specified Service Limitation
		• Example 1.5.10 QBI Deduction for Column 2 Scenario with Wage/Property Limitations
		• Example 1.5.11 QBI Deduction for Column 2 Scenario with Specified Service and Wage/Property Limitations
		• Practice Problem 1.5.1 Calculating Qualified Business Income 1
		• Practice Problem 1.5.2 Calculating Qualified Business Income 2

Tax Forms referenced in this chapter:

Form 1040	U.S. Individual Income Tax Return
Form 1040, Schedule C	Profit or Loss from Business
Form 1040, Schedule D	Capital Gains and Losses
Form 1041	U.S. Income Tax Return for Estates and Trusts
Form 1065	U.S. Return of Partnership Income
Form 1065-X	Amended Return or Administrative Adjustment Request (AAR)
Form 1120	U.S. Corporation Income Tax Return
Form 1120-S	U.S. Income Tax Return for an S Corporation
Form 1120-X	Amended U.S. Corporation Income Tax Return
Form 1139	Corporation Application for Tentative Refund
Form 4797	Sales of Business Property
Form 7004	Application for Automatic Extension of Time to File Certain Business Income Tax, Information, and Other Returns.
Form 8275	Disclosure Statement
Form 8275-R	Regulation Disclosure Statement
Form 8949	Sales and Other Dispositions of Capital Assets

1.1 Basics of Business Entity Taxation

LEARNING OBJECTIVE 1

Understand how income tax rules apply to various business entities.

VIDEO CONTENT

New business owners have many decisions to make when beginning and growing their venture. One of the best decisions they can make is to hire a tax professional to guide them through setting up the organization and choosing the best business entity to use. For example, the tax professional should know the owner's end goal for the business—which may seem unusual at this stage. Some business owners hope to grow a business and sell it within five to ten years. Others would like to build a business that will stay in their family for generations. Thinking through these issues places focus on the lifecycle of the business, which is our focus in this section. We begin by explaining how the income tax laws apply across the lifecycle of a business. Next, we review the types of entities that are discussed in this book.

Business Lifecycle

When you learned the income tax rules for individuals, most of the issues discussed focused on the taxation of transactions that occurred during the tax year. For example, you learned what types of income are taxable, which expenditures are deductible, and the tax consequences of selling or disposing of assets. These topics comprise approximately 80% or more of the income tax rules for individuals. For the income taxation of business entities, however, the composition of the topics you will learn is very different. The taxation of income and deduction transactions during the year comprises approximately 20% or less of the tax law for entities. So, what makes up the other 80% of the tax law for entities?

To address this question, let's look at the lifecycle of business entities, which has four main stages (**Illustration 1.1**). The first stage is the formation of the entity, when the owners

ILLUSTRATION 1.1 The Lifecycle of a Business Entity

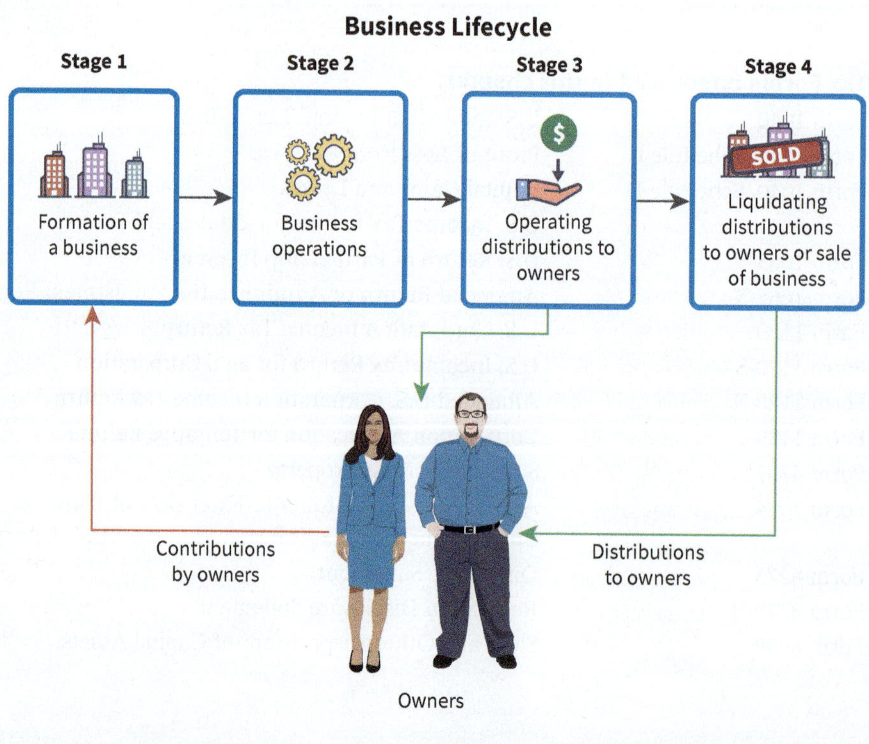

contribute cash or assets to the entity in exchange for an ownership interest such as stock or a partnership interest. The second stage is the taxation of the operations of the business. The third stage is the distribution of profits to the owners. The fourth stage is when the entity ends, which can be a liquidating distribution to the owners or a sale by the owners of the business.

Formation of a Business

A business entity must be created by the business owners. State laws must be followed to create a corporation or a limited liability company, and the partners in a partnership must come to an understanding of the co-ownership of the business and how profits and losses will be shared. Therefore, there are income tax laws that address the formation of a business entity. Consider an owner who is forming a new corporation with two other owners, with each contributing property to the corporation and receiving stock in return. Some of the tax issues that arise include:

- What is each shareholder's realized gain or loss from the transaction?
- Is each shareholder's realized gain or loss recognized?
- Does the corporation recognize any gains or losses?
- What basis does each shareholder have in their stock?
- What basis does the corporation have in the assets received?

These questions never have to be addressed with individual income taxation, but they are addressed in this text for the formation of corporations, partnerships, and limited liability companies. Individuals are subject to the income tax law because they are citizens of the United States, or they are conducting business or investment activities in the United States. There are no tax consequences related to "forming" an individual that needed to be discussed in your individual income tax course, but this is a key issue for business entities.

Business Operations

Once a business is formed, its operations are subject to the income tax laws. Income and expenses, as well as tax credits, must be reported on the appropriate tax form. While your individual income tax courses spent considerable time on these topics for individuals, you will discover that for business entities these topics are considerably shorter. The main reason for this is that the fundamental income tax rules related to income, deductions, and property transaction are generally the same rules as for individuals. Therefore, in this text for business entities, we focus on the income tax rules that differ from those for individuals. For example, some of the charitable contribution rules for corporations are the same as the rules for individuals, but some contributions rules differ. Additionally, corporations are allowed a deduction for the dividends received deduction, but this deduction is not available to individuals. These topics are discussed in detail in Chapter 3, Fundamentals of Corporate Taxation.

Operating Distributions to Owners

Under the entity theory, once a business entity has generated income, the income is owned by the entity. The business owners do not have access to the income until it is distributed to them, because of the entity theory. The **entity theory** provides that a business is a distinct entity from its owners. The entity theory is used by C corporations and for most S corporation transactions (except for the flow-through of income to S corporation shareholders).[3] Thus, under the entity theory, any time that cash or property passes between the entity and the owners, there are potential tax consequences. If an **operating distribution** is made to the owners, then the recipient continues to be an owner after the distribution. If a liquidating

[3]The competing theory to the entity theory is the *aggregate theory*, which is used for partnerships. The aggregate theory holds that the partnership does not exist as a separate entity from the partners. That is, a partnership is simply an aggregation of the partners. To determine the tax result of a partnership transaction using the aggregate theory, you should ask what the result would be if the partnership did not exist. The aggregate theory is also used for the flow-through of income for S corporations. See Chapter 6, LO3, Taxation of Partnership Income and Guaranteed Payments, for further discussion.

distribution is received, then the recipient is no longer an owner after the distribution. The entity will remain in existence as long as it has other owners. Some of the tax issues that must be addressed for distributions are as follows:

- Does the owner have a gain or loss from the operating distribution, and what is the character of the gain or loss?
- Does the entity have a gain or loss from the operating distribution, and what is the character of the gain or loss?
- What basis does the owner take in any property received in the distribution?
- What holding period does the owner have in any property received in the distribution?

Related exercises: Discussion Questions 1, 2

Liquidating Distributions or Sale of Business

The owners may decide that they want to completely terminate their interests in the business. This can be accomplished by either a liquidating distribution or by selling their ownership interests. If all owners receive a **liquidating distribution**, then the entity is dissolved. Some of the tax issues that must be addressed for distributions are as follows:

- Does the owner have a gain or loss from the liquidating distribution, and what is the character of the gain or loss?
- Does the entity have a gain or loss from the liquidating distribution, and what is the character of the gain or loss?
- What are the tax consequences if the owners sell their ownership interests?
- What are the tax consequences if two or more entities combine into one, or if one entity splits into two or more entities?

Legal Forms of Business

A business owner has several different legal entities to choose from when forming an entity. Remember that a sole proprietorship is not a separate business entity. The most common legal forms include:

- **Corporation** A **corporation** is a business that has met a state's requirements to organize as a legal entity that is distinct from its owners. In most states, the owners file articles of incorporation with the state and elect a board of directors.
- **General partnership** A **general partnership** is a business for which two or more owners agree to assume the responsibility for managing the business, and to share profits, losses, and liquidation proceeds. All partners in a general partnership are general partners. General partners have unlimited liability, meaning that their personal assets are at risk to creditors of the partnership. Unlimited liability includes malpractice judgments against the partnership even though the partner may not have been personally involved in the malpractice.
- **Limited partnership** A **limited partnership** is a business for which two or more taxpayers agree to own and operate the business, and to share profits, losses, and liquidation proceeds. The partnership must have at least one general partner and at least one limited partner. A limited partner's personal assets are not at risk with respect to debts of the partnership. A limited partner's losses from the partnership are limited to the amount the partner has invested and promised to invest in the partnership. A limited partner cannot participate in the active management of the partnership.
- **Limited liability partnership (LLP)** A **limited liability partnership (LLP)** differs from a general partnership in that with an LLP, a partner is not liable for damages resulting from the negligence, malpractice, or fraud committed by other partners. However, each partner is personally liable for other debts of the partnership, as well as debts arising from their own negligence, malpractice, or fraud. LLPs are often used by service providers

that may not be permitted to be a LLC, such as architects, accountants, attorneys, and physicians.

- **Limited liability company (LLC)** A **limited liability company (LLC)** is a formal business relationship for which articles of organization must be filed with the state in which the LLC is legally organized. Owners of an LLC are known as members. All members have limited liability. Many states do not allow professional service providers such as accountants and attorneys to organize as an LLC.
- **Business trust** A **business trust** is a legal entity that holds the rights to an individual's stake or interest in a business. The trust technically owns the business interest, and the trustee controls the interest. The trust can have multiple beneficiaries.

Tax Classifications for Businesses

Businesses generally report for federal income tax purposes as one of the business forms shown in **Illustration 1.2**.

The word *corporation* in this text always refers to a C corporation. An S corporation referenced in the text will always have an S designation.

ILLUSTRATION 1.2 Tax Classifications for Businesses

Tax classification	Description	Federal tax forms used
C Corporation (Chapters 3–5)	C corporation that has *not* elected to be taxed as an S corporation.	**Form 1120** (U.S. Corporation Income Tax Return)
Partnership* (Chapters 6–7)	General partnerships, limited partnerships, LLCs, and LLPs are all generally taxed as partnerships.	**Form 1065** (U.S. Return of Partnership Income)
S corporation (Chapter 8)	Incorporated entity that *has* elected to be taxed as an S corporation.	**Form 1120-S** (U.S. Income Tax Return for an S Corporation)
Sole proprietorship	If an owner does not create a separate business entity, then the owner will report as a sole proprietorship.	**Schedule C**** (Profit or Loss from Business)
Trust (Chapter 11)	Legal entity that holds the rights to an individual's stake or interest in a business.	**Form 1041** (U.S. Income Tax Return for Estates and Trusts)
Tax-exempt organization*** (Chapter 15)	A tax-exempt organization must pay tax on its unrelated business taxable income.	**Form 990-T** (Exempt Organization Business Income Tax Return)

*If there is more than one owner, and no separate entity is formally created, the business defaults to a partnership.
**As part of their Form 1040, U.S. Individual Income Tax Return.
***This will be discussed in more detail in Chapter 15, Tax-Exempt Organizations.

To determine which of these tax-reporting forms to use for a particular business, you must use the *check-the-box regulations* discussed in Chapter 6, LO1, Definitions Related to Partnerships.

Related exercises: Multiple Choice Questions 1, 2

PRACTICE PROBLEM 1.1.1
Formation of a Business

Provide three issues that arise when forming a business.

SOLUTION

When an entity is formed, possible issues include:

- What is each owner's realized gain or loss from the transaction?
- Is each owner's realized gain or loss recognized?
- Does the entity recognize any gains or losses?
- What basis does each owner have in the entity?
- What basis does the entity have in the assets received?

PRACTICE PROBLEM 1.1.2
Distributions

Describe the difference between an operating distribution and a liquidating distribution.

SOLUTION

If an operating distribution is made to the owners, then the recipient continues to be an owner after the distribution. If a liquidating distribution is received, then the recipient is no longer an owner after the distribution. The entity will remain in existence as long as it has other owners. If all owners receive liquidating distributions, then the entity is dissolved.

INTERACTIVE SELF-SCORING QUIZZES

1.2 Tax Compliance for Business Entities

LEARNING OBJECTIVE 2

Understand the compliance requirements for business entities

VIDEO CONTENT

Tax professionals need to ensure that their clients meet all compliance requirements. In this section, we review the most common penalties that business entities can incur for not filing appropriately or paying taxes in a timely manner. Most of the rules we cover in this section are for corporations, because partnerships, LLCs, and S corporations are not taxpaying entities.

Filing Requirements

If the proper tax forms are not filed by the required due date, the IRS can assess penalties. In this section, we first review the due dates for business entity returns, then cover the statute of limitations and explain the penalties for filing late.

Tax Return Due Dates and Tax Forms

The due dates for tax returns vary by type of business entity. If the due date falls on a weekend or holiday, the deadline is extended to the next weekday that is not a holiday.

- Corporate tax returns (other than those with a June 30 year-end) are due three and one-half months after the end of the tax year, which is April 15 for calendar-year corporations.

All business entities use the same form to request an extension of time to file the return, Form 7004, Application for Automatic Extension of Time to File Certain Business Income Tax, Information, and Other Returns. Corporations can request an extension of six months to file the tax return. The extension of time, though, is only to *file the return*. A business must pay the taxes due for the year by the original due date or the IRS will assess a late payment penalty. This provides businesses with more time to finalize their return for filing, but they do need to estimate their liability for the year to ensure they have paid in the appropriate amount by the original filing date.

- Corporate tax returns with a June 30 year-end are due two and one-half months after the end of the year, which is September 15. The extended due date is seven months after the due date, which is April 15 of the next year.[4]
- Partnership tax returns and S corporation tax returns are due two and one-half months after the end of the tax year, which is March 15 for a calendar-year business. Extensions for partnership and S corporations are for six months, which is September 15 for a calendar-year business.

Related exercises: Discussion Question 3
Multiple Choice Question 3

Statute of Limitations

Businesses that discover a mistake in a previously filed tax return usually need to file an amended return for that year to correct the error. Corporations file amended returns on Form 1120-X, Amended U.S. Corporation Income Tax Return. S corporations amend a return by filing another Form 1120-S, U.S. Income Tax Return for an S Corporation, and checking the box on line H(4) indicating amended return. The partnership rules for amended returns are more complicated. Generally, if the partnership is not required to e-file the amended return, it can file another Form 1065, U.S. Return of Partnership Income, and check the box on line G(5) indicating it is an amended return. If the amended return must be e-filed, the partnership uses Form 1065-X, Amended Return or Administrative Adjustment Request (AAR).[5]

The IRS audits certain returns to make sure businesses have complied with the law. The **statute of limitations** is the period that a taxpayer has to file an amended return or that the IRS has to assess a tax deficiency. The idea is to encourage the IRS and taxpayers to settle disputes in a timely way. If the statute of limitations has not expired for a return, then that year is an **open year**. If the statute of limitations has expired, that year is a **closed year**.

Here are key facts to remember when considering issues related to the statute of limitations as you work with a client:

- The primary statute of limitations is three years from the later of the due date of the tax return or the date the return was filed.
- The statute is extended to six years if more than 25% of the gross income is understated on the original tax return.
- The statute never expires if the taxpayer commits fraud or fails to file a return.

The period for a business to file a claim for refund is slightly different from the statute of limitations for amending a return. The statute of limitations for claiming a refund (on Form 1120-X, Amended U.S. Corporation Income Tax Return or Form 1139, Corporation Application for Tentative Refund) is the *later* of:

a. two years from the date the tax was paid, *or*
b. three years from the later of the due date of the tax return or the date the return was filed.

[4]For taxable years beginning after 2025 and ending on June 30, the due date will change to the same rule as for other corporations: three and one-half months after year-end for the due date (October 15) and a six-month extension (April 15 of the next year).
[5]To correct errors to partnership-related items, partnerships under the Bipartisan Budget Act (BBA) of 2015 must file an administrative adjustment request (AAR) instead of an amended return.

If no return was filed by the business, the claim must be filed within two years from the time the tax was paid.

> **Tax Planning Tip**
>
> **Even if your client is not required to file a tax return, it may be prudent to file a return so the statute of limitations will begin to run, and the year will eventually close for audit purposes.**

EXAMPLE 1.2.1
Statute of Limitations

Hornet, Inc., filed Form 1120 for 2025 on March 3, 2026.

Scenario 1: When will the statute of limitations for Hornet's 2025 return expire?
Scenario 2: When will the statute of limitations expire if Hornet filed its tax return on July 17, 2026?
Scenario 3: When will the statute of limitations expire if Hornet never filed its 2025 tax return?

SOLUTION

There are three different scenarios here to evaluate:

Scenario 1: Hornet filed its 2025 return on March 3, 2026. The due date of the return was April 15, 2026, so the later of the due date or the date the return was filed is April 15, 2026. Three years from then is April 15, 2029, which is when the statute of limitations will expire.

Scenario 2: Hornet filed its 2025 return on July 17, 2026. The due date of the return was April 15, 2026, so the later of the due date or the date the return was filed is July 17, 2026. Three years from then is July 17, 2029, which is when the statute of limitations will expire.

Scenario 3: Hornet never filed its 2025 return. If a business files a return late, the statute of limitations expires three years after the return is filed. If the business never files the return, the statute of limitations never begins running. So, the 2025 tax year will always be an open year that the IRS can audit.

Related exercises: Discussion Question 4
Multiple Choice Question 4
Application Problem 1

Taxpayer Penalties

In this section, we discuss the four major penalties businesses may have to pay. First, the law imposes a penalty if a business fails to file a required tax return on time (*failure to file*). Second, Congress imposes a penalty if a business fails to make adequate tax payments during the year (*underpayment of estimated tax*). Third, a penalty is imposed if a business fails to pay the tax reflected on the tax return by the due date (*failure to pay*). Finally, the law imposes a penalty if a business files an inaccurate tax return (*accuracy penalty*).

Failure to File

The tax law imposes a failure to file penalty on any business that is required to file a return if the return is not filed by the due date. If a business requests an automatic extension, this penalty does not apply unless the business files the tax return after the extended date.

Corporations The following is a summary of the failure to file penalties that might apply to corporations:

- The penalty for late filing is 5% per month (or portion thereof) of the tax due with the return. Thus, a tax return filed 32 days late will have a penalty rate of 10% (2 months × 5%), because even a small portion of the second month counts as a whole month. The maximum penalty is 25% of the tax due.

- The minimum penalty is the lesser of $525 (2025) or the amount of the tax due. The minimum penalty applies only if the corporation does not file the tax return within 60 days of the due date and the computed penalty amount is less than the minimum penalty.
- If the failure to file is intentional (a case of tax fraud), the penalty is increased to 15% per month up to a maximum of 75% of the tax due with the return.
- S corporations must also pay a penalty equal to $255 (2025) per shareholder for each month, or part of a month, that the return is late. The penalty is assessed for no more than 12 months.

Partnerships Partnerships must pay a penalty equal to $255 (2025) per partner for each month, or part of a month, that the return is late. The penalty is assessed for no more than 12 months.

The next two Examples show the computation of the failure to file penalty for a corporation and partnership.

EXAMPLE 1.2.2
Failure to File Penalty

Locust, Inc., did not file a request for an automatic extension (Form 7004) for its 2025 tax return, which was due on March 15, 2026.

Scenario 1: Locust filed its tax return on May 10, 2026, and owed tax of $10,000. How much is his failure to file penalty?

Scenario 2: How much is Locust's failure to file penalty if it filed on September 20, 2026?

SOLUTION

There are two different scenarios here to evaluate:

Scenario 1: Locust filed its 2025 return on May 10, 2026. Locust filed its return one full month and a portion of the second month late. The penalty rate is 10% (2 months × 5%), and the penalty is $1,000 ($10,000 tax due × 10%).

Scenario 2: Locust filed its 2025 return on September 20, 2026. Locust filed its return six full months and a portion of the seventh month late. The penalty rate is 25% (7 months × 5%, limited to 25%), and the penalty is $2,500 ($10,000 tax due × 25%).

EXAMPLE 1.2.3
Late-Filing Penalty for Partnership

Termite Partnership has a calendar year-end. Termite filed its Form 1065 for 2025 on November 17, 2026. Termite has 10 partners. What is Termite's penalty for late filing of its tax return?

SOLUTION

Termite's Form 1065 for 2025 was due on March 15, 2026, and it was filed on November 17, 2026, which is nine months late (eight full months and one partial month). Termite's penalty is computed as follows:

$$\$255 \times 10 \text{ partners} \times 9 \text{ months} = \$22{,}950$$

Related exercises: Multiple Choice Question 5
Brief Exercise 2

Tax Planning Tip

Because the penalty percentage for most penalties is multiplied by the amount of tax due, generally no penalty is imposed if no tax is due with the return, or the taxpayer is eligible for a refund. An exception to this is if partnerships or S corporations file a return late, because the penalty is based on the number of partners or shareholders.

Underpayment of Estimated Tax

Congress requires businesses to pay their federal tax liability throughout the tax year. They cannot postpone payment until the end of the tax year, or until the tax return is due. If they do not pay the appropriate amount of tax during the year, they are subject to a penalty for underpayment of estimated tax. This is the case even if the business has paid 100% of the tax liability by the due date of the return.

General Rules The due date for estimated tax payments for businesses is on the 15th of the applicable month unless the 15th is on a weekend or holiday, and then the due date is the next business day. Estimated tax payments for a calendar-year corporation are due on the following dates in 2025 for the periods shown (see the **Potential Pitfall**):

Payment 1	April 15, 2025	January 1–March 31
Payment 2	June 16, 2025	April 1–May 31
Payment 3	September 15, 2025	June 1–August 31
Payment 4	December 15, 2025	September 1–December 31

Each payment is equal to 25% of the required annual tax payment for the year. If the required annual tax payment is less than $500, then estimated tax payments are not required. Corporations must pay the estimated tax payments through the Electronic Federal Tax Payment System.

The underpayment penalty is an interest rate computed using the federal short-term rate plus three percentage points. The IRS sets these rates on a quarterly basis. The underpayment penalty applies from the date the payment was due until the earlier of when it was paid or the due date of the tax return.

Exceptions to the Underpayment Penalty Corporations can avoid being subject to the underpayment penalty by meeting one of four conditions:

1. The tax liability for the year is less than $500.
2. The tax payments made during the year were at least 100% of that year's taxes.
3. The tax payments made during the year were at least 100% of the past year's taxes (not available for the first year of the corporation).

   a. A corporation with $1 million or more of taxable income in any of its three preceding tax years can use the preceding year's tax exception only for its first installment. The other installments must be based on the current year's tax to avoid penalty.

   b. If a taxpayer had a net operating loss in the previous tax year, the previous year's tax liability exception cannot be used to avoid an underpayment penalty.

> **Tax Planning Tip**
>
> **For the first three exceptions, the taxes must be paid evenly throughout the tax year to satisfy the exception. For example, taxpayers cannot wait until the end of the tax year to pay 100% of the previous year's tax liability and avoid the underpayment penalty.**

4. The annualization exception has been met. To qualify for this exception, compute the actual income for each payment period, and then base each estimated tax payment on the income earned for that period. The annualization exception is computationally complex. It benefits taxpayers whose income fluctuates significantly throughout the tax year, particularly if they earn higher amounts of income later in the year. If a corporation does not meet one of the first three exceptions, always check to see if the annualization exception can reduce or eliminate the penalty.

The next Example shows how the underpayment penalty is computed when it applies.

EXAMPLE 1.2.4
Underpayment Penalty

Snail Corporation estimates that its federal income tax liability for 2025 will be $600,000. Snail's federal income tax liability for 2024 was $500,000. How much must Snail pay in estimated income taxes in 2025 to avoid an underpayment penalty for 2025? Assume the annualization exception is not beneficial to Snail.

SOLUTION

To avoid an underpayment penalty, Snail must pay estimated taxes at least equal to the lower of 100% of the 2025 tax liability or 100% of the 2024 tax liability. Therefore, Snail must pay at least $500,000 of estimated taxes. If Snail does so, and the 2025 tax liability is $600,000, Snail must pay the remaining $100,000 ($600,000 – $500,000) by the due date of the tax return.

Failure to Pay Penalty

If a business has not paid all the tax due by the filing deadline, the IRS will assess both interest and the failure to pay penalty. The IRS assesses interest on late payments beginning on the due date for filing and is calculated using the federal short-term interest rate plus three percentage points.[6] This penalty rate has been approximately 7% to 8% over the past two years.

The failure to pay penalty is 0.5% of the underpayment for each month (or portion thereof) the tax is paid after the filing deadline. The maximum penalty is 25%. The failure to pay penalty is 1/10 of the failure to file penalty (0.5% vs. 5%). If both the failure to pay penalty *and* the failure to file penalty potentially apply, the maximum penalty for both is limited to 5% of the tax due per month.

EXAMPLE 1.2.5
Failure to Pay Penalty and Interest

Earwig Corporation paid tax of $5,000 for its 2025 tax return on May 4, 2026, 49 days late (March 15–May 4). Assume the federal short-term interest rate is 4%. How much will the IRS assess Earwig for interest and penalties?

SOLUTION

The interest rate is the short-term interest rate of 4% plus 3%, or 7%. Earwig will pay interest of $47 ($5,000 × 7% × 49/365). Earwig's failure to pay penalty will be 1% (0.5% × 2 months), resulting in a penalty of $50 ($5,000 × 1%).

The IRS can waive the failure to file and the failure to pay penalties if a business has a reasonable cause for failing to file or failing to pay. A **reasonable cause** is one outside the control of a business, such as irregularities in mail delivery, death or serious illness, unavoidable absence, or disaster. A business generally has the burden of proving that failure was due to reasonable cause and not simply neglect.

[6] IRC §6621(a)(2).

EXAMPLE 1.2.6
Reasonable Cause

Assume that in Example 1.2.5 Earwig also did not file its tax return until May 4. What would Earwig's total penalties be? What would the penalties be if Earwig had failed to file a timely return and pay taxes because a fire destroyed its records?

SOLUTION

Earwig would pay 5% for each month (or portion thereof) that it filed and paid late. Earwig's total penalties would therefore be \$500 (\$5,000 × 5% × 2 months). Even though both penalties apply, the maximum penalty assessed for any month is 5%. If a fire had destroyed Earwig's records, this would qualify as a reasonable cause and excuse both penalties. Earwig would still owe interest on the underpayment.

Tax Planning Tip

Penalties paid to the IRS are not deductible by taxpayers. However, business entities can deduct interest paid because of late tax payments.

Why **Why is the failure to file penalty ten times larger than the failure to pay penalty?** Congress set the penalty rates in this fashion to strongly encourage taxpayers to file their tax returns on time, even if they do not have the cash to pay the tax at that point. The filing of the tax return in a timely manner establishes the taxpayer's official financial record for the tax year, and Congress has emphasized its importance through the penalty structure. The IRS has several different payment plans that taxpayers can use to pay the taxes in installments over a period of time (see the **Potential Pitfall**).

Related exercises: Discussion Question 5
Application Problems 2, 3, 4, 5, 6, 7

Potential Pitfall

Refer to Example 1.2.4. If Snail had paid estimated taxes during the year of \$500,000, it would have avoided the underpayment penalty because it would have paid 100% of the previous year's tax liability. What if the IRS later audits Snail's 2024 tax return and the actual tax liability for 2024 is changed to \$510,000? Now Snail did not pay in 2025 estimated taxes equal to 100% of the 2024 tax liability (\$500,000 was paid rather than \$510,000), so Snail is subject to the underpayment of estimated tax for 2025. However, the penalty is not based on the \$10,000 shortfall that caused the penalty. If your client does not meet one of the exceptions for the penalty, then the penalty is computed on the difference between the *total tax liability* and the amount of taxes paid, not the amount of taxes that would have been necessary to avoid the penalty. Therefore, the underpayment penalty is based on \$100,000, the difference in the liability of \$600,000 and the taxes paid of \$500,000.

Accuracy Penalties

The IRS may impose additional penalties if a business underpays the actual tax because of an inaccurate position taken on a tax return. An **inaccurate position** occurs when a taxpayer disregards the tax rules without reasonable cause. Before reviewing the penalties, let's look at the terminology used to determine whether the IRS can assess an accuracy penalty:

- A **reasonable basis** means that at least one primary authority supports the taxpayer's position and has not been overruled.[7]
- **Substantial authority** is based on the likelihood that a taxpayer's position would be supported if the matter were taken to court. While the law does not identify a specific percentage of success that represents substantial authority, it is well accepted that the likelihood does not need to exceed 40%.

Related exercise: Discussion Question 6

- The **more likely than not standard** means that a taxpayer has a greater than 50% chance of succeeding if the taxpayer takes the position to court.

Who determines the likelihood that a position would be sustained in a judicial proceeding? You must use professional judgment to estimate this likelihood based on your knowledge and experience and on input from others. The determination is subjective. You must clearly communicate the reasons for your estimate to your client because the client ultimately makes the decision about what position to report on the return. If the IRS audits the return, it will use its professional judgment to decide whether to assess a penalty if it disagrees with your reporting position. And if the matter goes to court, then a judge or jury makes the same subjective determination.

[7]Treas. Reg. §1.662-3(b).

ILLUSTRATION 1.3 Timeline of Payment Penalties for a Calendar-Year Corporation

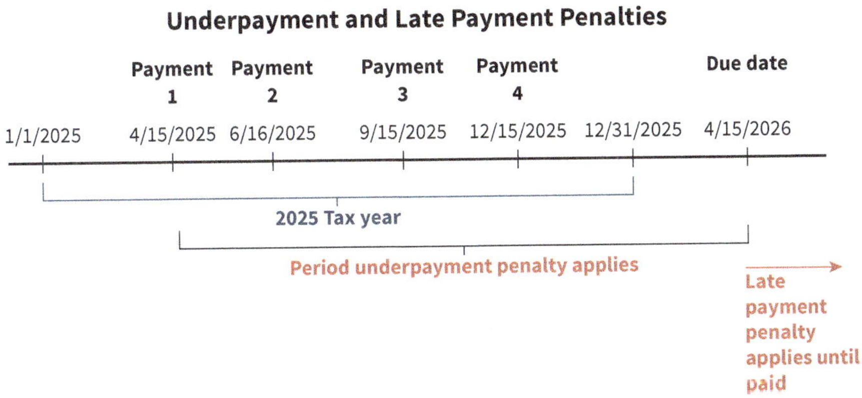

> **Potential Pitfall**
>
> Too many taxpayers confuse the late payment penalty with the underpayment of estimated tax penalty. Remember that the late payment penalty applies only to payments of tax made after the filing deadline. The underpayment penalty applies from the date the payment was due until the earlier of when it was paid or the March 15 filing deadline (for a calendar-year corporation). This timeline is shown in **Illustration 1.3**.

Accuracy penalties vary depending upon the nature of the noncompliance, as discussed in the rest of this section.

Negligence is defined as an intentional disregard of rules and regulations without intent to defraud. Congress imposes a penalty of 20% of the tax due to the inaccuracy if the taxpayer's position results from negligence. The IRS will not assess this penalty if there was substantial authority for the position taken, or if the position had a reasonable basis and the taxpayer adequately disclosed it on the tax return on Form 8275, Disclosure Statement, or Form 8275-R, Regulation Disclosure Statement.

EXAMPLE 1.2.7
Negligence

The IRS audited Centipede Inc.'s 2023 tax return this year and has assessed additional tax of $25,000. Centipede did not report a $100,000 lawsuit it won because it did not think it was taxable. Assuming Centipede's actions were negligent but not fraudulent, what is its accuracy penalty?

SOLUTION

Centipede is subject to the 20% penalty for negligence in underreporting its income. The penalty is 20% of the tax due, so the penalty is $5,000 (20% × $25,000).

Substantial understatement occurs when the additional tax due for an individual taxpayer exceeds the greater of $5,000 or 10% of the total tax on the return. For corporations, a substantial understatement results when the understatement exceeds the lesser of 10% of the tax required to be shown on the return (or $10,000 if that is greater) or $10 million. The tax law imposes a penalty of 20% of the tax due because of the inaccuracy if the taxpayer substantially understates the tax. As with the penalty for negligence, the IRS will waive this penalty if there was substantial authority for the position taken, or if the taxpayer adequately disclosed the position on the tax return.

Some penalties are imposed if there is a substantial or gross overstatement of the value or basis of any property. Those penalties are assessed as follows:

- A **substantial misvaluation** occurs if the property is valued on a tax return at 150% or more of the correct amount. The penalty is 20% of the tax understatement for a substantial misvaluation.
- A **gross misvaluation** occurs if the property is valued on a tax return at 400% or more of the correct amount. The penalty is 40% of the tax understatement for a gross misvaluation.

The most serious civil accuracy penalty the IRS can assess a taxpayer is for fraud. **Fraud** is a deliberate action by a taxpayer to conceal information, misrepresent information, or deceive tax authorities about a tax deficiency. The penalty for fraud is 75% of the underpayment, and the interest due on the underpayment is increased by an additional 50%.

Accuracy penalties are civil and financial penalties only, and do not include the possibility of a criminal record or imprisonment. However, criminal penalties *do* exist for tax fraud, in addition to civil penalties. The IRS uses its discretion to decide whether the fraud is at a level that warrants criminal sanctions. Generally, the maximum criminal penalty for tax fraud is five years in prison and/or a $100,000 fine.

EXAMPLE 1.2.8
Fraud

Jared owns 100% of Dragonfly Corporation, which does financial planning consulting. After completing Dragonfly's tax return this year, Jared realized that Dragonfly owed $42,000 in taxes. Instead of paying the taxes as owed, Jared added a $150,000 advertising expense that had not actually been made to the company's expenses. How would the IRS respond to this situation?

SOLUTION

If the IRS later audited Dragonfly's return and Jared could not produce any evidence that Dragonfly had made the expenditure, the IRS could assess a 75% fraud penalty against Dragonfly. If the IRS felt that it could prove beyond a reasonable doubt that Jared had intentionally and knowingly violated the tax law, it might also choose to pursue criminal sanctions against him.

Related exercises: Discussion Question 7
Brief Exercise 3

PRACTICE PROBLEM 1.2.1
Determining the Statute of Limitations Period

Zella Inc. is an art gallery showing work from various artists. Zella Inc. was not aware that it needed to file a tax return for its income. Its 2025 tax return was not filed until October 31, 2026. When will the statute of limitations expire for its 2025 tax return?

SOLUTION

The primary statute of limitations runs for three years from the later of the due date of the tax return or the date the return is filed. Zella Inc. filed its return on October 31, 2026, so the statute of limitations expires on October 31, 2029.

PRACTICE PROBLEM 1.2.2
Determining Penalties Due—C Corporation

Assume the same facts as in Practice Problem 1.2.1. Zella Inc. had never filed a tax return in the past because it had never sold any artwork; however, it had collected income from other sources. The 2025 tax return (filed October 31, 2026) showed a tax liability of $13,600. Zella Inc. paid the $13,600 when it filed its return. What penalties apply to Zella Inc.?

SOLUTION

Zella Inc. must pay failure to file and failure to pay penalties. It will not owe the underpayment of estimated tax penalty because it had never had a tax liability in the past. If both the failure to pay penalty and the failure to file penalty are imposed, the maximum penalty for both is limited to 5% of the tax due per month. Zella Inc. filed its return and paid the tax due seven months late. The penalty rate cannot exceed 25% (5 months). Zella Inc. must pay a penalty of $3,400 ($13,600 × 5% × 5 months).

PRACTICE PROBLEM 1.2.3
Determining Penalties Due—S Corporation

Clay Court is an S corporation with a calendar year-end. Clay Court filed its Form 1020-S for 2025 on November 28, 2026. Clay Court has 17 shareholders. What is Clay Court's penalty for late filing of its tax return?

SOLUTION

Clay Court's Form 1120-S for 2025 was due on March 15, 2026, and it was filed on November 28, 2026, which is nine months late (eight full months and one partial month). Clay Court's penalty is computed as follows:

$$\$255 \times 17 \text{ shareholders} \times 9 \text{ months} = \$39{,}015$$

INTERACTIVE SELF-SCORING QUIZZES

1.3 Review of Fundamentals of Property Transactions

LEARNING OBJECTIVE 3

Understand the fundamental rules for property transactions that apply to the taxation of business entities.

VIDEO CONTENT

In your previous tax course(s), you learned the fundamental rules that apply to property transactions and how these rules apply to transactions such as like-kind exchanges, involuntary conversions, and sale of a principal residence. In this text, we will cover many property transactions that apply to business entities, especially related to formations, distributions, and reorganizations. You cannot correctly determine the tax consequences of these types of transactions without knowing the fundamentals of property transactions, particularly the computation of *realized gains and losses* and *recognized gains and losses.*

It is also essential to remember that assets are classified into three mutually exclusive categories: *ordinary*, *capital*, and *Section 1231*. We review these rules, including the taxation of capital gains and losses, as well as how Section 1231 assets are taxed, including the depreciation recapture rules.

Gains and Losses from Sales and Dispositions

Businesses must compute a *realized gain or loss* every time they sell or dispose of property. The term **sale or disposition** includes sales, exchanges, trade-ins, casualties, condemnations, thefts, and retirements. When one of these events occurs, the taxpayer must compute the realized gain or loss.

Amount Realized

Conceptually, the **amount realized** represents the value that the owner of the property receives because of the disposition. Computing the amount realized is a four-step process, shown below (and in **Illustration 1.4**):

Step 1. Determine: **The amount of cash received.**

Step 2. Determine: **The fair market value (FMV) of any property and services received** and ADD it to the amount of cash received (see step 1).

Step 3. Calculate: **The liabilities assumed by the buyer, reduced by debts of the buyer assumed by the seller,** and ADD it to the amount calculated at the end of step 2.[8]

Step 4. Determine: **The selling or disposition expenses** and SUBTRACT this amount from the total calculated at the end of step 3.

ILLUSTRATION 1.4 The Steps in Determining Amount Realized

Determining Amount Realized

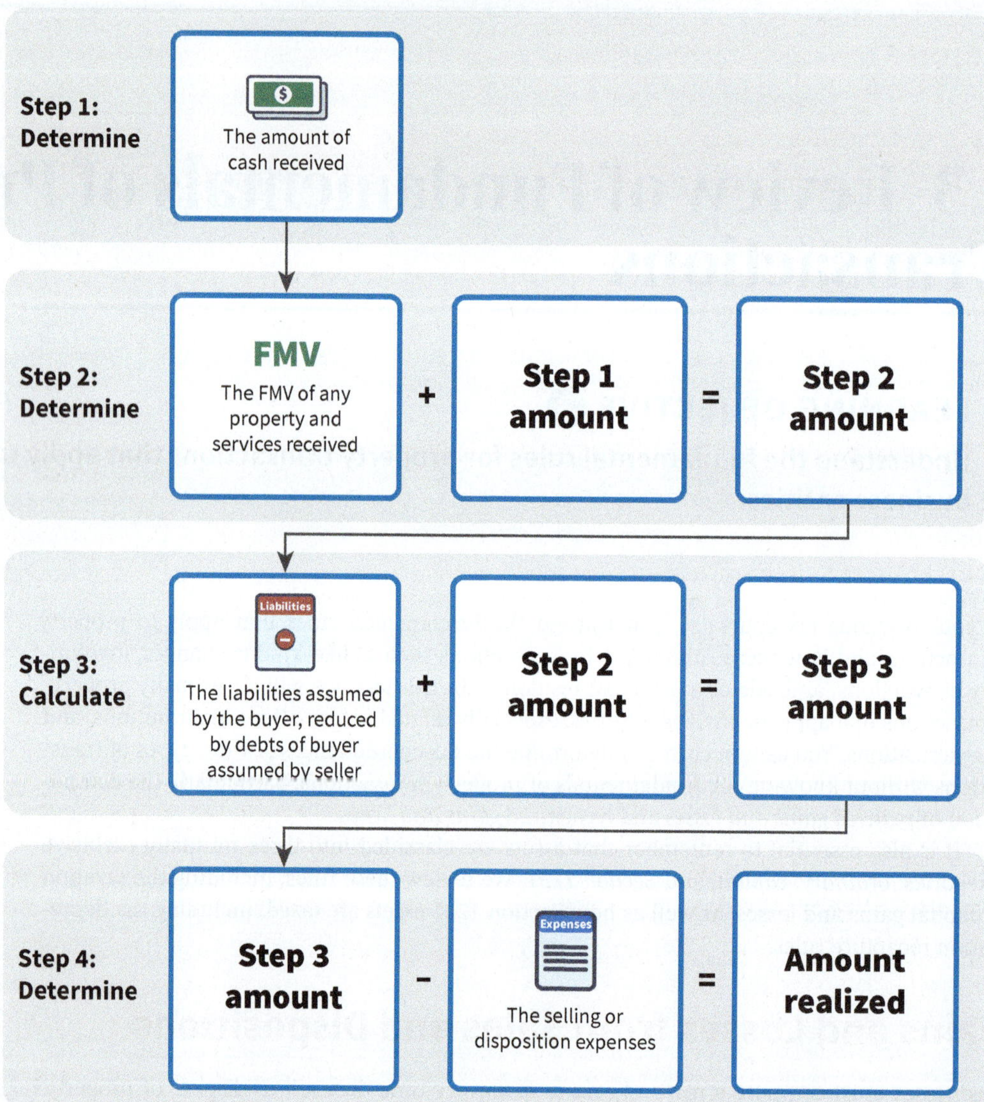

> **Potential Pitfall**
>
> Repairs to property to prepare it for sale are not selling costs. If the taxpayer is using the asset for business use, the repairs are deductible against business income.

Selling or disposition expenses include costs incurred by the property owner to complete the transaction, such as the following (also see the **Potential Pitfall**):

- Real estate commissions
- Transfer taxes
- Title policy for buyer

[8]The phrase "liabilities assumed by the buyer" is sometimes referred to as "debt relief." In a real estate transaction, debt relief is often the result of the buyer assuming the seller's mortgage on the property purchased.

- Attorney's fees
- Accounting fees

Adjusted Basis

For some assets, taxpayers must make changes to the asset's basis after its acquisition, and the result is known as the **adjusted basis**. The tax law defines *adjusted basis* as:

Original cost
Plus: Capital improvements
Less: Accumulated depreciation
Adjusted basis

Capital improvements are expenditures that either restore an asset, resulting in an increase in value, extend the asset's life, or adapt the asset to a new use. Let's take a look at calculating the adjusted basis for rental real estate.

EXAMPLE 1.3.1
Adjusted Basis

Rebecca bought a house in Year 1 for $120,000 and has used it for rental property. In Year 11, she sold the house for $190,000. Her accumulated depreciation at the time of sale was $40,000. In Year 5, she added a two-car garage onto the house at a cost of $25,000. The week before she sold the house, she spent $150 to repair the fence in the backyard. Rebecca has asked you to compute her adjusted basis in the house at the time it was sold.

SOLUTION

We can calculate Rebecca's adjusted basis as follows:

Original cost	$120,000
Plus: Capital improvements	25,000
Less: Accumulated depreciation	(40,000)
Adjusted basis	$105,000

The $150 fence repair does not affect adjusted basis because it is not a capital improvement. It is a repair expense that Rebecca can deduct in the period she incurs it.

Realized Gain or Loss

Once you have calculated the amount realized and the adjusted basis, you can compute the **realized gain or loss** as follows:

Amount realized
(Adjusted basis)
Realized gain/loss

Illustration 1.5 combines the formulas for amount realized and realized gain or loss.

ILLUSTRATION 1.5 Computation of Gains and Losses

Realized Gain or Loss Computation

Cash received
Plus: FMV of any property or services received
Plus: Liabilities assumed by buyer less debts of buyer assumed by seller
Less: Selling or disposition expenses
Amount realized
Less: Adjusted basis
Realized gain or loss

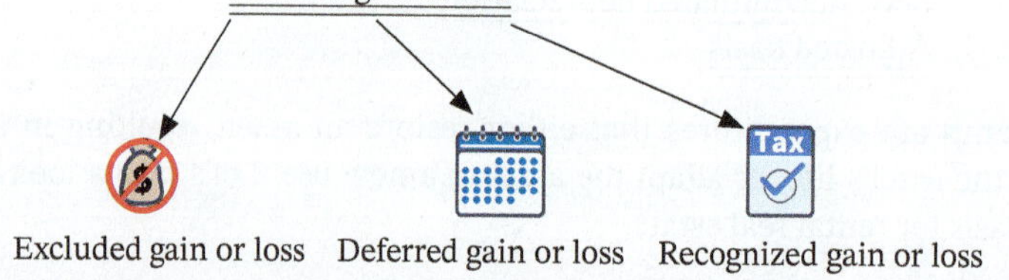

EXAMPLE 1.3.2 Sale of an Asset

Butterfly Company sells property with the following characteristics:

Adjusted basis	$15,000
Mortgage	$ 8,000
Selling expenses	$ 1,500

The buyer assumes the mortgage and pays cash of $17,000. Butterfly has asked you to compute its realized gain or loss.

SOLUTION

To determine Butterfly's realized gain or loss, we use the steps shown in Illustration 1.5:

Step 1.	Cash received	$17,000
Step 2.	Plus: FMV of any other property or services received	0
Step 3.	Plus: Debt relief	8,000
Step 4.	*Less*: Selling expenses	(1,500)
	Amount realized	$23,500
	Less: Adjusted basis	(15,000)
	Realized gain	$ 8,500

Related exercises: Discussion Question 8
Multiple Choice Question 6
Application Problem 8

Recognized Gains and Losses

All realized gains and losses are recognized by a business unless a tax law allows the gain or loss to be deferred or excluded. A **recognized gain or loss** is one the business includes in the computation of taxable income.

Deferred Gains and Losses

A business does not *recognize* all realized gains and losses. If a gain or loss is not recognized, it is either *excluded* or *deferred* (see **Illustration 1.5**). If it is an **excluded gain or loss**, the taxpayer never includes it in taxable income. If it is a **deferred gain or loss**, the taxpayer includes the gain or loss in taxable income in a later year. ***Assume your client must recognize all realized gains and losses unless a tax law provides otherwise.***

Related exercise: Discussion Question 9

Assume a business must recognize all realized gains and losses unless a tax law provides otherwise.

Tax Planning Tip

The recognized gain or loss will never exceed the realized gain or loss. The realized gain or loss is the maximum amount a taxpayer can recognize.

Why **Why does debt relief increase amount realized?** Taxpayers are sometimes confused about why debt relief increases the amount realized, and question whether this overstates the amount realized. It does not. Suppose Beetle Company owns a building with the following characteristics:

Fair market value	$350,000
Adjusted basis	$270,000
Mortgage	$225,000

Let's compare two scenarios, assuming Beetle sells the building.

Scenario One: The buyer pays Beetle $350,000 cash. Beetle's realized gain is:

Amount realized	$350,000
Less: Adjusted basis	(270,000)
Realized gain	$ 80,000

Beetle then uses $225,000 of the cash to pay off the mortgage and now has $125,000 cash remaining.

Scenario Two: The buyer assumes Beetle's mortgage of $225,000 and pays Beetle $125,000 cash. Beetle's realized gain is:

Cash received	$125,000
Plus: Debt relief	225,000
Amount realized	$350,000
Less: Adjusted basis	(270,000)
Realized gain	$ 80,000

The realized gain of $80,000 is the same for both scenarios. Beetle also has $125,000 of cash after each scenario. So these are two different ways to achieve the same economic result. Including the debt relief in the amount realized does not overstate it. Why? Because when the buyer assumes the seller's debt, the buyer reduces the cash payment to the seller by an equivalent amount.

Why **Why can certain gains and losses be deferred?** Congress allows certain realized gains and losses to be deferred for either of the following reasons:

- The transaction did not generate any cash for the business, so if the business did have to pay tax, the cash must come from other sources.
- The business's economic situation has not changed significantly because of the transaction, so Congress does not believe it is appropriate to tax such gains.

Related exercise: Discussion Question 10

Qualified Property When Congress permits businesses to defer gains and losses, some types of property will qualify for deferral and others will not. **Qualified property** is property meeting the specific requirements for a particular deferral transaction. **Boot** is any property exchanged that is not qualifying like-kind property, including cash. A business must recognize realized gains to the extent of the fair market value of the boot received. The recognized gain or loss is the *lower* of:

- realized gain or loss, *or*
- fair market value of boot received.

Boot received has no impact on the deferral of losses. A business that qualifies to defer a loss and receives boot can still defer all the realized loss.

Related exercise: Discussion Question 11

Deferred Gain or Loss When establishing a tax-deferred transaction, a business must know the amount of gain or loss that the law postpones or defers. This can be determined as follows:

Realized gain or loss
(Recognized gain or loss)
Deferred gain or loss

Basis in New Property Received You must also know the basis that your client has in the asset received in the tax-deferred transaction. You use the basis of the asset transferred to determine the basis of the asset received. The law labels this a **substituted basis** because the basis of the transferred asset substitutes for the basis of the asset received. In contrast, when there is no deferral and a business recognizes all realized gains or losses, the basis of the asset received is always its fair market value.

Basis in property received can be determined with two different formulas. Both always provide the same answer. Formula 1 better reflects what is included in the new basis, while Formula 2 is simpler to apply.

Formula 1: Adjusted basis in property transferred
Plus: Recognized gain
Less: Fair market value of boot received
Less: Debt relief
Basis in property received

Formula 2: Fair market value of property received
Less: Deferred gain
Plus: Deferred loss
Basis in property received

Basis of boot received is the boot's fair market value.

Holding Period of New Property For a tax-deferred transaction, the holding period of property received always includes the holding period of the property transferred. Because the business is deferring gain or loss that has accrued on the asset transferred, it also needs to include the period during which the postponed gain or loss accrued with the holding period of the asset received.

Related exercise: Discussion Question 12

Evaluating Tax Deferred Transactions There are seven steps to follow when determining whether a business meets the rules for deferral of gain or loss, and for computing the tax consequences. You will encounter many tax-deferred transactions throughout this book, such as corporate formations in Chapter 3 (LO1, Taxation of Corporate Formations) and corporate reorganizations in Chapter 5 (LO3, Corporate Reorganizations).

Step 1. Compute: The realized gain or loss from the exchange.

Cash
Plus: FMV of any property or services received
Plus: Liabilities assumed by buyer reduced by debts of buyer assumer by seller
Less: Selling or disposition expenses
Amount realized
Less: Adjusted basis
Realized gain or loss

Step 2. **Ask: Does the transaction meet the criteria for the taxpayer to *defer* the gain or loss?** If not, then you must recognize the realized gain or loss.

Step 3. **Determine: The recognized gain**. This amount is the *lower* of:

- the realized gain, *or*
- the fair market value of the boot received

Note that if the taxpayer is deferring a loss, boot received does not cause the taxpayer to recognize gain.

Step 4. **Determine: The deferred gain.** This amount can be calculated as follows:

Realized gain
Less: Recognized gain or loss
Deferred Gain

Step 5. **Calculate: The basis in the property received.** This amount can be determined with either of the following formulas (both always provide the same answer).

Formula 1:

Adjusted basis in property transferred
Plus: Recognized gain
Less: Fair market value of boot received
Less: Debt relief
Basis in property received

Formula 2:

Fair market value of property received
Less: Deferred gain
Plus: Deferred loss
Basis in property received

Step 6. **Determine: The basis in the boot received.** The basis in the boot received is the property's fair market value.

Step 7. **Determine: The holding period.** The holding period of the new asset includes the holding period of the exchanged asset.

Illustration 1.6 provides a flow chart showing these steps.

Example 1.3.3 considers the tax implications of a qualifying tax-deferred transaction in the context of a corporate formation. Do not concern yourself with the specific rules for corporation formations, as you will learn these in Chapter 3, LO1, Corporate Formations. The focus is on the seven steps for tax-deferred transactions, which are the same for all such transactions.

ILLUSTRATION 1.6 Seven Steps to Evaluate Tax-Deferred Transactions

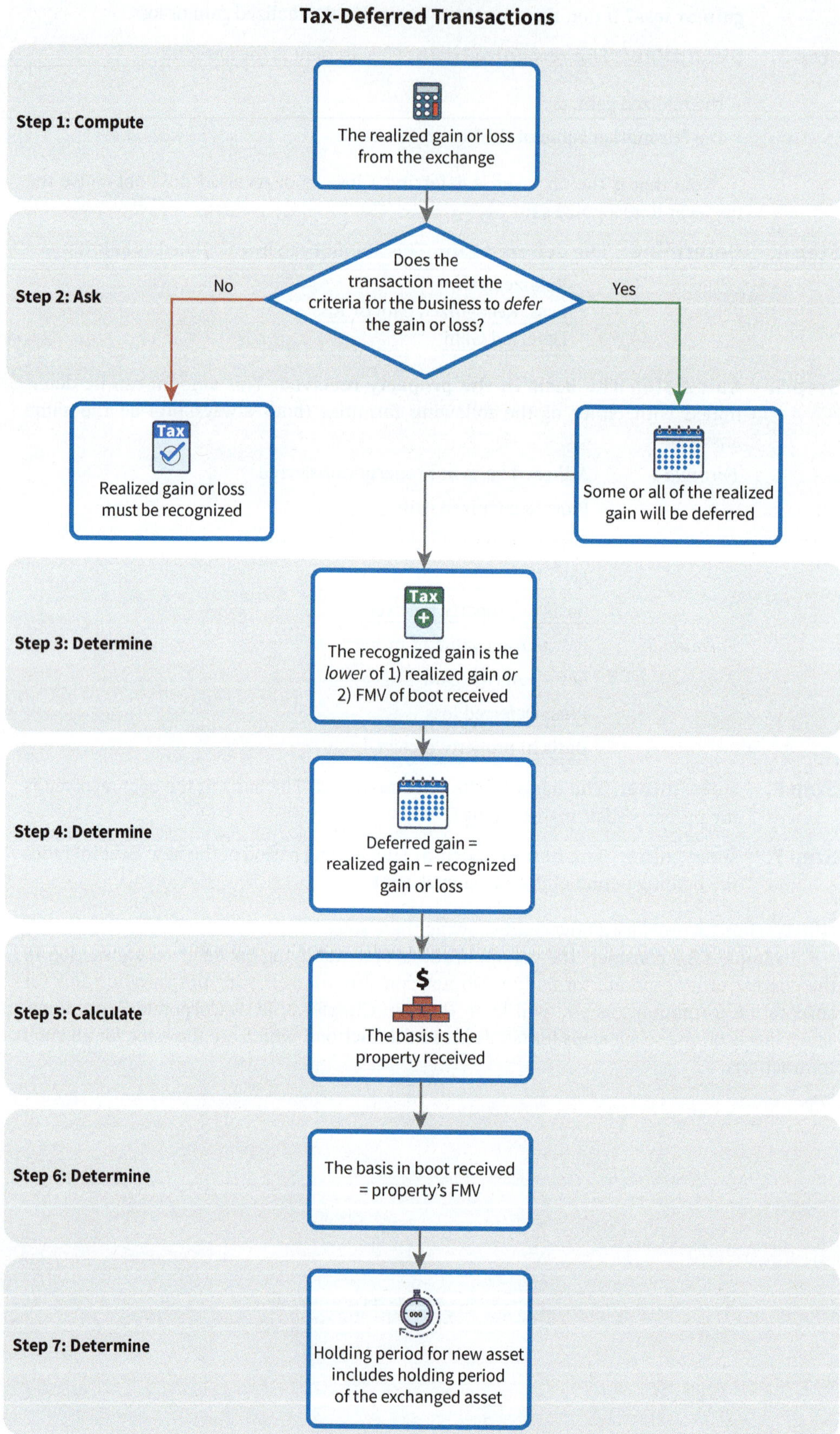

EXAMPLE 1.3.3 Tax-Deferred Transaction

Noah has owned Property A, a capital asset, for three years with an adjusted basis of $60,000 and a fair market value of $100,000. In a tax-deferred corporate formation, Noah transfers Property A to Bedbug Corporation in exchange for stock with a fair market value of $85,000 and cash of $15,000. The cash received is treated as boot. Compute the tax consequences for Noah of this tax-deferred transaction.

SOLUTION

To determine the tax implications of this transaction, we follow the steps outlined in Illustration 1.6.

Step 1. We first compute Noah's realized gain or loss from the exchange.

Cash	$ 15,000
Plus: FMV of any property or services received	85,000
Plus: Liabilities assumed by buyer reduced by debts of buyer assumed by seller	0
Less: Selling or disposition expenses	(0)
Amount realized	$ 100,000
Less: Adjusted basis	(60,000)
Realized gain or loss	$ 40,000

Step 2. Next, we ask if the transaction meets the criteria for Noah to defer the gain or loss. The problem states that this transaction does qualify, so we assume that the transaction meets the appropriate requirements to qualify for tax deferral.

Step 3: We then determine Noah's recognized gain by taking the *lower* of:

- realized gain ($40,000), *or*
- fair market value of boot received ($15,000).

Here, the recognized gain is $15,000.

Step 4. Next, we need to determine Noah's deferred gain, which we can calculate as follows:

Realized gain	$40,000
Less: Recognized gain or loss	(15,000)
Deferred gain	$25,000

Step 5. We now calculate Noah's basis in the stock received with either of two different formulas. Both always provide the same answer.

Formula 1:	Adjusted basis in property transferred	$60,000
	Plus: Recognized gain	15,000
	Less: Fair market value of boot received	(15,000)
	Less: Debt relief	0
	Basis in stock received	$60,000
Formula 2:	Fair market value of property received	$85,000
	Less: Deferred gain	(25,000)
	Plus: Deferred loss	0
	Basis in stock received	$60,000

Both formulas ensure that if Noah were to immediately sell the stock received, he would recognize the deferred gain of $25,000 ($85,000 amount realized less $60,000 adjusted basis).

Step 6. Next, we determine Noah's basis in the boot received, which is the fair market of the cash ($15,000).

Step 7. Finally, we determine Noah's holding period of stock, which will include the holding period of the exchanged asset. Noah's holding period in the stock is three years, because it includes the holding period of Property A.

Related exercises: Brief Exercise 4
Application Problem 9

Related-Party Losses

Another important part of property transactions is understanding how the related-party loss rules apply to business entities and their owners. Realized losses from the sale or disposition of an asset between related parties cannot be recognized, but the buyer may be able to benefit from the disallowed loss in the future. The term **related party** includes the following family members: spouse, children, grandchildren/other descendants, parents, grandparents/other ancestors, and brothers and sisters. Aunts, uncles, and cousins are not related parties, and neither are in-laws.[9]

Definitions for Businesses The related-party loss rules apply to many situations other than sales between family members. The definition of related party also includes relationships between individuals and business entities, and between certain business entities. Other examples of related parties include:[10]

- An individual and a corporation in which the individual owns, directly or indirectly, more than 50% of the corporation by value of the outstanding stock.
- A partner and a partnership in which the partner owns, directly or indirectly, more than 50% of the partnership's capital interest or profits interest.
- Two corporations, two partnerships, or two S corporations if the same individual owns more than 50% of the stock of both.
- A partnership and a corporation if the same owners own more than 50% of both.
- An S corporation and a C corporation if the same owners own more than 50% of both.

The disallowed loss from a related-party sale creates a **right of offset**, which taxpayers can use to reduce a gain upon the ultimate sale of the property to an unrelated taxpayer. The right of offset cannot create a loss, nor can it make a loss greater. Once the related-party buyer sells the asset to a third party, the related-party buyer permanently loses any unused right of offset.[11]

Why **Why are losses from related-party sales disallowed?** Luisa owns 500 shares of stock in LU Corporation, which she purchased on June 1, Year 1. She also owns 100% of Ant Corporation. Her adjusted basis in the LU stock is $150,000, and its current fair market value (FMV) is $180,000. Luisa has sold other investments during the current year, and her net capital gain from these sales is $30,000. She would rather not have to pay tax on the $30,000 gain, so she sells the 500 shares of LU stock to Ant for $120,000 on July 10, Year 9. This creates a $30,000 realized loss ($120,000 amount realized less $150,000 adjusted basis) that she intends to use to reduce her net capital gain to zero. However, because Luisa owns more than 50% of Ant, she cannot recognize the $30,000 loss, and her net capital gain remains at $30,000. The related-party loss rules exist to prevent this type of tax avoidance.

Luisa reduced her net worth by $30,000 when she sold the stock to LU because she sold it for less than its fair market value. Why would she be willing to do this? While individually Luisa has incurred a $30,000 loss, her corporation, Ant, still holds the stock.

Evaluating Related-Party Transactions There are four steps to solving all issues for a related-party transaction. **Illustration 1.7** provides a flow chart showing these steps.

Step 1. **Compute:** **The realized gain or loss from the transaction.** If a realized gain, then the taxpayer must recognize it. If a realized loss, go to step 2.

Step 2. **Ask:** **Are the buyer and seller related parties?** If NO, then you can recognize the realized loss. If YES, then you cannot recognize the realized loss, and must proceed to step 3.

Step 3. **Calculate:** **The right of offset is equal to the amount of the realized loss.**

[9]IRC §267(c)(4).

[10]IRC §267(b) and IRC §707(b)(1).

[11]IRC §267(d).

Step 4. **Determine:** **The holding period of the new owner of the asset.** This period begins on the day after the date the taxpayer purchased the property from the related party and does not include the holding period of the seller.

ILLUSTRATION 1.7 The Four Steps for Assessing Related-Party Transactions

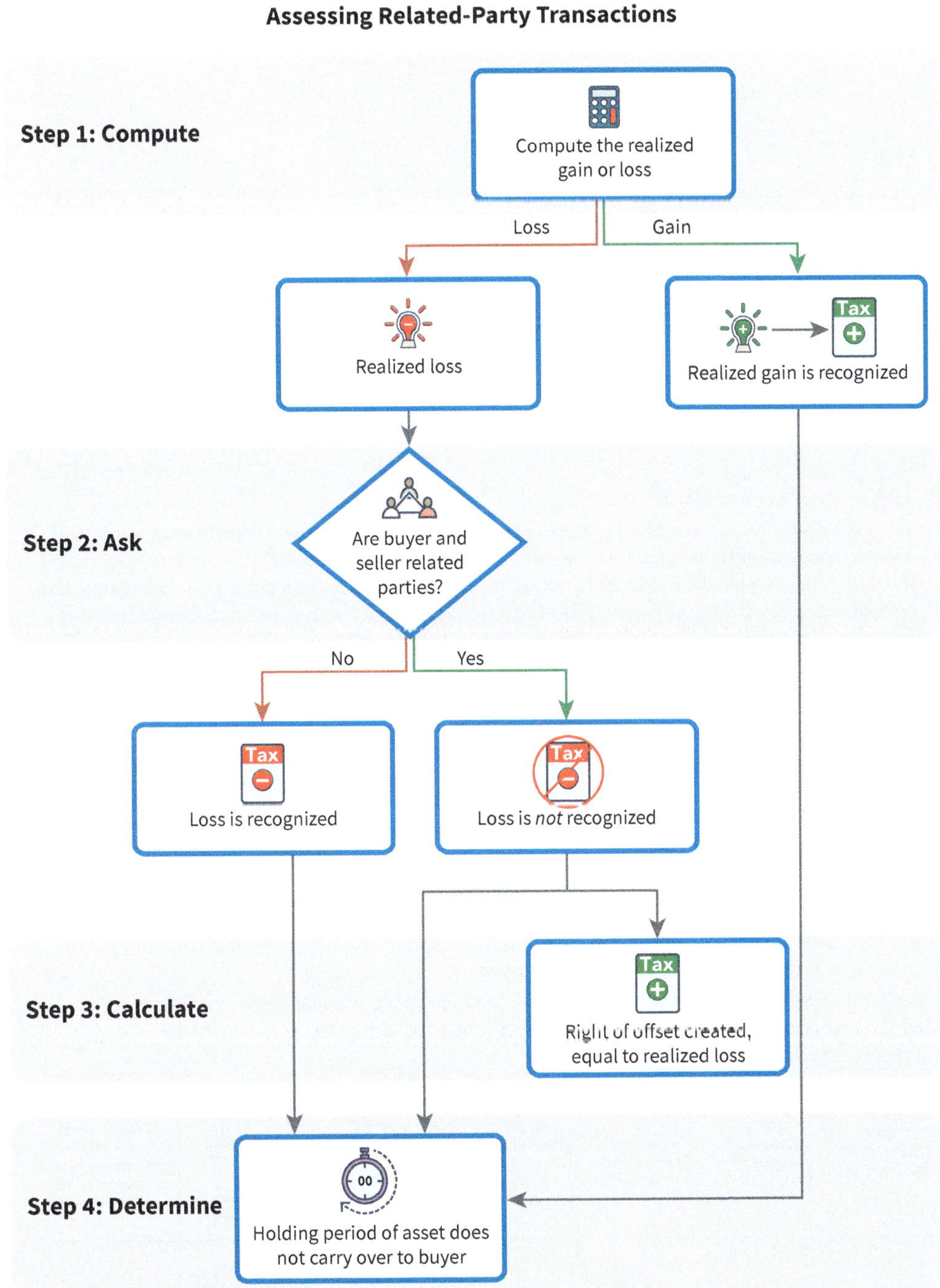

EXAMPLE 1.3.4
Related-Party Loss

Continue with the facts given for Luisa in the **Why** section above. Determine the realized gain or loss, the recognized gain or loss, the right of offset (if any), and the holding period for the new owner of the asset.

SOLUTION

Step 1. First, we compute Luisa's realized gain or loss.

Amount realized	$120,000
Less: Adjusted basis	(150,000)
Realized loss	($ 30,000)

Step 2. Next, we ask: Are the buyer and seller related parties? Luisa and Ant Corporation are related parties because she owns more than 50% of Ant, so the realized loss is not recognized. The deferred loss is $30,000.

Step 3. We then calculate the right of offset, which is equal to the amount of the realized loss. Here, the right of offset available for Ant to use in the future is $30,000.

Step 4. Finally, we determine the holding period of the new owner of the asset. Ant's holding period for the stock begins on July 11, the day after the date of the transaction.

Tax Return Guidance

Sales of capital assets are reported on Form 8949, Sales and Other Dispositions of Capital Assets (see Appendix B for a full copy of Form 8949). In Example 1.3.4, Luisa would report the sale of the stock as shown in Illustration 1.8. Her gain or loss is long-term because she owned the stock for eight years. The "L" in box (f) indicates that this is a nondeductible loss other than a wash sale. The amount of the disallowed loss is shown in box (g).

ILLUSTRATION 1.8 Form 8949 (Example 1.3.4)

Part II **Long-Term.** Transactions involving capital assets you held more than 1 year are generally long-term (see instructions). For short-term transactions, see page 1.

Note: You may aggregate all long-term transactions reported on Form(s) 1099-B showing basis was reported to the IRS and for which no adjustments or codes are required. Enter the totals directly on Schedule D, line 8a; you aren't required to report these transactions on Form 8949 (see instructions).

You *must* check Box D, E, *or* F below. Check only one box. If more than one box applies for your long-term transactions, complete a separate Form 8949, page 2, for each applicable box. If you have more long-term transactions than will fit on this page for one or more of the boxes, complete as many forms with the same box checked as you need.

☐ **(D)** Long-term transactions reported on Form(s) 1099-B showing basis was reported to the IRS (see **Note** above)
☑ **(E)** Long-term transactions reported on Form(s) 1099-B showing basis **wasn't** reported to the IRS
☐ **(F)** Long-term transactions not reported to you on Form 1099-B

1 (a) Description of property (Example: 100 sh. XYZ Co.)	(b) Date acquired (Mo., day, yr.)	(c) Date sold or disposed of (Mo., day, yr.)	(d) Proceeds (sales price) (see instructions)	(e) Cost or other basis See the **Note** below and see *Column (e)* in the separate instructions.	Adjustment, if any, to gain or loss If you enter an amount in column (g), enter a code in column (f). **See the separate instructions.** (f) Code(s) from instructions	(g) Amount of adjustment	(h) Gain or (loss) Subtract column (e) from column (d) and combine the result with column (g).
LU Corporation - 500 shares to Ant			120,000	150,000	L	30,000	0

Now let's examine the tax consequences for Ant Corporation's later sale of the stock.

EXAMPLE 1.3.5
Right of Offset

Assume the same facts as in Example 1.3.4 and the **Why** section above. Determine Ant's recognized gain or loss if it holds the stock for two years and then sells it to an unrelated party for $140,000. Alternatively, assume sales prices of $160,000 and $115,000.

SOLUTION

Once a related-party sale with a deferred loss has occurred, the buyer of the asset can use the right of offset to reduce gain when selling or disposing of the asset.

	A	B	C
Sales price	**$140,000**	**$160,000**	**$115,000**
Amount realized	$140,000	$160,000	$115,000
Less: Adjusted basis	(120,000)	(120,000)	(120,000)
Gain (loss) before right of offset	$ 20,000	$ 40,000	($ 5,000)
Less: Right of offset	(20,000)	(30,000)	0
Recognized gain (loss)	$ 0	$ 10,000	($ 5,000)

In scenario A, Ant can use only $20,000 of the right of offset because the right of offset cannot create a loss. In scenario B, the entire right of offset can reduce the gain. In scenario C, Ant cannot use any of the right of offset because it would increase a loss. In scenarios A and C, the unused right of offset cannot be used in the future.

A situation that may sometimes occur is that a related party has a qualified appraisal verifying that they sold the asset for its actual value and a loss is realized. In such cases, the loss is still disallowed, as we will see in the next Example.

EXAMPLE 1.3.6
Qualified Appraisal

How would the answer to Example 1.3.4 change if Luisa had a qualified appraisal that verified the fair market value of her shares was $120,000, rather than $180,000?

SOLUTION

The answer would not change. The related-party loss rules apply any time a realized loss occurs on a transaction between related parties, even if the seller uses the proper fair market value and is not using a false value to create a tax loss.

Related exercises: Discussion Questions 13, 14
Multiple Choice Questions 7, 8
Brief Exercises 5, 6
Application Problem 10
Tax Planning Problem 1

Classification of Assets

There are many areas of tax law in which you must classify assets correctly as either *ordinary*, *Section 1231*, or *capital* before you can develop appropriate tax planning recommendations. You also need to be able to classify assets as either *personalty* or *realty*. We cannot overemphasize how necessary it is for you to be able to properly classify assets for tax purposes.

Definition of Ordinary Assets, Capital Assets, and Section 1231 Assets

Ordinary assets produce ordinary income and ordinary loss when disposed of or sold. Individuals must pay tax on **ordinary income**, such as the distributive share that flows to a partner from a partnership, at their marginal tax rate, which currently ranges from 10% to 37%. **Ordinary losses** can reduce ordinary income and capital gains, whereas capital losses can reduce only capital gains and up to $3,000 ($1,500 for married filing separately) of ordinary income for individuals. For corporations, capital losses can offset only capital gains. Excess capital losses can be carried back three years and carried forward five years.

The more common types of ordinary assets are:

- Inventory, accounts receivable, and notes receivable
- Depreciable property and realty used in a trade or business that the taxpayer has owned for one year or less
- Copyrights and musical, artistic, and literary works, if held by the taxpayer who created the work (though a composer can elect to have their musical work treated as a capital asset instead)

> **Potential Pitfall**
>
> Assets that a business owns and uses for one year or less are ordinary assets. However, taxpayers often misclassify these as short-term capital assets.

Section 1231 assets are depreciable property and realty used in a trade or business that the business has owned for more than one year. For example, a florist's Section 1231 assets include the land and building where the shop is located, the refrigeration units used to store the flowers, and vans used to deliver flowers. (See the **Potential Pitfall**.)

The tax law defines a **capital asset** as any asset that is not an ordinary asset or a Section 1231 asset.[12] The most common types of capital assets are property held for investment use and property held for personal use. Goodwill is also a capital asset. Copyrights are capital assets when not held by the taxpayer who created the work.

Net long-term capital gains for individuals are taxed at a preferential rate of either 0%, 15%, or 20%. Corporations do not have a preferential tax rate for net long-term capital gains. LTCGs for corporations are taxed at a 21% rate, the same as ordinary income.

Related exercises: Discussion Question 15

The next two Examples show how to determine the character of an asset.

EXAMPLE 1.3.7
Copyrights

Cicada Corporation is a publisher focused on scientific research. Cicada has created a new Encyclopedia of Insects and has obtained a copyright for the book. Five years later, Cicada sells the copyright to National Geographic for $750,000. What type of asset is the copyright for Cicada and for National Geographic?

SOLUTION

In Cicada's hands, the copyright was an ordinary asset. National Geographic has purchased the copyright as part of a trade or business, because it hopes to sell enough copies of the Encyclopedia to produce a large profit. The copyright is a capital asset for National Geographic.

[12]IRC §1221.

EXAMPLE 1.3.8 Classification of Assets

Classify each of the following assets as ordinary, Section 1231, or capital.

a. Land held as an investment
b. Clothing held for sale in a retail store
c. Truck owned for four years and used in landscaping business
d. Patent owned by business that created the patent
e. Real estate owned by a partnership that is a dealer in land
f. Equipment used in restaurant and sold after being owned for eight months
g. Land owned for 10 years and used by hardware store as a parking lot
h. Land owned for 10 years but not used by the business for its operations

SOLUTION

a. Capital; all investments are capital assets.
b. Ordinary; this is inventory.
c. Section 1231; asset used in a business and owned for more than one year.
d. Ordinary; patents owned by the created are ordinary assets.
e. Ordinary; the real estate is inventory because it is held by a dealer in land.
f. Ordinary; asset used in a business and owned for one year or less.
g. Section 1231; asset used in a business and owned for more than one year.
h. Capital; because it is not used in a business, the land is an investment.

In classifying the assets above, you needed to know what type of activity applied in each case. For example, land owned for 10 years and used in a business activity is a Section 1231 asset, but if the landowner holds the same parcel of land as an investment, it is a capital asset.

Spotlight on the Law

Classification of an Asset: Sell Now or Later?

Emelio Estes is 100% shareholder in an S corporation that owns a popular theater downtown that offers live shows, a restaurant, and a gift shop. The S corporation purchased a plot of land near the theater to use for parking on January 2 of the current year for $85,000. It is now December 22, and the land has substantially appreciated in value, to $140,000. Emelio is considering selling the land instead of building on it. He would like to know if it is best to sell the land by December 31 or wait until the end of January of the following year. Emelio's marginal tax rate is 35%.

If a business-use asset is held for one year or less, it is an ordinary asset, and the sale would create ordinary income of $55,000. The S corporation would report the income, and it would flow through to Emelio, who would have a tax liability of $19,250 ($55,000 × 35%). If a business-use asset is held for more than one year, it is a Section 1231 asset, and the sale would create a Section 1231 gain of $55,000. The net Section 1231 gains for the S corporation would flow through to Emelio and be treated as a long-term capital gain on his tax return. Emelio would pay tax at a preferential rate of 15%. The tax liability would be $8,250 ($55,000 × 15%). Thus, if the S corporation holds the asset until January 3 of the following year, this will reduce Emelio's tax liability by $11,000 ($19,250 – $8,250).

Realty vs. Personalty

In addition to classifying all assets as ordinary, Section 1231, or capital, the tax law also categorizes them as either realty or personalty. **Realty** is land and any structure permanently attached to the land. The most common type of asset that is permanently attached to land is buildings, so realty is land and buildings. Other examples of realty include fences, silos, railroad tracks, and landscaping. Accountants sometimes refer to realty as "real property."

Personalty is any asset that is not realty. Taxpayers often refer to personalty as personal property. However, the term "personal property" can be misunderstood to mean property held for "personal use," which causes confusion and incorrect conclusions. Therefore, we use the term "personalty" throughout this book.[13]

Related exercise: Discussion Question 16

There are three categories of personalty. **Tangible property** has physical qualities and can be touched and moved. For example, cars and machinery are examples of tangible property. **Intangible property** does not have a physical form but is an abstraction that represents an ownership right. Patents, trademarks, copyrights, and goodwill are examples of intangible property. **Natural resources**, the third type of personalty, are a source of wealth that occurs in a natural state and has value, such as timber, mineral deposits, and water. Unextracted natural resources are considered to be attached to land and are treated as realty. Once a natural resource is extracted, it becomes personalty.

Related exercises: Multiple Choice Questions 9, 10, 11, 12

EXAMPLE 1.3.9
Personalty vs. Realty

Classify each of the following assets as realty, personalty (tangible asset), personalty (intangible asset), or personalty (natural resource).

a. Undeveloped land used/held as an investment
b. Desk and chair in a business office
c. Building used by retail stores near a mall
d. Projector in a classroom used to display images on a screen
e. Automobile
f. Boeing 747 airplane
g. Football stadium
h. Commercial office building
i. Extracted natural gas
j. Copyright for a book

SOLUTION

a. Realty; land is always realty.
b. Personalty (tangible asset); it is not land or a building, and it can be touched.
c. Realty; buildings are always realty.
d. Personalty (tangible asset); it is not land or a building, and it can be touched.
e. Personalty (tangible asset); it is not land or a building, and it can be touched.
f. Personalty (tangible asset); it is not land or a building, and it can be touched.
g. Realty; it is permanently attached to land.
h. Realty; buildings are always realty.
i. Personalty (natural resource); it exists in a natural state, has been extracted, and has value.
j. Personalty (intangible asset); it is not land or a building, and it cannot be touched.

Related Exercises: Application Problems 11, 12

[13] Law dictionaries routinely define "personalty" as personal property and "realty" as real property.

Holding Period

Before we leave the topic of asset classification, let's look at the concept of *holding period*. The **holding period** is the amount of time that a business has owned an asset. The holding period always begins the day after the business acquires the asset and ends on the day the asset is sold.

- A **long-term holding period** means that a business has owned the asset for more than one year.
- A **short-term holding period** means that a business has owned the asset for one year or less.

Holding period is relevant in two situations related to classification of assets.

- A business must own a capital asset for more than one year to be eligible for long-term capital gain treatment.
- A business owner must own an asset used in a trade or business for more than one year for it to be a Section 1231 asset. Otherwise, it is an ordinary asset. ***In this book, always assume business assets are owned for more than one year unless informed otherwise.***

In this book, always assume business assets are owned for more than one year unless informed otherwise.

Related exercises: Discussion Question 17
Brief Exercise 7

PRACTICE PROBLEM 1.3.1
Classification of Assets

Classify each of the following assets as ordinary, Section 1231, or capital.

a. 60-inch TV in a company's employee lounge, owned for two years
b. Sofas and loveseats held for resale in a furniture store
c. Heavy circular saw used in a construction business for four years
d. 500 shares of stock in Netflix
e. Equipment used for business and sold after three months
f. Storefront property used as an ice cream shop

SOLUTION

a. Section 1231; this is used in a trade or business and has been owned for more than one year.
b. Ordinary; this is inventory.
c. Section 1231; this is used in a trade or business and has been owned for more than one year.
d. Capital; this is an investment.
e. Ordinary; this is used in a trade or business and has been owned for one year or less.
f. Section 1231; this is used in a trade or business and has been owned for more than one year.

PRACTICE PROBLEM 1.3.2
Adjusted Basis Computation

Rumba Inc. purchased a building for its business in 2021 for $580,000. In 2025, Rumba expanded the building's office space at a cost of $55,000. The depreciation on the building has totaled $62,000. What is Rumba's adjusted basis in the building?

SOLUTION

Rumba's adjusted basis is computed as follows:

Original cost	$580,000
Plus: Capital improvements	55,000
Less: Accumulated depreciation	(62,000)
Adjusted basis	$573,000

PRACTICE PROBLEM 1.3.3 Computing Recognized Gain

Jamaica Partnership sold its rental property for cash of $100,000 and the assumption of its mortgage of $345,000. Jamaica paid a real estate commission of $23,000. It had purchased the rental property for $325,000 several years earlier. Jamaica remodeled the bathrooms last year for $15,000. The accumulated depreciation was $58,000 as of the date of sale. What is Jamaica's recognized gain?

SOLUTION

Jamaica's adjusted basis is computed as follows:

Original cost	$325,000
Plus: Capital improvements	15,000
Less: Accumulated depreciation	(58,000)
Adjusted basis	$282,000

We compute its recognized gain as follows:

Cash	$100,000
Plus: FMV of any property or services received	0
Plus: Liabilities assumed by buyer reduced by debts of buyer assumed by seller	345,000
Less: Selling or disposition expenses	(23,000)
Amount realized	$422,000
Less: Adjusted basis	(282,000)
Realized and recognized gain	$140,000

PRACTICE PROBLEM 1.3.4 Sale of Assets between Related Parties

Jamie owns an apartment building with an adjusted basis of $108,000 and fair market value of $90,000. She sells the building to Windy Inc. for $85,000. Jamie is a 75% shareholder in Windy. Windy Inc. then sells the building to an unrelated third party for $115,000.

a. What is Jamie's realized gain/loss and recognized gain/loss? What is Windy's basis in the building purchased?

b. What is Windy's realized gain/loss and recognized gain/loss?

c. Assume the same facts given except that Windy sells the building to an unrelated third party for $92,000. What is Windy's realized gain/loss and recognized gain/loss?

d. Assume the same facts given except that Windy sells the building to an unrelated third party for $76,000. What is Windy's realized gain/loss and recognized gain/loss?

SOLUTION

a. We will first determine if Jamie has a realized gain or loss on this transaction, as follows:

Amount realized	$ 85,000
Less: Adjusted basis	(108,000)
Realized loss	($ 23,000)

Because Jamie owns more than 50% of Windy Inc., Jamie and the corporation are related parties. Taxpayers cannot deduct realized losses from the sale or exchange of property between related parties. Jamie's recognized loss is $0. Windy's basis in the building purchased is its purchase price of $85,000.

b. Because Jamie cannot recognize the loss of $23,000 from the sale to Windy, this creates a right of offset of $23,000 that Windy can use to reduce any realized gain to zero when it sells the property. When Windy sells the building, we can determine its realized and recognized gains as follows:

Amount realized	$115,000
Less: Adjusted basis	(85,000)
Realized gain	$ 30,000
Less: Right of offset	(23,000)
Recognized gain	$ 7,000

Windy reduces its gain by the right of offset of $23,000. Therefore, Windy's recognized gain is $7,000.

c. Because Jamie cannot recognize the loss of $23,000 from the sale to Windy, this creates a right of offset of $23,000 that Windy can use to reduce any realized gain to zero when it sells the property. When Windy sells the building, we can determine its realized and recognized gain/loss as follows:

Amount realized	$92,000
Less: Adjusted basis	(85,000)
Realized gain	$ 7,000
Less: Right of offset	(7,000)
Recognized gain	$ 0

Windy reduces its gain by the right of offset, but only to the extent of its realized gain of $7,000. The right of offset cannot create or increase a loss. Windy's recognized gain is $0. The remaining $16,000 ($23,000 – $7,000) of the right of offset is forfeited.

d. Because Jamie cannot recognize the loss of $23,000 from the sale to Windy, this creates a right of offset of $23,000 that Windy can use to reduce any realized gain to zero when it sells the property. When Windy sells the building for $76,000, we can determine its realized and recognized gain/loss as follows:

Amount realized	$76,000
Less: Adjusted basis	(85,000)
Realized loss	($ 9,000)

The right of offset cannot create or increase a loss, so none of it can be used. Windy's recognized loss is $9,000. The $23,000 right of offset is forfeited.

INTERACTIVE SELF-SCORING QUIZZES

1.4 Review of Section 1231 Assets

LEARNING OBJECTIVE 4

Determine the tax consequences of disposing of Section 1231 assets.

VIDEO CONTENT

When Section 1231 assets have been sold, you must determine if any depreciation recapture exists, and you net all Section 1231 gains and Section 1231 losses at the end of the tax year. You determine the net Section 1231 gain or loss *before* the net capital gain or loss. (It is necessary to use this order because if there is a net Section 1231 gain, this amount is included in the netting of capital gains and losses.) We first review the netting rules for Section 1231 gains and losses, and then we summarize the depreciation rules.

Netting Section 1231 Gains and Losses

There are three steps to follow when netting Section 1231 gains and losses. Illustration 1.9 provides a flow chart showing these steps.

Step 1. Net: All casualty and theft gains and losses on business property held for more than one year.

- If the losses exceed gains, treat them as ordinary losses and gains and do not net them with other Section 1231 gains and losses.

Related exercise: Discussion Question 18

- If the gains exceed losses, the net gain is combined with other Section 1231 gains and losses.

ILLUSTRATION 1.9 The Three Steps in the Section 1231 Netting Process

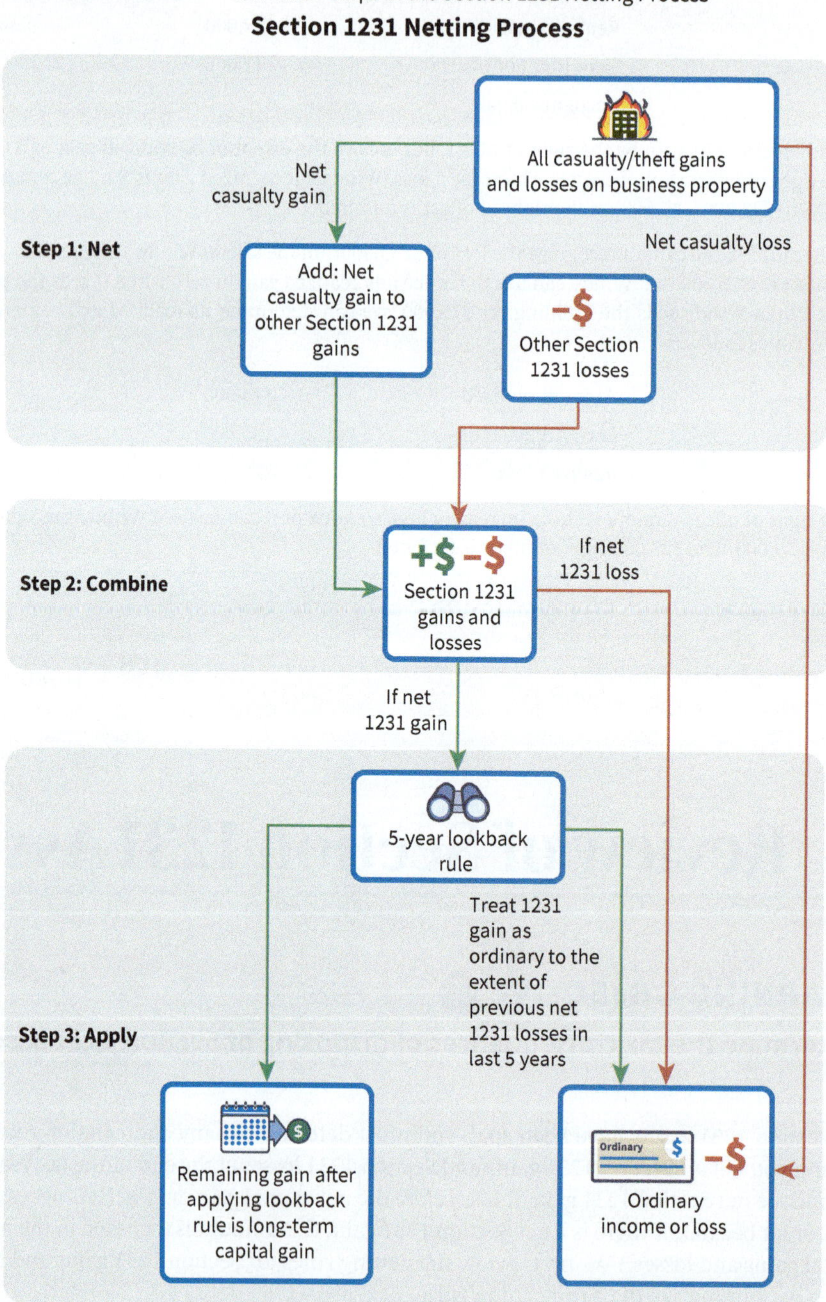

Step 2. **Combine: The net Section 1231 casualty and theft gain (if any) from step 1 with all other Section 1231 gains and losses recognized for the tax year.**

- To the extent that Section 1231 gains exceed Section 1231 losses, treat the net gain as a long-term capital gain (subject to the lookback rule; see step 3).
- If Section 1231 losses exceed Section 1231 gains, the net loss is deductible as an ordinary loss.

Related exercise: Application Problem 13

Step 3. **Apply: The lookback rule.** The **lookback rule** provides that net Section 1231 gains must be reduced by net Section 1231 losses from the five preceding tax years that have not already been recaptured. To the extent of these losses, the net Section 1231 gain is treated as ordinary income. Any remaining gain is treated as long-term capital gain.

Related exercise: Discussion Questions 19, 20

Potential Pitfall

The lookback rule applies *only* in years that have a net Section 1231 gain. Net Section 1231 losses from the previous *five years* can cause the gain to be taxed as ordinary income. The lookback rule never applies in years that have a net Section 1231 loss.

EXAMPLE 1.4.1
Netting Section 1231 Gains and Losses

Mayfly Partnership has the following transactions for the current tax year. It has not recognized any net Section 1231 losses in the last five years.

- Gain of $20,000 from the sale of land used in its business for the last five years
- Loss of $8,000 on the sale of depreciable property used in its business for seven years
- $3,000 loss when a car used in its business for the last 15 months was involved in a collision (the car was not insured)

Mayfly has asked you to identify the tax consequences of these transactions.

SOLUTION

Step 1. First, we net all casualty and theft gains and losses on business property held for more than one year. The net gain or loss from the casualty in this case is the $3,000 loss when the business vehicle was involved in a collision. That loss is treated as an ordinary loss.

Step 2. Next, we combine the net Section 1231 casualty and theft gain, if any, from step 1 with all other Section 1231 gains and losses recognized for the tax year. Mayfly has an $8,000 Section 1231 loss and a $20,000 Section 1231 gain. These net to a Section 1231 gain of $12,000 ($20,000 – $8,000). This gain is treated as a long-term capital gain and is combined with Mayfly's other capital gains and losses.

Step 3. The lookback rule does not apply because Mayfly has had no net Section 1231 losses in the last five years.

For these transactions, Mayfly has a $3,000 ordinary loss and a $12,000 long-term capital gain.

A net Section 1231 gain is netted with other capital gains and losses for the tax year, as shown in the next Example.

EXAMPLE 1.4.2
Net Section 1231 Gains

Assume the same facts as in Example 1.4.1 and note that Mayfly's only other capital transaction for the year resulted in a $7,000 net capital loss. Identify the tax consequences of these new circumstances.

SOLUTION

Mayfly can net the $7,000 capital loss with the $12,000 long-term capital gain from the Solution to Example 1.4.1 to produce a net long-term capital gain of $5,000.

Related exercise: Brief Exercise 8

The next Example demonstrates how to apply the lookback rule in step 3. When applying the lookback rule, begin the analysis with the year that is five years in the past, and then work forward. If you begin with the year just prior, you are moving in the wrong direction chronologically and will not arrive at the proper result.

EXAMPLE 1.4.3
Lookback Rule

Wasp LLC has had net Section 1231 gains and losses as follows since beginning its business in Year 1:

- $10,000 loss in Year 1
- $6,000 gain in Year 2
- $20,000 loss in Year 3
- $15,000 gain in Year 4

In Year 5, Wasp has a $30,000 net Section 1231 gain. Identify the tax consequences of this gain in Year 5.

SOLUTION

The tax consequences of each of Wasp's gains and losses are as follows:

Year 1: Wasp has a net Section 1231 loss of $10,000, which is an ordinary loss.

Year 2: Wasp has a net Section 1231 gain of $6,000. Wasp looks back to Year 1, and because it has recognized net Section 1231 losses in the previous five years of at least $6,000, the $6,000 is taxed as ordinary income. Year 1 has $4,000 of net Section 1231 losses remaining that can cause future Section 1231 gains to be ordinary income.

Year 3: Wasp has a net Section 1231 loss of $20,000, which is an ordinary loss.

Year 4: Wasp has a net Section 1231 gain of $15,000. Wasp looks back to Year 1, and the remaining $4,000 of Section 1231 loss causes $4,000 of the gain to be taxed as ordinary income. The remaining $11,000 of gain ($15,000 – $4,000) is taxed as ordinary income because of the $20,000 Section 1231 loss in Year 3. Year 3 has $9,000 ($20,000 – $11,000) of net Section 1231 losses remaining that can cause future Section 1231 gains to be ordinary income.

Year 5: The first $9,000 of Section 1231 gain in Year 5 is taxed as ordinary income due to the remaining Section 1231 loss in Year 3. The remaining $21,000 ($30,000 – $9,000) is taxed as long-term capital gain.

The calculations are tabulated as follows:

	Section 1231	Ordinary loss	Ordinary income	LTCG gain
Year 1	$10,000 loss	$10,000		
Year 2	$ 6,000 gain		$ 6,000	
			Recharacterized $6,000 loss from Year 1	
Year 3	$20,000 loss	$20,000		
Year 4	$15,000 gain		$15,000	
			Recharacterized $4,000 loss from Year 1	
			Recharacterized $11,000 loss from Year 3	
Year 5	$30,000 gain		$ 9,000	$21,000
			Recharacterized $9,000 loss from Year 3	

Potential Pitfall

Step 2 in Example 1.4.1 mentions that Mayfly has a $20,000 Section 1231 gain for the sale of land. Would you be correct if you had classified this as a $20,000 long-term capital gain? No, but this is a common mistake. When a Section 1231 asset is sold, the gain or loss from that transaction must be categorized as a Section 1231 gain or loss. The later characterization as ordinary loss or long-term capital gain does not happen until all Section 1231 gains and losses have been netted at the end of the year.

Why **Why does the lookback rule exist?** Assume a business that is managed by a sole proprietor owns two Section 1231 assets. Asset G has an unrealized gain of $100,000, and Asset L has an unrealized loss of $100,000. If the business sells both assets in the current year, the $100,000 Section 1231 gain and $100,000 Section 1231 loss will net to zero.

Alternatively, assume the following:

- Asset L is sold on December 31, Year 1, for a $100,000 Section 1231 loss.
- Asset G is sold on January 1, Year 2, for a $100,000 Section 1231 gain.
- The marginal tax rate for ordinary income is 37%.
- The marginal rate for long-term capital gains is 20%.

Year 1 would have a net Section 1231 loss of $100,000, treated as an ordinary loss. Year 1 tax savings from the deduction would be $37,000 ($100,000 × 37%). Year 2 would have a net Section 1231 gain of $100,000, which would be treated as a long-term capital gain if there were no lookback rule. The tax due for this sale in Year 2 would be $20,000 ($100,000 × 20%). For the two years combined, the entity would have positive cash flow from the tax results of $17,000 ($37,000 – $20,000), compared to no positive cash flow if the assets were sold in the same year. It is illogical for tax results to vary this much between two options, and for the law to reward taxpayers for selling their Section 1231 assets with losses in one year and those with gains in the next year.

The lookback rule exists to prevent this type of tax scheme. In Year 2, the lookback rule requires the business to treat the $100,000 of Section 1231 gain as ordinary income, because it had net Section 1231 losses in the previous five years. The tax due on the gain will be $37,000 ($100,000 × 37%), so the positive cash flow will be zero, just as if the business had sold the assets in the same year.

Related exercises: Multiple Choice Question 13
Application Problems 14, 15, 16, 17, 18

Tax Planning Tip

Even with the lookback rule, one planning opportunity exists for the timing of Section 1231 gains and losses. Taxpayers can sell their assets with Section 1231 gains in the year before selling the assets with Section 1231 losses. In the scenario above, what would be the results if the order of the sales were switched?

- **Asset G is sold on December 31, Year 1, for a $100,000 Section 1231 gain.**
- **Asset L is sold on January 1, Year 2, for a $100,000 Section 1231 loss.**

In Year 1, there would be a $100,000 long-term capital gain, with a tax due of $20,000, because there were no net Section 1231 losses in the preceding five years. In Year 2, the net Section 1231 loss will be an ordinary loss that results in $37,000 of tax savings.

The reason this order provides a different tax result is that the lookback rule does not apply in Year 2, because it does not apply to net Section 1231 losses. To use this strategy again, the taxpayer must wait more than five years, because the net Section 1231 loss in Year 2 will convert future gains to ordinary income under the lookback rule for the next five years.

It's therefore a good idea to evaluate a business's Section 1231 transactions several weeks before year-end. If there is a net Section 1231 gain for the year, consider whether selling Section 1231 assets with losses before year-end is appropriate to reduce the net gain.

Depreciation Recapture Rules

There are two sets of rules for depreciation recapture. Section 1245 recapture applies to personalty used in a trade or business, and Section 1250 recapture applies to buildings. We begin with the Section 1245 recapture rules.

Section 1245 Recapture

The character of the gain or loss from the sale of business assets will not always be Section 1231. Some of the gain will be taxed as ordinary income due to the depreciation recapture rules. Depreciation recapture applies to the sale of Section 1231 assets to potentially convert Section 1231 gain into ordinary income. Depreciation recapture is computed before Section 1231 gains and losses are netted, because recapture reduces the amount of Section 1231 gain. This section describes the depreciation recapture rules for Section 1245 assets—personalty used in a trade or business.

Why **Why does depreciation recapture exist?** Assume a solely owned S corporation purchases a machine for use in its business for $1,000, and the depreciation expense in the first two years is $300. The following steps illustrate the illogical tax consequences that would result *if there were no depreciation recapture.*

1. If the S corporation shareholder's tax bracket is 35%, the depreciation expense deduction saves taxes of $105 ($300 × 35%).
2. The adjusted basis for the machine is $700 ($1,000 – $300).
3. The machine is a Section 1231 asset because it is used in a trade or business, and it has been owned for more than one tax year.
4. If the S corporation sells the machine for $1,000, its gain is $300.

Amount realized	$1,000
Less: Adjusted basis	(700)
Recognized gain	$ 300

5. *Tax result with no depreciation recapture.* Section 1231 gains have the potential to be taxed as long-term capital gains. If that was the case and the shareholder's long-term capital gain rate was 20%, the shareholder would owe taxes of $60 on the gain ($300 × 20%).
6. The S corporation sold the asset for the same amount it paid for it, $1,000. There was no change in the economic value of the asset. Yet there is a positive cash flow of $45 when comparing the taxes saved from the depreciation ($105) and the taxes owed on the gain ($60). The $45 arises because the depreciation expense reduces ordinary income, which is taxed at ordinary rates, while the gain created by the reduction in basis due to the depreciation expense is taxed at LTCG rates.

To prevent taxpayers from creating cash flow when assets do not change in value, Congress added Section 1245, which taxes the $300 gain as ordinary income because it was created by the depreciation expense. Applying Section 1245, the $300 gain is taxed at 35% and the taxes owed are $105, the same amount of taxes saved by the depreciation expense.

Defining Section 1245 Assets **Section 1245 assets** include any tangible, depreciable, or amortizable property, other than land or buildings, that is used in a trade or business and that has been owned for more than one year. All Section 1231 assets (other than land and buildings) are Section 1245 assets, including:

- Certain livestock and crops
- Purchased patents
- Machinery and equipment
- Office furniture
- Business automobiles
- Assets used in rental real estate, such as a stove, refrigerator, and air conditioner

Section 1245 depreciation includes cost recovery, Section 179 immediate expensing, first-year bonus depreciation, and amortization of Section 197 intangibles. The recapture is the *lesser* of:

- the recognized gain, *or*
- all depreciation taken on the asset.

Gain in excess of the recaptured amount is treated as Section 1231 gain. Section 1245 recapture is taxed as ordinary income. The recapture rules do not apply to losses. So, if the asset is disposed of at a recognized loss, the loss is a Section 1231 loss, and no depreciation is recaptured.

Related exercise: Discussion Question 21

Evaluating Section 1245 Depreciation Recapture There are four steps to follow when determining Section 1245 depreciation recapture. Illustration 1.10 provides a flow chart showing these steps. We assume that all realized gains are recognized in this section.

Step 1. **Calculate: The recognized gain or loss from the sale.** This amount can be determined as follows:

Amount realized
Less: Adjusted basis (Cost less accumulated depreciation)
Recognized gain

Recapture applies only to recognized gains.

Step 2. **Ask: Is the asset sold a Section 1245 asset?** If the asset is a Section 1245 asset and was sold for a gain, the Section 1245 depreciation recapture rules apply. If the asset is a Section 1245 asset and was sold for a loss, Section 1245 depreciation

ILLUSTRATION 1.10 The Four Steps for Determining Section 1245 Depreciation Recapture

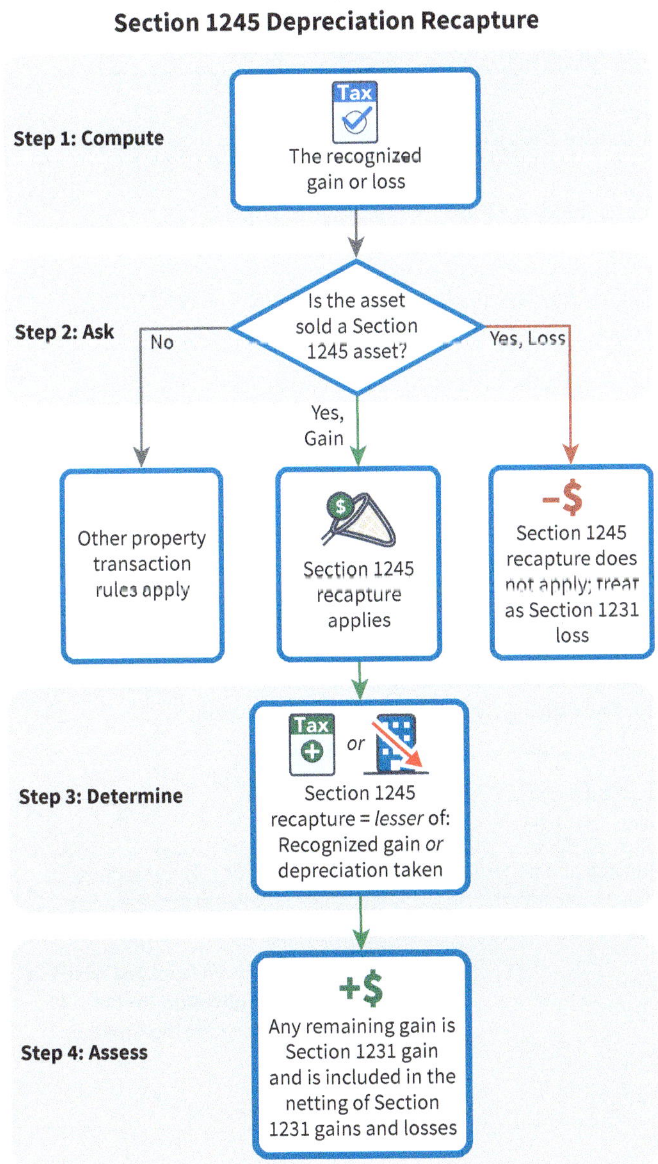

Potential Pitfall

Do not make the mistake of evaluating the lookback rule after step 4. At this point, you have computed the Section 1231 gain for one asset sale. The lookback rule is not used until all Section 1231 gains and losses are netted at the end of the tax year, and must be used if there is a net Section 1231 gain.

recapture does not apply, and the loss is treated as a Section 1231 loss. (If the asset sold is *not* a Section 1245 asset, then other transaction rules apply.)

Step 3. Determine: The Section 1245 recapture, which is the *lesser* of:

- the recognized gain, *or*
- all depreciation taken on the asset.

Step 4. Assess: Any remaining Section 1231 gain. Any remaining gain is considered a Section 1231 gain, because the asset was used in a trade or business and was owned for more than a year. The Section 1231 gain is included in the netting of all Section 1231 gains and losses at the end of the tax year.

The two following Examples explore different Section 1245 recapture situations.

EXAMPLE 1.4.4 Section 1245 Recapture, All Gain Is Ordinary

Bee Partnership sells a machine that has been used in its business for six years with the following characteristics:

- Original cost $10,000
- Accumulated depreciation $ 7,000
- Sales price $ 4,500

Bee has asked you to advise on the amount and character of any gain or loss.

SOLUTION

To determine the amount and character of Bee's gain or loss, we will follow the steps outlined in Illustration 1.10.

Step 1. First, we calculate Bee's recognized gain or loss from the sale, as follows:

Amount realized	$4,500	
Less: Adjusted basis	(3,000)	[Cost ($10,000) less accumulated depreciation ($7,000)]
Recognized gain	$1,500	

Step 2. Next, we need to determine whether the asset sold is a Section 1245 asset. A machine is not a building or land, so it is a Section 1245 asset.

Step 3. Now, we need to determine the Section 1245 depreciation recapture, which is the *lesser* of:

- the recognized gain ($1,500), *or*
- all depreciation taken on the asset ($7,000).

The recapture in this case is $1,500.

Step 4. Finally, we need to determine what gain, if any, remains after the recapture. Any such remaining gain would be a Section 1231 gain, because the asset was used in a trade or business and was owned for more than a year. We can calculate this as follows:

Recognized gain	$1,500
Less: Section 1245 recapture	(1,500)
Section 1231 gain	$ 0

Thus, Bee has $1,500 of ordinary income and no Section 1231 gain as a result of this transaction.

Related exercises: Brief Exercise 9
Application Problem 19
Tax Planning Problem 2

EXAMPLE 1.4.5 Section 1245 Recapture and Section 1231 Gain

Assume the same facts as in Example 1.4.4, except that the asset is sold for $11,000. What is the amount and character of any gain or loss now?

SOLUTION

To determine the amount and character of Bee's gain or loss in this new scenario, we will again follow the steps outlined in Illustration 1.10.

Step 1. First, we calculate Bee's recognized gain or loss from the sale:

Amount realized	$11,000
Less: Adjusted basis	(3,000) [Cost ($10,000) less accumulated depreciation ($7,000)]
Recognized gain	$ 8,000

Step 2. We know from the previous example that the machine Bee sold is a Section 1245 asset.

Step 3. Next, we calculate the Section 1245 recapture, which is the *lesser* of:

- the recognized gain ($8,000), *or*
- all depreciation taken on the asset ($7,000).

In this new situation, the lesser amount is $7,000, so this is the Section 1245 recapture.

Step 4. Finally, we need to determine what, if any, is the remaining Section 1231 gain.

Recognized gain	$8,000
Less: Section 1245 recapture	(7,000)
Section 1231 gain	$1,000

Thus, in this scenario, Bee has a Section 1231 gain of $1,000, and ordinary income (from the Section 1245 recapture) of $7,000.

Tax Planning Tip

In Example 1.4.5, the asset was purchased for $10,000 and appreciated in value to $11,000. The appreciation of $1,000 is the amount that is taxed as Section 1231 gain. This demonstrates that, to the extent that the asset appreciates, the gain from the sale of the asset will be Section 1231 gain, and the remaining gain will be Section 1245 recapture, taxed as ordinary income. Congress allows Section 1231 gain preferential treatment to the extent that the asset increases in value. However, it is very rare that a Section 1245 asset ever appreciates in value after it is purchased. Thus, in most situations, all of the gain from the sale of Section 1245 assets is recaptured as ordinary income.

The next Example illustrates that the recapture rules do not apply to losses.

EXAMPLE 1.4.6 Section 1245 Asset Sold at a Loss

Assume the same facts as in Example 1.4.4, except that the asset is sold for $2,500. What is the amount and character of any gain or loss now?

SOLUTION

To determine the amount and character of Bee's gain or loss in this new situation, we will again follow the steps outlined in Illustration 1.10.

Step 1. First, we calculate Bee's recognized gain or loss from the sale:

Amount realized	$2,500
Less: Adjusted basis	(3,000) [Cost ($10,000) less accumulated depreciation ($7,000)]
Recognized loss	($ 500)

Step 2. We know from the previous example that the machine Bee sold is a Section 1245 asset.
Step 3. We do not need to calculate the Section 1245 recapture in this situation, because the Section 1245 recapture rules do not apply to losses.
Step 4. The $500 recognized loss is thus a Section 1231 loss.

Related exercises: Multiple Choice Questions 14, 15, 16
Application Problem 20

The Section 1245 recapture rules also apply to the amortization claimed on Section 197 intangible assets. The rules operate in the same manner as for tangible personal property, as you will see in the following Example.

EXAMPLE 1.4.7
Section 197 Intangibles

Moth Corporation purchased the assets of LSU Corporation three years ago for $2,000,000. As part of the acquisition, Moth acquired four trademarks and assigned $200,000 of the purchase price to them. In the current year, Moth sells the trademarks for $270,000. Total amortization claimed on the trademarks at the date of sale was $40,000. Moth has asked you to calculate the tax consequences of this sale.

SOLUTION

To determine the tax consequences for Moth's sale, we will follow the steps outlined in Illustration 1.10.

Step 1. First, we calculate Moth's recognized gain or loss from the sale:

Amount realized	$270,000	
Less: Adjusted basis	(160,000)	[Cost ($200,000) less accumulated amortization ($40,000)]
Recognized gain	$110,000	

Step 2. Next, we determine whether the asset sold is a Section 1245 asset. A trademark purchased as part of a business acquisition is a Section 1245 asset.
Step 3. Next, we calculate the Section 1245 recapture, which is the *lesser* of:

- the recognized gain ($110,000), *or*
- all amortization taken on the asset ($40,000).

The lesser amount in this case is $40,000, so this is the Section 1245 recapture.

Step 4. Finally, we need to determine what, if any, is the remaining gain (which is a Section 1231 gain, because the asset was used in a trade or business and was owned for more than a year):

Recognized gain	$110,000
Less: Section 1245 recapture	(40,000)
Section 1231 gain	$ 70,000

In this situation, Moth has $40,000 of ordinary income and a Section 1231 gain of $70,000.

Related exercises: Discussion Question 22
Application Problem 21

Section 1250 Recapture

Section 1250 recapture applies to only one type of asset—buildings. Whereas gain from the sale of Section 1245 property can be taxed at two different rates (ordinary income and LTCG), three types of gain (discussed below) can apply to the sale of Section 1250 property. The Section 1250 recapture rules are different for regular corporations than for individuals, partnerships, LLCs, and S corporations. We first review the rules for individuals, partnerships, LLCs, and S corporations, and then for corporations.

Defining Section 1250 Assets **Section 1250 assets** are defined as depreciable buildings used in a trade or business and owned for more than one year. When determining Section 1250 recapture, you use the *lesser* of:

- the recognized gain, *or*
- the *excess depreciation.*

Excess depreciation is the depreciation claimed in excess of the amount that would have been claimed under the straight-line depreciation method.

Depreciation claimed
Less: Straight-line depreciation
Excess depreciation

IRC Section 1250 provides that excess depreciation is subject to being recaptured as ordinary income. The following rules also apply to Section 1250 gains and losses for individuals, partnerships, and S corporations:

- If the property is disposed of at a recognized loss, the loss is a Section 1231 loss. No depreciation is recaptured.
- Gain in excess of the recaptured amount is treated as either *unrecaptured Section 1250 gain* or Section 1231 gain. **Unrecaptured Section 1250 gain** is capital gain taxed at a maximum tax rate of 25% to the extent of accumulated straight-line depreciation claimed on the real estate. If the taxpayer's marginal tax rate for ordinary income is less than 25%, then the ordinary income rate is used.
- Section 1250 recapture also applies to rental real estate, because rental buildings are depreciable.

Related exercises: Discussion Questions 23, 24

Illustration 1.11 summarizes the three types of gain an individual, partnership, or S corporation can have when a building that is a Section 1231 asset is sold, and the gain is allocated to these categories in the order shown:

Step 1: Section 1250 recapture

Step 2: Unrecaptured Section 1250 gain

Step 3: Section 1231 gain

Potential Pitfall

For Section 1245 assets, all depreciation claimed is subject to being recaptured. For Section 1250 assets, only excess depreciation has the potential to be taxed as ordinary income. Be careful not to confuse these rules.

ILLUSTRATION 1.11 Types of Gain from Sale of a Building—Individuals, Partnerships, and S Corporations

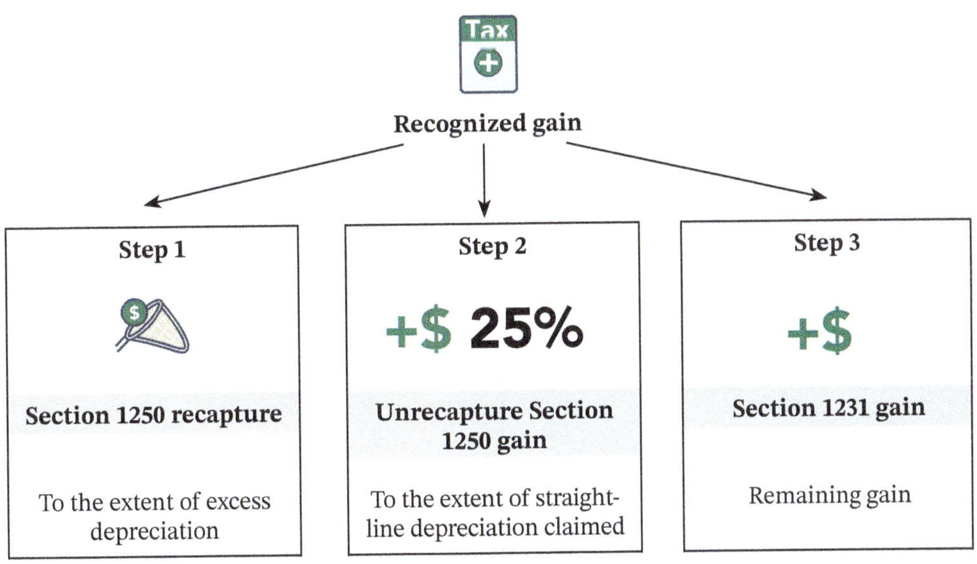

Tax Planning Tip

The only situation for which you may have Section 1250 recapture is for buildings placed in service before 1987. If a building is depreciated using straight-line depreciation, there will be no Section 1250 recapture because there is no excess depreciation. Accelerated depreciation is not available for buildings placed in service after 1986.

Evaluating Section 1250 Depreciation Recapture—Individuals, Partnerships, and S Corporations There are six steps to follow when determining Section 1250 depreciation recapture for individuals, partnerships, and S corporations. Illustration 1.12 provides a flow chart showing these steps.

Step 1. Calculate: The recognized gain or loss from the sale. This can be determined as follows:

Amount realized
Less: Adjusted basis (Cost less accumulated depreciation)
Recognized gain

Step 2. Ask: Is the asset sold a Section 1250 asset? If YES, then proceed to step 3. Otherwise, different property transaction rules apply.

Step 3. Calculate: Excess depreciation. This can be determined as follows:

Depreciation claimed
Less: Straight-line depreciation
Excess depreciation

Step 4. Determine: The Section 1250 recapture, which is the *lesser* of:

- the recognized gain, *or*
- the excess depreciation.

Step 5. Calculate: The gain remaining after step 4 is taxed as unrecaptured Section 1250 gain up to the amount of straight-line depreciation claimed. Unrecaptured Section 1250 gain, limited to the taxpayer's net capital gain as reported on Form 1040, Schedule D, is taxed at the *lower* of the taxpayer's ordinary income tax rate or 25%.

Step 6. Assess: Any remaining Section 1231 gain. Any remaining gain is considered Section 1231 gain, because the asset was used in a trade or business and was owned for more than a year.

Recognized gain
Less: Section 1250 recapture
Less: Unrecaptured Section 1250 gain
Section 1231 gain

The Section 1231 gain is included in the netting of all Section 1231 gains and losses at the end of the tax year.

ILLUSTRATION 1.12 The Six Steps in Determining Section 1250 Depreciation Recapture—Individuals, Partnerships, and S Corporations

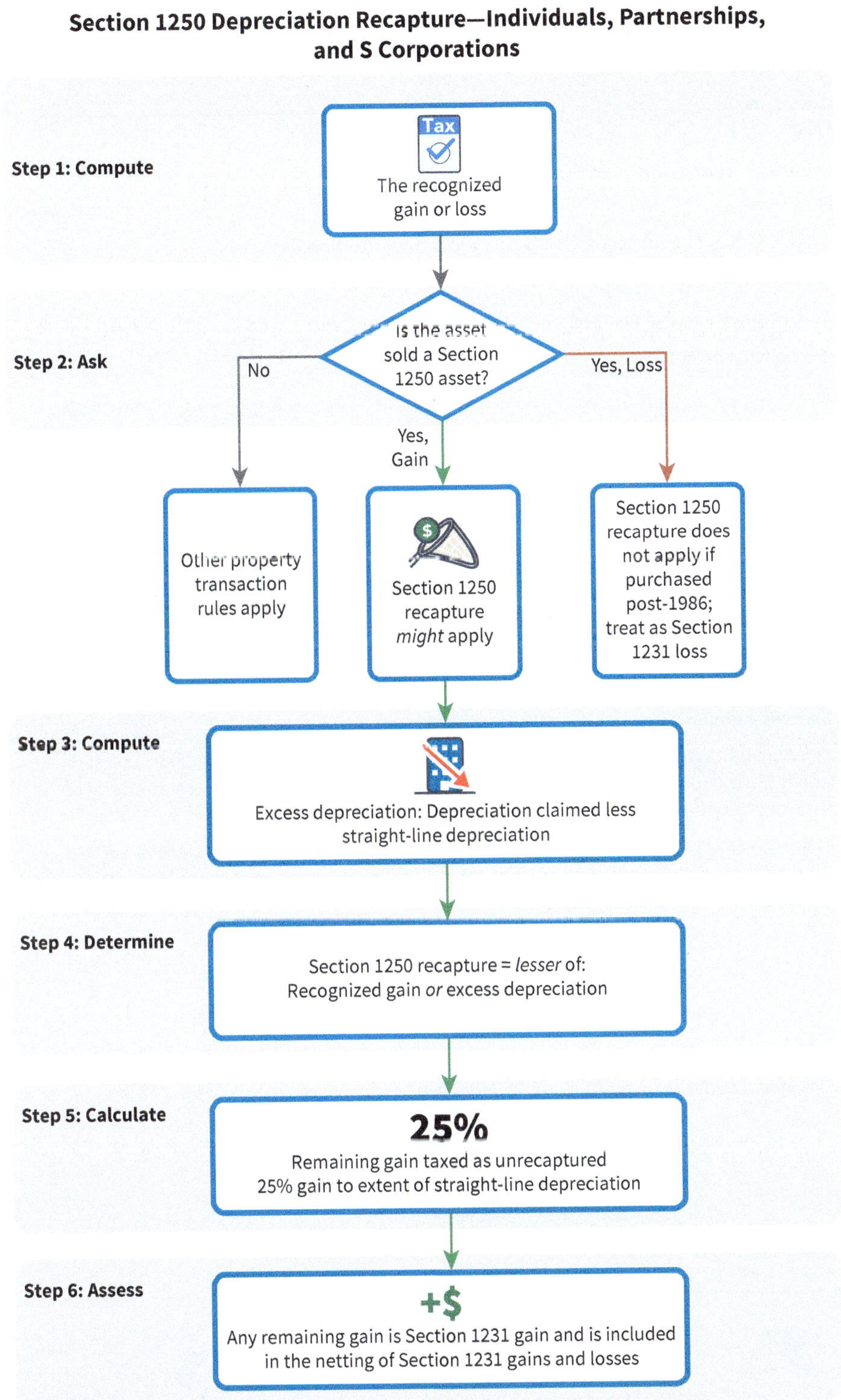

The two following Examples explore different Section 1250 depreciation scenarios.

EXAMPLE 1.4.8 Sale of a Building—Straight-Line Depreciation

Scorpion LLC sells a building that it has used in its business for the last 10 years. Scorpion's cost for the building was $500,000, and accumulated straight-line depreciation is $170,000. Scorpion sells the building for $600,000 in the current year. Assuming Scorpion has no sales of capital assets this year, compute the recognized gain or loss from this sale and determine its character.

SOLUTION

To determine the tax consequences for Scorpion's disposition, we will follow the steps outlined in Illustration 1.12.

Step 1. First, we calculate the recognized gain or loss from the disposition:

Amount realized	$600,000	
Less: Adjusted basis	(330,000)	[Cost ($500,000) less accumulated depreciation ($170,000)]
Recognized gain	$270,000	

Step 2. Next, we determine if the asset sold is a Section 1250 asset. Scorpion sold a depreciable building held for more than one year, so this is a Section 1250 asset.

Step 3. Now we calculate any excess depreciation, as follows:

Depreciation claimed	$170,000
Less: Straight-line depreciation	(170,000)
Excess depreciation	$ 0

Step 4. Next, we determine the Section 1250 recapture, which is the *lesser* of:

- the recognized gain ($270,000), *or*
- the excess depreciation ($0).

The lesser amount is $0, so this is the Section 1250 recapture.

Step 5. The remaining gain is next taxed as unrecaptured Section 1250 gain, up to the amount of straight-line depreciation claimed. Thus, $170,000 of the gain is taxed as unrecaptured Section 1250 gain at the *lower* of Scorpion's ordinary income rate or 25%.

Step 6. Finally, whatever gain from the disposition that remains (if any) is considered a Section 1231 gain, because the asset was used in a trade or business and was owned for more than a year. It can be calculated as follows:

Recognized gain	$270,000
Less: Section 1250 recapture	(0)
Less: Unrecaptured Section 1250 gain	(170,000)
Section 1231 gain	$100,000

The tax consequences of the disposition are summarized in the diagram below:

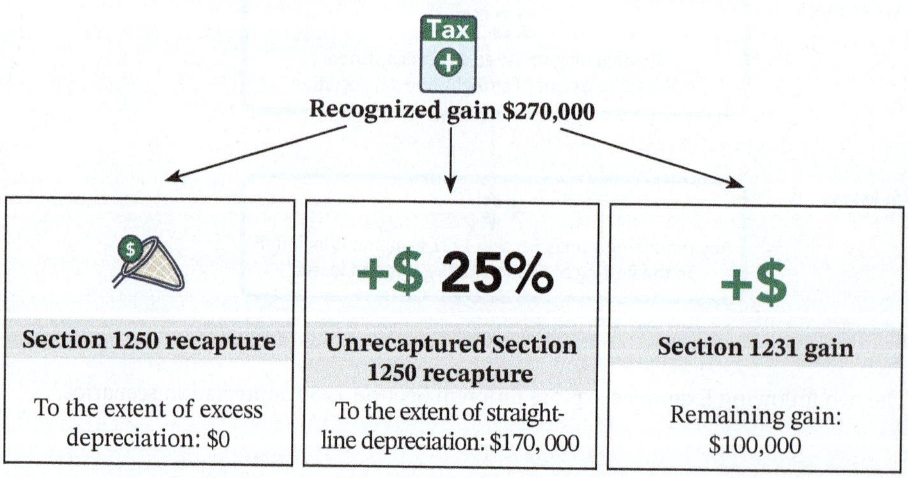

Related exercises: Application Problem 22
Tax Planning Problem 3

EXAMPLE 1.4.9 Sale of a Building—Accelerated Depreciation

In 1979, Thrips Company, an S corporation, purchased a building at a cost of $1,000,000 and elected to depreciate it using the 150% declining balance method with a useful life of 50 years. This year, Thrips sells the building for $2,400,000. Accumulated depreciation at the time of sale was $890,000. Straight-line depreciation would have been $800,000. Compute the recognized gain or loss from this sale and determine its character.

SOLUTION

To determine the tax consequences of Thrips's sale of the building, we will follow the steps outlined in Illustration 1.12.

Step 1. First, we'll calculate the recognized gain or loss from the sale, as follows:

Amount realized	$2,400,000	
Less: Adjusted basis	(110,000)	[Cost ($1,000,000) less accumulated depreciation ($890,000)]
Recognized gain	$2,290,000	

Step 2. Next, we determine whether the asset sold is a Section 1250 asset. Thrips sold a depreciable building owned for more than one year, so this is a Section 1250 asset.

Step 3. Next, we calculate any excess depreciation:

Depreciation claimed	$890,000
Less: Straight-line depreciation	(800,000)
Excess depreciation	$ 90,000

Step 4. Next, we determine the Section 1250 recapture, which is the *lesser* of:

- the recognized gain ($2,290,000), *or*
- the excess depreciation ($90,000).

The lesser amount is $90,000, so this is the Section 1250 recapture.

Step 5. The remaining gain is next taxed as unrecaptured Section 1250 gain, up to the amount of straight-line depreciation claimed. So $800,000 of the gain is taxed as unrecaptured Section 1250 gain at the lower of Thrips's ordinary income rate or 25%.

Step 6. Finally, whatever gain from the sale that remains (if any) is considered a Section 1231 gain, because the asset was used in a trade or business and was owned for more than a year. This can be calculated as follows:

Recognized gain	$2,290,000
Less: Section 1250 recapture	(90,000)
Less: Unrecaptured Section 1250 gain	(800,000)
Section 1231 gain	$1,400,000

The tax consequences of the disposition are summarized in the diagram below:

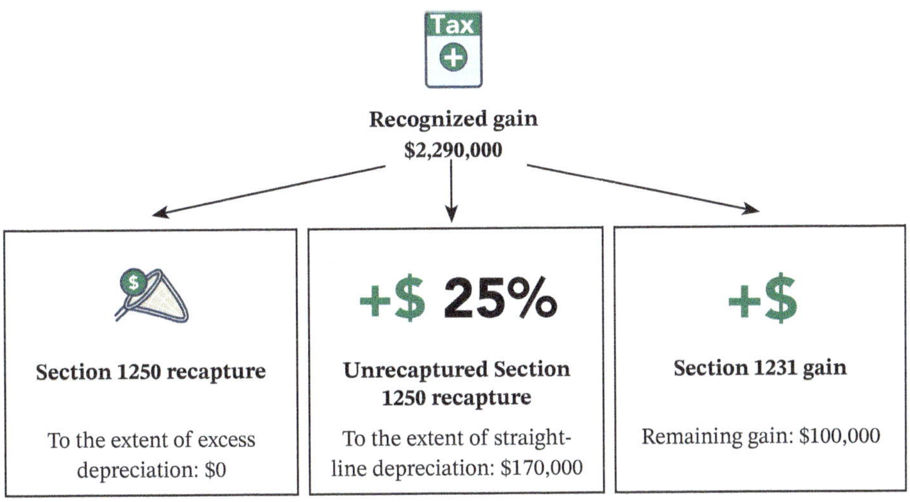

Just as with Section 1245 assets, to the extent that the asset appreciates [$1,400,000 for Thrips in Example 1.4.9 ($2,400,000 − $1,000,000)], the gain will be Section 1231 gain, and the remaining gain will be Section 1250 recapture or unrecaptured Section 1250 gain.

Related exercises: Multiple Choice Questions 17, 18
Application Problem 23
Tax Planning Problem 4

Tax Planning Tip

In contrast to the case for Section 1245 assets, when Section 1250 assets are sold, some of the gain is often taxed as Section 1231 gain. Whereas personal property rarely appreciates in value from its original cost, real property values tend to increase over time. Therefore, with Section 1250, most, if not all, of the gain is taxed either as unrecaptured Section 1250 gain or as Section 1231 gain. It is unusual that any of the gain is taxed as ordinary income, because the only situation for which you may have Section 1250 recapture is for buildings placed in service before 1987.

Evaluating Section 1250 Depreciation Recapture—Corporations For Section 1250 property (buildings) for corporations, the accumulated depreciation claimed in excess of straight-line depreciation is subject to being recaptured as ordinary income, just as with individuals, partnerships, and S corporations. However, the unrecaptured Section 1250 gain rule does *not* apply for corporations. Instead, **Section 291 depreciation recapture** applies and is computed by assuming the property is actually Section 1245 property, as follows:

Section 1245 recapture IF the property had been Section 1245 property
Less: Actual Section 1250 recapture
Excess amount
× 20%
Section 291 recapture

Section 291 recapture for C corporations is in addition to Section 1250 recapture and does not take the place of Section 1250 recapture. Step 5 of the evaluation for determining Section 1250 recapture is thus changed as follows for corporations.

Step 5. **Calculate: The remaining gain is next taxed as Section 291 recapture and is treated as ordinary income**, in addition to any Section 1250 recapture.

EXAMPLE 1.4.10 Sale of a Building—Corporations

Continue with the facts of Example 1.4.8 except that Scorpion is a corporation. Scorpion sells a building that it has used in its business for the last 10 years. Scorpion's cost for the building was $500,000, and accumulated straight-line depreciation is $170,000. Scorpion sells the building for $600,000 in the current year. Assuming Scorpion has no sales of capital assets this year, compute the recognized gain or loss from this sale and determine its character.

SOLUTION

To determine the tax consequences for Scorpion's disposition, we will follow the steps outlined in Illustration 1.12. Steps 1–4 are the same as in Example 1.4.8.

Step 1. First, we calculate the recognized gain or loss from the disposition:

Amount realized	$600,000	
Less: Adjusted basis	(330,000)	[Cost ($500,000) less accumulated depreciation ($170,000)]
Recognized gain	$270,000	

Step 2. Next, we determine if the asset sold is a Section 1250 asset. Scorpion sold a depreciable building held for more than one year, so this is a Section 1250 asset.

Step 3. Now, we calculate any excess depreciation, as follows:

Depreciation claimed	$170,000
Less: Straight-line depreciation	(170,000)
Excess depreciation	$ 0

Step 4. Next, we determine the Section 1250 recapture, which is the *lesser* of:

- the recognized gain ($270,000), *or*
- the excess depreciation ($0).

The lesser amount is $0, so this is the Section 1250 recapture.

Step 5. The remaining gain is next taxed as Section 291 recapture and is treated as ordinary income, in addition to any Section 1250 recapture. If the building had been Section 1245 property, the Section 1245 recapture would have been $170,000, which is the lower of the depreciation claimed of $170,000 or the recognized gain of $270,000. The Section 291 recapture is computed as follows:

Section 1245 recapture IF the property had been Section 1245 property	$170,000
Less: Actual Section 1250 recapture	0
Excess amount	$170,000
× 20%	× 20%
Section 291 recapture	$ 34,000

Step 6. Finally, whatever gain from the disposition that remains (if any) is considered a Section 1231 gain, because the asset was used in a trade or business and was owned for more than a year. It can be calculated as follows:

Recognized gain	$270,000
Less: Section 1250 recapture	(0)
Less: Section 291 recapture	(34,000)
Section 1231 gain	$236,000

The tax consequences of the disposition are summarized in the diagram below:

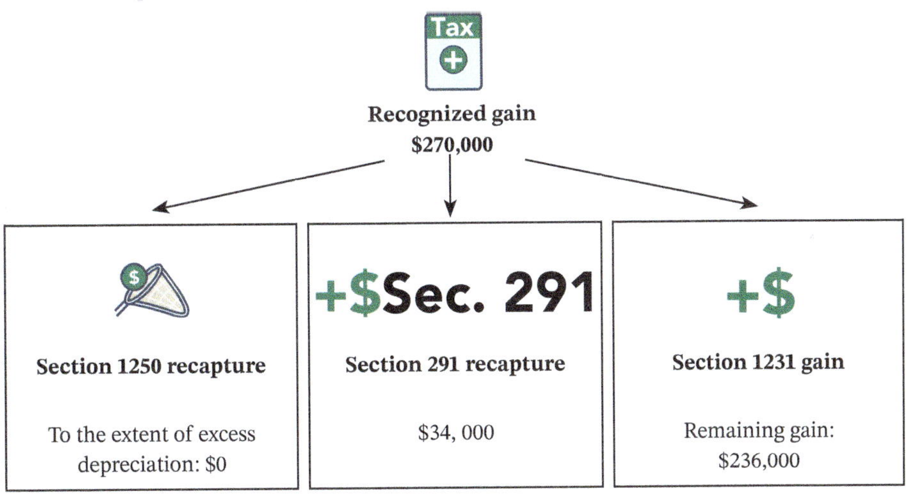

Related exercises: Multiple Choice Question 19
Application Problem 24

Reporting Sales of Business Assets: Form 4797

Business assets that a taxpayer sells or disposes of are reported on Form 4797, Sale of Business Property. The items discussed in this chapter are reported as follows.

- Part I reports Section 1231 gains and losses. For the gain or loss from the sale to be included in Part I, the business asset must have been held for more than one year when sold.
- If the business asset sold was *not* held for more than one year, then the gain or loss is reported in Part II. Part II reports ordinary income and loss from the sale of these assets. Part II also reports the recapture from Section 1245 and Section 1250 assets.
- Section 1245 and Section 1250 assets held for more than one year and sold at a gain are initially reported in Part III on page 2 of Form 4797. The depreciation recapture is reported as ordinary income and is transferred from Part III, Line 31 and included on Part II, Line 13 as ordinary income. The amount of gain taxed as Section 1231 gain is transferred from Part III, Line 32 to Part 1, Line 6.
- Section 1245 and Section 1250 assets sold at a loss are reported in Part I if held for more than one year, and in Part II otherwise.
- Unrecaptured Section 1250 gain is reported on Form 1040, Schedule D, Part III, Line 19.

These reporting rules are summarized in Illustration 1.13.

ILLUSTRATION 1.13 Where to Make First Entry on Form 4797 for Certain Business Gains and Losses

	Held one year or less	Held more than one year
Section 1245 and Section 1250 property:		
Sold at a gain	Part II	Part III
Sold at a loss	Part II	Part I
Land:		
Sold at a gain	Part II	Part I
Sold at a loss	Part II	Part I

Related exercise: Discussion Question 25

Dispositions That Do *Not* Trigger Depreciation Recapture

There are some transactions for which, if there is a sale or disposition of Section 1250 property, the recapture rules do *not* apply. Section 1245 also does not apply to these transactions. In some of these cases, the depreciation recapture potential stays with the property and carries over to the new owner. Examples of such transactions include:

- **Gifts:** recapture potential carries over to the donee
- **Death:** recapture potential is eliminated (does not carry over to the one who inherits the property)
- **Charitable transfers:** recapture potential reduces charitable contribution deduction
- **Certain tax-free exchanges, such as like-kind exchanges and involuntary conversions:** recapture potential carries over to the new owner with the property received in the exchange

Related exercises: Discussion Question 26
Brief Exercise 10
Application Problem 25
Tax Planning Problem 5

PRACTICE PROBLEM 1.4.1
Determining Net Section 1231 Gains and Losses

Pepe sold several assets used in his boat manufacturing business, operated as Pepe Inc., an S corporation. S corporations are flow-through entities, and the shareholders report their share of income and loss items on their tax returns, Pepe is the sole owner of Pepe Inc. Its total gains and losses are:

- Section 1231 gains $5,200
- Section 1231 losses $7,000

Pepe Inc. also sold stock at a loss of $3,500. What are the tax effects of these transactions?

SOLUTION

Pepe Inc. has a net Section 1231 loss of $1,800 ($5,200 gains – $7,000 losses). Net Section 1231 losses are treated as ordinary losses and are fully deductible against other items of income on Pepe's individual tax return as a separately stated flow-through item. The $3,500 stock sale loss is a capital loss because the stock is a capital asset to Pepe Inc. The $3,500 loss will be reported on Pepe's individual tax return as a separately stated flow-through item. Individual taxpayers are limited to a capital loss deduction of $3,000. Pepe will have a capital loss carryforward of $500.

PRACTICE PROBLEM 1.4.2
Applying the Lookback Rule

SEJ Inc. has been operating as a C corporation since Year 1. SEJ has reported the following:

Year 1: No Section 1231 gains or losses
Year 2: $4,500 net Section 1231 gain
Year 3: $8,000 net Section 1231 loss
Year 4: $2,500 net Section 1231 loss
Year 5: $6,000 net Section 1231 gain

In Year 6, SEJ has a net Section 1231 gain of $9,500. How should this gain be taxed to SEJ?

SOLUTION

We need to use the lookback rule for this problem to determine how SEJ's gain in Year 6 would be taxed:

Year 2: $4,500 net Section 1231 gain—treated as a long-term capital gain

Year 3: $8,000 net Section 1231 loss—treated as an ordinary loss

Year 4: $2,500 net Section 1231 loss—treated as an ordinary loss

Year 5: $6,000 net Section 1231 gain—treated as an ordinary gain, due to the $8,000 ordinary loss in Year 3. $2,000 of the loss from Year 3 ($8,000 – $6,000) remains available to recharacterize net Section 1231 gains for future years.

Year 6: $9,500 net Section 1231 gain—treated as an ordinary gain of $4,500 and a long-term capital gain of $5,000. Year 3 has $2,000 of ordinary losses remaining, and Year 4 has a $2,500 loss. The $4,500 combined from Year 3 and Year 4 will be used to partially recharacterize the Year 6 Section 1231 gain.

	Net Section 1231	Ordinary loss	Ordinary income	LTCG gain
Year 2:	$4,500 gain			$4,500
Year 3:	$8,000 loss	$8,000		
Year 4:	$2,500 loss	$2,500		
Year 5:	$6,000 gain		$6,000	
			Recharacterized $6,000 loss from Year 3	
Year 6:	$9,500 gain		$4,500	$5,000
			Recharacterized $2,000 loss from Year 3	
			Recharacterized $2,500 loss from Year 4	

PRACTICE PROBLEM 1.4.3
Sale of Tangible Business-Use Asset

Amara LLC has been a CPA firm since Year 1. In Year 6, Amara sells the office furniture for $10,000. It purchased the office furniture in Year 1 for $15,000 and has taken depreciation expense of $12,000. What is Amara's gain and its character?

SOLUTION

Following the steps outlined in Illustration 1.10 results in the following:

Amount realized	$10,000	
Less: Adjusted basis	(3,000)	[Cost ($15,000) – Accumulated depreciation ($12,000)]
Recognized gain	$ 7,000	

Office furniture is a Section 1245 asset. Section 1245 recapture is the *lesser* of:

Recognized gain	$ 7,000
Accumulated depreciation	$12,000

Thus, all the recognized gain of $7,000 is taxed as ordinary income.

PRACTICE PROBLEM 1.4.4
Sale of Realty by a Partnership

Cayton is a 70% partner in a partnership that owns a two-flat rental apartment building in Wrigleyville, Chicago, which it is selling for $1,200,000 in Year 7. The partnership purchased the building in Year 5 for $850,000 and has taken straight-line depreciation of $92,700. What is the partnership's gain and its character? How much of the gain flows to Cayton?

SOLUTION

We first calculate the recognized gain from the sale:

Amount realized	$1,200,000	
Less: Adjusted basis	(757,300)	[Cost ($850,000) – Accumulated depreciation ($92,700)]
Recognized gain	$ 442,700	

Because straight-line depreciation was taken on the building, there is no Section 1250 recapture. The unrecaptured Section 1250 gain of $92,700 is taxed at a maximum rate of 25%. The remaining $350,000 gain is a Section 1231 gain.

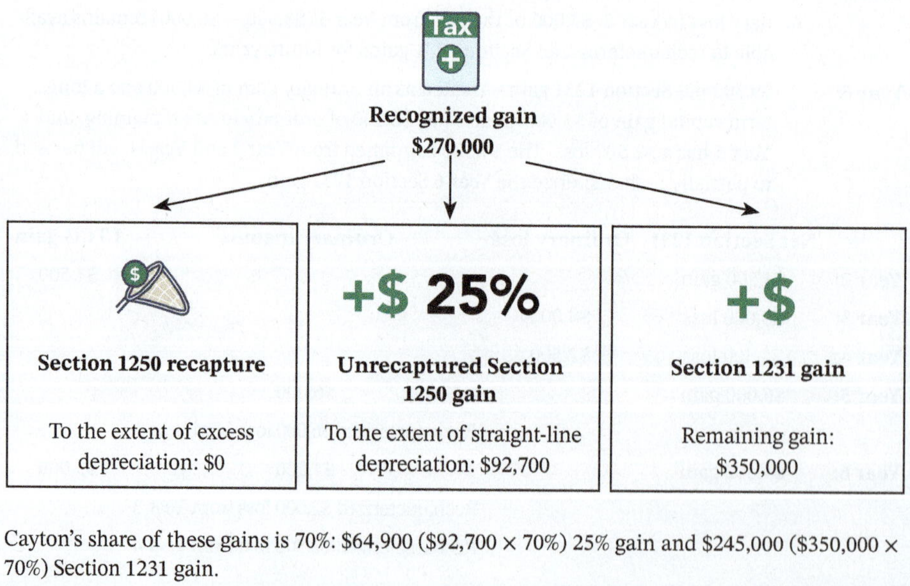

Cayton's share of these gains is 70%: $64,900 ($92,700 × 70%) 25% gain and $245,000 ($350,000 × 70%) Section 1231 gain.

PRACTICE PROBLEM 1.4.5
Sale of Realty by a Corporation

French Corporation purchased a strip mall on March 9, 2022, for $360,000 and sold the building on November 28, 2025, for $520,000. French deducted straight-line depreciation of $33,856 for years 2022–2025. Determine the recognized gain and its character.

SOLUTION

Following the steps outlined in Illustration 1.12 results in the following:

Step 1. First, we calculate the recognized gain or loss from the disposition:

Amount realized	$520,000	
Less: Adjusted basis	(326,144)	($360,000 − $33,856)
Recognized gain	$193,856	

Step 2. Next, we determine if the asset sold is a Section 1250 asset. French sold a depreciable building held for more than one year, so this is a Section 1250 asset.

Step 3. Now, we calculate any excess depreciation, as follows:

Depreciation claimed	$33,856
Less: Straight-line depreciation	(33,856)
Excess depreciation	$ 0

Step 4. Next, we determine the Section 1250 recapture, which is the *lesser* of:

- the recognized gain ($193,856), *or*
- the excess depreciation ($0).

The lesser amount is $0, so this is the Section 1250 recapture.

Step 5. The remaining gain is next taxed as Section 291 recapture and is treated as ordinary income, in addition to any Section 1250 recapture. If the building was Section 1245 property, the Section 1245 recapture would be $33,856, which is the lower of the depreciation claimed of $33,856 or the recognized gain of $193,856. The Section 291 recapture is computed as follows:

Section 1245 recapture IF the property had been Section 1245 property	$33,856
Less: Actual Section 1250 recapture	0
Excess amount	$33,856
× 20%	× 20%
Section 291 recapture	$ 6,771

Step 6. Finally, whatever gain from the disposition that remains (if any) is considered a Section 1231 gain, because the asset was used in a trade or business and was owned for more than a year. It can be calculated as follows:

Recognized gain	$193,856
Less: Section 1250 recapture	(0)
Less: Section 291 recapture	(6,771)
Section 1231 gain	$187,085

INTERACTIVE SELF-SCORING QUIZZES

1.5 Review of Qualified Business Income Deduction

LEARNING OBJECTIVE 5

Compute the qualified business income deduction.

Taxpayers can take advantage of the **qualified business income (QBI) deduction**, which is computed as 20% of the taxpayer's income from flow-through entities (partnerships, limited liability companies, and S corporations) and sole proprietorships. To qualify for the QBI deduction, the taxpayer must generally conduct business activity in the United States.[14]

Why **Why did Congress create the QBI deduction?** Congress created the QBI deduction for tax years after 2017 at the same time it changed the corporate income tax rate to a flat rate of 21%. The highest marginal income tax rate for individuals is 37%, meaning that income from sole proprietorships and flow-through entities taxed on individual returns could be taxed at 37%. On the other hand, business income generated by corporations is now taxed at 21%. This differential of 37% versus 21% seemed inequitable, so Congress created the QBI deduction. If a taxpayer is eligible for the QBI deduction, then only 80% of business income from sole proprietorships and flow-through entities is taxed on individual returns. This lowers the highest marginal tax rate on this income from 37% to 29.6%, reducing the disparity between this effective rate and the corporate rate of 21%.

It is important to note that the QBI deduction is not a deduction for adjusted gross income (AGI), nor is it an itemized deduction. Rather, the tax law provides that the QBI deduction is taken *from* adjusted gross income.

Related exercise: Multiple Choice Question 20

Qualified Business Income

QBI must be derived from a "qualified business," which includes businesses conducted as sole proprietorships and flow-through income from partnerships, limited liability companies, and S corporations. It does *not* include performance of services by an employee, guaranteed payments to a partner, investment income, or payments made to a partner in a capacity other than serving as a partner. It also does not include reasonable compensation paid to an owner or income earned in foreign countries. **Illustration 1.14** summarizes the types of income that qualify for this deduction.

Related exercise: Multiple Choice Question 21

ILLUSTRATION 1.14 Definition of Qualified Business Income

Qualified business income includes:	Qualified business income does *not* include:
Sole proprietorship income	Capital gains and capital losses
Partnership ordinary business income	Dividends
S corporation ordinary business income	Interest income
Rental real estate income if certain conditions are met	Certain other investment items
	Compensation earned by an employee or an owner
	Guaranteed payments made to a partner for services rendered

[14]IRC §199A.

Rental Real Estate

Income from rental real estate activities qualifies for the QBI deduction if the rental activity is a trade or business. We assume the activity is a trade or business if individuals complete at least 250 hours of service activities related to the rental real estate activity each year. Owners do not have to complete the rental services themselves; the 250 hours includes services completed by employees and contractors.[15]
Services included in the 250 hours are:

- Advertising to rent the real estate
- Negotiating and executing leases
- Verifying information in prospective tenant applications
- Collecting rent
- Conducting daily operation, maintenance, and repair
- Managing the real estate
- Purchasing materials
- Supervising employees and contractors

Services *not* included in the 250 hours are:

- Conducting financial or investment management activities
- Studying and reviewing financial statements
- Planning, managing, or constructing long-term capital improvements
- Traveling to and from the real estate

Determining the Qualified Business Income Deduction (Steps 1–5)

We will use **Illustration 1.15** to facilitate your understanding of how to compute the QBI deduction. As you can see in the illustration, there are three limitations that can reduce the QBI deduction. The limitations apply differently depending on whether the taxpayer's modified taxable income places them in Column 1, 2, or 3. Once you identify the proper column for a taxpayer, you will know which limitations apply.

ILLUSTRATION 1.15 QBI Limitations for Married Filing Jointly (MFJ), Married Filing Separately (MFS), and Other Filers (2025)

	COLUMN 1 2025 Modified taxable income	COLUMN 2 2025 Modified taxable income	COLUMN 3 2025 Modified taxable income
Filling status	MFJ: ≤ $394,600 MFS: ≤ $197,300 Other: ≤ $197,300	MFJ: > $394,600 and < $494,600 MFS: > $197,300 and < $247,300 Other: > $197,300 and < $247,300	MFJ: ≥ $494,600 MFS: ≥ $247,300 Other: ≥ $247,300
Wage/property limitation	Limitations does not apply	Limitations phased in; partially applies	Wage limitation fully phased in
Specified services limitation	Limitations does not apply; QBI deduction allowed	QBI deduction partially allowed	QBI deduction not allowed
20% of Taxable income limitation applies?	Yes	Yes	Yes

[15]Rev. Proc. 2019-38, 2019-42 IRB 942.

There are eight steps in determining the qualified business income deduction. The first five steps are as follows:

Step 1. **Compute: The qualified business income.** In general, the QBI is the owner's share of the net income from a business. To compute the qualified business income, you must first reduce the activity's taxable income by each of the following:

- 50% of the self-employment tax
- The self-employed health insurance deduction
- Any retirement plan contributions based on this income[16]

Related exercises: Brief Exercise 11
Application Problem 26

Step 2. **Calculate: The QBI deduction.** To calculate the QBI deduction before any limitations, the computation is:

$$\text{QBI} \times 20\% = \text{QBI deduction}$$

> **Potential Pitfall**
>
> The tax law usually affords architects and engineers the tax provisions that apply to those performing professional services. However, Congress did not include services performed by architects and engineers as a specified service trade or business, so architects and engineers are not subject to the same limitations on their QBI deduction as the professions listed.

Step 3. **Calculate: The taxpayer's modified taxable income.** The taxpayer's **modified taxable income (MTI)** is taxable income *before* the QBI deduction.

Step 4. **Ask: Is the trade or business a specified service trade or business?** If the answer is NO, then you can proceed to step 6. If the answer is YES, then whether the QBI deduction is limited will be determined in step 5. The business is a **specified service trade or business** if the owners perform services in the fields of:

- health
- law
- accounting
- actuarial sciences
- performing arts
- consulting
- athletics
- financial services
- brokerage services
- any business where the principal asset is the reputation of an employee or owner.

Illustration 1.16 summarizes the types of businesses Congress included as specified services.

Related exercises: Discussion Question 27
Multiple Choice Question 22

ILLUSTRATION 1.16 Specified Service Trades or Businesses

Specified service trades or businesses include any trade or business whose principal asset is the reputation of one or more of its employees or owners:

Health	Law	Accounting
Actuarial science	Performing arts	Consulting
Athletics	Financial services*	Brokerage services*

*Financial service and brokerage services include and investment management and trading or dealing in securities, partnerships interests, or commodities.

Illustration 1.17a provides a flowchart for all eight steps used to determine the QBI deduction, while **Illustrations 1.17b** and **1.17c** show details for steps 5 and 6.

[16]QBI from a particular activity is reduced by these items only to the extent that the individual's gross income from the trade or business activity is taken into account in calculating the allowable deduction, on a proportionate basis to the gross income received from the trade or business activity (see Treas. Reg. §1.199A-3(b)(1)(vi)).

ILLUSTRATION 1.17A Flowchart for QBI Deduction Computation

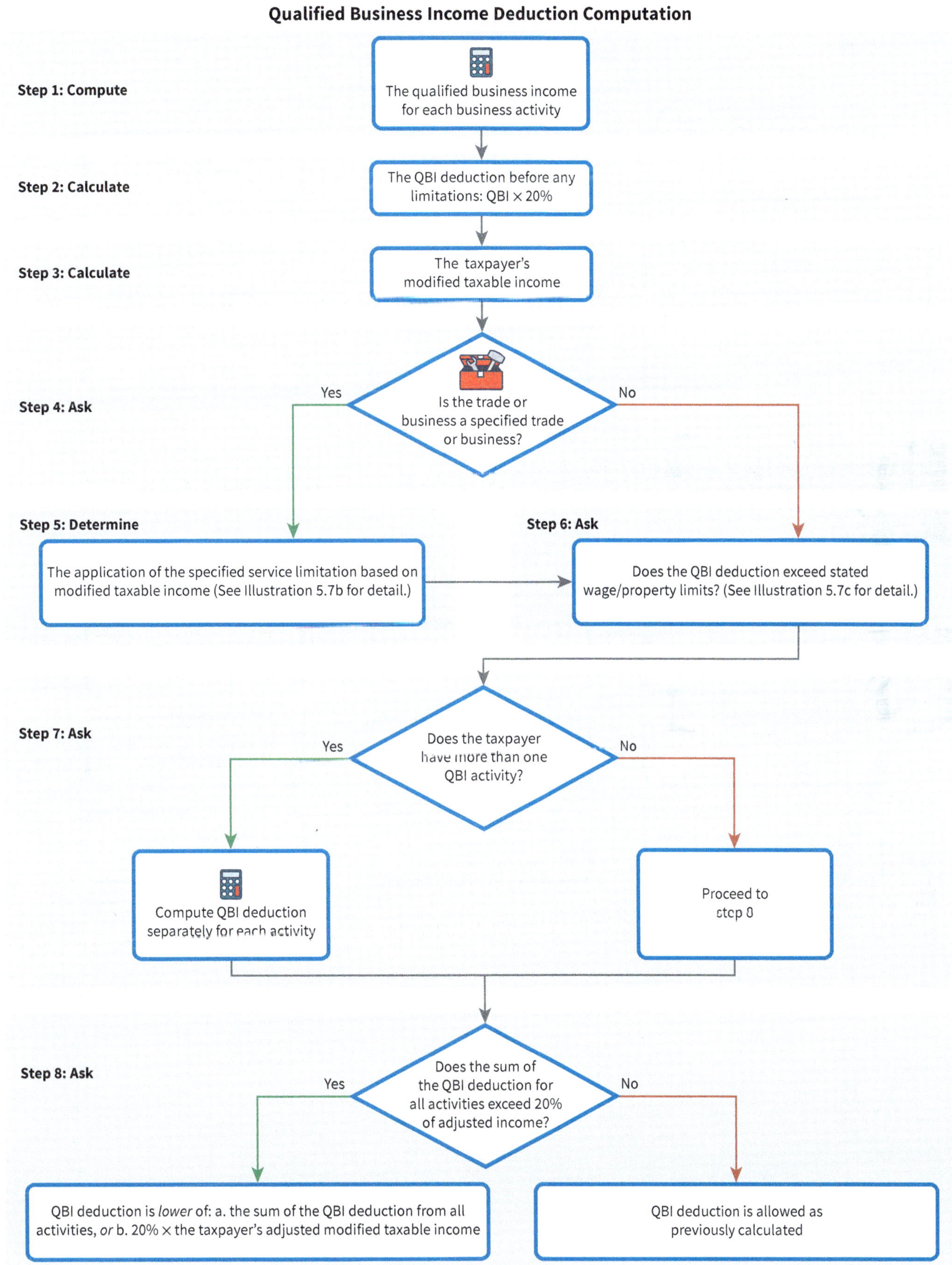

ILLUSTRATION 1.17B Detail for Step 5 for QBI Deduction Computation

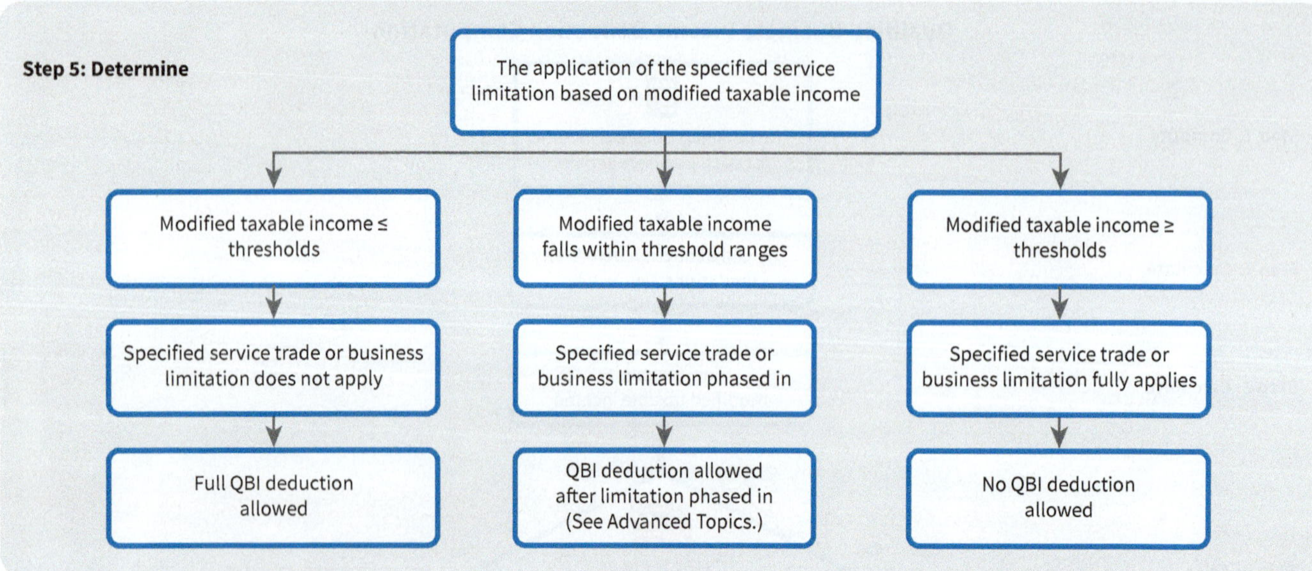

ILLUSTRATION 1.17C Detail for Step 6 for QBI Deduction Computation

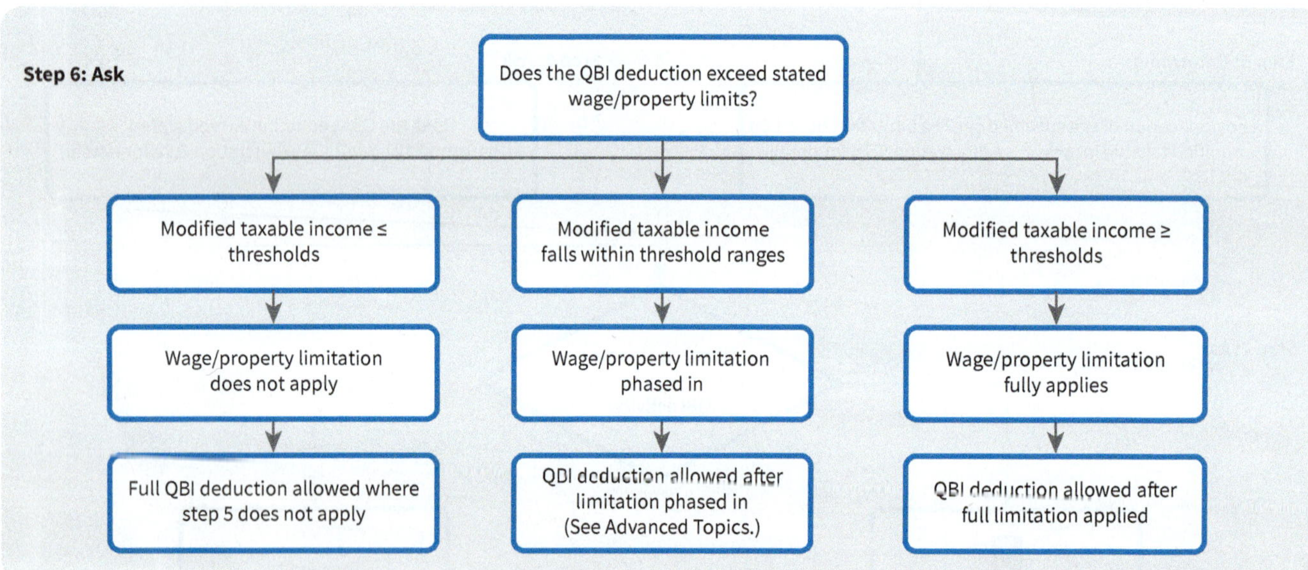

Step 5. Determine: The application of the specified service limitation based on the taxpayer's modified taxable income. (*Refer to Illustrations 1.15 and 1.17b for this step.*) Once you have calculated the taxpayer's modified taxable income (step 3) and answered step 4 as YES, limitation of the QBI deduction falls into one of three cases:

Case 1: The limitation described in step 4 does *not* apply to specified service trades or businesses if the modified taxable income of the taxpayer is *less than or equal to* the following thresholds (2025) (see Column 1 in Illustration 1.15):

Married filing jointly	$394,600
Married filing separately	$197,300
Other	$197,300

Case 2: If modified taxable income of the taxpayer falls into the range (2025) shown in Column 2 of Illustration 1.15:

Married filing jointly	> $394,600 and < $494,600 ($100,000 range)
Married filing separately	> $197,300 and < $247,300 ($50,000 range)
Other	> $197,300 and < $247,300 ($50,000 range)

and the QBI is from a specified service trade or business, then the computation of the QBI deduction is very complex and is discussed as an Advanced Topic at the end of this section.

Case 3: If the modified taxable income of the taxpayer *equals or exceeds* the thresholds (2025) shown below (see Column 3 in Illustration 1.15):

Married filing jointly	$494,600
Married filing separately	$247,300
Other	$247,300

and the QBI is from a specified service trade or business, then the QBI deduction is $0.

Before we proceed with the last three steps in determining the qualified business income deduction, let's look at some Examples of how the first five steps would apply in real-world situations.

EXAMPLE 1.5.1
QBI Deduction for Case 1 Scenarios

Marcos is single and owns a sole proprietorship that provides financial consulting, which is a specified service trade or business. For 2025, his QBI from the business is $150,000 and his modified taxable income is $159,200. Calculate his QBI deduction.

SOLUTION

Financial consulting is a specified trade or business. However, Marcos's modified taxable income is less than $197,300, so the limitation for specified service trades or businesses does not apply. His QBI deduction is calculated as follows:

QBI × 20% = QBI deduction

$150,000 × 20% = $30,000

Related exercises: Multiple Choice Question 23
Application Problem 27

EXAMPLE 1.5.2
QBI Deduction for Case 3 Scenarios

Assume the same facts as in Example 1.5.1, except that Marcos's modified taxable income is $250,000. Calculate his QBI deduction.

SOLUTION

Marcos's new modified taxable income amount places him into a Case 3 situation (the amount exceeds $247,300). Because of this, and the fact that his income is from a specified service trade or business, his QBI deduction amount would now be $0.

Illustration 1.18 summarizes the previous two Examples and shows how the specified service limitation applies in each of the three columns in Illustration 1.13 for a taxpayer who files as married filing jointly.

ILLUSTRATION 1.18 Specified Service Limitation for Married Filing Jointly

Modified Taxable Income		
$0	$394,600	$494,600
Full QBI deduction allowed	QBI deduction phased out	QBI deduction is $0
Column 1 (Case 1)	Column 2 (Case 2)	Column 3 (Case 3)
(Example 1.5.1)	(See Advanced Topics)	(Example 1.5.2)

Why **Why is the QBI deduction limited for specified service trades or businesses?** The tax law does not permit a QBI deduction for wages paid to an employee. The daily activities and responsibilities of those who deliver professional services through their own business look very similar to the activities of employees who work in their profession. For example, when you visit your medical doctor and she provides health services to you, her actions will appear the same whether she owns her own healthcare facility, or she is an employee of a facility. Therefore, Congress decided to limit the QBI deduction for those rendering specified services, but only if their modified taxable income exceeds certain thresholds. If your medical doctor's modified taxable income places her in step 5, Case 1, and she provides services through her sole proprietorship or flow-through entity, she will receive the full QBI deduction.

Determining the Qualified Business Income Deduction (Steps 6–7)

We'll now review the next two steps needed to determine the qualified business income deduction. Step 6 is summarized in **Illustration 1.17c**.

Step 6. **Ask: Does the QBI deduction exceed stated wage/property limits?** The second limitation on the QBI deduction is that the amount of the deduction cannot exceed the *greater* of:

1. 50% of the taxpayer's share of the W-2 wages paid by the business, *or*
2. 25% of the taxpayer's share of the W-2 wages paid by the business, plus 2.5% of the *unadjusted basis* of qualified property.

Potential Pitfall

Because the formula uses *unadjusted* basis, do not reduce the basis of the asset by depreciation, including bonus depreciation, when applying this formula.

Qualified property for QBI is tangible property subject to depreciation that the taxpayer used in the production of QBI. Taxpayers can include assets in this computation until the end of their depreciable life or 10 years, whichever is later.

The wage/property limitation is subject to the same conditions as Cases 1–3 in step 5:

Case 1: The wages/property limitation described in step 6 does *not* apply to taxpayers with modified taxable income *less than or equal to* the thresholds (2025) shown below (see Column 1 in Illustration 1.15):

Married filing jointly	\$394,600
Married filing separately	\$197,300
Other	\$197,300

Case 2: If modified taxable income of the taxpayer falls into the range (2025) shown in Column 2 of Illustration 1.15:

Married filing jointly	> \$394,600 and < \$494,600 (\$100,000 range)
Married filing separately	> \$197,300 and < \$247,300 (\$50,000 range)
Other	> \$197,300 and < \$247,300 (\$50,000 range)

the computation of the QBI deduction in this scenario is very complex and is discussed as an Advanced Topic at the end of this section.

Case 3: If the modified taxable income of the taxpayer *equals or exceeds* the thresholds (2025) shown below (see Column 3 in Illustration 1.15):

Married filing jointly	\$494,600
Married filing separately	\$247,300
Other	\$247,300

then the wage/property limitation fully applies.

Step 7. Ask: Does the taxpayer have more than one QBI activity? If so, compute the QBI deduction separately for each activity using the limitations discussed in steps 4–6.

Let's now look at some Examples of how steps 6 and 7 in determining the qualified business income deduction might apply in real-world situations.

EXAMPLE 1.5.3 Qualified Property

Denzel operates a sole proprietorship for which he purchased 7-year equipment this year at a cost of \$80,000. How should this equipment be considered when he calculates his QBI deduction?

SOLUTION

Denzel will include the full \$80,000 cost in the QBI wage/asset limitation computation for the next 10 years. After 10 years, he will not include any of this asset's cost in the computation.

EXAMPLE 1.5.4 Wage/Property Limitation for Case 1 Scenario

Una, a married taxpayer, operates a sole proprietorship selling outdoor supplies. She has one employee who is paid \$40,000 per year. During 2025, the taxable income of the business is \$120,000. Una's unadjusted basis in qualified property is \$100,000. Una and her spouse's tax return for the year reports modified taxable income of \$300,000. Compute Una's QBI deduction.

SOLUTION

Because Una and her spouse's taxable income does not exceed the threshold of \$394,600 for married filing jointly, the wage/property limitation does not apply in this situation. Una's QBI deduction is computed as follows:

$$\$120{,}000 \times 20\% = \$24{,}000$$

EXAMPLE 1.5.5 Wage/Property Limitation for Case 3 Scenario

Assume the same facts as in Example 1.5.4 except Una and her spouse's modified taxable income is $500,000. Calculate Una's QBI deduction.

SOLUTION

Because the couple's taxable income places them in a Case 3 scenario, the wage/property limitation fully applies and is the *greater* of:

1. 50% of the taxpayer's share of the W-2 wages paid by the business ($40,000), or $20,000 in this case, *or*
2. 25% of the taxpayer's share of the W-2 wages paid by the business ($40,000), plus 2.5% of the *unadjusted basis* of qualified property ($100,000). In this case:

$$(25\% \times \$40{,}000) + (2.5\% \times \$100{,}000) = \$10{,}000 + \$2{,}500 = \$12{,}500$$

Una's QBI deduction is then computed as the *lower* of:

- $120,000 × 20% = $24,000 *or*
- wage/property limitation of $20,000.

Una's QBI deduction is $20,000.

Why **Why does the wage/property limitation rule exist?** As mentioned previously, one reason Congress created the QBI deduction was to better align the top marginal rate on business income from corporations and other business forms. One important goal of Congress is to provide tax laws that incentivize job creation. Legislators want to provide the QBI deduction for higher-income taxpayers only if they are maintaining or creating jobs. Thus, the law limits the QBI deduction to a certain percentage of the W-2 wages paid to employees. Congress also included qualified property in the limitation for businesses that rely more on assets than on employees for their business activity, because the purchase of new assets also stimulates economic growth.

Determining the Qualified Business Income Deduction (Step 8)

The last step of the QBI computation is to apply the third limitation for the QBI deduction.

Step 8. **Ask: Does the sum of the QBI deduction for all activities exceed 20% of *adjusted* modified taxable income?** As shown in the last row of Illustration 1.15, this overall limitation applies to all modified taxable income levels (Columns 1, 2, and 3). Whether there is one QBI activity or more than one, the total QBI deduction reported on the tax return from all QBI activities cannot exceed 20% of the taxpayer's *adjusted* modified taxable income, computed as:

Modified taxable income
Less: Net capital gain
Less: Qualified dividend income
Adjusted modified taxable income

The QBI deduction is the *lower* of:

a. the sum of the QBI deduction from all activities, *or*
b. 20% × the taxpayer's adjusted modified taxable income.

Net positive QBI deductions that are limited because there is not sufficient *adjusted* modified taxable income cannot be carried forward to future years.

What happens if some QBI activities have a loss? If the net QBI deduction from all activities is negative, this net negative QBI deduction is carried forward to future years.[17]

The next two Examples demonstrate the application of Step 8.

EXAMPLE 1.5.6
Overall QBI Limitation—Scenario #1

Assume the same facts as in Example 1.5.1, except that Marcos has modified taxable income of $140,000. Calculate his QBI deduction.

SOLUTION

His QBI deduction will be $28,000, the *lower* of:

- $150,000 × 20% = $30,000, *or*
- $140,000 × 20% = $28,000

Related exercises: Brief Exercise 12
Application Problems 28, 29, 30

EXAMPLE 1.5.7
Overall QBI Limitation—Scenario #2

Fynn and Sarah are married, and their modified taxable income is $300,000. This amount includes $50,000 of net capital gains and $5,000 of qualified dividend income. They have qualified business income or losses from two separate businesses.

The QBI and QBI deduction for each activity, after considering the wage limitation and the specified service limitation, is:

	QBI	QBI deduction
• Partnership A	$156,000	$31,200
• S Corporation B	$104,000	$20,800

Calculate their QBI deduction.

SOLUTION

Their QBI deduction for the year before considering the overall limitation is $52,000 ($31,200 + $20,800). They must limit the deduction to 20% of *adjusted* modified taxable income:

Modified taxable income	$300,000
Less: Net capital gains	(50,000)
Less: Qualified dividend income	(5,000)
Adjusted modified taxable income	$245,000
× 20%	× 20%
Overall limitation	$ 49,000

We must limit their QBI deduction to $49,000. The $3,000 potential QBI deduction that is disallowed ($52,000 – $49,000) cannot be carried forward to future years.

Related exercise: Application Problem 31

[17]In some circumstances, a taxpayer can elect to aggregate businesses, which may result in increasing the QBI deduction. This topic is beyond the complexity level of this book.

Advanced Topics—Drilling Down

QBI Losses

If a QBI activity has a loss, the way we handle it depends on whether there are also QBI activities with income.

- If a QBI activity has a loss and there are no QBI activities with net income, the loss is carried forward and reduces QBI income in future years.
- If a QBI activity has a loss and there is one QBI activity with net income, we net the income and losses from the QBI activities.
- If a QBI activity has a loss and there is more than one activity with a gain, the activity with the loss must be allocated against the activities with income, in proportion to their positive QBI.

EXAMPLE 1.5.8
Overall QBI Limitation

Assume the same facts as in Example 1.5.7 except S Corporation B now has a loss of ($70,000) and modified taxable income is $200,000.

	QBI
• Partnership A	$156,000
• S Corporation B	($ 70,000)

Calculate the QBI deduction.

SOLUTION

The net QBI income for Partnership A is $86,000 ($156,000 − $70,000) after reduction for the loss from S Corporation B. Now the QBI deduction for both entities combined is $86,000 × 20% = $17,200. We must limit this amount to 20% of *adjusted* modified taxable income:

Modified taxable income	$200,000
Less: Net capital gains	(50,000)
Less: Qualified dividend income	(5,000)
Adjusted modified taxable income	$145,000
× 20%	× 20%
Overall limitation	$ 29,000

The 20% overall limitation is greater than $17,200, so the full $17,200 can be taken as the QBI deduction.

Related exercise: Tax Planning Problem 6

Phase-In of QBI Limitations

Let's return to Case 2 in steps 5 and 6. If a taxpayer is in Column 2 of Illustration 1.15, meaning that the specified service limitation and the wage/property limitation are being phased in, then the computation of QBI is very complicated. Case 2 applies when the modified taxable income of the taxpayer falls into the range (2025) shown in Column 2 of Illustration 1.15:

Married filing jointly	> $394,600 and < $494,600 ($100,000 range)
Married filing separately	> $197,300 and < $247,300 ($50,000 range)
Other	> $197,300 and < $247,300 ($50,000 range)

We use the following process in this computation:

1. If a taxpayer has qualified business income from a specified service trade or business, the taxpayer includes only the applicable percentage of QBI and adjusts the components of the wage/property limitation by the applicable percentage, as follows:
   a. *Determine the applicable percentage.*

      Applicable percentage =

      $$100\% - \frac{\text{Taxable income before the QBI deduction} - \text{Applicable threshold}}{\$100{,}000\ (\text{MFJ})\ \text{or}\ \$50{,}000\ (\text{Others})}$$

   b. *Determine reduced components of QBI deduction.* This can be determined as follows:
      1. 20% × QBI × applicable percentage
      2. Reduced components of the wage/property limitation are as follows, but not to exceed the greater of:
         - 50% × wages × applicable percentage, *or*
         - (25% × wages) + (2.5% × unadjusted basis of qualified property) × applicable percentage

      Note: If the specified service limitation does *not* apply, then the amounts do *not* have to be reduced by the applicable percentage.
2. If the taxpayer is in Column 2 of Illustration 1.15 and the wage/property limitation is reducing the deduction, the general QBI deduction is used, but reduced as follows:
   a. Determine the excess between the general 20% QBI deduction as reduced in 1b above and the full wage/property limitation.
   b. Determine the reduction ratio:

      $$\frac{\text{Taxable income before the QBI deduction} - \text{Applicable threshold}}{\$100{,}000\ (\text{MFJ})\ \text{or}\ \$50{,}000\ (\text{Others})}$$

   c. Determine the reduction in the wage/property limitation:

      Excess from part 2a × Reduction ratio from part 2b
3. Determine the final QBI deduction amount:

   General 20% QBI deduction amount from 1b

   Less: Reduction from 2c

   Final QBI amount
4. The final QBI deduction cannot exceed 20% × modified taxable income.

The next three Examples demonstrate the computation of QBI when the limitations are being phased in as follows:

	Specified service limitation applies?	**Wage/property limitation applies?**
Example 1.5.9	Yes	No
Example 1.5.10	No	Yes
Example 1.5.11	Yes	Yes

EXAMPLE 1.5.9
QBI Deduction for Column 2 Scenario with Specified Service Limitation

Rhys is a physician who files as married filing jointly in 2025. He and his wife have QBI of $380,000 from his medical practice and modified taxable income of $427,000. Rhys pays $300,000 of W-2 wages, so the wage/property limitation does not apply because the QBI deduction does not exceed 50% of W-2 wages. Calculate Rhys's QBI deduction.

SOLUTION

Rhys's modified taxable income falls into the range (2025) shown in Column 2 of Illustration 1.15:

Married filing jointly > \$394,600 and < \$494,600

This means that the specified service and wage/property limitations potentially need to be phased in. Therefore, the QBI deduction is computed as follows:

1. Because Rhys has qualified business income from a specified service trade or business, he includes only the *applicable percentage* of QBI and adjusts the components of the wages/property limitation by the applicable percentage, as follows:

   a. *Determine the applicable percentage.*

   Applicable percentage =

   $$100\% - \frac{\text{Taxable income before the QBI deduction} - \text{Applicable threshold}}{\$100{,}000\ (\text{MFJ})\ \text{or}\ \$50{,}000\ (\text{Others})}$$

   In Rhys's example, because he is in a specified service trade or business:

   $$\text{Applicable percentage} = 100\% - \frac{\$427{,}000 - \$394{,}600}{\$100{,}000} = 67.6\%$$

   b. *Determine reduced components of QBI deduction.* Because Rhys is in a specified service trade or business, the QBI deduction amount needs to be reduced by the applicable percentage.

   1. 20% × QBI × applicable percentage = 20% × \$380,000 × 67.6% = \$51,376
   2. Reduced components of the wage/property limitation are as follows, but not to exceed the *greater* of:
      - 50% × wages (\$300,000) × applicable percentage = \$150,000 × 67.6% = \$101,400, *or*
      - [25% × wages (\$300,000)] + [2.5% × unadjusted basis of qualified property (\$0)] × 67.6% = \$50,700

   Rhys's reduced QBI deduction is \$51,376. Rhys's reduced wage/property limitation is \$101,400.

2. If a taxpayer is in Column 2 of Illustration 1.15 and the wage/property limitation is reducing the deduction, the general QBI deduction is used, but reduced using a formula. Here, though, the wage/property limitation is not reducing Rhys's QBI deduction, so this part of the process is not used.

3. We can determine Rhys's final QBI deduction amount as follows:

General 20% QBI deduction amount from 1b	\$51,376
Less: Reduction from 2	(0)
Final QBI amount	\$51,376

4. Finally, we check whether Rhys's final QBI deduction of \$51,376 exceeds 20% × modified taxable income (\$427,000), or \$85,400. As it does not, Rhys's final QBI amount remains \$51,376.

EXAMPLE 1.5.10 QBI Deduction for Column 2 Scenario with Wage/Property Limitations

Continuing with the facts from Example 1.5.4, Una, a married taxpayer, operates a sole proprietorship selling outdoor supplies. She has one employee who is paid \$40,000 per year. During 2025, the taxable income of the business is \$120,000. Una's unadjusted basis in qualified property is \$100,000. Una and her spouse's tax return for the year reports modified taxable income of \$397,000. Determine Una's QBI deduction.

SOLUTION

The specified service limitation does *not* apply to Una. Una's modified taxable income falls into the range (2025) shown in Column 2 of Illustration 1.15:

Married filing jointly > $394,600 and < $494,600

This means that the specified service and wage/property limitations potentially need to be phased in. Therefore, the QBI deduction is determined as follows:

1. No reduction is necessary for this step because Una is *not* operating a specified trade or business, so the applicable percentage is not used to reduce the amounts.

   QBI deduction = 20% × QBI = 20% × $120,000 = $24,000

2. Because Una is in Column 2 and the wage/property limitation is reducing the deduction, the general QBI deduction is used, but reduced as follows:
   a. Determine the excess between Una's general 20% QBI deduction as shown in 1 above ($24,000) and her full wage/property limitation ($20,000): $4,000 ($24,000 – $20,000). (Shown in Example 1.5.5)
   b. Determine Una's reduction ratio:

   $$\frac{\text{Taxable income before the QBI deduction} - \text{Applicable threshold}}{\$100{,}000 \text{ (MFJ) or } \$50{,}000 \text{ (Others)}}$$

   $$\frac{(\$397{,}000 - \$394{,}600)}{\$100{,}000} = 2.4\%$$

   c. Determine the reduction in Una's wage/property limitation:

   Excess from part 2a ($4,000) × Reduction ratio from part 2b (2.4%) = $96

3. We can determine Una's final QBI deduction amount as follows:

General 20% QBI deduction amount from 1	$24,000
Less: Reduction from 2c	(96)
Final QBI amount	$23,904

4. Finally, we check whether UNA's final QBI deduction of $23,904 exceeds 20% × modified taxable income ($397,000), or $79,400. Because it does not, Una's final QBI amount remains $23,904

EXAMPLE 1.5.11 QBI Deduction for Column 2 Scenario with Specified Service and Wage/Property Limitations

Next, we continue with facts similar to those from Example 1.5.10, except that Una, a married taxpayer, is an attorney and operates a sole proprietorship providing legal services. She has one employee, who is paid $40,000 per year. During 2025, the taxable income of the business is $120,000. Una's unadjusted basis in qualified property is $100,000. Una and her spouse's tax return for the year reports modified taxable income of $397,000. Calculate Una's QBI deduction.

SOLUTION

The specified service limitation now applies because Una is providing legal services. Una's modified taxable income falls into the range (2025) shown in Column 2 of Illustration 1.15:

Married filing jointly > $394,600 and < $494,600

This means that the specified services and wage/property limitations potentially need to be phased in. Therefore, the QBI deduction is computed as follows:

1. Because Una has qualified business income from a specified service trade or business, she includes only the *applicable percentage* of QBI and adjusts the components of the wage/property limitation by the applicable percentage, as follows:

   a. *Determine the applicable percentage.*

   Applicable percentage =

   $$100\% - \frac{\text{Taxable income before the QBI deduction} - \text{Applicable threshold}}{\$100{,}000\ \text{(MFJ) or } \$50{,}000\ \text{(Others)}}$$

   In Una's example, because she is in a specified service trade or business:

   $$\text{Applicable percentage} = \frac{100\% - \$397{,}000 - \$394{,}600}{\$100{,}000 = 97.6\%}$$

   b. *Determine reduced components QBI deduction.* Because Una is in a specified service trade or business, the QBI deduction amount needs to be reduced by the applicable percentage.

      1. 20% × QBI × Applicable percentage = 20% × \$120,000 × 97.6% = \$23,424
      2. Reduced components of the wage/property limitation are as follows, but not to exceed the *greater* of:
         - 50% × wages (\$40,000) × applicable percentage = \$20,000 × 97.6% = \$19,520, *or*
         - [25% × wages (\$40,000)] + [2.5% × unadjusted basis of qualified property (\$100,000)] × 97.6% = \$12,200

   Una's reduced QBI deduction is \$23,424 after reduction for the specified service limitation. The reduced wage/property limitation is \$19,520.

2. Because Una is in Column 2 and the wage/property limitation is reducing the deduction, the general QBI deduction is used, but reduced as follows:

   a. Determine the excess between the general 20% QBI deduction as reduced in 1b1 above (\$23,424) and the full wage/property limitation as reduced in 1b2 (\$19,520): \$3,904 (\$23,424 – \$19,520).

   b. Determine Una's reduction ratio:

   $$\frac{\text{Taxable income before the QBI deduction} - \text{Applicable threshold}}{\$100{,}000\ \text{(MFJ) or } \$50{,}000\ \text{(Others)}}$$

   $$\frac{(\$397{,}000 - \$394{,}600)}{\$100{,}000} = 2.4\%$$

   c. Determine the reduction in Una's wage/property limitation:

   Excess from part 2a (\$3,904) × Reduction ratio (2.4%) = \$94

3. We can determine UNA's final QBI deduction amount as follows:

General 20% QBI deduction amount from 1b	\$23,424
Less: Reduction from 2c	(94)
Final QBI amount	\$23,330

4. Finally, we check whether Una's final QBI deduction of \$23,300 exceeds 20% × modified taxable income (\$397,000), or \$79,400. Because it does not, Una's final QBI amount remains \$23,330.

Related exercise: Application Problem 32

PRACTICE PROBLEM 1.5.1
Calculating Qualified Business Income 1

Chih-Chen owns a bicycle and repair shop as a sole proprietorship and has net revenue from operations of $57,000. What is her qualified business income? Assume that her deduction for self-employment tax is $4,027.

SOLUTION

Chih-Chen is allowed a self-employment tax deduction for adjusted gross income of $4,027. (The self-employment tax deduction is calculated as follows: $57,000 × 0.9235 × 0.153 × 50%.) Therefore, Chih-Chen's qualified business income is $57,000 – $4,027, or $52,973.

PRACTICE PROBLEM 1.5.2
Calculating Qualified Business Income 2

Novak is a single taxpayer who owns and operates a sporting goods store. He has no employees. In 2025, he reported qualified business income from the store of $98,000 and AGI of $105,000. He has no itemized deductions and claims the standard deduction of $15,000 on his 2025 Form 1040. What is Novak's qualified business income deduction?

SOLUTION

Novak's modified taxable income can be calculated as follows:

AGI – Standard deduction = Modified taxable income
$105,000 – $15,000 = $90,000

His QBI deduction can then be calculated as the *lower* of:

- 20% × QBI = 20% × $98,000 = $19,600, *or*
- 20% × adjusted modified taxable income = 20% × $90,000 = $18,000.

In this case, Novak's qualified business income deduction would be $18,000.

INTERACTIVE SELF-SCORING QUIZZES

Review and Practice

Chapter Summary

The income tax rules for business entities are similar to the income tax rules for individuals in the context of income, deductions, and property transactions. But there are also significant differences. We began this introductory chapter by providing the foundational principles for income taxation. We then discussed the business lifecycle. We followed with a discussion of the compliance responsibilities of all tax professionals. Finally, we reviewed the principles of income, deductions, and property transactions that are critical to your understanding of the material presented for business entities.

1 Understand how income tax rules apply to various business entities.

- For the income taxation of business entities, the composition of the topics you will learn is very different from that for the taxation of individuals.
- The taxation of income and deduction transactions during the year comprises approximately 20% or less of the tax law for business entities. The remaining 80% relates to transactions that occur the lifecycle of the business.
- The lifecycle has four main stages: the formation of the entity, the taxation of the operations of the business, the distribution of profits to the owners, and the dissolution of the business.

2 Understand the compliance requirements for business entities.

- Corporate tax returns (other than those with a June 30 year-end) are due three and one-half months after the end of the tax year, which is April 15 for calendar-year corporations. All business entities use the same form to request an extension of time to file the return, Form 7004, Application for Automatic Extension of Time to File Certain Business Income Tax, Information, and Other Returns. Corporations can request an extension of six months to file the tax return. The extension of time, though, is only to *file the return*. The taxpayer must pay the taxes due for the year by the original due date or the IRS will assess a late payment penalty. Corporate tax returns with a June 30 year-end are due two and one-half months after the end of the year, which is September 15. The extended due date is seven months after the due date, which is April 15 of the next year.
- Partnership tax returns and S corporation tax returns are due two and one-half months after the end of the tax year, which is March 15 for a calendar-year business. Extensions for partnerships and S corporations are for six months, which is September 15 for a calendar-year business.
- The primary **statute of limitations** runs for three years from the later of the due date of the tax return or the date the return is filed.
- There are four major tax penalties that corporations may have to pay. First, a penalty is imposed if the taxpayer fails to file a required tax return on time (failure to file). Second, a penalty is imposed if the taxpayer fails to make adequate tax payments during the year (underpayment of estimated tax). Third, a penalty is imposed if the taxpayer fails to pay the tax reflected on the tax return by the due date (failure to pay). Finally, a penalty is imposed if the taxpayer files an inaccurate tax return (accuracy penalty).
- S corporations must pay a penalty equal to $255 (2025) per shareholder for each month, or part of a month, that the return is late. The penalty is assessed for no more than 12 months. Partnerships must pay a penalty equal to $255 (2025) per partner for each month, or part of a month, that the return is late. The penalty is assessed for no more than 12 months.

3 Understand the fundamental rules for property transactions that apply to the taxation of business entities.

- You must compute a **realized gain or loss** every time there is a **sale or disposition** of property. The gain or loss may be either **recognized** and included in taxable income, **deferred**, or **excluded**. A taxpayer must recognize all realized gains and losses unless a tax law provides otherwise.
- The basis of the asset received is the same as the basis in the asset transferred to the extent that the taxpayer defers the realized gain or loss. For fully taxable transactions, the basis in the asset received is always the property's fair market value.
- For a tax-deferred transaction, the **holding period** of property received always includes the holding period of the property transferred. For a fully taxable transaction, the holding period of property received never includes the holding period of the property transferred.
- Realized losses from the sale or disposition of an asset between related parties cannot be recognized. The term **related party** includes the following family members: spouse, children, grandchildren/other descendants, parents, grandparents/other ancestors, and brothers and sisters. Aunts, uncles, and cousins are not related parties, and neither are in-laws. The related-party loss rules apply to many situations other than sales between family members. The definition of *related party* includes relationships between individuals and business entities, and between certain business entities.
- Every asset can be classified as:
  - either an **ordinary asset**, a **Section 1231 asset**, or a **capital asset**; *and*
  - either **personalty** or **realty**.

4 Determine the tax consequences of disposing of Section 1231 assets.

- A **Section 1231 asset** is an asset used in a trade or business and held for over one year (long-term). An **ordinary asset** is one that is used in a trade or business and that produces ordinary income or loss when disposed of or sold.
- All Section 1245 and Section 1250 assets are also Section 1231 assets.
- To the extent that Section 1231 gains exceed Section 1231 losses, the net gain is treated as a long-term capital gain (subject to the lookback rule). If Section 1231 losses exceed Section 1231 gains, the loss is deductible as an **ordinary loss**.
- The **lookback rule** provides that the net Section 1231 gains must be offset by net Section 1231 losses from the five preceding tax years that have not already been recaptured. To the extent of these losses, the net Section 1231 gain is treated as **ordinary income**.
- **Section 1245 assets** include all tangible depreciable or amortizable property used in a trade or business other than land or buildings. Section 1245 recapture is the *lesser* of:
  - the recognized gain, *or*
  - all depreciation taken on the asset.
- **Section 1250 assets** are defined as depreciable buildings used in a trade or business and owned for more than one year. **Excess depreciation** is the depreciation claimed in excess of the amount that would have been claimed under the straight-line depreciation method. The excess depreciation is subject to being recaptured as ordinary income under Section 1250. Section 1250 recapture is the *lesser* of:
  - the recognized gain, *or*
  - the excess depreciation.
- For individuals, gain in excess of the recaptured amount is treated as either unrecaptured Section 1250 gain or Section 1231 gain. **Unrecaptured Section 1250 gain** is gain taxed at a maximum tax rate of 25% to the extent of accumulated straight-line depreciation taken on the real estate.
- For corporations, gain in excess of the Section 1250 recapture amount is treated first as **Section 291 recapture**, and then as Section 1231 gain.

5 Compute the qualified business income deduction.

- Taxpayers can take advantage of the **qualified business income (QBI) deduction**, which is computed as 20% of the taxpayer's income from pass-through entities (partnerships, limited liability companies, and S corporations) and sole proprietorships.
- Three significant limitations can reduce the QBI deduction, depending on the taxpayer's modified taxable income.
- The first limitation affects **specified service trades or businesses**—those involved in the services of health, law, accounting, actuarial sciences, performing arts, consulting, athletics, financial services, brokerage services, or any business where the principal asset is the reputation of an employee or owner. Additional steps are required to determine the QBI deduction, if any, for owners of such trades or businesses.
- The second limitation is that the QBI deduction cannot exceed the *greater* of:
  - 50% of the taxpayer's share of the W-2 wages paid by the business, *or*
  - 25% of the taxpayer's share of the W-2 wages paid by the business, plus 2.5% of the unadjusted basis of qualified property.
- If a taxpayer has more than one QBI activity, we compute the QBI deduction separately for each activity using the limitations discussed above.
- The third limitation is that the total QBI deduction reported on the tax return from all QBI activities cannot exceed 20% of the taxpayer's modified taxable income.

Communication Application

Communication

Identifying Use of Asset and Character of Gain

(LO4) Fernando LLC has owned 10 acres of land in rural Arkansas for several years and is considering selling them. The land's adjusted basis is $100,000, and the fair market value is $230,000. Fernando LLC has requested that you explain how the gain would be reported on its tax return. Write a memo to Fernando LLC explaining your answer and requesting any additional information you may need.

Solution

Memo to Client

Dear Fernando LLC,

I am responding to your inquiry concerning the potential sale of your land in Arkansas. You have held the land for more than one year, which qualifies it as long term. The amount of your gain from a sale would be $130,000 ($230,000 realized − $100,000 adjusted basis). But the way that gain is treated on your tax return depends on how you have used the land, so I will need to know that information.

There are three possibilities:

- The LLC is a real estate dealer and holds this land as inventory along with other parcels of land for sale,
- The LLC has been using the land in a trade or business, *or*
- The LLC has held the land for investment planning for it to appreciate.

If the LLC held the land as inventory, then the gain will be ordinary gain and taxed at the members' marginal tax rate for ordinary income, possibly as high as 37%. If the land was used in a trade or business, the gain will be a Section 1231 gain. If the land is the only Section 1231 asset sold this year, then the gain will be a long-term capital gain and receive a preferential tax rate, not to exceed 20%. If the LLC held the land for investment, then it is a capital asset resulting in a long-term capital gain with a preferential tax rate, not to exceed 20%.

Please provide further information regarding the use of the land, and we can determine the gain's character and how it will be treated on your tax return.

Sincerely,
Carnes & Youngberg, CPAs

Ethics and Professional Responsibilities Application

Ethics

Correcting Errors

(LO1) Tommy "The Tattoo King" Tinker has a tattoo parlor in Tennessee operating as an S corporation. He has asked you to look at his online QuickBooks file and prepare his current-year tax return. While reviewing the file, you find some suspicious expenses. When you dig deeper, you realize that Tommy is paying his ex-wife's alimony, home mortgage interest expense, home real estate taxes, and various other personal expenses from his S corporation business checking account. Tommy says that because his business supports his wife's alimony and his other personal expenses, they should all be deductible. How should you respond to Tommy?

In addition to the chapter content, see *Statements on Standards for Tax Services* at www.aicpa-cima.com/resources/landing/statements-on- standards-for-tax-services, *Circular 230* at www.irs.gov/tax-professionals/office-of-professional-responsibility-and-circular-230, and Chapter 2, LO4, Tax Professional Responsibilities.

Solution

Deductions related to the taxpayer's personal life are not deductible as a business expense. Under IRC §162(a), expenses deductible for the business must be ordinary, necessary, and reasonable for the carrying on of that trade or business. As Tommy's tax accountant, per the AICPA *Statement on Standards for Tax Services* No. 1.2, Knowledge of Errors, you should advise him of the potential consequences of the error and recommend what corrective measures he should take. SSTS No. 1.2.6 states that a CPA "should promptly inform a taxpayer upon becoming aware of a taxpayer's failure to file a required return, an error in a previously filed return, [or] an error in a return that is the subject of an administrative proceeding." The CPA may provide the recommendation either orally or in writing. §10.21 of *Circular 230* imposes similar obligations on tax professionals.

You should tell Tommy that you will correct the QuickBooks file and the current-year tax return to properly reflect the expenses for the business.

Five-Year Lookback Rule

(LO4) Hogan Inc. is a C corporation and is a new client this year. The company has provided you with its tax returns from the last three years to help you prepare its current year's return. In the current year, Hogan Inc. sold several business assets, resulting in a net Section 1231 gain of $17,000. When you review the prior returns, you notice that your client has had net Section 1231 gains and losses in which the five-year lookback rule was not followed. You realize this will affect your preparation of the current year's return. Should you inform Hogan Inc. that you need to amend the previous returns, or leave them as filed because you have been hired to prepare only the current year's return?

In addition to the chapter content, see *Statements on Standards for Tax Services* at www.aicpa-cima.com/resources/landing/statements-on-standards-for-tax-services, *Circular 230* at www.irs.gov/tax-professionals/office-of-professional-responsibility-and-circular-230, and Chapter 2, LO4, Tax Professional Responsibilities.

Solution

Under AICPA *Statements on Standards for Tax Services* No. 1.2.6, Knowledge of Errors, "A member should promptly inform a taxpayer upon becoming aware of the taxpayer's failure to file a required return, [or] an error in a previously filed return." Therefore, you must inform Hogan Inc. of the earlier error before preparing the current year's return. Also, per *Circular 230* §10.21, if a practitioner has knowledge of an omission or error in a previously filed tax return, then the practitioner must notify the client of the noncompliance and offer suggestions to remedy the situation. If Hogan Inc. does not agree to amend the prior year's returns, you should consider walking away from the engagement. It is the CPA's professional responsibility to advise the client of appropriate treatment, but the CPA cannot inform the Internal Revenue Service of earlier errors and must keep the information confidential.

Key Terms

End-of-Chapter Assessment

Discussion Questions

1. **(LO1)** Describe the entity theory.

2. **(LO1)** Explain the difference between an operating distribution and a liquidating distribution.

3. **(LO2)** What is the due date for partnerships and S corporations to file their income tax returns?

4. **(LO2)** Define *statute of limitations* and explain how it applies to tax assessment and refunds.

5. **(LO2)** Describe the failure to pay penalty and the failure to file a tax return penalty.

6. **(LO2)** What is meant by the term *substantial authority*?

7. **(LO2)** Provide two examples of an accuracy-related penalty.

8. **(LO3)** What does the tax law include in *amount realized*?

9. **(LO3)** What is the difference between *realized gain or loss* and *recognized gain or loss*?

10. **(LO3)** Provide two reasons why realized gain might be deferred for tax purposes.

11. **(LO3)** Provide a definition for *boot*.

12. **(LO3)** How does a tax-deferred transaction impact the holding period of an asset?

13. **(LO3)** Define *related-party transaction*.

14. **(LO3)** Does the related-party loss disallowance rule apply even when the selling price is equal to the fair market value and can be substantiated by a qualified appraisal?

15. **(LO3)** Why is it important to differentiate among ordinary assets, Section 1231 assets, and capital assets?

16. **(LO3)** Distinguish between *realty* and *personalty*.

17. **(LO3)** When is an asset deemed long-term for holding-period purposes? Why is this important?

18. **(LO4)** If a business-use asset held long-term is sold at a loss, and it is the only business-use asset sold during the year, what is the character of that loss?

19. **(LO4)** Explain the five-year lookback rule regarding Section 1231 net gains.

20. **(LO4)** Does the lookback rule apply to both net Section 1231 gains and losses generated in the current year?

21. **(LO4)** What is a Section 1245 asset?

22. **(LO4)** If Section 197 intangible assets are purchased as part of an acquisition of a business, how are they treated when they are sold?

23. **(LO4)** What is a Section 1250 asset?

24. **(LO4)** What is unrecaptured Section 1250 gain?

25. **(LO4)** On what tax form does a taxpayer report the sale of business-use assets?

26. **(LO4)** Provide some examples where the recapture rules do not apply.

27. **(LO5)** What is a specified service business activity?

Multiple Choice Questions

1. **(LO1)** A C corporation files which tax form to report its income, expenses, and credits?
   - **a.** Form 1120
   - **b.** Form 1040
   - **c.** Form 1065
   - **d.** Form 1120-S

2. **(LO1)** Form 1041 is used to file a tax return for which entity?
   - **a.** Corporation
   - **b.** Partnership
   - **c.** Trust
   - **d.** Limited liability company

3. **(LO2)** On what day, in general, is Form 1120 due for a calendar year-end corporation, not including extensions and without incurring a possible penalty?
   - **a.** March 15
   - **b.** April 1
   - **c.** April 15
   - **d.** June 30

4. **(LO2)** If Burger Inc. (a calendar year-end corporation) filed its Year 3 tax return on February 14, Year 4, when does the statute of limitations expire for assessing additional tax?
   - **a.** February 14, Year 6
   - **b.** April 15, Year 6
   - **c.** February 14, Year 7
   - **d.** April 15, Year 7

5. **(LO2)** Heather Inc. inadvertently failed to e-file its Year 10 tax return on April 15, Year 11, but it did pay its balance due of $1,500 on time. Heather Inc. e-filed on June 3, Year 11. What late filing penalty does Heather Inc. incur?
   - **a.** $0
   - **b.** $150
   - **c.** $215
   - **d.** $500

6. **(LO3)** Rico Inc. sells a parcel of investment real estate and receives $120,000 cash and stock with a fair market value of $100,000 and basis of $60,000. Additionally, the $50,000 mortgage on the property is assumed by the buyer. Rico Inc. paid an attorney $1,000 to execute the sale. The week before the sale, Rico paid $75 to have a fence repaired on the property. The basis in the parcel of investment real estate is $200,000. What is Rico Inc.'s amount realized from selling the property?
   - **a.** $219,000
   - **b.** $268,925
   - **c.** $269,000
   - **d.** $270,000

7. **(LO3)** Which of the following fall under the related-party relationship rules for loss disallowance on sale of an asset? Select all that apply.
   - **a.** Two cousins
   - **b.** A shareholder who owns 60% of a corporation's stock
   - **c.** Brother and sister
   - **d.** Mother-in-law and daughter-in-law

8. **(LO3)** On April 16, Year 10, Alvin Inc. sold 200 shares of Chipmunk stock to its 100% shareholder, Tang, for $18,000. Alvin Inc. purchased the stock in Year 5 for $23,000. Tang sold the stock to Amber, an unrelated third party, for $30,000 on December 28, Year 10. What amount of gain from the sale of the stock to Amber should Tang report on his Year 10 income tax return?
   - **a.** $0
   - **b.** $2,000
   - **c.** $5,000
   - **d.** $7,000

9. **(LO3)** Which of the following is an ordinary asset?
   - **a.** Computer
   - **b.** Delivery truck
   - **c.** Accounts receivable
   - **d.** Equipment

10. **(LO3)** Which of the following assets would be classified as ordinary for purposes of determining the character of gain or loss?
    - I. Personal residence
    - II. Inventory
    - III. Asset sold by a business that had been owned for eight months
    - **a.** II
    - **b.** II, III
    - **c.** I, II
    - **d.** I, II, III

11. **(LO3)** Which of the following assets would be classified as capital for purposes of determining the character of gain or loss?
    - I. Equipment used in a business
    - II. Land owned by a dealer in real estate
    - III. Stock owned by a corporation
    - IV. Copyright owned by author of book
    - **a.** III
    - **b.** IV
    - **c.** II, III
    - **d.** I, II, III, IV

12. **(LO3)** Which of the following is an example of realty?
    - **a.** Storefront property
    - **b.** Land
    - **c.** Apartment building
    - **d.** Warehouse
    - **e.** All of these

13. **(LO4)** Wolf, Inc. had the following net Section 1231 gains/losses for its first four years of operations:

    Year 1 $10,000
    Year 2 $ 4,000
    Year 3 $12,000
    Year 4 ($18,000)

In Year 5, Wolf has a net Section 1231 gain of $30,000. How will this gain be taxed according to the following classification?

	Ordinary income	Long-term capital gain
a.	$18,000	$12,000
b.	$ 0	$30,000
c.	$30,000	$ 0
d.	$12,000	$18,000

14. **(LO4)** On January 1, Year 8, Whitehouse Corp. placed into service five-year MACRS equipment with an initial tax basis of $10,000. On December 31, Year 10, Whitehouse sold the property for $8,000, after having taken $6,000 in MACRS depreciation deductions. What amount of the gain should Whitehouse recapture as ordinary income under the Section 1245 recapture rules?
    - **a.** $0
    - **b.** $2,000
    - **c.** $4,000
    - **d.** $6,000

15. **(LO4)** Tanner Company purchased and placed into service seven-year furniture on March 15, Year 2. The furniture cost $3,600 and was sold in Year 4 for $4,000 after taking $1,711 in MACRS depreciation deductions. What amount should Tanner recapture as ordinary income under the Section 1245 recapture rules?
    - **a.** $0
    - **b.** $1,711
    - **c.** $1,889
    - **d.** $2,111

16. **(LO4)** Becker Company sold a business-use computer for $1,000 in December of the current year. Becker Company had purchased the computer several years earlier for $2,800 and had taken $1,500 of MACRS depreciation deductions as of the date of the sale. What amount is subject to Section 1245 depreciation recapture?
    - **a.** $0
    - **b.** $1,300
    - **c.** $1,500
    - **d.** ($300)

17. **(LO4)** Carmella LLC purchased a commercial building on June 1, Year 3, for $200,000. The building was depreciated using regular MACRS straight-line depreciation. The apartment building was sold on December 31, Year 8, for $330,000 when its adjusted tax basis was $160,000 (assume that $40,000 of depreciation had been claimed). How much gain from the sale of the building is subject to the 25% rate as unrecaptured Section 1250 gain, and how much gain qualifies as Section 1250 depreciation recapture?

	Unrecaptured Section 1250 gain at 25% rate	Section 1250 recapture
a.	$ 0	$170,000
b.	$ 40,000	$130,000
c.	$ 40,000	$ 0
d.	$170,000	$ 0

18. **(LO4)** Anthony Inc., an S corporation, purchased a rental apartment building for $325,000 in April 1984. The corporation elected to depreciate it using the 150% declining balance method with a useful life of 50 years, resulting in accelerated depreciation taken of $260,000. Straight-line depreciation would have been $220,000. Anthony Inc. sold the building in November 2025, for $400,000. What portion of the gain is subject to Section 1250 recapture?
    - **a.** $0
    - **b.** $40,000
    - **c.** $65,000
    - **d.** $335,000

19. **(LO4)** Section 291 recaptures applies to which of the following entity types?
    - **a.** S corporation
    - **b.** C corporation
    - **c.** LLC that has not elected to be treated as a corporation
    - **d.** Partnership

20. **(LO5)** Where does the QBI deduction appear on Form 1040?
    - **a.** It is an itemized deduction taken on Schedule A of Form 1040.
    - **b.** It is a deduction from AGI on Form 1040 taken after the deduction for the greater of itemized deductions or the standard deduction.
    - **c.** It is a business deduction and is taken on Schedule C of Form 1040.
    - **d.** It is a deduction that reduces self-employment income and is taken on Schedule SE of Form 1040.

21. **(LO5)** Abe is the sole shareholder and president of Lincoln, Inc., an S corporation that is a qualified trade or business. In 2025, Lincoln has net income of $330,000 after deducting Abe's salary of $75,000. What is Abe's qualified business income?
    - **a.** $0
    - **b.** $75,000
    - **c.** $330,000
    - **d.** $405,000

22. **(LO5)** Which of the following is not a specified service activity for the purpose of calculating the qualified business income deduction?
    - **a.** Accounting
    - **b.** Financial services
    - **c.** Athletics
    - **d.** Architecture

23. **(LO5)** In 2025, Cal, who is single, earns sole proprietor income of $245,000 generated from his law practice. He does not have any employees or qualified assets. Cal's modified taxable income is $285,000. How much is his QBI deduction?
    - **a.** $0
    - **b.** $49,000
    - **c.** $54,490
    - **d.** $57,000

Brief Exercises

1. **(LO1)** Describe the three foundational principles for property transactions.

2. **(LO2)** TennisNow is an S corporation with a calendar year-end. TennisNow filed its Form 1120-S for 2025 on December 26, 2026. TennisNow has eight shareholders. What is TennisNow's penalty for late filing of its tax return?

3. **(LO2)** Bennett owns 100% of Garrand Corporation, which does estate planning and consulting. After completing Garrand's tax return this year, Bennett realized that Garrand owed $24,000 in taxes. Instead of paying the taxes as owed, Bennett reduced Garrand's income by $100,000. How would the IRS respond to this situation?

4. **(LO3)** Shane Inc. exchanged its investment land (basis $43,000, FMV $56,000) for farming land (basis $44,000, FMV $51,000) and $5,000 cash. Assume this exchange qualifies as a tax-deferred transaction. What is Shane Inc.'s recognized gain, if any?

5. **(LO3)** Harriet owns 500 shares of Coca-Cola stock and paid $36 per share in 2018. She sold it in the current year for $30 per share to Ethyl Company, a partnership in which she has a capital interest of 35%. Ethyl Company later sold the stock to an unrelated third party for $50 per share. What is Harriet's recognized gain or loss on the sale? What is Ethyl Company's recognized gain or loss on the sale?

6. **(LO3)** Harriet owns 500 shares of Coca-Cola stock and paid $36 per share in 2018. She sold it in the current year for $30 per share to Ethan Company, a partnership in which she has a capital interest of 65%. Ethan Company later sold the stock for $50 per share. What is Harriet's recognized gain or loss on the sale? What is Ethan Company's recognized gain or loss on the sale?

7. **(LO3)** Tito Company purchased equipment to be used in its business on January 9 of the current year. In December, Tito is considering selling the equipment. If Tito sells in December, what is the asset's classification? If Tito sells it on January 10 of next year, what is the asset's classification?

8. **(LO4)** Daewoon Company owns a popular restaurant on Main Street. During the current year, it sold various assets, resulting in net Section 1231 gains of $22,000 and net Section 1231 losses of $11,000. Daewoon Company also sold stock, which generated a capital loss of $9,000. What is the net effect of these transactions?

9. **(LO4)** Toucan owns Fit for U (FFU), an exercise facility. FFU sells weightlifting equipment for $44,000. FFU purchased the equipment four years ago for $75,000 and has accumulated depreciation of $60,000. What is FFU's realized and recognized gain or loss? What is the character of the gain or loss?

10. **(LO4)** Giada received a building to expand her pizza restaurant business as a gift from her Uncle Joey. The building had a fair market value of $225,000 and an adjusted basis of $100,000. Is Joey subject to the recapture provisions on the gift? Is Giada subject to the recapture provisions if she decides to sell the gifted building?

11. **(LO5)** Enid operates, as a sole proprietor, an animal shelter that generates net revenue of $88,000. Enid has also made a self-employed health insurance payment of $6,000. What is Enid's qualified business income?

12. **(LO5)** Theo, single, is the sole shareholder of Theo's Tool and Dye, Inc., a tool and dye manufacturing company operating as an S corporation. Theo reports qualified business income of $118,000, and he has no employees. He also has qualified dividend income of $4,400. He has no itemized deductions and claims the standard deduction of $15,000 on his 2025 Form 1040. What is Theo's qualified business income deduction?

Application Problems

1. **(LO2)** Cain Inc. (a calendar year-end corporation) filed its 2025 Form 1120 on February 14, 2026.
   a. When will the statute of limitations for its 2025 return expire?
   b. When will the statute of limitations expire if it filed its tax return on August 15, 2026?
   c. When will the statute of limitations expire if Cain Inc. never filed its return?

2. **(LO2)** Granite Inc. filed its 2025 tax return on May 29, 2026, and never properly extended its tax return. Granite owed $6,400, which was paid on April 15, 2026.
   a. How much is its failure to file penalty?
   b. If it filed its return on December 15, 2026, what is its failure to file penalty?

3. **(LO2)** Granite Inc. filed its 2025 tax return on April 15, 2026. Granite Inc. owed $6,400 for its 2025 tax return, which was not paid when the return was filed.
   a. How much is Granite's failure to pay penalty if it filed its return on April 15, 202, and paid the balance due on May 29, 2026?
   b. If Granite filed its return on April 15, 2026, and paid the balance due on December 15, 2026, what is its failure to pay penalty?

4. **(LO2)** Granite Inc. filed its 2025 tax return late and never properly extended its tax return. Granite's failure to file its return on time was determined to be intentional and fraudulent. Granite owed $6,400 for its 2025 tax return.
   a. How much is its failure to file penalty if it filed its return on May 29, 2026?
   b. If it filed its return on December 15, 2026, what is its failure to file penalty?

5. **(LO2)** Asher Inc. is a medical supply corporation with a calendar year-end. Its tax liability is $56,000 for 2025 and $50,000 for 2024. How much must Asher Inc. pay in estimated income taxes in 2025 to avoid an underpayment penalty for 2025? Assume the annualization exception is not beneficial to Asher.

6. **(LO2)** Decker Corporation owes $18,500 in tax liability with its 2025 tax return due on April 15, 2026. Decker filed its return, but unfortunately, Decker was not able to pay its liability until July 1, 2026. Assume that the federal short-term interest rate is 4%. How much will the IRS assess Decker for interest and penalties?

7. **(LO2)** Enthusiasm Learning Center is a partnership with a calendar year-end. Enthusiasm filed its Form 1065 for 2025 on October 5, 2026. Enthusiasm has 24 limited partners and one general partner. What is Enthusiasm's penalty for late filing of its tax return?

8. **(LO3)** Elijah Inc. owns an apartment building that it purchased 10 years ago for $345,000. Its current adjusted basis is $220,000, and the outstanding mortgage is $250,000. Elijah Inc. sells the building for cash of $300,000 plus assumption of the mortgage. Elijah Inc. pays commissions on the sale of $30,000, title transfer fees of $500, and an attorney at closing $1,000. What is Elijah Inc.'s realized and recognized gain?

9. **(LO3)** Chase Company would like to exchange land that it owns (adjusted basis $140,000 and FMV of $172,000) for land in a neighboring county (adjusted basis $120,000 and FMV $142,000) plus cash of $30,000. Assume that the parcels of land are qualified property for treating this as a deferred transaction, and that the cash is boot.

a. What is Chase's realized gain?

b. What is Chase's recognized gain?

c. What is Chase's deferred gain?

d. What is Chase's basis in the property received?

e. What is Chase's holding period in the new property?

10. **(LO3)** Evan owns investment land with an adjusted basis of $52,000 and fair market value of $42,000. He sells the land to Stan Corporation, an S Corporation for which he is an 80% shareholder, for $39,000. Stan Corporation then sells the land to an unrelated third party for $65,000.

a. What is Evan's realized gain/loss and recognized gain/loss? What is Stan Corporation's basis in the land purchased?

b. What is Stan Corporation's realized gain/loss and recognized gain/loss?

c. Assume the same facts except Stan Corporation then sells the land to an unrelated third party for $45,000. What is Stan Corporation's realized gain/ loss and recognized gain/loss?

d. Assume the same facts except Stan Corporation then sells the land to an unrelated third party for $35,000. What is Stan's realized gain/loss and recognized gain/loss?

11. **(LO3)** Classify each of the following assets as realty, personalty (tangible), personalty (intangible asset), or natural resource.

a. Extracted coal

b. Covenant not to compete

c. Warehouse used to store chemicals

d. Trademark used to sell a product

e. Dump truck used at a construction site

f. Printer used in an office

12. **(LO3)** Classify each of the following assets as ordinary, Section 1231, or capital.

a. Notes receivable

b. One parcel of land held for investment

c. Automobile used 100% for business and held for three years

d. 1967 Ford Mustang owned for personal pleasure

e. Desk and chair used in business and sold after three months

f. Land used as a playground for a day care center

13. **(LO4)** Sven Inc. sold several business assets in the current year. The sales resulted in Section 1231 gains of $12,000 and Section 1231 losses of $15,000. What is the character of the Section 1231 gains and losses?

14. **(LO4)** Boris is the sole owner of a single-member LLC that reports its tax items on Schedule C. The LLC had several transactions during the year.

- Land held for investment for 13 months and sold at a gain of $45,000
- Inventory used in the LLC and sold for a loss of $23,000
- Casualty loss from a fire in the warehouse of $55,000
- Parking lot adjacent to the business sold at a gain of $20,000 after being held for more than one year

Determine the tax consequences of these transactions. Assume that the LLC had no prior Section 1231 losses in previous years and no other sales of Section 1231 assets this year.

15. **(LO4)** Daisy Company had several pieces of land that it sold in the current year:

Asset	Sales price	Cost	Holding period
Land held for Investment	$100,000	$ 74,000	Long-term
Land #1 used in its business	$135,000	$140,000	Short-term
Land #2 used in its business	$122,000	$115,000	Long-term

What are the tax consequences of the asset sales? Assume that Daisy Company does not have any net Section 1231 losses in prior years and that these are all the Section 1231 transactions for this year.

16. **(LO4)** Li Company started its ice cream parlor in Year 1. In Year 4, Li sold one business-use asset for a Section 1231 gain of $5,000 and sold another business-use asset for a Section 1231 loss of $2,200. If Li Company had a net Section 1231 loss of $1,000 in Year 3, what is the amount and character of the assets sold in Year 4?

17. **(LO4)** Rhys Inc. sold various business-use assets in Year 10 resulting in a net Section 1231 gain of $7,000. Rhys Inc. had the following net Section 1231 gains and losses in the previous years:

Year 4 ($2,000)
Year 5 ($1,500)
Year 6 $2,500
Year 7 $ 800
Year 8 ($4,500)
Year 9 $3,000

How is the Year 10 net Section 1231 gain of $7,000 treated?

18. **(LO4)** Sandra Company sold land that it used in its business for $125,000 in the current year. Sandra Company purchased the land several years ago for $138,000.

a. What is the amount and character of Sandra's recognized gain/loss?

b. What if Sandra Company sold the asset for $150,000? Assume it did not have any prior net Section 1231 losses in the past five years and that there were no other Section 1231 transactions this year.

19. **(LO4)** Sasha Inc. owns business-use equipment with an initial purchase price of $50,000. The asset's accumulated depreciation is

$30,000. Assume that Sasha Inc. sells the equipment for $25,000 and that its tax rate is 21%.

a. Compute Sasha Inc.'s tax gain or loss on the sale and the character of the gain or loss.

b. Compute Sasha Inc.'s after-tax cash flow from the sale.

20. **(LO4)** Bohai owns Dig Deep Company (DDC), specializing in manufacturing colonoscopy equipment. In the current year, DDC sold a machine for $28,000. DDC purchased the machine in 2021 for $38,000 and deducted depreciation expense of $23,000.

a. What is the amount and character of the gain/loss?

b. What if the machine was sold for $49,000?

c. What if the machine was sold for $12,000?

21. **(LO4)** MaryAnn Company purchased Tanger Corporation five years ago for $780,000. As part of the purchase, MaryAnn Company acquired two patents, which had a value of $50,000. In the current year, the company sells both patents for $65,000. Total amortization claimed on the patents through the date of sale was $16,800. What are the tax consequences of this sale?

22. **(LO4)** Daisy LLC has owned an apartment building since 1985, which it purchased for $232,000. Daisy LLC sold the apartment building in 1989 for $248,000. Accumulated depreciation as of the date of sale was $34,000, of which $6,000 was in excess of straight-line depreciation. How much of the gain is considered ordinary income?

23. **(LO4)** Eric LLC purchased a commercial building five years ago for $365,000. In the current year, Eric LLC sold the building for $100,000 cash and the buyer's assumption of Eric's debt on the building of $300,000. Through the date of sale, Eric LLC deducted $47,000 straight-line depreciation on the building. Compute Eric LLC's recognized gain on the sale and the character of the gain.

24. **(LO4)** Delgado Corporation purchased an apartment building on August 3, 2021, for $980,000 and sold the building on March 9, 2025, for $1,300,000. Delgado deducted straight-line depreciation of $127,689 for years 2021–2025. Determine the recognized gain and its character.

25. **(LO4)** Upon her death, Latif's grandmother bequeathed him the apartment building that she had rented out for the last 12 years. He does not want the hassle of maintaining the building, so he intends to sell the building right away. What are his tax consequences based on the following information?

- Fair market value as of the date of death was $625,000.
- Original cost was $400,000.
- Straight-line depreciation taken was $175,000 through the date of sale.
- Latif sells the building for $650,000.

26. **(LO5)** Susan owns a floral shop as a sole proprietorship and has net earnings of $100,000 on Schedule C. Susan is allowed a self-employment tax deduction for AGI of $7,065 ($100,000 × 0.9235 × 15.3% × 50%). What is her qualified business income?

27. **(LO5)** Roger, a single taxpayer, owns and operates a video game store. He does not have any employees and reported qualified business income of $125,000 through a sole proprietorship in 2025. Roger has AGI of $155,000, including $2,000 interest income, has no itemized deductions, and claimed the standard deduction of $15,000 on his 2025 Form 1040. His modified taxable income is $140,000 ($155,000 – $15,000). What is Roger's QBI deduction?

28. **(LO5)** Kate, a single taxpayer, owns and operates an ice cream shop. She does not have any employees and reported qualified business income of $125,000 through a sole proprietorship in 2025. Kate has AGI of $155,000, including $20,000 of net capital gain, has no itemized deductions, and claimed the standard deduction of $15,000 on her 2025 Form 1040. Her modified taxable income is $120,000 ($155,000 – $15,000 – $20,000). What is Kate's QBI deduction?

29. **(LO5)** Jaewoo is a CPA and operates his own CPA firm as a single-member LLC. His qualified business income from his accounting firm was $555,000 for 2025. Jaewoo paid wages of $162,000 this year, and the unadjusted basis of the property used in the LLC was $400,000. Jaewoo is married, and the taxable income before the QBI deduction is $500,000 for him and his spouse. What is Jaewoo's QBI deduction?

30. **(LO5)** Lexi, a single taxpayer, owns and operates a computer repair shop. She pays one employee $15,000 in wages and has no qualified property. Lexi reported qualified business income through a sole proprietorship of $145,000 in 2025. She has AGI of $285,000, has no itemized deductions, and claimed the standard deduction of $15,000 on her 2025 Form 1040. Her modified taxable income is $270,000 ($285,000 – $15,000).

a. What is Lexi's QBI deduction?

b. Assume Lexi has machinery and equipment with an unadjusted basis of $160,000. What is her QBI deduction?

31. **(LO5)** Grant, a single taxpayer, has qualified business income and the following qualified business deductions after considering the wage limitation and the specified services limitation:

Sunshine LLC	$25,000
Monsoon S Corporation	$18,000
Landslide LLP	$15,000

Grant's modified taxable income is $275,000, which includes net capital gains of $5,000 and qualified dividend income of $2,500. What is his allowable QBI deduction?

32. **(LO5 Advanced)** Alexander, a single taxpayer, owns and operates a fishing supply store. He pays one employee $15,000 in wages and has qualified property with an unadjusted basis of $160,000. He reported qualified business income through a sole proprietorship of $145,000 in 2025. Alexander has taxable income of $205,350, which is also his modified taxable income.

a. What is Alexander's QBI deduction?

b. If Alexander were a tennis professional, what would be his QBI deduction?

c. If Alexander were a tennis professional with a taxable income of $250,000, what would be his QBI deduction?

Tax Planning Problems

1. **(LO3)** Benjamin owns equipment that is used 100% in his business with a fair market value of $11,000 and an adjusted basis of $15,000. He would like to sell the equipment and is looking for the best net after-tax cash flow. His tax rate is 35%. Would it be better to sell the equipment to his dad for $11,000 or his best friend for $10,000? Why?

2. **(LO4)** Your client, Dwayne, owns Dwayne's Manufacturing Company, and is looking to sell and replace his entire line of machinery and equipment, which is used to manufacture rugs. The machinery and equipment originally cost $500,000 and is fully depreciated. Dwayne expects to sell the machinery and equipment for its fair market value of $500,000. He has told you that he assumes he will recognize no gain because he is selling the machinery and equipment for the same amount he paid for them. Explain how the sale will be treated and why Congress created the depreciation recapture rules. Assume that Dwayne's ordinary marginal tax rate is 37% and his LTCG rate is 20%.

3. **(LO4)** Barret Company has been in business since 2014 and has never sold a Section 1231 asset. Barret has a net profit before asset sales of $350,000 this year. Barret has owned the following assets since inception of the business but is trying to decide if it is the right time to sell the assets before the end of the year.

Asset	Sales price	Cost	Accumulated depreciation	Gain/loss
Furniture	$ 7,000	$10,000	$10,000	$ 7,000
Computers	$ 2,500	$ 4,000	$ 3,000	$ 1,500
Artwork	$ 10,000	$12,000		($ 2,000)
Machinery	$ 8,000	$12,000	$ 2,000	($ 2,000)
Building	$100,000	$75,000	$ 7,500	$32,500
Stock	$ 60,000	$33,000		$27,000

What is the character of the gains/losses, and what is Barret's profit after asset sales? Is there any advice you would give him with regard to the Section 1231 assets?

4. **(LO4)** DeMarcus owns and operates a sporting goods store as a single member LLC. He is considering selling several assets (used in the business and held long-term) and would like to know the most advantageous tax result. These would be the only Section 1231 assets sold this year. Assume DeMarcus is in a 37% tax bracket and has never sold an asset in the past. The following information will help you decide the best course of action. Should Demarcus sell the assets this year or wait until next year?

Asset	Sales price	Cost	Depreciation	Gain/loss
Building	$100,000	$75,000	$5,000	$ 30,000
Land	$ 25,000	$37,000	N/A	($ 12,000)

5. **(LO4)** Sanjay has asked your advice on how to treat an asset sale that he will have in the near future. Sanjay is very close to his uncle, who is critically ill. His uncle has listed several assets in his will that Sanjay will inherit upon the uncle's death. One of the assets is a warehouse that his uncle uses in his business and has owned for the last 10 years. Sanjay would like to know the tax consequences if the warehouse was gifted to him by his uncle or if he waits and receives it through inheritance. Calculate the gain, if any, and its character if Sanjay receives the gift today or if he waits until his uncle passes, based on the following information.

Fair market value today	$500,000
Original cost	$375,000
Straight-line depreciation claimed	$ 96,000

Assume that the uncle dies, Sanjay sells the warehouse for $550,000, and the fair market value as of date of death is $500,000.

6. **(LO5)** Candy Cane, single, owns and operates the following businesses in 2025. None of these are specified service businesses.

Business	QBI	W-2 wages	Property
Treetop Decorations	$100,000	$12,500	$0
Candy's Cookies	$ 65,000	$ 0	$0
Candy's Snow Supplies	($ 45,000)	$ 5,000	$0

Candy's modified taxable income is $400,000. Can she ignore the loss from Candy's Snow Supplies in calculating her QBI deduction?

Professional Development Skills

Communication Problem

Communication

1. **(LO4) Decision on When to Sell Business-Use Assets** Sylvia has owned her own beauty salon as a sole proprietorship in Alpharetta, Georgia, since 2017. The salon needs a makeover, and she is looking at selling her salon chairs, furniture, and pedicure basins. All of these assets have been held long-term. Sylvia has never sold any business assets in the past, and her current year AGI before the sale of assets is $150,000. Included in her AGI is a $10,000 short-term capital loss from the sale of stock that has been limited to $3,000. She would like your advice as to whether the sale of these assets will help utilize her entire $10,000 loss. She provides you with the following information:

Asset	Cost	Accumulated depreciation	FMV
Chairs	$48,000	$30,000	$24,000
Furniture	$25,000	$15,000	$ 8,000
Basins	$12,000	$ 3,000	$13,000

If Sylvia sells the assets at their fair market value (FMV), what will be the amount of recognized gain/loss and its character? Will the sale of assets help utilize her $10,000 short-term capital loss? Write a letter to Sylvia explaining your findings.

Ethics and Professional Responsibilities Problem

Ethics

1. **(LO1) Underreported Income** Anthony Johnson, who owns a local bar and works as its bartender, is a new client of yours and would like to meet to discuss his financial statements and tax return for the current year. He operates the bar as an S corporation and is the sole shareholder. Anthony indicates that business has been slow; he expects a loss and feels he shouldn't owe any taxes this year. While reviewing the manual business records and Anthony's personal tax information, you see that there are very few cash receipts and no recording of tips. Anthony also has a large mortgage on his home, generating $28,000 in mortgage interest expense, and $25,000 in property taxes. You continue to dig through previous tax returns for the S corporation and Anthony's Form 1040 and notice very little income for the last five years. You wonder how Anthony can afford such a nice home. During your next meeting, you ask him about the cash receipts, the tips, and his large mortgage and property taxes. Anthony is vague and says no one in his line of work reports all the cash receipts and tips. What should you do?

   In addition to the chapter content, see *Statements on Standards for Tax Services* at www.aicpa- cima.com/resources/landing/statements-on-standards-for-tax-services, *Circular 230* at www.irs.gov/tax-professionals/office-of-professional-responsibility-and-circular-230, and Chapter 2, LO4, Tax Professional Responsibilities.

2. **(LO1) Reliance on Workpapers of a Third Party** Your CPA firm, Carnes and Youngberg, has been hired to help a new client in resolving a dispute with the IRS for a prior year's tax return. Carnes and Youngberg did not prepare the return, and your client did not have the best record keeping in the past. When reviewing the correspondence from the IRS, as well as Form 4797, Form 8949, and Schedule D, you notice some discrepancies on the forms compared to the workpapers that your client did provide. You realize that the workpapers and tax return were prepared by Frank Fishy, an attorney who also prepares tax returns. With a little digging, you find out that Frank Fishy has been disbarred from practicing before the IRS, and this concerns you. May you ask for assistance from Frank or rely on his workpapers? What is your responsibility regarding representing the client before the IRS?

   In addition to the chapter content, see *Statements on Standards for Tax Services* at www.aicpa-cima.com/resources/landing/statements-on-standards-for-tax-services, *Circular 230* at www.irs.gov/tax-professionals/office-of-professional-responsibility-and-circular-230, and Chapter 2 LO4, Tax Professional Responsibilities.

Research Problems

Research

1. (LO2) **Timely Filing of Tax Return** Collins Inc. is a calendar year-end C corporation owned 100% by Chase Collins. Chase was out of the country on the due date for filing the 2025 tax return, so he asked his CPA to file an extension. The CPA properly completed the extension form and queued it up to file electronically with her software. Unfortunately, the CPA never hit the submit button and did not realize the error until October 15 when she wanted to electronically file the tax return at the extension due date. As a result, the Collins Inc. tax return was not timely filed, and the IRS assessed a late filing penalty of $83,650 against the corporation. Collins Inc. paid the penalty and have filed a case in District Court to have the penalty abated. Chase Collins states that he relied on his CPA to properly file the extension, and the corporation should not be assessed the penalty. Conduct research to determine if Collins Inc. has reasonable cause to have the penalty abated.

2. (LO4) **Potential Depreciation Recapture** Grandma Sally died on November 5 of the current year. In her will, she left her granddaughter, Sienna, several assets that Sally had used in her farming business, including:

	FMV at date of death	Sally's basis in the asset
Silo	$335,000	$145,000
Farming equipment	$ 80,000	$110,000

Sienna would like to sell the assets immediately for their FMV. Does the depreciation recapture provision apply to either Sally or Sienna?

Excel Problems

Technology

1. (LO3) **Related-Party Sale** Chike owns 100 shares of stock in Belvidere Corporation. He purchased the stock for $40,000 three years ago. Chike sells the shares to Naomi Inc. in the current year for $32,000, resulting in a realized loss of $8,000 to Chike. Chike owns 75% of Naomi Inc. Create an Excel spreadsheet to indicate the recognized gain if Naomi Inc. sells the stock to an outside third party for:

   1. $42,000
   2. $36,000
   3. $30,000

2. (LO4) **Lookback Rule** Elonzo Corporation sold various business-use assets in Year 20, resulting in a net Section 1231 gain of $12,000. Year 14 was the first year of operations. Elonzo Corporation had the following net Section 1231 gains and losses in the previous years:

   Year 14 $6,500

   Year 15 ($2,000)

   Year 16 ($4,500)

   Year 17 $5,000

   Year 18 ($2,500)

   Year 19 ($1,000)

   a. How is the Year 20 net Section 1231 gain of $12,000 treated?

   b. How would your answer change if the Year 14 amount was ($6,500)?

   c. Create an Excel spreadsheet that shows your results and that could also be used for the same question with different amounts.

Tax Compliance and Reporting Problem

Compliance

1. **(LO4) Sale of Assets** Victor E. Husky (SSN: 123-45-6789) owns and operates Husky Ice Arena and Pro Shop as a sole proprietor. During 2025, the following transactions occurred:

   1. A delivery truck used in the business was sold on January 2 for $3,500. The truck had been purchased on January 2, 2019, for $6,000. The asset was fully depreciated.
   2. Unimproved land (which is considered a business-use asset) adjacent to the Ice Arena was sold for $15,000 on February 1. This land had been purchased on November 28, 2003, for $40,000.
   3. Victor sold a rowing machine used by the hockey players at the ice arena on June 5 for $4,900. The rowing machine was purchased on July 29, 2016, for $5,200. The asset was fully depreciated.
   4. Victor sold an apartment building on September 1 for $300,000. The rental property had been purchased on September 1, 2022, for $150,000. As of the date of the sale, the adjusted basis was $133,637.
   5. A Zamboni used in the business was sold on October 10 for $85,000. The Zamboni had been purchased on October 10, 2023, for $100,000. As of the date of sale, the accumulated depreciation was $61,600.
   6. Ice equipment used in the business was sold on October 14 for $5,000. The ice equipment had been purchased on October 16, 2022, for $35,000. As of the date of the sale, accumulated depreciation was $26,936.

   Victor does not have any unrecovered Section 1231 lookback losses. Victor needs help completing his tax return in regard to these asset sales. Please complete Form 4797. The 2024 Form 4797 is used because it was the most recent form available at the time of publication.

CPA Exam Preparation: Task-Based Simulation

1. **(LO3) Calculation of Realized Gain** Hall Inc. is selling its current warehouse and purchasing another larger warehouse for its growing business. You will review a list of improvements provided by Hall Inc., as well as the settlement statements for purchase and sale, and determine the amount realized, adjusted basis, and realized gain on the sale.

   Go to Wiley's book companion site to complete the Task-Based Simulation.

2. **(LO4) Calculating Gain/Loss and Character on Sale of Assets** Harry Clarke and Russell Addison own Nutty for U (NFU), a partnership located on Waverly Avenue in Windy City, Illinois. NFU is a very popular store for nuts, popcorn, and candy, but its owners would like to move their location closer to a popular ballpark. NFU will be selling some of its assets and would like to know the tax implications of each sale. You will calculate the gain or loss for assets like inventory, equipment, and real estate, and determine the character of each gain or loss.

   Go to Wiley's book companion site to complete the Task-Based Simulation.

3. **(LO5) Saenz—Qualified Business Income** Javier and Maria Saenz, married filing jointly, have several business investments. Their adjusted gross income and taxable income for 2025 is $300,000 and $275,000, respectively, before any qualified business income deduction.

   Referencing information from two Schedule K-1 forms and one Schedule C form, you will calculate their qualified business income deduction for three different deduction scenarios.

   Go to Wiley's book companion site to complete the Task-Based Simulation.

CHAPTER 2

Taxation of Business Entities: Strategies and Planning

fizkes/Adobe Stock Photos

Chapter Introduction

VIDEO CONTENT

Serving as a tax professional is an exciting and rewarding career, in part because a tax professional serves as an advocate for the client. The role of a tax professional is very different from the role of an auditor. An auditor must be independent of the client, and the auditor's role is to protect the public interest by attesting to the client's financial statements. A tax professional, on the other hand, has a professional responsibility to make decisions that are in the best interest of the client, as long as the professional is being true to the tax law and acting ethically.

In this chapter, we begin by discussing the opportunities for tax planning and contrast this role with tax compliance. Next, we explain the distinction between tax avoidance and tax evasion, as the former is legal, but the latter can result in criminal sanctions for the taxpayer and the preparer. We then explain why the tax law varies from GAAP and remind you not to confuse the two accounting systems. Given that a CPA is a member of a profession, we next discuss the professional responsibilities of a CPA—the foundation that a tax professional must use for decision making. We conclude the chapter with a summary of the great career opportunities that are available in taxation.

LEARNING OBJECTIVES	TOPICS	PRACTICE OPPORTUNITIES

1 Explain the opportunities for tax planning.	**2.1 The Basics of Tax Planning**
	• Tax Planning: The Big Picture
	  • The IRS: An Uninvited Third Party
	  • The Goal of Tax Planning
	  • Considering Tax Costs and Non-Tax Costs
	• Tax Planning Opportunities
	  • Rates Vary across Time Periods
	  • Rates Vary across Jurisdictions
	  • Rates Vary across Types of Income
	  • Rates Vary across Different Types of Taxpayers
	  • Rates Vary within a Family
	  • Time Value of Money
		• Example 2.1.1 Maximizing After-Tax Income
		• Example 2.1.2 Changing Tax Rates
		• Example 2.1.3 Changing Tax Jurisdictions
		• Example 2.1.4 Rates Vary across Different Types of Income
		• Example 2.1.5 Rates Vary across Taxpayers
		• Example 2.1.6 Family Tax Planning
		• Example 2.1.7 Time Value of Money
		• Example 2.1.8 Time Value of Money—Deduction
		• Example 2.1.9 Time Value of Money—Income Taxes
		• Practice Problem 2.1.1 Determining Tax Consequences
		• Practice Problem 2.1.2 Determining Present Value

2 Differentiate between tax avoidance and tax evasion.	**2.2 Tax Avoidance vs. Tax Evasion** • Tax Evasion • Tax Ethics	• Example 2.2.1 Tax Avoidance • Practice Problem 2.2.1 Tax Evasion
3 Compare the appropriate accounting methods to use when complying with tax rules and with GAAP rules.	**2.3 Tax Rules vs. GAAP**	• Example 2.3.1 Tax Rules vs. GAAP • Practice Problem 2.3.1 Reporting Payments

4 Distinguish between professional and unprofessional actions related to tax professionals' role with clients.	**2.4 Tax Professional Responsibilities**
	• Circular 230
	  • Practice before the IRS
	  • Substantive Provisions of Circular 230
	  • Penalties and Procedures for Tax Professionals
	• Statements of Standards for Tax Services (SSTS)
		• Example 2.4.1 Error on Prior Return
		• Example 2.4.2 Working with Individuals Disbarred from Practicing before the IRS
		• Example 2.4.3 Return of Tax Records
		• Practice Problem 2.4.1 Representing a Client before the IRS
		• Practice Problem 2.4.2 Ethical Considerations when Preparing a Return

LEARNING OBJECTIVES	TOPICS	PRACTICE OPPORTUNITIES
5 Discuss career opportunities for tax professionals.	**2.5 Professional Taxation as a Career** • The Role of a Tax Professional • Characteristics of Successful Tax Professionals	• Practice Problem 2.5.1 Careers in Accounting

Tax Forms referenced in this chapter

Form 2848	Power of Attorney and Declaration of Representative

2.1 The Basics of Tax Planning

LEARNING OBJECTIVE 1

Explain the opportunities for tax planning.

VIDEO CONTENT

The study of federal income taxation is exciting, challenging, and rewarding. Careers in professional taxation are fulfilling because all taxpayers want to structure their transactions in a tax-efficient manner. If you like the idea of adding value to others, then you will enjoy being a tax advisor to individuals and businesses. You need a thorough understanding of federal income taxation rules to be an effective tax planner, but the job requires much more than that. A tax professional must also have excellent analytical skills, be creative, and be an effective problem-solver and communicator. The purpose of this text is to provide you with the knowledge and skills you need to be a tax professional, which will provide great career opportunities for you.

Tax Planning: The Big Picture

There are three big-picture items to consider when evaluating how best to execute tax efficient transactions for businesses. These can be viewed as the three legs of a stool that provides the foundation for effective tax planning, as shown in **Illustration 2.1**.

- The Internal Revenue Service (IRS) is a potential uninvited third party to *all* financial transactions, which means the tax implications for all transactions need to be considered.
- The goal of tax planning is not to minimize taxes, but to *maximize after-tax income*, given a business's spending and investing goals.
- Businesses should consider both tax costs and non-tax costs when evaluating transactions. While businesses often ignore the tax effects of a transaction because of a lack of knowledge, tax professionals should focus on both the tax costs and the relevant non-tax costs.

ILLUSTRATION 2.1 Foundation for Effective Tax Planning

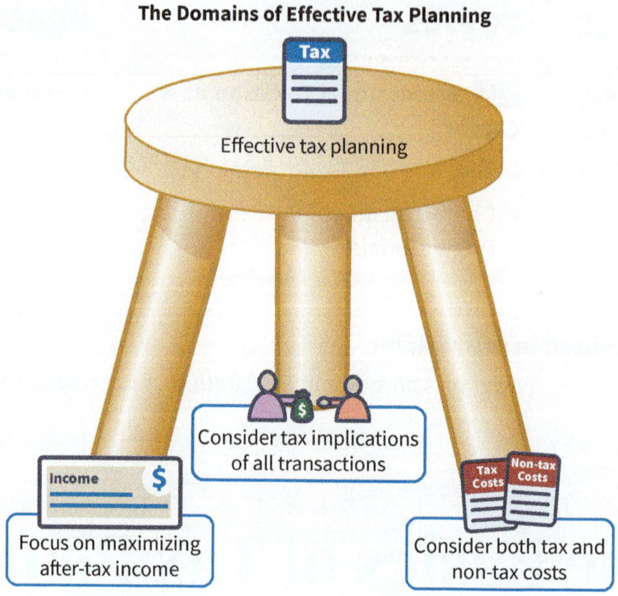

The IRS: An Uninvited Third Party

The services of tax professionals are in high demand because there is a potential tax effect for every business transaction, including transactions between business owners and their businesses. Thus, the Internal Revenue Service (IRS) is a potential uninvited third party to every financial transaction. If businesses do not understand the tax consequences of their transactions, poor decisions can result.

If a business knows the tax consequences *before* a transaction occurs, it has three options:

- If satisfied with the tax results, the business finalizes the transaction.
- If not satisfied with the tax results, the business seeks advice to find a more tax-efficient way to structure the transaction.
- If a satisfactory tax result is not possible, the business may decide not to pursue the transaction.

Once a business understands the tax consequences of a particular transaction, it can move on to the tax planning stage, which we discuss in the next section.

The Goal of Tax Planning

Is the outcome of appropriate tax planning for you to minimize a business's tax liability for the year? Were that the goal, then the ultimate success would be to reduce a business's tax liability to zero—actually an easy goal to meet. If a business had no income for the year, then it would have no tax liability, and you would have minimized its taxes. But the business's owners and shareholders would not be very happy, so this cannot be the proper goal.

The appropriate goal for tax planning is to maximize *after-tax income* given a business's operational circumstances. **After-tax income** is net income after reducing revenue for all expenses, including federal income taxes. Conceptually, the goal for any business is to make as much net profit as it can and, in the process, structure its transactions in the manner that is the most tax efficient.

Related exercise: Discussion Question 1

EXAMPLE 2.1.1 Maximizing After-Tax Income

Carolinda owns a large manufacturing company and plans to build a new manufacturing plant in either Florida or Ohio. Her chief financial officer presents her with the following annual projections for placing the plant in each state.

	Revenue	Non-income tax costs	Income tax
Florida	$800,000	$600,000	$ 80,000
Ohio	$900,000	$525,000	$150,000

Carolinda has told you that she is leaning toward choosing Florida because the income taxes are much lower than in Ohio. She asks for your advice.

SOLUTION

There are several ways to evaluate the two alternatives.

- Which choice maximizes revenue? Ohio: $900,000 vs. $800,000
- Which choice minimizes taxes? Florida: $80,000 vs. $150,000
- Which choice maximizes after-tax income?

Florida:	$120,000	($800,000 – $600,000 – $80,000)
Ohio:	$225,000	($900,000 – $525,000 – $150,000)

You should advise Carolinda that Ohio maximizes her company's after-tax income. The goal of tax minimization would have led to a suboptimal choice of Florida.

Related exercise: Brief Exercise 1

Considering Tax Costs and Non-Tax Costs

Both tax and non-tax costs must be considered when making financial and investment decisions. **Tax costs** include any type of tax paid to a local, state, federal, or foreign government. **Non-tax costs** include all expenses other than tax costs, as well as non-financial factors such as risk, location, brand reputation, and sustainability concerns. Let's focus first on the problems that can arise if you do not include the factors that determine tax costs in the decision-making process. While taxpayers often ignore the tax effects of a transaction, tax professionals can overweigh the tax consequences if they do not consider the relevant non-tax costs or non-financial factors. Effective tax planning requires consideration of both tax and non-tax costs. **Illustration 2.2** lists common types of tax costs, non-tax expenses, and non-financial factors.

ILLUSTRATION 2.2 Tax and Non-Tax Costs

Common Types of Tax and Non-Tax Costs

Tax costs	Non-tax expenses	Non-financial factors
• Federal, state, local, and foreign income taxes • State, local, and foreign property taxes • State, local, and foreign sales taxes • Foreign value-added taxes • Federal excise taxes • Federal, state, local, and foreign payroll taxes	• Salaries and fringe benefits • Land and buildings • Machinery, equipment, furniture, and fixtures • Energy costs • Shipping costs • Other operating costs	• Risk • Location • Brand reputation • Sustainability concerns

Tax Planning Opportunities

This section introduces a framework that you can use to identify tax planning opportunities. Certain situations are often useful for evaluating different tax planning alternatives and determining which is the most efficient. When evaluating tax planning alternatives, you should always use the *marginal tax rate*. The **marginal tax rate** is the tax rate applied to the next additional dollar of income earned.

Rates Vary across Time Periods

When marginal tax rates change across time periods, opportunities for tax planning are available.

- If rates are *increasing* in the future, it is best to accelerate income and defer deductions in the current year.
- If rates are *decreasing* in the future, it is best to accelerate deductions and defer income in the current year.

Rates can also vary across time periods because Congress changes the tax rates.

Related exercises: Discussion Questions 2, 3
Multiple Choice Question 1

The next Example shows how tax rate changes over time present tax planning opportunities.

EXAMPLE 2.1.2
Changing Tax Rates

Jiera is the sole shareholder of an S corporation and is in the 32% tax bracket for Year 20. Due to changes in her income, next year her tax bracket will be 37%. The S corporation plans to make a $100,000 donation to the College of Business at Jiera's alma mater. She has asked your advice about the timing of the donation. Assume that once the contribution flows to her from the S corporation, she can deduct the fair market value of the contribution on her return for the year it is made.

SOLUTION

Jiera's tax savings for the contribution will be determined by her marginal tax bracket.

	Year 20	**Year 21**
Contribution	$100,000	$100,000
× Marginal tax rate	× 32%	× 37%
Tax savings	$ 32,000	$ 37,000
Net cost of contribution	$ 68,000	$ 63,000

Jiera should wait until next year for the S corporation to make the contribution, because she will save $5,000 more in taxes ($68,000 – $63,000) than if the S corporation makes the contribution in Year 20. This reduces the cost of the contribution by 5% ($5,000/$100,000).

Related exercises: Application Problems 1, 2, 3, 4

Rates Vary across Jurisdictions

Rates can vary across different jurisdictions—whether at the local, state, or international levels. The tax laws and tax rates vary significantly across these jurisdictions. Forty-four states levy a corporate income tax, with rates ranging from a 2.5% flat rate in North Carolina to a 9.8% top marginal rate in Minnesota. Alaska, Illinois, Minnesota, and New Jersey also have corporate income tax rates of 9% or higher. Twelve states have corporate tax rates of 5% or less (Arizona, Arkansas, Colorado, Indiana, Kentucky, Mississippi, Missouri, North Carolina, North Dakota, Oklahoma, South Carolina, and Utah).[1]

The next Example shows the impact different tax rates in different jurisdictions can have on tax planning.

EXAMPLE 2.1.3 Changing Tax Jurisdictions

Atlas Corporation manufacturers engine components that are installed in Hyundai automobiles assembled in Alabama. Atlas is planning to build a new manufacturing plant and has narrowed the choices for its location to Minnesota and North Carolina. Which location would result in the lowest federal and state income taxes for Atlas?

SOLUTION

The federal corporate income tax rate is a flat 21% and would be the same in either Minnesota or North Carolina, so it is not a factor in the decision. The highest marginal tax rate in Minnesota is 9.8%, while North Carolina has a flat rate of only 2.5%. Therefore, Atlas's business income could be taxed at 7.3% less in North Carolina. While non-tax costs must also be considered in making the final choice, state income taxes would be substantially less in North Carolina.

Related exercise: Discussion Question 4

Corporations involved in global business activities must also consider international tax rates. For example, Barbados has a corporate income tax rate of 9%, while Puerto Rico has a rate of 37.5%. This compares to the flat corporate tax rate of 21% in the United States.[2]

Related exercise: Application Problem 5

Rates Vary across Types of Income

Different tax rates apply to different types of income. Often, a taxpayer's ordinary income is taxed at a higher rate than long-term capital gains, so tax professionals look for opportunities to convert ordinary income into long-term capital gains through the structure of a transaction. Qualified dividend income is also taxed at long-term capital gain rates. Certain types of income are not even taxed at all, such as municipal interest income (interest paid on state and local bonds). The following Example explores a scenario where taxpayers pay different tax rates depending on the type of income received.

[1]Laughead, Katherine. "State Corporate Income Tax Rates and Brackets, 2024." Tax Foundation. 23 Jan. 2024. taxfoundation.org/data/all/state/state-corporate-income-tax-rates-brackets-2024/.
[2]Enache, Cristina. "Corporate Tax Rates around the World, 2024." Tax Foundation. 17 Dec. 2024. taxfoundation.org/data/all/global/corporate-tax-rates-by-country-2024/.

EXAMPLE 2.1.4
Rates Vary across Different Types of Income

Jonathon and Anna are married, and each owns 50% of the stock of a corporation that operates a physical fitness center and spa. Each works at the facility 40 hours per week and receives an annual salary of $75,000. Once their total income is considered, their marginal tax rate is 37%. This year, the spa had an excellent year financially, earning taxable income of $500,000, and Jonathon and Anna plan to receive an additional $20,000 each from the corporation. How would this extra income be treated for tax purposes if it is salary compared to a qualified dividend?

SOLUTION

The additional payment will be taxed at the ordinary income rate of 37% if it is treated as salary. However, if it is a qualified dividend paid to them as shareholders, then the lower long-term capital gain rate of 20% applies. Jonathon and Anna may wish to structure the payment as a dividend for this reason. However, they also need to consider that dividends are not deductible by the corporation, but salaries are (see Example 2.1.5 for more detail).

Related exercise: Discussion Question 5

Rates Vary across Different Types of Taxpayers

Tax rates also can vary across different types of taxpayers. Individual income tax rates in the United States vary from 10% to 37%. Other entities also pay income taxes, such as corporations, which have a flat income tax rate of 21%. Corporations also pay a 21% tax rate on long-term capital gains, whereas individuals pay a rate of 0%, 15%, or 20%. Partnerships, limited liability companies, and S corporations are *flow-through entities.* Rather than paying income taxes themselves, **flow-through entities** flow income through to their owners, who report the income on their tax returns. Other entities, such as estates and trusts, also pay income taxes if they retain the income; their tax rates are the same rates that apply to individuals, but their income is taxed at the highest marginal rate of 37% at taxable income of only $15,650 in 2025.

Corporations have a significantly different tax rate structure than individuals. Corporate taxpayers pay a flat rate of 21%, regardless of the level of income or generally the type of income. Individuals in the highest marginal tax bracket of 37% may consider whether they would prefer to incorporate and have the income taxed at the corporate rate of 21%. The advantage of the lower corporate rate is partially offset, however, by the second level of tax on corporate income when it is distributed to a shareholder as a dividend. Choosing the best structure for a business is a complex decision that we cover extensively in Chapter 9, Choice of Business Entity.

EXAMPLE 2.1.5
Rates Vary Across Taxpayers

Return to the facts of Example 2.1.4. Is the corporate structure best for Jonathon and Anna's business from a tax perspective, or would a partnership be better?

SOLUTION

If Jonathon and Anna's business structure is a corporation, a corporate tax rate of 21% would apply to the $500,000 of business income. Further, the shareholders would be taxed on the dividends (20%) or salaries (37%) received. The corporation would be able to deduct the salaries but not the dividends.

If, however, their business structure is a flow-through entity like a partnership, the $500,000 of taxable income would flow through to Jonathan and Anna, and they would report it on their individual return and pay taxes on it at their marginal rate of 37%. If the partners each receive $20,000 of salary (called a guaranteed payment), the partnership could deduct this, reducing its income to $460,000. The salary and the flow-through income would be taxed at 37%. The tax computations for these scenarios are shown below.

Taxes owed if a corporation and qualified dividend is paid:

Corporate income tax	\$105,000 (\$500,000 × 21%) (no deduction allowed)
Individual income tax	8,000 (\$40,000 × 20%)
Total taxes paid	\$113,000

Taxes owed if a corporation and salary is paid:

Corporate income tax	\$ 96,600 ([\$500,000 − \$40,000] × 21%)
Individual income tax	14,800 (\$40,000 × 37%)
Total taxes paid	\$111,400

Taxes owed if a partnership and \$40,000 salary (guaranteed payment) is made:

Flow-through income	\$460,000 (\$500,000 − \$40,000)
Salary paid to partners	40,000
Total income	\$500,000
Marginal tax rate	× 37%
Total taxes paid	\$185,000

The total taxes paid in the corporate form are much less than the taxes paid as a partnership. The goal of this Example is only to show how tax rates vary across different business entities. The facts are too limited to conclude that the corporate form is better than the partnership form. In Chapter 9, Choice of Business Entity, we provide a comprehensive discussion of the factors that determine the best choice of business entity.

Related exercises: Discussion Question 6
Application Problem 6
Tax Planning Problem 1

Rates Vary within a Family

Tax rates vary across different individuals based on their levels of income. This presents opportunities for tax planning within a family. Many wealthy families are more concerned about the total tax paid by the entire family than they are about the tax paid by any one individual. Placing investment assets in the name of the family members who have lower marginal tax rates results in lower taxes for the family. The *kiddie tax* can reduce or eliminate these savings in some situations.[3]

EXAMPLE 2.1.6 Family Tax Planning

A mother is in the 37% tax bracket, and her 25-year-old son is in the 10% tax bracket. The mother gifts \$100,000 of bonds paying 8% interest to her son. What is the overall tax saving for the family in this scenario?

SOLUTION

The son will pay tax on the \$8,000 of interest income at a 10% rate, a saving of \$2,160 for the family (\$8,000 × [37% − 10%]). The family should also consider whether any gift tax would have to be paid because of the \$100,000 gift.

Related exercise: Brief Exercise 2

[3]If a dependent child has investment income that exceeds a base amount, the *kiddie tax* taxes a portion of the child's investment income at the parent's tax rate. Gift taxes are covered in Chapter 12, Estate and Gift Taxation.

Time Value of Money

The **time value of money** is the concept that funds available today are worth more than the identical sum in the future due to their earnings potential if they are invested. The time value of money presents tax planning opportunities even when there is no change in tax rates across varying time periods, jurisdictions, types of income, or types of taxpayers. Saving a dollar of taxes today is worth more than saving a dollar of taxes next year because of the time value of money. Similarly, paying a dollar of tax next year is better than paying a dollar of tax today.

EXAMPLE 2.1.7
Time Value of Money

Return to the facts of Example 2.1.2. Assume that Jiera's tax rate will be 32% in both Year 20 and Year 21, and that Jiera can earn 5% annually on her cash investments. Are the after-tax consequences the same if the $100,000 donation is made in Year 20 instead of Year 21?

SOLUTION

The amount of tax savings from the donation, $32,000 ($100,000 × 32%), will be the same whether the S corporation makes the contribution in Year 20 or Year 21. But because of the time value of money, reducing Jiera's taxes in Year 20 is better than reducing them in Year 21. If Jiera invests the $32,000 of tax savings from Year 20 and earns 5% interest, she will earn $1,600 ($32,000 × 5%) of interest income during Year 21. Will Jiera be able to keep the entire $1,600 of interest income? No, she must include this in her taxable income for Year 21 and will pay $512 of tax ($1,600 × 32%). So her net positive cash flow from making the contribution in Year 20 versus Year 21 will be $1,088 ($1,600 − $512).

Related exercise: Discussion Question 7

Illustration 2.3 shows how much $1 in the future is worth today at the *discount factor* shown. The **discount factor** is based on the rate of return to determine the present value of future income received or taxes owed. The present value of an amount to be received in the future is computed as:

$$\text{Present value} = \text{Discount factor} \times \text{Future amount to be received}$$

The discount factor for 1 year at 5% interest is 0.952 in Illustration 2.3. This means that with a 5% discount factor, $1,000 received one year from today has a present value of only $952 today (0.952 × $1,000).

The following two Examples explore the time value of money concept.

EXAMPLE 2.1.8
Time Value of Money—Deduction

Franklin Corporation is considering making a $250,000 cash donation to its favorite charity. Assume Franklin qualifies to deduct the full amount of the donation. Based on other cash flow needs for the next five years, Franklin will make the donation either this year or five years from now. Franklin asks you to compute the economic difference between these alternatives. Assume Franklin's marginal tax rate is 21% and the discount factor is 5%.

SOLUTION

The tax savings to Franklin from the donation is $52,500 ($250,000 × 21%). The discount factor for five years at a 5% rate is 0.784. A $52,500 deduction today will be worth only $41,160 ($52,500 × 0.784) if taken five years from now. Franklin's deduction is worth $11,340 more to the company this year ($52,500 − $41,160) than in five years.[4]

[4] If Franklin decides to make the contribution five years from now and invests the money during that time period, then the investments earnings will increase the $41,160 value from the net present value of the charitable contribution.

ILLUSTRATION 2.3 Present Value Table—Present Value of a Single Payment

	Interest rates									
Years	**1%**	**2%**	**3%**	**4%**	**5%**	**6%**	**7%**	**8%**	**9%**	**10%**
1	0.990	0.980	0.971	0.962	0.952	0.943	0.935	0.926	0.917	0.909
2	0.980	0.961	0.943	0.925	0.907	0.890	0.873	0.857	0.842	0.826
3	0.971	0.942	0.915	0.889	0.864	0.840	0.816	0.794	0.772	0.751
4	0.961	0.924	0.888	0.855	0.823	0.792	0.763	0.735	0.708	0.683
5	0.951	0.906	0.863	0.822	0.784	0.747	0.713	0.681	0.650	0.621
6	0.942	0.888	0.837	0.790	0.746	0.705	0.666	0.630	0.596	0.564
7	0.933	0.871	0.813	0.760	0.711	0.665	0.623	0.583	0.547	0.513
8	0.923	0.853	0.789	0.731	0.677	0.627	0.582	0.540	0.502	0.467
9	0.914	0.837	0.766	0.703	0.645	0.592	0.544	0.500	0.460	0.424
10	0.905	0.820	0.744	0.676	0.614	0.558	0.508	0.463	0.422	0.386
11	0.896	0.804	0.722	0.650	0.585	0.527	0.475	0.429	0.388	0.350
12	0.887	0.788	0.701	0.625	0.557	0.497	0.444	0.397	0.356	0.319
13	0.879	0.773	0.681	0.601	0.530	0.469	0.415	0.368	0.326	0.290
14	0.870	0.758	0.661	0.577	0.505	0.442	0.388	0.340	0.299	0.263
15	0.861	0.743	0.642	0.555	0.481	0.417	0.362	0.315	0.275	0.239
16	0.853	0.728	0.623	0.534	0.458	0.394	0.339	0.292	0.252	0.218
17	0.844	0.714	0.605	0.513	0.436	0.371	0.317	0.271	0.231	0.198
18	0.836	0.700	0.587	0.494	0.416	0.350	0.296	0.250	0.212	0.180
19	0.828	0.686	0.570	0.475	0.396	0.331	0.277	0.232	0.194	0.164
20	0.820	0.673	0.554	0.456	0.377	0.312	0.258	0.215	0.178	0.149

EXAMPLE 2.1.9
Time Value of Money—Income Taxes

Katrina Corporation uses the cash-basis method of accounting. Katrina can choose to invoice a customer for $50,000 during December Year 6 or during January Year 7. Katrina has a marginal tax rate of 21%, and the interest rate is 4%. The company has asked you what the tax benefit would be if customer did not pay until Year 7.

SOLUTION

Katrina's tax due on the $50,000 of revenue would be $10,500 ($50,000 × 21%) whether received in Year 6 or Year 7. Delaying the receipt of the income until Year 7 defers the payment of the tax on the income for a full year. A $10,500 payment in Year 7 only costs Katrina $10,101 ($10,500 × 0.962). The discount factor for 1 year with a 4% interest rate is 0.962. Deferring the revenue to Year 7 reduces the economic cost of the tax payment made by $399 ($10,500 − $10,101).

Related exercises: Discussion Question 8
Multiple Choice Questions 2, 3
Application Problem 7
Tax Planning Problem 2

PRACTICE PROBLEM 2.1.1
Determining Tax Consequences

Barry LLC is a lucrative law practice in New York City that produces a generous profit. Barry LLC members frequently take clients golfing and to New York Yankees games for entertainment. The members believe it is good business to maintain a professional and personal relationship with clients. Barry LLC's members do not understand the tax effect of these expenses and think that they are deductible. How would you advise Barry LLC regarding the tax consequences of these expenditures?

SOLUTION

As Barry LLC's tax accountant, it is your responsibility to determine if expenses incurred are deductible or not. Entertainment expenses are not deductible as a business expense. Therefore, you should advise Barry LLC that it needs to determine how much additional revenue it is generating from these activities compared with the after-tax cost of the entertainment. Because the company cannot deduct the expenses, perhaps it should reduce the amounts spent on these activities.

PRACTICE PROBLEM 2.1.2
Determining Present Value

Gunther owns 100% of a floral shop that operates as an S corporation. He projects that it will have net income of $65,000, $75,000, and $85,000 in Year 1, Year 2, and Year 3, respectively. Assume Gunther has a marginal tax rate of 24% for this net income and a 4% discount factor. Calculate his present value for the net income.

SOLUTION

We can determine the present value with the following calculation:

	Year 1	Year 2	Year 3
Net revenues	$65,000	$75,000	$85,000
Less: Tax at 24%	(15,600)	(18,000)	(20,400)
After-tax cash flow	$49,400	$57,000	$64,600
Discount factor (× 4%)		0.962	0.925
Present value	$49,400	$54,834	$59,755

Total present value is $163,989 ($49,400 + $54,834 + $59,755).

INTERACTIVE SELF-SCORING QUIZZES

2.2 Tax Avoidance vs. Tax Evasion

LEARNING OBJECTIVE 2

Differentiate between tax avoidance and tax evasion.

VIDEO CONTENT

As a tax professional, you must understand the difference between *tax avoidance* and *tax evasion*. **Tax avoidance** is structuring a transaction or arranging your financial affairs in a legal manner to maximize after-tax income. It is reasonable to expect individuals and businesses to avoid taxes, as expressed by a former senior judge of the United States Court of Appeals for the Second Circuit, Learned Hand:

> Anyone may arrange his affairs so that his taxes shall be as low as possible; he is not bound to choose that pattern which best pays the treasury. There is not even a patriotic duty to increase one's taxes. Over and over again the Courts have said that there is nothing sinister

in so arranging affairs as to keep taxes as low as possible. Everyone does it, rich and poor alike and all do right, for nobody owes any public duty to pay more than the law demands.[5]

Tax evasion is reducing tax liability illegally. Most situations are "black and white," meaning that the taxpayer (or tax professional) can clearly distinguish between tax avoidance and tax evasion. Timing a charitable donation (as discussed in several examples in the previous section) to achieve the most efficient tax outcome is tax avoidance. Alternatively, intentionally omitting $5,000 of cash income from a tax return is tax evasion. The more challenging situations for tax professionals are the "gray" issues where there is ambiguity concerning the appropriate tax outcome. Navigating these decisions requires experience, good judgment, and integrity, as we will see in this section.

Tax Evasion

Tax evasion can be intentional or inadvertent. Inadvertent tax evasion occurs when a business does not realize that the position taken on a tax return was impermissible. The IRS does distinguish between intentional and inadvertent tax evasion when assessing penalties against taxpayers (see Chapter 1, LO2, Tax Compliance for Business Entities, for more discussion). Tax evasion is a significant issue, particularly for income taxes. The IRS has estimated that $1 out of every $6 (about 16%) that should be paid as federal income taxes is not paid. This percentage resulted in underpayment of taxes of approximately $696 billion in 2022.[6] Many different types of income contribute to this underreporting tax gap, as shown in **Illustration 2.4**. The federal budget deficit was $1.4 trillion in 2022, meaning that underpaid taxes accounted for approximately 49% of the federal budget deficit that year.

Related exercise: Brief Exercise 3

ILLUSTRATION 2.4 Share of the Individual Income Tax Underreporting Tax Gap by Income Type (2022)[7]

Income type	Share of the individual income tax underreporting tax gap
Nonfarm proprietor income	31%
Partnership and S corp income	11%
Capital gains	8%
Income offsets	7%
Rents and royalties	7%
Earned income tax credit	6%
Other income	6%
Child tax credit and additional child tax credit	4%
Unallocated marginal effects	4%
Taxable Social Security benefits	3%
Farm income	2%
Filing status	2%
Pensions and annuities	2%
Wages, salaries, tips	2%
All other credits	1%
Education credits	1%
Form 4797 income	1%
Interest income, dividend income, state income tax refunds, and unemployment compensation	1%
Other taxes	1%

[5]*Gregory v. Helvering*, 69 F.2d 809, 810 (2d Cir. 1934).

[6]Department of the Treasury. *Federal Tax Compliance Research: Tax Gap Projections for Tax Years 2022*, Publication 5869 (Rev. 10-2024). Catalog Number 94404A. Page 11, Table 1. Internal Revenue Service, October 2024, www.irs.gov/pub/irs-pdf/p5869.pdf.

[7]Department of the Treasury. *Federal Tax Compliance Research: Tax Gap Projections for Tax Years 2022*, Publication 5869 (Rev. 10-2024). Catalog Number 94404A. Page 15, Table 4. Internal Revenue Service, October 20243, www.irs.gov/pub/irs-pdf/p5869.pdf.

Compliance with tax laws varies significantly across different types of income. It is highest when someone other than the taxpayer is required to report income to the IRS, such as corporations reporting dividends paid to shareholders on Form 1099-DIV, or employers reporting wages on Form W-2, Dividends and Distributions. **Illustration 2.5** shows an estimate of the percentage of income underreported by income type. The percentage ranges from near zero for wages to 64% for income from farms.[8] While the noncompliance rate for farmers is high, an analysis of IRS data shows that the average amount of underreported farm income was less than $4,500, which is significantly less than the amount from bars and restaurants.[9]

ILLUSTRATION 2.5 Percentage of Income Underreported by Income Type[10]

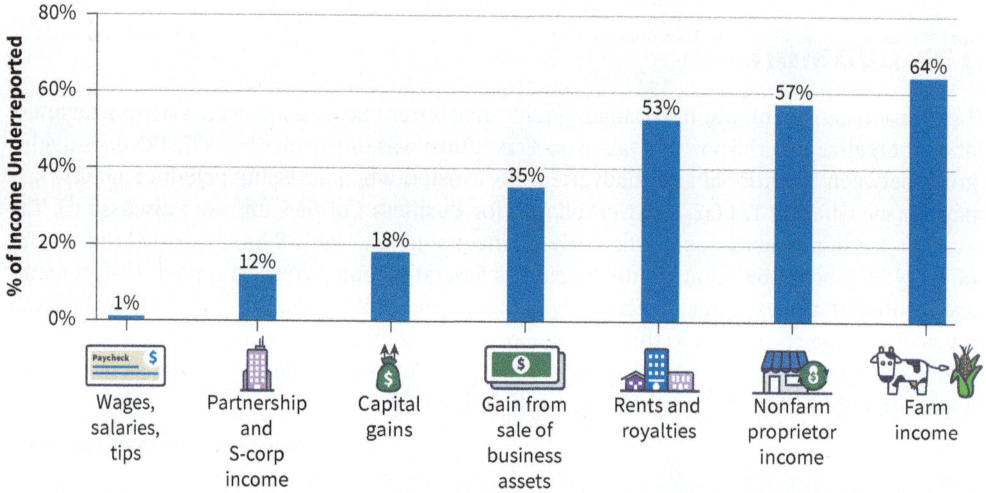

Income tax fraud is far too prevalent, and several celebrities and athletes have been involved in well-publicized cases after failing to pay the taxes they should have.

- Jeffrey Bruce Atkins, more commonly known as the rapper Ja Rule, pled guilty to not filing tax returns from 2004 to 2008. He owed over $1,000,000 in back taxes and penalties and was sentenced to 28 months in prison.
- The first reality TV show to capture the interest of America was *Survivor*, which first aired in 2000. The first winner, Richard Hatch, was well known to many people, as over 125 million viewers watched some part of that initial season. Richard Hatch was the lone survivor, but he could not survive the reach of the IRS when he failed to report his $1,000,000 prize as income. In May 2006, he was sentenced to 57 months in prison.
- Willie Nelson owed the IRS $16.7 million for back taxes, which his lawyer managed to negotiate down to $6 million. Because he lacked the funds to pay off the taxes, Nelson recorded the album, *The IRS Tapes: Who'll Buy My Memories?*, which was sold for the sole purpose of paying his IRS debt.
- *Jersey Shore* star Mike "The Situation" Sorrentino pled guilty to tax evasion in January 2018. He had failed to pay taxes on approximately $9 million in earnings from 2010 to 2012. He was sentenced to eight months in prison in October 2018.

Related exercise: Discussion Question 9

[8]Department of the Treasury. *Federal Tax Compliance Research: Tax Gap Estimates for Tax Years 2014-2016.* Publication 1415 (Rev. 10-2022). Catalog Number 10263H. Page 20, Table 5. Internal Revenue Service, October 2022, www.irs.gov/pub/irs-pdf/p1415.pdf.

[9]Key, Nigel. "Do Most U.S. Farms Really Lose Money? Taxation and Farm Income Underreporting." *Journal of Agriculture and Applied Economics.* 29 July 2019. *51*(4), 646–663. www.cambridge.org/core/journals/journal-of-agricultural-and-applied-economics/article/do-most-us-farms-really-lose-money-taxation-and-farm-income-underreporting/07973ADEDF444329591350988BA3D5B5.

[10]Department of the Treasury. *Federal Tax Compliance Research: Tax Gap Estimates for Tax Years 2014-2016.* Publication 1415 (Rev. 10-2022). Catalog Number 10263H. Page 20, Table 5. Internal Revenue Service, Oct. 2022, www.irs.gov/pub/irs-pdf/p1415.pdf.

Spotlight on the Law

Is the Tax Law Unconstitutional?

The Sixteenth Amendment of the Constitution, ratified in 1913, states that "Congress shall have power to lay and collect taxes on incomes, from whatever source derived, without apportionment among the several States, and without regard to any census or enumeration."

Nevertheless, many taxpayers argue that the imposition of income taxes is unconstitutional. Can taxpayers refuse to pay taxes based on religious or moral grounds by invoking the First Amendment? Can a taxpayer refuse to pay taxes because they believe that the Internal Revenue Service is not an agency of the United States? Can a taxpayer refuse to pay taxes because they believe that compelled compliance with the federal income tax laws is a form of servitude in violation of the Thirteenth Amendment?

Many claims have been made since 1913, but the courts have held firm that such claims are frivolous, and that the Sixteenth Amendment is constitutional. In *United States v. Lee*, 455 U.S. 252 (1982), the Supreme Court held that religious beliefs in conflict with the payment of taxes provide no basis for refusing to pay the tax, stating "The tax system could not function if denominations were allowed to challenge the tax system because tax payments were spent in a manner that violates their religious belief." Also, in *United States v. Fern*, 696 F.2d 1269 (11th Cir. 1983), the Eleventh Circuit declared, "Clearly, the Internal Revenue Service is a 'department or agency' of the United States." And courts have consistently found arguments that taxation constitutes a form of involuntary servitude to be frivolous and not in violation of the Thirteenth Amendment. In Rev. Rul. 2005-19, 2005-1 C.B. 819 and in Notice 2010-33, 2010-17 I.R.B. 609, the IRS discussed this frivolous argument in more detail and warned taxpayers against making such claims.

The tax law is constitutional. Taxpayers may disagree with its formation and results, but nonetheless, must comply and pay their taxes. It is, however, appropriate for taxpayers to hire tax professionals to assist them in structuring their transactions and businesses so they do not overpay their taxes.

Tax Ethics

Because taxpayers do not wish to pay fees for answers to black-and-white issues, your clients are more likely to ask for your assistance with gray issues. Tax professionals spend a significant percentage of their time addressing ambiguous areas of the tax law. The proper application of the tax law can be uncertain because either the facts are unclear, or the law is unclear, or both. If the facts are unclear, you must show proper diligence to clarify or find them (though, as you will learn, in some cases the facts are not available). When the law is unclear, you must apply the most relevant tax authority that exists to the current facts. We will discuss how to handle ambiguous issues in more detail in Chapter 16, LO2, Locating and Evaluating Authority. For now, realize that tax professionals spend significant time working in areas of uncertainty and must exercise proper professional judgment to represent their clients in an appropriate manner. Working with ambiguous tax issues creates an environment where tax professionals must be committed to ethical behavior. Tax professionals should serve as advocates for their clients within the parameters allowed by the law and their professional standards.

One of the characteristics of a profession is that it has a code of conduct. The accounting profession has the AICPA's *Code of Professional Conduct*, which applies to all CPAs, including those who are tax professionals. The AICPA disciplines members of the profession who do not adhere to the code. Because tax professionals so often must make judgments when providing tax advice, the ethical environment in which they operate is very complex. The business and legal communities expect them to make decisions that are reasonable given the circumstances. The Sixth Circuit Court of Appeals provided a helpful description of these expectations in a case from 2006:

> A taxpayer is not required to be perfect for this would be an unrealistic expectation. Even tax specialists cannot be perfect. The Code is complex. Reasonable minds can differ over tax reporting and sometimes the IRS disallows certain transactions. Every time a transaction is challenged or disallowed, the taxpayer is not liable for penalties. Only those taxpayers who fail to meet the applicable standard of care—to do what

a reasonable taxpayer would do under the circumstances—can be slapped with negligence penalties and interest. Again, perfection is not required, but when the predators are circling, no reasonable ostrich sticks its head in the sand.... The ostrich that does pays the penalty.[11]

To be confident of your decisions when dealing with complex tax scenarios, you need three traits (shown in **Illustration 2.6**):

- Excellent knowledge of the tax law
- Problem-solving and critical-thinking skills
- Integrity to anchor your decisions and judgments

ILLUSTRATION 2.6 Traits for Confident Tax Planning

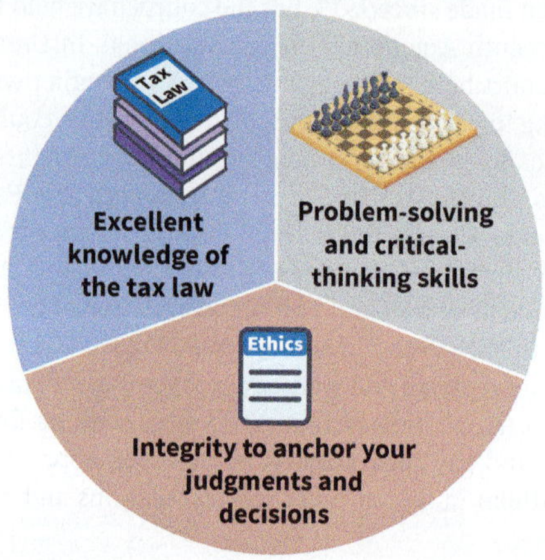

French philosopher Albert Camus said, "Integrity has no need of rules." Integrity will help you discern the difference between practicing tax avoidance and slipping into an aggressive mindset that can lead to tax evasion. In LO4, Tax Professional Responsibilities, we review the standards of professional responsibility that apply to tax professionals. Our goal is to help you develop the three traits listed above so you will have a prosperous and rewarding tax career.

EXAMPLE 2.2.1 Tax Avoidance

Tax avoidance is exemplified in which of the following situations?

a. Aztec Corporation made its fourth-quarter income tax payment in December.

b. Aztec Corporation elected Section 179 to expense the $850,000 it spent this year on tangible personalty.

c. Aztec Corporation structured the disposition of its business's storefront property in such a way as to defer paying income taxes in the current year.

d. Aztec Corporation is setting up a flexible spending arrangement (FSA) for its employees.

SOLUTION

The last three situations (**b–d**) are examples of ways for a taxpayer to reduce current taxes legally. Electing Section 179 is a legal method to reduce current income taxes An FSA allows employees to set aside funds for healthcare and dependent care on a tax-free basis. Making the fourth-quarter estimated tax payment in December is not an example of tax planning because that is when the payment due for corporation.

Related exercises: Discussion Question 10
Multiple Choice Questions 4, 5

[11]G.A. Mortensen, CA-6, 2006-1 USTC ¶50,194, 440 F3d 375, at 385. The ostrich was once thought to place its head in the sand to hide from danger, when this would actually create a more dangerous situation for survival.

PRACTICE PROBLEM 2.2.1
Tax Evasion

Which of the following is an example of tax evasion?

- **a.** Fred Inc. transposed a dividend income number on its Form 1120.
- **b.** Fred Inc. omitted $8 of interest earned from a savings account.
- **c.** Fred Inc. did not report cash receipts of $38,000 from its business.
- **d.** Fred Inc. reported a deduction that it had researched and had concluded was deductible, but the IRS determined it was not deductible.

SOLUTION

The correct answer is **c.** Fred Inc. must report all income. Omission of *de minimis* income is not considered to be tax evasion, but the amount involved here—$38,000—is not *de minimis*, and omitting it is tax evasion

INTERACTIVE SELF-SCORING QUIZZES

2.3 Tax Rules vs. GAAP

LEARNING OBJECTIVE 3

Compare the appropriate accounting methods to use when complying with tax rules and with GAAP rules.

VIDEO CONTENT

As an accounting major, you have spent many hours learning the generally accepted accounting principles (GAAP) that apply to financial reporting. **Do not extend the logic of GAAP to the tax laws. The reporting systems are for two diverse purposes, so many of the rules are different.** In this text, you will learn the tax accounting rules, many of which differ from GAAP. This may lead you to ask: Why is there not just one set of reporting standards for both financial accounting *and* tax accounting? That would be much less complex, not only for you as a student, but also for businesses.

Do not extend the logic of GAAP to the tax laws. The reporting systems are for two diverse purposes, so many of the rules are different.

Why **Why do the financial accounting rules and tax accounting rules differ?** The reason for the different rules is that they exist for very different purposes. The purpose of GAAP is to provide financial statements that are useful for decision-making by investors, creditors, employees, and other users. To be useful, the statements must be relevant. To be relevant, businesses must adhere to certain principles. The **matching principle** requires a business to record expenses incurred during the same period it recognizes the related revenue as earned. This ensures that the business does not overstate income. The **conservatism principle** requires that a business recognize expenses and liabilities as soon as possible, even when there is some uncertainty about the existence of the liability, but recognize revenues and assets only when they are assured of being received. Because outside investors rely on the financial statements to make important decisions, these principles protect the public trust.

The main purpose of the tax laws, by contrast, is to generate revenue to fund the federal government. This is a very different purpose from providing financial information useful to investors for decision-making. One important area where the tax rules differ from the rules for financial reporting is the timing of recognizing expenses. The tax law does not usually allow taxpayers to estimate expenses; rather, no expense is recorded until the taxpayer knows the amount of the expense with certainty.

Related exercise: Brief Exercise 4
Discussion Question 11

EXAMPLE 2.3.1
Tax Rules vs. GAAP

Akio's Laptops began business this year and manufactures and repairs computers. In the current year, laptop sales totaled $500,000. The laptops come with a three-year limited warranty. Akio reports on the accrual basis for both tax and financial reporting, and at year-end, he has accounts receivable of $60,000. Industry data shows that he will not collect approximately 8% of the receivables and that he will incur warranty expense equal to 10% of sales. The amount of bad debts Akio has written off this year is $2,000, and the amount of warranty expense he incurred is $8,000. Akio has asked you whether he should treat these items the same for financial reporting and the business's tax return. What should you tell Akio?

SOLUTION

Akio will report revenue of $500,000 for both financial reporting and taxes. Due to the matching and conservatism principles used for financial reporting, he will use the allowance method of reporting bad debts and will record bad debt expense of $4,800 ($60,000 × 8%). Similarly, Akio must create a warranty expense reserve of $50,000 ($500,000 × 10%). His financial reporting entries would be as follows:

Financial Reporting Entries:

Bad debt expense $4,800

    Allowance for doubtful accounts $4,800

Warranty expense $50,000

    Warranty reserve $50,000

The income tax law does not permit the use of the allowance method to report bad debt expense. The tax law requires use of the direct write-off method; that is, Akio cannot expense an account receivable until he knows the specific customer cannot pay the bill. He also cannot expense warranty repairs until incurred. His tax reporting entries would thus be as follows

Tax Reporting Entries:

Bad debt expense $2,000

    Accounts receivable $2,000

Warranty expense $8,000

    Cash $8,000

Understanding the different purposes of the financial reporting system and the tax laws will help you remember the most important differences in these rules.

PRACTICE PROBLEM 2.3.1
Reporting Payments

Nigel operates his own construction business and frequently makes payments to influence politicians and in that way to receive licenses and permits at a quicker pace than his competitors. Nigel spent $10,000 for these bribes in the current year. How are these payments handled for financial and tax reporting?

SOLUTION

Under GAAP, these payments are reported as a deduction on the income statement. However, the tax law does not allow a deduction for payments against public policy.

INTERACTIVE SELF-SCORING QUIZZES

2.4 Tax Professional Responsibilities

LEARNING OBJECTIVE 4

Distinguish between professional and unprofessional actions related to tax professionals' role with clients.

VIDEO CONTENT

Tax professionals have ethical and professional responsibilities to which they must adhere. There is a difference between a tax preparer and a tax professional in the context of professional responsibilities. Anyone who prepares a tax return for compensation is a **tax preparer** and is required to have a preparer tax identification number (PTIN). Failure to have a current PTIN could result in the imposition of a penalty ($65 per return, maximum of $32,500 per year; 2025) and also disciplinary action by the IRS. However, there are few requirements to qualify for a PTIN, the primary one being that you must be at least 18 years old.

An individual who is authorized to practice before the IRS (see below) is a **tax practitioner**. Generally, this right is limited to CPAs, attorneys, and enrolled agents. An **enrolled agent** is a person who has passed a three part comprehensive IRS test covering individual and business tax returns, or who has substantial experience as a former IRS employee.

In this section, we review the professional responsibilities provided by the IRS's *Circular 230* and the AICPA's *Statements on Standards for Tax Services* (SSTS).

Circular 230

Circular 230 contains the IRS's rules of practice governing CPAs, attorneys, enrolled agents, and others authorized to practice before the IRS. The government may censure, fine, suspend, or disbar tax advisors from practice before the IRS if they violate Circular 230's standards of conduct.

Related exercise: Discussion Question 12

Practice before the IRS

Circular 230 sets forth rules governing authority to practice before the IRS. An individual must belong to one of the following groups to practice before the IRS:

- Attorneys
- CPAs
- Enrolled agents
- Enrolled actuaries[12]
- Enrolled retirement plan agents[13]

CPAs may practice before the IRS by filing with the IRS a written declaration that they are currently qualified as a CPA and are authorized to represent taxpayers.

Practice before the IRS includes conducting all matters related to a presentation to the IRS or any of its officers or employees about a taxpayer's rights, privileges, or liabilities under IRS laws or regulations. These matters include but are not limited to:

- Preparing documents
- Filing documents

[12]Enrolled by the Joint Board for the Enrollment of Actuaries; their practice is generally limited to issues related to qualified retirement plans.

[13]Practice is limited to issues related to employee plans and to IRS forms in the 5300 and 5500 series.

- Corresponding and communicating with the IRS
- Rendering written advice about transactions that have the potential for tax avoidance or evasion
- Representing a client at conferences, hearings, and meetings

Related exercise: Multiple Choice Question 6

A tax professional must have a power of attorney from their client to represent the client before the IRS. A **power of attorney** gives one individual the legal right to represent another for the matters specified in the power, which usually include financial and/or medical issues. A power of attorney is granted by filing Form 2848, Power of Attorney and Declaration of Representative.

Substantive Provisions of Circular 230

The substantive provisions of Circular 230 are the professional responsibilities that CPAs and others must follow when practicing before the IRS. These are the most common:

- **Furnish information** A practitioner must promptly submit to the IRS any records or information that IRS agents and officers properly and lawfully request, unless the practitioner believes in good faith and on reasonable grounds that the records or information are privileged. **Privileged information** applies to communications between a tax practitioner and a taxpayer to the extent that the communication would be privileged if it were between an attorney and a taxpayer. This privilege for a tax professional is limited to noncriminal matters and does not apply to communications regarding tax shelters. A **tax shelter** is defined as a plan or arrangement where a significant purpose is the avoidance or evasion of federal income tax.[14]
- **Correct client's omission** What if you learn that your client has not complied with the laws or has made an error or omission on a tax return? Consistent with AICPA ethics guidelines, you must promptly notify the client of the error and its potential consequences. You may not notify the IRS of the error without your client's permission.

EXAMPLE 2.4.1 Error on Prior Return

Virginia has practiced as a CPA for the past 10 years. This year, she picked up a new client, Douglas, who owns a manufacturing company. Douglas provided Virginia with his tax returns for the past two years. While reviewing them, she discovered that he had been using an improper method to value inventory. Using the correct method would increase his taxable income by a total of $175,000 for the past two years. What are Virginia's responsibilities under Circular 230 regarding her discovery?

SOLUTION

Virginia must promptly inform Douglas of the error and encourage him to authorize her to file an amended return to correct it. Whether or not Douglas agrees to this, she cannot communicate the information to the IRS. If Douglas does not agree to amend the returns, Virginia needs to consider whether she should retain Douglas as a client.

- **Exercise due diligence and rely on others** Practitioners must exercise due diligence in all aspects of their tax practice. They can rely on the work of others if they use reasonable care in engaging, supervising, training, and evaluating them.
- **Avoid assistance from the disbarred** A practitioner should not accept even indirect assistance from any person disbarred or suspended from practice by the IRS.

[14]IRC §6662(d)(2)(C)(ii).

EXAMPLE 2.4.2 Working with Individuals Disbarred from Practicing before the IRS

Assume you are a CPA. Your former business partner violated IRS regulations and was disbarred from practicing before the IRS. He still needs a job and wants to continue to do the same work as before. He asks whether he can do work for you and have you sign off on everything, as you are still authorized to practice before the IRS. How should you respond to your former partner?

SOLUTION

Circular 230 clearly provides that you cannot receive any assistance, even indirect, from someone disbarred from practicing before the IRS. You must inform your former partner that you cannot agree to his request.

- **Correctly charge contingent fees** A practitioner may not charge a contingent fee for providing services before the IRS, with limited exceptions, such as when representing a client in an IRS examination or a judicial proceeding.
- **Return client records** A practitioner must promptly return all records needed for the client to comply with federal tax obligations. The practitioner may keep a copy.
- **Avoid conflicts of interest** A practitioner should not represent a client before the IRS if doing so would create a conflict of interest. Such a conflict exists if the representation of one client is harmful to the interests of another.
- **Practice ethical solicitation** False advertising is, of course, prohibited. But practitioners may publish accurate written schedules of fees and hourly rates. Unsolicited e-mails and letters are permissible.
- **Avoid negotiating checks** A practitioner who prepares tax returns may not endorse or otherwise negotiate any check issued to a client by the IRS.
- **Avoid practicing law** Tax accountants learn quite a bit of tax law, but Circular 230 is not meant to authorize persons who are not members of the bar to practice law.
- **Adhere to tax return standards** Practitioners must inform clients of reasonably likely penalties that could follow from positions taken. They may generally rely in good faith on information provided by their clients, but may not ignore inconsistent information that comes from their personal knowledge or other red flags that might appear.

EXAMPLE 2.4.3 Return of Tax Records

Joan has been your client for five years. This year, when you billed her for doing the preliminary work on her tax return, she became very angry about the amount and said she would not pay you. She has now informed you that she is taking her business to another CPA and asks that you return her tax information. You tell her that you will return her tax records as soon as she pays for the work you have already performed. Does your decision create any risk for you?

SOLUTION

Yes, this creates tremendous risk, because your action is in violation of Circular 230. You may keep a copy of her tax information, but, whether she pays you or not, you must promptly return all records Joan needs to comply with federal tax obligations.

Penalties and Procedures for Tax Professionals

Circular 230 authorizes the IRS to punish any tax professional who is incompetent or disreputable, who violates the Treasury Department's rules of practice, or who with intent to defraud willfully and knowingly misleads or threatens the person being represented.

The IRS can impose a monetary penalty on practitioners who have violated practice rules. The maximum penalty equals 100% of the gross income derived from the conduct and can be added to other penalties, such as suspensions and censures. This is in addition to the 50% of gross income penalty for taking an unreasonable position, meaning that the penalty could equal 150% of the income derived from an engagement. Unreasonable positions are discussed in Chapter 16, LO3, Tax Preparer Penalties.

Circular 230 lists numerous acts of incompetence or disreputable conduct that are sanctionable, including:

- Being convicted of any crime under federal tax laws
- Being convicted of any crime involving dishonesty or breach of trust
- Being convicted of any state or federal felony that renders the practitioner unfit to practice before the IRS
- Giving false or misleading information to tax officials
- Willfully evading taxes
- Being disbarred or suspended from practice as a CPA or an attorney
- Displaying contemptuous conduct before the IRS

Related exercise: Brief Exercise 5

Statements on Standards for Tax Services (SSTS)

The **Statements on Standards for Tax Services (SSTS)** are issued by the AICPA and provide a summary of the professional responsibilities to which CPAs must adhere when performing tax services. They were originally issued in 2000 and updated in 2009 and 2023. The preface to the SSTS states:

> Standards are the foundation of a profession. The AICPA aids its members in fulfilling their ethical responsibilities by instituting and maintaining standards against which their professional performance can be measured. Compliance with tax professional standards also reaffirms the public's awareness of the professionalism that is associated with CPAs as well as the AICPA....This publication sets forth enforceable tax practice standards for members of the AICPA, known as the Statements on Standards for Tax Services (SSTSs). These statements apply to all members providing tax services, regardless of the jurisdictions in which they practice.

If the AICPA determines that a CPA has violated these standards or other laws or ethical guidelines, the AICPA can do one of the following, depending on the nature of the offense (numbers in parentheses are the numbers of occurrences in 2021):[15]

- Expel or suspend the CPA (74)
- Admonish the CPA in a written public statement (66)
- Require corrective action, such as completing an additional 80 hours of continuing professional education (94)

[15]AICPA. *Annual Report of AICPA Disciplinary Activity, 2021*. www.aicpa-cima.com. For definitions of ethics sanctions and dispositions, see www.aicpa-cima.com/resources/article/definitions-of-ethics-sanctions-disposition. This is the last year for which data was available at the time of publication.

Before 2024, there were seven SSTS. The SSTS have been updated and reformatted, and there are now four, effective January 1, 2024. We present the main topics of each one below as provided in the SSTS. The complete SSTS are available on the AICPA's website.[16] The word "member" refers to a regular member of the AICPA who provides tax services.

SSTS #1: General Standards for Members Providing Tax Services

- A member should determine and comply with the standards, if any, that are imposed by the applicable taxing authority with respect to advising on tax positions.
- A member should promptly inform a taxpayer upon becoming aware of the taxpayer's failure to file a required return, [or] an error in a previously filed return.
- A member should make reasonable efforts to safeguard taxpayer data, including data transmitted or stored electronically.
- A member should exercise appropriate professional judgment and professional care when relying on a tool.

SSTS #2: Standards for Members Providing Tax Compliance Services, Including Tax Return Positions

- A member should determine and comply with the standards, if any, that are imposed by the applicable taxing authority with respect to preparing or signing a tax return.
- Before signing as preparer, a member should take reasonable steps to obtain from the taxpayer the information necessary to provide appropriate answers to all required questions on a tax return.
- When preparing or signing a return, or portion of a return, a member may, in good faith, rely on information furnished, without verification, by the taxpayer or by third parties. However, a member should not ignore the implications of information furnished and should make reasonable inquiries if the information furnished appears to be incorrect, incomplete, or inconsistent either on its face or on the basis of other facts known to the member.
- Unless prohibited by statute, administrative rule, or judicial holdings, a member may use estimates, whether from the taxpayer or other sources authorized by the taxpayer ... if it not practical to obtain exact data and if the member determines that the estimates are reasonable based on the facts and circumstances known to the member.

SSTS #3: Standards for Members Providing Tax Consulting Services

- A member should use professional judgment to ensure that tax advice provided in a tax consulting engagement is competent and based on applicable standards.
- A member has no professional obligation to communicate the impact of subsequent developments that affect advice previously provided to taxpayers, regardless of whether the taxpayers are current clients.

SSTS #4: Standards for Members Providing Tax Representation Services

- The member, and any individuals working with or for the member, should take steps to obtain technical competence in the subject matter involved.
- If, in connection with professional representation, a member becomes aware of taxpayer conduct that may be fraudulent or criminal in nature, the member should consider

[16]Full text available at: www.aicpa-cima.com/resources/download/revised-statements-on-standards-for-tax-services-no-1-4-1-1-2024.

whether to continue a professional or employment relationship with the taxpayer. A member may also recommend a legal consultation.

Related exercises: Multiple Choice Questions 7, 8, 9
Application Problems 8, 9, 10
Tax Planning Problem 3

PRACTICE PROBLEM 2.4.1
Representing a Client before the IRS

You took a tax class as part of the accounting program curriculum at your university. You are not a CPA, but you do prepare returns for compensation for family and friends. If the IRS audits one of your clients, can you represent your client?

SOLUTION

No, you cannot represent your client, because you are not a CPA, an attorney, or an enrolled agent. The other exceptions for practicing before the IRS also do not apply.

PRACTICE PROBLEM 2.4.2
Ethical Considerations when Preparing a Return

In preparing your client's tax return, you notice that you do not have the cost basis for various shares of stock that were sold. Your client gives you permission to call his stockbroker for this information. Can you rely on this third-party information?

SOLUTION

Yes, you may rely on information provided by the stockbroker. Under SSTS 2.3.2, a member has an obligation to examine or verify certain supporting data or to consider information related to another taxpayer when preparing a taxpayer's tax return.

INTERACTIVE SELF-SCORING QUIZZES

2.5 Professional Taxation as a Career

LEARNING OBJECTIVE 5

Discuss career opportunities for tax professionals.

VIDEO CONTENT

Students who choose a career in accounting have many different paths from which to select. The American Institute of Certified Public Accountants (AICPA) has often referred to these varied and rewarding careers as *360 Degrees of Opportunity.* One of these opportunities is a career in taxation. While the general public first thinks of "tax returns" and "compliance" when hearing the word "tax," this is a misperception of the role that many tax professionals play in businesses and accounting firms. Tax careers are more interesting, challenging, and rewarding than most would imagine.

The Role of a Tax Professional

Successful organizations understand that to build long-term business value they must include tax professionals in the strategic planning process. Directors of corporations have a responsibility to their shareholders to manage tax risk and tax strategies. Former IRS Commissioner Doug Shulman made the following comments to the National Association of Corporate Directors (NACD) Corporate Governance Conference.

> I realize that the IRS Commissioner has not customarily addressed the NACD's corporate governance conference, but what I want to discuss with you this afternoon is the important role that boards of directors can play in overseeing tax risk and tax strategies of corporations. After all, taxes are one of the biggest expenses of a corporation, so how they are managed is very important to most corporations.... I also understand that even with all of your sophistication, expertise and experience in business and financial affairs, it's difficult to understand the tax consequences of a complicated business transaction, such as a tax-free reorganization or a hedging transaction, let alone the corporation's overall tax profile as it relates to federal, state, and international taxes. That's why you need to have strong tax departments and outside tax advisors. After all, you have finance experts to help you understand the economic value of hedging transactions, and you need tax experts to help you understand the myriad and complex tax issues facing your company.[17]

Business owners who understand the value of structuring transactions in a tax-efficient way build more value for their investors. Tax professionals add value in a wide range of areas, such as:

- Business tax services
- Financial services
- Private wealth consulting
- Estate planning
- International tax
- State and local taxation
- Tax compliance
- Representing clients that have tax controversies
- Mergers and acquisitions

There are also many jobs in the government sector for tax professionals, including positions with the Internal Revenue Service and state revenue departments.

Characteristics of Successful Tax Professionals

Tax laws become more complex every year at the federal, state, local, and international levels. Building and maintaining a successful business has also become more challenging because the business environment changes so rapidly. At the same time, technological innovation presents new opportunities for analyzing tax data. Successful tax professionals are key strategic partners with business owners. To meet these opportunities and challenges, tax professionals need the following skills:

- Integrity
- Problem-solving skills
- Analytical skills
- Oral and written communication skills

[17]Shulman, Douglas H. *Prepared Remarks Before the 2009 National Association of Corporate Directors Corporate Governance Conference.* 19 Oct. 2009, Washington DC, www.irs.gov/pub/irs-news/ir-09-095.pdf.

- Listening skills
- Research skills
- Technology agility
- Conflict resolution skills

Related exercise: Brief Exercise 6

The most common undergraduate degree for an entry-level position in taxation is an accounting degree. Common graduate degrees for those working in taxation are:

- Master of Science in Taxation
- Master of Accounting with Specialization in Tax
- Doctor of Jurisprudence (J.D.)
- L.L.M. in Taxation (focused taxation degree that builds on J.D.)

Many accounting graduates sit for the CPA exam to become certified in their state. Licensed certified public accountants must maintain minimum continuing professional education credits to keep their license active. Each state has its own rules on how and when this is accomplished. Other certifications that an accounting graduate may obtain include:

- Certified Financial Planner
- Certified Estate Planner
- Enrolled Agent
- Certified Information Systems Analyst

All these certifications are valuable to tax professionals who want to build their reputation as full-service tax accountants who add value to individuals, firms, or businesses.

Related exercises: Discussion Question 13
Multiple Choice Questions 10, 11

PRACTICE PROBLEM 2.5.1
Careers in Accounting

Why is a career in accounting referred to as offering 360 degrees of opportunity?

SOLUTION

Accounting offers 360 degrees of opportunity because of the diversity of choices a student has when selecting a career path. The roles of an accountant vary across business types and industries and have great potential for growth.

INTERACTIVE SELF-SCORING QUIZZES

Review and Practice

Chapter Summary

In this chapter, we began by discussing the goals of tax planning and identified opportunities for tax planning. Next, we explained the distinction between tax avoidance and tax evasion, as the former is legal, but the latter can result in criminal sanctions for the taxpayer and the preparer. We then explained why the tax law varies from GAAP and reminded you not to confuse the two accounting systems. Given that a CPA is a member of a profession, we next discussed the professional responsibilities of a CPA—the foundation that the tax professional must use for decision making. We concluded the chapter with a summary of the great career opportunities that are available in taxation.

1 Explain the opportunities for tax planning.

- The Internal Revenue Service is a potential uninvited third party to *all* financial transactions.
- The goal of *tax planning* is not to minimize taxes but to maximize **after-tax income**.
- While taxpayers often ignore the tax effects of a transaction, tax professionals can overweigh the tax consequences if they do not consider the relevant non-tax costs.
- **Marginal tax rates** should always be used when evaluating tax planning alternatives.
- Variances in rates across time periods, jurisdictions, types of income, and types of taxpayers create tax planning opportunities.
- Saving a dollar of taxes today is worth more than saving a dollar of taxes next year—assuming tax rates are not changing—because of the **time value of money**. Similarly, paying a dollar of tax next year is better than paying a dollar of tax today.

2 Differentiate between tax avoidance and tax evasion.

- Tax professionals must understand the difference between **tax avoidance** and **tax evasion**.
- Integrity helps tax professionals discern the difference between practicing tax avoidance and slipping into an aggressive mindset that can lead to tax evasion.

3 Compare the appropriate accounting methods to use when complying with tax rules and with GAAP rules.

- Do not extend the logic of GAAP to the tax laws. The reporting systems are for two diverse purposes, so many of the rules are different.

4 Distinguish between professional and unprofessional actions related to tax professionals' role with clients.

- Individuals who are authorized to **practice before the IRS** are tax professionals. Generally, this right is limited to CPAs, attorneys, and enrolled agents. Professional responsibilities for tax practice are provided by the IRS's **Circular 230** and the AICPA's **Statements on Standards for Tax Services (SSTS)**.
- Circular 230 contains the IRS's rules of practice governing CPAs, attorneys, enrolled agents, and others authorized to practice before the IRS. The government may censure, fine, suspend, or disbar tax advisors from practice before the IRS if they violate Circular 230's standards of conduct. The Statements on Standards for Tax Services are issued by the AICPA and provide a summary of the professional responsibilities that CPAs must adhere to when performing tax services.

5 Discuss career opportunities for tax professionals.

- Students who choose a career in accounting have many different paths to take for their careers. The American Institute of Certified Public Accountants (AICPA) has often referred to these varied and rewarding careers as *360 Degrees of Opportunity*. One of these opportunities is a career in taxation. Tax careers are more interesting, challenging, and rewarding than most would imagine.

Communication Application

Communication

Maximizing After-Tax Income

(LO1) Do Good Corporation specializes in solar panel manufacturing. It is very concerned with sustainability and how the company's operations impact society. Do Good Corporation aligns its actions with its core value criteria of being green and providing consumers with the ability to use an alternative power source for their homes. Do Good currently has stores located in the Midwest but is looking to expand in the south, in particular, in either Alabama or Florida. The ESG (Environmental, Social, and Governance) officer of Do Good presents you with the following information:

	Revenue	Deductible expenses	Non-deductible expenses	Income tax
Florida	$1,430,000	$540,000	$410,000	$235,850
Alabama	$1,430,000	$490,000	$380,000	$258,500

As Do Good's tax accountant, prepare a memo to the ESG officer providing your suggestion on which state Do Good should choose for its new location.

Solution

Dear ESG Officer,

Thank you for allowing our firm to evaluate Do Good Corporation's option to open a store in Florida or Alabama. Based on the information you provided, we have prepared the following analysis:

	Florida	Alabama
Taxable revenue received	$1,430,000	$1,430,000
Less: Deductible expenses paid	(540,000)	(490,000)
Net taxable income	$ 890,000	$ 940,000
Less: Tax cost	(235,850)	(258,500)
After-tax taxable income	$ 654,150	$ 681,500
Less: Non-deductible expenses paid	(410,000)	(380,000)
After-tax net profit	$ 244,150	$ 301,500

Although Florida and Alabama would have the same gross revenue and Alabama has a slightly higher combined federal and state tax rate, Alabama's after-tax net profit would be greater than Florida's because non-deductible expenses would be lower in Alabama. I would like to discuss both alternatives with you, but we recommend that Do Good open a new location in Alabama.

Please let me know if you have any questions about this analysis or if we can help you with any other accounting and tax questions.

Sincerely,
Carnes and Youngberg, CPAs

Ethics and Professional Responsibility Application

Ethics

PTIN

(LO4) Denny Deviant passed the CPA exam about 30 years ago, but he has long since let his CPA license lapse. He continues to prepare clients' tax returns for payment and prepares about 100 individual tax returns per year. Denny has not bothered to register as a paid tax return preparer and has never had a PTIN in any previous year in which it was required. Can Denny prepare and sign the tax returns for payment?

In addition to the chapter content, see *Statements on Standards for Tax Services* at www.aicpa-cima.com/resources/landing/statements-on-standards-for-tax-services, *Circular 230* at www.irs.gov/tax-professionals/office-of-professional-responsibility-and-circular-230, and Chapter 2, LO4, Tax Professional Responsibilities.

Solution

No. *Circular 230* provides many rules that govern tax practice. Tax professionals must also adhere to the Internal Revenue Code and other Treasury regulations that provide requirements specific to tax professionals. Treas. Reg. §1.6109-2 requires that all paid tax return preparers apply for and receive a PTIN. Failure to include the PTIN on any return is currently subject to a $65 penalty per violation. Denny would thus be subject to a penalty of $6,500 ($65 × 100) for a year in which he prepared 100 individual tax returns. Also, in general, no preparer is required to file returns electronically in a calendar year unless the preparer is required to file at least 10 returns during that calendar year. Preparers required to file fewer than 10 returns during the calendar year may file electronically or on paper. A PTIN is required for a preparer to file electronically.

Key Terms

End-of-Chapter Assessment

Discussion Questions

1. **(LO1)** Describe the goal of tax planning.
2. **(LO1)** Explain why a taxpayer would want to delay receipt of income or accelerate expenses into the current year.
3. **(LO1)** In what circumstances would it be better to accelerate income into the current year?
4. **(LO1)** Discuss why the jurisdiction of a business might affect its after-tax cash flow.
5. **(LO1)** Why is it important to identify the type of income earned or losses incurred?
6. **(LO1)** Which taxpayer, an individual or a corporation, would pay more income tax on a net long-term capital gain of $10,000?
7. **(LO1)** Discuss the phrase "A dollar earned today is worth more than a dollar earned in the future."
8. **(LO1)** Name three tax planning opportunities that taxpayers need to be familiar with.
9. **(LO2)** Which term describes a legal method of reducing taxes?
10. **(LO2)** Why must a CPA be ethical when providing professional tax advice to others?
11. **(LO3)** Why are there two different sets of rules to govern the preparation of financial statements and the preparation of tax returns?
12. **(LO4)** What is Circular 230?
13. **(LO5)** Discuss the different specialty areas in which a person may work as a tax professional.

Multiple Choice Questions

1. **(LO1)** Which tax rate is best to use in tax planning?
   a. Marginal tax rate
   b. Average tax rate
   c. Effective tax rate
   d. None of the these

2. **(LO1)** Which of the following does *not* present a tax planning opportunity?
   a. Difference in tax rates across jurisdictions
   b. Difference in tax rates across time periods
   c. Difference in tax rates across entity types
   d. All are examples of tax planning opportunities.

3. **(LO1)** Which of the following is *not* an appropriate aspect of effective tax planning?
   a. Maximizing after-tax income
   b. Considering tax costs and non-tax costs
   c. Minimizing taxes paid
   d. Considering the tax effects of all financial transactions

4. **(LO2)** Which of the following is an example of tax evasion?
   a. Corporation A accelerates its deductible expenses into December of the current year because it anticipates that its tax rate will be lower next year.
   b. Corporation B purchases equipment in December so it can use Section 179 in the current year for the purchase.
   c. Corporation C owns a candy store (customers may only pay in cash) and does not report any of the $33,000 income received.
   d. Corporation D omits dividend income of $28 from its return because it did not realize it lost the Form 1099-DIV that reported it to the corporation.

5. **(LO2)** Which of the following statements is true concerning tax compliance?
   a. Taxpayers do not have to report income unless it is more than $100.
   b. Tax compliance is generally the same across all types of income.
   c. Tax compliance for farm income is higher than tax compliance for wages.
   d. Tax compliance for wages is higher than tax compliance for farm income.

6. **(LO4)** Which of the following may practice before the IRS?
   a. CPA
   b. Enrolled agent
   c. Attorney
   d. All of these

7. **(LO4)** CPA Rick has for many years prepared the corporate income tax returns for his client, Luka Inc. In preparing this year's return, Rick discovered a material error in last year's return that caused Luka Inc. to substantially underpay its taxes. Which of the following is the best course of action for Rick?
   a. Rick must promptly tell Luka Inc. of the error.
   b. Rick must promptly tell the IRS of the error.
   c. Rick should consider not preparing Luka Inc.'s tax returns in the future if Luka Inc. refuses to bring the error to the IRS's attention.
   d. Rick must promptly tell Luka Inc. of the error, and Rick should consider not preparing Luka's tax returns in the future if Luka Inc. refuses to bring the error to the IRS's attention.

8. **(LO4)** Which of the following statements related to professional responsibilities is false?
   a. IRS's Circular 230 applies only to IRS personnel and does not apply to CPAs representing clients.
   b. The AICPA's Code of Professional Conduct applies to all CPAs.
   c. Anyone who prepares a tax return for compensation must have a preparer tax identification number (PTIN).
   d. AICPA's *Statements on Standards for Tax Services* (SSTS) were updated in 2023.

9. **(LO4)** Which of the following is not an act of incompetence or disreputable conduct under Circular 230?
   a. Being convicted of any crime under federal tax laws
   b. Being convicted of a misdemeanor (driving without a license)
   c. Willfully evading taxes
   d. Giving false or misleading information to tax officials

10. **(LO5)** Which certification is most popular among tax accountants?
    a. Certified Financial Planner
    b. Certified Public Accountant
    c. Attorney
    d. Certified Estate Planner

11. **(LO5)** Which of the following is a possible career in taxation?
    a. Corporate accounting
    b. Public accounting
    c. Government accounting
    d. All of the these

Brief Exercises

1. **(LO1)** Narayani Corporation has taxable income in 2025 of $90,000. Narayani is considering opening a location in Illinois that will generate additional income of $20,000. What would Narayani's federal after-tax income be on the additional $20,000?

2. **(LO1)** Jasmine Inc. has a federal tax rate of 21%. Jasmine gifts stock to a key employee with a fair market value of $50,000 that earns non-qualified dividend income of $4,300 in 2025 (meaning that the dividend income is taxed at ordinary income rates). The employee is in the 12% marginal tax bracket. What is the overall tax saving in this scenario considering only the dividend income and not the gift?

3. **(LO2)** Discuss why tax evasion is a significant issue for the federal government.

4. **(LO3)** What is the main purpose of GAAP and the main purpose of the tax laws?

5. **(LO4)** List three acts of incompetence of a tax professional under Circular 230.

6. **(LO5)** List five characteristics of a successful tax professional.

Application Problems

1. **(LO1)** Sarah is a 20% owner/employee in an S corporation. She has asked for help in determining whether she should receive her $25,000 bonus check in the current year or next year. In the current year, her marginal tax rate is 24%, and she anticipates she will be in the 32% marginal tax bracket next year. What advice can you give Sarah?

2. **(LO1)** What is the after-tax income in the following situations for a corporation in 2025?

   a. Taxable income received of $100,000

   b. Taxable income received of $75,000, tax-exempt revenue received of $25,000

3. **(LO1)** What is the after-tax cost in the following situations if the corporation has additional deductions as stated?

   a. Deductible expense paid of $35,000

   b. Deductible expense paid of $25,000; non-deductible expense paid of $10,000

4. **(LO1)** Kratum Corporation has the following revenue and expenses. Calculate the after-tax net profit for Kratum.

Taxable revenue received	$125,000
Tax-exempt revenue received	$ 15,000
Deductible expenses paid	$ 22,000
Non-deductible expenses paid	$ 5,000

5. **(LO1)** Aroon Inc. will receive a significant increase in income due to the popularity of a new product. Aroon, which is currently located in State A, is considering moving to a new location in State B, which has a lower tax rate, but the store will not open until January of next year.

   However, the federal tax rate is increasing next year. You are able to determine the following information:

	Federal tax rate	State tax rate	Income received
Current year	21%	10% (State A)	$75,000
Next year	28%	5% (State B)	$80,000

   Should Aroon Inc. choose to move to the new location in State B next year and receive income after construction costs of $80,000 or remain in State A and receive income of $75,000?

6. **(LO1)** Butch, single, operates a sole proprietorship with net income of $145,000. Butch's taxable income is also $145,000, including the income from the sole proprietorship. Butch is considering incorporating his business. Calculate the income tax liability for Butch as a sole proprietor (ignoring self-employment tax) and as a corporation in 2025. List two other factors that Butch should consider before deciding to incorporate.

7. **(LO1)** Kurt Inc. has the opportunity to invest in a transaction that will generate $200,000 in before-tax cash flow and taxable income in Year 1.

   a. Calculate the after-tax cash flow.

   b. How does your answer change if Kurt Inc. could restructure the transaction in a way that results in before-tax cash flow and taxable income of $50,000 in Year 1, $100,000 in Year 2, and $50,000 in Year 3? Assume a discount factor of 4% and the same tax rate in Years 1–3.

8. **(LO4)** Alan is a CPA who works long hours at his accounting practice in the city. He has been researching two issues for his client and cannot find absolute tax law on how to treat the positions. Discuss what Alan needs to take a position on a tax return. What is his obligation under the AICPA's Statements on Standards for Tax Services?

9. **(LO4)** While reviewing a new client's prior-year tax returns, a CPA became aware that the client had not properly filed all required federal income tax returns in the past. What should the CPA do in this situation?

10. **(LO4)** Melba Company is a tax client of CPA Buck. Melba is not a great record keeper, and Buck would like to save Melba some money by using estimates rather than incurring great expense in recovering or reconstructing original records. Is this an allowable practice by Buck?

Tax Planning Problems

Planning

1. **(LO1)** Rafael is thinking of starting an office supplies business specializing in home and office delivery. He is not sure what entity type is best from a tax perspective and needs your help. He projects that he will generate net cash flow and taxable income of $50,000 in his first year.

   a. Compare and compute the difference in after-tax cash flow if Rafael structures his business as a C corporation, which has a 21% flat rate, or an S corporation, which has income flowing to him on his personal return at a 24% rate.

   b. What are some other concerns that Rafael should consider?

2. **(LO1)** McKeller Company would like to start a new venture. The owners of the company are currently in the 24% marginal tax bracket and use a 5% discount factor. The company projects that the venture will produce before-tax cash flows of $10,000 in Year 1, $20,000 in Year 2, and $30,000 in Year 3.

   a. Assume that taxable income and the before-tax cash flows are equal in the year received, and compute the present value of the cash flows.

   b. What if the company can defer receipt of cash flow from Year 1 and Year 2 until Year 3? Recompute the present value of cash flows.

   c. Assume the same facts in part a, except the company can delay paying any tax on cash flows from Year 1 and Year 2 until Year 3. Recompute the new present value of cash flows.

   d. Which option provides the best outcome?

3. **(LO4)** A husband prepared his own taxes as married filing separately. His wife hired a CPA to prepare her tax return as married filing separately and asked the CPA not to disclose the information to anyone. The CPA was not retained by the husband for any tax work. The husband believes that his wife's return was negligently prepared and that he was financially harmed. He hired an attorney, without his wife's consent, to pursue a negligence claim against the CPA. The CPA hired an attorney to defend against the negligence claim. To which party, if any, may the CPA disclose the wife's tax return information without the wife's consent?

Professional Development Skills

Communication Problem

Communication

1. **(LO5) Careers in Taxation** Being a full-time accountancy student is exciting and challenging. You are aware that there are many careers within accountancy to choose from, but your interest has been in taxation. Explain to your family why you would like to be a tax accountant and discuss the different career paths within taxation that you can explore.

Ethics and Professional Responsibilities Problem

Ethics

1. **(LO4) Preparing a Tax Return** A friend of yours has approached you about preparing his tax return. You are in your senior year of college taking a taxation course, and everyone keeps asking you questions and seeking your advice on how to prepare their tax returns and get the largest tax refund possible. You have told them that you have only taken one course so far and are not a CPA. Can you prepare your friend's tax return? Can you accept payment?

   In addition to the chapter content, see *Statements on Standards for Tax Services* at www.aicpa-cima.com/resources/landing/statements-on-standards-for-tax-services, *Circular 230* at www.irs.gov/tax-professionals/office-of-professional-responsibility-and-circular-230, and Chapter 2 LO4, Tax Professional Responsibilities.

Research Problem

1. **(LO4) Is the Tax Law Constitutional?** Peter "The Prophet" Verdad is a self-proclaimed prophet who claims that the end of times is near. He earns income as a guest lecturer, from the sale of prophecy books and videos, and as a host at a popular radio station. Peter did not file an income tax return for tax years 2017–2024, claiming that the federal income tax system is unconstitutional. He also claims that he shouldn't have to pay tax because he is essentially the same as a church. What would be your response to Peter if he were your client? Hint: See *Lloyd v. Commissioner*, T.C. Memo. 2020-92 (2020).

CHAPTER 3

Fundamentals of Corporate Taxation

Gorodenkoff/Adobe Stock

Before studying this chapter, you should know or, if necessary, review:

1.1 Basics of Business Entity Taxation

1.2 Fundamentals of Property Transactions

Chapter Introduction

VIDEO CONTENT

Olivia and Aiden are professors of data analytics at A&M University. They have been consulting with a few businesses for the last two years to assist them in creating problem-solving processes for their research and development work. They see significant opportunity to leave the university and do this work full-time. They are considering creating a corporation so that they can have the liability protection that is afforded corporate shareholders. They each plan to invest $400,000 in the business. They will also contribute technology, equipment, and certain intellectual property to the corporation. They have come to you seeking advice on the tax consequences of forming a corporation.

In this chapter, you will learn the tax rules for corporate formations, as well as the basic rules for computing taxable income for a corporation. We also present the most common rules for accounting methods and periods for a corporation, as well as two penalty taxes that a corporation may have to pay if it inappropriately accumulates income. We are not implying that a corporation would be the best business entity choice for Aiden and Olivia, but we do want you to see how the corporate tax laws could impact them.

LEARNING OBJECTIVES	TOPICS	PRACTICE OPPORTUNITIES

1 Compute the tax consequences to the shareholders for a corporate formation.	**3.1 Taxation of Corporate Formations**
	• Section 351 Requirements
	  • Property
	  • Stock
	  • Control Club
	• Receipt of Boot
	• Basis Issues
	  • Shareholder's Basis
	  • Corporation's Basis
	  • Basis Adjustment for Loss Property
	• Debt Relief
	• Holding Period Rules
	  • Shareholder's Holding Period
	  • Corporation's Holding Period
	• Capital Contributed, No Stock Received
	  • Shareholder
	  • Non-shareholder
		• Example 3.1.1 Formation of a Corporation
		• Example 3.1.2 Section 351 Requirements Not Met
		• Example 3.1.3 Property and Services Contributed for Stock
		• Example 3.1.4 Receipt of Boot
		• Example 3.1.5 Basis Issues Related to a Corporation Formation
		• Example 3.1.6 Basis Adjustment for Loss Property
		• Example 3.1.7 Debt Relief on Corporate Formation
		• Example 3.1.8 No Business Purpose for Debt Assumption
		• Example 3.1.9 Holding Period after a Corporate Formation
		• Example 3.1.10 Contribution of Property by a Non-shareholder
		• Practice Problem 3.1.1 Contribution of Property and Services
		• Practice Problem 3.1.2 Liability Assumed by the Corporation

2 Determine the tax consequences of organizational expenses, start-up costs, and syndication costs.	**3.2 Taxation of Costs Incident to Formation** • Organizational Expenses • Start-Up Costs • Syndication Costs	• Example 3.2.1 Determining Deductibility of Corporate Formation Costs • Practice Problem 3.2.1 Amortization of Organizational Costs

3 Compute taxable income for a corporation.	**3.3 Corporate Taxable Income**
	• Corporate Income Tax Formula
	• Corporate Deductions
	  • Charitable Contributions
	  • Dividends Received Deduction
	  • Research and Development Expenses
	  • Corporate Insurance Premiums
	  • Limitations on Deductions
		• Example 3.3.1 LTCG Property Contributions
		• Example 3.3.2 Property Not Used for Tax-Exempt Purpose
		• Example 3.3.3 Reduction for Ordinary Income or STCG
		• Example 3.3.4 Charitable Contribution of Loss Property
		• Example 3.3.5 Contribution of Inventory
		• Example 3.3.6 Timing of Charitable Contribution Deduction
		• Example 3.3.7 Taxable Income Limitation

LEARNING OBJECTIVES	TOPICS	PRACTICE OPPORTUNITIES
		• Example 3.3.8 DRD Holding Period Test • Example 3.3.9 Taxable Income Limit Applies • Example 3.3.10 Taxable Income Limit Applies and Limits Deduction • Example 3.3.11 Taxable Income Limit Applies and Does Not Limit Deduction • Example 3.3.12 Deductibility of Corporate Insurance Premiums • Practice Problem 3.3.1 Corporate Tax Formula • Practice Problem 3.3.2 Calculating a Corporation's Charitable Contribution Deduction • Practice Problem 3.3.3 Assessing DRD for a Corporation with a Foreign Affiliate

4 Apply other special rules for computing corporate taxable income.	**3.4 Other Corporate Tax Issues**
	• Capital Gains and Losses
	• Accounting Methods and Periods
	  • General Rules
	  • Prepaid Income
	  • Change in Accounting Method
	  • Prepaid Expenses
	  • Prepaid Interest
	  • Payments to a Related Party
	  • Inventory Accounting—Small Businesses
	  • Inventory Accounting—Large Businesses
	  • Reconciliation of Book Income and Taxable Income
	  • Net Operating Loss
	  • Reconciliation of Retained Earnings
	• Passive Loss Rules
	• Corporate Alternative Minimum Tax
	  • Applicable Corporation
	  • Adjusted Financial Statement Income
	  • Other Items
		• Example 3.4.1 Capital Gains and Losses
		• Example 3.4.2 Cash vs. Accrual Method
		• Example 3.4.3 Prepaid Service Income
		• Example 3.4.4 Prepaid Interest
		• Example 3.4.5 Prepaid Expenses—Cash Basis—12-Month Rule Not Met
		• Example 3.4.6 Prepaid Expenses—Cash Basis—12-Month Rule Met
		• Example 3.4.7 Prepaid Interest
		• Example 3.4.8 Related-Party Payments
		• Example 3.4.9 Inventory for Small Businesses
		• Example 3.4.10 Lower of Cost or Market
		• Example 3.4.11 M-1 Reconciliation
		• Example 3.4.12 NOL Carrybacks and Carryforwards
		• Example 3.4.13 NOL Computation
		• Example 3.4.14 NOL Carryforward
		• Example 3.4.15 Schedule M-2 Computation
		• Example 3.4.16 Passive Loss Rules
		• Practice Problem 3.4.1 Determining Taxable Income after Assessing Capital Gains and Losses
		• Practice Problem 3.4.2 Cash vs. Accrual Method of Accounting
		• Practice Problem 3.4.3 UNICAP Rules
		• Practice Problem 3.4.4 Calculating Taxable Income from Book Income

5 Calculate the penalty taxes that apply to corporations if earnings are inappropriately accumulated and not distributed to shareholders.	**3.5 Penalty Taxes**
	• Accumulated Earnings Tax (AET)
	• Computing the Accumulated Earnings Tax
	  • Adjustments to ATI
	  • Accumulated Earnings Credit
	• Personal Holding Company (PHC) Tax
	  • Defining a Personal Holding Company
	  • Computing the Personal Holding Company Tax
		• Example 3.5.1 Paying the Penalty Taxes
		• Example 3.5.2 Accumulated Earnings Credit
		• Example 3.5.3 Accumulated Earnings Tax
		• Example 3.5.4 Personal Holding Company Tests
		• Example 3.5.5 Computing the PHC Tax
		• Practice Problem 3.5.1 Calculating the Accumulated Earnings Tax
		• Practice Problem 3.5.2 Calculating the Personal Holding Company Tax

6 Compute the business tax credits available for a corporation.	**3.6 Business Tax Credits**
	• Foreign Tax Credit
	• General Business Credit
	  • Rehabilitation Credit
	  • Small Employer Health Insurance Credit
	  • Work Opportunity Tax Credit (WOTC)
	  • Research Credit
	  • Disabled Access Credit
	  • Employer-Provided Childcare Credit
	  • Employer-Paid Medical and Family Leave Credit
	• Business Energy Credits
		• Example 3.6.1 Foreign Tax Credit
		• Example 3.6.2 General Business Credit Limitation
		• Example 3.6.3 Rehabilitation Credit
		• Example 3.6.4 Work Opportunity Tax Credit
		• Example 3.6.5 Research Credit
		• Example 3.6.6 Disabled Access Credit
		• Example 3.6.7 Employer-Provided Childcare Credit
		• Example 3.6.8 Employer-Paid Medical and Family Leave Credit
		• Practice Problem 3.6.1 Determining the Foreign Tax Credit
		• Practice Problem 3.6.2 Calculating the General Business Credit
		• Practice Problem 3.6.3 Computing the Employer-Provided Childcare Credit

Tax Forms referenced in this chapter

Form 1040, Schedule J	Accumulated Earnings & Profits (E&P) of Controlled Foreign Corporation
Form 1116	Foreign Tax Credit
Form 1120	U.S. Corporation Income Tax Return
Form 1120, Schedule C	Dividends, Inclusions, and Special Deductions
Form 1120, Schedule M-1	Reconciliation of Income (Loss) per Books With Income per Return
Form 1120, Schedule M-2	Analysis of Unappropriated Retained Earnings per Books
Form 1120, Schedule M-3	Net Income (Loss) Reconciliation for Corporations With Total Assets of $10 Million or More
Form 1139	Corporation Application for Tentative Refund
Form 3115	Application for Change in Accounting Method
Form 3468	Investment Credit
Form 3800	General Business Credit
Form 5884	Work Opportunity Credit
Form 6765	Credit for Increasing Research Activities
Form 8826	Disabled Access Credit
Form 8882	Credit for Employer-Provided Child Care Facilities and Services
Form 8941	Credit for Small Employer Health Insurance Premiums
Form 8994	Employer Credit of Paid Family and Medical Leave

3.1 Taxation of Corporate Formations

LEARNING OBJECTIVE 1

Compute the tax consequences to the shareholders for a corporate formation.

VIDEO CONTENT

When business owners form a corporation, a property transaction occurs. Specifically, the owners contribute assets to the corporation, and, in return, they receive stock in the corporation. The owners realize gains and losses on the transaction to the extent that the fair market value of the property they contribute differs from the property's adjusted basis. Congress has provided some good news for the shareholders, in that—if they meet certain requirements—the realized gains and losses from the property transactions are not recognized. Corporations never recognize gains or losses as a result of a corporate formation. Returning to the chapter introduction, Olivia and Aiden would be very interested in learning how they could incorporate without incurring any tax liability from the formation.

Section 351 Requirements

Shareholders must satisfy the following three requirements for gains and losses to be deferred on a corporate formation (see **Illustration 3.1**):[1]

1. Contribute property to the corporation (rather than services)
2. Receive only stock in return from the corporation
3. The *control club* must own 80% or more of the voting power and number of shares of the corporation immediately after the exchange.[2]

The **control club** includes the shareholders who contributed property and received corporate stock. The *80% or more test* is often referred to as the **control test**. The control test is either met for all the shareholders or none of the shareholders.

ILLUSTRATION 3.1 Section 351 Requirements for Corporate Formation

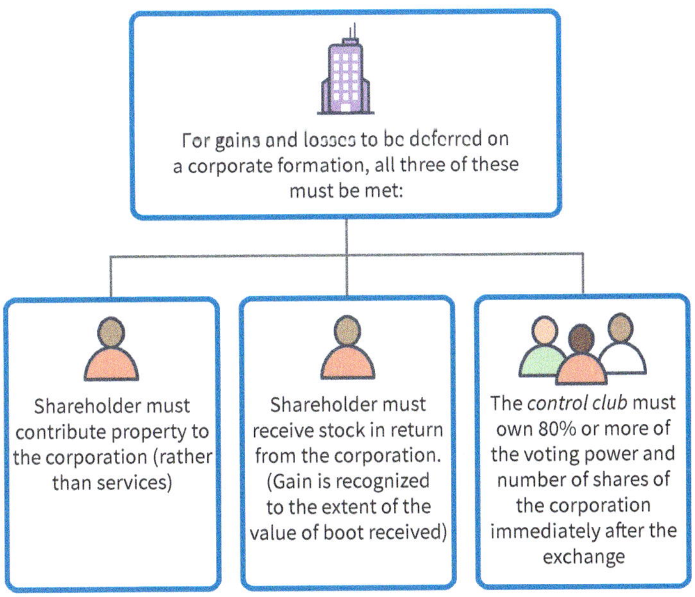

[1]IRC §351.

[2]IRC §368(c).

If these three conditions are met, then tax professionals often refer to the transaction as a **Section 351 formation**, because this is the section of the Internal Revenue Code that provides these rules. Let's look at each of these requirements in more detail.

Related exercises: Discussion Question 1
Multiple Choice Question 1

Property

Property is defined very broadly for purposes of the corporate formation rules. In addition to cash and tangible property, it includes intangible property such as trademarks, copyrights, customer lists, and secret formulas and processes. Therefore, the intellectual property that Aiden and Olivia donate to their corporation does qualify as property for the formation rules. The main item that is not included as property is services. If an individual performs services for a corporation and receives stock in return, this does not fall under Section 351 and the individual recognizes income equal to the fair market value of the stock received. The corporation generally recognizes an offsetting deduction equal to the fair market value of the services received.

Stock

The created corporation can issue common stock or preferred stock as part of a Section 351 formation, except *nonqualified preferred stock* is treated as *boot*. **Nonqualified preferred stock** exists if the holder of such stock has the right to require the issuer or a related person to redeem or purchase the stock, or if the dividend yield on such stock varies in whole or in part with reference to interest rates, commodity prices, or other similar indices. Preferred stock is not treated as nonqualified preferred stock if the corporation has to wait at least 20 years from the date the stock was issued to redeem it.[3] **Boot** is cash or property transferred to the shareholder from the corporation that is not common stock or preferred stock.

Control Club

Shareholders who contribute both property and services to the corporation for their stock are included in the control club only if they contribute more than a small amount of property. The IRS has ruled that the value of the property must be equal to *at least* 10% of the value of the services for the shareholder's stock ownership to be included. If this benchmark is met, then all the shareholder's stock is included in the control test, not just the stock received for property.[4]

Related exercises: Discussion Question 2
Multiple Choice Question 2
Brief Exercise 1

Why **Why does Congress permit tax-deferred corporation formations?** When one or more individuals create a corporation, they typically receive only stock in the new corporation in exchange for their property. If the shareholders had to recognize gain on the formation, they would need cash from another source to pay the tax liability. However, very little has changed economically. The shareholders still own the property they owned before the formation; the ownership is now indirect through their stock ownership.

The following Examples show how the corporation formation rules are applied.

[3]IRC §351(g).

[4]Treas. Reg. §1.351-1(a).

EXAMPLE 3.1.1
Formation of a Corporation

Wendell and Margarita decide to form a corporation, WeDeliver, that will deliver food, groceries, and other home supplies to individuals. Margarita contributes a building that she held as an investment to the corporation with the following tax characteristics:

Fair market value	$350,000
Adjusted basis	$214,000
Original cost	$270,000

Wendell contributes $350,000 of cash to the corporation. They each receive stock worth $350,000 from the corporation. What are the tax consequences of these transactions to Wendell, Margarita, and WeDeliver?

SOLUTION

Margarita does realize a gain/loss on the formation, as follows:

Amount realized	$350,000
Adjusted basis	(214,000)
Realized gain	$136,000

To determine if the gain is recognized, we need to check if the three requirements for a Section 351 formation have been satisfied.

- **Was property transferred to the corporation?** Yes, for both Margarita and Wendell.
- **Was stock received from the corporation?** Yes, for both Margarita and Wendell.
- **Does the control club own 80% or more of the corporation?** Yes. Margarita and Wendell own 100% of WeDeliver after the formation. Therefore, the control test is met.

Because all conditions are satisfied, Margarita does not recognize any gain on the formation, nor does Wendell or WeDeliver.

EXAMPLE 3.1.2
Section 351 Requirements Not Met

Continuing with the facts of Example 3.1.1, assume that instead of contributing cash to the corporation, Wendell contributed services in return for his stock of $350,000. Wendell agreed to develop all the software applications that WeDeliver would need for its operations. What are the tax consequences of these transactions to Wendell and Margarita?

SOLUTION

To determine if Margarita's gain is recognized, we need to check if the three requirements for a Section 351 formation have been satisfied.

- **Was property transferred to the corporation?** Yes, for Margarita, but no for Wendell. Therefore, Wendell will recognize income from the formation.
- **Was stock received from the corporation?** Yes, for both Margarita and Wendell.
- **Does the control club own 80% or more of the corporation?** No. Margarita is the only individual included in the control club because Wendell contributed services, and she owns 50% of the stock. Therefore, the 80% or more control test is not met.

Because all three requirements for a Section 351 formation are not met, this is a taxable transaction for Margarita and Wendell. Margarita's $136,000 capital gain is recognized on her individual tax return (Form 1040). Therefore, her basis in the stock is its fair market value of $350,000. Wendell has $350,000 of wage income for his services, and he will also have a basis in his stock of $350,000.

Related exercises: Application Problems 1, 2

Tax Planning Tip

In Example 3.1.2, whether the formation meets the Section 351 requirements has no impact on Wendell. He will have compensation income either way. Section 351 will potentially benefit only Margarita. If Wendell had received 20% or less of the stock of WeDeliver, then Margarita would have owned at least 80% of the corporation and her gain would be deferred.

EXAMPLE 3.1.3 Property and Services Contributed for Stock

Continuing with the facts from Example 3.1.2, assume that Margarita suggests to Wendell that he also contribute property to the corporation in addition to his services, so that they can include his stock ownership in the control test. Wendell contributes $50,000 to the corporation, and he reduces the value of the services that he will provide to $300,000. He still receives stock with a value of $350,000. What are the tax consequences of these transactions to Wendell and Margarita?

SOLUTION

To determine if the gain is recognized, we need to check if the three requirements for a Section 351 formation have been satisfied.

- **Was property transferred to the corporation?** Yes, for both Margarita and Wendell. Wendell also contributed services.
- **Was stock received from the corporation?** Yes, for both Margarita and Wendell.
- **Does the control club own 80% or more of the corporation?** Because Wendell contributed both property and services to the corporation, we must determine if the value of the property is material in relation to the services. Specifically, is the value of the property at least equal to 10% of the value of the services. The benchmark for Wendell is $30,000 ($300,000 × 10%). Because the value of his property contributed of $50,000 equals or exceeds the benchmark of $30,000, Wendell is included in the control club. His entire ownership of stock is included. Therefore, the control club owns 100% of the stock and the 80% or more control test is met.

Because all conditions are satisfied, Margarita does not recognize any gain on the formation. Wendell has $300,000 of wage income for the stock he received in return for his services.

Related exercises: Application Problem 3
Tax Planning Problem 1

Receipt of Boot

To the extent that a shareholder receives boot in a corporation, then their economic situation has changed because of the formation. Instead of converting the ownership of their property into corporate stock, they converted some of the property into cash or other forms of boot. Therefore, to the extent boot is received, Section 351 does not apply, and gain is recognized to the shareholder equal to the *lower* of:

1. The realized gain, *or*
2. The fair market value of the boot received.

The shareholder will always have a fair market value basis in the property received, because the boot received causes realized gain to be recognized

Potential Pitfall

The receipt of boot will never cause realized losses to be recognized. Boot only affects realized gains.

EXAMPLE 3.1.4
Receipt of Boot

Let's return to the basic facts of Example 3.1.1, with a few changes. Wendell and Margarita decide to form a corporation, WeDeliver, that will deliver food, groceries, and other home supplies to individuals. Margarita contributes a building to the corporation with the following tax characteristics:

Fair market value	$400,000
Adjusted basis	$214,000
Original cost	$270,000

Wendell contributes $350,000 of cash to the corporation. They each receive stock worth $350,000 from the corporation, and Margarita also receives bonds from the corporation with a fair market value of $50,000. What are the tax consequences of these transactions to Wendell and Margarita?

SOLUTION

Margarita realizes a gain/loss on the formation, as follows:

Amount realized:	
Stock received	$350,000
Bonds received	50,000
Total amount realized	$400,000
Less: Adjusted basis	(214,000)
Realized gain	$186,000

To determine if the gain is recognized, we need to check if the three requirements for a Section 351 formation have been satisfied.

- **Was property transferred to the corporation?** Yes, for both Margarita and Wendell.
- **Was stock received from the corporation?** Yes, for both Margarita and Wendell. Additionally, Margarita received $50,000 of bonds, which is boot.
- **Does the control club own 80% or more of the corporation?** Yes. Margarita and Wendell own 100% of WeDeliver after the formation. Therefore, the control test is met.

Because all conditions are satisfied, the corporate formation meets the requirements for Section 351. However, since Margarita received boot, her recognized gain is $50,000, the *lower* of:

1. the realized gain ($186,000), *or*
2. the fair market value of the boot received ($50,000).

Margarita's basis in the bonds received is $50,000.

Related exercise: Application Problem 4

Basis Issues

Another important consideration for a Section 351 formation is determining the shareholder's basis in their stock received and the corporation's basis in the assets received. Recall that when the tax law allows gains and losses to be deferred, the general rule is that tax basis stays the same. You will see that this is the starting point for both basis computations.

Shareholder's Basis

The shareholder's basis in the stock received from the corporation is:

The shareholder's basis in all property (including cash) transferred to the corporation
Plus: Gain recognized by shareholder
Less: Boot received by shareholder
Less: Shareholder debt that is assumed by the corporation
Shareholder's basis

An alternative method of computing the shareholder's basis in the stock received from the corporation is:

Fair market value of the stock received from the corporation
Less: The deferred gain on the formation
Plus: The deferred loss on the formation
Shareholder's basis

A shareholder who recognizes gain on a corporate formation because they rendered services to the corporation has a basis in their stock equal to the fair market value of the stock received because this is a taxable transaction. The corporation will receive a deduction for the stock transfer to the service provider. The deduction will be for wage expense unless the services rendered are organizational expenses or start-up costs (these items are covered later in the chapter).

Related exercise: Brief Exercise 2

Corporation's Basis

The corporation's basis in the assets received from the shareholders is:

The shareholder's basis in all property (including cash) transferred to the corporation
Plus: Gain recognized by shareholder
Corporation's basis

Tax Planning Tip

The formula for the corporation's basis in the assets received is the first two lines of the formula for the shareholder's basis in the stock received.

In the next Example, we show how basis is computed for the facts of Example 3.1.4.

EXAMPLE 3.1.5
Basis Issues Related to a Corporation Formation

Continuing with the facts of Example 3.1.4, what bases do Margarita and Wendell have in their stock, and what basis does WeDeliver have in the building contributed by Margarita?

SOLUTION

Margarita's basis in her stock is computed as follows:

The shareholder's basis in all property (including cash) transferred to the corporation	$214,000
Plus: Gain recognized by shareholder	50,000
Less: Boot received by shareholder	(50,000)
Less: Shareholder debt that is assumed by corporation	N/A
Total	$214,000

Margarita's deferred gain is $136,000, her realized gain of $186,000 reduced by her $50,000 recognized gain. Her basis can also be computed under the alternative formula as:

Fair market value of the stock received from the corporation	$350,000
Less: The deferred gain on the formation	(136,000)
Plus: The deferred loss on the formation	N/A
Total	$214,000

Margarita's basis in the bonds received is its fair market value of $50,000. Wendell's basis in his stock received is its fair market value of $350,000 because he contributed $350,000 of cash for his stock.

WeDeliver's basis in the building received is computed as:

The shareholder's basis in all property (including cash) transferred to the corporation	$214,000
Plus: Gain recognized by shareholder	50,000
Total	$264,000

Related exercise: Application Problem 5

Basis Adjustment for Loss Property

If the total basis of the property transferred by a shareholder is greater than the fair market value of the property, then the shareholder has an unrealized loss in the property. A basis adjustment is required to prevent both the shareholders and the corporation from benefiting from this unrealized loss. The downward basis adjustment is allocated proportionately among all assets contributed by the shareholder that had a basis in excess of FMV. Alternatively, the shareholder's stock basis can be reduced rather than the basis of the corporation's assets if both the shareholder and corporation agree to the election.

In the next Example, we illustrate how this loss adjustment works.

EXAMPLE 3.1.6 Basis Adjustment for Loss Property

Wang transferred Lossacre, with a FMV of $2,000 and a basis of $6,000, and Gainacre, with a fair market value of $5,000 and a basis of $4,000, to ABE Corporation in exchange for stock in a Section 351 formation. What is Wang's adjusted basis in his stock and ABE's basis in Lossacre and Gainacre?

SOLUTION

The following tables summarize this solution:

Before contribution

Asset contributed	Adjusted basis	Fair market value
Lossacre	$ 6,000	$ 2,000
Gainacre	$ 4,000	$ 5,000
Total	$10,000	$ 7,000

Basis after contribution if no election made to reduce basis of stock

Basis of Lossacre is reduced by $3,000 (excess of aggregate FMV over aggregate adjusted basis).

Asset contributed	Adjusted basis	
Lossacre	$ 3,000	($6,000 – $3,000)
Gainacre	$ 4,000	
Total	$ 7,000	

Basis of stock to Wang is the original adjusted basis of the assets contributed of $10,000.

Basis after contribution if election made to reduce basis of stock

Basis of Lossacre remains the same

Asset contributed	Adjusted basis
Lossacre	$ 6,000
Gainacre	$ 4,000
Total	$10,000

Basis of stock to Wang is $7,000, the original adjusted basis of the assets contributed of $10,000 reduced by $3,000 (excess of aggregate FMV over aggregate adjusted basis).

Related exercise: Application Problem 6

Why **Why does Congress require a basis adjustment for loss property?** In Example 3.1.6, if the loss adjustment was not required, Wang would have been able to take one asset with a built-in loss of $4,000 (Lossacre) and create two assets with losses. ABE Corporation would have a $6,000 basis in Lossacre so if it sold Lossacre for $2,000 it would have a recognized loss of $4,000. Additionally, if Wang sold his stock in ABE for its FMV of $7,000, he would have a loss of $3,000 because his basis would be $10,000. Congress was not keen on taxpayers in Wang's situation creating additional losses, so it requires a downward basis adjustment in either the asset's basis or the stock's basis.

It is interesting, though, that when a shareholder contributes an asset with a built-in gain to a corporation, Congress is not concerned that the potential future gain doubles. The unrecognized gain is still built into the basis for the corporation, and the shareholder also will have a gain built into their stock. However, this is consistent with the notion of double taxation for corporations.

Debt Relief

A contribution of property with debt attached to it requires that the transferor reduce the basis of the stock by the amount of debt assumed by the corporation, as shown in the shareholder's basis formula above. Generally, debt assumption by the corporation is not treated as boot received by the shareholder, even though this is an economic benefit received in addition to corporate stock.[5] However, there are two situations for which debt assumption by the corporation may cause gains to be recognized by the shareholder.

- If the total liabilities assumed by the corporation exceed the total adjusted basis of property transferred by the shareholder, then the shareholder must recognize gain as follows:[6]

  Gain recognized = Liabilities assumed − Basis of all property transferred

- If the principal purpose of the debt assumption was to avoid federal income tax or did not have a bona fide business purpose, then the corporate assumption will cause *all* the debt relief to be treated as boot.[7] This will cause gain to be recognized, but only to the extent of the shareholder's realized gain. If the shareholder's use of the borrowed funds was for personal purposes rather than business purposes, then the debt assumption does not likely have a bona fide purpose. Additionally, if the debt was incurred by the shareholder shortly before it was transferred to the corporation, this is likely to increase scrutiny from the IRS.

We review these rules for debt relief in the next two Examples.

EXAMPLE 3.1.7
Debt Relief on Corporate Formation

Let's use similar facts to Example 3.1.4 with the addition that Margarita has a mortgage on the building that is assumed by WeDeliver. Wendell and Margarita decide to form a corporation, WeDeliver, that will deliver food, groceries, and other home supplies to individuals. Margarita contributes a building to the corporation with the following tax characteristics:

Fair market value	$640,000
Adjusted basis	$214,000
Original cost	$270,000
Mortgage	$240,000

Wendell contributes $350,000 of cash to the corporation and the corporation assumes Margarita's mortgage. They each receive stock worth $350,000 from the corporation, and Margarita also receives bonds from the corporation with a fair market value of $50,000.

a. How much gain do Wendell and Margarita recognize?

b. What basis do Margarita and Wendell have in their stock?

c. What is Margarita's basis in the bonds she received?

d. What basis does WeDeliver have in the building contributed by Margarita?

[5]IRC §357(a).

[6]IRC §357(c).

[7]IRC §357(b).

SOLUTION

a. Margarita realizes a gain/loss on the formation, as follows:

Amount realized:	
Stock received	$350,000
Bonds received	50,000
Debt relief	240,000
Total amount realized	$640,000
Less: Adjusted basis	(214,000)
Realized gain	$426,000

To determine if the gain is recognized, we need to check if the three requirements for a Section 351 formation have been satisfied.

- **Was property transferred to the corporation?** Yes, for both Margarita and Wendell.
- **Was stock received from the corporation?** Yes, for both Margarita and Wendell. Additionally, Margarita received $50,000 of bonds, which is boot. She also received debt relief, but this is not considered boot received unless there was not a business purpose for the debt assumption. However, the debt relief of $240,000 is greater than the basis of the property contributed, $214,000, so Margarita has gain for the excess debt relief of $26,000 ($240,000 – $214,000).
- **Does the control club own 80% or more of the corporation?** Yes, Margarita and Wendell own 100% of WeDeliver after the formation. Therefore, the control test is met.

Because all conditions are satisfied, the corporate formation meets the requirements for Section 351. However, because Margarita received boot, her gain is $50,000, the *lower* of:

1. the realized gain ($426,000), *or*
2. the fair market value of the boot received ($50,000).

You compute Margarita's total gain on the corporation formation as follows:

Gain from boot received	$50,000
Plus: Gain from debt relief in excess of basis	26,000
Total	$76,000

b. Margarita's basis in her stock is computed as follows:

The shareholder's basis in all property (including cash) transferred to the corporation	$214,000
Plus: Gain recognized by shareholder	76,000
Less: Boot received by shareholder	(50,000)
Less: Shareholder debt that is assumed by corporation	(240,000)
Total	$ 0

c. Margarita's basis in the bonds received is its fair market value of $50,000. Wendell's basis in his stock received is its fair market value of $350,000 because he contributed $350,000 of cash for his stock.

d. WeDeliver's basis in the building received is computed as:

The shareholder's basis in all property (including cash) transferred to the corporation	$214,000
Plus: Gain recognized by shareholder	76,000
Total	$290,000

Related exercise: Application Problem 7

EXAMPLE 3.1.8
No Business Purpose for Debt Assumption

Let's use similar facts to Example 3.1.7 except that Margarita's mortgage on the building is $150,000. Margarita took the mortgage out two months before the corporate formation and used the funds as a down payment on a new personal residence. Wendell and Margarita decide to form a corporation, WeDeliver, that will deliver food, groceries, and other home supplies to individuals. Margarita contributes a building to the corporation with the following tax characteristics:

Fair market value	$550,000
Adjusted basis	$214,000
Original cost	$270,000
Mortgage	$150,000

Wendell contributes $350,000 of cash to the corporation and the corporation assumes Margarita's mortgage. They each receive stock worth $350,000 from the corporation, and Margarita also receives bonds from the corporation with a fair market value of $50,000. How much gain does Margarita recognize?

SOLUTION

Margarita realizes a gain/loss on the formation, as follows:

Amount realized:	
Stock received	$350,000
Bonds received	50,000
Debt relief	150,000
Total amount realized	$550,000
Less: Adjusted basis	(214,000)
Realized gain	$336,000

Margarita did not use the $150,000 of loan proceeds for a business purpose because she used the funds to purchase a personal residence. Therefore, the entire debt of $150,000 is treated as boot. Margarita also received $50,000 of boot for her receipt of the bonds. Therefore, her total boot received is $200,000 ($150,000 + $50,000), and her recognized gain is $200,000, the *lower* of:

1. the realized gain ($336,000), *or*
2. the fair market value of the boot received ($200,000).

You compute Margarita's total gain on the corporation formation as follows:

Gain from boot received	$200,000
Plus: Gain from debt relief in excess of basis	0
Total	$200,000

Related exercise: Application Problem 8

Holding Period Rules

When gains and losses are deferred for a property transaction, the general rule is that the holding period of the assets involved do not start over, and that is the case with Section 351 formations.[8]

[8]IRC §1221.

Shareholder's Holding Period

For the shareholder, the stock received from the corporation may or may not include the amount of time the shareholder held the property given to the corporation.

- If the property transferred was a capital asset or Section 1231 asset, then the property's holding period is tacked on to the stock's holding period. For example, if the shareholder contributed a parcel of land that had been held for four years as an investment, the four years are included in the stock's holding period.
- For all other property, meaning ordinary income property such as inventory and accounts receivable, the holding period of the property contributed does not tack on for the stock. Rather, the holding period for stock begins on day after the transfer.

Related exercises: Discussion Question 3
Multiple Choice Question 3

The best way to remember this distinction for holding period is to note that it has significance only for capital assets (holding period must be longer than one year to be long-term) and Section 1231 assets (must be held for more than one year). Holding period has no significance for ordinary income assets.

Corporation's Holding Period

The holding period rule for the corporation is simpler than for the shareholder. The holding period of the property received by the corporation *always* includes the period that the shareholder held the property before the formation. This is for all assets: ordinary, capital, and Section 1231.

EXAMPLE 3.1.9 Holding Period After a Corporate Formation

Return to the basic facts of Example 3.1.1, except that Wendell contributes property to the corporation rather than cash. Wendell and Margarita decide to form a corporation, WeDeliver, that will deliver food, groceries, and other home supplies to individuals. Margarita contributes a building to the corporation with the following tax characteristics:

Fair market value	$350,000
Adjusted basis	$214,000
Original cost	$270,000

Margarita had owned the building for three years at the time of contribution. She held the building as investment property. Wendell contributes inventory to the corporation with an adjusted basis of $230,000 and FMV of $350,000. He had held the inventory in his business for four months. They each receive stock worth $350,000 from the corporation.

a. What holding period does Margarita have in her stock?

b. What holding period does Wendell have in his stock?

c. What holding period does WeDeliver have in the assets received?

SOLUTION

a. Margarita held the building as investment property. Therefore, it is a capital asset to her. If the property transferred is a capital asset or Section 1231 asset, then the property's holding period is tacked on to the stock's holding period. Therefore, Margarita's holding period in her stock is three years on the day of the formation.

b. Wendell held his property as inventory, which means that the holding period of the property contributed does not tack on for the stock. Therefore, Wendell's holding period for his stock begins on the day after the formation.

c. The holding period of the property received by the corporation *always* includes the period that the shareholder held the property before the formation. Therefore, WeDeliver's basis in the building is three years and in the inventory is four months.

Capital Contributed, No Stock Received

There are situations where a taxpayer may contribute assets to a corporation but receive no stock in return. The tax consequences for these transactions depends on whether the contributor is a shareholder or non-shareholder.

Shareholder

If a shareholder contributes property to a corporation and does not receive additional stock in return, there is no gain or loss recognized to the shareholder or to the corporation. The corporation's basis in the asset will be the same basis that the shareholder had in it. The shareholder will increase their basis in their stock by the basis of the property contributed.

Non-shareholder

If a non-shareholder contributes property to a corporation and does not receive any stock in return, there are important tax consequences. The corporation will recognize a gain equal to the fair market value of the property received, and it will have a fair market value basis in the property. A good question to ask is why someone would give property to a corporation and not ask for stock or anything else in return. Individuals do not usually make such contributions. Rather, these are made by state and/or local governments that are encouraging companies to locate their businesses in their communities for economic development purposes, as we explore in the next Example.

EXAMPLE 3.1.10
Contribution of Property by a Non-shareholder

The city of Florence, Alabama, wants to attract a large defense contractor to build a new facility in Florence. The local economic development authority has estimated that the facility would bring over 200 high-paying jobs to the north Alabama region. Florence offers the company 50 acres of land valued at $500,000 if it will build the facility in Florence. Florence also offers $1,000,000 of cash as an additional incentive. What are the tax consequences of these transactions for the defense contractor, and what is its basis in the property received?

SOLUTION

The defense contractor must recognize a gain of $1,500,000 ($500,000 + $1,000,000) because it was given property but did not provide stock to the contributor. It will have a basis of $500,000 in the land and a basis of $1,000,000 with the property that is purchased with the cash of $1,000,000.

Related exercise: Brief Exercise 3

PRACTICE PROBLEM 3.1.1
Contribution of Property and Services

Simone contributed gymnastics equipment with an adjusted basis of $64,000 and a fair market value of $75,000 for 75% of the stock Tumbler Corporation. Nadia rendered services to Tumbler with a value of $20,000 and also contributed $5,000 cash for the remaining 25% ownership interest. What are the tax consequences to Simone and Nadia on this transaction?

SOLUTION

To determine if the gain is recognized, we need to check if the three requirements for a Section 351 formation have been satisfied.

- **Was property transferred to the corporation?** Yes, for both Simone and Nadia. Nadia also contributed services.
- **Was stock received from the corporation?** Yes, for both Simone and Nadia.

- **Does the control club own 80% or more of the corporation?** Because Nadia contributed both property and services to the corporation, we must determine if the value of the property is material in relation to the services. Specifically, is the value of the property at least equal to 10% of the value of the services. The benchmark for Nadia is $2,000 ($20,000 × 10%). Because the value of her property contributed of $5,000 equals or exceeds the benchmark of $2,000, Nadia is included in the control club. Her entire ownership of stock is included. Therefore, the control club owns 100% of the stock and the 80% or more control test is met.

Because all conditions are satisfied, Simone does not recognize any gain on the formation. Nadia has $20,000 of wage income for the stock she received in return for her services.

PRACTICE PROBLEM 3.1.2
Liability Assumed by the Corporation

Felix and Tiger contributed property when forming a corporation in exchange for stock during the current tax year. Felix contributed $60,000 cash for 50% of the stock and Tiger contributed land with an adjusted basis of $42,000 and a fair market value of $60,000 for 50% of the stock. The land had a $48,000 mortgage attached that was assumed by the corporation. What is Tiger's recognized gain on this transaction?

SOLUTION

This transaction meets the criteria for Section 351 formation. Property was transferred in exchange for stock and at least 80% ownership was acquired. Because Tiger contributed land with a mortgage that was assumed by the corporation that is in excess of his basis, Tiger must recognize gain of $6,000 ($48,000 mortgage − $42,000 basis).

INTERACTIVE SELF-SCORING QUIZZES

3.2 Taxation of Costs Incident to Formation

LEARNING OBJECTIVE 2

Determine the tax consequences of organizational expenses, start-up costs, and syndication costs.

VIDEO CONTENT

When taxpayers form a business entity, there are three types of costs that may be incurred that are not deductible as regular ordinary and necessary business expenses. Each type is not deductible for a different reason, as discussed below. Recall that the general rule is that business expenses are deductible if they:

- are incurred while operating a trade or business, *and*
- are ordinary, necessary, and reasonable.[9]

If these requirements are satisfied, the expenses are known as **Section 162 expenses**. *Organizational expenses* and *start-up costs* are potentially deductible under specialized rules. *Syndication costs* are not deductible at all. In this section, we define these three types of costs, explain why they are not deductible as Section 162 business expenses, and describe how you treat them for tax purposes. The rules for these costs are summarized in **Illustration 3.2**.

[9]IRC §162(a).

ILLUSTRATION 3.2 Business Expenses Incurred in First Year

Types of Business Expenses Incurred During Corporation's First Tax Year			
Type of cost	**Definition**	**Tax consequences**	**Examples**
Section 162 expenses	Expenses incurred while operating a trade or business and are ordinary, necessary, and reasonable.	Deductible	• Advertising expense • Wages paid • Depreciation expense • Office expense
Organizational expenses	Expenses incurred in connection with the organization of a corporation.	• Maximum amount deductible in year of formation is $5,000 • $5,000 is reduced dollar for dollar once total is in excess of $50,000 • Amortize remaining costs over 180 months beginning with month business begins operations	• Legal services and accounting services to incorporate • Organizational meetings of directors and shareholders that are related to organization • Fees paid to incorporate
Start-up costs	Expenses that would be deductible as ordinary and necessary business expenses if a business had already begun, including investigation expenses, advertising, training employees, and rent paid before the business officially begins.	• Maximum amount deductible in year of formation is $5,000 • $5,000 is reduced dollar for dollar once total is in excess of $50,000 • Amortize remaining costs over 180 months beginning with month business begins operations	Paid before operations begin: • Rent expense • Utilities paid • Wages paid • Contractor fees
Syndication costs	Expenses related to issuing and selling stock.	Not deductible	• Brokerage fees • Stock registration fees • Underwriter fees • Printing costs of the prospectus

Organizational Expenses

Organizational expenses are expenditures incurred in connection with the organization of a corporation. Typical organizational expenses are legal services, accounting services, organizational meetings of directors and shareholders that are related to the organization, and fees paid to incorporate. Organizational expenses are not deductible as Section 162 expenses because they will benefit the corporation over its entire life. Therefore, they must be capitalized. However, the owners do not know how long the corporation will remain in existence; it could be six months, six years, or even 60 years. This creates a problem for the corporation because the tax law does not allow an asset to be amortized if it has an indeterminable life.

Congress has addressed this problem by providing a path for corporations to procure a tax benefit from organizational expenses, as follows:[10]

- The maximum amount of these expenses that can be deducted in the year of formation is $5,000.
- The $5,000 deduction is reduced by the amount of expenditures incurred that exceed $50,000. The reduction is dollar-for-dollar, so once total organizational expenses incurred reaches $55,000, the $5,000 deduction is reduced to zero.
- Organization expenses not deducted must be capitalized, and amortized over 180 months, beginning with the month that the corporation begins its business operations, unless an election is filed not to do so.
- Generally, the corporation begins its business operations when it begins to earn revenue. The *beginning business* date is a different standard to meet than the date that the corporation *comes into existence*.[11]

[10]IRC §248.

[11]Treas. Reg. §1.248-1(d).

- To be deducted and/or amortized, organization expenses must be *incurred* before the end of the taxable year that business begins. They do not have to be paid by the end of the first taxable year, even if on the cash basis.
- If the corporation does not incur organizational expenses by the end of the first tax year, they are not eligible to be deducted or amortized under this special rule. In that case, you must capitalize them as an intangible asset on the corporation's balance sheet, and they cannot be amortized.

Start-Up Costs

Start-up costs are expenses that would be deductible as ordinary and necessary business expenses if a business had already begun, including investigation expenses, advertising, training employees, and rent paid before the business officially begins. Because the corporation has not yet started its trade or business operation, start-up costs are not deductible as Section 162 expenses. For example, if a new restaurant pays its employees while management is training them, but before it opens for business, these salary payments are start-up costs. Other typical start-up costs include rent expense and utilities incurred before business operations begin.

The deduction and amortization rules for start-up costs are identical to the rules for organizational expenses.[12]

Syndication Costs

Syndication costs are expenses related to issuing and selling stock. Typical syndication costs include brokerage fees, stock registration fees, underwriter fees, and printing costs of the prospectus and other selling or promotional material. Like organizational costs, syndication costs cannot be deducted as Section 162 expenses because they benefit the corporation for its entire life. Unfortunately, Congress has not provided another means to deduct syndication costs. Therefore, the corporation must capitalize them as an intangible asset on the balance sheet, but they cannot be amortized.

Related exercise: Discussion Question 4

Returning to the chapter introduction, if Aiden and Olivia decide to incorporate, they will likely incur organization costs. They will probably not have start-up costs because their business was operating before it was incorporated. Whether they have any syndication costs will be a function of whether they try to sell stock to others. We demonstrate the computation for these expense in the next Example.

Potential Pitfall

Do not confuse syndication costs with the regular marketing and advertising costs for the corporation that are encouraging customers to buy their products or services. Such costs are deductible as Section 162 expenses if the corporation's business has begun. Syndication costs relate to the promotion and selling of the corporation's *stock*, not its products or services.

EXAMPLE 3.2.1
Determining Deductibility of Corporate Formation Costs

Caleb recently completed his undergraduate degree in computer science with a minor in business. While in college, Caleb began developing a software product that would revolutionize the way companies could protect their networks and systems from computer viruses and software. He entered several business idea competitions and has won $125,000 in prize money to invest in his company. Caleb is ready to take the next step to incorporate his business, and he wants to raise at least $1,000,000 in capital. He files articles of incorporation with the state on June 1 of the current year. He leases office space beginning July 1 and begins business operations on November 1. Caleb paid the following expenses during the year:

Rent expense for office (per month)	$ 4,000
Utilities (per month)	$ 900
Attorney's fees for incorporation	$ 4,500
Printing costs for prospectus	$ 3,500
Incorporation fees	$ 2,980
Staff salaries for August through December (per month)	$11,000
Commissions to investment firm for selling stock to investors	$30,000

[12]IRC §248.

In addition, Caleb incurred fees of $4,000 from an accounting firm to facilitate with the incorporation, but he had not paid these fees by the end of the year. How will Caleb treat these expenses on his tax return for the current year? Caleb uses the cash method of accounting.

SOLUTION

To determine the tax consequences for these costs, we must identify them as organizational expenses, start-up costs, syndication costs, or Section 162 expenses.

Organizational expenses

Attorney's fees for incorporation	$ 4,500
Incorporation fees	2,980
Accounting fees	4,000
Total	$11,480

The accounting fees of $4,000 are included as an organizational expense even though not paid and the corporation is cash basis. Costs can be deducted or amortized as organizational expenses if they are *incurred* by the end of the corporation's first tax year.

The corporation can deduct $5,000 of these costs. The remaining $6,480 ($11,480 – $5,000) is amortized over 180 months, beginning November 1, the day that business begins. The amortization expense for the current year is $72 ($6,480 × 2 months/180 months).

Start-up costs

Rent expense for office (July through October; 4 months × $4,000)	$16,000
Utilities (July through October; 4 months × $900)	3,600
Staff Salaries (August through October; 3 months × $11,000)	33,000
Total	$52,600

The corporation cannot deduct the entire $5,000 of start-up costs of $52,600 because the total exceeds $50,000. The excess costs of $2,600 ($52,600 – $50,000) reduces the deduction to $2,400 ($5,000 – $2,600). The remaining $50,200 ($52,600 – $2,400) is amortized over 180 months, beginning November 1, the day that business begins. The amortization expense for the current year is $558 ($50,200 × 2 months/180 months; rounded to nearest dollar).

Syndication fees

Printing costs for prospectus	$ 3,500
Commissions to investment firm for selling stock to investors	30,000
Total	$33,500

The syndication fees cannot be deducted or amortized.

Section 162 expenses

Rent expense for office (November and December; 2 months × $4,000)	$ 8,000
Utilities (November and December; 2 months × $900)	1,800
Staff salaries (November and December; 2 months × $11,000)	22,000
Total	$31,800

The Section 162 expenses of $31,800 are fully deductible for the current year.

Related exercises: Multiple Choice Questions 4, 5
Brief Exercise 4
Application Problem 9

Spotlight on the Law

When to Capitalize Organizational Expenses

Fanny is a nutritionist specializing in farm to table produce. She filed for Articles of Incorporation on November 10, Year 22 for her corporation, Green Earth, Inc. Green Earth incurred organizational expenses such as legal services, accounting services, and fees paid to the state of incorporation of $8,800 in Year 22. Green Earth also incurred expenses of $4,100 on January 20, Year 23 for organizational expenses related to an organizational meeting of directors and shareholders. Green Earth opened its business on March 3, Year 23. When can Green Earth deduct the organizational costs and how much can be expensed?

Under IRC §248(a)(1) and (2), a corporation can elect to expense up to $5,000 of organizational costs if the total is less than or equal to $50,000, and it can amortize the remaining costs over 180 months beginning in the month in which the corporation begins business. The expenses must be incurred by the end of the corporation's first tax year to qualify under IRC §248. If Green Earth did not begin its business until March, Year 23, what happens to the $8,800 incurred in Year 22?

IRC §248(a)(1)(a) further states that "the corporation shall be allowed a deduction for the taxable year in which the corporation begins business in an amount equal to the lesser of—

(A) the amount of organizational expenditures with respect to the taxpayer

(B) $5,000, reduced (but not below zero) by the amount by which such organizational expenditures exceed $50,000."

IRC §248(b) states "The term "organizational expenditures" means any expenditure which—

(1) is incident to the creation of the corporation;

(2) is chargeable to capital account; and

(3) is of a character which, if expended incident to the creation of a corporation having a limited life, would be amortizable over such life."

Because Green Earth's expenses meet all these conditions as an organizational cost, Green Earth can deduct $5,000 in Year 23 and amortize the remaining amount of $7,900 ($12,900 – $5,000) over 180 months beginning in March, Year 23. An entire month of amortization is allowed for the month business begins.

PRACTICE PROBLEM 3.2.1

Amortization of Organizational Costs

Morton is starting his own business and has filed his articles of incorporation on March 15. He has incurred total organizational costs of $53,500 on May 1, and he opened his business on August 1. How will Morton treat these expenses on his tax return for the current year?

SOLUTION

The corporation cannot deduct the entire $5,000 of organizational costs of $53,500 because the total exceeds $50,000. The excess costs of $3,500 ($53,500 – $50,000) reduces the deduction to $1,500 ($5,000 – $3,500). The remaining $52,000 ($53,500 – $1,500) is amortized over 180 months, beginning August 1, the day that business begins. The amortization expense for the current year is $1,444 ($52,000 × 5 months/180 months; rounded to nearest dollar).

INTERACTIVE SELF-SCORING QUIZZES

3.3 Corporate Taxable Income

LEARNING OBJECTIVE 3

Compute taxable income for a corporation.

VIDEO CONTENT

In this section, we review the formula for computing the corporate federal income tax, including the completion of Schedule M-1 and Schedule M-3 for the book income to taxable income reconciliation required by Form 1120, U.S. Corporate Income Tax Return.

Corporate Income Tax Formula

The general rules for income and deductions that you have learned for individuals are the starting point for computing corporate taxable income. For example, the following rules for income are the same for individuals and for corporations:

- Income will be taxable if the taxpayer's wealth has increased, the taxpayer has realized this increase in wealth, and the law does not provide a specific exclusion for this type of income.
- Prepaid revenue is generally included in income when received, even for accrual-basis taxpayers.
- Municipal interest income is exempt from taxation.
- Long-term capital gains are gains from the sale of capital assets held for more than one year.

Similarly, the basic rules for deductions are the same for individuals and corporations:

- Business expenses are deductible if they are paid or incurred in operating a business and are ordinary, necessary, and reasonable.
- Expenditures that are a violation of public policy are not deductible.
- Prepaid interest expense is deducted over the period the interest relates to, not when paid, even for cash-basis taxpayers.
- Net operating losses are generated only by business losses and casualty losses.
- Entertainment expenses are not deductible.

The word *corporation* in this textbook always references a C corporation. An S corporation referenced in this textbook will always have the *S* designation.

Related exercise: Discussion Question 5

Nevertheless, there are several important differences in the computation of income and deductions for corporations, and those are the focus of this section. Tax professionals often refer to a corporation subject to the corporate income tax as a *C corporation* because the rules governing corporate taxation are provided in Subchapter C of the Internal Revenue Code.

Corporations report their taxable income or loss on page 1 of Form 1120, U.S. Corporation Income Tax Return (see **Illustration 3.3**; we use the 2024 form because it was the most recent form available at the time of publication). Corporate returns are due on the 15th day of the fourth month after the tax year-end. A six-month extension can be requested to file the return, but the due date to pay the taxes cannot be extended. For a calendar-year corporation, the due date is April 15, and the extended due date is October 15.[13]

[13]For corporations with a June 30 year-end, the due date is September 15 which is the 15th day of the 3rd month after year-end.

ILLUSTRATION 3.3 Corporate Income Tax Return

DOWNLOAD DOCUMENTS & TEMPLATES

Form **1120** Department of the Treasury Internal Revenue Service

U.S. Corporation Income Tax Return

For calendar year 2024 or tax year beginning ________, 2024, ending ________, 20 ____

Go to *www.irs.gov/Form1120* for instructions and the latest information.

OMB No. 1545-0123

2024

A Check if:	TYPE OR PRINT		
1a Consolidated return (attach Form 851) ☐		Name	**B Employer identification number**
b Life/nonlife consolidated return ☐		Number, street, and room or suite no. If a P.O. box, see instructions.	**C** Date incorporated
2 Personal holding co. (attach Sch. PH) ☐		City or town, state or province, country, and ZIP or foreign postal code	**D** Total assets (see instructions) $
3 Personal service corp. (see instructions) ☐			
4 Schedule M-3 attached ☐	**E** Check if: **(1)** ☐ Initial return **(2)** ☐ Final return **(3)** ☐ Name change **(4)** ☐ Address change		

Income	1a	Gross receipts or sales	1a			
	b	Returns and allowances	1b			
	c	Balance. Subtract line 1b from line 1a			1c	
	2	Cost of goods sold (attach Form 1125-A)			2	
	3	Gross profit. Subtract line 2 from line 1c			3	
	4	Dividends and inclusions (Schedule C, line 23)			4	
	5	Interest			5	
	6	Gross rents			6	
	7	Gross royalties			7	
	8	Capital gain net income (attach Schedule D (Form 1120))			8	
	9	Net gain or (loss) from Form 4797, Part II, line 17 (attach Form 4797)			9	
	10	Other income (see instructions—attach statement)			10	
	11	**Total income.** Add lines 3 through 10			11	
Deductions (See instructions for limitations on deductions.)	12	Compensation of officers (see instructions—attach Form 1125-E)			12	
	13	Salaries and wages (less employment credits)			13	
	14	Repairs and maintenance			14	
	15	Bad debts			15	
	16	Rents			16	
	17	Taxes and licenses			17	
	18	Interest (see instructions)			18	
	19	Charitable contributions			19	
	20	Depreciation from Form 4562 not claimed on Form 1125-A or elsewhere on return (attach Form 4562)			20	
	21	Depletion			21	
	22	Advertising			22	
	23	Pension, profit-sharing, etc., plans			23	
	24	Employee benefit programs			24	
	25	Energy efficient commercial buildings deduction (attach Form 7205)			25	
	26	Other deductions (attach statement)			26	
	27	**Total deductions.** Add lines 12 through 26			27	
	28	Taxable income before net operating loss deduction and special deductions. Subtract line 27 from line 11			28	
	29a	Net operating loss deduction (see instructions)	29a			
	b	Special deductions (Schedule C, line 24)	29b			
	c	Add lines 29a and 29b			29c	
Tax, Refundable Credits, and Payments	30	**Taxable income.** Subtract line 29c from line 28. See instructions			30	
	31	Total tax (Schedule J, line 12)			31	
	32	Reserved for future use			32	
	33	Total payments and credits (Schedule J, line 23)			33	
	34	Estimated tax penalty. See instructions. Check if Form 2220 is attached ☐			34	
	35	**Amount owed.** If line 33 is smaller than the total of lines 31 and 34, enter amount owed			35	
	36	**Overpayment.** If line 33 is larger than the total of lines 31 and 34, enter amount overpaid			36	
	37	Enter amount from line 36 you want: **Credited to 2025 estimated tax**		**Refunded**	37	

Sign Here

Under penalties of perjury, I declare that I have examined this return, including accompanying schedules and statements, and to the best of my knowledge and belief, it is true, correct, and complete. Declaration of preparer (other than taxpayer) is based on all information of which preparer has any knowledge.

Signature of officer | Date | Title

May the IRS discuss this return with the preparer shown below? See instructions. ☐ **Yes** ☐ **No**

Paid Preparer Use Only	Print/Type preparer's name	Preparer's signature	Date	Check ☐ if self-employed	PTIN
	Firm's name			Firm's EIN	
	Firm's address			Phone no.	

For Paperwork Reduction Act Notice, see separate instructions. Cat. No. 11450Q Form **1120** (2024)

Corporations are subject to a flat 21% tax rate as compared to the progressive tax rate structure for individuals. **Illustration 3.4** shows the computation of taxable income for a corporation.

Related exercises: Multiple Choice Questions 6, 7, 8
Brief Exercise 5

ILLUSTRATION 3.4 Corporate Income Tax Formula

Corporate Income Tax Computation	
(Line references are for Form 1120, U.S. Corporation Income Tax Return page 1, unless noted otherwise.)	
Gross receipts or sales	(Line 1a)
Less: Returns and allowances	(Line 1b)
Net receipts or sales	(Line 1c)
Less: Cost of goods sold	(Line 2)
Gross profit	(Line 3)
Plus: Other income	(Lines 4–10)
Total income	(Line 11)
Less: Other business deductions	(Lines 12–27)
Taxable income before net operating loss (NOL) and special deduction	(Line 28)
Less: NOL	(Line 29a)
Less: Special deductions	(Line 29b)
Taxable income	(Line 30)
× Tax rate (21%)	
Gross tax	
Plus: Other taxes	
Less: Tax credits	
Total tax	(From Schedule J and Line 31)
Less: Estimated tax payments	(Line 33)
Tax due/overpayment	(Lines 35 and 36)

Related exercises: Brief Exercise 6
Application Problem 10

Corporate Deductions

There are some corporate deductions that have different rules than the corresponding individual deductions, such as for charitable contributions. There are also deductions that are permitted for corporations that are not allowed for individuals, such as the *dividends received deduction*. We discuss these deductions in more detail in this section.

Charitable Contributions

The corporate charitable contribution rules are the same as for individuals, with a few exceptions. Cash contributions are deductible based on the amount of cash given, subject to a taxable income limitation discussed below. For contributions of property, there are different rules for long-term capital gain (LTCG) property and all other property. LTCG property is property that, if sold, would generate a LTCG. Corporations also have special rules for contributions of inventory and for the timing of when the contribution is made.

Donation of LTCG Property The full fair market value (FMV) of contributions of LTCG property is deductible. Additionally, the donor does not have to recognize the unrealized gain in the asset, which is the difference in the asset's fair market value and adjusted basis when the owner contributes the property. If the LTCG property contributed is tangible personalty and the charitable organization does not use the property in a manner that is related to its tax-exempt purpose, the donor can deduct only the adjusted basis of the property. This rule applies only if the deduction is more than $5,000.[14]

We review scenarios featuring LTCG property and charitable contributions in the next two Examples.

EXAMPLE 3.3.1
LTCG Property Contributions

Wren Corporation owns land that it has held as an investment for the last 12 years. Wren's basis in the land is $50,000 and its current FMV is $120,000. Wren contributes the land to a local charitable organization to build a community recreation center. What is Wren's charitable contribution, and how much gain does Wren recognize because of the contribution?

SOLUTION

If Wren sold the land, it would have a LTCG of $70,000 ($120,000 amount realized – $50,000 adjusted basis). However, because Wren is donating the land, it can deduct the FMV of $120,000 as a charitable contribution. Wren does not recognize any gain due to the contribution.

Related exercises: Brief Exercise 8
Application Problem 11

EXAMPLE 3.3.2
Property Not Used for Tax-Exempt Purpose

Blue Jay Corporation owns a famous painting by a contemporary artist that has been appraised for $650,000. Blue Jay's adjusted basis in the painting is $320,000, and Blue Jay has owned the painting for six years. Blue Jay donates the painting to a local art museum. Instead of displaying the painting for visitors to see, the museum immediately sold the painting for $575,000 to raise cash to pay off debt. How much can Blue Jay deduct for this contribution, assuming there are no taxable income limitations on the deduction?

SOLUTION

The property is LTCG property so the general rule is that Blue Jay can deduct the FMV of $650,000. However, the museum sold the painting and did not use it in a manner consistent with its tax-exempt purposes. Therefore, Blue Jay's deduction is limited to its adjusted basis of $320,000.

Related exercise: Application Problem 12

Donation of All Other Property For all other property, the deduction is:

$$\left(\begin{array}{c}\text{FMV of}\\ \text{the Property}\end{array}\right) - \left(\begin{array}{c}\text{The ordinary income or short-term}\\ \text{capital gain (STCG) that would be recognized if}\\ \text{the taxpayer sold the property}\end{array}\right)$$

Ordinary income property includes ordinary income due to depreciation recapture, as shown in the next Example.

[14]IRC §170(e).

EXAMPLE 3.3.3 Reduction for Ordinary Income or STCG

Sparrow Corporation owns machinery with a fair market value of $125,000 and an adjusted basis of $90,000. Depreciation claimed is $27,000. How much could Sparrow deduct as a charitable contribution if it contributed the machine to a qualified charity?

SOLUTION

If Sparrow sold the machine, the total gain would be $35,000 ($125,000 amount realized – $90,000 adjusted basis), of which Sparrow would recapture $27,000 as ordinary income. If Sparrow contributed this property to a qualified charitable organization, the deduction would be $98,000 ($125,000 – $27,000).

Related exercise: Application Problem 13

If the fair market value of the property is less than its adjusted basis, the deduction is limited to the fair market value, as shown in the next Example.

EXAMPLE 3.3.4 Charitable Contribution of Loss Property

Presume that Heron Corporation contributed IBM stock that it had owned for 11 months to a local university that is a qualified charity. Heron's basis in the stock was $36,500 and the stock's fair market value was $24,000. How much can Heron deduct for the charitable contribution?

SOLUTION

If Heron had sold the stock to an unrelated third party, it would have a short-term capital loss of $12,500 ($24,000 amount realized – $36,500 adjusted basis). The tax law limits Heron's deduction to the FMV of $24,000.

Tax Planning Tip

In Example 3.3.4, Heron should have sold the stock, rather than donating it, so it could recognize the $12,500 short-term capital loss (STCL). Heron could then donate the $24,000 cash received from the sale to the university. Given a marginal tax rate of 21%, the $12,500 STCL can produce tax savings of $2,625 ($12,500 × 21%) when it offsets other capital gains.

Donation of Inventory If an individual donates inventory to a qualified charity, the deduction is limited to the lower of the adjusted basis or fair market value of the property. However, a corporation's contribution of inventory, depreciable personalty, or realty used in its trade or business results in a deduction that is greater than the property's adjusted basis if the following conditions are met:

- The charity uses the property in a manner related to its exempt purpose, *and*
- Solely for the care of the ill, needy, or infants, *or*
- For research purposes under specified conditions.

If these conditions are met, the deduction of the adjusted basis is increased by 50% of the appreciation in the property. However, the deduction can never exceed twice the adjusted basis.[15] The formula for the deduction is the *lower* of the:

- Adjusted basis of the property (AB) + [50% × (FMV – AB)], *or*
- 2 × AB.

[15]IRC §170(e)(3).

The next Example shows how the formula is applied.

EXAMPLE 3.3.5
Contribution of Inventory

Redbird Corporation is a book publisher and contributes 100 children's books to a shelter for people experiencing homelessness that is a qualified charity. The books will be given to children when they come to the shelter. The books sell for $24 each and Redbird's cost basis in the books is $11 each. How much can Redbird deduct for this contribution?

SOLUTION

Because Redbird's contribution consists of inventory that is used for the needy, it can deduct more than the adjusted basis of the property, as follows:

The deduction is the *lower* of the:

- $1,100 + [50% × ($2,400 – $1,100)] = $1,750, *or*
- 2 × $1,100 = $2,200

Therefore, Redbird can deduct $1,750 for the contribution of the 100 books.

If the inventory is *wholesome* food inventory and is contributed by corporations or other businesses to charities that use the food in an appropriate manner, the contribution can be deducted up to 15% of taxable income from the food operations.

Related exercises: Discussion Question 7
Application Problem 14

Potential Pitfall

The food inventory rule applies to all businesses, not just corporations.

Timing Cash-basis corporations deduct charitable contributions in the year that the contribution is paid. An accrual-basis corporation can elect to deduct accrued contributions, if the corporation's board has approved the contribution before year-end, and it has been paid within the first 3½ months following its tax year-end, which is April 15 for calendar-year corporations.[16] For corporations with a June 30 year-end, the deadline is 2½ months following year-end, which is September 15.

We show how the timing rule applies in the next Example.

EXAMPLE 3.3.6
Timing of Charitable Contribution Deduction

Albatross, Inc., is a calendar-year, accrual-basis taxpayer. On December 18 of Year 1, Albatross's board authorized a donation of $2 million to the local city library to expand its existing building. Albatross paid the $2 million as follows:

December 30, Year 1	$500,000
March 1, Year 2	$300,000
September 1, Year 2	$400,000
January 10, Year 3	$600,000
July 1, Year 3	$200,000

How much can Albatross deduct in Year 1, Year 2, and Year 3, assuming no taxable income limitations and that Albatross wants to deduct the contributions as early as possible? Alternatively, how much can Albatross deduct if it is a cash-basis taxpayer?

[16] IRC §170(a)(2).

SOLUTION

If Albatross is an accrual-basis taxpayer, it can deduct contributions that were board approved by December 31, Year 1 as long as these are paid by April 15, Year 2. Therefore, Albatross can deduct \$800,000 in Year 1 (\$500,000 + \$300,000). For Year 2, Albatross can deduct \$400,000, and for Year 3, the deduction is \$800,000 (\$600,000 + \$200,000). The \$600,000 payment on January 10, Year 3, was paid before April 15, Year 3, but this was approved by the board in Year 1, not Year 2, so the 3½ month rule does not apply.

If Albatross is a cash-basis taxpayer, the deduction for Year 1 would be limited to \$500,000. For Year 2, the deduction would be \$700,000 (\$300,000 + \$400,000), and \$800,000 for Year 3 (\$600,000 + \$200,000).

Related exercises: Discussion Question 6
Multiple Choice Questions 9, 10
Brief Exercises 7, 9
Application Problem 15

Why **Why are accrued contributions deductible only if paid within 3½ months after the end for the tax year?** Charitable contributions are voluntary payments that corporations choose to make for various reasons. If an accrual-basis corporation did not have a time limit on how long it has to pay the contribution, the corporation's board could approve a large contribution before the end of the year to create a large deduction, but then wait several months, or even years, to pay the contribution. This would create a large deduction without a corresponding cash outlay in the near future. To prevent corporations from having this discretion, the 3½ month rule for payment was put in place.

Limit on Charitable Deduction The maximum amount that can be deducted for charitable contributions each year is 10% of taxable income (before deducting charitable contributions, the dividends received deduction (see next section), and carrybacks).[17] Cash contributions by corporations are deducted up to 10% of taxable income. Any excess charitable contribution above the 10% limit can be carried forward for five years. There is no carryback for excess charitable contributions. The deductions rules for charitable contributions for a corporation are summarized in **Illustration 3.5**.

ILLUSTRATION 3.5 Corporate Charitable Contribution Deductions

Corporate Charitable Contributions Rules	
Asset donated	**Deduction**
LTCG property	FMV
LTCG property—Not used for tax-exempt purpose	Adjusted basis (if more than \$5,000)
Other property	FMV − (ordinary income or STCG if sold)
Inventory—For ill, needy, infants, or research	Adjusted basis + (50% × appreciation), not to exceed twice adjusted basis
Overall limitation	10% of taxable income before contribution, dividends received deduction, and carryforwards

We show how the 10% overall limitation applies in the next Example.

Related exercise: Application Problem 16

[17]IRC §170(b)(2).

EXAMPLE 3.3.7
Taxable Income Limitation

The financial statements of Finch Corporation, a calendar-year, accrual-basis corporation, disclose net income for the current year of $350,000 after deducting a charitable contribution of $125,000. The contribution was paid on August 15 of the current year. How much can Finch deduct in the current year for this contribution?

SOLUTION

The allowable charitable contribution deduction for the current year is limited to 10% of taxable income computed before the charitable contribution deduction. The deduction is computed as follows:

Net income after the charitable contribution	$350,000
Plus: Charitable contributions	125,000
Taxable income before charitable contribution	$475,000
Limitation	× 10%
Deductible contribution	$ 47,500

Finch can deduct $47,500 of the contribution in the current year. The remaining contribution of $77,500 ($125,000 – $47,500) is carried forward for up to five years.

Dividends Received Deduction

Corporations are allowed a **dividends received deduction (DRD)** to offset some or all the dividend income it receives from other corporations. S corporations cannot claim the DRD. This section deals with dividends received from domestic corporations. Separately, a 100% deduction is allowed by U.S. corporations for the foreign-source portion of dividends received from the earnings and profits of 10% or more-owned foreign affiliates. This deduction completely offsets the income from the foreign subsidiary.[18]

The domestic DRD is either 50%, 65%, or 100% of the qualifying dividend received. The percentage used to compute the DRD depends on the percentage of stock owned in the dividend-paying corporation, as shown in **Illustration 3.6**.

ILLUSTRATION 3.6 Dividends Received Deduction Percentages

DRD Percentages by Ownership Percentage	
Ownership interest in dividend-paying corporation	**DRD percentages**
< 20%	50%
≥ 20% and < 80%	65%
≥ 80%	100%

There are two requirements that must be met for the corporation to qualify for the DRD with respect to a specific dividend: generally, it must be received from a domestic corporation, and it must pass the holding period test.

Domestic Corporation The dividend must be received from a corporation that is legally incorporated in the United States. Foreign corporations that are traded on a U.S. stock exchange are treated as domestic corporations for purposes of this rule. Additionally, certain treaties with foreign countries permit dividends from corporations organized in the foreign country to be treated as a qualified dividend for the DRD.

Holding Period Test To be eligible for the DRD, the stock must have been held by the corporation for at least 46 days within a 91-day window. The 91-day window begins 45 days before the ex-dividend date and ends 45 days after the ex-dividend date, as shown in **Illustration 3.7**.

[18]IRC §245A.

The ex-dividend date is one day after the record date for the dividend. All shareholders who own stock on the record date receive the dividend when it is paid.

> **Potential Pitfall**
>
> Recall that the holding period for an asset begins on the day after the asset is purchased. If a taxpayer purchases an asset on January 7, the first day of the holding period is January 8.

ILLUSTRATION 3.7 Holding Period Test for DRD

46-Day DRD Holding Period Requirement

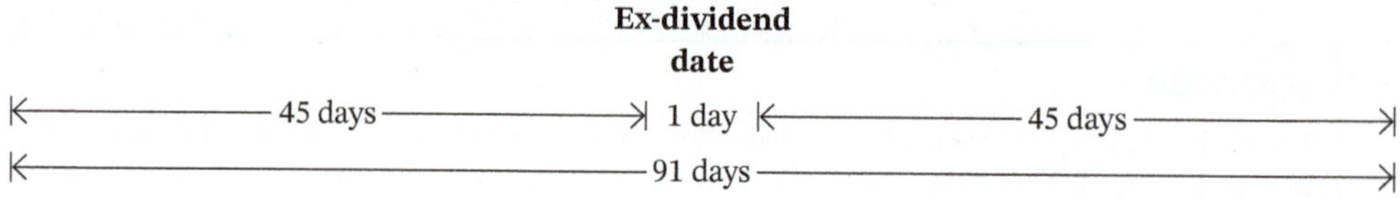

Related exercises: Multiple Choice Question 10
Brief Exercise 9

The next Example demonstrates how the holding period test works.

EXAMPLE 3.3.8 DRD Holding Period Test

Raven, Inc. purchased 10,000 shares of stock in General Motors on April 16 of the current tax year and received a dividend of $40,000 on May 12 of the current tax year. The ex-dividend date was May 1 of the current year. Raven sold the stock on May 28 of the current year. Does Raven qualify for the DRD with respect to this dividend?

SOLUTION

Because the ex-dividend date is May 1, the 91-day period runs from March 16 to June 15. To qualify for the DRD, Raven must own the stock for at least 46 days during this period. Because Raven owned the stock for only 42 days, Raven does not qualify for the DRD.

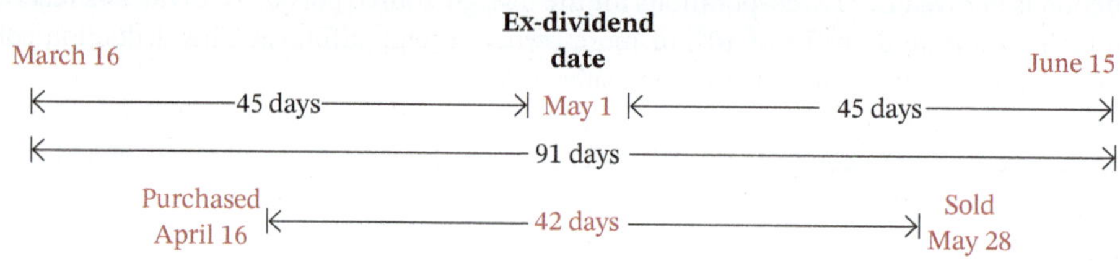

Related exercise: Tax Planning Problem 2

Computing the DRD The DRD is limited by taxable income before the DRD and before any NOL carryforwards or capital loss carrybacks. However, this limitation does not apply if the DRD creates or adds to an NOL. There are four steps to computing the DRD. These steps are also shown in the flowchart in **Illustration 3.8**.

> **Potential Pitfall**
>
> If the ownership percentage in another corporation is exactly 20%, the DRD is 65%. Similarly, if the ownership percentage is exactly 80%, the DRD is 100%. Do not confuse these rules by assuming the thresholds are more than 20% or more than 80%.

Step 1. **Determine:** The ownership interest in the dividend-paying corporation and the applicable DRD percentage.

Step 2. **Compute:** The full DRD, assuming no limitations apply, as follows:

$$\text{Dividend income} \times \text{Applicable DRD percentage}$$

Step 3. **Subtract:** The full DRD from the corporation's taxable income determined before the DRD, capital loss carrybacks, and any NOL carryforwards. If this results in a taxable loss, then the taxable income limit test does not apply. If this does not result in a loss, then go to step 4.

Step 4. **Analyze:** The DRD cannot exceed the following:

$$\left(\begin{array}{c}\text{Taxable income before the}\\ \text{DRD, capital loss carrybacks, and NOL carryforwards}\end{array}\right) \times \left(\begin{array}{c}\text{The applicable}\\ \text{DRD percentage from step 1}\end{array}\right)$$

ILLUSTRATION 3.8 Dividends Received Deduction Flowchart

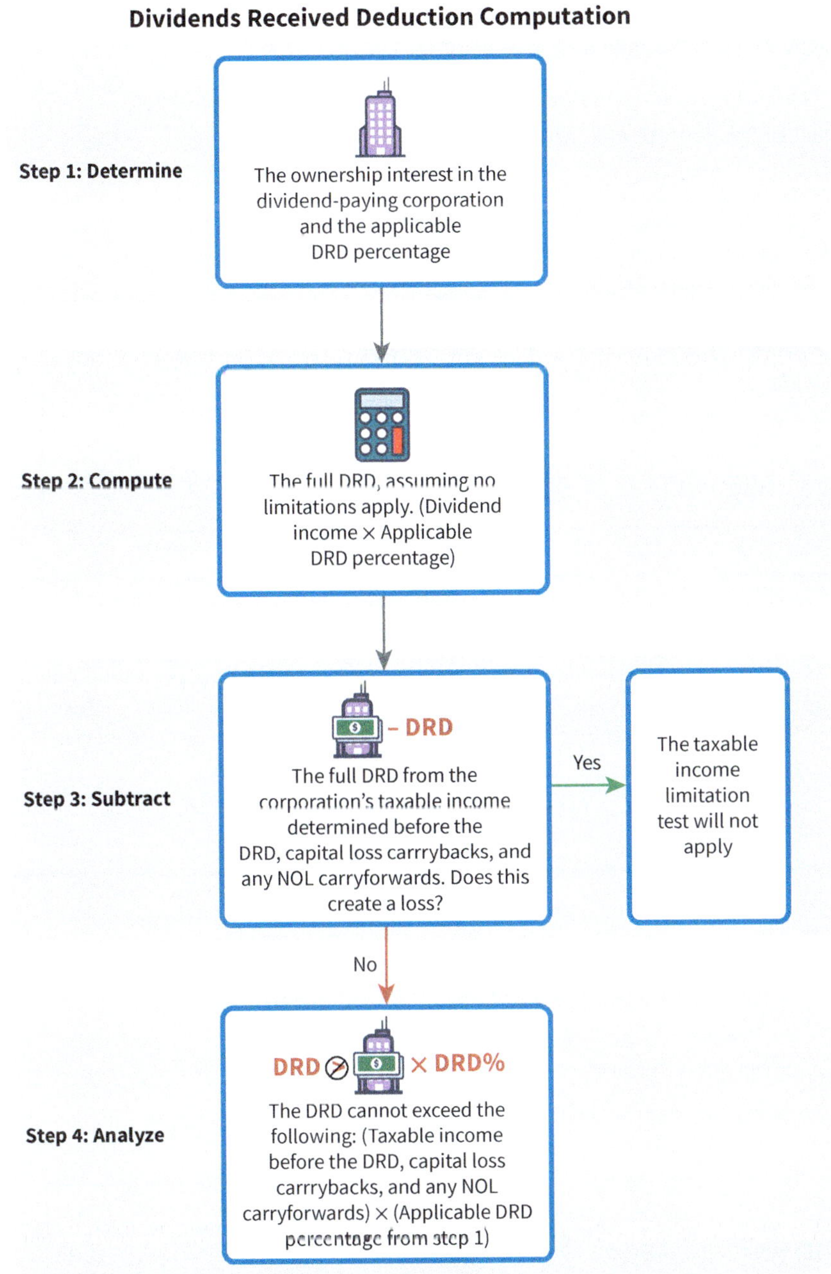

The next three Examples demonstrate the DRD computation.

EXAMPLE 3.3.9
Taxable Income Limit Applies

Eagle, Inc. owns 1% of the stock of Home Depot. Eagle has the following information this year, before deducting the DRD:

Revenue from operations	$1,450,000
Dividend—Home Depot	$ 100,000
Operating expenses	$ 800,000

What is Eagle's taxable income after the DRD?

SOLUTION

We apply the steps shown in Illustration 3.8 to compute the DRD:

Step 1: The ownership percentage in Home Depot is 1%, so the DRD percentage is 50%.

Step 2: The full DRD is $50,000 ($100,000 × 50%).

Step 3: If the full DRD is subtracted, Eagle has taxable income of $700,000, so a loss is not created. Therefore, the taxable income limit test applies.

Revenue from operations	$1,450,000
Plus: Dividend—Home Depot	100,000
Less: Operating expenses	(800,000)
Taxable income before the DRD	$ 750,000
Less: DRD	(50,000)
Taxable income after DRD	$ 700,000

Step 4: The taxable income limit is $750,000 × 50%, or $375,000. This is greater than or equal to the full DRD of $50,000, so the full DRD is allowed.

Related exercises: Multiple Choice Question 11
Brief Exercise 10

EXAMPLE 3.3.10 Taxable Income Limit Applies and Limits Deduction

Eagle, Inc. owns 1% of the stock of Home Depot. Eagle has the following information this year, before deducting the DRD:

Revenue from operations	$1,450,000
Dividend—Home Depot	$ 100,000
Operating expenses	$1,490,000

What is Eagle's taxable income after the DRD?

SOLUTION

We apply the steps shown in Illustration 3.8 to compute the DRD:

Step 1: The ownership percentage in Home Depot is 1%, so the DRD percentage is 50%.

Step 2: The full DRD is $50,000 ($100,000 × 50%).

Step 3: If the full DRD is subtracted, Eagle has taxable income of $10,000, so a loss is not created. Therefore, the taxable income limit test applies.

Revenue from operations	$1,450,000
Plus: Dividend—Home Depot	100,000
Less: Operating expenses	(1,490,000)
Taxable income before the DRD	$ 60,000
Less: DRD	(50,000)
Taxable income after DRD	$ 10,000

Step 4: The taxable income limit is $60,000 × 50%, or $30,000. Because $30,000 is less than the full DRD of $50,000, the DRD is limited to $30,000, and Eagle's taxable income is $30,000.

Revenue from operations	$ 1,450,000
Plus: Dividend—Home Depot	100,000
Less: Operating expenses	(1,490,000)
Taxable income before the DRD	$ 60,000
Less: DRD	(30,000)
Taxable income after DRD	$ 30,000

EXAMPLE 3.3.11 Taxable Income Limit Applies and Does Not Limit Deduction

Eagle, Inc. owns 1% of the stock of Home Depot. Eagle has the following information this year, before deducting the DRD:

Revenue from operations	$1,450,000
Dividend—Home Depot	$ 100,000
Operating expenses	$1,520,000

What is Eagle's taxable income after the DRD?

SOLUTION

We apply the steps shown in Illustration 3.8 to compute the DRD:

Step 1: The ownership percentage in Home Depot is 1%, so the DRD percentage is 50%.

Step 2: The full DRD is $50,000 ($100,000 × 50%).

Step 3: If the full DRD is subtracted, Eagle would recognize a loss of $20,000. Therefore, the taxable income limit test does not apply, and step 4 is not used.

Revenue from operations	$1,450,000
Plus: Dividend—Home Depot	100,000
Less: Operating expenses	(1,520,000)
Taxable income before the DRD	$ 30,000
Less: DRD	(50,000)
Taxable Loss after DRD	($ 20,000)

Related exercises: Application Problem 17, 18, 19

Why Why does Congress allow the DRD? One of the major disadvantages of corporations is that the income is taxed twice, once to the corporation on Form 1120 and a second time when the earnings are distributed to shareholders. While double taxation is a significant disadvantage for corporations, when a corporation owns stock in another corporation, there is a possibility of triple taxation, as shown in **Illustration 3.9**. Assume that Ricky owns 100% of Corporation B and that Corporation B owns 100% of Corporation A. Corporation A has taxable income of $100,000 this year. Corporation A pays 100% of its after-tax income as a dividend to Corporation B. Corporation B pays 100% of its after-tax income to Ricky. If the dividend is a qualified dividend and Ricky's LTCG rate is 20%, what are Ricky's after-tax proceeds?

ILLUSTRATION 3.9 Potential Triple Taxation of Corporate Earnings

With No Dividends Received Deduction for Corporation B

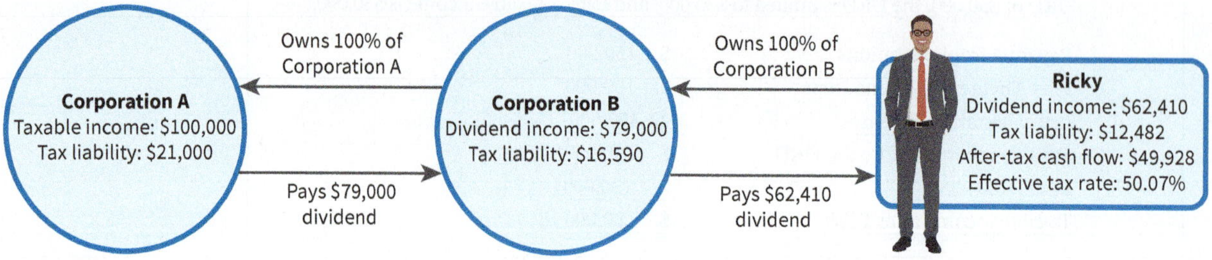

With 100% Dividends Received Deduction for Corporation B

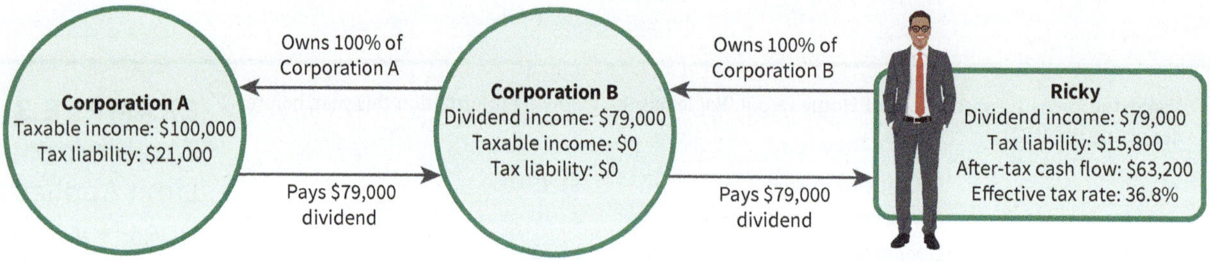

Corporation A will pay federal income tax of $21,000 ($100,000 × 21%), which results in after-tax proceeds of $79,000. Corporation B thus has dividend income of $79,000 and a federal tax liability of $16,590 ($79,000 × 21%). Corporation B then pays a dividend to Ricky of $62,410 ($79,000 – $16,590). Because this is a qualified dividend, it is taxed at Ricky's LTCG rate of 20%, resulting in a tax liability of $12,482. Ricky's after-tax proceeds are $49,928 ($62,410 – $12,482). The original income of $100,000 is reduced to $49,928 by the time the cash ends up in the hands of an individual shareholder because of the triple taxation. The triple taxation results in an effective tax rate of 50.07% ($100,000 – $49,928)/$100,000). If state income taxes are considered, the effective tax rate could be even higher.

The DRD was created by Congress to mitigate or eliminate triple taxation of corporate earnings. Corporation B would receive a 100% DRD because it owns 100% of the stock of Corporation A, which eliminates completely the second level of tax above. If the DRD percentage is 50% or 65%, then the triple taxation is not completely eliminated, but it is mitigated. If Corporation B receives a 100% DRD, then it has no tax liability for the $79,000 dividend. When Corporation B pays the $79,000 dividend to Ricky, he will have a $79,000 LTCG that is taxed at 20% and a tax liability of $15,800 ($79,000 × 20%). With the DRD, the total tax liability paid is $36,800 ($21,000 + $15,800) which reduces the total effective tax rate to 36.8% ($36,800/$100,000). Ricky's after-tax cash flow has increased to $63,200.

Related exercise: Discussion Question 8

Research and Development Expenses

Research and development expenses are costs that are incident to the development or improvement of a product in the experimental or laboratory sense. Expenditures qualify as research and development costs in the experimental or laboratory sense if they are for activities intended to discover information that eliminates uncertainty as to the development or improvement of a product.[19] Research and development expenses incurred after 2021 must be amortized over 60 months. For the year that these expenses are incurred, they can be amortized for six months regardless of when incurred during the year.[20]

[19]Treas. Reg. §1.274-2(a)(1).

[20]IRC §174(a)(2).

Corporate Insurance Premiums

A corporation may deduct insurance premiums paid for casualty insurance, employee health or accident insurance, and life insurance coverage for its employees and their beneficiaries. Premiums paid on life insurance policies in which the corporation itself is the beneficiary are not deductible because any insurance proceeds received later will not be taxable.

EXAMPLE 3.3.12
Deductibility of Corporate Insurance Premiums

Moss Corporation's income statement for the current year showed the following expenses for life insurance premiums:

Group-term life insurance premiums paid on employees' lives with the employees' dependents as beneficiaries	$10,000
Term life insurance premiums paid on life insurance policy on the life of the president of Moss Corporation with Moss Corporation named as beneficiary	$7,000

How much should Moss Corporation deduct for life insurance premiums?

SOLUTION

The life insurance premiums paid on the life of the president of Moss Corporation are not deductible because Moss Corporation is the beneficiary of the life insurance policy. Its deduction is $10,000 because the group term life insurance premiums for the benefit of the employees are deductible.

Limitations on Deductions

The following expenses have limitations attached to them that affect their deductibility.

Deduction for compensation payments to the principal executive officer, principal financial officer, and the three other highest compensated executives are limited to $1,000,000 each for publicly traded companies. Compensation paid under performance-based contracts are included in the $1,000,000 limitation.[21]

Corporations, as well as other businesses, are limited in the amount of business interest expense they can deduct each year if their average gross receipts for the previous three years are greater than or equal to $31 million (2025). In that case, the deduction for business interest expense cannot exceed the sum of:

- Business interest income,
- 30% of the taxpayer's adjusted taxable income, *and*
- The taxpayer's **floor plan financing interest** for the tax year, which is defined as interest paid or accrued on debt used to finance motor vehicles held for sale or lease, and which is secured by that same inventory.[22]

[21] IRC §162(m).

[22] IRC §163(j).

PRACTICE PROBLEM 3.3.1
Corporate Tax Formula

Glee Inc. has the following for the current year:

Gross receipts	$680,000
Cost of goods sold	$190,000
Interest income	$ 500
Short-term capital gain	$ 15,000
Salaries expense	$260,000
Other operating expenses	$225,000

Glee paid federal estimated tax payments of $5,000. What is Glee's tax refund/owed?

SOLUTION

We compute Glee's taxable income as follows:

Gross receipts	$ 680,000
Cost of goods sold	(190,000)
Interest income	500
Short-term capital gain	15,000
Salaries expense	(260,000)
Other operating expenses	(225,000)
Taxable income	$ 20,500

Glee has a corporate tax liability of $4,305 ($20,500 × 21%). Therefore, Glee's refund is $695 ($5,000 – $4,305).

PRACTICE PROBLEM 3.3.2
Calculating a Corporation's Charitable Contribution Deduction

Titans Corporation is a calendar-year corporation and made several charitable contributions to qualified charities by the end of the year. Titans made cash contributions of $23,000, contributed Walmart stock with an adjusted basis of $4,500 and fair market value of $6,900, and contributed Disney stock with an adjusted basis of $10,000 and a fair market value of $8,500. Both stocks had been held for several years. If Titan's taxable income before the charitable contribution is $350,000, what is Titan's allowable charitable contribution deduction?

SOLUTION

Because the stocks contributed are LTCG assets, Titan can deduct the fair market value of these stocks. Therefore, total charitable contributions are $38,400 ($23,000 + $6,900 + $8,500). The allowable charitable contribution deduction is limited to 10% of taxable income computed before the charitable contribution deduction, and determined as follows:

Taxable income before charitable contribution	$350,000
Charitable contribution limitation	× 10%
Deductible contribution	$ 35,000

The remaining contribution of $3,400 ($38,400 – $35,000) is carried forward for up to five years.

Astro Inc. owns the following stocks and received the following dividend income:

Stock	Percent ownership	Dividend income
Sanrusky Inc.	5%	$ 2,000
Stargazer Inc.	25%	$10,000
Saare Inc.	15%	$ 8,000

Both Sanrusky and Stargazer are domestic corporations and Saare is a foreign affiliate. If Astro's taxable income before the dividends received deduction is $100,000, what is Astro's taxable income after the dividends received deduction?

PRACTICE PROBLEM 3.3.3
Assessing DRD for a Corporation with a Foreign Affiliate

SOLUTION

We must first compute the percentage that applies for the DRD for each dividend. A 100% DRD is allowed for Saare Inc. because it is a foreign entity and at least 10% is owned by Astro. Next, we compute the taxable income limitation, which is $100,000 multiplied by the DRD percentage.

Stock	% ownership	Dividend income	DRD%	DRD	Taxable income limitation
Sanrusky Inc.	5%	$ 2,000	50%	$ 1,000	$ 50,000
Stargazer Inc.	25%	$10,000	65%	$ 6,500	$ 65,000
Saare Inc.	15%	$ 8,000	100%	$ 8,000	$100,000
				$15,500	

The taxable income limitation does not limit the DRD for any of the dividends. Therefore, Astro's DRD is $15,500. Astro's taxable income after the DRD is $84,500 ($100,000 – $15,500).

INTERACTIVE SELF-SCORING QUIZZES

3.4 Other Corporate Tax Issues

LEARNING OBJECTIVE 4

Apply other special rules for computing corporate taxable income.

In addition to the special corporation deductions discussed in the previous section, there are other areas of the corporate tax law that differ from the individual taxation rules. In this section, we cover:

VIDEO CONTENT

- Capital gains and losses
- Accounting methods and periods
- Reconciliation of book income and taxable income
- Net operating losses (NOLs)
- Reconciliation of retained earnings
- Passive losses
- Corporate alternative minimum tax

Capital Gains and Losses

Recall that for individuals, net long-term capital gains are taxed at preferential rates, and net capital losses are limited to $3,000 per year, with an unlimited carryforward. While the netting rules for capital gains and losses are the same for individuals and corporations, the tax consequences are quite different.

- Corporations do not have a preferential tax rate for LTCGs. Rather, ordinary income, STCGs, and LTCGs are taxed at the same tax rate, 21%.

Related exercise: Discussion Question 10

- Deductible capital losses are offset against recognized capital gains, but there is no deduction for a net capital loss. Rather, a net capital loss is carried back three years and forward five years to offset capital gains in other years, as shown in **Illustration 3.10.**[23]

Related exercise: Discussion Question 9

ILLUSTRATION 3.10 Net Capital Losses

Capital Loss Carryback and Carryforward

|← 3-year carryback →| Current year |← 5-year carryforward →|

We show how the rules apply for capital losses in the next Example.

EXAMPLE 3.4.1
Capital Gains and Losses

Goose Corporation had the following transactions for the current tax year:

Operating net income	$82,000
STCG	$ 6,000
STCL	$11,000
LTCG	$ 3,000

What are the tax consequences of these transactions?

SOLUTION

The STCL of $11,000 offsets the STCG of $6,000 and the LTCG of $3,000, which results in a net capital loss of $2,000 ($11,000 STCL – $6,000 STCG – $3,000 LTCG). The $2,000 net capital loss cannot offset the $82,000 of operating income because net capital losses are not deductible for corporations. The $2,000 net capital loss can be carried back three years and carried forward five years.

Related exercises: Multiple Choice Question 12
Brief Exercise 11
Application Problem 20

Tax Planning Tip

Because corporations do not have a preferential LTCGs rate, it is not uncommon for students to wonder why Congress requires corporations to separate the gains from ordinary assets and capital assets. The reason solely relates to losses. Corporations can offset capital losses only against capital gains. If this limitation did not exist, then corporations would not need to keep up with the tax character of gains and losses.

[23]IRC §1211.

Accounting Methods and Periods

Corporations have certain rules related to accounting methods and periods that they must follow. In this section, you will learn the most common rules of this nature.

General Rules

The accounting method rules that apply for other businesses also apply for corporations.[24] Additionally, the following rules govern corporate accounting methods.

- A corporation can designate any month for its tax year-end. While many corporations have a calendar year-end, this is not required.

Related exercises: Discussion Question 11
Multiple Choice Question 13

- Corporations must use the accrual method of accounting unless the entity qualifies as a **small business corporation.** To be a small business corporation, the corporation's average gross receipts over the last three tax years cannot exceed $31 million (2025).[25]

Related exercise: Discussion Question 12

- Passive loss limits do not apply to regular corporations because they exist to operate a business and make a profit.

The next Example demonstrates the application of the cash-method versus accrual-method test.

EXAMPLE 3.4.2
Cash vs. Accrual Method

Hummingbird, Inc. began business five years ago in Year 1. They have used the cash basis method of accounting since inception. Hummingbird's gross receipts over the last five years are as follows:

Year 1	$ 9,000,000
Year 2	$12,000,000
Year 3	$31,000,000
Year 4	$33,000,000
Year 5	$30,000,000

Can Hummingbird continue to use the cash method in Year 6 (assume Year 6 is 2025)?

SOLUTION

Hummingbird must compute its average gross receipts over the last three years, determined as follows:

$$\frac{(\$31,000,000 + \$33,000,000 + \$30,000,000)}{3} = \$31,333,333$$

Because the average gross receipts of $31,333,333 exceeds the benchmark of $31,000,000 Hummingbird cannot use the cash method for Year 6 and must use the accrual basis.

Related exercise: Application Problem 21

[24]More detail can be found in *Fundamentals of Taxation—Individuals and Business Entities*, Chapter 5, LO3, Accounting Methods and Periods—Income; Chapter 8, LO4, Accounting Methods for Deductions; and Chapter 8, LO6, Accounting for Inventories.

[25]IRC §448.

Prepaid Income

The major exception to the general accrual method for income tax purposes is that taxpayers usually recognize prepaid income, including prepaid interest, when received. If the prepayment is for services the taxpayer will render in the future, a special **deferral rule** applies. In general, the taxpayer must include it in gross income when received. However, the taxpayer can elect to defer prepaid service income to the following tax year if the taxpayer treats it the same way for financial reporting purposes. Prepaid service income can never be deferred beyond the end of the tax year following the year it is received. This deferral rule does not apply if the taxpayer does not have audited financial statements or similar records.

The following two Examples explore tax situations related to prepaid income.

EXAMPLE 3.4.3
Prepaid Service Income

Buzz owns his own business providing landscaping services for residences and small businesses. For tax and financial reporting, he uses the accrual basis. On December 1, Year 12, Buzz offered a customer a substantial discount in return for prepaying 18 months of service (through May 31, Year 14). The customer accepted the offer and paid Buzz $1,800 on December 1, Year 12. How should Buzz treat this situation for tax purposes?

SOLUTION

In his financial statements, Buzz reports only $100 of income in Year 12 for this contract ($1,800/18 months). Because Buzz has deferred the inclusion of the other 17 months of income for financial reporting purposes, he is not required to report this income in Year 12. For tax purposes, he must include the remaining $1,700 in income in Year 13, because the prepayments cannot be deferred beyond the end of Year 13.

EXAMPLE 3.4.4
Prepaid Interest

Oscar loaned a friend $100,000 so the friend could build an addition on to his house. Oscar charges his friend 9.6% interest annually, which is $800 per month, and the loan must be repaid within 10 years. In December of Year 2, his friend prepays interest of $4,800 for the first six months of Year 3. Is the $4,800 of interest income taxable in Year 2 or Year 3? Would your answer be different if Oscar were in the trade or business of lending money and uses the accrual method of accounting?

SOLUTION

Oscar's loan to his friend is a personal activity so the cash method of accounting applies. Therefore, Oscar recognizes the $4,800 of prepaid interest income in Year 2 when he receives it. The answer is the same if Oscar is in the trade or business of lending money. Even under the accrual method, prepaid interest income is taxed in Year 2 when it is received.

Related exercises: Application Problems 22, 23

Change in Accounting Method

Once a taxpayer has selected a method of accounting, it cannot be changed without the consent of the IRS. The IRS must consent even if the taxpayer is changing from an impermissible method to a permissible method. The following steps should be followed if your client wishes to change their accounting method:

- The taxpayer makes the request on Form 3115, Application for Change in Accounting Method.
- The IRS provides automatic consent for some changes. For such changes, once the Form 3115 is correctly filed, then the consent is deemed to have taken place.[26] For nonautomatic changes, the taxpayer must wait for the IRS's written consent before making the change.

[26]The list of automatic changes is provided in Rev. Proc. 2019-43, 2019-48 IRB 1107.

- The taxpayer takes any negative adjustment to income into account in the year they make the accounting method change.
- The taxpayer spreads any positive adjustment to income required due to a voluntary change in accounting method over four years, beginning with the year of change. A voluntary change includes changing from an incorrect to a correct method. If the adjustment is less than $25,000, the taxpayer can elect to include all income in the year of change. If the IRS initiates the change in accounting method due to an IRS examination, the taxpayer must include any positive adjustment in the earliest tax year under examination and cannot spread the income over four years.

Related exercises: Discussion Question 13
Multiple Choice Question 14

Prepaid Expenses

A taxpayer using the cash method can take an immediate deduction for prepaid business expenses when paid, as long as the benefits from those expenses do not extend beyond the *earlier* of:

- 12 months after benefits first begin, *or*
- The end of the year after the year in which the taxpayer made the payment.

If the benefits from the prepayment extend beyond this period, the taxpayer must spread the deduction over the period for which the expenses apply. This **12-month rule** does not affect the timing of the deduction for accrual-basis taxpayers because in that case the taxpayer must also meet the economic performance rules. Congress provided the economic performance rule to prevent taxpayers from claiming current deductions while delaying the payment of the amounts owed far into the future. **Economic performance** occurs when the taxpayer receives services or property or uses property another party provided. The law does not permit a deduction until the taxpayer has performed what has been promised under the contract.

We demonstrate the application of the prepaid expenses rule in the next two Examples.

EXAMPLE 3.4.5 Prepaid Expenses—Cash Basis—12-Month Rule Not Met

On December 1, Year 8, LeBron Corporation pays a $10,000 insurance premium for automobiles that it uses in its business. The premium is for a 1-year term that begins on February 1, Year 9. Can LeBron deduct the entire $10,000 premium in Year 8 if the corporation is a cash-basis taxpayer?

SOLUTION

As a cash-basis taxpayer, LeBron must first determine the *earlier* of:

- 12 months after benefits first begin (February 1, Year 10), *or*
- The end of the year after the year in which the taxpayer made the payment (December 31, Year 9)

The earlier date is December 31, Year 9. Because the benefit from the premium extends to January 31, Year 10 (which is after December 31, Year 9), LeBron does not meet the 12-month rule. The corporation must therefore capitalize the $10,000 in Year 8, and the premium will be deductible over the period to which it relates. It can deduct $9,167 ($10,000 × 11 months/12 months) in Year 9 and $833 ($10,000 × 1 month/12 months) in Year 10.

EXAMPLE 3.4.6
Prepaid Expenses—Cash Basis—12-Month Rule Not Met

Assume the same facts as in Example 3.4.5 except that the policy has a term beginning on December 15, Year 8, and ending December 14, Year 9.

SOLUTION

LeBron Corporation first determines the *earlier* of:

- 12 months after benefits first begin (December 15, Year 9), *or*
- The end of the year after the year in which the taxpayer made the payment (December 31, Year 9).

The earlier date is December 15, Year 9. Because the benefit from the premium extends to December 14, Year 9, which is not after December 15, Year 9, then LeBron meets the 12-month rule. It can deduct the entire $10,000 in Year 8.

Why **Why does the 12-month rule exist for prepaid expenses?** If the 12-month rule did not exist, cash-basis taxpayers could reduce their income by prepaying large expenses near the end of the tax year. Presume that a sole proprietorship knew in December of the current tax year that it was going to be in the 37% tax bracket because of some large sales this year. Next year, it expects to be in the 24% tax bracket. So, if it accelerates expenses into the current year, it will save $37 in taxes for every $100 of deductions, whereas next year it would save only $24 of taxes for the same payment.

Such a situation raises an interesting question: Should you advise the business to prepay expenses this year? Yes, you should, but within certain limits. It must ensure that the benefit the business receives from the prepayment will not extend beyond 12 months from when benefits begin, and in no case should it extend beyond the end of the following tax year. In that case, it can deduct the prepayment! But if it gets greedy and prepays expenses for which the benefit will continue past 12 months, then none of the prepayment may be deductible in the current year. The intent of Congress with the 12-month rule is to make sure that taxpayers will not get a deduction in the current year for prepaying expenses that are not due for more than one year in the future.

Related exercises: Discussion Question 14
Application Problem 24

Prepaid Interest

While it is reasonable for you to assume the 12-month rule applies to *any* prepaid expenses, this is *not* the case. Taxpayers must always amortize prepaid interest over the life of the loan.

EXAMPLE 3.4.7
Prepaid Interest

On December 1, Year 8, Maria Corporation prepays 12 months of business interest for the period December 1, Year 8, through November 30, Year 9. Maria Corporation owns a restaurant and reports on the cash basis. Its payment to ABC Bank is $12,000, representing $1,000 per month. How much of the prepayment can Maria Corporation deduct in Year 8?

SOLUTION

Taxpayers must deduct prepaid interest over the life of the loan, so Maria Corporation can deduct only $1,000 in Year 8 for the $12,000 paid in Year 8. The other $11,000 of interest accrued in Year 9 and Maria Corporation must deduct it in Year 9.

Related exercises: Multiple Choice Question 15
Application Problem 25

Payments to a Related Party

There are restrictions on when a business entity can deduct a payment to someone who owns more than 50% of the business entity, in which case the business owner and the entity are related parties.[27] This rule applies when the business uses the accrual basis of accounting, and the recipient of the payment uses the cash basis. In such a case, the accrual-basis business cannot deduct the payment until the cash-basis recipient includes the payment in income.[28] This ensures that the deduction and the income both occur in the same tax year for the related parties. As shown in **Illustration 3.11**, if a payment of this nature is accrued in Year 1, but not paid until Year 2, the recipient will not have income until the payment is received in Year 2. Therefore, the corporation cannot deduct the payment until Year 2.

ILLUSTRATION 3.11 Related-Party Payments

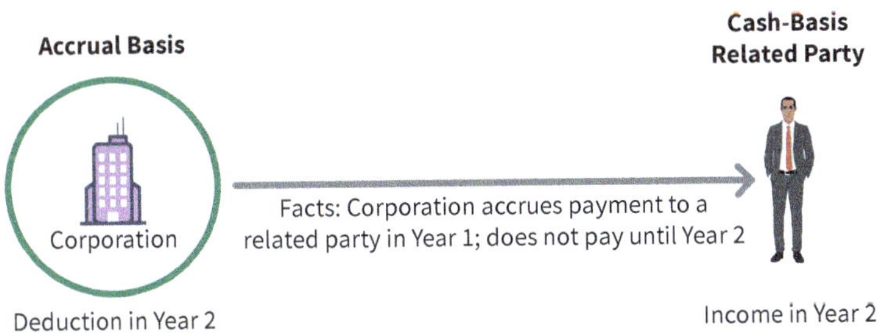

This rule applies more broadly for partnerships and S corporations. For those entities, this rule applies to all payments between an accrual-basis entity and a cash-basis partner or shareholder. Even if the ownership interest of the partner or shareholder receiving the payment was very small, such as less than 1%, this deferral rule would still apply.[29]

Related exercises: Discussion Question 15
Application Problem 26

EXAMPLE 3.4.8
Related-Party Payments

Antonio is a 10% owner of Banners, Inc., and he also serves as CEO. Banners, Inc. reports on the accrual basis of accounting. In December, Year 8, Banners approved a $75,000 bonus for Antonio that Banners paid in January, Year 9. What are the tax effects of this transaction? How would the result change if Banners was an S corporation?

SOLUTION

The special timing rules for related-party payments discussed above does not apply because Antonio does not own more than 50% of the stock of Banners. Therefore, Banners can deduct $75,000 in Year 8 and Antonio would report $75,000 of income in Year 9.

If Banners is an S corporation, then the timing rule *does* apply and Banners cannot deduct the $75,000 payment until Year 9, when Antonio reports income.

Why **Why does the related-party timing rule exist?** Without the special timing rule provided for this payment, an owner of a business entity could intentionally create situations each year where the accrual-basis business entity accrues the deduction to save taxes in the current year, but the cash-basis recipient does not have income until the payment is received in the following year, so their payment of taxes is deferred. Congress does not want to allow such timing schemes to work.

[27]There are other relationships that can be related parties for this rule, but they are beyond the scope of this book.

[28]IRC §267(a)(2).

[29]IRC §267(e).

Inventory Accounting—Small Businesses

Small businesses (gross receipts do not exceed $31 million [2025]) do not have to account for inventories under the accrual method of accounting. Rather, they can:

- deduct the cost of inventory in the year sold or the year purchased, whichever is later, *or*
- report inventory in the same manner as on the taxpayer's financial accounting statement.[30]

Related exercises: Discussion Question 16
Multiple Choice Question 16

Inventory costs can be allocated between ending inventory and cost of goods sold using one of the following methods:

- FIFO,
- LIFO,
- weighted average, *or*
- specific identification.

A business can use LIFO *only* if it also uses LIFO for financial reporting. During a period of rising prices, LIFO produces a higher cost of goods sold and lower taxable income. Congress does not want corporations to be able to lower their taxable income by using LIFO but keep financial reporting high by using FIFO for books.

Related exercise: Multiple Choice Question 17

Taxpayers can value inventory at the **lower of cost or market** unless they are using LIFO, in which case the business must value inventory at cost. Congress defines *market* as replacement cost or reproduction cost.

EXAMPLE 3.4.9
Inventory for Small Businesses

Prisha Inc. owns a children's clothing store and its gross receipts for each of the last three years has been less than $1,000,000. At the beginning of the year, its inventory had a value of $80,000. Prisha purchased inventory during the year of $340,000, and its ending inventory has a value of $105,000. If Prisha uses the cash basis of accounting for its business, how much can Prisha deduct this year for its inventory?

SOLUTION

Because Prisha is a small business, it can deduct the cost of inventory in the year it is sold. Prisha purchased $340,000 of inventory this year, but it cannot deduct this amount, even though the company is a cash-basis taxpayer. Rather, it must deduct the cost of inventory in the year sold if that is later than when Prisha purchased it. You compute the amount of inventory sold as follows:

Beginning inventory	$ 80,000
Plus: Purchases	340,000
Inventory available for sale	$420,000
Less: Ending inventory	(105,000)
Inventory sold during the year	$315,000

Prisha Inc.'s deduction for cost of goods sold is $315,000.

Related exercise: Application Problem 27

[30] IRC §471(c)(1)(B).

EXAMPLE 3.4.10
Lower of Cost or Market

RST Company is a global supplier of fertilizer. At the end of the current tax year, its inventory had the following values:

Cost using uniform capitalization rules	$5,260,000
Market value, using replacement cost	$4,970,000

RST uses the FIFO method to value its inventory. What value should RST use for the inventory for tax purposes? How would your answer change, if at all, if RST uses the LIFO method?

SOLUTION

RST can use the lower of cost or market method to value inventory if it is using FIFO, so the inventory is valued at $4,970,000. If RST used LIFO, it must value the inventory at its cost of $5,260,000.

Related exercises: Application Problems 28, 29

Inventory Accounting—Large Businesses

Large businesses (gross receipts of more than $31 million, 2025) *must* use the accrual method of accounting for all tax reporting, including inventory. In addition to the accrual method mandate, certain large businesses must use the uniform capitalization rules. The **uniform capitalization rules (UNICAP)** provide the rules for valuing inventory including direct and indirect costs for property produced and property bought for resale. Manufacturers and certain retailers and wholesalers must use the uniform capitalization method to capitalize all the direct and indirect costs allocable to property they produce and for property bought for resale.[31] These costs are then allocated to ending inventory and property sold during the year, which usually results in an increase in the basis of the inventory for tax purposes. A higher level of ending inventory will result in a decrease in the deduction for cost of goods sold. **Illustration 3.12** summarizes the costs that must be capitalized as inventory under the uniform capitalization rules. UNICAP rules apply to realty and tangible personalty produced by the taxpayer or acquired by the taxpayer for resale.

ILLUSTRATION 3.12 UNICAP Rules

Capitalized	Not Capitalized
Direct material costs	Mixed service and indirect costs including:
Direct labor costs	• Marketing
Indirect costs including:	• Selling
• Indirect labor costs	• Advertising
• Employee benefit expenses	• Income taxes
• Indirect material costs	• Tax services
• Indirect purchasing and handling costs	• Distribution
• Storage costs, rent, taxes, insurance, utilities	• Research and experimental
• Depreciation	• Warranty
• Engineering and design costs	
• Tools and equipment	
• Interest, licensing, and franchise costs	

The uniform capitalization rules do not apply to costs incurred in certain farming businesses and in raising and harvesting crops and timber; certain creative expenses incurred by freelance photographers, artists, and writers; personal use property; intangible drilling and development costs; natural gas acquired for resale; and research and experimental expenditures.

[31] IRC §263A.

The tax law requires direct materials and direct labor, and virtually all indirect production costs (such as utilities, repairs, rent, and depreciation) to be capitalized under the uniform capitalization rules. The business must capitalize storage costs to the extent that they can be traced to an off-site storage or warehouse facility. The taxpayer does not have to capitalize storage costs attributed to an on-site storage facility. The tax law does not require marketing, selling, advertising, and distribution expenses to be capitalized under the uniform capitalization rules. General and administrative expenses also do not have to be capitalized.

Related exercise: Brief Exercise 12

Reconciliation of Book Income and Taxable Income

Corporations must comply with different reporting rules for tax purposes and for GAAP (generally accepted accounting principles). On Schedule M-1 of Form 1120 (shown in **Illustration 3.13**), corporations must reconcile their book income and taxable income by showing the timing and permanent differences that account for the different measures of income. Schedule M-1 reconciles to taxable income before the dividends received and net operating loss deductions. Corporations with total assets of $10 million or more are required to file Schedule M-3 (see Appendix B), rather than Schedule M-1, which requires significantly more detail than Schedule M-1.

Related exercise: Multiple Choice Question 18

ILLUSTRATION 3.13 Schedule M-1 (Form 1120)

DOWNLOAD DOCUMENTS & TEMPLATES

Schedule M-1 **Reconciliation of Income (Loss) per Books With Income per Return**

Note: The corporation may be required to file Schedule M-3. See instructions.

1 Net income (loss) per books		7 Income recorded on books this year not included on this return (itemize): Tax-exempt interest $	
2 Federal income tax per books			
3 Excess of capital losses over capital gains .			
4 Income subject to tax not recorded on books this year (itemize):		8 Deductions on this return not charged against book income this year (itemize):	
5 Expenses recorded on books this year not deducted on this return (itemize):		a Depreciation . . $	
a Depreciation . . . . $		b Charitable contributions $	
b Charitable contributions . $			
c Travel and entertainment . $			
		9 Add lines 7 and 8	
6 Add lines 1 through 5		10 Income (page 1, line 28)—line 6 less line 9	

M-1 Items Differences between book income and taxable income fall into four distinct categories. We list some of the more common differences below.

- Expenses deducted for book income that are not deductible for taxable income:
  - Federal tax expense
  - Net capital losses
  - Charitable contributions that exceed the 10% of taxable income limit
  - Entertainment expenses
  - 50% of meals
  - Fines, penalties, and other expenses in violation of public policy
  - Life insurance premiums on lives of key employees (corporation is beneficiary)

- Income not included in book income that is included in taxable income:
  - Prepaid income
- Income included in book income that is not included in taxable income:
  - Municipal interest income
  - Life insurance proceeds due to death of the insured
- Expenses not deducted for book income that are deducted for taxable income:
  - Tax depreciation in excess of book depreciation, including Section 179 expense and bonus depreciation
  - Charitable contributions carried forward from a previous year

Related exercise: Discussion Question 17

Computing Schedule M-1 To complete Schedule M-1, use the following steps:

Step 1. Ask: Is the item treated differently for book purposes and tax purposes?

- If the answer is NO, then this is not a Schedule M-1 item.
- If the answer is YES, then proceed to step 2.

Step 2. Determine: Whether the adjustment increases or decreases book income. This step is sometimes confusing to students. To avoid mistakes, follow the logic of the diagram in Illustration 3.14.

ILLUSTRATION 3.14 Schedule M-1 (Form 1120) Adjustments

	Determining the Direction of Schedule M-1 Adjustments		
	Is this included in book income computation?	Should it be included in taxable income computation?	Adjustment needed to book income
Federal tax expense	Yes	No	Positive (increase book income for the amount of the deduction)
Prepaid income	No	Yes	Positive (increase book income for the prepaid income)
Municipal interest income	Yes	No	Negative (decrease book income for the non-taxable income)
Excess tax depreciation	No	Yes	Negative (decrease book income for the expense)

For additional information on the M-1 computation, see Chapter 10, LO4, Disclosures in the Tax Return. The following Example illustrates how book income is reconciled to taxable income.

EXAMPLE 3.4.11
M-1 Reconciliation

Oriole, Inc. has book income after federal income tax expenses of $270,000. Oriole is an accrual-basis taxpayer for both book reporting and tax reporting. Compute Oriole's taxable income given the information below:

Federal income tax	$55,000
Book depreciation	$41,000
Tax depreciation	$56,000
Prepaid rental revenue	$18,000
Net capital loss	$ 7,000
Municipal interest income	$ 4,000
Charitable contributions in excess of 10% limit	$ 6,000
Entertainment expenses	$ 2,000

SOLUTION

We compute taxable income as follows:

Book income after taxes	$270,000
• Plus: Expenses deducted for book income that are not deductible for taxable income:	
Federal income tax expense	55,000
Net capital loss	7,000
Charitable contributions in excess of 10% limit	6,000
Entertainment expenses	2,000
• Plus: Income not included in book income that is included in taxable income:	
Prepaid rental revenue (not taxed for book under accrual method)	18,000
• *Less*: Income included in book income that is not included in taxable income:	
Municipal interest income	(4,000)
• *Less*: Expenses not deducted for book income that are deducted for taxable income:	
Tax depreciation in excess of book depreciation ($56,000 – $41,000)	(15,000)
Taxable income	$339,000

Related exercises: Brief Exercise 13
Application Problem 30

Schedule M-3 A corporation with total assets of at least $10 million must file Schedule M-3 instead of Schedule M-1. Certain large S corporations and partnerships must also file Schedule M-3 (see Appendix B). Schedule M-3 is divided into three sections:[32]

- Part I provides certain financial information and reconciles worldwide consolidated net income on the book financial statements to book income for the entities included on the corporate tax return.
- Part II reconciles the book income computed in Part I to the taxable income shown on the Form 1120. For each reconciling item, the effect due to permanent differences and timing differences must be shown.
- Part III provides a breakdown of the expense/deduction items that affect the reconciliation of book income to taxable income in Part II. This total is carried to Part II and combined with the income items listed in Part II.

[32]Rev. Proc. 2004-45, §2004-31 IRB 140.

Net Operating Losses

The **net operating loss (NOL)** rules for corporations are very similar to the rules for individuals. An NOL occurs when certain deductible expenditures exceed taxable revenue for a year. Corporations can carry NOLs forward to offset future income, and, in the recent past, some NOLs could be carried back.[33]

There are currently three sets of rules for net operating losses, depending on the year the corporation incurred the loss:

- Pre-2018 NOLs
- NOLs incurred in 2018, 2019, and 2020
- Post-2020 NOLs

We summarize the differences in these rules in **Illustration 3.15**.

ILLUSTRATION 3.15 Differences in NOL Rules

Year of loss	Carryback	Carryforward	Offset
Pre 2018 NOLs	2 years	20 years	100% of Taxable income (TI)
2018–2020 NOLs	5 years	Indefinitely	100% of pre-2021 TI, 80% of post-2020 TI
Post-2020 NOLs	No	Indefinitely	80% of post-2020 TI

Pre-2018 NOLs NOLs that taxpayers incurred before 2018 could be carried back 2 years and forward 20 years. The NOL had to be carried back unless the taxpayer elected to not do so. Pre-2018 NOLs can offset up to 100% of the taxable income for the year the taxpayer uses them. These rules still have relevance because these NOLs can be carried forward for up to 20 years.

NOLs in 2018, 2019, and 2020 NOLs incurred in 2018, 2019, or 2020 can be carried back for the five years preceding the year of the loss. If they are not completely used during those five years, then they can be carried forward indefinitely. NOLs that were carried forward to 2020 can offset 100% of taxable income. NOL carryforwards that are used for years after 2020 can offset only 80% of the taxable income for the year the NOL is used.

Post-2020 NOLs Taxpayers cannot carry back NOLs incurred after 2020. The taxpayer can carry them forward indefinitely, and they can offset only 80% of the taxable income for the year the NOL is used.

Related exercises: Discussion Questions 18, 19

Why **Why can NOLs offset income in other tax years?** The NOL rules ensure that over time businesses pay taxes on the income that they earned over the life of the business. Taxpayers must report income every 12 months, and the income or loss is determined for each 12-month period. However, if the reporting period were different, such as 6 months or 24 months, the income or loss reported would differ. Regardless of the reporting period, the total income reported over the life of the business should be the same. The NOL rules ensure that is the case by providing that losses from one reporting period can offset income in other years.

The following Example demonstrates the use of NOL carrybacks and carryforwards.

[33]IRC §172.

EXAMPLE 3.4.12
NOL Carrybacks and Carryforwards

Robin Corporation has been your client for the last 10 years and operates a chain of fitness centers. In a certain tax year, Robin Corporation incurred a significant loss for the fitness center due to a severe recession. Its net operating loss for that year was $67,000.

a. If the NOL year was 2016 and the NOL was not completely used before 2020, how much of the NOL could Robin Corporation use to offset income for 2020? When will the 2016 NOL expire?
b. Assess the same situation as in part a, but with the NOL year as 2018.
c. If the NOL year was 2025, can it be carried back to 2024? When will the NOL expire, and how much income can it offset when carried forward?

SOLUTION

a. The 2016 NOL can offset 100% of the income for 2020. Robin Corporation can carry forward the NOL for 20 years, so it will expire in 2036.
b. The 2018 NOL can offset 100% of the income for 2020. Robin Corporation can carry forward the NOL indefinitely because it never expires.
c. An NOL incurred in 2025 is not eligible for Robin Corporation to carry back. Robin Corporation can use the NOL in future years, and it will never expire. It can offset only 80% of the income in future tax years.

If the NOL is carried back to a prior year, the taxpayer deducts the NOL against income in that year and can receive a refund of previously paid taxes by filing an amended return. A corporation can also obtain a refund by filing Form 1139, Corporation Application for Tentative Refund.

NOL Computation Only business losses and casualty losses can create an NOL. The current year carryover ignores carryovers created in other years. Multiple carryovers to one year are used in a FIFO (first-in, first-out) order. Charitable contributions are not allowed in computing the NOL. The following two Examples deal with situations involving a corporate NOL.

EXAMPLE 3.4.13
NOL Computation

Pigeon Corporation has a $71,000 taxable loss for 2025 after deducting 100% of a $47,000 NOL carryforward from 2016. What is Pigeon's NOL for 2025 and how can it be used?

SOLUTION

Pigeon's NOL for 2025 is computed as follows:

Taxable loss after NOL carryforward	($71,000)
Plus: NOL carryforward from 2016	47,000
Net operating loss for 2025	($24,000)

The $24,000 net operating loss cannot be carried back. It is carried forward indefinitely and used to offset 80% of taxable income in future years.

EXAMPLE 3.4.14
NOL Carryforward

Assume the same facts as in Example 3.4.13. Additionally, Pigeon has a $14,000 charitable contribution carryforward from 2025. In 2026, Pigeon has taxable income before NOL of $54,000. How much of the 2016 and 2025 NOLs can be utilized in 2026?

SOLUTION

Pigeon's 2016 NOL can offset 100% of future income, so the $47,000 NOL reduces the 2026 income to $7,000 ($54,000 − $47,000). Pigeon can use the 2025 NOL to offset 80% of the remaining $7,000 of taxable income in 2026, which is $5,600 ($7,000 × 80%). Pigeon can also use the $14,000 charitable contribution carryforward to offset up to 10% of its taxable income after the NOL carryforwards. Pigeon's 2026 income after NOLs is $1,260, as shown below:

2026 income before NOLs	$ 54,000	
Less: 2016 NOL	(47,000)	
Remaining income	$ 7,000	
Less: 2025 NOL	(5,600)	(80% × $ 7,000)
2026 income after NOLs	$ 1,400	
Less: Charitable contribution	(140)	(limited to 10% × $ 1,400)
Taxable income	$ 1,260	

The remaining 2025 NOL of $18,400 ($24,000 − $5,600) is carried forward indefinitely. The remaining charitable contribution from 2025 of $13,860 ($14,000 − $140) is carried forward for four more years (2027–2030). Any contribution not deducted by 2030 is lost forever.

Related exercises: Multiple Choice Question 19
Brief Exercise 14
Application Problem 31

Reconciliation of Retained Earnings

Schedule M-2 of Form 1120 (see **Illustration 3.16**) analyzes changes in a corporation's unappropriated retained earnings per books between the beginning and end of the year. The computation is as follows:

Balance at beginning of year
Plus: Net income per books
Plus: Other increases
Less: Distributions to shareholders
Less: Other decreases
Balance at end of year

ILLUSTRATION 3.16 Schedule M-2 (Form 1120)

Schedule M-2 Analysis of Unappropriated Retained Earnings per Books (Schedule L, Line 25)

1	Balance at beginning of year		5	Distributions: **a** Cash	
2	Net income (loss) per books			**b** Stock	
3	Other increases (itemize):			**c** Property	
			6	Other decreases (itemize):	
			7	Add lines 5 and 6	
4	Add lines 1, 2, and 3		8	Balance at end of year (line 4 less line 7)	

In the following Example, we demonstrate the computation used to complete Schedule M-2.

EXAMPLE 3.4.15
Schedule M-2 Computation

Warbler Corporation, which reports on a calendar-year basis, has the following information for the current tax year:

Retained earnings, January 1	$419,000
Cash dividend paid	$ 43,000
Net income per books	$337,000
Net taxable income	$265,000
Treasury bonds distributed as a dividend	$ 28,000

The treasury bonds have a basis to Warbler of $28,000. What is Warbler Corporation's retained earnings at the end of the tax year?

SOLUTION

There is no gain to Warbler on the distribution of the bonds because the fair market value of the bonds is the same as its adjusted basis. Warbler's ending retained earnings is computed as follows:

Retained earnings, January 1	$419,000
Plus: Net income per books	337,000
Plus: Other increases	N/A
Less: Distributions to shareholders ($43,000 + $28,000)	(71,000)
Less: Other decreases	N/A
Retained earnings, December 31	$685,000

Related exercise: Application Problem 32

Passive Loss Rules

Individuals cannot offset passive losses against active income or portfolio income. Individuals can offset passive losses only against passive income. However, the rules are quite different for corporations. In general, the passive loss limits do not apply to corporations. However, there are exceptions for *personal service corporations* and *closely held corporations*.

A **personal service corporation** is a corporation whose principal activity is the performance of personal services performed by employees who own 95% or more of the corporation's stock, such as a medical corporation whose owners are also the doctors providing the medical services.[34] For purposes of the passive loss rules, personal service corporations are treated just like individuals. That is, their passive losses cannot offset active income or portfolio income.

A **closely held corporation** exists if at any time during the last half of the taxable year more than 50% of the value of its outstanding stock is owned, directly or indirectly, by not more than five individuals. Closely held corporations can use passive losses to offset active corporate income but not portfolio income.

EXAMPLE 3.4.16
Passive Loss Rules

Shoals, Inc. is a C corporation that has the following information for the current year:

Operating income	$100,000
Investment income	$ 30,000
Passive loss	($ 40,000)

What is Shoals's taxable income? How would your answer change if Shoals was a personal service corporation or a closely held corporation?

[34] Treas. Reg. 1.488-2(e).

SOLUTION

If Shoals is a regular C corporation, then the passive loss rules do not apply. Therefore, the $40,000 passive loss can offset its other income, and taxable income is $90,000 ($100,000 + $30,000 – $40,000).

If Shoals is a personal service corporation, then the passive loss cannot offset operating income or investment income, so taxable income is $130,000 ($100,000 + $30,000).

If Shoals is a closely held corporation, then the passive loss can offset the $100,000 operating income but not the investment income, so taxable income is $90,000 ($100,000 – $40,000 + $30,000).

Related exercise: Application Problem 33

Corporate Alternative Minimum Tax

Similar to the federal income taxation of individuals, Congress had provided a corporate alternative minimum tax (AMT) beginning in 1987. The *Tax Cuts and Jobs Act of 2017* repealed the corporate AMT, so it was not in effect from 2018 to 2022. *The Inflation Reduction Act of 2022* reinstated the corporate AMT, but it is a much different type of tax than in the past and applies to a very small number of corporations.[35] The Joint Committee on Taxation has estimated that the new corporate AMT will apply to no more than 150 of the Fortune 500 companies.

The new corporate AMT is effective for tax years beginning after 2022, and includes a 15% tax on the *adjusted financial statement income of applicable corporations*. The minimum tax applies only to the extent that it exceeds the taxpayer's regular tax, including its base erosion tax and anti-abuse tax for the tax year.[36]

Applicable Corporation

An **applicable corporation** for a tax year that ends after December 31, 2022, is a corporation whose average annual adjusted financial statement income for a 3-tax-year period that ends after December 31, 2021, (determined without regard to loss carryovers) exceeds $1 billion. This rule does not apply to S corporations, regulated investment companies, or real estate investment trusts.[37]

Adjusted Financial Statement Income

Adjusted financial statement income is the net income or loss of the taxpayer as presented in the taxpayer's *applicable financial statements*. Various adjustments are made to determine adjusted financial statement income. Certain items are taken into account on a tax basis, rather than on a financial statement (book) income basis.[38] Generally, an **applicable financial statement** is one that meets the following criteria:[39]

- A financial statement certified as being prepared in accordance with generally accepted accounting principles (GAAP) and that is one of the following:
  - a Form 10–K
  - an audited financial statement of the corporation that is used for credit purposes

[35]IRC §55.

[36]Congress created the Base Erosion and Anti-Abuse Tax (BEAT) in 2017 to prevent foreign and domestic corporations operating in the United States from avoiding domestic tax liability by shifting profits outside the United States. See Chapter 13, LO6, U.S. Taxation of Foreign Corporations and Foreign Persons, for more detail.

[37]IRC §59(k).

[38]IRC §56A.

[39]IRC §453(b)(3).

- A financial statement prepared in accordance with international financial reporting standards (IFRS), is certified as such, and is *either*
  - filed by the taxpayer with an agency of a foreign government that is equivalent to the U.S. Securities and Exchange Commission (SEC) and has reporting standards not less stringent than the standards required by the SEC, *or*
  - an audited financial statement of the taxpayer that is used for credit purposes.

Other Items

There are several other parts of the corporate AMT computation:

- A domestic corporation can use a corporate AMT foreign tax credit for the direct foreign taxes that are taken into account on the corporation's applicable financial statement and paid or accrued by the applicable corporation.
- In years where the regular tax is higher than the minimum tax, a corporation can carry forward a credit for the net minimum tax for all prior tax years beginning after 2022 to reduce the corporation's regular tax, including the base erosion anti-abuse tax.[40]

PRACTICE PROBLEM 3.4.1 Determining Taxable Income after Assessing Capital Gains and Losses

Dancer Inc. has taxable income before capital gains and losses of $50,000. Dancer has the following capital transactions:

Short-term capital gain	$1,000
Short-term capital loss	$3,000
Long-term capital gain	$5,500
Long-term capital loss	$2,000

What is Dancer's taxable income after the capital transactions, and what is Dancer's tax liability?

SOLUTION

The capital transactions must first be netted to find the net capital gain or loss. Dancer has a net short-term capital loss of $2,000 ($1,000 STCG – $3,000 STCL) and a net long-term capital gain of $3,500 ($5,500 LTCG – $2,000 LTCL), resulting in a net capital gain of $1,500. The taxable income after the capital transactions is $51,500 ($50,000 + $1,500), and Dancer's tax liability is $10,815 ($51,500 × 21%). Corporations do not receive a preferential tax rate for net long-term capital gain.

PRACTICE PROBLEM 3.4.2 Cash vs. Accrual Method of Accounting

Derrick owns a manufacturing facility which has produced annual gross receipts for the last three years of $24,400,000, $27,800,000, and $42,000,000. Can Derrick's business use the cash method of accounting?

SOLUTION

No, because Derrick's business gross receipts for the last three years average more than $31 million ($31,400,000 = [($24,400,000 + $27,800,000 + $42,000,000)/3).] He must use the accrual method of accounting.

[40]IRC §53(e).

PRACTICE PROBLEM 3.4.3
UNICAP Rules

Wilson Manufacturing Company (WMI) manufacturers small tools used in landscaping and nurseries. Randall is an employee in charge of purchasing inventory. Randall earns $80,000 a year and he spends about 15% of his time acquiring inventory and the remaining time working on projects for WMI. Assuming WMI was *required* to apply the UNICAP rules, how would WMI allocate Randall's salary under the UNICAP rules?

SOLUTION

If the UNICAP rules applied to WMI, it would allocate $12,000 ($80,000 × 15%) of Randall's salary to the cost of the inventory WMI acquired this year.

PRACTICE PROBLEM 3.4.4
Calculating Taxable Income from Book Income

Skull Inc. has book income of $456,000 for the current year. Included in book income are the following:

Municipal interest income	$1,500
Fines and penalties paid	$1,350
Book depreciation	$6,800
Entertainment expense	$4,200

Skull also has tax depreciation of $8,900 and paid life insurance premiums of $3,000 for a policy on its CEO, for which Skull is the beneficiary. What is Skull's taxable income and tax liability?

SOLUTION

Municipal interest income is tax-exempt and should not be included in taxable income. Fines and penalties and entertainment expenses are not deductible for tax purposes. Premiums paid on life insurance for a key officer where the corporation is the beneficiary of the policy are not deductible for tax purposes. Skull is allowed to deduct the excess tax depreciation. We compute Skull's taxable income as follows:

Book income	$456,000
Less: Municipal interest income	(1,500)
Less: Excess tax depreciation	(2,100)
Plus: Entertainment expense	4,200
Plus: Fines and penalties paid	1,350
Plus: Life insurance premiums paid	3,000
Taxable income	$460,950
Tax liability at 21%	$ 96,800

INTERACTIVE SELF-SCORING QUIZZES

3.5 Penalty Taxes

LEARNING OBJECTIVE 5

Calculate the penalty taxes that apply to corporations if earnings are inappropriately accumulated and not distributed to shareholders.

VIDEO CONTENT

In addition to the federal income tax, corporations may be subject to paying two excise taxes, the *accumulated earnings tax* and the *personal holding company tax*. Congress created these taxes to discourage certain corporate strategies that it deemed to be inconsistent with the intent of the corporate tax law. Therefore, they are often referred to as *penalty taxes*. Returning to the chapter introduction, if Delta Consulting began to accumulate significant amounts of income to avoid paying dividends, it could be subject to one of these penalty taxes.

Tax Planning Tip

The tax rate for both the *accumulated earnings tax* and the *personal holding company tax* is 20%. A corporation would never pay both taxes, because a personal holding company is not subject to the accumulated earnings tax. Because these excise taxes are in addition to the federal income tax, the total tax rate for a corporation who pays one of these is 41% (21% for federal income tax and 20% for excise tax). Both excise taxes are easy to avoid, so it is important for corporations to plan properly so they can avoid these additional tax burdens.

Tax Return Guidance

Corporations often do not report the *accumulated earnings tax* or the *personal holding company tax* because they are not aware they are owed. If the taxes are assessed as the result of an audit, the company still has an opportunity to pay a *deficiency dividend* to its shareholders for prior years to avoid the tax.

Accumulated Earnings Tax

An **accumulated earnings tax (AET)** of 20% is imposed on undistributed *accumulated taxable income*. Conceptually, **accumulated taxable income (ATI)** measures the corporation's ability to pay a dividend. Personal holding companies, tax-exempt corporations, and S corporations are not subject to the AET.[41]

Why **Why does the accumulated earnings tax exist?** Under the current tax law, the highest individual tax rate is 37% while the highest corporate tax rate is only 21%. This creates an incentive for individual business owners to use the corporate tax form rather than a flow-through entity like a limited liability company or S corporation, for which the income is taxed at individual rates. The use of the corporate form to reduce tax rates is beneficial only if the income remains in the corporation; that is, if the corporation does not pay dividends to its shareholders. If the corporation pays a dividend, then it is subject to the individual tax and no tax savings is realized. Congress designed the accumulated earnings tax to mitigate the use of the corporate form to shelter business earnings from the higher individual income tax rates by not paying dividends. Unnecessarily high levels of accumulated taxable income trigger this penalty tax, and it operates by imposing a penalty tax on any undistributed income.

The accumulated earnings tax can be avoided either by documenting business reasons for accumulating income, or by distributing income as dividends.

EXAMPLE 3.5.1 Paying the Penalty Taxes

Martin Corporation computed the following taxes for the current year:

Regular tax liability	$320,000
Accumulated earnings tax	$ 83,000
Personal holding company tax	$ 71,000

What is Martin's total tax liability for the year?

SOLUTION

A personal holding company does not have to pay the accumulated earnings tax. Therefore, Martin's total tax liability is the sum of the regular tax and the personal holding company tax, or $391,000 ($320,000 + $71,000).

[41] IRC §§531 and 532.

Computing the Accumulated Earnings Tax (AET)

In order to compute the AET, a corporation must first determine its ATI. ATI is computed by adjusting taxable income to reflect the corporation's dividend paying ability.

Adjustments to ATI

There are several modifications made to taxable income to compute ATI.[42] **Illustration 3.17** shows the complete formula for computing the AET.

ILLUSTRATION 3.17 Accumulated Earnings Tax Computation

Formula for Computation of the Accumulated Earnings Tax
Begin with taxable income
Add: Capital loss carryforwards or carrybacks
Add: Net operating loss carryforwards
Add: Dividends received deduction
Add: Charitable contribution carryforwards
Less: Federal income taxes and foreign taxes paid
Less: Net capital losses
Less: Charitable contribution in excess of percentage limitation
Less: Net capital gains after tax
Less: Accumulated earnings credit
Less: Dividends paid including consent dividends
Accumulated taxable income
× AET rate (20%)
Accumulated earnings tax

Carryforwards or Carrybacks The corporation's taxable income could be decreased by net operating loss carryforwards, capital loss carrybacks, and capital loss carryforwards. If so, the corporation must *add* these back to taxable income when computing ATI.

Dividends Received Deduction The DRD reduces taxable income, even though it is not a cash expenditure. Therefore, the DRD is *added back* to taxable income when computing ATI. After this add-back, ATI reflects the full amount of the dividend received, as it should because the corporation can use these funds to pay a dividend to its shareholders.

Charitable Contribution Carryforwards If a corporation deducted a charitable contribution carryforward in the current tax year, it must be *added back* to taxable income when computing ATI. The corporation deducted the full amount of the charitable contribution from ATI, even any carryforward, in the year it was made. Thus, the carryforward cannot reduce ATI a second time.

Federal Income Taxes To the extent that the corporation has paid, or will pay, federal income taxes on its taxable income and foreign taxes, those amounts are not available to pay a dividend. So, the corporation must *reduce* ATI for federal income taxes and foreign taxes because the corporation did not deduct these taxes when computing taxable income.

Net Capital Losses Corporations can deduct capital losses only to the extent of its capital gains. No deduction is allowed for net capital losses. Nevertheless, the net capital loss is an economic loss for the corporation and a dividend cannot be paid from those losses. Therefore, net capital losses *reduce* taxable income when computing ATI.

Excess Charitable Contributions As discussed previously in this chapter, the tax law limits a corporation's charitable contribution deduction to 10% of taxable income. The amount of contributions to charity in excess of 10% of taxable income has already been paid to the

Potential Pitfall

State income taxes are not an adjustment for ATI. Why are state income taxes and federal income taxes treated differently when computing ATI? ATI should be reduced for both federal and state income taxes because a dividend cannot be paid from these funds. However, state income taxes are deductible for federal income tax, so they have already reduced taxable income. Thus, a reduction to taxable income for state income taxes is not necessary or allowed when computing ATI.

[42] IRC §535(a) and (b).

[43] IRC §563. For a C corporation with a tax year ending on June 30, the period to pay a dividend that qualifies as a deduction in the previous year must be made within two-and-a-half months after the end of the year.

charity, but this excess did not reduce taxable income. Therefore, a dividend cannot be paid from this excess, and it is *deducted* from taxable income to compute ATI.

Net Capital Gains After Tax A corporation can accumulate net capital gains after tax and not be subject to the AET. The net capital gains are included in taxable income so the net capital (reduced by the federal income tax due on the gain) *reduces* taxable income when computing ATI.

Dividend Distributions Dividend distributions *reduce* ATI because income is not accumulated once it is paid to shareholders as a dividend. For purposes of the accumulated earnings tax, dividends include *consent dividends* and dividends paid within three-and-a-half months of year-end.[43] **Consent dividends** are hypothetical dividends that are treated as if they were paid to shareholders on the last day of the corporation's taxable year. A corporation can declare a consent dividend at any time if the corporation has a reasonable basis to believe that it may be subject to the AET.[44] There are two tax effects of consent dividends for shareholders:

- The shareholder must include the dividend income in their gross income.
- Because the corporation did not actually distribute the dividend to its shareholders, shareholders increase their stock basis by the amount of consent dividends included in their gross income.

Accumulated Earnings Credit

Potential Pitfall

The term *credit* is a misnomer when considering the accumulated earnings credit, because it functions as a *deduction* that reduces ATI, rather than a credit.

Corporations can also reduce ATI with the **accumulated earnings credit**. This credit permits corporations to accumulate at least a minimum amount of business income and not be subject to the AET, even if there is no business purpose for the accumulation. The corporation also earns a credit for income accumulated for the **reasonable needs of the business**.[45]

For income accumulations to be included in reasonable needs of the business, the corporation's board of directors must formally approve accumulations for this purpose. Thus, it is not sufficient just that the corporation has a need; the corporation must have specific plans to meet that need. While determining the reasonable needs of the business is a subjective determination that requires judgment, in the past, reasonable business needs have existed for amounts to:

- Finance business expansion (actual or planned)
- Provide working capital
- Retire liabilities
- Set aside funds required by creditors
- Build up appropriate working capital

Reasonable needs of the business do *not* include amounts for:

- Unrealistic needs
- Loans to shareholders
- Accumulated for concerns about general economic conditions, rather than specific financial concerns about the corporation.

The accumulated earnings credit is the *greater* of:

- $250,000 ($150,000 for service corporations) less the *accumulated earnings and profits* at the close of the preceding year, (see Chapter 4, LO2, Earnings & Profits, for the definition of this term), *or*
- The reasonable needs of the business.[46]

[44]Treas. Reg. §1.565-1(a).

[45]IRC §533.

[46]IRC §535(c).

Service corporations are corporations that provide services in the areas of health, law, engineering, architecture, accounting, actuarial science, performing arts, or consulting.

Tax Planning Tip

Because the credit is the greater of these two items, there is no maximum on the credit if reasonable business needs support it.

The following two Examples illustrate the computation of the accumulated earnings credit and the accumulated earnings tax.

EXAMPLE 3.5.2
Accumulated Earnings Credit

Big Bird Corporation manufactures neck braces and has the following information for the current tax year:

Earnings and profits at the close of the preceding tax year	$156,000
Board approved set aside to retire corporate bonds	$128,000
Board approved set aside because a recession might begin soon	$140,000
Board approved set aside to replace manufacturing equipment	$ 93,000

What is Big Bird's accumulated earnings credit for the current tax year?

SOLUTION

We begin by computing Big Bird's reasonable needs of the business. The set asides for the retirement of corporate bonds and replacing manufacturing equipment qualify to be included as reasonable business needs, and these total $221,000 ($128,000 + $93,000). The set aside because of a general concern about the economy cannot be included in the reasonable business needs.

The accumulated earnings credit is $221,000, the *greater* of:

- $94,000 [$250,000 (Big Bird is a manufacturing company) less $156,000 (the *accumulated earnings and profits* at the close of the preceding year)], *or*
- $221,000 (the reasonable needs of the business).

EXAMPLE 3.5.3
Accumulated Earnings Tax

Continuing with the facts in Example 3.5.1, Big Bird Corporation also has the following tax items for the current tax year:

Taxable income	$340,000
Excess charitable contributions	$ 18,000
Long-term capital gains	$ 62,000
Short-term capital losses	$ 75,000
Dividends received deduction	$ 48,000
Cash dividend paid	$ 33,000
NOL carryforward	$ 41,000

a. How much is Big Bird's accumulated earnings tax?

b. What actions could Big Bird take, if any, to reduce the accumulated earnings tax to zero?

SOLUTION

a. To determine Big Bird's accumulated earning tax, we must first compute accumulated taxable income. We computed the accumulated earnings credit of $221,000 in Example 3.5.1.

Taxable income	$340,000
Less: Excess charitable contributions	(18,000)
Less: Net capital losses*	(13,000)
Plus: Dividends received deduction	48,000
Plus: NOL carryforward	41,000
Less: Cash dividends paid	(33,000)
Less: Accumulated earnings credit	(221,000)
Adjusted taxable income	$144,000

*Big Bird's net capital loss is computed as:

Long-term capital gains	$ 62,000
Short-term capital losses	(75,000)
Net capital loss	($ 13,000)

ATI is multiplied by 20%, as follows:

Adjusted taxable income	$144,000
	× 20%
Accumulated earnings tax	$ 28,800

b. Big Bird can avoid the AET by paying an additional dividend of $144,000, or declaring a consent dividend of $144,000. In either case, Big Bird's shareholders will recognize dividend income of $144,000.

Related exercises: Discussion Question 20
Multiple Choice Question 20
Brief Exercise 15
Application Problem 34

Personal Holding Company (PHC) Tax

The **personal holding company (PHC) tax** is similar to the AET in that it is a penalty tax that the IRS assesses if a corporation accumulates excess income, and in this case, specifically investment income.[47] The PHC tax of 20% is imposed only on corporations qualifying as personal holding companies. Banks, insurance, and finance companies are exempt from the tax because their business purpose is to manage investments. The tax base for the PHC tax is taxable income adjusted to reflect retained economic income. The PHC tax can be avoided either by keeping investment income levels relatively low, or (as with the accumulated earnings tax) by distributing income as dividends.

Why **Why does the personal holding company tax exist?** Corporations are sometimes used to hold investments because corporations are entitled to deduct either 50%, 65%, or 100% of the dividends received. Therefore, the corporation is taxed on 50%, 35%, or 0% of the dividend. Hence, corporations pay less tax on dividend income than individuals, so investors may create a corporation with the primary purpose of having it hold investment assets. The PHC tax mitigates the use of the corporate form to hold investment assets by imposing this penalty tax if the corporation has high levels of investment income that have not been distributed to shareholders.

Defining a Personal Holding Company

A corporation is a PHC if it meets the *income test* and the *ownership test.*[48]

[47]IRC §541.

[48]IRC §542.

Income Test The **income test** is met if *personal holding company income* constitutes 60% or more of *adjusted ordinary gross income* (AOGI), expressed as:

$$\text{PHC income} \geq 60\% \times \text{AOGI}$$

The following definitions are key to computing the PHC tax. These definitions are quite complex, and we provide only a basic description of them in this text.

Personal holding company income includes taxable:[49]

- dividends (before the dividends received deduction),
- interest,
- rental income, unless more than 50% of the corporation's gross income is from rents,
- amounts a corporation receives for providing personal services if the services are performed by a shareholder owning more than 25% of the stock, *and*
- certain royalties, including adjusted income from mineral, oil, and gas interests, and copyright royalties.

The following adjustments also must be made when computing PHC income:[50]

- Reduce by accrued income taxes, excess charitable contributions, and net capital gains (after tax), *and*
- Increase for the dividends received deduction and the carryover for net operating losses from the year prior to the previous tax year.

Adjusted ordinary gross income (AOGI) is computed as follows:[51]

Gross Income (after reduction for cost of goods sold)
Less: Net capital gains and net Section 1231 gains
Ordinary Gross Income
Less: Certain rental expenses
Adjusted ordinary gross income

Ownership Test For the purposes of the PHC tax, the **ownership test** is met if more than 50% of the value of the stock is owned directly or indirectly by five or fewer individuals at any time during the last half of the year. The indirect ownership rules define ownership to include a proportionate share of the stock held by a corporation, partnership, trust, or estate. Indirect ownership also includes stock owned by brothers and sisters, spouse, ancestors, and lineal descendants.[52]

> **Tax Planning Tip**
> **A corporation with 10 or more equal and unrelated shareholders will never qualify as a PHC because it will not pass the ownership test.**

If either the income test or the ownership test is not met, then the corporation is not a personal holding company and the PHC tax does not apply.

[49]IRC §543(a).
[50]IRC §545(b).
[51]IRC §543(b).
[52]IRC §544(a).

EXAMPLE 3.5.4
Personal Holding Company Tests

Egret, Inc. is owned by seven equal shareholders and has the following information for the current tax year:

Personal holding company income	$480,000
Adjusted ordinary gross income	$600,000

Does Egret qualify as a personal holding company?

SOLUTION

To be a personal holding company, Egret must meet the income test and the ownership test. The income test is met because the personal holding company income is 80% of the adjusted ordinary gross income ($480,000/$600,000) which is greater than or equal to the 60% benchmark. The ownership test is met since each shareholder owns approximately 14.29% of the company, meaning that five shareholders own 71.43%, which is greater than 50%. Egret does qualify as a PHC.

Computing the Personal Holding Company Tax

The PHC tax is imposed on undistributed PHC income. Dividends paid reduce PHC income, but only if paid to every shareholder pro-rata based on their ownership interest. The following types of dividends can *reduce* PHC income:

- Dividends paid during the year
- Consent dividends
- Dividends paid within 3½ months of year-end (limited to 20% of dividends actually paid during year)
- Deficiency dividends

A corporation declares a **deficiency dividend** to avoid the PHC tax. It must be paid within 90 days of the imposition of the tax by the IRS or a court decision.[53]

The following Example illustrates how dividends reduce the PHC tax.

EXAMPLE 3.5.5
Computing the PHC Tax

The following information pertains to Egret, Inc., a personal holding company, for the current tax year:

Undistributed PHC income	$145,000
Dividends paid this year	$ 80,000
Consent dividends reported to shareholders but not paid	$ 40,000

Compute Egret's PHC tax for the year.

SOLUTION

Egret's PHC tax is computed as follows:

Undistributed PHC income	$145,000
Less: Dividends paid	(80,000)
Less: Consent dividends declared	(40,000)
	$ 25,000
	× 20%
PHC tax	$ 5,000

Related exercises: Discussion Question 21
Multiple Choice Question 21
Brief Exercise 16
Application Problem 35

[53]IRC §547.

PRACTICE PROBLEM 3.5.1
Calculating the Accumulated Earnings Tax

Carnes & Youngberg, Inc. (CY) is a public accounting firm that has $144,000 of taxable income for the current year. CY had earnings and profits at the close of the preceding year of $147,000. At a recent board meeting, CY decided to set aside $50,000 to open a new office location. CY has the following tax items for the current year:

Taxable income	$144,000
Federal taxes paid	$ 30,500
Excess capital loss	$ 7,700
Excess charitable contributions	$ 6,900
Cash dividends paid	$ 50,000

How much is CY's accumulated earnings tax?

SOLUTION

We begin by calculating CY's accumulated earnings tax credit. The accumulated earnings credit is $50,000, the *greater* of:

- $3,000 [$150,000 (CY is a personal service corporation) less $147,000 (the accumulated earnings and profits at the close of the preceding year)], *or*
- $50,000 (the reasonable needs of the business).

Next, we compute the accumulated earnings tax.

Taxable income	$144,000
Less: Federal taxes paid	(30,500)
Less: Excess capital loss	(7,700)
Less: Excess charitable contributions	(6,900)
Less: Accumulated earnings credit	(50,000)
Less: Cash dividends paid	(50,000)
Adjusted taxable income (loss)	($ 1,100)

CY does not have an accumulated earnings tax because its ATI is negative.

PRACTICE PROBLEM 3.5.2
Calculating the Personal Holding Company Tax

Autumn Inc., a PHC, paid $21,000 in federal income taxes on $100,000 of taxable income after special deductions. The taxable income included $8,000 of dividend income from a stock held with 5% ownership. Autumn, Inc. also had a long-term capital gain of $6,600, on which $1,386 of tax was paid. Autumn's Board of Directors declared and paid $5,000 of dividends this year to its shareholders. How much, if any, is the PHC tax?

SOLUTION

The computation of the PHC tax is as follows:

Taxable income	$100,000
Less: Federal income tax paid	(21,000)
Less: Net capital gain after tax	(5,214)
Plus: Dividends received deduction*	4,000
Adjusted taxable income	$ 77,786
Less: Dividends paid	(5,000)
Undistributed PHC income	$ 72,786
× Rate	× 20%
PHC tax	$ 14,557

*The DRD percentage is 50% since the stock ownership is less than 20%.

INTERACTIVE SELF-SCORING QUIZZES

3.6 Business Tax Credits

LEARNING OBJECTIVE 6

Compute the business tax credits available for a corporation.

The corporate income tax liability can be decreased by business tax credits. With over 40 tax credits available, a discussion of all these credits is beyond the scope of our focus. We discuss the following common business credits in this section:

- Foreign tax credit
- General business credit (includes the credits shown below):
  - Rehabilitation credit
  - Small employer health insurance credit
  - Work opportunity tax credit (WOTC)
  - Research credit
  - Disabled access credit
  - Employer-provided childcare credit
  - Employer-paid medical and family leave credit
- Business energy credits

Foreign Tax Credit

The United States includes income from all sources in taxable income, including income from foreign countries. Because income earned in a foreign country may also be taxed in that country, the purpose of the **foreign tax credit** is to mitigate the double taxation of foreign income.[54] Foreign income taxes that are creditable include taxes imposed that are *in lieu* of an income tax. The credit is limited to the *lower* of:

1. Foreign income tax paid, *or*
2. $\text{U.S. tax on worldwide income} \times \dfrac{\text{Foreign source taxable income}}{\text{Worldwide taxable income}}$

The second part of this formula is referred to as the **foreign tax credit limitation**. The limitation is applied separately for each country. The excess of the foreign taxes paid in excess of the foreign tax credit limitation can be carried back one year and carried forward for 10 years. The foreign tax credit is claimed on Form 1116, Foreign Tax Credit. We show how the foreign tax credit limitation is applied in the next Example.

EXAMPLE 3.6.1
Foreign Tax Credit

Woodpecker, Inc. has $830,000 of U.S. source income, $210,000 of foreign source income, and Woodpecker paid foreign taxes of $43,500. Assume that the U.S. income tax liability before the foreign tax credit is $205,000. How much is Woodpecker's foreign tax credit? How much is Woodpecker's foreign tax credit carryback/carryforward, if any?

SOLUTION

Woodpecker's foreign tax credit is limited to the *lower* of:

1. Foreign tax paid ($43,500), *or*

[54]IRC §901.

2. U.S. tax on worldwide income $\times \frac{\text{Foreign source taxable income}}{\text{Worldwide taxable income}}$

$$\$205{,}000 \times \frac{\$210{,}000}{(\$830{,}000 + \$210{,}000)} = \$41{,}394$$

Therefore, Woodpecker's foreign tax credit is limited to $41,394. Woodpecker has a foreign tax credit carryback/carryforward of $2,106 ($43,500 – $41,394).

Why **Why is the foreign tax credit limited by the foreign tax credit limitation?** The foreign tax credit limitation is based on the proportion of worldwide income that is foreign-sourced. In other words, the foreign tax credit cannot exceed what the U.S. tax liability would be on the same income. That proportion is multiplied by the U.S. tax liability on worldwide income. For example, if 24% of the worldwide income is foreign-sourced, then the foreign tax credit cannot exceed 24% of the U.S. tax liability on worldwide income. The foreign tax credit limitation limits the credit when the effective foreign tax rate on foreign-sourced income exceeds the U.S. statutory rate of 21%.

Related exercises: Discussion Question 22
Application Problem 36

General Business Credit

The **general business credit** consists of a combination of credits designed to subsidize certain activities. While each credit is calculated independently, the combination of credits is subject to an overall limit. Unused credits are carried back one year and then forward 20 years.[55] The general business credit is computed on Form 3800, General Business Credit. There are over 30 tax credits that make up the general business credit, each having its own rules, including the following:

- Rehabilitation credit
- Small employer health insurance credit
- Work opportunity tax credit (WOTC)
- Research credit
- Disabled access credit
- Employer-provided childcare credit
- Employer-paid family and medical leave credit

We explore these credits in more detail in this section below.

The general business credit is the sum of selected individual credits, subject to a limitation. The essence of the general business credit limitation is that the credit cannot offset all of the regular tax if the liability exceeds $25,000. The formula for the general business credit limitation is as follows:

$$\text{Taxpayer's net income tax} - [(\text{Net regular tax liability} - \$25{,}000) \times 25\%]$$

Net income tax is the sum of the regular tax liability, reduced by certain nonrefundable tax credits such as the foreign tax credit. Carrybacks and carryforwards of the general business tax credit are used in FIFO order. This benefits the taxpayer because older credits can be used before they expire and before more recent credits are used.

The next Example illustrates how the general business credit is computed.

[55] IRC §38; certain energy credits that are part of the general business credit can be carried back three years and carried forward 22 years.

EXAMPLE 3.6.2
General Business Credit Limitation

Warbler Corporation's general business credit for the year before limitation is $90,000. Warbler's net regular tax liability is $110,000. Assume that Warbler has no other tax credits. How much of the general business credit can Warbler utilize this year, what is Warbler's tax liability after the credit, and what happens to any remaining credit?

SOLUTION

To compute the amount of general business credit that Warbler can use this year, we must compute the general business credit limitation, as follows:

Taxpayer's net income tax – [(Net regular tax liability – $25,000) × 25%]

$110,000 – [($110,000 – $25,000) × 25%] =

$110,000 – $21,250 = $88,750

Warbler's general business credit is limited to $88,750, so Warbler's tax liability is $21,250 ($110,000 – $88,750). The unused general business credit is $1,250 ($90,000 – $88,750), and can be carried back one year and then carried forward 20 years.

Related exercises: Discussion Question 23
Multiple Choice Question 22
Application Problem 37

Rehabilitation Credit

A **rehabilitation credit** is allowed for companies that rehabilitate certified historic buildings. The building must be a certified historic structure by the National Park Service, the building must be "substantially rehabilitated" during specified time periods, and completion of the work must be certified following specific requirements. The rehabilitation credit is equal to 20% of the rehabilitation expenditures, not including costs to purchase the building.[56]

The credit is claimed on a straight-line basis over a five-year period. To qualify for the credit, the building must be depreciated using straight-line depreciation or the ADS (alternative depreciation system). The credit reduces the property's adjusted basis, eliminating any double benefit. The credit is claimed on Form 3468, Investment Credit, which flows to the General Business Credit Form 3800.

To qualify for the credit, buildings must be substantially rehabilitated. A building has been **substantially rehabilitated** if qualified rehabilitation expenditures during a 24-month period exceed the *greater* of:

- The property's adjusted basis before the rehabilitation expenditures, *or*
- $5,000.

If the project is determined to be done in phases before the rehabilitation begins, then the 24-month period is extended to 60 months. Qualified rehabilitation expenditures do *not* include the cost of acquiring a building, the cost of facilities related to a building (such as a parking lots), and the cost of enlarging an existing building. An application of the rehabilitation credit is shown in the next Example.

[56] IRC §47.

EXAMPLE 3.6.3
Rehabilitation Credit

Quail Corporation spent $900,000 during the last 12 months to substantially rehabilitate a certified historic structure. Quail's basis in the building before the rehabilitation project began was $800,000. How much is Quail's rehabilitation credit for the current year, and what is the basis of the building after the credit?

SOLUTION

Because this is a certified historic structure, the credit percentage is 20%. Therefore, the total rehabilitation credit is $180,000 ($900,000 × 20%). The credit must be spread evenly over five years, so the credit claimed for the current year is $36,000 ($180,000/5). Quail's adjusted basis in the building must be reduced by the amount of the credit, so the basis after the credit is $1,520,000 ($800,000 + $900,000 − $180,000).

Related exercise: Application Problem 38

Small Employer Health Insurance Credit

An eligible small employer (ESE) can claim a **small employer health insurance credit** equal to 50% of its nonelective contributions for health insurance for its employees.[57] The criteria for the credit are as follows:

- The ESE contributes at least 50% of the cost of the employee's insurance premiums under a contribution arrangement offered through a small business health options program (SHOP) exchange.
- An ESE can only claim the credit in two consecutive tax years.
- The full amount of the credit is available only to an ESE with 10 or fewer full-time equivalent employees and whose employees have average annual full-time equivalent wages of less than $33,300 (2025). The credit is fully phased out once the number of full-time employees reaches 25 and/or the average wages reach $66,600 (2025).[58]
- For purposes of the credit, business owners and specified relatives are not treated as employees, and thus no credit is allowed for the employer contributions for the health insurance of those employees. Specified relatives include:
    - a child and descendants of a child
    - sibling or stepsibling
    - a parent, or ancestor of a parent
    - a stepparent
    - a niece or nephew
    - an aunt or uncle
    - a son-in-law, daughter-in-law, father-in-law, mother-in-law, brother-in-law, sister-in-law, *or*
    - a spouse of any of the family members listed above.
- Employers claiming the credit must reduce their deduction for health insurance premiums paid by the amount of the credit.
- Tax-exempt employers may claim a 35% credit that offsets the employers' payroll taxes.
- The credit is claimed on Form 8941, Credit for Small Employer Health Insurance Premiums.

[57]IRC §45R.

[58]For more information see www.irs.gov/affordable-care-act/employers/small-business-health-care-tax-credit-and-the-shop-marketplace.

Work Opportunity Tax Credit (WOTC)

The **work opportunity tax credit** is calculated on the amount of wages paid per eligible employee during the first year of employment. The credit is 40% of qualified wages with maximum wages of $6,000, so the maximum credit is $2,400.[59] Key criteria for this credit are as follows:

- The credit is elective.
- The credit is targeted at the following groups:
  - Veterans (qualified wages are a maximum of $12,000 for veterans with a disability, $14,000 if unemployed for the last six months, or $24,000 if both requirements are met)
  - Recipients of long-term unemployment
  - Members of families receiving Targeted Assistance for Needy Families or Supplemental Nutritional Assistance Program (qualified wages are a maximum of $10,000 for first year and $5,000 for second year)
  - Summer youth employees (qualified wages are limited to $3,000)
  - Individuals living in empowerment zones or rural renewal communities
  - Individuals having a physical or mental disability
  - Supplemental Security Income (SSI) recipients
  - Individuals previously convicted of a felony
- The deduction for wages must be reduced by the amount of the WOTC.

To qualify for the WOTC, the employee must be certified by a designated local agency as being a member of one of the targeted groups. Additionally, the employee must have completed at least 400 hours of service to the employer. If an employee does not work at least 400 hours but works a minimum of 125 hours, the WOTC is allowed, but the credit percentage is reduced from 40% to 25%. The WOTC is claimed on Form 5884, Work Opportunity Credit. We show how the WOTC is computed in the following Example.

EXAMPLE 3.6.4
Work Opportunity Tax Credit

During the current tax year, Pelican, Inc. hired the following individuals, each of whom worked at least 400 hours during the year, and paid them wages as shown:

Veteran with a disability	$32,000
Summer youth employee	$ 4,200
Person previously convicted of a felony	$14,000

Compute Pelican's work opportunity tax credit for the current year.

SOLUTION

The WOTC is computed as follows for Pelican, using the 40% rate for all individuals:

Targeted group	Maximum qualified wages	Credit
Veteran with a disability	$12,000	$4,800
Summer youth employee	3,000	1,200
Person previously convicted of a felony	6,000	2,400
Total credit		$8,400

Why **Why is the work opportunity tax credit allowed?** Critics of the WOTC argue that the credit is not large enough to encourage employers to create new jobs and hire additional employees. This is likely true, but misses the point of the WOTC. A one-year credit of $2,400 is not sufficient to justify creating a new position for one's business. However, the WOTC is targeted at employers who have already decided to add a new position, or who have an existing

[59]IRC §51.

position that is not filled. Those employers are encouraged to hire individuals who typically have difficulty finding employment, and by doing so, the employers receive a one-time credit to offset some of their federal income tax liability.

Related Exercise: Application Problem 39

Research Credit

To encourage businesses to invest in research and development, *incremental* research expenditures are eligible for a 20% **research credit.** Research expenditures qualify for the credit if companies are developing new or improved business components, including products, processes, computer software, formulas or inventions, that result in new or improved functionality or quality.[60] The credit is allowed for two different types of expenses, basic research payments (BRPs) and qualified research expenses (QREs). The difference between BRPS and QREs are as follows:

	BRPs	QREs
Must the expense relate to an original investigation?	Yes	No
Must the expense advance scientific knowledge?	Yes	No
Must the expense have a specific commercial objective?	No	Yes

While the IRS has not published statistics on business credits since 2013, historically most research credits have related to QREs.

Other criteria for the research credit include:

- The credit only applies to *incremental* expenses exceeding a base amount determined by the amount spent on research during the past three years.
- The research must be conducted within the United States and does not apply to research for commercial production, surveys, or social science research.
- No deduction is allowed for research expenditures used to compute the research credit.
- If the research is contracted to others outside the taxpayer's business, only 65% of the amount paid qualifies for the credit.
- The research credit is claimed on Form 6765, Credit for Increasing Research Activities.

Taxpayers may elect to use an alternative simplified research credit. This is equal to 14% of the excess of qualified research expenses over 50% of the average research expenses for the last three years.

Some small businesses may not have enough income to take advantage of their research credit. Therefore, qualified small businesses can use the research credit to offset up to $500,000 of the employer's match for Social Security and Medicare taxes due on employee's wages. A qualified small business is a corporation, S corporation, or partnership with gross receipts of less than $5,000,000 and that is less than five years old.

We demonstrate the computation of the research credit in the next Example.

EXAMPLE 3.6.5
Research Credit

Loon Corporation pays the following expenses this year related to qualifying research activities:

In-house wages	$120,000
Technology	$ 43,000
Supplies	$ 11,000

Loon's base amount for past research expenses is $118,000. How much is Loon's research credit for the current year?

[60] IRC §41.

SOLUTION

Loon's qualifying research expenses for the year are $174,000 ($120,000 + $43,000 + 11,000). Loon's research credit is $11,200, computed as follows:

Qualifying research expenses	$ 174,000
Less: Base research expenses	(118,000)
Incremental research expenses	$ 56,000
Credit percentage	× 20%
Research credit	$ 11,200

Related Exercise: Application Problem 40

Disabled Access Credit

The **disabled access credit** is available to an eligible small business for expenditures incurred to make the business accessible to individuals with disabilities. The amount of this credit is equal to 50% of the amount of the eligible access expenditures for a year, to the extent that they exceed a base of $250 up to a maximum of $10,250 in expenditures.[61] The credit is claimed on Form 8826, Disabled Access Credit. Criteria for the credit include the following:

- An eligible small business is one that *either* had:
  - gross receipts for the preceding tax year that did not exceed $1 million, *or*
  - no more than 30 full-time employees during the preceding tax year.
- Eligible access expenditures are amounts incurred to comply with the requirements of the Americans with Disabilities Act of 1990 and include amounts incurred for the purpose of removing architectural, communication, physical, or transportation barriers that prevent a business from being accessible to, or usable by, individuals with disabilities; amounts incurred to provide qualified readers to persons with vision impairments; and amounts incurred to acquire or modify equipment or devices for individuals with disabilities.
- The building must have been placed in service before November 6, 1990, to qualify for the credit.
- Expenses paid or incurred in connection with new construction are not eligible for the credit.
- The property's tax basis is reduced by the amount of the credit.
- The business must elect to use the credit.

The next Example demonstrates the computation of the disabled access credit.

EXAMPLE 3.6.6
Disabled Access Credit

Hawk Corporation had gross receipts last year of $760,000. Hawk made $8,000 of improvements to a building that was originally placed in service in 1985 to improve accessibility for individuals with disabilities. How much is Hawk's disabled access credit this year, and how does this impact the basis of the building?

SOLUTION

Hawk is an eligible small business because it had gross receipts of $1,000,000 or less in the previous year. The expenses that qualify for the credit that are greater than $250 but not greater than $10,250 are $7,750 ($8,000 – $250). Therefore, the disabled access credit is $3,875 ($7,750 × 50%). The basis of the building is increased by $4,125, the difference in the capital improvements of $8,000 less the credit of $3,875.

Related exercises: Brief Exercise 17
Application Problem 41

[61] IRC §44.

Employer-Provided Childcare Credit

Employers that provide childcare services to its employees can deduct such expenses. Alternatively, employers may prefer to claim the **employer-provided childcare credit** on Form 8882, Credit for Employer-Provided Child Care Facilities and Services, for expenses paid or incurred to provide childcare facilities to their employees during normal working hours.[62] The credit is equal to:

- 25% of qualified childcare expenditures, *and*
- 10% of qualified childcare resource and referral expenditures.

Qualified childcare expenditures include amounts paid or incurred to acquire, construct, and rehabilitate property that is to be used as a qualified childcare facility, including:

- training costs of employees,
- scholarship programs, *and*
- compensation for employees with high levels of childcare training.

Qualified childcare resource and referral expenditures include amounts paid or incurred under a contract to provide childcare resource and referral services to an employee. Other criteria for the credit include:

- The maximum credit is $150,000 per year.
- If a childcare facility ceases to be used in a qualified manner within 10 years of being placed in service, the taxpayer must recapture a portion of the credit previously claimed.
- The basis of qualifying property is reduced by the amount of the credit claimed, and the amount of qualifying expenditures that would otherwise be deductible must be reduced by the amount of the credit claimed.

The following Example shows how the employer-provided childcare credit is computed.

EXAMPLE 3.6.7
Employer-Provided Childcare Credit

Goldfinch Corporation constructed a childcare facility this year for $350,000 that employees can use for their children while the parents are at work. Goldfinch incurred $75,000 of costs this year for training and salaries for childcare workers. How much is Goldfinch's employer-provided childcare credit? What are the other tax consequences of the credit?

SOLUTION

The qualified childcare expenditures for Goldfinch are $425,000 ($350,000 + $75,000). Therefore, the credit is $106,250 ($425,000 × 25%). The basis of the childcare facility is reduced to $262,500 ($350,000 – [$350,000 × 25%]). The deduction for training and salaries is reduced to $56,250 ($75,000 – [$75,000 × 25%]).

Related exercises: Multiple Choice Question 23
Application Problem 42

Employer-Paid Medical and Family Leave Credit

Certain employers are required under federal law to provide medical and family leave to employees in certain circumstances. However, they are not required to pay employees during the leave. Therefore, a credit is provided as an incentive to employers to pay for at least a portion of the leave. Businesses can claim an **employer-paid medical and family leave credit** equal to 12.5% of wages paid to qualifying employees while on family and medical leave. The 12.5% is increased by 0.25 percentage points for each percentage point by which the wages paid exceed 50% of the employee's wages. The credit percentage can never exceed 25%.[63] The credit is claimed on Form 8994, Employer Credit for Paid Family and

[62] IRC §45F.

[63] IRC §45S.

Medical Leave. To qualify for the credit, the employer must have a written plan that meets the following conditions:

- The employee must receive at least 50% of the wages normally paid to an employee.
- All qualifying employees must receive at least two weeks of annual paid family and medical leave.
- The credit is limited to 12 weeks of paid family and medical leave per employee per year.

The computation for this credit is demonstrated in the next Example.

EXAMPLE 3.6.8
Employer-Paid Medical and Family Leave Credit

Dove Corporation has a written qualifying family and medical leave policy in place for its employees. Dove pays 80% of the employees' normal salary for up to four weeks while on medical and family leave. This year, 30 employees took paid family and medical leave for the four weeks, and total wages of $120,000 were paid for this leave. How much is Dove's employer-paid medical and family leave credit this year?

SOLUTION

To compute this credit, we must first determine the percentage of wages that is eligible for the credit. The minimum credit of 12.5% is increased by 0.25 percentage points for each percentage point by which the wages paid exceed 50%. Dove's credit percentage is computed as follows:

Percent of wages paid for medical and family leave	80%
Less: Minimum percentage required	(50%)
Excess percentage paid	30%
	× 0.25
	7.5%
Plus: Minimum credit allowed	12.5%
Credit percentage allowed	20.0%

To compute Dove's credit, 20% is multiplied by the qualifying wages paid. Dove's credit is $24,000 ($120,000 × 20%).

Related exercise: Application Problem 43

Business Energy Credits

Congress created the business energy credit as a tax incentive to encourage the production and use of, or conversion to, business equipment using energy sources other than oil or gas as a primary source of industrial or agricultural energy.[64] The business energy credit is claimed on Form 3468, Investment Credit, and is comprised of numerous credits with various percentages, such as:

- Qualified fuel cell property
- Solar energy equipment property
- Qualified small wind energy property
- Waste energy recovery property
- Geothermal property
- Qualified microturbine property
- Combined heat and power system property
- Geothermal heat systems property[65]

Related exercise: Discussion Question 24

[64]S. Rept. No. 95-529 (PL 95-618) p. 71; S. Rept. No. 96-394 (PL 96-223) p. 1.

[65]IRC §48(a).

The *Inflation Reduction Act of 2022* added a new advanced manufacturing credit. The credit is 25% of the investment in tangible depreciable property that is either constructed, re-constructed or erected by the taxpayer, or is new property acquired by the taxpayer. The tangible property can include, in addition to equipment, buildings or building portions if they are not used for office space, administrative functions, or other functions not related to manufacturing. The investment has to be made in a facility whose primary purpose is the manufacture of semiconductors or semiconductor manufacturing equipment.[66]

PRACTICE PROBLEM 3.6.1
Determining the Foreign Tax Credit

Migration, Inc. has $410,000 of U.S. source income, $90,000 of foreign source income, and Migration paid foreign taxes of $15,000. Assume that the U.S. income tax liability before the foreign tax credit is $96,000. How much is Migration's foreign tax credit? How much is Migration's foreign tax credit carryback/carryforward, if any?

SOLUTION

Migration's foreign tax credit is limited to the *lower* of:

1. Foreign tax paid of $15,000, *or*
2. $\text{U.S. tax on worldwide income} \times \dfrac{\text{Foreign source taxable income}}{\text{Worldwide taxable income}}$

$$\$96,000 \times \frac{\$90,000}{(\$410,000 + \$90,000)} = \$17,280$$

Therefore, Migration's foreign tax credit is $15,000. Migration has no foreign tax credit carryback/carryforward.

PRACTICE PROBLEM 3.6.2
Calculating the General Business Credit

Midterm Inc.'s general business credit for the year before limitation is $85,000. Midterm's net regular tax liability is $99,000. Assume that Midterm has no other tax credits. How much of the general business credit can Midterm utilize this year, what is Midterm's tax liability after the credit, and how can Midterm use any remaining credit?

SOLUTION

The general business tax credit is computed as follows:

$$\text{Taxpayer's net income tax} - [(\text{Net regular tax liability} - \$25,000) \times 25\%]$$

$$\$99,000 - [(\$99,000 - \$25,000) \times 25\%] =$$

$$\$99,000 - \$18,500 = \$80,500$$

Midterm's general business credit is limited to $80,500, so Midterm's tax liability is $18,500 ($99,000 – $80,500). The unused general business credit is $4,500 ($85,000 – $80,500), and it can be carried back one year and then carried forward 20 years.

PRACTICE PROBLEM 3.6.3
Computing the Employer-Provided Childcare Credit

Reindeer Inc. provides childcare to its employees on the employer's premises. Reindeer paid $125,000 in salaries this year directly related to the childcare facility. How much is Reindeer's employer-provided childcare credit? What are the other tax consequences of the credit?

SOLUTION

The qualified childcare expenditures for Reindeer are $125,000. Therefore, the credit is $31,250 ($125,000 × 25%). The deduction for salaries is reduced by the amount of the credit to $93,750 ($125,000 – $31,250).

INTERACTIVE SELF-SCORING QUIZZES

[66] IRC §48D.

Review and Practice

Chapter Summary

In this chapter, we reviewed the tax rules for corporate formations, computing taxable income, and penalty taxes that are levied for inappropriate accumulations of income.

1 Compute the tax consequences to the shareholders for a corporate formation.

- Shareholders must satisfy the following three requirements for gains and losses to be deferred on a corporate formation:

  1. Contribute property to the corporation (rather than services)

  2. Receive only stock in return from the corporation

  3. The *control club* must own 80% or more of the voting power and number of shares of the corporation immediately after the exchange

- The **control club** includes the shareholders who contributed property and received corporate stock. The *80% or more test* is often referred to as the **control test**. The control test is either met for all the shareholders or none of the shareholders.
- Individuals who contribute only services to the corporation are not members of the control club. Control is defined as at least 80% of the voting power and number of shares of the corporation immediately after the exchange.
- To the extent **boot** is received, Section 351 does not apply, and gain is recognized to the shareholder equal to the *lower* of:

  1. The realized gain, *or*

  2. The fair market value of the boot received.

- The shareholder's basis in the stock received from the corporation is:

  The shareholder's basis in all property (including cash) transferred to the corporation

  Plus: Gain recognized by shareholder

  Less: Boot received by shareholder

  Less: Shareholder debt that is assumed by the corporation

  Shareholder's basis

  An alternative method of computing the shareholder's basis in the stock received from the corporation is:

  Fair market value of the stock received from the corporation

  Less: The deferred gain on the formation

  Plus: The deferred loss on the formation

  Shareholder's basis

- The corporation's basis in the assets received from the shareholders is:

  The shareholder's basis in all property (including cash) transferred to the corporation

  Plus: Gain recognized by shareholder

  Corporation's basis

- If the total liabilities assumed by the corporation exceed the total adjusted basis of property transferred by the shareholder, then the shareholder must recognize gain as follows:

  Gain recognized =

  Liabilities assumed − Basis of all property transferred

- If a non-shareholder contributes property to a corporation and does not receive any stock in return, there are important tax consequences. The corporation will recognize gain equal to the fair market value of the property received, and it will have a fair market value basis in the property.

2 Determine the tax consequences of organizational expenses, start-up costs, and syndication costs.

- **Organizational expenses** are expenditures incurred in connection with the organization of a corporation. Typical organizational expenses are legal services, accounting services, organizational meetings of directors and shareholders that are related to organization, and fees paid to incorporate.
- Organizational expenses are not deductible as **Section 162 expenses** because they will benefit the corporation over its entire life. Therefore, they must be capitalized and are treated as follows:
  - The maximum amount of these expenses that can be deducted in the year of formation is $5,000.
  - The $5,000 deduction is reduced by the amount of expenditures incurred that exceed $50,000. The reduction is dollar-for-dollar, so once total organizational expenses incurred reaches $55,000, the $5,000 deduction is reduced to zero.
  - Organizational expenses not deducted must be capitalized, and amortized over 180 months, beginning with the month that the corporation begins its business operations, unless an election is filed not to do so.
- **Start-up costs** are expenditures that would be deductible as regular operating expenses, except that the corporation has not yet started its trade or business operation, so they do not meet the criteria for deductibility. For example, if a new restaurant pays its employees while management is training them, but before it opens for business, these salary payments are start-up costs. Other typical start-up costs include rent expense and utilities incurred before business operations begin. The deduction and amortization rules for start-up costs are identical to the rules for organizational expenses.

- **Syndication costs** are expenses related to issuing and selling stock. Typical syndication costs include brokerage fees, stock registration fees, underwriter fees, and printing costs of the prospectus and other selling or promotional material. Like organizational costs, syndication costs cannot be deducted as Section 162 expenses because they benefit the corporation for its entire life. Unfortunately, Congress has not provided another means to deduct syndication costs. Therefore, the corporation must capitalize them as an intangible asset on the balance sheet, but they cannot be amortized.

3 Compute taxable income for a corporation.

- The general rules for income and deductions that you have learned for individuals is the starting point for computing corporate taxable income. Nevertheless, there are several important differences in the computation of income and deductions for corporations. Corporations report their taxable income or loss on Form 1120, U.S. Corporate Income Tax Return. Corporate returns are due on the 15th day of the fourth month after tax year-end. Corporations are subject to a flat 21% tax rate as compared to the progressive tax rate structure for individuals.
- The maximum amount that can be deducted for charitable contributions each year is 10% of taxable income (before deducting charitable contributions, the dividends received deduction, and carrybacks). Any excess charitable contribution above the 10% limit can be carried forward for five years. There is no carryback for excess charitable contributions.
- Corporations are allowed a **dividends received deduction (DRD)** to offset some or all the dividend income it receives from other corporations.
    - The domestic DRD is either 50%, 65%, or 100% of the qualifying dividend received.
    - There are two requirements that must be met for the corporation to qualify for the DRD with respect to a specific dividend: generally, it must be received from a domestic corporation, and it must pass the holding period test.
    - The DRD is limited by taxable income before the DRD and before any NOL carrybacks or carryforwards or capital loss carrybacks. However, this limitation does not apply if the DRD creates or adds to an NOL.
    - A 100% deduction is allowed by U.S. corporations for the foreign-source portion of dividends received from the earnings and profits of 10%-or-more-owned foreign affiliates. This deduction completely offsets the income from the foreign subsidiary.

4 Apply other special rules for computing corporate taxable income.

- Corporations do not have a preferential tax rate for LTCGs. Rather, ordinary income, STCGs, and LTCGs are taxed at the same tax rate, 21%.
- Deductible capital losses are offset against recognized capital gains, but there is no deduction for a net capital loss. Rather, a net capital loss is carried back three years and forward five years to offset against capital gains in other years.
- Corporations can designate any month for its tax year-end. While many corporations have a calendar year-end, this is not required.
- Corporations must use the accrual method of accounting unless the entity qualifies as a **small business corporation.** To be a small business corporation, the corporation's average gross receipts over the last three tax years cannot $31 million (2025).
- A taxpayer using the cash method and following the **12-month rule** can take an immediate deduction for prepaid business expenses when paid, as long as the benefits from those expenses do not extend beyond the *earlier* of:
    - 12 months after benefits first begin, *or*
    - The end of the year after the year in which the taxpayer made the payment.
- **Small business corporations** (gross receipts do not exceed $31 million [2025]) do not have to account for inventories under the accrual method of accounting. Rather, they can deduct the cost of inventory in the year sold or the year purchased, whichever is later, *or* report inventory in the same manner as on the taxpayer's financial accounting statement.
- On Schedule M-1 of the Form 1120, corporations must reconcile their book income and taxable income by showing the timing and permanent differences that account for the different measures of income. Schedule M-1 reconciles to taxable income before the dividends received and net operating loss deductions. Corporations with total assets of $10 million or more are required to file Schedule M-3 rather than Schedule M-1.
- Taxpayers cannot carryback NOLs incurred after 2020. The taxpayer can carry them forward indefinitely, and they can offset only 80% of the taxable income for the year the NOL is used.
- Large businesses (gross receipts of more than $31 million [2025]) *must* use the accrual method of accounting for all tax reporting, including inventory. In addition to the accrual method mandate, certain large businesses must use the uniform capitalization rules. The **uniform capitalization rules (UNICAP)** provide the rules for valuing inventory including direct and indirect costs for property produced and property bought for resale.

5 Calculate the penalty taxes that apply to corporations if earnings are inappropriately accumulated and not distributed to shareholders.

- An **accumulated earnings tax (AET)** of 20% is imposed on undistributed **accumulated taxable income (ATI)**. Conceptually, accumulated taxable income measures the corporation's ability to pay a dividend. Personal holding companies, tax-exempt corporations, and S corporations are not subject to the AET.
- AET is computed as follows:

Begin with taxable income
Add: Capital loss carryforwards or carrybacks
Add: Net operating loss carryforwards
Add: Dividends received deduction
Add: Charitable contribution carryforwards
Less: Federal income taxes and foreign taxes paid
Less: Net capital losses
Less: Charitable contribution in excess of percentage limitation
Less: Net capital gains after tax
Less: Accumulated earnings credit
Less: Dividends paid including consent dividends
Accumulated taxable income
× AET rate (20%)
Accumulated earnings tax

- Corporations can also reduce ATI by the accumulated earnings credit. This credit permits corporations to accumulate at least a minimum amount of business income and not be subject to the AET, even if there is no business purpose for the accumulation. The corporation also earns a credit for income that is accumulated for the reasonable needs of the business. The accumulated earnings credit is the *greater* of:
  - $250,000 ($150,000 for service corporations) less the *accumulated earnings and profits* at the close of the preceding year, *or*
  - The reasonable needs of the business.
- The **personal holding company (PHC) tax** of 20% is imposed only on corporations qualifying as personal holding companies. Banks, insurance, and finance companies are exempt from the tax because their business purpose is to manage investments. The tax base for the PHC tax is taxable income adjusted to reflect retained economic income. Like the accumulated earnings tax, the PHC tax can be avoided by paying dividends.
- A corporation is a PHC if it meets the income test and the ownership test. The **income test** is met if **personal holding company income** constitutes 60% or more of **adjusted ordinary gross income**. The **ownership test** is met if more than 50% of the value of the stock is owned directly or indirectly by five or fewer individuals at any time during the last half of the year.

6 Compute the business tax credits available for a corporation.

The corporate income tax liability can be decreased by business tax credits. We discuss the following common business credits in this section:

- **Foreign tax credit**
- General business credit (includes the credits shown below):
  - **Rehabilitation credit**
  - **Small employer health insurance credit**
  - **Work opportunity tax credit (WOTC)**
  - **Research credit**
  - **Disabled access credit**
  - **Employer-provided childcare credit**
  - **Employer-paid medical and family leave credit**
- Business energy credits

Communication Application

Communication

Dividend Received Deduction

(LO3) Dirkson Drum owns 100% of Tambourine Corporation, an accrual-based, calendar-year corporation, that manufactures musical instruments. Tambourine owns 75% of Loud Noise, Inc. In the current year, Loud Noise paid a dividend to Tambourine of $10,000. Dirkson has hired you as his tax accountant and would like to know how the dividend will be taxed. Dirkson thinks that because Tambourine is a majority owner in Loud Noise, the dividend is not taxable to Tambourine. Explain the dividends received deduction, and how the dividend will be taxed to Tambourine.

Solution

Memo to Client

Hello Mr. Drum,

Thank you for allowing me to prepare your tax return this year and address your questions about the dividend that Tambourine Corporation received from Loud Noise, Inc.

The $10,000 of dividend income is taxable to Tambourine and will be reported as taxable income on its Form 1120. However, Tambourine is allowed a dividends received deduction of 65% as a special deduction on its Form 1120. When a corporation owns stock in another corporation, a dividends received deduction is allowed to the receiving corporation to help mitigate the inherent double taxation of corporate earnings and distributions at this time. When the corporation that received the dividend pays the dividend to an individual shareholder, the second level of taxation will occur for this income. Because Tambourine owns at least 20% but not at least 80% of Loud Noise, the dividend received deduction is limited to 65%. If Tambourine owned at least 80% of Loud Noise, then it would be allowed a dividends received deduction of 100%.

I know you were hoping that because Tambourine had a majority ownership in Loud Noise, it would be allowed a 100% dividend received deduction, but that is not the case. Please let me know if I can answer any further questions you might have.

Sincerely,
Carnes & Youngberg, CPAs

Tax memo to the file

Facts: Dirkson Drum owns 100% of Tambourine Corporation, an accrual-based, calendar-year corporation, that manufactures musical instruments. Tambourine owns 75% of Loud Noise, Inc. In the current year, Loud Noise paid a dividend to Tambourine of $10,000.
Issue: What is the net amount of dividend included in gross income when a corporation owns 75% of another corporation that has issued dividends?
Conclusion: The $10,000 of dividend income is taxable to Tambourine and will be reported as taxable income on its Form 1120. However, Tambourine is allowed a dividends received deduction of 65% as a special deduction on its Form 1120.
Analysis: Corporations must report all dividend income received from another corporation. To help mitigate triple taxation of the income for the corporation that received the dividend, corporations are allowed a dividends received deduction under IRC §243(a) as a special tax deduction on its tax return. Because Tambourine owns at least 20% but not at least 80% of Loud Noise, the dividends received deduction is limited to 65% [IRC §243(c)]. If Tambourine owned at least 80% of Loud Noise, then it would be allowed a dividends received deduction of 100% [IRC §243(a)(3)].

Ethics and Professional Responsibility Application

Ethics

Net Operating Losses

(LO4) Chestnut, Inc. is an accrual-based, calendar year-end corporation. Chestnut's specialty is harvesting organically grown nuts in Georgia. Due to tremendous flooding in the area, Chestnut incurred a net operating loss in 2024. You have been hired to prepare the 2025 Form 1120. While reviewing the 2024 return, you noticed that Chestnut's prior accountant carried back the 2024 NOL five years and amended Chestnut's 2019 Form 1120 and utilized the loss. This carryback of the NOL provided Chestnut with a large refund on the amended return. What is your advice to Chestnut, Inc.?

In addition to the chapter content, see *Statements on Standards for Tax Services* at www.aicpa-cima.com/resources/landing/statements-on-standards-for-tax-services, *Circular 230* at www.irs.gov/tax-professionals/circular-230-tax-professionals, and Chapter 2, LO4, Tax Professional Responsibilities.

Solution

Chestnut Inc. should not have filed an amended return for 2019. NOLs incurred in 2024 can only be carried forward. They can be carried forward indefinitely, and their use is limited to 80% of the income in the carryforward year. Under *Circular 230* §10.21, Knowledge of Client's Omission, "A practitioner who, having been retained by a client with respect to a matter administered by the Internal Revenue Service, knows that the client has not complied with the revenue laws of the United States or has made an error in or omission from any return, document, affidavit, or other paper which the client submitted or executed under the revenue laws of the United States, must advise the client promptly of the fact of such noncompliance, error, or omission. The practitioner must advise the client of the consequences as provided under the Code and regulations of such noncompliance, error, or omission."

As the practitioner for Chestnut, Inc., you must inform Chestnut of the error and advise them of the consequences. Depending on the amount of income that Chestnut has for the carryforward year in 2025, the NOL can possibly be utilized in 2025.

Key Terms

End-of-Chapter Assessment

Discussion Questions

1. **(LO1)** Describe the three requirements needed to qualify a transaction as a Section 351 formation.

2. **(LO1)** Define the control club requirement.

3. **(LO1)** Explain whether the holding period in the stock received in a corporate formation includes the holding period of the property contributed.

4. **(LO2)** Explain the difference between an organizational cost, start-up cost, and a syndication cost. What are the tax consequences of each?

5. **(LO3)** Discuss at least three similarities between the computation of corporate taxable income and individual taxable income.

6. **(LO3)** Explain when a charitable contribution is deducted using the cash method of accounting and the accrual method of accounting.

7. **(LO3)** Are all charitable contributions deducted based on an asset's fair market value? If not, briefly describe the rules used when the deduction is and is not measured by the fair market value.

8. **(LO3)** Explain why Congress allows the dividends received deduction.

9. **(LO3, 4)** Discuss at least three differences between the computation of corporate taxable income and individual taxable income.

10. **(LO4)** Is a corporate net long-term capital gain taxed at a preferential rate? If not, what rate do corporations pay on net capital gains?

11. **(LO4)** What year-end can a C corporation have for tax reporting?

12. **(LO4)** When must a corporation use the accrual method of accounting?

13. **(LO4)** Which form is used to file a voluntary request to change an accounting method?

14. **(LO4)** When can a business deduct a prepaid expense under the cash method of accounting?

15. **(LO4)** Hank has his own construction business which uses the accrual method of accounting with a calendar year-end. Hank agreed on December 31, Year 2, to pay his employees a bonus on February 1, Year 3. Should Hank's business take a deduction for the bonus payment in Year 2 or Year 3?

16. **(LO4)** Do small businesses have to account for inventory under the accrual method of accounting?

17. **(LO4)** Provide and explain five different book income to taxable income adjustments that are reported on Schedule M-1.

18. **(LO4)** What are the rules pertaining to the use of a corporate NOL incurred in 2025?

19. **(LO4)** Sharp Corporation had a net operating loss of $44,000 in 2020. What is the earliest year to which Sharp can carryback this NOL? How much of this NOL can be used in 2025, assuming Sharp has $50,000 of taxable income in 2025?

20. **(LO5)** Describe the accumulated earnings tax and why it exists.

21. **(LO5)** Describe the personal holding company tax and why it exists.

22. **(LO6)** Briefly explain the concept of taxing worldwide income and the foreign tax credit.

23. **(LO6)** Briefly explain the general business credit.

24. **(LO6)** Identify four business energy credits.

Multiple Choice Questions

1. **(LO1)** In order to meet the control requirement for a Section 351 formation, a shareholder must own at least what percent of the voting power and number of shares of the corporation immediately after the exchange?
   - **a.** 50%
   - **b.** 80%
   - **c.** 100%
   - **d.** None of the above

2. **(LO1)** Shareholders who contribute both property and services to the corporation for their stock are included in the control club only if they contribute more than a small amount of property. What percentage of the value of the services rendered must the value of the property be to satisfy this rule?
   - **a.** 0%
   - **b.** 10%
   - **c.** 50%
   - **d.** 80%

3. **(LO1)** Frank and Benita contributed property to a corporation in exchange for stock during the current tax year. Frank contributed $45,000 cash for 50% of the stock and Benita contributed land held for investment property with an adjusted basis of $33,000 and a fair market value of $45,000 for the remaining 50% of the stock of the corporation. Benita had owned the land for three years. What is Benita's holding period in his stock after this transaction, and what is the corporation's holding period in the land?
   - **a.** Stock – 0 years; Land – 0 years
   - **b.** Stock – 0 years; Land – 3 years
   - **c.** Stock – 3 years; Land – 0 years
   - **d.** Stock – 3 years; Land – 3 years

4. **(LO2)** Jackson Corporation, a calendar year taxpayer, organized in the current year and began business operations on July 1. Jackson incurred the following expenditures during the year:

Legal fees to organize the corporation	$54,000
Commissions paid to underwriter	$32,000

   What can Jackson Corporation deduct for syndication expenses (including any amortization expenses) for the current year?
   - **a.** $0
   - **b.** $5,000
   - **c.** $10,000
   - **d.** $32,000

5. **(LO2)** Which of the following is an organizational cost?
   - **a.** Wages paid after operations have begun
   - **b.** Attorney fees to draft articles of incorporation
   - **c.** Utilities paid before operations began
   - **d.** Printing cost of the prospectus

6. **(LO3)** What is the current tax rate for a corporation?
   - **a.** 10%
   - **b.** 20%
   - **c.** 21%
   - **d.** 35%

7. **(LO3)** What tax rate structure does a corporation follow?
   - **a.** Regressive
   - **b.** Progressive
   - **c.** Cumulative
   - **d.** Proportionate (flat)

8. **(LO3)** A for-profit corporate tax return is filed on which tax form?
   - **a.** Form 1120
   - **b.** Form 1065
   - **c.** Form 1040
   - **d.** Form 990

9. **(LO3)** Reindeer Inc. uses the cash method of accounting and has a calendar year-end. Reindeer's board of directors has agreed to pay a charitable contribution of $4,500 on December 15 of the current year and $2,300 on January 28 of the following year. How much can Reindeer deduct in the current year, assuming no taxable income limitation?
   - **a.** $0
   - **b.** $2,300
   - **c.** $4,500
   - **d.** $6,800

10. **(LO3)** Greco Insurance Inc. has taxable income before the charitable contribution deduction of $425,000 in the current year. Greco contributed $50,000 to a qualified charitable organization. What is Greco's charitable contribution deduction in the current year?
    - **a.** $0
    - **b.** $42,500
    - **c.** $50,000
    - **d.** $106,250

11. **(LO3)** Sailor Inc. owns 35% of Navy Corporation. Sailor received dividend income of $35,000 from Navy. What is Sailor's dividends received deduction, assuming that Sailor has taxable income of $125,000?
    - **a.** $8,750
    - **b.** $17,500
    - **c.** $22,750
    - **d.** $35,000

12. (LO4) Birdie Inc. had the following transactions in the current year:

- Short term capital gain $10,000
- Short term capital loss ($ 6,400)
- Long term capital gain $ 8,000
- Long term capital loss ($ 2,000)

If Birdie has taxable income of $100,000 before considering the capital transactions, what is Birdie's taxable income after the capital transactions?

a. $97,000
b. $100,000
c. $109,600
d. $118,000

13. (LO4) Which of the following is an allowable year-end for C corporations?

a. December 31
b. March 31
c. September 30
d. All of these

14. (LO4) Which of the following statements is correct with regard to changes in accounting methods for federal income tax purposes?

a. A taxpayer can never change a method of accounting except when changing from an incorrect to a correct method.
b. A taxpayer does not need the permission of the Internal Revenue Service to change accounting methods.
c. Any adjustment to income required due to a voluntary change in accounting method is spread over five years beginning with the year of change.
d. If the change is initiated by an Internal Revenue Service examination and it increases income, 100% of the change must be included in income for the year of the change.

15. (LO4) Sanjay took out a loan on November 1, Year 1, for $100,000 to purchase inventory for his clothing store, which he operates as a cash basis sole proprietorship. His annual interest rate is 6%. On December 31, Year 1, he pays the $1,000 of interest due for Year 1 and also prepays $3,000 of interest for the first six months of Year 2. What is his deduction on his Year 1 tax return for interest expense?

a. $0
b. $1,000
c. $3,000
d. $4,000

16. (LO4) The cash basis method of accounting is allowed when

a. average gross receipts do not exceed $31 million.
b. assets do not exceed $31 million.
c. inventory does not exceed $31 million.
d. None of these.

17. (LO4) A business can use LIFO in identifying inventory costs when

a. FIFO is used for financial reporting purposes.
b. LIFO is used for financial reporting purposes.
c. Specific identification method is used for financial reporting purposes.
d. None of these.

18. (LO4) Only corporations with total assets of $10 million or more are required to file which of the following forms?

a. Schedule M-1
b. Schedule M-3
c. Schedule P-1
d. Schedule M-2

19. (LO4) Raven Inc. has a net operating loss (NOL) of $26,000 from 2025. If Raven's taxable income in 2026 is $30,000 before considering the NOL carryforward from 2025, what is its taxable income for 2026 after considering the NOL carryforward from 2025?

a. $4,000
b. $6,000
c. $15,000
d. $26,000

20. (LO5) What is the accumulated earnings tax rate?

a. 10%
b. 20%
c. 25%
d. 30%

21. (LO5) The corporation will not be subject to the personal holding company tax if rental income is in excess of what percent of the corporation's gross income?

a. 10%
b. 25%
c. 50%
d. 80%

22. (LO6) The general business tax credit is computed on which form?

a. Form 1120
b. Form 8800
c. Form 4562
d. Form 3800

23. (LO6) The maximum amount for the employer-provided child-care credit per year is?

a. $0
b. $25,000
c. $100,000
d. $150,000

Brief Exercises

1. **(LO1)** Dana contributed property with an adjusted basis of $70,000 and a fair market value of $80,000 for 80% of the stock of Lilac Corporation. Monique rendered services to Lilac and received 20% of Lilac's stock with a value of $20,000. What are the tax consequences to Dana and Monique?

2. **(LO1)** Jakur and Allison contributed property to a corporation in exchange for stock during the current tax year. Jakur contributed $25,000 cash for 50% of the stock and Allison contributed property with an adjusted basis of $17,500 and a fair market value of $25,000 for 50% of the stock. What is Allison's adjusted basis in her stock?

3. **(LO1)** The city of St. Charles, IL, wants to attract a large food distributor to build a new warehouse in St. Charles. The city planning board has estimated that the warehouse would bring over 100 new jobs to the Tri Cities area. St. Charles offers the company 30 acres of land valued at $2,100,000 if it will build the facility in St. Charles. St. Charles also offers $900,000 of cash as an additional incentive and property tax abatement of $5,000 per year for the first five years. What are the tax consequences of these transactions for the food distributor, and what is its basis in the property received?

4. **(LO2)** Crokus Inc., a calendar-year taxpayer, organized in the current year and began business operations on July 1. Crokus incurred the following expenditures during the year:

Legal fees to organize the corporation	$54,000
Commissions paid to an underwriter	$32,000

What can Crokus Inc. deduct for organizational expenses (including any amortization expenses) for the current year?

5. **(LO3)** Sparty Corporation has taxable income of $166,000. What is Sparty's tax liability?

6. **(LO3)** Twizzler Corporation has gross receipts of $590,000, cost of goods sold of $135,000, interest income of $2,200, operating expenses of $240,000, and an NOL carryforward of $12,000. What is Twizzler's taxable income?

7. **(LO3)** Tiger Inc. uses the accrual method of accounting and has a calendar year-end. Tiger's board of directors have agreed to pay a charitable contribution of $6,500 on December 10 of the current year, $3,800 on February 2 of the following year, and $5,250 on April 27 of the following year. How much can Tiger deduct in the current year assuming the taxable income limitation does not apply?

8. **(LO3)** Cyber Security Systems Inc. (CSSI) made the following contributions by the end of the current year:

American Cancer Society	$2,750
United Way	$1,000
Fair market value of Walmart stock to Salvation Army (adjusted basis $1,800)	$2,600

The Walmart stock was purchased three years ago. Assuming no taxable income limitation, what is CSSI's charitable contribution deduction?

9. **(LO3)** Tasma Inc. has taxable income of $620,000 after deducting a $185,000 charitable contribution in the current year. How much can Tasma deduct on its corporate tax return for the charitable contribution in the current year?

10. **(LO3)** Dolphins Inc. reports the following for the current year:

Gross receipts	$100,000
Cost of goods sold	$ 33,000
Dividend income	$ 12,000
Operating expenses	$ 35,000

Dolphins Inc. owns 15% of the dividend-paying corporation. What is Dolphins' dividend received deduction and taxable income for the current year?

11. **(LO4)** Eagle Inc. had the following transactions in the current year:

Short term capital gain	$10,000
Short term capital loss	($ 6,400)
Long term capital gain	$ 8,000
Long term capital loss	($15,000)

If Eagle's taxable income before capital transactions is $100,000, what is its taxable income after the net capital gain or loss?

12. **(LO4)** UNICAP rules apply to what types of assets? Provide three examples of costs that must be capitalized under the UNICAP rules.

13. **(LO4)** Gold Star Inc.'s book income of $267,000 included municipal interest income of $1,400 and entertainment expense of $2,200. Charitable contributions of $3,900 were carried forward from a prior year into the current year. What is Gold Star's taxable income based on this information?

14. **(LO4)** Pepper Corporation had a net operating loss (NOL) of $10,000 in 2025. If Pepper had a marginal tax rate of 21% in 2024, what is Pepper's tax savings from carrying back the 2025 NOL to 2024?

15. **(LO5)** Maria owns 100% of Salt Corporation. The Board of Directors has decided to declare and pay $5,000 in dividends to Maria on October 31. The Board of Directors has also decided to declare a $7,500 dividend on December 31 that it will pay out on January 31 of the next year. Maria agrees to a consent dividend for the current year of $10,000. What is the tax effect to Maria for these dividends?

16. **(LO5)** Tanker Corporation computed the following taxes for the current year:

Regular tax liability	$222,000
Accumulated earnings tax	$ 47,000
Personal holding company tax	$ 68,000

What is Tanker's total tax liability for the year?

17. **(LO6)** Stormcast Corporation had gross receipts last year of $1,150,000. Stormcast made $5,500 in improvements to a building that was originally placed in service in 1989 to improve accessibility for individuals with disabilities. How much is Stormcast's disabled access credit this year, and how does this impact the basis of the building?

Application Problems

1. **(LO1)** Desiree contributed property with an adjusted basis of $36,000 and a fair market value of $50,000 for 50% of the stock of Huskie Corporation. Charles rendered services to Huskie and received 50% of Huskie stock with a value of $50,000. What are the tax consequences to Desiree and Charles?

2. **(LO1)** Fabio and Coco create a new secret formula for aging cream that will dramatically reduce wrinkles in one week. They incorporate the business and call it Fountain of Youth Corporation (FYC). Fabio contributes a delivery truck to the corporation with the following tax characteristics:

Fair market value	$50,000
Adjusted basis	$38,000
Original cost	$60,000

Coco contributes $50,000 of cash to FYC. They each receive stock worth $50,000 from FYC. What are the tax consequences of these transactions to Fabio, Coco, and FYC?

3. **(LO1)** Gus and Hunan form Green Weed Relief, Inc. (GWR), a fertilizer and pesticide business using organic products. Gus contributes $100,000 cash. Hunan contributes services worth $90,000 and machinery with an adjusted basis of $8,200 and a fair market value of $10,000. Both Gus and Hunan receive stock with a fair market value of $100,000. What are the tax consequences of these transactions to Gus and Hunan?

4. **(LO1)** Ari and Holly form Musicians for Hire, Inc. (MFH), specializing in providing traveling performers for special events. Ari contributes $125,000 cash and Holly contributes musical instruments with an adjusted basis of $85,000 and a fair market value of $145,000. In return, they each receive $125,000 stock in MFH, and Holly receives cash of $20,000 from MFH. What are the tax consequences to Ari and Holly?

5. **(LO1)** Ari and Holly form Musicians for Hire, Inc. (MFH), specializing in providing traveling performers for special events. Ari contributes $125,000 cash and Holly contributes musical instruments with an adjusted basis of $85,000 and a fair market value of $145,000. In return, they each receive $125,000 stock in MFH, and Holly receives cash of $20,000 from MFH. Assuming Holly's recognized gain is $20,000, what basis do Ari and Holly have in their stock, and what basis does MFH have in the musical instruments contributed by Holly?

6. **(LO1)** Yannick transferred land with a FMV of $10,000 and a basis of $16,000 and equipment with a fair market value of $8,000 and a basis of $6,000 to Blue Sky Corporation in exchange for all of its stock in a Section 351 formation. What is Yannick's adjusted basis in his stock and Blue Sky's basis in the land and equipment?

7. **(LO1)** Newt and Giselle decide to form a corporation, Food on Wheels, which will sell meals through a food truck in various neighborhoods. Newt contributes a truck to the corporation with the following tax characteristics:

Fair market value	$125,000
Adjusted basis	$ 38,000
Original cost	$135,000
Truck Loan	$ 50,000

Giselle contributes $65,000 of cash to the corporation and the corporation assumes Newt's $50,000 loan on the truck. They each receive stock worth $65,000 from the corporation, and Newt also receives $10,000 in cash from the corporation.

a. How much gain do Newt and Giselle recognize?

b. What basis do Newt and Giselle have in their stock, and what basis does Food on Wheels have in the truck contributed by Newt?

8. **(LO1)** Cayton and Garfield decide to form a corporation, CG Inc., which will sell paint supplies. Cayton contributes land to the corporation with the following tax characteristics:

Fair market value	$175,000
Adjusted basis	$ 72,000
Original cost	$ 72,000
Mortgage	$ 50,000

Cayton took out the mortgage on the land six months ago to purchase a personal automobile. Garfield contributes $100,000 of cash to the corporation and the corporation assumes Cayton's mortgage. They each receive stock worth $100,000 from the corporation, and Cayton also receives cash from the corporation with a fair market value of $25,000. How much gain do Cayton and Garfield recognize?

9. **(LO2)** Ahana is a successful photographer and is opening a studio in Boulder, CO. She files articles of incorporation with the state of Colorado on January 1 of the current year. She leases studio space beginning February 1 and begins business operations on May 1. Ahana paid the following expenses during the year:

Rent expense for studio (per month)	$4,800
Utilities (per month)	$1,100
Insurance expense (per month)	$ 900
Artist fees paid to decorate studio in March	$5,000
Attorney's fees for incorporation	$1,200
Organizational meetings incident to organization	$4,400
Printing costs for prospectus	$1,800
Incorporation fees for state of Colorado	$1,000
Instructor salaries for February through December (per month)	$9,000
Underwriter fees	$4,800

How will Ahana treat these expenses on her tax return for the current year? Ahana uses the cash method of accounting.

10. **(LO3)** Based on the following information, calculate Blitzen Corporation's taxable income and tax liability.

Gross receipts	$1,425,000
Interest income	$ 2,200
Municipal interest income	$ 1,600
Capital gains	$ 16,800
Cost of goods sold	$ 580,000
Advertising expense	$ 12,000
Depreciation expense	$ 42,000
Rent expense	$ 36,000
Wages paid	$ 225,000
Utilities	$ 6,000
Entertainment expense	$ 10,000
Fines and penalties	$ 800
Other operating expenses	$ 18,000

11. **(LO3)** Lazarus Corporation owns a small building in the city with a fair market value of $325,000 and an adjusted basis of $216,000. Lazarus has owned this building for three years. Lazarus has decided to gift the building to a qualified charitable organization to build a shelter for people experiencing homelessness. What is Lazarus's charitable contribution and how much gain does Lazarus recognize because of the contribution?

12. **(LO3)** Arthur's Automotive Inc. (AAI) purchases and refurbishes old cars. AAI contributes a refurbished Honda SUV with a fair market value of $32,000 and adjusted basis of $30,000 to a senior center that qualifies as a charitable organization. AAI has owned the SUV for three years. Instead of using the SUV to transport the seniors, the senior center sold the SUV to pay for a new kitchen. How much can AAI deduct for this contribution, assuming there are no taxable income limitations on the deduction?

13. **(LO3)** Poinsettia Corporation owns equipment with a fair market value of $105,000 and an adjusted basis of $70,000. Depreciation claimed is $30,000. How much can Poinsettia deduct as a charitable contribution if it contributed the equipment to a qualified charity?

14. **(LO3)** Uniforms Plus Inc. (UPI) manufacturers and sells uniforms to businesses and schools. In the current year, UPI contributes 200 school uniforms to St. Matthew's Church, a qualified charity, to be given to children from families with low incomes. The uniforms have a fair market value of $35 each and cost basis to UPI is $5 each. How much can UPI deduct for this contribution?

15. **(LO3)** Greensville, Inc. is a calendar-year, accrual-basis taxpayer. On December 5 of Year 1, Greensville's board approved a donation of $1.25 million to the local city to build a youth recreation center. Greensville paid the $1.25 million as follows:

December 28, Year 1	$300,000
April 1, Year 2	$250,000
June 1, Year 2	$275,000
December 10, Year 2	$300,000
January 15, Year 3	$125,000

a. How much can Greensville deduct in Year 1, Year 2, and Year 3, assuming no taxable income limitations and that Greensville wants to deduct the contributions as early as possible?

b. Alternatively, how much can Greensville deduct in Year 1, Year 2, and Year 3 if it is a cash-basis taxpayer?

16. **(LO3)** Crator Inc., an accrual-based, calendar-year corporation, has taxable income for the current year of $468,000 after deducting a charitable contribution of $79,000 and a dividend received deduction (DRD) of $51,000. How much can Crator deduct in the current year for this contribution?

17. **(LO3)** Frank N Beans Inc. (FNBI) owns 15% of Hotdog Inc. FNBI has the following information this year, before deducting the DRD:

Revenue from operations	$775,000
Dividend income—Hotdog Inc.	$ 5,000
Capital gains	$ 2,500
Operating expenses	$125,000

What is FNBI's taxable income after the DRD?

18. **(LO3)** Shepards Inc. owns 38% of Pie Inc. Shepards has the following information this year, before deducting the DRD:

Revenue from operations	$297,000
Dividend income—Pie Inc.	$ 54,000
Capital gains	$ 9,000
Operating expenses	$315,000

What is Shepard's taxable income after the DRD?

19. **(LO3)** Framer Inc. owns 10% of Pictures Inc. Framer has the following information this year, before deducting the DRD:

Revenue from operations	$550,000
Dividend income—Pictures Inc	$ 66,000
Capital gains	$ 5,000
Operating expenses	$600,000

What is Framer's taxable income after the DRD?

20. **(LO4)** Maverick Corporation had the following transactions for the current tax year:

Operating net income	$95,000
STCG	$ 8,000
STCL	$ 7,000
LTCG	$ 6,000
LTCL	$10,000

What are the tax consequences of these transactions?

21. **(LO4)** Kerber, Inc. began business seven years ago in Year 1. They have used the cash basis method of accounting since inception. Kerber's gross receipts over the last 7 years are as follows:

Year 1	$ 3,500,000
Year 2	$ 9,800,000
Year 3	$22,000,000
Year 4	$26,000,000
Year 5	$32,500,000
Year 6	$29,000,000
Year 7	$32,000,000

Can Kerber continue to use the cash method in Year 8?

22. **(LO4)** Jensen loaned his brother Jackson $60,000 for college and charged him an annual interest rate of 4%, or $200 per month. Jackson paid Jensen $800 on December 25 of Year 1 for the first 4 months of interest in Year 2. Should Jensen report the interest as income in Year 1 or Year 2?

23. **(LO4)** In late November, Year 4, Javi received $4,050 in advance from a customer for monthly painting lessons that were to begin in December, Year 4, and run through May, Year 6. When must Javi recognize income from the 18 months of advance payment of services:

a. under the cash method of accounting?

b. under the accrual method, assuming he defers the income for financial reporting purposes until it is earned?

24. **(LO4)** On November 2, 2025, Dirty Company, a calendar year, cash-basis taxpayer, paid an $9,900 premium to acquire a casualty insurance policy on its business assets.

a. If the policy has a one-year term from December 1, 2025, through November 30, 2026, what is the insurance deduction for Dirty Company in 2025?

b. If the policy has a one-year term from February 1, 2026, through January 31, 2027, what is the insurance deduction for Dirty Company in 2025?

c. If the policy has a three-year term from January 1, 2026, through December 31, 2028, what is the insurance deduction for Dirty Company in 2025?

25. **(LO4)** On November 1, 2025, Pablo Company, which is a calendar year, cash-basis taxpayer, borrowed $200,000 from National Bank at 3.2% interest per year. On December 22, 2025, Pablo Company paid $6,400 to the bank for the first year's interest on the loan. How much can Pablo Company deduct in 2025 for the interest paid?

26. **(LO4)** GridIron Company, a calendar year business, employs 75 employees. On December 1, 2025, it decided that it would pay bonuses to all its employees. Each employee will receive their $2,000 bonus on February 14, 2025. One of the owners who owns 65% of the company will receive his bonus of $20,000 on February 14, 2026, as well.

   a. How much can GridIron Company deduct for the bonuses on their 2025 tax return?

   b. If the employee bonuses were paid on March 25, 2026, when are the bonuses deductible?

27. **(LO4)** Bones and Talus, Inc is an orthopedic specialist medical provider. The corporation also sells crutches, wheelchairs, arm slings, and other medical devices to their patients. The corporation's average gross receipts in 2025 was $8 million.

   a. What method of accounting may Bones and Talus use to value its inventory?

   b. If Bones and Talus purchased $67,000 of medical devices on December 1, 2025, had beginning inventory of $33,000, and had $43,000 on hand on December 31, 2025, how much can the corporation deduct on its 2025 tax return?

28. **(LO4)** Jermaine owns an auto body shop and has average gross receipts of $1,200,000 for the last three years. At the beginning of the current year, his inventory had a value of $165,000. He purchased inventory during the year of $275,000, and his ending inventory has a value of $135,000. Assuming that he uses the cash basis of accounting for his business, how much can he deduct this year for his inventory?

29. **(LO4)** BB Company is a manufacturer of guns. At the end of the current tax year, its inventory had the following values:

Cost using uniform capitalization rules	$4,780,000
Market value, using replacement cost	$5,860,000

BB uses the FIFO method to value its inventory. What value should be used for the inventory for tax purposes? How would your answer change, if at all, if BB uses the LIFO method?

30. **(LO4)** Cashiers Inc. has book income after federal income tax expenses of $520,000. Cashiers is an accrual-basis taxpayer for both book reporting and tax reporting. Compute Cashiers's taxable income given the information below:

Federal income tax	$109,200
Book depreciation	$ 66,000
Tax depreciation	$ 78,000
Charitable contribution carryforward	$ 10,000
Net capital loss	$ 3,000
Municipal interest income	$ 1,000
Entertainment expenses	$ 4,500

31. **(LO4)** Jaryn Corporation has a $102,000 taxable loss for 2025 after deducting 100% of an NOL carryforward from 2018 of $38,000.

   a. What is Jaryn's NOL for 2025 and how can it be used?

   b. In 2026, Jaryn has taxable income before the NOL of $45,000. How much of the NOL can be utilized in 2026?

32. **(LO4)** Cancun Inc., which reports on the calendar year, has the following information for the current tax year:

Retained earnings, January 1	$327,000
Cash dividend paid	$ 35,000
Net income per books	$285,000
Net taxable income	$245,000
Treasury bonds distributed as a dividend	$ 16,000

What is Cancun's retained earnings at the end of the tax year?

33. **(LO4)** TVA, Inc. is a C corporation that has the following information for the current year:

Operating income	$ 25,000
Investment income	$ 15,000
Passive loss	($45,000)

What is TVA's taxable income? How would your answer change if TVA was a personal service corporation or a closely held corporation?

34. **(LO5)** Roadrunner, Inc. manufactures car parts and has $200,000 of taxable income for the current year. Roadrunner had earnings and profits at the close of the preceding year of $188,000. The Board of Directors decided to set aside $52,000 for expansion of its business in the Midwest. Roadrunner has the following tax items for the current year:

Taxable income	$200,000
Federal taxes paid	$ 42,000
Excess capital loss	$ 4,500
Excess charitable contributions	$ 7,800
Dividends received deduction	$ 11,000

   a. How much is Roadrunner's accumulated earnings tax?

   b. What actions could Roadrunner take, if any, to reduce the accumulated earnings tax to zero?

35. **(LO5)** Creamery Inc., a PHC, paid $26,250 in federal income taxes on $125,000 of taxable income. The taxable income included $10,000 of dividend income from a stock held with 5% ownership. Creamery also had a Section 1231 gain of $12,000 on which $2,520 of tax was paid. Creamery's Board of Directors declared and paid $12,500 of dividends this year to its shareholders. How much is the PHC tax for Creamery, if any?

36. **(LO6)** Blizzard Corporation has $445,000 of U.S. source income, $108,000 of foreign source income, and Blizzard paid foreign taxes of $31,000. Assume that the U.S. income tax liability before the foreign tax credit is $116,130.

   a. How much is Blizzard's foreign tax credit?

   b. How much is Blizzard's foreign tax credit carryback/carryforward, if any?

37. **(LO6)** Workman Corporation's general business credit for the year before limitation is $98,000. Workman's net regular tax liability is $110,000. Assume that Workman has no other tax credits.

   a. How much of the general business credit can Workman utilize this year?

   b. What is Workman's tax liability after the credit?

   c. What can Workman do with any remaining credit?

38. **(LO6)** The Downtown Corporation spent $390,000 in the past year to rehabilitate an old theater that was built in 1890 and that is a certified historic structure. Downtown's basis in the building before the rehabilitation project began was $325,000. How much is Downtown's rehabilitation credit for the current year, and what is the basis of the building after the credit?

39. **(LO6)** During the current tax year, Grease, Inc. hired the following individuals and paid them wages as shown:

Long-term unemployment recipient	$45,000
Individual having a physical or mental disability	$12,000
Member of family receiving Targeted Assistance for Needy Families	$14,000

Compute Grease's work opportunity credit for the current year.

40. **(LO6)** Tadpole Inc. has contracted an outside firm to research the effect of a product that has been developed to convert river water to clean drinking water. Tadpole paid the outside firm $200,000 in the current year. Tadpole's base amount for past research expenses is $105,000. How much is Tadpole's research credit for the current year?

41. **(LO6)** HealthNow Corporation had gross receipts last year of $550,000. HealthNow made $4,900 in improvements to a building that was originally placed in service in 1988 to improve accessibility for individuals with disabilities. How much is HeathNow's disabled access credit this year, and how does this impact the basis of the building?

42. **(LO6)** Mandella Corporation constructed a childcare facility this year for $465,000 that employees can use for their children while the parents are at work. Mandella incurred $88,000 of costs this year on training and salaries for childcare workers. How much is Mandella's employer-provided childcare credit? What are the other tax consequences of the credit?

43. **(LO6)** Tutu Inc. has a written qualifying family and medical leave policy in place for its employees. Tutu pays 75% of the employees' normal salary for up to three weeks while on medical and family leave. This year 25 employees took paid family and medical leave for the three weeks, and total wages of $150,000 were paid for this leave. How much is Tutu's employer-paid medical and family leave credit this year?

Tax Planning Problems

Planning

1. **(LO1)** Garret and Frank form a corporation in the current year. Garret contributes property with an adjusted basis of $143,000 and a fair market value of $166,000. Frank can either contribute services of $166,000 or cash of $166,000.
   a. If the objective is to minimize overall taxes for the current year, should Frank contribute services or property?
   b. If Frank contributes $166,000 of services, how much property should he contribute to minimize overall taxes on this transaction?

2. **(LO3)** Heirloom, Inc. purchased 2,000 shares of stock in Walmart on February 10 of the current tax year and received a dividend of $12,000 on March 30 of the current tax year. The ex-dividend date was March 15 of the current year. If Heirloom would like to qualify for the DRD with respect to this dividend, when can Heirloom sell the stock and still qualify?

Professional Development Skills

Communication Problem

Communication

1. **(LO1) Formation of a Corporation** Jan and Suzanne are forming a new corporation, Grandmas for Hire, Inc., a calendar-year, accrual-based corporation, which focuses on providing childcare services. Jan is contributing cash of $20,000 and a passenger van with an adjusted basis of $15,000 and a fair market value of $26,000 in exchange for her 50% interest in the corporation. Suzanne is contributing $1,000 cash and services as a bookkeeper worth $45,000 in exchange for her 50% interest in the corporation. They would like to understand what, if any, are the tax consequences of creating this corporation and who will be liable for tax on the earnings from the corporation. Please write a memo to Jan and Suzanne and a memo to the file that addresses their concerns. Do you have any suggestions to provide Jan and Suzanne that would help the transaction be tax-deferred?

Ethics and Professional Responsibilities Problem

Ethics

1. **(LO3) Charitable Contribution Deduction Limit** Tariq owns 100% of Flip Corporation and has handled his own accounting records and tax preparation in previous years. He has prepared Flip's Form 1120 for 2025 and would like you to review it because of several transactions that he is not sure how to handle. While reviewing his tax return, you notice that he has a deduction for charitable contributions that exceeds the amount allowed for 2025. Tariq has reported a deduction of 25% of taxable income before the charitable contribution deduction. The current law for 2025 indicates that the limit is 10% of taxable income instead of 25%. What is your advice to Tariq?

   In addition to the chapter content, see *Statements on Standards for Tax Services* at www.aicpa-cima.com/resources/landing/statements-on-standards-for-tax-services, *Circular 230* at www.irs.gov/tax-professionals/circular-230-tax-professionals, and Chapter 2, LO4, Tax Professional Responsibilities.

Research Problem

Research

1. (LO5) **Accumulated Earnings Tax** Annabelle owns 100% of Buford Corporation, an accrual-based, calendar-year corporation. The business has been profitable in recent years, and Annabelle has increased her salary accordingly. Unfortunately, Annabelle's five-year-old daughter has contracted a rare illness and the medical bills are mounting. Annabelle has instructed the Board of Directors to issue her an open loan so that Annabelle can easily access money to pay the medical bills. The tax accountant for Buford is concerned that the money being used for the shareholder loan will be considered accumulating money beyond the reasonable needs of the business and Buford will be subject to the accumulated earnings tax. Research IRC §531 & §537 and Treasury Regulation §1.537-1 to provide guidance and determine if the shareholder loan is allowed as a reasonable need for accumulating earnings.

Tax Compliance and Reporting Problem

Compliance

1. (LO1, 2, 3) **Form 1120 and Schedule C** Axel Corporation (FEIN: 36-1234567) is a regular C corporation with a calendar year-end. In the current year, Axel reported the following information on its income statement.

Gross revenue	$1,750,000
Municipal interest income	$ 1,250
Dividend income from Dart Corp.	$ 3,300
Long-term capital gain	$ 12,000
Cost of goods sold	$ 330,000
Advertising	$ 14,000
Wages paid	$ 238,000
Depreciation	$ 76,000
Charitable contributions	$ 120,000
Utilities	$ 22,000
Office expense	$ 4,900
Insurance expense	$ 19,000
Entertainment expense	$ 4,000

Axel owned 5% of Dart Corporation. Axel Corporation's address is 100 State Street, Chicago, IL 60606. The corporation paid $200,000 in federal estimated payments. Complete Form 1120 pages 1 and 2.

Excel Problem

Technology

1. (LO3) **Dividends Received Deduction** Cherry, Inc. would like to know their dividend received deduction (DRD) in each of the following cases. Assume all dividends received were from a domestic corporation.

Case	Ownership in dividend-paying corporation	Dividends received	Cherry's net income before DRD
1	12%	$10,000	$15,000
2	25%	$10,000	$ 9,000
3	32%	$10,000	$ 6,000

Create an Excel spreadsheet to develop your solution.

CPA Exam Preparation: Task-Based Simulation

1. **(LO3) Calculating the Dividends Received Deduction** Sunshine Inc., a calendar-year corporation, has been profitable in recent years. In 20XX, Sunshine has gross income from sales operations of $125,000 and expenses from operations of $65,000. Sunshine has made investments in four other corporations and has received dividend income from each. Sunshine's ownership percentage of each corporation is as follows:

GetFit, Inc.	5%
Yellow Inc.	19%
Sol, Inc.	5%
Orange, Inc.	10%

Please refer to the Exhibits tab to access the following resources:

- Form 1099—DIV GetFit, Inc.
- Form 1099—DIV Yellow, Inc.
- Form 1099—DIV Sol, Inc.
- Form 1099—DIV Orange, Inc.

For each item in column A, calculate the requested information and enter it in the associated cell in column B.

Go to Wiley's book companion site to complete the Task-Based Simulation.

2. **(LO4) Reconciliation of Book to Taxable Income** Practical Publishing Corporation (PPC) has operated as an accrual-based C corporation since 2013. PPC has a calendar year-end and has provided its financial income statement for tax year 2025. PPC has also provided additional information:

- In December 2025, PPC received $13,500 from a company that will lease excess space in the warehouse from PPC from January 1 through October 31, 2026.
- PPC has $1,500 of bad debt expense under the direct write-off method.
- PPC has total cost recovery for tax purposes on assets purchased of $120,000.

Review the Exhibits provided and complete all applicable lines on the Schedule M-1 Excel worksheet. A sample Schedule M-1 has been provided for your reference.

Go to Wiley's book companion site to complete the Task-Based Simulation.

CHAPTER 4

Corporate Taxation:

Distributions, Redemptions, and Liquidations

Andrey Popov/Adobe Stock

Before studying this chapter, you should know or, if necessary, review:

3.3 Corporate Taxable Income

Chapter Introduction

VIDEO CONTENT

Delta Consulting, Inc. was formed nine years ago by Olivia and Aiden to provide data analytics advice to businesses, including developing systems to capture and manage their data. Olivia and Aiden each invested $400,000 in Delta, and Delta borrowed an additional $900,000 in the first year of business. Delta has performed extremely well over the last nine years, so during that period there have been times that they each wanted to receive a distribution from Delta, including the following:

- In six of the nine years, they each received a cash dividend ranging from $5,000 to $38,000 each year.
- Four years ago, Olivia received a distribution of land from Delta.
- Three years ago, they each received a 40% stock dividend.
- Two years ago, Aiden sold 25% of her stock to Delta for $165,000.

In the current year, they are considering whether to liquidate Delta and form a new corporation, or sell their stock in Delta to a third party.

Transactions of this nature are common between corporations and its shareholders, and the resulting tax consequences can have significant influence on whether the transaction should be pursued. In this chapter, you will learn how such transactions are taxed to the corporation and the shareholders. When shareholders receive distributions from a corporation, the transactions can be classified as a dividend, redemption, or liquidation, as shown in the Illustration on the next page.

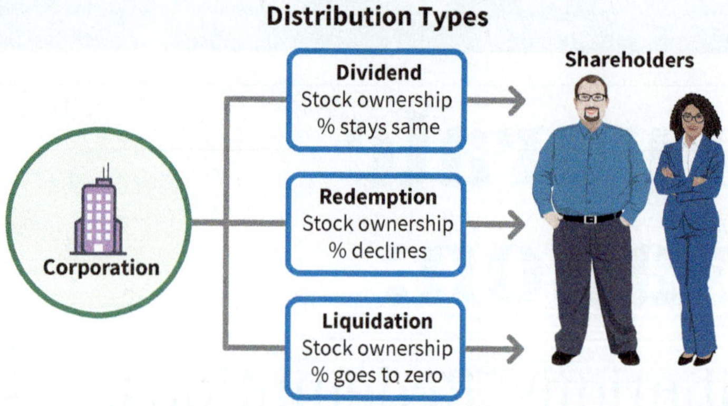

LEARNING OBJECTIVES	TOPICS	PRACTICE OPPORTUNITIES

1 Determine the tax consequences of shareholder distributions taxed as dividends.	**4.1 Distributions Taxed as Dividends**
	• Dividend Rules for Shareholders
	  • Qualified Dividend Income
	  • Evaluating the Tax Consequences for Shareholders of Dividend Distributions
	  • Stock Dividends
	  • Constructive Dividends
		• Example 4.1.1 Form 1099-DIV
		• Example 4.1.2 Dividend Record Date
		• Example 4.1.3 Qualified Dividend Income
		• Example 4.1.4 Dividends: Earnings & Profits and Basis
		• Example 4.1.5 Nontaxable Common Stock Dividend
		• Example 4.1.6 Preferred Stock Dividend
		• Example 4.1.7 Constructive Dividends
		• Practice Problem 4.1.1 Tax Consequences of a Dividend Distribution
		• Practice Problem 4.1.2 Stock Dividends and Basis

2 Evaluate a corporation's earnings and profits to determine the shareholder's dividend income from a corporate distribution.	**4.2 Earnings & Profits** • Earnings & Profits Computation • Using E&P to Determine the Amount of Dividends • Allocation of E&P to Distributions	• Example 4.2.1 E&P Computation • Example 4.2.2 Evaluating E&P • Example 4.2.3 Allocation of Accumulated E&P and Positive Current E&P • Example 4.2.4 Allocation of Accumulated E&P and Negative Current E&P • Practice Problem 4.2.1 Calculation of E&P • Practice Problem 4.2.2 Distribution with Deficit in Accumulated E&P • Practice Problem 4.2.3 Timing of Distributions

3 Determine the tax consequences of property distributions to the corporation and the shareholder.	**4.3 Property Distributions**
	• Property Distributions—Corporate Tax Consequences
	  • Recognition of Gain or Loss
	  • Effect of E&P
	• Property Distributions—Shareholder Tax Consequences
	• Property Distributions—Liability Greater than FMV
		• Example 4.3.1 Corporate Distribution of Appreciated Property
		• Example 4.3.2 Corporate Distribution of Loss Property
		• Example 4.3.3 Property Distributions—E&P
		• Example 4.3.4 Shareholder Consequences of Property Distributions
		• Example 4.3.5 Shareholder Consequences of Property Distributions—Liabilities Exceed FMV
		• Practice Problem 4.3.1 Distribution of Appreciated Property
		• Practice Problem 4.3.2 Effect of a Property Distribution
		• Practice Problem 4.3.3 Property Distribution's Effect on Earnings and Profits

LEARNING OBJECTIVES	TOPICS	PRACTICE OPPORTUNITIES

4 Compute the tax consequences of a redemption for a shareholder of a corporation.	**4.4 Stock Redemptions**
	• Redemption Consequences vs. Dividend Consequences
	• Qualified Redemptions
	  • Substantially Disproportionate Redemption
	  • Not Essentially Equivalent to a Dividend (NEED)
	  • Constructive Ownership of Stock
	• Advanced Topics—Drilling Down
	  • Reattribution
	  • Complete Termination of a Shareholder's Interest
	• Tax Consequences to Corporations
	  • Corporate Gain or Loss
	  • Earnings & Profits
	• Partial Liquidation
	  • Subjective Test for Partial Liquidation
	  • Objective Test for Partial Liquidation
	• Advanced Topic—Drilling Down
	  • Redemption Used to Pay Estate Taxes
		• Example 4.4.1 Redemption or Dividend
		• Example 4.4.2 Substantially Disproportionate Test
		• Example 4.4.3 Not Essentially Equivalent to a Dividend
		• Example 4.4.4 Family Attribution Rules
		• Example 4.4.5 Corporation to Shareholder Attribution
		• Example 4.4.6 Partnership to Partner Attribution
		• Example 4.4.7 Shareholder Attribution to Corporation
		• Example 4.4.8 Partner Attribution to Partnership
		• Example 4.4.9 Reattribution of Stock
		• Example 4.4.10 Complete Termination of Interest
		• Example 4.4.11 Tax Effects to Corporations for Qualified Redemptions—Gain
		• Example 4.4.12 Tax Effects to Corporations for Qualified Redemptions—Loss
		• Example 4.4.13 Partial Liquidation
		• Example 4.4.14 Redemption to Pay Estate Taxes
		• Practice Problem 4.4.1 Stock Redemption
		• Practice Problem 4.4.2 Constructive Ownership
		• Practice Problem 4.4.3 Stock Redemption Effect on E&P

5 Compute the tax consequences of a corporate liquidation for the shareholder and the corporation.	**4.5 Corporate Liquidations**
	• Tax Effects for Shareholders
	  • Related-Party Losses
	  • Liabilities Assumed by the Shareholder
	• Tax Effects for Corporations
	• Limitations on a Corporation's Loss Recognition
	  • Distributions of Loss Property to Related-Party Shareholders
	  • Distributions of Disqualified Property to Shareholders
	• Parent-Subsidiary Liquidations
		• Example 4.5.1 Shareholder's Gain or Loss on Liquidation
		• Example 4.5.2 Corporation's Gain or Loss on Liquidation
		• Example 4.5.3 Loss Disallowance to Corporations for Related-Party Distributions
		• Example 4.5.4 Loss Disallowance to Corporations for Distributions of Disqualified Property
		• Example 4.5.5 Liquidation of a Subsidiary
		• Practice Problem 4.5.1 Tax Consequences of a Liquidation
		• Practice Problem 4.5.2 Loss Recognition in Complete Liquidation

Tax Forms referenced in this chapter

Form 1040, Schedule B	Interest and Ordinary Dividends
Form 1099-DIV	Dividends and Distributions

4.1 Distributions Taxed as Dividends

LEARNING OBJECTIVE 1

Determine the tax consequences of shareholder distributions taxed as dividends.

VIDEO CONTENT

Aiden and Olivia each received six cash distributions from Delta during the last nine years. What are the typical tax consequences of distributions of this nature? Generally, the law taxes any distribution of cash or property from a corporation to its shareholders as **dividend** income if the distribution is made from the corporation's earnings and profits.[1] In this section, we first review the cash dividend rules for shareholders, and then we describe the tax consequences of *stock dividends* and *constructive dividends*.

Potential Pitfall

The definitions for ordinary and qualified dividends often create confusion when one reviews Form 1099-DIV (shown in **Illustration 4.1**), which is the form that corporations send to shareholders to report their dividend income for the year. Box 1a is for *Total Ordinary Dividends* and box 1b is for *Qualified Dividends*. The word *total* for box 1a means *all* dividends are shown in the box, even qualified dividends. Box 1b shows how much of the total ordinary dividends the shareholder treats as qualified dividends.

Dividend Rules for Shareholders

Ordinary dividends are taxed using two different rate structures:

- Regular **ordinary dividends** are distributions from a corporation's *earnings and profits* that are taxed at ordinary income rates.
- Ordinary dividends that are **qualified dividends** are taxed at long-term capital gain rates.

ILLUSTRATION 4.1 Form 1099-DIV

☐ CORRECTED (if checked)

PAYER'S name, street address, city or town, state or province, country, ZIP or foreign postal code, and telephone no. Netflix Los Gatos, CA 95030		1a Total ordinary dividends $ 2,200 1b Qualified dividends $ 1,500	OMB No. 1545-0110 Form **1099-DIV** (Rev. January 2024) For calendar year 2025	**Dividends and Distributions**
		2a Total capital gain distr. $	2b Unrecap. Sec. 1250 gain $	**Copy B** **For Recipient**
PAYER'S TIN 36-1234567	RECIPIENT'S TIN 123-45-6789	2c Section 1202 gain $	2d Collectibles (28%) gain $	
		2e Section 897 ordinary dividends $	2f Section 897 capital gain $	
RECIPIENT'S name Xavier James		3 Nondividend distributions $	**4 Federal income tax withheld** $	This is important tax information and is being furnished to the IRS. If you are required to file a return, a negligence penalty or other sanction may be imposed on you if this income is taxable and the IRS determines that it has not been reported.
Street address (including apt. no.) 100 South Street		5 Section 199A dividends $	6 Investment expenses $	
		7 Foreign tax paid $	8 Foreign country or U.S. possession	
City or town, state or province, country, and ZIP or foreign postal code Florence, AL 35630		9 Cash liquidation distributions $	10 Noncash liquidation distributions $	
	11 FATCA filing requirement ☐	12 Exempt-interest dividends $	13 Specified private activity bond interest dividends $	
Account number (see instructions)		14 State / 15 State identification no.	16 State tax withheld $ $	

Form **1099-DIV** (Rev. 1-2024) (keep for your records) www.irs.gov/Form1099DIV Department of the Treasury - Internal Revenue Service

[1]IRC §316.

EXAMPLE 4.1.1
Form 1099-DIV

Xavier James is a shareholder in Netflix. Assume that he received a Form 1099-DIV with the following information:

Total ordinary dividends, Box 1a	$2,200
Qualified dividends, Box 1b	$1,500

What is the total amount of Xavier's ordinary dividends? Of his qualified dividends?

SOLUTION

Xavier's total dividends (shown in Box 1a) are $2,200 for the year. Of this amount, $1,500 are qualified dividends (shown in Box 1b). He will pay tax using ordinary income rates on the difference of $700 ($2,200 total – $1,500 qualified). Illustration 4.1 shows how these dividends are reported on Form 1099-DIV.

To determine the tax implications of a corporate distribution to a shareholder, the company's earnings and profits need to be known. *Earnings and profits (E&P)* is the cumulative earnings for a corporation that it has never distributed as a dividend or a redemption.[2]

Dividends have three important dates: *declaration date*, *record date*, and the *payment date*, defined as follows:

- **Declaration date**: Date that a corporation announces it will pay a dividend, the amount of the dividend, and other important details.
- **Record date**: Date that a corporation determines who owns the stock for purposes of paying the dividend.
- **Payment date**: Date that a corporation pays a dividend.

Cash-basis taxpayers recognize income for dividends when received, while accrual-basis taxpayers do so as of the record date (see Tax Planning Tip).

Tax Planning Tip

Once a corporation declares a dividend and announces the record date, a shareholder who sells the stock before the record date will not receive the dividend on the payment date. Make sure your clients are aware of this so they can time the sale of their stock appropriately.

The **ex-dividend date** is the day after the record date. The stock begins trading on the ex-dividend date at a reduced price for the value of the dividend.

EXAMPLE 4.1.2
Dividend Record Date

Samuel, a cash-basis taxpayer, owns 100 shares of stock in NIU Corporation. The corporation declared a dividend of $1 per share on March 6 of the current tax year. Shareholders who own stock as of March 13, the record date, will be eligible to receive the dividend, which NIU will pay on March 20. Samuel sells his stock to Robin on March 14. Who receives the dividend, Samuel or Robin?

SOLUTION

On March 20, NIU will pay the dividend to Samuel because he was the shareholder of record on March 13. Samuel has dividend income as of March 20 because he is a cash-basis taxpayer.

Related exercise: Discussion Question 1

[2]IRC §312.

Other rules related to dividends are:

- Dividends issued by credit unions and mutual savings banks are taxed as interest income rather than dividend income.
- Mutual funds characterize their distributions as either ordinary dividends, qualified dividends, or capital gains. Taxpayers must treat capital gain distributions as long-term capital gains. You can find the capital gain distributions in box 2a of Form 1099-DIV (see Illustration 4.1).

Qualified Dividend Income

In this section, we take a closer look at qualified dividends. The major advantage of qualified dividends for individuals is that they are taxed at the same rates as long-term capital gains (LTCG) for individuals. The LTCG rate is 0% if the individual is in lower tax brackets, such as the 10% bracket. For higher tax brackets, such as the 37% bracket, the LTCG rate is 15% or 20%.[3]

Related exercises: Discussion Questions 2 and 3
Application Problem 1

> **Potential Pitfall**
> A taxpayer does not have to own stock for more than one year for a qualified dividend to be taxed at LTCG rates. The taxpayer just needs to meet the 61-day holding period rule.

To qualify for this lower LTCG rate, the dividend must satisfy two requirements:

1. Taxpayers must receive the dividend from a domestic corporation. Dividends from foreign corporations are eligible only if:
   - The foreign corporation's stock is tradable on an established U.S. securities market,
   - The foreign entity is incorporated in a U.S. possession, *or*
   - The foreign entity is incorporated in a country that has a treaty with the United States providing for qualified dividend treatment. More than 50 countries have such treaties, including Canada, China, Mexico, Switzerland, and the United Kingdom.[4]
2. Taxpayers must hold the stock for more than 60 days during the 121-day period beginning 60 days before the ex-dividend date.

The following Example illustrates the requirements for qualified dividend income.

EXAMPLE 4.1.3 Qualified Dividend Income

Terri purchases 200 shares of STY stock on January 7 of the current year. On February 1, STY declares a dividend of $2 per share that it will pay on February 28 to the shareholders of record on February 15. The ex-dividend date is February 16. How long must Terri hold her stock for the dividend to be considered qualified dividend income?

SOLUTION

Terri must hold the stock for more than 60 days during the 121-day period beginning on December 18, which is 60 days before the ex-dividend date (February 16) and ending April 16 of the current year for the dividend to be qualified. Terri's holding period begins on January 8, the day after she purchased the stock. As of February 16, she has owned the stock for 40 days. She must hold the stock until March 8 of the current year, 21 more days, to meet the 61-day holding period requirement for the dividend to qualify for long-term capital gain rates.

December 18	**February 16**	**April 16**
← 60 days →	1 day	← 60 days →
	121 days	

[3] IRC §1(h)(11).
[4] Notice 2011-64, 2011-37 IRB 231.

Evaluating the Tax Consequences for Shareholders of Dividend Distributions

Having received a dividend, the taxpayer must determine the tax consequences of the distribution. There are four steps in determining if dividend income should be taxed at ordinary income rates or long-term capital gain rates. **Illustration 4.2** provides a flow chart showing these steps.

Step 1. Determine: The fair market value of the cash and property distributed to the shareholder.

Step 2. Determine: To what extent the dividend distribution comes from the corporation's earnings and profits. You treat the distribution as dividend income to the extent of the corporation's earnings and profits. The dividend is taxed as ordinary income unless it is a qualified dividend, in which case it is taxed as long-term capital gain.

Potential Pitfall

Qualified dividends for individuals are *not* treated as LTCGs. That is, they are not included in the netting process of capital gains and losses. Rather, they are taxed at LTCG rates. Do not make the mistake of including them in the capital gain and loss netting process.

ILLUSTRATION 4.2 Determining the Taxation of Dividends

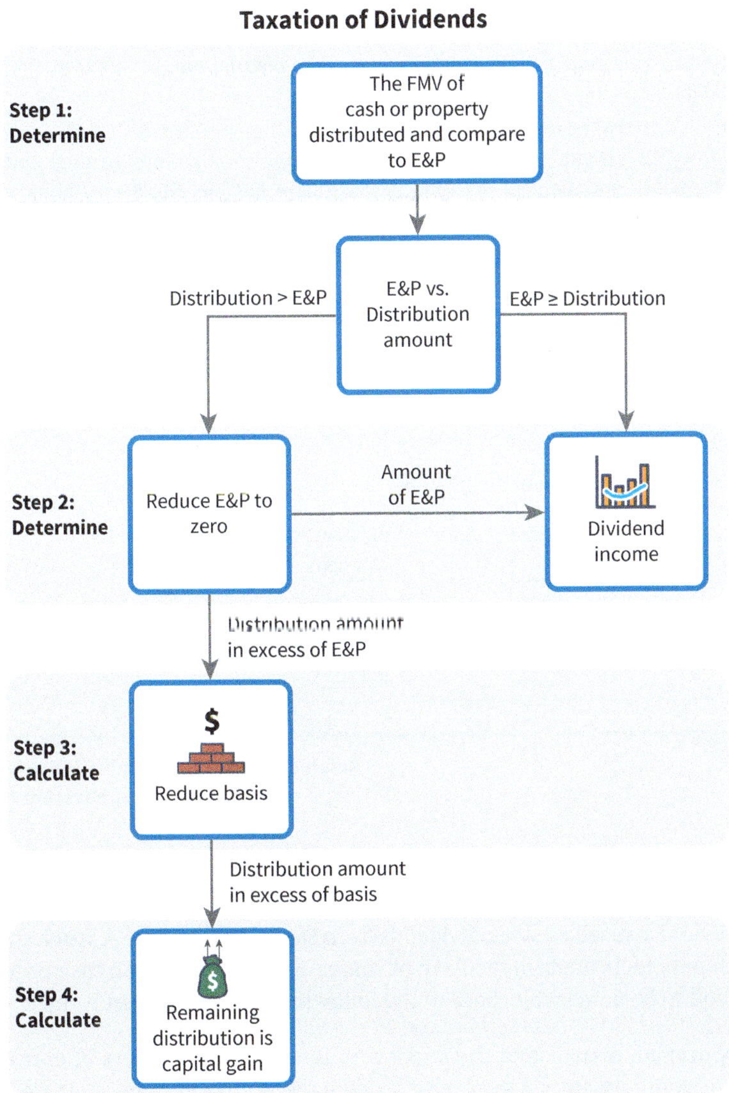

Step 3. **Calculate: The portion of the dividend distribution (if any) that exceeds a corporation's earnings and profits and reduces the shareholder's basis in the stock.**

Step 4. **Calculate: The portion of the dividend distribution (if any) that remains after the stock basis is reduced to zero.** Once a shareholder has reduced their stock basis to zero, the remaining amount of the distribution is a capital gain. It will be long-term capital gain if the shareholder has owned the stock for more than one year.

This four-step process for determining the taxation of distributions from corporations is demonstrated in the following Example.

EXAMPLE 4.1.4
Dividends: Earnings & Profits and Basis

Juan purchases 1,000 shares of stock in UTK, Inc., a domestic corporation, in Year 3 for $12,000. In January, Year 5, the corporation distributes $20,000 in cash to him. Juan's share of the corporation's earnings and profits at the end of Year 5 is $6,000. He still owns the stock at the end of Year 5. What are the tax effects of the $20,000 distribution?

SOLUTION

To determine the tax effects of Juan's dividend distribution, we follow the steps outlined in Illustration 4.2:

Step 1. First, we determine the fair market value of the distribution. In this case, the value is $20,000.

Step 2. Next, we determine to what extent the dividend income comes from UTK's earnings and profits. Juan's dividend income, to the extent of the corporation's earnings and profits, is $6,000. It is a qualified dividend because Juan has met the 61-day holding period requirement and the stock is from a domestic corporation.

Step 3. Next, we calculate the portion of the dividend distribution (if any) that exceeds UTK's earnings and profits and use it to reduce the basis in the stock. Here, the remaining $14,000 of the dividend distribution reduces Juan's basis in the stock from $12,000 to zero.

Step 4. Finally, we calculate the portion of the dividend distribution (if any) that remains after the stock basis is reduced to zero. After Juan reduces his stock basis to zero, there is still $2,000 remaining from the distribution. Juan treats this remainder ($2,000) as a long-term capital gain because Juan has owned the stock for more than one year.

Here is the complete calculation of all the steps:

Step 1	$20,000
Step 2	(6,000)
Step 3	14,000
Step 4	(12,000)
LTCG	$ 2,000

Related exercises: Multiple Choice Question 1
Application Problem 2

Stock Dividends

Aiden and Olivia also received stock dividends from Delta Corporation. A **stock dividend** is a payment to shareholders made in the form of shares of stock rather than cash or property. For a stock dividend to be nontaxable, both of the following conditions must be met:[5]

1. **The corporation must issue the stock dividend to only holders of common stock.** Holders of common stock can receive a dividend of either common or preferred stock and the dividend is nontaxable. A stock dividend paid to preferred stock shareholders is always taxable.

[5]IRC §305.

2. **The stock dividend must be proportionate.** This means that all shareholders receive the same percentage of the stock dividend as the percentage of stock they currently own. For example, if every shareholder receives a 15% stock dividend, meaning 15% of the current number of shares owned by each individual shareholder, this is a proportionate dividend.

Related exercises: Discussion Question 4
Brief Exercise 1

Other rules regarding stock dividends are as follows:

- The existence of an option to receive cash in lieu of stock (whether exercised or not) triggers recognition of dividend income.
- A nontaxable stock dividend requires the taxpayer to adjust the basis per share of their stock. The total basis of the stock remains the same, but the basis per share decreases because the number of shares owned has increased.

Related exercise: Application Problem 3

Why **Why are most stock dividends not taxable?** Most stock dividends are not taxable because corporations ensure that they meet the rules stated above. Shareholders do not receive an increase in their net worth by receiving a proportionate stock dividend. Assume that you and 19 of your classmates each own five shares of stock in GameGo Corporation and the total number of shares outstanding are 100. Each shareholder owns 5% of the corporation. The current value is $10 per share, which means the total value of your holdings is $50. GameGo declares a 20% stock dividend, meaning that each shareholder receives one additional share of stock (5 shares × 20% = 1 share). Now, you and your classmates own six shares each, but you each still own 5% of the company (6 shares/120 shares = 5%). The value of the shares will drop proportionately to $8.333 per share ($10 × 5/6), because nothing has happened to change the value of the company. The value of your shares is still $50 ($8.33 × 6 shares). Thus, the stock dividend did not increase your wealth, so there should not be any taxable income.

The following Example discusses the tax implications for stock dividends.

EXAMPLE 4.1.5
Nontaxable Common Stock Dividend

Moses owns 50 shares in UAB Corporation purchased at a cost of $10 per share ($500 total). He received an additional 30 shares as a nontaxable stock dividend. What are the tax implications for Moses on this stock dividend?

SOLUTION

Moses's total stock basis of $500 does not increase because he has not recognized any income as a result of the stock dividend. His basis per share, however, is now $6.25 ($500 divided by 80 shares).

A common stock shareholder who receives a nontaxable preferred stock dividend must allocate the basis of the original stock between the common shares and the preferred shares based on their fair market values, using the following formulas:

For Common Stock

$$\text{Basis in common stock} \times \frac{\text{FMV common shares}}{\text{FMV preferred shares} + \text{FMV common shares}} = \text{Common stock allocation}$$

$$\text{New basis per share in common stock} = \frac{\text{Common stock allocation}}{\text{Number of common shares}}$$

For Preferred Stock

$$\text{Basis in preferred stock} \times \frac{\text{FMV preferred shares}}{\text{FMV preferred shares} + \text{FMV common shares}} = \text{Preferred stock allocation}$$

$$\text{New basis per share in preferred stock} = \frac{\text{Preferred stock allocation}}{\text{Number of preferred shares}}$$

We apply these formulas in the following Example.

EXAMPLE 4.1.6
Preferred Stock Dividend

Ted acquired 100 shares of MU Corporation common stock in Year 2 for $12,000. In Year 7, he received a nontaxable distribution of 10 MU Corporation preferred shares. On the date of distribution, the FMV of Ted's 100 common shares was $15,000, and the FMV of his 10 new preferred shares was $5,000. How does Ted allocate the basis of his original stock between his common and preferred shares?

SOLUTION

Ted allocates the $12,000 basis to the preferred and common shares as follows.

$$\text{Preferred stock} = \$12{,}000 \times \frac{\$5{,}000}{\$5{,}000 + \$15{,}000} = \$3{,}000$$

Basis is $300 per share ($3,000/10).

$$\text{Common stock} = \$12{,}000 \times \frac{\$15{,}000}{\$5{,}000 + \$15{,}000} = \$9{,}000$$

Basis is $90 per share ($9,000/100).

Related exercises: Multiple Choice Question 2
Application Problem 4

Tax Planning Tip

When a company declares a stock dividend, it should always be proportionate to ensure that it is tax-free. The corporation should not give any shareholder the opportunity to receive cash or some other benefit in lieu of the additional shares of the stock if it wants the stock dividend to be tax-free. If just one shareholder receives a benefit other than shares of stock, that shareholder's ownership percentage will decrease, and the percentage will increase for every shareholder who receives additional shares. The stock dividend would then not be proportionate, and it would be taxable for all shareholders.[6]

Related exercise: Application Problem 5

Constructive Dividends

Constructive dividends are benefits paid to shareholders in a form other than cash, property, or stock with no expectation of repayment.[7] The law treats these benefits as ordinary income. Constructive dividends include:

- Shareholders' use of company aircraft or other corporate assets for personal reasons.
- Shareholders' sale of assets to the corporation above their fair market value.
- Shareholders' receipt of an amount greater than fair market value for services provided to the corporation.
- Amounts paid to a family member that were in excess of the value of services the family member rendered.
- Payment by a corporation of expenses of a shareholder without expectation of repayment.
- An advance to a shareholder that is not a *bona fide* loan.

[6]Even if a shareholder chooses to receive stock and not the other benefit, the dividend is taxable for all shareholders because the shareholder *had the opportunity* not to receive stock.

[7]*Wortham Machinery Co v. U.S.*, (1975, CA10) 36 AFTR 2d 75-5607, 521 F2d 160, 75-2 USTC ¶9665.

The constructive dividend rules also apply to family members of shareholders. The tax law defines family members as the shareholder's spouse, children, grandchildren, and parents.[8] The dividend is taxed to the shareholder even if the family member receives all the economic benefit.

At times, a corporation provides benefits such as those listed above to shareholders but do not treat them as a dividend, often because they do not realize that the benefit should be treated as a dividend. If the IRS reclassifies the benefit as a dividend, the shareholder recognizes ordinary income, and the corporation does not receive a deduction for the outlay because dividends are not deductible by corporations.

Related exercises: Multiple Choice Question 3
Application Problem 6

The next Example explores the tax implications of constructive dividends.

EXAMPLE 4.1.7
Constructive Dividends

April is a 30% shareholder in UNA Corporation. Her daughter's family uses the corporate condominium in Colorado for a two-week ski vacation. The normal rental rate for the condo during ski season is $2,500 per week. What are the tax implications of this event for April?

SOLUTION

April has received a $5,000 constructive dividend (2 weeks × market rental rate of $2,500 per week).

Tax Return Guidance

- **Corporations report dividends to the taxpayer annually on Form 1099-DIV.**
- **Taxpayers must use Schedule B if either interest or dividends exceed $1,500. Otherwise, they report the dividends only on Form 1040, line 3. The amount of total dividends is reported on line 3b and the amount representing qualified dividends is reported of line 3a.**
- **If total dividends exceed $1,500, the taxpayer must complete a series of questions in Part III about whether the taxpayer earns dividends from foreign accounts.**

PRACTICE PROBLEM 4.1.1
Tax Consequences of a Dividend Distribution

Darshanna owns 100% of Utica, Inc., a domestic corporation, which she purchased 11 months ago on January 31 for $1,000. Utica, Inc. pays a cash dividend on December 31 to Darshanna of $3,750 when Utica's earnings and profits (E&P) were $1,800. What is the tax effect to Darshanna from the receipt of the cash dividend?

SOLUTION

To determine the tax effects of Darshanna's dividend distribution, we follow the Steps outlined in Illustration 4.2:

Step 1: The fair market value of the distribution is $3,750.

Step 2: This is treated as dividend income to the extent of the corporation's earnings and profits, which is $1,800. It is a qualified dividend because the 61-day holding period requirement is met and the dividend is from a domestic corporation.

Step 3: The remaining $1,950 of the distribution reduces the basis of the stock, but not below zero. Darshanna's basis is $1,000, and it is reduced to zero.

Step 4: The remainder of the distribution, $950, is treated as short-term capital gain because Darshanna has owned the stock for less than one year.

---

[8]IRC §318(a)(1).

PRACTICE PROBLEM 4.1.2
Stock Dividends and Basis

Elsa and Anna each own a percentage of Frozen Enterprises. Elsa owns 25% (250 shares of the 1,000 common shares outstanding) and Anna owns 75% (750 shares). Elsa has a stock basis of $2,500 and Anna has a stock basis of $7,500. Frozen Enterprises declares a proportionate, 100% common stock dividend.

a. Is this a taxable event for Elsa and Anna?

b. What is the tax basis of each share of Frozen Enterprises stock now held by Elsa and Anna?

SOLUTION

a. Because the stock distribution is pro rata to the shareholders and is paid to common stock shareholders, it is not a taxable event to Elsa and Anna.

b. Elsa's original stock basis was $2,500 for 250 shares. It is now divided among 500 shares providing Elsa with a per share basis of $5 ($2,500/500). Anna's original stock basis was $7,500 for 750 shares. It is now divided among 1,500 shares providing Anna with a per share basis of $5 ($7,500/1,500).

INTERACTIVE SELF-SCORING QUIZZES

4.2 Earnings & Profits

LEARNING OBJECTIVE 2

Evaluate a corporation's earnings and profits to determine the shareholder's dividend income from a corporate distribution.

VIDEO CONTENT

In this section, we discuss earnings and profits (E&P) in more detail and explain four areas of the dividend rules that affect corporations:

- The computation of earnings and profits (E&P).
- The manner in which *accumulated E&P* and *current E&P* impacts the amount of the distribution that is classified as a dividend.
- How the tax consequences of property distributions vary from cash distributions.
- The effect of the distribution on E&P.

Returning to the chapter introduction, Olivia and Aiden will need to know Delta's E&P to determine the consequences of the distributions they received.

Earnings & Profits Computation

Earnings and profits (E&P) is the cumulative earnings for a corporation that it has never distributed as a dividend or a redemption. Conceptually, E&P is very similar to retained earnings, but it is computed based on the tax law rather than financial reporting rules. Earnings and profits is a corporate-level account, not a shareholder account. There are two types of E&P:

- **Accumulated E&P** is the E&P as of the beginning of the tax year.
- **Current E&P** is the E&P generated during the tax year.

Current E&P is computed by adjusting taxable income for tax items that are treated differently for purpose of taxable income versus E&P. In determining these adjustments, you should remember that E&P represents the corporation's ability to pay a dividend.[9] Depreciation

[9]Treas. Reg. §1.316-2.

expense for E&P purposes is computed using the straight-line method under the alternate depreciation system (ADS). Bonus depreciation is not allowed for computing E&P. Section 179 expenses are taken into account for E&P on a pro rata basis over five years.

Differences between taxable income and E&P fall into four distinct categories.[10]

1. Expenses deducted for taxable income that do not reduce E&P are added back to taxable income:
   - The dividends received deduction (DRD) does not represent a cash outlay, so it is added back to taxable income.
   - MACRS tax depreciation in excess of depreciation allowed for E&P.
   - The amount deducted under Section 179 for regular tax must be deducted ratably over five years for computing E&P. For the year Section 179 is claimed, 80% of that amount must be added back to taxable income.
   - Bonus depreciation is not allowed when computing E&P.
   - Deductions claimed for charitable contribution and capital loss carryforwards from previous years must be added back to taxable income (because these items reduced E&P in the year they first occurred).
2. Income items not included in taxable income that are included in E&P are added back to taxable income:
   - Municipal interest income
   - Proceeds from corporate life insurance policy (less cash surrender value)
   - Deferred portion of gain from a current installment sale.
3. Income items included in taxable income that are not included in E&P are subtracted from taxable income:
   - Income recognized this year from an installment sale that occurred in a prior year.
4. Expenses not deducted for taxable income that do reduce E&P are subtracted from taxable income:
   - Federal income tax (net of credits)
   - Related party losses
   - Penalties and fines
   - Lobbying expenses
   - Life insurance premiums for a policy on corporate-owned policies for executives or officers
   - Entertainment expenses
   - Disallowed portion of business meals
   - E&P depreciation in excess of MACRS depreciation
   - Net capital losses
   - Charitable contributions that exceed the 10% of taxable income limit
   - 20% of the original Section 179 expense for years two through five that the expense is being ratably deducted for E&P.

Rather than memorizing the list above, as long as you understand that E&P measures the capacity of the corporation to pay a dividend, you can compute E&P using the following steps:

Step 1. Ask: Is the item treated differently for computing taxable income versus E&P? If the answer is NO, then the tax item is not included as an adjustment. If the answer is YES, then proceed to step 2.

Step 2. Determine: Whether the adjustment increases or decreases E&P. This step is sometimes confusing to students. To avoid mistakes, follow the logic of the diagram in Illustration 4.3. In this illustration, we provide one example for each of the four situations that can result in an adjustment.

> **Potential Pitfall**
>
> Earnings and profits can be negative if the corporation has had losses. However, a distribution can never create a loss in E&P or make a loss larger.

[10] IRC §312.

ILLUSTRATION 4.3 Schedule M-1 Adjustments

Determining the Direction of Schedule M-1 Adjustments				
Category	**Example**	**Is this included in taxable income computation?**	**Should it impact E&P?**	**Adjustment needed to taxable income**
1. Expenses deducted for taxable income	Dividends received deduction	Yes	No (not a cash outlay so does not reduce ability to pay a dividend)	Positive (increase taxable income for the DRD)
2. Income items *not* included in taxable income	Municipal interest income	No	Yes (funds are available to pay a dividend)	Positive (increase taxable income for the municipal interest income)
3. Income items included in taxable income that are *not* included in E&P	Income this year from a prior year's installment sale	Yes	No (this income was included in E&P in year of sale)	Negative (decrease taxable income for this income)
4. Expenses *not* deducted for taxable income that *do* reduce E&P	Federal tax expense	No	Yes (funds are not available to pay a dividend)	Negative (decrease taxable income for the amount of the expense)

The following Example illustrates how a corporation adjusts taxable income to compute E&P.

EXAMPLE 4.2.1
E&P Computation

XYZ, Inc. has taxable income of $339,000 and is an accrual-basis taxpayer. Compute XYZ's E&P given the information below for the current tax year:

Federal income tax	$55,000
E&P depreciation	$41,000
Tax depreciation	$56,000
Dividend income	$18,000
Dividends received deduction	$ 9,000
Net capital loss	$ 7,000
Municipal interest income	$ 4,000
Charitable contributions in excess of 10% limit	$ 6,000
Entertainment expenses	$ 2,000
Installment sale income received from a sale that occurred last year	$10,000

SOLUTION

XYZ's E&P is computed as follows, beginning with taxable income:

Taxable income	$339,000
• **Plus:** Expenses deducted for taxable income that do not reduce E&P:	
Dividends received deduction	$ 9,000
Tax depreciation in excess of E&P depreciation ($56,000 – $41,000)	$ 15,000
• **Plus:** Income items not included in taxable income that are included in E&P:	
Municipal interest income	$ 4,000
• ***Less***: Income items included in taxable income that are not included in E&P:	
Installment sale income received from a sale that occurred last year	($ 10,000)
• ***Less:*** Expenses not deducted for taxable income that do reduce E&P:	
Federal income tax expense	($ 55,000)
Excess capital loss	($ 7,000)
Charitable contributions in excess of 10% limit	($ 6,000)
Entertainment expenses	($ 2,000)
Earnings & Profits	$287,000

An adjustment is not needed for dividends received because they are included in taxable income and E&P.

Related exercises: Discussion Questions 5, 6
Multiple Choice Questions 4, 5
Brief Exercise 2
Application Problem 7

Using E&P to Determine the Amount of Dividends

Once E&P is computed, both current and accumulated E&P are used to determine whether a distribution is a dividend. E&P is negative if the corporation has had losses in the past and/or in the current year. Recall that distributions can never create or increase a deficit in E&P. Because E&P can be positive or negative, there are four different combinations of E&P that can occur, as we discuss below.

	Accumulated E&P	Current E&P
Scenario #1	Positive	Positive
Scenario #2	Negative	Negative
Scenario #3	Negative	Positive
Scenario #4	Positive	Negative

Scenario #1—Accumulated E&P: Positive/Current E&P: Positive. The distribution is taxed as dividend income to the extent of the total of both. Once current E&P is depleted, then distributions reduce accumulated E&P.

Scenario #2—Accumulated E&P: Negative/Current E&P: Negative. A distribution is a return of capital, meaning that it is tax-free up to the shareholder's adjusted basis of their stock, with any excess treated as a capital gain. None of the distribution is taxed as dividend income.

Scenario #3—Accumulated E&P: Negative/Current E&P: Positive. A distribution is a dividend only to the extent of current E&P.

Scenario #4—Accumulated E&P: Positive/Current E&P: Negative. The accumulated and current E&P are netted. If the net amount is positive, the distribution is a dividend to that extent. If the net amount is a negative, then none of the distribution is taxed as dividend income.

EXAMPLE 4.2.2
Evaluating E&P

Aletta owns 100% of DEF Corporation and she receives a distribution of $40,000 in the current tax year. This is the only distribution made by DEF this year. Aletta purchased her stock five years ago for $13,000. Determine Aletta's tax consequences for each of the scenarios below.

	Accumulated E&P	Current E&P
Scenario #1	$30,000	$15,000
Scenario #2	($30,000)	($15,000)
Scenario #3	($30,000)	$15,000
Scenario #4	$30,000	($21,000)

SOLUTION

- **Scenario #1**—The total E&P available is $45,000 ($30,000 + $15,000), so the $40,000 distribution is taxed as dividend income. The accumulated E&P as of the beginning of next year is $5,000 ($45,000 – $40,000).
- **Scenario #2**—Because both accumulated and current E&P are negative, none of the distribution is taxed as dividend income. The first $13,000 of the distribution reduces the basis in Aletta's stock to zero and is not taxable. The remaining $27,000 ($40,000 – $13,000) of the distribution is a long-term capital gain because she has owned the stock for more than one year. Accumulated E&P as of the beginning of the next tax year is ($45,000).
- **Scenario #3**—Because accumulated E&P is negative and current E&P is positive, the distribution is taxed as dividend income to the extent of the current E&P of $15,000. This reduces the current E&P to zero. The remaining $25,000 of the distribution ($40,000 – $15,000) is treated as a return of capital of $13,000 and reduces the basis of her stock to zero. This $13,000 is not taxable. The remaining distribution of $12,000 ($25,000 – $13,000) is taxed as long-term capital gain. The accumulated E&P as of the beginning of next year is ($30,000). Note that a distribution does not increase the amount of negative E&P.
- **Scenario #4**—When accumulated E&P is positive and current E&P is negative, they are netted together which results in positive E&P of $9,000. The distribution is taxed as dividend income to the extent of $9,000. This reduces the accumulated E&P to zero as of the beginning of the next tax year. The remaining $31,000 of the distribution ($40,000 – $9,000) is treated as a return of capital of $13,000 and reduces the basis of her stock to zero. This $13,000 is not taxable. The remaining distribution of $18,000 ($31,000 – $13,000) is taxed as long-term capital gain.

Related exercises: Brief Exercise 3
Application Problems 8, 9, 10, 11, 12

Allocation of E&P to Distributions

The manner in which E&P is allocated to distributions varies based on whether the E&P is:

- Accumulated or current, *and*
- Positive or negative.

The following rules are used for these allocations:[11]

- Accumulated E&P is always used in chronological order.
- A positive current E&P balance is prorated among the distributions based on the amount of the distributions.
- A deficit in current E&P is allocated ratably during the year based on time, even if there is only one distribution for the year.
- When more than one shareholder receives a distribution, E&P is allocated to the shareholders based on their proportionate ownership of the corporation.

Potential Pitfall

Do not confuse the allocation rules for *positive* current E&P (allocated based on amount of distributions) and *negative* current E&P (allocated based on time).[12]

[11] Treas. Reg. §1.316-2.

[12] Assume that a corporation has one distribution during the year of $20,000 made on June 30. If the corporation has positive current E&P of $25,000, all the current E&P would be allocated to that distribution because it was the only distribution during the year. However, if the corporation has negative current E&P of $25,000 for the year, only $12,500 of the negative current E&P would be allocated to it because the distribution was made six months into the year. Had the distribution been made on December 31 of the year, then the entire $25,000 of negative current E&P would be allocated to the distribution.

The following two Examples illustrate the application of these allocation rules.

EXAMPLE 4.2.3 Allocation of Accumulated E&P and Positive Current E&P

Santanu owns 60% of BCD Corporation, a calendar-year corporation, and Joy owns the remaining 40%. They have each owned their stock for 4 years. Santanu has a basis in his stock of $60,000 and Joy's basis is $10,000. As of January 1, accumulated E&P was $50,000. Current E&P this year is $20,000. Santanu and Joy receive the following distributions this year:

	Total	Santanu	Joy
March 1	$ 70,000	$42,000	$28,000
October 15	30,000	18,000	12,000
Total	$100,000	$60,000	$40,000

How are these distributions taxed to Santanu and Joy?

SOLUTION

The accumulated E&P is allocated chronologically to the distributions, so all the $50,000 of accumulated E&P is allocated to the March distribution of $70,000. The current E&P is allocated based on the amount of the distributions, so $14,000 ($70,000/$100,000 × $20,000) is allocated to the March distribution, and $6,000 ($30,000/$100,000) is allocated to the October distribution. Earning and profits must also be allocated proportionately to Santanu and Joy based on their stock ownership (60% and 40%, respectively). The allocations are summarized as follows:

	Total E&P		Santanu (60%)			Joy (40%)		
	Accumulated	Current	Accumulated	Current	Total	Accumulated	Current	Total
March 1	$50,000	$14,000	$30,000	$ 8,400	$38,400	$20,000	$5,600	$25,600
October 15	0	6,000	0	3,600	3,600	0	2,400	2,400
Total	$50,000	$20,000	$30,000	$12,000	$42,000	$20,000	$8,000	$28,000

The tax consequences to Santanu are as follows:

Santanu	**March 1**	**October 15**		**Stock basis**
Distribution	$42,000	$18,000	Distribution	$60,000
Dividend income to extent of E&P	(38,400)	(3,600)		
	$ 3,600	$14,400		
Recovery of basis	(3,600)	(14,400)	Recovery of basis	(18,000)
Capital gain	$ 0	$ 0	Basis	$42,000

For the March distribution, Santanu has $38,400 of dividend income and a recovery of basis of $3,600. For the October distribution, Santanu has $3,600 of dividend income and a recovery of basis of $14,400. His stock basis after both distributions is $42,000.

The tax consequences to Joy are as follows:

Joy	**March 1**	**October 15**		**Stock basis**
Distribution	$28,000	$12,000	Distribution	$10,000
Dividend income to extent of E&P	(25,600)	(2,400)		
	$ 2,400	$ 9,600		
Recovery of basis	(2,400)	(7,600)	Recovery of basis	(10,000)
Capital gain	$ 0	$ 2,000	Basis	$ 0

For the March distribution, Joy has $25,600 of dividend income and a recovery of basis of $2,400. For the October distribution, Joy has $2,400 of dividend income and a recovery of basis of $7,600. She has a capital gain of $2,000 that is long-term because she has owned her stock for more than one year. Her stock basis after both distributions is $0.

EXAMPLE 4.2.4 Allocation of Accumulated E&P and Negative Current E&P

Assume the same facts as in Example 4.2.3, except that the current E&P has a deficit of $20,000. Santanu and Joy receive the following distributions this year:

	Total	Santanu	Joy
March 1	$ 70,000	$42,000	$28,000
October 15	30,000	18,000	12,000
Total	$100,000	$60,000	$40,000

How are these distributions taxed to Santanu and Joy?

SOLUTION

The accumulated E&P is allocated chronologically to the distributions, so all of the $50,000 of accumulated E&P is allocated to the March distribution of $50,000. The current E&P is allocated based on the time of the year that the distribution was made, as follows:

March 1 distribution was made two month after the beginning of the tax year:

$$2 \text{ months}/12 \text{ months} \times (\$20,000) = (\$3,333)$$

October 15 distribution was made 7.5 months after the March distribution:

$$7.5 \text{ months}/12 \text{ months} \times (\$20,000) = (\$12,500)$$

The remaining ($4,167) of the current E&P is not allocated to a distribution. Earning and profits must also be allocated proportionately to Santanu and Joy based on their stock ownership (60% and 40%, respectively). The allocations are summarized as follows:

	Total E&P		Santanu (60%)			Joy (40%)		
	Accumulated	Current	Accumulated	Current	Total	Accumulated	Current	Total
March 1	$50,000	($ 3,333)	$30,000	($2,000)	$28,000	$20,000	($1,333)	$18,667
October 15	0	(12,500)	0	(7,500)	(7,500)	0	(5,000)	(5,000)
Total	$50,000	($15,833)	$30,000	($9,500)	$20,500	$20,000	($6,333)	$13,667

The tax consequences to Santanu are as follows:

Santanu	March 1	October 15		Stock basis
Distribution	$42,000	$ 18,000	Distribution	$60,000
Dividend income to extent of E&P	(28,000)	(0)		
	$14,000	$ 18,000		
Recovery of basis	(14,000)	(18,000)	Recovery of basis	(32,000)
Capital gain	$ 0	$ 0	Basis	$28,000

For the March distribution, Santanu has $28,000 of dividend income and a recovery of basis of $14,000. For the October distribution, Santanu has no dividend income and a recovery of basis of $18,000. His stock basis after both distributions is $28,000.

The tax consequences to Joy are as follows:

Joy	March 1	October 15		Stock basis
Distribution	$28,000	$12,000	Distribution	$10,000
Dividend income to extent of E&P	(18,667)	(0)		
	$ 9,333	$12,000		
Recovery of basis	(9,333)	(667)	Recovery of basis	(10,000)
Capital gain	$ 0	$11,333	Basis	$ 0

For the March distribution, Joy has $18,667 of dividend income and a recovery of basis of $9,333. For the October distribution, Joy has no dividend income and a recovery of basis of $667. She has a capital gain of $11,333 that is long-term because she has owned her stock for more than one year. Her stock basis after both distributions is $0.

Related exercises: Application Problems 13, 14

PRACTICE PROBLEM 4.2.1
Calculation of E&P

Drummond, Inc. has taxable income of $482,000 and is an accrual-basis taxpayer. Compute Drummond's earnings and profits given the following information for the current year:

Federal income tax	$102,000
E&P depreciation	$ 36,000
Tax depreciation	$ 19,000
Charitable contributions in excess of 10% limit	$ 3,300
Municipal interest income	$ 2,200
Dividends received deduction	$ 10,000
Net capital losses	$ 2,500
Proceeds from corporate owned life insurance policy	$100,000
Life insurance premiums paid on a corporate owned policy on executives and officers	$ 2,400

SOLUTION

Drummond's E&P is computed as follows, beginning with taxable income:

Taxable income		$482,000
Plus: Expenses deductible for taxable income that do not reduce E&P:		
Dividends received deduction	$10,000	$ 10,000
Plus: Income items not included in taxable income that are included in E&P:		
Municipal interest income	$2,200	
Proceeds from corporate life insurance policy	100,000	$102,200
Less: Expenses not deducted for taxable income but do reduce E&P:		
Federal income tax expense	$102,000	
E&P depreciation in excess of tax depreciation ($36,000 − $19,000)	17,000	
Charitable contributions in excess of 10%	3,300	
Net capital losses	2,500	
Life insurance premiums paid on a corporate owned policy on executives and officers	2,400	($127,200)
Earnings and profits		$467,000

PRACTICE PROBLEM 4.2.2
Distribution with Deficit in Accumulated E&P

At the beginning of the current year, Shaker, Inc., an accrual-basis C corporation, had a $58,000 deficit in earnings and profits (E&P). For the current year, Shaker had E&P of $22,000 and made a $34,000 cash distribution to its stockholders. What amount of the distribution is taxable as dividend income to Shaker's stockholders?

SOLUTION

Corporate distributions to shareholders are taxable to the shareholder as dividend income to the extent of E&P, current and accumulated. Distributions in excess of E&P are treated as return of capital that are nontaxable unless the distribution exceeds the shareholder's basis in their stock. Because Shaker had current E&P of $22,000, the shareholders will report dividend income of $22,000. The remaining $12,000 of the distribution is treated as a return of capital because accumulated E&P is negative. You do not net current E&P and accumulated E&P in this scenario.

PRACTICE PROBLEM 4.2.3
Timing of Distributions

Periwinkle Corporation is a calendar-year, accrual-basis corporation. Periwinkle had a deficit in current E&P of $18,000 for January 1 through June 30 and a positive E&P of $29,000 from July 1 through December 31. Periwinkle Corporation made a distribution of $8,000 on July 1 of the current year. What amount of the distribution is classified as dividend income to Periwinkle's shareholders?

SOLUTION

Although Periwinkle Corporation had a deficit in E&P on the date of the distribution (July 1), the E&P on this date is irrelevant. Instead, we look at Periwinkle's current E&P as of December 31 to determine if current E&P is positive or negative for the year. Because Periwinkle has positive E&P on December 31 of $11,000 ($29,000 – $18,000), the $11,000 is allocated to the July 1 distribution because it was the only distribution made this year. Therefore, the entire $8,000 distribution is reported as dividend income.

INTERACTIVE SELF-SCORING QUIZZES

4.3 Property Distributions

LEARNING OBJECTIVE 3

Determine the tax consequences of property distributions to the corporation and the shareholder.

VIDEO CONTENT

Returning to Olivia in the introduction, she received a distribution of land four years ago. If property other than cash or stock is distributed to shareholders as a dividend, there are additional rules to know to determine the tax consequence. In this section, we address these rules for both the corporation and the shareholder.

Property Distributions—Corporate Tax Consequences

There are two primary implications to corporations for property distributions:

- the potential for the recognition of gain or loss, *and*
- the effect on E&P.

Recognition of Gain or Loss

If a corporation distributes appreciated property to a shareholder, it is treated as if the corporation sold the property for its fair market value, and the realized gain from the sale is recognized. However, if the corporation distributes property that has a fair market value *less* than its adjusted basis, the corporation *cannot* recognize a loss.[13]

Tax Planning Tip

An important phrase to remember with corporate distributions of property is *gains but not losses*. The corporation recognizes gains for distributions of appreciated property, but cannot recognize losses for property that would have a realized loss if sold. Therefore, corporations should not distribute loss property because the loss disappears. Rather, the corporation should sell the property so it can recognize the loss, and then it can distribute the cash from the sale to the shareholders as a dividend.

[13] IRC §311(a) and (b).

The next two Examples illustrate these rules for corporation property distributions.

EXAMPLE 4.3.1
Corporate Distribution of Appreciated Property

NOP Corporation owns land with a fair market value of $100,000 and an adjusted basis of $73,000. There is a mortgage attached to the land of $60,000. If NOP distributes the land to a shareholder and the shareholder assumes the mortgage, how much gain, if any, is recognized by NOP?

SOLUTION

Because NOP distributed land, it is treated as if NOP sold the land for its fair market value, as follows:

Amount realized	$100,000
(Adjusted basis)	(73,000)
Realized gain	$ 27,000

NOP must recognize the gain of $27,000.

Related exercises: Multiple Choice Question 6
Application Problem 15

EXAMPLE 4.3.2
Corporate Distribution of Loss Property

NOP Corporation owns land with a fair market value of $65,000 and an adjusted basis of $73,000. There is a mortgage attached to the land of $60,000. If NOP distributes the land to a shareholder and the shareholder assumes the mortgage, what is the amount of the distribution to the shareholder and how much gain, if any, is recognized by NOP?

SOLUTION

The amount distributed to the shareholder is $5,000, which is the fair market value of $65,000 reduced by the $60,000 mortgage assumed by the shareholder. Because NOP distributed land, it is treated as if NOP sold the land for its fair market value, as follows:

Amount realized	$65,000
(Adjusted basis)	(73,000)
Realized loss	($ 8,000)

NOP cannot recognize the realized loss of $8,000. The tax benefit of the loss is permanently lost.

Related exercises: Discussion Questions 7, 8
Application Problems 16, 17, 18
Tax Planning Problem 1

Effect on E&P

When a corporation distributes property as a dividend, E&P is reduced by the *greater* of the adjusted basis or fair market value of the property.[14] If there is a liability attached to the property that the shareholder assumes, this amount is reduced by the amount of the liability. So, the formula for the E&P reduction is:

(Greater of adjusted basis or FMV) – Liability that shareholder assumes.[15]

[14]The adjusted basis used is the basis for E&P purposes, which will be different for tax purposes because deprecation is computed differently for tax versus E&P. For simplicity purposes, the problems in this chapter assume that tax basis and E&P basis are the same. However, that would only be the case if the taxpayer elected to use ADS depreciation for tax purposes. Recall that ADS depreciation is required for computing E&P.

[15]IRC §312(a) and (b).

In the next Example, we demonstrate how E&P is reduced for corporate distributions of property.

EXAMPLE 4.3.3
Property Distributions—E&P

NOP Corporation owns land with a fair market value of $100,000 and an adjusted basis of $73,000. There is a mortgage attached to the land of $60,000. E&P is $168,000 before the distribution. If NOP distributes the land to a shareholder and the shareholder assumes the mortgage, what is the amount of E&P after the distribution?

SOLUTION

NOP must recognize a gain of $27,000 because of the distribution ($100,000 − $73,000), which also increases E&P. E&P is reduced by $40,000 because of the distribution:

[Greater of adjusted basis ($73,000) or FMV ($100,000)] − Liability assumed by shareholder ($60,000) = $100,000 − $60,000 = $40,000

Therefore, E&P is computed as follows:

E&P before the distribution	$168,000
Plus: Gain from distribution	27,000
Less: Distribution	(40,000)
E&P after the distribution	$155,000

Related exercise: Application Problem 19

Potential Pitfall

If a corporation distributes appreciated property, the corporation must recognize gain for the appreciation. This gain will also increase E&P. Do not forget to increase E&P for the gain in this situation, unless the problem tells you that the E&P as given already accounts for the gain.

Property Distributions—Shareholder Tax Consequences

There are three steps to determining the tax consequences of property distributions to shareholders. These steps are simple, and can be used for all property distributions to determine the tax results for the shareholder. **Illustration 4.4** provides a flow chart showing these steps.

Step 1: Determine: The amount of the distribution. The amount is measured as the fair market value of the property less any debt attached to the property that is assumed by the shareholder.[16]

Amount distributed = FMV − Debt assumed by shareholder

Step 2: Determine: The tax effects of the distribution. We use the same three-step process as for cash distributions:[17]

a. Dividend income to the extent of E&P.

b. Once E&P is exhausted, a nontaxable reduction in the basis of the shareholder's stock.

c. Once the basis of the stock is reduced to zero, the remainder of the distribution is taxed as a capital gain.

Step 3: Determine: The shareholder's basis in the property distributed. This amount is always the property's fair market value.[18]

Related exercises: Multiple Choice Question 7
Brief Exercise 4

The next Example illustrates how these steps for property distributions received from the corporation apply to shareholders.

[16]IRC §301(b).
[17]IRC §301(c).
[18]IRC §301(d).

ILLUSTRATION 4.4 Determining the Tax Consequences of Property Distribution for Shareholders

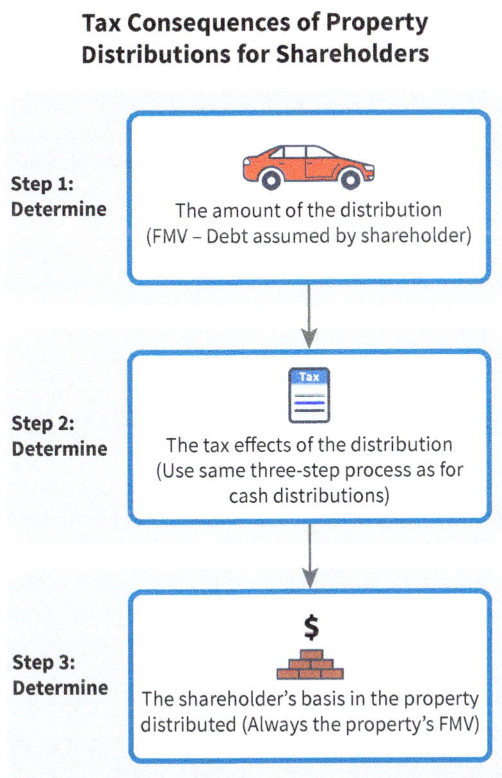

EXAMPLE 4.3.4 Shareholder Consequences of Property Distributions

NOP Corporation owns land with a fair market value of $100,000 and an adjusted basis of $85,000. There is a mortgage attached to the land of $60,000. E&P is $20,000 before the distribution. NOP distributes the land to Wendy, a shareholder, and she assumes the mortgage. Wendy's basis in her stock is $145,000. Answer the following questions with regard to this distribution.

1. How much gain or loss does NOP recognize?
2. What is NOPs E&P after the distribution?
3. What is the amount distributed to Wendy?
4. How is the distribution taxed to Wendy?
5. What is Wendy's basis in the land?

SOLUTION

1. Because NOP distributed land, it is treated as if NOP sold the land for its fair market value, as follows:

Amount realized	$100,000
(Adjusted basis)	(85,000)
Realized gain	$ 15,000

Therefore, NOP recognizes a gain of $15,000.

2. We calculate the reduction in E&P from the distribution as follows:

[Greater of adjusted basis ($85,000) or FMV ($100,000)] – Liability assumed by shareholder ($60,000) = $100,000 – $60,000 = $40,000. Therefore, E&P is computed as follows:

E&P before the distribution	$20,000
Plus: Gain from distribution	15,000
Less: Distribution*	(35,000)
E&P after the distribution	$ 0

*A distribution can never reduce E&P below zero. Therefore, only $35,000 of the distribution is used to reduce E&P to zero.

3. The amount distributed is the land's fair market value of $100,000 reduced by the $60,000 mortgage that Wendy assumed, which is $40,000.
4. The $40,000 amount distributed is taxed as dividend income to Wendy to the extent of the corporation's E&P, which we computed above to be $35,000 after it is increased for the recognized gain of $15,000. Therefore, Wendy has dividend income of $35,000. The remaining $5,000 of the distribution reduces the basis in her stock to $140,000 ($145,000 – $5,000).
5. Wendy's basis in the land is $100,000, its fair market value.

Related exercises: Application Problems 20, 21

Property Distributions—Liability Greater than FMV

A special rule applies if the liability attached to distributed property is greater than the property's FMV. In that case, the tax law creates a *hypothetical* FMV equal to the amount of the liability, and the *hypothetical* FMV is used to determine the tax consequences to the corporation and to the shareholder.[19] The *actual* FMV is not used for the computations.

The next Example uses the facts of Example 4.3.4 except the amount of the liability is increased.

EXAMPLE 4.3.5 Shareholder Consequences of Property Distributions—Liabilities Exceed FMV

NOP Corporation owns land with a fair market value of $100,000 and an adjusted basis of $85,000. There is a mortgage attached to the land of $115,000. E&P is $20,000 before the distribution. NOP distributes the land to Wendy, a shareholder, and she assumes the mortgage. Wendy's basis in her stock is $145,000. Answer the following questions with regard to this distribution.

1. How much gain or loss does NOP recognize?
2. What is NOP's E&P after the distribution?
3. What is the amount distributed to Wendy?
4. How is the distribution taxed to Wendy?
5. What is Wendy's basis in the land?

SOLUTION

To compute this solution, you must use the amount of the liability, $115,000, as the *hypothetical* FMV because it exceeds the actual FMV of $100,000.

1. Because NOP distributed land, it is treated as if NOP sold the land for its hypothetical fair market value of $115,000, as follows:

Amount realized	$115,000
(Adjusted basis)	(85,000)
Realized gain	$ 30,000

Therefore, NOP recognizes a gain of $30,000.

2. We calculate the reduction in E&P from the distribution as follows:

[Greater of adjusted basis ($85,000) or hypothetical FMV ($115,000)] – liability assumed by shareholder ($115,000) = $115,000 – $115,000 = $0. Therefore, E&P is computed as follows:

E&P before the distribution	$20,000
Plus: Gain from distribution	30,000
Less: Distribution	(0)
E&P after the distribution	$50,000

[19] IRC §336(b).

3. The amount distributed is the land's hypothetical fair market value of $115,000 reduced by the $115,000 mortgage that Wendy assumes, which is $0.
4. Wendy has no income because the amount distributed to her is $0.
5. Wendy's basis in the land is $115,000, its hypothetical fair market value.

Related exercise: Application Problem 22

Tax Planning Tip

You may wonder why Wendy would accept a distribution of property with a FMV of $100,000 if she must assume the liability of $115,000 that is attached to it. This reduces her net worth by $15,000. Clearly, Wendy would not do this unless there is a business purpose for doing so. However, it is important for you to realize that Wendy can recognize a loss when she sells the property. If she sold the property the day after she received it for its actual FMV of $100,000, her adjusted basis in the property is its hypothetical FMV of $115,000. Thus, she would recognize a $15,000 loss on the sale.

PRACTICE PROBLEM 4.3.1

Distribution of Appreciated Property

Bones, Inc. owns a warehouse with a fair market value of $162,500 and an adjusted basis of $77,000. If Bones distributes the warehouse to a shareholder, how much gain, if any, must Bones recognize on the distribution?

SOLUTION

Because Bones distributed the building, it is treated as if Bones had sold the building for its fair market value:

Amount realized	$162,500
Less: Adjusted basis	(77,000)
Realized gain	$85,500

PRACTICE PROBLEM 4.3.2

Effect of a Property Distribution

Lily, the sole shareholder in Lilac, a C corporation, has a tax basis of $55,000 in her stock in Lilac. Lilac has $38,000 of accumulated earnings and profits at the beginning of the year and $12,000 of current earnings and profits. At year end, Lilac distributed land with an adjusted basis of $34,000 and a fair market value of $41,000 to Lily. The land has an outstanding mortgage of $4,000 that Lily must assume.

a. What is Lilac Corporation's recognized gain or loss?
b. What is Lily's dividend income?
c. What is Lily's basis in the land after the distribution?

SOLUTION

a. Lilac will recognize a gain of $7,000 ($41,000 FMV – $34,000 adjusted basis). Gains, but not losses, are recognized by a corporation on the distribution of property to shareholders.
b. Lily's dividend income is $37,000. The amount distributed is $37,000, the FMV of the distribution ($41,000) less any liability assumed ($4,000) by Lily. Because the earnings and profits are $57,000 after adding gain of $7,000, and in excess of the amount distributed of $37,000, the distribution is taxed as dividend income.
c. Lily's basis in the land is equal to the FMV of the property received, $41,000.

PRACTICE PROBLEM 4.3.3
Property Distribution's Effect on Earnings and Profits

Sunny Corporation was organized and commenced operations in 2008. On December 31 of the current year, Sunny had total earnings and profits of $23,000 before any dividend declaration and distribution. On December 31 of the current year, Sunny distributed cash of $11,000 and a vacant parcel of land to June, Sunny's only stockholder. At the date of the distribution, the land had a basis of $6,500 and a fair market value of $33,000.

a. What is the effect on Sunny's earnings and profits from these distributions?

b. What is June's taxable dividend income in the current year from these distributions?

SOLUTION

a. The distribution of appreciated property increases a corporation's earnings and profits by the difference between the distributed property's FMV and the corporation's adjusted basis in the distributed property.

Thus, while Sunny Corporation had E&P totaling $23,000 before the distribution, the corporation's E&P will increase by the gain recognized by Sunny of $26,500 ($33,000 FMV – $6,500 adjusted basis). Additionally, E&P will be reduced by the greater of the FMV ($44,000) or adjusted basis ($17,500) of all assets distributed.

Final E&P after the distribution will be:

E&P before the distribution	$23,000
Plus: Gain from the distribution	26,500
Less: FMV from the distribution	(44,000)
E&P after the distribution	$ 5,500

b. June's dividend income is $44,000. There is dividend income on the FMV of the distribution ($44,000) less any liability assumed by June ($0). Because E&P is $49,500 after adding the gain recognized by the corporation, the dividend income is $44,000.

INTERACTIVE SELF-SCORING QUIZZES

4.4 Stock Redemptions

LEARNING OBJECTIVE 4

Compute the tax consequences of a redemption for a shareholder of a corporation.

VIDEO CONTENT

Returning to the facts for Delta Corporation in this chapter's Introduction, two years ago Aiden sold 25% of her stock to Delta for $165,000, which is an example of a stock redemption. A **stock redemption** occurs when a corporation purchases stock from a shareholder. If the purchase qualifies as a redemption for tax purposes, the transaction is treated as a property transaction and the shareholder will have a capital gain or loss.[20] However, in some situations, the economic consequences of a sale of stock by a stockholder may more closely resemble a dividend than a property transaction. Hence, Congress has created laws to ensure that transactions that are very similar to a dividend will not qualify for redemption treatment.

Related exercise: Discussion Question 9

[20]IRC §302(a).

Redemption Consequences vs. Dividend Consequences

Why does it matter to an individual shareholder if a transaction is treated as a dividend or as a property transaction? There are two advantages to a sale of stock by a shareholder being treated as a property transaction (see **Illustration 4.5**):

1. Shareholders can recover their basis in their stock before the sales proceeds result in gain recognition, *and*
2. Any gain from the transaction is a capital gain, which will qualify for preferential tax treatment if it is a LTCG.

ILLUSTRATION 4.5 Differences in the Characteristics of Redemptions and Dividends

Characteristics of Redemptions and Dividends		
	Reduced by redemption?	**Reduced by dividend?**
Voting power	Yes	No
Ability to share in profits	Yes	No

Related exercise: Discussion Question 10

Alternatively, when a shareholder receives a dividend:

1. The shareholder cannot reduce the amount received by the shareholder's basis in the stock, *and*
2. The amount received is taxed as dividend income to the extent of the corporation's E&P. If the dividend is a qualified dividend, then LTCG rates will apply, but otherwise, the dividend is taxed as ordinary income.

To determine whether a shareholder's sale of stock to the corporation more closely resembles a redemption or a dividend, you need to understand the basic rights that a shareholder has, which are the right to share in profits and the right to vote. Assume that a corporation has 100 shares of stock outstanding and shareholder Donna owns 15 shares, so she owns 15% of the corporation. If Donna receives a $10,000 dividend, after the dividend, she still has 15% of the corporation's voting power and the right to share in 15% of future profits. Thus, the dividend did not reduce her shareholder's rights.

Alternatively, assume that Donna sells 5 of her shares back to the corporation. Her ownership interest is reduced to 10.53% [(15 – 5)/(100 – 5)], so the sale has reduced her voting power and right to share in future profits. You can see that the key in determining whether a shareholder's sale of stock to the corporation is a redemption or a dividend is the change in the shareholder's ownership interest.

The following Example demonstrates the different tax effects of a redemption and a dividend.

EXAMPLE 4.4.1 Redemption or Dividend

Theron owns 100 shares of EFG Corporation which represents all of the outstanding shares. His basis in each share is $15. Theron sells 30 of his shares to EFG for $50 per share. What are the tax consequences of this sale to Theron, assuming that EFG has significant E&P?

SOLUTION

EFG pays Theron $1,500 ($50 × 30 shares) and his basis in the shares is $450 ($15 × 30 shares). Theron owns 100% of EFG before the sale, and also 100% after the sale because he owns all 70 shares that remain outstanding. Theron's voting power and his right to share in future profits did not change at all because of the sale. Therefore, this transaction is treated as a dividend, and Theron has $1,500 of dividend income.

Related exercise: Multiple Choice Question 8

Qualified Redemptions

If a transaction meets one of the statutory rules provided by Congress that allow redemption treatment, then the shareholder's sale of stock to the corporation will be treated as a property transaction.[21] In this section, we review three of these provisions (see **Illustration 4.6**):

1. Substantially disproportionate
2. Not essentially equivalent to a dividend
3. Complete termination of the shareholder's interest (Advanced Topic)

ILLUSTRATION 4.6 Qualified Stock Redemptions

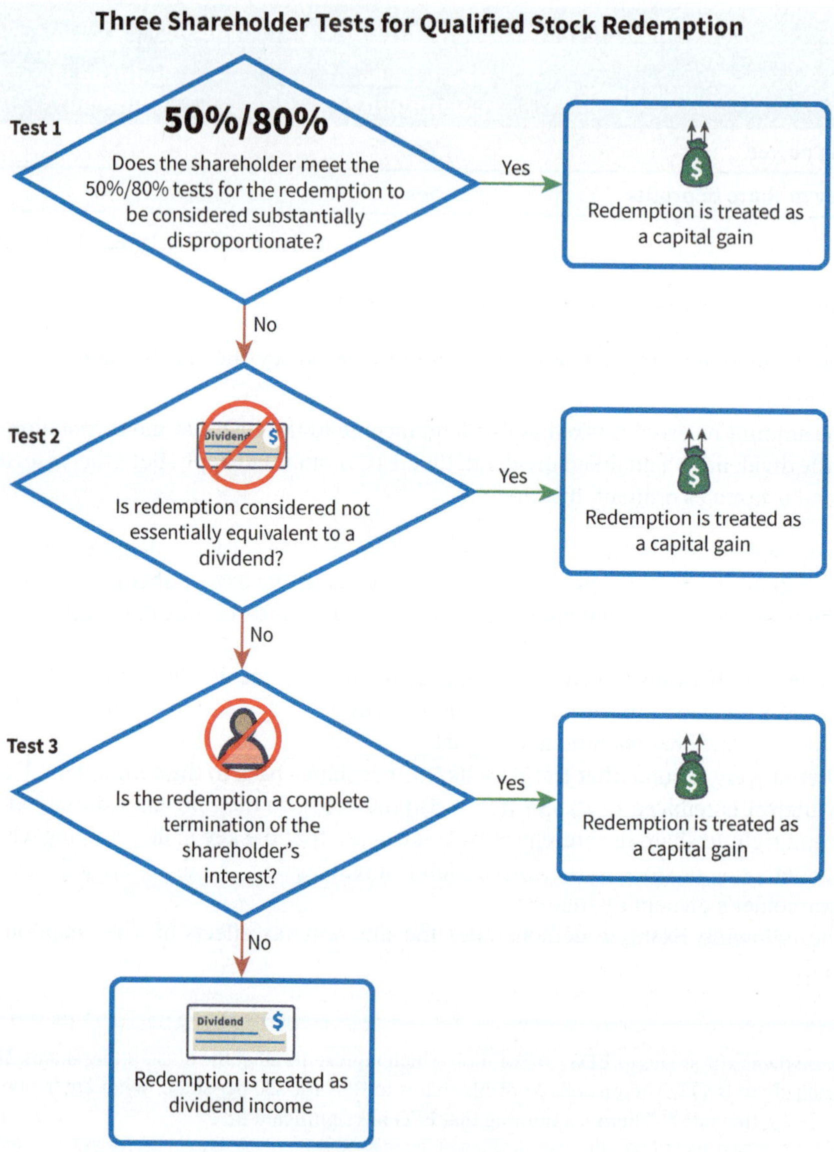

Potential Pitfall

When computing the stock ownership percentage after the sale of stock, don't forget to reduce the total number of shares outstanding in the denominator by the number of shares sold back to the corporation. This is a common mistake that you want to avoid.

We also cover the constructive ownership rules in this section as those must be used when computing the percentage of stock ownership for a shareholder.

Substantially Disproportionate Redemption

For a shareholder's sale of stock to the corporation to be treated as a property transaction, there must be a reduction in the shareholder's voting rights and the right to share in future profits. Congress has provided an objective test that is straightforward to use for this determination

[21] IRC §302(b).

called the *substantially disproportionate* test. The stock sale is **substantially disproportionate** if:

- the shareholder owns less than 50% of the voting power of the stock after the sale, *and*
- the shareholder's ownership of the corporation's voting stock after the sale is less than 80% of their voting stock ownership before the sale.

Both of these conditions must be satisfied for the substantially disproportionate test to be met. The starting point for this test is to compute the shareholder's voting stock ownership percentage before the sale of stock and after the sale of stock. The following Example shows how to apply this test.

Related exercise: Multiple Choice Question 9

EXAMPLE 4.4.2 Substantially Disproportionate Test

Mateo owns 100 shares of voting stock of LMN Corporation that he purchased three years ago. The corporation has 400 shares of voting stock outstanding. Mateo sells 40 shares of stock to LMN for $18,000. His basis in the shares sold is $6,500. What are the tax consequences of the sale to Mateo?

SOLUTION

To determine Mateo's tax consequences, we must first decide whether this sale is a substantially disproportionate redemption. The first step in this analysis is to compute Mateo's ownership interest in LMN's voting stock before and after the sale.

Ownership interest.

Before the sale: 100 shares/400 shares = 25%

After the sale: 60 shares/(400 – 40 shares) = 16.67%

We next determine whether both the 50% and 80% tests are met.

50% Test: Met. After the sale, Mateo owns 16.67% of the voting stock.

80% Test: Met. 25% × 80% = 20%. Mateo's post-sale ownership of 16.67% is less than 20%.

Because both the 50% and 80% tests are met, Mateo's sale of stock to LMN is treated as a property transaction, and his tax consequences are as follows:

Amount realized	$18,000
Adjusted basis	($ 6,500)
Capital gain	$11,500

The gain is a long-term capital gain because Mateo had owned the stock for more than one year.

Tax Planning Tip

Because both the 50% and 80% rules must be met for the substantially disproportionate test to apply, any shareholder who owns more than 50% of the corporation's voting stock after selling stock to the corporation will not meet the substantially disproportionate test.

Related exercises: Brief Exercise 5
Application Problems 23, 24
Tax Planning Problem 2

Not Essentially Equivalent to a Dividend (NEED)

As explained above, the economic consequences of a dividend and a redemption are very different, so Congress has provided a subjective test which provides that the stock sale will be treated as a redemption as long as it is **not essentially equivalent to a dividend (NEED)**. The Supreme Court has ruled that the NEED standard can be satisfied only if there is a *meaningful reduction* in the redeemed shareholder's proportionate interest in the distributing corporation.[22] A meaningful reduction occurs if there is an appropriate reduction in the shareholder's voting interest and right to share in profits. This is a subjective test, and it does not need to be used unless the shareholder does not meet the substantially disproportionate test. The next Example illustrates a potential application of the NEED test.

EXAMPLE 4.4.3 Not Essentially Equivalent to a Dividend

Tierra owns 1,200 shares of voting stock of XYZ Corporation that she purchased ten years ago. The corporation has 2,000 shares of voting stock outstanding. Tierra sells 460 shares of stock to XYZ for $13,800. Her basis in the shares sold is $2,800. What are the tax consequences of the sale to Tierra?

SOLUTION

To determine Tierra's tax consequences, we must first decide whether this sale is a substantially disproportionate redemption. The first step in this analysis is to compute Tierra's ownership interest in XYZ's voting stock before and after the sale.

Ownership interest:

Before the sale: 1,200 shares/2,000 shares = 60%

After the sale: 740 shares/(2,000 − 460 shares) = 48.05%

We next determine whether both the 50% and 80% tests are met.

50% Test: Met. After the sale, Tierra owns 48.05% of the voting stock.

80% Test: Not met. 60% × 80% = 48%. Tierra's post-sale ownership of 48.05% is *not* less than 48%.

Because the 80% test is not met, Tierra's sale of stock to XYZ does not meet the substantially disproportionate test. However, before concluding that the sale is treated as a dividend, we should consider the NEED test.

Tierra's stock ownership declined from 60% to 48.05%, so she no longer has the majority voting interest for XYZ, which is a substantial change for her. While her overall ownership of voting stock did not decline by more than 20%, it declined by 19.92% (11.95%/60%). The key question then is whether the decline of 19.95%, when combined with her voting rights falling below 50%, is a *meaningful reduction* in her interests as a shareholder. Because this is a subjective determination, for an actual taxpayer you would need to gather other facts that could impact the decision. However, in many situations similar to this Example's fact pattern, it would be appropriate to treat this as a meaningful reduction in her shareholder rights. In that case, this would be treated as a property transaction and her tax consequences would be as follows:

Amount realized	$13,800
Adjusted basis	($ 2,800)
Capital gain	$11,000

The gain is a long-term capital gain because Tierra had owned her stock for 10 years.

Related exercise: Application Problem 25

[22] *U.S. v. Davis, Maclin*, (1970, S Ct) 25 AFTR 2d 70-827, 397 U.S. 301, 25 L Ed 2d 323, 70-1 USTC ¶9289, 1970-1 CB 62, revg & remg (1969, CA6) 23 AFTR 2d 69-1028, 408 F2d 1139, 69-1 USTC ¶9303, reh den (1970, S Ct) 397 U.S. 1071, 25 L Ed 2d 695.

Spotlight on the Law

Which Is Better—Qualified Stock Redemption or Dividend? It Depends!

Horn Corporation (HC) is a calendar-year, accrual-basis C corporation. Dom Ram, who is in a 32% tax bracket for ordinary income and 15% bracket for LTCG, purchased his 40% ownership in HC ten years ago for $40,000. In the current year, HC redeems all of Ram's shares for $100,000 while HC has earnings and profits of $500,000. If this transaction is a qualified stock redemption, Ram will have a long-term capital gain of $60,000 ($100,000 – $40,000), and he will pay tax of $9,000 ($60,000 × 15%). If the transaction does not qualify as a stock redemption, then Ram will pay tax of $15,000 ($100,000 × 15%) on his dividend income.

What if Ram is a corporation and not an individual? Because of the dividends received deduction (DRD) for corporations, Ram would prefer the transaction be a dividend. If it is a qualified stock redemption, then Ram will have a long-term capital gain of $60,000 ($100,000 – $40,000), and it will pay tax of $12,600 ($60,000 × 21%). On the other hand, if the transaction does not qualify as a stock redemption, then Ram will have a dividends received deduction (see Chapter 3, LO3, Corporate Taxable Income) on the dividend income received. Ram's DRD will be $65,000 ($100,000 × 65%), so only $35,000 of the dividend payment will be taxed. Therefore, Ram will pay tax of $7,350 ($35,000 × 21%) on its dividend income.

As you can see, shareholders may want different outcomes depending on their entity type. Individual shareholders favor a qualified stock redemption to receive the preferential rate on their long-term capital gain and the ability to use their basis to offset the payment received. Corporate shareholders favor a dividend treatment, because it can use the dividends received deduction.

Constructive Ownership of Stock

The **constructive ownership** of stock rules must be used when determining the shareholder's ownership of voting stock before and after the sale of stock to the corporation. The constructive ownership rules provide that a shareholder is deemed to own stock owned by those related to the shareholder, in addition to the shares held directly by the shareholder. There are three sets of constructive ownership rules that apply to redemptions:[23]

- Family attribution
- Entity-to-owner attribution
- Owner-to-entity attribution

Why **Why are the constructive ownership rules needed in evaluating the redemptions rules?** Assume that Pablo owns 50 shares of BCE Corporation, representing 50% of the voting stock, and his wife, Paige, owns the other 50 shares. Pablo sells 30 shares of his stock to BCE. Let's apply the substantially disproportionate rules to this transaction, both with and without the constructive ownership rules.

Ownership interest (without the constructive ownership rules):

Before the sale: 50 shares/100 shares = 50%

After the sale: 20 shares/(100 – 30 shares) = 28.6%

We next determine whether both the 50% and 80% tests are met.

50% Test: Met. After the sale, Pablo owns 28.6% of the voting stock.

80% Test: Met. 50% × 80% = 40%. Pablo's post-sale ownership of 28.6% is less than 40%.

If we do not use the constructive ownership rules, both the 50% and 80% tests are met, and this will be treated as a property transaction for Pablo, so he will recognize a capital gain or loss from the sale. However, because the remaining shares of stock are owned by his wife, Pablo could still control the corporation through his remaining shares and influencing Paige's

[23]IRC §318.

> **Potential Pitfall**
>
> The family definition for the constructive ownership rules is much narrower than most definitions of family. For related-party losses, family members are defined as one's spouse, ancestors, descendants, and brothers and sisters. The definition is even more narrow for constructive ownership, including only spouses, children, adopted children, grandchildren, and parents. It is important to not confuse these rules when applying the tax laws.

votes for her shares. Therefore, Congress requires the constructive ownership rules to be used when evaluating the 50% and 80% tests. Before and after the sale, Pablo owns his shares and indirectly owns Paige's 50 shares.

Ownership interest (with the constructive ownership rules):

Before the sale: 100 shares (50 + 50)/100 shares = 100%

After the sale: 70 shares (20 + 50)/(100 − 30 shares) = 100%

With the constructive ownership rules, Pablo owns 100% of BCE before and after the sale. Because his ownership interest did not change at all, this is not treated as a property transaction, and Pablo will report the amount received from the corporation as a dividend. You can see that the constructive ownership rules produce a result that is consistent with the economic reality that Pablo and his wife have complete control of BCE both before and after the sale of stock. Also note that if Paige had sold some of her stock to BCE rather than Pablo, the result would be the same, because Paige would own 100% of the stock, directly and indirectly, before and after the sale.

Family Attribution Rules Under the **family attribution** rules, an individual is deemed to indirectly own the stock owned by the individual's spouse, children, grandchildren, and parents.[24] An individual is not attributed shares from former spouses. The same stock can be attributed to more than one family member. For example, if husband, wife, and daughter each own 10 shares of stock of a corporation directly, then each of them is deemed to own 30 shares. We apply the family attribution rule in the next Example.

EXAMPLE 4.4.4 Family Attribution Rules

Tyler owns 100 shares of PQR Corporation, and the remaining shares are owned as follows:

Tyler's wife	100 shares
Tyler's uncle	50 shares
Tyler's daughter	200 shares
Tyler's brother	50 shares
Tyler's grandson	100 shares
Tyler's grandmother	500 shares

How many shares does Tyler own using the constructive ownership rules?

SOLUTION

Tyler is deemed to own the shares owned by his wife, daughter, and grandson, so his total ownership is as follows:

Tyler	100 shares
Tyler's wife	100 shares
Tyler's daughter	200 shares
Tyler's grandson	100 shares
Total shares	500 shares

He is not attributed the shares owned by his uncle, brother, and grandmother.

Related exercises: Multiple Choice Question 10
Brief Exercise 6

Entity Attribution If an individual has an ownership interest in a business entity, then the individual may be deemed to own stock that the business entity owns. This is known as **entity-to-owner attribution**. The rules vary based on the type of business entity. Alternatively, a business entity may be deemed to own a portion of the stock held by one of its owners.

[24]IRC §318(a)(1).

This is known as **owner-to-entity attribution**. We describe the attribution rules for corporations, partnerships/LLCs, and estates and trusts in the following sections.

Corporation to Shareholder Attribution A shareholder is attributed stock owned by a corporation only if the shareholder owns 50% or more of the stock of the corporation. In that case, the shareholder is deemed to own a proportionate interest in any stock owned by that corporation based on the shareholder's stock ownership percentage. If the shareholder owns less than 50% of the corporation, then there is no attribution from the corporation.[25]

EXAMPLE 4.4.5 Corporation to Shareholder Attribution

LUV Corporation has 1,000 shares of stock outstanding. Daryl owns 600 shares and Willow owns 400 shares. LUV owns 400 shares of stock in Exxon Corporation. Daryl owns 200 shares of Exxon and Willow owns 100 shares. How many total shares of Exxon are Daryl and Willow deemed to own under the constructive ownership rules?

SOLUTION

Daryl owns 60% of LUV and Willow owns 40%. Therefore, Daryl is attributed a pro rata share of the Exxon stock owned by LUV, but Willow is not. Daryl is deemed to own 60% of the Exxon stock owned by LUV, or 240 shares (400 shares × 60%). His total ownership in Exxon, directly and indirectly, is 440 shares (200 + 240). Willow owns only the 100 shares in Exxon that she owns directly.

Partnership/Estate/Trust to Owner Attribution The attribution rules for other business entities to their owners is different than the rules for corporate attribution. All partners in a partnership are attributed stock owned by the partnership proportionately based on the partner's ownership interest. Thus, the attribution to partners occurs for *all* partners, not just those owning 50% or more of the partnership. The attribution rules are the same as the partnership rules for beneficiaries of estates and trusts. The next Example applies the constructive ownership rules for partnerships.[26]

Potential Pitfall

For attribution of stock ownership to a corporate shareholder from a corporation, you are attributing stock that the corporation owns as an investment in other corporations.

EXAMPLE 4.4.6 Partnership to Partner Attribution

Continuing with similar facts to Example 4.4.5, assume that LUV Partnership has two partners, Daryl and Willow. Daryl owns 60% of the partnership and Willow owns 40%. LUV owns 400 shares of stock in Exxon Corporation. Daryl owns 200 shares of Exxon and Willow owns 100 shares. How many total shares of Exxon are Daryl and Willow deemed to own under the constructive ownership rules?

SOLUTION

Daryl and Willow are both attributed Exxon stock from LUV because all partners are attributed stock based on their proportionate ownership interest. Daryl is deemed to own 60% of the Exxon stock owned by LUV, or 240 shares (400 shares × 60%). His total ownership in Exxon, directly and indirectly, is 440 shares (200 + 240). Willow is deemed to own 40% of the Exxon stock owned by LUV, or 160 shares (400 shares × 40%). Her total ownership in Exxon, directly and indirectly, is 260 shares (100 + 160).

Related exercises: Discussion Question 11
Application Problem 26

Shareholder to Corporation Attribution Stock owned by a 50% or greater shareholder is deemed to be owned in full (100%) by the corporation. If the shareholder owns less than 50% of the corporation, there is no attribution from the shareholder to the entity.[27]

[25]IRC §318(a)(2)(C).
[26]IRC §318(a)(2)(A) and (B).
[27]IRC §318(a)(3)(C).

EXAMPLE 4.4.7
Shareholder Attribution to Corporation

Continuing with similar facts to Example 4.4.5, LUV Corporation has 1,000 shares of stock outstanding. Daryl owns 600 shares and Willow owns 400 shares. Daryl owns 500 shares of Walmart Corporation and Willow owns 300 shares of Target Corporation. How many total shares of Walmart and Target is LUV deemed to own under the constructive ownership rules?

SOLUTION

Because Daryl owns 50% or more of LUV, LUV is deemed to own all (500) of his shares of Walmart. Willow owns less than 50% of LUV, so LUV is not attributed any of her stock in Target.

Related exercise: Brief Exercise 7

Partner/Beneficiary Attribution to Partnership/Estate or Trust Stock owned by a partner is deemed to be owned in full by the partnership. Note that this attribution applies to stock owned by all partners, not just partners who own 50% or more. The same rule applies to stock owned by beneficiaries of an estate or trust. The partnership or estate/trust is deemed to own all of the shares owned by the beneficiary.[28]

EXAMPLE 4.4.8
Partner Attribution to Partnership

Continuing with similar facts to Example 4.4.6, assume that LUV Partnership has two partners, Daryl and Willow. Daryl owns 60% of the partnership and Willow owns 40%. Daryl owns 500 shares of Walmart Corporation and Willow owns 300 shares of Target Corporation. How many total shares of Walmart and Target is LUV deemed to own under the constructive ownership rules?

SOLUTION

Stock owned by partners is deemed to be owned in full by the partnership. This applies for all partners, regardless of the amount of the partnership that is owned. Therefore, LUV is deemed to own the 500 shares of Walmart that is owned by Daryl, and the 300 shares of Target that is owned by Willow.

Related exercise: Application Problem 27

Advanced Topic—Drilling Down

Reattribution

Reattribution is when stock that is attributed from one taxpayer to a second taxpayer is then reattributed to a third taxpayer. However, stock constructively owned by a person under the family attribution rules cannot be reattributed to another individual. Additionally, stock that has been attributed to a corporation, partnership, estate or trust cannot be reattributed to another taxpayer.[29] The next Example provides an application of the reattribution rule.

Related exercise: Discussion Question 12

EXAMPLE 4.4.9
Reattribution of Stock

Chris owns 65% of HIJ Corporation and 10% of AAA Partnership. HIJ owns 100 shares of Meta, Inc. stock. How do the attribution rules apply to Chris, HIJ, and AAA?

SOLUTION

Because Chris owns 50% or more of the stock of HIJ, he is deemed to own a proportionate share of any stock owned by HIJ. Therefore, Chris is deemed to own 65 shares (100 × 65%) of the Meta stock that is owned by HIJ. Because Chris constructively owns 65 shares of Meta, this ownership is also attributed to AAA because he is a partner in AAA. Consequently, AAA is reattributed the 65 shares of Meta stock that are constructively owned by Chris.

[28] IRC §318(a)(3)(A) and (B).
[29] IRC §318(a)(5).

Complete Termination of a Shareholder's Interest

If a shareholder completely terminates their interest in a corporation by selling all of their stock to the corporation, this will be treated as a qualified redemption, and therefore a property transaction. At first glance, this rule may appear to be redundant with the substantially disproportionate rule above. The 50% and 80% rules will clearly be met if a shareholder sells 100% of their stock. So there must be more to this rule, and there is.

The constructive ownership rules must be applied when determining if there has been a complete termination of ownership of a shareholder's interest. If *any* stock is constructively owned by a shareholder because a family member or entity related to them also owns stock in the corporation, then it is not possible for the shareholder to completely terminate their interest. The *complete termination rule* provides a means for a shareholder who constructively owns stock to be eligible for qualified redemption treatment. This provision allows the *family attribution* rules to be waived for the shareholder if *all* the following requirements are met:

- The shareholder executes an agreement with the IRS providing that the shareholder will not directly reacquire any ownership interest in the corporation or exercise management influence for the next 10 years.
- The individual cannot be an employee, director, or officer during this prohibited period.
- The individual can be a creditor of the corporation during the 10-year period.
- The selling shareholder must agree to notify the IRS if they reacquire stock in the corporation at any time during the next 10 years.
- If stock is acquired by inheritance during the 10-year period, that is not treated as a prohibited transaction.

If the shareholder violates the agreement during the 10-year prohibition period by participating in management and/or acquiring prohibited stock, then the waiver of the family attribution rules is voided. Most likely this will cause the complete termination sale of the stock to be recharacterized as a dividend, and the taxpayer will be responsible for paying any additional tax due, including interest, from the day of the original transaction.

We apply the complete termination of interest rule in the following Example.

EXAMPLE 4.4.10
Complete Termination of Interest

TUV Corporation has 1,000 shares of stock outstanding. The stock of TUV is owned as follows:

Rosa	200 shares
Rosa's husband	400 shares
Rosa's daughter	100 shares
XYZ Corporation	300 shares

Rosa also owns 60% of XYZ Corporation. Rosa sells her 200 shares to TUV Corporation for $30,000. Does this sale constitute a complete termination of Rosa's stock interest for purposes of the redemption rules, assuming Rosa files the proper paperwork with the IRS? If not, will the sale be treated as a qualified redemption?

SOLUTION

Before Rosa's sale of stock, she is deemed to own the following shares of stock in TUV:

Rosa	200 shares
Rosa's husband	400 shares
Rosa's daughter	100 shares
XYZ Corporation	180 shares
Total	880 shares

Rosa is deemed to own her husband's shares and her daughter's shares under the family attribution rules. However, if she executes an agreement with the IRS stating that she agrees to not acquire stock in TUV or exercise management influence for the next 10 years, then she can waive the attribution of these shares under the family attribution rules. Nevertheless, this would not be a qualified redemption under the qualified termination rule because Rosa would still be deemed to own 180 shares (300 shares × 60%) of TUV through XYZ corporation, because Rosa owns 50% or more of XYZ.

We next need to determine if Rosa's sale qualifies as a substantially disproportionate reduction in her ownership interest. Before the sale, Rosa owned 88% (880 shares/1,000 shares) of TUV, directly and indirectly. After the sale, Rosa owns 680 shares of TUV (attributed from her husband, daughter, and XYZ). With 680 shares, she owns 85% of TUV (680 shares/800 shares) so her constructive ownership increased. Therefore, this is not a substantially disproportionate reduction in her ownership interest, and the sale will be treated as a dividend.

Related exercises: Multiple Choice Questions 11, 12
Brief Exercise 8
Application Problem 28

Tax Consequences to Corporations

There are two questions that must be answered to determine the tax consequences to a corporation of a qualified redemption:

1. Does the corporation recognize a gain or loss if it pays for the redemption with property?
2. What is the impact on the corporation's E&P from the redemption?

Corporate Gain or Loss

The tax consequences for a corporation for distributing property to a shareholder as part of redemption are the same as for a dividend: corporations recognize gains but not losses. If a corporation uses appreciated property as part of a redemption, the appreciation is recognized as gain to the corporation. But, if the corporation uses loss property, the loss is not recognized.[30]

Tax Planning Tip

Corporations should never use loss property to pay a shareholder for stock that is being redeemed. Should the corporation do so, the loss is not deferred, but excluded, and any tax benefit from that loss completely disappears.

Earnings & Profits

A corporation could have two adjustments to E&P because of a redemption:[31]

1. If a corporation recognizes gain because of distributing appreciated property, the first step in the E&P adjustment is to increase E&P for such gain. The starting point for computing E&P is the corporation's taxable income, so the gain will increase taxable income and E&P.
2. Corporations must reduce their E&P after completing a redemption because the corporation has less stock outstanding. The reduction is the *lower* of:
   - the corporation's E&P × the percentage of stock redeemed, *or*
   - the redemption price.

[30]IRC §311(a) and (b).
[31]IRC §312.

If the redemption is treated as a dividend, then E&P is reduced based on the rules for dividends: the greater of the adjusted basis or FMV of the property distributed, less any liability assumed by the shareholder.

Related exercise: Discussion Question 13

The following two Examples illustrate the tax effects of qualified redemptions to corporations.

EXAMPLE 4.4.11 Tax Effects to Corporations for Qualified Redemptions—Gain

Continuing with the facts of Example 4.4.2, Mateo owns 100 shares of voting stock of LMN Corporation that he purchased three years ago. The corporation has 400 shares of voting stock outstanding. Mateo sells all 100 shares of stock to LMN for $18,000. His basis in the shares sold is $6,500. LMN pays for the stock by distributing land to Mateo with a FMV of $18,000 and an adjusted basis of $7,000. LMN's total E&P before the redemption was $80,000. What are the tax consequences of the sale to LMN?

SOLUTION

As described in Example 4.4.2, this is a qualified redemption. LMN redeemed 25% of its shares (100 shares/400 shares). LMN will recognize a gain for the redemption of $11,000 due to the distribution of the land ($18,000 FMV − $7,000 adjusted basis). LMN's E&P will be adjusted as follows for the redemption:

E&P before the redemption	$80,000
Gain from the redemption	11,000
Adjusted E&P	$91,000
*E&P Reduction	(18,000)
E&P after the redemption	$73,000

*E&P is reduced by the *lower* of:

- the corporation's E&P ($91,000) × the percentage of stock redeemed (25%) which is $22,750, *or*
- the redemption price of $18,000.

EXAMPLE 4.4.12 Tax Effects to Corporations for Qualified Redemptions—Loss

Continuing with the facts of Example 4.4.11, Mateo owns 100 shares of voting stock of LMN Corporation that he purchased three years ago. The corporation has 400 shares of voting stock outstanding. Mateo sells all 100 shares of stock to LMN for $25,000. His basis in the shares sold is $6,500. LMN pays for the stock by distributing land to Mateo with a FMV of $25,000 and an adjusted basis of $28,000. LMN's total E&P before the redemption was $80,000. What are the tax consequences of the sale to LMN?

SOLUTION

As described in Example 4.4.11, this is a qualified redemption. LMN redeemed 25% of its shares (100 shares/400 shares). LMN will *realize* a loss for the redemption of $3,000 due to the distribution of the land ($25,000 FMV − $28,000 adjusted basis). However, the loss cannot be recognized. LMN's E&P will be adjusted as follows for the redemption:

E&P before the redemption	$80,000
Loss from the redemption	0
Adjusted E&P	$80,000
*E&P Reduction	(20,000)
E&P after the redemption	$60,000

*E&P is reduced by the *lower* of:

- the corporation's E&P ($80,000) × the percentage of stock redeemed (25%) which is $20,000, *or*
- the redemption price of $25,000.

Related exercises: Application Problems 29, 30

1% Tax on Stock Buyouts

Publicly traded companies must pay a 1% excise tax on the fair market value of any stock that is repurchased by the corporation. The tax applies to repurchases of both common stock and preferred stock. The excise tax does not apply to aggregate repurchases that do not exceed $1 million for the tax year, nor to tax-free reorganizations (discussed in Chapter 5, LO3, Corporate Reorganizations).

Partial Liquidations

A **partial liquidation** occurs when a corporation that has more than one distinct line of business terminates one of those lines. The corporation remains in existence and continues to operate the remaining lines of business. If the necessary requirements are met for this to be a qualified redemption, then noncorporate shareholders are treated as if they sold their stock and have capital gain or loss. Corporate shareholders are treated as if they received a dividend, which is usually more beneficial to them because they may qualify for the dividends received deduction. There are two different ways for corporations to meet the partial liquidation rules: a *subjective test* and an *objective test*.[32]

Related exercise: Discussion Question 14

Potential Pitfall

The *not essentially equivalent to a dividend* test for partial liquidations is very different from the NEED test for other redemptions. For a partial liquidation, the test is focused on the contraction of the corporation's business, whereas for redemptions the test focuses on the reduction in stock ownership by a shareholder.

Tax Planning Tip

To determine if a partial liquidation qualifies as a qualified redemption, you must analyze the effect at the corporate level, rather than at the shareholder level as we have done with the three tests for qualified redemptions so far in this chapter.

Subjective Test for Partial Liquidation

The **subjective test (partial liquidation)** provides that a transaction is a partial liquidation if the transaction is *not essentially equivalent to a dividend* and there is a *contraction of the corporate business*.[33] The following rules apply for partial liquidations under the subjective test:

- A **contraction of the corporate business** occurs when there is a significant reduction in the level of business activities, such as the number of employees, services, income or assets. A reduction in inventory because of depressed market conditions does not qualify as a partial contraction of the business.[34]
- The partial liquidation must occur during the year that the liquidation plan is adopted or the following tax year.
- A contraction has *not* occurred when a corporation distributes assets but does not reduce the level of its business activities. For example, if a corporation distributed assets it used in its business to a shareholder, and then rented the assets back from the shareholder, this would not be a contraction of the corporate business.

Objective Test for Partial Liquidation

The **objective test (partial liquidation)** provides that the corporation must have at least two qualifying trades or businesses before the partial liquidation, and at least one qualifying trade or business after the partial liquidation. The objective test provides a more certain outcome for the shareholders if it is met than the subjective test. The following rules apply for partial liquidations under the objective test:

- A **qualifying trade or business (partial liquidation)** is one that the corporation has operated for at least five years.

[32]IRC §302(b)(4).
[33]IRC §302(e)(1).
[34]Rev. Rul. 78-55, 1978-1 CB 118.

- If the corporation acquired the business during the five-year period in a tax-free transaction, the business is still a qualifying business as long it had been active during the entire five-year period.
- If the business was acquired in a taxable or partially taxable transaction, then the current owner must have operated the business itself for five years; operational time before the acquisition does not count in the five years.

We demonstrate the qualification rules for partial liquidations in the next Example.

EXAMPLE 4.4.13
Partial Liquidation

Corporation MNO has been in existence for 25 years. MNO has some individual shareholders and some corporate shareholders. During this time, it has established three active businesses that sell the following items as shown below:

Construction equipment	25 years
Lawn and garden equipment	8 years
Automobile parts	4 years

a. During the current year, MNO distributes all the assets in the construction equipment business to its shareholders in return for 40% of their MNO stock. Is this treated as a partial liquidation? What are the tax consequences to the shareholders?

b. During the current year, MNO distributes all the assets in the construction equipment and lawn and garden equipment businesses to its shareholders in return for 70% of their MNO stock. Is this treated as a partial liquidation? What are the tax consequences to the shareholders?

SOLUTION

To determine if these transactions are a partial liquidation, we use the objective test because it provides a more certain outcome for the shareholders than the subjective test.

a. MNO has two qualifying businesses because the construction equipment and the lawn and garden equipment businesses have been operated as active businesses for at least five years. After the transaction, MNO still has at least one qualifying business (lawn and garden). Therefore, this is a partial liquidation, and the individual shareholders of MNO will have capital gain or loss on the transaction. The corporate shareholders will have dividend income.

b. MNO has two qualifying businesses because the construction equipment and the lawn and garden equipment businesses have been operated as active businesses for at least five years. However, after the transaction, MNO does not have any qualifying businesses because the auto parts sales business has been owned for only four years. Therefore, this is not a partial liquidation. The distribution of the assets to the shareholders, both individuals and corporate, is treated as a dividend distribution.

Related exercise: Brief Exercise 9

Advanced Topic—Drilling Down

Redemption Used to Pay Estate Taxes

A redemption of stock to pay estate taxes can qualify as a sale or exchange of stock if *both* of the following requirements are met:[35]

- The value of the stock of the redeeming corporation included in the shareholder's gross estate must exceed 35% of the value of the gross estate after reduction for expenses, indebtedness, and losses related to the estate.
- The amount treated as a sale or exchange of stock cannot exceed the sum of the estate and inheritance taxes (including any interest) imposed on the estate, plus the amount of funeral and administration expenses allowed as deductions for the estate.

[35]IRC §303.

Why **Why are redemptions of stock used to pay estate taxes treated as a sale of exchange of stock for the shareholder (i.e., the decedent's estate)?** When shareholders own stock in a valuable corporation, the value of this stock may constitute a significant percentage of the estate's value. If estate or other taxes are owed, the estate may have to sell some of the stock to generate cash to pay the taxes. Also recall that when an individual dies, the bases of the individual's assets are increased or decreased to the fair market of each asset on the date of death (or the alternate valuation date if elected by the executor of the estate). Thus, the estate's basis in the stock is the stock's FMV. If the redemption of the stock is treated as a property transaction, and therefore a sale of the stock, the estate should have minimal, if any, capital gain because its basis in the stock was increased to the FMV. If the redemption was treated as a dividend, the estate could have significant dividend income on which it would have to pay income taxes. Congress added this provision to the redemption rules to benefit the estate of the deceased, and the family of the deceased, in such circumstances.

EXAMPLE 4.4.14
Redemption to Pay Estate Taxes

Kanesha passed away on August 5th of the current tax year. The value of her estate at the date of her death, after reduction for expenses, indebtedness, and losses, is $16,000,000. Kanesha had started a corporation, UVW, 35 years before her death. This stock was valued at $8,500,000 (100,000 shares @ $85 per share) on the date of her death. Kanesha's executor has completed all federal and state returns related to her death that must be filed. Her total estate taxes are $1,900,000. To generate cash to pay these taxes, her executor redeemed $2,000,000 of UVW stock from the corporation. UVW stock had a fair market value of $100 per share on the day of the redemption. The estate also paid $40,000 of funeral and administration expenses. What are the tax consequences of this redemption for Kanesha's estate?

SOLUTION

We must first determine if this is a qualified redemption that permits sale or exchange treatment for the redemption. There are two requirements that must be met for this to be a qualified redemption:

- The value of the stock of the redeeming corporation included in the shareholder's gross estate must exceed 35% of the value of the gross estate after reduction for expenses, indebtedness, and losses related to the estate. This is met because 35% of the gross estate is $5,600,000 (35% × $16,000,000), and the $8,500,000 value of the UVW stock in the estate exceeds this amount.
- The amount treated as a sale or exchange of stock cannot exceed $1,940,000, the sum of ($1,900,000) the estate, inheritance, legacy, and succession taxes (including any interest) imposed on the estate, plus ($40,000) the amount of funeral and administration expenses allowed as deductions for the estate.

Therefore, $1,940,000 of the redemption is treated as being from the sale or exchange of stock, and the remaining $60,000 is treated as a dividend to the estate, assuming UVW has sufficient E&P. The capital gain from the sale of the stock is computed as follows:

Amount realized	$1,940,000
**Less*: Adjusted basis	(1,649,000)
Long-term capital gain	$ 291,000

*The adjusted basis is computed as: Total value of UVW stock on redemption date: 100,000 shares × $100 = $10,000,000. The percentage of stock deemed to be sold is 19.4% ($1,940,000/$10,000,000). The basis per share is the FMV of the stock on the date of death, or $85. The basis in the shares sold is $1,649,000 (19.4% × $8,500,000).

The holding period for the stock is long-term because all inherited assets are deemed to be held long-term. Therefore, the estate has a LTCG of $291,000 and dividend income of $60,000.

Related exercise: Application Problem 31

PRACTICE PROBLEM 4.4.1
Stock Redemption

Fung has owned 1,500 voting shares of Urban Corporation for four years. His basis per share is $105. Urban has 2,000 shares outstanding. In the current year, Fung sells 800 shares of his stock back to Urban for $130 per share. What are the tax consequences of the sale to Fung?

SOLUTION

To determine the tax consequences to Fung, we must first decide whether this sale is a substantially disproportionate redemption. The first step in this analysis is to compute Fung's ownership interest in Urban's voting stock before and after the sale.

Ownership interest:
Before the sale: 1,500 shares/2,000 shares = 75%
After the sale: 700 shares/ (2,000 – 800) = 58%

We next determine whether both the 50% and 80% tests are met.
50% test: Not met. After the sale, Fung owns 58% of the voting stock.
80% test: Met. 75% × 80% = 60%. Fung's post sale ownership of 58% is less than 60%.

Because only the 80% test was met, Fung's sale of stock to Urban is not a qualified stock redemption. Fung must report dividend income of $104,000 ($130 × 800 shares sold).

PRACTICE PROBLEM 4.4.2
Constructive Ownership

Galewind Partnership has two partners, Windy and Stormy. Windy owns 75% of the partnership and Stormy owns 25%. Windy owns 130 shares of Sky Corporation and Stormy owns 700 shares of Rain Corporation. How many total shares of Sky and Rain is Galewind deemed to own under the constructive ownership rules?

SOLUTION

Stock owned by partners is deemed to be owned in full by the partnership. This applies for all partners regardless of the amount of the partnership that is owned. Therefore, Galewind is deemed to own the 130 shares of Sky Corporation that is owned by Windy and the 700 shares of Rain Corporation that is owned by Stormy.

PRACTICE PROBLEM 4.4.3
Stock Redemption Effect on E&P

Jafar owns 160 shares of voting stock of Middle Corporation that he purchased three years ago. The corporation has 1,000 shares of voting stock outstanding. Jafar sells all 160 shares of stock to Middle for $28,800. His basis in the shares sold is $17,600. Middle pays for the stock by distributing land to Jafar with a FMV of $28,800 and an adjusted basis of $33,000. Middle's total E&P before the redemption was $57,000. What are the tax consequences of the sale to Middle Corporation? How will Middle's E&P be adjusted after the sale?

SOLUTION

Middle Corporation redeemed 16% of its shares (160/1,000). Middle will *realize* a loss for the redemption of $4,200 due to the distribution of the land ($28,800 FMV – $33,000 adjusted basis). However, the loss cannot be recognized. Middle's E&P will be adjusted as follows for the redemption:

E&P before the redemption	$57,000
Loss from the redemption	$ 0
Adjusted E&P	$57,000
*E&P reduction	($ 9,120)
E&P after the redemption	$47,880

*E&P is reduced by the *lower* of:
1. The corporation's E&P ($57,000) × the percentage of stock redeemed (16%) which is $9,120, *or*
2. The redemption price of $28,800.

INTERACTIVE SELF-SCORING QUIZZES

4.5 Corporate Liquidations

LEARNING OBJECTIVE 5

Compute the tax consequences of a corporate liquidation for the shareholder and the corporation.

VIDEO CONTENT

Returning to the chapter introduction, Delta Consulting has indicated that it may consider liquidating. To serve your client effectively, you need to be able to discuss with them the tax effects of liquidations to both the shareholders and the corporation. A **corporate liquidation** occurs when a corporation dissolves and distributes any remaining assets to the shareholders. A complete liquidation is similar to a redemption in that the shareholders are receiving cash and/or property in return for their stock. However, the tax implications for complete liquidations are different than for redemptions. When a complete liquidation occurs, there are three key groups that you need to know the tax results for:

- shareholders,
- the corporation, *and*
- minority shareholders.

Generally, gain or loss is recognized on a corporate liquidation at both the corporate and the shareholder level, reflecting the double taxation of income that is a characteristic of corporations. We review the tax consequences of liquidations in this section, including the specialized rules for when a parent liquidates a subsidiary.

Tax Effects for Shareholders

The general rule for shareholders who surrender their shares in a complete liquidation is that gains and losses are recognized.[36] The gain or loss is computed as follows:

FMV of assets received from the corporation
Less: Adjusted basis of stock
Shareholder's gain or loss

Other important tax effects to the shareholder include:

- The shareholder's gain or loss is capital as long as the shareholder holds the stock as an investment.
- The shareholder's basis in the assets received by the corporation is the FMV of the assets on the date distributed.

There are two other issues that could affect the shareholder's gain or loss on a corporate liquidation: related-party loss rules, and corporate liabilities assumed by the shareholder.

Related-Party Losses

It is not unusual for a corporate shareholder to own, directly and indirectly, more than 50% of the corporation's stock, meaning that the corporation and shareholder are related parties. In general, losses generated on transactions between related parties cannot be recognized.

[36]IRC §331.

However, the related-party loss disallowance rule does *not* apply to shareholders in the corporate liquidation setting.[37]

Liabilities Assumed by the Shareholder

If the shareholder assumes debt of the corporation as part of the liquidation, the FMV of the assets received by the shareholder are reduced by the debt assumed. This reduces the amount of gain recognized, or increases the amount of loss recognized, by the shareholder.

EXAMPLE 4.5.1 Shareholder's Gain or Loss on Liquidation

IJK Corporation adopts a plan of liquidation during the current tax year. IJK has two shareholders, Tasha and Kimone. Tasha owns 70% of the stock and Kimone owns 30%. Before the liquidation, IJK's assets had a FMV of $3,200,000. IJK distributed $2,800,000 of the assets pro rata to Tasha ($1,960,000) and Kimone ($840,000). IJK used the remaining cash of $400,000 to pay the income taxes due at the corporate level on the distribution. Tasha and Kimone each assumed the liability attached to the land that was distributed to them, $350,000 and $150,000, respectively. Tasha and Kimone's basis in their stock, respectively, is $700,000 and $300,000. They had formed IJK seven years ago. Compute the shareholder's gain or loss, and their basis in the assets received.

SOLUTION

Tasha's and Kimone's gain or loss is computed as follows:

	Tasha	Kimone
FMV of assets received from the corporation	$1,960,000	$840,000
Less: Liability assumed by shareholder	(350,000)	(150,000)
Less: Adjusted basis of stock	(700,000)	(300,000)
Shareholder's gain	$ 910,000	$390,000

Tasha has a long-term capital gain of $910,000 and a basis in the assets she received of $1,960,000. Kimone has a long-term capital gain of $390,000 and a basis in the assets she received of $840,000.

Related exercises: Brief Exercise 10
Application Problem 32

Potential Pitfall

For distributions treated as dividends and redemptions, you learned the phrase *gains but not losses*, meaning that when property was distributed for these transactions, gains for the assets were recognized, but losses were not. For complete liquidations, the general rule is different. In general, losses embedded in assets are recognized by the corporation for a complete liquidation. However, in some situations, the loss recognition will be limited, as discussed below.

Tax Effects for Corporations

Corporations recognize gains and losses on a distribution in complete liquidation as if they had sold each distributed asset for its fair market value.[38] The FMV is reduced by the adjusted basis of each asset to determine the corporate gain or loss on the distribution. Other tax consequences to the liquidating corporation include:

- When the corporation distributes assets to the shareholders in a complete liquidation, it will need to retain enough cash to pay the taxes due on the liquidation at the corporate level.
- The nature of the gain or loss depends on whether the asset is capital, Section 1231, or ordinary.
- If the property distributed is encumbered by a liability that the shareholder assumes, then the FMV of the property cannot be less than the amount of the liability. For example, if property with a FMV of $100 is distributed in complete liquidation, and it is encumbered by debt of $120 that the shareholder assumes, then the FMV is presumed to be $120 for purposes of the liquidation.

[37]IRC §267(a)(1).
[38]IRC §336(a).

EXAMPLE 4.5.2 Corporation's Gain or Loss on Liquidation

Continuing with some of the facts from Example 4.5.1, IJK Corporation adopts a plan of liquidation during the current tax year. IJK has two shareholders, Tasha and Kimone. Tasha owns 70% of the stock and Kimone owns 30%. Before the liquidation, IJK's assets had a FMV of $3,200,000 and an adjusted basis of $2,600,000, as follows:

	Adjusted basis	Fair market value
Cash	$ 500,000	$ 500,000
Inventory	$ 630,000	$ 800,000
Equipment	$ 270,000	$ 230,000
Land	$1,200,000	$1,670,000

The land was purchased by IJK three years ago and is held for investment purposes. The equipment was purchased five years ago. IJK distributed $2,800,000 of the assets pro rata to Tasha ($1,960,000) and Kimone ($840,000). IJK used the remaining cash of $400,000 to pay the income taxes due at the corporate level on the distribution. Tasha and Kimone each assumed the liability attached to the land that was distributed to them, $350,000 and $150,000 respectively. What are the tax consequences of this distribution to IJK?

SOLUTION

IJK's gain or loss on the distribution of the assets in complete liquidation is computed as if each asset had been sold for its FMV as follows:

	Adjusted basis	Fair market value	Gain or loss	Character
Cash	$ 500,000	$ 500,000	$ 0	N/A
Inventory	$ 630,000	$ 800,000	$170,000	Ordinary
Equipment	$ 270,000	$ 230,000	($ 40,000)	Section 1231
Land	$1,200,000	$1,670,000	$470,000	Capital

The loss of $40,000 for the distribution is recognized by IJK. You will learn below that this is because the equipment was distributed pro-rata to the shareholders, and it was not contributed to IJK in a tax-free incorporation in the last two years. In other situations, the loss may not be recognized.

Related exercises: Discussion Question 15
Application Problem 33

Limitations on a Corporation's Loss Recognition

When a corporation has a realized loss from a complete liquidation, there are three situations for which loss recognition may be not allowed, or at least limited. These limitations are summarized in the flowchart in Illustration 4.7.

ILLUSTRATION 4.7 Loss Limitations to a Liquidating Corporation

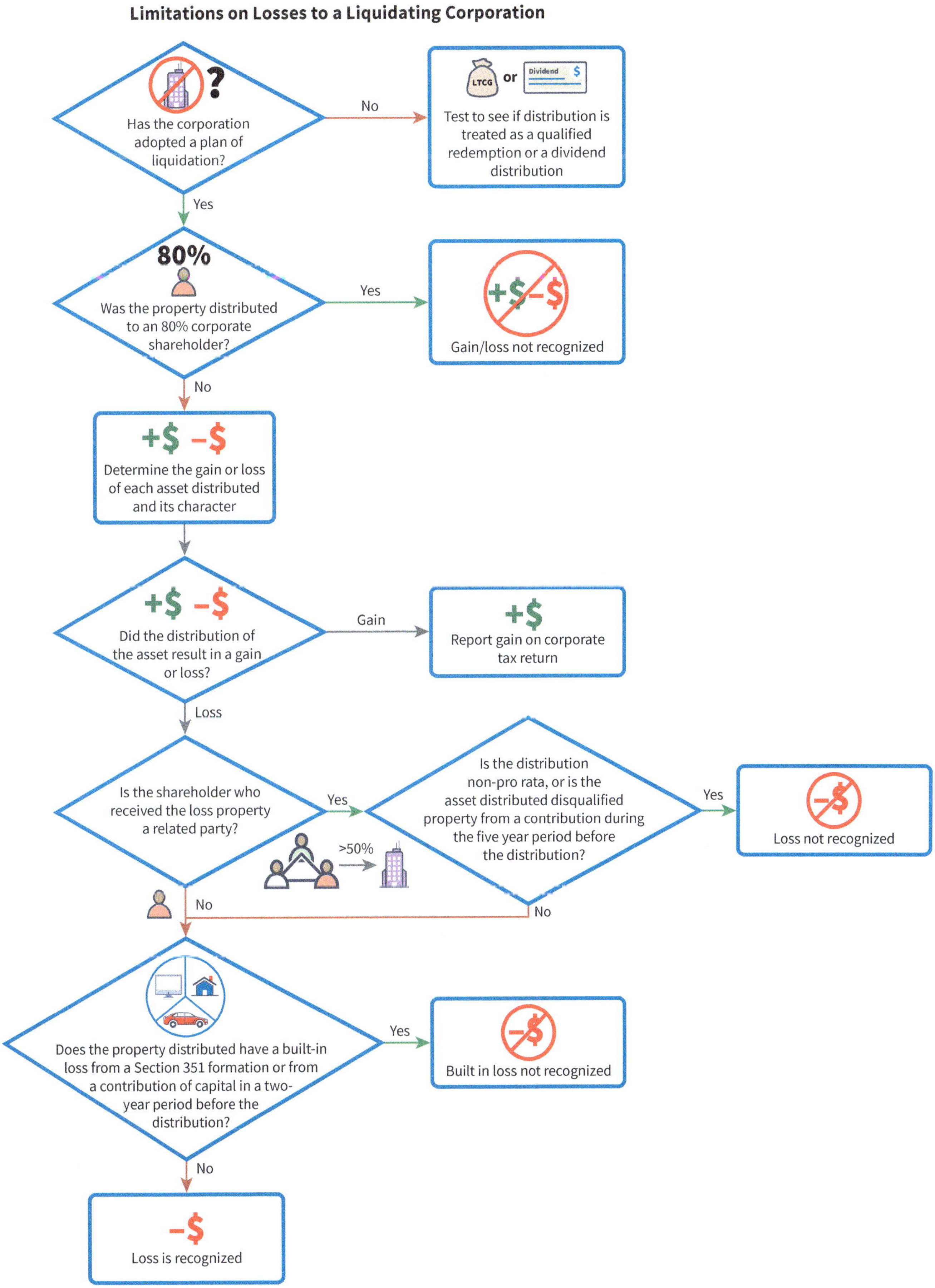

Why **Why does Congress limit the opportunity for corporations to recognize losses on corporate liquidations?** Congress limits corporate loss recognition only when it believes there are opportunities for corporations to use the tax law to create tax losses that may not be true economic losses. This can happen if the shareholder who receives the loss property is a related party, or if the loss property is *disqualified property*, meaning that it had been contributed to the corporation recently in a tax-deferred transaction or as a contribution to capital. Thus, the motivation for Congress to limit these losses in certain circumstances is to prevent corporations and shareholders from receiving unintended benefits.

Distributions of Loss Property to Related-Party Shareholders

In the context of a complete liquidation, a related party is a shareholder who owns, directly and/or indirectly, more than 50% of the corporation. The corporate loss limitations can occur for one of the following two reasons for distributions to related parties:[39]

- The loss property was distributed to a related party, and the property distributed in complete liquidation is **disqualified property**, meaning that the property was contributed to the corporation in a tax-deferred corporate formation under IRC §351, or a contribution to capital, during the five-year period ending when the property was distributed.

  Tax effect. In this circumstance, the loss is disallowed, even if it would be recognized had the asset been sold for its FMV on the date it was distributed to the related party.
- The loss property was distributed to a related party, and the property was *not* distributed pro rata to each shareholder (e.g., meaning that a 60% shareholder would not have received exactly 60% of the loss property).

  Tax effect. In this scenario, the loss is disallowed, even if it would be recognized had the asset been sold for its FMV on the date it was distributed to the related party.

The following Example is a comprehensive problem that demonstrates the application of these loss disallowance rules.

EXAMPLE 4.5.3 Loss Disallowance to Corporations for Related-Party Distributions

Continuing with the facts from Example 4.5.2, IJK Corporation adopts a plan of liquidation during the current tax year. IJK has two shareholders, Tasha and Kimone. Tasha owns 70% of the stock and Kimone owns 30%. Before the liquidation, IJK's assets had a FMV of $3,200,000 and an adjusted basis of $2,600,000, as follows:

	Adjusted basis	Fair market value
Cash	$ 500,000	$ 500,000
Inventory	$ 630,000	$ 800,000
Equipment	$ 270,000	$ 230,000
Land	$1,200,000	$1,670,000

The land was purchased by IJK three years ago and is held for investment purposes. The equipment was purchased five years ago. Tasha and Kimone each assumed the liability attached to the land that was distributed to them, $350,000 and $150,000, respectively.

a. IJK distributed the assets as follows to Tasha and Kimone. IJK used the remaining cash of $400,000 to pay the income taxes due at the corporate level on the distribution. What are the tax consequences to IJK?

	Adjusted basis	Fair market value	Distributed to Tasha	Distributed to Kimone
Cash	$ 500,000	$ 500,000	$ 1,000	$ 99,000
Inventory	$ 630,000	$ 800,000	$ 560,000	$240,000
Equipment	$ 270,000	$ 230,000	$ 230,000	$ 0
Land	$1,200,000	$1,670,000	$1,169,000	$501,000

[39]IRC §336(d).

b. Assume the same facts as in part **a.** except IJK distributed the assets as follows to Tasha and Kimone.

	Adjusted basis	Fair market value	Distributed to Tasha	Distributed to Kimone
Cash	$ 500,000	$ 500,000	$ 70,000	$ 30,000
Inventory	$ 630,000	$ 800,000	$ 560,000	$240,000
Equipment	$ 270,000	$ 230,000	$ 0	$230,000
Land	$1,200,000	$1,670,000	$1,330,000	$340,000

c. Assume the same set of facts as in part **a.** except IJK distributed the assets as follows to Tasha and Kimone.

	Adjusted basis	Fair market value	Distributed to Tasha	Distributed to Kimone
Cash	$ 500,000	$ 500,000	$ 58,500	$ 41,500
Inventory	$ 630,000	$ 800,000	$ 560,000	$240,000
Equipment	$ 270,000	$ 230,000	$ 172,500	$ 57,500
Land	$1,200,000	$1,670,000	$1,169,000	$501,000

SOLUTION

We must determine if any of the loss limitation rules apply to these distributions.

a. The $170,000 gain on the distribution of the inventory is recognized, as well as the $470,000 gain on the land. All of the equipment, the loss asset, was distributed to Tasha, who is a related party. The loss cannot be recognized by IJK because it was not distributed on a pro rata basis to the shareholders. The equipment was purchased five years ago, so it was not contributed in a Section 351 transaction.

b. The $170,000 gain on the distribution of the inventory is recognized, as well as the $470,000 gain on the land. The land was not distributed on a pro rata basis, but that does not prevent realized gains from being recognized in a complete liquidation. All of the equipment (the loss property) was distributed to Kimone, who is not a related party. Therefore, the $40,000 loss on the equipment can be recognized by IJK. The only other reason that the loss could be disallowed is if it was contributed to IJK in the last two years in a tax-free contribution (see next section), but that is not the case, because the equipment was purchased five years ago.

c. The $170,000 gain on the distribution of the inventory is recognized, as well as the $470,000 gain on the land. The equipment was distributed 75% to Tasha and 25% to Kimone. Because these ratios are different than their stock ownership ratios (70%/30%), the loss on the equipment cannot be recognized if it was distributed to a related party. Therefore, $30,000 of the loss, representing the 75% of the asset that was distributed to Tasha, cannot be recognized. The other $10,000 of the loss, representing the 25% of the asset that was distributed to Kimone, can be recognized.

Related exercises: Discussion Question 16
Application Problem 34

Distributions of Disqualified Property to Other Shareholders

Corporations can also have losses disallowed if the property distributed to shareholders who are not related parties in a complete liquidation is disqualified property, meaning that the property had been contributed to the corporation in a tax-deferred corporate formation under IRC §351, or a contribution to capital during the two-year period ending when the property was distributed.

Tax effect: Only the built-in loss is disallowed. The **built-in loss** is the loss that would have been recognized had the asset been sold for its FMV on the date it was *contributed to the corporation* during the previous two years.

The following Example illustrates this loss disallowance rule.

EXAMPLE 4.5.4
Loss Disallowance to Corporations for Distributions of Disqualified Property

QRS Corporation was formed by Luis and Armand in a tax-deferred Section 351 formation. Luis contributed $4,800,000 cash for an 80% interest, and Armand contributed land with a FMV of $1,200,000 and an adjusted basis of $1,340,000 for a 20% interest. Luis decided to completely liquidate QRS Corporation 18 months later, and as part of the liquidation, the land is distributed to Armand when it had a FMV of $1,150,000 and the adjusted basis is still $1,340,000. What are the tax effects of this distribution to QRS?

SOLUTION

When the property is distributed to Armand in complete liquidation, QRS realizes a loss of $190,000 ($1,150,000 FMV – $1,340,000 adjusted basis). The land was not distributed to a related party, but it is disqualified property because it had been contributed to the corporation in the last two years in a tax-deferred transaction. Therefore, the built-in loss at the time the property was contributed is disallowed to QRS. The built-in loss is $140,000 ($1,200,000 FMV – $1,340,000 adjusted basis). QRS can recognize a loss of $50,000, determined as follows:

Realized loss	$190,000
Disallowed built-in loss	(140,000)
Recognized loss	$ 50,000

Related exercise: Brief Exercise 11

Parent–Subsidiary Liquidations

There is a significant limitation to the recognition of gain or loss rule for corporate liquidations that applies to the corporation and to some shareholders. If the following two conditions are met, no gain or loss may be recognized to a parent corporation when liquidating a subsidiary corporation:[40]

- The parent owns 80% or more of the voting stock of the subsidiary and 80% or more of the value of all stock of the subsidiary, *and*
- The subsidiary distributes all of its assets within three years from the end of the tax year that the first distribution of assets as part of the liquidation occurs.

There are four main tax effects of the parent-subsidiary liquidation:

1. No gain or loss is recognized to the parent corporation.
2. If the subsidiary corporation distributes property to minority shareholders as part of the liquidation, gain is recognized, but not losses, by the subsidiary. A minority shareholder is any shareholder other than the parent corporation.
3. The parent corporation takes the same basis in the assets received from the subsidiary as the subsidiary had in them.
4. The parent corporation inherits the tax attributes of the subsidiary, such as net operating losses, earnings and profits, and credit carrybacks and carryforwards.

[40] IRC §337.

EXAMPLE 4.5.5 Liquidation of a Subsidiary

FGH Corporation is owned 90% by WXY Corporation and 10% by Kyrone. FGH owned the following assets:

	Adjusted basis	Fair market value
Cash	$100,000	$100,000
Accounts receivable	65,000	65,000
Inventory	220,000	300,000
Equipment	195,000	150,000
Land	120,000	185,000
Total	$700,000	$800,000

FGH adopted a plan of liquidation in the current year. All of its assets were distributed to its shareholders by the end of the tax year, as follows:

	Adjusted basis	Fair market value	WXY	Kyrone
Cash	$100,000	$100,000	$ 63,000	$ 7,000
Accounts receivable	65,000	65,000	58,500	6,500
Inventory	220,000	300,000	270,000	30,000
Equipment	195,000	150,000	135,000	15,000
Land	120,000	185,000	166,500	18,500
Total	$700,000	$800,000	$693,000	$77,000

FGH retained $30,000 of cash to pay its corporate tax liability on the liquidation. Kyrone's basis in his stock is $60,000 and WXY's basis is $600,000. Both shareholders acquired their stock seven years ago. What are the tax consequences to FGH and the shareholders, and what basis does WXY and Kyrone have in the distributed assets?

SOLUTION

This liquidation qualifies as a parent-subsidiary liquidation because WXY owns more than 80% of FGH and the liquidation was finalized within three years of the end of the tax year during which the first distribution was made. Therefore, the tax consequences are as follows:

- WXY, the parent corporation, recognizes no gain or loss.
- Kyrone recognizes a LTCG of $17,000 ($77,000 – $60,000 basis in stock)
- FGH, the subsidiary, recognizes no gain or loss for the assets distributed to WXY. FGH realizes gains and losses for the assets distributed to Kyrone, as follows:

	Adjusted basis	Fair market value	Realized gain or loss
Cash	$ 7,000	$ 7,000	$ 0
Accounts receivable	6,500	6,500	0
Inventory	22,000	30,000	8,000
Equipment	19,500	15,000	(4,500)
Land	12,000	18,500	6,500

  FGH must recognize $8,000 of ordinary income for the distribution of the inventory and $6,500 of capital gain for the distribution of the land. The $4,500 loss for the distribution of the equipment is not recognized.

- WXY has the same basis in the assets it received from FGH as FGH had in them (90% of FGH's basis in all the assets). Kyrone's basis in the assets received is the fair market value of the assets, because distributions to minority shareholders in liquidation are taxable.

	Adjusted basis—WXY	Adjusted basis—Kyrone
Cash	$ 63,000	$ 7,000
Accounts receivable	58,500	6,500
Inventory	198,000	30,000
Equipment	175,500	15,000
Land	108,000	18,500
Total	$603,000	$77,000

Related exercises: Multiple Choice 13
Application Problem 35

PRACTICE PROBLEM 4.5.1

Tax Consequences of a Liquidation

Redbird Corporation has two shareholders, Heather (25%) and Ashton (75%). Heather and Ashton formed the business eight years ago. Redbird adopts a plan of liquidation in the current year. Before the liquidation, Redbird's assets had a FMV of $333,000. Redbird distributed $263,000 of the assets pro rata to Heather ($65,750) and Ashton ($197,250). Redbird used the remaining cash of $70,000 to pay the income taxes at the corporate level on the distribution. Heather and Ashton each assumed the liability attached to the land that was distributed to them, $25,000 and $75,000 respectively. Heather and Ashton's basis in their stock, respectively, is $35,000 and $22,000. Compute the shareholder's gain or loss and their basis in the assets received.

SOLUTION

Heather and Ashton's gain is computed as follows:

	Heather	Ashton
FMV of assets received from Redbird	$ 65,750	$197,250
Less: Liability assumed by the shareholder	(25,000)	(75,000)
Less: Adjusted basis of the stock	(35,000)	(22,000)
Shareholder's gain	$ 5,750	$100,250

Heather has a long-term capital gain of $5,750 and a basis in the assets she received of $65,750. Ashton has a long-term capital gain of $100,250 and a basis in the assets she received of $197,250.

PRACTICE PROBLEM 4.5.2

Loss Recognition in Complete Liquidation

Moab Corporation was formed by Naomi and Ruth in a tax-deferred Section 351 formation. Naomi contributed $130,000 cash for a 65% interest, and Ruth contributed land with a FMV of $70,000 and an adjusted basis of $85,000 for a 35% interest. Naomi decides to completely liquidate Moab Corporation 20 months later, and, as part of the liquidation, the land is distributed to Ruth when it had a FMV of $61,000 and the adjusted basis is still $85,000. What are the tax effects of this distribution to Moab?

SOLUTION

When the property is distributed to Ruth in a complete liquidation, Moab realizes a loss of $24,000 ($61,000 FMV – $85,000 adjusted basis). The land was not distributed to a related party, but it is disqualified property because it had been contributed to the corporation in the last two years in a tax-deferred transaction. Therefore, the built-in loss at the time the property was contributed is disallowed to Moab. The built-in loss is $15,000 ($70,000 FMV – $85,000 adjusted basis). Moab can recognize a loss of $9,000, determined as follows:

Realized loss	$24,000
Less: Disallowed built-in loss	(15,000)
Recognized loss	$ 9,000

INTERACTIVE SELF-SCORING QUIZZES

Review and Practice

Chapter Summary

In this chapter, you have learned the tax consequences, for the shareholders and the corporation, of dividends, redemptions, and liquidations.

1 Determine the tax consequences of distributions to shareholders that are taxed as dividends.

- Ordinary dividends are taxed using two different rate structures:
  - Regular **ordinary dividends** are distributions from a corporation's *earnings and profits* that are taxed at ordinary income rates.
  - Ordinary dividends that are **qualified dividends** are taxed at long-term capital gain rates.
- For a dividend to be a qualified dividend:
  - Taxpayers must receive the dividend from a domestic corporation. Dividends from foreign corporations are eligible in certain circumstances.
  - Taxpayers must hold the stock for more than 60 days during the 121-day period beginning 60 days before the ex-dividend date.
- Having received a dividend, the taxpayer must determine the tax consequences of the distribution. There are four steps in determining if dividend income should be treated as ordinary income or as long-term capital gain.

  Step 1. **Determine: The fair market value of the cash and property distributed to the shareholder.**

  Step 2. **Determine: To what extent the dividend distribution comes from the corporation's earnings and profits.**

  Step 3. **Calculate: The portion of the dividend distribution (if any) that exceeds a corporation's earnings and profits and reduces the shareholder's basis in the stock.**

  Step 4. **Calculate: The portion of the dividend distribution (if any) that remains after the stock basis is reduced to zero.** Once a shareholder has reduced their stock basis to zero, the remaining amount of the distribution is a capital gain.

2 Evaluate a corporation's earnings and profits to determine the shareholder's dividend income from a corporate distribution.

- **Earnings and profits (E&P)** is the cumulative earnings for a corporation that it has never distributed as a dividend or a redemption. Conceptually, E&P is very similar to retained earnings, but is computed based on the tax law rather than financial reporting rules. Earnings and profits is a corporate-level account, not a shareholder account. There are two types of E&P:
  - **Accumulated E&P** is a corporation's E&P as of the beginning of the tax year.
  - **Current E&P** is a corporation's E&P generated during the tax year.
- Current E&P is computed by adjusting taxable income for tax items that are treated differently for purpose of taxable income versus E&P. In determining these adjustments, you should remember that E&P represents the corporation's ability to pay a dividend.
- Once E&P is computed, both current and accumulated E&P are used to determine whether a distribution is a dividend. E&P is negative if the corporation has had losses in the past and/or in the current year. Recall that distributions can never create or increase a deficit in E&P. Because E&P can be positive or negative, there are four different combinations of E&P that can occur:

	Accumulated E&P	Current E&P
Scenario #1	Positive	Positive
Scenario #2	Negative	Negative
Scenario #3	Negative	Positive
Scenario #4	Positive	Negative

- The following rules are used to allocate E&P to distributions:
  - Accumulated E&P is always used in chronological order.
  - A positive current E&P balance is prorated among the distributions based on the amount of the distributions.
  - A deficit in current E&P is allocated ratably during the year based on time, even if there is only one distribution for the year.
  - When more than one shareholder receives a distribution, E&P is allocated to the shareholders based on their proportionate ownership of the corporation.

3 Determine the tax consequences of property distributions to the corporation and the shareholder.

- If a corporation distributes appreciated property to a shareholder, it is treated as if the corporation sold the property for its fair market value, and the realized gain from the sale is recognized. However, if the corporation distributes property that has a fair market value *less* than its adjusted basis, the corporation *cannot* recognize a loss.

- When a corporation distributes property as a dividend, E&P is reduced by the *greater* of the adjusted basis or fair market value of the property. If there is a liability attached to the property that the shareholder assumes, this amount is reduced by the amount of the liability.
- The amount of the distribution to a shareholder is measured as the fair market value of the property less any debt attached to the property that is assumed by the shareholder.
- A special rule applies if the liability attached to distributed property is greater than the property's FMV. In that case, the tax law creates a *hypothetical* FMV equal to the amount of the liability, and the *hypothetical* FMV is used to determine the tax consequences to the corporation and to the shareholder. The *actual* FMV is not used for the computations.

4 Compute the tax consequences of a redemption for a corporate shareholder.

- A **stock redemption** occurs when a corporation purchases stock from a shareholder. If the purchase qualifies as a redemption for tax purposes, the transaction is treated as a property transaction and the shareholder will have a capital gain or loss. However, in some situations, the economic consequences of a sale of stock by a stockholder may more closely resemble a dividend than a property transaction. Hence, Congress has created laws to ensure that transactions that are very similar to a dividend will not qualify for redemption treatment.
- For a shareholder's sale of stock to the corporation to be treated as a property transaction, there must be a reduction in the shareholder's voting rights and the right to share in future profits. Congress has provided an objective test that is straightforward to use for this determination called the substantially disproportionate test. The stock sale is **substantially disproportionate** if:
  - the shareholder owns less than 50% of the voting power of the stock after the sale, *and*
  - the shareholder's ownership of the corporation's voting stock after the sale is less than 80% of their voting stock ownership before the sale.
- Congress has provided a subjective test which provides that the stock sale will be treated as a redemption as long as it is **not essentially equivalent to a dividend (NEED)**. The Supreme Court has ruled that the NEED standard can be satisfied only if there is a *meaningful reduction* in the redeemed shareholder's proportionate interest in the distributing corporation.
- The **constructive ownership** of stock rules must be used when determining the shareholder's ownership of voting stock before and after the sale of stock to the corporation. The constructive ownership rules provide that a shareholder is deemed to own stock owned by those related to the shareholder, in addition to the shares held directly by the shareholder. There are three sets of constructive ownership rules that apply to redemptions:
  - **Family attribution**
  - **Entity-to-owner attribution**
  - **Owner-to-entity attribution**
- The *complete termination rule* provides a means for a shareholder who constructively owns stock to be eligible for qualified redemption treatment. This provision allows the *family attribution* rules to be waived for the shareholder if all the following requirements are met:
  - The shareholder executes an agreement with the IRS providing that the shareholder will not directly reacquire any ownership interest in the corporation or exercise management influence for the next 10 years.
  - The individual cannot be an employee, director, or officer during this prohibited period.
  - The individual can be a creditor of the corporation during the 10-year period.
  - The selling shareholder must agree to notify the IRS if they reacquire stock in the corporation at any time during the next 10 years.
  - If stock is acquired by inheritance during the 10-year period, that is not treated as a prohibited transaction.
- The tax consequences for a corporation for distributing property to a shareholder as part of a redemption are the same as for a dividend: corporations recognize gains but not losses. If a corporation uses appreciated property as part of a redemption, the appreciation is recognized as gain to the corporation. But, if the corporation uses loss property, the loss is not recognized.
- Corporations must reduce their E&P after completing a redemption because the corporation has less stock outstanding. The reduction is the *lower* of:
  - the corporation's E&P × the percentage of stock redeemed, *or*
  - the redemption price.
- A **partial liquidation** occurs when a corporation that has more than one distinct line of business terminates one of those lines. The corporation remains in existence and continues to operate the remaining lines of business. If the necessary requirements are met for this to be a qualified redemption, then noncorporate shareholders are treated as if they sold their stock and have capital gain or loss. Corporate shareholders are treated as if they received a dividend, which is usually more beneficial to them because they may qualify for the dividends received deduction.
- The **objective test** for a partial liquidation provides that the corporation must have at least two qualifying trades or businesses before the partial liquidation, and at least one qualifying trade or business after the partial liquidation.

5 Compute the tax consequences of a corporate liquidation for the shareholder and the corporation.

- A **corporate liquidation** occurs when a corporation dissolves and distributes any remaining assets to the shareholders. A complete liquidation is similar to a redemption in that the shareholders are receiving cash and/or property in return for their stock. However, the tax implications for complete liquidations are different than for redemptions.
- The general rule for shareholders who surrender their shares in a complete liquidation is that gains and losses are recognized.
- If the shareholder assumes debt of the corporation as part of the liquidation, the FMV of the assets received by the

shareholder are reduced by the debt assumed. This reduces the amount of gain recognized, or increases the amount of loss recognized, by the shareholder.

- Corporations recognize gains and losses on a distribution in complete liquidation as if they had sold each distributed asset for its fair market value. However, losses may not be recognized by the corporation in certain situations.
- The corporate loss limitations can occur for one of the following two reasons for distributions to related parties:
  - The loss property was distributed to a related party, and the property distributed in complete liquidation is *disqualified property*, meaning that the property had been contributed to the corporation in a tax-deferred corporate formation under IRC §351, or a contribution to capital, during the five-year period ending when the property was distributed.

    Tax effect. In this circumstance, the loss is disallowed, even if it would be recognized had the asset been sold for its FMV on the date it was distributed to the related party.
  - The loss property was distributed to a related party, and the property was not distributed pro rata to each shareholder (e.g., meaning that a 60% shareholder would not have received exactly 60% of the loss property).

    Tax effect. In this circumstance, the loss is disallowed, even if it would be recognized had the asset been sold for its FMV on the date it was distributed to the related party.
- Corporations can also have losses disallowed if the property distributed to shareholders who are not related parties in complete liquidation is disqualified property, meaning that the property had been contributed to the corporation in a tax-deferred corporate formation under IRC §351, or a contribution to capital during the *two-year* period ending when the property was distributed,

  Tax effect: Only the built-in loss is disallowed. The built-in loss is the loss that would have been recognized had the asset been sold for its FMV on the date it was *contributed to the corporation* during the previous two years.
- No gain or loss is recognized to a parent corporation if a subsidiary corporation is liquidated if two conditions are met:
  - The parent must own 80% or more of the voting stock of the subsidiary and 80% or more of the value of all stock of the subsidiary, and
  - The subsidiary must distribute all of its assets within three years from the end of the tax year that the first distribution of assets as part of the liquidation occurs.
- If the subsidiary corporation distributes property to minority shareholders as part of the liquidation, gain is recognized, but not losses, by the subsidiary. A minority shareholder is any shareholder other than the parent corporation.

Communication Application

Communication

Property Distribution

(LO2) Rory owns 100% of Hole in One, Inc., an accrual-based calendar-year corporation. Hole in One would like to distribute a golf cart that it is no longer using in the business to Rory. The golf cart has a fair market value of $4,500 and an adjusted basis of $8,800. Rory indicated to you that the corporation will be able to offset the loss against its existing capital gains on its tax return.

What is your advice to Rory? Write a memo to Rory.

Solution

Hello Rory,

I really enjoyed playing golf with you last Saturday. The course was challenging! I am happy to assist you with any accounting and tax questions that you have for Hole in One and yourself as its 100% shareholder.

The corporation is planning on distributing a golf cart to you that has a fair market value that is less than its adjusted basis, creating a realized loss of $4,300 ($8,800 – $4,500). Unfortunately, if the corporation distributes property that has a fair market value that is less than its adjusted basis, the corporation cannot recognize the loss. Hole in One will not be able to use the loss to help offset its existing capital gains.

I would suggest having Hole in One sell the golf cart. The corporation would be able to recognize the loss and partially offset its existing capital gains. The corporation could then distribute the cash to you as a cash dividend.

If you have any questions, please let me know. I am more than happy to assist you. And if you ever need a fourth for your Saturday tee time, I am willing!

Sincerely,
Carnes & Youngberg, CPAs

Ethics and Professional Responsibilities Application

Ethics

Constructive Dividend

(LO2) Milana owns a day care center called Milana's Minutes, Inc. Milana is a 100% shareholder, and she handles all of the hiring, training, and bookkeeping. While shopping for her day care center, she frequently purchases personal items for her home on the corporate credit card. You have been hired to prepare the tax return and have reviewed the corporation's QuickBooks file. You noticed the personal purchases and ask Milana for more information about those purchases. Milana's answers were vague, but she finally admits that sometimes she charges personal items to the corporate credit card. Milana says she owns 100% of the business so it shouldn't matter because it is all her money anyway. What is your advice to Milana?

In addition to the chapter content, see *Statements on Standards for Tax Services* at www.aicpa-cima.com/resources/landing/statements-on-standards-for-tax-services, *Circular 230* at https://www.irs.gov/tax-professionals/office-of-professional-responsibility-and-circular-230, and *Taxation of Business Entities*, Chapter 2, LO4, Tax Professional Responsibilities.

Solution

While reviewing the QuickBooks file, it was noticed that some items purchased have been confirmed as being used for personal purposes. None of the items purchased for personal use are deductible by the corporation. Expenses must be related to the trade or business and must be ordinary, necessary, and reasonable to be deductible. Because the corporation paid for these personal expenses, the purchase price will be considered a constructive dividend to Milana. Constructive dividends are benefits paid to shareholders in a form other than cash, property, or stock. The law treats these benefits as ordinary income. A constructive dividend can include payment by a corporation of expenses of a shareholder without expectation of repayment.

According to *Circular 230* §10.22 Diligence as to accuracy, "A practitioner must exercise due diligence—(1) In preparing or assisting in the preparation of, approving, and filing of tax returns, documents, affidavits, and other papers relating to other Internal Revenue Service matters;" Also, the *Statement on Standards for Tax Services* No. 2.3.3 indicates that "if the tax law or regulations impose a condition with respect to deductibility or other tax treatment of an item, such as taxpayer maintenance of books and records or substantiating documentation to support the reported deduction or tax treatment, a member should make appropriate inquiries to determine to the member's satisfaction whether such condition has been met." Milana does not want to report the purchases as a constructive dividend, but as a tax professional you must follow the guidance of *Circular 230* and *SSTS* No. 2.

Key Terms

Accumulated E&P 4-12
Built-in Loss (Corporate Liquidation) 4-47
Constructive Dividends 4-10
Constructive Ownership 4-31
Contraction of the Corporate Business (Partial Liquidation) 4-38
Corporate Liquidation 4-42
Current E&P 4-12
Declaration Date 4-5
Disqualified Property (Corporate Liquidation) 4-46
Dividend 4-4
Earnings and Profits (E&P) 4-12
Entity-to-Owner Attribution 4-32
Ex-dividend Date 4-5
Family Attribution 4-32
Not Essentially Equivalent to a Dividend (NEED) 4-29
Objective Test (Partial Liquidation) 4-38
Ordinary Dividends 4-4
Owner-to-Entity Attribution 4-33
Partial Liquidation 4-38
Payment Date 4-5
Qualified Dividends 4-4
Qualifying Trade or Business (Partial Liquidation) 4-38
Reattribution 4-34
Record Date 4-5
Stock Dividend 4-8
Stock Redemption 4-26
Subjective Test (Partial Liquidation) 4-38
Substantially Disproportionate 4-29

End-of-Chapter Assessment

Discussion Questions

1. **(LO1)** Briefly describe the definition for a dividend's date of declaration, date of record, and ex-dividend date.

2. **(LO1)** Explain the difference between an ordinary dividend and a qualified dividend.

3. **(LO1)** At what tax rate is a qualified dividend income taxed for an individual taxpayer?

4. **(LO1)** Is the receipt of a stock dividend typically a taxable event for a taxpayer? Why?

5. **(LO2)** What is earnings and profits (E&P)?

6. **(LO2)** Describe the four categories of differences between taxable income and earnings and profits?

7. **(LO3)** What does the phrase "gains, but not losses" refer to in regard to a property distribution?

8. **(LO3)** If a corporation is considering distributing an asset to a shareholder, should the corporation distribute an asset if the fair market value is less than the adjusted basis?

9. **(LO4)** What is a stock redemption and how is it typically treated for tax purposes?

10. **(LO4)** What are two advantages to a sale of stock by a shareholder being treated as a property transaction?

11. **(LO4)** What is constructive ownership?

12. **(LO4 Advanced)** Describe reattribution.

13. **(LO4)** Explain the adjustment to earnings and profits that is necessary because of a property distribution using appreciated property that is treated as a qualified redemption.

14. **(LO4)** How is a partial liquidation treated for a noncorporate shareholder versus a corporate shareholder?

15. **(LO5)** In general, what are the tax consequences for a corporation that adopts a plan of liquidation?

16. **(LO5)** In the context of a complete liquidation, what is the definition of a related party?

Multiple Choice Questions

1. **(LO1)** Hubie is the sole shareholder of EW Enterprises, Inc. His basis in the EW stock is $100,000. On December 31 of the current year, EW distributed $175,000 cash to Hubie. EW has current and accumulated earnings and profits, in total, of $60,000. How will this distribution be treated for federal income tax purposes?
   - **a.** Dividend income of $60,000 and capital gain of $15,000
   - **b.** Dividend income of $75,000
   - **c.** Dividend income of $60,000 and capital gain of $115,000
   - **d.** Dividend income of $175,000

2. **(LO1)** Louise owns 100 shares of Social, Inc. common stock that she purchased for $1,500. On May 29 of the current year, Social issued a 10% proportionate common stock dividend and Louise received an additional 10 shares, each of which has a value of $18. How much income does Louise report for this dividend?
   - **a.** $0
   - **b.** $180
   - **c.** $1,500
   - **d.** $1,800

3. **(LO1)** Which of the following is considered a constructive dividend? Select all that apply.
   - **a.** A loan to a shareholder at a below-market interest rate.
   - **b.** Excessive compensation that is above a reasonable rate.
   - **c.** Use by shareholders of corporate property at less than fair market value.
   - **d.** Assumption of shareholder debt by the corporation.
   - **e.** Payments made to others for the benefit of the shareholder.

4. **(LO2)** Which one of the following reduces earnings and profits but does not reduce taxable income?
   - **a.** Fines and penalties
   - **b.** Federal income tax
   - **c.** Entertainment expenses
   - **d.** All of the above

5. **(LO2)** Which one of the following items reported on a C corporation's tax return would not require an adjustment to taxable income when computing earnings and profits?
   - **a.** Straight-line depreciation
   - **b.** Installment sale income
   - **c.** Amortization of organizational expenses
   - **d.** Entertainment expenses

6. **(LO3)** Spartan, Inc. owns 1,000 shares of Illini Corporation stock that it bought in 2004 for $10 per share. In the current year, when the fair market value of Illini stock was $22 per share, Spartan distributed this stock to a noncorporate shareholder. Spartan's recognized gain on the distribution is:
   - **a.** $22,000
   - **b.** $12,000
   - **c.** $10,000
   - **d.** $0

7. **(LO3)** A distribution from a C corporation to a shareholder cannot be treated by the shareholder as which of the following classifications?

a. Dividend income

b. Nontaxable return of capital

c. Capital gain

d. Capital loss

8. **(LO4)** Mia is a 100% shareholder in APLUS, Inc. and owns all 1,000 shares outstanding. Her basis in each share is $40. Mia sells 400 shares to APLUS for $65 per share. Assuming that APLUS has earnings and profits of $250,000, what are the tax consequences to Mia?

a. No income recognized

b. $26,000 capital gain

c. $10,000 capital gain

d. $26,000 dividend income

9. **(LO4)** A stock sale is substantially disproportionate if:

a. The shareholder owns less than 50% of the voting power of the stock after the sale.

b. The shareholder's ownership of the corporation's voting stock after the sale is less than 80% of their voting stock ownership before the sale.

c. Neither a. nor b.

d. Both a. and b.

10. **(LO4)** Under the family attribution rules, Jouri is not deemed to indirectly own the stock owned by which of the following?

a. Jouri's spouse

b. Jouri's mother

c. Jouri's grandson

d. Jouri's ex-wife

11. **(LO4)** For the family attribution rules to be waived, a shareholder who completely terminates their interest must not reacquire any shares within how many years?

a. 1 year

b. 2 years

c. 10 years

d. 20 years

12. **(LO4)** Lilac Corporation, a C corporation with earnings and profits, redeemed shares of stock from an individual shareholder. The distribution in redemption of stock will likely result in dividend income treatment to the redeeming shareholder if:

a. The redemption is proportionate with respect to the shareholder.

b. The redemption is due to a complete liquidation of the corporation.

c. The redemption is due to a partial liquidation of the corporation.

d. The redemption results in a complete termination of the shareholder's interest in the corporation.

13. **(LO5)** No gain or loss is recognized by a parent corporation if a subsidiary corporation is liquidated if which of the following two conditions are met?

I. The parent must own 80% or more of the voting stock of the subsidiary and 80% or more of the value of all stock of the subsidiary.

II. The parent must own 50% or more of the voting stock of the subsidiary and 50% or more of the value of all stock of the subsidiary.

III. The subsidiary must distribute all of its assets within three years from the end of the tax year that the first distribution of assets as part of the liquidation occurs.

IV. The subsidiary must distribute all of its assets within two years from the end of the tax year that the first distribution of assets as part of the liquidation occurs.

a. I & III

b. I & IV

c. II & III

d. II & IV

Brief Exercises

1. **(LO1)** Doud received dividend income from the following sources:

Met Life Insurance Company	$1,450
Mexico Manufacturing Company	$1,100
Schwab mutual fund	$ 660
Fair market value common stock dividend	$2,000

How much is includible in Doud's taxable income?

2. **(LO2)** White Inc. has taxable income of $444,000 and is an accrual-basis taxpayer. Compute White's earnings and profits given the following information for the current year:

Installment sale income reported in the current year; the sale occurred last year	$60,000
Federal income tax	$95,000
Lobbying expenses	$12,000
Bonus depreciation deducted in the current year in excess of allowable ADS depreciation	$23,000
Municipal interest income	$ 5,000

3. **(LO2)** Bruster, Inc. had a deficit in accumulated earnings and profits of $45,000 at the beginning of the year and had current earnings and profits of $9,000. At year end, Bruster paid a dividend of $16,000 to its sole shareholder. What amount of the dividend is reported as income?

4. **(LO3)** Webster, a C corporation, has $70,000 of accumulated earnings and profits and no current earnings and profits. Webster distributes $20,000 cash and property with a fair market value and adjusted basis of $60,000 to its shareholders. What amount should the shareholders report as dividend income?

5. **(LO4)** Yao is a 40% shareholder in Hover, Inc. He sells 50 shares of his stock to Hover for $100,000. His basis in his shares sold was $65,000. After the sale, Yao owns 30% of Hover, Inc. How much income does Yao recognize?

6. **(LO4)** Abraham owns 200 shares of Canaan Corporation, and the remaining shares are owned by the following:

Sarah (Abraham's wife)	100 shares
Hagar (Abraham's maid who lives with Abraham and Sarah)	50 shares
Isaac (Abraham's son)	25 shares
Ishmael (Abraham's son)	25 shares
Terah (Abraham's father)	150 shares
Jacob (Abraham's grandson)	25 shares

How many shares does Abraham own using the constructive ownership rules?

7. **(LO4)** Concrete Corporation has 5,000 shares of stock outstanding. Sebastian owns 75% or 3,750 shares of Concrete, and Matus owns 25% or 1,250 shares of Concrete. Sebastian owns 200 shares of Sand, Inc. and Matus owns 1,000 shares of Rock Inc. How many total shares of Sand and Rock is Concrete deemed to own under the constructive ownership rules?

8. **(LO4)** Dogs R Us Corporation (DRU) has 500 shares outstanding. The DRU stock is owned by the following:

Sergio	150 shares
Sergio's father	100 shares
Sergio's son	125 shares
Kitten Partnership	125 shares

Sergio owns 20% of Kitten Partnership. Sergio sells his 150 shares to DRU Corporation for $15,000. Does this sale constitute a complete termination of Sergio's stock interest for purposes of the redemption rules, assuming Sergio files the proper paperwork with the IRS?

9. **(LO4)** Dance Academy Inc. has been in existence for ten years. During this time, it has established four active businesses that sell the following items or services as shown below:

Leasing studio space	6 years
Selling of dance clothing	7 years
Instructor training and competitions	10 years
Set design	4 years

During the current year, Dance Academy Inc. distributes all the assets in the selling of dance clothing and set design businesses to its shareholders for 55% of their Dance Academy stock. Is this treated as a partial liquidation?

10. **(LO5)** Good For You, Inc. (GFY) has two shareholders, Sanjay (45%) and Amit (55%). Sanjay and Amit formed the business 12 years ago. GFY adopts a plan of liquidation in the current year. Before the liquidation, GFY's assets had a FMV of $555,000. GFY distributed $400,000 of the assets pro rata to Sanjay ($180,000) and Amit ($220,000). GFY used the remaining cash of $155,000 to pay the income taxes due at the corporate level on the distribution. Sanjay and Amit's basis in their stock, respectively, is $185,000 and $190,000. Compute the shareholder's gain or loss, and their basis in the assets received.

11. **(LO5)** Bewitched Corporation was formed by Samantha and Darrin in a tax-deferred Section 351 formation. Samantha contributed $120,000 cash for a 60% interest, and Darrin contributed land with a FMV of $80,000 and an adjusted basis of $95,000 for a 40% interest. Samantha decides to completely liquidate Bewitched Corporation 15 months later, and as part of the liquidation, the land is distributed to Darrin when it had a FMV of $72,000 and the adjusted basis is still $95,000. What are the tax effects of this distribution to Bewitched?

Application Problems

1. **(LO1)** Kathy and Tom, who file as married filing jointly, received Form 1099-DIV from Coca-Cola, Inc., showing ordinary dividends of $2,300 and qualified dividends of $1,800. Kathy and Tom have taxable income of $100,000. Their marginal tax bracket is 22%. What is the tax liability on the dividend income received?

2. **(LO1)** Dicky owns 100% of Kernals, Inc. stock, which he purchased 9 months ago on March 31 for $2,800. Kernals, Inc. distributed cash of $7,000 to Dicky on December 31, when its earnings and profits (E&P) were $3,800. What is the tax effect to Dicky from the payment of the cash distribution?

3. **(LO1)** Bane and Bruce each own a percentage of Wayne Enterprises. Bane owns 40% (400 shares of the 1,000 shares outstanding) and Bruce owns 60% (600 shares of the 1,000 shares outstanding). Bane has a stock basis of $4,000 and Bruce has a stock basis of $6,000. Wayne Enterprises declares a proportionate, 100% common stock dividend.

   a. Is this a taxable event for Bane and Bruce?

   b. What is the tax basis of each share of Wayne Enterprises stock held by Bane and Bruce after the dividend?

4. **(LO1)** Hank owns 1,000 shares of common stock of Jasper Corporation and has a $4,400 basis in his shares. Jasper Corporation declares a 400% stock dividend for every shareholder that owns common stock.

   a. Is this a taxable event for Hank?

   b. What is the tax basis of each share of Jasper Corporation stock held by Hank after the distribution?

5. **(LO1)** Adam owns 1,000 shares of Green Corporation common stock that was acquired in Year 3 for $15,000. In Year 6, Adam received a nontaxable dividend of 100 Green Corporation preferred shares. On the date of distribution, the FMV of the common shares was $20,000, and the FMV of the preferred shares was $8,000. What is the basis of the preferred shares and the common shares after the stock dividend?

6. **(LO1)** Jamie has owned and operated her own clothing boutique, Style, Inc., since Year 5. Jamie's daughter, Nicole, has had a string of bad luck with her employment. Jamie hires Nicole to perform cashier work for Style, Inc. In the current year, Year 8, Style, Inc. paid Nicole $125,000. The average salary for cashier work in their area is $42,000. Style, Inc. took a salary deduction of $125,000 for payment to Nicole. Is the $125,000 payment a valid salary deduction for Style, Inc.?

7. **(LO2)** Pink Inc. has taxable income of $925,000 and is an accrual-basis taxpayer. Compute Pink's earnings and profits given the following information for the current year:

Installment sale income reported in the current year; the sale occurred last year	$ 38,000
Federal income tax	$132,000
E&P depreciation	$ 22,000
Tax depreciation	$ 18,000
Charitable contributions in excess of 10% limit	$ 9,000
Municipal interest income	$ 3,500
Net capital losses	$ 5,500
Proceeds from corporate life insurance policy	$200,000
Life insurance premiums for a policy on corporate owned policies for executives or officers	$ 4,800

8. **(LO2)** At the beginning of the year, Billions, Inc., an accrual-basis C corporation, had a $33,000 deficit in earnings and profits (E&P). For the current year, Billions Inc. had current E&P of $18,000 and made a $22,000 cash distribution to its shareholders. What amount of the distribution is taxable as dividend income to Billions' stockholders?

9. **(LO2)** Tomato Inc., a calendar-year, accrual-basis corporation, had $22,000 of accumulated E&P as of the beginning of the current year. During the current year, Tomato had $14,000 of current E&P and made four quarterly distributions of $2,000 each to its shareholders. What amount of the distribution is taxable as dividend income to Tomato's shareholders?

10. **(LO2)** On January 1 of the current year, Chain Corporation, a calendar-year, accrual-basis C corporation, had $42,000 of accumulated E&P. For the current year, Chain had current E&P of $32,000 and made two $38,000 cash distributions to its shareholders, one in April and one in September. What amount of the distribution is taxable as dividend income to Chain's shareholders?

11. **(LO2)** Tank Corporation is a calendar-year, accrual-basis corporation. Tank had an E&P deficit of $16,000 for January 1 through June 30 of the current year and positive E&P of $22,000 for July 1 through December 31 of the current year. Tank Corporation made a distribution of $5,000 on July 1 of the current year. What amount of the distribution is taxable as dividend income to Tank's shareholders?

12. **(LO2)** Jamison owns 100% of Backstreet Corporation, and he receives a distribution of $55,000 in the current tax year. This is the only distribution made by Backstreet this year. Jamison purchased his stock three years ago for $22,000. Determine Jamison's tax consequences for each of the scenarios below:

	Accumulated E&P	Current E&P
Scenario 1	$40,000	$20,000
Scenario 2	($40,000)	($20,000)
Scenario 3	($40,000)	$20,000
Scenario 4	$40,000	($19,000)

13. **(LO2)** TennisNow, Inc. is a calendar-year, accrual-basis C corporation that has $19,000 of accumulated E&P as of the beginning of the year. TennisNow has $44,000 of current E&P in the current year and made four quarterly distributions of $18,000 each. How are the distributions treated for tax purposes to the shareholders?

14. **(LO2)** Dainty, Inc., a calendar-year, accrual-basis C corporation, has accumulated E&P of $67,000 at the beginning of the year. Dainty had a deficit in current E&P for the current year of $38,000 and made a $22,000 distribution on April 1 and October 1 of the current year. How are the distributions treated for tax purposes to the shareholders?

15. **(LO3)** Discreet Inc. owns a warehouse with a fair market value of $233,000 and an adjusted basis of $88,000. If Discreet distributes the warehouse to a shareholder, how much gain, if any, must Discreet recognize on the distribution?

16. **(LO3)** Ocampa Corporation has earnings and profits of $127,000 when it distributes an asset to its shareholder. The asset has a fair market value of $45,000 and an adjusted basis of $52,000. There is a mortgage attached to the asset of $35,000 which the shareholder will assume.

   a. What is the tax effect to the shareholder?

   b. What is the tax effect to Ocampa Corporation?

17. **(LO3)** Hope Corporation, a C corporation, distributes land to its sole shareholder, Charlie, with a fair market value of $40,000 and an adjusted basis of $25,000. Hope has total earnings and profits of $500,000.

   a. What is Hope's recognized gain or loss?

   b. What is Charlie's dividend income?

   c. What is Charlie's basis in the land?

18. **(LO3)** Fox, the sole shareholder in Fall Corporation, has a tax basis of $60,000 in Fall. Fall has $40,000 of accumulated earnings and profits at the beginning of the year and $10,000 of current earnings and profits for the current year. At year end, Fall distributed land with an adjusted basis of $30,000 and a fair market value of $38,000 to Fox. The land has an outstanding mortgage of $3,000 that Fox must assume.

   a. What is Fall Corporation's recognized gain/loss?

   b. What is Fox's dividend income?

   c. What is Fox's basis in the land after the distribution?

19. **(LO3)** Dahl Corporation was organized and commenced operations in 2012. On December 31 of the current year, Dahl had total accumulated and current earnings and profits of $19,000 before any dividend declaration and distribution. On December 31 of the current year, Dahl distributed cash of $9,000 and a vacant parcel of land to

Green, Dahl's only stockholder. At the date of the distribution, the land had a basis of $5,000 and a fair market value of $40,000.

a. What is the effect on Dahl's earnings and profits from these distributions?

b. What is Green's taxable dividend income in the current year from these distributions?

20. **(LO3)** Drum Corporation owns a vacant lot with a fair market value of $233,000 and an adjusted basis of $165,000. There is a mortgage attached to the lot of $98,000. Earnings and profits is $154,000 before the distribution. Drum distributes the lot to Bubba, a shareholder, and he assumes the mortgage. Bubba's basis in his stock is $138,000. Answer the following questions with regard to this distribution.

a. How much gain or loss does Drum Corporation recognize?

b. What is Drum's E&P after the distribution?

c. What is the amount distributed to Bubba?

d. How is the distribution taxed to Bubba?

e. What is Bubba's basis in the lot?

21. **(LO3)** Drum Corporation owns a vacant lot with a fair market value of $233,000 and an adjusted basis of $165,000. There is a mortgage attached to the lot of $98,000. Earnings and profits is $54,000 before the distribution. Drum distributes the lot to Bubba, a shareholder, and he assumes the mortgage. Bubba's basis in his stock is $138,000. Answer the following questions with regard to this distribution.

a. How much gain or loss does Drum Corporation recognize?

b. What is Drum's E&P after the distribution?

c. What is the amount distributed to Bubba?

d. How is the distribution taxed to Bubba?

e. What is Bubba's basis in the lot?

22. **(LO3)** Drum Corporation owns a vacant lot with a fair market value of $233,000 and an adjusted basis of $165,000. There is a mortgage attached to the lot of $244,000. Earnings and profits is $154,000 before the distribution. Drum distributes the lot to Bubba, a shareholder, and he assumes the mortgage. Bubba's basis in his stock is $138,000. Answer the following questions with regard to this distribution.

a. How much gain or loss does Drum Corporation recognize?

b. What is Drum's E&P after the distribution?

c. What is the amount distributed to Bubba?

d. How is the distribution taxed to Bubba?

e. What is Bubba's basis in the lot?

23. **(LO4)** Two years ago, Sabrina purchased 50 shares of voting stock in Witch, Inc. for $5,000. Witch Inc. has 500 shares outstanding. In the current year, Sabrina sells 15 shares of her stock back to Witch for $1,800. What are the tax consequences of the sale to Sabrina?

24. **(LO4)** Terrell has owned 750 voting shares of City Corporation for five years. His basis per share is $100. City has 1,000 shares outstanding. In the current year, Terrell sells 400 shares of his stock back to City for $125 per share. What are the tax consequences of the sale to Terrell?

25. **(LO4)** Deacon owns 730 shares of Electric Company's 1,175 shares outstanding. His basis per share is $15. Deacon has owned Electric for several years. In the current year, Deacon sells 290 shares of his stock to Electric for $7,250. What are the tax consequences of the sale to Deacon? (Round to two decimal places in your calculation.)

26. **(LO4)** Hamad has ownership in several businesses:

- 80% ownership in Circle Corporation (800 shares) which owns 400 shares of Square Inc.
- 35% ownership in Oval Corporation (350 shares) which owns 100 shares in Rectangle Inc.
- 55% ownership in Triangle Partnership which owns 500 shares of Rhombus Inc.
- 20% ownership in Pentagon Partnership which owns 600 shares in Octagon Inc.

How many total shares is Hamad deemed to own directly and indirectly under the constructive ownership rules for each of these corporations?

27. **(LO4)** Red Partnership has two partners, Frank and Joseph. Frank owns 70% of the partnership and Joseph owns 30%. Frank owns 150 shares of Hawk Corporation and Joseph owns 800 shares of Eagle Corporation. How many total shares is Red deemed to own under the constructive ownership rules?

28. **(LO4)** Grass Courts, Inc. has 1,500 shares outstanding. The Grass Courts stock is owned by the following:

Tiafo	800 shares
Tiafo's mother	300 shares
Tiafo's cousin	150 shares
Clay Courts Corporation	250 shares

Tiafo owns 70% of Clay Courts Corporation. Tiafo sells his 800 shares to Grass Courts Corporation for $6,000. Does this sale constitute a complete termination of Tiafo's stock interest for purposes of the redemption rules, assuming Tiafo files the proper paperwork with the IRS? If not, will the sale be treated as a qualified redemption?

29. **(LO4)** Autumn owns 250 shares of voting stock of Fern Corporation that she purchased four years ago. The corporation has 1,000 shares of voting stock outstanding. Autumn sells all 250 shares of stock to Fern for $50,000. Her basis in the shares sold is $22,000. Fern pays for the stock by distributing land to Autumn with a FMV of $50,000 and an adjusted basis of $27,000. Fern's total E&P before the redemption was $66,000. What are the tax consequences of the sale to Fern Corporation?

30. **(LO4)** Autumn owns 250 shares of voting stock of Fern Corporation that she purchased four years ago. The corporation has 1,000 shares of voting stock outstanding. Autumn sells all 250 shares of stock to Fern for $50,000. Her basis in the shares sold is $22,000. Fern pays for the stock by distributing land to Autumn with a FMV of $50,000 and an adjusted basis of $55,000. Fern's total E&P before the redemption was $66,000. What are the tax consequences of the sale to Fern Corporation?

31. **(LO4 Advanced)** Yoon died during the current year. The value of his estate at the date of his death, after reduction for expenses, indebtedness, and losses is $12,300,000. Yoon was a 100% shareholder in Havel Corporation. This stock was valued at $4,500,000 (90,000 shares @ $50 per share) on the date of his death. Yoon's executor has completed all federal and state tax returns related to his death that must be filed. His total estate taxes are $1,476,000. To generate cash to pay these taxes, his executor redeemed $1,550,000 of Havel stock from the corporation. Havel stock had a FMV of $65 per share on the day of redemption. The estate also paid $30,000 of funeral and administration expenses. What are the tax consequences of this redemption for Yoon's estate?

32. **(LO5)** Canyon Corporation has two shareholders, Heath (35%) and Suni (65%). Heath and Suni formed the business ten years ago.

Canyon adopts a plan of liquidation in the current year. Before the liquidation, Canyon's assets had a FMV of $888,000. Canyon distributed $700,000 of the assets pro rata to Heath ($245,000) and Suni ($455,000). Canyon used the remaining cash of $188,000 to pay the income taxes due at the corporate level on the distribution. Heath and Suni each assumed liability attached to the land that was distributed to them, $35,000 and $65,000 respectively. Heath and Suni's basis in their stock, respectively, is $125,000 and $200,000. Compute each shareholder's gain or loss and their basis in the assets received.

33. **(LO5)** Canyon Corporation has two shareholders, Heath (35%) and Suni (65%). Heath and Suni formed the business ten years ago. Canyon adopts a plan of liquidation in the current year. Before the liquidation, Canyon's assets had a FMV of $888,000 and an adjusted basis of $750,000 as follows:

Asset	FMV	Adjusted basis
Cash	$ 12,000	$ 12,000
Accounts receivable	$125,000	$125,000
Machinery	$400,000	$444,000
Land	$307,000	$537,000

The land was purchased by Canyon four years ago and is held for investment purposes. The machinery was purchased three years ago. Canyon distributed $700,000 of the assets pro rata to Heath ($245,000) and Suni ($455,000). Canyon used the remaining cash of $188,000 to pay the income taxes due at the corporate level on the distribution. Heath and Suni each assumed liability attached to the land that was distributed to them, $35,000 and $65,000 respectively. Heath and Suni's basis in their stock, respectively, is $125,000 and $200,000. What are the tax effects of this distribution to Canyon Corporation?

34. **(LO5)** Brave Corporation adopts a plan of liquidation during the current tax year. Brave has two shareholders, Chipper (60%) and Maddox (40%). Before the liquidation, Brave's assets had a FMV of $1,135,000 and an adjusted basis of $800,000 as follows:

Asset	Adjusted basis	FMV
Cash	$160,000	$160,000
Inventory	$115,000	$325,000
Machinery	$165,000	$100,000
Land	$360,000	$550,000

The land was purchased by Brave six years ago and is held for investment purposes. The machinery was purchased four years ago.

a. Brave distributed the assets as follows to Chipper and Maddox:

Asset	Adjusted basis	FMV	Distributed to Chipper	Distributed to Maddox
Cash	$160,000	$160,000	$ 11,000	$ 74,000
Inventory	$115,000	$325,000	$195,000	$130,000
Machinery	$165,000	$100,000	$100,000	$ 0
Land	$360,000	$550,000	$330,000	$220,000

Brave used the remaining cash of $75,000 to pay the income taxes due at the corporate level on the distribution. What are the tax consequences to Brave?

b. Brave distributed the assets as follows to Chipper and Maddox:

Asset	Adjusted basis	FMV	Distributed to Chipper	Distributed to Maddox
Cash	$160,000	$160,000	$ 41,000	$ 44,000
Inventory	$115,000	$325,000	$195,000	$130,000
Machinery	$165,000	$100,000	$ 0	$100,000
Land	$360,000	$550,000	$400,000	$150,000

Brave used the remaining cash of $75,000 to pay the income taxes due at the corporate level on the distribution. What are the tax consequences to Brave?

c. Brave distributed the assets as follows to Chipper and Maddox:

Asset	Adjusted basis	FMV	Distributed to Chipper	Distributed to Maddox
Cash	$160,000	$160,000	$ 31,000	$ 54,000
Inventory	$115,000	$325,000	$195,000	$130,000
Machinery	$165,000	$100,000	$ 80,000	$ 20,000
Land	$360,000	$550,000	$330,000	$220,000

Brave used the remaining cash of $75,000 to pay the income taxes due at the corporate level on the distribution. What are the tax consequences to Brave?

35. **(LO5)** Cherub, Inc. and Anton own Cupid Corporation, 85% and 15% respectively. Cherub's basis in its stock is $140,000 and Anton's basis is $30,000. Both shareholders acquired their stock five years ago. Cupid owns the following assets:

Asset	Adjusted basis	FMV
Cash	$60,000	$60,000
Inventory	$33,000	$45,000
Machinery	$85,000	$72,000
Land	$45,000	$50,000

Cupid adopted a plan of liquidation in the current year. All of its assets were distributed to its shareholders by the end of the following tax year, as follows:

Asset	Adjusted basis	FMV	Cherub, Inc.	Anton
Cash	$60,000	$60,000	$25,500	$ 4,500
Inventory	$33,000	$45,000	$38,250	$ 6,750
Machinery	$85,000	$72,000	$61,200	$10,800
Land	$45,000	$50,000	$42,500	$ 7,500

Cupid retained $30,000 of cash to pay its corporate tax liability on the liquidation. What are the tax consequences to Cupid, Cherub, and Anton? What basis does Cherub and Anton have in the distributed assets?

Tax Planning Problems

Planning

1. **(LO3)** Dimitri is the sole shareholder of Oros Corporation. The following assets are being considered for distribution to Dimitri from Oros:

Asset	Fair market value	Adjusted basis
Truck	$26,000	$ 0
Office furniture	$ 8,500	$12,500
Computer	$ 2,600	$ 3,200
Land	$45,000	$28,000

Which assets should be distributed to Dimitri, and what is the tax effect to Oros?

2. **(LO4)** Gunther owns 600 shares of Deutsche Inc. Deutsche has 900 voting shares outstanding. Gunther is considering selling some of his shares, and he would like to receive capital gain treatment on the sale. How many shares must Gunther sell to achieve this result?

Professional Development Skills

Communication Problem

Communication

1. **(LO1) Treatment of Cash Distribution** Denzel has owned 100% of Hollywood Corporation, an accrual-based, calendar-year corporation, for the last several years. Denzel has a $6,600 basis in Hollywood. At the beginning of the current year, Hollywood has accumulated earnings and profits of $12,000. During the current year, Hollywood incurs a $22,000 deficit in its current earnings and profits that accrues ratably. On July 1 of the current year, Hollywood distributes $10,000 cash to Denzel. Denzel has asked for your advice on the tax treatment of the cash distribution. Write a memo to Denzel.

Ethics and Professional Responsibilities Problem

Ethics

1. **(LO4) Family Attribution and Qualified Stock Redemption Rules** Kiera owned 40% of Halter Corporation. Jamal, Kiera's husband, owned 40% of Halter, and Lee, Kiera's son, owned 20% of Halter. Halter redeemed all Kiera's shares for its fair market value, leaving Jamal and Lee as the remaining shareholders. Kiera received long-term capital gain treatment on the redemption. At the time, Kiera agreed to not hold or acquire any interest in Halter for ten years, and she also filed a statement agreeing to notify the IRS if she does reacquire a prohibited interest.

In the current year, Lee would like to leave the family business and sell his shares. Kiera and Jamal would like to keep the shares inside the family. Halter redeems all of Lee's shares making Jamal a 100% owner. Because Jamal cannot handle all the responsibilities of Halter, Kiera becomes a director and employee of Halter. Kiera does not notify the IRS of this change because Kiera did not purchase any Halter stock. What is your responsibility in this situation as their tax accountant?

In addition to the chapter content, see *Statements on Standards for Tax Services* at www.aicpa-cima.com/resources/landing/statements-on-standards-for-tax-services, *Circular 230* at https://www.irs.gov/tax-professionals/office-of-professional-responsibility-and-circular-230, and *Taxation of Business Entities*, Chapter 2, LO4, Tax Professional Responsibilities.

Research Problem

Research

1. **(LO4 Advanced) Redemption to Pay Estate Taxes** Sandy Corporation is owned by Kareem (35%), Julianna (40%), and Danielle (25%), who are all related shareholders. Sandy has a life insurance policy on all three shareholders and has been paying the premiums to date. In the current year, Kareem died. Kareem's adjusted gross estate is $16.82 million and the estate taxes, funeral costs, and related administrative expenses total $2,100,000. Kareem had acquired his Sandy Corporation shares seven years ago for $550,000. Kareem's estate would like to sell some of Kareem's shares back to Sandy for $2,000,000. The value of Sandy shares in Kareem's estate is equal to $6,728,000. How will this transaction be treated for tax purposes for Sandy and Kareem? Does Kareem's estate actually have to use the proceeds from the stock sale for the estate taxes, funeral expenses, and related administrative costs to qualify for stock redemption? Hint: Consider IRC §303, §101(a), and §264(a)(1).

Excel Problem

Excel

1. **(LO2) Cash Distributions** Freida owns 100% of Feline Corporation, and she receives a distribution of $47,000 in the current tax year. This is the only distribution made by Feline this year. Freida purchased her stock six years ago for $17,500. Determine Freida's tax consequences for each of the scenarios below:

	Accumulated E&P	Current E&P
Scenario #1	$38,000	$22,000
Scenario #2	($38,000)	($22,000)
Scenario #3	($38,000)	$22,000
Scenario #4	$38,000	($18,000)

CPA Exam Preparation: Task-Based Simulation

1. **(LO2) Cash Distribution** Chicago Corporation has one shareholder, Ernie, who owns 100% of the stock. Ernie has a basis in his stock of $18,000. Chicago Corporation has accumulated earnings and profits of ($18,500) and current earnings and profits of $13,600.

Assume that on December 31st, Chicago Corporation distributes $35,000 cash to Ernie. Enter your answer in the following data entry boxes.

1. How much dividend income must Ernie report because of the distribution, if any?	$
2. What is Ernie's ending stock basis after the distribution?	$
3. How much capital gain must Ernie report because of the distribution, if any?	$
4. What is Chicago's ending accumulated earnings and profits after the distribution?	$

Go to Wiley's book companion site to complete the Task-Based Simulation.

CHAPTER **5**

Corporate Taxation:

Related Corporations and Reorganizations

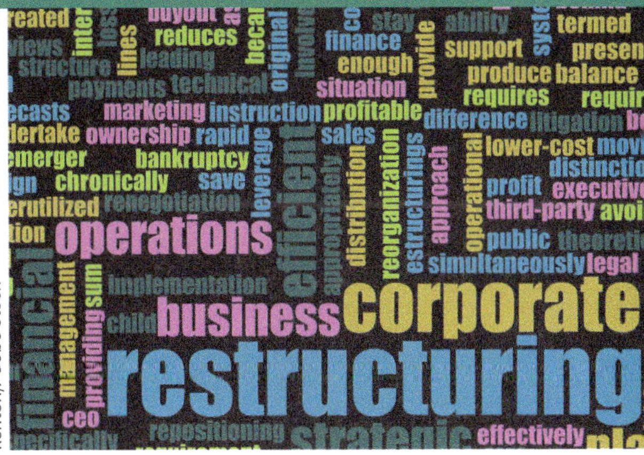

kentoh/Acobe Stock

Before studying this chapter, you should know or, if necessary, review:

1.2 Fundamentals of Property Transactions

3.1 Taxation of Corporate Formations

Chapter Introduction

VIDEO CONTENT

Looking back to Chapter 4, recall that Delta Consulting, Inc. was formed nine years ago by Olivia and Aiden to provide data analytics advice to businesses, including developing systems to capture and manage their data. Olivia and Aiden each invested $400,000 in Delta, and they borrowed an additional $900,000 in the first year of business. Delta has performed extremely well over the last nine years. A next step for Olivia and Aiden could be to expand their business operations. This could be done by starting additional business ventures or acquiring other businesses. Should they do so, this could result in the creation of related businesses. Common ownership of more than one business can create an opportunity for the related corporations to file as a consolidated group. Common ownership could also result in the related corporations being part of a controlled group, which can lead to restrictions on the group's ability to use certain beneficial tax attributes. The tax implications of these transactions are covered in the first two sections of this chapter.

If this growth activity results in the acquisition of another corporation, the owners usually prefer for the acquisition to be structured in such a way that realized gains from the transaction are deferred. For deferral to occur, the acquisition needs to be structured as a qualified reorganization, of which there are seven types (Type A, Type B, Type C, Type D, Type E, Type F, and Type G). In the chapter's third section, we review the qualification requirements and tax implications of these reorganization types. In the final section of the chapter, you will learn about how tax attributes of an acquired business may carry over to the acquiring business.

LEARNING OBJECTIVES	TOPICS	PRACTICE OPPORTUNITIES

1 Apply appropriate restrictions to tax benefits for controlled groups.	**5.1 Controlled Groups**
	• Limitations on Controlled Groups
	  • Accumulated Earnings Credit
	  • Section 179
	  • Lower Corporate Tax Rates
	• Other Characteristics of Controlled Groups
	  • Related-Party Loss Limitations
	  • Gain from Sale of Depreciable Property
	  • Allocation of Tax Benefit Among Controlled Group
	• Parent-Subsidiary (P-S) Controlled Groups
	  • Evaluating Parent-Subsidiary Controlled Groups
	• Brother-Sister (B-S) Controlled Groups
	  • Evaluating Brother-Sister Controlled Groups
		• Example 5.1.1 Parent-Subsidiary Controlled Group Rules (Scenario 1)
		• Example 5.1.2 Parent-Subsidiary Controlled Group Rules (Scenario 2)
		• Example 5.1.3 Brother-Sister Controlled Group
		• Practice Problem 5.1.1 Parent-Subsidiary Controlled Group
		• Practice Problem 5.1.2 Brother-Sister Controlled Group

2 Apply rules for filing consolidated tax returns.	**5.2 Affiliated Groups and Consolidated Returns**
	• Definition of Affiliated Groups
	  • Evaluating Affiliated Groups
	• The Consolidation Process
	  • Ineligible Corporations
	  • Consolidation Rules
	  • Affiliated Groups that Do Not Consolidate
	• Advantages and Disadvantages of Electing to Consolidate
	  • Advantages of Consolidated Returns
	  • Disadvantages of Consolidated Returns
	• Computing Consolidated Taxable Income
	• Stock Basis of Subsidiary
	  • Computing Stock Basis
	  • Excess Loss Account
	  • Net Operating Losses
		• Example 5.2.1 Identifying Affiliated Groups (Scenario 1)
		• Example 5.2.2 Identifying Affiliated Groups (Scenario 2)
		• Example 5.2.3 Identifying Affiliated Groups (Scenario 3)
		• Example 5.2.4 Consolidation Requirements
		• Example 5.2.5 Decision to Consolidate
		• Example 5.2.6 Computing Consolidated Taxable Income
		• Example 5.2.7 Stock Basis of Subsidiary
		• Practice Problem 5.2.1 Identifying an Affiliated Group
		• Practice Problem 5.2.2 Computing Consolidated Taxable Income
		• Practice Problem 5.2.3 Calculating Stock Basis of a Subsidiary

LEARNING OBJECTIVES	TOPICS	PRACTICE OPPORTUNITIES

3 Determine the tax consequences of a reorganization for the acquiring corporation, acquired corporation, and the acquired corporation's shareholders.	**5.3 Corporate Reorganizations**
	• Types of Reorganizations
	  ◦ Taxable Purchase of Target's Assets by Acquiring
	  ◦ Tax-Deferred Purchase of Target's Assets by Acquiring with Acquiring's Stock
	  ◦ Taxable Purchase of Target's Stock by Acquiring
	  ◦ Tax-Deferred Purchase of Target's Stock by Acquiring
	• Types of Qualified (Tax-Deferred) Reorganizations
	  ◦ Acquisitive Reorganizations (Types A, B, C)
	  ◦ Divisive Reorganizations (Type D)
	  ◦ Other Reorganizations (Types E, F, G)
	• Judicial Doctrines
	  ◦ Business Purpose
	  ◦ Continuity of Interest
	  ◦ Continuity of Business Enterprise
	  ◦ Step Transaction
	• Tax Consequences of Qualified Reorganizations
	  ◦ Acquiring Corporation
	  ◦ Target Corporation
	  ◦ Target's Shareholders
		• Example 5.3.1 Type A Reorganization (Scenario 1)
		• Example 5.3.2 Type A Reorganization (Scenario 2)
		• Example 5.3.3 Type B Reorganization (Scenario 1)
		• Example 5.3.4 Type B Reorganization (Scenario 2)
		• Example 5.3.5 Type C Reorganization (Scenario 1)
		• Example 5.3.6 Type C Reorganization (Scenario 2)
		• Example 5.3.7 Type D Reorganization
		• Example 5.3.8 Judicial Doctrines
		• Example 5.3.9 Gain to Acquiring Corporation
		• Example 5.3.10 Gain to Target Corporation
		• Example 5.3.11 Gain to Target's Shareholders
		• Example 5.3.12 Loss to Target's Shareholders
		• Practice Problem 5.3.1 Type A Reorganization
		• Practice Problem 5.3.2 Type B Reorganization
		• Practice Problem 5.3.3 Gain to Target's Shareholder

4 Determine the required limitations that apply to an acquiring corporation's ability to use the earnings and profits and net operating losses of the target corporation after a qualified reorganization.	**5.4 Preservation of Tax Attributes**
	• Earnings & Profits Limitation
	• NOL Limitations
	  ◦ NOL Limitation for Year of Acquisition
	  ◦ Greater than 50% Change in Ownership
		• Example 5.4.1 Determining Tax Characteristics of a Target Corporation after Reorganization
		• Example 5.4.2 Limitation on Earnings & Profits
		• Example 5.4.3 Determining NOL Limitation for Year of Acquisition
		• Example 5.4.4 NOL Limited by Ownership Change
		• Practice Problem 5.4.1 Use of Charitable Contribution Carryforward

Tax Forms referenced in this chapter

Form 851	Affiliations Schedule
Form 1122	Authorization and Consent of Subsidiary Corporation to be Included in a Consolidated Income Tax Return

5.1 Controlled Groups

LEARNING OBJECTIVE 1

Apply appropriate restrictions to tax benefits for controlled groups.

VIDEO CONTENT

If Olivia and Aiden expand their business operations by forming or acquiring new businesses, they will need to determine whether or not the *controlled group* rules apply. A **controlled group** is two or more corporations that have a certain level of common ownership among them. There are three types of controlled groups: parent-subsidiary groups, brother-sister groups, and certain insurance companies.[1] In this section, you will learn the definitions of *parent-subsidiary groups* and *brother-sister groups*, and the tax limitations that Congress has placed on them.

Related exercise: Discussion Question 1

Why **Why are there tax limitations placed on controlled groups?** Recall the accumulated earnings credit from Chapter 3, LO5, Penalty Taxes. The accumulated earnings tax (AET) imposes a penalty tax on corporations that accumulate too much earnings, rather than distributing it to the shareholders. Congress allows corporations to accumulate at least $250,000 ($150,000 for service corporations) each year of earnings without a valid business purpose and not be subject to the AET. The $250,000 is known as the accumulated earnings credit. Assume that Anita owns 100% of A-Corp, a small manufacturing company, and that she does not want to distribute any earnings to herself so she can avoid paying tax on the dividends. As of the end of the current year, she has accumulated $240,000 of earnings, so she knows that once she accumulates an additional $10,000 of earnings next year, she will have to pay the AET unless she has a valid business purpose. To avoid this problem, Anita created B-Corp and begins to divide the revenue and expenses between A-Corp and B-Corp so that B-Corp has most of the profits. She does this because she thinks that B-Corp will have an additional accumulated earnings credit of $250,000. However, as you will see below, A-Corp and B-Corp will have to share one $250,000 accumulated earnings credit due to the restrictions on controlled groups. Congress needed to restrict certain types of related companies from benefitting more than once from tax provisions. Otherwise, owners like Anita would create as many corporations as needed to achieve their desired result.

Limitations on Controlled Groups

There are three limitations placed on controlled groups by the tax law: accumulated earnings credit, Section 179, and the use of certain corporate tax rates.

Accumulated Earnings Credit

As explained above, the $250,000/$150,000 accumulated earnings credit can be used only one time each year by all the corporations in the controlled group. The credit can be allocated among the corporations in any manner preferred by the corporations.[2]

Section 179

Section 179 allows eligible businesses to elect to expense the cost of qualifying property in the year of purchase, rather than depreciating the cost over the property's useful life. The Section 179 deduction is capped at $1,250,000 (2025) for the controlled group. The $1,250,000

[1]IRC §1563(a).
[2]IRC §1561.

cap begins to phase out when purchases of qualified property from the entire group exceed $3,130,000 (2025). The deduction can be allocated among the corporations in any manner preferred by the corporations.

Lower Corporate Tax Rates

Before 2018, the corporate income tax rates were progressive with the following specific rates: 15%, 25%, 34%, and 35%. The 15% rate applied to the first $50,000 of taxable income and the 25% rate applied to the next $25,000. To prevent business owners from creating multiple corporations to take advantage of the 15% and 25% rates more than once, controlled groups could use the 15% rate one time for $50,000 of income and the 25% rate one time for $25,000 of income. The current corporate income tax rate is a flat rate of 21%. Therefore, there is now no advantage of using multiple corporations to take advantage of lower tax rates. If the corporate tax rates become progressive again in the future, then Congress will likely restore this restriction for controlled groups.

Other Characteristics of Controlled Groups

There are several other important tax implications of controlled groups, which we discuss below.

Related-Party Loss Limitations

The corporations in a controlled group are related parties for purposes of the loss disallowance rule.[3] This means that realized losses from the sales of assets between corporations in the group cannot be recognized until the asset is sold outside the group.

Gain from Sale of Depreciable Property

Any gain that is recognized from the sale of depreciable property between corporations in the controlled group is treated as ordinary income.[4]

Allocation of Tax Benefit Among Controlled Group

If the controlled group rules limit a tax benefit for the group, the benefit can be spread among the group in any manner that the group prefers. Assume that corporations R, S, and T are part of a controlled group and must share a $250,000 accumulated earnings credit. Some examples of how the credit could be shared are:

- $83,333 each to R, S, and T.
- $250,000 to R, and none to S and T.
- $50,000 to R, $75,000 to S, and $125,000 to T.

Any other allocations are acceptable, as long as the total allocation does not exceed $250,000.

Related exercise: Multiple Choice Question 1

Parent-Subsidiary (P-S) Controlled Groups

The focus for *parent-subsidiary (P-S) controlled groups* is on corporations owning other corporations. A **parent-subsidiary (P-S) controlled group** exists if *both* of these conditions are met:

- **80% Test (Controlled Group)** One or more of the other corporations in the group possess at least 80% of the voting power of all classes of stock entitled to vote, *or* at least 80% of the total value of all classes of stock of each of the corporations (except the common parent), *and*

[3] IRC §267(f).
[4] IRC §1239(c).

> **Potential Pitfall**
>
> You must identify the largest group of corporations that meet the P-S rules, because the purpose of the rule is to limit the applicable tax benefit so that it applies only once to the whole group.

- **Common Parent Test (Controlled Group)** The common parent owns stock possessing at least 80% of the total combined voting power of all classes of stock entitled to vote, *or* at least 80% of the total value of shares of all classes of stock of at least one of the other corporations in the group.

These tests must be met on the last day of the tax year.[5] Nonvoting preferred stock and treasury stock are not included when applying these tests.

Related exercises: Discussion Question 2
Multiple Choice Question 2
Tax Planning Problem 1

Evaluating Parent-Subsidiary Controlled Groups

Use the following steps to determine if a P-S controlled group exists. These steps are also shown in **Illustration 5.1**.

ILLUSTRATION 5.1 Parent-Subsidiary Controlled Groups

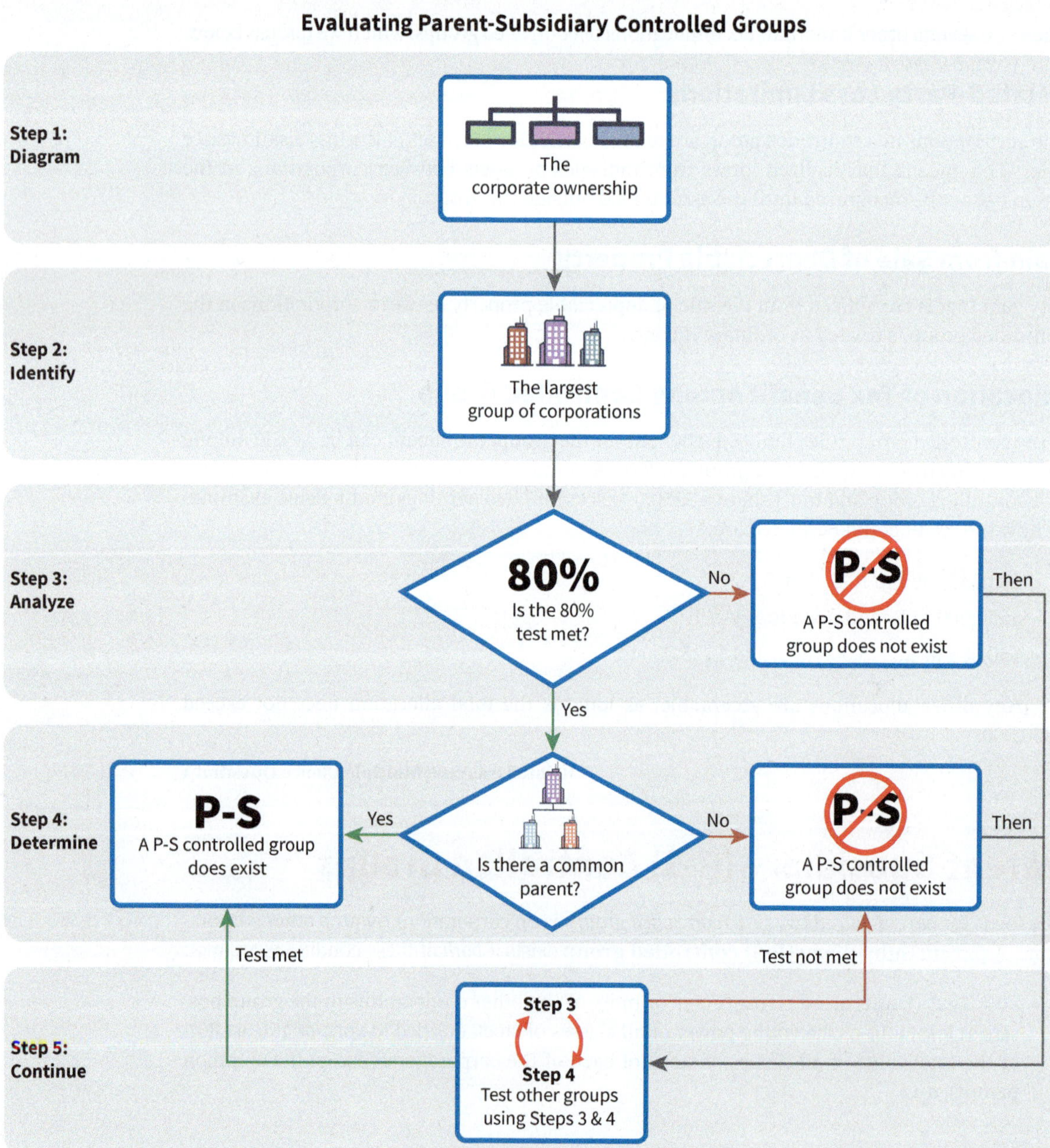

[5]IRC 1561(a)(1).

Step 1. **Diagram:** **The corporate ownership to ensure you understand the structure.**

Step 2. **Identify:** **The largest group of corporations that might meet the P-S rules.**

Step 3. **Analyze:** **Is 80% test met?** (*Either* the 80% voting *or* 80% value test must be met.) If YES, go to step 4. If NO, go to step 5.

Step 4. **Determine:** **Is there is a common parent?** If YES, the group is a parent-subsidiary controlled group. If NO, go to step 5.

Step 5. **Continue (if needed):** **Test other groups of corporations until a parent-subsidiary group is found or all possible groups have been tested**, keeping in mind that your goal is to find the largest group of corporations that meet the test.

The following two Examples illustrate the application of the P-S controlled group rules.

EXAMPLE 5.1.1
Parent-Subsidiary Controlled Group Rules (Scenario 1)

Red Corporation owns stock in the following corporations:

- 90% of the stock of Green Corporation
- 80% of the stock of Blue Corporation
- 70% of the stock of Purple Corporation

Identify the P-S controlled group, if one exists.

SOLUTION

We apply the steps shown in Illustration 5.1 to determine if a P-S control group exists.

Step 1. **Diagram the corporate ownership to ensure you understand the structure.**

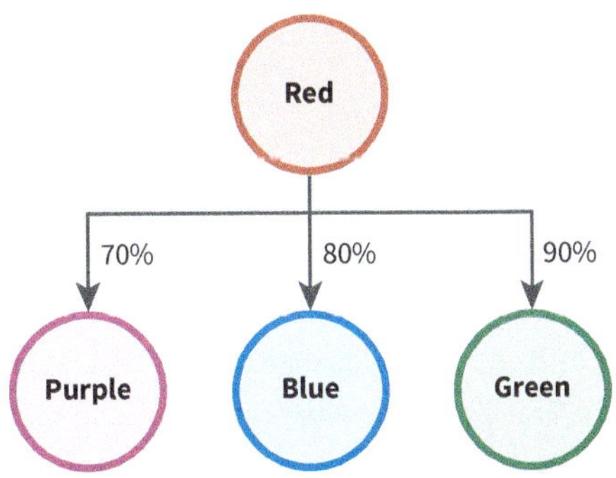

Step 2. **Identify the largest group of corporations that might meet the P-S rules.** The largest group of corporations to test first includes all four corporations (Red, Green, Blue, and Purple).

Step 3. **Analyze if the 80% test is met.** Green and Blue are owned at least 80% or more by Red. Purple is not owned 80% or more by Red, Green, and Blue, so Purple fails the 80% test.

Step 4. **Determine if there is a common parent.** Red is the common parent because it owns 80% or more of at least one other corporation in the controlled group (Green and Blue).

Step 5. Not needed.

Therefore, Red, Green, and Blue are part of a P-S controlled group because the 80% test and common parent tests are met.

Potential Pitfall

For Example 5.1.1, if you concluded that Red and Green constituted a controlled group, that would be incorrect. It is true that the 80% test and Common Parent test are met for Red and Green. However, a controlled group with more than just Red and Green exists that includes Blue. The largest controlled group is always the correct answer.

EXAMPLE 5.1.2
Parent-Subsidiary Controlled Group Rules (Scenario 2)

The following corporations are owned as shown:

Corporation A:	Owned 100% by an individual
Corporation B:	Owned 80% by Corporation A and 20% by individuals
Corporation C:	Owned 92% by Corporation A and 8% by individuals
Corporation D:	Owned 60% by Corporation B, 20% by Corporation C, and 20% by individuals
Corporation E:	Owned 79% by Corporation B and 21% by individuals

Identify the P-S controlled group, if one exists.

SOLUTION

We apply the steps shown in Illustration 5.1 to determine if a P-S control group exists.

Step 1. Diagram the corporate ownership to ensure you understand the structure, as follows:

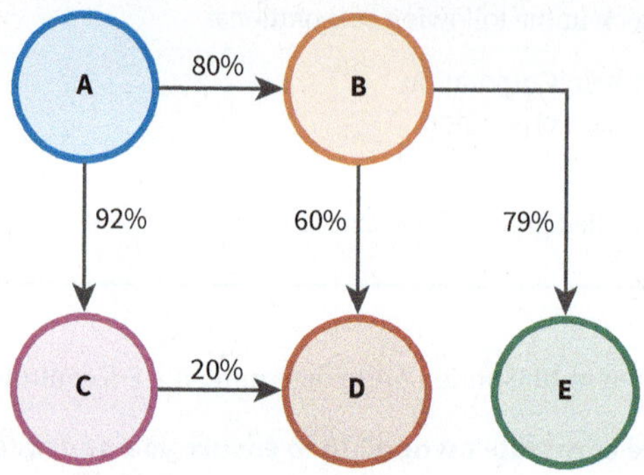

Step 2. Identify the largest group of corporations that might meet the P-S rules, which is A, B, C, D, and E.

Step 3. Analyze if the 80% test is met:

A is not owned at least 80% by the other corporations in the group.

B is owned 80% by A, so the 80% test is met.

C is owned 92% by A, so the 80% test is met.

D is owned 80% by B and C combined, so the 80% test is met.

E is not owned at least 80% by the other corporations in the group.

The 80% test is met for corporations B, C, and D.

Step 4. Determine if there is a common parent. The common parent must own at least 80% of at least one of the other companies.

- A meets the test because it owns 80% or more of both B and C (although one would be sufficient).
- E does not meet the test because it does not own 80% or more of at least one of the other corporations.

Step 5. Not needed.

Therefore, A is the common parent. The group A, B, C, and D is a P-S controlled group. E is not part of the group because E is not a common parent, and it does not meet the 80% test.

Related exercises: Application Problems 1, 2

Brother-Sister (B-S) Controlled Groups

The focus for **brother-sister (B-S) controlled groups** is on common ownership by individuals for a group of corporations. A B-S controlled group exists if *all* the following conditions are met:[6]

- **Shareholder Test** Two or more corporations are owned by five or fewer persons (individuals, estates, or trusts)
- **50% Test** The corporations have common ownership of more than 50% of the total combined voting powers of all classes of stock entitled to vote, *or* more than 50% of the total value of shares of all classes of stock of each corporation, *and*
- **80% Test (Brother-Sister Controlled Group)** The corporations possess stock representing at least 80% of the voting power of all classes of stock entitled to vote, *or* at least 80% of the total value of all classes of stock of each the corporations. An individual's ownership is counted for the 80% test only if the individual contributes to the common ownership used for the 50% test.

The 80% test does not apply for determining brother-sister corporations for the limitation on the accumulated earnings credit. It *does* apply for limiting the Section 179 deduction.

Related exercise: Discussion Question 3

Potential Pitfall

A corporation in a brother-sister controlled group can have more than five shareholders. For example, there could be a brother-sister controlled group that has four corporations in it, and each corporation has between seven and ten shareholders. The key is that there is a *common group* of five or fewer shareholders who meet the 50% test and 80% test.

Evaluating Brother-Sister Controlled Groups

You use the following steps to determine if a B-S controlled group exists. These steps are also shown in Illustration 5.2.

Step 1. **Diagram: The corporate ownership to ensure you understand the structure.**

Step 2. **Analyze: Is the shareholder test met?** Ensure that you do not include the stock ownership of more than five individuals in the analysis.

Step 3. **Identify: The largest group of corporations that could meet the B-S rules to begin the analysis.**

Step 4. **Analyze: The 50% test first.** If the 50% test is met, then the limitation on the accumulated earnings credit will apply and you should proceed to step 6 for the 80% test. If the 50% test is not met, go to step 5.

Step 5. **Continue (if needed): Test other groups, using steps 3 and 4 if the 50% test is not met for the tested group of corporations.** Remember that your goal is to find the largest group of corporations that meet the test. If the 50% test is not met for any group of corporations, then no tax limitations will be imposed on the tested corporations. If the 50% test is met, then the limitation on the accumulated earnings credit will apply and you should proceed to step 6 for the 80% test.

Step 6. **Analyze: The 80% test, if a group of corporations meet the 50% test.** If the 80% test is met, then the Section 179 limit will also be imposed on the corporations. If the 80% test is not met, go back to step 5 and test other groups, keeping in mind that your goal is to find the largest group of corporations that meet the test. If the 50% test and 80% test are not both met for a group of corporations, then each of the tested corporations can fully utilize the Section 179 benefit.

In the next Example, we show how you determine if a brother-sister controlled group exists.

Potential Pitfall

The 80% test for both P-S and B-S controlled groups is 80% *or more* of the stock of the corporation. However, the 50% test for B-S controlled groups is *more than* 50%. The 50% test is not met if the common ownership of the shareholders is exactly 50%.

[6] IRC §1563(a)(2).

ILLUSTRATION 5.2 Brother-Sister Controlled Groups

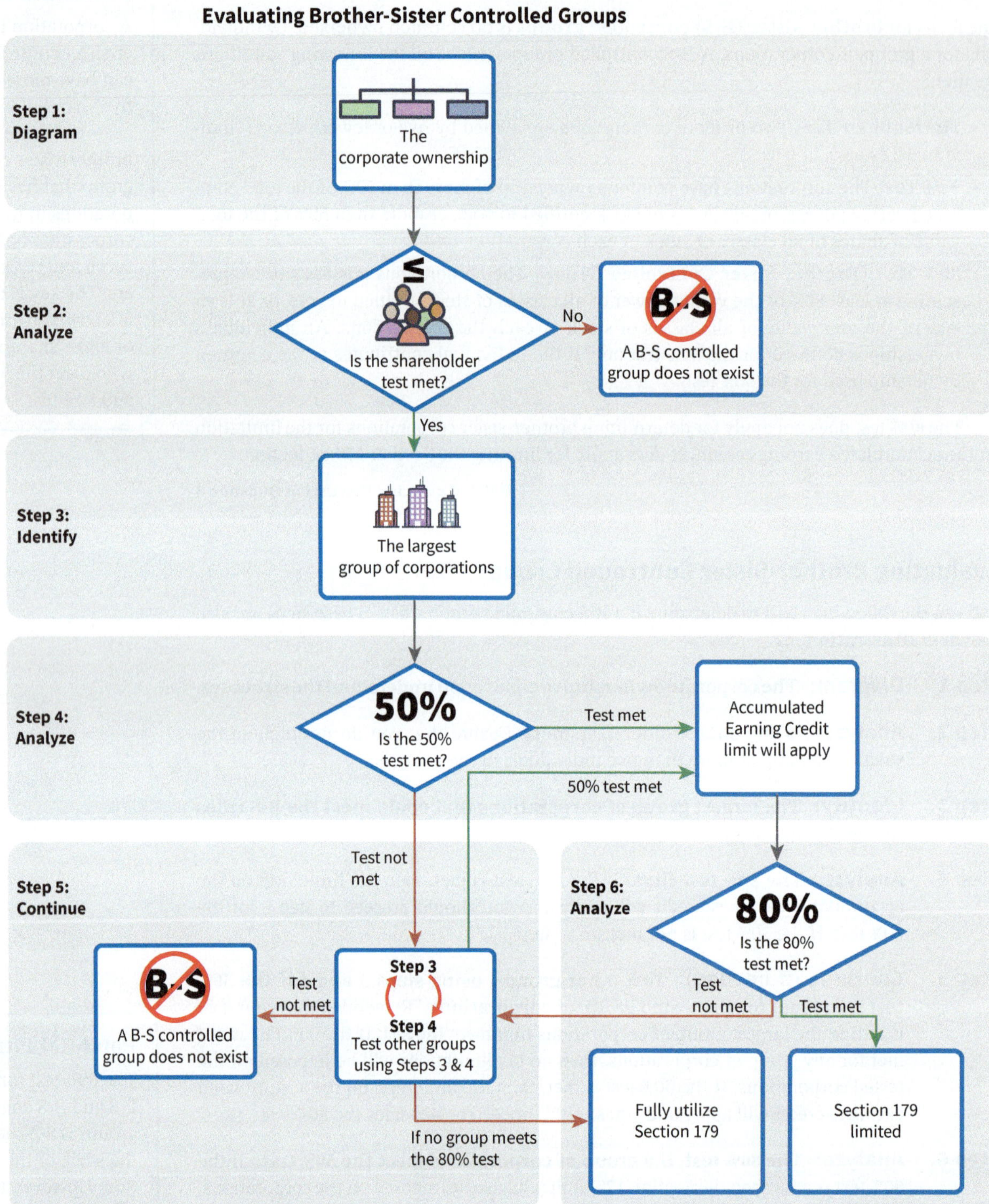

EXAMPLE 5.1.3
Brother-Sister Controlled Group

Individuals 1, 2, 3, 4, and 5 own the following percentages of the only class of outstanding stock of Corporations N, O, P, Q, and R:

	Corporations/Percent of stock owned				
Individual	**N**	**O**	**P**	**Q**	**R**
1	40%	40%	40%	40%	40%
2	20%	0%	10%	20%	30%
3	10%	10%	20%	20%	10%
4	30%	0%	30%	10%	0%
5	0%	50%	0%	10%	0%

Which corporations are members of a brother-sister controlled group?

SOLUTION

We apply the steps shown in Illustration 5.2 to determine which (if any) of the corporations are part of a B-S controlled group.

Step 1. Diagram the corporate ownership to ensure you understand the structure. This is given to you in the problem.

Step 2. Analyze if the shareholder test is met. Ensure that you do not include the stock ownership of more than five individuals in the following analysis of the 50% test and 80% test.

Step 3. Identify the largest group of corporations that meet the B-S rules. The largest group includes all five corporations, N, O, P, Q, and R.

Step 4. Analyze if the 50% test is met first. If the 50% test is not met for at least one group of two or more corporations, then a B-S controlled group does not exist.

	Corporations/Percent of stock owned					
Individual	**N**	**O**	**P**	**Q**	**R**	**Common ownership**
1	40%	40%	40%	40%	40%	40%
2	20%	0%	10%	20%	30%	0%
3	10%	10%	20%	20%	10%	10%
4	30%	0%	30%	10%	0%	0%
5	0%	50%	0%	10%	0%	0%
						50%

The common ownership that each individual has in N, O, P, Q, and R is the lowest amount of ownership for these five companies. These amounts are shown in the common ownership column and are highlighted in green. The 50% test is failed because the total common ownership of individuals 1, 2, 3, 4 and 5 does not exceed 50%.

Step 5. Continue to test other groups using steps 3 and 4. Identify the next largest group of corporations that should be tested. This would be groups that have four of the five corporations in them. Because there are three companies that at least one of the shareholders does not have any ownership interest in, none of these groups meet the 50%. To help you understand this, we show the result for N, O, P, and Q:

	Corporations/Percent of stock owned				
Individual	**N**	**O**	**P**	**Q**	**Common ownership**
1	40%	40%	40%	40%	40%
2	20%	0%	10%	20%	0%
3	10%	10%	20%	20%	10%
4	30%	0%	30%	10%	0%
5	0%	50%	0%	10%	0%
					50%

Once again, the 50% test is not met because the common ownership that the five individuals have in NOPQ is not more than 50%.

Step 5. **(repeat): Continue to test other groups using steps 3 and 4.** You next need to test groups of three corporations to determine if one of them meets the 50% test. While there are several iterations of groups of three corporations, we will test N, P, and Q. We are eliminating corporation O first because two individuals have no ownership in it, so this should increase the likelihood of meeting the 50% test.

	Corporations/Percent of stock owned			
Individual	**N**	**P**	**Q**	**Common ownership**
1	40%	40%	40%	40%
2	20%	10%	20%	10%
3	10%	20%	20%	10%
4	30%	30%	10%	10%
5	0%	0%	10%	0%
				70%

The 50% test is met for N, P, and Q because the common ownership of the five individuals is 70%. Therefore, N, P, and Q will be limited to one accumulated earnings credit.

Step 6. **Analyze the 80% test, if a group of corporations meet the 50% test.** For the 80% test to be met for N, P, and Q, each corporation must be owned at least 80% by five or fewer individuals. An individual must have contributed to the common ownership test to be included in the 80% test. So individual 5 is not included in the 80% test. The 50% test has to be done before the 80% test to determine which individuals can be used for the 80% test.

	Corporations/Percent of stock owned			
Individual	**N**	**P**	**Q**	**Common ownership**
1	40%	40%	40%	40%
2	20%	10%	20%	10%
3	10%	20%	20%	10%
4	30%	30%	10%	10%
5	0%	0%	10%	0%
	100%	100%	90%	70%

N, P, and Q are all owned 80% or more by the individuals, so the 80% test is met and N, P, and Q is a B-S corporation. Therefore, N, P, and Q can use only one accumulated earnings credit this year as a group. They also can only use Section 179 expensing up to its maximum level this year.

Potential Pitfall

Even though you are analyzing the ownership of the shareholders to determine if a B-S controlled group exists, the conclusion has nothing to do with the shareholders. The conclusion is that corporations N, P, and Q comprise a B-S controlled group.

Related exercises: Brief Exercise 1
Application Problem 3

PRACTICE PROBLEM 5.1.1
Parent-Subsidiary Controlled Group

Brick Corporation owns stock in the following corporations:

- 60% of the stock of Mortar Corporation
- 75% of the stock of Rock Corporation
- 90% of the stock of Stone Corporation

Identify the P-S controlled group, if one exists.

SOLUTION

Step 1. Diagram the corporate ownership to ensure you understand the structure.

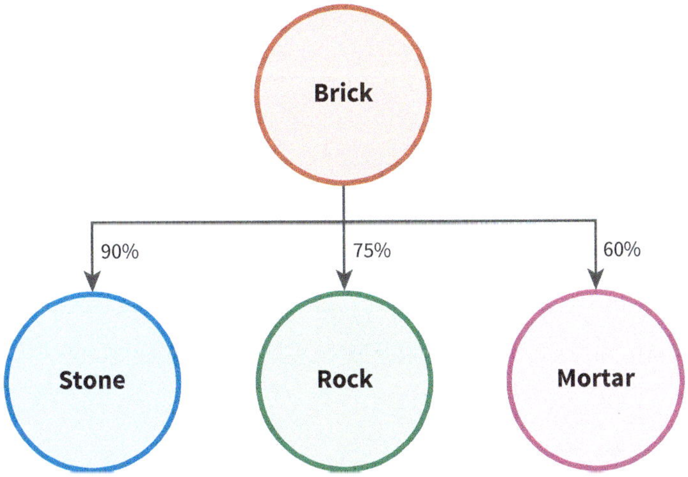

Step 2. Identify the largest group of corporations that might meet the P-S rules. The largest group of corporations to test first includes all four corporations, BMRS.

Step 3. Analyze if the 80% rule is met. Stone is owned at least 80% or more by Brick. Mortar and Rock are not owned 80% or more by Brick or Stone, so Mortar and Rock fail the 80% test.

Step 4. Determine if there is a common parent. Brick is the common parent because it owns 80% or more of at least one other corporation in the controlled group (Stone).

Step 5. Not needed.

Brick and Stone are part of a P-S controlled group because the 80% and common parent tests are met.

PRACTICE PROBLEM 5.1.2
Brother-Sister Controlled Group

Corporations Cubs, Braves, and Orioles are owned by Ernie, Greg, and Brooks as follows:

Owner	Cubs	Braves	Orioles
Ernie	55%	10%	10%
Greg	20%	65%	35%
Brooks	25%	25%	55%

Which corporations are members of a brother-sister controlled group for all purposes of the corporate tax law?

SOLUTION

Because five or fewer individuals own stock in the corporations in the group being analyzed, we next look for common ownership.

Owner	Cubs	Braves	Orioles	Common ownership
Ernie	55%	10%	10%	10%
Greg	20%	65%	35%	20%
Brooks	25%	25%	55%	25%
Total	100%	100%	100%	55%

The common ownership is 55%, so the 50% test is met. Next, we look to see if each corporation is owned at least 80% by the three individuals. Because all three are owned at least 80% by Ernie, Greg, and Brooks, the Cubs, Braves, and Orioles are a brother-sister controlled group.

INTERACTIVE SELF-SCORING QUIZZES

5.2 Affiliated Groups and Consolidated Returns

LEARNING OBJECTIVE 2

Apply rules for filing consolidated tax returns.

VIDEO CONTENT

In this section, we cover the following topics related to affiliated groups and consolidated returns.

- Definition of affiliated groups
- The consolidation process
- Computing consolidated taxable income
- Parent's stock basis in its subsidiary

We begin by defining an *affiliated group*, and then describe how the election to consolidate is made and the *consolidation* process. We then provide a template for computing consolidated taxable income that will make a fairly complicated process more understandable. We close this section by explaining the purpose of the parent having stock basis in the subsidiary and how the basis is computed. If Olivia and Aiden do expand their business operations and own corporations in additional to Delta Consulting, they will need to determine if they have an affiliated group.

Definition of Affiliated Groups

Affiliated groups can elect to file a consolidated return. An **affiliated group** exists if *both* of the conditions below are met:

- **80% Test (Affiliated Group)** One or more of the other corporations in the group possess stock with at least 80% of the voting power of all classes of stock entitled to vote, *and* at least 80% of the total value of shares of all classes of stock of each of the corporations (except the common parent), *and*
- **Common Parent Test (Affiliated Group)**: The common parent owns stock possessing at least 80% of the total combined voting power of all classes of stock entitled to vote, *and* at least 80% of the total value of shares of all classes of stock of at least one of the other corporations in the group.[7]

Related exercise: Discussion Question 4

[7]IRC §1504(a).

While the definitions of P-S controlled groups and affiliated groups are similar, there are two distinct differences:

- The tests for controlled groups must be met only on the last day of the tax year, whereas the test for affiliated groups must be met on *every* day of the tax year.
- For controlled groups, *either* the 80% voting *or* 80% value test must be met. But for affiliated groups, *both* the 80% voting *and* 80% value test must be met.

These differences make it more difficult to qualify as an affiliated group than a controlled group.

Evaluating Affiliated Groups

Use the following steps to determine if an affiliated group exists. These steps are also shown in **Illustration 5.3**.

ILLUSTRATION 5.3 Determining if an Affiliated Group Exists

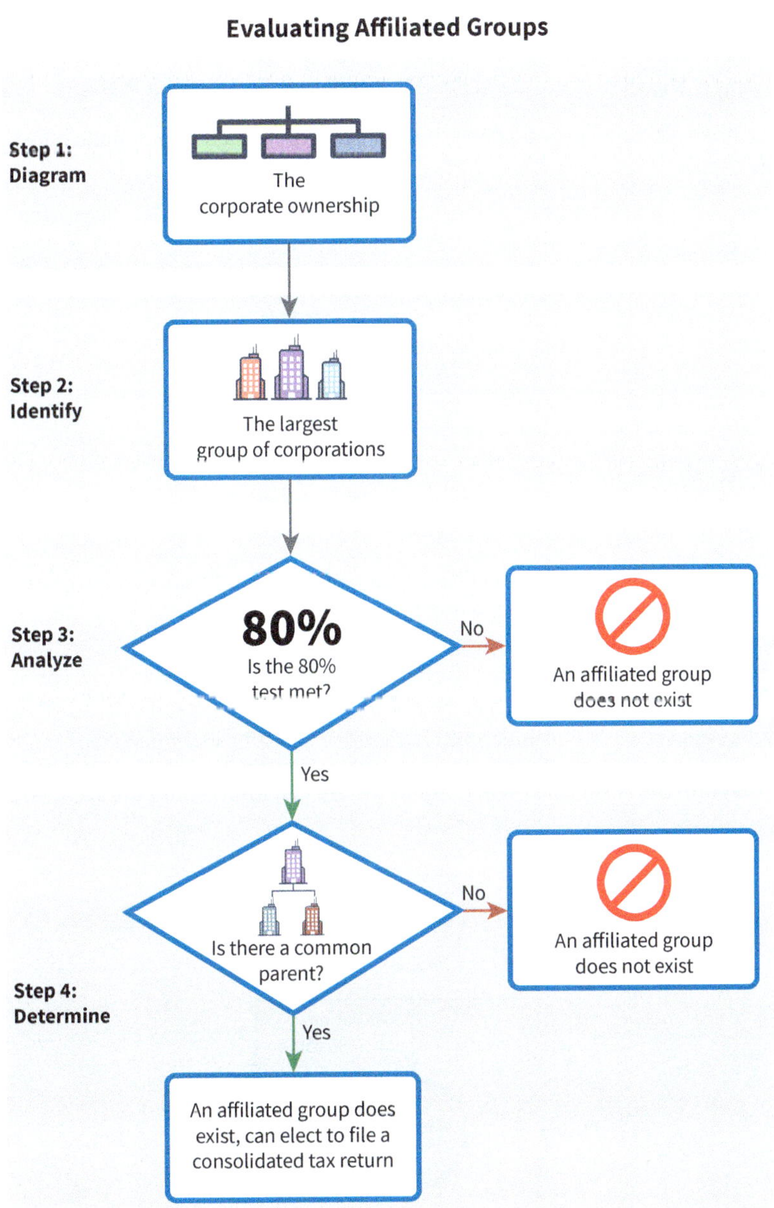

Step 1. Diagram: The corporate ownership to ensure you understand the structure.

Step 2. Identify: The largest group of corporations that might meet the affiliated group rules.

Step 3. Analyze: If the 80% test is met. (*Both* the 80% voting *and* 80% value test must be met.) If NO, then an affiliated group does not exist. If YES, go to step 4.

Step 4. Determine: Is there is a common parent? If NO, an affiliated group does not exist. If YES, there is an affiliated group.

Why **Why did Congress make it more difficult to qualify as an affiliated group than a controlled group?** To understand the reason for these differences you must realize that the implications for being a P-S controlled group versus an affiliated group are very different, as follows:

- Only negative effects result from being a P-S controlled group. The effect is that all corporations in the controlled group can use certain tax benefits only once. Therefore, Congress has made it less difficult to qualify as a controlled group.
- Only positive effects result from being an affiliated group. The effect is that the affiliated group has the option to elect to file a consolidated return, but it does not *require* the group to do so. The affiliated group can take the action that it believes is best.

Because of an affiliated group's favorable tax benefits, Congress has made it more difficult to qualify as one.

Related exercise: Discussion Question 5

The following three Examples demonstrate the process for determining if an affiliated group exists.

EXAMPLE 5.2.1
Identifying Affiliated Groups (Scenario 1)

Red Corporation owns stock in the following corporations:

- 90% (voting and value) of the stock of Green Corporation
- 80% of the voting and 77% of the value of the stock of Blue Corporation
- 70% (voting and value) of the stock of Purple Corporation

Determine the largest group of corporations that qualify as an affiliated group, assuming that these ownership percentages are for every day of the tax year.

SOLUTION

We follow the steps shown in Illustration 5.3 to determine if an affiliated group exists.

Step 1. Diagram the corporate ownership to ensure you understand the structure.

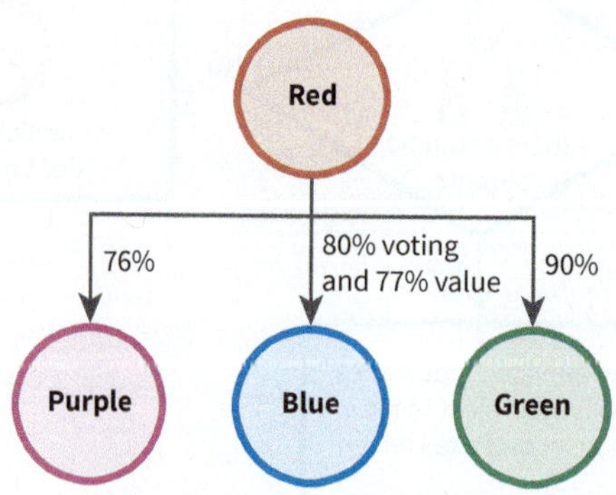

Step 2. **Identify the largest group of corporations that might meet the affiliated group rules.** The first group to test is Red, Green, Blue, and Purple.

Step 3. **Analyze if the 80% test is met.** (*Both* the 80% voting *and* 80% value test must be met.)

- Purple does not meet the 80% test because only 70% of its stock is owned by the other corporations.
- Blue does not meet the test because Red owns only 77% of Blue's value, so it does not own more than 80% of both Blue's voting stock and its value.
- Green does meet the test because 90% of its stock (voting and value) is owned by Red.

Step 4. **Determine if there is a common parent.** Red's stock is not owned more than 80% by the other corporations, but it qualifies as the common parent because it owns more than 80% of at least one of the corporations.

Therefore, Red and Green qualify as an affiliated group, and the group can decide whether it wants to elect to file a consolidated tax return.

EXAMPLE 5.2.2 Identifying Affiliated Groups (Scenario 2)

Pear Corporation owns 80% (voting and value) of the stock of Apricot Corporation, 50% (voting and value) of the stock of Banana Corporation, and 45% (voting and value) of the stock of Cherry Corporation. Apricot Corporation owns 40% (voting and value) of the stock of Banana Corporation. Determine the largest group of corporations that qualify as an affiliated group, assuming that these ownership percentages are for every day of the tax year.

SOLUTION

We follow the steps shown in Illustration 5.3 to determine if an affiliated group exists.

Step 1. **Diagram the corporate ownership to ensure you understand the structure.**

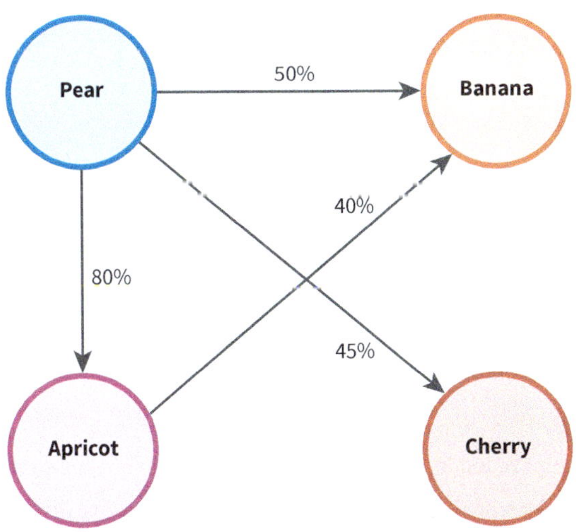

Step 2. **Identify the largest group of corporations that might meet the affiliated group rules.** The first group to test is Pear, Apricot, Banana, and Cherry.

Step 3. **Analyze if the 80% test is met.** (*Both* the 80% voting *and* 80% value test must be met.) Apricot meets the 80% test because 80% of its voting stock and 80% of its value is owned by Pear. Banana meets the 80% test because 90% of its voting stock and 90% of its value is owed by Pear and Apricot. However, Cherry does not meet the 80% test because only 45% of its stock is owned by the other corporations.

Step 4. **Determine if there is a common parent.** Pear's stock is not owned more than 80% by the other corporations, but it qualifies as the common parent because it owns more than 80% of at least one of the corporations (Apricot).

Therefore, Pear, Apricot, and Banana qualify as an affiliated group, and the group can decide whether it wants to elect to file a consolidated tax return.

EXAMPLE 5.2.3 Identifying Affiliated Groups (Scenario 3)

Acorn Corporation owns 65% (voting and value) of Pecan Corporation and 25% (voting and value) of Cashew Corporation. Pecan Corporation owns 75% (voting and value) of Cashew Corporation, while Cashew owns 20% (voting and value) of Pecan. Determine the largest group of corporations that qualify as an affiliated group, assuming that these ownership percentages are for every day of the tax year.

SOLUTION

We follow the steps shown in Illustration 5.3 to determine if an affiliated group exists.

Step 1. **Diagram the corporate ownership to ensure you understand the structure.**

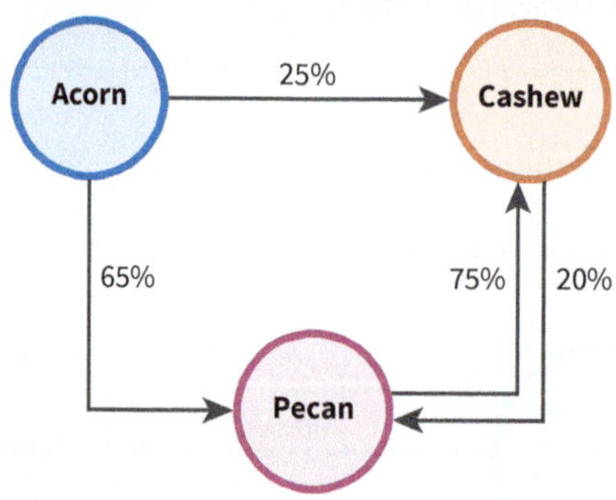

Step 2. **Identify the largest group of corporations that might meet the affiliated group rules.** The first group to test is Acorn, Cashew, and Pecan.

Step 3. **Analyze if the 80% test is met.** (*Both* the 80% voting *and* 80% value test must be met.) Pecan meets the 80% test because it is owned 85% by Acorn and Cashew. Cashew meets the 80% test because it is owned 100% by Acorn and Pecan.

Step 4. **Determine if there is a common parent.** Acorn is not owned at least 80% by Pecan and Cashew, which means that it must be the common parent if the three corporations qualify as an affiliated group. However, Acorn does not own at least 80% of at least one corporation in the group. Therefore, it cannot be the common parent.

Acorn, Cashew, and Parent are not an affiliated group because there is not a common parent. There is also not an affiliated group of two corporations because none of the corporations are owned 80% or more by only one of the other corporations.

Related exercises: Brief Exercise 2
Application Problem 4

If the affiliated group rules are met, the members in the group must decide whether they want to elect to file a consolidated tax return, which we discuss next.

The Consolidation Process

Eligible affiliated corporations can elect to file a consolidated return. A **consolidated return** is a tax return that includes the taxable income of more than one corporation. Even though the corporations are legally separate entities, for tax purposes, they file only one return.

Ineligible Corporations

The following corporations are *not* eligible to file a consolidated tax return:[8]

- Foreign corporations
- Tax-exempt corporations
- Regulated investment companies
- S corporations
- Insurance companies
- Partnerships, limited liability companies, estates, trusts, and other noncorporate entities

Related exercises: Multiple Choice Questions 3, 4

Consolidation Rules

There are several important rules related to the decision to consolidate.

Election

- The election to consolidate must be unanimous by all the corporations in the affiliated group, and it is binding on future returns. The group must make the election by the extended due date for the parent's return. The extended due date is typically five months after the due date.
- The election creates a joint and several tax liability for each corporation included in the election, meaning that the IRS can collect the tax for the entire group from any of the included corporations, should it choose to do so.
- The election can be revoked only if a member leaves the group, or with the permission of the IRS. Permission must be requested no later than 90 days before the extended due date of the return.
- Generally, if a subsidiary leaves the group, it cannot return to the group for five years.
- The election to consolidate may not apply for state tax purposes. The tax laws for each applicable state should be consulted to determine how the related corporations' rules apply for state filings.

Filing

- As with all corporations, the due date of the return is the 15th day of the fourth month after the end of the tax year, which is April 15 for a calendar-year corporation. A six-month extension to October 15 is available.
- Estimated tax payments must be made on a consolidated tax basis, except for the first two tax years that the consolidated return is filed. For those years, each corporation can make estimated tax payments if it prefers.[9]

[8] IRC §1504(b).
[9] Treas. Reg. 1.1502-5(a)(1).

Accounting Methods and Periods

- The members of the group must conform their tax year to the parent's tax year. Corporations in the group that must change their tax year-end will file a short-year tax return for their last non-consolidated return. A short-year tax return is a return that covers less than 12 months.
- Earnings & profits (E&P) are not computed on a consolidated basis. The parent and each subsidiary compute their own E&P, adjusting it each year for its pro rata share of the consolidated taxable income. E&P is adjusted for each corporation for the intercompany gains and losses, and it is reduced for the allocable share of the consolidated federal income tax liability.
- Each corporation can use its own accounting methods. These do not need to be conformed to the parent's methods. However, if the consolidated gross receipts exceed $31 million (2025), then all of the corporations must use the accrual method.[10]

Related exercise: Multiple Choice Question 5

The next Example explains how these consolidation requirements can impact corporate planning.

EXAMPLE 5.2.4
Consolidation Requirements

Blue Corporation is the common parent for an affiliated group that includes Red Corporation and Green Corporation. Blue has a calendar year-end while Red and Green both have June 30 year-ends. The shareholders of Green Corporation approach you to determine if there are any concerns they should have about agreeing to the election to file a consolidated tax return for Year 4.

SOLUTION

Green Corporation will have two immediate effects from agreeing to this election. The tax year for the consolidated return will be Blue's year of December 31 because Blue is the common parent. Green's most recent tax return was for the year ended June 30, Year 3. Green will file as part of the consolidated group for Year 4 including its results from January 1 to December 31 of Year 4. Green will have to file a short-year return for the six-month period from July 1 to December 31, Year 3. The short-year will be included as a full-year for carryforwards (see Disadvantages of Consolidated Returns section below).

You should also inform the shareholders of Green that Green has joint and several liability for the consolidated income tax liability. For example, if the income tax liability for a year is $550,000 and it is not paid with the consolidated tax return, the IRS could collect the entire $550,000 from Green, if it chose to do so.

Affiliated Groups that Do Not Consolidate

If an affiliated group does *not* elect to file as a consolidated group, then the limitations that apply to controlled groups discussed in LO1, Controlled Groups, will apply to the corporations, because they will qualify as a controlled group. **Illustration 5.4** summarizes the key differences that exist between electing to file as a consolidated return or not.

[10]IRC §448(a) and (c).

ILLUSTRATION 5.4 Filing Rules for Consolidated Return vs. Controlled Groups

Differences in Consolidating and Filing as Controlled Group		
Item	**Affiliated group that elects to file a consolidated return**	**Controlled group where separate returns are filed**
80% test	Must be met on every day of the year and *both* the 80% voting *and* 80% value test must be met.	Must be met only on the last day of the tax year and *either* the 80% voting *or* 80% value test must be met.
Accounting method	Each corporation can use its own accounting methods.	Each corporation can use its own accounting methods.
Tax year	The members of the group must conform their tax year to the parent's tax year.	The members of the group do not need to conform their tax year to the parent's tax year.
Tax liability	The election creates a joint and several tax liability for each corporation.	Each corporation is liable for only its own tax.
Accumulated earnings credit	Can be used only one time by all the corporations.	Can be used only one time by all the corporations.
Section 179, NOLs, Section 1231 gains/losses, charitable contribution deduction, dividends received deduction, etc.	Computed on a consolidated basis.	Computed separately for each corporation.
Related-party gains/losses	Gains and losses on intercompany sales are deferred until disposition outside the group.	Realized gains/losses from the sales of assets between corporations in the group can be recognized.
Intercompany dividend	Eliminated and not taxed.	Included in taxable income but dividends received deduction allowed.
Basis of parent's investment	Adjustments made for Subsidiary's operating gains/losses, distributions, and taxes.	No adjustments allowed.

Tax Return Guidance

A Form 1122, Authorization and Consent of Subsidiary Corporation to be Included in a Consolidated Income Tax Return, must be signed by each member of the consolidated return and attached to the first consolidated tax return. Form 851, Affiliations Schedule, must be included with the tax return every year.

Advantages and Disadvantages of Electing to Consolidate

There are important advantages and disadvantages of filing on a consolidated basis, and these must be carefully weighed to ensure that the best decision is made, especially given that the election is permanent. The decision to not consolidate is not permanent, meaning that if an affiliated group does not make the election for its first year as an affiliated group, it can always choose to make the election in the future. Therefore, uncertainty for the election might best be handled by deferring the election to a future year.

> **Potential Pitfall**
>
> The criteria that have to be met to consolidate are different for financial reporting purposes than for tax purposes. Therefore, do not assume that corporations that file consolidated financial statements also file a consolidated tax return.

Advantages of Consolidated Returns

There are several advantages which can result from filing a consolidated return. The circumstances vary for each affiliated group so each must be reviewed carefully to determine if an election to consolidate will be beneficial. For the situations described below, assume that two corporations, Rock and Roll, are an affiliated group and elect to file a consolidated return. Some of the more common advantages include:

Netting Capital Gains and Losses Assume Rock has net capital gains of $10,000 and Roll has net capital losses of $9,000. If they did not consolidate, Rock would pay tax on the $10,000 capital gain and Roll would not be able to deduct the capital loss in the current year. However, these items would net on a consolidated return and reduce the consolidated capital gain to $1,000 ($10,000 – $9,000).

Netting Income and Losses Assume that Rock has $1,000,000 net income and Roll has a $1,000,000 net operating loss. If they did not consolidate, Rock would pay tax on the $1,000,000 income and Roll would carryforward the net operating loss of $1,000,000. However, these items would net to zero on a consolidated return, so the $1,000,000 NOL would provide a tax benefit immediately.

Deferral of Gains from the Sale of Assets If Rock sells an asset to Roll that has a fair market value of $50,000 and adjusted basis of $15,000, the $35,000 gain imbedded in the asset is not recognized. That gain is not recognized until the asset is sold outside the affiliated group.

Avoiding Limitations on Deductions Based on Taxable Income Assume that Rock's charitable contributions are equal to 14% of its taxable income and that Roll did not make any charitable contributions this year. If Rock files its own return, the charitable contribution deduction will be limited to 10% of taxable income. However, on the consolidated return, Roll's taxable income can also be used in the 10% computation to increase the charitable contribution deduction. The same advantage can exist for the taxable income limitation for the dividends received deduction.

Disadvantages of Consolidated Returns

There are also several disadvantages to filing consolidated tax returns that taxpayers should consider before making the election to consolidate, including:

Election Is Binding for Future Tax Years Once made, the election to file a consolidated return is binding for all tax years. The affiliated group does not have the option to decide each year whether it is to its advantage to consolidate. The only exceptions to this rule are that the election can be changed with the approval of the IRS commissioner, or if the composition of the affiliated group changes.

Creation of Short-Tax Years If the subsidiaries have a different tax year than the parent, when they switch to the parent's year-end, this will create a short-tax year. Short-tax years count as a full year for purposes of carryforwards such as for charitable contributions and capital losses, so this can cause a carryforward to expire more quickly.

Deferral of Losses from the Sale of Assets If Rock sells an asset to Roll that has a fair market value of $50,000 and adjusted basis of $75,000, the $25,000 loss imbedded in the asset is not recognized. The loss is not recognized until the asset is sold outside the affiliated group.

Complexity of Tax Return The consolidated tax rules are very complex, so this can increase administrative costs for the corporations.

Illustration 5.5 summarizes the advantages and disadvantages of electing to consolidate.

ILLUSTRATION 5.5 The Decision to Consolidate

Advantages and Disadvantages of Electing to Consolidate	
Advantages	**Disadvantages**
Netting capital gains and losses across group members	Election is binding for future tax years
Netting income and losses against income of other group members	Creation of short-tax years
Deferral of gains from sale of assets to other group members	Deferral of losses from sale of assets to other group members
Avoiding limitations on deductions based on taxable income by using income from all group members	Complexity of tax return

Some of the factors that influence the decision to consolidate are investigated in the next Example.

EXAMPLE 5.2.5 Decision to Consolidate

Based on just the information given, would it be advantageous for the corporations in each of the scenarios below to elect to file a consolidated tax return?

- **Scenario A:** Cornhusker Corporation has unused capital losses of $5,300,000 that will expire in two more years. Terrapin Corporation expects to generate capital gains of $8,000,000 over the next two years. Cornhusker owns 85% of Terrapin.
- **Scenario B:** Bluegrass Corporation owns a building with a fair market value of $13,000,000 and an adjusted basis of $17,000,000. Bluegrass owns 90% of Peach Corporation but they have not elected in the past to file a consolidated tax return. Bluegrass is considering selling the building to Peach this year and may also elect to begin filing a consolidated tax return with Peach.
- **Scenario C:** Buckeye Corporation plans to contribute $1,000,000 per year for the next three years to qualified charitable organizations that support economic development efforts in its region. Buckeye expects to have taxable income of approximately $6,000,000 per year during this period. Wolverine Corporation should generate at least $5,000,000 of taxable income over the next three years, and it does not plan to make any charitable contributions. Wolverine owns 90% of Buckeye.

SOLUTION

- **Scenario A:** Cornhusker and Terrapin should consider electing to file a consolidated tax return because the $5,300,000 of capital losses from Cornhusker can reduce the capital gains of $8,000,000 to $2,700,000. Cornhusker can carry forward the capital losses for only two more years and if not used by then, they will expire.
- **Scenario B:** You should advise Bluegrass to not elect to file a consolidated return with Peach. If it did file a consolidated return, when the building is sold to Peach, Bluegrass's loss of $4,000,000 ($13,000,000 – $17,000,000) cannot be recognized until the building is sold outside of the consolidated group.
- **Scenario C:** Buckeye and Wolverine will make a smart tax decision if they elect to file a consolidated tax return. Buckeye's charitable contribution deduction will be limited to $600,000 each year ($6,000,000 of taxable income × 10%), so $400,000 ($1,000,000 contribution – $600,000) of the contribution each year will be carried forward. However, contributions can be carried forward for only five years. Consolidated taxable income would be $11,000,000 ($6,000,000 + $5,000,000) and charitable contributions of up to $1,100,000 ($11,000,000 × 10%) could be deducted each year.

Related exercises: Brief Exercises 3, 4

We next explain how consolidated taxable income is computed.

Computing Consolidated Taxable Income

The filing of consolidated returns is one of the most complicated processes in the federal income tax law, and most of these laws are beyond the scope of this text. We provide an explanation of a few of the basic rules below. Computing consolidated taxable income requires four steps. The flowchart in **Illustration 5.6** also details these steps.

Step 1. **Compute:** **Taxable income** separately for each corporation in the group.

Step 2. **Remove:** **Group items** that are computed on an aggregate basis for the group, including:[11]

- Net capital gain and losses
- Charitable contributions

ILLUSTRATION 5.6 Computing Consolidated Taxable Income

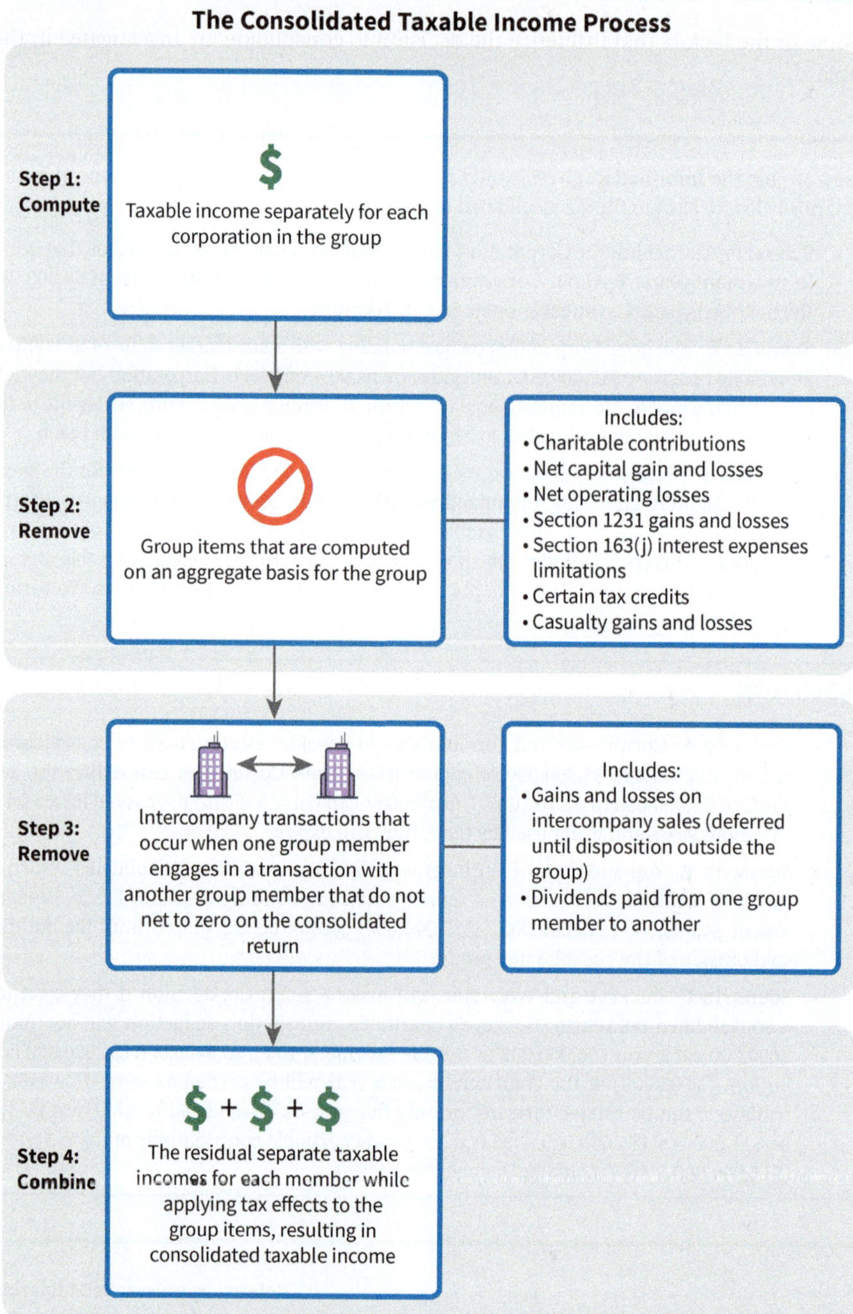

[11] Treas. Reg. § 1.1502-11(a).

- Net operating losses
- Section 1231 gains and losses
- Section 163(j) interest expenses limitations
- Certain tax credits
- Casualty gains and losses

Step 3. Remove: Intercompany transactions that occur when one group member engages in a transaction with another group member that do not net to zero on the consolidated return. Most intercompany transactions are not removed from the members' separate taxable incomes because the effect of these transactions usually nets to zero on the consolidated tax return.

For example, if Parent pays Subsidiary $1,000 for consulting services rendered by Subsidiary, Subsidiary will have $1,000 of income and Parent will have an expense of $1,000. These will net to zero on the consolidated return. However, there are some intercompany transactions which must be removed from the separate taxable incomes, such as:

- Gains and losses on intercompany sales are deferred until disposition outside the group. These gains and losses will be recognized at the time of the eventual disposition outside the consolidated firm. The nature of the gain or loss is determined by the use of the property at the time of the intercompany sale.
- Dividends paid from one group member to another are ignored, so neither dividend income nor the dividends received deduction is included in consolidated taxable income.

Step 4. Combine: The residual separate taxable incomes for each member while applying tax effects to the group items, resulting in consolidated taxable income.

The template shown in **Illustration 5.7** should be helpful for computing consolidated taxable income. You must include a separate column for each subsidiary in the group.

ILLUSTRATION 5.7 Template for Computing Consolidated Taxable Income

Consolidated Taxable Income Computation				
	Parent	**Subsidiary One**	**Subsidiary Two**	**Consolidated**
Separate taxable income				
Remove group items:				
Net capital gain and losses				
Charitable contributions				
Net operating losses				
Section 1231 gains and losses				
Section 163(j) interest limit				
Certain tax credits				
Casualty gains and losses				
Remove intercompany transactions if included in income				
Adjusted separate taxable income				
Consolidated taxable income before group items:				
Net capital gain and losses				
Charitable contributions				
Net operating losses				
Section 1231 gains and losses				
Section 163(j) interest limit				
Certain tax credits				
Casualty gains and losses				
Consolidated taxable income				

We apply this template to compute consolidated taxable income in the next Example.

EXAMPLE 5.2.6 Computing Consolidated Taxable Income

Parent owns 100% of Subsidiary. Parent reports on the accrual basis and Subsidiary reports on the cash basis. Their tax information for the current year is as follows:

Parent taxable income	$200,000
Subsidiary loss	($ 80,000)

Parent's income includes a $17,000 long-term capital gain and a charitable contribution deduction of $14,000. Parent rented equipment from Subsidiary during the year for $35,000. Parent paid $20,000 of the rental fee in the current year but did not pay the other $15,000 until the following year. Subsidiary's loss includes a short-term capital loss of ($24,000). Subsidiary paid a dividend to Parent of $12,000. Parent recorded dividend income and a dividends received deduction. Compute the consolidated taxable income for the year.

SOLUTION

We can use the template shown in Illustration 5.7 to help determine the consolidated taxable income:

	Consolidated taxable income computation		
	Parent	Subsidiary	Consolidated
Separate taxable income	$200,000	($ 80,000)	
Remove group items:			
Net capital gain and losses (1)	(17,000)	0	
Charitable contributions (2)	14,000		
Remove intercompany transactions if included in taxable income:			
Rental fee (3)	15,000		
Dividend (4)	0		
Adjusted separate taxable income	$212,000	($ 80,000)	
Consolidated taxable income before group items:			$132,000
Net capital gain and losses (5)			0
Charitable contributions (6)			(13,200)
Consolidated taxable income			$118,800

(1) Net capital gains and losses must be removed from separate taxable income. Parent's LTCG of $17,000 is removed by subtracting it. Subsidiary's STCL of ($24,000) did not reduce its taxable income because net capital losses cannot be deducted, so it does not need to be added back.

(2) Charitable contributions must be deducted based on consolidated taxable income, so Parent's contribution must be added back to its separate taxable income.

(3) The $20,000 rental fee that was paid this year is an intercompany transaction that does not need an adjustment. Parent deducted the $20,000 and Subsidiary reported $20,000 of revenue, so this nets to zero on the consolidated return. However, Subsidiary would not have included the other $15,000 of revenue in its income because it reports on the cash basis and the income has not been received. Parent is on the accrual basis so it would usually deduct the $15,000 this year. However, because these are related corporations, Parent cannot deduct the payment until Subsidiary includes it in income, which will be in Year 2. So, the $15,000 cannot be deducted by Parent until Year 2.

(4) Parent recorded $12,000 of dividend income and a DRD of $12,000. Because this nets to zero on Parent's separate return, no adjustment is needed.

(5) The consolidated net capital loss is ($7,000) ($17,000 LTCG – $24,000 STCL). They cannot deduct this loss on the consolidated return, but it can be carried back three years and forward five years.

(6) The charitable contribution deduction is limited to $13,200, which is 10% of consolidated taxable income of $132,000.

Related exercises: Application Problems 5, 6, 7

Parent corporations must adjust their stock basis in a subsidiary if they consolidate, something that is not usually done for other investors in stock. We next explain this computation.

Stock Basis of Subsidiary

When a parent corporation acquires a subsidiary, the parent records its investment in a stock basis account for the subsidiary.

Computing Stock Basis

The parent's stock basis is adjusted on the last day of each tax year as follows:[12]

- **Plus:** The parent's allocable share of the consolidated income
- **Plus:** The parent's allocable share of the capital loss of the subsidiary if the subsidiary could not use it in a carryback year
- ***Less*:** The parent's allocable share of the consolidated loss
- ***Less*:** The parent's allocable share of any capital loss that was a carryforward to the current year and has not previously reduced the stock basis
- ***Less*:** Dividends paid to the parent from the subsidiary's earnings & profits

Why **Why does the parent corporation adjust its stock basis in the subsidiary?** In general, shareholders do not adjust the basis in their stock for income or losses of the corporation, because the shareholder does not pay taxes on the earnings of the corporation unless they are later paid out as a dividend. However, a parent corporation is treated differently because it is taxed on the subsidiary's earnings on the consolidated tax return. Therefore, the parent corporation can adjust its stock basis in the subsidiary, so the parent does not recognize this income a second time if it sells the subsidiary in the future. If the subsidiary has a loss for the year, the decrease in the stock basis prevents the parent from benefiting from the loss twice.

Excess Loss Account

The allocable share of losses cannot reduce the parent's stock basis below zero, even though the entire loss can reduce the consolidated income. The parent must add any loss that cannot reduce the basis to the **excess loss account**. If the parent sells the subsidiary's stock, or the group is deconsolidated, while an excess loss exists, the parent must recognize the amount in the excess loss account as a capital gain.[13]

Net Operating Losses

One advantage of electing to file a consolidated return is that losses from one member can be used to offset income from another member. The general NOL rules for corporations also apply to consolidated groups, such as:

- NOLs incurred in the current tax year cannot be carried back and can be carried forward indefinitely.
- When NOLs incurred after 2017 are carried forward, they can offset only 80% of taxable income before the NOL in the carryforward year.
- NOLs incurred before 2018 can be carried forward for only 20 years and can offset 100% of taxable income in the carryforward year.

When computing the consolidated NOL, the following items must be removed from consolidated income because they have separate carryback and/or carryforward rules:

- Charitable contributions
- Capital gains and losses

Related exercise: Brief Exercise 5

[12]Treas. Reg. §1.1502-32.
[13]Treas. Reg. §§1.1502-19(a).

Limitations on the use of NOLs are discussed in LO4, Preservation of Tax Attributes. The next Example applies the rules for computing the parent's stock basis in a subsidiary.

EXAMPLE 5.2.7
Stock Basis of Subsidiary

Parent Corporation purchased all the stock of Subsidiary in Year 1 for $320,000. Subsidiary's operating results were as follows:

Year 1	($260,000)
Year 2	($100,000)
Year 3	$ 70,000
Year 4	($ 20,000)

Compute Parent's stock basis in Subsidiary at the end of each year. What would be the result if Parent sold the stock of Subsidiary at the end for Year 2 for $260,000?

SOLUTION

The beginning stock basis in Subsidiary is $320,000, and it is adjusted as follows:

Investment	Income/loss	Stock basis	Excess loss account
		$320,000	
Year 1	($260,000)	(260,000)	
Year 2	($100,000)	(60,000)	($ 40,000)
		$ 0	($ 40,000)
Year 3	$ 70,000	30,000	40,000
		$ 30,000	$ 0
Year 4	($ 20,000)	(20,000)	
		$ 10,000	$ 0

For Year 2, the loss of ($100,000) cannot reduce the stock basis below zero. The first ($60,000) of loss reduces the basis to zero, and the remaining ($40,000) is added to the excess loss account.

For Year 3, the income of $70,000 is first used to increase the excess loss account to zero. The remaining income of $30,000 increases the basis account.

If Parent sold the stock of Subsidiary at the end of Year 2, the gain would be a $300,000 capital gain, computed as follows:

Amount realized	$260,000
Adjusted basis	0
Gain before excess loss	$260,000
Plus: Excess loss account	40,000
Recognized gain	$300,000

Related exercise: Application Problem 8

PRACTICE PROBLEM 5.2.1
Identifying an Affiliated Group

Venus Corporation owns stock in the following corporations:

- 60% (voting and value) of the stock of Mercury Corporation
- 85% of the voting and 75% of the value of the stock of Jupiter Corporation
- 85% (voting and value) of the stock of Mars Corporation

Determine the largest group of corporations that qualify as an affiliated group, assuming that these ownership percentages are for every day of the tax year.

SOLUTION

We use the following steps from Illustration 5.3 to determine if an affiliated group exists.

Step 1. Diagram the corporate ownership to ensure you understand the structure.

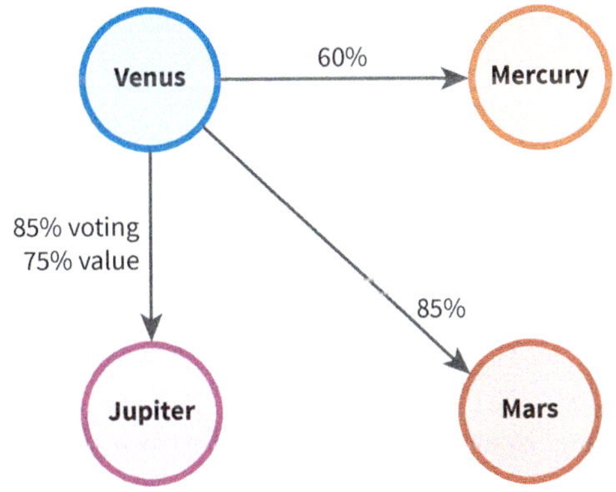

Step 2. Identify the largest group of corporations that might meet the affiliated group rules. The first group to test is Venus, Jupiter, Mercury, and Mars.

Step 3. Analyze if the 80% test is met. (*Both* the 80% voting *and* 80% value test must be met.) Mercury does not meet the 80% test because only 60% of its stock is owned by the other corporations. Jupiter does not because Venus owns 75% of Jupiter's value, so it does not own more than 80% of both Jupiter's voting stock and its value. Mars does meet the test because 85% of its stock (voting and value) is owned by Venus.

Step 4. Determine if there is a common parent. Venus's stock is not owned more than 80% by the other corporations, but it qualifies as the common parent because it owns more than 80% of at least one of the corporations.

Therefore, Venus and Mars qualify as an affiliated group, and the group can decide whether it wants to elect to file a consolidated tax return.

PRACTICE PROBLEM 5.2.2
Computing Consolidated Taxable Income

Paper Corporation owns 100% of Scissors Corporation in the current year. Scissors paid Paper a $38,000 cash dividend on December 31. Including the dividend income, Paper has separate taxable income of $222,000 and Scissors reported separate taxable income of $133,000. What is the consolidated taxable income for the two corporations?

SOLUTION

Paper Corporation included the dividend received in its separate taxable income, but it did not claim a dividends received deduction. The dividend income must be eliminated in calculating consolidated taxable income. No elimination is required for Scissors because dividend payments are not deductible. Therefore, consolidated taxable income is as follows:

Paper separate taxable income	$222,000
Scissors separate taxable income	133,000
Intercompany adjustment	(38,000)
Consolidated taxable income	$317,000

PRACTICE PROBLEM 5.2.3 Calculating Stock Basis of a Subsidiary

Pink Corporation purchased all the stock of Scarlet Corporation in Year 1 for $85,000. Scarlet's operating results were as follows:

Year 1	($55,000)
Year 2	$40,000
Year 3	($78,000)
Year 4	$45,000

Compute Pink's stock basis in Scarlet at the end of each year. What would be the result if Pink sold the stock of Scarlet at the end of Year 3 for $60,000?

SOLUTION

The beginning stock basis in Scarlet is $85,000, and it is adjusted as follows:

Investment	Income/loss	Stock basis	Excess loss account
		$85,000	
Year 1	($55,000)	(55,000)	
		$30,000	
Year 2	$40,000	40,000	
		$70,000	
Year 3	($78,000)	(70,000)	($8,000)
		$ 0	($8,000)
Year 4	$45,000	37,000	8,000
		$37,000	$ 0

For Year 3, the loss of ($78,000) cannot reduce the stock basis below zero. The first ($70,000) of loss reduces the basis to zero, and the remaining ($8,000) is added to the excess loss account.

For Year 4, the income of $45,000 is first used to increase the excess loss account to zero. The remaining income of $37,000 increases the basis account.

If Pink sold the stock of Scarlet at the end of Year 3, the gain would be $68,000 computed as follows:

Amount realized	$60,000
Adjusted basis	0
Gain before excess loss	$60,000
Excess loss account	8,000
Recognized gain	$68,000

INTERACTIVE SELF-SCORING QUIZZES

5.3 Corporate Reorganizations

LEARNING OBJECTIVE 3

Determine the tax consequences of a reorganization for the acquiring corporation, acquired corporation, and the acquired corporation's shareholders.

VIDEO CONTENT

A **reorganization** occurs when one or more corporations rearrange their legal ownership structure to merge two or more corporations into one entity (*acquisitive reorganizations*), or to divide a corporation into two or more entities (*divisive reorganizations*). Reorganizations can be taxable or tax-deferred. If the changes in the nature of the business operations and the substance of the ownership structure are not significant, then realized gains and losses from the transaction are usually deferred. Throughout this section, we will use the terms *Acquiring* and *Target* to represent the corporations involved in the reorganization.

Related exercise: Discussion Question 6

Types of Reorganizations

We can separate acquisitive corporate reorganizations into four distinct types. The general tax consequences for each type are also provided.

Taxable Purchase of Target's Assets by Acquiring

A taxable purchase of Target's assets has the following tax consequences:

- Target will recognize gain or loss based on the difference in the FMV and basis of its assets.
- Acquiring will have a FMV basis in the purchased assets.
- If Target is liquidated, the shareholders of Target will have gain or loss based on the difference in the value of the assets they receive and their stock basis.
- Target's shareholders will have a FMV basis in the assets received from Acquiring.

Tax-Deferred Purchase of Target's Assets by Acquiring with Acquiring's Stock

A tax-deferred purchase of Target's assets has the following consequences:

- Target will generally not recognize gain or loss.
- Acquiring will have a carryover basis in the assets of Target.
- Target's shareholders will recognize any realized gain only to the extent that they receive assets other than stock of Acquiring. Target's shareholders will never recognize a loss.
- Target's shareholders' basis in the stock of Acquiring will be the basis they had in their old Target stock plus any gain they recognized.

Taxable Purchase of Target's Stock by Acquiring

A taxable purchase of Target's stock has the following tax consequences:

- Target will not recognize gain or loss. Target still owns its assets with the same basis as before the transaction.
- Acquiring will have a FMV basis in the purchased stock of Target.
- Target's shareholders will recognize gain or loss based on the difference in the FMV received and the basis of their stock.
- Target's shareholders will have a FMV basis in the assets received from Acquiring.

Related exercise: Discussion Question 7

Tax-Deferred Purchase of Target's Stock by Acquiring

A tax-deferred purchase of Target's stock has the following tax consequences:

- Target will not recognize gain or loss. Target still owns its assets with the same basis as before the transaction.
- Acquiring will not recognize gain or loss.
- Target's shareholders will not recognize gain or loss.
- Target's shareholders' basis in the new stock of Acquiring will be the same basis they had in their old stock of Target.

The remainder of this section describes the seven types of qualified reorganizations and reviews the tax consequences of such tax deferred reorganizations.

> **Spotlight on the Law**
>
> **Friendly Fire or Hostile Takeover?**
>
> There are many types of corporate reorganizations, and they can occur for a variety of reasons. But what if the merger is not wanted, but in fact, considered a hostile takeover? How does a target corporation block an attempted raid?
>
> Back in 1983, Sam Snyder, assistant general counsel for Union Oil (known as Unocal and eventually acquired by Chevron), wrote a memo outlining potential defenses against such an attack. In the late 1970s and 1980s, T. Boone Pickens, Jr. had a reputation for taking over big oil companies and making millions in the process. Snyder wanted to protect Unocal and its CEO, Fred L. Hartley, from such an attack. Snyder's best defense strategy was to involve the executives and current shareholders at Unocal and not surrender prematurely to Pickens's attack. It was risky to ask Unocal shareholders to approve an internal corporate restructuring that would approve keeping current management under Hartley to thwart a takeover bid by Pickens. But in 1983, the Unocal shareholders did approve such a restructuring, making it harder for Pickens to take over Unocal.
>
> But Pickens was not ready to give up, and in 1984 began buying Unocal stock once again, as well as Phillips Petroleum stock. In the end, Phillips succumbed and agreed to a recapitalization and stock repurchase plan that gave Pickens an $89 million profit on his Phillips shares. Pickens' claim was that his takeover attempts would boost the value for all oil company shareholders. Pickens continued to purchase Unocal stock. After several unsuccessful negotiations and restructuring offerings, the two sides settled. Unocal remained intact but also had to incur astronomical attorney fees and buy back costs. Hartley claimed that he would never sell to Pickens. Although Hartley won the war, it was at a huge cost.
>
> As learned from this case, not all mergers and acquisitions are friendly. In the end, it can be very costly to defend against a hostile takeover.
>
> *Source:* Whitefield, Debra and Rivera, Nancy. "Takeover Ware: Unocal Saw Pickens Bid, Trumped It." *Los Angeles Times,* 2 June 1985, www.latimes.com/archives/la-xpm-1985-06-02-mn-15382-story.html.

Types of Qualified (Tax-Deferred) Reorganizations

Congress has provided seven different types of qualified reorganizations, all of which allow most realized gains and losses to be deferred. They are classified as follows:

- **Acquisitive Reorganizations**: Types A, B, and C
- **Divisive Reorganization**: Type D
- **Other Reorganizations**: Types E, F, and G

Acquisitive reorganizations occur when two or more corporations are merged or consolidated into one organization. In a **merger**, the acquired corporation (target) dissolves into another corporation (the acquiring corporation). In a **consolidation**, both the acquired and acquiring corporations dissolve into a new (surviving) corporation. **Divisive reorganizations** occur when one corporation divides into two or more corporations.

Acquisitive Reorganizations (Types A, B, C)

Acquisitive stock-for-asset reorganizations can generally be viewed as follows (and as shown in **Illustration 5.8**):

- Acquiring exchanges its stock for the assets of Target. Acquiring may also provide assets other than stock, which is treated as boot.
- Target then exchanges with its shareholders the stock and assets it received from Acquiring for the stock of Target.
- Target then usually dissolves.

ILLUSTRATION 5.8 Acquisitive Reorganizations

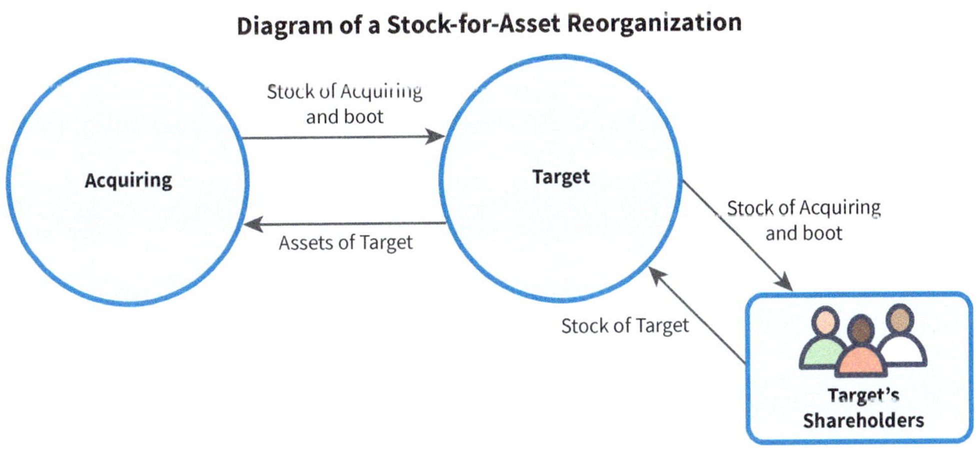

Type A Reorganization This is a stock-for-asset reorganization, meaning that Acquiring exchanges its stock for Target's assets. A **Type A reorganization** must meet the following requirements:

- The transaction must qualify as a statutory merger. A **statutory merger** is a merger or consolidation that complies with the laws of the applicable state.
- Acquiring corporation can transfer voting or nonvoting stock to Target.
- Boot can be transferred, but the value of the boot cannot exceed 50% of the consideration provided to Target by Acquiring. **Boot** for a qualified reorganization is any consideration provided to Target other than qualifying stock. In some situations, the IRS and courts have allowed as much as 60% of the acquisition price to be boot, meaning that the value of the stock transferred could be as low as 40%.
- Acquiring must assume all the liabilities of Target.
- Target must dissolve.

The next two Examples apply these requirements for a Type A reorganization.

EXAMPLE 5.3.1
Type A Reorganization (Scenario 1)

As part of a statutory merger, Acquiring Corporation transfers $170,000 of nonvoting stock and $30,000 cash to Target Corporation in return for assets of Target that have a fair market value of $270,000, adjusted basis of $180,000, with liabilities attached of $70,000. Acquiring assumes Target's liabilities. Target distributes the nonvoting stock and cash to its shareholders in return for their stock. Does this qualify as a Type A reorganization?

SOLUTION

Yes, this does qualify as a Type A reorganization. The following requirements are satisfied:

- The transaction is a statutory merger.
- The stock transferred by Acquiring is at least 50% of the total consideration transferred. The $170,000 of stock is 85% ($170,000/$200,000) of the consideration transferred.
- Acquiring assumed all the liabilities of Target.
- Target dissolves.

EXAMPLE 5.3.2
Type A Reorganization (Scenario 2)

Continuing with facts similar to Example 5.3.1, as part of a statutory merger, Acquiring Corporation transfers $170,000 of nonvoting stock and $40,000 cash to Target Corporation in return for assets of Target that have a fair market value of $270,000, adjusted basis of $180,000, with liabilities attached of $70,000. Acquiring assumes $60,000 of Target's liabilities. Target distributes the nonvoting stock and cash to its shareholders in return for their stock. Does this qualify as a Type A reorganization?

SOLUTION

No, this does not qualify as a Type A reorganization because Acquiring did not assume all the liabilities of Target. Acquiring assumed only $60,000 of Target's liabilities. Therefore, all realized gains and losses will be recognized by Acquiring, Target, and Target's shareholders.

Related exercises: Brief Exercise 6
Application Problem 9

Type B Reorganization A **Type B reorganization** is a stock-for-stock reorganization, meaning that Acquiring exchanges its stock for Target stock. The following requirements must be met for a Type B reorganization:

- Acquiring can transfer only its voting stock to Target. It cannot transfer nonvoting stock or boot.
- Acquiring must own at least 80% of the stock of Target (voting power and value) after the transaction.

The next two Examples apply these requirements for a Type B reorganization.

Potential Pitfall

Acquiring does not have to acquire at least 80% of Target's stock in the transaction for it to qualify as a Type B reorganization. It just needs to own at least 80% of Target after the transaction. If Acquiring owned 65% of Target before the transaction, then it would need to purchase 15% more of Target to reach the 80% threshold.

EXAMPLE 5.3.3 Type B Reorganization (Scenario 1)

Acquiring Corporation owns 500 shares of Target Corporation's voting stock. Acquiring has 20,000 shares of voting stock outstanding while Target has 1,000 shares of voting stock outstanding. Acquiring transfers 50 shares of its voting stock for 300 additional shares of Target's voting stock. Does this transaction qualify as a Type B reorganization?

SOLUTION

Yes, this does qualify as a Type B reorganization because the following requirements are met:

- Acquiring transferred only voting stock to Target. It did not use nonvoting stock or boot.
- After the transaction, Acquiring owns 800 shares of Target's 1,000 outstanding shares, so it owns at least 80% of Target.

EXAMPLE 5.3.4 Type B Reorganization (Scenario 2)

Acquiring Corporation owns 500 shares of Target Corporation's voting stock. Target has 1,000 shares of voting stock outstanding. Acquiring transfers 45 shares of its voting stock and $23,000 for 300 additional shares of Target's voting stock. Does this transaction qualify as a Type B reorganization?

SOLUTION

This does not qualify as a Type B reorganization. Acquiring does own at least 80% of Target after the transaction. However, Acquiring transferred $23,000 of cash to Target so it did not transfer only voting stock. Therefore, all realized gains and losses are recognized for Acquiring, Target, and Target's shareholders.

Related exercises: Multiple Choice Question 6
Brief Exercise 7
Application Problem 10

Type C Reorganization This is a stock-for-asset reorganization, meaning that Acquiring exchanges its stock for Target's assets. A **Type C reorganization** must meet the following requirements:

- Acquiring can use only voting stock in the transfer. Nonvoting stock is not permitted.
- The voting stock that Acquiring transfers to Target must be at least 80% of the consideration provided. If Acquiring transfers boot to Target, the boot cannot exceed 20% of the total consideration provided by Acquiring.
- If liabilities secured by Target's assets are assumed by Acquiring, this liability relief is not considered as boot (and therefore not subject to the 20% test) unless other boot is also given. If Acquiring provides other boot to Target, then the total amount of boot and liability relief cannot exceed 20% of the consideration.
- Acquiring must own *substantially all* the assets of Target after the transaction. **Substantially all** the assets is defined by the IRS as 90% of net asset value and 70% of gross asset value.[14]
- Acquiring does not have to assume all the liabilities of Target.
- Target does not have to dissolve, although it can.

Potential Pitfall

In Example 5.3.3, does it matter that Acquiring transferred only 2.5% (50 shares/20,000 shares) of its shares to Target? No, it does not. There is no requirement for what percentage of Acquiring's stock must be owned by Target. The reason that Acquiring needed to use only 2.5% of its shares in return for 30% (300 shares/1,000 shares) of Target's shares is that Acquiring is valued at a much higher amount than Target.

[14] Rev. Proc. 77-37, 1977-2 CB 568.

When evaluating reorganizations, it is often a good idea to start by diagramming the transaction, so that the relationship between the entities is clear. The next Example applies the qualifying rules for a Type C reorganization.

EXAMPLE 5.3.5
Type C Reorganization (Scenario 1)

Acquiring Corporation transferred voting stock worth $1,000,000 to Target in return for Target's assets with the following information:

	Total	Transferred to Acquiring	Retained by Target
Fair market value	$1,200,000	$1,100,000	$100,000
Adjusted basis	$ 300,000	$ 250,000	$ 50,000
Liabilities attached	$ 150,000	$ 100,000	$ 50,000

Target remains in existence after the transaction. The shareholders of Target receive $1,000,000 of Acquiring stock in return for $1,000,000 of Target stock. Does this transaction qualify as a Type C reorganization?

SOLUTION

We begin by diagramming the transaction.

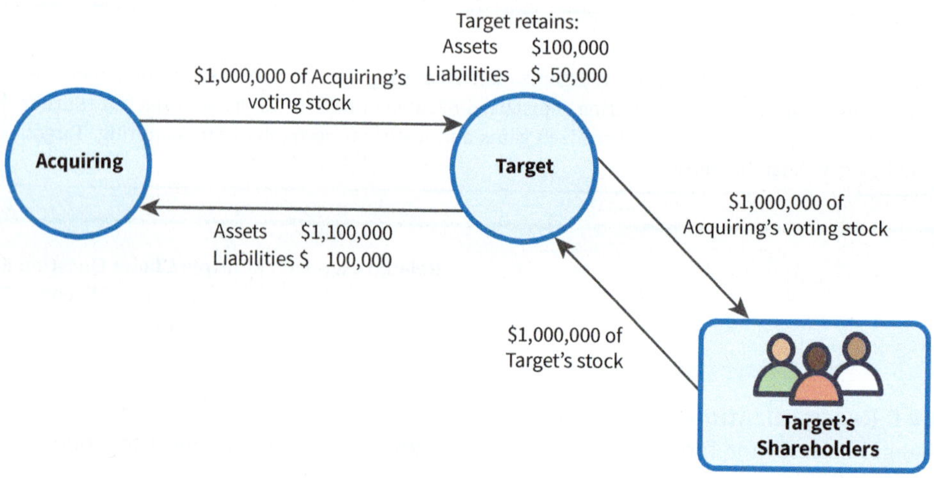

We next need to make sure the requirements for a Type C reorganization are met:

- Voting stock is used as consideration by Acquiring, so that requirement is met.
- There is no boot transferred by Acquiring, so the 20% boot limitation is met. The liability relief is not considered boot for Target because Acquiring did not transfer any assets to Target other than voting stock.
- Target must transfer at least 90% of net asset value and 70% of gross asset value to Acquiring.
  - Minimum net asset value needed in transfer from Target to Acquiring:

    $$(\$1,200,000 - \$150,000) \times 90\% = \$945,000.$$

    Target transferred $1,000,000 ($1,100,000 – $100,000) of net assets so Acquiring meets this test.
  - Minimum gross asset value needed in transfer from Target to Acquiring:

    $$\$1,200,000 \times 70\% = \$840,000.$$

    Target transferred $1,100,000 of gross assets so Acquiring meets this test.

Therefore, this is a qualified Type C reorganization. Target's shareholders do not recognize any gain because they did not receive boot. Acquiring and Target do not recognize gain.

EXAMPLE 5.3.6
Type C Reorganization (Scenario 2)

Assume the same facts as in Example 5.3.5, except that Acquiring also transfers boot to Target. Acquiring Corporation transferred voting stock worth $850,000 and bonds worth $150,000 (adjusted basis of $150,000) to Target in return for Target's assets with the following information:

	Total	Transferred to Acquiring	Retained by Target
Fair market value	$1,200,000	$1,100,000	$100,000
Adjusted basis	$ 300,000	$ 250,000	$ 50,000
Liabilities attached	$ 150,000	$ 100,000	$ 50,000

Target remains in existence after the transaction. The shareholders of Target receive $850,000 of Acquiring stock and $150,000 of bonds in return for $1,000,000 of Target stock. Does this transaction qualify as a Type C reorganization?

SOLUTION

Just as in Example 5.3.5, the voting stock requirement and the 90%/70% value tests are met. We must check the boot limitation of 20% for these facts. The $100,000 of debt relief for Target is considered boot for this example because Acquiring did transfer assets other than voting stock to Target. Therefore, the total amount of the boot received by Target is:

Bonds	$150,000
Debt relief	$100,000
Total	$250,000

The total consideration transferred by Acquiring is $1,100,000 ($850,000 + $150,000 + $100,000), so the maximum amount of boot allowed is $220,000 ($1,100,000 × 20%). The total boot is $250,000 which exceeds $220,000, so the 20% boot limit is not met and this does not qualify as a Type C reorganization. All realized gains and losses are recognized for Acquiring, Target, and Target's shareholders.

Related exercise: Application Problem 11

Divisive Reorganizations (Type D)

A **Type D reorganization** is a divisive reorganization meaning that a parent corporation divides into two corporations by transferring assets to a subsidiary in exchange for shares of the subsidiary. The parent then has three options:

- In a **spin-off**, the parent distributes the subsidiary shares to its shareholders.
- In a **split-off**, the parent uses the subsidiary to redeem shares of the parent (i.e., buy shares of the parent).
- In a **split-up**, the parent is liquidated into two new corporations and the parent no longer exists.

In all events, the parent corporation must receive and distribute control of the subsidiary in the exchange, defined as 80% of the voting and other classes of stock. An example of a Type D reorganization is Abbot Laboratories in 2013. Abbott spun off its branded pharmaceutical business to a new subsidiary named AbbVie, Inc. In its first year, AbbVie had over 21,000 employees, operated in 170 countries, and had more than $18 billion in sales. Abbott spun-off AbbVie so that investors could more directly invest in branded pharmaceuticals if that was their preference, while Abbot focused on generic pharmaceuticals, medical devices, and diagnostics.[15]

Related exercise: Multiple Choice Question 8

[15]"AbbVie Spins off from Abbott." *Genetic Engineering & Biotechnology News*, 2 Jan. 2013, www.genengnews.com/news/abbvie-spins-off-from-abbott/

EXAMPLE 5.3.7
Type D Reorganization

Titans Corporation creates a subsidiary, Bears Corporation, and contributes an office building to Bears in exchange for all of its shares. Titans then distributes the Bears shares to its shareholders. What type of qualified Type D reorganization is this?

SOLUTION

This transaction qualifies as a spin-off. The shareholders of Titans would defer any realized gains and losses on the distribution, as would Titans and Bears.

Other Reorganizations (Types E, F, G)

A **Type E reorganization** involves only one corporation that is adjusting its capital structure. For example, it may be adjusting the percentage of its capital that is in stock versus bonds. A **Type F reorganization** is a mere change in identity, form, or place of organization of one corporation. A **Type G reorganization** is used as a part of a reorganization necessitated by a bankruptcy filing[16].

Judicial Doctrines

In addition to meeting the specific reorganization rules described above, tax-free reorganizations must comply with the following judicial doctrines:

- Business Purpose
- Continuity of Interest
- Continuity of Business Enterprise
- Step Transaction

Business Purpose

The transaction must be motivated by a valid **business purpose.** In a 1935 decision, the U.S. Supreme Court held that a qualified reorganization did not occur, but that a series of transactions, though consistent with the terms of the reorganization statute, was "an elaborate and devious form of conveyance masquerading as a corporate reorganization" with no business purpose. The taxpayer devised a scheme where her corporation transferred assets to a newly formed corporation, and then spun off the stock of the newly formed corporation. The taxpayer then liquidated the newly formed corporation and sold the assets. The transaction was ruled to not be a qualified reorganization because it had no business purpose.[17]

Continuity of Interest

The **continuity of interest** doctrine requires that a substantial amount of the consideration that Acquiring gives to Target must be stock in Acquiring. This ensures that the shareholders of Target have a significant ownership interest in Parent after the transaction, hence ensuring the continuity of their investment. If at least 50% of the consideration is Acquiring stock, then this test is met for a Type A reorganization. For a Type C reorganization, the percentage must be at least 80%. The IRS has ruled that in certain circumstances the percentage can be as low as 40% to satisfy the continuity of interest requirement.[18]

[16]IRC §368(a)(1)(E), (F), and (G).
[17]*Gregory, Evelyn v. Helvering*, (1935, S Ct) 14 AFTR 1191, 293 U.S. 465, 79 L Ed 596, 35-1 USTC ¶9043.
[18]IRS Letter Ruling 200644008; IRS Letter Ruling 200611004; IRS Letter Ruling 200610007.

Continuity of Business Enterprise

The **continuity of business enterprise** doctrine requires that the acquiring corporation must either continue the historic business of the target corporation, or use a significant portion of target's assets in the continuing business of acquiring corporation.[19] Whether the assets used are significant is generally determined by the relative importance of the assets to the operation of the business.

Step Transaction

The **step transaction** doctrine permits multiple steps to be collapsed into a single step when the steps are so interdependent on one another that one would not have occurred without the other(s). Collapsing these steps may lead to a tax result other than that desired by the taxpayer.[20]

EXAMPLE 5.3.8
Judicial Doctrines

Dollar Warehouse, Inc. is interested in acquiring some of the retail stores owned by Dollar Bargains, Inc. Dollar Warehouse only wants to pursue the transaction if it can be done in a tax-deferred manner with a qualified stock-for-asset reorganization. Dollars Bargains owns 120 retail stores, but Dollar Warehouse only wants to keep 30 of the stores that are in the best markets. Dollar Warehouse transfers 35% of its voting stock to Dollar Bargains's shareholders in return for all their retail stores. Before this transaction was finalized, Dollar Warehouse negotiated with Family Stores that it would buy the 90 Dollar Bargains's locations that Dollar Warehouse does not want to retain from Dollar Warehouse for cash. Does this transaction qualify as a tax-deferred reorganization?

SOLUTION

Because this is a stock-for-asset reorganization, to be tax-deferred, it would need to qualify as a Type A or a Type C reorganization. Technically, Dollar Warehouse acquired all of Dollar Bargains's stores in one step. However, in a separate step, Dollar Warehouse had a contractual obligation to sell 75% of the Dollar Bargains's locations to Family Stores. After both steps are completed, Dollar Warehouse owns only 25% of Dollar Bargains's locations. Because the second step would happen only if the first step occurred, it is likely that the step transaction doctrine should be applied and collapse these two steps into one. After this collapse, the continuity of business enterprise test would not be met, because Dollar Warehouse retained only 25% of the stores that Dollar Bargains owned before the reorganization. Therefore, this would not be a tax-deferred reorganization.

Related exercises: Discussion Question 8
Multiple Choice Question 7

Tax Consequences of Qualified Reorganizations

Generally, a qualified reorganization does not require income recognition at the corporate level or the shareholder level. However, the corporations and the shareholders of Target corporation may have to recognize income *but not losses* in certain situations, even when the reorganization is qualified. In this section, we review the circumstances that can cause these gains to be recognized. We also review the rules for computing the basis of assets.

Acquiring Corporation

In a qualified reorganization, the Acquiring corporation does not recognize gain or loss on the transfer of its stock for the Target corporation's assets. An exception to this rule occurs if the Acquiring corporation distributes appreciated property to Target in addition to Acquiring's

[19] Treas. Reg. 1.368-1(b).

[20] *Helvering v. Alabama Asphaltic Limestone Co*, (1942, S Ct) 28 AFTR 567, 315 U.S. 179, 86 L Ed 775, 42-1 USTC ¶9245; Treas. Reg. 1.368-1(a).

stock. The appreciated property will trigger gain recognition to the Acquiring corporation just as if the Acquiring firm sold the assets.

The basis that the Acquiring corporation takes in the assets received is:

Basis in property to Target + Gain recognized by Target

In the next Example, we review the computation of gain for Acquiring and the computation of its basis in the assets received by Target.

EXAMPLE 5.3.9
Gain to Acquiring Corporation

Continuing with facts similar to Example 5.3.2, as part of a statutory merger, Acquiring Corporation transfers $170,000 of nonvoting stock and land with a FMV of $40,000 (adjusted basis is $23,000) to Target Corporation in return for assets of Target that have a fair market value of $280,000, adjusted basis of $180,000, and liabilities attached of $70,000. Acquiring assumes $70,000 of Target's liabilities. Target distributes the nonvoting stock and cash to its shareholders in return for their stock. This qualifies as a Type A reorganization.

a. Does Acquiring recognize any gain as a result of this transaction, and what is Acquiring's basis in the asset received from Target?

b. How would the answer change if Acquiring's adjusted basis in the land was $47,000?

SOLUTION

a. Yes, Acquiring does recognize gain, even though this is a qualified Type A reorganization. Because Acquiring transferred appreciated property to Target, the appreciation in the land of $17,000 ($40,000 FMV – $23,000 adjusted basis) must be recognized by Acquiring.

Acquiring's basis in the assets received from Target is $180,000, the same basis that Target had in the assets.

b. If Acquiring's basis in the land was $47,000, then if Acquiring sold the land it would recognize a loss of $7,000 ($40,000 FMV – $47,000 adjusted basis). However, such losses cannot be recognized as part of a qualified reorganization.

Acquiring's basis in the asset received from Target is $180,000, the same basis that Target had in the assets.

Related exercise: Application Problem 12

Target Corporation

In a qualified reorganization, the acquired corporation does not generally recognize gain or loss. However, if Target distributes its own appreciated property to shareholders in connection with the reorganization, this will trigger gain recognition by Target. Target cannot recognize a loss if it distributes property to its shareholders for which it has an unrealized loss.

In the following Example, we review the computation of gain for Target.

EXAMPLE 5.3.10
Gain to Target Corporation

Continuing with facts similar to Example 5.3.5, Acquiring Corporation transferred voting stock worth $1,000,000 to Target in return for Target's assets with the following information:

	Total	Transferred to Acquiring	Retained by Target
Fair market value	$1,200,000	$1,100,000	$100,000
Adjusted basis	$ 300,000	$ 250,000	$ 50,000
Liabilities attached	$ 150,000	$ 100,000	$ 50,000

Target remains in existence after the transaction. The shareholders of Target receive $1,000,000 of Acquiring stock in return for $1,000,000 of Target stock. One of the assets retained by Target is land with a FMV of $38,000 and adjusted basis of $25,000, and Target distributes this land to its shareholders.

a. Does Target recognize any gain as a result of this transaction?

b. How would the answer change if Target's basis in the land is $45,000?

SOLUTION

a. Yes, Target does recognize gain, even though this is a qualified Type A reorganization. Because Target transferred appreciated land to its Target shareholders, the appreciation in the land of $13,000 ($38,000 FMV – $25,000 adjusted basis) must be recognized.

b. If Target's basis in the land was $45,000, then if Acquiring had sold the land instead of distributing it, Target would recognize a loss of $7,000 ($38,000 FMV – $45,000 adjusted basis). However, such losses cannot be recognized as part of a qualified reorganization.

Related exercise: Application Problem 13

Tax Planning Tip

Whenever a corporation distributes appreciated property (property with a value in excess of adjusted basis), the corporation will recognize the gain. This applies regardless of whether the distribution is related to a reorganization, dividend, redemption, or liquidation.

Target's Shareholders

No gain or loss is recognized by the shareholders of Target for a qualified reorganization if they receive only stock in Acquiring for their stock in Target. If the shareholders receive other property in addition to stock, this property is treated as boot and gain is recognized equal to the *lower* of the:

1. Realized gain, *or*
2. FMV of the boot received.

Any gain recognized by Target's shareholders will be dividend income to the extent of the shareholder's proportionate share of Target's earnings & profits (E&P). Any remaining gain is capital gain.

The basis to the shareholder in the stock received is:

- Basis in stock surrendered
- Plus: Gain recognized by shareholder
- *Less*: FMV of boot received by shareholder

The next two Examples demonstrate the effect of boot on the tax consequences for a Target's shareholders.

EXAMPLE 5.3.11
Gain to Target's Shareholders

Similar to the facts of Example 5.3.1, as part of a statutory merger, Acquiring Corporation transfers $170,000 of nonvoting stock and $30,000 cash to Target Corporation in return for assets of Target that have a fair market value of $270,000, adjusted basis of $180,000, and liabilities attached of $70,000. Acquiring assumes Target's liabilities. Target distributes the nonvoting stock and cash to its sole shareholder, Maya. Maya's basis in her stock is $145,000. Target Corporation has E&P of $16,000. Assuming that this transaction qualifies as a Type A reorganization, what are the tax consequences to Maya?

SOLUTION

Maya's realized gain or loss is computed as follows:

Amount realized	$200,000	($170,000 stock + $30,000 cash)
Less: Adjusted basis	(145,000)	
Realized gain or loss	$ 55,000	

Maya's recognized gain is $30,000, the *lower* of the:

1. Realized gain ($55,000) *or*
2. FMV of the boot received ($30,000).

The character of the $30,000 is dividend income to extent of the E&P of $16,000. The remaining $14,000 of income is taxed as capital gain.

Maya's basis in her new Acquiring stock is computed as follows:

Basis in Target stock	$145,000
Plus: Gain recognized by shareholder	30,000
Less: FMV of boot received by shareholder	(30,000)
Basis in Acquiring stock	$145,000

EXAMPLE 5.3.12 Loss to Target's Shareholders

Similar to the facts of Example 5.3.11, as part of a statutory merger, Acquiring Corporation transfers $170,000 of nonvoting stock and $30,000 cash to Target Corporation in return for assets of Target that have a fair market value of $270,000, adjusted basis of $180,000, and liabilities attached of $70,000. Acquiring assumes Target's liabilities. Target distributes the nonvoting stock and cash to its sole shareholder, Maya. Maya's basis in her stock is $245,000. Target Corporation has E&P of $16,000. Assuming that this transaction qualifies as a Type A reorganization, what are the tax consequences to Maya?

SOLUTION

Maya's realized gain or loss is computed as follows:

Amount realized	$200,000	($170,000 stock + $30,000 cash)
Less: Adjusted basis	(245,000)	
Realized gain or loss	($ 45,000)	

Maya's realized loss is not recognized because this is a qualified Type A reorganization. Boot does not cause realized losses to be recognized.

Maya's basis in her new Acquiring stock is computed as follows:

Basis in Target stock	$245,000
Plus: Gain recognized by shareholder	0
Less: FMV of boot received by shareholder	(30,000)
Basis in Acquiring stock	$215,000

Related exercises: Application Problems 14, 15

In the next section, we review what happens to target's tax attributes as the result of a qualified reorganization.

PRACTICE PROBLEM 5.3.1
Type A Reorganization

As part of a statutory merger, Kiwi Corporation transfers $46,000 of voting stock and land with a fair market value of $51,000 to Tree Corporation in return for assets of Tree that have a fair market value of $127,000, adjusted basis of $45,000, with liabilities attached of $30,000. Kiwi assumes Tree's liabilities. Tree distributes the voting stock and land to its shareholders in return for their stock. Tree Corporation dissolves. Does this qualify as a Type A reorganization? Explain.

SOLUTION

Kiwi Corporation can transfer voting or nonvoting stock to Tree in a Type A reorganization. Boot can also be transferred, but the value of the boot cannot exceed 50% of the consideration provided to the target corporation by the acquiring corporation. Boot for a qualified reorganization is any consideration provided to a target corporation other than qualifying stock. Because the value of the land which is boot ($51,000) is more than 50% of the value of the consideration ($97,000), this transaction does not qualify as a Type A reorganization.

PRACTICE PROBLEM 5.3.2
Type B Reorganization

Abiud Corporation owns 200 shares of Tamar Corporation's voting stock. Abiud has 5,000 shares of voting stock and 3,000 shares of nonvoting stock outstanding while Tamar has 1,000 shares of voting stock outstanding. Abiud transfers 1,000 shares of its nonvoting stock for 600 additional shares of Tamar's voting stock. Does this transaction qualify as a Type B reorganization? Explain.

SOLUTION

This transaction does not qualify as a Type B reorganization because both requirements have not been met. After the transaction, Abiud owns 800 shares of Tamar's 1,000 outstanding shares, so it owns at least 80% of Tangerine. However, Abiud transferred nonvoting stock instead of voting stock to Tamar in the transaction. Therefore, the transaction does not qualify as a Type B reorganization.

PRACTICE PROBLEM 5.3.3
Gain to Target's Shareholder

Abraham exchanges stock that he owns in Dry Corporation with a value of $175,000 for stock in Wet Corporation. The stock he received from Wet Corporation had a value of $150,000 when received. In addition, he received land with a fair market value of $25,000 and an adjusted basis of $11,000 from Wet Corporation. This exchange is pursuant to a qualified Type A reorganization. Abraham had purchased his stock from Dry Corporation five years ago for $66,000. How much gain or loss does Abraham recognize on this transaction?

SOLUTION

Abraham has a realized gain of $109,000 calculated as follows:

Amount realized	175,000 ($150,000 stock + $25,000 FMV land)
Adjusted basis	(66,000)
Realized gain	$109,000

Recognized gain = *Lesser* of	1. Realized gain	$109,000 *or*
	2. Boot received	$ 25,000

Abraham's recognized gain is $25,000.

INTERACTIVE SELF-SCORING QUIZZES

5.4 Preservation of Tax Attributes

LEARNING OBJECTIVE 4

Determine the required limitations that apply to an acquiring corporation's ability to use the earnings and profits and net operating losses of the target corporation after a qualified reorganization.

VIDEO CONTENT

Another important aspect of tax-free reorganizations is what happens to the *tax attributes* of the target corporation. **Tax attributes** are the tax characteristics of the corporation. The most common attributes are as follows:

- adjusted basis of assets
- earnings and profits of the corporation
- carryforwards, including net operating losses, capital losses, and excess charitable contributions
- accounting methods, including depreciation methods, *and*
- tax credit carryforward.

Some examples of how the tax attributes are handled in Type A–G reorganizations are:

- The tax attributes of the Target firm carryover to Acquiring in Type A and Type C reorganizations if the Target firm dissolves.
- The Target firm does not dissolve in Type B, Type E, and Type F reorganizations, so its tax attributes do not carryover to Acquiring.
- In a Type D spin-off or split-off, the original corporation retains its tax attributes except for a pro rata amount of E&P that carryovers to the new corporation.
- In a Type D split-up, the tax attributes of the original corporation disappear.[21]

The carryover rules for tax attributes are summarized in **Illustration 5.9**.

ILLUSTRATION 5.9 Carryover of Tax Attributes for Reorganizations

Tax Attribution Rules for Reorganizations

Reorganization type	Target survive?	Which corporation can use target's tax attributes?
A	No	Acquiring
B	Yes	Target
C—Target dissolves	No	Acquiring
C—Target continues	Yes	Target
D—Spin-off	N/A	Original
D—Split-off	N/A	Original
D—Split-up	N/A	None
E	Yes	Target
F	Yes	Target
G	N/A	New

[21]IRC §381.

If the Acquiring corporation purchases the stock of Target corporation in a taxable acquisition and operates the Target as a subsidiary, Target's tax attributes created before the acquisition survive, but they are trapped in the Target firm. Acquiring can use Target's tax attributes created after the acquisition if they elect to file a consolidated tax return.

EXAMPLE 5.4.1 Determining Tax Characteristics of a Target Corporation after Reorganization

On September 30 of the current year, Acquiring Corporation and Target Corporation finalize a qualified Type A reorganization and Target dissolves. Acquiring has a calendar year-end and uses the accrual method of accounting. Before the transaction, Target has the following tax characteristics:

- Year-end of September 30
- Cash method of accounting
- MACRS depreciation including bonus depreciation
- Assets with a FMV of $3,500,000 and an adjusted basis of $1,800,000
- Foreign tax credit carryforward of $34,000
- Net operating loss carryforward of $1,530,000
- Accumulated earnings and profits of ($1,280,000)
- Current earnings and profits of ($60,000)

What happens to these tax characteristics of Target after the reorganization?

SOLUTION

The September 30 year-end for Target and its cash method of accounting do not transfer to Acquiring. Acquiring will continue to file on a calendar-year basis, and continue to use the accrual method of accounting. All the remaining tax characteristics transfer to Acquiring and are available for Acquiring to use.

Related exercises: Discussion Question 9
Multiple Choice Question 9

The use of certain tax attributes by a surviving corporation or a parent is limited through the application of provisions designed to limit tax incentives for corporate acquisitions. In the next section, we review the tax limitations for earnings and profits and for net operating losses.

Earnings & Profits Limitation

While the E&P of Target carries over to Acquiring, if Target has a deficit in E&P, that deficit can be used to offset only future earnings of the combined companies. In other words, the E&P of Acquiring earned *before* the acquisition cannot be reduced by Target's deficit E&P.

EXAMPLE 5.4.2 Limitation on Earnings & Profits

Acquiring Corporation purchased all the assets of Target Corporation as part of a Type A reorganization on September 1 of the current year. Target then liquidated. Acquiring and Target have the following information:

	Acquiring	Target
Accumulated E&P	$1,500,000	($345,000)
Current E&P as of September 1	$ 145,000	($ 65,000)
Current E&P for September 1 through December 31	$ 22,000	

How much of Target's E&P can be used this year to offset Acquiring's E&P?

SOLUTION

Target's total deficit in E&P as of September 1 is ($410,000) ($345,000 + $65,000). Acquiring can use this deficit in E&P to offset E&P earned only after September 1. Therefore, Acquiring can use $22,000 of Target's deficit E&P to offset its E&P earned from September 1 through December 31. The remaining E&P deficit of ($388,000) ($410,000 – $22,000) can be used to offset E&P earned after this year, but it can never be used to offset the $1,645,000 ($1,500,000 + $145,000) of E&P that was earned before September 1 of the current year.

Why **Why does Congress limit the use of Target's deficit earnings and profits?** Acquiring Corporation could benefit from Target's deficit in E&P because this would reduce the amount of dividend income that its shareholders would have for future distributions. If the dividends would be taxed at ordinary income rates, then Acquiring's shareholders would benefit from reducing its E&P. However, if the dividends would be qualified dividends that are taxed at LTCG rates, then this incentive is reduced for Acquiring. Additionally, if the shareholder was a corporation, it would prefer distributions to be taxed as dividends so it could use the dividends received deduction.

Related exercises: Brief Exercise 8
Application Problem 16

NOL Limitations

Congress has also placed limitations on Acquiring's ability to use Target's NOLs to offset income of Acquiring. There are two limitations, one of which always applies in the year of the reorganization, and the other of which can apply in the year of acquisition and future years if certain conditions are met. If both limitations apply in the year of the reorganization, then the one that allows the lowest amount of Target's NOL to be used applies.

NOL Limitation for Year of Acquisition

The use of Target's NOL is limited as follows for Acquiring's first tax return after the reorganization:

$$\text{NOL limitation} = \text{Income of Acquiring} \times \frac{(\text{\# of days in year after transfer})}{365 \text{ days}}$$

We explore this limitation in the following Example.

EXAMPLE 5.4.3
Determining NOL Limitation for Year of Acquisition

Acquiring Corporation acquired Target Corporation in a Type A statutory merger on October 19, Year 9. The former Target shareholders received 40% of Acquiring's stock with a value of $700,000. Acquiring reports on the cash basis. Assume the following additional information:

- Target has a Year 8 NOL carryforward of $150,000.
- Acquiring has taxable income, before the NOL deduction, of $91,500.

How much of Target's NOL can Acquiring use in Year 9 to reduce Acquiring's income?

SOLUTION

The number of days in Acquiring's taxable year after the acquisition is determined as follows:

	Days
October 20–31	12
November	30
December	31
Total	73

The amount of Target's \$150,000 NOL carryforward that Acquiring can deduct for Year 9 is limited to \$18,300, determined as follows:

$$\text{Income of Acquiring (\$91,500)} \times \frac{\text{(\# of days in year after transfer) (73)}}{\text{365 days}}$$

Recall that the NOL carryforward that Acquiring can use is also limited to 80% of Acquiring's income for the year.

NOL Limitation for Greater than 50% Change in Ownership

The use of the NOLs of Target will also be limited if there is a significant change in the ownership of Target, generally determined as a greater than 50% change in ownership over a three-year period. If this occurs, the amount of Target's NOL that Acquiring can use for each year in the future is limited as follows:[22]

$$\text{FMV of Target's stock before the change} \times \text{Long-Term tax-exempt rate for the month of purchase}$$

This limitation is known as the Section 382 limitation because these rules are provided in Section 382 of the Internal Revenue Code. If the Section 382 limitation applies, it does so for the year of acquisition as well as all future years.

The long-term tax-exempt rate used in the computation is the highest of the adjusted Federal long-term rates in effect for any month in the three-calendar-month period ending with the month in which the stock ownership change becomes greater than 50% over the preceding three years. The IRS publishes the current long-term exempt rate each month and that is the amount used in the computation.[23]

Why **Why does Congress limit Acquiring Corporation's use of Target's net operating losses?** Congress put these limits in place in the 1980s to stop NOL shopping, which was the purchase of a corporation with large NOLs for the *sole* purpose of using the NOLs to reduce Acquiring's tax liability. In those times, the top corporate tax rate was 40%. Assume that Acquiring had annual taxable income of \$100,000,000 and Target had total NOLs of \$20,000,000. The NOLs could reduce Acquiring taxes by \$8,000,000 (\$20,000,000 × 40%), so Acquiring would be willing to pay up to approximately \$8,000,000 to Target's shareholders to purchase Target. Congress felt it was dysfunctional to reward Target's shareholder in this manner when their business had no value other than the NOLs.

This helps you understand the logic of the limitation using the long-term tax-exempt rate. The amount of NOL that can be used each year by Acquiring is limited to what Acquiring would have earned if, instead of purchasing Target, it had invested the same amount in long-term tax-exempt bonds.

[22]IRC §382.
[23]www.irs.gov/applicable-federal-rates.

Tax Planning Tip

Determining whether there has been a greater than 50% change in the ownership of Target can be confusing if not considered carefully. For example, if Target's shareholders receive 30% of the stock in Acquiring for 100% of their stock in Target, there would be a greater than 50% change in the ownership of Target. Assume that Target had 100 shares outstanding and Acquiring has 500 shares of stock outstanding. Acquiring would transfer 150 (500 × 30%) shares of its stock for Target's assets, and Target would retire its 100 shares of stock. The former Target shareholders would now own 30% of Acquiring. Consider who owns Target's assets before and after the transaction.

- **Before the transaction, Target's shareholders owned 100% of Target's assets.**
- **After the transaction, Target's shareholders own 30% of Target's assets (that are now inside Acquiring) while the original Acquiring shareholders own the other 70%.**

Thus, there has been a greater than 50% change in the ownership of Target.

On the other hand, consider if Target's shareholders received 80% of the stock of Acquiring. After the transaction, Target's shareholders would own 80% of Target's assets and the original shareholders of Acquiring would own only 20% of Target's assets. So, this would not be a greater than 50% change in the ownership of Target.

EXAMPLE 5.4.4
NOL Limited by Ownership Change

Continuing with the facts of Example 5.4.3, would the amount of Target's NOL that can be used by Acquiring be further limited by the NOL ownership rule? Assume that the long-term tax-exempt rate for the month of the acquisition is 4%.

SOLUTION

The Section 382 limitation does apply. Target's shareholders received 40% of Acquiring's stock so the change in ownership of Target is 60%. The Section 382 limitation is computed as follows:

FMV of Target's stock before the change × Long-Term tax-exempt rate for the month of purchase

$700,00 × 4% = $28,000

Acquiring can use $18,300 of Target's NOL in Year 9 because this limitation is less than the Section 382 limitation of $28,000. Beginning in Year 10 and all future years, the Section 382 restriction will limit the use of Target's NOLs by Acquiring to $28,000.

To summarize, Target's $150,000 NOL will be used as follows (assuming it is not limited in any year by 80% of Acquiring's income for the year).

Year 9	$18,300
Year 10	$28,000
Year 11	$28,000
Year 12	$28,000
Year 13	$28,000
Year 14	$19,700

Related exercises: Application Problem 17
Tax Planning Problem 2

PRACTICE PROBLEM 5.4.1

Use of Charitable Contribution Carryforward

On October 31 of the current year, Aluminum Corporation and Tin Corporation finalize a qualified Type A reorganization and Tin dissolves. Aluminum has a calendar year-end and uses the accrual method of accounting. Before the transaction, Tin has the following tax characteristic:

Charitable contribution carryforward	$28,000

If Aluminum has current year taxable income of $270,000 before considering charitable contributions, what happens to this tax characteristic of Tin after the reorganization?

SOLUTION

The tax characteristic transferred to Aluminum is available for Aluminum to use. In the current year, Aluminum can use $27,000 ($270,000 × 10%) of the $28,000 charitable contribution carryforward. The remaining $1,000 is carried forward.

INTERACTIVE SELF-SCORING QUIZZES

Featured Tax Professional: Matthew Harris

Matt has worked in accounting for seven years and is a CPA and Senior Manager, Consulting Solutions, Tax Reporting & Strategy for PricewaterhouseCoopers (PwC) U.S. He specializes in operational tax strategy and consulting, and assists clients with transformation efforts specifically aimed to improve people, process, data, and technology aspects of corporate tax functions.

From Classroom to Career Non-U.S. income tax reporting can be a challenge for many tax departments supporting U.S.-based multinational corporations. The process required to design, build, train, and execute such tax reporting takes careful planning and can involve ever-changing technology.

One challenging aspect involves the collection, centralization, and validation of data. The first step for some teams is to define and assess all upstream data sources (for example, trial balances), including the supplier of such data and at what interval the data will be received. The next decision point is how to centralize and standardize the data for preparation purposes. Some companies are using Extract, Transform, Load (ETL) tools to pre-populate, refresh, and validate various data sources within standard collection packages. After the packages have been prepared, visualization tools can assist tax professionals by providing targeted data analytics, which help reviewers focus on areas of higher value and/or higher risk to the overall consolidated tax reporting results.

Professional Skills Building and leveraging a network of trusted colleagues is a key skill to succeed as a tax professional. Tax accounting is fraught with complexity based on the ever-changing nature of both its technical rules as well as the technology which enables timely and accurate reporting. Tax accounting professionals should individually pursue both skills (technical as well as technological) but more importantly, form and develop a team which embodies this holistic skillset.

Future Tax Landscape The future ways of working will impact professionals entering Tax. In the past, professionals were developed through in-person projects and training, which involved informal ways to cultivate relationships. The shift to a hybrid or remote model of working requires tax professionals (and managers) to be extremely proactive in pursuing virtual training sessions and hosting virtual meetings with direct reports to allow for virtual collaboration (such as screen sharing and providing real-time feedback). These virtual trainings/meetings should focus both on technical aspects of tax (application of rules, tax law changes, etc.) as well as technology ranging from research tools, to reporting software, to data automation tools such as Extract, Transform, Load (ETL), Robotic Process Automation (RPA), and visualization.

Review and Practice

Chapter Summary

Common ownership of more than one business can create an opportunity for the related corporations to file as a consolidated group. The common ownership could also result in the related corporations being part of a controlled group, which can lead to restrictions on the group's ability to use certain beneficial tax attributes. If growth of the business results in the acquisition of another corporation, the owners usually prefer for the acquisition to be structured in such a way that realized gains from the transaction are deferred. For deferral to occur, the acquisition needs to be structured as a qualified reorganization.

1 Apply appropriate restrictions to tax benefits for controlled groups.

There are three limitations placed on **controlled groups** by the tax law: accumulated earnings credit, Section 179, and the use of certain corporate tax rates.

- A **parent-subsidiary controlled group** exists if *both* of these conditions are met:
  - **80% Test (Controlled Group)** One of more of the other corporations in the group possess at least 80% of the voting power of all classes of stock entitled to vote, *or* at least 80% of the total value of all classes of stock of each of the corporations (except the common parent), *and*
  - **Common Parent Test (Controlled Group)** The common parent owns stock possessing at least 80% of the total combined voting power of all classes of stock entitled to vote, *or* at least 80% of the total value of shares of all classes of stock of at least one of the other corporations in the group.

  These tests must be met on the last day of the tax year.
- The focus for **brother-sister controlled groups** is on common ownership by individuals for a group of corporations. A B-S controlled group exists if all the following conditions are met:
  - **Shareholder Test** Two or more corporations are owned by five or fewer persons (individuals, estates, or trusts)
  - **50% Test** The corporations have a common ownership of more than 50% of the total combined voting powers of all classes of stock entitled to vote, *or* more than 50% of the total value of shares of all classes of stock of each corporation, *and*
  - **80% Test (Brother-Sister Controlled Group)** The corporations possess stock representing at least 80% of the total combined voting power of all classes of stock entitled to vote, *or* at least 80% of the total value of shares of all classes of each corporation. An individual's ownership is counted for the 80% test only if the individual contributes to the common ownership used for the 50% test.

The 80% test does not apply for determining brother-sister corporations for the limitation on the accumulated earnings credit. It *does* apply for limiting the Section 179 deduction.

2 Apply rules for filing consolidated tax returns.

- Affiliated groups can elect to file a consolidated return. An **affiliated group** exists if *both* of the conditions below are met:
  - **80% Test** One or more of the other corporations in the group possess stock with at least 80% of the voting power of all classes of stock entitled to vote, *and* at least 80% of the total value of shares of all classes of stock of each of the corporations (except the common parent), *and*
  - **Common Parent Test (Affiliated Group)** The common parent owns stock possessing at least 80% of the total combined voting power of all classes of stock entitled to vote, *and* at least 80% of the total value of shares of all classes of stock of at least one of the other corporations in the group.
- Advantages of consolidated returns:
  - Netting capital gains and losses across group members.
  - Netting income and losses.
  - Deferral of gains from the sale of assets to other group members.
  - Avoiding limitations on deductions based on taxable income.
- Disadvantages of consolidated returns:
  - Election is binding for future tax years.
  - Creation of short-tax years.
  - Deferral of losses from sale of assets to other group members.
  - Complexity of tax return.
- The parent's stock basis is adjusted on the last day of each tax year as follows:
  - **Plus:** The parent's allocable share of the consolidated income
  - **Plus:** The parent's allocable share of the capital loss of the subsidiary if the subsidiary could not use it in a carryback year
  - ***Less:*** The parent's allocable share of the consolidated loss
  - ***Less:*** The parent's allocable share of any capital loss that was a carryforward to the current year and has not previously reduced the stock basis
  - ***Less:*** Dividends paid to the parent from the subsidiary's earnings & profits

3 Determine the tax consequences of a reorganization for the acquiring corporation, acquired corporation, and the acquired corporation's shareholders.

- Congress has provided seven different types of qualified **reorganizations**, all of which allow most realized gains and losses to be deferred. They are classified as follows:
  - **Acquisitive Reorganizations**: Types A, B, and C
  - **Divisive Reorganization**: Type D
  - **Other Reorganizations:** Types E, F, and G
- **Type A Reorganization** This is a stock-for-asset reorganization, meaning that Acquiring exchanges its stock for Target's assets. A Type A reorganization must meet the following requirements:
  - The transaction must qualify as a statutory merger. A **statutory merger** is a **merger** or **consolidation** that complies with the laws of the applicable state.
  - Acquiring corporation can transfer voting or nonvoting stock to Target.
  - Boot can be transferred also, but the value of the boot cannot exceed 50% of the consideration provided to Target by Acquiring. **Boot** for a qualified reorganization is any consideration provided to Target other than qualifying stock. In some situations, the IRS and courts have allowed as much as 60% of the acquisition price to be boot, meaning that the value of the stock transferred could be as low as 40%.
  - Acquiring must assume all the liabilities of Target.
  - Target must dissolve.
- **Type B Reorganization** A Type B reorganization is a stock-for-stock reorganization, meaning that Acquiring exchanges its stock for Target stock. The following requirements must be met for a Type B reorganization:
  - Acquiring can transfer only its voting stock to Target. It cannot transfer nonvoting stock or boot.
  - Acquiring must own at least 80% of the stock of Target (voting power and value) after the transaction.
- **Type C Reorganization** This is a stock-for-asset reorganization, meaning that Acquiring exchanges its stock for Target's assets. A Type C reorganization must meet the following requirements:
  - Acquiring can use only voting stock in the transfer. Nonvoting stock is not permitted.
  - The voting stock that Acquiring transfers to Target must be at least 80% of the consideration provided. If Acquiring transfers boot to Target, the boot cannot exceed 20% of the total consideration provided by Acquiring.
  - If liabilities secured by Target's assets are assumed by Acquiring, this liability relief is not considered as boot (and therefore not subject to the 20% test) unless other boot is also given. If Acquiring provides other boot to Target, then the total amount of boot and liability relief cannot exceed 20% of the consideration.
  - Acquiring must own *substantially all* the assets of Target after the transaction. **Substantially all** the assets is defined by the IRS as 90% of net asset value and 70% of gross asset value.
  - Acquiring does not have to assume all the liabilities of Target.
  - Target does not have to dissolve, although it can.
- In addition to meeting the specific reorganization rules described above, tax-free reorganizations must comply with the following judicial doctrines:
  - **Business Purpose**
  - **Continuity of Interest**
  - **Continuity of Business Enterprise**
  - **Step Transaction**
- In a qualified reorganization, the acquiring corporation does not recognize gain or loss on the transfer of its stock for the acquired corporation's assets. An exception to this rule occurs if the acquiring corporation distributes appreciated property to Target, in addition to Acquiring's stock. The appreciated property will trigger gain recognition to the Acquiring corporation just as if the Acquiring firm sold the assets.

  The basis that the Acquiring corporation takes in the assets received is:

  Basis in property to Target + Gain recognized by Target

- In a qualified reorganization, the Target corporation does not generally recognize gain or loss. However, if Target distributes its own appreciated property to shareholders in connection with the reorganization, this will trigger gain recognition by Target. Target cannot recognize a loss if it distributes property to its shareholders for which it has an unrealized loss.
  - No gain or loss is recognized by the shareholders of Target for a qualified reorganization if they receive only stock in Acquiring for their stock in Target. If the shareholders receive other property in addition to stock, this property is treated as boot and gain is recognized equal to the *lower* of the:

    1. Realized gain, *or*
    2. FMV of the boot received.

    The basis to the shareholder in the stock received is:

    Basis in stock surrendered
    Plus: Gain recognized by shareholder
    Less: FMV of boot received by shareholder

4 Determine the required limitations that apply to an acquiring corporation's ability to use the earnings and profits and net operating losses of the target corporation after a qualified reorganization.

- **Tax attributes** are the tax characteristics of the corporation. The most common attributes are as follows:
  - adjusted basis of assets
  - earnings and profits of the corporation
  - carryforwards, including net operating losses, capital losses, and excess charitable contributions

- accounting methods, including depreciation methods, *and*
- tax credit carryforward.

- While the E&P of Target carries over to Acquiring, if Target has a deficit in E&P, that deficit can be used to offset only future earnings of the combined companies. In other words, the E&P of Acquiring earned *before* the acquisition cannot be reduced by Target's deficit E&P.
- The use of Target's NOL is limited as follows for Acquiring's first tax return after the reorganization:

NOL Limitation =

$$\text{Income of Acquiring} \times \frac{(\text{\# of days in year after transfer})}{365 \text{ days}}$$

- The use of the NOLs of Target will also be subject to the Section 382 limitation if there is a significant change in the ownership of Target, generally determined as a greater than 50% change in ownership over a three-year period. If this occurs, the amount of Target's NOL that Acquiring can use for each year in the future is limited as follows:

$$\text{FMV of Target's stock before the change} \times \text{Long-term tax-exempt rate for the month of purchase}$$

Communication Application

Communication

Continuity of Business Enterprise

(LO3) Rocky Corporation would like to acquire Bullwinkle Corporation in a tax-free reorganization. The Board of Directors has hired you for advice on how to structure the transaction to obtain a tax-free result. Bullwinkle Corporation has the following lines of business:

1. Production of cruelty-free soap, shampoo, cleaning supplies, etc. (FMV of assets $500,000)
2. Pet supplies and food (FMV of assets $330,000)
3. Animal rescue services (FMV of assets $250,000)

Once the assets are acquired, Rocky Corporation plans to continue to use the assets only in the production of its cruelty-free products business. The transaction will not qualify as a statutory merger under state law. Based on the information provided, write a letter to the client and a memo to the tax file with your conclusion.

Solution

Memo to Client

Board of Directors,

Thank you for giving me the opportunity to discuss a plan of reorganization that will result in a tax-free transaction. In order for this result to occur, the statutory requirements must be met as well as satisfying the relevant judicial doctrines. Because the transaction will not qualify as a statutory merger under state law, it cannot qualify as a Type A reorganization. In a Type C reorganization, the acquiring corporation obtains substantially all of the target corporation's assets in exchange for the acquiring corporation's voting stock and a limited amount of other property. *Substantially all* the assets is defined by the IRS as 90% of net asset value and 70% of gross asset value. The target corporation must distribute all assets received in the reorganization, as well as any of its own property retained. The target corporation then can liquidate but it does not have to.

The continuity of business enterprise judicial doctrine must be satisfied as well. The target corporation's business operations must continue in some capacity. This test requires the acquiring corporation to either continue the target corporation's historic business or use a significant portion of the target corporation's assets in its business. The term "significant" is based on facts and circumstances.

If Rocky acquires all of the assets of all three lines and continues the production of its cruelty-free products business line, this will meet the historic business use test and the significant use of the target corporation's assets test. The tax law does not indicate that at least 50% of the FMV of assets be used, but rather just a significant portion. Because 46% ($500,000/$1,080,000) of the assets acquired will be used and are important to the operation of the business, the significant use test is satisfied.

I recommend moving forward with the acquisition of Bullwinkle. Please let me know if you have any questions.

Sincerely,
Carnes & Youngberg, CPAs

Tax memo to the file

Facts: Rocky Corporation would like to acquire Bullwinkle Corporation in a tax-free reorganization. Bullwinkle Corporation has the following lines of business:

1. Production of cruelty-free soap, shampoo, cleaning supplies, etc. (FMV of assets $500,000)
2. Pet supplies and food (FMV of assets $330,000)
3. Animal rescue services (FMV of assets $250,000)

Rocky Corporation would like to continue only the production of cruelty-free products business.

Issue: Will this transaction qualify for tax-free corporate reorganization treatment?

Conclusion: Under IRC §368(a)(1)(c), a tax-free reorganization can be accomplished.

Analysis: Because the transaction will not qualify as a statutory merger under state law, it cannot qualify as a Type A reorganization. In a Type C reorganization, the acquiring corporation obtains substantially all of the target corporation's assets in exchange for acquiring corporation voting stock and a limited amount of other property. *Substantially all* the assets is defined by the IRS as 90% of net asset value and 70% of gross asset value. The target corporation must distribute all assets received in the reorganization, as well as any of its own property retained. The target corporation then can liquidate but it does not have to.

To ensure that the target corporation continues, the continuity of business enterprise judicial doctrine must be satisfied. The target corporation's business operations must continue in some capacity. This test requires the acquiring corporation to either continue the target corporation's historic business or use a significant portion of the target corporation's assets in its business. The term "significant" is based on facts and circumstances.

If Rocky acquires the assets of all three lines and continues the production of its cruelty-free products business line, this will meet the historic business use test and the significant use of the target corporation's assets test. The tax law does not indicate that at least 50% of the FMV of assets be used, but rather just a significant portion. Because 46% ($500,000/$1,080,000) of the assets acquired will be used and are important to the operation of the business, the significant use test is satisfied. Treas. Reg §1.368-1(d)(1-3).

Ethics and Professional Responsibilities Application

Ethics

Privileged Documents and the IRS

(LO2) Pop Corporation and Soda Corporation filed consolidated tax returns in 2023, 2024, and 2025. The IRS is auditing these tax returns and believe that Pop and Soda were not eligible to file a consolidated tax return in 2023, the year the acquisition took place. Your CPA firm has been hired to provide consultation. In reviewing the documents between the corporations and its attorney at the time, you discover documentation that might be detrimental to Pop and Soda. What is your obligation to your client and to the IRS if the IRS is requesting that all information be furnished?

In addition to the chapter content, see *Statements on Standards for Tax Services* at www.aicpa-cima.com/resources/landing/statements-on-standards-for-tax-services, *Circular 230* at https://www.irs.gov/tax-professionals/office-of-professional-responsibility-and-circular-230, and Chapter 2, LO4, Tax Professional Responsibilities.

Solution

A CPA has certain duties relating to its practice before the IRS. Under *Circular 230* §10.20 Information to be furnished, (a) To the Internal Revenue Service. (1) "A practitioner must, on a proper and lawful request by a duly authorized officer or employee of the Internal Revenue Service, promptly submit records or information in any matter before the Internal Revenue Service unless the practitioner believes in good faith and on reasonable grounds that the records or information are privileged."

If the CPA believes the requested material is privileged, then the CPA does not have to immediately comply with the IRS request. The documentation that was discovered that might be detrimental is between the corporations and its attorney. If the documents are subpoenaed, then the CPA must comply with the request and turn over the documents requested.

Key Terms

50% Test (Brother-Sister Controlled Group) 5-9
80% Test (Affiliated Group) 5-14
80% Test (Brother-Sister Controlled Group) 5-9
80% Test (Controlled Group) 5-5
Affiliated Group 5-14
Acquisitive Reorganizations 5-33
Boot (Corporate Reorganization) 5-5
Brother-Sister Controlled Group 5-9
Business Purpose 5-38
Common Parent Test (Affiliated Group) 5-14
Common Parent Test (Controlled Group) 5-6
Consolidated Return 5-19
Consolidation 5-23
Continuity of Business Enterprise 5-39
Continuity of Interest 5-38
Controlled Group 5-4
Divisive Reorganizations 5-33
Excess Loss Account 5-27
Merger 5-23
Parent-Subsidiary Controlled Group 5-5
Reorganization 5-37
Shareholder Test (Brother-Sister Controlled Group) 5-9
Spin-Off 5-37
Split-Off 5-37
Split-Up 5-37
Statutory Merger 5-33
Step Transaction 5-39
Substantially All 5-35
Tax Attributes (Corporation) 5-44
Type A Reorganization 5-33
Type B Reorganization 5-34
Type C Reorganization 5-35
Type D Reorganization 5-37
Type E Reorganization 5-38
Type F Reorganization 5-38
Type G Reorganization 5-38

End-of-Chapter Assessment

Discussion Questions

1. **(LO1)** Define a controlled group.

2. **(LO1)** Describe the two conditions that must be met for a controlled group to be considered a parent-subsidiary controlled group.

3. **(LO1)** Define a brother-sister controlled group.

4. **(LO2)** What are the two tests that must be met in order for two corporations to be considered an affiliated group?

5. **(LO2)** Explain why Congress made it more difficult to qualify as an affiliated group than a controlled group.

6. **(LO3)** Define a corporate reorganization.

7. **(LO3)** If the Acquiring corporation purchases the stock of Target corporation in a taxable transaction, who must report gain or loss, if any?

8. **(LO3)** Briefly describe the judicial doctrines that must be satisfied in order for a transaction to be considered a tax-free reorganization.

9. **(LO4)** What is a tax attribute? Provide three examples of a tax attribute?

Multiple Choice Questions

1. **(LO1)** Corporations F, U, and R are part of a controlled group and must share the $250,000 accumulated earnings credit. Which of the following is an acceptable allocation?
   - **a.** $250,000 to R and none to the rest
   - **b.** $10,000 to F and $120,000 to U and R
   - **c.** $83,333 to each of F, U, and R
   - **d.** All of the above

2. **(LO1)** Corporations S, T, and Y are part of a controlled group. Which of the following is a false statement?
   - **a.** The Section 179 can be allocated solely to any member of the controlled group.
   - **b.** $250,000 of the accumulated earnings credit can be allocated solely to any member of the controlled group.
   - **c.** In order for a parent-subsidiary controlled group to exist, only one corporation must own at least 80% of another corporation.
   - **d.** All of the above are true statements.

3. **(LO2)** Which of the following are eligible to file a consolidated tax return?
   - **a.** S Corporations
   - **b.** Tax exempt organizations
   - **c.** Partnerships
   - **d.** None of the above

4. **(LO2)** Franz, an individual, owns 85% and 90% of the total value and voting power of A and B Corps., which in turn own the following (both value and voting power):

	Ownership	
Property	A Corp	B Corp
C Corp	90%	—
D Corp	—	80%

All companies are C corporations except B Corp., which had elected S status since inception. Which of the following statements is correct with respect to the companies' ability to file a consolidated return?

a. A, C, and D may file as a group.

b. A and C may not file as a group, and B and D may not file as a group.

c. A and C may file as a group, and B and D may file as a group.

d. A and C may file as a group, and B and D may not file as a group.

5. **(LO2)** Which of the following is a true statement?

a. The election to consolidate must be unanimous by all the corporations in the affiliated group.

b. If a subsidiary leaves the group, in general, it cannot return to the group for until four years has passed.

c. Each corporation must conform to the accounting method used by the parent.

d. The due date of the consolidated return is the 15th day of the third month after the end of the tax year.

6. **(LO3)** North Corporation owns 200 shares of South Corporation. South Corporation has 2,000 shares of stock outstanding. North wants to acquire more shares of South in a tax-free Type B reorganization. Which of the following statements is true?

a. North Corporation must obtain at least 1,600 additional shares of South's voting stock.

b. North Corporation must obtain at least 1,200 additional shares of South's voting stock.

c. North Corporation can transfer assets to South's shareholders in addition to voting stock.

d. North must give South's shareholders only voting stock in North Corporation.

7. **(LO3)** Which of the following statements is false assuming that BIG Corporation acquires Small Corporation in a stock for asset reorganization?

a. Shareholders of Small Corporation must recognize their realized gains to the extent they receive boot.

b. If this is a Type C reorganization, then BIG Corporation can transfer both voting and non-voting stock to Small's shareholders.

c. If this is a Type A reorganization, then Small Corporation must dissolve.

d. The continuity of interest test requires that the shareholders of Small Corporation acquire stock in BIG that has a value of at least 50% (40% in some circumstances) of the value of Small Corporation stock before the transfer in a Type A reorganization.

8. **(LO3)** Which of the following is not an example of a divisive reorganization?

a. Spin-off

b. Split-up

c. Split-off

d. None of the above

9. **(LO4)** Which of the following is a tax attribute of a corporation?

a. Charitable contribution carryforward

b. MACRS depreciation including bonus depreciation

c. Foreign tax credit carryforward

d. All of the above

Brief Exercises

1. **(LO1)** Corporations Alpha, Beta, and Chi are owned by Terrance, Zeke, and Vance as follows:

Owner	Alpha	Beta	Chi
Terrance	40%	30%	60%
Zeke	35%	15%	30%
Vance	25%	25%	10%

Which corporations are members of a brother-sister controlled group for all purposes of the corporate tax law?

2. **(LO2)** Happy Corporation owns stock in the following corporations:

- 79% (voting and value) of the stock of Mad Corporation
- 75% of the voting and 85% of the value of the stock of Fear Corporation
- 60% (voting and value) of the stock of Excited Corporation

Determine the largest group of corporations that qualify as an affiliated group, assuming that these ownership percentages are for every day of the tax year.

3. **(LO2)** Price Corporation plans to contribute $55,000 per year for the next four years to qualified charitable organizations that support Price Corporation's mission to improve its impact on ESG (Environmental, Social, and Corporate Governance). Price expects to have taxable income of approximately $400,000 per year during this period. Dollar Corporation should generate at least $750,000 of taxable income over the next four years, and it does not plan to make any charitable contributions. Based on just the information given, would it be advantageous for the corporations to elect to file a consolidated tax return?

4. **(LO2)** Assume that Hamburger Corporation and Hot Dog Inc. are members of an affiliated group. Hamburger Corporation has $650,000 net income and Hot Dog Inc. has a $700,000 net operating loss. What are the tax consequences if Hamburger and Hot Dog file separate tax returns? A consolidated tax return?

5. **(LO2)** ParentCo, SubOne, and SubTwo have filed consolidated returns since their inception. The members reported the following taxable incomes (losses) for the year:

ParentCo	$55,000
SubOne	(65,000)
SubTwo	(45,000)

No member reported a capital gain or loss or charitable contributions. What is the amount of the consolidated net operating loss?

6. **(LO3)** As part of a statutory merger, Aline Corporation transfers $60,000 of voting stock and land with a fair market value of $65,000 to Trucker Corporation in return for assets of Trucker that have a fair market value of $135,000, adjusted basis of $20,000, with liabilities attached of $10,000. Aline assumes Trucker's liabilities. Trucker distributes the voting stock and land to its shareholders in return for their stock. Does this qualify as a Type A reorganization? Explain.

7. **(LO3)** Grapefruit Corporation owns 100 shares of Tangerine Corporation's voting stock. Grapefruit has 2,500 shares of voting stock and 1,500 shares of nonvoting stock outstanding while Tangerine has 500 shares of voting stock outstanding. Grapefruit transfers 500 shares of its nonvoting stock for 300 additional shares of Tangerine's voting stock. Does this transaction qualify as a Type B reorganization? Explain.

8. **(LO4)** Antelope Corporation purchased all the assets of Tiger Corporation as part of a Type A reorganization on May 1 of the current year. Tiger then liquidated. Antelope and Tiger have the following information:

	Antelope	Tiger
Accumulated E&P	$765,000	($200,000)
Current E&P as of May 1	$222,000	($ 46,000)
Current E&P for May through December	$173,000	

How much of Tiger's E&P can be used this year to offset Antelope's E&P?

Application Problems

1. **(LO1)** Old McDonald Corporation owns stock in the following corporations:

- 95% of the stock of Horse Corporation
- 85% of the stock of Pig Corporation
- 60% of the stock of Goat Corporation

Identify the parent-subsidiary controlled group, if one exists.

2. **(LO1)** The following corporations are owned as shown:

Corporation Sun:	Owned 100% by an individual
Corporation Rain:	Owned 85% by Corporation Sun and 15% by individuals
Corporation Cloudy:	Owned 95% by Corporation Sun and 5% by individuals
Corporation Hail:	Owned 50% by Corporation Rain, 15% by Corporation Cloudy, and 35% by individuals
Corporation Windy:	70% by Corporation Rain and 30% by individuals

Identify the parent-subsidiary controlled group, if one exists.

3. **(LO1)** Individuals 1, 2, 3, 4, and 5 own the following percentages of the only class of outstanding stock of Corporations V, W, X, Y, and Z:

	Corporations/Percent of stock owned				
Individual	V	W	X	Y	Z
1	35%	35%	35%	35%	35%
2	15%	0%	15%	25%	25%
3	15%	15%	25%	25%	15%
4	35%	0%	25%	10%	0%
5	0%	50%	0%	5%	0%

Which corporations are members of a brother-sister controlled group?

4. **(LO2)** Gold Corporation owns 85% (voting and value) of the stock of Silver Corporation, 55% (voting and value) of the stock of Platinum Corporation, and 35% (voting and value) of the stock of Copper Corporation. Silver Corporation owns 45% (voting and value) of the stock of Copper Corporation. Determine the largest group of corporations that qualify as an affiliated group, assuming that these ownership percentages are for every day of the tax year.

5. **(LO2)** Pumpkin Corporation owns 100% of Stalk Corporation in the current year. Pumpkin provided web development services to Stalk in the current year. Pumpkin uses the cash method of accounting and Stalk uses the accrual method. The services rendered have a value of $40,000 and will be paid to Pumpkin in the following year. Including the intercompany transactions, Pumpkin's separate taxable income is $135,000. Stalk's separate taxable income is $188,000. What is the consolidated taxable income for the two corporations?

6. **(LO2)** Potato Corporation owns 100% of Soup Corporation in the current year. Soup paid Potato a $25,000 cash dividend on December 31. Including the dividend income, Potato has separate taxable income of $334,000 and Soup reported separate taxable income of $120,000. What is the consolidated taxable income for the two corporations?

7. **(LO2)** Pudding Corporation owns 100% of Soufflé Corporation. Pudding reports on the cash basis and Soufflé reports on the accrual basis. Their tax information for the current year is as follows:

Pudding taxable income	$187,000
Soufflé loss	($ 63,000)

Pudding's income includes a $4,000 Section 1231 gain and a charitable contribution deduction of $13,000. Soufflé's loss includes a short-term capital loss of ($3,500). Soufflé paid a dividend to Pudding of $15,000. Pudding recorded dividend income and a dividends received deduction. Compute the consolidated taxable income for the year.

8. **(LO2)** Porpoise Corporation purchased all the stock of Shark Corporation in Year 1 for $190,000. Shark's operating results were as follows:

Year 1	($120,000)
Year 2	$ 60,000
Year 3	($140,000)
Year 4	$ 35,000

Compute Porpoise's stock basis in Shark at the end of each year. What would be the result if Porpoise sold the stock of Shark at the end of Year 3 for $110,000?

9. **(LO3)** As part of a statutory merger, Aqua Corporation transfers $280,000 of nonvoting stock and land with a FMV of $52,000 (adjusted basis of $25,000) to Teal Corporation in return for assets of Teal that have a fair market value of $360,000, adjusted basis of $200,000, and liabilities attached of $28,000. Aqua assumes $28,000 of Teal's liabilities. Teal distributes the nonvoting stock and cash to its shareholders in return for their stock.

a. Does this qualify as a Type A reorganization?

b. Does Aqua recognize any gain as a result of this transaction, and what is Aqua's basis in the asset received from Teal?

c. How would the answer change if Aqua's basis in the land was $58,000?

d. What are the tax consequences to Teal?

10. (LO3) Anger Corporation owns 600 shares of Timid Corporation's voting stock. Anger has 10,000 shares of voting stock outstanding while Timid has 1,000 shares of voting stock outstanding. Anger transfers 100 shares of its voting stock for 250 additional shares of Timid's voting stock. Does this transaction qualify as a Type B reorganization?

11. (LO3) Aardvark Corporation transferred voting stock worth $500,000 to Tiger Corporation in return for Tiger's assets with the following information:

	Total	Transferred to Aardvark	Retained by Tiger
Fair market value	$600,000	$550,000	$50,000
Adjusted basis	$150,000	$125,000	$25,000
Liabilities attached	$ 75,000	$ 50,000	$25,000

Tiger remains in existence after the transaction. The shareholders of Tiger receive $500,000 of Aardvark stock in return for $500,000 of Tiger stock. Does this transaction qualify as a Type C reorganization?

12. (LO3) Abern Corporation transferred voting stock worth $500,000 to Tangent Corporation in return for Tangent's assets with the following information:

	Total	Transferred to Abern	Retained by Tangent
Fair market value	$600,000	$550,000	$50,000
Adjusted basis	$150,000	$125,000	$25,000
Liabilities attached	$ 75,000	$ 50,000	$25,000

Tangent remains in existence after the transaction. The shareholders of Tangent receive $500,000 of Abern stock in return for $500,000 of Tangent stock. One of the assets retained by Tangent is land with a FMV of $28,000 and adjusted basis of $15,000, and Tangent distributes this land to its shareholders.

a. Does Tangent recognize any gain as a result of this transaction?

b. How would the answer change if Tangent's basis in the land is $38,000?

13. (LO3) Grigor exchanges stock that he owns in Hard Corporation with a value of $23,500 for stock in Easy Corporation. The stock he received from Easy Corporation had a value of $20,000 when received. In addition, he received land with a fair market value of $3,500 and an adjusted basis of $1,000 from Easy Corporation. This exchange is pursuant to a qualified type A reorganization. Grigor had purchased his stock from Hard Corporation five years ago for $10,000. How much gain or loss does Grigor recognize on this transaction?

14. (LO3) Affa Corporation transfers $380,000 of nonvoting stock and $90,000 cash to Titan Corporation in return for assets of Titan that have a fair market value of $540,000, adjusted basis of $220,000, and liabilities attached of $70,000. Affa assumes Titan's liabilities. Titan distributes the nonvoting stock and cash to its sole shareholder, Venus. Venus's basis in its stock is $290,000. Titan Corporation has E&P of $66,000. Assuming that this transaction qualifies as a Type A reorganization, what are the tax consequences to Venus?

15. (LO3) Affa Corporation transfers $380,000 of nonvoting stock and $90,000 cash to Titan Corporation in return for assets of Titan that have a fair market value of $540,000, adjusted basis of $220,000, and liabilities attached of $70,000. Affa assumes Titan's liabilities. Titan distributes the nonvoting stock and cash to its sole shareholder, Venus. Venus's basis in its stock is $500,000. Titan Corporation has E&P of $66,000. Assuming that this transaction qualifies as a Type A reorganization, what are the tax consequences to Venus?

16. (LO4) Apple Corporation purchased all the assets of Tangerine Corporation as part of a Type A reorganization on August 1 of the current year. Tangerine then liquidated. Apple and Tangerine have the following information:

	Apple	Tangerine
Accumulated E&P	$830,000	($190,000)
Current E&P as of August 1	$445,000	($ 35,000)
Current E&P for August through December	$ 65,000	

a. How much of Tangerine's E&P can be used this year to offset Apple's E&P?

b. If Tangerine's accumulated E&P is a positive $225,000, how are Tangerine's accumulated E&P and current E&P treated by Apple?

17. (LO4) Astronomy Corporation purchased Telescope Corporation in a Type A reorganization on September 25, Year 5. The former Telescope shareholders received 30% of Astronomy's stock with a value of $500,000. Astronomy reports on the cash basis. Assume the following additional information:

- Telescope has a Year 4 NOL carryforward of $68,000.
- Astronomy has taxable income, before the NOL deduction, of $55,000.

a. How much of Telescope's NOL can Astronomy use in Year 5 to reduce Astronomy's income?

b. Would the amount of Telescope's NOL that can be used by Astronomy be further limited by the NOL ownership rule? Assume that the long-term tax-exempt rate for the month of the acquisition is 5%.

Tax Planning Problems

Planning

1. (LO1) Pixie Corporation is considering purchasing 90% of Skittle Corporation on June 1 of the current year. Skittle is considering selling the following assets to Pixie in the current year:

	FMV	Adjusted basis
Asset 1	$22,000	$26,000
Asset 2	$55,000	$60,000

Would you recommend the sale of these assets from Skittle to Pixie?

2. (LO2, 4) Periwinkle Corporation, a calendar-year corporation, owns 70% of Saffron Corporation. Periwinkle is considering purchasing more of Saffron Corporation on January 1 of next year in order to use Saffron's net operating loss carryforward of $44,000. What percentage does Periwinkle need to purchase in order to use Saffron's NOL? How much income must Saffron earn in the coming year in order for Periwinkle to use the entire NOL carryforward assuming Periwinkle has $225,000 of separate taxable income? Assume none of the NOL was carried back.

Professional Development Skills

Communication Problem

Communication

1. (LO2, 4) **Decision to File a Consolidated Tax Return** Purple Corporation owns 75% of Silver Corporation and is considering purchasing another 5% on January 1, Year 25. Purple Corporation has been very profitable, and the CEO of Purple would like to use Silver Corporations NOLs that have been generated. Neither Purple nor Silver has made any charitable contributions or incurred any capital transactions in the last three years. The following is a list of the corporations' taxable income reported on a separate year tax return. All tax years occur after 2020.

Year	Purple Corporation taxable income	Silver Corporation taxable income
22	$238,000	$ 60,000
23	$335,000	($ 45,000)
24	$384,000	($120,000)
25	$400,000	$ 50,000

If Purple Corporation purchases an additional 5% of the voting power/total value of all classes of stock, will Purple Corporation be able to utilize all $165,000 of Silver Corporation losses on the consolidated tax return in Year 25? Write a memo to the CEO of Purple Corporation.

Ethics and Professional Responsibilities Problem

Ethics

1. (LO1) **Use of Section 179 in a Controlled Group** You are a new staff accountant in the tax department of Carnes and Youngberg, CPAs. Your senior manager asks you to review the 2025 tax return for a new client, Glorify, Inc. that manufactures religious items for sale in churches across the world. Glorify owns 85% of Praise Corporation, and the corporations are owned 50% each by Joseph and Mary. When reviewing the separate tax returns for Glorify and Praise, you notice that both corporations claimed a Section 179 deduction of $1,250,000 in 2025. What is your recommendation to Joseph and Mary concerning the preparation of the 2025 tax returns?

   In addition to the chapter content, see *Statements on Standards for Tax Services* at www.aicpa-cima.com/resources/landing/statements-on-standards-for-tax-services, *Circular 230* at www.irs.gov/tax-professionals/office-of-professional-responsibility-and-circular-230, and Chapter 2, LO4, Tax Professional Responsibilities.

Research Problem

Research

1. (LO3) **Type C Reorganization and the "Substantially All" Test** Takeover Inc. would like to acquire the assets of Bullseye Corporation in a Type C reorganization. Bullseye has assets with a total fair market value of $500,000 and has liabilities of $80,000. If all other conditions are met for a Type C reorganization, what percent of Bullseye assets need to be acquired by Takeover, Inc.? Hint: See Rev. Proc. 77-37, 1977-2 CB 568 and Rev. Rul. 78-47, 1978-1 CB 113.

Part II (Chapters 3-5): Comprehensive Tax Return Problems

1. **Fit4You 1120** Complete Form 1120 pages 1–3, 6 (Schedule M-1), Schedule D, and Form 8949 for Fit4You, an accrual-basis, calendar-year corporation that operates several fitness centers. Use 2025 tax law in preparing the forms. Our solution uses 2024 forms as they were the most current forms available at the time of publication.

Go to Wiley's book companion site for the complete Comprehensive Tax Return Problem for Part II (Chapters 3-5).

2. **Huskies 1120** Complete Form 1120 pages 1–3, 6 (Schedule M-1), Schedule D, and Form 8949 for Huskies, Inc., an accrual-basis, calendar-year corporation that operates five local pet stores. Use 2025 tax law in preparing the forms. Our solution uses 2024 forms as they were the most current forms available at the time of publication.

Go to Wiley's book companion site for the complete Comprehensive Tax Return Problem for Part II (Chapters 3-5).

CHAPTER 6

Partnership Taxation:

Formation, Basis, and Income

Nancy Honey/Getty Images

Before studying this chapter, you should know or, if necessary, review

1.1 Business Entities: Business Lifecycle and Operations

1.2 Fundamentals of Property Transactions

Chapter Introduction

VIDEO CONTENT

Aletta has operated a hair salon for the last seven years as a sole proprietorship. She owns the building that she uses for her business, as well as the equipment in her shop. She has recently learned that her current business structure as a sole proprietorship is very risky for her because she has unlimited liability. For example, if one of her customers is injured in her salon her personal financial assets could be put at risk. She considered incorporating her business so that she can have the liability protection that is afforded corporate shareholders. However, she is concerned about the potential for double taxation with corporations. Therefore, she has asked you whether she should organize her business as a partnership, or possibly a limited liability company (LLC).

To form a partnership or an LLC, she would have to bring in at least one additional owner. This would be to her advantage only if others have capital or expertise that would benefit the business. Aletta could form a single-member LLC, but if so, it would not be taxed as a partnership and would most likely be taxed as a sole proprietorship on Schedule C of her Form 1040.

Thirty-seven percent (37%) of small businesses are organized as LLCs or partnerships.[1] LLCs are much more popular today than partnerships for reasons that we will describe in this chapter. Most small business owners prefer to be either an LLC or partnership, with S corporations running a close second at 33%. In this chapter, we discuss the characteristics of partnerships, the tax implications of forming a partnership, the flow-through of income to the partners and how this affects the partner's basis in the partnership interest, limitations on the use of partnership losses, the required tax year for partnerships, and a few special related-party rules.

[1] Taylor, D.P. "2023 Small Business Ownership Statistics." *The Ascent: A Motley Fool* Service. Updated 5 Aug. 2022, www.fool.com/the-ascent/small-business/articles/small-business-statistics/

LEARNING OBJECTIVES	TOPICS	PRACTICE OPPORTUNITIES
1 Recall definitions related to partnerships and partners.	**6.1 Definitions Related to Partnerships** • Characteristics of Partnerships • Limited Liability Companies • Check-the-Box Regulations	• Example 6.1.1 Partnership Characteristics • Example 6.1.2 Check-the-Box Regulations • Practice Problem 6.1.1 Debt Responsibility • Practice Problem 6.1.2 Entity Type
2 Compute the tax consequences of partnership formations.	**6.2 Taxation of Partnership Formations** • Qualifications to Defer Gains and Losses • Receipt of Boot • Receipt of a Profits Interest • Basis • Holding Period and Other Tax Characteristics	• Example 6.2.1 Partnership Interest Received for Property • Example 6.2.2 Partnership Interest Received for Services • Example 6.2.3 Boot Received on a Partnership Formation • Example 6.2.4 Special Rules for Carried Interest • Example 6.2.5 Basis and Holding Period • Practice Problem 6.2.1 Services Contributed in Exchange for Partnership Interest • Practice Problem 6.2.2 Recognition of Gain/Loss on Partnership Formation • Practice Problem 6.2.3 Basis and Holding Period with Partnership Formation

3 Compute the adjustment to partner's bases for partnership debt.	**6.3 Impact of Partnership Debt on Partner's Basis in Partnership Interest**
	• Transactions that Affect Debt Basis
	• Allocating Recourse Debt and Nonrecourse Debt
	  • Recourse Debt
	  • Nonrecourse Debt
	• Temporary Benefit of Debt Basis
		• Example 6.3.1 Partnership Assumption of Partner Debt
		• Example 6.3.2 Gain Recognized Due to Debt Relief
		• Example 6.3.3 Allocation of Recourse and Nonrecourse Debt to Basis
		• Practice Problem 6.3.1 Liability Assumed by Partnership
		• Practice Problem 6.3.2 Liability Assumption Effect on Basis

4 Compute the ordinary business income or loss and separately stated items for a partnership.	**6.4 Taxation of Partnership Income and Guaranteed Payments**
	• Timing of Income to Partners
	• Guaranteed Payments
	• Fringe Benefits for Partners
	• Character of Partnership Tax Items
	• Basis in Partnership Interest and Capital Account
	  • Basis Computation
	  • Order of Adjustments to Basis in Partnership Interest
	  • Capital Interest in Partnership
		• Example 6.4.1 Death of a Partner
		• Example 6.4.2 Guaranteed Payments
		• Example 6.4.3 Character of Partnership Items
		• Example 6.4.4 Partnership Partner's Income
		• Example 6.4.5 Single Taxation for Partners
		• Example 6.4.6 Basis in Partnership Interest vs. Capital Account
		• Practice Problem 6.4.1 Identification of Bucket Items and Separately Stated Items
		• Practice Problem 6.4.2 Calculating Ending Basis in a Partnership

Learning Objective	Section	Examples and Practice Problems

5 Determine the partner's share of partnership losses that can be currently deducted and that is suspended.	**6.5 Use of Partnership Losses**
	• Basis Hurdle
	• At-Risk Hurdle
	  • Defining At-Risk Amount
	  • At-Risk for Real Estate
	• Passive Loss Hurdle
	  • Material Participation
	• Combining the Three Hurdles: Basis, At-Risk, and Passive Loss
	• Excess Business Losses
		• Example 6.5.1 At-Risk Limitation
		• Example 6.5.2 Material Participation
		• Example 6.5.3 Loss Limitations
		• Example 6.5.4 Excess Business Losses
		• Practice Problem 6.5.1 Hurdles for Loss Limitations
		• Practice Problem 6.5.2 Determining Excess Business Loss

6 Identify the required tax year for partnerships and other optional tax years.	**6.6 Permitted Tax Years for Partnerships**
	• Required Tax Year
	• Exceptions to Required Tax Year
	  • Natural Business Year
	  • Business Purpose
	  • Section 444 Election
	• Advanced Topic—Drilling Down
	  • Least Aggregate Deferral Method
		• Example 6.6.1 Timing of Flow-Through of Income to Partners
		• Example 6.2.2 Required Tax Year
		• Example 6.6.3 Principal Partner Test
		• Example 6.6.4 Natural Business Year
		• Example 6.6.5 Least Aggregate Deferral Method
		• Practice Problem 6.6.1 Permitted Tax Year
		• Practice Problem 6.6.2 Natural Business Year End

7 Apply the related-party rules to partnership transactions.	**6.7 Related-Party Rules** • Disallowance of Related-Party Losses • Evaluating Related-Party Transactions • Preservation of Unrealized Ordinary Income • Payments to a Partner	• Example 6.7.1 Related-Party Loss • Example 6.7.2 Right of Offset • Example 6.7.3 Sale of Asset Between Partnerships • Example 6.7.4 Payments to a Partner • Practice Problem 6.7.1 Related-Party Loss

Tax Forms referenced in this chapter

Form 1040, Schedule E	Supplemental Income or Loss
Form 1065	U.S. Return of Partnership Income
Form 1065, Schedule K-1	Partner's Share of Income, Deductions, Credits, etc.
Form 1120	U.S. Corporation Income Tax Return
Form 1128	Application to Adopt, Change or Retain a Tax Year
Form 8832	Entity Classification Election

6.1 Definitions Related to Partnerships

LEARNING OBJECTIVE 1

Recall definitions related to partnerships and partners.

VIDEO CONTENT

A **partnership** is an association of two or more taxpayers to operate a business that has an objective to make a profit that is not taxed as a corporation. Additionally, there must be an intent to share profits among the partners. Just the co-ownership of property does not necessarily create a partnership, nor does the sharing of only expenses.

Characteristics of Partnerships

Potential Pitfall

LLCs are taxed as partnerships for federal income tax purposes. In this chapter we refer to partnerships most of the time. You should assume the same rules apply to LLCs unless we provide different rules for LLCs.

The major tax advantage for partnerships is single taxation, contrasted with double taxation for C corporations. Partnership income is reported on Form 1065, U.S. Return of Partnership Income, but the partnership does not pay tax on this income. Rather, the income flows through to the partners, regardless of whether it has been distributed, and the partners pay tax on the income on their returns. The partners' share of each tax item is reported to each partner on their Schedule K-1 (Form 1065).

Related exercise: Discussion Question 1

Another advantage of partnerships is the flexibility that partners have in how they arrange their economic relationship. The partners can determine how profits and losses are shared among the partners. For example, two partners, A and B could share:

- Profits 50% to A and 50% to B, and losses 70% to A and 30% to B.
- Profits 50% to A and 50% to B for Year 1, changing to 20% to A and 80% to B for Year 2.
- All tax items 50% to A and 50% to B, except for one tax time such as depreciation which could be 100% to A and 0% to B.

The only limitation on partners' flexibility in allocating tax items among the partners is that the allocation must have substantial economic effect under IRC §704(b). **Substantial economic effect** means that there must be economic consequences for the allocations to be respected for tax purposes. Other characteristics of partnerships include the following:

- **General partners** can participate in management and have unlimited liability, so they are personally liable for partnership debt. All partnerships must have at least one general partner.
- **Limited partners** have limited liability and can lose only what they have invested and promised to invest in the partnership. Limited partners cannot participate in the management of the partnership.
- All the partners in a **general partnership** are general partners and their personal assets are at risk to creditors of the partnership. A **limited partnership** must have at least one general partner and at least one limited partner.

Related exercise: Discussion Question 2

Limited Liability Companies

All 50 states have passed laws that allow a business owner to form a **limited liability company (LLC)** by filing articles of organization with the appropriate secretary of state's office. Unless the owners of the LLC elect to be taxed as a corporation, an LLC is taxed as a partnership and files a Form 1065. In that case, LLCs are taxed like partnerships. The important differences between an LLC and a partnership are from a legal perspective, not a tax perspective, including the following:

- Owners of an LLC are known as members, rather than partners.
- All owners of an LLC have limited liability, whereas all partnerships must have at least one general partner that has unlimited liability.
- All owners of an LLC can participate in management (but are not required to), whereas limited partners cannot participate in management.

In the following Example, we review how the limited liability rules apply to owners of partnerships and LLCs.

Potential Pitfall

We use the term *SMLLC* to refer to an LLC with one member. We use *LLC* to refer to a multi-member LLC.

EXAMPLE 6.1.1
Partnership Characteristics

Which of the following is true for partnerships?

a. General partners, limited partners, and LLC members all have limited liability.
b. LLC members have limited liability, but general partners and limited partners do not.
c. LLC members and limited partners have limited liability, but general partners do not.
d. General partners, limited partners, and LLC members all have unlimited liability.

SOLUTION

The correct answer is **c**. Of these three types of business owners, only general partners do not have limited liability.

Related exercise: Multiple Choice Question 1

Check-the-Box Regulations

The **check-the-box regulations** determine how a business entity is taxed for federal income tax purposes, and we show these rules in a flowchart in **Illustration 6.1**.[2] The main premise of the check-the-box regulations is that unincorporated entities may choose to be taxed as a corporation or a partnership.

- C corporations and S corporations, also known as *per se* corporations, will always be taxed as corporations. That is, they do not have an option to be taxed as a partnership. Many foreign business entities also qualify as *per se* corporations.
- If the business is not incorporated and has two or more owners, the default classification of the entity is a partnership. For the purposes of our limited discussion, this default rule typically applies to partnerships and limited liability companies (LLCs). If a partnership or LLC prefers to be taxed as a corporation, it can file Form 8832, Entity Classification Election (see Appendix B), and check a box to be taxed as a corporation.[3]
- If an entity is not incorporated and has only one owner, then the default classification is that the entity is disregarded for federal income tax purposes. The entity that this applies to for our discussion is a **single-member limited liability company (SMLLC)**. A disregarded SMLLC that is owned by an individual reports its tax items on Schedule C as part of the individual's Form 1040.[4] A disregarded entity that is owned by a corporation reports its tax items on the corporation's Form 1120. A SMLLC can also elect to be taxed as a corporation by filing Form 8832.
- An election under the check-the-box regulations is effective for the current year if filed within the first 75 days of the tax year.
- Any entity that is publicly traded is taxed as a corporation. Certain publicly traded partnerships (i.e., certain master limited partnerships) are taxed as corporations.[5]

Related exercise: Multiple Choice Question 2

[2]Treas. Reg. §§301.7701-1, 301.7701-2, and 301.77-1-3.

[3]The rules for this section are for U.S.-based entities. Different rules apply for foreign entities.

[4]If the SMLLC owns a rental activity, then the tax results are reported on Schedule E.

[5]IRC §7704. Publicly traded eligible entities are taxable as corporations, unless at least 90% of their gross income is from certain passive sources. Publicly traded partnerships, such as master limited partnerships (MLPs), often qualify for the gross income exception.

ILLUSTRATION 6.1 Check-the-Box Regulations Flowchart

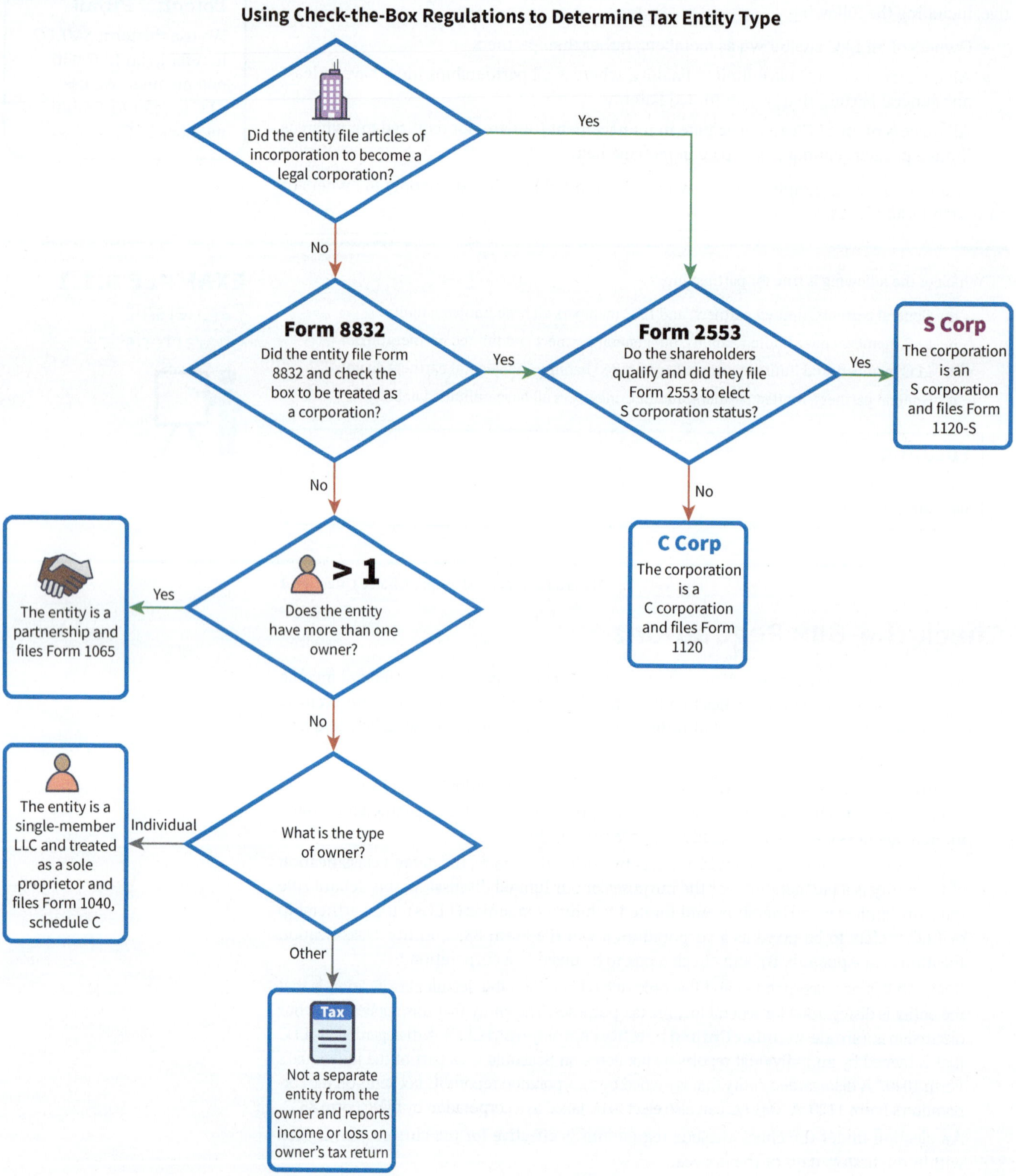

The next Example relates to the rules for the check-the-box regulations.

EXAMPLE 6.1.2
Check-the-Box Regulations

Which of the following statements is true with regard to the check-the-box regulations?

a. C corporations can elect to be taxed as partnerships.

b. A single-member LLC can elect to be taxed as a corporation.

c. An S corporation can elect to be taxed as a partnership.

d. A partnership can elect to be disregarded.

SOLUTION

The correct answer is **b**. The default classification for a SMLLC is to be disregarded, but it can elect to be taxed as a corporation. Responses **a** and **c** are incorrect because incorporated businesses must be taxed as either a C corporation or an S corporation. They cannot elect to be taxed as a partnership. Response **d** is incorrect because a partnership's default classification is to be taxed as a partnership, or it can elect to be taxed as a corporation; disregarded status is not an option.

PRACTICE PROBLEM 6.1.1
Debt Responsibility

Tracy invested $4,000 in TNT Partnership to become a 20% limited partner. Nellie and Theresa are each 40% general partners who invested $8,000 each. If the partnership has debt of $12,000, which partner(s) are liable for this debt?

SOLUTION

Nellie and Theresa are general partners and are liable for the debt. General partners can participate in management and have unlimited liability, so they are personally liable for partnership debt. Tracy can lose only the $4,000 that she invested because she is a limited partner.

PRACTICE PROBLEM 6.1.2
Entity Type

Sierra and Nicole would like to start a home healthcare business together. They know they will have significant upfront costs and expect to incur losses for the first three years. They would like advice as to what entity type would be best for their business.

SOLUTION

If Sierra and Nicole expect losses in the first three years, they should consider forming a partnership or an LLC. The income/loss flows through to the partners, regardless of whether it has been distributed, and is reported on their individual tax returns. Loss limitations rules may apply and are discussed in more detail in LO5, Use of Partnership Losses. (We discuss in Chapter 8 the reasons why they may also wish to consider forming an S corporation.)

INTERACTIVE SELF-SCORING QUIZZES

6.2 Taxation of Partnership Formations

LEARNING OBJECTIVE 2

Compute the tax consequences of partnership formations.

VIDEO CONTENT

Returning to the chapter introduction, if Aletta does decide to form a partnership or LLC, she will want to ensure that the transaction is not taxable. For example, if the building she owns has appreciated in value, she does not want the partnership formation to result in gain recognition for the appreciation. The good news for Aletta is that the tax rules for tax-deferred partnership formations are much more flexible than the rules for corporate formations because there is no 80% control test for partners to qualify for tax deferral (see Chapter 3, LO1, Taxation of Corporate Formations). In this section, we first discuss the requirements to qualify for tax deferral. We then discuss the basis rules and holding period rules related to partnership formations.

Qualifications to Defer Gains and Losses

The rules are simple to qualify for deferral of realized gains and losses for a partnership formation.[6] These rules are summarized in **Illustration 6.2**.

- If a taxpayer contributes property in exchange for a capital interest in a partnership, the realized gains and losses for the partner are not recognized.
- On the other hand, if a taxpayer provides services in return for the partnership interest, then the partner has ordinary income (known as a *guaranteed payment*, which we discuss later) equal to the fair market value of the capital interest received. The partnership can deduct the guaranteed payment made to the service partner.
- The partnership never recognizes a gain or loss because of a partnership formation.

ILLUSTRATION 6.2 Partnership Formation

Tax Consequences of a Partnership Formation

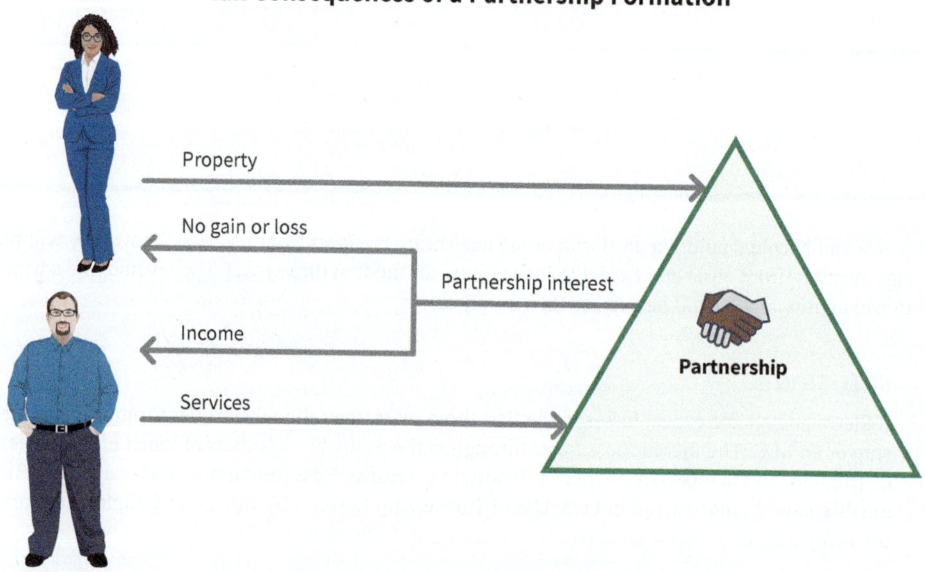

[6]IRC §721. The deferral rules for gains and losses do not apply to partnerships formed solely for investment purposes.

The absence of an 80% control test to defer gains and losses for partnership formations presents planning opportunities that do not exist for corporations. For example:

- If a taxpayer receives a partnership interest in return for services, the other partners who received an interest in return for property can defer gains and losses regardless of the ownership interest of the service partner. This would be true even if the service partner owns 90% or more the partnership. However, for corporations, if the service shareholder owns more than 20% of the corporation, then the shareholders contributing property cannot meet the 80% control test.
- If an existing partnership desires to add a new partner who wants to contribute appreciated property to the partnership, the new partner can defer the realized gain on the contribution regardless of the new partner's ownership interest, even if the ownership is 1% or less. However, for corporations, the new shareholder, together with others contributing property in exchange for stock, must own at least 80% of the corporation.

The next two Examples illustrate the rules for partnership formations.

EXAMPLE 6.2.1
Partnership Interest Received for Property

Will and Mallory formed the WM Partnership this year. Will contributed cash of $40,000 for a 40% capital interest. Mallory contributed a building with a fair market value of $60,000 and an adjusted basis of $45,000 for a 60% capital interest. What are the tax consequences to Will, Mallory, and WM?

SOLUTION

Will does not have a gain because he contributed cash. Mallory has a realized gain of $15,000 on the formation (Amount realized $60,000 – Adjusted basis $45,000). Her recognized gain is $0. WM Partnership does not recognize a gain or loss on the formation.

EXAMPLE 6.2.2
Partnership Interest Received for Services

Continue with the same facts of Example of 6.2.1, except that Mallory rendered services to the partnership and received a capital interest with a value of $60,000. What are the tax consequences to Will, Mallory, and WM?

SOLUTION

Will does not have a gain because he contributed cash. Mallory has a guaranteed payment of $60,000 which is taxed as ordinary income to her. WM Partnership does not recognize a gain or loss on the formation. WM can deduct $60,000 for the guaranteed payment made to Mallory.

Related exercises: Brief Exercises 1, 2
Application Problem 1

Receipt of Boot

Boot is any property received by a partner in a partnership formation other than a partnership interest. If boot is received, the recognized gain by the partner is the *lower* of:

- Realized gain, *or*
- Fair market value of the boot received.

The following Example explores the effect of boot on a partnership formation.

EXAMPLE 6.2.3
Boot Received on a Partnership Formation

Pablo and Jeffrey formed the PJ Partnership. Pablo contributed $180,000 cash for a 60% interest in the partnership. Jeffrey contributed a patent that has an adjusted basis of $5,000 and FMV of $150,000. In return, Jeffrey received a 40% partnership interest with a value of $120,000 and $30,000 cash. How much gain or loss is recognized by Pablo and Jeffrey, if any?

SOLUTION

Pablo and Jeffrey each received a partnership interest in return for property, so the general rule is that they do not recognize any gain or loss. However, because Jeffrey received boot (i.e., cash) in addition to his partnership interest, we must compute his realized gain and determine if any of it is recognized.

	Jeffrey
Partnership interest	$120,000
Cash	30,000
Amount realized	$150,000
Less: Adjusted basis	(5,000)
Realized gain or loss	$145,000

Jeffrey's recognized gain ($30,000) is the *lower* of:

- Realized gain ($145,000), *or*
- Fair market value of the boot received ($30,000).

Related exercise: Application Problem 2

Receipt of a Profits Interest

Occasionally a partner will receive only a profits interest in a partnership. For example, a partner may have a 20% interest in profits, 0% interest in losses, and a 0% capital interest. This means that when the partnership liquidates, the partner will not receive any partnership assets because they have no capital interest. However, if the partnership has ordinary business income of $500,000 for a tax year, the partner would be allocated $100,000 ($500,000 × 20%) of income.

In general, a partner recognizes no income when they receive only a profits interest in a partnership. Rather, the partner is taxed each year when their share of the partnership income is reported to them on their Schedule K-1.[7]

Special rules apply to profits interest that are:

- Received in return for services, *and*
- Held in partnerships that have significant assets in investments or real estate.

These interests are often referred to as **carried interest**. If both of these conditions are met, then the following special rules apply for the partner holding the carried interest:

- Gains from the sale of the investments or real estate are treated as long-term capital gain only if the assets were held for more than three years before being sold.
- Gain from the sale of the partnership profits interest is treated as long-term only if the interest is held for more than three years before being sold.[8]

[7]Exceptions to this rule are provided in Rev. Proc. 93-27, 1993-2 CB 343; clarified by Rev. Proc. 2011-43, 2011-2 CB 191.

[8]IRC §1061(a).

The following Example illustrates the specialized rules that apply for carried interests.

EXAMPLE 6.2.4
Special Rules for Carried Interest

An investment fund manager holds a profits interest in a partnership that was received in connection with the performance of services. For the current year, the manager's separately stated net long-term capital gain in connection with that interest is $20 million. However, only $12 million of that amount is attributable to underlying investments that have been held for more than three years. What are the tax consequences to the manager?

SOLUTION

The manager will receive LTCG treatment only for assets held more than three years. Therefore, the manager has $12 million of long-term capital gain that will be taxed at capital gains rates and $8 million of short-term capital gain that will be taxed at ordinary income tax rates.

Basis

As with all tax-deferred transactions, basis stays the same for a tax-deferred partnership formation. This leads to two consequences:

- The partner's basis in the partnership interest received is equal to the basis of the cash plus all property contributed to the partnership. This is also known as a **substituted basis.**[9] If the partner does recognize gain as a result of the partnership formation, the partner's basis in the partnership interest is increased by the gain.
- The partnership's basis in an asset received from the partner is the same basis as the partner had in the asset. This is also known as a **carryover basis.**[10]

The total basis of all assets on the partnership's balance sheet is the **inside basis**.

Holding Period and Other Tax Characteristics

Special holding period rules exist for tax-deferred transactions. The specific rules for tax-deferred partnership formations are as follows:[11]

- The holding period in the partnership interest includes the holding period of the contributed asset for contributions of capital assets and Section 1231 assets. For other assets, the holding period starts when the contribution is received by the partnership.
- The holding period that the partner has in the asset before contribution always transfers to the partnership, regardless of the type of asset contributed.

Other tax characteristics of the assets also carryover from the partner to the partnership, including:

- The depreciation method used for the asset.
- Potential depreciation recapture under Section 1245 and Section 1250 in the asset.

[9] IRC §722.
[10] IRC §723.
[11] IRC §1223.

We explore the determination of basis and holding period in the following Example.

EXAMPLE 6.2.5
Basis and Holding Period

Mia and Paul formed the MP Partnership to open a new fitness center. They contributed the following assets in return for a 50% partnership interest each:

		Adjusted basis	FMV
Mia:			
	Cash	$ 60,000	$ 60,000
	Equipment	$240,000	$300,000
	Accounts receivable	$ 40,000	$ 40,000
Paul:			
	Building	$450,000	$400,000

Mia owned her own fitness center that she had operated for four years. The equipment had a holding period of two years. The equipment had originally been purchased for $380,000. The accounts receivable has been outstanding for 90 days. Paul owned the building as an investment for six years before the partnership formation. What are the tax consequences of the partnership formation including the tax characteristics of the assets?

SOLUTION

The realized gain or loss for Mia and Paul is computed as follows:

	Mia	Paul
Amount realized	$400,000	$400,000
Adjusted basis	(340,000)	(450,000)
Realized gain or loss	$ 60,000	($ 50,000)

Because Mia and Paul contributed property in exchange for their partnership interests, their recognized gain and loss is zero. There is no gain or loss for MP Partnership.

The tax characteristics of relevance are basis, holding period, and depreciation recapture.

Basis

Basis for Mia, Paul, and MP Partnership is computed as follows:

- Mia's basis in her partnership interest is $340,000, the sum of the cash and the adjusted basis of the property she contributed.
- Paul's basis in his partnership interest is $450,000, the adjusted basis of the property he contributed.
- MP's basis in the assets received are equal to the basis the partner had in them:

Cash	$ 60,000
Equipment	240,000
Accounts receivable	40,000
Building	450,000
Total	$790,000

Holding Period

The holding period for Mia, Paul, and MP Partnership is determined as follows:

- The equipment that Mia contributed was a Section 1231 asset because she used it in her trade or business and owned it for more than one year. She received 75% of her interest in the partnership ($300,000/($60,000 + $300,000 + $40,000) for the equipment so her holding period is two years for 75% of her interest.
- The cash and accounts receivable that Mia contributed are not Section 1231 assets or capital assets, so her holding period for 25% of her interest [($60,000 + $40,000)/$400,000] begins at the time of formation.
- The building that Paul contributed was a capital asset because he held it as an investment, so his holding period in his partnership interest is six years.

- The holding period of the partners always carries over to the partnership, so MP's holding periods are as follows:

Cash	Not applicable
Equipment	Two years
Accounts receivable	90 days
Building	Six years

Depreciation Recapture

If Mia had sold the equipment rather than contributing it to the partnership, she would have recognized Section 1245 depreciation recapture of $60,000. Her realized gain would have been $60,000 (Amount realized $300,000 – Adjusted basis $240,000). The equipment was purchased for $380,000 so the accumulated depreciation claimed for it was $140,000 ($380,000 – $240,000). The depreciation recapture is the *lower* of the realized gain of $60,000 *or* the accumulated depreciation of $140,000 (see Chapter 1, LO3, Section 1231 Assets). The depreciation recapture is *not* recognized due to the formation, but the recapture potential does carryover to the partnership.

Related exercises: Discussion Question 3
Multiple Choice Questions 3, 4, 5
Brief Exercises 3, 4
Application Problem 3

PRACTICE PROBLEM 6.2.1
Services Contributed in Exchange for Partnership Interest

Rajeev is an attorney who provided services to help organize a partnership in the current year. Rajeev received a 10% interest in the partnership in return for the services which have a fair market value of $10,000. His regular charge for similar legal services is $9,000. How much income should Rajeev recognize for the receipt of the partnership interest?

SOLUTION

Rajeev must report $10,000 of ordinary income for the services rendered in exchange for the value of the partnership interest received.

PRACTICE PROBLEM 6.2.2
Recognition of Gain/Loss on Partnership Formation

Dray contributed property that has an adjusted basis of $14,000 and FMV of $28,000 to the DMV Partnership. In return, Dray received a 20% partnership interest with a value of $23,000 and $5,000 cash. How much gain or loss is recognized by Dray, if any?

SOLUTION

Dray received a partnership interest in return for property, so the general rule is that he does not recognize any gain or loss. However, because Dray received boot (i.e., cash) in addition to his partnership interest, we must compute his realized gain and determine if any of it is recognized.

	Dray
Partnership interest	$23,000
Cash	5,000
Amount realized	$28,000
Less: Adjusted basis	(14,000)
Realized gain or loss	$14,000

Dray's recognized gain ($5,000) is the *lower* of:

- Realized gain ($14,000), *or*
- Fair market value of the boot received ($5,000).

PRACTICE PROBLEM 6.2.3
Basis and Holding Period with Partnership Formation

As part of forming a partnership, Shea contributed cash of $8,000 and a delivery truck with a basis of $32,000 and a fair market value of $35,000, in exchange for a 30% partnership interest. The delivery truck was used in her floral shop and had a holding period of 18 months. What is Shea's basis and holding period in her partnership interest?

SOLUTION

Shea's basis in her partnership interest is $40,000, the sum of the cash ($8,000) and the adjusted basis of the property ($32,000) she contributed. The delivery truck that Shea contributed was a Section 1231 asset because she used it in her trade or business and owned it for more than one year. She received 81% of her interest in the partnership ($35,000/$43,000) for the delivery truck, so her holding period is 18 months for 81% of her interest. The cash that Shea contributed is not a Section 1231 asset or capital asset, so her holding period for 19% of her interest ($8,000/$43,000) begins at the time of formation.

INTERACTIVE SELF-SCORING QUIZZES

6.3 Impact of Partnership Debt on Partner's Basis in Partnership Interest

LEARNING OBJECTIVE 3

Compute the adjustment to partner's bases for partnership debt.

VIDEO CONTENT

One of the major advantages of partnerships over other business entities is that partners may be able to increase the basis of their partnership interest for their share of partnership debt. This additional debt basis allows partners to flow more losses through to their tax returns and decreases the potential for gain upon partnership distributions of a sale of the partnership interest.

In this section, we first review the basic transactions that can increase or decrease debt basis. We next review how the allocation of debt rules vary for *recourse* and *nonrecourse debt.* We close this section by emphasizing the temporary benefit of debt basis to partners.

Transactions that Affect Debt Basis

The transactions that can affect debt basis fall into four categories:[12]

Category 1: An increase in the partnership's liabilities (e.g., loan from a bank, increase in accounts payable) is considered to be a contribution of money by each partner and increases each partner's basis in the partnership by each partner's share of the increase.

Category 2: Any decrease in the partnership's liabilities is considered to be a distribution of money to each partner and reduces each partner's basis in the partnership by each partner's share of the decrease.

Category 3: Any decrease in a partner's individual liability by reason of the assumption by the partnership of such individual liabilities is considered to be a distribution of money to the partner by the partnership. Thus, the partner's basis is decreased.

[12]IRC §752.

Category 4: Any increase in a partner's individual liability by reason of the assumption by the partner of partnership liabilities is considered to be a contribution of money to the partnership by the partner. Thus, the partner's basis is increased.

There are two important consequences that flow from these rules. First, if there is a debt transaction under Category 3 or 4 above, the computation of the effect on the partner's basis is a two-step process (**Illustration 6.3**). If the partnership assumes the debt of the partner, the steps are as follows:

Step 1: Partner's basis is reduced by the amount of debt that the partnership assumed.

Step 2: The partnership now has new debt added to its balance sheet, so all the partners' bases are increased by their respective share of the partnership debt.

If the partner assumes debt of the partnership, the steps are as follows:

Step 1: Partner's basis is increased by the amount of debt that the partner assumed.

Step 2: The partnership now has less debt on its balance sheet, so all the partners' bases are deceased by their respective share of the partnership debt.

ILLUSTRATION 6.3 Impact of Debt Assumption on Partner's Basis

	Partnership assumes debt of partner	**Partner assumes debt of partnership**
Step 1	***Decrease*** partner's basis by the debt assumed	***Increase*** partner's basis by the debt assumed
Step 2	***Increase*** all other partners' bases by respective share of the debt	***Decrease*** all other partners' bases by respective share of debt

We illustrate this two-step process in the following Example.

EXAMPLE 6.3.1
Partnership Assumption of Partner Debt

Jose is a 25% partner in a partnership, and he transfers a warehouse to the partnership. The warehouse has an adjusted basis to Jose of $120,000 and a fair market value of $160,000. There is a mortgage attached to the warehouse of $80,000 that the partnership assumes. Jose's basis in his partnership interest before the transfer is $95,000. What is Jose's basis after this transaction?

SOLUTION

We use the two-step process described above to compute Jose's basis:

Basis in partnership interest before the transaction	$ 95,000
Basis in warehouse	120,000
Step 1: Decrease for debt the partnership assumed ($80,000)	(80,000)
Step 2: Increase for Jose's share of the new partnership debt ($80,000 × 25%)	20,000
Jose's basis after the transaction	$155,000

For step 2, the other partners will collectively increase the bases of their partnership interests by $60,000 ($80,000 × 75%). The fair market value of the warehouse ($160,000) does not affect these computations.

Related exercises: Brief Exercise 4
Application Problem 4

Recall that a partner's basis in the partnership cannot be reduced below zero. Therefore, the second consequence of the debt allocation rules is that if the net change in basis in the partnership interest because of debt being assumed by the partnership exceeds the partner's basis in their partnership interest before the debt assumption, the partner must recognize gain equal to that excess to prevent negative basis from occurring.

The following Example explores a situation where a partner's basis is reduced to zero because of debt assumption.

EXAMPLE 6.3.2
Gain Recognized Due to Debt Relief

Amanda became a 25% partner by contributing property to the partnership with an adjusted basis of $20,000, FMV of $50,000, and a liability of $30,000 which the partnership assumed. How does this transaction affect the basis of Amanda and the other partners?

SOLUTION

Amanda's basis is first increased by $20,000 for the basis of the property contributed, and then is decreased by $30,000 for the debt assumption. However, because the partnership debt increased by $30,000 and Amanda is allocated 25% of the debt, her basis is increased by $7,500 ($30,000 × 25%). The net effect on Amanda's basis for the debt assumption is a decrease of $22,500 ($30,000 – $7,500) reflecting that she shifted 75% of the responsibility of the debt to the other partners. We use the two-step process described above to compute Amanda's basis:

Amanda's basis in property contributed	$20,000
Step 1: Decrease for debt partnership assumed ($30,000)	(30,000)
Step 2: Increase for Amanda's share of the new partnership debt ($30,000 × 25%)	7,500
Amanda's basis after the transaction	($ 2,500)
Recognized gain	2,500
Basis after contribution	$ 0

Amanda must recognize the gain so that her basis in her partnership interest will not be negative. For step 2, the other partners will collectively increase the bases of their partnership interests by $22,500 ($30,000 × 75%).

Related exercise: Application Problem 5

Potential Pitfall

The determination of whether debt is recourse or nonrecourse is not made by looking only at the loan document. Other binding commitments and agreements must be considered also. For example, if a partner personally guarantees nonrecourse debt, that partner now has an economic risk of loss for that debt, so the debt is classified as recourse for tax purposes. This is so even though the loan document itself will continue to indicate that the loan is nonrecourse.

Allocating Recourse Debt and Nonrecourse Debt

In the Examples above, we assumed that debt was allocated based on ownership percentage. This is a simplistic assumption because the debt allocation rules are much more complex than this, and vary based on whether the debt is recourse debt or nonrecourse debt. **Recourse debt** is debt for which at least one of the partners, or a person related to a partner, has the potential for an economic risk of loss with respect to the debt. **Nonrecourse debt** is debt for which no partner, or a person related to a partner, has an economic risk of loss. If the borrower defaults on the repayment of nonrecourse debt, the creditor's only recourse is to take the property back that is secured by the loan.[13]

Recourse Debt

For recourse debt, each partner's share of debt is measured by his or her economic risk of loss assuming a constructive liquidation scenario occurred. The detailed rules for a constructive liquidation scenario are beyond the scope of this book.[14] In general, limited partners and LLC

[13]Treas. Reg. §1.752-1.

[14]Treas. Reg. §1.752-2.

members are not allocated any recourse debt for debt basis purposes because they have no economic risk of loss for the debt. ***For problems in this book, you should allocate recourse debt according to the loss sharing ratio, if given, in the problem. Otherwise, you should use the ownership ratio.*** While the loss ratio does not provide the precise correct answer in some situations, it is a reasonable approximation of the results from the constructive liquidation scenario.

Potential Pitfall

For problems in this book, you should allocate recourse debt according to the loss sharing ratio if given in the problem. Otherwise, you should use the ownership ratio.

Nonrecourse Debt

Just as with recourse debt, the allocation of nonrecourse debt is beyond the scope of this book.[15] You should be aware that nonrecourse debt is often allocated based on the partners' profit-sharing ratios. Also, contrasted with recourse debt, general partners, limited partners, and LLC members can be allocated nonrecourse debt.

The following Example explores how to allocate recourse and nonrecourse debt to basis.

EXAMPLE 6.3.3
Allocation of Recourse and Nonrecourse Debt to Basis

Sophie owns 70% of the FS Partnership as a general partner and Fatima owns 30% as a limited partner. At the beginning of the year, Sophie's basis in her partnership interest is $64,000 and Fatima's basis is $47,000. During the year, the partnership secures new recourse debt of $50,000 and new nonrecourse debt of $80,000. Assume that Sophie and Fatima also share profits and losses 70%/30%.

a. Compute their bases in their partnership interests after the debt is incurred.

b. What is the effect to their bases if $30,000 of the nonrecourse debt is paid back in the following tax year.

SOLUTION

You cannot allocate any of the recourse debt to Fatima because she is a limited partner. Therefore, 100% of the recourse debt is allocated to Sophie because she is the only general partner. You can allocate the nonrecourse debt to both partners, and it is allocated using the profit-sharing ratio of 70%/30%.

a. Their bases after the debts are incurred are as follows:

	Sophie	Fatima
Beginning basis	$ 64,000	$47,000
Recourse debt allocation	50,000	-0-
Nonrecourse debt allocation	56,000	24,000
Ending basis	$170,000	$71,000

b. If $30,000 of the nonrecourse debt is paid back next year, then their bases are decreased because this is treated as a cash distribution to them. The bases are decreased using the profit-sharing ratios.

	Sophie	Fatima
Beginning basis	$170,000	$71,000
Nonrecourse debt reduction of $30,000	(21,000)	(9,000)
Ending basis	$149,000	$62,000

Related exercises: Discussion Question 4
Multiple Choice Questions 6, 7
Application Problems 6, 7

Temporary Benefit of Debt Basis

As mentioned above, debt basis provides several benefits to partners including the ability to flow more losses through to the taxpayer's return. For example, assume that Hai's basis in her partnership interest is $10,000, and it is then increased by $50,000 due to debt basis. Her total

[15] Treas. Reg. §1.752-3.

basis is now $60,000. In Year 1, her share of the partnership loss is $25,000 and in Year 2, her share is $35,000. These losses reduce her basis to $0 as shown below:

Beginning basis	$10,000
Debt basis	50,000
Total basis before losses	$60,000
Year 1 loss	(25,000)
Year 2 loss	(35,000)
Basis at end of Year 2	$ 0

Although Hai has received tax benefits from $60,000 of losses, Hai invested only $10,000 in the partnership. Therefore, only $10,000 of her tax benefits are permanent. The tax benefits from the $50,000 of losses that Hai deducted because of the debt basis are temporary, meaning that Hai will recognize $50,000 of gain in the future to offset these losses. Hai could recognize the additional $50,000 of gain for several different reasons, including:

- Hai could sell her partnership interest for no consideration except that the buyer assumes her $50,000 partnership debt. The debt relief will result in an amount realized of $50,000. Because Hai now has no basis in her partnership interest, her recognized gain would be $50,000.
- The partnership could pay the debt back to the creditor. This would be treated as a $50,000 cash distribution to Hai. You will learn in more detail in Chapter 7 that this would create $50,000 gain for Hai because the cash distributed would exceed her basis by $50,000.

The temporary nature of the tax benefit from debt basis does not necessarily mean that debt basis is not an advantage for partnerships. The magnitude of the advantage depends on how much time passes before the additional $50,000 gain is recognized. If debt basis allows an additional $50,000 loss to be recognized now but the $50,000 gain does not materialize for many years, then this is a significant benefit. However, if the $50,000 gain is recognized within a couple of years of the loss, then the advantage is not as much. The main point for you to remember from this discussion is that the tax benefits from debt basis are *temporary*, because many taxpayers believe they are *permanent*.

Related exercise: Tax Planning Problem 1

PRACTICE PROBLEM 6.3.1
Liability Assumed by Partnership

June is a 15% partner in April Partnership and contributed property with an adjusted basis of $120,000, fair market value of $143,000, and a liability attached of $75,000 that April assumed. What is the effect on June's basis in the partnership?

SOLUTION

June's basis is first increased by $120,000 for the basis of the property contributed, and then is decreased by $75,000 for the debt assumption. However, because the partnership debt increased by $75,000 and June is allocated 15% of the debt, her basis is increased by $11,250 ($75,000 × 15%). The net effect on June's basis for the debt assumption is a decrease of $63,750 ($75,000 – $11,250) reflecting that she shifted 85% of the responsibility of the debt to the other partners.

June's basis in property contributed	$120,000
Step 1: Decrease for debt partnership assumed ($75,000)	(75,000)
Step 2: Increase for June's share of the new partnership debt ($75,000 × 15%)	11,250
Change in June's basis due to contribution	$ 56,250

PRACTICE PROBLEM 6.3.2
Liability Assumption Effect on Basis

Cho owns 80% of the CA Partnership as a general partner and Aki owns 20% as a limited partner. At the beginning of the year, Cho's basis in his partnership interest is $44,000 and Aki's basis is $33,000. During the year, the partnership secures new recourse debt of $18,000 and new nonrecourse debt of $32,000. Assume that Cho and Aki also share profits and losses 80%/20%. Compute their bases in their partnership interests after the debt is incurred.

SOLUTION

You cannot allocate any of the recourse debt to Aki because he is a limited partner. Therefore, 100% of the recourse debt is allocated to Cho because he is the only general partner. You can allocate the nonrecourse debt to both partners, and it is allocated using the profit-sharing ratio of 80%/20%.

Their bases after the debts are incurred are as follows:

	Cho	Aki
Beginning basis	$44,000	$33,000
Recourse debt allocation	18,000	-0-
Nonrecourse debt allocation	25,600	6,400
Ending basis	$87,600	$39,400

INTERACTIVE SELF-SCORING QUIZZES

6.4 Taxation of Partnership Income and Guaranteed Payments

LEARNING OBJECTIVE 4

Compute the ordinary business income or loss and separately stated items for a partnership.

VIDEO CONTENT

Single taxation of income is one of the major advantages of partnerships. Referring back to the chapter introduction, Aletta will need to understand how and when the partnership income is taxable to her if she decides to form a partnership. In this section, you will learn how the flow-through rules for partnerships, combined with the basis rules, ensure that partnership income is taxed only once.

Timing of Income to Partners

As shown in **Illustration 6.4**, partnership income is reported on Form 1065, U.S. Return of Partnership Income, and the income flows through to the partners on the last day of the partnership tax year, regardless of whether it has been distributed, on the partner's Schedule K-1 (Form 1065). Partnership returns are due on the 15th day of the third month after year-end, which is March 15 for calendar-year partnerships. A six-month extension is available until September 15.

ILLUSTRATION 6.4 Timing of Flow-Through to Partners

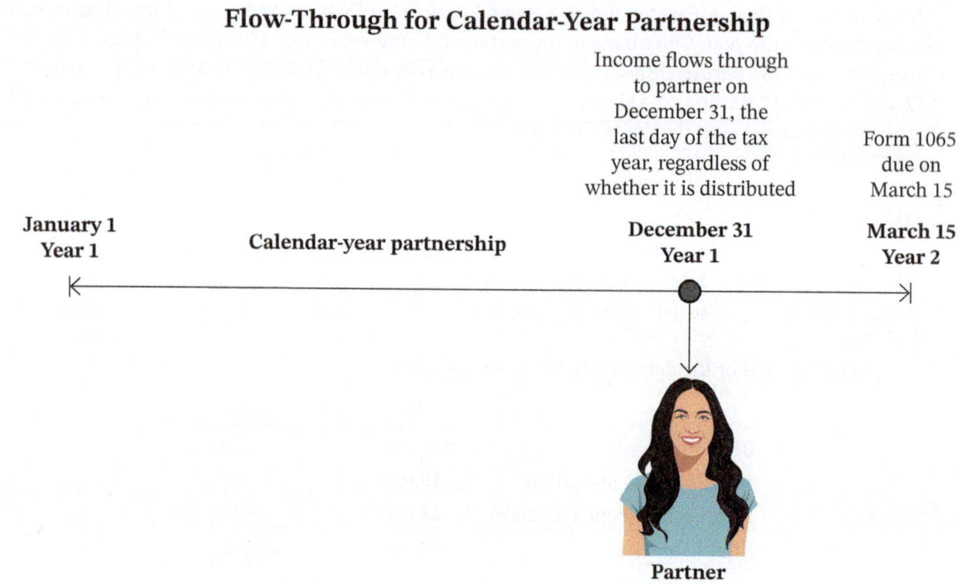

There are two situations where the tax year will close with respect to a partner before the end of the tax year. Both situations result in the partnership share of income flowing through to the partner before the last day of the partnership's tax year:

1. A partner who sells their *entire* interest in the partnership has their tax year close on the sale date.
2. A deceased partner's partnership tax year closes as of date of death.

The following Example demonstrates the timing of the flow-through when a partner dies.

EXAMPLE 6.4.1
Death of a Partner

Sophie is a one-third partner in the NIU Partnership that uses a calendar year-end. Sophie died on April 30, Year 9. She bequeaths her one-third interest in the partnership to her son. The partnership's ordinary business income is $360,000 for Year 9. How and when is this income reported to Sophie and her son?

SOLUTION

One-third of the partnership income is $120,000 ($360,000 × 1/3). The partnership year closes with respect to Sophie on April 30, the date of her death. On that date, a pro rata share of income flows to her and will be reported on her final Form 1040. Her share of the income is $40,000 ($120,000/12 months × 4 months). Her son's income flows to him on the last day of the partnership year which is December 31. His share of the income is $80,000 ($120,000/12 months × 8 months).

Guaranteed Payments

Partners who work for the partnership are not considered to be employees. Therefore, they do not receive a salary; rather their compensation is known as a **guaranteed payment**. A guaranteed payment is not based on the income of the partnership. Guaranteed payments can also be received for the use of capital owned by the partner, such as a building. Here are a few characteristics of guaranteed payments:

- Guaranteed payments are ordinary income to the partner.
- The guaranteed payment is deemed to flow to the partner on the last day of the partnership tax year regardless of when payment was actually made[16]

[16]IRC §706(a).

- Guaranteed payments received for services, but not capital, are subject to self-employment taxes.
- Guaranteed payments are reported to the partner on Schedule K-1 (Form 1065).
- Guaranteed payments are an ordinary deduction to the partnership, and as such, are reported on page 1 of Form 1065. Therefore, the payments reduce each partner's distributive share of ordinary business income.

Why **Why can't a partner be an employee of a partnership?** The theory that governs most of partnership taxation is the aggregate theory. The **aggregate theory** holds that the partnership does not exist as a separate entity from the partners. That is, a partnership is simply an aggregation of the partners. To determine the tax result of a partnership transaction using the aggregate theory, you should ask what the result would be if the partnership did not exist. The aggregate theory is visualized in **Illustration 6.5**, showing that the partnership is just an aggregation of the partners. We also show the visualization of the entity theory, which is the theory used by C corporations and for most S corporation transactions. The **entity theory** holds that a business is a distinct entity from its owners. Thus, any time that cash or property passes between the entity and the owners, there are potential tax consequences.

> **Potential Pitfall**
>
> When will a partner receive a Form W-2, Wage and Tax Statement, from a partnership? The answer is never. However, this is a frequent mistake made by partnerships. Employers issue W-2s to employees but a partner is not an employee. A partner's distributive share and guaranteed payments are reported to the partner on Schedule K-1 (Form 1065).

ILLUSTRATION 6.5 Aggregate Theory vs. Entity Theory

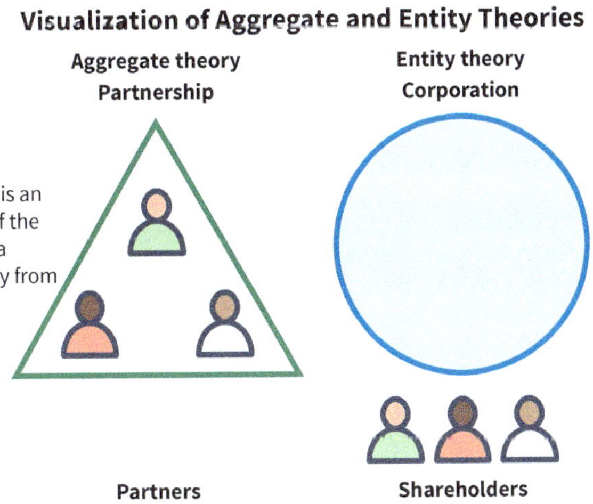

Under the aggregate theory, the partner cannot be an employee of the partnership because the partnership is assumed not to exist separate from the partners. On the other hand, shareholders of C corporations and S corporations can be employees because they are considered to be distinct entities from the business.

EXAMPLE 6.4.2
Guaranteed Payments

Tori is a 20% partner in the LU Partnership. She provides consulting services for the partnership and the partnership has agreed to pay her $80,000 per year in addition to her 20% profit share. LU is a cash-basis taxpayer that had a December 31 year-end. LU had cash flow problems during Year 1 and did not pay Tori her guaranteed payment until January 31 of Year 2.

a. Will Tori be taxed on the $80,000 guaranteed payment in Year 1 or Year 2? On what day will the income flow to her?

b. What would your answers be if the partnership reported on the accrual basis?

SOLUTION

a. LU is a cash-basis taxpayer, so the guaranteed payment is reported on the partnership tax return for Year 2, the year that it was paid. Therefore, it flows to Tori on the last day of Year 2, which is December 31, Year 2. Tori will report the $80,000 guaranteed payment on her Year 2 Form 1040. It will also be subject to self-employment tax for Year 2.

b. If LU is an accrual-basis taxpayer, then the guaranteed payment is reported on the partnership tax return for Year 1, because it was incurred in Year 1. It does not matter when the $80,000 is paid because LU accrued the expense in Year 1. Therefore, it flows to Tori on the last day of the year, which is December 31, Year 1, and is included on her Year 1 tax return.

Related exercises: Discussion Question 5
Multiple Choice Question 8
Brief Exercise 6
Tax Planning Problem 2

Spotlight on the Law

Guaranteed Payments in Relation to the QBI Deduction

The tax law has long focused on reasonable compensation for officers for a corporation. However, only recently have guaranteed payments been discussed in detail for partners in a partnership. The Tax Cuts and Jobs Act (TCJA), P.L. 115-97, added IRC §199A, which allows an individual a qualified business income (QBI) deduction on income from pass-through entities. However, under IRC §199A(c)(4)(B), a guaranteed payment (GP) is not allowed when calculating the QBI deduction. Because the guaranteed payment is allowed as a deduction for the partnership in calculating ordinary business income (OBI), this dollar amount, therefore, reduces the tax benefit of the partner's QBI deduction.

For example, Jamie is a surgical podiatrist in a successful group medical practice operating as a partnership. She files married filing jointly with her spouse. The partnership has ordinary business income (OBI) of $500,000 divided evenly among four partners which includes a $70,000 guaranteed payment to Jamie. Under this scenario (without regard to any other limitation included in §199A), Jamie would realize taxable income of $195,000 ($125,000 OBI + $70,000 GP), but the QBI would only be $125,000 with a corresponding $25,000 ($125,000 ×20%) QBI deduction on her individual tax return.

What if instead Jamie receives $70,000 as a priority profit allocation distribution based on allocation of profits and not as a guaranteed payment? The partnership does not receive a deduction for the guaranteed payment so the OBI is $570,000 ($500,000 + $70,000). Jamie would receive the first $70,000 as a priority profit allocation distribution with the remaining $500,000 would be divided evenly among the four partners ($125,000 to each). Jamie would still receive $195,000 of taxable income but would now have $195,000 of QBI with a corresponding $39,000 ($195,000 × 20%) QBI deduction on her individual tax return.

In order to be certain that the priority profit allocation is not considered a guaranteed payment, the partnership agreement should be amended to remove this wording and insert priority profit allocation. Under IRC §761(c), a partnership may amend its partnership agreement, but it must be timely to be effective. Another item to consider is whether the partnership will have enough profits each year to make the priority profit allocation. If the partnership has a loss, there will be no priority profit allocation so this is a risk for Jamie if the partnership amends the partnership agreement.

Fringe Benefits for Partners

Because partners are generally not considered to be employees, the value of most fringe benefits that are tax-free to employees is taxable to partners. For example, the following common fringe benefits are taxable if a partnership pays this for the benefit of a partner:

- Premium for $50,000 of group-term life insurance
- Premiums or benefits under an employer accident or health plan
- Value of meals and lodging provided for the convenience of the employer
- Benefits under a cafeteria plan

The cost of a partner's fringe benefits paid by the partnership are deductible by the partnership as guaranteed payments and must be included as ordinary income to the partner on Schedule K-1 (Form 1065). The partner can deduct the cost of premiums paid for health insurance by the partnership as a deduction for AGI if the other requirements for this deduction are satisfied (such as the partner and partner's spouse are not eligible to participate in an employer-subsidized health insurance plan).

There are a few fringe benefits that partners can exclude from income, including:

- Educational assistance plans
- Dependent care assistance plans
- Qualified employee discounts
- Working condition fringe benefits
- No additional cost services
- *De minimis* benefits

Character of Partnership Tax Items

The character of partnership tax items is determined at the partnership level. **Recall** from Chapter 1, LO2, Fundamentals of Property Transactions, that the character of tax gains and losses will be *either*:

- Ordinary income or loss,
- Section 1231 gain or loss, *or*
- Capital gain or loss.

Once the tax character is determined at the partnership level, the character stays the same when it flows from the partnership to the partners.[17] We illustrate this concept in the following Example.

EXAMPLE 6.4.3 Character of Partnership Items

Theron purchases a 10% partnership interest on October 1 of the current tax year. The partnership has been in existence for 10 years. On December 10 of the current year, the partnership sells stock in Exxon corporation that it has owned for three years and has a long-term capital gain (LTCG) of $80,000. How much of the gain flows to Theron, and what will be the character of the gain for Theron?

SOLUTION

10% of the gain flows to Theron for the 91 days (October 2–December 31) he owns his partnership interest or $1,995 ($80,000 × 10% × 91/365). The partnership will report this to Theron as LTCG even though he has been a partner for less than three months at the time the stock was sold. The LTCG character is determined at the partnership level, and the character stays the same when it flows through to Theron.

[17] IRC §702.

The tax items that comprise partnership income or loss are divided into two categories: *separately stated items* and *nonseparately stated items*. **Separately stated items** are tax items that could potentially impact partners' tax liabilities in different ways. Some of the more common separately stated items and the reason they are separately stated are as follows:

- Net capital gains and losses, because the partner must net the partnership capital gains and losses with other capital gains and loss reported on the partner's tax return.
- Section 1231 gains and losses, because the partner must net the partnership Section 1231 gains and losses with other Section 1231 gains and losses on the partner's tax return.
- Other types of investment income, such as dividends and interest, because partners need these amounts to compute net investment income for various purposes.
- Charitable contributions, because individual partners must apply various limitations to determine their charitable contribution deduction, such as the 60% of AGI limit for cash contributions.
- Section 179 expense, because partners are limited in the amount of Section 179 expense that they can deduct in any given year.

Other separately stated items are shown on Schedule K-1 (see **Illustration 6.6**; we use the 2024 Schedule K-1 because it was the most recent form available at the time of publication).

Any items of income or loss not separately stated are reported on page 1 of Form 1065, U.S. Return of Partnership Income (see **Illustration 6.7**; we use the 2024 Form 1065 because it was the most recent form available at the time of publication) as **nonseparately stated items**. These are items characterized as ordinary income or loss and that have no special rules that need to be applied at the partner level. The full Form 1065 is shown in Appendix B.

ILLUSTRATION 6.6 Schedule K-1 (Form 1065)

DOWNLOAD DOCUMENTS & TEMPLATES

651123

☐ Final K-1 ☐ Amended K-1 OMB No. 1545-0123

Schedule K-1 (Form 1065) **2024**
Department of the Treasury
Internal Revenue Service

For calendar year 2024, or tax year

beginning / / 2024 ending / /

Partner's Share of Income, Deductions, Credits, etc. **See separate instructions.**

Part I Information About the Partnership

A Partnership's employer identification number

B Partnership's name, address, city, state, and ZIP code

C IRS center where partnership filed return:

D ☐ Check if this is a publicly traded partnership (PTP)

Part II Information About the Partner

E Partner's SSN or TIN (Do not use TIN of a disregarded entity. See instructions.)

F Name, address, city, state, and ZIP code for partner entered in E. See instructions.

G ☐ General partner or LLC member-manager ☐ Limited partner or other LLC member

H1 ☐ Domestic partner ☐ Foreign partner

H2 ☐ If the partner is a disregarded entity (DE), enter the partner's:

TIN ______ Name ______

I1 What type of entity is this partner? ______

I2 If this partner is a retirement plan (IRA/SEP/Keogh/etc.), check here . ☐

J Partner's share of profit, loss, and capital (see instructions):

	Beginning	Ending
Profit	%	%
Loss	%	%
Capital	%	%

Check if decrease is due to:

☐ Sale or ☐ Exchange of partnership interest. See instructions.

K1 Partner's share of liabilities:

	Beginning	Ending
Nonrecourse . .	$	$
Qualified nonrecourse financing . . .	$	$
Recourse . . .	$	$

K2 Check this box if item K1 includes liability amounts from lower-tier partnerships ☐

K3 Check if any of the above liability is subject to guarantees or other payment obligations by the partner. See instructions . . . . . ☐

L **Partner's Capital Account Analysis**

Beginning capital account . . . . $ ______

Capital contributed during the year . . $ ______

Current year net income (loss) . . . $ ______

Other increase (decrease) (attach explanation) $ ______

Withdrawals and distributions . . . $ (______)

Ending capital account . . . . $ ______

M Did the partner contribute property with a built-in gain (loss)?

☐ **Yes** ☐ **No** If "Yes," attach statement. See instructions.

N **Partner's Share of Net Unrecognized Section 704(c) Gain or (Loss)**

Beginning . . . . $ ______

Ending . . . . $ ______

Part III Partner's Share of Current Year Income, Deductions, Credits, and Other Items

1 Ordinary business income (loss)

2 Net rental real estate income (loss)

3 Other net rental income (loss)

4a Guaranteed payments for services

4b Guaranteed payments for capital

4c Total guaranteed payments

5 Interest income

6a Ordinary dividends

6b Qualified dividends

6c Dividend equivalents

7 Royalties

8 Net short-term capital gain (loss)

9a Net long-term capital gain (loss)

9b Collectibles (28%) gain (loss)

9c Unrecaptured section 1250 gain

10 Net section 1231 gain (loss)

11 Other income (loss)

12 Section 179 deduction

13 Other deductions

14 Self-employment earnings (loss)

15 Credits

16 Schedule K-3 is attached if checked . . . . . ☐

17 Alternative minimum tax (AMT) items

18 Tax-exempt income and nondeductible expenses

19 Distributions

20 Other information

21 Foreign taxes paid or accrued

22 ☐ More than one activity for at-risk purposes*

23 ☐ More than one activity for passive activity purposes*

*See attached statement for additional information.

For IRS Use Only

For Paperwork Reduction Act Notice, see the Instructions for Form 1065. www.irs.gov/Form1065 Cat. No. 11394R **Schedule K-1 (Form 1065) 2024**

ILLUSTRATION 6.7 Form 1065, U.S. Return of Partnership Income

DOWNLOAD DOCUMENTS & TEMPLATES

Form **1065**

Department of the Treasury
Internal Revenue Service

U.S. Return of Partnership Income

For calendar year 2024, or tax year beginning ________, 2024, ending ________, 20 ___.

Go to *www.irs.gov/Form1065* for instructions and the latest information.

OMB No. 1545-0123

2024

	Type or Print		
A Principal business activity		Name of partnership	D Employer identification number
B Principal product or service		Number, street, and room or suite no. If a P.O. box, see instructions.	E Date business started
C Business code number		City or town, state or province, country, and ZIP or foreign postal code	F Total assets (see instructions) $

G Check applicable boxes: **(1)** ☐ Initial return **(2)** ☐ Final return **(3)** ☐ Name change **(4)** ☐ Address change **(5)** ☐ Amended return

H Check accounting method: **(1)** ☐ Cash **(2)** ☐ Accrual **(3)** ☐ Other (specify): ________

I Number of Schedules K-1. Attach one for each person who was a partner at any time during the tax year: ________

J Check if Schedules C and M-3 are attached . . . ☐

K Check if partnership: **(1)** ☐ Aggregated activities for section 465 at-risk purposes **(2)** ☐ Grouped activities for section 469 passive activity purposes

Caution: Include **only** trade or business income and expenses on lines 1a through 23 below. See instructions for more information.

Income	1a	Gross receipts or sales ________ **b** Less returns and allowances ________ **c** Balance	1c	
	2	Cost of goods sold (attach Form 1125-A)	2	
	3	Gross profit. Subtract line 2 from line 1c	3	
	4	Ordinary income (loss) from other partnerships, estates, and trusts (attach statement)	4	
	5	Net farm profit (loss) (attach Schedule F (Form 1040))	5	
	6	Net gain (loss) from Form 4797, Part II, line 17 (attach Form 4797)	6	
	7	Other income (loss) (attach statement)	7	
	8	**Total income (loss).** Combine lines 3 through 7	8	
Deductions (see instructions for limitations)	9	Salaries and wages (other than to partners) (less employment credits)	9	
	10	Guaranteed payments to partners	10	
	11	Repairs and maintenance	11	
	12	Bad debts	12	
	13	Rent	13	
	14	Taxes and licenses	14	
	15	Interest (see instructions)	15	
	16a	Depreciation (if required, attach Form 4562) — 16a		
	b	Less depreciation reported on Form 1125-A and elsewhere on return — 16b	16c	
	17	Depletion **(Do not deduct oil and gas depletion.)**	17	
	18	Retirement plans, etc.	18	
	19	Employee benefit programs	19	
	20	Energy efficient commercial buildings deduction (attach Form 7205)	20	
	21	Other deductions (attach statement)	21	
	22	**Total deductions.** Add the amounts shown in the far right column for lines 9 through 21	22	
	23	**Ordinary business income (loss).** Subtract line 22 from line 8	23	
Tax and Payment	24	Interest due under the look-back method—completed long-term contracts (attach Form 8697)	24	
	25	Interest due under the look-back method—income forecast method (attach Form 8866)	25	
	26	BBA AAR imputed underpayment (see instructions)	26	
	27	Other taxes (see instructions)	27	
	28	**Total balance due.** Add lines 24 through 27	28	
	29	Elective payment election amount from Form 3800	29	
	30	Payment (see instructions)	30	
	31	**Amount owed.** If the sum of line 29 and line 30 is smaller than line 28, enter amount owed	31	
	32	**Overpayment.** If the sum of line 29 and line 30 is larger than line 28, enter overpayment	32	

Sign Here

Under penalties of perjury, I declare that I have examined this return, including accompanying schedules and statements, and to the best of my knowledge and belief, it is true, correct, and complete. Declaration of preparer (other than partner or limited liability company member) is based on all information of which preparer has any knowledge.

Signature of partner or limited liability company member | Date

May the IRS discuss this return with the preparer shown below? See instructions. ☐ **Yes** ☐ **No**

Paid Preparer Use Only				
Print/Type preparer's name	Preparer's signature	Date	Check ☐ if self-employed	PTIN
Firm's name			Firm's EIN	
Firm's address			Phone no.	

For Paperwork Reduction Act Notice, see separate instructions. Cat. No. 11390Z Form **1065** (2024)

For the remaining discussion, we refer to the nonseparately stated items as the *bucket items*, to emphasize that these items are all mixed together, or netted, and result in one measure known as the **ordinary business income or loss** for the partnership. The bucket items include wages, depreciation, supplies, and the other items shown in **Illustration 6.8**.

Related exercises: Discussion Question 6
Multiple Choice Questions 9, 10, 11
Brief Exercises 7, 8, 9

ILLUSTRATION 6.8 Taxation of Partnership Income

Reporting of Partnership Tax Items

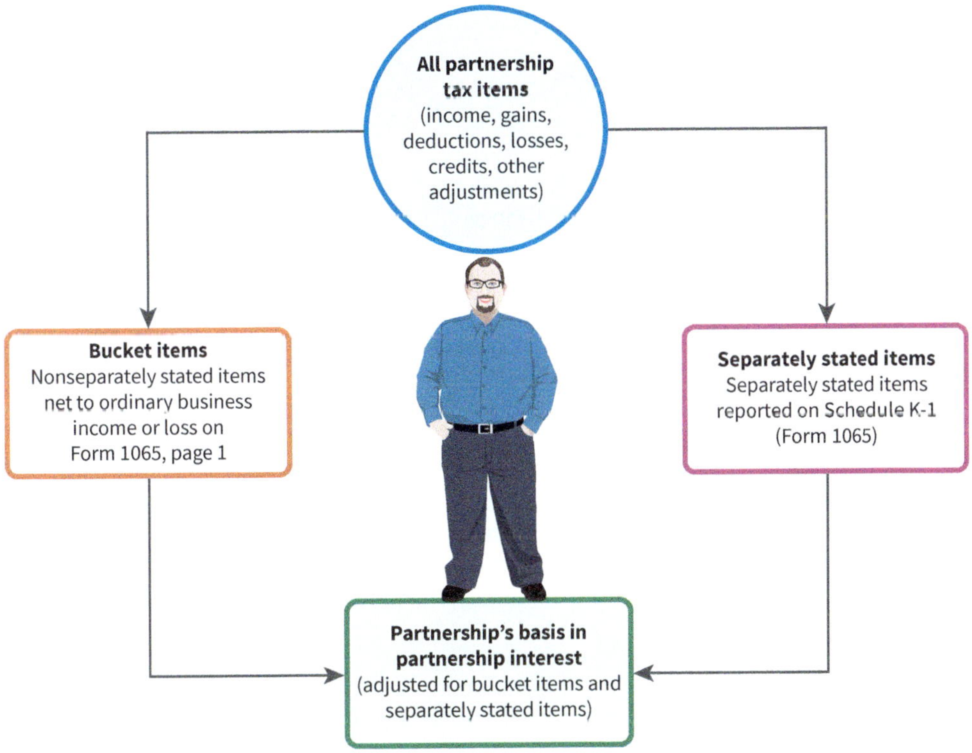

The separation of partnership tax items between the bucket and the separately stated items is shown in the next Example.

EXAMPLE 6.4.4
Partnership Partner's Income

Crackle, Inc., is a partnership that has four partners. Benjamin owns 25% of Crackle. He also works at Crackle, and Crackle pays him $60,000 per year for his services as a guaranteed payment. The following items were reported on Crackle's Form 1065 this year:

Gross receipts less cost of goods sold	$1,700,000
Interest income	$ 13,000
Net long-term capital gain	$ 28,000
Salaries and wages	$ 385,000
Guaranteed payment	$ 60,000
Repairs and maintenance	$ 43,000
Net Section 1231 loss	$ 41,000
Rent expense	$ 117,000
Charitable contributions	$ 42,000
Advertising	$ 38,000
Interest expense	$ 26,000
Depreciation	$ 61,000
Section 179 expense	$ 59,000

How would these amounts be reported on Benjamin's Schedule K-1, and how would his guaranteed payment be reported to him?

SOLUTION

We begin by splitting these tax items into the bucket items and the separately stated items and using the bucket items to compute ordinary business income:

Bucket items		Separately stated items	
Gross receipts less cost of goods sold	$1,700,000	Interest income	$13,000
Less: Salaries and wages	(385,000)	Net LTCG	$28,000
Repairs and maintenance	(43,000)	Net Section 1231 loss	$41,000
Rent expense	(117,000)	Charitable contributions	$42,000
Advertising	(38,000)	Section 179 expense	$59,000
Interest expense	(26,000)		
Guaranteed payment	(60,000)		
Depreciation	(61,000)		
Ordinary business income	$ 970,000		

Crackle's ordinary business income is $970,000. Benjamin's Schedule K-1 would reflect 25% of the ordinary business income and each separately stated item, as follows:

	Total	Benjamin's allocation (25%)
Ordinary business income	$970,000	$242,500
Interest income	$ 13,000	$ 3,250
Net long-term capital gain	$ 28,000	$ 7,000
Net Section 1231 loss	$ 41,000	$ 10,250
Charitable contributions	$ 42,000	$ 10,500
Section 179 expense	$ 59,000	$ 14,750

Benjamin's guaranteed payment of $60,000 would be reported to him on his Schedule K-1 (Form 1065) from Crackle.

Basis in Partnership Interest and Capital Account

A partner's initial basis in their partnership interest is determined based on how the interest was acquired. If a partner receives a partnership interest as part of a tax-deferred partnership formation, the partner's basis is equal to the cash plus basis of the property the partner contributed to the partnership. If the partner bought the partnership interest, then they will have a cost basis.

A partner's basis in their partnership interest represents their investment in the partnership for tax purposes and is a culmination of their contributions, distributions, and their distributive share of partnership income and losses. A partner's basis is sometimes referred to as their **outside basis** in the partnership, and it is used to:

- Compute the partner's gain or loss on the sale of their partnership interest,
- Determine the tax consequences of distributions to the partner as well as the partner's tax basis in assets distributed to them, *and*
- Determine the amount of partnership loss that can be deducted on the partner's tax return.

Potential Pitfall

A partner's basis in the partnership interest can never be *negative*.

Basis Computation

Partners adjust their outside basis for partnership transactions each year, as follows:

- Outside basis is *increased* by a partner's proportionate share of:
  1. Income and gains,
  2. Tax-exempt income, *and*
  3. Increases in partnership debt.
- Outside basis is *decreased* by a partner's proportionate share of:
  1. Expenses and losses,
  2. Nondeductible expenses that are not capital expenditures, *and*
  3. Decreases in partnership debt.

The partner's proportionate share of these items is reported to the partner on their Schedule K-1 and they flow to the partner on the last day of the partnership year. The basis increase for the partner's share of income ensures that the income will not be taxed again when it is distributed to the partner. It is the partner's basis that prevents the double taxation of partnership income, as shown in the next Example.

EXAMPLE 6.4.5
Single Taxation for Partners

Micah and Taylor are each 50% partners in the MT partnership which has a calendar year-end. They organized the partnership this year by each contributing cash of $40,000. MT has ordinary business income of $68,000 this year. Micah receives a cash distribution of $33,000 from MT on December 20. How is this income reported to Micah, what are her tax consequences, and what is the basis in her partnership interest at the end of the tax year?

SOLUTION

The tax consequences of these events are as follows:

- Micah's initial basis in her partnership interest is $40,000 when the partnership is formed.
- $34,000 ($68,000 × 50%) of ordinary business income is reported to Micah on her Schedule K-1.
- Micah reports the $34,000 of income on Schedule E, page 2 of her Form 1040.
- Her basis in her partnership interest is increased for the $34,000 of income to $74,000 ($40,000 + $34,000). This basis increase ensures that she will not be taxed on the $34,000 again when it is distributed to her.
- The $33,000 distribution is not taxable to Micah, and it reduces the basis of her partnership interest to $41,000 ($74,000 − $33,000).

Order of Adjustments to Basis in Partnership Interest

At the end of the tax year, the partners' bases in their partnership interests are adjusted in the following order:[18]

- First, contributions to capital increase the partner's adjusted basis. Recall that increases in the partner's share of partnership liabilities are treated as cash contributions.
- Second, the partner's share of income, including tax-exempt income, increases the partner's adjusted basis.
- Third, distributions to the partner from the partnership decrease the partner's adjusted basis. Recall that decreases in the partner's share of partnership liabilities are treated as cash distributions.
- Fourth, the partner's share of loss (including nondeductible expenses) decreases the partner's adjusted basis.

[18] Treas. Reg. §1.704-1(d)(2).

Illustration 6.9 details the computation of a partner's basis and shows the order that adjustments are taken into account. Distributions and losses can never reduce a partner's basis below zero. Loss allocations that exceed the partner's basis are suspended and carried forward to future tax years. Cash distributions that exceed a partner's basis in their partnership interest create gain to the partner equal to the excess.

ILLUSTRATION 6.9 Basis in Partnership Interest Computation

Ordering Rules for Basis in Partnership Interest Adjustments		
Initial basis		
Plus:	Additional contributions	
	Partner's share of increase in partnership liabilities	
	Partner's share of:	Ordinary business income
		Separately stated income items
		Tax-exempt income
Less:	Cash distributions	
	Basis of property distributed	
	Partner's share of decrease in partnership liabilities	
	Partner's share of:	Nondeductible expenses
		Ordinary business loss
		Separately stated expenses and loss items
Adjusted basis		

Related exercises: Discussion Question 7
Multiple Choice Question 12
Application Problems 8, 9, 10, 11, 12

Capital Interest in Partnership

A partner's **capital account** represents the liquidation proceeds that a partner should receive when the partnership liquidates. Therefore, the capital account should reflect the fair market value of the partner's interest in the partnership. We compute basis and capital account in a similar fashion, *except*:

- Liabilities of the partnership do not affect the capital account, *and*
- The capital account is adjusted by the fair market value of assets contributed and assets distributed, whereas the basis in the partnership interest is adjusted by the tax basis of these assets.

The next Example illustrates the differences in the computations of basis and capital account.

EXAMPLE 6.4.6
Basis in Partnership Interest vs. Capital Account

Luis contributes land with an adjusted basis of $35,000 and fair market value of $80,000 for a 40% interest in the Play Partnership. The partnership borrows $100,000 from Trust Bank and Luis's share of the debt is 40%. What is Luis's basis in his partnership interest and the balance in his capital account after these transactions?

SOLUTION

Luis's tax basis and capital account are computed as follows:

	Tax basis	Capital account
Land contribution	$35,000	$80,000
Trust loan	40,000	N/A
Ending amount	$75,000	$80,000

To understand partnership taxation, it is imperative to recognize that the tax basis and capital account are two separate accounting systems. For every transaction that a partnership has, you must determine whether an accounting entry is needed for each system. For example, the journal entries for the partnership in Example 6.4.6 would be as follows for the land contribution:

Tax basis			**Capital account**		
Land	$35,000		Land	$80,000	
Luis, Tax basis		$35,000	Luis, Capital account		$80,000

Tax basis financial statements can be generated for partnerships, as well as financial statements based on the capital account reporting rules.

Related exercises: Brief Exercise 10
Application Problem 13

PRACTICE PROBLEM 6.4.1
Identification of Bucket Items and Separately Stated Items

Identify the following as either bucket items (BI) or separately stated items (SSI):

a. Advertising expense
b. Sales revenue
c. Charitable contributions
d. Section 1231 gains
e. Dividend income
f. Rent expense
g. Depreciation expense
h. Section 179 expense

SOLUTION

a. Advertising expense—BI
b. Sales revenue—BI
c. Charitable contributions—SSI
d. Section 1231 gains—SSI
e. Dividend income—SSI
f. Rent expense—BI
g. Depreciation expense—BI
h. Section 179 expense—SSI

PRACTICE PROBLEM 6.4.2
Calculating Ending Basis in a Partnership

Tully is a 25% general partner in TKGL Partnership. Tully's beginning basis is $18,000, and TKGL has the following tax items for the current year:

Ordinary business loss	$50,000
Municipal interest income	$ 1,200
Interest income	$ 1,000
Section 1231 gain	$ 5,000

Tully received a distribution of $4,000 during the year. TKGL's debt increased by $10,000 this year. What is Tully's ending basis?

SOLUTION

We compute Tully's basis as follows, using the ordering rules discussed above (income, distributions, losses):

Beginning basis	$18,000	
Plus: Municipal interest income	300	($1,200 × 25%)
Plus: Interest income	250	($1,000 × 25%)
Plus: Section 1231 gain	1,250	($5,000 × 25%)
Plus: Increase in debt	2,500	($10,000 × 25%)
Available basis	$22,300	
Less: Distributions	(4,000)	
Available basis	$18,300	
Less: Ordinary business loss	(12,500)	($50,000 × 25%)
Ending basis	$ 5,800	

INTERACTIVE SELF-SCORING QUIZZES

6.5 Use of Partnership Losses

LEARNING OBJECTIVE 5

Determine the partner's share of partnership losses that can be currently deducted and that is suspended.

VIDEO CONTENT

We discussed in LO4, Taxation of Partnership Income and Guaranteed Payments, that a partner can deduct their share of partnership losses only to the extent of the partner's basis in their partnership interest. There are additional hurdles that the loss may have to clear before being deducted in the current year, as follows:

- Basis hurdle
- At-risk hurdle
- Passive loss hurdle (if the loss is a passive loss)
- Limitation on business losses for individuals

While Aletta from the chapter introduction plans to have profits, her business may have losses in some years. If that is the case, and she has organized her business as a partnership, the loss will be deductible by her only if she meets the rules described in this section.

Basis Hurdle

Recall that basis represents the amount that a partner has invested in an asset. The **basis hurdle** limits the amount of losses and deductions that a partner can deduct related to a particular investment to the partner's tax basis. Losses in excess of basis can be carried forward and used in future years when the partner has sufficient basis in their partnership interest.

Why **Why does the basis hurdle limitation exist?** If a partner buys a depreciable asset for $10,000, then the maximum amount of loss that the partner can claim on the asset is $10,000. Basis can never be negative so a partner cannot recover more than the basis in their partnership interest. There are limited exceptions for which a taxpayer can recover more than their basis, such as percentage depletion and contribution of LTCG property to a qualified charitable organization.[19]

At-Risk Hurdle

The amount of the loss that clears the basis hurdle is next evaluated under the at-risk hurdle. The **at-risk hurdle** limits deductions incurred in a trade or business or in the production of income to the amount a partner has *at risk* in a partnership interest.

Defining At-Risk Amount

The at-risk rules apply to all trade or business activities and production of income activities for individuals. The at-risk amount is calculated using the following formula:[20]

1. The cash and adjusted basis of property contributed by the partner, *plus*
2. Liabilities for which the partner is personally liable (i.e., recourse debt).

[19]Treas. Reg. 1.613A-3(e)(1) and IRC §704(d)(3)(B).
[20]IRC §465.

Partners carry forward losses not deductible because of the at-risk amount indefinitely and are deducted when the at-risk amount has been increased.

At-Risk for Real Estate

Special rules exist for computing the at-risk amount for real estate activities.

- For real estate activities, a partner's amount at risk includes *qualified nonrecourse debt* secured by the real property used in the activity. A debt is **qualified nonrecourse debt** if it is borrowed from a lender engaged in the business of making loans (such as banks and savings and loan associations), provided that the lender is not the seller of the property, or a party related to either. Qualified nonrecourse debt also includes money borrowed from or guaranteed by any federal, state, or local government.
- Nonrecourse financing obtained from a qualified lender who has an equity interest in the venture is treated as an amount at-risk, if the terms of the financing are commercially reasonable.
- The nonrecourse financing must not be convertible into stock, and no person can be personally liable for repayment.

EXAMPLE 6.5.1
At-Risk Limitation

Wendy invested $60,000 cash and land in a general partnership that manufactures appliances this year for a 50% capital interest. On the investment date, the land had a fair market value of $20,000 and an adjusted basis of $12,000. At the end of the current tax year, the partnership has no income or loss, and it has recourse debt of $100,000. If the partnership does not pay the debt, Wendy is personally liable for 50% of it. The partnership also has $40,000 of nonrecourse debt.

a. What is Wendy's at-risk amount at the end of the tax year?

b. How would your answer change if the nonrecourse debt is qualified nonrecourse debt?

SOLUTION

a. We can compute Wendy's at-risk amount using the formula from above:

1. The cash ($60,000) and adjusted basis of property contributed by the partner ($12,000), *plus*
2. Liabilities for which the partner is personally liable ($100,000 × 50% = $50,000).

Because Wendy is not at risk for paying the nonrecourse debt, it does not increase her at-risk amount. Her at-risk amount is thus $122,000 ($60,000 + $12,000 + $50,000).

b. If the nonrecourse debt is qualified nonrecourse debt, then Wendy can increase her at-risk basis by $20,000 ($40,000 × 50%). Her at-risk amount is then $142,000 ($60,000 + $12,000 + $50,000 + $20,000).

Related exercises: Discussion Question 8
Brief Exercises 11, 12

Passive Loss Hurdle

The amount of loss that clears the at-risk hurdle is next evaluated under the passive loss rules if the loss is a passive loss. The passive loss must clear the **passive loss hurdle**, which means that the loss is deducted only to the extent of passive income. There are three baskets of income, as shown in **Illustration 6.10**: *passive, portfolio,* and *active*.

- **Passive income** is income earned by a profit-seeking activity in which the taxpayer does not materially participate in its management. If the loss is a passive loss, it can only offset passive income. Passive losses cannot offset active income or portfolio income.

- **Portfolio income** is investment income such as interest, dividends, annuities, and royalties that one does not derive from a trade or business, and capital gains from selling property that generates investment income.
- **Active income** is any income that is not passive income or portfolio income.

Related exercise: Discussion Question 9

ILLUSTRATION 6.10 The Three Baskets of Income

Material Participation

If a partner does not want a trade or business activity to be passive, they need to meet the **material participation** requirement. If a partner meets one of the following seven tests, they are considered to materially participate in an activity.[21] Limited partners can use only Tests 1, 5, and 6. We categorize these tests in **Illustration 6.11**.

1. The partner participates in the activity for more than 500 hours during the tax year.
2. The partner's activity is substantially all of the participation in such activity by all partners, including non-partners, for the tax year.
3. The partner participates in the activity for more than 100 hours during the tax year, and the participation is not less than any other partner's participation for the year.
4. The activity is a *significant participation activity*, and the partner's participation in all significant participation activities during the tax year exceeds 500 hours. A **significant participation activity** is any trade or business activity in which the partner participated for more than 100 hours during the year.
5. The partner materially participated in the activity for any five of the immediately preceding ten tax years.
6. The partner materially participated for any three preceding tax years in any personal service activity.
7. Based on all the facts and circumstances, the partner participates in the activity on a regular, continuous, and substantial basis during the tax year.

Related exercises: Multiple Choice Question 13
Application Problem 14

[21]Treas. Reg. §1.469-5T.

ILLUSTRATION 6.11 Material Participation Test

To materially participate in an activity, a partner must meet one of the following seven tests:
(*Limited partners can use only these three tests)

Current participation

*1. The partner participates in the activity for more than 500 hours during the tax year

2. The partner's activity is substantially all of the participation in such activity by all partners, including non-partners, for the tax year

3. The partner participates in the activity for more than 100 hours during the tax year, and the participation is not less than any other partner's participation in the activity for the year

4. The activity is a *significant participation activity* where the partner's participation exceeds 100 hours during the year, and the hours for all "significant participation activities" for the partner is greater than 500 hours for the tax year

Past participation

*5. The partner materially participated in the activity for any five of the immediately preceding ten taxable years

*6. The partner materially participated for any three preceding tax years in any personal service activity

Facts and circumstances

7. Based on the facts and circumstances, the partner participates in the activity on a regular, continuous, and substantial basis during the tax year

A limited partner has limited liability with regard to partnership debts and cannot participate in the management of the partnership. There is an exception to this rule for limited partners if the partner meets the 1st, 5th, or 6th material participation tests in Illustration 6.11 above. To meet these rules, the limited partner must have worked in the partnership for more than 500 hours in the current year or multiple years in the past, so this is a difficult threshold to meet because limited partners cannot manage the business.

EXAMPLE 6.5.2 Material Participation

Huey, Dewey, and Louie are general partners in the HDL Partnership that operates a marina in Missouri. This is Louie's second year as a partner. They worked the following hours this year in partnership activities:

Huey	1,400
Dewey	685
Louie	450

Which of the partners materially participated in the partnership?

SOLUTION

Huey and Dewey are material participants because each worked more than 500 hours in the partnership. Louie worked more than 100 hours, but the participation was not at least as much as any other individual. Louie is, therefore, not a material participant. The income and losses from HDL are active for Huey and Dewey but are passive for Louie.

Related exercises: Multiple Choice Question 14
Application Problem 15

Combining the Three Hurdles: Basis, At-Risk, and Passive Loss

Now that you understand the impact of the basis hurdle, at-risk hurdle, and passive loss hurdle on loss deductions, we'll demonstrate how these rules work together. If a passive loss flows through to an owner from a partnership or an LLC, it must clear all three of these hurdles before the owner can deduct the loss. There are two key rules for applying these hurdles to flow-through losses:

1. Losses must clear each hurdle in the specified order: basis, at-risk, and passive loss. Losses that do not clear a hurdle are suspended and carried forward to the future.
2. Losses must clear each hurdle only once and the losses do not have to clear all hurdles in the same year.

Illustration 6.12 depicts the ordering rule for clearing these hurdles. If the owner's basis in the partnership is less than their distributive share of the loss, then not all of the loss will clear the basis hurdle. If the at-risk rules and passive loss rules also limit the loss, then the amount of loss that the owner can deduct is reduced at each level. The loss that clears the passive loss hurdle is the loss that the taxpayer deducts on the return, assuming the excess business loss rule does not apply.

ILLUSTRATION 6.12 Loss Limitations

Hurdles for Partnership Losses

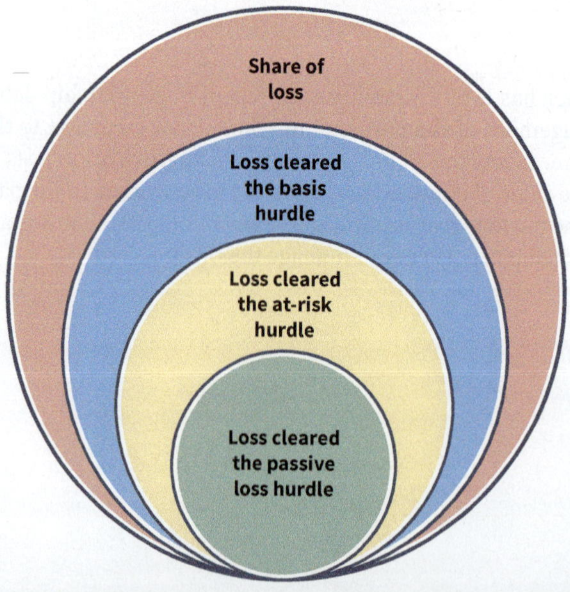

EXAMPLE 6.5.3
Loss Limitations

Jose's share of Partnership JAK's loss is $50,000. Other relevant tax information is as follows:

Basis in partnership interest	$ 40,000
At-risk amount	$ 35,000
Passive income	$ 20,000

a. How much loss from the partnership can Jose deduct on this year's tax return if the excess business loss rule (discussed below) does not apply?

b. For the losses that are suspended, what must occur in future years for them to be deducted?

SOLUTION

a. To determine the loss that can be deducted, we will apply the basis hurdle, at-risk hurdle, and passive loss hurdle in the correct order, as follows:

Basis hurdle: $40,000 of the loss clears the basis hurdle. The remaining $10,000 of the $50,000 loss is suspended at the basis level.

At-risk hurdle: $40,000 of the loss made it to the at-risk hurdle. $35,000 of the loss clears the at-risk hurdle. The remaining $5,000 of the loss is suspended at the at-risk level.

Passive loss hurdle: $35,000 of the loss made it to the passive loss hurdle. $20,000 of this loss can offset $20,000 of passive income on Jose's tax return. The remaining $15,000 of loss is suspended at the passive loss hurdle.

	Cleared hurdle	Suspended
Basis hurdle	$40,000	$10,000
At-risk hurdle	$35,000	$ 5,000
Passive loss hurdle	$20,000	$15,000
		$30,000

Jose can deduct $20,000 of the loss and $30,000 is suspended.

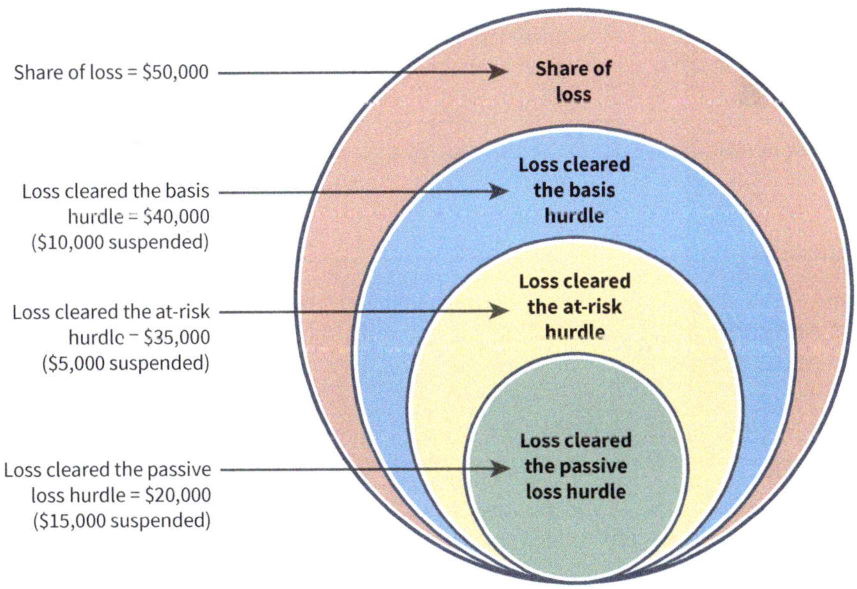

b. For Jose to be able to deduct the $10,000 loss suspended at the basis level in the future, it must clear the basis, at-risk, and passive loss hurdles.

For Jose to be able to deduct the $5,000 loss suspended at the at-risk level in the future, it must clear the at-risk and passive loss hurdles.

For Jose to be able to deduct the $15,000 loss suspended at the passive loss level in the future, it must clear only the passive loss hurdle, which will happen when Jose has $15,000 of passive income.

Related exercises: Application Problems 16, 17, 18, 19

Excess Business Losses

Congress has limited the amount of *business* losses that an individual can deduct each tax year.[22] The limitation on excess business losses applies to noncorporate taxpayers for losses from sole proprietorships, partnerships, S corporations, and limited liability companies. Wages and capital gains cannot be used to reduce the amount of the excess business loss. The deductibility of business losses is limited according to the following rules:

- The disallowance applies to business losses that exceed $626,000/$313,000 (married filing jointly/other) for 2025.
- The disallowed amount is added to the taxpayer's NOL carryforward.
- This limitation applies after application of the *passive loss rules.*

Why **Why is there a limitation on the deduction of business losses?** Congress has placed a limit on the amount of business losses that an individual taxpayer can deduct for a tax year. Even though the losses are legitimate business deductions, Congress believes that there should be a limit on the amount of losses that can offset other income and reduce the individual's tax liability for a given year.

EXAMPLE 6.5.4 Excess Business Losses

Robin is single and has the following results from her trades and businesses for 2025:

Horse-breeding sole proprietorship	($290,000)
Partnership distributive share	($ 75,000)
S corporation distributive share	$ 50,000

How much can she deduct for these business losses, assuming that the losses are not passive and that she has sufficient basis and at-risk amount to deduct the losses?

SOLUTION

The aggregate net loss from all of Robin's trades and businesses is $315,000 ($50,000 – $290,000 – $75,000). She must limit her business loss deduction for 2025 to $313,000. She includes the remaining loss of $2,000 as part of her NOL for 2025 that she can carry forward indefinitely to future tax years.

Related exercise: Application Problem 20

PRACTICE PROBLEM 6.5.1 Hurdles for Loss Limitations

Betty has a basis of $35,000 in her partnership interest at the beginning of the tax year. Her at-risk amount is $20,000. Betty has a passive loss from the partnership of $52,000 in the current year. She also has passive income from another source of $12,000. How much of the partnership loss may she deduct on her individual tax return for the current year?

SOLUTION

To determine the loss that can be deducted, we will apply the basis hurdle, at-risk hurdle, and passive loss hurdle in the correct order, as follows:

Basis hurdle: $35,000 of the loss clears the basis hurdle. The remaining $17,000 of the $52,000 loss is suspended at the basis level.

At-risk hurdle: $35,000 of the loss made it to the at-risk hurdle. $20,000 of the loss clears the at-risk hurdle. The remaining $15,000 of the loss is suspended at the at-risk level.

Passive loss hurdle: $20,000 of the loss made it to the passive loss hurdle. $12,000 of this loss can offset $12,000 of passive income on Betty's tax return. The remaining $8,000 of loss is suspended at the passive loss hurdle.

[22] IRC §461(l).

	Cleared hurdle	Suspended
Basis hurdle	$35,000	$17,000
At-risk hurdle	$20,000	$15,000
Passive loss hurdle	$12,000	$ 8,000
		$40,000

Betty can deduct $12,000 of the loss and $40,000 is suspended.

PRACTICE PROBLEM 6.5.2
Determining Excess Business Losses

Barkley and Jin are married and file a joint tax return. The following results are from their trades and businesses for 2025:

Pet grooming sole proprietorship	$125,000
Partnership distributive share	($440,000)
S corporation distributive share	($360,000)

How much can they deduct for these business losses, assuming that the losses are not passive and that they have sufficient basis and at risk amount to deduct the losses?

SOLUTION

The aggregate net loss from all of Barkley and Jin's trades and businesses is $675,000 ($125,000 − $440,000 − $360,000). They must limit their business loss deduction for 2025 to $626,000. They include the remaining loss of $49,000 as part of their NOL for 2025 that they can carry forward indefinitely to future tax years.

INTERACTIVE SELF-SCORING QUIZZES

6.6 Permitted Tax Years for Partnerships

LEARNING OBJECTIVE 6

Identify the required tax year for partnerships and other optional tax years.

VIDEO CONTENT

Congress has placed significant limitations on partnerships for their choice of tax years. Each partnership has a *required tax year* that it must use unless it qualifies to use one of a few limited exceptions.

Why **Why does Congress limit the year-end that partnerships can use?** If a partnership could choose any tax year it desired, as C corporations can, the partnership would choose the year-end that would permit the maximum deferral of income for the partners. Recall that all the partnership income flows to the partners on the last day of the partnership tax year.[23] Assume that a partnership had three individual partners so they each have a calendar year-end. To maximize deferral of income, the partnership would select a year-end of January 31, as shown in **Illustration 6.13**. The partner would report their share of the January 31, Year 2, income on their return for the year ended December 31, Year 2. This results in an 11-month deferral of reporting the income, because 11 months of partnership income earned in Year 1 (from February 1 to December 31, Year 1) is not reported by the partner until Year 2.

[23]IRC §706(a).

ILLUSTRATION 6.13 Timing of Income to Partners

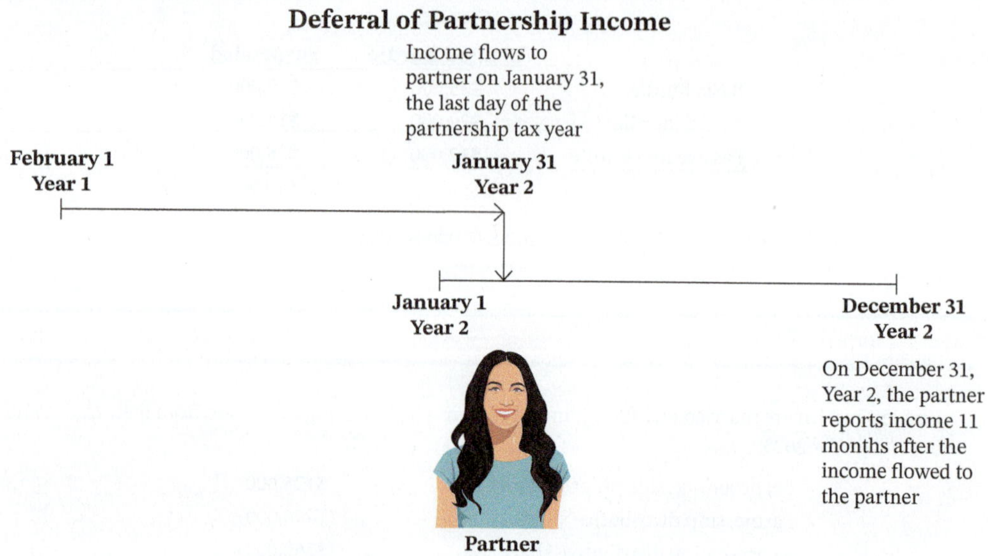

EXAMPLE 6.6.1 Timing of Flow-Through of Income to Partners

ABC is a partnership with a June 30 fiscal year-end. Partner A owns a 1/3 interest and has a calendar year-end. ABC has ordinary business income as follows:

July 1, Year 1 to June 30, Year 2	$24,000
July 1, Year 2 to December 31, Year 2	$ 9,000

How much income must Partner A report on their Year 2 Form 1040?

SOLUTION

Partner A will report partnership income for Year 2 for any tax year of the partnership that ends between January 1 and December 31 of Year 2. Partner A is allocated $8,000, 1/3 of the $24,000 ordinary income, on his Schedule K-1 for the year ended June 30, Year 2, and reports the income on their Form 1040 for Year 2. Partner A does not report any of the $9,000 earned during the last six months of Year 2 because that income will flow to the partners on June 30, Year 3.

Related exercise: Discussion Question 10

Required Tax Year

To prevent partners from maximizing the deferral of income with the choice of year-end, the general rule is that partnerships must use their required tax year. The **required tax year** is the year-end that meets one of the following tests, that must be applied in the order shown:[24]

1. ***Majority Interest Test*** Partnerships must use the same year-end as its majority interest partner(s). The **majority interest test** is met if partners having the same tax year own *more than 50%* of partnership capital and profits. If the partnership does not meet this test, then the 2nd test is used.
2. ***Principal Partner Test*** The **principal partner test** requires that a partnership must use the same year-end that all its principal partners have. A **principal partner** is one that owns *at least a 5%* interest in either partnership capital or profits. If the partnership does not meet this test, then the 3rd test is used.

[24]IRC §706(b)(1)(B).

3. ***Least Aggregate Deferral Method*** If neither the majority interest test nor principal partner test is met, the required tax year is determined by using the **least aggregate deferral method**. This method is computationally intensive, but determines the year-end which will provide the least amount of deferral for the entire partnership group. This test is described in the Advanced Topic section below.

The purpose of these tests is to minimize the aggregate deferral of income for the partners as a group. When the partners do not all have the same year-end, the required year-end will result in some deferral for one or more (but not all) partners. The number of months of deferral is the time from the partnership's year-end to the partner's year-end.

Tax Planning Tip

Some tax professionals incorrectly believe that all partnerships have a December 31 year-end. They have reached this conclusion because all partnerships they have been involved with have had a December 31 year-end. A very high percentage of partners in partnerships are individuals who must have a December 31 year-end. If all partners are individuals, then the majority interest test will always result in a required year-end of December 31. However, be aware that if one or more partners do not have a December 31 year-end, then the partnership may not either, depending on the outcome of the three tests.

The next two Examples illustrate the determination of the required tax year.

Potential Pitfall

One can easily confuse some of the requirements for the majority interest test and principal partner test, so make sure you know the details. Note these two differences:

- Majority interest test is *greater than* 50%, while principal partner test is *greater than or equal to* 5%.
- Majority interest is measured by capital *and* profits interest, while the principal partner test is measured by capital *or* profits interest.

EXAMPLE 6.6.2
Required Tax Year

A partnership has the following ownership structure:

	Capital interest	Profits interest	Year-end
Corporation XYZ	55%	55%	March 31
Mia Company	30%	30%	January 31
Paul	15%	15%	December 31

What is the required year-end for the partnership?

SOLUTION

The required year-end is March 31 under the majority interest test. Corporation XYZ owns more than 50% of the capital and profits interests, so its year-end becomes the required year-end. This results in there being no deferral of income for Corporation XYZ. While Mia and Paul do have some deferral of income (from March 31 to January 31 for Mia and from March 31 to December 31 for Paul), this deferral of income is for only 45% of the profits while 55% of the profits has no deferral.

EXAMPLE 6.6.3
Principal Partner Test

Partnership TNT has the following ownership structure with 23 partners:

	Capital interest	Profits interest	Year-end
11 corporations (each)	4%	4%	June 30
Pablo LLC	12%	12%	September 30
11 individuals (each)	4%	4%	December 31

What is the required year-end for Partnership TNT?

SOLUTION

We apply the three tests for the required year-end of a partnership to these facts. The 11 corporate partners with a June 30 year-end own 44% of the partnership and the 11 individuals with a December 31 year-end also own 44%. Because there is not a group of partners with the same year-end who own more than 50% of the capital and profits interest, the majority interest test is not met.

We next evaluate the principal partner test. Pablo LLC is the only partner who owns 5% or more of the partnership and is the only principal partner. Because all of the principal partners have the same year-end, the required tax year for the partnership is Pablo's year-end of September 30.

Related exercise: Brief Exercise 13

Exceptions to Required Tax Year

If a partnership does not want to use the required tax year, there are three exceptions that a partnership may be able to elect to use a different year-end:

- Natural business year
- Business purpose
- Section 444 election

Natural Business Year

Businesses often prefer to have a year-end that is at the end of their heaviest sales season because this is when inventory is at its lowest so it represents an end to a business cycle. The natural business year exception is consistent with this preference. A **natural business year** is a year in which 25% or more of the gross receipts occur in the last two months of the year being tested for three consecutive years. For example, if the June 30, Year 7, year-end was being tested, the total receipts would be determined for July 1, Year 6, to June 30, Year 7, and 25% or more of the gross receipts would have to be earned in May and June Year 7. Once this criterion is met for three years, then the partnership can switch to the natural business year for the following year by filing Form 1128, Application to Adopt, Change or Retain a Tax Year.

EXAMPLE 6.6.4
Natural Business Year

Breckenridge Partnership has a required year-end of December 31. Breckenridge operates a ski resort, and it earns most of its revenue in the winter months. Breckenridge would prefer to have a year-end of April 30. Gross receipt information is as follows for the last three years:

	Year ended April 30, Year 2	Year ended April 30, Year 3	Year ended April 30, Year 4
12 months receipts	$1,000,000	$1,600,000	$2,100,000
March and April receipts	$ 280,000	$ 460,000	$ 680,000

Can Breckenridge use April 30 for its year-end? If so, what is the first year that it can do so?

SOLUTION

Breckenridge must use the natural business year exception to use a year-end of April 30. To do so, it must for three consecutive years earn at least 25% of its gross receipts in March and April for year ended April 30. The computation is as follows:

	Year ended April 30, Year 2	Year ended April 30, Year 3	Year ended April 30, Year 4
March and April receipts	$ 280,000	$ 460,000	$ 680,000
12 months receipts	$1,000,000	$1,600,000	$2,100,000
Percentage	28%	28.75%	32.38%

Breckenridge does meet the 25% test for three consecutive years. It can use the new year-end for its year ended April 30, Year 5. Breckenridge will use December 31 for its year ending on December 31, Year 4, and its first tax return with the year-end of April 30 will be a short year return for January–April Year 5.

Related exercise: Application Problem 21

Business Purpose

A partnership can choose any year-end if it has a business purpose for doing so and the IRS approves the change. However, this is an extremely difficult definition to satisfy.[25] Deferral of income is not considered a business purpose.

Section 444 Election

A third exception to the required tax year is that under IRC Section 444, partnerships may elect a year-end with no more than three months of deferral. However, a deposit with the IRS is required to compensate the government for the otherwise deferred tax benefits to the partners if the deferred benefit exceeds $500. A detailed discussion of this election is beyond the scope of this book, but there are two basic rules that you should know:

- For a partnership with a required year-end of December 31, the Section 444 election allows a year-end of September, October, or November to be selected. A September year-end would result in three months of deferral of income to the partners.
- The deposit that is required to be made with the Section 444 election is *not* a prepayment of tax for the partners. The partners cannot use this deposit to reduce the taxes owned on their tax returns. The deposit remains with the IRS and is adjusted up or down each year depending on the estimated tax deferral each year.

Related exercise: Multiple Choice Question 15

Advanced Topic—Drilling Down

Least Aggregate Deferral Method

The least aggregate deferral method must be used to determine the required tax year if the majority interest and principal partner test are not met. The least aggregate deferral method will always provide a required year-end. Each year-end that at least one partner has is tested to determine an aggregate deferral measurement for each possibility. The number of months of deferral is the time from the partnership's year-end to the partner's year-end. The number of months' deferral that a partner has for the year being tested is multiplied by the partner's profits interest. This weighted deferral for each partner is then added together. The year-end that produces the least aggregate deferral is the required tax year. If more than one option has the same deferral measurement that is the lowest amount, the partnership can choose between one of those year-ends.[26]

[25]IRC §706(b)(1)(C). Rev. Proc. 2006-46, 2006-2 CB 859.

[26]Treas. Reg. 1.706-1(b)(3)(i).

The following Example illustrates the least aggregate deferral method computation.

EXAMPLE 6.6.5
Least Aggregate Deferral Method

The USC Partnership has the following ownership structure:

	Capital interest	Profits interest	Year-end
Dexter	30%	30%	December 31
DIS Corporation	45%	45%	June 30
ORL Corporation	25%	25%	October 31

What is the required year-end for USC Partnership?

SOLUTION

We apply the three tests for the required year-end of a partnership to these facts. The majority interest test is not met because one or more partners who have the same year-end do not own more than 50% of the capital and profits interest. The principal partner test is also not met. There are three principal partners, but they do not all have the same tax year. Therefore, the least aggregate deferral method must be used to determine the required tax year.

The number of months of deferral is the time from the partnership's year-end to the partner's year-end. We test June, October, and December to determine which produces the least amount of aggregate deferral for the partners.

June

	Year-end	Months of deferral	Profits interest	Months of deferral × Profits interest
Dexter	December 31	6	30%	1.8
DIS	June 30	0	45%	0.0
ORL	October 31	4	25%	1.0
			Aggregate deferral	2.8

October

	Year-end	Months of deferral	Profits interest	Months of deferral × Profits interest
Dexter	December 31	2	30%	0.6
DIS	June 30	8	45%	3.6
ORL	October 31	0	25%	0.0
			Aggregate deferral	4.2

December

	Year-end	Months of deferral	Profits interest	Months of deferral × Profits interest
Dexter	December 31	0	30%	0.0
DIS	June 30	6	45%	2.7
ORL	October 31	10	25%	2.5
			Aggregate deferral	5.2

The required year-end is June 30 because it produces the least deferral (2.8) of the three possible year-ends.

Related exercise: Application Problem 22

PRACTICE PROBLEM 6.6.1
Permitted Tax Year

Park Partnership has the following ownership structure:

	Capital interest	Profits interest	Year-end
City Corporation	70%	70%	August 31
Drey	20%	20%	December 31
Pasquel	10%	10%	December 31

What is the required year-end and result for the partnership?

SOLUTION

We apply the three tests for the required year-end of a partnership to these facts. The required year-end is August 31 under the majority interest test. City Corporation owns more than 50% of the capital and profits interests, so its year-end becomes the required year-end. This results in there being no deferral of income for City Corporation. While Drey and Pasquel do have four months of deferral of income (from August 31 to December 31), this deferral of income is for only 30% of the profits while 70% of the profits have no deferral.

PRACTICE PROBLEM 6.6.2
Natural Business Year End

Holiday Partnership has a required year-end of March 31. Holiday operates a toy manufacturing business, and it earns most of its revenue during the Christmas season. Holiday would prefer to have a year-end of December 31. Holiday has met the natural business year gross receipts test for Years 1 & 2, in which 25% or more of the gross receipts occur in the last two months of that year for three consecutive years. Their gross receipts for Year 3 are $465,000. What amount of gross receipts need to be collected in November and December in Year 3 to be able to use December 31 as their year-end beginning December 31, Year 4?

SOLUTION

Holiday must use the natural business year exception to use a year-end of December 31. To do so, it must earn at least 25% of its gross receipts in November and December for the year ended December 31 for three consecutive years. Holiday must collect at least $116,250 ($465,000 × 25%) in Year 3 to use December 31 as their year-end.

INTERACTIVE SELF-SCORING QUIZZES

6.7 Related-Party Rules

LEARNING OBJECTIVE 7

Apply the related-party rules to partnership transactions.

VIDEO CONTENT

Congress usually places restrictions on transactions between related parties, and the partnership rules are no exception to this. In fact, because of the flexibility of partnerships, there are more related-party transaction rules for partnerships than for other business entities. In this section, we cover three of the most common related-party rules:

- Disallowance of related-party losses
- Preservation of unrealized ordinary income
- Payments to a partner

Disallowance of Related-Party Losses

If an asset is sold between a partnership and a partner who owns, directly and indirectly, more than 50% of the capital or profits interest of the partnership, any realized loss is disallowed. The same rule applies if an asset is sold at a loss between two partnerships if more than 50% of the ownership of each partnership is the same.[27]

The disallowed loss from a related-party sale creates a **right of offset**, which taxpayers can use to reduce a gain upon the ultimate sale of the property to an unrelated taxpayer. The right of offset cannot create a loss, nor can it make a loss greater. Once the related-party buyer sells the asset to a third party, the related-party buyer permanently loses any unused right of offset.[28]

Related exercise: Discussion Question 11

Why **Why are losses from related-party sales disallowed?** Marcos owns 95% of the capital in UK Partnership, which he started eight years ago with his best friend from college. Marcos owns some land outside the partnership that has an adjusted basis of $150,000 and its current fair market value (FMV) is $180,000. Marcos has sold other investments during the current year, and his net capital gain from these sales is $30,000. If he sells the land, he would rather not have to pay tax on the $30,000 gain, so he sells the land to UK Partnership for $120,000 on June 10. This creates a $30,000 realized loss ($120,000 amount realized less $150,000 adjusted basis) that he intends to use to reduce his net capital gain to zero. However, because UK is related to him, Marcos cannot recognize the $30,000 loss, and his net capital gain remains at $30,000. The related-party loss rules exist to prevent this type of tax avoidance. Marcos reduced his net worth by $30,000 when he sold the land to UK because he sold it for less than its FMV. Why would he be willing to do this? While individually Marcos has incurred a $30,000 loss, the partnership that he owns 95% of still owns the land, so he can recover most of this loss when the partnership sells the property for its true FMV.

Evaluating Related-Party Transactions

There are four steps to solving all issues for a related-party transaction. **Illustration 6.14** provides a flow chart showing these steps

Step 1. **Compute: The realized gain or loss from the transaction.** If a realized gain, then the taxpayer must recognize it. If a realized loss, go to step 2.

Step 2. **Ask: Are the buyer and seller related parties**? If NO, then you can recognize the realized loss. If YES, then you cannot recognize the realized loss, and must proceed to step 3.

Step 3. **Calculate: The right of offset is equal to the amount of the realized loss.**

Step 4. **Determine: The holding period of the new owner of the asset.** It begins on the day after the date the taxpayer purchased the property from the related party and does not include the holding period of the seller.

[27]IRC §707(b)(1).

[28]IRC §267(d).

ILLUSTRATION 6.14 The Four Steps for Assessing Related-Party Transactions

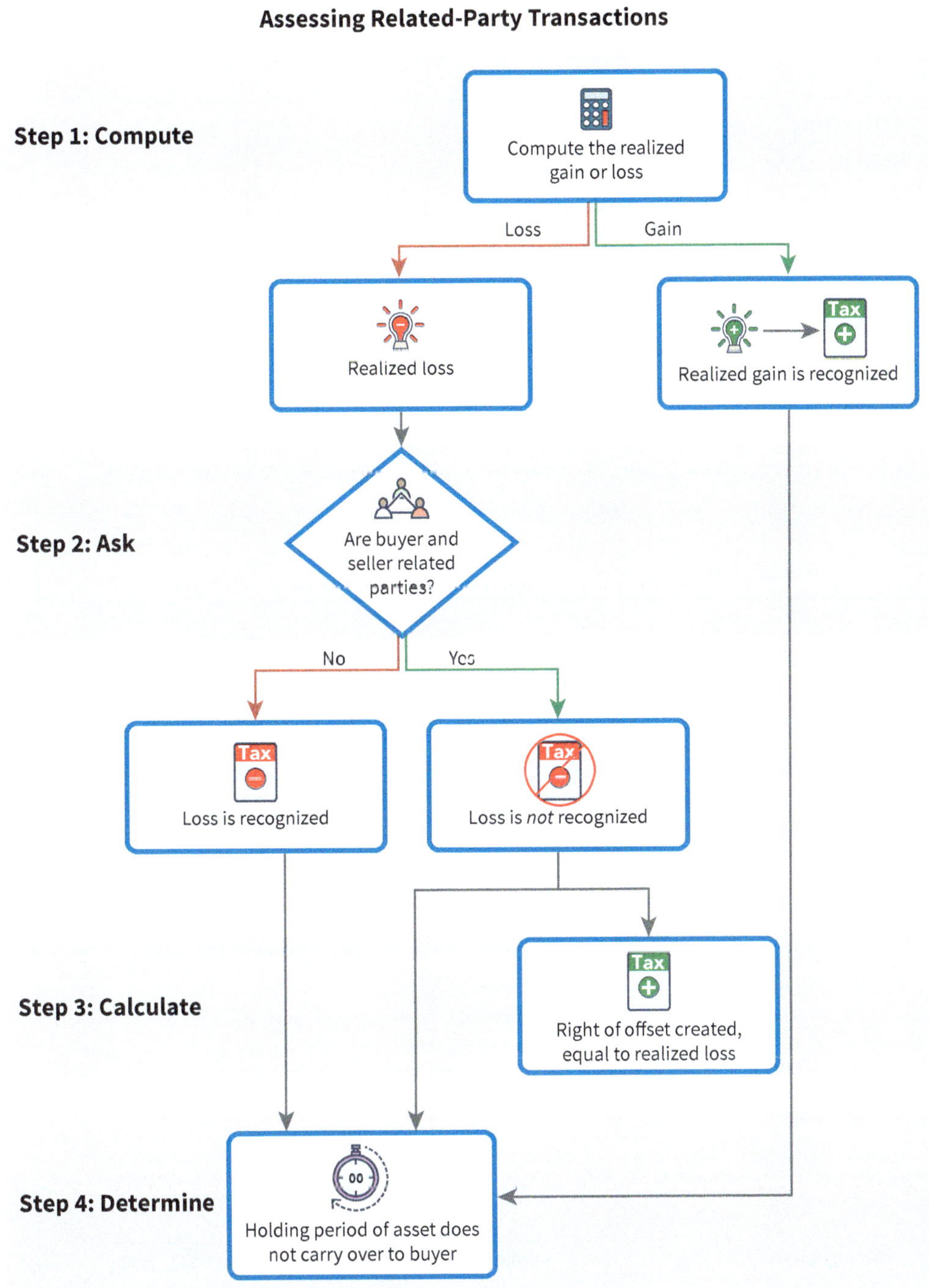

To determine the tax consequences for Marcos from this transaction, we will follow the Steps outlined in Illustration 6.14 in the following example.

EXAMPLE 6.7.1
Related-Party Loss

Continue with the facts for Marcos from the **Why** section above. Determine the realized gain or loss, the recognized gain or loss, the right of offset (if any), and the holding period for the new owner of the asset.

SOLUTION

Step 1. First, we compute Marcos's realized gain or loss.

Amount realized	$120,000
Less: Adjusted basis	(150,000)
Realized loss	($ 30,000)

Step 2. Next, we ask: Are the buyer and seller related parties? Marcos and UK Partnership are related parties because Marcos owns more than 50% of the capital, so the realized loss is not recognized. The deferred loss is $30,000.

Step 3. We then calculate the right of offset, which is equal to the amount of the realized loss. Here, the right of offset available for UK Partnership to use in the future is $30,000.

Step 4. Finally, we determine the holding period of the new owner of the asset. UK's holding period for the stock begins on June 11, the day after the date of the transaction.

Tax Planning Tip

If a taxpayer owns an asset that would create a loss if sold, the taxpayer should not sell the asset to a related party because the loss cannot be recognized.

Now let's examine the tax consequences for when UK Partnership later sells the stock in the following Example.

EXAMPLE 6.7.2
Right of Offset

Assume the same facts as in Example 6.7.1 and the **Why** section above. Determine UK's recognized gain or loss if it holds the land for two years and then sells it to an unrelated party for $140,000. Alternatively, assume the sales price is $160,000, and $115,000.

SOLUTION

Once a related-party sale with a deferred loss has occurred, the buyer of the asset can use the right of offset to reduce gain when the buyer sells or disposes of the asset.

	A	B	C
Sales Price	**$140,000**	**$160,000**	**$115,000**
Amount realized	$140,000	$160,000	$115,000
Less: Adjusted basis	(120,000)	(120,000)	(120,000)
Gain (loss) before right of offset	$ 20,000	$ 40,000	($ 5,000)
Less: Right of offset	(20,000)	(30,000)	-0-
Recognized gain (loss)	$ - 0 -	$ 10,000	($ 5,000)

In scenario A, UK can use only $20,000 of the right of offset because the right of offset cannot create a loss. In scenario B, the entire right of offset can reduce the gain. In scenario C, UK cannot use any of the right of offset because it would increase a loss. In scenarios A and C, the unused right of offset cannot be used in the future.

Related exercises: Multiple Choice Question 16
Brief Exercise 14
Application Problem 23
Tax Planning Problem 3

Preservation of Unrealized Ordinary Income

A gain recognized on a sale or exchange of property between a partnership and a person owning, directly or indirectly, more than 50% of the capital or profits interests in such partnership, will be treated as ordinary income if the property is not a capital asset in the hands of the transferee. The same rule applies for a sale or exchange of property between two partnerships in which the same persons own, directly or indirectly, more than 50% of the capital or profits interests.

Why **Why does the preservation of unrealized ordinary income rule exist?** Assume that Shinika and Rachel own equal interests in five acres of land that were inherited 20 years ago. Their combined basis in the land is $50,000. A real estate development company has offered to pay them $500,000 for the land. If accepted, they would have a combined LTCG of $450,000 ($500,000 – $50,000) that would be subject to the 20% LTCG rate. After further investigation, they discover that if they subdivided the land into one-half acre residential lots, they could sell the 10 lots for $125,000 each, or $1,250,000 in total. Shinika's son, who is a tax whiz in his university taxation course this semester, warns her that if they subdivide the land, then they will become dealers in real estate, and the land will be inventory to them. Therefore, their $1,200,000 ($1,250,000 – $50,000) profit will be taxed as ordinary income to them at a maximum rate of 37%.

Shinika and Rachel would like to increase their profit from $450,000 to $1,200,000 by subdividing the land, but they would also like to have as much of the gain as possible taxed at the 20% LTCG rate. Therefore, they form a partnership, and they are each 50% partners. The partnership buys the land from them for $700,000, resulting in (they hope!) a $650,000 ($700,000 – $50,000) LTCG. The partnership then subdivides the land and, when it sells the lots, it will have ordinary income to the extent the sales proceeds exceed the partnership's basis of $700,000.

If this strategy worked as they hoped, Shinika and Rachel would be able to use a partnership to lock in their capital *gain* before they convert that asset to inventory. However, this will not work, because the land is an ordinary asset in the hands of the partnership immediately after the sale. Therefore, Shinika's and Rachel's gain of $650,000 is treated as ordinary income to them.

The next Example applies this ordinary income rule to the sale of an asset between two partnerships under common control.

EXAMPLE 6.7.3
Sale of Asset Between Partnerships

Moe, Larry, and Curly are equal partners in the Stooge Partnership. The partnership owns a valuable piece of real estate in New York that has an adjusted basis of $350,000 and FMV of $2,000,000. Moe and Larry created a new partnership of which they are equal partners, Comic Films Partnership. Stooge then sells the land to Comic Films for $2,000,000. Comic Films plans to subdivide the land into 10 parcels that will be sold for commercial development. What are the tax consequences to Stooge Partnership for the sale?

SOLUTION

Stooge and Comic Films are commonly controlled partnerships because more than 50% of the stock of each is owned by Moe and Larry. Moe and Larry own 67% of Stooge and 100% of Comic Film. The profit from the sale of land is $1,650,000 ($2,000,000 – $350,000) and is treated as ordinary income to Stooge because the land in the hands of Comic Films is inventory. Comic Films is a dealer in real estate.

Related exercise: Brief Exercise 15
Application Problem 24

Payments to a Partner

There are restrictions on when a partnership can deduct an accrued expense to a cash-basis partner.[29] In such a case, the accrual-basis partnership cannot deduct the payment until the cash-basis partner includes the payment in income. This ensures that the deduction and the income both occur in the same tax year for the partner and the partnership. As shown in **Illustration 6.15**, if a payment of this nature is accrued in Year 1, but not paid until Year 2, the partner will not have income until the payment is received in Year 2. Therefore, the partnership cannot deduct the payment until Year 2.

Related exercise: Discussion Question 12

ILLUSTRATION 6.15 Payments to a Partner

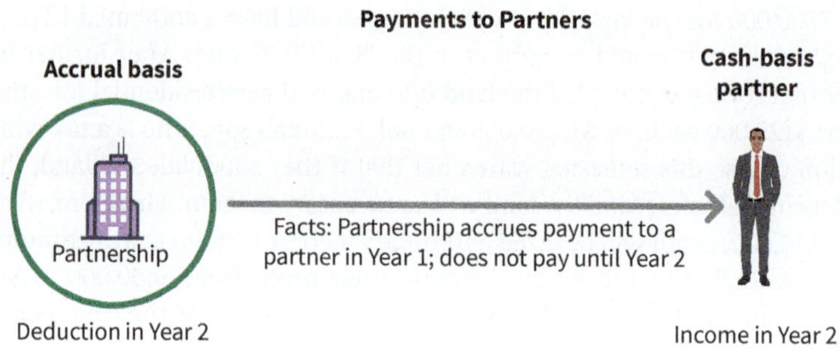

The next Example applies this timing rule for partnership.

EXAMPLE 6.7.4
Payments to a Partner

Antonio is a 10% partner of Sand Partnership and he also serves as CEO. Sand reports on the accrual basis of accounting. During Year 2, Antonio loaned Sand $500,000. The interest owed to Antonio for Year 2 is $16,000, but it is not paid until Year 3. What are the tax effects of this transaction?

SOLUTION

The special timing rules for partners discussed above does apply because Antonio is a cash-basis taxpayer and Sand is accrual basis. Therefore, Sand can deduct $16,000 in Year 3, the same year that Antonio must recognize the interest income.

Why **Why does the related-party timing rule exist?** Without the special timing rule provided for this payment, an owner of a business entity could intentionally create situations each year where the accrual-basis business entity accrues the deduction to save taxes in the current year, but the cash-basis recipient does not have income until the payment is received in the following year, so the payment of taxes is deferred. Congress does not want to allow such timing schemes to work.

Related exercise: Application Problem 25

[29]IRC §267(a)(2) and (e).

PRACTICE PROBLEM 6.7.1
Related-Party Loss

Janelle owns an apartment building with an adjusted basis of $100,000 and fair market value of $85,000. She sells the building to Sunshine Partnership for $80,000. Janelle owns 90% of Sunshine. Sunshine then sells the building to an unrelated third party for $105,000.

a. What is Janelle's realized gain/loss and recognized gain/loss? What is Sunshine's basis in the building purchased?

b. What is Sunshine's realized gain/loss and recognized gain/loss?

c. Assume the same facts except Sunshine then sells the building to an unrelated third party for $90,000. What is Sunshine's realized gain/loss and recognized gain/loss?

d. Assume the same facts except Sunshine then sells the building to an unrelated third party for $78,000. What is Sunshine's realized gain/loss and recognized gain/loss?

SOLUTION

a. We will first determine if Janelle has a realized gain or loss on this transaction, as follows:

Amount realized	$ 80,000
Less: Adjusted basis	(100,000)
Realized loss	($ 20,000)

Because Janelle owns more than 50% of Sunshine Partnership, they are related parties. You cannot deduct realized losses from the sale or exchange of property between related parties. Janelle's recognized loss is $0. Sunshine's basis in the building purchased is its purchase price of $80,000.

b. Because Janelle cannot recognize the loss of $20,000 from the sale to Sunshine, this creates a right of offset of $20,000 that Sunshine can use to reduce to zero any realized gain when it sells the property. When Sunshine sells the building, we can determine its realized and recognized gains as follows:

Amount realized	$105,000
Less: Adjusted basis	(80,000)
Realized gain	$ 25,000
Less: Right of offset	(20,000)
Recognized gain	$ 5,000

Sunshine reduces its gain by the right of offset of $20,000. Therefore, Sunshine's recognized gain is $5,000.

c. Because Janelle cannot recognize the loss of $20,000 from the sale to Sunshine, this creates a right of offset of $20,000 that Sunshine can use to reduce to zero any realized gain when it sells the property. When Sunshine sells the building, we can determine its realized and recognized gain/loss as follows:

Amount realized	$90,000
Less: Adjusted basis	(80,000)
Realized gain	$10,000
Less: Right of offset	(10,000)
Recognized gain	$ 0

Sunshine reduces its gain by the right of offset, but only to the extent of its realized gain of $10,000. The right of offset cannot create or increase a loss. Sunshine's recognized gain is $0. The remaining $10,000 ($20,000 – $10,000) of the right of offset is forfeited.

d. Because Janelle cannot recognize the loss of $20,000 from the sale to Sunshine, this creates a right of offset of $20,000 that Sunshine can use to reduce to zero any realized gain when it sells the property. When Sunshine sells the building for $78,000, we can determine its realized and recognized gain/loss as follows:

Amount realized	$78,000
Less: Adjusted basis	(80,000)
Realized loss	($ 2,000)

The right of offset cannot create or increase a loss, so none of it can be used. Sunshine's recognized loss is $2,000. The $20,000 right of offset is forfeited.

INTERACTIVE SELF-SCORING QUIZZES

Review and Practice

Chapter Summary

Thirty-seven percent (37%) of small businesses are organized as LLCs or partnerships. LLCs are much more popular today than partnerships for reasons that we describe in the chapter. Most small business owners prefer to be an LLC or partnership, with S corporations running a close second at 33%. In this chapter, we discuss the characteristics of partnerships, the tax implications of forming a partnership, the flow-through of income to the partners and how this affects the partner's basis in the partnership interest, limitations on the use of partnership losses, the required tax year for partnerships, and a few special related-party rules.

1 Recall definitions related to partnerships and partners.

- A **partnership** is an association of two or more taxpayers to operate a business that has an objective to make a profit that is not taxed as a corporation. Additionally, there must be an intent to share profits among the partners. Just the co-ownership of property does not necessarily create a partnership, nor does the sharing of only expenses.
- The major tax advantage for partnerships is single taxation, contrasted with double taxation for C corporations. Partnership income is reported on Form 1065, U.S. Return of Partnership Income, but the partnership does not pay tax on this income. Rather, the income flows through to the partners, regardless of whether it has been distributed, and the partners pay tax on the income on their returns. The partners' share of each tax item is reported to each partner on their Schedule K-1 (Form 1065).
- The important differences between a **limited liability company (LLC)** and a partnership are from a legal perspective, not a tax perspective, including the following:
    - Owners of an LLC are known as members, rather than partners.
    - All owners of an LLC have limited liability, whereas all partnerships must have at least one general partner that has unlimited liability.
    - All owners of an LLC can participate in management (but are not required to), whereas limited partners cannot participate in management.
- The **check-the-box regulations** determine how a business entity is taxed for federal income tax purposes. The main premise of the check-the-box regulations is that unincorporated entities may choose to be taxed as a corporation or a partnership. If an entity is not incorporated and has only one owner, then the default classification is that the entity is disregarded for federal income tax purposes.

2 Compute the tax consequences of partnership formations.

- If a taxpayer contributes property in exchange for a capital interest in a partnership, then realized gains and losses for the partner are not recognized.
- On the other hand, if a taxpayer provides services in return for the partnership interest, then the partner has ordinary income (known as a *guaranteed payment*) equal to the fair market value of the capital interest received. The partnership can deduct the guaranteed payment made to the service partner.
- The partnership never recognizes a gain or loss because of a partnership formation.
- **Boot** is any property received by a partner in a partnership formation other than a partnership interest. If boot is received, the recognized gain by the partner is the *lower* of:
    - Realized gain, *or*
    - Fair market value of the boot received.
- As with all tax-deferred transactions, basis stays the same for a tax-deferred partnership formation.
- The holding period in the partnership interest includes the holding period of the contributed asset for contributions of capital assets and Section 1231 assets. For other assets, the holding period starts when the contribution is received by the partnership.
- The holding period that the partner has in the asset before contributed always transfers to the partnership, regardless of the type of asset contributed.

3 Compute the adjustment to partner's bases for partnership debt.

- The transactions that can affect debt basis fall into four categories:

Category 1: An increase in the partnership's liabilities (e.g., loan from a bank, increase in accounts payable) is considered to be a contribution of money by each partner and increases each partner's basis in the partnership by each partner's share of the increase.

Category 2: Any decrease in the partnership's liabilities is considered to be a distribution of money to each partner and reduces each partner's basis in the partnership by each partner's share of the decrease.

Category 3: Any decrease in a partner's individual liability by reason of the assumption by the partnership of such individual liabilities is considered to be a distribution of money to the partner by the partnership. Thus, the partner's basis is decreased.

Category 4: Any increase in a partner's individual liability by reason of the assumption by the partner of partnership liabilities is considered to be a contribution of money to the partnership by the partner. Thus, the partner's basis is increased.

- If the net change in basis in the partnership interest because of debt being assumed by the partnership exceeds the partner's basis in their partnership interest before the debt assumption, the partner must recognize gain equal to that excess to prevent negative basis from occurring.
- **Recourse debt** is debt for which at least one of the partners, or a person related to a partner, has the potential for an economic risk of loss with respect to the debt. **Nonrecourse debt** is debt for which no partner, or a person related to a partner, has an economic risk of loss. If the borrower defaults on the repayment of nonrecourse debt, the creditor's only recourse is to take the property back that is secured by the loan.
- In general, limited partners and LLC members are not allocated any recourse debt for debt basis purposes because they have no economic risk of loss for the debt. Nonrecourse debt is often allocated based on the partners' profit-sharing ratios. Also, contrasted with recourse debt, general partners, limited partners, and LLC members can be allocated nonrecourse debt.

4 Compute the ordinary business income or loss and separately stated items for a partnership.

- Partnership income is reported on Form 1065, U.S. Return of Partnership Income, and the income flows through to the partners on the last day of the partnership tax year, regardless of whether it has been distributed, on the partner's Schedule K-1 (Form 1065).
- Partners have significant flexibility in how they choose to share economic gains and losses.
- Partners who work for the partnership are not considered to be employees. Therefore, they do not receive a salary; rather their compensation is known as a guaranteed payment. A **guaranteed payment** is not based on the income of the partnership. Guaranteed payments can also be received for the use of capital owned by the partner, such as a building. Guaranteed payments are ordinary income to the partner.
- Because partners are generally not considered to be employees, the value of most fringe benefits that are tax-free to employees is taxable to partners.
- The character of partnership tax items is determined at the partnership level. Once the tax character is determined at the partnership level, the character stays the same when it flows from the partnership to the shareholders.
- The tax items that comprise partnership income or loss are divided into two categories: *separately stated items* and *nonseparately stated items*. **Separately stated items** are tax items that could potentially impact partners' tax liabilities in different ways. We refer to the **nonseparately stated items** as the *bucket items*, to emphasize that these items are all mixed together, or netted, and result in one measure known as the **ordinary business income or loss** for the partnership.
- In addition to contributions and distributions, partners adjust their outside basis for partnership transactions each year, as follows:
  - Outside basis is *increased* by a partner's proportionate share of:
    1. Income and gains,
    2. Tax-exempt income, *and*
    3. Increases in partnership debt.
  - Outside basis is *decreased* by a partner's proportionate share of:
    4. Expenses and losses,
    5. Nondeductible expenses that are not capital expenditures, *and*
    6. Decreases in partnership debt
- A partner's **capital account** represents the liquidation proceeds that a partner should receive when the partnership liquidates. Therefore, the capital account should reflect the fair market value of the partner's interest in the partnership.

5 Determine the partner's share of partnership losses that can be currently deducted and that is suspended.

If a passive loss flows through to an owner from a partnership or an LLC, it must clear the **basis hurdle**, **at-risk hurdle**, and **passive loss hurdle** before the taxpayer can deduct the loss on the partner's tax return. There are two key rules for applying these hurdles to flow-through losses:

1. Losses must clear each hurdle in the specified order: basis, at-risk, and passive. Losses that do not clear a hurdle are suspended and carried forward to the future.
2. Losses must clear each hurdle only once and the losses do not have to clear all hurdles in the same year.

- Congress has limited the amount of business losses that an individual can deduct each tax year. The limitation on excess business losses applies to noncorporate taxpayers for losses from sole proprietorships, partnerships, S corporations, and limited liability companies. Wages and capital gains cannot be used to reduce the amount of the excess business loss. The deductibility of business losses is limited according to the following rules:
  - The disallowance applies to business losses that exceed \$626,000/\$313,000 (married filing jointly/other) for 2025.
  - The disallowed amount is added to the taxpayer's NOL carryforward.
  - This limitation applies after application of the passive loss rules.

6 Identify the required tax year for partnerships and other optional tax years.

- Congress has placed significant limitations on partnerships for their choice of tax years. Each partnership has a **required tax year** that it must use unless it qualifies to use one of a few limited exceptions. The required tax year is the year-end that meets one of the following tests, that must be applied in the order shown:

  1. ***Majority Interest Test*** Partnerships must use the same year-end as its majority interest partner(s). The **majority interest test** is met if partners having the same tax year own *more than 50%* of

partnership capital and profits. If the partnership does not meet this test, then the 2nd test is used.

2. ***Principal Partner Test*** The **principal partner test** requires that a partnership must use the same year-end that all its principal partners have. A **principal partner** is one that owns *at least a 5%* interest in either partnership capital or profits.

3. ***Least Aggregate Deferral Method*** If neither the majority interest test nor principal partner test is met, the required tax year is determined by using the **least aggregate deferral method**.

- If a partnership does not want to use the required tax year, there are three exceptions that a partnership may be able to elect to use a different year-end:
  - **Natural business year**
  - Business purpose
  - Section 444 election

7 Apply the related-party rules to partnership transactions.

- If an asset is sold between a partnership and a partner who owns, directly and indirectly, more than 50% of the capital or profits interest, directly and indirectly, of the partnership, any realized loss is disallowed. The same rule applies if an asset is sold at a loss between two partnerships if more than 50% of the ownership of each partnership is the same.
- The disallowed loss from a related-party sale creates a **right of offset**, which taxpayers can use to reduce a gain upon the ultimate sale of the property to an unrelated taxpayer. The right of offset cannot create a loss, nor can it make a loss greater.
- A gain recognized on a sale or exchange of property between a partnership and a person owning, directly or indirectly, more than 50% of the capital or profits interests in such partnership, will be treated as ordinary income if the property is not a capital asset in the hands of the transferee. The same rule applies for a sale or exchange of property between two partnerships in which the same persons own, directly or indirectly, more than 50% of the capital or profits interests.
- There are restrictions on when a partnership can deduct an accrued expense to a cash-basis partner. In such a case, the accrual-basis partnership cannot deduct the payment until the cash-basis partner includes the payment in income. This ensures that the deduction and the income both occur in the same tax year for the partner and the partnership.

Communication Application

Communication

Taxability of Partnership Income

(LO4) Maverick, Cayton, and Autumn have formed the MCA Partnership as equal general partners. This is their first year in business and MCA has been quite profitable, generating ordinary business income of $300,000. Each partner has received a distribution of $25,000. All three partners were under the impression that they would only pay tax on the $25,000 received. Prepare a memo to the partners and to the tax file explaining the taxability of partnership income.

Solution

Memo to Client

Hello Maverick, Cayton, and Autumn,

Thank you for giving me an opportunity to work with you and help you understand the taxability of partnership income. A partnership is a flow-through entity and does not pay tax on its earnings. Instead, the partners pay tax on items of income flowing to them from the partnership on their individual income tax return. MCA Partnership will file Form 1065 and include Schedule K-1 for each partner showing the amount that is taxable to each of you. Although the distribution to each of you was only $25,000, you will pay tax on your share of partnership income, $100,000 each. Each of you will also pay self-employment tax of 15.3% on the $100,000 because you are all general partners.

To ensure that there is only a single level of taxation, your basis in the partnership will adjust each year based on the items reported on your Schedule K-1. Your basis will increase for the $100,000 of ordinary business income to each of you and decrease for the distribution of $25,000 to each of you. The good news is that the distribution of $25,000 is not taxable to you because it does not exceed your basis in your partnership interest.

I hope this clears up your questions regarding the taxability of partnership income. I would be happy to prepare your individual tax returns as well as the partnership tax return. Please let me know if you have any more questions.

Sincerely,
Carnes & Youngberg, CPAs

Tax memo to the file

Facts: Maverick, Cayton, and Autumn have formed the MCA partnership acting as equal general partners. This is their first year in business and MCA has been quite profitable, having ordinary business income of $300,000. Each partner has received a distribution of $25,000. All three partners were under the impression that they would only pay tax on the $25,000 received.

Issue: How is partnership income and distributions taxed to the partners?

Conclusion: Each partner will pay tax on their share of partnership income, $100,000 each. Each of them will also pay self-employment tax of 15.3% on the $100,000 because they are all general partners.

Analysis: Under IRC §701, a partnership is a flow-through entity and does not pay tax on its earnings. Instead, the partners pay tax on items of income flowing from the partnership on their individual income tax return. MCA Partnership will file Form 1065 and include Schedule K-1 for each partner showing what is taxable to each partner.

To ensure that there is only a single level of taxation, each partner's basis in the partnership will adjust each year based on the items reported on their Schedule K-1. The basis will increase for the $100,000 of ordinary business income to each partner and decrease for the distribution of $25,000 to each partner.

Ethics and Professional Responsibilities Application

Ethics

Loss Limitation Rule

(LO5) Ahanu became a 25% general partner in Rainforest Partnership three years ago by contributing $25,000 cash. He has prepared his own individual tax return since he became a partner. For Year 3, Ahanu has asked you to prepare his tax return. Ahanu's Year 3 Schedule K-1 (Form 1065) reflects income of $10,000. While reviewing the last two years' tax returns and supporting information, you notice that his Schedule K-1s from Rainforest reflect an ordinary business loss in both years. On Ahanu's individual tax return, he deducted the full losses on Schedule E, page 2. The loss reported on his Schedule K-1 for Year 1 was $22,000 and for Year 2 was $18,000. Due to the rule limiting losses to the partner's basis in the partnership interest, Ahanu should have deducted only $3,000 of the loss in Year 2 with a suspended loss of $15,000 to carry forward to Year 3. When you explain this to Ahanu, he says to not amend the previous tax returns but to file the return correctly for Year 3. What is your response to Ahanu?

In addition to the chapter content, see *Statements on Standards for Tax Services* at www.aicpa-cima.com/resources/landing/statements-on-standards-for-tax-services, *Circular 230,* at https://www.irs.gov/tax-professionals/office-of-professional-responsibility-and-circular-230, and *Taxation of Business Entities*, Chapter 2, LO4, Tax Professional Responsibilities.

Solution

Ahanu incorrectly deducted the $18,000 loss for Year 2. Due to the loss limitation rule, Ahanu can deduct losses only to the extent of his basis. But in Year 3, his basis increases by the $10,000 of income. The Year 2 suspended loss of $15,000 can be used to the extent of this $10,000 increase in basis, as shown below. Ahanu's remaining suspended loss from Year 2 is $5,000 which can be carried forward to Year 4.

Beginning basis	$25,000
Year 1 loss	(22,000)
Remaining basis	$ 3,000
Year 2 loss	(3,000)
Remaining basis	$ 0
Year 3 income	10,000
Year 2 suspended loss	(10,000)
Ending basis	$ 0

Under *Circular 230* §10.22, Diligence as to Accuracy, "a practitioner must exercise due diligence—(1) In preparing or assisting in the preparation of, approving, and filing tax returns, documents, affidavits, and other papers relating to Internal Revenue Service matters." This is not the result Ahanu was looking for, but you have an obligation to inform your client of the law and prepare his tax return in accordance with the law.

Also under *Circular 230* §10.21, Knowledge of Client's Omission, "A practitioner who, having been retained by a client with respect to a matter administered by the Internal Revenue Service, knows that the client has not complied with the revenue laws of the United States or has made an error in or omission from any return, document, affidavit, or other paper which the client submitted or executed under the revenue laws of the United States, must advise the client promptly of the fact of such noncompliance, error, or omission. The practitioner must advise the client of the consequences as provided under the Code and regulations of such noncompliance, error, or omission." You must inform Ahanu that his Year 2 individual tax return was prepared incorrectly, and an amended return should be filed immediately. The good news is that the suspended loss can be carried forward and used to offset future income. If Ahanu refuses to amend the prior year's tax return, then you should discuss disengaging from Ahanu with the other partners of your firm and Ahanu.

Tax Compliance Application

Compliance

Preparation of Form 1065 and Schedule K-1

(LO2, 3, 4) Praise LLC (FEIN: 98-1234567) is a limited liability company using the accrual method that has two members. Joy Stevens (SSN: 123-45-6789) owns 40% of Praise. The following items were reported on Praise's Form 1065 this year:

Gross receipts	$1,390,000	Net Section 1231 gain	$ 22,000
U.S. treasury bond interest income	$ 1,000	Rent expense	$166,000
Municipal interest income	$ 800	Charitable contributions	$ 15,000
Qualified dividend income	$ 3,300	Advertising	$ 12,000
Net long-term capital gain	$ 4,500	Insurance expense	$ 25,000
Cost of goods sold	$ 235,000	Depreciation	$ 55,000
Salaries and wages paid	$ 190,000	Section 179 expense	$ 32,000
Guaranteed payment to Joy	$ 100,000	Entertainment expense	$ 4,150
Utilities	$ 36,000		

How would these amounts be reported on Joy's Schedule K-1, and how would her guaranteed payment be reported to her? Prepare Form 1065 pages 1 and 5 and Schedule K-1 for Joy. The 2024 Form 1065 and Schedule K-1 are used because they were the most current forms available at the time of publication.

Solution

We begin by dividing the tax items into the bucket items and the separately stated items and using the bucket items to compute ordinary business income of $571,000.

Bucket items		**Separately stated items**	
Gross receipts	$1,390,000	U.S. treasury interest income	$ 1,000
Less:		Municipal interest income	$ 800
COGS	(235,000)	Net LTCG	$ 4,500
Salaries and wages	(190,000)	Net Section 1231 gain	$22,000
Guaranteed payment	(100,000)	Qualified dividend income	$ 3,300
Utilities	(36,000)	Charitable contributions	$15,000
Rent expense	(166,000)	Section 179 expense	$32,000
Advertising	(12,000)	Entertainment expense	$ 4,150
Insurance expense	(25,000)		
Depreciation	(55,000)		
Ordinary business income	$ 571,000		

Joy's Schedule K-1 will reflect 40% of the ordinary business income and each separately stated item, as follows:

	Total	Joy's allocation (40%)
Ordinary business income	$571,000	$228,400
U.S. treasury interest income	$ 1,000	$ 400
Municipal interest income	$ 800	$ 320
Net long-term capital gain	$ 4,500	$ 1,800
Net Section 1231 gain	$ 22,000	$ 8,800
Qualified dividend income	$ 3,300	$ 1,320
Charitable contributions	$ 15,000	$ 6,000
Section 179 expense	$ 32,000	$ 12,800
Entertainment expense	$ 4,150	$ 1,660

Joy's guaranteed payment of $100,000 will be reported to her on her Schedule K-1 from Praise, and she will report it on her Form 1040, Schedule E page 2.

The entertainment expense is not deductible.

Form **1065** — Department of the Treasury, Internal Revenue Service

U.S. Return of Partnership Income

OMB No. 1545-0123 — **2024**

For calendar year 2024, or tax year beginning ________, 2024, ending ________, 20 ____.

Go to *www.irs.gov/Form1065* for instructions and the latest information.

	Type or Print	
A Principal business activity	Name of partnership: Praise LLC	D Employer identification number: 98-1234567
B Principal product or service	Number, street, and room or suite no. If a P.O. box, see instructions.: 109 Cooper Street	E Date business started
C Business code number	City or town, state or province, country, and ZIP or foreign postal code: DeKalb, IL 60112	F Total assets (see instructions) $

G Check applicable boxes: (1) ☐ Initial return (2) ☐ Final return (3) ☐ Name change (4) ☐ Address change (5) ☐ Amended return

H Check accounting method: (1) ☐ Cash (2) ☑ Accrual (3) ☐ Other (specify): ________

I Number of Schedules K-1. Attach one for each person who was a partner at any time during the tax year: ________

J Check if Schedules C and M-3 are attached ☐

K Check if partnership: (1) ☐ Aggregated activities for section 465 at-risk purposes (2) ☐ Grouped activities for section 469 passive activity purposes

Caution: Include **only** trade or business income and expenses on lines 1a through 23 below. See instructions for more information.

Income	1a	Gross receipts or sales	1,390,000	b Less returns and allowances ____ c Balance	1c	1,390,000
	2	Cost of goods sold (attach Form 1125-A)			2	235,000
	3	Gross profit. Subtract line 2 from line 1c			3	1,155,000
	4	Ordinary income (loss) from other partnerships, estates, and trusts (attach statement)			4	
	5	Net farm profit (loss) (attach Schedule F (Form 1040))			5	
	6	Net gain (loss) from Form 4797, Part II, line 17 (attach Form 4797)			6	
	7	Other income (loss) (attach statement)			7	
	8	**Total income (loss).** Combine lines 3 through 7			8	1,155,000
Deductions (see instructions for limitations)	9	Salaries and wages (other than to partners) (less employment credits)			9	190,000
	10	Guaranteed payments to partners			10	100,000
	11	Repairs and maintenance			11	
	12	Bad debts			12	
	13	Rent			13	166,000
	14	Taxes and licenses			14	
	15	Interest (see instructions)			15	
	16a	Depreciation (if required, attach Form 4562)	16a	55,000		
	b	Less depreciation reported on Form 1125-A and elsewhere on return	16b		16c	55,000
	17	Depletion **(Do not deduct oil and gas depletion.)**			17	
	18	Retirement plans, etc.			18	
	19	Employee benefit programs			19	
	20	Energy efficient commercial buildings deduction (attach Form 7205)			20	
	21	Other deductions (attach statement)			21	73,000
	22	**Total deductions.** Add the amounts shown in the far right column for lines 9 through 21			22	584,000
	23	**Ordinary business income (loss).** Subtract line 22 from line 8			23	571,000
Tax and Payment	24	Interest due under the look-back method—completed long-term contracts (attach Form 8697)			24	
	25	Interest due under the look-back method—income forecast method (attach Form 8866)			25	
	26	BBA AAR imputed underpayment (see instructions)			26	
	27	Other taxes (see instructions)			27	
	28	**Total balance due.** Add lines 24 through 27			28	
	29	Elective payment election amount from Form 3800			29	
	30	Payment (see instructions)			30	
	31	**Amount owed.** If the sum of line 29 and line 30 is smaller than line 28, enter amount owed			31	
	32	**Overpayment.** If the sum of line 29 and line 30 is larger than line 28, enter overpayment			32	

Sign Here

Under penalties of perjury, I declare that I have examined this return, including accompanying schedules and statements, and to the best of my knowledge and belief, it is true, correct, and complete. Declaration of preparer (other than partner or limited liability company member) is based on all information of which preparer has any knowledge.

Signature of partner or limited liability company member ________ Date ________

May the IRS discuss this return with the preparer shown below? See instructions. ☐ Yes ☐ No

Paid Preparer Use Only

Print/Type preparer's name	Preparer's signature	Date	Check ☐ if self-employed	PTIN
Firm's name			Firm's EIN	
Firm's address			Phone no.	

For Paperwork Reduction Act Notice, see separate instructions. Cat. No. 11390Z Form **1065** (2024)

Form 1065 (2024) Page 5

Schedule K **Partners' Distributive Share Items**

Section	Line	Item		Total amount
Income (Loss)	1	Ordinary business income (loss) (page 1, line 23)	1	571,000
	2	Net rental real estate income (loss) (attach Form 8825)	2	
	3a	Other gross rental income (loss) . . . 3a		
	b	Expenses from other rental activities (attach statement) . . . 3b		
	c	Other net rental income (loss). Subtract line 3b from line 3a	3c	
	4	Guaranteed payments: a Services 4a 100,000 b Capital 4b		
		c Total. Add lines 4a and 4b	4c	100,000
	5	Interest income	5	1,000
	6	Dividends and dividend equivalents: a Ordinary dividends	6a	3,300
		b Qualified dividends 6b 3,300 c Dividend equivalents 6c		
	7	Royalties	7	
	8	Net short-term capital gain (loss) (attach Schedule D (Form 1065))	8	
	9a	Net long-term capital gain (loss) (attach Schedule D (Form 1065))	9a	4,500
	b	Collectibles (28%) gain (loss) . . . 9b		
	c	Unrecaptured section 1250 gain (attach statement) . . . 9c		
	10	Net section 1231 gain (loss) (attach Form 4797)	10	22,000
	11	Other income (loss) (see instructions) Type:	11	
Deductions	12	Section 179 deduction (attach Form 4562)	12	32,000
	13a	Cash contributions	13a	15,000
	b	Noncash contributions	13b	
	c	Investment interest expense	13c	
	d	Section 59(e)(2) expenditures: (1) Type: (2) Amount:	13d(2)	
	e	Other deductions (see instructions) Type:	13e	
Self-Employment	14a	Net earnings (loss) from self-employment	14a	671,000
	b	Gross farming or fishing income	14b	
	c	Gross nonfarm income	14c	
Credits	15a	Low-income housing credit (section 42(j)(5))	15a	
	b	Low-income housing credit (other)	15b	
	c	Qualified rehabilitation expenditures (rental real estate) (attach Form 3468, if applicable)	15c	
	d	Other rental real estate credits (see instructions) Type:	15d	
	e	Other rental credits (see instructions) Type:	15e	
	f	Other credits (see instructions) Type:	15f	
International	16	Attach Schedule K-2 (Form 1065), Partners' Distributive Share Items—International, and check this box to indicate that you are reporting items of international tax relevance ☐		
Alternative Minimum Tax (AMT) Items	17a	Post-1986 depreciation adjustment	17a	
	b	Adjusted gain or loss	17b	
	c	Depletion (other than oil and gas)	17c	
	d	Oil, gas, and geothermal properties—gross income	17d	
	e	Oil, gas, and geothermal properties—deductions	17e	
	f	Other AMT items (attach statement)	17f	
Other Information	18a	Tax-exempt interest income	18a	800
	b	Other tax-exempt income	18b	
	c	Nondeductible expenses	18c	4,150
	19a	Distributions of cash and marketable securities	19a	
	b	Distributions of other property	19b	
	20a	Investment income	20a	
	b	Investment expenses	20b	
	c	Other items and amounts (attach statement)		
	21	Total foreign taxes paid or accrued	21	

Form **1065** (2024)

651123

☐ Final K-1 ☐ Amended K-1 OMB No. 1545-0123

Schedule K-1 (Form 1065) **2024**

Department of the Treasury
Internal Revenue Service

For calendar year 2024, or tax year

beginning / / 2024 ending / /

Partner's Share of Income, Deductions, Credits, etc.

See separate instructions.

Part I Information About the Partnership

A Partnership's employer identification number
98-1234567

B Partnership's name, address, city, state, and ZIP code
Praise LLC
109 Cooper Street, DeKalb, IL 60112

C IRS center where partnership filed return:

D ☐ Check if this is a publicly traded partnership (PTP)

Part II Information About the Partner

E Partner's SSN or TIN (Do not use TIN of a disregarded entity. See instructions.)
123-45-6789

F Name, address, city, state, and ZIP code for partner entered in E. See instructions.
Joy Stevens
112 E. Madison Ave, Decatur, IL 62501

G ☒ General partner or LLC member-manager ☐ Limited partner or other LLC member

H1 ☒ Domestic partner ☐ Foreign partner

H2 ☐ If the partner is a disregarded entity (DE), enter the partner's:
TIN ______ Name ______

I1 What type of entity is this partner? Individual

I2 If this partner is a retirement plan (IRA/SEP/Keogh/etc.), check here ☐

J Partner's share of profit, loss, and capital (see instructions):

	Beginning	Ending
Profit	40 %	40 %
Loss	40 %	40 %
Capital	40 %	40 %

Check if decrease is due to:
☐ Sale or ☐ Exchange of partnership interest. See instructions

K1 Partner's share of liabilities:

	Beginning	Ending
Nonrecourse	$	$
Qualified nonrecourse financing	$	$
Recourse	$	$

K2 Check this box if item K1 includes liability amounts from lower-tier partnerships ☐

K3 Check if any of the above liability is subject to guarantees or other payment obligations by the partner. See instructions ☐

L **Partner's Capital Account Analysis**

Beginning capital account	$
Capital contributed during the year	$
Current year net income (loss)	$
Other increase (decrease) (attach explanation)	$
Withdrawals and distributions	$ ( )
Ending capital account	$

M Did the partner contribute property with a built-in gain (loss)?
☐ **Yes** ☐ **No** If "Yes," attach statement. See instructions.

N **Partner's Share of Net Unrecognized Section 704(c) Gain or (Loss)**
Beginning $
Ending $

Part III Partner's Share of Current Year Income, Deductions, Credits, and Other Items

Line	Item	Amount
1	Ordinary business income (loss)	228,400
2	Net rental real estate income (loss)	
3	Other net rental income (loss)	
4a	Guaranteed payments for services	100,000
4b	Guaranteed payments for capital	
4c	Total guaranteed payments	100,000
5	Interest income	400
6a	Ordinary dividends	1,320
6b	Qualified dividends	1,320
6c	Dividend equivalents	
7	Royalties	
8	Net short-term capital gain (loss)	
9a	Net long-term capital gain (loss)	1,800
9b	Collectibles (28%) gain (loss)	
9c	Unrecaptured section 1250 gain	
10	Net section 1231 gain (loss)	8,800
11	Other income (loss)	
12	Section 179 deduction	12,800
13	Other deductions	A 6,000
14	Self-employment earnings (loss)	328,400
15	Credits	
16	Schedule K-3 is attached if checked ☐	
17	Alternative minimum tax (AMT) items	
18	Tax-exempt income and nondeductible expenses	A 320 C 1,660
19	Distributions	
20	Other information	
21	Foreign taxes paid or accrued	

22 ☐ More than one activity for at-risk purposes*
23 ☐ More than one activity for passive activity purposes*
*See attached statement for additional information.

For IRS Use Only

For Paperwork Reduction Act Notice, see the Instructions for Form 1065. www.irs.gov/Form1065 Cat. No. 11394R **Schedule K-1 (Form 1065) 2024**

Key Terms

End-of-Chapter Assessment

Discussion Questions

1. **(LO1)** Briefly provide the definition of partnership.
2. **(LO1)** Discuss two advantages of being a partnership.
3. **(LO2)** Discuss the holding period rules for tax-deferred partnership formations.
4. **(LO3)** What is nonrecourse debt for partnership tax purposes?
5. **(LO4)** How does the tax treatment for a guaranteed payment differ from a salary payment?
6. **(LO4)** Briefly explain what a separately stated item is and provide two examples.
7. **(LO4)** If a partner's proportionate share of ordinary business income is $45,000 and the partner receives a cash distribution of $55,000, how much will the partner report as income on their individual income tax return, assuming their basis in the partnership interest is $150,000?
8. **(LO5)** Describe the difference between a partner's basis in the partnership interest and the at-risk amount.
9. **(LO5)** Briefly define passive income, portfolio income, and active income.
10. **(LO6)** Why does Congress limit the year-end that partnerships can use?
11. **(LO7)** Describe the loss disallowance rules in regard to losses reported on a partner's Schedule K-1 (Form 1065).
12. **(LO7)** Why is there a restriction on when a partnership can deduct an accrued expense to a cash-basis partner?

Multiple Choice Questions

1. **(LO1)** Which of the following statements is true with regard to the federal income taxation of partnerships?
   a. A limited liability company is generally taxed as a partnership and files Form 1065.
   b. All partnerships must have at least one general partner that has unlimited liability.
   c. All owners of an LLC can participate in management but are not required to.
   d. All of the above

2. **(LO1)** Which of the following statements is *false* with regard to the federal income taxation of partnerships?
   a. A limited partner cannot actively manage the business of the partnership.
   b. Under the check-the-box regulations, limited liability companies generally are disregarded if they have one owner.
   c. Under the check-the-box regulations, entities that are incorporated may elect to be taxed as a partnership.
   d. Limited liability company owners are referred to as members.

3. **(LO2)** Calvin contributed land with a basis of $12,000 and a fair market value of $15,000 to the Waverly Partnership. He also contributed services with a value of $20,000. In return, Calvin received a partnership interest in Waverly with a value of $35,000. What is Calvin's basis in his partnership interest?

   a. $0

   b. $12,000

   c. $32,000

   d. $35,000

4. **(LO2)** The partner's basis in the partnership interest received is known as:

   a. Substituted basis

   b. Carryover basis

   c. Inside basis

   d. None of the above

5. **(LO2)** The partnership's basis in the assets received from a contributing partner is known as:

   a. Substituted basis

   b. Carryover basis

   c. Outside basis

   d. None of the above

6. **(LO3)** Nonrecourse debt may be allocated to the following:

   a. General partner

   b. Limited partner

   c. Member of an LLC

   d. All of the above

7. **(LO3)** At the beginning of Year 7, Pablo owned a 30% interest in Dairy Partnership. During Year 7, a new partner was admitted, and Pablo's interest was reduced to 20%. The partnership liabilities at January 1, Year 7, were $160,000, but decreased to $125,000 at December 31, Year 7. Pablo's and the other partner's capital accounts are in proportion to their respective interests. Disregarding any income, loss, or distributions for Year 7, the basis of Pablo's partnership interest at December 31, Year 7, compared to the basis of his interest at January 1, Year 7 was:

   a. Decreased by $25,000

   b. Increased by $25,000

   c. Decreased by $23,000

   d. Decreased by $3,500

8. **(LO4)** Which of the following is a true statement?

   a. A general partner must pay self-employment tax on their share of ordinary business income.

   b. A general partner must pay self-employment tax on their guaranteed payment regardless if it is for payment of services rendered or for use of capital.

   c. A limited partner does not have to pay tax on their guaranteed payment.

   d. None of these

9. **(LO4)** Which of the following is a separately stated item?

   a. Advertising

   b. Qualified dividend income

   c. Rent expense

   d. Sales revenue

10. **(LO4)** Which of the following is a nonseparately stated item?

    a. Municipal interest income

    b. Section 1231 gains

    c. MACRS depreciation

    d. Charitable contributions

11. **(LO4)** A partnership files which of the following tax return forms to report its income/loss?

    a. Form 1065

    b. Form 1120

    c. Form 1040

    d. Form 990

12. **(LO4)** Greg and Suzanne form the GS Partnership. Greg contributes $35,000 of cash in exchange for his 50% interest in GS capital and profits. During the first year of operations, the following occurred:

GS Partnership Ordinary Business Income	$ 8,000
Greg received a cash distribution	$ 5,000
GS increased partnership debt	$40,000

    What is Greg's ending outside basis?

    a. $34,000

    b. $35,000

    c. $39,000

    d. $54,000

13. **(LO5)** How many current year hours are needed to definitely be a material participant for an activity?

    a. 250

    b. 500

    c. 501

    d. 1,000

14. **(LO5)** Which of the following tests can a limited partner use to determine if they have materially participated in a partnership activity?

    a. The individual participates in the activity for more than 500 hours during the tax year.

    b. The individual materially participated in the activity for any five of the immediately preceding ten tax years.

    c. The individual materially participated for any three preceding tax years in any personal service activity.

    d. All of the above

15. **(LO6)** Which one of the following statements regarding a partnership's tax year is correct?

    a. A partnership formed on April 1 is required to adopt a tax year ending on March 30.

    b. A partnership may elect to have a tax year other than the generally required tax year if the deferral period for the tax year elected does not exceed three months and the proper election is made under Section 444.

    c. A "valid business purpose" can no longer be claimed as a reason for adoption of a tax year other than the generally required tax year.

    d. Within 60 days after a partnership has established a tax year, a form must be filed with the IRS as notification of the tax year adopted.

16. **(LO7)** On April 16, Year 10, Alvin sold 200 shares of Chipmunk stock to Tang Partnership, for $18,000. Alvin has a 65% interest in Tang. Alvin had purchased the stock in Year 5 for $23,000. Tang sold the stock to Amber, an unrelated third party, for $30,000 on December 28, Year 10. What amount of gain from the sale of the stock to Amber should Tang report on the Year 10 partnership tax return?

   a. $0
   b. $2,000
   c. $5,000
   d. $7,000

Brief Exercises

1. **(LO2)** Ron and Willie form the equal RW Partnership as part of a tax-deferred partnership formation. Ron contributes cash of $50,000 and Willie contributes land with a fair market value of $50,000 and adjusted basis of $35,000. What is Willie's basis in her partnership interest?

2. **(LO2)** Shrek and Fiona form the Shrek Swamp Partnership (SSP) as part of a tax-deferred partnership formation. Shrek contributed $90,000 cash for a 90% partnership interest valued at $90,000. Fiona rendered services worth $10,000 for a 10% partnership interest valued at $10,000. What are the tax consequences to Fiona?

3. **(LO2)** An accountant holds a profits interest in a partnership that was received in connection with the performance of services. The partnership has significant real estate investments. For the current year, the accountant's separately stated net long-term capital gain in connection with that interest is $100,000. However, only $33,000 of that amount is attributable to underlying investments that have been held for more than three years. What are the tax consequences to the accountant?

4. **(LO2)** Norton and Richard are equal members in Orange, an LLC. Norton contributes $9,000 cash and Richard contributes a machine with a basis of $6,000 and a fair market value of $10,000, subject to a liability of $1,000. What is Orange's basis for the machine?

5. **(LO3)** Ren is a 10% partner in Argon Partnership and contributed land with an adjusted basis of $7,500, fair market value of $10,000, and a liability of $2,000 that Argon assumed. What is the effect on Ren's basis in the partnership?

6. **(LO4)** Jamie is a 30% partner in the JNY Partnership. During the current year, the partnership reported ordinary business income of $300,000 before any permitted deductions for guaranteed payments and distributions to partners. The JNY Partnership made a current cash distribution of $35,000 to Jamie and paid guaranteed payments to partners Jamie, Nicole, and Yun of $25,000 each ($75,000 total guaranteed payments). How much will Jamie's adjusted gross income increase as a result of these items? How will Jamie's basis change as a result of these items?

7. **(LO4)** Kalani purchases 25% of a partnership on August 1 of the current tax year. The partnership has been in existence for 5 years. Kalani and the selling partner agree to split income for the year on a pro rata basis. On December 31 of the current year, the partnership receives qualified dividend income of $1,000. How much of the dividend income flows to Kalani, and what will be the character of the income for Kalani?

8. **(LO4)** Ursula is a 25% partner in the UNA Partnership that uses a calendar year-end. Ursula died on July 31, Year 32. She bequeaths her 25% interest in the partnership to her daughter. The partnership's ordinary business income is $100,000 for Year 32. How and when is this income reported to Ursula and her daughter, assuming that it is divided on a pro rata basis?

9. **(LO4)** Mark is a 70% partner in the MMM Partnership. During the year, MMM reported gross receipts of $280,000. MMM paid charitable contributions of $45,000 and office expenses of $75,000. In addition, MMM distributed $25,000 each to partners Margo and Michelle, and MMM paid Margo $20,000 for administrative services. How much ordinary business income and separately stated items would Mark report on his individual tax return?

10. **(LO4)** Sabo contributes property with an adjusted basis of $13,200 and fair market value of $22,400 for a 30% interest in the Danger Partnership. The partnership borrows $50,000 from Cherish Bank and Sabo's share of the debt is 30%. What is Sabo's basis in his partnership interest and the balance in his capital account after these transactions?

11. **(LO5)** Kelly invested $33,000 cash and property in a general partnership this year for a 20% capital interest. On the investment date, the property had a fair market value of $18,000 and an adjusted basis of $10,000. At the end of the current tax year, the partnership has no income or loss, and it has recourse debt of $80,000. Kelly is personally liable for 20% of the debt. The partnership also has $20,000 of nonrecourse debt.

   a. What is Kelly's basis and at-risk amount at the end of the tax year?
   b. How would you answer change if the nonrecourse debt is qualified nonrecourse debt?

12. **(LO5)** Roberto is a 10% partner in the RS Partnership. His outside basis in his RS interest is $60,000 before any debt or loss allocation. Roberto's share of qualified nonrecourse debt is $30,000. If Roberto's current year Schedule K-1 reflects an ordinary nonpassive business loss of $100,000, how much of this loss can Roberto deduct on his individual tax return?

13. **(LO6)** A partnership has the following ownership structure:

	Capital interest	Profits interest	Year-end
Party Corporation	60%	60%	July 31
Cake, Inc.	20%	20%	December 31
Lily	20%	20%	December 31

   a. What is the required year-end for the partnership?
   b. What method would be used to determine the required year-end if Party Corporation has a capital and profits interest of 50% and Cake has a capital and profits interest of 30%?

14. **(LO7)** Harriet owns 55% of Cola Partnership. Harriet owns a delivery truck with an adjusted basis of $20,000 and a fair market value of $16,000. Harriet purchased the delivery truck three years ago for another business activity. What is Harriet's recognized gain or loss and deferred gain or loss if Harriet sells the delivery truck to Cola Partnership on March 9 of the current year? What is Cola's holding period in the truck after the sale?

15. **(LO7)** Jekyll and Hyde are equal partners in the Strange Partnership. The partnership owns an investment in a valuable piece of literature that has an adjusted basis of $5,000 and FMV of $8,500. Jekyll and Hyde create a new partnership of which they are equal partners, Evil Partnership. Evil Partnership is an eclectic bookstore that maintains an inventory of unique books for sale. Strange sells the literature to Evil Partnership for $8,500. What are the tax consequences to Strange Partnership for the sale?

Application Problems

1. **(LO2)** Gregor and Astro form the equal GA Partnership as equal partners. Gregor renders services of $35,000 and Astro contributes land with a fair market value of $35,000 and adjusted basis of $22,000. What are the tax consequences to Gregor, Astro, and GA Partnership?

2. **(LO2)** Mya and Veda formed the MV Partnership. Mya contributed $65,000 cash for a 65% interest in the partnership. Veda contributed land that has an adjusted basis of $15,000 and FMV of $45,000. In return, Veda received a 35% partnership interest with a value of $35,000 and $10,000 cash. How much gain or loss is recognized by Mya and Veda, if any?

3. **(LO2)** Amar and Kanan formed the AK Partnership to open a nursery and greenery. They contributed the following assets in return for a 50% partnership interest:

	Adjusted basis	FMV
Amar:		
Cash	$50,000	$50,000
Machinery	$15,000	$25,000
Inventory	$10,000	$10,000
Kanan:		
Land	$95,000	$85,000

Amar owned his own landscaping business that he had operated for six years. The machinery had a holding period of three years. The machinery had originally been purchased for $20,000. The inventory has been held for 60 days. Kanan owned the land as an investment for four years before the partnership formation. What are the tax consequences of the partnership formation including the tax characteristics of the assets?

4. **(LO3)** Ralph and Wayne form the equal RW Partnership. Ralph contributes cash of $50,000 and Wayne contributes land with a fair market value of $70,000 and adjusted basis of $35,000. The land has a $20,000 recourse mortgage attached to it that is assumed by RW Partnership. What are Ralph and Wayne's bases in their partnership interests?

5. **(LO3)** Derrick owns a 45% interest in Bulls Partnership. Derrick contributes property with an adjusted basis of $12,000, fair market value of $37,000, and a liability of $26,000 which the partnership assumed. His outside basis in his partnership interest before the contribution of property is $1,200. How does this transaction affect the basis of Derrick and the other partners?

6. **(LO3)** Elijah owns 60% of the EL Partnership as a general partner and Levi owns 40% as a limited partner. At the beginning of the year, Elijah's basis in his partnership interest is $23,000 and Levi's basis is $18,000. During the year, the partnership secures new recourse debt of $10,000 and new nonrecourse debt of $30,000. Assume that Elijah and Levi also share profits and losses 60%/40%.

   a. Compute their bases in their partnership interests after the debts are incurred.

   b. What is the effect to their bases if $17,000 of the nonrecourse debt is paid back in the following tax year.

7. **(LO3)** The Volunteers Partnership (TVP) is a partnership that has two partners, Peyton and Greg. Peyton's profit sharing ratio is 70% and his loss-sharing ratio is 65%. Greg's profit-sharing ratio is 30% and his loss-sharing ratio is 35%. During Year 1, TVP takes out a $50,000 recourse loan and a $20,000 nonrecourse loan.

   a. How do these debts impact Peyton's and Greg's bases in their partnership interest, assuming the loss sharing ratio is used to allocate the recourse debt?

   b. If $20,000 of the nonrecourse loan is paid off in Year 2, how are the bases affected?

8. **(LO4)** The Cattle Ranch Partnership had the following tax information for the current tax year:

Revenue	$88,000
Interest income	$ 2,000
Insurance expense	$ 4,800
Salaries paid	$12,000
Section 1231 gain	$ 4,000
Charitable contributions	$ 1,500

What is the ordinary business income for Cattle Ranch Partnership?

9. **(LO4)** Lily is a 40% partner in Blooming Gardens Partnership. Blooming has the following tax items this year:

Ordinary business income	$100,000
Dividend income	$ 5,000
Long-term capital loss	$ 12,000
Decrease in partnership debt	$ 45,000

Lily's basis in her partnership interest at the beginning of the year was $88,000 and Lily received a cash distribution during the year of $35,000. What is Lily's basis in her partnership interest at the end of the tax year?

10. **(LO4)** Gadzook is a 60% partner in Bear Enterprises. Bear has the following tax items this year:

Ordinary business loss	$48,000
Interest income	$ 1,000
Dividend income	$ 2,200
Charitable contributions	$ 1,800

Gadzook's basis in his partnership interest at the beginning of the year is $16,000, and Gadzook received a cash distribution during the year of $20,000. What is Gadzook's basis at the end of the tax year? What is the tax effect of the distribution?

11. **(LO4)** Stefanie's outside basis in her 35% interest in SEJ LLC at the beginning of the year was $400,000. Her allocable share of partnership items on her Schedule K-1 are as follows:

Ordinary business loss	$220,000
Tax exempt interest income	$ 8,000
Long-term capital gain	$ 4,500

In addition, the LLC distributed $50,000 of cash to Stefanie at the end of the year. During the year, Stefanie's share of partnership debt also increased by $18,000. What is Stefanie's ending outside basis in her LLC interest?

12. **(LO4)** Moose LLC is a limited liability company using the accrual method that has two members. Yukon owns 30% of Moose. The following items were reported on Moose's Form 1065 this year:

Gross receipts	$2,220,000
Municipal interest income	$ 600
Qualified dividend income	$ 2,300
Cost of goods sold	$ 330,000
Salaries and wages paid	$ 225,000
Guaranteed payment to Yukon	$ 125,000
Utilities	$ 48,000
Net Section 1231 gain	$ 11,000
Rent expense	$ 120,000
Advertising	$ 24,000
Insurance expense	$ 28,000
Depreciation	$ 45,000
Section 179 expense	$ 32,000
Entertainment expense	$ 5,600

a. How would these amounts be reported on Yukon's Schedule K-1, and how would his guaranteed payment be reported to him?

b. If Yukon's beginning basis is $60,000, what is his ending basis?

13. **(LO4)** At the beginning of the year, Maverick's capital account balance in the Top Gun Partnership was $95,000 and his basis in his partnership interest was $70,000. During the year, Maverick contributed property with a basis of $7,500 and a fair market value of $12,000. His share of Top Gun ordinary income and separately stated items was $40,000. At the end of the year, Top Gun distributed $22,000 cash to Maverick. In addition, Top Gun allocated $12,000 of recourse debt and $10,000 of nonrecourse debt to Maverick for new debt incurred during the year. What is Maverick's ending basis and capital account balance?

14. **(LO5)** Which of the following independent situations qualify as material participation?

a. Randy is a retired partner and receives a Schedule K-1 from his former law firm reporting a $12,000 loss. Randy retired two years ago from a law firm where he had been a partner for 25 years.

b. Dominique is a partner in an activity where she provides 375 hours of service, and the other two partners provide 200 hours each.

c. Adeline is a 25% partner and works 300 hours and her partners work 525 hours each.

15. **(LO5)** Sherlock, Watson, and Bond are general partners in the SWB Partnership that operates a detective agency in New York City. This is the second year of the partnership. They worked the following hours this year in partnership activities:

Sherlock	300
Watson	250
Bond	450

Which of the partners materially participated in the partnership, if any?

16. **(LO5)** Timone has a 25% partnership interest in TGIF Partnership. His beginning outside basis is $44,000. His Schedule K-1 from TGIF reflects dividend income of $2,200, tax-exempt interest income of $500, and ordinary business loss of $45,000. TGIF also distributed $3,000 to Timone at the end of the year. What is Timone's ending outside basis if the excess business loss rule does not apply?

17. **(LO5)** Chenglei's share of Partnership Blue's loss is $48,000. Chenglei does not materially participate in the partnership. Other relevant tax information is as follows:

Basis in partnership interest	$32,000
At-risk amount	$27,000
Passive income	$19,000

How much loss from the partnership can Chenglei deduct on this year's tax return if the excess business loss rule does not apply?

18. **(LO5)** Asif and Hussain each have a 50% interest in AH Partnership. Both contributed $5,000 cash to form the partnership. The AH Partnership has the following for its first year of operations:

	Total	Asif	Hussain
Ordinary business income (After the guaranteed payment)	$100,000	$50,000	$50,000
Interest income	800	400	400
Short-term capital gain	1,500	750	750
Guaranteed payment	40,000	25,000	15,000
Cash distributions	10,000	6,000	4,000

a. Calculate Asif and Hussain's ending basis for Year 1.

b. If in Year 2, AH Partnership reported an ordinary business loss of $110,000 and interest income of $1,000. Calculate Asif and Hussain's ending basis for Year 2.

c. If in Year 3, AH Partnership has ordinary business income of $25,000 and interest income of $800. Calculate Asif and Hussain's ending basis for Year 3.

19. **(LO5)** Jerome has the following from his investments:

Moon Partnership ordinary business income	$66,000
Sun Partnership ordinary business loss	$55,000
Passive income from other sources	$38,000

Assume Jerome's basis in each activity is $100,000, he is a passive investor in Sun Partnership, and the excess business loss rule does not apply. What income/loss must Jerome report on his individual income?

20. **(LO5)** Carly and Russell are married and file a joint tax return. They have the following results from their trades and businesses for 2025:

Landscaping sole proprietorship	$ 78,000
Partnership distributive share	$ 75,000
S corporation distributive share	($850,000)

How much can they deduct for these business losses, assuming that the losses are not passive and that they have sufficient basis and at-risk amount to deduct the losses?

21. **(LO6)** Royal Fox Partnership has a required year-end of December 31. Royal Fox operates a farm, and it earns most of its revenue in the late summer months. Royal Fox would prefer to have a year-end of September 30. Gross receipt information is as follows for the last three years:

	Year ended Sept. 30, Year 1	Year ended Sept. 30, Year 2	Year ended Sept. 30, Year 3
12 months receipts	$500,000	$650,000	$700,000
August & Sept. receipts	$150,000	$227,500	$224,000

Can Royal Fox use Sept. 30 for its year-end? If so, what is the first year that it can do so?

22. **(LO6 Advanced)** Lilac, Inc., Daisy, Inc., and Rose, Inc. form the Three Flowers Partnership on January 1 of the current year. Lilac is a 40% partner and Daisy and Rose are each 30% partners. For reporting purposes, Lilac uses a fiscal year with a March 31 year-end, Daisy uses a fiscal year with an October 31 year-end, and Rose uses a calendar year-end. What year-end must Three Flowers Partnership use?

23. **(LO7)** Evan owns investment land with an adjusted basis of $52,000 and fair market value of $42,000. He sells the land to Stan Partnership, for $39,000. Evan owns 85% of Stan Partnership. Stan Partnership later sells the land to an unrelated third party for $65,000.

   a. What is Evan's realized gain/loss and recognized gain/loss? What is Stan Partnership's basis in the land purchased?

   b. What is Stan Partnership's realized gain/loss and recognized gain/loss?

   c. Assume the same facts except Stan Partnership sells the land to an unrelated third party for $45,000. What is Stan Partnership's realized gain/loss and recognized gain/loss?

   d. Assume the same facts except Stan Partnership sells the land to an unrelated third party for $35,000. What is Stan Partnership's realized gain/loss and recognized gain/loss?

24. **(LO7)** Nico owns 50 acres of land that he has held as an investment for the last 23 years. His basis in the land is $50,000. It was recently announced that a new interstate will be built within one mile of his property. Nico decides to subdivide the land into 100 lots for residential homes and believes that he can sell each lot for $45,000. Nico creates a partnership, Lucky Homes, for which he owns a 95% partnership interest, and his son owns the remaining 5%. Nico sells the 50 acres to Lucky Homes for $4,500,000. Lucky Homes plans to subdivide the lots and sell them for residential homes. What are the tax consequences of this sale to Nico?

25. **(LO7)** Desiree is a 60% partner of Action Partnership and she also serves as CEO. Action reports on the accrual basis of accounting. Desiree personally owns a warehouse that was used in a previous business activity. During Year 8, Desiree rented warehouse space to Action for $120,000. The rent accrued as of December 31 is $120,000, but it is not paid to Desiree until January 15, Year 9.

   a. What are the tax effects of this transaction?

   b. How would the answer to part **a** change if Desiree owned 6% of Action Partnership rather than 60%?

Tax Planning Problems

Planning

1. **(LO3)** Tristan owns a 25% interest as a general partner in Bear Partnership and has a beginning basis of $2,000, not including any debt basis. Recourse debt of $8,500 has been allocated to him based on his ownership percentage. The partnership anticipates losses of $20,000 in Year 1 and $22,000 in Year 2. If Tristan is in a 15% tax bracket for LTCGs and plans to sell his interest on January 1 of Year 3 for no consideration, would this sale be advantageous to Tristan? He is in the 35% marginal tax bracket for other income. Discuss the consequences of the debt allocation, loss deductibility, and the sale of the partnership interest. Assume Bear Partnership does not have any inventory or accounts receivables on its balance sheet.

2. **(LO4)** Brooks Kelly, single, graduated from college majoring in law and passed the Bar Exam shortly after graduation. He was hired by a large law firm and worked his way up to Senior Manager, earning $150,000 per year as an employee. Because of his outstanding work ethic, knowledge of law, and ability to bring in new clients, Brooks was offered the position of general partner beginning January 1 of his seventh year (2025) at the firm. Brooks will receive a guaranteed payment of $200,000 and 1% of ordinary business income each year. He is not aware of the tax implications of switching from an employee to a partner. Provide Brooks with his total tax liability, including self-employment tax and the additional Medicare tax, if the firm's ordinary business income was $5 million, and Brooks has taxable income of $210,000 in 2025.

3. **(LO7)** Benjamin owns equipment that is used 100% in his business with a fair market value of $11,000 and an adjusted basis of $15,000. He would like to sell the equipment and is looking for the best net after-tax cash flow. His tax rate is 35%. Would it be better to sell the equipment for $11,000 to Utah Partnership, of which Benjamin owns 75%, or his best friend for $10,000? Why?

Professional Development Skills

Communication Problem

Communication

1. (LO5) **Passive Loss Limitation** Mateo, Santiago, and Julian form the MSJ Partnership in the current year contributing cash of $45,000, $45,000, and $10,000, respectively. Mateo and Santiago own 45% each as general partners and Julian owns 10% as a limited partner. Julian does not participate in management decisions. At the end of the year, MSJ reported the following on its Schedule K and Julian's Schedule K-1:

	MSJ Schedule K	Julian's Schedule K-1
Ordinary business loss	($120,000)	($12,000)
Interest income	$ 500	$ 50
Dividend income	$ 1,200	$ 120

Julian hires you to prepare his tax return. He does not have any other business activities, but he does have a W-2 as an employee. Julian tells you that you have made a mistake because he does not see the loss reported anywhere on the return. Prepare your response to Julian and to the tax file supporting your answer.

Ethics and Professional Responsibilities Problem

Ethics

1. (LO4) **Taxation of Guaranteed Payments** Mickey, Minnie, and Goofy formed the Disney Partnership. Mickey and Minnie are general partners and Goofy is a limited partner. In the current year, Disney Partnership has ordinary business income of $600,000. All three perform services for the partnership and receive guaranteed payments of $50,000 each. You were hired to prepare the Disney Partnership tax return as well as the individual tax returns for the three partners. While meeting with the three partners, Goofy questions why he has to pay self-employment tax on his guaranteed payment because he is a limited partner. The tax accountant in prior years did not include the guaranteed payment as self-employment income on Goofy's prior years' tax returns. What is your response to Goofy?

In addition to the chapter content, see *Statements on Standards for Tax Services* at www.aicpa-cima.com/resources/landing/statements-on-standards-for-tax-services, *Circular 230* at https://www.irs.gov/tax-professionals/office-of-professional-responsibility-and-circular-230, and Chapter 2, LO4, Tax Professional Responsibilities.

Research Problem

Research

1. (LO6) **Permitted Tax Years for Partnerships** Tarik and Daniel, individual taxpayers with a calendar year-end, form the TD Partnership on January 7, Year 4. Both Tarik and Daniel contributed $50,000 cash. They expect the partnership to perform well and generate income of $80,000 in each of the first five years. They would like to have a January 31 year-end. Explain the rules regarding choosing an allowable year-end for a partnership.

CHAPTER 7

Partnership Taxation:

Distributions, Sales, and Advanced Topics

Prostock-studio/Adobe Stock

Before studying this chapter, you should know or, if necessary, review

6.1 Definitions Related to Partnerships

Chapter Introduction

VIDEO CONTENT

Recall the situation that was presented for Aletta in Chapter 6. Aletta has owned a hair salon for the past seven years, which includes a building and equipment. Her current business structure as a sole proprietorship results in unlimited liability for her. She considered incorporating her business so that she can have limited liability, but she is concerned about the potential for double taxation with corporations. Therefore, she has asked you whether she should organize her business as a partnership, or possibly a limited liability company (LLC). To form a partnership or an LLC, she would have to bring in at least one additional owner. Aletta could form a single-member LLC, but it would not be taxed as a partnership and would most likely be taxed as a sole proprietorship on Schedule C of her Form 1040.

If Aletta did organize her business as a partnership, there are several situations that could occur for which partnerships have special tax rules. For example:

- Aletta or other partners could contribute assets that would have had recognized gain or loss if sold rather than contributed. These built-in gains and built-in losses have many special rules that apply, some of which you will learn in this chapter.
- Aletta will likely want to receive distributions from the partnership. The tax consequences of partnership distributions are much better than the rules for corporate distributions. The partnership will never recognize gain or loss on a distribution, and partners recognize gains and losses only in unusual situations.
- If Aletta wants to sell her partnership interest in the future, there are special rules that apply that may cause the gain or loss to not be a capital gain or capital loss.

In this chapter, you will learn how to address these situations so you will be equipped to provide effective tax planning for your partnership clients.

LEARNING OBJECTIVES	TOPICS	PRACTICE OPPORTUNITIES

1 Compute the tax consequences of assets with built-in gains and losses contributed to a partnership.	**7.1 Built-In Gains and Losses**
	• Tax Consequences of Built-In Gains and Losses
	• Tax Reporting of Built-In Gains and Losses
	• Character of Gain or Loss on Sale of Certain Contributed Assets
	  • Unrealized Receivables
	  • Inventory
	  • Capital Loss Property
	• Combining the BIG/BIL Rule with the Contributed Asset Rules
		• Example 7.1.1 Allocation of Built-In Gain
		• Example 7.1.2 Built-In Gain Allocation Limited to Recognized Gain
		• Example 7.1.3 Allocation of Built-In Losses
		• Example 7.1.4 Unrealized Receivables and Inventory
		• Example 7.1.5 Capital Loss Property
		• Practice Problem 7.1.1 Built-In Gain Allocation
		• Practice Problem 7.1.2 Unrealized Receivables and Inventory

2 Determine the tax consequences of a distribution from a partnership to a partner.	**7.2 Distributions from a Partnership**
	• Tax Consequences to Partnerships for Distributions
	• Ordering Rules for Partnership Distributions
	• Tax Consequences to Partners for Current Distributions
	  • Gain and Loss for Current Distributions
	  • Basis Issues for Current Distributions
	• Tax Consequences to Partners for Liquidating Distributions
	  • Gain and Loss for Liquidating Distributions
	  • Basis Issues for Liquidating Distributions
	• Holding Period Rules for Partnership Distributions
	• Character of Gain or Loss for Distributed Assets
		• Example 7.2.1 Tax Consequences to Partnerships for Distributions
		• Example 7.2.2 Current Distributions
		• Example 7.2.3 Liquidating Distribution
		• Example 7.2.4 Basis Increase on a Liquidating Distribution
		• Example 7.2.5 Sale of Distributed Ordinary Income Assets
		• Practice Problem 7.2.1 Tax Consequences to Partnerships for Distributions
		• Practice Problem 7.2.2 Current Distributions
		• Practice Problem 7.2.3 Sale of Distributed Ordinary Income Assets

Learning Objective	Topic	Examples and Practice Problems

3 Compute the tax consequences of a retirement distribution to a partner.	**7.3 Retirement Distributions**
	• Section 736(a) vs. Section 736(b) Payments
	  • Effect of Capital on Classification of Payments
	  • Unrealized Receivables and Unstated Goodwill
	• Evaluating Retirement Distributions
	• Tax Consequences of Section 736(a) and Section 736(b) Payments
		• Example 7.3.1 Unrealized Receivables and Unstated Goodwill
		• Example 7.3.2 Taxation of Retirement Distributions—Capital Intensive
		• Example 7.3.3 Retirement Distribution—Service Partnership with Unstated Goodwill
		• Example 7.3.4 Retirement Distribution—Service Partnership with Stated Goodwill
		• Practice Problem 7.3.1 Unrealized Receivables and Unstated Goodwill
		• Practice Problem 7.3.2 Taxation of Retirement Distributions

4 Compute the tax consequences of the disposition of a partnership interest.	**7.4 Sale of a Partnership Interest**
	• Assets that Affect the Character of Gain/Loss from Sale of a Partnership Interest
	  • Hot Assets—Unrealized Receivables & Depreciation Recapture
	  • Hot Assets—Inventory
	  • Look-Through Rule: Collectible Gain
	  • Look-Through Rule: Unrecaptured Section 1250 Gain
	• Partner's Gain or Loss on Sale of Partnership Interest
	• Other Dispositions of Partnership Interests
	  • Death of a Partner
	  • Gift of a Partnership Interest
	  • Sale of a Carried Interest
		• Example 7.4.1 Partner's Gain or Loss on Sale of Partnership Interest
		• Example 7.4.2 Recharacterized Gain Greater than Recognized Gain
		• Example 7.4.3 Death of a Partner
		• Example 7.4.4 Gift of a Partnership Interest
		• Practice Problem 7.4.1 Partner's Gain or Loss on Sale of Partnership Interest

5 Determine the tax effects of a disproportionate distribution.	**7.5 Advanced Topic (Drilling Down)—Disproportionate Distributions** • Hot Assets for Partnership Distributions • Testing for Substantial Appreciation • Testing to Determine if the Distribution Is Proportionate • Tax Consequences of a Disproportionate Distribution • Comparing a Proportionate and Disproportionate Distribution	• Example 7.5.1 Identifying Hot Assets for Partnership Distributions • Example 7.5.2 Proportionate Distribution • Example 7.5.3 Disproportionate Distribution • Example 7.5.4 Tax Consequences of a Disproportionate Distribution • Practice Problem 7.5.1 Proportionate Distributions • Practice Problem 7.5.2 Disproportionate Distribution

6 Determine how a Section 754 election affects the basis of partnership assets.	**7.6 Advanced Topic (Drilling Down)—Optional Adjustment to Basis of Partnership Assets (Section 754 Elections)**
	• Section 754 Election
	• Section 754 and Sales of Partnership Interests
	  • Section 754 Not Elected by Partnership
	  • Section 754 Elected by Partnership
	  • Special Two-Year Rule When Section 754 Is Not Elected
	• Section 754 and Partnership Distributions
	  • Gain on a Distribution
	  • Loss on a Distribution
	  • Basis Reduction for Partnership Assets
	  • Basis Increase for Partnership Assets
	• Substantial Built-In Losses
	• Allocation of Basis Adjustments
	  • Ordinary Income Assets vs. All Other Assets
		• Example 7.6.1 Section 754 Election
		• Example 7.6.2 Section 754 and Sale of a Partnership Interest
		• Example 7.6.3 Special Two-Year Rule for Certain Distributions
		• Example 7.6.4 Section 754 and Distributions from a Partnership
		• Example 7.6.5 Substantial Built-In Loss from Sale of Partnership Interest
		• Example 7.6.6 Substantial Basis Reduction on Partnership Distribution
		• Example 7.6.7 Allocation of Section 743(b) Adjustment
		• Example 7.6.8 Allocation of Section 734(b) Adjustment for a Gain: One Capital Asset
		• Example 7.6.9 Allocation of Section 734(b) Adjustment for a Gain: Three Capital Assets
		• Practice Problem 7.6.1 Section 754 and Sale of a Partnership Interest
		• Practice Problem 7.6.2 Section 754 and Distributions from a Partnership
		• Practice Problem 7.6.3 Substantial Built-In Loss from Sale of Partnership Interest

7 Compute the tax consequences of distributions related to built-in gain property.	**7.7 Advanced Topic (Drilling Down)—Distributions of Built-In Gain Property** • Distribution of Built-In Gain Property • Distribution of Other Property to BIG Partner	• Example 7.7.1 Distribution of Built-In Gain Property • Example 7.7.2 Distribution of Other Property to Built-In Gain Partner • Practice Problem 7.7.1 Distribution of Built-In Gain Property • Practice Problem 7.7.2 Distribution of Other Property to Built-In Gain Partner

Tax Forms referenced in this chapter

Form 1065, Schedule K-1 Partner's Share of Income, Deductions, Credits, etc.

7.1 Built-In Gains and Losses

LEARNING OBJECTIVE 1

Compute the tax consequences of assets with built-in gains and losses contributed to a partnership.

One of the most important topics in the partnership tax law is built-in gains and losses. A **built-in gain or loss** occurs when a partner contributes an asset that has a different fair market value (FMV) from its adjusted basis in exchange for a partnership interest. For example, if a partner contributes an asset with a FMV of $100 and an adjusted basis of $65, then there is a built-in gain of $35. Alternatively, if the asset has an adjusted basis of $125 then there is a built-in loss of $25.

VIDEO CONTENT

Potential Pitfall

Built-in gains and losses are also known as **precontribution gains and losses** or **Section 704(c) gains and losses**. We refer to them as built-in gains (or BIGs) and built-in losses (or BILs). We refer to partners who contribute assets with BIGs as BIG partners, or with BILs as BIL partners.

Tax Consequences of Built-In Gains and Losses

Built-in gains (BIG) and losses (BIL) must be allocated back to the contributing partner when the asset with the BIG or BIL is sold or disposed of by the partnership. This prevents the BIG or BIL from being shifted to another partner. The amount of BIG or BIL that is allocated to the BIG partner can never exceed the partnership's recognized gain from the sale or disposition of the asset. Therefore, the BIG that is allocated to a BIG partner is the *lower* of:

1. The recognized gain from the sale or disposition of the asset, *or*
2. The BIG.[1]

We show how to compute the BIG allocation in the next two Examples.

EXAMPLE 7.1.1
Allocation of Built-In Gain

Hendon became a 40% partner in the Orange partnership by contributing land with a FMV of $60,000 and an adjusted basis of $42,000. If the partnership sells the asset three years later for $68,000, how is the gain on the sale allocated to the partners?

SOLUTION

The recognized gain by the partnership for the sale is computed as follows:

Amount realized	$68,000
Adjusted basis	(42,000)
Recognized gain	$26,000

Hendon is a BIG partner who has BIG of $18,000 ($60,000 – $42,000). Hendon's BIG allocation is $18,000, the *lower* of:

1. The recognized gain from the sale or disposition of the asset ($26,000), *or*
2. The BIG ($18,000).

The remaining gain of $8,000 ($26,000 – $18,000) is allocated to the partners based on their profit-sharing ratios as follows:

Hendon (40%)	$3,200
Other partners (60%)	$4,800

[1] IRC §704(c)(1)(A).

The gain allocation is summarized as follows:

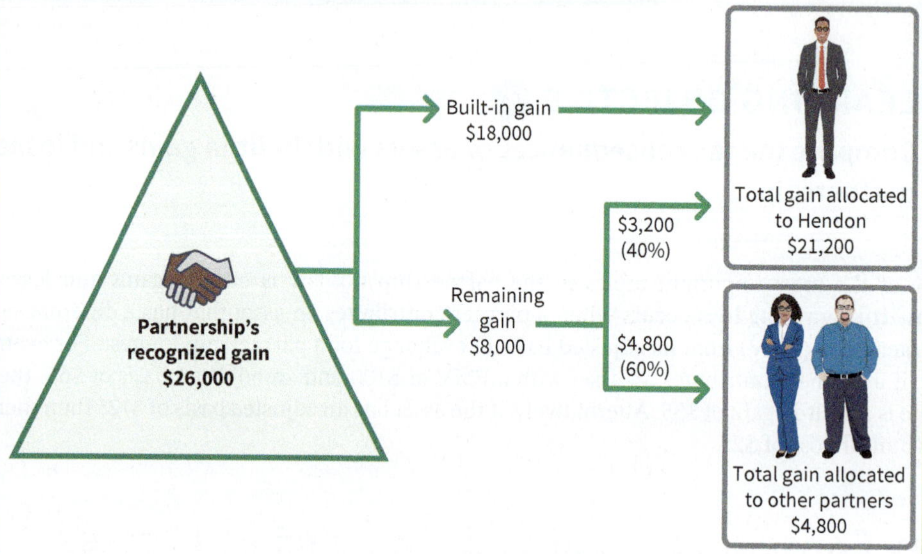

EXAMPLE 7.1.2
Built-In Gain Allocation Limited to Recognized Gain

Assume the same facts as in Example 7.1.1 except that the partnership sells the land for $56,000. How is the gain on the sale allocated to the partners?

SOLUTION

The recognized gain by the partnership for the sale is computed as follows:

Amount realized	$56,000
Adjusted basis	(42,000)
Recognized gain	$14,000

Hendon is a BIG partner who has BIG of $18,000 ($60,000 − $42,000). Hendon's BIG allocation is thus $14,000, the *lower* of:

1. The recognized gain from the sale or disposition of the asset ($14,000), *or*
2. The BIG ($18,000).

The gain allocation is summarized as follows:

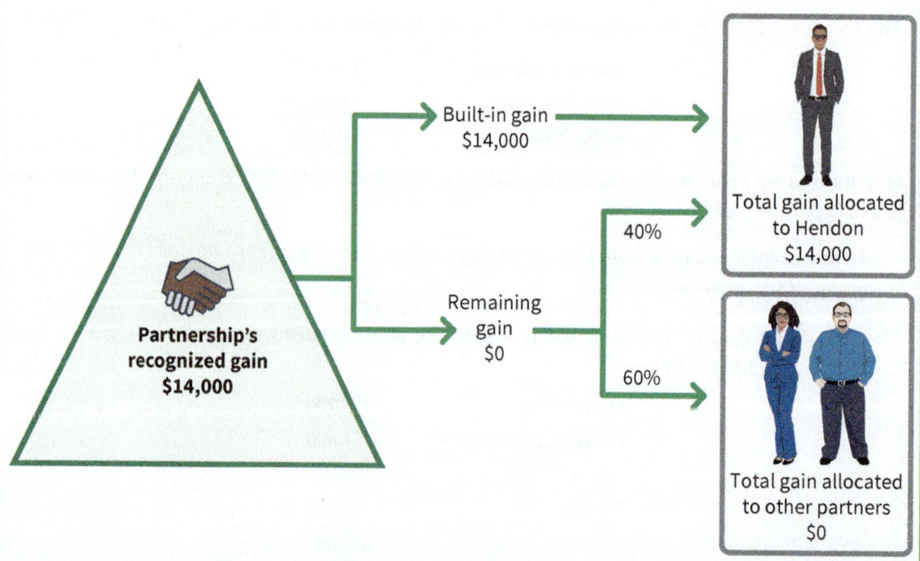

In the next Example, we demonstrate how BILs are computed.

EXAMPLE 7.1.3
Allocation of Built-In Losses

Jesse became a 25% partner in the Green partnership by contributing land with a FMV of $60,000 and an adjusted basis of $72,000. If the partnership sells the asset eight years later for $52,000, how is the loss on the sale allocated to the partners?

SOLUTION

The recognized loss by the partnership for the sale is computed as follows:

Amount realized	$52,000
Adjusted basis	(72,000)
Recognized loss	($20,000)

Jesse is a BIL partner who has a BIL of $12,000 ($60,000 – $72,000). Jesse's BIL allocation is $12,000, the *lower* of:

1. The recognized loss from the sale or disposition of the asset ($20,000), *or*
2. The BIL ($12,000).

The remaining loss of $8,000 ($20,000 – $12,000) is allocated to the partners based on their loss-sharing ratios as follows:

Jesse (25%)	($2,000)
Other partners (75%)	($6,000)

The loss allocation is summarized as follows:

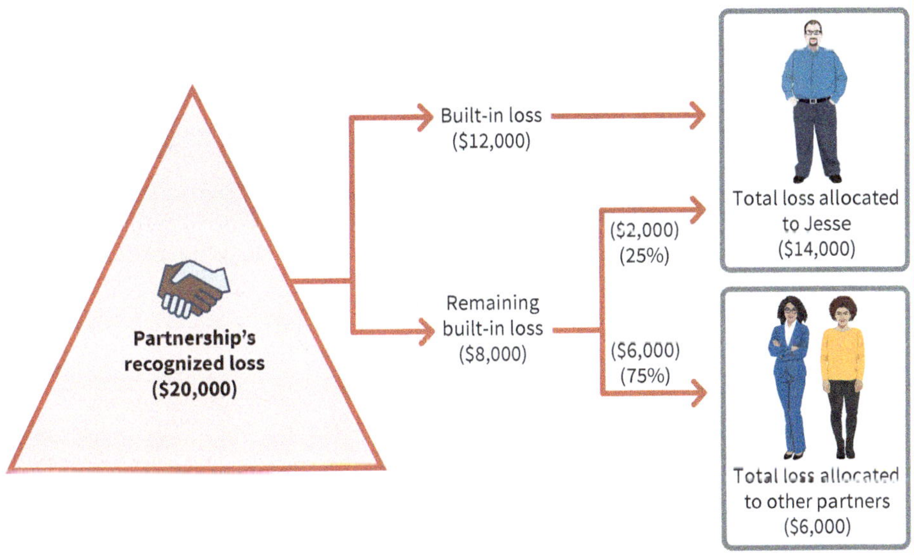

Tax Reporting of Built-In Gains and Losses

There are reporting requirements on a partner's Schedule K-1 if the partner has contributed assets with BIGs or BILs, as shown in **Illustration 7.1**. The partnership must report whether:

- The partner contributed BIG or BIL property during the current year, and
- The partner's cumulative net unrecognized BIG or BIL at the beginning and end of the year.

ILLUSTRATION 7.1 Schedule K-1 (Form 1065) Built-In Gain and Loss Reporting

Schedule K-1, Partner's Share of Income, Deductions, Credits, etc.: BIG and BIL Items

M	Did the partner contribute property with a built-in gain (loss)? ☐ **Yes** ☐ **No** If "Yes," attach statement. See instructions.
N	**Partner's Share of Net Unrecognized Section 704(c) Gain or (Loss)** Beginning . . . . $ Ending . . . . $

Character of Gain or Loss on Sale of Certain Contributed Assets

The partnership tax law has special rules concerning the character of gain or loss when certain contributed assets are sold.[2] These rules apply to assets which, in the hands of the partners, were:

- Unrealized receivables
- Inventory
- Capital assets with a built-in loss (capital loss property)

In each situation, the law prevents partners from using a partnership to convert the character of the gain or loss to a type that is more favorable. **Illustration 7.2** summarizes the differences in the contributed asset rules for unrealized receivables, inventory, and capital loss property.

ILLUSTRATION 7.2 Special Rules for Certain Contributed Assets

Comparing Unrealized Receivables, Inventory, and Capital Loss Property

Asset	Applies to	Character when sold by partnership	Time period for recharacterization
Unrealized receivables	Gains and losses	Ordinary	No time period
Inventory	Gains and losses	Ordinary	Five years
Capital loss property	Built-in losses	Capital	Five years

Unrealized Receivables

If a partner contributes an *unrealized receivable* to a partnership, when the partnership collects or sells the receivable, it will have ordinary income. An **unrealized receivable** is an account receivable of a cash-basis taxpayer. There is no time limit on this provision, although receivables are usually collected over a short time frame.

Inventory

If a partner contributes inventory to a partnership, the partnership will have ordinary income or loss if it sells or disposes of the asset during the next five years. This is the case even if the partnership uses the asset as a Section 1231 asset or a capital asset.

Why **Why does the unrealized receivables and inventory rule exist?** Buzz is a dealer in land, and he owns a three-acre plot that is zoned for manufacturing use. He contributes the land to Brown Partnership in return for an 80% partnership interest which qualifies as a tax-deferred formation. The land has an adjusted basis of $170,000 and a FMV of $300,000. Brown will build a manufacturing plant and warehouse on the land. Brown Partnership uses the land as a Section

[2]IRC §724.

1231 asset because it is using the land in its trade or business. If Buzz had sold the land to the partnership, he would have had ordinary income of $130,000 ($300,000 − $170,000). Because he contributed the land to the partnership, he now has a BIG of $130,000. If the partnership sold the land two months later for $300,000, it would have a gain of $130,000 that would all be allocated to Buzz because of his BIG.

If the unrealized receivables and inventory rules did not exist, the gain would be Section 1231 gain because the partnership used the property in its business. Stepping back and seeing the big picture, Buzz would have converted $130,000 of ordinary income in the land into $130,000 of Section 1231 gain by contributing it to a partnership. This would be an easy way for taxpayers to convert ordinary income into income with a character with better tax consequences. Because of the five-year inventory rule, Brown would also have $130,000 of ordinary income when it sells the land.

Tax Planning Tip

In the example above with Buzz, if Brown Partnership held the land for more than five years before selling it, then the gain when Brown sells the land would be Section 1231 gain. And because of the BIG rule, the first $130,000 of Section 1231 gain would be allocated to Buzz. So, converting the gain in the land from ordinary income to Section 1231 gain is possible if the partnership holds the asset for more than five years before selling it. This planning idea does not apply to unrealized receivables because there is no time limit for treating the gain or loss from unrealized receivables as ordinary.

Capital Loss Property

If a partner contributes a capital asset with a built-in loss to a partnership, the partnership will have a capital loss when it sells the asset, regardless of how the partnership uses the asset. There are two important restrictions on the capital loss rule. First, it applies only for the five years after the partner contributes the asset to the partnership. Second, the capital loss treatment applies only to the extent of the BIL at the time of contribution.

Why **Why does the capital loss property rule exist?** While individual taxpayers like capital assets when they have long-term capital gains, they do not like capital losses because net capital losses can be deducted only to the extent of $3,000, with a carryforward of the remaining loss. Therefore, individuals who have capital assets with a loss in them may contribute them to a partnership so the partnership could use the asset as an ordinary or Section 1231 asset. The hope is that when the partnership sells the asset, the loss that would be allocated back to the BIL partner would no longer be capital loss. However, the capital loss property rule prevents taxpayers from benefiting from this tax maneuver, unless the partnership holds the asset for more than five years before selling it.

Combining the BIG/BIL Rule with the Contributed Asset Rules

It is easy to confuse the application of the rules for BIGs and BILs with the rules for the character of gain or loss on contributed assets. Use these two steps to keep this simple.

Step 1. **Apply:** The contributed asset rule for unrealized receivables, inventory, and capital loss property first, to determine the *character* of the gain or loss.

Step 2. **Determine:** The BIG or BIL, if any, and how much of the gain or loss is allocated to each partner.

The following Example explains the application of these steps.

EXAMPLE 7.1.4 Unrealized Receivables and Inventory

Rashmi has owned a clothing company for the past nine years, and in Year 1, she contributes the following assets to the Rose Partnership in return for a 30% interest:

	Adjusted basis	Fair market value
Unrealized receivable	$ 0	$23,000
Inventory	$49,000	$67,000
Land (investment)	$80,000	$62,000

Rose Partnership collects the $23,000 receivable two months later. Rose sells the inventory and land as follows:

	Sales price	Year sold
Inventory	$72,000	Year 4
Land (investment)	$54,000	Year 4

Rose uses the land as a Section 1231 asset. What are the tax consequences for these three assets?

SOLUTION

Rashmi has the following BIG or BIL after her contributions:

	Adjusted basis	Fair market value	BIG/(BIL)
Unrealized receivable	$ 0	$ 23,000	$23,000
Inventory	$ 49,000	$ 67,000	$18,000
Land (investment)	$ 80,000	$ 62,000	($18,000)

We use the two steps above for each asset to determine the tax consequences.

Unrealized receivable

Step 1. Rose has $23,000 of ordinary income for the collection of the unrealized receivable.

Step 2. All the income is allocated to Rashmi because her BIG was $23,000.

Inventory

Step 1. Rose has $23,000 of ordinary income ($72,000 – $49,000). The ordinary income is not limited to the BIG of $18,000. All the income or loss will be ordinary if the inventory is not held for more than five years after the partnership received it.

Step 2. The first $18,000 of income is allocated to Rashmi because of the BIG rule. The remaining income of $5,000 is allocated according to the profit-sharing ratios: $1,500 ($5,000 × 30%) for Rashmi, $3,500 ($5,000 × 70%) for the other partners. Rashmi's total income is $19,500 ($18,000 + $1,500).

Land

Step 1. Rose has a loss of $26,000 from the sale of the land ($54,000 amount realized – $80,000 basis). Rose holds the land as a Section 1231 asset, but it was contributed as capital loss property within the past five years. Therefore, the loss is a capital loss to the extent of the built-in loss ($18,000). The remaining loss of $8,000 is a Section 1231 loss because that loss occurred after the land was contributed to the partnership.

Step 2. The first $18,000 of loss is allocated to Rashmi because of the BIL rule. The remaining loss of $8,000 is allocated according to the loss sharing ratios: $2,400 ($8,000 × 30%) for Rashmi; $5,600 ($8,000 × 70%) for the other partners.

The loss allocation is summarized as follows:

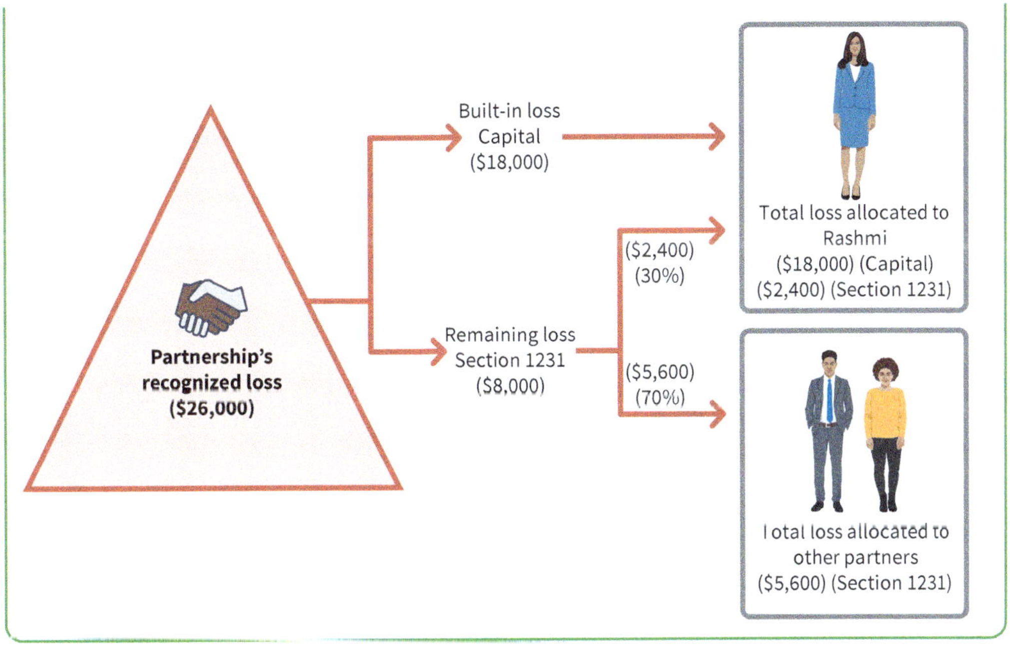

EXAMPLE 7.1.5
Capital Loss Property

In Example 7.1.4, how would the answer change if the partnership had held the land for more than five years before selling it?

SOLUTION

In this case, the contributed asset rule would not apply for the character of the loss of the capital loss property. Therefore, the $26,000 loss would be a Section 1231 loss because that is how Rose holds the property. The allocation of the BIL to the partners is the same as in Example 7.1.4. The first $18,000 of loss is allocated to Rashmi because of the BIL rule. The remaining loss of $8,000 is allocated according to the loss sharing ratios: $2,400 ($8,000 × 30%) for Rashmi; $5,600 ($8,000 × 70%) for the other partners.

Related exercises: Discussion Questions 1, 2
Multiple Choice Question 1
Brief Exercise 1
Application Problems 1, 2, 3, 4, 5
Tax Planning Problem 1

PRACTICE PROBLEM 7.1.1
Built-In Gain Allocation

Rob became a 30% partner in the Dallas partnership by contributing property with a FMV of $55,000 and an adjusted basis of $40,000. If the partnership sells the asset two years later for $52,000, how is the gain on the sale allocated to the partners?

SOLUTION

The recognized gain by the partnership for the sale is computed as follows:

Amount realized	$52,000
Adjusted basis	(40,000)
Recognized gain	$12,000

Rob is a BIG partner who has BIG of $15,000 ($55,000 – $40,000). Rob's BIG allocation is $12,000, the *lower* of:

1. The recognized gain from the sale or disposition of the asset ($12,000), *or*
2. The BIG ($15,000).

There is no remaining gain to allocate to the other partners.

PRACTICE PROBLEM 7.1.2

Unrealized Receivables and Inventory

Chandra has owned a sports equipment company for the past five years, and in Year 1, he contributes the following assets to the Earth Partnership in return for a 25% interest:

	Adjusted basis	Fair market value
Unrealized receivable	$ 0	$19,000
Inventory	$42,000	$62,000
Land (investment)	$75,000	$57,000

Earth Partnership collects the $19,000 receivable three months later. Earth sells the inventory and land as follows:

	Sales price	Year sold
Inventory	$67,000	Year 3
Land (investment)	$48,000	Year 5

Earth uses the land as a Section 1231 asset. What are the tax consequences for these three assets?

SOLUTION

Chandra has the following BIGs or BILs after his contributions:

	Adjusted basis	Fair market value	BIG/(BIL)
Unrealized receivable	$ 0	$19,000	$19,000
Inventory	$42,000	$62,000	$20,000
Land (investment)	$75,000	$57,000	($18,000)

We use the two steps above for each asset to determine the tax consequences.

Unrealized receivable

Step 1. Earth has $19,000 of ordinary income for the collection of the unrealized receivable.

Step 2. All the income is allocated to Chandra because his BIG was $19,000.

Inventory

Step 1. Earth has $25,000 of ordinary income ($67,000 – $42,000). The ordinary income is not limited to the BIG of $20,000. All the income or loss will be ordinary if the inventory is not held for more than five years after the partnership received it.

Step 2. The first $20,000 of income is allocated to Chandra because of the BIG rule. The remaining income of $5,000 is allocated according to the profit-sharing ratios: $1,250 ($5,000 × 25%) for Chandra; $3,750 ($5,000 × 75%) for the other partners. Chandra's total income is $21,250 ($20,000 + $1,250).

Land

Step 1. Earth has a loss of $27,000 from the sale of the land ($48,000 amount realized – $75,000 basis). Earth holds the land as a Section 1231 asset, but it was contributed as capital loss property within the past five years. Therefore, the loss is a capital loss to the extent of the built-in loss ($18,000). The remaining loss of $9,000 is a Section 1231 loss because that loss occurred after the land was contributed to the partnership.

Step 2. The first $18,000 of loss is allocated to Chandra because of the BIL rule. The remaining loss of $9,000 is allocated according to the loss sharing ratios: $2,250 ($9,000 × 25%) for Chandra; $6,750 ($9,000 × 75%) for the other partners.

INTERACTIVE SELF-SCORING QUIZZES

7.2 Distributions from a Partnership

LEARNING OBJECTIVE 2

Determine the tax consequences of a distribution from a partnership to a partner.

VIDEO CONTENT

The rules for the taxation of partnership distributions vary significantly from the rules for distributions from corporations. In general, the partnership rules are more taxpayer friendly than the corporate rules. While it is possible for a corporation to recognize gain if it distributes appreciated property to a shareholder, a partnership will not if it distributes appreciated property to a partner. Additionally, it is very likely that shareholders will recognize income when they receive a distribution (See Chapter 4, LO1, Distributions Taxed as Dividends), but it is unlikely that partners will recognize income when they receive a distribution from a partnership, as we will explain below.

The rules for distributions for partnerships vary based on the answers to these two questions:

- Is this a current distribution or a liquidating distribution?
- Is the distribution proportionate or disproportionate?

We cover the rules for current distributions and liquidating distributions in this section. A **current distribution** is a distribution where the partner continues to be a partner after the distribution. A **liquidating distribution** means that the partnership is dissolving, and the partner will no longer hold a partnership interest. All distributions in the main part of the chapter are proportionate distributions.[3] We explain the rules for disproportionate distributions in an Advanced Topic section later in this chapter.

Related exercise: Discussion Question 3

Tax Consequences to Partnerships for Distributions

Partnerships do not recognize gain or losses for distributions to partners.[4] This rule applies for both current and liquidating distributions. This is the case whether the distribution is cash or property. Recall that corporations must recognize a gain when they distribute appreciated property to shareholders. The lack of gain recognition upon a distribution of appreciated property is a major advantage of partnerships.

Tax Planning Tip

If property owned by a business is expected to appreciate significantly, then the business owners may not want to use the corporate form of business. If the appreciated asset is later sold by the corporation or is distributed to shareholders, then there could be two levels of tax: one at the corporate level and one at the shareholder level. If a partnership distributes similar appreciated property, there is no gain to the partnership or the partners. If the partnership sells the appreciated property, there will be one level of tax only—that being at the partnership level.

[3]If one partner is liquidating their interest but the partnership is not dissolving, the partner is considered to have retired from the partnership. The tax rules for retiring partners are covered in LO3, Retirement Distributions.

[4]IRC §731(b).

The following Example explores the tax consequences of a typical distribution from a partnership.

EXAMPLE 7.2.1
Tax Consequences to Partnerships for Distributions

Kiwi Partnership owns a building that has a fair market value of $1,250,000 and an adjusted basis of $300,000. Kiwi originally purchased the building for $375,000. During the current year, Kiwi distributed the building to Hideo who owns a 70% interest in the partnership.

a. What are the tax consequences of the distribution to Kiwi?

b. What are the tax consequences to Kiwi if the fair market value of the building is $225,000?

c. How would the tax consequences vary for parts **a** and **b** if Kiwi was a corporation?

SOLUTION

a. Kiwi Partnership has a realized gain of $950,000 when it distributes the building to Hideo. However, Kiwi does not recognize the gain.

b. Kiwi Partnership has a realized loss of $75,000 ($225,000 amount realized − $300,000 adjusted basis), but the loss is not recognized.

c. If Kiwi was a corporation, for the scenario in **a,** it would recognize a gain of $950,000 if the FMV was $1,250,000. For the scenario in **b,** if the FMV was $225,000, it would not be allowed to recognize the $75,000 realized loss.

Related exercises: Discussion Question 4
Application Problem 6

Ordering Rules for Partnership Distributions

If the partner receives more than one item of property in the distribution, then the following ordering rules are used to reduce the partner's basis:[5]

- First, the partner's adjusted basis is allocated to cash distributions and deemed cash (reductions in liabilities).
- Second, the partner's adjusted basis is allocated to distributions of unrealized receivables and inventory in an amount equal to the partnership's basis in these assets.
- Finally, the partner's adjusted basis is allocated to other assets distributed. The other assets are capital assets and Section 1231 assets.

For purposes of the partnership tax laws, inventory is defined differently than it is for financial accounting. The typical definition for financial accounting is that inventory consists of goods held for sale in the ordinary course of a trade or business. However, for partnership taxation, **inventory** is defined more broadly, and includes all assets other than cash, capital assets, and Section 1231 assets.[6] Therefore, for partnership tax law inventory includes:

- Goods held for sale in the ordinary course of a trade or business
- Unrealized receivables
- Accounts receivables

[5]IRC §732(c).

[6]IRC §751(d).

Tax Consequences to Partners for Current Distributions

It is important to understand the rules for gain and loss recognition for partners when receiving a current distribution, and also the effect on the partner's basis in the partnership interest.

Gain and Loss for Current Distributions

If a partner receives a current distribution, the tax consequences are as follows:[7]

- The partner recognizes gain only to the extent that the *cash* distributed to the partner exceeds their basis in their partnership interest.
- If the partner's share of partnership debt decreases, or if the partnership assumes the partner's debt, the amount of debt relief is identified as **deemed cash** and is treated as a cash distribution to the partner.
- Marketable securities received by the partner are considered to be the same as cash. However, the marketable securities will not cause gain to be recognized unless the partner receives more than the partner's pro rata share of the securities.[8]
- If the partner receives a distribution of property, the partner will never recognize a gain.[9]
- A partner never recognizes a loss upon the receipt of a current distribution.

Basis Issues for Current Distributions

The rules for the basis of property received in a current distribution are as follows:[10]

- The general rule for the effect of partnership distributions on the partner's basis is that the basis is reduced by the amount of cash distributed or the basis of the property distributed.
- The basis in the partnership interest can never be reduced below zero. Therefore, if the total basis of all the assets distributed is greater than the partner's basis in the partnership interest, the reduction in basis is limited to the partner's basis. If that is the case, the partner's basis in the asset received is *less* than the partnership's basis in that asset before the distribution.

The next Example demonstrates the tax consequences of a current distribution from a partnership.

EXAMPLE 7.2.2
Current Distributions

On August 1, the REK Partnership, a calendar-year partnership, distributes to each of its equal partners the following assets: $12,000 cash and land with a fair market value of $8,000 and a basis of $4,000. Robert, Esther, and Kareem have outside bases in their partnership interest of $21,000, $13,000, and $7,000, respectively. The partnership had the following assets prior to the distribution:

Assets	Adjusted basis	Fair market value
Cash	$60,000	$60,000
Accounts receivable	0	15,000
Inventory	22,000	32,000
Land	33,000	63,000
Building	14,000	54,000

a. What are the tax consequences of the distribution to Robert, Esther, and Kareem, assuming that the distributions are proportionate?

b. How would the solution change if each partner received debt relief of $12,000 instead of a cash distribution of $12,000?

[7]IRC §731.

[8]IRC §731(c).

[9]There are some advanced topics involving Section 704(c) built-in gain property that are exceptions to this general rule.

[10]IRC §732 and IRC §733.

SOLUTION

a. The starting point for computing the tax consequences of the distribution is the partner's basis in their partnership. Using the ordering rules discussed above, we consider the effect of cash first, and then the land. Refer to this table as you read the analysis.

	Robert	Esther	Kareem
Starting basis	$21,000	$13,000	$ 7,000
Cash	(12,000)	(12,000)	(12,000)
	$ 9,000	$ 1,000	($5,000)
Gain			5,000
			0
Land	(4,000)	($1,000)	0
Ending basis	$ 5,000	0	0

Robert: Robert's basis of $21,000 is reduced to $9,000 by the cash received of $12,000. His basis is next reduced to $5,000 by the land's basis of $4,000. Robert's ending basis in his partnership interest is $5,000. He takes a $4,000 basis in the land, the same basis that the partnership had in the land.

Esther: Esther's basis of $13,000 is reduced to $1,000 by the cash received of $12,000. Her basis is next reduced to $0 for the distribution of the land. Esther cannot reduce her basis by the full $4,000 basis of the land because that would result in a negative basis of ($3,000) in her partnership interest, but basis can never be negative. Esther's ending basis in her partnership interest is $0. Her basis in the land is $1,000, which is the lower of the $4,000 basis the partnership had in the land or her remaining basis of $1,000 before the land distribution.

Kareem: Kareem's basis of $7,000 is reduced to $0 by the cash received of $12,000. He recognizes $5,000 of gain because the cash distributed exceeds the basis in this partnership interest. The $5,000 gain increases his basis to zero so that his basis is not negative. Kareem had no basis remaining to allocate to the land, so he reduced his basis by $0 for the land distribution. Kareem's ending basis in his partnership interest is $0. His basis in the land is $0, which is the lower of the $4,000 basis the partnership had in the land or his remaining basis of $0 before the land distribution.

b. If the partners received $12,000 of debt relief instead of a $12,000 cash distribution, the solution would be the same. Debt relief is treated as a cash distribution to the partner.

Tax Planning Tip

Each parcel of land in Example 7.2.2 had $4,000 of unrealized appreciation in it when distributed. The appreciation in the land is not recognized by the partnership when distributed. Rather, the unrealized gain goes with the property to the partner. For example, if Robert sells his parcel of land the day after he receives it, he will have a recognized gain of $4,000 (amount realized $8,000 – $4,000 adjusted basis).

If Esther and Kareem sell their land for $8,000, their gain will be more than $4,000. The additional gain they recognize is because they did not have enough basis in their partnership interest to assign $4,000 of basis to the land. Esther's gain would be $7,000 (amount realized $8,000 – $1,000 adjusted basis) and Kareem's would be $8,000 (amount realized $8,000 – $0 adjusted basis).

Related exercises: Brief Exercises 2, 3
Application Problems 7, 8, 9

Tax Consequences to Partners for Liquidating Distributions

It is also important to understand the rules for gain and loss recognition for partners when receiving a liquidating distribution, and the effect on the partner's basis in the partnership interest. The rules in this section apply when the partnership is liquidating, so none of the partners will remain partners after the distribution. In the next section (LO3), we discuss the retirement of a partner from the partnership where the partnership continues in existence.

Gain and Loss for Liquidating Distributions

If a partner receives a liquidating distribution, the tax consequences are generally the same as for current distributions. One difference is that in certain situations, the partner can recognize a loss for a liquidating distribution. The rules for liquidating distributions include:

- A partner recognizes gain only to the extent that the sum of the *cash* and *deemed cash* distributed to the partner exceeds the partner's basis in the partnership interest.
- If the partner receives a distribution of only property, the partner will never recognize a gain.[11]
- A partner recognizes a loss on the receipt of a distribution if the following three conditions are satisfied:[12]

  1. The distribution is liquidating,
  2. The distribution consists only of cash, unrealized receivables, and inventory, *and*
  3. The outside basis of the partner's interest exceeds the sum of cash plus the basis of the receivables and inventory. In other words, the partner has some basis left in their partnership interest after subtracting the basis of the cash, inventory, and unrealized receivables.

Related exercises: Discussion Question 5
Multiple Choice Questions 2, 3

Basis Issues for Liquidating Distributions

The basis that a partner has in their partnership interest after a liquidating distribution must be zero. Keep the following three guidelines in mind for liquidating distributions:

- The general rule for the effect of partnership distributions on the partner's basis is that the basis is reduced by the amount of cash distributed and/or the basis of the property distributed.
- The ending basis in the partnership interest after the liquidation distribution must be zero. To meet this rule, in some situations the partner's basis in an asset distributed is *greater* than the partnership's basis in the asset.
- The basis in the partnership interest can never be reduced below zero. Therefore, if the total basis of all the assets distributed is greater than the partner's basis in the partnership interest, the reduction in basis is limited to the partner's basis. If that is the case, the partner's basis in the asset received is less than the partnership's basis in that asset before the distribution.

The next two Examples illustrate the tax consequences of liquidating distribution.

[11]There are some distributions involving Section 704(c) built-in gain property that are exceptions to this general rule, see LO6, Advanced Topic (Drilling Down)—Optional Adjusted to Basis of Partnership Assets (Section 754 Elections).

[12]IRC §731(a)(2).

EXAMPLE 7.2.3 Liquidating Distribution

The TAN partnership has the following balance sheet as of April 1 of the current year.

Assets	Adjusted basis	Fair market value	Partners' capital	Adjusted basis	Fair market value
Cash	$120,000	$120,000	Teo	$ 92,000	$ 90,000
Inventory	12,000	30,000	Ann	92,000	90,000
Land	144,000	120,000	Nigel	92,000	90,000
	$276,000	$270,000		$276,000	$270,000

a. In liquidation of her interest in the partnership, Ann receives one-third of the inventory and two-thirds of land. What are the tax consequences of this distribution to Ann and the partnership?

b. Same as part **a**, except that Ann receives one-third of the inventory and $80,000 cash. What are the tax consequences of this distribution to Ann and the partnership?

SOLUTION

a. To compute the tax results for the distribution, you begin with Ann's basis in her partnership interest before the distribution. Following the ordering rules, the inventory reduces the basis before the land.

Adjusted basis	$92,000
One-third of inventory (basis = $4,000; FMV = $10,000)	(4,000)
Basis before land distribution	$88,000

Her basis is next reduced for the distribution of the land.

Two-thirds of land (basis = $96,000; FMV = $80,000)	(88,000)
Ending basis	$ 0

Ann cannot reduce her basis by the $96,000 basis of the land because that would result in a basis of ($8,000) in her partnership interest, but basis can never be negative. Ann's ending basis in her partnership interest is $0. Her basis in the land is $88,000, which is the lower of the $96,000 basis the partnership had in the land or her remaining basis of $88,000 before the land distribution. Ann's ending basis in her partnership interest is zero and no gain or loss is recognized to Ann or the partnership.

To summarize, her basis in the inventory is $4,000 and her basis in the land is $88,000. The $6,000 of unrealized gain in the inventory at the partnership level has transferred to Ann. The basis of the land is reduced from $96,000 in the hands of the partnership to $88,000 in Ann's hands.

b. Once again, begin with Ann's basis in her partnership interest before the distribution. Following the ordering rules, the cash reduces her basis before the inventory.

Adjusted basis	$92,000
Cash	(80,000)
Basis before inventory distribution	$12,000
One-third of inventory (basis = $4,000; FMV = $10,000)	(4,000)
Basis after distributions	$ 8,000

Ann's ending basis in her partnership interest is zero and no gain or loss is recognized by the partnership.

Loss	(8,000)
Ending basis	$ 0

Ann recognized a capital loss of $8,000 because the three conditions for a loss are met:

- It is a liquidating distribution.
- Capital assets and Section 1231 assets were not distributed.
- There is basis in the partnership remaining after it is reduced for the cash and the basis of the inventory received.

Her basis in the inventory is $4,000. The $6,000 of unrealized gain in the inventory at the partnership level has transferred to Ann.

One of the peculiar aspects of partnership distributions is that the fair market value of the property distributed does not affect the tax consequences of the distribution. For example, assume the same facts as in Example 7.2.3b except that the inventory is worth $120,000 rather than $30,000, and the value of each partner's interest increases from $90,000 to $120,000. The balance sheet now appears as follows:

Assets	**Adjusted basis**	**Fair market value**	**Partners' capital**	**Adjusted basis**	**Fair market value**
Cash	$120,000	$120,000	**Teo**	$ 92,000	$120,000
Inventory	12,000	120,000	**Ann**	92,000	120,000
Land	144,000	120,000	**Nigel**	92,000	120,000
	$276,000	$360,000		$276,000	$360,000

However, the tax implications would be exactly the same, because the values changed were not used in computing the solution to Example 7.2.3.

It is also possible that the basis of an asset distributed in a liquidating distribution could increase. This is because the ending basis in the partnership interest must be $0, as shown in the next Example.

EXAMPLE 7.2.4
Basis Increase on a Liquidating Distribution

The TAN partnership has the following balance sheet as of April 1 of the current year. The items in **red** changed from Example 7.2.3.

Assets	**Adjusted basis**	**Fair market value**	**Partners' capital**	**Adjusted basis**	**Fair market value**
Cash	$120,000	$120,000	**Teo**	**$ 64,000**	$ 90,000
Inventory	12,000	30,000	**Ann**	**64,000**	90,000
Land	**60,000**	120,000	**Nigel**	**64,000**	90,000
	$192,000	$270,000		**$192,000**	$270,000

In liquidation of her interest, Ann receives one-third of the inventory and two-thirds of land. What are the tax consequences of this distribution to Ann and the partnership?

SOLUTION

To compute the tax results for the distribution, you begin with Ann's basis in her partnership interest before the distribution. Following the ordering rules, the inventory reduces the basis before the land.

Adjusted basis	$64,000
One-third of inventory (basis = $4,000; FMV = $10,000)	(4,000)
Basis before land distribution	$60,000
Two-thirds of land (basis = $40,000; FMV = $80,000)	(60,000)
Ending basis	$ 0

Ann's ending basis in her partnership interest is zero and no gain or loss is recognized to Ann or the partnership. Her basis in the inventory is $4,000 and her basis in the land is $60,000 because her ending basis in her partnership interest must be zero. The basis of the land is increased from $40,000 in the hands of the partnership to $60,000 in Ann's hands.

Related exercises: Brief Exercise 4
Application Problems 10, 11, 12

Illustration 7.3 compares the tax consequences of current and liquidating distributions.

ILLUSTRATION 7.3 Summarizing Partnership Distribution Rules

Tax Consequences of Current Distributions and Liquidating Distributions

Tax item	Current distributions	Liquidating distributions
Gain Recognition for Cash Distributions	Partners recognize gain only to the extent cash distributed exceeds their basis in their partnership interest.	Partners recognize gain only to the extent cash distributed exceeds their basis in their partnership interest.
Partner's Liability Relief/ Deemed Cash	If the partner's share of partnership debt decreases, or if the partnership assumes the partner's debt, the amount of net debt relief is identified as deemed cash and is treated as a cash distribution to the partner.	If the partner's share of partnership debt decreases, or if the partnership assumes the partner's debt, the amount of net debt relief is identified as deemed cash and is treated as a cash distribution to the partner.
Gain Recognition for Property Distributions	Partner does not recognize gain if they receive only a property distribution.	Partner does not recognize gain if they receive only a property distribution.
Loss Recognition for Distributions	A partner never recognizes a loss upon the receipt of a current distribution.	A partner recognizes a loss on the receipt of a distribution if the following three conditions are satisfied: **1.** The distribution is liquidating. **2.** The distribution consists of only cash, unrealized receivables, and inventory. **3.** The outside basis of the partner's interest exceeds the sum of cash plus the basis of the receivables and inventory.
Reduction in Basis of Partnership Interest	Basis is reduced by the amount of cash distributed and the basis of the property distributed. The basis can never be reduced below zero.	Basis is reduced by the amount of cash distributed and the basis of the property distributed. The ending basis in the partnership must be zero. The basis can never be reduced below zero.

Holding Period Rules for Partnership Distributions

The holding period of partnership property that is distributed to a partner goes with the property to a partner.[13] This applies regardless of whether the property is an ordinary, capital, or Section 1231 asset. For example, in Example 7.2.4, if TAN Partnership had held the land for six years before it was distributed to her, then Ann's holding period would be six years for the land on the day she received it.

Related exercise: Discussion Question 6

[13]IRC §735(b).

Character of Gain or Loss for Distributed Assets

Certain ordinary income assets that are distributed to partners carry the ordinary income taint with them to the partner, regardless of whether the partner holds the asset as an ordinary, capital, or Section 1231 asset. This taint applies to assets that, in the hands of the partnership, are:

- Unrealized receivables, *or*
- Inventory[14]

When a partner recognizes income on an unrealized receivable distributed by a partnership, the income will always be ordinary. When a partner sells or disposes of inventory distributed by a partnership within five years of the distribution date, the gain or loss recognized by the partner is ordinary. If the partner has owned the inventory for more than five years since distributed, then the character of the gain or loss is determined based on how the partner used the asset.

> **Potential Pitfall**
>
> The ordinary income taint for unrealized receivables received from a partnership has no time limitation, while the taint for inventory lasts for only five years in the hands of the partner.

Why **Why do ordinary income assets retain their ordinary income taint for the partner?** Individual taxpayers would prefer to have long-term capital gain or Section 1231 gain rather than ordinary income. Congress does not want taxpayers to change the character of unrealized income in an ordinary income asset by distributing the asset to a partner because ordinary income is often taxed at higher rates than other income.

EXAMPLE 7.2.5
Sale of Distributed Ordinary Income Assets

The Purple Partnership is a dealer in land. Priya, an engineer, receives a current distribution of land from Purple on October 15 of Year 10. The basis of the land to the partnership is $20,000 and its fair market value at the date of distribution is $24,000. Priya's basis in her partnership interest before the distribution is $45,000. Priya uses the land as an investment.

a. On December 12, Year 10, Priya sells the land for $33,000. What is the amount and character of Priya's gain?

b. In **a.** above, how do the results change if Priya sold the land on November 15, Year 15?

SOLUTION

a. We first compute the tax effect of the distribution of the land to Priya.

Basis in partnership interest	$45,000
Basis in land to partnership	(20,000)
Ending basis in partnership interest	$25,000

Priya's basis in the land is $20,000, and she recognized no gain or loss from the distribution. Purple is a dealer in land, so the land is inventory. Therefore, if Priya sells the land within five years of receiving it, her gain or loss will be ordinary. She sold the land less than two months after receiving it, so her gain of $13,000 ($33,000 − $20,000) is ordinary income.

b. Priya sold the land on November 15, Year 15, which is more than five years after she received it, so the character of the $13,000 gain is determined based on the manner in which Priya held the property. This is a capital asset to Priya because it is an investment, so the $13,000 is a long-term capital gain.

Related exercise: Application Problem 13

[14]IRC §735.

Spotlight on the Law

The Flexibility of Partnerships

In Chapter 6, you learned that partnership formations are rarely taxable because there is not an 80% control test like corporations have. You have just learned that partnership distributions are rarely taxable. Gain is recognized to the partner only if the cash distributed exceeds the partner's basis in their partnership interest. Further, gain or loss is never recognized to the partnership for a distribution. Distributions to corporate shareholders are treated very differently. For example, if appreciated property is distributed to a shareholder, the corporation must recognize gain for the appreciation, and the shareholder will likely have dividend income. What a terrible result—double taxation for corporate distributions! Whereas the same distribution to a partner usually is not taxed to the partner, and never to the partnership. You should start to see how flexible partnerships are, and how much better the overall tax treatment is for partnerships over corporations. Congress created partnerships so business owners can usually get into the partnership tax-free, and out of the partnership tax-free. This is why partnerships and limited liability companies are used so often for new start-ups and joint ventures. We compare all aspects of partnerships to corporations in Chapter 9, Choice of Business Entity.

PRACTICE PROBLEM 7.2.1

Tax Consequences to Partnerships for Distributions

Cloudy Partnership owns a warehouse that has a fair market value of $850,000 and an adjusted basis of $225,000. Cloudy originally purchased the building for $300,000. During the current year, Cloudy distributed the building to Viola who owns a 60% interest in the partnership.

a. What are the tax consequences of the distribution to Cloudy?

b. What are the tax consequences if the fair market value of the building is $180,000?

c. How would the tax consequences vary for parts **a** and **b** if Cloudy was a corporation?

SOLUTION

a. Cloudy Partnership has a realized gain of $625,000 ($850,000 – $225,000) when it distributes the building to Viola. However, Cloudy does not recognize the gain.

b. Cloudy Partnership has a realized loss of $45,000 ($180,000 amount realized – $225,000 adjusted basis), but the loss is not recognized.

c. If Cloudy was a corporation, it would recognize a gain of $625,000 if the FMV was $850,000. If the FMV was $180,000, it would not be allowed to recognize the $45,000 realized loss.

PRACTICE PROBLEM 7.2.2

Current Distributions

On September 1, the QU Partnership, a calendar-year partnership, distributes the following assets to each of its equal partners: $9,000 cash, and land with a value of $5,000 and a basis of $3,300. Quin and Ursula have outside bases in their partnership interest of $15,000 and $8,000, respectively. The partnership had the following assets prior to the distribution:

Assets	Adjusted basis	Fair market value
Cash	$42,000	$42,000
Accounts receivable	0	13,000
Inventory	18,000	26,000
Land	19,000	40,000
Building	10,000	34,000

What are the tax consequences of the distribution to Quin and Ursula assuming that the distributions are proportionate?

SOLUTION

The starting point for computing the tax consequences of the distribution is the partner's basis in their partnership. Using the ordering rules discussed above, we consider the effect of cash first, and then the land.

Quin: Quin's basis of $15,000 is reduced to $6,000 by the cash received of $9,000. His basis is next reduced to $2,700 by the land's basis of $3,300. Quin's ending basis in his partnership interest is $2,700. He takes a $3,300 basis in the land, the same basis that the partnership had in the land.

Ursula: Ursula's basis of $8,000 is reduced to $0 by the cash received of $9,000. She recognizes $1,000 of gain because the cash distributed exceeds the basis in her partnership interest. The $1,000 gain prevents her basis from being negative. Ursula has no basis remaining to allocate to the land, so she reduces her basis by $0 for the land distribution. Ursula's ending basis in her partnership interest is $0. Her basis in the land is $0, which is the lower of the $3,300 basis the partnership had in the land or her remaining basis of $0 before the land distribution.

PRACTICE PROBLEM 7.2.3 Sale of Distributed Ordinary Income Assets

The Bluegrass Partnership is a dealer in real estate. Serge, a salesperson, receives a current distribution of land from Bluegrass on April 15 of Year 12. The basis of the land to the partnership is $12,000 and its fair market value at the date of distribution is $17,000. Serge's basis in his partnership interest before the distribution is $32,000. Serge uses the land as an investment.

a. On October 15, Year 12, Serge sells the land for $29,000. What is the amount and character of Serge's gain?

b. In part **a** above, how do the results change if Serge sold the land on June 15, Year 17?

SOLUTION

a. We first compute the tax effect of the distribution of the land to Serge.

Basis in partnership interest	$32,000
Basis in land to partnership	(12,000)
Ending basis in partnership interest	$20,000

Serge's basis in the land is $12,000, and he recognizes no gain or loss from the distribution. Bluegrass is a dealer in real estate, so the land is inventory. Therefore, if Serge sells the land within five years of receiving it, his gain or loss will be ordinary. He sold the land less than two months after receiving it, so his gain of $17,000 ($29,000 − $12,000) is ordinary income.

b. Serge sold the land on June 15, Year 17, which is more than five years after he received it, so the character of the $17,000 gain is determined based on the manner in which Serge held the property. This is a capital asset to Serge because it is an investment, so the $17,000 is a long-term capital gain.

INTERACTIVE SELF-SCORING QUIZZES

7.3 Retirement Distributions

LEARNING OBJECTIVE 3

Compute the tax consequences of a retirement distribution to a partner.

VIDEO CONTENT

You should assume that all distributions in this chapter are proportionate unless told differently.

In the previous section, we discussed the tax consequences of liquidating distributions when the partnership is liquidating. If the interest of only one partner is liquidated, and the partnership continues in existence, this is known as a **retirement distribution**. These rules also apply to a partner who is deceased. Everything you learned about liquidating distributions previously still applies to a retirement distribution, but there is an additional layer of rules that you also must use. ***You should assume that all distributions in this chapter are proportionate unless told differently***.

Related exercise: Discussion Question 7

Section 736(a) vs. Section 736(b) Payments

The first step in determining the tax consequences of a retirement distribution is to separate the distributions to the retiring partner into Section 736(a) payments and Section 736(b) payments. You will learn new rules for how to treat Section 736(a) payments. You treat the Section 736(b) payments the same as you learned in LO2, Distributions from a Partnership. That is, Section 736(b) payments are treated as being in exchange for the partnership interest and result in a capital gain or loss to the partner.

Effect of Capital on Classification of Distributions

The first issue when determining if a distribution is classified as Section 736(a) or Section 736(b) is whether capital is a material income-producing factor for the partnership. If the partnership only provides services such as engineering, law, accounting, consulting, or medical, then capital is *not* a material income-producing factor. Capital is ordinarily a material income-producing factor if the operation of the business requires substantial inventories or a substantial investment in plant, machinery, or other equipment.[15]

Related exercise: Discussion Question 8

Potential Pitfall

If capital is a material income-producing factor for the partnership and the retiring partner is a limited partner, then none of the distribution is treated as a Section 736(a) payment. Therefore, the entire retirement distribution for a limited partner is always treated as a Section 736(b) payment.

Unrealized Receivables and Unstated Goodwill

If capital *is* a material income-producing factor for the partnership and the partner is a general partner, and the retirement distributions are in return for unrealized receivables or *unstated goodwill*, then those distributions are Section 736(a) payments. The excess of the value of the retirement distributions over the partner's share of the partnership's assets is known as goodwill. **Unstated goodwill** is goodwill that is not provided for in the partnership agreement. **Stated goodwill** is goodwill that is defined in and allowed by the partnership agreement.

Related exercise: Multiple Choice Question 4

[15] Treas. Reg. §1.704-1(e)(1)(iv).

EXAMPLE 7.3.1
Unrealized Receivables and Unstated Goodwill

Orange Partnership manufactures fancy chocolates and has the following assets on its balance sheet at the end of the current year:

	Adjusted basis	Fair market value
Cash	$345,000	$345,000
Unrealized receivables	$ 0	$ 30,000
Inventory	$ 70,000	$ 70,000
Equipment	$ 27,000	$ 36,000
Buildings	$ 50,000	$300,000
Land	$100,000	$125,000
Goodwill	$ 0	$ 90,000
Total	$592,000	$996,000

Orlando is a one-third general partner in the Orange Partnership who retired as of December 31 of the current year. What is Orlando's share of the unrealized receivables and the goodwill?

SOLUTION

Because Orlando is a one-third partner in Orange, his share of these assets is as follows:

	Adjusted basis	Fair market value
Unrealized receivables	$0	$10,000
Goodwill	$0	$30,000

Evaluating Retirement Distributions

The following steps break down the process general partners use to determine if retirement distributions are Section 736(a) or Section 736(b) payments.

Step 1. **Ask: Does the partnership only provide services?** If YES, go to step 3. If NO, proceed to step 2.

Step 2. **Ask: Is capital a material income-producing factor for the partnership?** If YES, all distributions are classified as Section 736(b). If NO, proceed to step 3.

Step 3. **Ask: Does the partnership have unrealized receivables?** If YES, the retirement distributions are treated as Section 736(a) payments to the extent of the retiring partner's share of the unrealized receivables. Whether YES or NO, go to step 4.

Step 4. **Ask: Does the partnership have unstated goodwill?** If YES, then the retirement distributions are treated as Section 736(a) payments to the extent of the retiring partner's share of the unstated goodwill.

Step 5. **Compute:** The remainder of the retirement distribution is treated as a Section 736(b) payment, and any gain or loss recognized is a capital gain or loss.

Illustration 7.4 provides a flowchart that shows the flow of the rules for retirement distributions.

ILLUSTRATION 7.4 Retirement Distributions

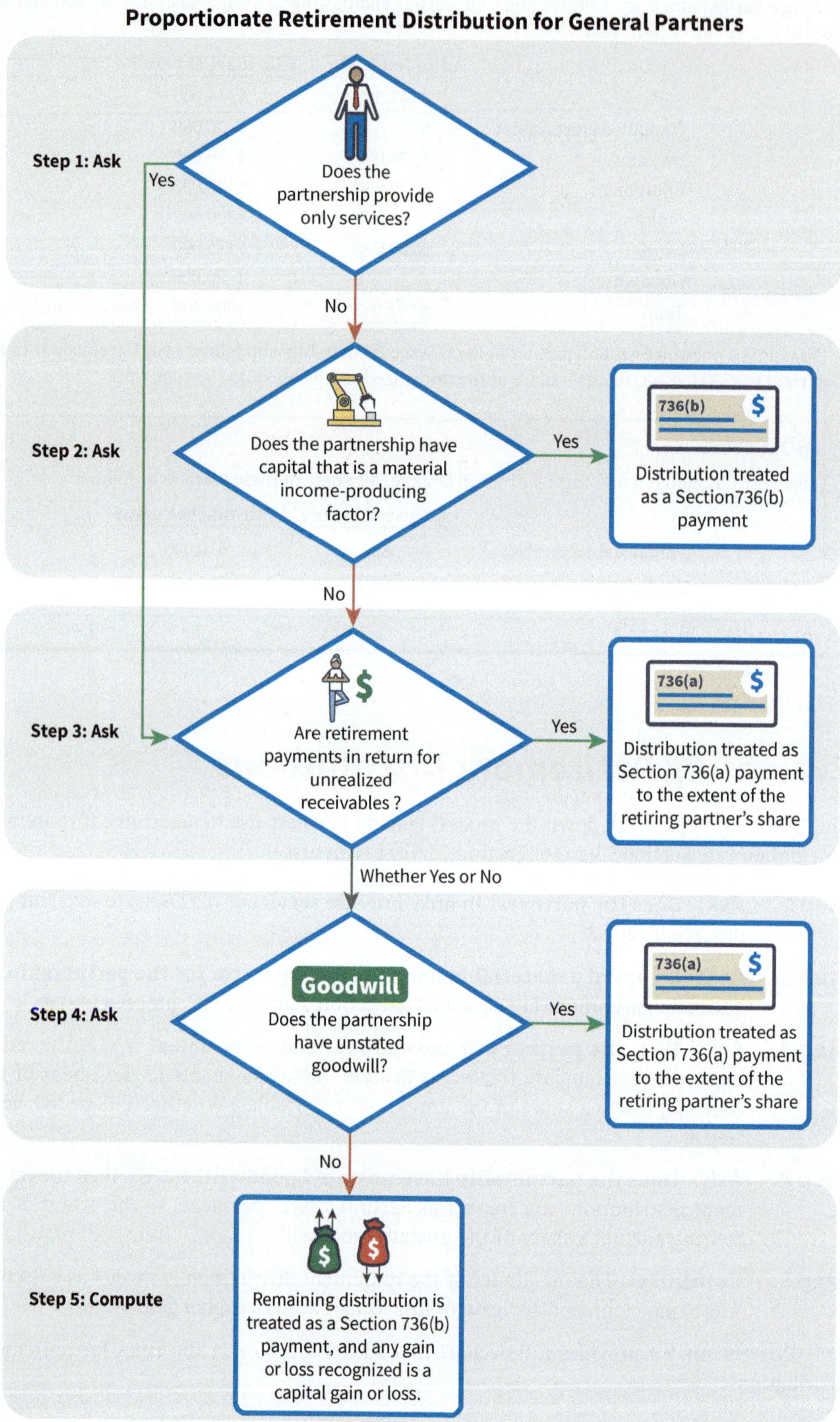

Tax Consequences of Section 736(a) and Section 736(b) Payments

Once the retirement distribution is divided into the Section 736(a) and Section 736(b) groups, you need to determine the tax consequences of each group. Section 736(a) payments are treated as guaranteed payments to the partner and taxed as ordinary income. Guaranteed payments are deductible by the partnership, which is a benefit for the remaining partners. The Section 736(b) payments are treated as being in exchange for the partner's interest in the partnership and are taxed according to the rules discussed in LO2, Distributions from a Partnership. Any gain or loss recognized is capital gain or loss assuming that the distribution is proportionate.

The next three Examples illustrate the taxation of retirement distributions. The first Example involves a capital-intensive business that has unrealized receivables but does not have unstated goodwill.

EXAMPLE 7.3.2 Taxation of Retirement Distributions—Capital Intensive

Continuing with Example 7.3.1, Orlando receives $332,000 in assets when he retires from the partnership. His basis in his partnership interest immediately before the distribution is $220,000. Assume that the distribution is proportionate. Recall that his share of unrealized receivable and stated goodwill are as follows:

	Adjusted basis	Fair market value
Unrealized receivables	$0	$10,000
Goodwill	$0	$30,000

How is the distribution to Orlando divided into Section 736(a) and Section 736(b) payments, and what are the tax consequences to Orlando?

SOLUTION

To determine the tax consequences to Orlando, we will follow the steps described in Illustration 7.4.

Step 1. We first need to ask if the partnership only provides services. Here, the answer is no, because Orange is a manufacturing company, so we proceed to step 2.

Step 2. Next, we need to ask if capital is a material income-producing factor for the partnership. Because Orange is a manufacturer, the answer is yes, so all distributions are classified as Section 736(b). We do not need to use steps 3, 4, and 5.

The Section 736(b) payment to Orlando is $332,000 and is in exchange for his partnership interest. The Section 736(b) $332,000 cash payment exceeds his basis in the partnership of $220,000 by $112,000, so Orlando has a capital gain of $112,000.

The next Example demonstrates the effect of unstated goodwill on the tax consequences for a service-oriented partnership.

EXAMPLE 7.3.3 Retirement Distribution—Service Partnership with Unstated Goodwill

Brown Partnership provides allergy treatments for patients and capital is not a material income-producing factor. It receives 10% of its revenue from selling prescription medication. Bree is a 20% general partner, and she receives a retirement distribution of $90,000. Bree's basis in her partnership interest is $40,000. Assume that the distribution is proportionate. Brown has the following balance sheet immediately before the distribution:

	Adjusted basis	Fair market value
Cash	$200,000	$200,000
Unrealized receivables	0	140,000
Inventory	5,000	12,000
Land	90,000	60,000
Total	$295,000	$412,000

What are the tax consequences of the retirement distribution to Bree?

SOLUTION

To determine the tax consequences to Bree, we will follow the steps described in Illustration 7.4.

Step 1. We first need to ask if the partnership only provides services. Here, the answer is no, because Brown does have a small amount of inventory (prescription medicine), so we proceed to step 2.

Step 2. Next, we need to ask if capital is a material income-producing factor for the partnership. Because Brown mainly provides medical services and the operation of the business does not require a substantial inventory of prescription medication, here the answer is no. We next proceed to step 3.

Step 3. Now, we need to ask if the partnership has unrealized receivables. Brown does have unrealized receivables, with a FMV of $140,000. Thus, the retirement distributions are treated as Section 736(a) payments to the extent of Bree's share of the unrealized receivables, which is $28,000 ($140,000 × 20%). Whether the answer in step 3 was yes or no, we next go to step 4.

Step 4. We ask if the partnership has unstated goodwill. If there is, then the retirement distribution is treated as a Section 736(a) payment to the extent of the retiring partner's share of the unstated goodwill. Here, the partnership does have unstated goodwill, because Bree's 20% share of the assets is $82,400 ($412,000 × 20%) while her retirement distribution is $90,000. Her share of the unstated goodwill is $7,600 ($90,000–$82,400). Therefore, $7,600 of her retirement distribution is a Section 736(a) payment.

Step 5. Because the partnership has unstated goodwill, there are no Section 736(b) payments due to any stated goodwill.

Bree's total Section 736(a) payment is $35,600 ($28,000 + $7,600). This is considered a guaranteed payment of $35,600, which is taxed as ordinary income. Brown can deduct the $35,600 guaranteed payment. The remaining distribution of $54,400 ($90,000 − $35,600) is treated as a Section 736(b) payment. Her basis in her partnership interest is $40,000, so she has a capital gain of $14,400 ($54,400 − $40,000)*.

*The hot asset rules discussed in an Advanced Topic below could change the character of a portion of the capital gain.

The last Example in this section shows the tax consequences of a retirement distribution for a service-oriented partnership with stated goodwill.

EXAMPLE 7.3.4

Retirement Distribution—Service Partnership with Stated Goodwill

Assume the same facts as in Example 7.3.3, except the partnership agreement now provides for the statement of goodwill. Brown Partnership provides allergy treatments for patients and capital is not a material income-producing factor. It receives 10% of its revenue from selling prescription medication. Bree is a 20% partner, and she receives a retirement distribution of $90,000. Bree's basis in her partnership interest is $40,000. Assume that the distribution is proportionate. Brown has the following balance sheet immediately before the distribution:

	Adjusted basis	Fair market value
Cash	$200,000	$200,000
Unrealized receivables	0	140,000
Inventory	5,000	12,000
Land	90,000	60,000
Goodwill	0	30,400
Total	$295,000	$442,400

What are the tax consequences of the retirement distribution to Bree?

SOLUTION

To determine the tax consequences to Bree, we will again follow the steps described in Illustration 7.4.

Step 1. We first need to ask if the partnership only provides services. Here, the answer is no, because the partnership does have a small amount of inventory, so we proceed to step 2.

Step 2. Next, we need to ask if capital is a material income-producing factor for the partnership. Because Brown mainly provides medical services and the operation of the business does not requires substantial inventory, here the answer is no. We next proceed to step 3.

Step 3. Now, we need to ask if the partnership has unrealized receivables. Brown does have unrealized receivables, with a FMV of $140,000. Thus, the retirement distributions are treated as Section 736(a) payments to the extent of Bree's share of the unrealized receivables, which is $28,000 ($140,000 × 20%). Whether the answer in step 3 was yes or no, we next go to step 4.

Step 4. Finally, we ask if the partnership has unstated goodwill. In this case, the answer is no, so the distribution Bree receives for the goodwill is not considered to be a Section 736(a) payment.

Step 5. The remaining distribution of $62,000 ($90,000 – $28,000) is treated as a Section 736(b) payment.

To summarize, Bree's Section 736(a) payment is $28,000. This is considered a guaranteed payment of $28,000, which is taxed as ordinary income. Brown can deduct the $28,000 guaranteed payment. The remaining distribution of $62,000 ($90,000 – $28,000) is treated as a Section 736(b) payment. Her basis in her partnership interest is $40,000, so she has a capital gain of $22,000 ($62,000 – $40,000).*

*The hot asset rules discussed in an Advanced Topic below could change the character of a portion of the capital gain.

Related exercises: Multiple Choice Question 5
Brief Exercise 5
Application Problems 14, 15, 16

PRACTICE PROBLEM 7.3.1
Unrealized Receivables and Unstated Goodwill

Watch Partnership has the following assets on its balance sheet at the end of the current year:

	Adjusted basis	Fair market value
Cash	$295,000	$295,000
Unrealized receivables	$ 0	$ 40,000
Inventory	$ 60,000	$ 60,000
Machinery	$ 19,000	$ 38,000
Buildings	$ 45,000	$280,000
Land	$125,000	$145,000
Goodwill	$ 0	$ 80,000
Total	$544,000	$938,000

Yara is a 50% general partner in the Watch Partnership who retired as of December 31 of the current year. What is Yara's share of the unrealized receivables and the goodwill?

SOLUTION

Because Yara is a 50% partner in Watch, her share of these assets is as follows:

	Adjusted basis	Fair market value
Unrealized receivables	$0	$20,000
Goodwill	$0	$40,000

PRACTICE PROBLEM 7.3.2
Taxation of Retirement Distributions

Continuing with Practice Problem 7.3.1, Yara receives $228,000 when she retires from the partnership. Her basis in her partnership interest immediately before the distribution is $110,000. Assume that the distribution is proportionate. Yara's share of unrealized receivable and stated goodwill are as follows:

	Adjusted basis	Fair market value
Unrealized receivables	$0	$20,000
Goodwill	$0	$40,000

How is the distribution to Yara divided into Section 736(a) and Section 736(b) payments, and what are the tax consequences to Yara?

SOLUTION

Step 1. First, we need to ask if the partnership only provides services. The answer is no, so we proceed to step 2.

Step 2. Next, we need to ask if capital is a material income-producing factor for the partnership, The answer is yes, so all distributions are Section 736(b) payments.

The $228,000 retirement distribution is a Section 736(b) payment and is in exchange for her partnership interest. The Section 736(b) $228,000 cash payment exceeds the basis in her partnership of $110,000 by $118,000, so Yara has a capital gain of $118,000.

INTERACTIVE SELF-SCORING QUIZZES

7.4 Sale of a Partnership Interest

LEARNING OBJECTIVE 4

Compute the tax consequences of the disposition of a partnership interest.

VIDEO CONTENT

In Chapter 6, LO4, Taxation of Partnership Income and Guaranteed Payments, you learned the difference between the aggregate and entity theories of partnership taxation. Both theories come into play when determining the tax consequences of a sale of a partnership interest; although the aggregate theory by far carries the most weight. IRC §742 states:

> In the case of a sale or exchange of an interest in a partnership, gain or loss shall be recognized to the transferor partner. Such gain or loss shall be considered as gain or loss from the sale or exchange of a capital asset, except as otherwise provided in section 751 (relating to unrealized receivables and inventory items).

The general rule for IRC §742 indicates that this is a sale of a capital asset, which means that the result is a capital gain or loss. This result reflects the entity theory, which treats the partnership as a separate entity from the partner, meaning that the partner can sell their ownership interest. The aggregate theory is reflected in the statement *except as otherwise provided in section 751 (relating to unrealized receivables and inventory items).* If a partner sells a one-third interest in a partnership, but the partnership did not exist, as assumed by the aggregate theory, then the partner would have, in effect, sold one-third of each asset on the partnership's balance sheet, with the partner's gain or loss having the character of each asset sold. This is generally how we treat the gain of loss from the sale of a partnership interest.

Assets that Affect the Character of Gain/Loss from Sale of a Partnership Interest

There are four types of assets on the balance sheet that can influence the character of gain or loss from the sale of a partnership interest. We first define these and then show how to apply them when considering the sale of a partnership interest. **Illustration 7.5** provides a table that summarizes these rules for each asset.

ILLUSTRATION 7.5 Sale of a Partnership Interest

Types of Gain from Sale of a Partnership Interest

Asset type	Rule
Hot asset: Unrealized receivables* and depreciation recapture	Treat as ordinary income.
Hot asset: Inventory	Treat as ordinary income.
Collectible gain	Taxed at a maximum rate of 28%.
Unrecaptured Section 1250 gain	Taxed at a maximum 25% rate.
Residual is capital gain/loss	Include in capital gain/loss netting process.

*Unrealized receivables are included as a separate category, even though the definition of inventory (all assets other than cash, capital assets and Section 1231 assets) is broad enough to include unrealized receivables. The reason for this has to do with disproportionate distributions, which are discussed in LO 5.5 as an Advanced Topic

Hot Assets—Unrealized Receivables & Depreciation Recapture

Hot assets are assets on the balance sheet that have ordinary income potential. An unrealized receivable is a receivable owned by a cash-basis taxpayer. The receivable has no tax basis because no income has been recognized yet. The partnership law includes many additional assets in the definition of unrealized receivables. The most important one for our purposes is depreciation recapture under Section 1245 and Section 1250.[16] **Recall** from Chapter 1, LO3, Section 1231 Assets that Section 1245 recapture applies to personalty (personal property) and Section 1250 to buildings. Section 1245 and Section 1250 are assets used in a trade or business that have been owned for more than one year, so they are classified as Section 1231 assets. Only the depreciation recapture component imbedded in the Section 1231 asset is treated as an unrealized receivable. To illustrate, assume that a partnership owns equipment with the following characteristics:

Fair market value	$80,000
Cost	$76,000
Accumulated depreciation	$32,000
Adjusted basis	$44,000 ($76,000 – $32,000)

If the partnership sold the asset, the tax consequences would be as follows:

Amount realized	$80,000
Less: Adjusted basis	(44,000)
Gain	$36,000

$32,000 Section 1245 recapture (Ordinary income)

$4,000 Section 1231 gain

Because there is $32,000 of Section 1245 recapture imbedded in the equipment, then for hot asset purposes, the asset is treated as follows:

	Total	Unrealized receivable	Section 1231 asset
Fair market value	$80,000	$32,000	$48,000
Adjusted basis	$44,000	$ 0	$44,000

If a partner sold their partnership interest when this equipment was on the balance sheet, $32,000 of the equipment would be treated as an unrealized receivable with no basis.

While the unrealized receivables definition applies also to Section 1250 property, recall that buildings placed in service after 1986 are not subject to Section 1250 recapture, because they are depreciated using straight-line MACRS.

[16]IRC §751(c).

Hot Assets—Inventory

Recall that for the partnership tax law, *inventory* includes all assets other than cash, capital assets, and Section 1231 assets. Therefore, for tax purposes, inventory includes:[17]

- Goods held for sale in the ordinary course of a trade or business
- Unrealized receivables
- Accounts receivables

Look-Through Rule: Collectible Gain

Gains from collectibles are taxed at a maximum rate of 28%. A **collectible** is tangible personal property such as coins, art, gold, silver, and antiques purchased for investment purposes. This asset rule and the next rule are known as **look-through rules**, because the partner must look through the partnership to the assets on the balance sheet to determine how the partner treats the gain from the sale of the interest.[18]

Look-Through Rule: Unrecaptured Section 1250 Gain

Unrecaptured Section 1250 gain is capital gain taxed at a maximum rate of 25% to the extent of accumulated straight-line depreciation claimed on the real estate. If a partnership has a building on its balance sheet, then this 25% gain will come into play for the selling partner if the partnership would have a gain if it sold the building.[19]

Partner's Gain or Loss on Sale of Partnership Interest

If a partner sells a partnership interest and hot assets or look-through assets are on the balance sheet, then some of the partner's gain from the sale of the partnership interest may be characterized as ordinary income, 28% collectible gain, or unrecaptured 25% gain. The amount of the gain that is characterized for each type of income would be the income or gain that would have been allocated to the partner if the partnership had sold the asset just before the partnership interest was sold.

An additional consideration for the sale of a partnership interest is to make sure that debt relief is included in the selling partner's amount realized. The buying partner will take over responsibility for the selling partner's share of the partnership debt, so this will increase the amount realized for the sale.

We explore these considerations in the following Example.

EXAMPLE 7.4.1
Partner's Gain or Loss on Sale of Partnership Interest

PINK Partnership has had four equal partners for the past five years—Paul, Izzy, Ngu, and Kabir. Paul sold his partnership interest to Paulette for $82,500 cash. PINK uses the cash basis of accounting. The partnership has the following balance sheet on the date of the sale:

Assets	Adjusted basis	FMV	Debt and partners' capital	Adjusted basis	FMV
Cash	$ 50,000	$ 50,000	Debt	$ 0	$ 80,000
Inventory	75,000	115,000	Paul	55,000	82,500
Accounts receivable	0	60,000	Izzy	55,000	82,500
Collectibles	15,000	45,000	Ngu	55,000	82,500
Building*	80,000	140,000	Kabir	55,000	82,500
Total	$220,000	$410,000	Total	$220,000	$410,000

*Original cost was $120,000. All depreciation was straight-line.

What was Paul's gain or loss from this sale?

[17]IRC §751(d).

[18]IRC §1(h)(5)(B).

[19]IRC §1(h)(9).

SOLUTION

We first compute Paul's recognized gain or loss, and then we determine the character of the gain or loss.

Cash	$ 82,500
Plus: Debt relief	20,000
Amount realized	$102,500
Less: Adjusted basis	(55,000)
Recognized gain	$ 47,500

Paul's share of the partnership's debt is $20,000 ($80,000 × 25%). His basis of $55,000 already includes his share of the debt, because the basis of the debt on the balance sheet is $0. That means it has already been allocated to the partners' bases.

We next determine the character of the $47,500 gain by determining whether there are any assets on the balance sheet that can change the character:

Unrealized receivables: If the unrealized receivables had been collected by the partnership before Paul sold his interest, $15,000 of ordinary income would have been allocated to Paul [($60,000 – $0 basis) × 25%)]. Therefore, $15,000 of the gain is ordinary income.

Inventory: If the inventory had been sold by the partnership before Paul sold his interest, $10,000 of ordinary income would have been allocated to Paul [($115,000 – $75,000 basis) × 25%)]. Therefore, $10,000 of the gain is ordinary income.

Collectibles: If the collectibles had been sold by the partnership before Paul sold his interest, $7,500 of ordinary income would have been allocated to Paul [($45,000 – $15,000 basis) × 25%)]. Therefore, $7,500 of the gain is treated as 28% capital gain.

Unrecaptured Section 1250 gain: If the building had been sold by the partnership before Paul sold his interest, there would have been $10,000 of unrecaptured Section 1250 gain allocated to Paul, computed as follows:

Amount realized	$140,000
Less: Adjusted basis	(80,000)
Recognized gain	$ 60,000
Less: Section 1250 recapture	0
Less: Unrecaptured Section 1250 gain	(40,000)
Section 1231 gain	$ 20,000

There is no Section 1250 recapture because straight-line depreciation was used for the building. The gain is classified as unrecaptured Section 1250 gain to the extent of the straight-line depreciation claimed, which is $40,000 ($120,000 cost – $80,000 basis). The remaining $20,000 of gain is Section 1231 gain. Therefore, $10,000 of unrecaptured Section 1250 gain would have been allocated to Paul ($40,000 × 25%) if the building has been sold before Paul sold his interest. Therefore, $10,000 of the gain is unrecaptured Section 1250 gain.

Summary: Paul's recognized gain of $47,500 is taxed as follows:

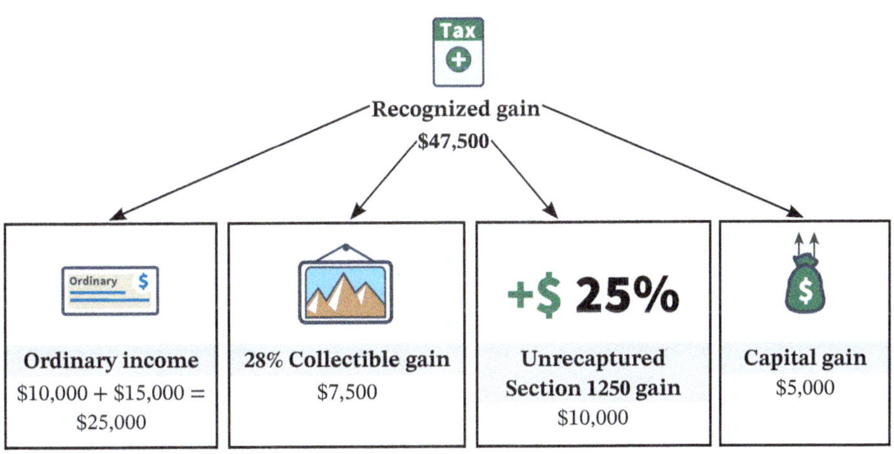

The residual gain of $5,000 is long-term capital gain because Paul owned his partnership interest for more than a year.

Why **Why does Congress not allow all gain on the sale of a partnership interest to be capital gain?** If a shareholder in a corporation sells their stock at a gain, the gain is treated as capital gain because stock is an investment. However, a partnership interest is also an investment. So why does Congress treat partners differently from shareholders when they sell their ownership interest? Review the following simple spreadsheet.

Assets	Adjusted basis	Fair market value	Partners' capital	Adjusted basis	Fair market value
Cash	$50,000	$ 50,000	A	$25,000	$ 75,000
Accounts receivable	$ 0	$100,000	B	$25,000	$ 75,000
Total	$50,000	$150,000	Total	$50,000	$150,000

Partner A's partnership interest has a basis of $25,000 and a fair market value of $75,000. Assume that A sold her partnership interest to C for $75,000, and that the hot asset rules did not exist. A's gain of $50,000 ($75,000 – $25,000) would be a capital gain because the partnership interest is an investment. Alternatively, assume that the partnership collects the receivable the day before A sells her partnership interest. This would generate $100,000 of ordinary income for the partnership, and $50,000 would flow to both A and B. After the collection of the receivable the balance sheet appears as follows:

Assets	Adjusted basis	Fair market value	Partners' capital	Adjusted basis	Fair market value
Cash	$150,000	$150,000	A	$ 75,000	$ 75,000
			B	$ 75,000	$ 75,000
Total	$150,000	$150,000	Total	$150,000	$150,000

If partner A sells to C now for $75,000, A's gain is $0 ($75,000 – $75,000) from the sale of the partnership interest.

Comparing the results from these two alternatives, A has $50,000 of income from both. If A sells her partnership interest before the receivable was collected, she has capital gain (if no hot asset rule). If A sells her partnership after the receivable is collected, she has ordinary income. Should it be that simple to change the character of the gain from ordinary to capital—by selling the partnership interest one day earlier? Clearly that is not logical, which is why the hot asset rule exists. With the hot asset rule, A would have ordinary income even if she sells her partnership interest before the receivable was collected, which provides the same result as if the partnership interest was sold after the receivable was collected.

Another important point with the hot asset and look-through rules is that the amount of gain whose character is changed from capital gain is not limited to the overall recognized gain from the sale. This is illustrated in the next Example.

EXAMPLE 7.4.2 Recharacterized Gain Greater than Recognized Gain

Isadora is a 30% partner in the Mauve Partnership. She sells her partnership interest and recognizes a $12,000 gain. The partnership has inventory on its balance sheet, and if the inventory was sold, Isadora's share of it would be $15,000. What are the tax consequences for Isadora?

SOLUTION

Due to the inventory on the balance sheet, Isadora's ordinary income is not limited to the overall recognized gain of $12,000. Rather, she has ordinary income of $15,000. Therefore, she has a residual capital loss of $3,000 that she deducts ($12,000 gain – $15,000 ordinary income). The ordinary income of $15,000 and the residual capital loss of $3,000 nets to an overall gain of $12,000.

Related exercises: Discussion Questions 9, 10
Multiple Choice Questions 6, 7, 8
Brief Exercise 6
Application Problems 17, 18, 19
Tax Planning Problem 2

Other Dispositions of Partnership Interests

In addition to a sale of a partnership interest, a partnership interest can be terminated because of the death of the partner, or it can be transferred by gift. We discuss these transactions in this section, as well as special rules related to a carried interest.

Death of a Partner

When a partner dies, the partnership tax year closes on the date of death, but only with respect to the deceased partner.[20] The deceased partner's share of income for the year is determined based on the pro rata method, unless the partnership elects to close the book and compute the actual income. The remaining income for the year related to the deceased partner's interest flows to the new owner of the partnership interest, which could be the estate of the deceased partner or a beneficiary of the partner's estate.

The beneficiary who receives the decedent's partnership interest will have a FMV basis in the interest under the estate tax rules. The next Example demonstrates the tax effects related to the death of a partner.

EXAMPLE 7.4.3
Death of a Partner

Charles was a 30% partner in Navy Partnership, a calendar-year partnership. Charles died on September 30 of the current year and his partnership interest was transferred to his son Jeff. The partnership income for the year is $120,000. The FMV of Charles's interest on the date of death was $50,000. What are the tax consequences of these transactions?

SOLUTION

The death of Charles is not a taxable event, so there is no gain or loss on the transfer of his partnership interest to Jeff. The partnership tax year closes on September 30 with respect to Charles. A pro rata share of income, $27,000 ($120,000 × 9/12 × 30%) flows to Charles on September 30. The $27,000 of income will be reported on his final Form 1040.

The remaining income allocated to the 30% interest, $9,000 ($120,000 × 3/12 × 30%) flows to Jeff on December 31, the last day of the partnership tax year. Jeff's initial basis in the partnership interest is its FMV of $50,000.

If a partner had suspended losses at the time of death, their treatment depends on the reason the losses were suspended.

- **Insufficient basis** If suspended due to insufficient basis, they are deductible to the extent the basis of the partnership interest is increased for the year of death. If not used in the year of death, they are lost forever.
- **Insufficient at-risk basis** If suspended due to insufficient at risk amount, they are deductible to the extent the at-risk amount of the partnership interest is increased for the year of death. If not used in the year of death, they are lost forever.
- **Insufficient passive income** If suspended due to insufficient passive income, they are deductible to the extent the partner has passive income for the year of death. They can also be deducted to the extent that the value of the partner's interest exceeds its basis in the interest.[21] If not used in the year of death, they are lost forever.

Gift of a Partnership Interest

If a partner gifts their partnership interest, the partner does not recognize any gain or loss on the transfer. The effect on the donee's basis in the partnership interest is determined as follows:

- The basis in the partnership interest is determined under the basis rules for gifts.
- The gain basis is the partner's basis in the partnership interest.
- The loss basis is the lower of the FMV of the interest or its basis.[22]

[20] IRC §706(c).

[21] IRC §469(g)(2).

[22] IRC §1015.

EXAMPLE 7.4.4
Gift of a Partnership Interest

Suzanne has owned a partnership interest for 12 years. The interest has a FMV of $49,000 and her basis in the interest is $64,000. Suzanne gifts the partnership interest to Roberta. What is Roberta's basis in the partnership interest? How much gain or loss will Roberta have if she sells the partnership interest for $45,000 two weeks after receiving it?

SOLUTION

Roberta's gain basis in the partnership interest is Suzanne's basis of $64,000. Roberta's loss basis is $49,000, the lower of the FMV or the adjusted basis. Roberta can recognize a loss only to the extent that she sells the interest for less than her loss basis.

Amount realized	$45,000
Loss basis	(49,000)
Recognized loss	($4,000)

Suzanne's unrealized loss of ($25,000) cannot be transferred to Roberta.

Sale of a Carried Interest

A **carried interest** is a profits interest that is received in return for services, *and* held in partnerships that have significant assets in investments or real estate. The gain from the sale of a carried interest is treated as a long-term capital gain only if it has been held for more than three years.[23]

Related exercises: Discussion Question 11
Brief Exercise 7
Application Problem 20

PRACTICE PROBLEM 7.4.1
Partner's Gain or Loss on Sale of Partnership Interest

Sunny Partnership has two equal partners—Darius and Darlee. Darius sold his partnership interest to Maxwell for $41,250 cash. Sunny uses the cash basis of accounting. The partnership has the following balance sheet on the date of the sale:

Assets	Adjusted basis	FMV	Debt and partners' capital	Adjusted basis	FMV
Cash	$12,500	$ 12,500	Debt	$ 0	$ 20,000
Inventory	18,750	28,750	Darius	27,500	41,250
Accounts receivable	0	15,000	Darlene	27,500	41,250
Collectibles	3,750	11,250			
Building*	20,000	35,000			
Total	$55,000	$102,500	Total	$55,000	$102,500

*Original cost was $30,000. All depreciation was straight-line.

What was Darius's gain or loss from this sale?

SOLUTION

We first compute Darius's recognized gain or loss, and then we determine the character of the gain or loss.

Cash	$41,250
Plus: Debt relief	10,000
Amount realized	$51,250
Less: Adjusted basis	(27,500)
Recognized gain	$23,750

[23]IRC §1061(a).

Darius's share of the partnership's debt is $10,000 ($20,000 × 50%). His basis of $27,500 already includes his share of the debt, because the basis of the debt on the balance sheet is $0, which means it has already been allocated to the partners' bases.

We next determine the character of the $23,750 gain by determining whether there are any assets on the balance sheet that can change the character:

Unrealized receivables: If the unrealized receivables had been collected by the partnership before Darius sold his interest, $7,500 of ordinary income would have been allocated to Darius [($15,000 – $0 basis) × 50%)]. Therefore, $7,500 of the gain is ordinary income.

Inventory: If the inventory had been sold by the partnership before Darius sold his interest, $5,000 of ordinary income would have been allocated to Darius [($28,750 – $18,750 basis) × 50%)]. Therefore, $5,000 of the gain is ordinary income.

Collectibles: If the collectibles had been sold by the partnership before Darius sold his interest, $3,750 of ordinary income would have been allocated to Darius [($11,250 – $3,750 basis) × 50%)]. Therefore, $3,750 of the gain is treated as 28% capital gain.

Unrecaptured Section 1250 gain: If the building had been sold by the partnership before Darius sold his interest, there would have been $5,000 of unrecaptured Section1250 gain allocated to Darius, computed as follows:

Amount realized	$35,000
Less: Adjusted basis	(20,000)
Recognized gain	$15,000
Less: Section 1250 recapture	0
Less: Unrecaptured Section 1250 gain	(10,000)
Section 1231 gain	$ 5,000

There is no Section 1250 recapture because straight-line depreciation was used for the building. The gain is classified as unrecaptured Section 1250 gain to the extent of the straight-line depreciation claimed which is $10,000 ($30,000 cost– $20,000 basis). The remaining $5,000 of gain is Section 1231 gain. Therefore, $5,000 of unrecaptured Section 1250 gain would have been allocated to Darius ($10,000 × 50%) if the building has been sold before Darius sold his interest. Therefore, $5,000 of the gain is unrecaptured Section 1250 gain.

Summary: Darius's recognized gain of $23,750 is taxed as follows:

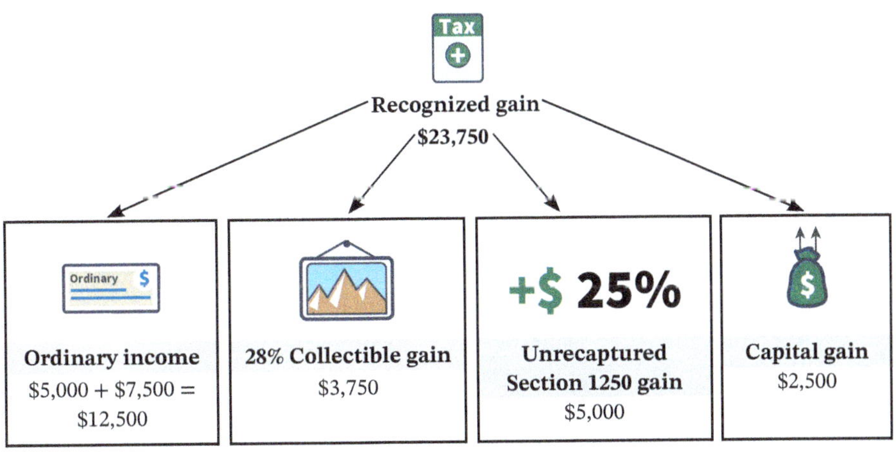

INTERACTIVE
SELF-SCORING QUIZZES

7.5 Advanced Topic (Drilling Down)—Disproportionate Distributions

LEARNING OBJECTIVE 5

Determine the tax effects of a disproportionate distribution.

VIDEO CONTENT

You have previously learned in this chapter that the partnership tax law goes to great lengths to ensure that each partner is taxed on their proportionate share of the income potential in ordinary assets. This focus also applies to partnership distributions. In LO2, Distributions from a Partnership, we limited our discussion to proportionate distributions. In this section, you will learn the tax consequences of a disproportionate distribution.

Potential Pitfall

Unrealized receivables must be included in the 20% appreciation test for inventory. This may surprise you, because unrealized receivables are defined as a hot asset separate from inventory. Furthermore, unrealized receivables do not have a substantial appreciation test. Nevertheless, the question to be asked is whether unrealized receivables are defined as *cash, capital assets, or Section 1231 assets*. The answer is no, of course, so unrealized receivables are included in the definition of inventory.

Hot Assets for Partnership Distributions

The hot asset rules for distributions are the same as for sales of a partnership interest with two differences:

- For inventory to be a hot asset in a distribution, it must be **substantially appreciated inventory**. The inventory is substantially appreciated if its FMV exceeds its adjusted basis by more than 20%.[24]

Related exercise: Multiple Choice Question 9

- With sales of partnership interests, the existence of hot assets always leads to some of the gain from the sale being characterized as ordinary income. However, the presence of hot assets on the balance sheet does not necessarily mean that the distribution is disproportionate. The distribution is proportionate if the partner's interest in the hot assets is the same before and after the distribution.

Testing for Substantial Appreciation

Recall that inventory consists of all assets other than cash, capital assets, and Section 1231 assets. Therefore, all these assets must be included when testing for more than 20% appreciation.

EXAMPLE 7.5.1
Identifying Hot Assets for Partnership Distributions

Navy Partnership has the following assets on its balance sheet.

	Adjusted basis	Fair market value
Cash	$ 35,000	$ 35,000
Accounts receivables	22,000	22,000
Inventory	60,000	70,000
Equipment	50,000	35,000
Accumulated depreciation	(42,000)	0
Land	200,000	300,000
Total	$325,000	$462,000

Which of these assets qualify as hot assets for the partnership distribution rules?

[24] IRC §751(b)(3).

SOLUTION

The only item that meets the definition of an unrealized receivable is the depreciation recapture potential in the equipment. If the equipment was sold, the recognized gain would be $27,000:

Amount realized	$35,000	
Less: Adjusted basis	(8,000)	($50,000 – $42,000)
Recognized gain	$27,000	

The $27,000 gain would be recaptured as Section 1245 ordinary income. The recapture is treated as unrealized receivable with an adjusted basis of $0 and fair market value of $27,000.

For the inventory to be a hot asset, the inventory must be substantially appreciated. The inventory listed by name on the balance sheet is not substantially appreciated because $60,000 × 120% = $72,000 and the inventory's FMV is $70,000.

However, inventory is defined as all assets other than cash, capital assets, and Section 1231 assets. Therefore, the proper test for substantial appreciation is as follows:

Inventory:

Accounts receivable	$22,000	$ 22,000
Plus: Inventory	$60,000	$ 70,000
Plus: Recapture potential	$ 0	$ 27,000
Total	$82,000	$119,000

The test for substantial appreciation is whether $119,000 exceeds $82,000 × 120% ($98,400), which it does. Therefore, the inventory is a hot asset.

To summarize, the hot assets fall into the following categories:

	Basis	FMV
Unrealized receivables:		
Recapture potential	$ 0	$27,000
Inventory:		
Accounts receivable	$22,000	$22,000
Inventory	$60,000	$70,000

Related exercise: Brief Exercise 8

Tax Planning Tip

Unrealized receivables are always treated as a hot asset for the distribution rules, whether the inventory is substantially appreciated or not. When the unrealized receivables are included in the inventory test, this will always make it more likely that the substantial appreciation test will be met because unrealized receivables, by definition, have an adjusted basis of $0.

Testing to Determine if the Distribution Is Proportionate

If the partnership has hot assets, the distribution is **proportionate** if the partner who receives the distribution has the same interest in the ordinary income potential in the hot assets before and after the distribution. Otherwise, the distribution is **disproportionate**.

Related exercise: Discussion Question 12

The following two Examples illustrate how the partner's ordinary income potential in the hot assets is determined.

EXAMPLE 7.5.2
Proportionate Distribution

The Lavender Partnership has the following cash and hot assets on its balance sheet:

	Adjusted basis	Fair market value	Ordinary income potential
Cash	$25,000	$25,000	$ 0
Unrealized receivables	$ 0	$20,000	$20,000
Inventory	$30,000	$45,000	$15,000

Raymond is a 30% partner who receives a liquidating distribution of $10,500 of the unrealized receivables and $19,500 of cash. Is this a proportionate distribution?

SOLUTION

To determine if the distribution is proportionate, you compare Raymond's share of the income potential before and after distribution.

Ordinary income potential before the distribution: $35,000 × 30% = $10,500

Ordinary income potential after the distribution: When the $10,500 of receivables are sold or collected, Raymond will have $10,500 of ordinary income.

The distribution is proportionate because Raymond has a $10,500 ordinary income interest in the hot assets both before and after the distribution.

EXAMPLE 7.5.3
Disproportionate Distribution

Assume the same facts as Example 7.5.2, except that Raymond receives a liquidating distribution of $5,000 of the unrealized receivables and $25,000 of cash. Is this a proportionate distribution?

SOLUTION

To determine if the distribution is proportionate, you compare Raymond's share of the income potential before and after distribution.

Ordinary income potential before the distribution: $35,000 × 30% = $10,500

Ordinary income potential after the distribution: When the $5,000 of receivables are sold or collected, Raymond will have $5,000 of ordinary income.

This is a disproportionate distribution because Raymond's share of the ordinary income potential in the hot assets declined from $10,500 before the distribution to $5,000 after the distribution.

Related exercise: Application Problem 21

Tax Consequences of a Disproportionate Distribution

If a partner receives a disproportionate distribution, you assume that the following transactions occurred (these are hypothetical, but the resulting tax consequences are real):[25]

Step 1. **Identify:** The amount of the asset that the partner did not receive enough of (deficit asset), contrasted to if the distribution had been proportionate.

Step 2. **Assume:** The deficit asset identified in step 1 is distributed to the partner. This is a hypothetical distribution because it did not actually occur, but its tax consequences are real.

[25]Treas. Reg. §1.751-1(b)(2).

Step 3. **Assume:** The partner sells the deficit asset received in step 1 back to the partnership and is paid with the asset that the partner received too much of (excess asset). This is a property transaction that will produce a recognized gain. Once again, this is hypothetical, but the tax consequences must be reported.

Step 4. **Assume:** The partner receives a distribution of the remaining assets needed to ensure that, economically, the partner has received all the assets actually distributed to them by the partnership.

Illustration 7.6 summarizes the logic used when working through the steps of a disproportionate distribution.

ILLUSTRATION 7.6 Tax Consequences of a Disproportionate Distribution

Logic Used in Hypothetical Steps for Disproportionate Distribution

Step 1. Identify whether the partner received more than or less than their proportionate share of the hot assets. If the partner received less than their proportionate share of the hot assets (deficit asset), that means the partner received more than their proportionate share of the non-hot assets (excess asset). Or, the non-hot assets could be the deficit asset and the hot assets could be excess asset. Determine the excess property amount that the partner received of either the hot assets or non-hot assets. The excess asset is the amount received over the proportionate share of that asset. The deficit asset is the proportionate share of the asset less the amount received.

Step 2. Assume the excess asset is distributed to the partners. Reduce the basis of the partner's partnership interest by the basis of the excess asset.

Step 3. Assume the partner sells the excess property back to the partnership and recognizes any gain or loss on the sale.

Step 4. Assume the partnership distributes remaining property needed so that economically the distributee partner ends up with the same assets received in the actual distribution. Remember that some of these assets are assumed to be received from the partnership when the partnership buys the excess property back from the partner.

We demonstrate these steps in the following Example.

EXAMPLE 7.5.4
Tax Consequences of a Disproportionate Distribution

Nala, Talib, and Harrison are equal partners in a partnership that has the following assets:

	Adjusted basis	Fair market value
Cash	$90,000	$90,000
Inventory	60,000	90,000
Land	75,000	90,000

Assume that Nala has a basis in her partnership interest of $75,000 and that her entire interest is redeemed in exchange for $90,000 cash. What are the tax consequences to Nala and the partnership?

SOLUTION

The partnership has substantially appreciated inventory because the $90,000 exceeds $60,000 × 120% ($72,000). Therefore, the partnership has hot assets. For this distribution to be proportionate, Nala must receive one-third of the hot assets, which would be $30,000 of the inventory ($90,000 × 1/3). However, Nala did not receive any of the hot assets. The tax consequences flow as follows:

Step 1. For the distribution to be proportionate, Nala should have received one-third of the inventory with a FMV of $30,000 and an adjusted basis of $20,000.

Step 2. We assume that one-third of the inventory was distributed to Nala. This distribution reduces the basis of her partnership interest by $20,000 from $75,000 to $55,000. Nala's basis in the inventory is $20,000.

Step 3. Assume that Nala sells the inventory to the partnership. The partnership pays for the inventory with the assets actually given to Nala in the distribution, which is cash of $30,000. Nala recognizes $10,000 of ordinary income from this sale, as follows:

Amount realized	$30,000
Less: Adjusted basis	(20,000)
Ordinary income	$10,000

Step 4. The partnership is then deemed to distribute the remaining cash ($60,000) to Nala.

	Nala
Basis in interest	$75,000
Less: Inventory	(20,000)
	$55,000
Less: Cash distribution	(60,000)
	(5,000)
Capital gain	5,000
Ending basis	$ 0

In summary, Nala has $10,000 of ordinary income and $5,000 of capital gain.

Partnership: There is no gain or loss to the partnership. However, the basis of the inventory is increased by $10,000 to $70,000 due to the purchase of the inventory from Nala for $30,000.

	Inventory
Original basis	$60,000
Distributed to Nala	(20,000)
Purchase from Nala	30,000
New basis	$70,000

Related exercise: Application Problem 22

In this textbook, we discuss only the situation for which a partner does not receive enough hot assets. However, there are other scenarios which are also disproportionate, such as the distributee partner receiving too many hot assets. This would mean that the partners remaining in the partnership have had a decrease in their share of hot assets. These additional scenarios are beyond the scope of this book.

Comparing a Proportionate and Disproportionate Distribution

In Example 7.5.4 the disproportionate distribution resulted in $10,000 of ordinary income and $5,000 of capital gain, both of which are recognized immediately. Let's think through what the result would have been for a proportionate distribution. Nala would have received one-third of the inventory ($30,000 with a basis of $20,000) for a proportionate distribution and the other $60,000 would be cash, land, or a combination of the two. Assuming she receives $60,000 of cash, the tax consequences are as follows:

	Nala
Basis in interest	$75,000
Less: Cash	(60,000)
	$15,000
Less: Inventory	(15,000)
Ending basis	$ 0

Nala has no gain or loss at the time of distribution, and her basis in the inventory is $15,000. The partnership's basis in the inventory of $20,000 is stepped down to $15,000. When Nala sells the inventory, she will have a gain of $15,000 if it is sold for $30,000 ($30,000 – $15,000 basis). The gain will be ordinary if she sells the inventory within the next five years. If she holds the inventory for more than five years, the character of the gain will depend on how she uses the property.

One of the consequences of the disproportionate distribution is that Nala recognized ordinary income at the time of distribution that is equal to the unrealized income in her share of the hot assets that were not distributed to her. If she had received a proportionate distribution, her gain would have been deferred until she sold or disposed of the inventory, which could be many years in the future.

Tax Planning Tip

If disproportionate distributions always accelerate the recognition of ordinary income, why do partners receive them? In many situations, a partner like Nala does not want to receive assets that are not liquid and may be hard to dispose of. From an economic perspective, they prefer to receive cash. So, they may be willing to bear the ordinary income recognition in order to receive the assets they prefer.

PRACTICE PROBLEM 7.5.1

Proportionate Distributions

The SleepWell Partnership has the following cash and hot assets on its balance sheet:

	Adjusted basis	Fair market value	Ordinary income potential
Cash	$50,000	$50,000	$ 0
Unrealized receivables	$ 0	$40,000	$40,000
Inventory	$60,000	$90,000	$30,000

Darnell is a 25% partner who receives a liquidating distribution of $17,500 of the unrealized receivables and $13,000 of cash. Is this a proportionate distribution?

SOLUTION

To determine if the distribution is proportionate, you compare Darnell's share of the income potential before and after distribution.

Ordinary income potential before the distribution: $70,000 × 25% = $17,500

Ordinary income potential after the distribution: When the $17,500 of receivables are sold or collected, Raymond will have $17,500 of ordinary income.

The distribution is proportionate because Darnell has a $17,500 ordinary income interest in the hot assets both before and after the distribution.

PRACTICE PROBLEM 7.5.2

Disproportionate Distribution

Assume the same facts as Practice Problem 7.5.1 except that Darnell receives a liquidating distribution of $10,000 of the unrealized receivables and $42,000 of cash. Is this a proportionate distribution?

SOLUTION

To determine if the distribution is proportionate, you compare Darnell's share of the income potential before and after distribution.

Ordinary income potential before the distribution: $70,000 × 25% = $17,500

Ordinary income potential after the distribution: When the $10,000 of receivables are sold or collected, Darnell will have $10,000 of ordinary income.

This is a disproportionate distribution because Darnell's share of the ordinary income potential in the hot assets declined from $17,500 before the distribution to $10,000 after the distribution.

INTERACTIVE SELF-SCORING QUIZZES

7.6 Advanced Topic (Drilling Down)—Optional Adjustment to Basis of Partnership Assets (Section 754 Elections)

LEARNING OBJECTIVE 6

Determine how a Section 754 election affects the basis of partnership assets.

VIDEO CONTENT

If the partnership has made a **Section 754 election**, then the partnership may be required to adjust the basis for its assets when a partnership interest is sold or when a partner receives a distribution of property. If the Section 754 election is not in effect, then the adjustments are not made. However, that can result in inequities to certain partners.

Section 754 Election

Section 754 elections are made by the partnership. The election can initially be made for any tax year, but once made it is irrevocable without the permission of the IRS. The election applies to all sales of partnership interests and all distributions that occur during the year the partnership makes the election, and all future years.

Related exercise: Multiple Choice Question 10

A Section 754 election is the best route for a partnership to take because it keeps the balance sheet balanced and therefore ensures that partners are taxed on the proper amount of income. However, many partnerships provide in their partnership agreements that they will not make a Section 754 election, especially large partnerships that have many partners and assets. The record keeping requirements for Section 754 elections can be very burdensome because the increase in basis for each asset due to Section 754 has to be separately recorded. For sales of partnership interests, the partnership must also maintain records showing to which partner the Section 754 basis is allocated. Further, if the basis of a depreciable asset is increased, then separate depreciation must be computed for that portion of the basis.

If a Section 754 election is in effect, the adjustment to the inside basis of assets due to the sale of a partnership interest is known as a **Section 743(b) adjustment**. An adjustment due to the distribution of an asset is known as a **Section 734(b) adjustment**.

Related exercise: Discussion Question 13

EXAMPLE 7.6.1
Section 754 Election

Black Partnership has five equal shareholders. Barney sells his 20% partnership interest to Sheila this year. Lorraine receives a cash distribution this year from Black that results in her recognizing a gain. Sheila would like for the partnership to make a Section 754 election, but Lorraine prefers that Black not do so. Can the partnership make a Section 754 election for Sheila's purchase, but not for Lorraine's distribution?

SOLUTION

Black cannot make the Section 754 election with respect to only Sheila's purchase of the partnership interest. The election applies to all sales and distributions for the year it is made, and all future years.

Related exercise: Brief Exercise 9

Section 754 and Sales of Partnership Interests

The issues for which a Section 754 election are helpful when related to a sale of a partnership interest are explained in the following example. Assume that the ABC Partnership has three equal partners and only one asset on its balance sheet, as follows:

Assets	Adjusted basis	Fair market value	Partners' capital	Adjusted basis	Fair market value
Land	$120,000	$180,000	A	$ 40,000	$ 60,000
			B	40,000	60,000
			C	40,000	60,000
Total	$120,000	$180,000	Total	$120,000	$180,000

Section 754 Not Elected by Partnership

A sells her partnership interest to D for $60,000 when A's basis in her partnership interest is $40,000. The partnership has not made a Section 754 election. Partner A recognizes a gain of $20,000 on the sale ($60,000 amount realized – $40,000 adjusted basis). Because D paid $60,000 for their partnership interest, they have a basis of $60,000. If the land had been sold by the partnership before A's sale to D, the partnership would have had a recognized gain of $60,000 ($180,000 amount realized – $120,000 adjusted basis) that would have been allocated $20,000 each to A, B, and C.

After the sale by partner A, the balance sheet is as follows:

Assets	Adjusted basis	Fair market value	Partners' capital	Adjusted basis	Fair market value
Land	$120,000	$180,000	B	$ 40,000	$ 60,000
			C	40,000	60,000
			D	60,000	60,000
Total	**$120,000**	$180,000	Total	**$140,000**	$180,000

The balance sheet is no longer in balance. The basis of the assets is $120,000 while the basis of the partners' capital accounts is $140,000. Your financial accounting professors taught you that if the balance sheet does not balance, then an error needs to be corrected. However, for partnership tax accounting, an error has *not* been made in this case. If a Section 754 election is not in effect, the balance sheet will not balance after one partner sells their partnership interest.

Next, assume that the partnership sells the land for $180,000. The partnership would recognize a gain of $60,000 ($180,000 amount realized – $120,000 adjusted basis) that is allocated $20,000 each to B, C, and D. This allocation, while correct, is not equitable to partner D. When Partner D paid $60,000 for their partnership interest, that price was based on one-third of the value of the land. In effect, they bought one-third of the land for $60,000 when they bought their partnership interest from A. But now, they must recognize $20,000 of gain when the land is sold by the partnership, even though the fair market value of their partnership interest is still $60,000. D must recognize $20,000 of tax gain even though their economic gain is $0. D has the right to be quite upset about this!

There is one consolation for D. Because $20,000 of the gain from the land sale flows to them, they do increase the basis in their partnership interest by $20,000 to $80,000 ($60,000 + $20,000). However, the value of the interest is still $60,000. Thus, when D sells their partnership interest, they will have a loss of $20,000 (or their gain will be $20,000 less) due to the $20,000 of gain recognition this year. So, eventually, the gain from the land sale and the loss from the sale of their partnership interest will offset one another. If D sells their interest a few months after the land sale, then the Section 754 effect is not extreme. But if the sale of their interest is many years later, the inequitable recognition of the $20,000 gain from the land is quite unfair.

Section 754 Elected by Partnership

The good news is that this inequitable result to D can be corrected with a Section 754 election. The Section 743(b) adjustment is computed as follows:

New partner's basis in partnership interest – New partner's share of inside basis of assets

$60,000 – ($120,000 × 1/3) = $20,000

The Section 754 election allows the partnership to increase the basis of the land by $20,000. This additional $20,000 inside basis is allocated entirely to partner D. The balance sheet is as follows after A's sale to D as follows with a Section 754 election:

Assets	Adjusted basis	Fair market value	Partners' capital	Adjusted basis	Fair market value
Land	$140,000	$180,000	B	$ 40,000	$ 60,000
			C	40,000	60,000
			D	60,000	60,000
Total	**$140,000**	$180,000	Total	**$140,000**	$180,000

There are two outcomes of the Section 754 election in this situation. First, the balance sheet now balances, which is preferred. Second, when the partnership sells the land, D will not be taxed on one-third of the appreciation in the land that existed when they purchased their partnership interest. If the partnership sells the land for $180,000, it is treated as if each partner sold one-third of the asset, as follows:

	Total	B	C	D
Amount realized	$180,000	$60,000	$60,000	$60,000
Original adjusted basis	(120,000)	(40,000)	(40,000)	(40,000)
Section 754 basis	(20,000)			(20,000)
Gain	$ 40,000	$20,000	$20,000	$ 0

Because the Section 754 basis of $20,000 is allocated to D, D has no tax gain on the sale of the land, which is consistent with D having no economic gain.

EXAMPLE 7.6.2

Section 754 and Sale of a Partnership Interest

Ira and Jala form the equal partnership Saffron. Ira and Jala each contribute $5,000 cash which the partnership uses to purchase land for $10,000. After a year, Ira sells her partnership interest to Tamara for $8,000. Immediately before the transfer of the partnership interest to Tamara, the balance sheet is as follows:

Assets	Adjusted basis	Fair market value	Partners' capital	Adjusted basis	Fair market value
Land	$10,000	$16,000	Ira	$ 5,000	$ 8,000
			Jala	$ 5,000	$ 8,000
Total	$10,000	$16,000	Total	$10,000	$16,000

a. Assuming that a Section 754 election is in effect, what is the inside basis of the assets to the partnership after the sale to Tamara, and how is this allocated to Jala and Tamara? Show the balance sheet after the sale to Tamara.

b. If the partnership later sells the land for $20,000, how is the gain allocated to the partners?

SOLUTION

a. We begin by computing the Section 743(b) adjustment. Tamara's basis in her partnership interest is her cost of $8,000. Tamara's share of the inside basis of the assets is $5,000 ($10,000 × 50%). Therefore, the adjustment needed for the basis of the assets is $3,000:

New partner's basis in partnership interest – New partner's share of inside basis of assets

$8,000 – ($5,000) = $3,000

The balance sheet is as follows:

Assets	Adjusted basis	Fair market value	Partners' capital	Adjusted basis	Fair market value
Land	$10,000	$16,000	Tamara	$ 8,000	$ 8,000
Land—Section 743(b)	$ 3,000		Jala	$ 5,000	$ 8,000
Total	$13,000	$16,000	Total	$13,000	$16,000

b. If the land is sold by the partnership for $20,000, the gain is allocated as follows:

	Total	Tamara	Jala
Amount realized	$20,000	$10,000	$10,000
Original adjusted basis	(10,000)	(5,000)	(5,000)
Section 743(b) basis	(3,000)	(3,000)	
Gain	$ 7,000	$ 2,000	$ 5,000

The land appreciated by $4,000 after Tamara bought her partnership interest and her share of that gain is $2,000 ($4,000 × 50%). She is not taxed on the unrealized appreciation in the land at the time she bought her interest.

Related exercise: Application Problem 23

Special Two-Year Rule When Section 754 Is Not Elected

As discussed above, if a partner buys an interest in an existing partnership and the partnership has appreciated assets, the partner is placed in an inequitable position if Section 754 has *not* been elected. This can be particularly harsh for a partner who then receives a distribution of property that would have had a higher basis if Section 754 was in effect, because the partner generally takes the same basis in the asset that the partnership had. The partner would recognize more gain in the future when the asset is disposed of because the basis was not increased under Section 754.

Congress has provided a relief measure for a partner in this situation. In this situation, if the partner receives a distribution of property within two years of buying their partnership interest, the partner can elect to assume that the basis of the property received is the amount it would have been had Section 754 been in effect.[26] The next Example demonstrates how this rule is applied.

EXAMPLE 7.6.3 Special Two-Year Rule for Certain Distributions

Jamal has a basis in his one-third interest in the profits, losses, and capital account of the Jade partnership of $50,000. He bought his interest in the prior year from a retiring partner. The partnership does not have a Section 754 election in effect. Jade makes a current distribution to Jamal of an asset with a basis of $12,000. At the time Jade bought his interest, the asset was worth $42,000, his share was $14,000, and Jade would have been allocated a $4,500 basis adjustment if Section 754 had been in effect. What are the tax consequences to Jamal on a current distribution of the asset?

SOLUTION

Jamal can elect to increase the basis of the asset received by $4,500, resulting in a basis of $16,500 ($12,000 + $4,500). Therefore, Jamal's basis in his partnership interest is reduced to $33,500 ($50,000 – $16,500). Jamal had no gain or loss and his basis in the asset received is $16,500, which is the basis the asset would have had if Section 754 had been elected.

[26] IRC §732(d).

Section 754 and Partnership Distributions

If Section 754 has been elected by the partnership, then it can also apply to partnership distributions. If the Section 754 election has *not* been made, then the balance sheet will not balance after certain distributions. However, whether the Section 754 election has been made has no immediate effect on the distributee partner. The election's effect is for the partners who remain in the partnership (and possibly future partners).

The Section 754 election has an effect on the inside basis of partnership assets for the following four types of distributions:

- The distributee partner recognizes a gain on the distribution.
- The distributee partner recognizes a loss on the distribution.
- The distributee partner's basis in the partnership interest is less than the basis of the assets distributed.
- The distributee partner's basis in the partnership is greater than the basis of the assets distributed, the distribution is liquidating, and the partner receives a Section 1231 or capital asset.

The adjustment made to the basis of assets due to a distribution when a Section 754 election is in effect is known as a Section 734(b) adjustment.

Section 734(b) basis adjustments arising because a gain or loss is recognized by the partner are made to the remaining capital assets and Section 1231 assets on the balance sheet. Other Section 734(b) basis adjustments are made to the remaining assets of the same character as the asset distributed. If the asset distributed was an ordinary asset, then Section 734(b) adjustments are allocated to the remaining ordinary assets on the balance sheet. If the partnership does not have an asset with the appropriate character for the Section 734(b) adjustment, the adjustment is held until such an asset is acquired.[27] These adjustments are summarized in **Illustration 7.7**.

ILLUSTRATION 7.7 Section 734(b) Basis Adjustments

Section 734(b) Basis Adjustments to Partnership Assets*

Reason for section 734(b) adjustment	Assets whose basis is adjusted
Gain recognized by partner on distribution	Capital assets/Section 1231 assets
Loss recognized by partner on distribution	Capital assets/Section 1231 assets
Other Section 734(b) adjustments due to distribution of ordinary assets	Ordinary assets
Other Section 734(b) adjustments due to distribution of non-ordinary assets	Capital assets/Section 1231 assets

*If the partnership does not have an asset with the appropriate character for the Section 734(b) adjustment, the adjustment is held until such an asset is acquired.

Gain on a Distribution

Assume that a partner's basis in their partnership interest is $10,000 and the partner receives a cash distribution of $11,000. The partner will recognize a $1,000 capital gain, because the cash distributed exceeds the basis in the partnership interest. The effect on the partnership balance sheet is as follows:

Assets		Liabilities and equity	
Cash	($11,000)	Partner's basis	($10,000)

If a Section 754 election is in effect, then the basis of other capital assets and Section 1231 assets on the balance sheet are increased by $1,000, as shown below:

[27]IRC §755.

Assets		Liabilities and equity	
Cash	($11,000)	Partner's basis	($10,000)
Section 754 basis	1,000		
Total	($10,000)		

With the Section 754 election, the balance sheet remains in balance. If a Section 754 election is not in effect, then the balance sheet will no longer balance. The assets decreased by $11,000, but the partner's tax basis decreased by only $10,000 because basis cannot be negative. The advantage of the Section 754 election for the remaining partners is that when these assets are sold in the future, there will be $1,000 less gain recognized because of the basis increase.

Loss on a Distribution

In the example above, if the distribution had been a liquidating distribution of $9,000 cash, then the partner would have recognized a loss of $1,000 because the basis in the partnership interest was $10,000. The effect on the partnership balance sheet is as follows:

Assets		Liabilities and equity	
Cash	($9,000)	Partner's basis	($10,000)

If a Section 754 election is in effect, then the basis of other capital assets and Section 1231 assets on the balance sheet is decreased by $1,000, as shown below:

Assets		Liabilities and equity	
Cash	($ 9,000)	Partner's basis	($10,000)
Section 754 basis	(1,000)		
Total	($10,000)		

With the Section 754 election, the balance sheet remains in balance. If a Section 754 election is not in effect, then the balance sheet will no longer balance. The assets decreased by $9,000, but the partner's tax basis decreased by $10,000 because the partner's ending basis in the partnership interest must be $0 for a liquidating distribution.

The decrease in basis of the assets means that the partnership will have an additional $1,000 of gain in the future.

Basis Reduction for Partnership Assets

Assume that a partner's basis in their partnership interest is $10,000 and the partner receives a liquidating distribution of land, which is a Section 1231 asset, with an adjusted basis of $11,000 and a FMV of $15,000. The partner will reduce their basis in their partnership interest from $10,000 to $0, will not recognize a gain, and will have a basis of $10,000 in the land. The effect on the partnership balance sheet is as follows:

Assets		Liabilities and equity	
Land	($11,000)	Partner's basis	($10,000)

The basis of the land was decreased by $1,000, from $11,000 to $10,000 as a result of the distribution. If a Section 754 election is in effect, then the basis of other capital assets or Section 1231 assets on the balance sheet are increased by $1,000, as shown below:

Assets		Liabilities and equity	
Land	($11,000)	Partner's basis	($10,000)
Section 754 basis (Section 1231 assets)	1,000		
Total	($10,000)		

With the Section 754 election, the balance sheet remains in balance. The advantage of this for the remaining partners is that when the other capital/Section 1231 assets are sold in the future, there will be $1,000 less gain recognized because of the basis increase.

If a Section 754 election is not in effect, then the balance sheet will no longer balance. The assets decreased by $11,000, but the partner's tax basis decreased by only $10,000 because basis cannot be negative.

Basis Increase for Partnership Assets

In the example above, assume that the land had a basis to the partnership of $9,000 and a FMV of $13,000. The partner will reduce their basis in their partnership interest from $10,000 to $0, will not recognize a loss because a Section 1231 asset was received, and will have a basis of $10,000 in the land. The effect on the partnership balance sheet is as follows:

Assets		Liabilities and equity	
Land	($9,000)	Partner's basis	($10,000)

The basis of the land was increased by $1,000, from $9,000 to $10,000 as a result of the distribution. If a Section 754 election is in effect, then the basis of other capital assets and Section 1231 assets on the balance sheet are decreased by $1,000, as shown below:

Assets		Liabilities and equity	
Land	($ 9,000)	Partner's basis	($10,000)
Section 754 basis (Section 1231 assets)	(1,000)		
Total	($10,000)		

With the Section 754 election, the balance sheet remains in balance. If a Section 754 election is not in effect, then the balance sheet will no longer balance. The assets decreased by $9,000, but the partner's tax basis decreased by $10,000 because basis in the partnership interest must be $0 after a liquidating distribution.

EXAMPLE 7.6.4
Section 754 and Distributions from a Partnership

Sonny had a basis of $30,000 in his partnership interest. He received a liquidating distribution consisting of $11,000 cash and inventory with a basis of $12,000. The partnership has a Section 754 election in effect. What are the tax consequences of the distribution to Sonny and the partnership?

SOLUTION

The tax consequences of the distribution for Sonny are as follows:

Basis in partnership interest	$30,000
Less: Cash	(11,000)
	$19,000
Less: Inventory	(12,000)
	$ 7,000
Loss	(7,000)
Ending basis	$ 0

Sonny has a capital loss of $7,000. The partnership has a Section 743(b) adjustment of $7,000 that will be allocated to other capital assets.

Related exercise: Application Problem 24

Substantial Built-In Losses

The adjustment allowed under Section 754 is required if a substantial built-in loss occurs because of the sale or transfer of the partnership interest. A **substantial built-in loss** exists if the partnership's adjusted basis in its property exceeds its fair market value by more than $250,000.[28] Similarly, an adjustment is required if there would be a substantial basis reduction of more than $250,000 due to the distribution of partnership assets.[29] In both cases, the rules of Section 754 are applied even though the Section 754 election has not been made.

We apply these adjustments in the next two Examples.

[28]IRC §743(d)(1)(b).

[29]IRC §734(d)(1).

EXAMPLE 7.6.5
Substantial Built-In Loss from Sale of Partnership Interest

Madeline is a 40% partner in Gold Partnership. She sells her partnership interest to Corey for $400,000. The assets on the partnership's balance sheet have a FMV of $1,000,000 and an adjusted basis of $1,800,000. The partnership does not have a Section 754 election in effect. What are the tax effects of this sale for Gold Partnership?

SOLUTION

If a Section 754 election *was* in effect, the Section 743(b) adjustment would be computed as follows:

New partner's basis in partnership interest	– New partner's share of inside basis of assets	
$400,000	– ($1,800,000 × 40%)	= ($320,000)

The ($320,000) is a substantial built-in loss because it exceeds $250,000. Therefore, even though a Section 754 election is not in effect, the partnership must reduce the basis of its assets by $320,000.

Related exercise: Application Problem 25

EXAMPLE 7.6.6
Substantial Basis Reduction on Partnership Distribution

Chunsheng has a basis of $2,400,000 in his partnership interest. The partnership does not have a Section 754 election in effect. He receives a liquidating distribution of land, which is a Section 1231 asset, from the partnership having a fair market value of $3,400,000 and a basis of $1,800,000. What are the tax consequences of this distribution to Chunsheng and the partnership?

SOLUTION

Chunsheng does not recognize a loss on the liquidating distribution, because he received a Section 1231 asset. The effect on his basis is computed as follows:

Basis in partnership interest	$2,400,000
Land	(2,400,000)
Ending basis	$ 0

Chunsheng's basis in the land is $2,400,000. The basis of the land to the partnership was $1,800,000, so it has been increased by $600,000. If Section 754 was in effect, the partnership would reduce the basis of its other assets by $600,000. Because the basis reduction exceeds $250,000, this is a substantial basis reduction that must be done even though Section 754 is not in effect.

Allocation of Basis Adjustments

You now are prepared to compute the Section 743(b) adjustment for sales of a partnership interest and the Section 734(b) adjustment for distributions. Up to now, we have kept the allocation of these adjustments to other assets simple, by using only one asset for the allocation. Of course, these adjustments with actual partnerships are much more complicated. The adjustments are governed by Section 755. Keep these two broad principles in mind when computing these allocations:

- If a partnership does not have additional assets to increase or decrease for the allocation, then the adjustment is carried forward.
- The basis of an asset can never be reduced below zero.

In this section, we will review the basics of the allocation process under Section 755. However, we keep this discussion very basic because a complete discussion of these rules is beyond the scope of a fundamentals of tax accounting textbook.

Ordinary Income Assets vs. All Other Assets

One important theme that runs throughout the partnership tax law is that each partner needs to eventually be taxed on their share of the partnership's ordinary income. This theme also applies to basis adjustments under Section 755, which are done in the following steps:

- First, the Section 743(b) or Section 734(b) adjustment is allocated into two parts: the portion allocated to ordinary income assets and the portion allocated to other assets. Ordinary income assets consist of unrealized receivables and inventory. Because inventory is defined as all assets other than Section 1231 assets and capital assets, the other asset category consists of only Section 1231 assets and capital assets. We refer to this latter category as capital assets for this discussion.
- Next, the adjustment for ordinary assets is allocated among the specific ordinary assets, and the adjustment allocated to the capital assets is allocated among all the capital assets.

Section 743(b) adjustments due to the sale of a partnership interest are allocated as shown in **Illustration 7.8**.

ILLUSTRATION 7.8 Allocation of Section 743(b) Adjustment

Step 1. **Allocate** first to ordinary income any property, based on the appreciation or depreciation of each asset.

Step 2. **Allocate** next to capital assets, based on the appreciation or depreciation of each asset, limited to the amount of appreciation or depreciation.

Step 3. **Allocate** any remaining adjustment to capital property, based on the relative FMV of the assets.

The next Example demonstrates the allocation of the Section 743(b) adjustment across multiple assets.

EXAMPLE 7.6.7 Allocation of Section 743(b) Adjustments

Assume that the GRAY Partnership has the following balance sheet:

Assets	Adjusted basis	FMV	Partners' capital	Adjusted basis	FMV
Cash	$ 30,000	$ 30,000	G	$ 74,000	$130,800
Inventory	60,000	52,000	R	37,000	65,400
Accounts receivable	0	60,000	A	37,000	65,400
Capital asset 1	15,000	45,000	Y	37,000	65,400
Capital asset 2	80,000	140,000			
Total	$185,000	$327,000	Total	$185,000	$327,000

G has a 40% interest in the partnership and the other partners have a 20% interest. G sells her interest in the partnership to P for $130,800, recognizing a gain of $56,800 ($130,800 − $74,000). GRAY Partnership made a Section 754 two years ago. Compute the adjustment to the inside basis of GRAY's assets, if any.

SOLUTION

P's basis in the partnership interest is its cost of $130,800, but his share of the inside basis of the assets is $74,000 ($185,000 × 40%). The Section 743(b) adjustment is computed as follows:

New partner's basis in partnership interest – New partner's share of inside basis of assets
$130,800 – (74,000) = $56,800

We follow the steps outlined in Illustration 7.8 to allocate the $56,800 adjustment to the partnership assets.

Step 1. There are two ordinary income assets. The inventory has an $8,000 ($52,000 FMV – $60,000 adjusted basis) unrealized loss in it. If sold, $3,200 ($8,000 × 40%) of this loss would have been allocated to G, the selling partner. The unrealized receivable has $60,000 of unrealized appreciation in it ($60,000 FMV – $0 adjusted basis). If sold, $24,000 ($60,000 × 40%) of this income would have been allocated to G. To summarize, $20,800 ($24,000 – $3,200) of the $56,800 adjustment is allocated to the ordinary income assets. This leaves $36,000 ($56,800 – $20,800) of the adjustment to allocate.

Step 2. Capital asset 1 has $30,000 of unrealized appreciation in it ($45,000 FMV – $15,000 adjusted basis). If sold, $12,000 ($30,000 × 40%) of this gain would have been allocated to G. Capital asset 2 has $60,000 of unrealized appreciation in it ($140,000 FMV – $80,000 adjusted basis). If sold, $24,000 ($60,000 × 40%) of this gain would have been allocated to G. To summarize, $36,000 ($12,000 + $24,000) of the $56,800 adjustment is allocated to the ordinary income assets.

Step 3. All the Section 743(b) adjustment was allocated in steps 1 and 2.

The balance sheet is as follows after the Section 743(b) adjustment is allocated. The adjustment amounts are all allocated to new partner P.

Assets	Adjusted basis	FMV	Partners' capital	Adjusted basis	FMV
Cash	$ 30,000	$ 30,000	P	$130,800	$130,800
Inventory	60,000	52,000	R	37,000	65,400
Inventory—734(b)	(3,200)				
Accounts receivable	0	60,000	A	37,000	65,400
A/R—734(b)	24,000				
Capital asset 1	15,000	45,000	Y	37,000	65,400
CA 1—734(b)	12,000				
Capital asset 2	80,000	140,000			
CA 2—734(b)	24,000				
Total	$241,800	$327,000	Total	$241,800	$327,000

Section 734(b) adjustments are allocated only to Section 1231 assets and capital assets if the adjustment is because the partner recognized gain or loss on the distribution. The adjustment is allocated to these assets as follows:

If adjustment is positive:

Step 1. Allocate: The adjustment first to assets that have appreciated in value, based on the amount of appreciation in each asset.

Step 2. Allocate: Any remaining adjustment to the Section 1231 assets and capital assets, based on relative FMVs.

If adjustment is negative:

Step 1. Allocate: The adjustment first to assets that have depreciated in value, based on the amount of depreciation in each asset.

Step 2. Allocate: Any remaining adjustment to the Section 1231 assets and capital assets, based on the relative adjusted bases of each asset after step 1.

We demonstrate the application of these rules in the next Example.

EXAMPLE 7.6.8
Allocation of Section 734(b) Adjustment for a Gain: One Capital Asset

Tan Partnership has the following assets:

	Basis	FMV
Cash	$12,000	$ 12,000
Inventory	24,000	36,000
Capital asset	30,000	55,000
Total	$66,000	$103,000

Assume that Tan has a Section 754 election in effect and is required to allocate a positive Section 734(b) adjustment due to a partner recognizing a gain of $3,000 on a distribution of cash. How is the adjustment allocated to the assets?

SOLUTION

The inside basis of assets must be increased by $3,000 because the partner recognized a $3,000 gain on the distribution. Section 734(b) adjustments due to gains and losses on distributions are allocated only to capital assets. Therefore, the basis of the capital asset is increased to $33,000 ($30,000 + $3,000).

Related exercise: Application Problem 26

Section 734(b) adjustments are allocated to assets that have the same character as the distributed property. If there are no such assets, the adjustment is carried forward until such assets are acquired. The adjustment is allocated to these assets as follows:

If adjustment is positive:

Step 1. Allocate: The adjustment first to assets of the same character of the distributed property that have appreciated in value, based on the amount of appreciation in each asset.

Step 2. Allocate: Any remaining adjustment is allocated to assets of the same character of the distributed property, based on relative FMVs.

If adjustment is negative:

Step 1. Allocate: The adjustment first to assets of the same character of the distributed property that have depreciated in value, based on the amount of depreciation in each asset.

Step 2. Allocate: Any remaining adjustment is allocated to assets of the same character of the distributed property based on the relative adjusted bases of each asset after step 1.

We demonstrate the application of these rules in the next Example.

EXAMPLE 7.6.9
Allocation of Section 734(b) Adjustment for a Gain: Three Capital Assets

White Partnership has the following assets:

	Basis	FMV
Cash	$ 12,000	$ 12,000
Inventory	24,000	36,000
Capital asset 1	30,000	55,000
Capital asset 2	67,000	40,000
Capital asset 3	18,000	25,000
Total assets	$151,000	$168,000

Assume that White has a Section 754 election in effect and it distributed capital asset 3 to a partner in a liquidating distribution. The partner's basis in their interest before the distribution was $30,000. How is the Section 734(b) adjustment allocated to the assets?

SOLUTION

We first need to determine if a Section 734(b) adjustment is required. The tax effects to the liquidating partner are as follows:

Basis in partnership interest	$30,000
Less: Capital asset 3	(30,000)
Ending basis in interest	$ 0

The partner stepped-up the basis of capital asset 3 from $18,000 to $30,000. Therefore, a negative Section 734(b) adjustment of $12,000 is required. The reduction must be allocated to other capital assets.

Step 1 (negative adjustment). The $12,000 negative adjustment must be allocated to assets that have an unrealized loss in them. Only capital asset 2 has an unrealized loss and the unrealized loss is greater than $12,000 [$40,000 – $67,0000 = ($27,000)], so the entire $12,000 adjustment is allocated to this asset. The basis of capital asset 2 is reduced to $55,000 ($67,000 – $12,000). Step 2 is not needed.

The asset balances are as follows after the distribution:

	Basis	FMV
Cash	$ 12,000	$ 12,000
Inventory	24,000	36,000
Capital asset 1	30,000	55,000
Capital asset 2	55,000	40,000
Total assets	$121,000	$143,000

PRACTICE PROBLEM 7.6.1

Section 754 and Sale of a Partnership Interest

Sven and Liam form the equal partnership, Lucia. Sven and Liam each contribute $8,000 cash which the partnership uses to purchase land for $16,000. After a year, Sven sells his partnership interest to Elsa for $11,000. Immediately before the transfer of the partnership interest to Elsa, the balance sheet is as follows:

Assets	Adjusted basis	Fair market value	Partners' capital	Adjusted basis	Fair market value
Land	$16,000	$22,000	Sven	$ 8,000	$11,000
			Liam	$ 8,000	$11,000
Total	$16,000	$22,000	Total	$16,000	$22,000

a. Assuming that a Section 754 election is in effect, what is the inside basis of the assets to the partnership after the sale to Elsa, and how is this allocated to Liam and Elsa? Show the balance sheet after the sale to Elsa.

b. If the partnership later sells the land for $25,000, how is the gain allocated to the partners?

SOLUTION

a. We begin by computing the Section 743(b) adjustment. Elsa's basis in her partnership interest is her cost of $11,000. Elsa's share of the inside basis of the assets is $8,000 ($16,000 × 50%). Therefore, the adjustment needed for the basis of the assets is $3,000:

New partner's basis in partnership interest	– New partner's share of inside basis of assets	
$11,000	– ($8,000)	= $3,000

The balance sheet is adjusted as follows:

Assets	Adjusted basis	Fair market value	Partners' capital	Adjusted basis	Fair market value
Land	$16,000	$22,000	Elsa	$11,000	$11,000
Land—Section 743(b)	$ 3,000		Liam	$ 8,000	$11,000
Total	$19,000	$22,000	Total	$19,000	$22,000

b. If the land is sold by the partnership for $25,000, the gain is allocated as follows:

	Total	Elsa	Liam
Amount realized	$25,000	$12,500	$12,500
Original adjusted basis	(16,000)	(8,000)	(8,000)
Section 743(b) basis	(3,000)	(3,000)	
Gain	$ 6,000	$ 1,500	$ 4,500

The partnership reports a gain of $6,000 which is allocated to the partners. The land appreciated by $3,000 after Elsa bought her partnership interest and her share of that gain is $1,500 ($3,000 × 50%). She is not taxed on the unrealized appreciation in the land at the time she bought her interest.

PRACTICE PROBLEM 7.6.2
Section 754 and Distributions from a Partnership

Sela had a basis of $28,000 in her partnership interest. She received a liquidating distribution consisting of $8,000 cash and inventory with a basis of $11,000. The partnership has a Section 754 election in effect. What are the tax consequences of the distribution to Sela and the partnership?

SOLUTION

The tax consequences of the distribution for Sela are as follows:

Basis in partnership interest	$28,000
Less: Cash	(8,000)
	$20,000
Less: Inventory	(11,000)
	$ 9,000
Loss	(9,000)
Ending basis	$ 0

Sela has a capital loss of $9,000. The partnership has a Section 743(b) adjustment of $9,000 that will be allocated to other capital assets.

PRACTICE PROBLEM 7.6.3
Substantial Built-In Loss from Sale of Partnership Interest

Mei is a 30% partner in Aqua Partnership. She sells her partnership interest to Feng for $310,000. The assets on the partnership's balance sheet have a FMV of $1,200,000 and an adjusted basis of $1,900,000. The partnership does not have a Section 754 election in effect. What are the tax effects of this sale for Aqua Partnership?

SOLUTION

If a Section 754 election was in effect, the Section 743(b) adjustment would be computed as follows:

New partner's basis in partnership interest	– New partner's share of inside basis of assets	
$310,000	– ($1,900,000 × 30%)	= ($260,000)

The ($260,000) is a substantial built-in loss because it exceeds $250,000. Therefore, even though a Section 754 election is not in effect, the partnership must reduce the basis of its assets by $260,000.

INTERACTIVE SELF-SCORING QUIZZES

7.7 Advanced Topic (Drilling Down)—Distributions of Built-In Gain Property

LEARNING OBJECTIVE 7

Compute the tax consequences of distributions related to built-in gain property.

VIDEO CONTENT

There are two situations related to distributions that can cause built-in gain to be allocated to the BIG contribution partner. Both of these rules have a time stipulation—they apply for only seven years after the partner contributed the BIG property to the partnership. The distributions at issue are:

- A distribution of the BIG property to a partner other than the contributing partner within seven years of the contribution date.[30]
- A distribution of a different asset to the contributing partner within seven years of the contribution date.[31]

Related exercises: Discussion Question 14
Multiple Choice Question 11

> **Potential Pitfall**
>
> The gain recognized by the contribution is *not the total gain* that would be allocated if the BIG property was sold for its FMV. Rather, it is just the BIG.

Distribution of Built-In Gain Property

If the BIG property is distributed to a partner other than the BIG partner within seven years of the contribution date, the tax consequences are as follows:

- On the date of distribution, it is assumed that the partnership sold the property for its current FMV, and the amount of BIG that would be allocated to the contribution partner from such a sale is taxed to the contribution partner.
- The BIG partner increases their basis in their partnership interest by the recognized BIG.
- The basis of the BIG property that was distributed is increased by the amount of gain recognized by the BIG partner.

We demonstrate these three tax effects in the following Example.

> **Potential Pitfall**
>
> The increase in basis of the BIG property for the BIG recognized is deemed to occur just before the property was distributed. This seems illogical, because it is the distribution that triggers these tax consequences. However, this ensures that the partner who receives the asset has a stepped-up basis for the asset.

EXAMPLE 7.7.1
Distribution of Built-In Gain Property

Corporation C contributed land (FMV $100,000 and basis $60,000) to Beige Partnership in exchange for a 25% interest in Beige. Three years later, Beige distributed the land to individual partner Pippa, thereby terminating Pippa's 30% interest in Beige. Immediately prior to the distribution, the land was worth $110,000 and Pippa's outside basis in her interest was $200,000. What are the tax consequences of the distribution?

SOLUTION

Corporation C has a built-in gain for the contributed land of $40,000 ($100,000 FMV – $60,000 basis). Because the distribution of this land to Pippa is within seven years of the date of contribution, Corporation C must recognize gain equal to the amount of BIG it would have recognized if the land had been sold. If sold, the partnership would have recognized a gain of $50,000 ($110,000 amount realized – $60,000 adjusted basis), $40,000 of which would have been allocated to Corporation C under the BIG rule. Thus, Corporation C has a gain of $40,000.

[30] IRC §704(c)(1)(B).

[31] IRC §737.

Corporation C's basis in its partnership interest increases by $40,000. Pippa is deemed to have received land with a basis of $100,000 ($60,000 + $40,000 [gain]) and a fair market value of $110,000. Pippa's basis in her interest was $200,000 and this distribution is a liquidating distribution. Therefore, Pippa takes a basis of $200,000 in the land.

Why **Why does this distribution rule exist for BIG property?** Before Congress put the 7-year rule into effect for the BIG property, taxpayers could avoid the general BIG rule on the sale of property by distributing the BIG property to another partner. Because the property was not sold, then the general BIG rule did not apply. Thus, partnerships could transfer the BIG on the property from the BIG partner to the distributee partner. The 7-year rule was created to prevent this tax planning strategy from working. However, this strategy can still work if the partnership is willing to wait more than seven years before distributing the BIG property.

Related exercises: Brief Exercise 10
Application Problem 28

Distribution of Other Property to BIG Partner

The next rule applies if the partnership distributes other property to the BIG partner within seven years of the contribution of the BIG property. Congress also created this law to minimize the success of some other tax-avoidance schemes. The tax consequences are as follows:

- The BIG partner recognizes gain equal to the *lower* of the:
  1. FMV of distributed property – Basis in partnership interest, *or*
  2. the BIG that would be recognized if the BIG property had been sold.
- The BIG partner increases their basis in their partnership interest by the recognized BIG.
- The basis of the BIG property that was distributed is increased by the amount of gain recognized by the BIG partner.

The next Example shows how to compute the tax consequences in this situation.

EXAMPLE 7.7.2
Distribution of Other Property to BIG Partner

Four years ago, Babou contributed investment land with a basis of $16,000 and FMV of $22,000 in exchange for a 20% capital and profits interest in the Silver Partnership. In the current year, when Babou had a basis in his partnership interest of $38,000, he received a current distribution of machinery with a basis of $27,000 and fair market value of $42,000. The FMV of the investment land at this time was $21,000. Babou had not recognized any of his BIG prior to the distribution. What are the tax consequences of the distribution?

SOLUTION

Upon contribution of the land, Babou has a built-in gain of $6,000 ($22,000 FMV – $16,000 basis). Because Babou received the distribution of another piece of property within seven years of his contribution of the land, he must recognize gain equal to the *lower* of:

1. FMV of distributed property – Basis in partnership interest, ($42,000 – $38,000 = $4,000), *or*
2. the BIG that would be recognized if the BIG property had been sold ($21,000 – $16,000 – $5,000).

If the investment land had been sold, the recognized gain would have been $5,000, all of which would be BIG allocated to Babou because the BIG is $6,000. The lower of these two amounts is

$4,000. Therefore, Babou must recognize a gain of $4,000. Babou's ending basis in his partnership interest is computed as:

Basis in partnership interest before the distribution	$38,000
Gain recognized	4,000
Basis of machinery	(27,000)
Ending basis in partnership interest	$15,000

Also note that the land, which is still owned by the partnership, receives a basis increase of $4,000 from $16,000 to $20,000.

Related exercise: Application Problem 27

PRACTICE PROBLEM 7.7.1
Distribution of BIG Property

Montana Corporation contributed land (FMV of $90,000 and basis of $45,000) to Colorado Partnership in exchange for a 30% interest in Colorado. Four years later, Colorado distributed the land to individual partner Bubba, thereby terminating Bubba's 30% interest in Colorado. Immediately prior to the distribution, the land was worth $102,000 and Bubba's outside basis in his interest was $190,000. What are the tax consequences of the distribution?

SOLUTION

Montana Corporation has a built-in gain for the contributed land of $45,000 ($90,000 FMV − $45,000 basis). When this land is distributed to Bubba, since the distribution is within seven years of the date of contribution, Montana Corporation must recognize gain equal to the amount of BIG it would have recognized if the land had been sold. If sold, the partnership would have recognized a gain of $57,000 ($102,000 amount realized − $45,000 adjusted basis), $45,000 of which would have been allocated to Montana Corporation under the BIG rule. Thus, Montana Corporation has a gain of $45,000.

Montana Corporation's basis in its partnership interest increases by $45,000. Bubba is deemed to have received land with a basis of $90,000 ($45,000 + $45,000 [gain]) and a fair market value of $102,000. Bubba's basis in his interest was $190,000 and this distribution is a liquidating distribution. Therefore, Bubba takes a basis of $190,000 in the land.

PRACTICE PROBLEM 7.7.2
Distribution of Other Property to BIG Partner

Two years ago, Redmond contributed investment land with a basis of $21,000 and FMV of $28,000 in exchange for a 25% capital and profits interest in the Elias Partnership. In the current year, when Redmond had a basis in his partnership interest of $42,000, he received a current distribution of equipment with a basis of $29,000 and fair market value of $43,000. The FMV of the investment land at this time was $26,000. Redmond had not recognized any of his BIG prior to the distribution. What are the tax consequences of the distribution?

SOLUTION

Upon contribution of the land, Redmond has a built-in gain of $7,000 ($28,000 FMV − $21,000 basis). Because Redmond received the distribution of another piece of property within seven years of his contribution of the land, he must recognize gain equal to the *lower* of:

1. FMV of distributed property – Basis in partnership interest, ($43,000 − $42,000 = $1,000), *or*
2. the BIG that would be recognized if the BIG property had been sold ($26,000 − $21,000 = $5,000).

If the investment land had been sold, the recognized gain would have been $5,000, all of which would be BIG allocated to Redmond because the BIG is $7,000. The lower of these two amounts is $5,000. Therefore, Redmond must recognize a gain of $5,000. Redmond's ending basis in his partnership interest is computed as:

Basis in partnership interest before the distribution	$42,000
Plus: Gain recognized	5,000
Less: Basis of equipment	(29,000)
Ending basis in partnership interest	$18,000

Also note that the land, which is still owned by the partnership, receives a basis increase of $5,000 from $21,000 to $26,000.

INTERACTIVE SELF-SCORING QUIZZES

Review and Practice

Chapter Summary

This chapter reviews additional topics related to the taxation of partnerships. The focus is on built-in gains and losses, nonliquidating and liquidating distributions, and the sale of a partnership interest. We include discussion of several advanced topics including disproportionate distributions and Section 754 elections.

1 Compute the tax consequences of assets with built-in gains and losses contributed to a partnership.

- A **built-in gain or loss** occurs when a partner contributes an asset to a partnership that has a different fair market value from its adjusted basis in exchange for a partnership interest. Built-in gains and losses must be allocated back to the BIG partner when the asset with the BIG or BIL is sold or disposed of by the partnership. This prevents the BIG or BIL from being shifted to another partner. The amount of BIG or BIL that is allocated to the BIG partner can never exceed the partnership's recognized gain from the sale of the asset.
- The partnership tax law has special rules concerning the character of gain or loss when certain contributed assets are sold. These rules apply to assets which in the hands of the partners were:
  - Unrealized receivables
  - Inventory
  - Capital assets with a built-in loss
- In each situation, the law prevents partners from using a partnership to convert the character to a type that is more favorable.

2 Determine the tax consequences of a distribution from a partnership to a partner.

- Partnerships do not recognize gain or losses for distributions to partners. This rule applies for both current and liquidating distributions. This is the case whether the distribution is cash or property. If the partner receives more than one item of property in the distribution, then the following ordering rules are used to reduce the partner's basis:
  - First, the partner's adjusted basis is allocated to cash distributions and deemed cash (reductions in liabilities).
  - Second, the partner's adjusted basis is allocated to distributions of unrealized receivables and inventory in an amount equal to the partnership's basis in these assets.
  - Finally, the partner's adjusted basis is allocated to other assets distributed. The other assets are capital assets and Section 1231 assets.
- If a partner receives a **current distribution**, the tax consequences are as follows:
  - The partner recognizes gain only to the extent that the *cash* distributed to the partner exceeds their basis in their partnership interest.

   - If the partner's share of partnership debt decreases, or if the partnership assumes the partner's debt, the amount of debt relief is identified as **deemed cash** and is treated as a cash distribution to the partner.
   - Marketable securities received by the partner are considered to be the same as cash. However, the marketable securities will not cause gain to be recognized unless the partner receives more than the partner's pro rata share of the securities.
   - If the partner receives a distribution of property, the partner will never recognize a gain.
   - A partner never recognizes a loss upon the receipt of a current distribution.
- The rules for the basis of property received in a current distribution are as follows:
   - The general rule for the effect of partnership distributions on the partner's basis is that the basis is reduced by the amount of cash distributed or the basis of the property distributed.
   - The basis in the partnership interest can never be reduced below zero. Therefore, if the total basis of all the assets distributed is greater than the partner's basis in the partnership interest, the reduction in basis is limited to the partner's basis. If that is the case, the partner's basis in the asset received is *less* than the partnership's basis in that asset before the distribution.
- The rules for **liquidating distributions** include:
   - A partner recognizes gain only to the extent that the sum of the *cash* and *deemed cash* distributed to the partner exceeds the partner's basis in the partnership interest.
   - If the partner receives a distribution of only property, the partner will never recognize a gain.
   - A partner recognizes a loss on the receipt of a distribution if the following three conditions are satisfied:
     1. The distribution is liquidating.
     2. The distribution must consist only of cash, unrealized receivables, and inventory.
     3. The outside basis of the partner's interest exceeds the sum of cash plus the basis of the receivables and inventory. In other words, the partner has some basis left in their partnership interest after subtracting the basis of the cash, inventory, and unrealized receivables.
   - The basis that a partner has in their partnership interest after a liquidating distribution must be zero.

3 Compute the tax consequences of a retirement distribution to a partner.

- If the interest of only one partner is liquidated, and the partnership continues in existence, this is known as a **retirement distribution**. These rules also apply to a partner who is deceased.
- If the partner is a general partner and capital is not a material income-producing factor for the partnership, then the next step is to determine if any of the retirement distributions are in return for unrealized receivables or unstated goodwill. If so, then those distributions are Section 736(a) payments. **Unstated goodwill** is goodwill that is not provided for in the partnership agreement. **Stated goodwill** is goodwill that is defined in and allowed by the partnership agreement.
- Section 736(a) payments are treated as guaranteed payments to the partner and taxed as ordinary income. The Section 736(b) payments are treated as being in exchange for the partner's interest in the partnership.

4 Compute the tax consequences of the disposition of a partnership interest.

- The general rule for IRC §742 indicates that this is a sale of a capital asset, which means that the result would be a capital gain or loss. There are four types of assets on the balance sheet that can influence the character of gain or loss from the sale of a partnership interest.

Asset type	Rule
Hot asset: Unrealized receivables and depreciation recapture	Treat as ordinary income.
Hot asset: Inventory	Treat as ordinary income.
Collectible gain	Taxed at a maximum rate of 28%.
Unrecaptured Section 1250 gain	Taxed at a maximum 25% rate.
Residual is capital gain/loss	Include in capital gain/loss netting process.

- When a partner dies, the partnership tax year closes on the date of death but only with respect to the deceased partner. The deceased partner's share of income for the year is determined based on the pro rata method, unless the partnership elects to close the book and compute the actual income.

5 Determine the tax effects of a disproportionate distribution.

- The hot asset rules for distributions are the same as for sales of a partnership interest with two differences:
   - For inventory to be a **hot asset**, it must be **substantially appreciated inventory**. The inventory is substantially appreciated if its FMV exceeds its adjusted basis by more than 20%.
   - With sales of partnership interests, the existence of hot assets always leads to some of the gain from the sale being characterized as ordinary income. However, the presence of hot assets on the balance sheet does not necessarily mean that the distribution is disproportionate. The distribution is proportionate if the partner's interest in the hot assets is the same before and after the distribution.
- If the partnership has hot assets, the distribution is **proportionate** if the partner who receives the distribution has the same interest in the ordinary income potential in the hot assets before and after the distribution. Otherwise, the distribution is **disproportionate**.

- If a partner receives a disproportionate distribution, you assume that the following steps occurred:

  Step 1. **Identify:** The amount of the asset that the partner did not receive enough of (deficit asset), contrasted to if the distribution had been proportionate.

  Step 2. **Assume:** The deficit asset identified in step 1 is distributed to the partner. This is a hypothetical distribution because it did not actually occur, but its tax consequences are real.

  Step 3. **Assume:** The partner sells the deficit asset received in step 1 back to the partnership and is paid with the asset that the partner received too much of (excess asset). This is a property transaction that will produce a recognized gain. Once again, this is hypothetical, but the tax consequences must be reported.

  Step 4. **Assume:** The partner receives a distribution of the remaining assets needed to ensure that, economically, the partner has received all the assets actually distributed to them by the partnership.

6 Determine how a Section 754 election affects the basis of partnership assets.

- If the partnership has made a **Section 754 election**, then the partnership may be required to adjust the basis for its assets when a partnership interest is sold or when a partner receives a distribution of property. If the Section 754 election is not in effect, then the adjustments are not made. However, that can result in inequities to certain partners.
- Section 754 elections are made by the partnership. Once made, the election is irrevocable without the permission of the IRS. The election applies to all sales of partnership interests and all distributions that occur during the year the partnership makes the election, and all future years. The adjustment allowed under Section 754 is required if a substantial built-in loss occurs because of the sale or transfer of the partnership interest. A substantial built-in loss exists if the partnership's adjusted basis in its property exceeds its fair market value by more than $250,000.
- The Section 754 election has an effect on the inside basis of partnership assets for the following four types of distributions:
  - The distributee partner recognizes a gain on the distribution.
  - The distributee partner recognizes a loss on the distribution.
  - The distributee partner's basis in the partnership interest is less than the basis of the assets distributed.
  - The distributee partner's basis in the partnership is greater than the basis of the assets distributed, the distribution is liquidating, and the partner receives a Section 1231 or capital asset.

7 Compute the tax consequences of distributions related to built-in gain property.

- There are two situations related to distributions that can cause built-in gain to be allocated to the BIG contribution partner. Both of these rules have a time stipulation—they apply for only seven years after the partner contributed the BIG property to the partnership. The distributions at issue are:
  - A distribution of the BIG property to a partner other than the contributing partner within seven years of the contribution date.
  - A distribution of a different asset to the contributing partner within seven years of the contribution date.

Communication Application

Communication

Built-In Gain

(LO1) The Yellowstone Partnership is a general partnership formed in the current year. When the Yellowstone Partnership was started, partner Dutton contributed land with a fair market value of $100,000 and a tax basis of $60,000 in exchange for a one-third interest in the partnership. The Yellowstone partnership agreement specifies that each partner will share equally in the partnership's profits and losses. During its second year of operation, Yellowstone sold the land to an unrelated third party for $160,000. Mr. Dutton would like to know what the proper tax treatment is for the sale. Write a memo to the Yellowstone Partnership in care of Mr. Dutton and to the tax file.

Solution

Memo to client

Dear Mr. Dutton,

Thank you for asking me to provide guidance on the sale of land by the Yellowstone Partnership. As we discussed during our last meeting, the land will be sold to an unrelated third party for $160,000. Because the land's basis is $60,000, there is a recognized gain of $100,000 on the sale. The partnership is a flow through entity and the partners will report the gain on their tax returns.

When the land was contributed by you to Yellowstone, a pre-contribution gain of $40,000 existed which is the difference between the land's fair market value ($100,000) and the land's basis ($60,000) at the time of the contribution. Therefore, the first $40,000 of gain is allocated to you, and the remaining gain of $60,000 is shared equally by all the partners in the partnership. Your total gain will be $60,000 ($40,000 pre-contribution gain + $20,000 allocated gain). The other two partners in Yellowstone will report $20,000 gain each.

Please let me know if you have any questions.

Sincerely,
Carnes & Youngberg, CPAs

Tax memo to the file

Facts: The Yellowstone Partnership is a general partnership formed in the current year. When the Yellowstone Partnership was started, partner Dutton contributed land with a fair market value of $100,000 and a tax basis of $60,000 in exchange for a one-third interest in the partnership. The Yellowstone partnership agreement specifies that each partner will share equally in the partnership's profits and losses. During its second year of operation, Yellowstone sold the land to an unrelated third party for $160,000.

Issue: How will the gain be allocated to the partners of Yellowstone?

Conclusion: There is a recognized gain of $100,000 ($160,000 – $60,000) from the sale of the land. The partnership is a flow through entity and the partners will report the gain on their tax returns. The first $40,000 of gain is allocated to Mr. Dutton, and the remaining gain of $60,000 is shared equally by all the partners in the partnership.

Analysis: According to IRC Section 704(c), pre-contribution gain exists when a partner contributes property where the fair market value is greater than its adjusted basis on the date of contribution. When the land was contributed by Mr. Dutton to Yellowstone, a pre-contribution gain of $40,000 existed, which is the difference between the land's fair market value ($100,000) and the land's basis ($60,000) at the time of the contribution. Therefore, the first $40,000 of gain is allocated to Mr. Dutton, and the remaining gain of $60,000 is shared equally by all the partners in the partnership. Mr. Dutton's total gain will be $60,000 ($40,000 pre-contribution gain + $20,000 allocated gain). The other two partners in Yellowstone will report $20,000 gain each.

Ethics and Professional Responsibility Application

Ethics

Potential Loss on a Liquidating Distribution

(LO2) Sunny Partnership made a proportionate liquidating distribution of $12,500 cash and land with an adjusted basis of $9,000 and a fair market value of $22,000 to Tamara, a 40% partner. The land was a Section 1231 asset for Sunny. At the time of the distribution, Tamara's basis in Sunny was $28,000. When Tamara filed her tax return, she reported a loss of $6,500, computed as follows:

Basis in partnership interest	$28,000
Less: Cash	(12,500)
Less: Land	(9,000)
Remaining basis	$ 6,500
Loss	(6,500)
Ending basis	$ 0

You are reviewing her tax return and have discovered that she was not allowed to deduct a loss. What advice do you offer to Tamara? In addition to the chapter content, see *Statements on Standards for Tax Services* at www.aicpa-cima.com/resources/landing/statements-on-standards-for-tax-services, *Circular 230* at https://www.irs.gov/tax-professionals/office-of-professional-responsibility-and-circular-230, and Chapter 2, LO4, Tax Professional Responsibilities.

Solution

Tamara's ending basis in her partnership interest is zero and no gain or loss is recognized to Tamara or the partnership. Tamara's basis in Sunny of $28,000 is reduced to $15,500 by the cash received of $12,500. A partner recognizes a loss on the receipt of a distribution if the following three conditions are satisfied:

1. The distribution is liquidating.
2. The distribution must consist only of cash, unrealized receivables, and inventory.
3. The outside basis of the partner's interest exceeds the sum of cash plus the basis of the receivables and inventory. In other words, the partner has some basis left in their partnership interest after subtracting the basis of the cash, inventory, and unrealized receivables.

Tamara received a Section 1231 asset, so she was not eligible to recognize a loss. Her basis in the land is $15,500 because her ending basis in her partnership interest must be zero after a liquidating distribution.

Because Tamara incorrectly reported a loss on her tax return, she must amend her tax return. Under *Circular 230* §10.22, Diligence as to Accuracy, "a practitioner must exercise due diligence—(1) In preparing or assisting in the preparation of, approving, and filing tax returns, documents, affidavits, and other papers relating to Internal Revenue Service matters." Also under *Circular 230*, §10.21 Knowledge of client's omission, a practitioner who "knows that the client has not complied with the revenue laws of the United States or has made an error in or omission from any return, document, affidavit, or other paper which the client submitted or executed under the revenue laws of the United States, must advise the client promptly of the fact of such noncompliance, error, or omission. The practitioner must advise the client of the consequences..." Tamara could incur penalties for not properly complying with the tax law.

Key Terms

End-of-Chapter Assessment

Discussion Questions

1. **(LO1)** When does a built-in gain or loss occur?
2. **(LO1)** Why does the tax law have the built-in gain or loss rule?
3. **(LO2)** Distinguish between a current distribution and a liquidating distribution.
4. **(LO2)** What is the tax consequence to a partnership when it makes a distribution to a partner?
5. **(LO2)** Can a partner recognize a loss on a liquidating distribution?
6. **(LO2)** Discuss the holding period rules for distributions.
7. **(LO3)** What is a retirement distribution?
8. **(LO3)** When is capital considered a material income-producing factor?
9. **(LO4)** Describe a hot asset.
10. **(LO4)** Even though a partnership interest is typically considered an investment asset that produces capital gain or loss when sold, explain when income might result from the sale of a partnership interest that is not taxed at regular capital gain rates?
11. **(LO4)** If a partner had suspended losses at the time of death due to insufficient passive income, what happens to the suspended losses?
12. **(LO5 Advanced)** When does a disproportionate distribution occur?
13. **(LO6 Advanced)** Discuss the tax effect of a Section 754 election.
14. **(LO7 Advanced)** Does the built-in gain rules apply if the contributing partner with the BIG receives a different asset through distribution?

Multiple Choice Questions

1. **(LO1)** Which of the following is a true statement regarding built-in gain or loss transactions?
   - **a.** All income generated from a built-in gain or loss transaction is ordinary income.
   - **b.** The contributing partner will recognize all the gain or loss when the asset is sold.
   - **c.** The contributing partner will recognize some or all the gain or loss when the asset is sold.
   - **d.** Other partners will never recognize any gain or loss when the asset is sold.

2. **(LO2)** Partner C receives three assets from Partnership CY as part of a current distribution. He receives cash, accounts receivable, and machinery used in the business for four years. What is the correct ordering that these assets should be considered in when determining the tax consequences of this distribution?
   - **a.** Machinery, accounts receivable, cash
   - **b.** Accounts receivable, cash, machinery
   - **c.** Cash, machinery, and accounts receivable
   - **d.** Cash, accounts receivable, and machinery

3. **(LO2)** A loss might be recognized on a liquidating distribution in which of the following circumstances?
   - **a.** A loss can never be recognized
   - **b.** If only cash and capital assets are distributed
   - **c.** If only Section 1231 assets are distributed
   - **d.** If only cash, unrealized receivables, and inventory are distributed

4. **(LO3)** In which of the following circumstances might a distribution be considered a Section 736(a) payment?
   - **a.** A retirement distribution when the partnership provides only services.
   - **b.** A retirement distribution when the partnership does not have capital that is a material income-producing factor.
   - **c.** A retirement distribution from the partnership in return for unrealized receivables and/or unstated goodwill.
   - **d.** All of the above.

5. **(LO3)** If a partner receives a proportionate retirement distribution from a partnership that provides only services and has assets of only cash and unrealized receivables, which of the following is true if the distribution is $45,000, her share of the unrealized receivables is $45,000, and her basis in the partnership is $23,000?
   - **a.** The $45,000 payment is treated as a Section 736(a) payment, and she has a guaranteed payment of $45,000 and a capital loss of $23,000.
   - **b.** The $45,000 payment is treated as a Section 736(a) payment, and she has a capital gain of $22,000.
   - **c.** The $45,000 payment is treated as a Section 736(b) payment, and she has a capital gain of $22,000.
   - **d.** The $45,000 payment is treated as a Section 736(a) payment, and she has a capital gain of $45,000.

6. **(LO4)** Which of the following is not a hot asset for a sale or exchange of a partnership interest?
   - **a.** Land held for investment
   - **b.** Accounts receivable of a cash-basis taxpayer
   - **c.** Accounts receivable of an accrual-basis taxpayer
   - **d.** Land held by a real estate developer

7. **(LO4)** Hot assets of a partnership include which of the following?
   - **a.** Cash
   - **b.** Section 1245 depreciation recapture
   - **c.** Section 1231 assets
   - **d.** Capital assets

8. **(LO4)** Partner M has been a 50% partner in the MJ Partnership for three years and has a basis in his partnership interest of $110,000, including his share of partnership debt (his share is $35,000). Dan buys M's partnership interest for $160,000 cash. What is M's gain from this sale?
   - **a.** $0
   - **b.** $35,000
   - **c.** $85,000
   - **d.** $160,000

9. **(LO5 Advanced)** Substantially appreciated inventory is inventory that has a fair market value in excess of what percentage of the partnership's adjusted basis for the inventory?
   - **a.** 110%
   - **b.** 120%
   - **c.** 125%
   - **d.** 150%

10. **(LO6 Advanced)** Which of the following can make a Section 754 election?
    - **a.** Partners in a partnership
    - **b.** Partnership
    - **c.** Corporation
    - **d.** All of the above

11. **(LO7 Advanced)** If a partner contributes property with a built-in gain in exchange for a partnership interest, how long does the partnership have to wait to distribute the asset in order for the contributing partner to not recognize the built-in gain?
    - **a.** 3 years
    - **b.** 5 years
    - **c.** 7 years
    - **d.** There is no holding period requirement

12. **(LO7 Advanced)** Tori contributes property to a partnership with a built-in gain of $40,000 on June 3, Year 4, and received a 50% partnership interest. The partnership distributes the land to another partner on September 10, Year 10, when the value of the land has increased by $8,000. How much gain is allocated to Tori because of the distribution?
    - **a.** $0
    - **b.** $40,000
    - **c.** $44,000
    - **d.** $48,000

Brief Exercises

1. **(LO1)** Chase contributes land to a partnership in return for a 35% interest in the partnership. The land has an adjusted basis of $13,000 and a fair market value of $22,000. Three years later, the partnership sells the land for $28,000. How much of the gain from this sale is allocated to Chase?

2. **(LO2)** Jahari is a 25% partner in the JHI Partnership. Jahari's basis in JHI Partnership is $69,000. JHI makes a proportionate nonliquidating cash distribution of $50,000. What is Jahari's gain or loss and the basis in JHI after the distribution?

3. **(LO2)** Partnership XYZ makes a proportionate current cash distribution of $23,000 to Partner Z who has a $16,000 basis in her partnership interest. What is Z's gain or loss and basis in her interest after the distribution?

4. **(LO2)** Dallas Partnership makes a proportionate liquidating distribution of $13,500 cash and land with an adjusted basis of $8,000 and a fair market value of $27,500 to Veena, a 25% partner. Dallas held the land as an investment. At the time of the distribution, Veena's basis in Dallas was $24,000. What is Veena's gain or loss, if any? What is the basis in her interest after the distribution?

5. **(LO3)** Tinker Partnership has the following assets on its balance sheet at the end of the current year:

	Adjusted basis	Fair market value
Cash	$225,000	$225,000
Unrealized receivables	0	24,000
Inventory	30,000	30,000
Machinery	17,000	26,000
Buildings	75,000	325,000
Land	55,000	125,000
Goodwill	0	60,000
Total	$402,000	$815,000

Carmen is a one-third partner in the Tinker Partnership who retired as of December 31 of the current year. What is Carmen's share of the unrealized receivables and the goodwill?

6. **(LO4)** On December 31, Year 28, after receipt of his share of partnership income, partner Desmond sold his interest in a limited partnership for $40,000 cash and relief of all liabilities. On that date, the basis in Desmond's partnership interest was $50,000, consisting of his capital account of $15,000, and his share of the partnership liabilities of $35,000. Assume the partnership has no unrealized receivables or inventory. What is Desmond's gain or loss on the sale of his partnership interest?

7. **(LO4)** Damien has owned a partnership interest for eight years. The interest has a FMV of $22,000 and her basis in the interest is $43,000. Damien gifts the partnership interest to Jody. What is Jody's basis in the partnership interest? How much gain or loss will Jody have if she sells the partnership interest for $20,000 one month after receiving it?

8. **(LO5 Advanced)** Tank Partnership has the following assets on its balance sheet.

	Adjusted basis	FMV
Cash	$ 22,000	$ 22,000
Accounts receivables	13,000	13,000
Equipment	48,000	33,000
Accumulated depreciation	(28,800)	--
Land	100,000	160,000
Total	$154,200	$228,000

Which of these assets qualify as hot assets for the partnership distribution rules?

9. **(LO6 Advanced)** Rain Partnership has four equal shareholders. June sells her 25% partnership interest to April this year. Ella receives a cash distribution this year from Rain that results in her recognizing a gain. April would like for the partnership to make a Section 754 election, but Ella prefers that Rain not do so. Can the partnership make a Section 754 election for April's purchase, but not for Ella's distribution?

10. **(LO7 Advanced)** Partner G contributed land (FMV $200,000 and basis $120,000) to Fuchsia Partnership in exchange for a 30% interest in Fuchsia. Four years later, Fuchsia distributed the land to individual partner S, thereby terminating S's 25% interest in Fuchsia. Immediately prior to the distribution, the land was worth $220,000 and partner S's outside basis in her interest was $400,000. What are the tax consequences of the distribution?

Application Problems

1. **(LO1)** When the QU Partnership was formed, partner Q contributed land with a fair market value of $120,000 and an adjusted basis of $64,000 in exchange for a 50% interest in the partnership. The QU Partnership agreement specifies that each partner will share equally in the partnership's profits and losses. During the second year of operation, QU sold the land to an unrelated third party for $145,000. What is the gain that Q must report on his tax return?

2. **(LO1)** When the QU Partnership was formed, partner Q contributed land with a fair market value of $120,000 and an adjusted basis of $64,000 in exchange for a 50% interest in the partnership. The QU Partnership agreement specifies that each partner will share equally in the partnership's profits and losses. During the second year of operation, QU sold the land to an unrelated third party for $110,000. What is the gain that Q must report on his tax return?

3. **(LO1)** When the QU Partnership was formed, partner U contributed inventory with a fair market value of $36,000 and an adjusted basis of $40,000 in exchange for a 50% interest in the partnership. The QU Partnership agreement specifies that each partner will share equally in the partnership's profits and losses. During the second year of operation, QU sold the inventory to an unrelated third party for $32,000. What is the loss that Q must report on his tax return?

4. **(LO1)** Ernie and Fergie form the Cubs Partnership as equal partners in the current year. Ernie contributes a capital asset with an adjusted basis of $16,000 and a fair market value of $11,000. The partnership will use the asset as inventory. Two years later, Cubs Partnership sells the asset to an unrelated third party for $8,000.

   a. What is the loss that Ernie must report on his tax return and what is the character of the loss?

b. How would the answer change if the Cubs sold the asset six years after it was contributed?

5. (LO1) Candace and A'ja form the Aces Partnership as equal partners. Candace contributes land that is held as inventory with an adjusted basis of $170,000 and a fair market value of $300,000. The partnership will use the land as a Section 1231 asset. Three years later, Aces Partnership sells the land for $360,000.

a. What is the gain that Candace must report on her tax return and what is the character of the gain?

b. How would the answer change if the Aces sold the asset eight years after it was contributed?

6. (LO2) Braves Partnership owns a building that has a fair market value of $875,000 and an adjusted basis of $290,000. Braves originally purchased the building for $370,000. During the current year, Braves distributed the building to Chipper who owns a 60% interest in the partnership before and after the distribution. Assume the distribution is proportionate.

a. What are the tax consequences of the distribution to Braves?

b. What are the tax consequences to Braves if the fair market value of the building is $235,000?

c. How would the tax consequences vary for parts **a** and **b** if Braves was a corporation?

7. (LO2) Partnership VOL makes a proportionate current distribution of $24,000 cash and land to Partner Lucy. Lucy's basis in her partnership interest before the distribution is $44,000. The land has an adjusted basis of $18,000 and a fair market value of $33,000. What is Lucy's gain or loss, if any, and basis in the land after the distribution?

8. (LO2) The Windy City Partnership makes a proportionate current distribution of $20,000 cash and land to partner Wendy. Wendy's basis in her partnership interest before the distribution is $50,000. The land has an adjusted basis of $40,000 and a fair market value of $35,000. What is Wendy's gain or loss, if any, and basis in the land after the distribution?

9. (LO2) Red Rock Partnership makes a proportionate current distribution of $23,000 cash and property to partner Greg. Greg's basis in his partnership interest before the distribution is $16,500. The property has an adjusted basis of $9,000 and a fair market value of $11,500. What is Greg's gain or loss, if any, and basis in the property after the distribution?

10. (LO2) Javier is a 25% partner in Lily Partnership and his basis is $42,000 in Lily. In a liquidating distribution, Javier received $29,000 cash, inventory with a basis of $3,300 and a fair market value of $4,000, and a truck with a basis of $8,200 and a fair market value of $15,000.

a. What are the tax consequences of this distribution to Javier and the partnership?

b. How would Javier's results differ if this was a current distribution?

11. (LO2) Jin is a 40% partner in the Evergreen Partnership and his basis is $28,000 in Evergreen. In a liquidating distribution, Jin received $25,000 cash and inventory with a basis of $2,000 and a fair market value of $4,000. What are the tax consequences of this distribution to Jin and the partnership?

12. (LO2) Amara is a 30% partner in the Downtown Partnership and her basis is $19,000 in Downtown. In a liquidating distribution, Amara received $15,000 cash and a Section 1231 asset with a basis of $2,000 and a fair market value of $8,000. What are the tax consequences of this distribution to Amara and the partnership?

13. (LO2) The DriveNow Partnership is a dealer in high-end automobiles. Ying, an engineer, receives a current distribution of a Jaguar from DriveNow on June 15 of Year 25. The basis of the Jaguar to the partnership is $51,000 and its fair market value at the date of distribution is $72,000. Ying's basis in her partnership interest before the distribution is $65,000. Ying uses the automobile as a collectible investment.

a. On December 8, Year 28, Ying sells the Jaguar for $82,000. What is the amount and character of Ying's gain?

b. In part **a** above, how do the results change if Ying sold the Jaguar on November 15, Year 30?

14. (LO3) World Partnership has the following assets on its balance sheet at the end of the current year:

	Adjusted basis	Fair market value
Cash	$333,000	$333,000
Unrealized receivables	0	20,000
Inventory	80,000	80,000
Machinery	15,000	25,000
Buildings	95,000	285,000
Land	50,000	120,000
Goodwill	0	100,000
Total	$573,000	$963,000

Tiafoe is a 25% partner in the World Partnership who retired as of December 31 of the current year. What is Tiafoe's share of the unrealized receivables and the goodwill?

15. (LO3) World Partnership has the following assets on its balance sheet at the end of the current year:

	Adjusted basis	Fair market value
Cash	$333,000	$333,000
Unrealized receivables	0	20,000
Inventory	80,000	80,000
Machinery	15,000	25,000
Buildings	95,000	285,000
Land	50,000	120,000
Goodwill	0	100,000
Total	$573,000	$963,000

Assume that capital is a material income-producing factor. Tiafoe is a 25% general partner in the World Partnership who retired as of December 31 of the current year. Tiafoe receives $240,750 as a retirement distribution. His basis in his partnership interest immediately before the distribution is $125,000. Assume that the distribution is proportionate, so you can ignore the impact of the hot asset rules. His share of unrealized receivables and stated goodwill are as follows:

	Adjusted basis	Fair market value
Unrealized receivables	$0	$ 5,000
Goodwill	$0	$25,000

How is the distribution to Tiafoe divided into Section 736(a) and Section 736(b) payments, and what are the tax consequences to Tiafoe?

16. (LO3) Relax Partnership provides physical therapy and massage treatments for patients. It provides only services, and capital is not a material income-producing factor. Nellie is a 25% partner, and she receives a retirement distribution of $95,000. Nellie's basis in her partnership interest is $45,000. Assume that the distribution is proportionate. Relax has the following balance sheet immediately before the distribution:

	Adjusted basis	Fair market value
Cash	$180,000	$180,000
Unrealized receivables	$ 0	$120,000
Land	$ 50,000	$ 40,000
Total	$230,000	$340,000

a. What are the tax consequences of the retirement distribution to Nellie?

b. How would the tax consequences change if the partnership had stated goodwill of $40,000 and the FMV of the partnership assets increased to $380,000 ($340,000 + $40,000)?

17. **(LO4)** Darius, Enrique, and Francis are one-third partners in the DEF Partnership. DEF had the following balance sheet on December 31, Year 30:

Assets	Adjusted basis	FMV	Debt and partners' capital	Adjusted basis	FMV
Cash	$120,000	$120,000	Note payable	$ 90,000	$ 90,000
Accounts receivable	0	390,000	Darius	10,000	140,000
			Enrique	10,000	140,000
			Francis	10,000	140,000
Total	$120,000	$510,000	Total	$120,000	$510,000

Francis sold his partnership interest to Geraldo, an unrelated third party, for $140,000 cash on January 1, Year 31. In addition, Geraldo assumed Francis's share of partnership liability.

a. What is the amount realized by Francis on the sale of the partnership interest?

b. What is the recognized gain by Francis?

c. What is the character of the gain?

18. **(LO4)** April, May, and June are one-third partners in the AMJ Partnership. AMJ had the following cash-basis balance sheet on December 31, Year 32:

Assets	Adjusted basis	FMV	Debt and partners' capital	Adjusted basis	FMV
Cash	$ 60,000	$ 60,000	Note payable	$ 0	$ 66,000
Accounts receivable	0	120,000	April	34,000	84,000
Collectibles	12,000	48,000	May	34,000	84,000
Building	30,000*	90,000	June	34,000	84,000
Total	$102,000	$318,000	Total	$102,000	$318,000

*Original cost was $51,000. All depreciation was straight-line.

June sold her partnership interest to Autumn, an unrelated third party, for $84,000 cash on January 1, Year 33. In addition, Autumn assumed June's share of partnership liability.

a. What is the amount realized by June on the sale of the partnership interest?

b. What is the recognized gain by June?

c. What is the character of the gain?

19. **(LO4)** Taylor is a 20% partner in the Groove Partnership. He sells his partnership interest and recognizes a $20,000 gain. The partnership has inventory on its balance sheet, and if the inventory was sold, Taylor's share of it would be $24,000. What are the tax consequences for Taylor?

20. **(LO4)** Roberto was a 25% partner in Bush Partnership, a calendar-year partnership. Roberto died on August 31 of the current year, and his partnership interest was transferred to his daughter, Maria. The partnership income for the year is $150,000. The FMV of Roberto's interest on the date of death was $65,000. What are the tax consequences of these transactions?

21. **(LO5 Advanced)** The Aqua Partnership has the following cash and hot assets on its balance sheet:

	Adjusted basis	Fair market value	Ordinary income potential
Cash	$50,000	$50,000	$ 0
Unrealized receivables	$ 0	$40,000	$40,000
Inventory	$60,000	$90,000	$30,000

Marco is a 25% partner who receives a liquidating distribution of $17,500 of the unrealized receivables and $22,000 of cash. Is this a proportionate distribution?

22. **(LO5 Advanced)** Brook is a 40% partner in a partnership that has the following assets:

	Adjusted basis	Fair market value
Cash	$200,000	$200,000
Inventory	60,000	100,000
Land	75,000	300,000

Assume that Brook has a basis in her partnership interest of $160,000 and that her entire interest is redeemed in exchange for $200,000 cash. What are the tax consequences to Brook and the partnership?

23. **(LO6 Advanced)** Bashir and Abbas form the equal partnership, Canyon. Bashir and Abbas each contribute $10,000 cash which the partnership uses to purchase land for $20,000. After a year, Bashir sells his partnership interest to Imran for $16,000. Immediately before the transfer of the partnership interest to Imran, the balance sheet is as follows:

Assets	Adjusted basis	Fair market value	Partners' capital	Adjusted basis	Fair market value
Land	$20,000	$32,000	Bashir	$10,000	$16,000
			Abbas	$10,000	$16,000
Total	$20,000	$32,000	Total	$20,000	$32,000

a. Assuming that a Section 754 election is in effect, what is the inside basis of the assets to the partnership after the sale to Imran, and how is this allocated to Bashir and Imran? Show the balance sheet after the sale to Imran.

b. If the partnership later sells the land for $40,000, how is the gain allocated to the partners?

24. **(LO6 Advanced)** Cami had a basis of $60,000 in her partnership interest. She received a liquidating distribution consisting of $22,000 cash and inventory with a basis of $24,000. The partnership has a Section 754 election in effect. What are the tax consequences of the distribution to Cami and the partnership?

25. **(LO6 Advanced)** Feng is a 40% partner in Silver Partnership. He sells his partnership interest to Yuan for $560,000. The assets on the partnership's balance sheet have a FMV of $1,400,000 and an adjusted basis of $2,520,000. The partnership does not have a Section 754 election in effect. What are the tax effects of this sale for Silver Partnership?

26. **(LO6 Advanced)** Cream Partnership has the following assets:

	Basis	FMV
Cash	$ 36,000	$ 36,000
Inventory	72,000	108,000
Capital Asset	90,000	165,000
Total	$198,000	$309,000

Assume that Cream has a Section 754 election in effect and is required to allocate a positive Section 734(b) adjustment due to a partner recognizing a gain of $9,000 on a distribution of cash. How is the adjustment allocated to the assets?

27. **(LO7 Advanced)** Two years ago, Mia contributed investment land with a basis of $32,000 and FMV of $44,000 in exchange for a 25% capital and profits interest in the Road Partnership. In the current year, when Mia had a basis in her partnership interest of $76,000, she received a current distribution of machinery with a basis of $54,000 and fair market value of $84,000. The FMV of the investment land at this time was $42,000. Mia had not recognized any of her BIG prior to the distribution. What are the tax consequences of the distribution?

28. **(LO7 Advanced)** Two years ago, Mia contributed investment land with a basis of $32,000 and FMV of $44,000 in exchange for a 25% capital and profits interest in the Road Partnership. In the current year, when Mia had a basis in her partnership interest of $76,000, the partnership distributed the investment land to Eli, another partner in the partnership. The FMV of the investment land at this time was $42,000. Mia had not recognized any of her BIG prior to the distribution. Eli's basis in his partnership interest immediately before the distribution was $56,000.

a. What are the tax consequences of the distribution?

b. What would the tax consequences be if the land was distributed to Eli 10 years after Mia contributed it?

Tax Planning Problems

Planning

1. **(LO1)** Carrie and Jermaine form the Coyote Partnership as equal partners on January 1, Year 1. Carrie contributes a capital asset with an adjusted basis of $22,000 and a fair market value of $16,000. The partnership will use the asset as inventory. In December Year 5, Coyote Partnership is considering selling the asset for $13,000. Should Coyote sell the asset in Year 5 or Year 6 to provide the best outcome for Carrie?

2. **(LO4)** Enrique has a 60% interest in the Sol Partnership. Enrique wants to sell his interest to Jorge for $45,000. Enrique's basis in Sol is $20,000, and the partnership has the following assets on its current balance sheet:

	Adjusted basis	Fair market value
Cash	$ 8,300	$ 8,300
Notes receivable	0	2,200
Accounts receivable	0	4,400
Land	9,900	15,000
Inventory	2,500	3,800
Total assets	$20,700	$33,700

Enrique would like to know what the tax consequences of the sale will be on his individual tax return and to Sol Partnership.

Professional Development Skills

Communication Problem

Communication

1. **(LO3) Effect of a Liquidating Distribution** Gulde's tax basis in Chyme Partnership was $26,000 at the time Gulde received a liquidating distribution of $12,000 cash and land with an adjusted basis to Chyme of $10,000 and a fair market value of $30,000. The land was a Section 1231 asset for Chyme. Chyme did not have unrealized receivables, appreciated inventory, or properties that had been contributed by its partners. What is the amount of Gulde's basis in the land? Prepare a memo to Gulde and to the tax file.

Ethics and Professional Responsibilities Problem

Ethics

1. **(LO1) Incorrectly Reporting Built-In Gains** Sebastian, Marco, and Manuel formed the SMM Partnership in Year 4. Sebastian contributed land with an adjusted basis of $44,000 and a fair market value of $72,000 in Year 3. In Year 7, SMM sold the land to an outside third party for $75,000. The Year 7 tax return showed all the gain being allocated proportionately to each of the partners. You are the new accountant hired in Year 8. What advice would you offer to Sebastian and SMM?

In addition to the chapter content, see *Statements on Standards for Tax Services* at www.aicpa-cima.com/resources/landing/statements-on-standards-for-tax-services, *Circular 230* at https://www.irs.gov/tax-professionals/office-of-professional-responsibility-and-circular-230, and Chapter 2, LO4, Tax Professional Responsibilities.

Research Problem

Research

1. (LO4) **What Is a Hot Asset?** When a partner disposes of his partnership interest, he may assume that his gain will be a capital gain because the interest is considered an investment which is a capital asset (IRC §742). Because of IRC §751, all or a portion of the gain may be recharacterized as ordinary income. Provide three examples of a hot asset under §751 besides unrealized receivables and inventory. Hint: §751(b) and §751(c).

Excel Problem

Technology

1. (LO1) **Built-In Gain/Loss Scenarios** Abraham contributes land to a partnership in return for a 40% interest in the partnership. Create an Excel spreadsheet that shows the gain/loss to be reported by Abraham in each independent scenario when the partnership sells the land four years later.

	Scenario 1	Scenario 2	Scenario 3	Scenario 4
Adjusted basis at date of contribution	$10,000	$10,000	$10,000	$10,000
FMV at date of contribution	$15,000	$17,000	$ 8,000	$ 6,000
Sales proceeds	$17,000	$15,000	$ 6,000	$ 8,000

CPA Exam Preparation: Task-Based Simulation

1. (LO4) **Sale of a Partnership Interest** Jamie and Lucas contribute cash and property to form the JL partnership in April 2025. See the JL Partnership Agreement. In addition to any liabilities mentioned in the JL Partnership Agreement, the partnership took out a bank loan and had accounts payable on December 31, 2025, of $10,000. Jamie sold her partnership interest on January 1, 2026, for $50,000. Lucas agreed to this sale. At the date of the sale, the JL partnership balance sheet reflected inventory with a fair market value of $10,000 and an adjusted basis of $6,000.

For each item in column A, calculate the requested information and enter it in the associated shaded cell in column B.

1	What is Jamie Berg's basis in JL Partnership on April 3, 2025?	
2	What is Lucas Tree's basis in JL Partnership on April 3, 2025?	
3	What is Jamie Berg's basis in JL Partnership on December 31, 2025?	
4	What is the gain/loss recognized on the sale of Jamie Berg's partnership interest on January 1, 2026?	
5	What amount of the gain (loss) on the sale of Jamie Berg's partnership interest on January 1, 2026, is ordinary?	
6	What amount on the sale of Jamie Berg's partnership interest on January 1, 2026, is a capital gain (loss)?	

Go to Wiley's book companion site to complete the Task-Based Simulation.

Part III (Chapters 6-7): Comprehensive Tax Return Problem

Complete Form 1065 pages 1 & 4, Schedule D, and Form 8949 for Fit4You, LLC, an accrual-basis, calendar-year LLC that operates several fitness centers. Use 2025 tax law in preparing the forms. Our solution uses 2024 forms as they were the most current forms available at the time of publication.

Go to Wiley's book companion site for the complete Comprehensive Tax Return Problem for Part III (Chapters 6-7).

CHAPTER 8

Taxation of S Corporations

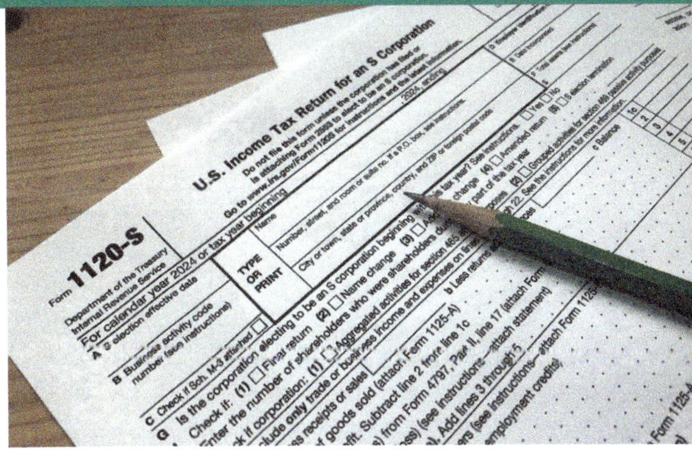

Before studying this chapter, you should know or, if necessary, review

1.1 Basics of Business Entities Taxation

1.2 Fundamentals of Property Transactions

Chapter Introduction

VIDEO CONTENT

Aletta has operated a hair salon for the past seven years as a sole proprietorship. She owns the building that she uses for her business as well as the equipment in her shop. She recently learned that her current business structure as a sole proprietorship is very risky for her because she has unlimited liability. For example, if one of her customers is injured in her salon, her personal financial assets could be put at risk. She considered incorporating her business so that she can have the liability protection that is afforded corporate shareholders. However, she is concerned about the potential for double taxation with corporations. In Chapter 6, we discussed the consequences of Aletta organizing her business as a partnership or LLC. She has also asked how the S corporation rules would apply to her situation. In this chapter, we review the tax laws for S corporations and shareholders, such as Aletta.

In 1946, the Department of Treasury first suggested that Congress should consider creating a business entity that had single taxation and limited liability for owners. In 1958, President Dwight Eisenhower suggested that S corporations be created with these characteristics, and Congress did that to encourage the creation of small businesses. In hindsight, this was a wise decision, as there are over 5 million S corporations today.[1] S corporations are legally organized under state law in the same manner as C corporations. Once incorporated, the shareholders elect to be taxed as an S corporation by filing Form 2553, Election by a Small Business Corporation. The major tax advantage for S corporations over C corporations is that S corporations have single taxation, contrasted with double taxation for C corporations.

S corporation income is reported on Form 1120-S, U.S. Income Tax Return for an S Corporation, but the S corporation does not pay tax on this income. Rather, the income flows through to the S corporation shareholders, regardless of whether it has been distributed, and the shareholders pay tax on the income on their returns. The shareholders' share of each tax item is reported to each shareholder on their Schedule K-1 (Form 1120-S). Form 1120-S is due on the 15th day of the third month after the tax year-end.

[1]S Corporation Association. "The History and Challenges of America's Dominant Business Structure." *S Corp*, 2018, https://s-corp.org/our-history/.

Potential Pitfall

The default tax rules for S corporations are the same as the C corporation rules. Many taxpayers, and even tax professionals, say that "S corporations are taxed like partnerships." That statement is true with respect to the flow-through of income from the business entity to the owner, because S corporation and partnership income are both subject to single taxation. However, for most other aspects of the taxation of S corporations, S corporations are taxed more similarly to C corporations than to partnerships.[2]

Other characteristics of S corporations include the following:

- Shareholders have limited liability and are not liable for corporate debt.
- The adjusted basis of shareholders' stock is adjusted each year for the shareholders' share of income and losses as reported on their Schedule K-1.
- Shareholders recognize income based on pro rata share of ownership. Distributions must be pro rata to all shareholders.
- Shareholders do not recognize income when they receive distributions to the extent that the fair market value (FMV) of the distribution does not exceed their adjusted stock basis.
- Shareholders who work for the S corporation are employees who are subject to payroll taxes (Social Security and Medicare). The distributive share of income to shareholders is not subject to self-employment taxes.
- S corporations are generally required to use a calendar year for tax purposes.

Related exercises: Discussion Questions 1, 2
Multiple Choice Question 1

LEARNING OBJECTIVES	TOPICS	PRACTICE OPPORTUNITIES

1 Determine if a corporation is eligible to elect to be taxed as an S corporation.	**8.1 Eligibility Rules and Shareholder Requirements**
	• Eligibility Rules
	• Shareholder and Other Requirements
	  • 100-Shareholder Limit
	  • Individuals
	  • Nonresident Aliens
	  • Business Entities
	  • Estates and Trusts
	  • Charitable and Tax-Exempt Organizations
	  • One Class of Stock
		• Example 8.1.1 Family-Owned Shares
		• Example 8.1.2 Shareholder Limits
		• Example 8.1.3 Preferred Distributions
		• Practice Problem 8.1.1 Identifying S Corporation Shareholders
		• Practice Problem 8.1.2 S Corporation Violation

2 Apply the rules for electing S corporation status and terminating S corporation status.	**8.2 Election Requirements and Terminations**
	• Election Requirements
	  • Specific Rules
	  • Late Elections
	• Termination of the S Election
	  • Voluntary Termination
	  • Violation of Eligibility Requirement
	  • Passive Investment Income
		• Example 8.2.1 S Corporation Election
		• Example 8.2.2 Late Election
		• Example 8.2.3 Termination of S Corporation
		• Practice Problem 8.2.1 S Corporation Election
		• Practice Problem 8.2.2 S Corporation Termination

[2]IRC §1371(a).

LEARNING OBJECTIVES	TOPICS	PRACTICE OPPORTUNITIES
3 Compute S corporation income and its flow-through to the shareholders.	**8.3 Taxation of S Corporation Income** • Timing of Income to Shareholders • Amount of Tax Items Reported to Shareholders • Character of S Corporation Tax Items • Reasonable Compensation	• Example 8.3.1 Allocation of Tax Items to Shareholder • Example 8.3.2 Character of S Corporation Items • Example 8.3.3 S Corporation Shareholder's Income • Practice Problem 8.3.1 Determining Income Reported on Schedule K-1 • Practice Problem 8.3.2 Reporting S Corporation Income and Expenses

4. Compute a shareholder's basis in their stock and the limitations on the deductibility of flow-through losses.	**8.4 Shareholder's Basis in S Corporation Stock and Loss Limitations**
	• Order of Adjustments to Stock Basis
	• Debt Basis
	Spotlight on the Law: Is Gain Recognized When a Loan Is Repaid to a Shareholder?
	• At-Risk Basis and Passive Losses
	  • At-Risk Basis
	  • Passive Losses
	• Excess Business Losses
	• Advanced Topic—Drilling Down
	  • Charitable Contributions of Appreciated Property
		• Example 8.4.1 Single Taxation for S Corporation Shareholders
		• Example 8.4.2 S Ordering Rules for Shareholder's Basis
		• Example 8.4.3 Debt Basis
		• Example 8.4.4 Excess Business Losses
		• Example 8.4.5 Charitable Contributions of Appreciated Property
		• Practice Problem 8.4.1 Determining Ending Basis In an S Corporation
		• Practice Problem 8.4.2 Determining Ending Basis in an S Corporation with an Ordinary Business Loss
		• Practice Problem 8.4.3 Debt Basis

5. Determine the tax effects of S corporation distributions to the shareholder and the corporation.	**8.5 Taxation of S Corporation Distributions**
	• Tax Consequences of Distributions for the Corporation
	  • Corporate Gain or Loss
	  • Effect of Distribution on AAA and E&P
	  • AAA Computation
	• Tax Consequences of Distributions for the Shareholder
	  • Earnings and Profits
	  • No Earnings and Profits
	• AAA Bypass Election
	• Post-Termination Transition Period
		• Example 8.5.1 Gain for S Corporation on Distributions
		• Example 8.5.2 Loss for S Corporation on Distributions
		• Example 8.5.3 Distributions of E&P
		• Example 8.5.4 Accumulated Adjustments Account and Other Adjustments Account
		• Example 8.5.5 Four-Step Formula When E&P Exists
		• Example 8.5.6 Distribution When Corporation Has E&P
		• Example 8.5.7 Distributions by Corporations with E&P and Insufficient AAA
		• Example 8.5.8 Distribution When Corporation Has No E&P
		• Example 8.5.9 AAA Bypass Election
		• Example 8.5.10 Post-Termination Transition Period
		• Example 8.5.11 Distributions During the Post-Termination Transition Period
		• Example 8.5.12 Use of Losses During the Post-Termination Transition Period
		• Practice Problem 8.5.1 Calculation of Ending AAA and OAA
		• Practice Problem 8.5.2 Distribution When E&P Exists

LEARNING OBJECTIVES	TOPICS	PRACTICE OPPORTUNITIES

6. Compute the taxes that an S corporation may have to pay.	**8.6** S Corporation Taxes
	• Built-In Gains Tax
	  • Definitions
	  • Quick Review
	  • Accounts Receivable and Accounts Payable
	• Net Passive Investment Income Tax
	  • Definitions and Computation
	  • Tax Planning
	• LIFO Recapture Tax
		• Example 8.6.1 Built-In Gains Tax
		• Example 8.6.2 Built-In Gains and Buil-In Losses
		• Example 8.6.3 Overall Limitation on BIG
		• Example 8.6.4 Limitation of Corporation's Net Income
		• Example 8.6.5 Accounts Receivable and Accounts Payable
		• Example 8.6.6 Net Passive Investment Income Tax
		• Practice Problem 8.6.1 Built-In Gains Tax
		• Practice Problem 8.6.2 Net Passive Investment Income Tax

Tax Forms referenced in this chapter

Form 1120	U.S. Corporation Income Tax Return
Form 1120-S	U.S. Income Tax Return for an S Corporation
Form 1120-S, Schedule K-1	Shareholder's Share of Income, Deduction, Credits, etc.
Form 2553	Election by a Small Business Corporation
Form 7203	S Corporation Shareholder Stock and Debt Basis Limitations

8.1 Eligibility Rules and Shareholder Requirements

LEARNING OBJECTIVE 1

Determine if a corporation is eligible to elect to be taxed as an S corporation.

VIDEO CONTENT

Congress created an attractive business entity with the S corporation rules, given that all shareholders have both single taxation and limited liability. However, Congress also put strict limitations on the types of corporations that can benefit from these advantages. These limitations are of two types:

- Certain types of corporations are *not* eligible to elect to be an S corporation.
- Shareholders of eligible corporations must meet several requirements.[3]

Eligibility Rules

The eligibility rules for S corporations are quite strict, which results in S corporations being very inflexible compared to other business entities. The following corporations are not eligible to elect S corporation status:[4]

[3]See Chapter 9, Choice of Business Entity, for a discussion of the advantages and disadvantages of S corporations compared to other business entities.
[4]IRC §1361(b)(2).

- Foreign corporations
- Banks if they use the reserve method of accounting for bad debts
- A domestic international sales corporation (DISC)[5]
- Insurance companies
- Certain members of affiliated groups (see Chapter 5, LO2, Affiliated Groups and Consolidated Returns)

S corporations may own:

- an interest in a C corporation, *or*
- a **qualified subchapter S subsidiary (QSSS)**, which is a corporation that meets all requirements for subchapter S status and is owned 100% by a parent S corporation.[6]

Tax Planning Tip

While a C corporation may not own stock in an S corporation, an S corporation can own stock in a C corporation or other business entity, as shown in Illustration 8.1. Additionally, while in general, an S corporation cannot own stock in another S corporation, an S corporation may own a qualified subchapter S subsidiary.

ILLUSTRATION 8.1 Corporate Ownership Rules

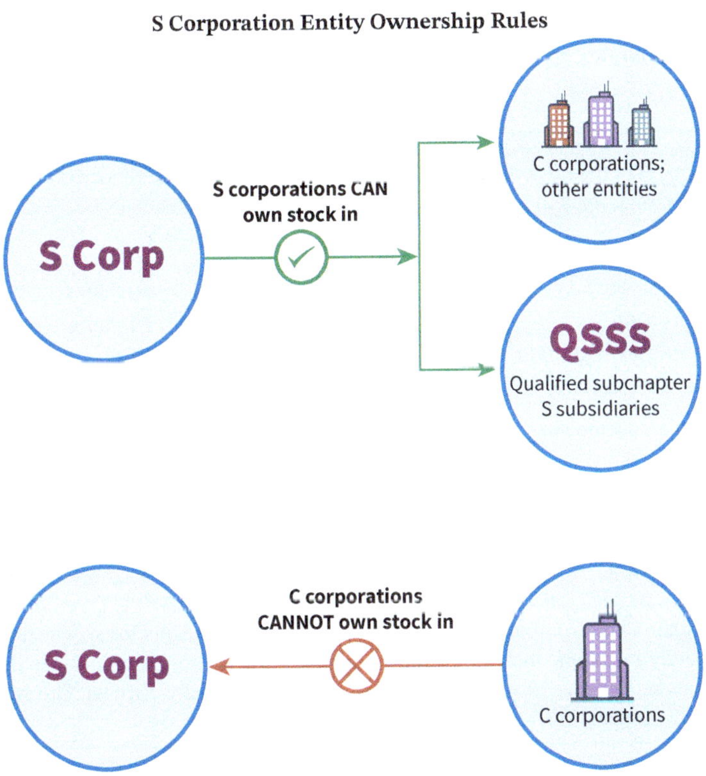

Shareholder and Other Requirements

There are strict requirements on who can be a shareholder in an S corporation.[7]

100-Shareholder Limit

The number of shareholders in an S corporation is limited to 100.[8] The theoretical purpose of the shareholder limit is to restrict the size of an S corporation. In general, S corporations

[5]A DISC provides tax benefits to businesses that export U.S.-made goods.
[6]IRC §1361(d).
[7]IRC §1361(b).
[8]IRC §1361(c)(1).

are considered to be small corporations. However, there are no restrictions on the total assets or total revenue of an S corporation, so S corporations can be very large. If one or more of the shareholders is very wealthy, such as Bill Gates or Warren Buffett, then the S corporation could have billions in assets and revenue, even though there are few shareholders. For example, over 4,500 S corporations have total assets of $100,000,000 or more, and more than 2,000 S corporations have revenues exceeding $250,000,000.[9] More than 4,700,000 S corporation tax returns were filed in the most recent year that the IRS has provided data.

While S corporations can have as many as 100 shareholders, they tend to have a much smaller number. In fact, only 4.3% of S corporations have more than three shareholders. Almost 65% of S corporations have only one shareholder, and 91% have two or fewer shareholders. The reason for the low number of shareholders is that S corporations do not provide the flexibility needed to meet the goals of many investors.

All in One Family More than 100 individuals can invest in an S corporation because all members of a family and their estates are treated as a single shareholder. **Family members** are defined as lineal descendants of a *common ancestor*, and the spouses (or former spouses) of the common ancestor and lineal descendants. The family members cannot be more than six generations removed from the common ancestor.[10] Thus, a shareholder, Barry, could identify his great-grandmother as the common ancestor, and then all lineal descendants for six generations are included as family members, as shown in **Illustration 8.2**. This would include, among others, Barry's great-grandparents, grandparents, aunts and uncles, cousins, siblings, nieces and nephews, and children and grandchildren. Adopted children and foster children also qualify, as do spouses and former spouses of these individuals, so the number of individuals who can be included as one family member is surprisingly large.

EXAMPLE 8.1.1 Family-Owned Shares

Dena owns 200 shares of the stock of Bluebird Corporation, a calendar-year S corporation. The following individuals also own stock in Bluebird:

Dena's brother	100 shares
Dena's adopted daughter	80 shares
Dena's son	50 shares
Dena's great-grandmother	35 shares
Dena's friend who lives with her for the entire year	25 shares

How many shares are included as part of Janice's shares as a family member?

SOLUTION

Family members are defined as lineal descendants of a *common ancestor*, and the spouses (or former spouses) of the common ancestor and lineal descendants. The family members cannot be more than six generations removed from the common ancestor.[11] If Dena identifies her great-grandmother as the common ancestor, then all lineal descendants for six generations are included as family members, including adopted children. Therefore, Dena includes the shares of all individuals listed above except for her friend, who is not a family member. The total shares deemed owned by Dena is 465.

[9]U.S. Department of the Treasury. *SOI Tax Stats - S corporation statistics*. Table 2.4. Internal Revenue Service, www.irs.gov/statistics/soi-tax-stats-s-corporation-statistics#basictables. This data is from the IRS Statistics of Income for 2017, the most recent year for which data is available.

[10]IRC §1361(c).

[11]IRC §1361(c).

ILLUSTRATION 8.2 Definition of Family Member for S Corporations

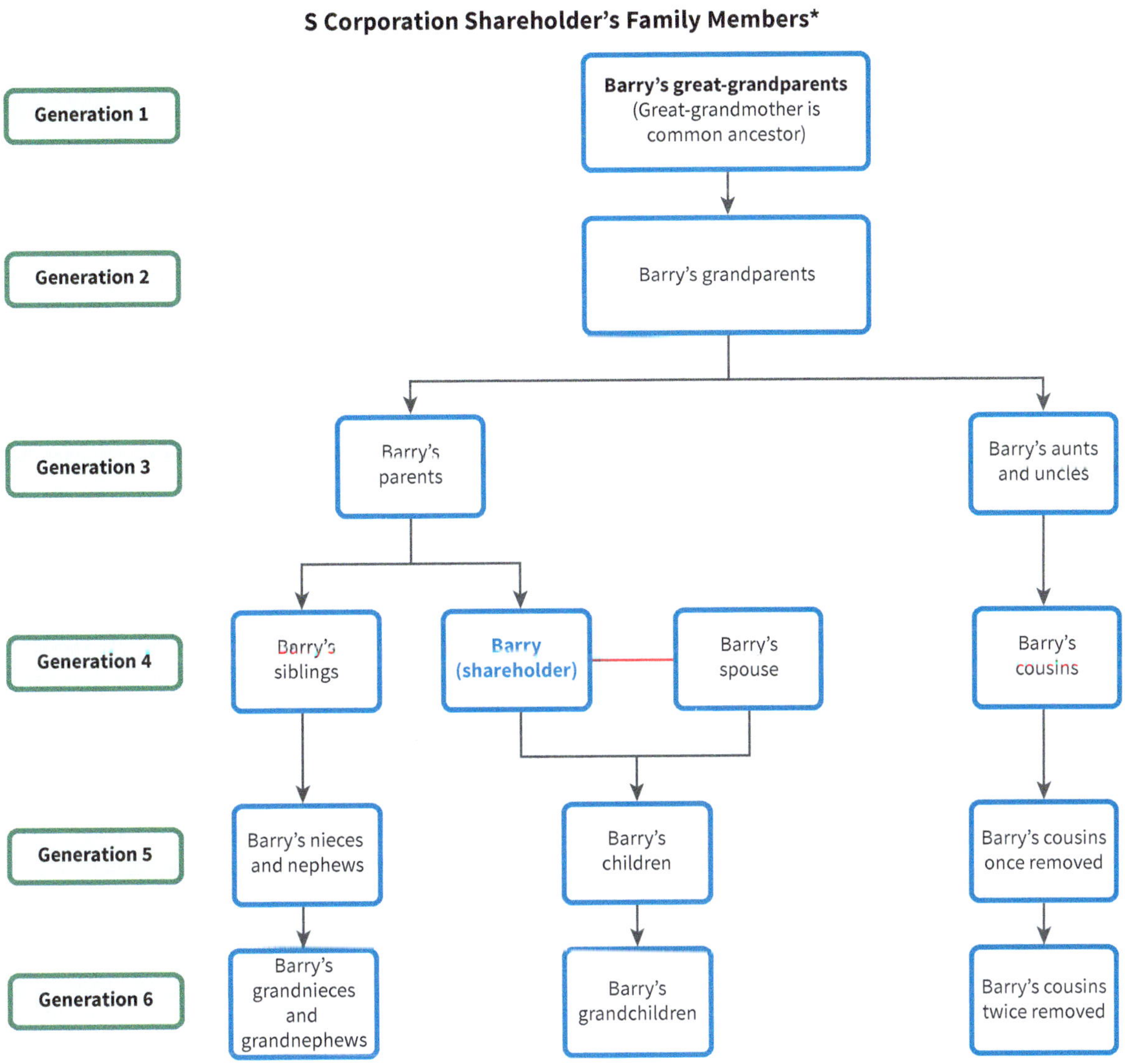

*Spouses and former spouses of all individuals shown are included.

Individuals

Individuals and single-member LLCs are allowed to be shareholders. Co-owners of stock each count as separate shareholders unless the co-owners are family members.

Nonresident Aliens

Nonresident aliens are individuals who are not citizens or residents of the United States. They *cannot* be shareholders of an S corporation, because it would be difficult for the government to collect taxes from them.[12]

Business Entities

C corporations, S corporations, partnerships, and multimember limited liability companies (LLCs) *cannot* be shareholders in an S corporation. If they could, it would be easy to circumvent the 100-shareholder limit because these business entities can have many owners that would count as only one shareholder of an S corporation.[13]

[12]IRC §1361(b)(1)(C).
[13]IRC §1361(b)(1)(B).

Estates and Trusts[14]

Estates, either bankruptcy or testamentary, can be shareholders. Trusts can also be shareholders. The types of trusts that can be shareholders include *grantor trusts*[15] and *testamentary trusts*. A **testamentary trust** is created when an individual dies based on the decedent's will. This type of trust can be a shareholder for only two years after the death of the shareholder. All beneficiaries of the trusts must be eligible to be S corporation shareholders, and each beneficiary counts toward the 100-shareholder limit. Special stock voting trusts and qualified S corporation trusts can be shareholders if all beneficiaries are qualified and elect to be treated as shareholders.

Charitable and Tax-Exempt Organizations

Charitable organizations that are qualified under Section 501(c)(3) can own stock in an S corporation. Tax-exempt entities are also allowed as shareholders.[16]

We emphasize these eligibility rules in the following Example.

Example 8.1.2
Shareholder Limits

Which of the following statements is false concerning an S corporation?

a. A citizen of Germany who is a resident in the United States can be a shareholder in an S corporation.

b. A partnership can be a shareholder in an S corporation as long as it has only two partners.

c. When an individual S corporation shareholder dies, the individual's estate can be a shareholder in the S corporation for up to two years.

d. In certain limited circumstances, a trust can be a shareholder in an S corporation.

SOLUTION

Statement **b.** is false. A partnership can never be a shareholder in an S corporation. The German citizen can be a shareholder because the individual is a resident of the United States. A testamentary estate can be a shareholder for up to two years. Special stock voting trusts, qualified S corporation trusts, and small business trusts that so elect can be shareholders of an S corporation.

Related exercises: Multiple Choice Question 2
Discussion Question 3
Brief Exercise 1

One Class of Stock

An S corporation can have only one class of stock. Thus, an S corporation cannot have both common stock and preferred stock. This requirement creates significant inflexibility for owners because when S corporations make distributions, each shareholder must receive a pro rata share of the distribution. Thus, a shareholder who owns 42% of an S corporation must receive 42% of each distribution. A distribution of more or less than that percentage could terminate the S election.

Other rules related to the one-class-of-stock requirement are as follows:

- Shares that vary solely in voting rights are not considered two classes of stock. Thus, an S corporation can have voting and nonvoting stock.
- Convertible debt does not violate the requirement unless and until it is converted into a second class of stock.

[14]See Chapter 11, LO1, Overview of Income Taxation of Trusts and Estates for a general description of trusts and estates.

[15]Special rules apply to the income taxation of a grantor trust. A **grantor trust** is a trust controlled by the grantor through retained powers or the possibility that the property in the trust will revert to the grantor. Grantor trusts are discussed in Chapter 11, LO3, Taxable Income for Trusts and Estates.

[16] IRC §1361(c)(6).

- Unissued treasury stock does not violate the requirement.
- A safe harbor exists for shareholder debt to prevent these securities from being treated by the IRS as a second class of stock. To meet the safe harbor requirements and be classified as **straight debt**, the debt must be evidenced by a written promise where the interest rate and interest payment dates are not contingent on profits. The debt cannot be convertible into stock. Straight debt will never be reclassified as equity by the IRS. Unwritten debt will not be considered to be a second class of stock as long as it does not exceed $10,000 at any time during the tax year.[17]

Related exercises: Multiple Choice Questions 3, 4
Application Problem 1

We illustrate the limitation imposed by the one-class-of-stock rule in the next Example.

Example 8.1.3
Preferred Distributions

Govind and Clay are equal shareholders in an S corporation. They each have a basis in their stock of $80,000. This year, Clay would like to receive a $25,000 distribution to use as a down payment on a new house. Govind has no interest in receiving a distribution this year. The corporation distributes $25,000 to Clay on October 7 and provides a written confirmation to Govind that he can receive a $25,000 distribution whenever he requests it in the future. Govind does not request a distribution this year. How do these transactions affect the eligibility of the S corporation?

SOLUTION

Unfortunately, these transactions could cause the S corporation election to be terminated, because the S corporation has inadvertently issued a second class of stock. Clay received a preferred distribution, which means his stock ownership has different rights than Govind's stock ownership. This is the case even though Govind could have taken a distribution had he so desired. Assuming that the S corporation does not request relief from the IRS (as described below), the S election is terminated as of the date of the $25,000 distribution to Clay.

Lack of Flexibility The requirement that S corporations can have one class of stock significantly limits the flexibility of S corporations. Regular corporations often issue preferred stock because not all shareholders have the same goals when investing in a corporation. The one-class-of-stock requirement means that S corporations can never have preferred distributions. If a distribution is made, each shareholder must receive their pro rata share of the distribution, which is based on the shareholder's stock ownership percentage.

To understand the significance of this limitation, consider the following scenario:

Darius has a net worth of $15,000,000 but does not have any promising ideas for new businesses. Camila has a great business idea for a process that will produce more energy-efficient businesses. However, she needs $1,500,000 to launch this business, and her net worth is only $120. She currently has an engineering job and makes $70,000 per year. Separately, Darius and Camila cannot launch a new business, but if they learn of each other's situation and form a joint venture, then together they could possibly make significant profits.

Assuming Darius and Camila do form a joint venture, they are investing very different things in the S corporation, and they also want very different things from the S corporation, as follows:

Darius

- He will invest $1,500,000 in the business but will provide limited services. This is an investment for him, not a job.
- He wants to recoup his $1,500,000 as quicky as possible, so he would like to have a 75% profit-sharing ratio.
- He wants limited liability so his other wealth will not be at risk with this business.

[17]IRC §1361(c)(5).

- He wants single taxation on the earnings.
- He would like to earn a total return of 50% on this investment over the next five years and hopes he can exit the business at that time.

Camila

- She needs a guaranteed salary because she must resign from her engineering job to start this business.
- Because she will be working 60–80 hours per week to launch this business, she believes her profit sharing should be 60%.
- She is not as concerned about limited liability as Darius since her net worth is so small.
- She wants single taxation on the earnings.
- She would like to grow this business for the next 30 years before selling it or giving it to her children.

There is a stark contrast between Camila's and Darius's situations. An S corporation will not allow preferential distributions to satisfy Darius's desire to recoup his investment quickly. Furthermore, each of them believes that they deserve more than 50% of profits, which is impossible to satisfy.

A limited partnership or an LLC does provide the flexibility needed to meet both Camila's and Darius's needs. These entities do allow preferential distributions. A typical structure for this type of business would be as follows:

Darius receives 100% of the profits until he recoups his $1,500,000 investment. After that, profits and losses are shared 50% each. Darius receives preferred distributions until he receives $1,500,000, which could not be done with an S corporation. Other characteristics of the structure would be:

- Camila would receive a guaranteed payment to compensate her fairly for the work she is performing for the business.
- If the business is organized as a limited partnership, Camila would be the general partner and Darius, the limited partner, because he needs liability protection.
- If the business is organized as an LLC, both partners would have limited liability.

As this Example demonstrates, the one-class-of-stock rule significantly limits S corporations' ability to create innovative structures to meet the needs of shareholders.

PRACTICE PROBLEM 8.1.1 Identifying S Corporation Shareholders

Which of the following is allowed as an S corporation shareholder?

a. An individual

b. Single-member LLC

c. Qualified charitable organization

d. All of the above

SOLUTION

The correct answer is **d**. Individuals and single-member LLCs are allowed to be shareholders. Estates, either bankruptcy or testamentary, can be shareholders. Charitable organizations that are qualified under Section 501(c)(3) can own stock in an S corporation. Tax-exempt entities are also allowed as shareholders.

PRACTICE PROBLEM 8.1.2
S Corporation Violation

Which of the following would violate the one-class-of-stock rule?

a. Voting and nonvoting stock
b. Unwritten shareholder debt less than $10,000
c. Unissued treasury stock
d. None of the above would violate the one-class-of-stock rule

SOLUTION

The correct answer is **d**. Shares that vary solely in voting rights are not considered two classes of stock. Unwritten debt will not be considered to be a second class of stock as long as it does not exceed $10,000 at any time during the tax year. Unissued treasury stock does not violate the requirement.

INTERACTIVE SELF-SCORING QUIZZES

8.2 Election Requirements and Terminations

LEARNING OBJECTIVE 2

Apply the rules for electing S corporation status and terminating S corporation status.

VIDEO CONTENT

Returning to the chapter introduction, if Aletta decides she wants her business organized as an S corporation, she will need to make a valid and timely election. She also needs to be aware of the ways in which an S corporation election can be voluntarily and involuntarily terminated.

Election Requirements

The shareholders of the corporation must make a qualifying election to become an S corporation, using Form 2553, Election by a Small Business Corporation. We show the first two pages of Form 2553 in **Illustration 8.3**, and the entire Form 2553 is in Appendix B. The unanimous consent of the shareholders is required for the election, not simply a majority vote. Thus, if just one shareholder refuses to agree to the S election, even a 1% shareholder, then the S election cannot be made. In such a case, the other shareholders may try to buy the stock of the holdout shareholder.

ILLUSTRATION 8.3 Election by a Small Business Corporation

DOWNLOAD DOCUMENTS & TEMPLATES

Form **2553** (Rev. December 2017) Department of the Treasury Internal Revenue Service

Election by a Small Business Corporation

(Under section 1362 of the Internal Revenue Code)
(Including a late election filed pursuant to Rev. Proc. 2013-30)
▶ **You can fax this form to the IRS. See separate instructions.**
▶ **Go to *www.irs.gov/Form2553* for instructions and the latest information.**

OMB No. 1545-0123

Note: This election to be an S corporation can be accepted only if all the tests are met under *Who May Elect* in the instructions, all shareholders have signed the consent statement, an officer has signed below, and the exact name and address of the corporation (entity) and other required form information have been provided.

Part I Election Information

Type or Print	Name (see instructions)	**A Employer identification number**
	Number, street, and room or suite no. If a P.O. box, see instructions.	**B** Date incorporated
	City or town, state or province, country, and ZIP or foreign postal code	**C** State of incorporation

D Check the applicable box(es) if the corporation (entity), after applying for the EIN shown in **A** above, changed its ☐ name or ☐ address

E Election is to be effective for tax year beginning (month, day, year) (see instructions) . . . . ▶ ______
Caution: A corporation (entity) making the election for its first tax year in existence will usually enter the beginning date of a short tax year that begins on a date other than January 1.

F Selected tax year:
(1) ☐ Calendar year
(2) ☐ Fiscal year ending (month and day) ▶ ______
(3) ☐ 52-53-week year ending with reference to the month of December
(4) ☐ 52-53-week year ending with reference to the month of ▶ ______
If box (2) or (4) is checked, complete Part II.

G If more than 100 shareholders are listed for item J (see page 2), check this box if treating members of a family as one shareholder results in no more than 100 shareholders (see test 2 under *Who May Elect* in the instructions) ▶ ☐

H Name and title of officer or legal representative whom the IRS may call for more information	Telephone number of officer or legal representative

I If this S corporation election is being filed late, I declare I had reasonable cause for not filing Form 2553 timely. If this late election is being made by an entity eligible to elect to be treated as a corporation, I declare I also had reasonable cause for not filing an entity classification election timely and the representations listed in Part IV are true. See below for my explanation of the reasons the election or elections were not made on time and a description of my diligent actions to correct the mistake upon its discovery. See instructions.

Sign Here

Under penalties of perjury, I declare that I have examined this election, including accompanying documents, and, to the best of my knowledge and belief, the election contains all the relevant facts relating to the election, and such facts are true, correct, and complete.

▶ Signature of officer | Title | Date

For Paperwork Reduction Act Notice, see separate instructions. Cat. No. 18629R Form **2553** (Rev. 12-2017)

ILLUSTRATION 8.3 *(continued)*

DOWNLOAD DOCUMENTS & TEMPLATES

Form 2553 (Rev. 12-2017) Page **2**

Name	**Employer identification number**

Part I **Election Information** *(continued)* **Note:** If you need more rows, use additional copies of page 2.

J Name and address of each shareholder or former shareholder required to consent to the election. (see instructions)	**K** **Shareholder's Consent Statement** Under penalties of perjury, I declare that I consent to the election of the above-named corporation (entity) to be an S corporation under section 1362(a) and that I have examined this consent statement, including accompanying documents, and, to the best of my knowledge and belief, the election contains all the relevant facts relating to the election, and such facts are true, correct, and complete. I understand my consent is binding and may not be withdrawn after the corporation (entity) has made a valid election. If seeking relief for a late filed election, I also declare under penalties of perjury that I have reported my income on all affected returns consistent with the S corporation election for the year for which the election should have been filed (see beginning date entered on line E) and for all subsequent years.		**L** Stock owned or percentage of ownership (see instructions)		**M** Social security number or employer identification number (see instructions)	**N** Shareholder's tax year ends (month and day)
	Signature	Date	Number of shares or percentage of ownership	Date(s) acquired		

Form **2553** (Rev. 12-2017)

Specific Rules

Other requirements for the election include:[18]

- In its initial year, a corporation must make the S election on or before the 15th day of the third month after commencing business for it to be effective for the entire year.
- For C corporations that want to change their status to S corporation, the election is valid for the current year if it is made on or before the 15th day of the third month of the tax year, as shown in **Illustration 8.4**. The eligibility requirements have to be met beginning with the first day of the tax year. For a retroactive election of this nature, all shareholders who owned stock in the corporation at any time during the year must consent to the election, even if they are no longer shareholders at the time the election is filed.
- An election made on or before the 15th day of the third month that is not valid will take effect at the beginning of the next tax year if eligibility requirements are met at that time. An election that is made after this date is effective as of the beginning of the next year unless a different prospective date in the current year is specified. For elections taking effect at the beginning of the next year, those becoming shareholders after the election was filed do not have to consent to the election.[19]
- The corporation must meet all eligibility requirements at the time the election is effective. If the election is effective retroactively to the beginning of the tax year, then the corporation must meet the eligibility requirements for the entire tax year.
- If stock is jointly owned, all owners must consent to the election. All individuals treated as one shareholder under the one-shareholder family ownership rule must consent to the election.

ILLUSTRATION 8.4 S Corporation Election Timeline

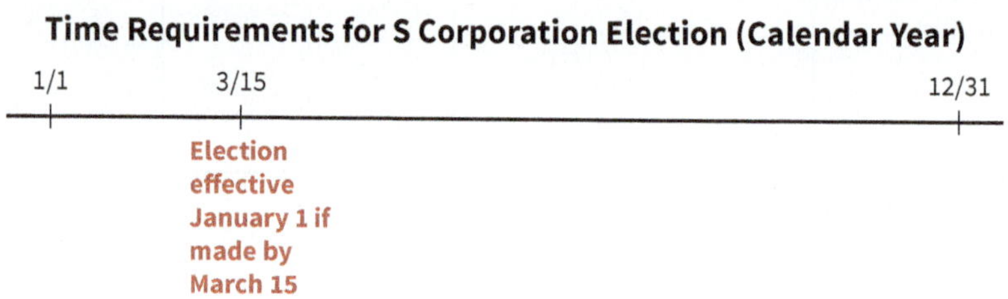

The next Example reviews the requirements for making a valid S corporation election.

Example 8.2.1 S Corporation Election

Seagull Corporation was incorporated in 2015 and has been a regular, calendar-year corporation since that time. In the current year, Seagull files a Form 2553 on March 10 electing to be taxed as an S corporation effective January 1 of the current year. There are seven shareholders of Seagull on March 10, and each has signed the Form 2553 consenting to the election. An eighth shareholder, Obstinate, sold his 5% interest in the corporation to the other seven shareholders on January 12 of the current year because he was not in support of the S election. Obstinate refuses to sign the Form 2553 because he is no longer a shareholder. When will Seagull's S corporation election be effective?

SOLUTION

An S election is effective only if 100% of the shareholders affected by the election agree to it and sign the Form 2553. Because the election affected Obstinate for the 12 days he owned stock in the current year, the S election is not valid for the current year. Therefore, Seagull remains a C corporation for the current year. Assuming all eligibility requirements continue to be met as of January 1 of the next year, Seagull will become an S corporation at that time. If Seagull has any new shareholders as of January 1 of the next year, the new shareholders do not have to consent to the election. Practically, they should be told about the prospective election before they buy their stock.

[18]IRC §1362.

[19]Treas. Reg. §1.1362-6(b)(3)(i)

Tax Planning Tip

It is essential that the shareholders of an S corporation can prove that the Form 2553 was filed on time. Therefore, mailed S elections should always be sent by certified or registered mail with return receipt requested. The receipt received from the post office is *prima facie* evidence that the election was delivered to the IRS.[20]

Related exercises: Discussion Question 4
Multiple Choice Question 5
Brief Exercise 2

Late Elections

There are two relief measures that corporations may use if the S election rules are not met in a timely manner.

- If any shareholder consents are filed late, the corporation can request an extension of time from the IRS if there is a reasonable cause for the delay.[21]
- Relief can also be requested for late S corporation elections if the election is filed within 3 years and 75 days from when the election was initially due.[22] The request must explain the reason for the delay, and the corporation must demonstrate that it acted quickly to correct the error once the missed filing deadline was discovered. It is essential that the corporation and its shareholders reported all income and paid all taxes due as if the S election had been in effect. If relief is granted by the IRS, the S election is effective on its original intended date.

We demonstrate the application of the relief measures for late elections in the following Example.

Example 8.2.2
Late Election

Cardinal Corporation incorporated on May 1, Year 1, and files using the calendar year. The shareholders intended for the corporation to be an S corporation from May 1, but there was confusion as to who had the responsibility to file the Form 2553. In April, Year 2, the shareholders realized that the Form 2553 had not been filed. Cardinal applied for relief by filing a Form 2553 and a statement asking for relief. When will Cardinal's S election be effective?

SOLUTION

The IRS can accept the application for relief and allow Cardinal Corporation to be an S corporation from May 1, Year 1, because Cardinal requested relief within 3 years and 75 days of May 1, Year 1. It is essential that Cardinal Corporation and its shareholders reported all income and paid all taxes due since May 1, Year 1, as if the S election had been in effect. While it is likely that the IRS would grant the application for relief, if it did not, the S election would be effective as of January 1, Year 3.

Tax Planning Tip

Shareholders should never use the late election relief provisions as a reason for procrastination of filing the Form 2553. Shareholders and their tax professionals should do everything necessary to ensure that the S corporation election is filed on time. If, in spite of these best efforts, it is later discovered that the S election was not filed in a timely manner, then the relief measures are an avenue that may be helpful to correct the mistake.

[20]Treas. Reg. §301.7502-1(d)(1).

[21]Treas. Reg. §1.1362-6(b)(3)(iii).

[22]Rev. Proc. 2013-30, 2013-36 IRB 173.

Termination of the S Election

An election to be an S corporation remains in effect until it is terminated. Termination of the election can occur through three circumstances, some voluntary and some involuntary.[23] Once terminated, the S corporation cannot elect S status without IRS permission for five years.

Voluntary Termination

A voluntary termination occurs with a majority vote of all shareholders specifying a prospective year. The shareholders can make the termination election retroactive to the beginning of the tax year if made before the 15th day of the third month of the current tax year. For a termination vote, all shareholders must be allowed to vote, including nonvoting shareholders.

Related exercise: Multiple Choice Question 6

A revocation can specify any date in the future as the effective date, and the S corporation election will terminate as of that date. For a calendar-year S corporation, a revocation not specifying a revocation date that is made on or before March 15 is effective as of January 1 of that year. A revocation not specifying a revocation date that is made after March 15 is effective as of January 1 the following year.

Violation of Eligibility Requirement

An involuntary termination occurs through a violation of an eligibility requirement, and this termination is effective on the date of the violation. An involuntary termination caused by a violation of an eligibility requirement will generally create a short S year and a short C year. A **short tax year** is a tax year consisting of less than 12 months. For example, assume that a calendar-year S corporation issues a second class of stock on June 4. The S corporation election is terminated as of June 4, and the corporation becomes a C corporation on that date. The corporation would have to file two tax returns for that year:

- An 1120-S for an S corporation from January 1 to June 3 of the year
- An 1120 for a C corporation from June 4 to December 31 of the year

If an S corporation election is terminated inadvertently, the shareholders can request relief from the IRS. The IRS is more likely to grant relief and allow the corporation to continue to be taxed as an S corporation if the shareholders corrected the situation that violated an eligibility requirement as quickly as possible.[24]

Passive Investment Income

An involuntary termination can occur if passive investment income (PII) exceeds 25% of gross receipts for three consecutive years. This termination is effective on the first day of the fourth consecutive year. This provision applies only if the S corporation has earnings and profits from previous C corporation years on its balance sheet. The S corporation also must pay the passive investment income tax for each year in which the PII exceeds 25% of gross receipts. This tax is discussed in detail in LO6, S Corporation Taxes.

[23]IRC §1362(c) and (d).

[24]Reg. §1.1362-4(a).

EXAMPLE 8.2.3
Termination of S Corporation

Blackbird Corporation has been a calendar-year S corporation for the last six years and is owned 100% by Shinika. Shinika decides that she wants to terminate her S corporation election. When would the termination election take effect in the following circumstances?

Situation 1: Shinika makes the termination election on February 17 effective as of January 1 of the current year.

Situation 2: Shinika makes the termination election on February 17 and does not specify a revocation date.

Situation 3: Shinika makes the termination election on April 17 and does not specify a revocation date.

Situation 4: Shinika makes the termination election on April 17 and specifies May 1 of the current year as the effective date.

SOLUTION

Situation 1: Because Shinika made the election by March 15 of the current year, she can make it retroactive to January 1.

Situation 2: Because Shinika made the election by March 15 of the current year, it will be effective on January 1 of the current year because a revocation date was not provided.

Situation 3: Because Shinika did not make the election by March 15 of the current year, it will be effective on January 1 of the following year.

Situation 4: Because Shinika made the election effective for a prospective date, it will take effect on the date specified, May 1 of the current year.

Related exercises: Brief Exercise 3
Application Problem 2

PRACTICE PROBLEM 8.2.1
S Corporation Election

Daydream Inc. is a calendar-year C corporation that would like to become an S corporation. Determine when the S election would be effective in the following situations:

a. Daydream files Form 2553 on March 8 of the current year.
b. Daydream files Form 2553 on November 8 of the previous year.
c. Daydream files Form 2553 on May 10 of the current year.

SOLUTION

a. The S election would be valid for the current year, January 1–December 31.
b. The S election would be valid for the current year, January 1–December 31.
c. The S election would be valid for the following year, January 1–December 31.

For C corporations that want to change their status to an S corporation, the election is valid for the current year if it is made on or before the 15th day of the third month of the tax year.

PRACTICE PROBLEM 8.2.2
S Corporation Termination

Ant Corporation has been a calendar-year S corporation for the last six years. It has $125,000 of earnings and profits from when it was previously a C corporation. Ant's passive investment income exceeds 25% of gross receipts Year 11 and Year 12. If Ant Corporation's passive investment income exceeds 25% of gross receipts for Year 13, when will its S election terminate?

SOLUTION

An involuntary termination can occur if passive investment income exceeds 25% of gross receipts for three consecutive years. This termination is effective on the first day of the fourth consecutive year, January 1, Year 14. This provision applies only if the S corporation has earnings and profits from previous C corporation years on its balance sheet.

INTERACTIVE SELF-SCORING QUIZZES

8.3 Taxation of S Corporation Income

LEARNING OBJECTIVE 3

Compute S corporation income and its flow-through to the shareholders.

VIDEO CONTENT

If Aletta decides to form an S corporation, the S corporation and Aletta are subject to single taxation. It is important to understand both the timing of income to the shareholders and the amount of each S corporation tax item that is reported to the shareholder.

Timing of Income to Shareholders

As shown in **Illustration 8.5**, S corporation income is reported on Form 1120-S, U.S. Income Tax Return for an S Corporation, and the income flows through to the S corporation shareholders on the last day of the corporate tax year, regardless of whether it has been distributed, on the shareholder's Schedule K-1 (Form 1120-S). In general, S corporations use the calendar year for tax reporting. S corporation returns are due on the 15th day of the third month after year-end, which is March 15 for calendar-year corporations. A six-month extension is available until September 15.

Related exercises: Discussion Question 5
Multiple Choice Question 7

ILLUSTRATION 8.5 Timing of Flow-Through to Shareholders

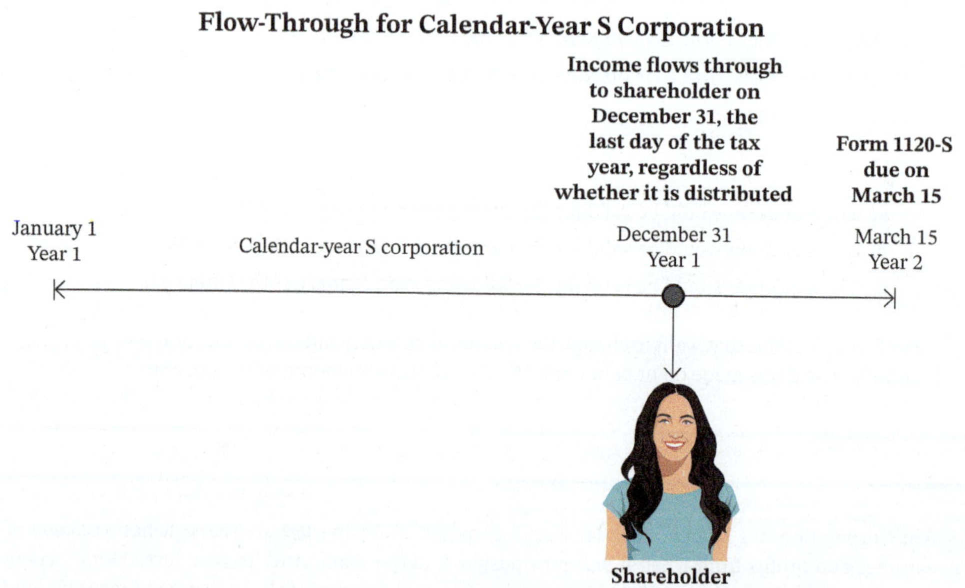

Amount of Tax Items Reported to Shareholders

The shareholder's proportionate share of each tax item is reported on their Schedule K-1 (Form 1120-S), determined by the shareholder's stock ownership percentage on a per day basis, using the following formula:

$$\text{Amount on Form 1120-S} \times \text{Stock ownership \%} \times \frac{\text{\# of days owned this year}}{\text{365 days}} = \text{Proportionate share of tax item}$$

If stock ownership changes during the year, then the computation of the shareholder's share of each tax item will need to be done for each ownership level.

A shareholder who owns 60% of the S corporation will be allocated 60% of each tax item on the shareholder's Schedule K-1. The S corporation law does not allow shareholders to choose their profit and loss sharing ratios, nor special allocations of tax items (as the partnership tax law does). Other reporting rules for S corporations include:

- S corporations may use the cash-basis method of accounting unless the corporation is a tax shelter. See Chapter 3, LO4, Other Corporate Tax Issues for additional rules if the S corporation has inventory.
- S corporations are not allowed a dividends received deduction.

EXAMPLE 8.3.1
Allocation of Tax Items to Shareholder

As of January 1 of this year, Rosa owned all 100 shares of a calendar-year S corporation, Falcon Corporation. On February 9, the 40th day of this year, Rosa sold 25 shares to Caitlyn. Falcon reported $73,000 in ordinary business income for the entire year to the shareholders and made no distributions. What amount of income should the S corporation report to Rosa on her Schedule K-1?

SOLUTION

Rosa's income allocation is computed as follows:

$$\text{Amount on Form 1120-S} \times \text{Stock ownership \%} \times \frac{\text{\# of days owned this year}}{\text{365 days}} = \text{Proportionate share of tax item}$$

<u>January 1–February 9</u>

$$\$73{,}000 \times 100\% \times \frac{\text{40 days}}{\text{365 days}} = \$8{,}000$$

<u>February 10–December 31</u>

$$\$73{,}000 \times 75\% \times \frac{\text{325 days}}{\text{365 days}} = \$48{,}750$$

Rosa's income allocation is thus $56,750 ($8,000 + $48,750).

Related exercises: Multiple Choice Question 8
Brief Exercise 4
Application Problem 3

Character of S Corporation Tax Items

The character of S corporation tax items is determined at the S corporation level. **Recall** from Chapter 1, LO3, Review of Fundamentals of Property Transactions, that the character of tax gains and losses will be *either*:

- Ordinary income or loss,
- Section 1231 gain or loss, *or*
- Capital gain or loss.

Once the tax character is determined at the S corporation level, the character stays the same when it flows from the S corporation to the shareholders.[25]

[25]IRC §1366(b).

We illustrate this concept in the following Example.

EXAMPLE 8.3.2
Character of S Corporation Items

Theron purchases 10% of an S corporation on October 1 of the current tax year. The S corporation has been in existence for 10 years. On December 10 of the current year, the S corporation sells stock in Exxon corporation that it has owned for three years and has a long-term capital gain (LTCG) of $80,000. How much of the gain flows to Theron, and what will be the character of the gain for Theron?

SOLUTION

10% of the gain flows to Theron for the 91 days he owns the stock, which amounts to $1,995 ($80,000 × 10% × 91/365). The S corporation will report this to Theron as LTCG even though he was a shareholder for less than three months at the time the stock was sold. The LTCG character is determined at the S corporation level, and the character stays the same when it flows through to Theron.

The tax items that comprise S corporation income or loss are divided into two categories: *separately stated items* and *nonseparately stated items*. **Separately stated items** are tax items that could potentially impact a shareholder's tax liabilities differently.[26] Separately stated items are reported on Schedule K. Each owner's share is reported on Schedule K-1. Some of the more common separately stated items and the reason they are separately stated are as follows:

- Net capital gains and losses, because the shareholder must net the S corporation capital gains and losses with other capital gains and losses reported on the shareholder's tax return.
- Section 1231 gains and losses, because the shareholder must net the S corporation Section 1231 gains and losses with other Section 1231 gains and losses on the shareholder's tax return.
- Other types of investment income, such as dividends and interest, because shareholders need these amounts to compute net investment income for various purposes.
- Charitable contributions, because individual shareholders must apply various limitations to determine their charitable contribution deduction, such as the 60% of AGI limit for cash contributions.
- Section 179 expense, because shareholders are limited in the amount of Section 179 expense that they can deduct in any given year.

Other separately stated items are shown on Schedule K-1 (see **Illustration 8.6**; we use the 2024 Form 1120-S Schedule K-1 because it was the most recent form available at the time of publication).

Any item of income or loss that is not separately stated is reported on page 1 of Form 1120-S (see **Illustration 8.7**; we use the 2024 Form 1120-S because it was the most recent form available at the time of publication). These are items characterized as ordinary income or loss and have no special rules that need to be applied at the shareholder level. For the remaining discussion, we refer to the **nonseparately stated items** as the *bucket items*, to emphasize that these items are all mixed together, or netted, and result in one measure known as the *ordinary business income or loss* for the S corporation. The bucket items include wages, depreciation, supplies, and the other items shown on page 1 of Form 1120-S in Illustration 8.7. The flow of these S corporation tax items to the shareholder is shown in **Illustration 8.8**.

Related exercises: Discussion Question 6
Multiple Choice Question 9
Application Problem 4

[26]IRC §1366(a).

ILLUSTRATION 8.6 Schedule K-1 (Form 1120-S)

DOWNLOAD DOCUMENTS & TEMPLATES

671124

☐ Final K-1 ☐ Amended K-1 OMB No. 1545-0123

Schedule K-1 (Form 1120-S) **2024**

Department of the Treasury
Internal Revenue Service

For calendar year 2024, or tax year

beginning / / 2024 ending / /

Shareholder's Share of Income, Deductions, Credits, etc.

See separate instructions.

Part I Information About the Corporation

A Corporation's employer identification number

B Corporation's name, address, city, state, and ZIP code

C IRS Center where corporation filed return

D Corporation's total number of shares

Beginning of tax year . . . . . . ________

End of tax year . . . . ________

Part II Information About the Shareholder

E Shareholder's identifying number

F1 Shareholder's name, address, city, state, and ZIP code

F2 If the shareholder is a disregarded entity, a trust, an estate, or a nominee or similar person, enter the individual or entity responsible for reporting:

TIN ________ Name ________

F3 What type of entity is this shareholder? ________

G Current year allocation percentage . . . ________ %

H Shareholder's number of shares

Beginning of tax year . . . . . . ________

End of tax year . . . . ________

I Loans from shareholder

Beginning of tax year . . . . . . $ ________

End of tax year . . . . $ ________

For IRS Use Only

Part III Shareholder's Share of Current Year Income, Deductions, Credits, and Other Items

1	Ordinary business income (loss)	13	Credits
2	Net rental real estate income (loss)		
3	Other net rental income (loss)		
4	Interest income		
5a	Ordinary dividends		
5b	Qualified dividends	14	Schedule K-3 is attached if checked . . . . . ☐
6	Royalties	15	Alternative minimum tax (AMT) items
7	Net short-term capital gain (loss)		
8a	Net long-term capital gain (loss)		
8b	Collectibles (28%) gain (loss)		
8c	Unrecaptured section 1250 gain		
9	Net section 1231 gain (loss)	16	Items affecting shareholder basis
10	Other income (loss)		
		17	Other information
11	Section 179 deduction		
12	Other deductions		

18 ☐ More than one activity for at-risk purposes*

19 ☐ More than one activity for passive activity purposes*

* See attached statement for additional information.

For Paperwork Reduction Act Notice, see the Instructions for Form 1120-S. www.irs.gov/Form1120S Cat. No. 11520D **Schedule K-1 (Form 1120-S) 2024**

ILLUSTRATION 8.7 Form 1120-S, Page 1

DOWNLOAD DOCUMENTS & TEMPLATES

Form **1120-S**

Department of the Treasury
Internal Revenue Service

U.S. Income Tax Return for an S Corporation

Do not file this form unless the corporation has filed or is attaching Form 2553 to elect to be an S corporation.
Go to *www.irs.gov/Form1120S* for instructions and the latest information.

OMB No. 1545-0123

2024

For calendar year 2024 or tax year beginning , 2024, ending , 20

	TYPE OR PRINT	
A S election effective date	Name	**D Employer identification number**
B Business activity code number (see instructions)	Number, street, and room or suite no. If a P.O. box, see instructions.	**E** Date incorporated
C Check if Sch. M-3 attached ☐	City or town, state or province, country, and ZIP or foreign postal code	**F** Total assets (see instructions) $

G Is the corporation electing to be an S corporation beginning with this tax year? See instructions. ☐ Yes ☐ No

H Check if: **(1)** ☐ Final return **(2)** ☐ Name change **(3)** ☐ Address change **(4)** ☐ Amended return **(5)** ☐ S election termination

I Enter the number of shareholders who were shareholders during any part of the tax year . . . .

J Check if corporation: **(1)** ☐ Aggregated activities for section 465 at-risk purposes **(2)** ☐ Grouped activities for section 469 passive activity purposes

Caution: Include **only** trade or business income and expenses on lines 1a through 22. See the instructions for more information.

Income	1a	Gross receipts or sales ______ **b** Less returns and allowances ______ **c** Balance	1c	
	2	Cost of goods sold (attach Form 1125-A)	2	
	3	Gross profit. Subtract line 2 from line 1c	3	
	4	Net gain (loss) from Form 4797, Part II, line 17 (attach Form 4797)	4	
	5	Other income (loss) (see instructions—attach statement)	5	
	6	**Total income (loss).** Add lines 3 through 5	6	
Deductions (see instructions for limitations)	7	Compensation of officers (see instructions—attach Form 1125-E)	7	
	8	Salaries and wages (less employment credits)	8	
	9	Repairs and maintenance	9	
	10	Bad debts	10	
	11	Rents	11	
	12	Taxes and licenses	12	
	13	Interest (see instructions)	13	
	14	Depreciation from Form 4562 not claimed on Form 1125-A or elsewhere on return (attach Form 4562)	14	
	15	Depletion **(do not deduct oil and gas depletion)**	15	
	16	Advertising	16	
	17	Pension, profit-sharing, etc., plans	17	
	18	Employee benefit programs	18	
	19	Energy efficient commercial buildings deduction (attach Form 7205)	19	
	20	Other deductions (attach statement)	20	
	21	**Total deductions.** Add lines 7 through 20	21	
	22	**Ordinary business income (loss).** Subtract line 21 from line 6	22	
Tax and Payments	23a	Excess net passive income or LIFO recapture tax (see instructions) — 23a		
	b	Tax from Schedule D (Form 1120-S) — 23b		
	c	Add lines 23a and 23b (see instructions for additional taxes)	23c	
	24a	Current year's estimated tax payments and preceding year's overpayment credited to the current year — 24a		
	b	Tax deposited with Form 7004 — 24b		
	c	Credit for federal tax paid on fuels (attach Form 4136) — 24c		
	d	Elective payment election amount from Form 3800 — 24d		
	z	Add lines 24a through 24d	24z	
	25	Estimated tax penalty (see instructions). Check if Form 2220 is attached ☐	25	
	26	**Amount owed.** If line 24z is smaller than the total of lines 23c and 25, enter amount owed	26	
	27	**Overpayment.** If line 24z is larger than the total of lines 23c and 25, enter amount overpaid	27	
	28	Enter amount from line 27: **Credited to 2025 estimated tax** **Refunded**	28	

Sign Here

Under penalties of perjury, I declare that I have examined this return, including accompanying schedules and statements, and to the best of my knowledge and belief, it is true, correct, and complete. Declaration of preparer (other than taxpayer) is based on all information of which preparer has any knowledge.

Signature of officer | Date | Title

May the IRS discuss this return with the preparer shown below? See instructions. ☐ **Yes** ☐ **No**

Paid Preparer Use Only	Print/Type preparer's name	Preparer's signature	Date	Check ☐ if self-employed	PTIN
	Firm's name			Firm's EIN	
	Firm's address			Phone no.	

For Paperwork Reduction Act Notice, see separate instructions. Cat. No. 11510H Form **1120-S** (2024)

ILLUSTRATION 8.8 Taxation of S Corporation Shareholder

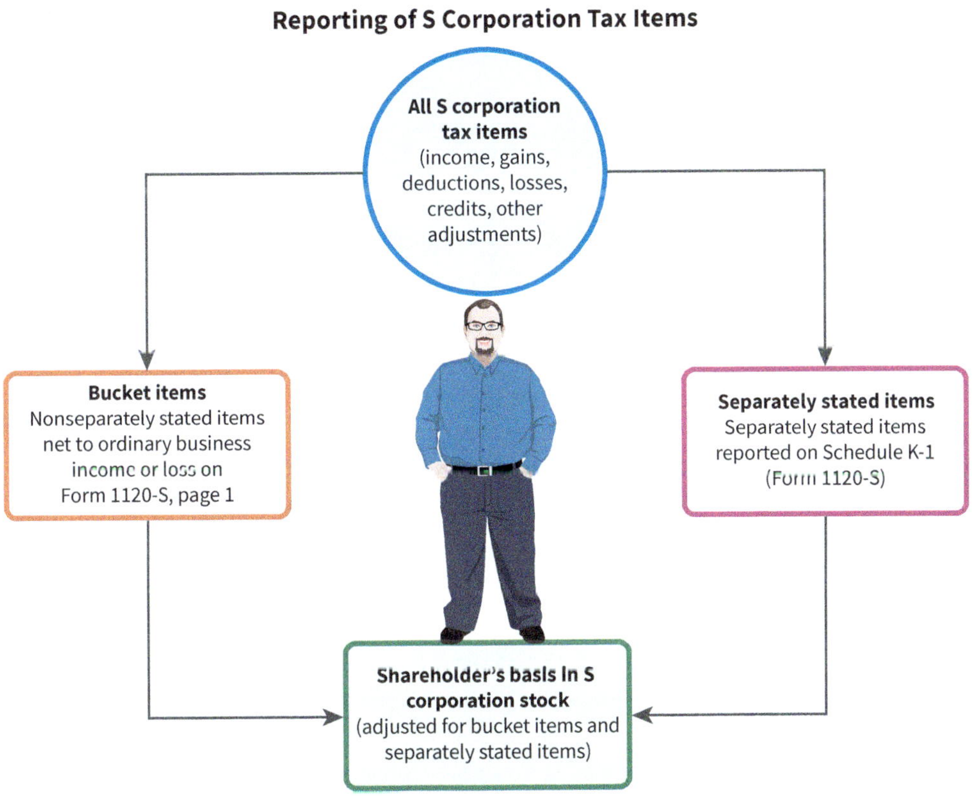

The separation of S corporation tax items between the bucket items and the separately stated items is shown in the next Example.

EXAMPLE 8.3.3
S Corporation Shareholder's Income

Grackle, Inc. is an S corporation that has four shareholders. Benjamin owns 25% of Grackle. He also works at Grackle and is paid $75,000 per year for his services. The following items were reported on Grackle's Form 1120-S this year:

Gross receipts less cost of goods sold	$1,980,000
Interest income	$ 4,000
Net long-term capital gain	$ 18,000
Salaries and wages (including $75,000 to Benjamin)	$ 490,000
Repairs and maintenance	$ 27,000
Net Section 1231 loss	$ 26,000
Rent expense	$ 133,000
Charitable contributions	$ 30,000
Advertising	$ 68,000
Interest expense	$ 31,000
Depreciation	$ 47,000
Section 179 expense	$ 39,000

How would these amounts be reported on Benjamin's K-1, and how would his salary be reported to him?

SOLUTION

We begin by splitting these tax items into the bucket items and the separately stated items and using the bucket items to compute ordinary business income:

Bucket items		**Separately stated items**	
Gross receipts less cost of goods sold	$ 1,980,000	Interest income	$ 4,000
Less: Salaries and wages	(490,000)	Net LTCG	$18,000
Repairs and maintenance	(27,000)	Net Section 1231 loss	$26,000
Rent expense	(133,000)	Charitable contributions	$30,000
Advertising	(68,000)	Section 179 expense	$39,000
Interest expense	(31,000)		
Depreciation	(47,000)		
Ordinary business income	$ 1,184,000		

Grackle's ordinary business income is $1,184,000. Benjamin's K-1 would reflect 25% of the ordinary business income and each separately stated item, as follows:

	Total	**Benjamin's allocation (25%)**
Ordinary business income	$1,184,000	$296,000
Interest income	$ 4,000	$ 1,000
Net long-term capital gain	$ 18,000	$ 4,500
Net section 1231 loss	$ 26,000	$ 6,500
Charitable contributions	$ 30,000	$ 7,500
Section 179 expense	$ 39,000	$ 9,750

Benjamin's salary of $75,000 would be reported to him on his W-2 from Grackle.

Related exercise: Application Problem 5

Reasonable Compensation

We previously noted that an S corporation shareholder's distributive share is not subject to self-employment tax. An S corporation shareholder who is also an employee has wage income, and those wages are subject to Social Security and Medicare withholding. These two rules combined provide an incentive for S corporation shareholders who are also employees to minimize the amount of wages that the S corporation pays them. This reduces the amount of Social Security and Medicare taxation. Of course, the lower wages increase the ordinary business income of the S corporation, but because the shareholder's distributive share is not subject to self-employment tax, the lower wages result in overall tax savings for the shareholder.

Because of this incentive, the IRS pays close attention to the salaries paid to S corporation shareholders to ensure that they are reasonably compensated for the services they provide. If the compensation paid to the shareholders is unreasonably low, the IRS can assess penalties against the shareholder.

PRACTICE PROBLEM 8.3.1

Determining Income Reported on Schedule K-1

As of January 1 of this year, Keisha owned all 500 shares of a calendar-year S corporation, Gallery Corporation. On June 25, the 176th day of this year, Keisha sold 50 shares to Diedre. Gallery reported $135,000 of ordinary business income for the entire year and made no distributions. What amount of income should the S corporation report to Keisha on her Schedule K-1? What amount of income should the S corporation report to Diedre on her Schedule K-1?

SOLUTION

Keisha's income allocation can be computed as follows:

$$\text{Amount on Form 1120-S} \times \text{Stock ownership \%} \times \frac{\text{\# of days owned this year}}{365\text{ days}} = \text{Proportionate share of tax item}$$

<u>January 1–June 25</u>

$$\$135{,}000 \times 100\% \times \frac{176\text{ days}}{365\text{ days}} = \$65{,}096$$

<u>June 26–December 31</u>

$$\$135{,}000 \times 90\% \times \frac{189\text{ days}}{365\text{ days}} = \$62{,}914$$

Keisha's income allocation is thus $128,010 ($65,096 + $62,914).

Diedre's income allocation is computed as follows:

<u>June 26–December 31</u>

$$\$135{,}000 \times 10\% \times \frac{189\text{ days}}{365\text{ days}} = \$6{,}990$$

Diedre's income allocation is $6,990.

PRACTICE PROBLEM 8.3.2

Reporting S Corporation Income and Expenses

Trellis Inc. is an S corporation 100% owned by Trevor. In the current year, Trellis had the following:

Gross receipts	$750,000
Interest income	$ 3,200
Dividend income	$ 5,500
Long-term capital gain	$ 4,800
Salaries paid (including $66,000 salary paid to Trevor)	$230,000
Insurance expense	$ 12,000
Office expense	$ 6,000
Section 179 expense	$ 18,000
Charitable contributions	$ 7,500

How would these amounts be reported on Trevor's Schedule K-1, and how would his salary be reported to him?

SOLUTION

We must separate the tax items into the bucket items used to compute ordinary business income or loss and the separately stated items. Ordinary business income is determined as follows:

Gross receipts	$750,000
Salaries paid (including $66,000 salary paid to Trevor)	(230,000)
Insurance expense	(12,000)
Office expense	(6,000)
Ordinary business income	$502,000

Trevor would report $502,000 ordinary business income, salary paid to him of $66,000, and the following separately stated items:

Interest income	$ 3,200
Dividend income	$ 5,500
Long-term capital gain	$ 4,800
Section 179 expense	$ 18,000
Charitable contributions	$ 7,500

INTERACTIVE SELF-SCORING QUIZZES

8.4 Shareholder's Basis in S Corporation Stock and Loss Limitations

LEARNING OBJECTIVE 4

Compute a shareholder's basis in their stock and the limitations on the deductibility of flow-through losses.

VIDEO CONTENT

A shareholder's basis in their stock tracks their investment in the business, and it is adjusted each year for the shareholder's distributive share of tax items, as shown above in Illustration 8.8. It is also increased for contributions made by the shareholder and decreased by the fair market value of distributions received by the shareholder.

It is the shareholder's basis that prevents the double taxation of S corporation income, as shown in the next Example.

EXAMPLE 8.4.1 Single Taxation for S Corporation Shareholders

Samantha is the sole owner of Parrot Inc., a calendar-year S corporation. She began the corporation this year with an investment of $100,000. Parrot has ordinary business income of $38,000 this year. Samantha receives a cash distribution of $27,000 from Parrot on December 20. How is this income reported to Samantha, what are her tax consequences, and what is the basis in her stock at the end of the tax year?

SOLUTION

The tax consequences of these events are as follows:

- Samantha's initial basis in her stock is $100,000 when the corporation is formed.
- The $38,000 of ordinary business income is reported to Samantha on her Schedule K-1, and it flows through to her on December 31.
- Samantha reports the $38,000 of income on Schedule E of her Form 1040.
- Her basis in her stock is increased for the $38,000 of income to $138,000 ($100,000 + $38,000). This basis increase ensures that she will not be taxed on the $38,000 again when it is distributed to her.
- The $27,000 distribution is not taxable to Samantha, and it reduces the basis of her stock to $111,000 ($138,000 – $27,000).

Order of Adjustments to Stock Basis

At the end of the tax year, the shareholder's basis in their stock is adjusted in the following order:[27]

- First, contributions to capital increase the shareholder's adjusted basis.
- Second, the shareholder's share of income, including tax-exempt income, increases the shareholder's adjusted basis.
- Third, distributions to the shareholder from the accumulated adjustments account (defined below) decrease the shareholder's adjusted basis.
- Fourth, the shareholder's share of loss (including nondeductible expenses) decreases the shareholder's adjusted basis.

[27]IRC §1367(a).

Illustration 8.9 details the computation of an S corporation shareholder's basis and shows the order in which adjustments are taken into account.

ILLUSTRATION 8.9 Basis in S Corporation Stock Computation

Ordering Rules for Stock Basis Adjustments		
Initial basis		
Plus:	Additional contributions	
	Shareholder's share of:	Ordinary business income (bucket items)
		Separately stated income items
		Tax-exempt income
Less:	Distributions from AAA (accumulated adjustments account)	
	Shareholder's share of:	Nondeductible expenses
		Ordinary business loss
		Separately stated expense and loss items
Adjusted basis		

Distributions and losses can never reduce a shareholder's stock basis below zero. Distributions that exceed the stock basis are treated as a capital gain. Losses that exceed the shareholder's basis are suspended and carried forward to future tax years.

The following Example illustrates the computation of an S corporation shareholder's basis.

EXAMPLE 8.4.2
S Ordering Rules for Shareholder's Basis

A calendar-year S corporation has tax-exempt interest income of $4,000 and an ordinary business loss of $6,000 for the current year. Its sole shareholder, Huong, had a stock basis of $8,000 on January 1. She received a cash distribution during the year of $7,000. What is Huong's basis in her stock at the end of the year? How much of the ordinary loss can she deduct on her Form 1040?

SOLUTION

Huong's stock basis at the end of the year is computed as follows, using the ordering rules described above:

Basis at the beginning of the year	$ 8,000
Plus: Tax-exempt interest income	4,000
	$12,000
Less: Cash distribution	(7,000)
	$ 5,000
Less: Ordinary business loss	($ 5,000)
Basis at the end of the year	$ 0

Huong can deduct only $5,000 of the ordinary business loss on her Form 1040. The other $1,000 of loss is suspended and carried forward to future years.

Related exercises: Discussion Question 7
Multiple Choice Question 10
Brief Exercise 5
Application Problems 6, 7, 8

Potential Pitfall

S corporation shareholders cannot increase their stock basis by debt on the balance sheet of the S corporation, because they have limited liability and are not personally liable for corporate debts. In contrast, owners of partnerships and limited liability companies can increase the basis of their ownership interest for entity debt in some situations.

Debt Basis

If a shareholder's allocated losses exceed their stock basis, the shareholder can also deduct losses against their *debt basis*. S corporation shareholders have **debt basis** to the extent that the shareholder has loaned money directly to the S corporation. Guarantees of corporate debt are not sufficient to create debt basis. Debt basis is significant to the shareholder because once a shareholder has exhausted their stock basis, losses can be deducted to the extent of debt basis. Other key points about debt basis include:[28]

- Debt basis can never be reduced below zero.
- Once debt basis has been reduced for losses, future positive adjustments to basis are first allocated to debt basis until restored to the principal amount of the debt outstanding.
- Debt basis is never reduced for distributions. It can be reduced only by losses.
- When the debt is repaid by the corporation, the shareholder will recognize gain to the extent that the repayment exceeds the shareholder's basis in the debt.

We demonstrate the debt basis rules in the next Example.

EXAMPLE 8.4.3
Debt Basis

Meghan is a 50% shareholder in an S corporation, and her share of the ordinary business loss for Year 3 is $20,000. Meghan's stock basis at the beginning of Year 3 is $11,000, and she personally loaned the S corporation $15,000 this year. Assuming that Meghan's loss deduction is not limited by the passive loss rules or the at-risk rules (discussed below), how much of the $20,000 loss can she deduct on her tax return for Year 3? If Meghan's share of the S corporation income in Year 4 was $10,000, how would this affect her stock basis and debt basis?

SOLUTION

Before the loss, Meghan has stock basis of $11,000 and debt basis of $15,000. Meghan's $20,000 share of the loss reduces her basis as follows:

	Stock basis	Debt basis
	$11,000	$15,000
Loss allocation, Year 3	(11,000)	(9,000)
Basis, December 31, Year 3	$ 0	$ 6,000

Her stock basis is reduced to $0, and her debt basis is reduced to $6,000. She can deduct the $20,000 loss on her Year 3 Form 1040.

For Year 4, her share of the income first increases her debt basis by $9,000 to the original $15,000 principal amount of the loan, and the remaining income of $1,000 ($10,000 – $9,000) increases her stock basis:

	Stock basis	Debt basis
Basis, December 31, Year 3	$ 0	$ 6,000
Income allocation, Year 4	1,000	9,000
Basis, December 31, Year 4	$1,000	$15,000

Related exercises: Multiple Choice Question 11
Brief Exercise 6
Application Problem 9
Tax Planning Problem 1

[28]IRC §1367(b).

Spotlight on the Law

Is Gain Recognized When a Loan Is Repaid to a Shareholder?

A shareholder's basis in their stock tracks their investment in the business, and it is adjusted each year for the shareholder's distributive share of tax items. It is also increased for contributions made by the shareholder and decreased by the fair market value of distributions received by the shareholder. If a shareholder's allocated losses exceed their stock basis, the shareholder can also deduct losses against their debt basis. Debt basis for the shareholder is created when the shareholder has loaned money directly to the S corporation. If the debt is repaid in full to the shareholder when the basis of the debt is less than the amount repaid, the shareholder will recognize gain for the excess. If the debt is partially repaid, to the extent partial repayments exceed a pro rata portion of the basis in the debt, gain will be recognized.*

For example, let's assume that Ernie is a shareholder of Cubby Corporation. In Year 3, Ernie's basis in Cubby Corporation is $0, and Ernie loans Cubby $50,000. The loan is a written debt instrument with repayment and interest clearly identified. In Year 4, Ernie's K-1 reflects an ordinary business loss of $22,000. Due to the available debt basis, the ordinary business loss was fully utilized in Year 4 on Ernie's Form 1040. This utilization reduces Ernie's debt basis to $28,000 ($50,000 – $22,000).

In Year 5, Cubby repaid 30% of the loan, or $15,000. What is the tax result for Ernie? Ernie has a potential gain of $22,000 ($50,000 loan outstanding – $28,000 debt basis). Because a partial repayment of the loan was provided to Ernie, only a portion of the gain needs to be recognized on a pro rata basis. The income from the repayment is $6,600, calculated as follows: ([$50,000 face amount – $28,000 basis] ÷ $50,000 face amount) × $15,000 repayment = $6,600. The repayment is made up of a long-term capital gain of $6,600 and a nontaxable return of basis of $8,400. Ernie's remaining debt basis equals $19,600 ($28,000 – $8,400).

One tax planning strategy to avoid the tax on the gain from repayment of a reduced-basis written note is to offset the capital gain with capital losses. Disposition of personal assets or investment assets such as stock can be sold to generate capital losses to offset the capital gain.

*Rev. Rul. 64-162 and Rev. Rul. 68-537

At-Risk Basis and Passive Losses

Once an allocated loss has cleared the stock basis and debt basis hurdles, the loss deduction could be limited by the at-risk rules or passive loss rules.

At-Risk Basis

Shareholders may only deduct losses to the extent that they are *at risk* for investments in the corporation. The S corporation shareholders' at-risk basis is equal to their stock basis plus any funds loaned to the S corporation. Debt of the S corporation is not included in the shareholders' at-risk amounts because they are not liable for the debt. Therefore, any loss that clears the stock basis and debt basis hurdles will also clear the at-risk hurdle.[29]

Passive Losses

If the shareholder does not materially participate in the S corporation, then the loss is a passive loss. Passive losses can be deducted only to the extent of passive income. Losses that are not deducted because of the passive loss limitation are carried forward and can be deducted when there is sufficient passive income in the future. Any unused passive losses at the time the S corporation stock is sold can be deducted in the year of sale.[30]

Related exercise: Discussion Question 8

[29] IRC §465.
[30] IRC §469.

Tax Return Guidance

If a shareholder deducts a loss from the S corporation, the shareholder must report their stock basis and debt basis (defined below) on Form 7203, S Corporation Shareholder Stock and Debt Basis Limitations, including any limitations on the ability to use deductions or credits on the shareholder's tax return. Form 7203 must also be completed if the shareholder sells shares in the S corporation.

Excess Business Losses

Congress has limited the amount of *business* losses that an individual can deduct each tax year.[31] The limitation on excess business losses applies to noncorporate taxpayers for losses from sole proprietorships, partnerships, S corporations, and limited liability companies. Wages and capital gains cannot be used to reduce the amount of the excess business loss. The deductibility of business losses is limited according to the following rules:

- The disallowance applies to business losses that exceed $626,000/$313,000 (married filing jointly/other) for 2025.
- The disallowed amount is added to the taxpayer's net operating loss (NOL) carryforward.
- This limitation applies after application of the *passive loss rules*.

Why **Why is there a limitation on the deduction of business losses?** Congress has placed a limit on the amount of business losses that an individual taxpayer can deduct for a tax year. Even though the losses are legitimate business deductions, Congress believes that there should be a limit on the amount of losses that can offset other income and reduce the individual's tax liability for a given year.

EXAMPLE 8.4.4
Excess Business Losses

Myles is single and has the following results from his trades and businesses for 2025:

Sole proprietorship	($325,000)
Partnership distributive share	$ 60,000
S corporation distributive share	($ 75,000)

How much can he deduct for these business losses, assuming that the losses are not passive and that he has sufficient basis and at risk amount to deduct the losses?

SOLUTION

The aggregate net loss from all of Myles's trades and businesses is $340,000 ($60,000 – $325,000–$75,000). He must limit his business loss deduction for 2025 to $313,000. He includes the remaining loss of $27,000 as part of his NOL for 2025 that he can carry forward indefinitely to future tax years.

Related exercise: Application Problem 10

Advanced Topic—Drilling Down

Charitable Contributions of Appreciated Property

If an S corporation contributes appreciated property to a charitable organization, the corporation can pass through the fair market value of the property as a deduction. However, S corporation shareholders reduce their basis by only the contributed property's basis. Further, the rule that limits the deduction of losses and deduction to the shareholder's stock basis does not apply for the deduction of charitable contribution property to the extent of the excess, if any, of the shareholder's pro rata share of the appreciation in the property.[32]

[31] IRC §461(l).

EXAMPLE 8.4.5 Charitable Contributions of Appreciated Property

Denzel is a 100% shareholder in an S corporation. In the current year, the S corporation contributes long-term capital gain property to a qualified charity with an adjusted basis of $10,000 and a FMV of $14,000.

a. What are the tax consequences of this contribution to Denzel and the S corporation if Denzel's basis in his stock before the contribution is $22,000?

b. What are the tax consequences of this contribution to Denzel and the S corporation if Denzel's basis in his stock before the contribution is $0.

SOLUTION

a. The S corporation reports a charitable contribution of $14,000 because the property is LTCG property. This is a separately stated item that flows through to Denzel. However, Denzel reduces his basis in his stock by the $10,000 basis of the property. Denzel's ending basis is $12,000 ($22,000 − $10,000).

b. The corporation's deduction is still $14,000, and it flows through to Denzel. If this was any other deduction item, Denzel would not be allowed to reduce his taxable income for the deduction because he has no basis in his stock. However, there is an exception to this rule for charitable contributions of appreciated property. Denzel can deduct the contribution up to his share of the appreciation ($4,000) even though his stock basis is zero. His stock basis remains zero because it cannot be negative.

Related exercise: Application Problem 11

PRACTICE PROBLEM 8.4.1 Determining Ending Basis in an S Corporation

Motors Corporation is an S corporation owned solely by Neil. Neil's beginning stock basis was $44,000, and he had the following items on his Schedule K-1 from Motors:

Ordinary business income	$12,000
Dividend income	$ 1,000
Charitable contributions	$ 2,200
Distributions	$25,000

The corporation's debt increased by $3,300 this year. What is Neil's ending stock basis in his S corporation interest?

SOLUTION

Neil's basis is computed as follows:

Beginning basis	$44,000
Plus:	
Ordinary business income	12,000
Dividend income	1,000
Available basis	$57,000
Less: Distributions	(25,000)
Less: Charitable contributions	(2,200)
Ending basis	$29,800

Neil's basis is not affected by the change of debt because this is an S corporation, not a partnership.

PRACTICE PROBLEM 8.4.2
Determining Ending Basis in an S Corporation with an Ordinary Business Loss

Francine owns 50% of Railway, an S corporation. At the beginning of the year, Francine's basis in Railway was $50,000. Railway reported the following items from operations during the current year:

Ordinary business loss	$120,000
Municipal interest income	$ 4,000
Section 1231 gain	$ 6,000
Dividend income	$ 8,000

What is Francine's basis in Railway at year-end?

SOLUTION

Beginning basis	$ 50,000
Plus:	
Municipal interest income	2,000
Section 1231 gain	3,000
Dividend income	4,000
Available basis	$ 59,000
Less: Ordinary business loss	(59,000)
Ending basis	$ 0

Francine's suspended loss of $1,000 ($60,000 – $59,000) is carried forward to the next year.

PRACTICE PROBLEM 8.4.3
Debt Basis

ABCD is an S corporation that has been in existence for seven years. A is a 25% shareholder and has a basis in her S corporation stock at the beginning of the year of $160,000. Because the corporation was having cash flow problems this year, A loaned the S corporation $130,000. The S corporation has an ordinary loss for the year of $1,200,000. How much of this loss may A deduct on her return, assuming it is not a passive loss?

SOLUTION

Shareholder A's share of the loss is $300,000 ($1,200,000 × 25%). First, A will use the loss against her stock basis. Then, A can use the loss against her debt basis because it was a direct loan from A.

	Stock	Debt
Beginning basis	$160,000	$130,000
Deductible loss	(160,000)	(130,000)
Ending basis	$ 0	$ 0

Due to basis limitations, the total deductible loss equals $290,000 ($160,000 + $130,000). The suspended loss is $10,000 ($300,000 – $290,000).

INTERACTIVE SELF-SCORING QUIZZES

8.5 Taxation of S Corporation Distributions

LEARNING OBJECTIVE 5

Determine the tax effects of S corporation distributions to the shareholder and the corporation.

VIDEO CONTENT

If Aletta forms an S corporation, it is likely that she will need to take distributions from the corporation at some time in the future. If Aletta wants to reinvest profits back into the S corporation, then a distribution is not needed. However, if she needs access to the profits to pay personal expenses, invest in other businesses, or for other reasons, then distributions will be needed. There can be tax consequences at both the corporate level and the shareholder level, and we discuss each of these in this section. We also discuss the tax consequences of both cash distributions and property distributions. The focus of this section is on non-liquidating distributions. The tax consequences of liquidating distributions for corporations are discussed in Chapter 4, LO5, Corporate Liquidations.

Remember from our previous discussion in this chapter that S corporations cannot have preferential distributions to shareholders because this would create a second class of stock and the S election would be terminated. Therefore, distributions must be pro rata to each shareholder based on the fair market value of the property being distributed.

Tax Consequences of Distributions for the Corporation

The two main tax consequences that a corporation must consider for a distribution are:

- the possible recognition of gain or loss if property is distributed, *and*
- the effect of the distribution on the corporation's *accumulated adjustments account* (AAA) and earnings and profits (E&P), if any.

Related exercise: Discussion Question 9

Corporate Gain or Loss

If an S corporation distributes cash to its shareholders, the corporation will not recognize any gain or loss. If the S corporation distributes appreciated property, the corporation must recognize gain as if it had sold the property for its fair market value. On the other hand, if the S corporation distributes loss property, the loss cannot be recognized. Thus, the phrase *gains but not losses* that applied frequently to regular corporations also applies to S corporations.

Tax Planning Tip

Both C corporations and S corporations must recognize gains if appreciated property is distributed, but neither can recognize losses if loss property is distributed. However, the taxation of the gain is handled differently. A C corporation will pay tax on the gain on its Form 1120. However, an S corporation will report the gain on its Form 1120-S, it will flow through to the shareholder, and the shareholder will pay tax on the gain. Recall that partnerships do not recognize gains or losses when property is distributed.

The following two Examples illustrate the application of these rules for an S corporation.

EXAMPLE 8.5.1
Gain for S Corporation on Distributions

An S Corporation distributes land to its sole shareholder. If the land has a value of $12,000 and an adjusted basis of $7,500 on the date of distribution, what are the tax consequences to the corporation?

SOLUTION

The S corporation must recognize a gain of $4,500 ($12,000 value – $7,500 basis). The gain will be passed through to the shareholder and taxed on the shareholder's tax return.

EXAMPLE 8.5.2
Loss for S Corporation on Distributions

An S Corporation distributes land to its sole shareholder. If the land has a value of $12,000 and an adjusted basis of $17,500 on the date of distribution, what are the tax consequences to the corporation?

SOLUTION

The S corporation has a realized loss on the distribution of $5,500 ($12,000 value – $17,500 basis). However, the loss cannot be recognized.

Tax Planning Tip

A corporation should not distribute loss property to a shareholder because the loss disappears. In Example 8.5.2, the corporation should have sold the property so it could have recognized the loss of $5,500 and then passed that loss through to the shareholder. The shareholder would then have received a tax benefit from the loss.

Related exercise: Tax Planning Problem 2

Effect of Distribution on AAA and E&P

AAA and E&P represent the retained earnings of an S corporation. The **accumulated adjustments account (AAA)** represents an S corporation's accumulated earnings that have never been distributed to shareholders for the years it has been an S corporation. All items of income, deductions, gains, and losses are included in AAA, *except* for tax-exempt income and expenses relating to production of tax-exempt income. In addition, if the S corporation was previously a C corporation, federal taxes relating to C corporation years are excluded. E&P represents undistributed cumulative earnings from any prior years in which an S corporation was a C corporation. When a C corporation makes an S election, the tax characteristics of the corporation, such as E&P, carry over to the S corporation. Once the S election is made, losses from the S corporation will not reduce E&P. Rather, E&P will be reduced only by distributions to shareholders.

Related exercise: Discussion Question 10

EXAMPLE 8.5.3
Distributions of E&P

Redbird, Inc. has one shareholder, Shandale, and it elected S status on January 1 of the current tax year, when it had E&P of $60,000. Redbird had an ordinary business loss of $50,000 this year. Redbird distributed $25,000 to Shandale this year. What are the tax consequences of this distribution to Shandale?

SOLUTION

Redbird does not have a positive balance in its AAA because this is its first year as an S corporation and it had a $50,000 loss. The loss cannot reduce E&P because the loss was incurred when Redbird was an S corporation. Therefore, the $25,000 distribution comes from Redbird's E&P and is taxed as dividend income to Shandale and E&P is reduced to $35,000.

Distributions from the AAA are not taxable to the shareholders, because S corporations have single taxation, and this income was taxed when it flowed to the shareholders in the year it was earned. Distributions from AAA also reduce a shareholder's stock basis. However, distributions from E&P are generally taxed as dividend income to the shareholders, and do not reduce a shareholder's stock basis.

For example, assume that a C corporation made an S election five years ago. At that time. the corporation had $32,000 of E&P. The corporation now has a balance in its AAA account of $68,000. Its total retained earnings are $100,000, as shown in **Illustration 8.10**.

ILLUSTRATION 8.10 Retained Earnings

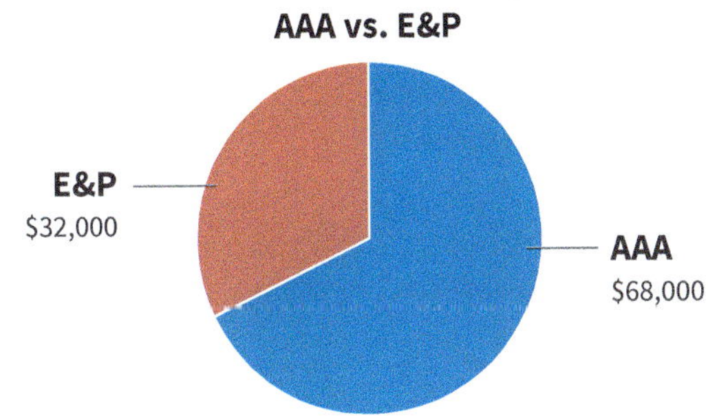

If the S corporation distributes $20,000 of cash to its shareholders, which category of retained earnings does it come from? Or is the distribution deemed to be pro rata from both AAA and E&P? The tax consequences vary significantly depending on the answer to that question.

The good news for taxpayers is that Congress has provided that distributions are deemed to come from the AAA until it is exhausted. Once AAA is exhausted, the distribution comes from E&P. This order works well for the shareholders because distributions from AAA are not taxable.

AAA Computation

The AAA is computed in much the same way as the shareholder's basis in stock, but there are a few significant differences. All items of income, deductions, gains, and losses are included in AAA, *except* for:[33]

- Tax-exempt income
- Expenses relating to production of tax-exempt income
- Federal taxes relating to a C corporation year

Related exercises: Multiple Choice Questions 12, 13

[33]IRC §1368(e).

The three items above make up the **other adjustments account (OAA)**. The OAA is included with AAA in the equity section of the balance sheet. All the items in the AAA and the OAA are included when adjusting the basis in the shareholder's stock at the end of the tax year.

Recall that distributions from the AAA account reduce the shareholder's basis in their stock as well. Distributions cannot reduce the AAA below zero, nor can distributions increase a negative balance in AAA. The AAA can be negative if the corporation has had cumulative losses in the past. **Illustration 8.11** summarizes the differences in how AAA and the shareholder's basis are computed.

ILLUSTRATION 8.11 Differences in Computing AAA and Stock Basis

Stock Basis vs. AAA

Characteristic	Stock basis	AAA
Ordering rules	Income, Distributions, Losses	Income, Losses, Distributions
Tax-exempt income	Increases	No effect
Expenses related to tax-exempt income	Decreases	No effect
Federal taxes related to C corp year	Decreases	No effect
Can be negative?	No	Yes (due to losses)

We review the computation of the AAA and OAA accounts in the next Example.

EXAMPLE 8.5.4 Accumulated Adjustments Account and Other Adjustments Account

Will is a 100% shareholder of Osprey Inc., an S corporation. Osprey has the following tax items this year:

Ordinary business income	$81,000
Tax-exempt interest income	$ 8,000
Expenses related to tax-exempt income	$ 2,500
Net long-term capital gains	$ 3,000
Charitable contributions	$ 4,500
AAA, January 1	$57,000
OAA, January 1	$ 3,500

Will's basis in his stock at the beginning of the year is $60,000. What is Will's basis at the end of the tax year, and what are the balances in the AAA and the OAA?

SOLUTION

We compute Will's basis and the AAA and the OAA as follows:

	Basis	AAA	OAA
Balances at beginning of year	$ 60,000	$ 57,000	$ 3,500
Plus:			
Ordinary business income	81,000	81,000	
Net long-term capital gains	3,000	3,000	
Tax-exempt interest income	8,000		8,000
Less:			
Expenses related to tax-exempt income	(2,500)		(2,500)
Charitable contributions	(4,500)	(4,500)	
Balances at end of year	$145,000	$136,500	$ 9,000

Related exercises: Brief Exercise 7
Application Problem 12

Tax Consequences of Distributions for the Shareholder

Distributions to shareholders of previously taxed earnings are not taxable to the shareholders. The amount of the distribution is equal to the cash plus the FMV of property distributed (less any debt on the property assumed by the shareholder). The AAA determines the amount of previously taxed earnings that have not been distributed, so if the distribution is from AAA, it is not taxable. The steps to determine the tax consequences for the shareholder depend on whether the corporation has earnings and profits. The amount of a distribution is the amount of cash plus the *value* of any property distributed.

Earnings and Profits

Assuming the corporation does have E&P, the steps for determining the tax consequences of distributions to shareholders are as follows (see flowchart in **Illustration 8.12**):

Step 1. **Evaluate:** Distributions are tax-free to the extent of AAA (recall that distributions from AAA also reduce stock basis).

Step 2. **Verify:** Dividend income to the extent of E&P

Step 3. **Ascertain:** Distributions are tax-free to the extent of stock basis (reduced for distributions from AAA in step 1).

Step 4. **Assess:** Any remaining distribution is a capital gain.

Debt basis is not a part of these steps because debt basis cannot be reduced for distributions.

ILLUSTRATION 8.12 Determining the Tax Consequences of S Corporation Distributions

Taxation of S Corporation Distributions

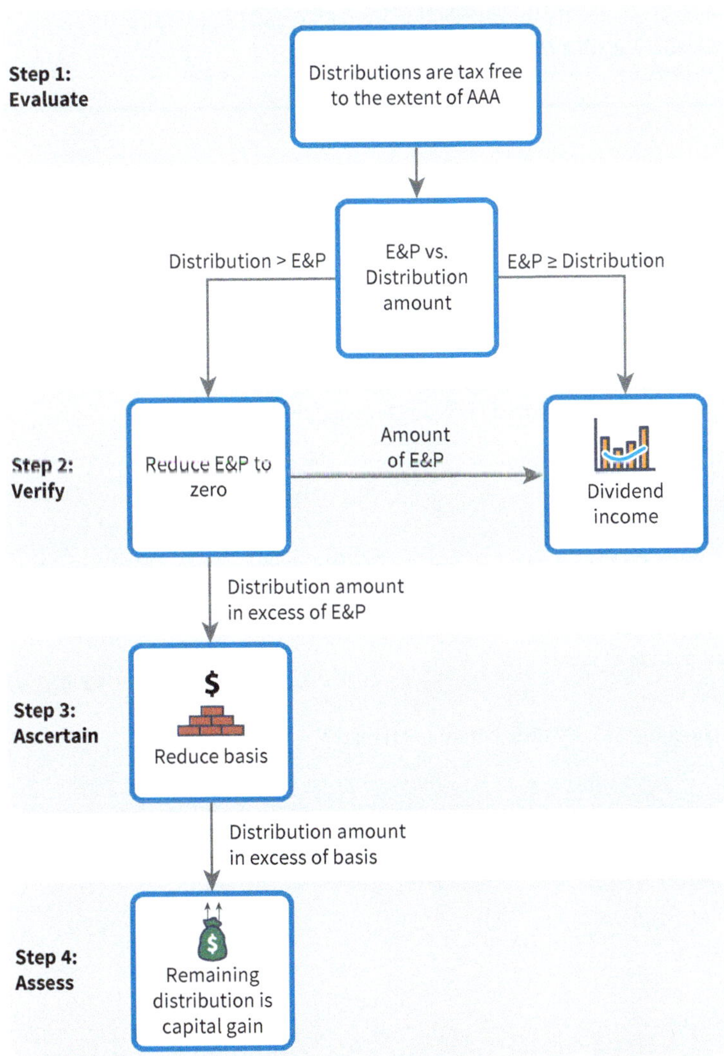

Potential Pitfall

In evaluating distributions to S corporation shareholders when the corporation has E&P, remember to also reduce the stock basis (before you get to step 3) for distributions from AAA in step 1.

The next Example demonstrates the four-step approach for S corporation distributions when there is E&P.

EXAMPLE 8.5.5
Four-Step Formula When E&P Exists

Condor Corporation was originally formed as a C corporation, and after five years it made an S election. It has been an S corporation for three years and has one shareholder, Frederick. The following information applies for Condor and Frederick as of the end of the current tax year:

Stock basis	$40,000
AAA	$30,000
E&P	$ 8,000

Frederick received a $50,000 distribution this year. What are the tax consequences of this distribution?

SOLUTION

We apply the four-step formula from Illustration 8.12 that is used when the S corporation has E&P to determine the tax consequences:

Step 1.	Tax-free to the extent of AAA	$30,000
Step 2.	Dividend income to the extent of E&P	$ 8,000
Step 3.	Tax-free to the extent of stock basis ($40,000 – $30,000 distribution from AAA)	$10,000
Step 4.	The remaining distribution is a capital gain ($50,000 – $30,000 – $8,000 – $10,000)	$ 2,000

Frederick has $8,000 of dividend income for the distribution from E&P, and he has a $2,000 LTCG. The basis of his stock after the distribution is $0.

The following Example shows how to analyze the tax consequences of a distribution to an S corporation shareholder when the AAA needs to be computed.

EXAMPLE 8.5.6
Distribution When Corporation Has E&P

Dove Corporation, a calendar-year corporation, made an S election effective on January 1 of the current year when it had E&P of $24,000. Melinda is the sole shareholder of Dove, and her basis was $16,000 at the beginning of the year. For the current tax year, Dove had the following items:

Ordinary business income	$67,000
Tax-exempt interest	$ 2,000
Net Section 1231 gain	$ 7,000
Charitable contribution	$ 3,000
Expenses related to tax-exempt income	$ 400
Disallowed portion of meals	$ 750
Distribution	$15,000

What are the tax consequences of the $15,000 distribution to Melinda?

SOLUTION

Because Dove has E&P, the corporate level AAA and E&P balances must be computed before Melinda's tax consequences can be determined.

	AAA	E&P
Balance, January 1	$ 0	$24,000
Ordinary business income	67,000	
Plus: Net Section 1231 gain	7,000	
Balance after income additions	$74,000	
Less: Charitable contribution	(3,000)	
Less: Disallowed portion of meals	(750)	
Balance before distributions	$70,250	
Less: Distributions	(15,000)	
Balance, December 31	$55,250	$24,000

Melinda's ending stock basis is computed as follows:

	Stock basis
Basis, January 1	$16,000
Plus:	
Ordinary business income	67,000
Net Section 1231 gain	7,000
Tax-exempt interest	2,000
Balance before distributions	$92,000
Less: Distributions from AAA	(15,000)
Basis after distributions	$77,000
Less:	
Charitable contribution	(3,000)
Expenses related to tax-exempt income	(400)
Disallowed portion of meals	(750)
Ending basis	$72,850

Because there is a sufficient balance in the AAA and sufficient stock basis, the $15,000 distribution is not taxable to her. The E&P is not changed by the income and loss items, and it is not reduced by the distribution because there is a sufficient balance in the AAA for the distribution.

The next Example demonstrates the tax consequences when the corporation has E&P and not enough in the AAA for the entire distribution.

EXAMPLE 8.5.7
Distributions by Corporations with E&P and Insufficient AAA

Assume the same facts as in Example 8.5.6 except that the distribution to Melinda is $80,000. What are the tax consequences of the distribution to Melinda?

SOLUTION

The solution approach is the same as in the previous example except the amount of the distribution changes, and there is not a sufficient AAA balance to absorb the entire loss.

	AAA	E&P
Balance, January 1	$ 0	$24,000
Plus:		
Ordinary business income	67,000	
Net Section 1231 gain	7,000	
Balance after income additions	$74,000	
Charitable contribution	3,000)	
Less: Disallowed portion of meals	(750)	
Balance before distributions	$70,250	
Less: Distributions	(70,250)	(9,750)
Balance, December 31	$ 0	$14,250

Melinda's ending stock basis is computed as follows:

	Stock basis
Basis, January 1	$16,000
Plus:	
Ordinary business income	67,000
Net Section 1231 gain	7,000
Tax-exempt interest	2,000
Basis before distributions	$92,000
Less: Distributions from AAA	(70,250)
Basis after distributions	$21,750
Less:	
Charitable contribution	(3,000)
Expenses related to tax-exempt income	(400)
Disallowed portion of meals	(750)
Ending basis	$17,600

Because there is not a sufficient balance in the AAA to absorb the distribution, only $70,250 of the distribution comes from AAA. The remaining distribution of $9,750 comes from E&P. Melinda has dividend income of $9,750, and her ending stock basis is $17,600.

Related exercises: Brief Exercises 8, 9
Application Problem 13

No Earnings and Profits

If there is no E&P, then only the last steps from above are needed to determine the tax consequences of a distribution:

Step 1. Evaluate: Distributions are tax-free to the extent of stock basis.

Step 2. Assess: The remaining distribution is a capital gain.

Tax Planning Tip

If an S corporation does not have E&P, then you do not need to use AAA to determine the tax consequences of distributions for shareholders. However, the AAA is still reduced for the distribution.

EXAMPLE 8.5.8
Distribution When Corporation Has No E&P

Antonio owns 100% of Parrot Corporation. Parrot Corporation was organized three years ago as an S corporation. Information for Antonio and Parrot is as follows as of the end of the current tax year:

Antonio's stock basis	$13,000
AAA	$12,000

Antonio receives a distribution of $15,000 from Parrot at the end of the tax year. What are the tax consequences of the distribution to Antonio?

SOLUTION

Because Parrot has no E&P, we can use the two-step formula to determine the tax consequences:

Distribution	$15,000
Step 1. Tax-free to the extent of stock basis	(13,000)
Step 2. The remaining distribution is a capital gain	$ 2,000

Antonio has a LTCG gain of $2,000 because he has owned the stock for more than one year. His basis in the stock is reduced to zero. The AAA account is reduced to $0.

Related exercise: Multiple Choice Question 14

AAA Bypass Election

An S corporation can elect to distribute its E&P before its AAA, known as the **AAA bypass election**.[34] All shareholders who will be affected by the election must consent to it. The election is made annually and applies to all distributions for that year. If the election is made, then the four-step formula for S corporation distributions is as follows:

Step 1. E&P

Step 2. AAA

Step 3. Basis in stock

Step 4. Capital gain

The bypass election is most often used if an S corporation wants to remove E&P from its balance sheet to avoid the potential application of the passive investment income tax (discussed below).

EXAMPLE 8.5.9
AAA Bypass Election

Return to the facts of Example 8.5.6. What would the tax consequences of the distribution be to Melinda if Dove Corporation made the AAA bypass election?

SOLUTION

The computation of AAA would be the same except for the distribution. However, the $15,000 distribution would come from E&P, and Melinda would have $15,000 of dividend income. The ending balances in the accounts would be computed as follows:

	AAA	E&P
Balance, January 1	$ 0	$24,000
Plus:		
Ordinary business income	67,000	
Net Section 1231 gain	7,000	
Balance after income additions	$74,000	
Less:		
Charitable contribution	(3,000)	
Disallowed portion of meals	(750)	
Balance before distributions	$70,250	
Less: Distributions	(0)	(15,000)
Balance, December 31	$70,250	$ 9,000

[34] IRC §1368(e)(3).

Melinda's ending stock basis is computed as follows:

	Stock basis
Basis, January 1	$16,000
Plus:	
Ordinary business income	67,000
Net Section 1231 gain	7,000
Tax-exempt interest	2,000
Basis before distributions	$92,000
Less: Distributions from AAA	(0)
Basis after distributions	$92,000
Less:	
Charitable contribution	(3,000)
Expenses related to tax-exempt income	(400)
Disallowed portion of meals	(750)
Ending basis	$87,850

Melinda's stock basis is not reduced for the $15,000 distribution because it came from E&P and not AAA.

Related exercise: Application Problem 14

Post-Termination Transition Period

The **post-termination transition period (PTTP)** is generally the one-year period following the termination of an S corporation. More specifically, the PTTP begins on the day the S election is terminated, and it ends as of the *later* of:

1. one year later,
2. the date of the final S corporation return (including extensions), *or*
3. 120 days after it is determined that the S election was terminated.

EXAMPLE 8.5.10
Post-Termination Transition Period

A calendar-year S corporation's election terminated as of November 10, Year 10. When does the PTTP end for this S corporation?

SOLUTION

Because the S election is terminated on November 10, the last day of the S corporation year is November 9. The PTTP begins on November 10, Year 10, and ends on November 9, Year 11, which is the *later* of 1) one year later, *or* 2) October 15, Year 11 (the due date of final S corporation return including extension).

Two key benefits can occur during the PTTP:

- Distributions of cash during the PTTP are treated as a tax-free recovery of stock basis to the extent the cash distributions do not exceed the AAA balance.[35]
- Losses and/or deductions that were suspended as of the termination of the S election due to insufficient basis can be deducted at the end of the PTTP if basis has increased.[36]

[35]IRC §1371(d).
[36]IRC §1366(d).

Why **Why do the special rules apply during the PTTP?** An S corporation shareholder's stock basis and the AAA include income that has already been taxed to the shareholder but not distributed. When the earnings are later distributed, they are not taxed again. However, once the S corporation election is terminated, then the C corporation rules apply, and distributions of earnings would typically be taxed as dividend income. Additionally, the shareholder could have suspended losses that have not been deducted because of insufficient basis in their stock. Congress has provided a one-year transition period for shareholders to receive tax-free their previously taxed S corporation income, as long as it is received in cash. This provides relief for an S corporation whose S election terminates unexpectedly because it did not have time to plan to exhaust the AAA or deduct suspended losses.

Tax Planning Tip

Property should not be distributed to a shareholder during the PTTP, because the value of the property is potentially taxable to the shareholder. The special rule for the PTTP applies only to cash distributions.

The following Example demonstrates the use of cash distributions during the PTTP.

EXAMPLE 8.5.11
Distributions During the Post-Termination Transition Period

Owl Corporation has been an S corporation for seven years, but the shareholders voted to terminate the S election as of January 1, Year 9. At the end of the year, there was a balance in the AAA of $23,000. Prisha, the sole shareholder, had a basis in her stock of $36,000. During Year 9, Prisha received a distribution of $15,000 cash and equipment with a FMV of $8,000 and adjusted basis of $15,000. Owl has E&P of $38,000 at the end of Year 9. What are the tax consequences of the distributions to Owl and Prisha?

SOLUTION

The last day that Owl was an S corporation was December 31, Year 8, so the PTTP for Owl runs from December 31, Year 8 to December 31, Year 9. Owl has a realized loss of $7,000 from the distribution of the equipment ($8,000 FMV – $15,000 basis), but the loss cannot be recognized. Prisha's receipt of the $15,000 is not taxable to her because it is a cash distribution during the PTTP, and it comes from AAA. The cash distribution reduces Owl's AAA account to $8,000 ($23,000 – $15,000) and reduces Prisha's stock basis to $21,000 ($36,000 – $15,000). However, the equipment distribution is treated as an $8,000 dividend to Prisha because property distributions cannot come from AAA during the PTTP. The remaining balance of $8,000 in the AAA disappears since it cannot be used by Owl after the PTTP ends on December 31, Year 9.

We demonstrate the use of suspended losses during the PTTP in the next Example.

EXAMPLE 8.5.12
Use of Losses During the Post-Termination Transition Period

Matt is a 100% shareholder of an S corporation whose S election terminated on November 1, Year 5. At the time of the termination, Matt had suspended losses from the S corporation of $56,000 that he has not deducted on his Form 1040 because the basis in his stock is $0. Are any planning opportunities available to Matt with respect to the suspended losses?

SOLUTION

Yes, Matt does have a planning opportunity during the PTTP, which runs from November 1, Year 5 to October 31, Year 6. Matt can deduct the suspended losses to the extent that he increases his stock basis during the PTTP. His stock basis cannot increase because of income from the corporation during the PTTP because the corporation is now a C corporation. However, he can contribute cash of $56,000 to the corporation, which would increase his basis to $56,000. Matt will then be able to deduct the $56,000 of losses on his Year 6 Form 1040, and this will decrease his stock basis back to $0.

Related exercises: Discussion Question 11
Application Problem 15

PRACTICE PROBLEM 8.5.1
Calculation of Ending AAA and OAA

Coco is a 100% shareholder of Melon Inc., an S corporation. Melon has the following tax items this year:

Ordinary business income	$58,000
Tax-exempt interest income	$ 1,300
Expenses related to tax-exempt income	$ 300
Dividend income	$ 4,400
Section 179 expense	$13,000
AAA, January 1	$60,000
OAA, January 1	$ 2,100

Coco's basis in her stock at the beginning of the year is $55,000. What is Coco's basis at the end of the tax year, and what are the balances in the AAA and the OAA?

SOLUTION

Coco's basis and the AAA and the OAA are calculated as follows:

	Basis	AAA	OAA
Balances at beginning of year	$ 55,000	$ 60,000	$ 2,100
Plus:			
Ordinary business income	58,000	58,000	
Dividend income	4,400	4,400	
Tax-exempt interest income	1,300		1,300
Less:			
Expenses related to tax-exempt income	(300)		(300)
Section 179	(13,000)	(13,000)	
Balances at end of year	$105,400	$109,400	$ 3,100

PRACTICE PROBLEM 8.5.2
Distribution When E&P Exists

Queen Corporation was originally formed as a C corporation. After two years, it made an S election. It has now been an S corporation for three years, and it has one shareholder, Duchess. The following information applies for Queen and Duchess as of the end of the current tax year:

Stock basis	$37,000
AAA	$28,000
E&P	$ 6,000

Duchess received a $55,000 distribution this year. What are the tax consequences of this distribution?

SOLUTION

We apply the four-step formula that is used when the S corporation has E&P to determine the tax consequences:

Step 1.	Tax-free to the extent of AAA	$28,000
Step 2.	Dividend income to the extent of E&P	$ 6,000
Step 3.	Tax-free to the extent of stock basis ($37,000 – $28,000 distribution from AAA)	$ 9,000
Step 4.	The remaining distribution is a capital gain ($55,000 – $28,000 – $6,000 – $9,000)	$12,000

Duchess has $6,000 of dividend income for the distribution from E&P, and she has a $12,000 LTCG. The basis of her stock after the distribution is $0.

INTERACTIVE SELF-SCORING QUIZZES

8.6 S Corporation Taxes

LEARNING OBJECTIVE 6

Compute the taxes that an S corporation may have to pay.

VIDEO CONTENT

While in general all items of income, gain, loss, and deduction flow through to an S corporation's shareholders and the shareholders pay any resulting tax liability, there are three taxes that an S corporation may have to pay. If these taxes apply, they are paid by the S corporation when Form 1120-S is filed. The three taxes are:

- Built-in gains (BIG) tax
- Net passive investment income tax
- LIFO recapture tax

These taxes can apply only to S corporations that previously were C corporations. Therefore, a corporation that has always been an S corporation is not subject to these taxes.

Related exercise: Discussion Question 12

Built-In Gains Tax

The *built-in gain (BIG) tax* may be assessed on a C corporation that makes an S election. When a C corporation makes an S election, it must measure the built-in gains and losses on the election date for all its assets and liabilities. If there is a net built-in gain on the election date, and the S corporation recognizes some or all of this built-in gain over the next five years, the S corporation must pay a **built-in gains (BIG) tax** at a 21% rate on the recognized built-in gain.[37]

Why **Why does the BIG tax exist?** One of the most important differences between a C corporation and an S corporation is that upon liquidation, a C corporation has double taxation, but an S corporation has single taxation. For a liquidation of a C corporation, gains and losses can be recognized at both the corporate and shareholder levels. However, for an S corporation that liquidates, all gains and losses are taxed at the shareholder level. Therefore, a creative tax strategy for a C corporation that plans to liquidate would be to make an S election and then liquidate to avoid double taxation.

Congress created the BIG tax to thwart this strategy by imposing a second level of tax on an S corporation that liquidates if it was previously a C corporation. The BIG tax potentially applies if such an S corporation sells assets with a BIG within five years of the effective date of the S election. Therefore, this tax strategy can work if the S corporation waits more than five years before selling the BIG assets.

Definitions

The starting point for computing the BIG tax is to measure the built-in gain (BIG) or built-in loss (BIL) for each asset on the day the S election is effective. The **built-in gain** is the excess of the fair market value over the adjusted basis of an asset. The **built-in loss** is the excess of the adjusted basis of the asset over its fair market value.

Quick Review

The following is a summary of a few rules for the BIG tax:

- The built-in gains tax is not imposed on a corporation that has always been an S corporation.

[37] IRC §1374.

- The tax is imposed at the highest corporate rate (21%) and is multiplied by the realized BIG for a given tax year.
- The tax can only be imposed for a period of five years after the S election is made.
- The maximum recognized BIG over the five-year recognition period is limited to the net amount of net unrealized built-in gain at the time of election. The **net unrealized built-in gain** is the excess of the BIGs over the BILs on the election date.
- When an asset with a BIG is sold, the recognized BIG is the *lower* of:
  1. the remaining unrealized BIG,
  2. the BIG for this asset on the election date, *or*
  3. the recognized gain on the sale date.
- In the year that BIG property is sold, if property is also sold that had built-in losses at the date of the S election, these built-in losses can offset the built-in gains.
- The total built-in gain subject to this tax in any year is also limited to the S corporation's taxable income for that year computed as if the S corporation were still a C corporation. Any BIG not recognized because of the taxable income limitation carries forward to other years in the five-year recognition period. If there is not enough taxable income to use the BIG by the end of the five-year period, then it will never be recognized.
- If the C corporation has unused NOLs or capital loss carryforwards at the time of the S election, these carryforwards can be used to offset recognized BIG income.
- The amount of built-in gains tax paid passes through on the S corporation tax return as an expense. To the extent the tax results from built-in gains on capital assets, the tax passes through as a capital loss.

The following Example demonstrates the basic rules of the BIG tax.

EXAMPLE 8.6.1
Built-In Gains Tax

Condor Corporation had been a C corporation for three years and made an S election this year. Condor owns one asset, which is land held for investment. On the effective date of the S election, the land has a FMV of $1,000,000 and an adjusted basis of $100,000. Assume that the S corporation's net income computed as if it were a C corporation is $1,500,000.

a. Assuming Condor sells the land two years after the S election date for $1,200,000, compute the BIG tax, if any.

b. Alternatively, what if Condor sells the land seven years after the S election date?

c. In part **a**, what would the result be if Condor sold the land for $800,000?

SOLUTION

The maximum amount of BIG is computed on the effective date of the S election, and that is $900,000 ($1,000,000 FMV – $100,000 basis).

a. When the land is sold two years later, the recognized BIG is taxed at a rate of 21% to Condor, as follows:

Amount realized	$1,200,000
Adjusted basis	(100,000)
Recognized gain	$1,100,000

The recognized BIG is $900,000, the *lower* of:

1. the remaining unrealized BIG ($900,000),
2. the BIG for this asset on the election date ($900,000), *or*
3. the recognized gain on the sale date ($1,100,000).

Therefore, the BIG tax is $189,000 ($900,000 × 21%). The tax effects are:

- Condor pays the BIG tax of $189,000 when it files its Form 1120-S.
- The $189,000 tax flows through to the shareholders as a capital loss because the land was an investment asset.
- The recognized gain of $1,100,000 flows through to the shareholders as a LTCG.

You now see that the $900,000 BIG is taxed twice, just as would have been the case if the land had been sold when the corporation was a C corporation. The $200,000 appreciation in the land after the S election date ($1,100,000 – $900,000) is taxed only once.

b. Because the land was sold more than five years after the S election date, the BIG tax does not apply. The $1,100,000 recognized gain flows through to the shareholders. Condor does not pay any tax.

c. When the land is sold two years later, the recognized BIG is taxed at a rate of 21% to Condor, as follows:

Amount realized	$800,000
Adjusted basis	(100,000)
Recognized gain	$700,000

The recognized BIG is $700,000, the *lower* of:

1. the remaining unrealized BIG ($900,000),
2. the BIG for this asset on the election date ($900,000), *or*
3. the recognized gain on the sale date ($700,000).

Therefore, the BIG tax is $147,000 ($700,000 × 21%). The $700,000 gain also flows through and is taxed to the shareholders. The $200,000 of BIG that was not taxed because the land declined in value will never be subject to the BIG tax.

Related exercise: Brief Exercise 10

The next Example combines BIGs and BILs in one problem.

Ibit Corporation was a C corporation for 12 years and made an S election this year. Ibit owns the following assets on the effective date of the S election:

	Adjusted basis	FMV
Land	$500,000	$800,000
Warehouse	$700,000	$500,000

a. Assuming Ibit sells the land four years after the S election date for $750,000, compute the BIG tax, if any. Ibit's taxable income computed as if it were a C corporation is $125,000.

b. Same as part **a**, except that Ibit also sells the warehouse four years later for $420,000 when it has a basis of $600,000.

SOLUTION

We begin by computing the BIG or BIL for each asset and the net unrealized BIG on the election date:

	Adjusted basis	FMV	BIG/(BIL)
Land	$500,000	$800,000	$300,000
Warehouse	$700,000	$500,000	(200,000)
Net unrealized BIG			$100,000

a. The recognized gain from the sale of the land is computed as follows:

Amount realized	$750,000
Adjusted basis	(500,000)
Recognized gain	$250,000

The recognized BIG is $100,000, the *lower* of:

1. the remaining unrealized BIG ($100,000),
2. the BIG for this asset on the election date ($300,000), *or*
3. the recognized gain on the sale date ($250,000).

Therefore, the BIG tax is $21,000 ($100,000 × 21%). The $250,000 gain also flows through and is taxed to the shareholders.

b. The recognized gain from the sale of the land is still $250,000, and this is also a recognized BIG because it is lower than the $300,000 BIG for the land on the election date. The recognized loss from the sale of the warehouse is computed as:

Amount realized	$420,000
Adjusted basis	(600,000)
Recognized loss	($180,000)

The recognized BIL for the warehouse is $180,000 because this is less than the total BIL for the warehouse on the election date of $200,000.

The recognized BIG and recognized BIL are netted together:

Recognized BIG	$250,000
Recognized BIL	(180,000)
Net recognized BIG for the year	$ 70,000

The BIG tax is computed on $70,000, the *lower* of:

1. the remaining unrealized BIG ($100,000), *or*
2. the net recognized BIG for the year ($70,000).Therefore, the BIG tax is $14,700 ($70,000 × 21%). The $250,000 gain and $180,000 loss also flows through to the shareholders.

Related exercise: Application Problem 16

The following Example reminds you that the total BIG recognized can never exceed the net unrealized BIG on the S election date.

EXAMPLE 8.6.3 Overall Limitation on BIG

Sandpiper, Inc. had been a C corporation for seven years when it made an S corporation election effective at the beginning of Year 13. At the time of the election, Sandpiper had the following assets:

	Adjusted basis	FMV
Cash	$ 45,000	$ 45,000
Inventory	$ 90,000	$140,000
Land	$ 70,000	$145,000
Equipment	$460,000	$400,000

In Year 13, after the S election, Sandpiper sold the inventory for $145,000. In Year 14, Sandpaper sold the land for $150,000. What is Sandpiper's BIG tax for Year 14?

SOLUTION

The first step in approaching this problem is to determine the net unrealized BIG on the effective date of the S election.

	Adjusted basis	FMV	BIG/(BIL)
Cash	$ 45,000	$ 45,000	$ 0
Inventory	$ 90,000	$140,000	50,000
Land	$ 70,000	$145,000	75,000
Equipment	$460,000	$400,000	(60,000)
Net unrealized BIG			$ 65,000

Next, we compute the recognized BIG for Years 13 and 14. The recognized income for the sale of inventory in Year 13 is computed as:

Amount realized	$145,000
Adjusted basis	(90,000)
Recognized income	$ 55,000

The recognized BIG is $50,000, the *lower* of:

1. the remaining unrealized BIG ($65,000),
2. the BIG for this asset on the election date ($50,000), *or*
3. the recognized gain on the sale date ($55,000).

The BIG tax for Year 13 is $10,500 ($50,000 × 21%). At the beginning of Year 14, the remaining net unrealized BIG is $15,000 ($65,000 – $50,000).

The gain on the sale of the land in Year 14 is computed as follows:

Amount realized	$150,000
Adjusted basis	(70,000)
Recognized gain	$ 80,000

The recognized BIG is $15,000, the *lower* of:

1. the remaining unrealized BIG ($15,000),
2. the BIG for this asset on the election date ($75,000), *or*
3. the recognized gain on the sale date ($80,000).

For Year 14, the recognized BIG is only $15,000 because $50,000 of the original unrealized BIG was recognized in Year 13. The BIG tax for Year 14 is $3,150 ($15,000 × 21%).

Related exercise: Application Problem 17

The final Example in this series demonstrates how the net recognized BIG is limited to the S corporation's net income computed as if the corporation were a C corporation.

EXAMPLE 8.6.4 Limitation of Corporation's Net Income

Assume the same facts as in Example 8.6.2 (part **b**), except that the S corporation's income for the year, computed as if Ibit were a C corporation, is $56,000. What is the BIG tax?

SOLUTION

The net recognized BIG of $70,000 cannot exceed the corporation's income of $56,000. Therefore, the BIG tax is $11,760 ($56,000 × 21%).

Accounts Receivable and Accounts Payable

One other tax item that creates a BIG on the date of the S election is accounts receivable of a cash-basis taxpayer. The BIG is the fair market value of the accounts receivable. Additionally, accounts payable of a cash-basis taxpayer creates a BIL equal to the amount of the accounts payable. These items do not create BIGs or BILs for accrual-basis taxpayers.

EXAMPLE 8.6.5
Accounts Receivable and Accounts Payable

Vulture Corporation, a cash-basis C corporation for four years, elects to become an S corporation effective for Year 10. At the time of the election, Vulture's balance sheet includes the following items:

	Adjusted basis	FMV
Cash	$15,000	$15,000
Accounts receivable	$ 0	$30,000
Inventory	$42,000	$65,000
Accounts payable	$ 0	$17,000

In Year 10, after the effective date of the S election, Vulture collected the accounts receivable and paid the accounts payable. What is the BIG tax for Year 10, if any?

SOLUTION

The first step in solving this problem is to determine the net unrealized BIG on the effective date of the S election.

	Adjusted basis	FMV	BIG/(BIL)
Cash	$15,000	$15,000	$ 0
Accounts receivable	$ 0	$30,000	30,000
Inventory	$42,000	$65,000	23,000
Accounts payable	$ 0	$17,000	(17,000)
Net unrealized BIG			$36,000

In Year 10, the net recognized BIG is computed as:

Accounts receivable	$30,000
Accounts payable	(17,000)
Net recognized BIG	$13,000

The BIG tax for Year 10 is $2,730 ($13,000 × 21%). The unrealized BIG at the end of Year 10 is $23,000 ($36,000 – 13,000).

Potential Pitfall

Remember that for accrual-basis taxpayers, accounts receivable are *not* BIGs, nor are accounts payable BILs.

Tax Planning Tip

If a cash-basis C corporation is planning to make an S election, it should manage its accounts receivable and accounts payable before the election date to minimize the net unrealized BIG. The corporation can encourage customers to pay off their receivables, and it can reduce its payables by paying them before the effective date of the S election. Additionally, the S corporation needs to ensure that it pays any remaining payables in the same year that the receivables are collected so they can offset each other.

Net Passive Investment Income Tax

As discussed previously in this chapter, an involuntary termination can occur if passive investment income (PII) exceeds 25% of gross receipts for three consecutive years. In addition to the possibility of a termination of the S election, for any year that this occurs, the excess net passive investment income is taxed at a 21% rate to the S corporation.[38] This provision applies only if the S corporation has earnings and profits from previous C corporation years on its balance sheet. The S corporation reduces the flow-through of passive investment income by the net PII tax paid.

Definitions and Computation

You must know four important definitions to compute the PII tax:

- **Gross receipts** include receipts from active operations and investment income (including tax-exempt interest). Only the net gain from the disposition of capital assets (other than stocks and securities) is included in gross receipts. For stocks and securities, all capital gains are included in gross receipts.
- **Passive investment income (PII)** includes interest (including tax-exempt interest), dividends (except dividends from a subsidiary to the extent that the subsidiary is conducting an active trade or business), royalties, rents (unless substantial extra services are provided to the tenants), and annuities.
- **Net passive investment income** is PII reduced by expenses incurred to produce the PII.
- **Excess net passive investment income** is net passive income in excess of 25% of gross receipts. Excess net PII cannot exceed the S corporation's taxable income for the year computed as if were a C corporation.[39]

The **net passive investment income tax** rate is the highest corporate income tax rate, which is currently 21%. The PII tax is computed as follows:

$$\frac{\text{Excess net passive investment income}}{\text{Passive investment income}} \times \text{Net passive investment income} \times 21\%$$

The following Example computes the net passive investment income tax.

EXAMPLE 8.6.6
Net Passive Investment Income Tax

Eagle Corporation, an S corporation, has the following tax information for the current tax year:

Revenue from operations	$40,000
Interest income	$12,000
Municipal interest income	$ 4,000
Dividend income	$ 9,000

Expenses related to the production of the passive income are $4,000. Eagle has $27,000 of E&P from when it was a C corporation. What is Eagle's passive investment income tax for the year?

SOLUTION

Because Eagle does have E&P, it is potentially subject to the PII tax. We begin by computing the amounts needed to determine the tax:

Gross receipts are $65,000 ($40,000 + $12,000 + $4,000 + $9,000). Municipal interest income is included in gross receipts and passive investment income.

PII is:

Interest income	$12,000
Municipal interest income	4,000
Dividend income	9,000
Passive investment income	$25,000

[38]IRC §1375.
[39]IRC §1375(b)(1)(b).

Net PII is $21,000 ($25,000 PII – $4,000 investment expenses).
Excess net PII is $4,750, the net PII of $21,000 in excess of $16,250 ($65,000 × 25%).
Eagle's PII tax is $838 (rounded), computed as follows:

$$\frac{\text{Excess net PII (\$4,750)}}{\text{PII (\$25,000)}} \times \text{Net PII (\$21,000)} \times 21\% = \$838$$

Tax Planning

S corporations can eliminate or reduce their exposure to the PII tax in several ways. One method is to eliminate the corporation's E&P by making an AAA bypass election and paying the E&P to shareholders as a dividend. Once the E&P is eliminated, then the PII tax will no longer apply.

If it is not possible to eliminate the corporation's E&P, then the corporation can reduce the amount of passive investment income that is earned and/or increase its active gross receipts. The corporation could sell its investment assets or distribute the assets to its shareholders.

Related exercises: Discussion Question 13
Multiple Choice Questions 15, 16
Application Problem 18

LIFO Recapture Tax

A C corporation using LIFO that converts to an S corporation must recapture any amount by which the inventory's value under FIFO exceeds its value under LIFO as of the close of its last tax year as a C corporation. The LIFO recapture is included in the C corporation's gross income, and the tax attributable to its inclusion is payable in four equal installments. The first installment must be paid by the due date of the tax return for the last C corporation year, with the three remaining installments due by the due dates of the tax returns for the three succeeding taxable years.

PRACTICE PROBLEM 8.6.1
Built-In Gains Tax

Buckeye Corporation had been a regular C corporation for eight years when it made an S election three years ago. On the date of the S election, Buckeye owned land with an adjusted basis of $190,000 and a FMV of $240,000. In the current year, three years after the S election, Buckeye sells the land for $260,000. How much of the $260,000 is subject to the built-in gains tax?

SOLUTION

The maximum amount of BIG is computed on the effective date of the S election, and that is $50,000 ($240,000 FMV – $190,000 basis). When the land is sold three years later, the recognized BIG is taxed at a rate of 21% to Buckeye, as follows:

Amount realized	$260,000
Adjusted basis	(190,000)
Recognized gain	$ 70,000

The recognized BIG is $50,000, the *lower* of:

1. the remaining unrealized BIG ($50,000),
2. the BIG for this asset on the election date ($50,000), *or*
3. the recognized gain on the sale date ($70,000).

Therefore, the BIG tax is $10,500 ($50,000 × 21%). The tax effects are:

- Buckeye pays the BIG tax of $10,500 when it files its Form 1120-S.
- The $10,500 tax flows through to the shareholders as a capital loss because the land was an investment asset.
- The recognized gain of $70,000 flows through to the shareholders as a LTCG.

PRACTICE PROBLEM 8.6.2
Net Passive Investment Income Tax

Queso Corporation is an S corporation that has the following tax information for the current tax year:

Revenue from operations	$39,000
Interest income	$ 9,000
Municipal interest income	$ 2,000
Dividend income	$ 7,000

Expenses related to the production of the passive income are $2,500. Queso has $21,000 of E&P from when it was a C corporation. What is Queso's passive investment income tax for the year?

SOLUTION

Because Queso does have E&P, then it is potentially subject to the PII tax. We begin by computing the amounts needed to determine the tax:

Gross receipts are $57,000 ($39,000 + $9,000 + $2,000 + $7,000). Municipal interest income is included in gross receipts and passive investment income. PII is:

Interest income	$ 9,000
Municipal interest income	2,000
Dividend income	7,000
Passive investment income	$18,000

Net PII is $15,500 ($18,000 PII − $2,500 investment expenses).

Excess net PII is $1,250, the net PII of $15,500 in excess of $14,250 ($57,000 × 25%).

Queso's PII tax is $226 (rounded), computed as follows:

$$\frac{\text{Excess net PII (\$1,250)}}{\text{PII (\$18,000)}} \times \text{Net PII (\$15,500)} \times 21\% = \$226$$

INTERACTIVE SELF-SCORING QUIZZES

Review and Practice

Chapter Summary

S corporations are legally organized under state law in the same manner as C corporations. Once incorporated, the shareholders elect to be taxed as an S corporation by filing Form 2553, Election by a Small Business Corporation. The major tax advantage for S corporations over C corporations is that S corporations have single taxation.

1 Determine if a corporation is eligible to elect to be taxed as an S corporation.

The eligibility rules for S corporations are quite strict, which results in S corporations being very inflexible when compared to other business entities.

- The number of shareholders in an S corporation is limited to 100. More than 100 individuals can invest in an S corporation because all members of a family and their estates are treated as a single shareholder.
- Individuals and single-member LLCs are allowed to be shareholders. **Nonresident aliens** are individuals who are not citizens or residents of the United States, and they are not allowed to be shareholders. C corporations, S corporations, partnerships, and multi-member limited liability companies (LLCs) cannot be shareholders in an S corporation.

- An S corporation can have only one class of stock. Thus, an S corporation cannot have both common stock and preferred stock. Shares that vary solely in voting rights are not considered two classes of stock. Thus, an S corporation can have voting and nonvoting stock.

2 Apply the rules for electing S corporation status and terminating S corporation status.

The shareholders of the corporation must make a qualifying election to become an S corporation using Form 2553. Unanimous consent of the shareholders is required for the election, not simply a majority vote.

- In its initial year, a corporation must make the S election on or before the 15th day of the third month after commencing business for it to be effective for the entire year. An election made on or before the 15th day of the third month that is not valid will take effect at the beginning of the next tax year if eligibility requirements are met at that time. An election that is made after this date is effective as of the beginning of the next year unless a different prospective date in the current year is specified.
- An election to be an S corporation remains in effect until it is terminated. Termination of the election can occur through four circumstances, some of which are voluntary and some involuntary. Once terminated, the S corporation cannot elect S status without IRS permission for five years.
- A voluntary termination occurs with a majority vote of all shareholders specifying a prospective year
- An involuntary termination occurs through a violation of an eligibility requirement, and this termination is effective on the date of the violation. An involuntary termination can occur if passive investment income (PII) exceeds 25% of gross receipts for three consecutive years.

3 Compute S corporation income and its flow-through to the shareholders.

- S corporation income is reported on Form 1120-S, U.S. Income Tax Return for an S Corporation, and the income flows through to the S corporation shareholders on the last day of the corporate tax year, regardless of whether it has been distributed, on the shareholder's Schedule K-1 (Form 1120-S).
- In general, S corporations use the calendar year for tax reporting. S corporation returns are due on the 15th day of the third month after year-end, which is March 15 for calendar-year corporations. A six-month extension is available until September 15.
- The shareholder's proportionate share of each tax item is reported on their Schedule K-1 (Form 1120-S), determined by the shareholder's stock ownership percentage on a per day basis.
- The character of S corporation tax items is determined at the S corporation level. Once the tax character is determined at the S corporation level, the character stays the same when it flows from the S corporation to the shareholders.
- The tax items that comprise S corporation income or loss are divided into two categories: *separately stated items* and *nonseparately stated items*. **Separately stated items** are tax items that could potentially impact shareholders' tax liabilities differently.

4 Compute a shareholder's basis in their stock and the limitations on the deductibility of flow-through losses.

- At the end of the tax year, the shareholder's basis in their stock is adjusted in the following order:
  - First, contributions to capital increase the shareholder's adjusted basis.
  - Second, the shareholder's share of income, including tax-exempt income, increases the shareholder's adjusted basis.
  - Third, distributions to the shareholder from the accumulated adjustments account decrease the shareholder's adjusted basis.
  - Fourth, the shareholder's share of loss (including nondeductible expenses) decreases the shareholder's adjusted basis.
- Distributions and losses can never reduce a shareholder's stock basis below zero. Distributions that exceed the stock basis are treated as a return of capital. Losses that exceed the shareholder's basis are suspended and carried forward to future tax years.
- If a shareholder's allocated losses exceed their stock basis, the shareholder can also deduct losses against their *debt basis*. **Debt basis** for the shareholder is created when the shareholder has loaned money directly to the S corporation.
- Once an allocated loss has cleared the stock basis and debt basis hurdles, the loss deduction could be limited by the at-risk rules or passive loss rules.

5 Determine the tax effects of S corporation distributions to the shareholder and the corporation.

- If an S corporation distributes cash to its shareholders, the corporation will not recognize any gain or loss. If the S corporation distributes appreciated property, the corporation must recognize gain as if it had sold the property for its fair market value. On the other hand, if the S corporation distributes loss property, the loss cannot be recognized.
- The **accumulated adjustments account (AAA)** shows accumulated earnings that have not been distributed to shareholders during the years the S corporation has been classified as an S corporation. Distributions from the AAA are not taxable to the shareholders because S corporations have single taxation, and this income was taxed when it flowed to the shareholders in the year it was earned. Distributions from AAA also reduce the shareholder's stock basis.
- Assuming the corporation does have earnings and profits (E&P), the steps for determining the tax consequences are as follows:

  Step 1. Evaluate: Distributions are tax-free to the extent of AAA (recall that distributions from AAA also reduce stock basis).

  Step 2. Verify: Dividend income to the extent of E&P

  Step 3. Ascertain: Distributions are tax-free to the extent of stock basis (reduced for distributions from AAA in step 1).

  Step 4. Assess: Any remaining distribution is a capital gain.
- If there is no E&P, then only the last steps from above are needed to determine the tax consequences:

  Step 1. Evaluate: Distributions are tax-free to the extent of stock basis.

  Step 2. Assess: The remaining distribution is a capital gain.

6 **Compute the taxes that an S corporation may have to pay.**

- The **built-in gain (BIG) tax** may be assessed on a C corporation that makes an S election. Generally, if the S corporation sells property within five years of the S election and the property had a BIG on the date of the S election, then the BIG tax may apply.
  - A built-in gains tax is not imposed on a corporation that has always been an S corporation.
  - The tax is imposed at the highest corporate rate (21%) and is multiplied by the realized BIG for a given tax year.
  - The tax can only be imposed for a period of five years after the S election is made.
  - The maximum recognized BIG over the five-year recognition period is limited to the net amount of net unrealized built-in gain at the time of election. The **net unrealized built-in gain** is the excess of the BIGs over the BILs on the election date.
- If **passive investment income (PII)** exceeds 25% of gross receipts, the excess net passive investment income is taxed at a 21% rate to the S corporation. This provision applies only if the S corporation has earnings and profits from previous C corporation years on its balance sheet. The **net passive investment income tax** is computed as follows:

$$\frac{\text{Excess net PII}}{\text{PII}} \times \text{Net PII} \times 21\%$$

- A C corporation using LIFO that converts to an S corporation must recapture any amount by which the inventory's value under FIFO exceeds its value under LIFO as of the close of its last tax year as a C corporation.

Communications Application

Communication

S Corporation Built-In Gains Tax

(LO6) Gus is a 100% shareholder of Valencia Corporation, an accrual-based calendar-year S corporation. Valencia was a C corporation for eight years, until two years ago, when Gus and the corporation elected S status. At the time of the election, Valencia had the following assets:

	Fair market value	Adjusted basis	Built-in gain/loss
Cash	$ 6,600	$ 6,600	$ 0
Accounts receivable	4,300	4,300	0
Land (investment)	75,000	50,000	25,000
Delivery truck	8,000	10,000	(2,000)
Machinery	2,000	7,500	(5,500)
Totals	$95,900	$78,400	$17,500

In the current year, Valencia sold the land for $100,000. If Valencia had been a C corporation in the current year, its taxable income would be $222,000. What are the tax consequences to Valencia Corporation and Gus? Prepare a memo to Valencia care of Gus and a memo to the tax file.

Solution

Memo to Client

Hello Gus,

Thank you for contacting me regarding your tax question involving the sale of Valencia Corporation's land. When the S election was filed, your corporation had a net unrealized built-in gain on its assets of $17,500. This represents the difference between the assets' fair market values and adjusted bases. If assets owned on the effective date of the S election are sold within five years of the date of conversion to S status, it is possible that a built-in gains tax must be paid. The net recognized built-in gain for any year is limited to the *lesser* of:

1. The net of the recognized built-in gains and losses for the year,
2. The net unrealized built-in gains as of the S election date less the net recognized built-in gains in previous years, *or*
3. The corporation's taxable income for the year excluding the dividends received deduction and the net operating loss deduction.

The recognized gain from the sale of the land is computed as follows:

Amount realized	$100,000
Adjusted basis	50,000
Recognized gain	$ 50,000

Therefore, Valencia Corporation must pay a built-in gains tax of $3,675 ($17,500 × 21%). The recognized BIG is the *lesser* of:

1. $25,000 (recognized built-in gain on land),
2. $17,500 (initial net unrealized gain), *or*
3. $222,000 (taxable income computed as if Valencia was a C corporation in the current year)

Valencia reports a capital loss of $3,675, which represents the built-in gains tax due to the land sale. It is a capital loss because the land was a capital asset.

Please let me know if you have any questions.

Sincerely,
Carnes & Youngberg, CPAs

Tax Memo to the File

Facts: Gus is a 100% shareholder of Valencia Corporation, an accrual-based calendar-year S corporation. Valencia was a C corporation for eight years, until two years ago, when Gus and the corporation elected S status. At the time of the election, Valencia had the following assets:

	Fair market value	Adjusted basis	Built-in gain/loss
Cash	$ 6,600	$ 6,600	$ 0
Accounts Receivable	4,300	4,300	0
Land (investment)	75,000	50,000	25,000
Delivery truck	8,000	10,000	(2,000)
Machinery	2,000	7,500	(5,500)
Totals	$95,900	$78,400	$17,500

In the current year, Valencia sold the land for $100,000. If Valencia had been a C corporation in the current year, its taxable income would be $222,000.

Issue: What are the tax consequences to Valencia Corporation and Gus?

Conclusion: Valencia Corporation has a built-in gains tax of $3,675. The built-in gains tax will be considered a capital loss and allocated to Gus as its 100% shareholder.

Analysis: Under IRC §1374(a), "if for any taxable year beginning in the recognition period an S corporation has a net recognized built-in gain, there is hereby imposed a tax (computed under subsection (b)) on the income of such corporation for such taxable year."

When the S election was filed, Valencia corporation had a net unrealized built-in gain on its assets of $17,500. This represents the difference between the assets' fair market values and adjusted bases. If assets owned on the effective date of the S election are sold within five years of the date of conversion to S status, it is possible that a built-in gains tax must be paid. The net recognized built-in gain for any year is limited to the *lesser* of:

1. The net of the recognized built-in gains and losses for the year,
2. The net unrealized built-in gains as of the S election date less the net recognized built-in gains in previous years, *or*
3. The corporation's taxable income for the year exclusive of the dividends received deduction and the net operating loss deduction.

Therefore, Valencia Corporation must pay a built-in gains tax of $3,675 ($17,500 × 21%). on the recognized BIG is the *lesser* of:

1. $25,000 (recognized built-in gain on land),
2. $17,500 (initial net unrealized gain), or
3. $222,000 (taxable income computed as if Valencia was a C corporation in the current year)

Because the built-in gains tax was due to the sale of land, the $3,675 is a capital loss allocated 100% to Gus.

Ethics and Professional Responsibility Application

Ethics

S Corporation—Basis Adjustments

(LO4) Timone is a 35% shareholder in Lion King Corporation, an accrual-based calendar-year S corporation. Timone's basis in his S corporation interest was $18,900 at the beginning of the year. Timone's current year Schedule K-1 indicated an ordinary business loss of $14,000, dividend income of $1,200, and a distribution to Timone of $10,000. Timone prepared his Form 1040 for the current year and would like you to review his work. Upon review, Timone had reported an ordinary business loss on his Schedule E, page 2, of $14,000. What is your responsibility and advice to Timone? In addition to the chapter content, see *Statements on Standards for Tax Services* at www.aicpa-cima.com/resources/landing/statements-on-standards-for-tax-services, *Circular 230* at www.irs.gov/tax-professionals/office-of-professional-responsibility-and-circular-230, and Chapter 2, LO4, Tax Professional Responsibilities.

Solution

Timone's Form 1040, Schedule E, page 2, incorrectly deducted an ordinary business loss of $14,000. The correct calculation for Timone's ending basis and entries on his tax return are as follows:

Beginning basis	$18,900
Dividend income	1,200
Available basis	$20,100
Less: Distributions	(10,000)
Available basis	$10,100
Less: Ordinary business loss	(10,100)
Ending basis	$ 0

Timone must report dividend income of $1,200 on Form 1040, Schedule B, and an ordinary business loss of $10,100 on Form 1040, Schedule E, page 2. Timone's distribution reduces his stock basis, and his loss of $14,000 is limited to his stock basis after adjusting for dividend income and the distribution. Timone has a suspended loss carryforward of $3,900 ($14,000 – $10,100).

Under *Circular 230* §10.21, Knowledge of Client's Omission, "A practitioner who, having been retained by a client with respect to a matter administered by the Internal Revenue Service, knows that the client has not complied with the revenue laws of the United States or has made an error in or omission from any return, document, affidavit, or other paper which the client submitted or executed under the revenue laws of the United States, must advise the client promptly of the fact of such noncompliance, error, or omission. The practitioner must advise the client of the consequences as provided under the Code and regulations of such noncompliance, error, or omission." Also, under *Circular 230* Section 10.22, Diligence as to Accuracy, "a practitioner must exercise due diligence—(1) In preparing or assisting in the preparation of, approving, and filing tax returns, documents, affidavits, and other papers relating to Internal Revenue Service matters."

It is your responsibility as the tax practitioner to report all items of income and loss correctly on the tax return. You must advise Timone of the corrections and of the consequences if he does not comply and correct the return.

Tax Compliance Application

Compliance

Preparation of Form 1120-S and Schedule K-1

(LO3) Oak Creek Inc. (FEIN: 98-1234567) is an S corporation using the accrual method that has two shareholders. John (SSN: 123-45-6789) owns 70% of Oak Creek. The following items were reported on Oak Creek's Form 1120-S this year:

Gross receipts	$1,888,000
U.S. treasury bond interest income	$ 2,100
Municipal interest income	$ 300
Qualified dividend income	$ 2,800
Net short-term capital gain	$ 3,300
Cost of goods sold	$ 520,000
Salaries paid to other employees	$ 230,000
Salary paid to John	$ 100,000
Utilities	$ 36,000
Net Section 1231 gain	$ 14,000
Rent expense	$ 175,000
Charitable contributions	$ 25,000
Advertising	$ 12,000
Insurance expense	$ 24,000
Depreciation	$ 38,000
Section 179 expense	$ 32,000
Entertainment expense	$ 5,000
Business meals	$ 4,400
Fines and penalties	$ 1,200

How would these amounts be reported on John's Schedule K-1, and how would his salary be reported to him? Prepare Form 1120-S page 1, page 3, and Schedule K-1 for John. We use the 2024 Form 1120-S and Schedule K-1 because these were the most recent forms available at the time of publication.

Solution

We begin by separating these tax items into the bucket items and the separately stated items and using the bucket items to compute ordinary business income of $750,800.

Bucket items		**Separately stated items**	
Gross receipts	$1,888,000	U.S. treasury interest income	$ 2,100
Less:		Municipal interest income	$ 300
COGS	(520,000)	Net STCG	$ 3,300
Salaries paid to employees	(230,000)	Net Section 1231 gain	$14,000
Salary to John	(100,000)	Qualified dividend income	$ 2,800
Utilities	(36,000)		
Rent expense	(175,000)	Charitable contributions	$25,000
Advertising	(12,000)	Section 179 expense	$32,000
Insurance expense	(24,000)	Entertainment expense	$ 5,000
Depreciation	(38,000)	Business meals (50%)	$ 2,200
Business meals (50%)	(2,200)	Fines and penalties	$ 1,200
Ordinary business income	$ 750,800		

John's Schedule K-1 will reflect 70% of the ordinary business income and each separately stated item, as follows:

	Total	**John's allocation (70%)**
Ordinary business income	$750,800	$525,560
U.S. treasury interest income	$ 2,100	$ 1,470
Muni. interest income	$ 300	$ 210
Net STCG	$ 3,300	$ 2,310
Net Section 1231 gain	$ 14,000	$ 9,800
Qualified dividend income	$ 2,800	$ 1,960
Charitable contributions	$ 25,000	$ 17,500
Section 179 expense	$ 32,000	$ 22,400
Entertainment expense	$ 5,000	$ 3,500
Business meals	$ 2,200	$ 1,540
Fines and penalties	$ 1,200	$ 840

John's salary of $100,000 will be reported to him on his W-2 from Oak Creek, and it would be included on his Form 1040, page 1.

The entertainment expense and fines and penalties are not deductible. Business meals are 50% deductible.

Form **1120-S** — Department of the Treasury, Internal Revenue Service

U.S. Income Tax Return for an S Corporation

Do not file this form unless the corporation has filed or is attaching Form 2553 to elect to be an S corporation.
Go to *www.irs.gov/Form1120S* for instructions and the latest information.

OMB No. 1545-0123 — **2024**

For calendar year 2024 or tax year beginning , 2024, ending , 20

A S election effective date: 1/1/2024	Name: Oak Creek, Inc.	**D** Employer identification number: 98-1234567
B Business activity code number (see instructions)	TYPE OR PRINT — Number, street, and room or suite no. If a P.O. box, see instructions.: 100 Rock Drive	**E** Date incorporated: 1/1/2024
C Check if Sch. M-3 attached ☐	City or town, state or province, country, and ZIP or foreign postal code: Oak Creek, AZ 86341	**F** Total assets (see instructions): $

G Is the corporation electing to be an S corporation beginning with this tax year? See instructions. ☐ Yes ☐ No

H Check if: **(1)** ☐ Final return **(2)** ☐ Name change **(3)** ☐ Address change **(4)** ☐ Amended return **(5)** ☐ S election termination

I Enter the number of shareholders who were shareholders during any part of the tax year . . . 2

J Check if corporation: **(1)** ☐ Aggregated activities for section 465 at-risk purposes **(2)** ☐ Grouped activities for section 469 passive activity purposes

Caution: Include **only** trade or business income and expenses on lines 1a through 22. See the instructions for more information.

Income	1a	Gross receipts or sales 1,888,000 — **b** Less returns and allowances — **c** Balance			1c	1,888,000
	2	Cost of goods sold (attach Form 1125-A)			2	520,000
	3	Gross profit. Subtract line 2 from line 1c			3	1,368,000
	4	Net gain (loss) from Form 4797, Part II, line 17 (attach Form 4797)			4	
	5	Other income (loss) (see instructions—attach statement)			5	
	6	**Total income (loss).** Add lines 3 through 5			6	1,368,000
Deductions (see instructions for limitations)	7	Compensation of officers (see instructions—attach Form 1125-E)			7	100,000
	8	Salaries and wages (less employment credits)			8	230,000
	9	Repairs and maintenance			9	
	10	Bad debts			10	
	11	Rents			11	175,000
	12	Taxes and licenses			12	
	13	Interest (see instructions)			13	
	14	Depreciation from Form 4562 not claimed on Form 1125-A or elsewhere on return (attach Form 4562)			14	38,000
	15	Depletion **(do not deduct oil and gas depletion)**			15	
	16	Advertising			16	12,000
	17	Pension, profit-sharing, etc., plans			17	
	18	Employee benefit programs			18	
	19	Energy efficient commercial buildings deduction (attach Form 7205)			19	
	20	Other deductions (attach statement)			20	62,200
	21	**Total deductions.** Add lines 7 through 20			21	617,200
	22	**Ordinary business income (loss).** Subtract line 21 from line 6			22	750,800
Tax and Payments	23a	Excess net passive income or LIFO recapture tax (see instructions)	23a			
	b	Tax from Schedule D (Form 1120-S)	23b			
	c	Add lines 23a and 23b (see instructions for additional taxes)			23c	
	24a	Current year's estimated tax payments and preceding year's overpayment credited to the current year	24a			
	b	Tax deposited with Form 7004	24b			
	c	Credit for federal tax paid on fuels (attach Form 4136)	24c			
	d	Elective payment election amount from Form 3800	24d			
	z	Add lines 24a through 24d			24z	
	25	Estimated tax penalty (see instructions). Check if Form 2220 is attached ☐			25	
	26	**Amount owed.** If line 24z is smaller than the total of lines 23c and 25, enter amount owed			26	
	27	**Overpayment.** If line 24z is larger than the total of lines 23c and 25, enter amount overpaid			27	
	28	Enter amount from line 27: **Credited to 2025 estimated tax** **Refunded**			28	

Sign Here

Under penalties of perjury, I declare that I have examined this return, including accompanying schedules and statements, and to the best of my knowledge and belief, it is true, correct, and complete. Declaration of preparer (other than taxpayer) is based on all information of which preparer has any knowledge.

Signature of officer — Date — Title

May the IRS discuss this return with the preparer shown below? See instructions. ☐ **Yes** ☐ **No**

Paid Preparer Use Only

Print/Type preparer's name	Preparer's signature	Date	Check ☐ if self-employed	PTIN
Firm's name			Firm's EIN	
Firm's address			Phone no.	

For Paperwork Reduction Act Notice, see separate instructions. Cat. No. 11510H Form **1120-S** (2024)

Form 1120-S (2024) Page **3**

Schedule B **Other Information** (see instructions) *(continued)*

		Yes	No
12	During the tax year, did the corporation have any non-shareholder debt that was canceled, was forgiven, or had the terms modified so as to reduce the principal amount of the debt?		
	If "Yes," enter the amount of principal reduction . . . $		
13	During the tax year, was a qualified subchapter S subsidiary election terminated or revoked? If "Yes," see instructions .		
14a	Did the corporation make any payments that would require it to file Form(s) 1099?		
b	If "Yes," did or will the corporation file required Form(s) 1099?		
15	Is the corporation attaching Form 8996 to certify as a Qualified Opportunity Fund?		
	If "Yes," enter the amount from Form 8996, line 15 . . . $		
16	At any time during the tax year, did the corporation: (a) receive (as a reward, award, or payment for property or services); or (b) sell, exchange, or otherwise dispose of a digital asset (or a financial interest in a digital asset)? See instructions		

Schedule K **Shareholders' Pro Rata Share Items**

Section	Line	Description	Sub-line	Sub-amount	Line	Total amount
Income (Loss)	1	Ordinary business income (loss) (page 1, line 22)			1	750,800
	2	Net rental real estate income (loss) (attach Form 8825)			2	
	3a	Other gross rental income (loss)	3a			
	b	Expenses from other rental activities (attach statement)	3b			
	c	Other net rental income (loss). Subtract line 3b from line 3a			3c	
	4	Interest income			4	2,100
	5	Dividends: a Ordinary dividends			5a	2,800
		b Qualified dividends	5b	2,800		
	6	Royalties			6	
	7	Net short-term capital gain (loss) (attach Schedule D (Form 1120-S))			7	
	8a	Net long-term capital gain (loss) (attach Schedule D (Form 1120-S))			8a	
	b	Collectibles (28%) gain (loss)	8b			
	c	Unrecaptured section 1250 gain (attach statement)	8c			
	9	Net section 1231 gain (loss) (attach Form 4797)			9	14,000
	10	Other income (loss) (see instructions) . . . Type:			10	
Deductions	11	Section 179 deduction (attach Form 4562)			11	32,000
	12a	Cash charitable contributions			12a	25,000
	b	Noncash charitable contributions			12b	
	c	Investment interest expense			12c	
	d	Section 59(e)(2) expenditures . . . Type:			12d	
	e	Other deductions (see instructions) . . . Type:			12e	
Credits	13a	Low-income housing credit (section 42(j)(5))			13a	
	b	Low-income housing credit (other)			13b	
	c	Qualified rehabilitation expenditures (rental real estate) (attach Form 3468, if applicable)			13c	
	d	Other rental real estate credits (see instructions) Type:			13d	
	e	Other rental credits (see instructions) . . . Type:			13e	
	f	Biofuel producer credit (attach Form 6478)			13f	
	g	Other credits (see instructions) . . . Type:			13g	
International	14	Attach Schedule K-2 (Form 1120-S), Shareholders' Pro Rata Share Items—International, and check this box to indicate you are reporting items of international tax relevance ☐				
Alternative Minimum Tax (AMT) Items	15a	Post-1986 depreciation adjustment			15a	
	b	Adjusted gain or loss			15b	
	c	Depletion (other than oil and gas)			15c	
	d	Oil, gas, and geothermal properties—gross income			15d	
	e	Oil, gas, and geothermal properties—deductions			15e	
	f	Other AMT items (attach statement)			15f	
Items Affecting Shareholder Basis	16a	Tax-exempt interest income			16a	300
	b	Other tax-exempt income			16b	
	c	Nondeductible expenses			16c	8,400
	d	Distributions (attach statement if required) (see instructions)			16d	
	e	Repayment of loans from shareholders			16e	
	f	Foreign taxes paid or accrued			16f	

Form **1120-S** (2024)

671124

☐ Final K-1 ☐ Amended K-1 OMB No. 1545-0123

Schedule K-1 (Form 1120-S) **2024**

Department of the Treasury
Internal Revenue Service

For calendar year 2024, or tax year

beginning / / 2024 ending / /

Shareholder's Share of Income, Deductions, Credits, etc.

See separate instructions.

Part I Information About the Corporation

A Corporation's employer identification number
98-1234567

B Corporation's name, address, city, state, and ZIP code
Oak Creek, Inc.
100 Rock Drive
Oak Creek, AZ 86341

C IRS Center where corporation filed return

D Corporation's total number of shares
Beginning of tax year 1,000
End of tax year 1,000

Part II Information About the Shareholder

E Shareholder's identifying number
123-45-6789

F1 Shareholder's name, address, city, state, and ZIP code
John Wood
222 Slim Road
Oak Creek, AZ 86341

F2 If the shareholder is a disregarded entity, a trust, an estate, or a nominee or similar person, enter the individual or entity responsible for reporting:
TIN ________ Name ________

F3 What type of entity is this shareholder? ________

G Current year allocation percentage . . . 70 %

H Shareholder's number of shares
Beginning of tax year 700
End of tax year 700

I Loans from shareholder
Beginning of tax year . . . . $ ________
End of tax year . . . . $ ________

For IRS Use Only

Part III Shareholder's Share of Current Year Income, Deductions, Credits, and Other Items

Line	Item	Amount
1	Ordinary business income (loss)	525,560
2	Net rental real estate income (loss)	
3	Other net rental income (loss)	
4	Interest income	1,470
5a	Ordinary dividends	1,960
5b	Qualified dividends	1,960
6	Royalties	
7	Net short-term capital gain (loss)	2,310
8a	Net long-term capital gain (loss)	
8b	Collectibles (28%) gain (loss)	
8c	Unrecaptured section 1250 gain	
9	Net section 1231 gain (loss)	9,800
10	Other income (loss)	
11	Section 179 deduction	22,400
12 A	Other deductions	17,500
13	Credits	
14	Schedule K-3 is attached if checked . . . . . ☐	
15	Alternative minimum tax (AMT) items	
16	Items affecting shareholder basis	
A		210
C		5,880
17	Other information	

18 ☐ More than one activity for at-risk purposes*
19 ☐ More than one activity for passive activity purposes*

* See attached statement for additional information.

Key Terms

End-of-Chapter Assessment

Discussion Questions

1. **(LO1)** Does an S corporation owe tax with Form 1120-S? Explain.
2. **(LO1)** Describe three facts or characteristics of an S corporation.
3. **(LO1)** Can more than 100 individuals own stock in an S corporation? Explain.
4. **(LO2)** PIC Corporation has been a regular C corporation for the last 10 years, filing on a calendar-year basis. All shareholders are individuals. For the current tax year (Year 11), all shareholders agree to sign an S election. For the election to be effective for the current tax year, it must be filed by what date?
5. **(LO3)** Explain the timing of the reporting of income to S corporation shareholders.
6. **(LO3)** Why are items separately stated in determining reportable income for an S corporation shareholder?
7. **(LO4)** What is the shareholder's basis in an S corporation, and why is it important to track this amount?
8. **(LO4)** Discuss the basis, at-risk, and passive loss hurdles involved in deducting a loss for an S corporation shareholder.
9. **(LO5)** Discuss the possible tax consequences to the S corporation of distributions.
10. **(LO5)** What does the accumulated adjustments account represent?
11. **(LO5)** When does the post-termination transition period (PTTP) end?
12. **(LO6)** What are the three taxes that an S corporation might be subject to?
13. **(LO6)** How is the net passive investment income tax computed?

Multiple Choice Questions

1. **(LO1)** A calendar-year S corporation must file its tax return without extensions by which date?
   - **a.** March 15
   - **b.** April 15
   - **c.** May 15
   - **d.** Any of these dates
2. **(LO1)** An S corporation cannot have more than how many shareholders?
   - **a.** 100
   - **b.** 50
   - **c.** 25
   - **d.** 10
3. **(LO1)** Which of the following characteristics would violate the eligibility requirements for an S corporation?
   - **a.** Issuing both common and preferred stock
   - **b.** Issuing both voting and nonvoting stock
   - **c.** Having stock owned by more than 50 shareholders
   - **d.** Having a shareholder who is a resident of the United States but not a citizen
4. **(LO1)** Which of the following is *not* a characteristic of an S corporation?
   - **a.** Shareholders have unlimited liability.
   - **b.** An S corporation can have only one class of stock.
   - **c.** Shareholders can work in the business as employees.
   - **d.** Income flows through and is taxed to the shareholders.

5. **(LO2)** Which of the following forms is used to file an S election?

   a. Form 4562

   b. Form 2553

   c. Form 2120

   d. Form 7004

6. **(LO2)** An S Corporation has 10,000 shares of voting common stock and 8,000 shares of nonvoting common stock issued and outstanding. The S election can be revoked voluntarily with the consent of the shareholders holding how many shares on the day of the revocation?

	Shares of voting stock	Shares of nonvoting stock
a.	6,000	2,000
b.	4,000	5,000
c.	5,000	5,000
d.	9,000	0

7. **(LO3)** If Dozer Inc. is a calendar S corporation, when is Form 1120-S due?

   a. February 15th of the next year

   b. March 15th of the next year

   c. April 15th of the next year

   d. None of the above

8. **(LO3)** If Sherique received a distribution of $10,000 and her S corporation K-1 reflected ordinary business income of $6,000, what amount is correctly reported as income on Sherique's Form 1040? Assume Sherique's basis in the S corporation is $20,000.

   a. $6,000

   b. $10,000

   c. $16,000

   d. None; Sherique is not taxed on income from an S corporation.

9. **(LO3)** Which of the following is *not* a separately stated item in calculating income for an S corporation?

   a. Interest income

   b. Dividend income

   c. Capital gains

   d. Gross receipts from sales

10. **(LO4)** Dimitri has a basis at the beginning of the year of $12,000 in an S corporation. His K-1 for the year reflects dividend income of $2,000, a distribution of $7,000, and an ordinary business loss of $10,000. What is Dimitri's ending basis?

   a. $0

   b. $14,000

   c. $7,000

   d. ($3,000)

11. **(LO5)** Spartan Company is an S corporation that has an $80,000 recourse loan on its balance sheet. Shareholder Sparty has $45,000 basis in his stock before considering the recourse loan. What is Sparty's basis in his S corporation stock after considering the recourse loan?

   a. ($35,000)

   b. $45,000

   c. $80,000

   d. $125,000

12. **(LO5)** The accumulated adjustments account includes which of the following?

   a. Tax-exempt income

   b. Expenses relating to production of tax-exempt income

   c. Federal taxes relating to a C corporation year

   d. None of the above

13. **(LO5)** Which of the following is *not* included in the accumulated adjustments account?

   a. Section 1231

   b. Long-term capital loss

   c. Charitable contributions

   d. Tax-exempt interest income

14. **(LO5)** Patrice owns 100% of Quilt Corporation. Quilt Corporation was organized three years ago as an S corporation. Information for Patrice and Quilt is as follows as of the end of the current tax year:

Patrice's stock basis	$18,000
AAA	$15,000

Patrice receives a distribution of $20,000 from Quilt at the end of the tax year. What is Patrice's reportable income, if any, and ending stock basis?

   a. Dividend income $2,000; stock basis $0

   b. Dividend income $20,000; stock basis $18,000

   c. Capital gain $2,000; stock basis $0

   d. Capital gain $20,000; stock basis $18,000

15. **(LO6)** Passive investment income includes all of the following *except*:

   a. Interest income

   b. Dividend income

   c. Sales revenue

   d. Annuities

16. **(LO6)** Which of the following statements is *not* true regarding the taxation of S corporation income?

   a. Some S corporation income items are separately stated when flowing through to its shareholders.

   b. An S corporation shareholder can have a 15% profit sharing ratio and a 25% loss sharing ratio.

   c. In limited circumstances, an S corporation may be required to pay certain taxes.

   d. An S corporation with only individuals as shareholders will have a required tax year ending on December 31.

Brief Exercises

1. **(LO1)** Janice owns 100 shares of stock of Royal Corporation, a calendar-year S corporation. The following individuals also own stock in Royal.

Janice's husband	100 shares
Janice's daughter	100 shares
Janice's mother	50 shares
Janice's cousin	25 shares
Janice's niece	25 shares

How many shares are included as part of Janice's shares as a family member?

2. **(LO2)** Sunny Inc. is a calendar-year C corporation that would like to become an S corporation. Determine when the S election would be effective in the following situations:

   a. Sunny files Form 2553 on February 14 of the current year.

   b. Sunny files Form 2553 on December 10 of the previous year.

   c. Sunny files Form 2553 on April 10 of the current year.

3. **(LO2)** Hans owns 60% of Timber Inc., a calendar-year S corporation. Tyler owns 20%, and Bridgett owns 20%. If Hans sells 40% to Debbye, will this result in a termination of the S election? Explain.

4. **(LO3)** As of January 1 of this year, Aisha owned all 1,000 shares of a calendar-year S corporation, Diamond Inc. On October 31, the 304th day of this year, Aisha sold 400 shares to Derek. Diamond reported $128,000 in ordinary business income for the entire year and made no distributions. What amount of income should Diamond report to Aisha on her Schedule K-1?

5. **(LO4)** Fulmer, an individual, owns 50% of Roadhouse, an S corporation. At the beginning of the year, Fulmer's basis in his stock in Roadhouse was $50,000. Roadhouse reported the following items from operations during the current year:

Ordinary loss	$20,000
Municipal interest income	$ 4,000
Section 1231 gain	$ 6,000
Dividend income	$ 8,000

What was Fulmer's basis in his stock in Roadhouse at year-end?

6. **(LO4)** LKM Company is an S corporation that has a $90,000 recourse loan on its balance sheet. Kate owns 100% of LKM and has a $40,000 basis in her stock before considering the recourse loan. What is Kate's basis in her S corporation stock?

7. **(LO5)** Declan is a 100% shareholder of Clover Inc., an S corporation. Clover has the following tax items this year:

Ordinary business income	$66,000
Tax-exempt interest income	$ 1,200
Expenses related to tax-exempt income	$ 500
Dividend income	$ 3,300
Section 179 expense	$15,000
AAA, January 1	$75,000
OAA, January 1	$ 2,200

Declan's basis in his stock at the beginning of the year is $50,000. What is Declan's basis at the end of the tax year, and what are the balances in the AAA and the OAA?

8. **(LO5)** Lion Inc. is an S corporation whose sole shareholder is Ella. After considering the current year's income, Ella has a basis in her stock of $130,000, and Lion has $220,000 in its AAA. On the last day of the tax year, Lion distributes property to Ella with a FMV of $35,000 and an adjusted basis of $75,000. How much income does Ella recognize on this distribution?

9. **(LO5)** Badger Corporation is a calendar-year S corporation that is owned 100% by Bucky. At the end of the tax year, after considering all current income and losses, Bucky has a basis in his stock of $80,000, and Badger has $60,000 of E&P and $40,000 in its AAA. Badger distributes cash of $75,000 to Bucky on the last day of the tax year. How much taxable income does Bucky have from this distribution?

10. **(LO6)** Volunteer Corporation had been a regular C corporation for seven years when it made an S election three years ago. On the date of the S election, Volunteer owned land with an adjusted basis of $90,000 and a FMV of $140,000. In the current year, three years after the S election, Volunteer sells the land for $160,000. How much of the $160,000 is subject to the built-in gains tax, and what is the BIG tax, if any?

Application Problems

1. **(LO1)** John owns 40% of FastTrack, Inc., a calendar-year S corporation. John receives the following from FastTrack:

   - $30,000 cash of $100,000 distributed to FastTrack shareholders
   - Proportionate distribution of 100 shares of nonvoting stock
   - A loan of $5,000 with appropriate terms and interest rate

   Which of these results in a termination of the S corporation?

2. **(LO2)** Answer the provided question for each of the independent situations below. Assume all corporations are S corporations.

   a. 40% of the shareholders of Almighty Inc., a calendar-year S corporation, would like to terminate the S election. If they elected on March 10 to terminate, when would the election be effective?

   b. Assume that Nashville Corporation issues a second class of stock on September 10. What are the tax consequences for Nashville?

   c. Drummer Inc. has passive investment income that exceeds 25% of gross receipts for three consecutive years. Drummer has earnings and profits from previous C corporation years. When will the S election terminate?

3. **(LO3)** As of January 1 of this year, Colin owned 500 shares of the 1,000 shares outstanding of a calendar-year S corporation, Baker Corporation. On March 8, the 67th day of this year, Colin sold 100 shares to Ronaldo. Baker reported $188,000 in ordinary business loss for the entire year to the shareholders and made no distributions. What amount of loss should the S corporation report to Colin on his Schedule K-1?

4. **(LO3)** Identify whether each of the following items is part of calculating ordinary business income (a nonseparately stated item) or a separately stated item:

   a. Short-term capital gain
   b. Municipal interest income
   c. Rent paid
   d. Insurance expense
   e. Section 179
   f. Charitable contributions
   g. Section 1231 loss
   h. Depreciation expense
   i. Qualified dividend income
   j. General business credit
   k. Wages paid
   l. Section 1245 depreciation recapture

5. **(LO3)** Beeker, Inc. is an S corporation that has two shareholders. Alvin owns 35% of Beeker. He also works at Beeker, and Beeker paid him $130,000 this year for his services. The following items were reported on Beeker's Form 1120-S this year:

Gross receipts	$2,600,000
Municipal interest income	$ 1,200
Net short-term capital gain	$ 8,800
Cost of goods sold	$ 569,000
Salaries and wages (including $130,000 to Alvin)	$ 515,000
Utilities	$ 38,000
Net Section 1231 gain	$ 22,000
Rent expense	$ 178,000
Charitable contributions	$ 39,000
Advertising	$ 15,000
Insurance expense	$ 26,000
Depreciation	$ 72,000
Section 179 expense	$ 33,000

How would these amounts be reported on Alvin's Schedule K-1, and how would his salary be reported to him?

6. **(LO4)** Shuchang Lee owns 20% of Lee Corporation, a calendar-year S corporation. His beginning basis in his stock is $44,500, and his Schedule K-1 reflects the following items for the current year:

Ordinary business income	$29,000
Interest income	$ 1,100
Long-term capital gain	$12,500
Section 179	$ 5,200
Nondeductible entertainment expenses	$ 600
Distributions	$13,000

What is Shuchang's ending basis in his stock for the current year in Lee Corporation?

7. **(LO4)** Lucille Kudrow owns 25% of Kudrow Corporation, a calendar-year S corporation. Her beginning basis in her stock is $50,000, and her Schedule K-1 reflects the following items for the current year:

Ordinary business income	$22,000
Municipal interest income	$ 1,000
Short-term capital gain	$ 8,000
Distributions	$85,000

What is Lucille's ending basis in her stock for the current year in Kudrow Corporation?

8. **(LO4)** Mark Davenport owns 40% of Davenport Corporation, a calendar-year S corporation. His beginning basis in his stock is $33,000, and his Schedule K-1 reflects the following items for the current year:

Ordinary business loss	$25,000
Dividend income	$ 4,000
Section 1231 gain	$ 6,000
Distributions	$20,000

What is Mark's ending basis in his stock for the current year in Davenport Corporation? How much of Mark's loss is deductible?

9. **(LO4)** JKLM is an S corporation that has been in existence for seven years. J is a 25% shareholder and has a basis of $60,000 in his stock at the beginning of the year. Because the corporation was having cash flow problems this year, J loaned it $30,000. The corporation has an ordinary loss for the year of $400,000. How much of this loss may J deduct on his return, assuming it is not a passive loss?

10. **(LO4)** Carly and Russell are married and file a joint tax return. They have the following results from their trades and businesses for 2024:

Landscaping sole proprietorship	$ 78,000
Partnership distributive share	$ 75,000
S corporation distributive share	($782,000)

How much can they deduct for these business losses, assuming that the losses are not passive and that they have sufficient basis and at-risk amount to deduct the losses?

11. **(LO4 Advanced Topic)** Kelly is a 100% shareholder in an S corporation. In the current year, the S corporation contributes long-term capital gain property to a qualified charity with an adjusted basis of $13,000 and a FMV of $18,000.

    a. What are the tax consequences of this contribution to Kelly and the S corporation if Kelly's basis in her stock before the contribution is $23,000?
    b. What are the tax consequences of this contribution to Kelly and the S corporation if Kelly's basis in her stock before the contribution is $0.

12. **(LO5)** Tyrone is a 100% shareholder of Pigskin Inc., an S corporation. Pigskin has the following tax items this year:

Ordinary business income	$295,000
Life insurance proceeds from death of key officer	$100,000
Premiums paid on life insurance of key officer	$ 12,000
Dividend income	$ 5,500
Fines and penalties	$ 10,000
AAA, January 1	$175,000
OAA, January 1	$ 12,700

Pigskin Inc. is the beneficiary of the life insurance policy. Tyrone's basis in his stock at the beginning of the year is $40,000. What is Tyrone's basis at the end of the tax year, and what are the balances in the AAA and the OAA?

13. **(LO5)** Dew is a calendar-year S corporation that is owned 100% by Deacon. At the end of the tax year, after considering all current year income and losses, Deacon has a basis in his stock of $60,000. Dew has $40,000 of E&P and $20,000 in its AAA. Dew distributes cash of $55,000 to Deacon on the last day of the tax year. After the distribution, what balance does Dew have in its E&P and AAA? What are the tax consequences to Deacon?

14. **(LO5)** Chipper Corporation, a calendar-year C corporation, made an S election effective on January 1 of the current year, when it had E&P of $74,000. Rosemary is the sole shareholder of Chipper, and her basis was $42,000 at the beginning of the year. For the current tax year, Chipper had the following items:

Ordinary business income	$88,000
Tax-exempt interest	$ 1,000
Short-term capital gain	$ 6,000
Charitable contribution	$ 4,000
Expenses related to tax-exempt income	$ 500
Fines paid	$ 750
Distribution	$40,000

What are the tax consequences of the $40,000 distribution to Rosemary if the AAA bypass election is made?

15. **(LO5)** Buffalo Corporation has been an S corporation for ten years, but the shareholders voted to terminate the S election as of January 1, Year 11. At the end of Year 10, there was a balance in the AAA of $32,000. Hank, the sole shareholder, had a basis in his stock of $47,000. During Year 11, Hank received a distribution of $19,000 cash and machinery with a FMV of $7,000 and adjusted basis of $11,000. Buffalo has E&P of $39,000 at the end of Year 11. What are the tax consequences of the distributions to Buffalo and Hank?

16. **(LO6)** Neon Corporation had been a C corporation for 13 years and made an S election this year. Neon owns the following assets on the effective date of the S election:

	Adjusted basis	FMV
Land	$100,000	$200,000
Building	$400,000	$360,000

a. Assuming Neon sells the land three years after the S election date for $180,000, compute the BIG tax, if any.

b. Same as part a, except that Neon also sells the building three years later for $335,000, when it has a basis of $350,000.

17. **(LO6)** Crabapple, Inc. had been a C corporation for six years when it made an S corporation election effective at the beginning of Year 15. At the time of the election, Crabapple had the following assets and BIGs and BILs:

	Adjusted basis	FMV
Cash	$ 60,000	$ 60,000
Inventory	$100,000	$130,000
Land	$ 85,000	$155,000
Machine	$220,000	$180,000

In Year 15, after the S election, Crabapple sold the inventory for $145,000. In Year 16, Crabapple sold the land for $150,000. What is Crabapple's BIG tax for Year 16?

18. **(LO6)** Lane Corporation is an S corporation that has the following tax information for the current tax year:

Revenue from operations	$55,000
Interest income	$11,000
Municipal interest income	$ 3,000
Dividend income	$10,500

Expenses related to the production of the passive income are $2,000. Lane has $23,000 of E&P from when it previously was a C corporation. What is Lane's passive investment income tax for the year?

Tax Planning Problems

Planning

1. **(LO4)** Tanker Corporation is a calendar-year S corporation. Tucker owns 100% of Tanker Corporation. Tucker's basis in his stock is $55,000, and Tanker has the following in the current year:

Ordinary business loss	$65,000
Short-term capital gain	$ 5,000

Tucker would like to receive a distribution this year. What advice can you give Tucker?

2. **(LO5)** Acre is an S corporation whose sole shareholder is Amy. After considering the current year's income, Amy has a basis in her stock of $100,000, and Acre has $175,000 in its AAA. Acre is considering distributing property to Amy on the last day of the tax year with an adjusted basis of $82,000 and FMV of $60,000. Should Acre distribute this property? What advice can you provide?

Professional Development Skills

Communication Problem

Communication

1. (LO1) **S Corporation—Number of Shareholders** Umbrella Inc. is a calendar-year S corporation with 100 shareholders. Your clients, Jose and Hermella Taquira, are each shareholders in Umbrella Inc., and they inform you that they are divorcing by year-end. They have asked you to provide advice as to the tax consequences of their divorce as it relates to the S corporation. Prepare a memo to the Taquieras explaining the tax consequences.

Ethics and Professional Responsibilities Problem

Ethics

1. (LO4) **S Corporation—Reasonable Salary** Jake is a 100% owner of Corporate Risk Insurance Company (CRIC), a calendar-year S corporation. In its first two years of operations, CRIC did not pay Jake a salary for the work he performed. Instead, Jake received a distribution. Jake has hired you to prepare this year's Form 1120-S and his Form 1040. Jake would like to continue receiving distributions instead of a salary to avoid having to pay any payroll taxes. What is your responsibility and your advice to Jake?

In addition to the chapter content, see Statements on Standards for Tax Services at www.aicpa-cima.com/resources/landing/statements-on-standards-for-tax-services, Circular 230 at www.irs.gov/tax-professionals/office-of-professional-responsibility-and-circular-230, and Chapter 2, LO4, Tax Professional Responsibilities.

Research Problem

Research

1. (LO2) **Revocation of S Corporation Status** Chain, Inc., was a calendar-year C corporation that properly executed Form 2553 by the 15th day of the third month of the tax year to be an S corporation in its year of formation. All shareholders consented to have the corporation be an S corporation. When Chain filed its current tax return, it completed and filed Form 1120 to be treated as a C corporation. Is Chain a C corporation or an S corporation?

Tax Compliance and Planning Problem

Compliance Planning

1. (LO3) **Form 1120-S and Schedule K-1** Volunteer Inc. (FEIN: 98-1234567) is an S corporation using the accrual method that has two shareholders. Smokey (SSN: 123-45-6789) owns 60% of Volunteer. The following items were reported on Volunteer's Form 1120-S this year:

Gross receipts	$1,480,000
U.S. treasury bond interest income	$ 1,500
Municipal interest income	$ 600
Qualified dividend income	$ 2,400
Net long-term capital gain	$ 4,800
Cost of goods sold	$ 380,000
Salaries paid to other employees	$ 180,000
Salary paid to Smokey	$ 100,000
Utilities	$ 24,000
Net Section 1231 gain	$ 16,000
Rent expense	$ 166,000
Charitable contributions	$ 20,000

Advertising	$ 12,000
Insurance expense	$ 36,000
Depreciation	$ 45,000
Section 179 expense	$ 30,000
Entertainment expense	$ 5,500
Business meals	$ 4,600

How would these amounts be reported on Smokey's Schedule K-1, and how would his salary be reported to him? Prepare Form 1120-S page 1, page 3, and Schedule K-1 for Smokey.

Excel Problem

Excel

1. **(LO4) Calculation of Basis** Hudson owns 100% of River Corporation, a calendar-year S corporation. In the following independent situations, determine Hudson's ending basis and tax results. Create an Excel spreadsheet to show your results and calculations.

	Scenario 1	Scenario 2	Scenario 3
Beginning basis	$10,000	$10,000	$10,000
Dividend income	$ 3,000	$ 3,000	$ 3,000
Tax-exempt interest	$ 1,200	$ 1,200	$ 1,200
Distribution	$10,000	$10,000	$15,000
Ordinary business loss	($ 3,000)	($ 5,000)	($ 5,000)

CPA Exam Preparation: Task-Based Simulations

1. **(LO3) Form 1120-S—Ordinary Business Income** Cloud 9 Corporation is an accrual-basis, calendar-year S corporation that manufactures and sells computers and parts. It also has begun to lease servers and provide cloud services. The income statement and Form 1120-S, U.S. Income Tax Return for an S Corporation, has been prepared by the in-house accountant, who would like you to review Form 1120-S for accuracy. After reviewing the Exhibits, you will identify whether all line items entered are correct or incorrect and enter the correct entries onto a spreadsheet that is provided.

Go to Wiley's book companion site to complete the Task-Based Simulation.

2. **(LO4) Calculation of Ordinary Business Income (OBI) and Basis** Stefanie, Jamie, and Lydia own Classic Brides, a calendar-year S corporation, in Chicago. Stefanie and Jamie each own 30%, and Lydia owns 40%. Classic Brides is a boutique bridal shop that has been serving brides, bridesmaids, and mothers of the bride and groom since Year 1. It has always been an S corporation. Its book income is $52,800 for Year 3; see the book income calculation in the Exhibits tab. Lydia's beginning stock basis is $10,000. She also made a loan to Classic Brides of $5,000. The beginning Accumulated Adjustments Account (AAA) for Classic Brides is $30,000. You will be asked to calculate ordinary business income for Classic Brides, Lydia's ending stock basis, and the ending AAA for Year 3, as well as what Lydia's ending loan basis is if she receives a certain cash distribution.

Go to Wiley's book companion site to complete the Task-Based Simulation.

3. **(LO4) Formation and Distributions from an S Corporation** Dikembe and Kofi formed a calendar-year S corporation in May, Year 31. Dikembe and Kofi are equal shareholders. You will be presented with five *independent* questions and asked to select an answer for each.

Go to Wiley's book companion site to complete the Task-Based Simulation.

4. **(LO5) Distributions and Basis Adjustments** Kalani formed a calendar-year C corporation, Moondrop Inc., in August, Year 38. Kalani is sole shareholder of Moondrop. In January, Year 39, Kalani completed Form 2553 and elected S corporation status for Moondrop beginning in January, Year 39. You will be presented with five *independent* questions and asked to select an answer for each.

Go to Wiley's book companion site to complete the Task-Based Simulation.

CHAPTER 9

Choice of Business Entity

iQoncept/Shutterstock

Before studying this chapter, you should know or, if necessary, review

Chapter 3 Fundamentals of Corporate Taxation
Chapter 4 Corporate Taxation: Distributions, Redemptions, and Liquidations
Chapter 5 Corporate Taxation: Related Corporations and Reorganizations
Chapter 6 Partnerships: Formations, Basis, and Reporting of Income
Chapter 7 Partnership Taxation: Distributions, Sales, and Advanced Topics
Chapter 8 S Corporations

Chapter Introduction

VIDEO CONTENT

In previous chapters, you were introduced to Aletta. Aletta has operated a hair salon for the last seven years as a sole proprietorship. She owns the building that she uses for her business, as well as the equipment in her shop. She has recently learned that her current business structure as a sole proprietorship is very risky for her because she has unlimited liability. Aletta has learned that each business entity form (corporations, partnerships, limited liability companies [LLCs], and S corporations) has certain strengths and weaknesses. A friend who is a long-time business owner has recommended that she organize her business as a partnership, as this will give her single taxation. A family member, though, has told her that her business will have unlimited liability as a partnership so she should organize it as a corporation. However, she has read on the internet that corporations are subject to double taxation and that a limited liability company would be the best choice. With these conflicting opinions, she is not sure which form is best for her, but she is convinced that she should not be operating as a sole proprietorship. Aletta would like to see an analysis of the pros and cons of each business entity form before making a final decision.

In this chapter, we build on what you have already learned so far in this book and summarize the factors that should be considered by business owners like Aletta when choosing the best entity form for their business. The number of businesses that use four major entity types is shown in the following illustration:[1]

[1]Information is from the most recent IRS data available. Data is for 2021 except for S corporations, which is from 2017, and C corporations, which is from 2020. U.S. Internal Revenue Service, *Statistics of Income: Corporate Income Tax Returns*, Publication 5655, Catalog Number 931611, U.S. Department of the Treasury, Rev. Sept. 2023, www.irs.gov/pub/irs-pdf/p5655.pdf; *Tax Stats - Partnership statistics by sector or industry*. Statistics of Income Division, Partnerships, U.S. Department of the Treasury, May 2023, www.irs.gov/pub/irs-soi/21pa01.xlsx; U.S. Internal Revenue Service, *SOI Tax Stats - S Corporation statistics*, Statistics of Income Division: 2017, U.S. Department of the Treasury, Table 2.4, Publication 16, Sept. 2020, www.irs.gov/pub/irs-soi/17co24ccr.xlsx; U.S. Internal Revenue Service, *SOI Tax Stats - Nonfarm sole proprietorship statistics*, Statistics of Income Division, Sole Proprietorship Returns 2020, U.S. Department of the Treasury, Nov. 2023, www.irs.gov/pub/irs-soi/21sp01br.xls.

	C corporations	S corporations	Partnerships	Sole proprietorships
Number of tax returns filed	6,400,000	4,725,684	4,467,584	29,075,643

Single-member LLCs are included as sole proprietorships in these numbers. There are more C corporations than either S corporations or partnerships, with the number of S corporations and partnerships being similar.

This chapter is divided into four main sections:

- Identifying the legal forms available to business owners
- Reviewing the key characteristics that influence the choice of entity
- Summarizing the advantages and disadvantages of partnerships/limited liability companies versus S corporations
- Comparing the tax consequences of sales of ownership interest and liquidating distributions across different business entities

LEARNING OBJECTIVES	TOPICS	PRACTICE OPPORTUNITIES

1 Identify the legal forms available to business owners.	**9.1 Business Structures**
	• Legal Forms of Business
	• Tax Classifications for Businesses
	  • Check-the-Box Regulations
	  • *Per Se* Corporations
	  • Other Entities
	  • Other Check-the-Box Rules
		• Example 9.1.1 Using a Business Entity to Implement a Tax Strategy
		• Example 9.1.2 Check-the-Box Regulations
		• Practice Problem 9.1.1 Sole Proprietorship
		• Practice Problem 9.1.2 Sole Owner

2 Understand the tax and non-tax characteristics for each business entity.	**9.2 Characteristics of Tax Entities**
	• Ability to Raise Capital
	• Limited Liability
	• Double Taxation of Income
	• Retaining Income at Lower Current Tax Cost
	• Entity Formation
	• Taxation of Distributions: Gain to Owner and Entity
	• Owner's Basis for Entity-Level Debt
	  • Temporary Benefit of Debt Basis
	• Taxation of Fringe Benefits
	• Application of Passive Loss Rules
	• Alternative Minimum Tax
	  • Corporations
	  • S Corporations, Limited Liability Companies, Partnerships, and Sole Proprietorships
	• Eligibility for QBI Deduction
		• Example 9.2.1 A One-Owner Business
		• Example 9.2.2 Retaining Income at a Lower Tax Cost
		• Example 9.2.3 Tax-Deferred Entity Formation
		• Example 9.2.4 80% Control Test with Service Shareholder
		• Example 9.2.5 Distribution Rules for Partnerships vs. S Corporations
		• Example 9.2.6 Taxation of Fringe Benefits
		• Practice Problem 9.2.1 Ability to Raise Capital
		• Practice Problem 9.2.2 Tax Consequences from Contribution of Property
		• Practice Problem 9.2.3 Tax Consequences from Distribution of Property

LEARNING OBJECTIVES	TOPICS	PRACTICE OPPORTUNITIES

3 Compare the tax characteristics of partnerships/LLCs and S corporations.	**9.3 Comparison of Partnerships/Limited Liability Companies and S Corporations**
	• Similarities between Tax Laws for Partnerships/LLCs and S Corporations
	• Differences between Tax Laws for Partnerships/LLCs and S Corporations
	  • Allocation of Profits and Losses
	  • Formation of Entity
	  • Limited Liability
	  • Payroll Taxes and Self-Employment Tax
	• Spotlight on the Law: S Corporations and Self-Employment Tax
	  • Basis Increase for Entity Debt
	  • Preferential Distributions
	  • Distributions Taxable to Owners
	  • Distribution of Appreciated Property: Taxable to Entity
	  • Section 704(c) Gains
	  • Hot Asset Rules
		• Example 9.3.1 Profit- and Loss-Sharing Ratios
		• Example 9.3.2 Self-Employment Tax and Payroll Tax
		• Example 9.3.3. The Effects of the Absence of a Section 704(c) Rule for S Corporations
		• Practice Problem 9.3.1 Advantage of an S Corporation over a Partnership
		• Practice Problem 9.3.2 Partnership vs. S Corporation—Flexibility
		• Practice Problem 9.3.3 Application of 704(c) Rule

LEARNING OBJECTIVES	TOPICS	PRACTICE OPPORTUNITIES

4 Distinguish the tax consequences from disposing of partnership interests, corporate stock, or S corporation stock.	**9.4 Dispositions of Ownership Interests and Conversions to Other Entity Types**
	• Sale of an Ownership Interest
	• Liquidation of an Ownership Interest
	  • Corporate Liquidations
	    • Shareholders
	    • Corporation
	  • S Corporation Liquidations
	    • Shareholders
	      • Earnings and Profits
	      • No Earnings and Profits
	    • S Corporation
	  • Partnership Liquidations
	    • Partners
	    • Partnership
	• Converting from One Entity Form to Another Entity Form
	  • Sole Proprietorships
	    • Partnership
	    • Corporation
	  • C Corporations
	    • Sole Proprietorship or Partnership
	    • S Corporation
	  • S Corporations
	    • Sole Proprietorship or Partnership
	    • C Corporation
	  • Partnerships
		• Example 9.4.1 Comparing the Tax Consequences of the Sale of Ownership Interests
		• Example 9.4.2 Comparing the Tax Consequences of Liquidating Distributions
		• Practice Problem 9.4.1 Unrealized Receivable
		• Practice Problem 9.4.2 S Corporation Liquidation
		• Practice Problem 9.4.3 Converting from a Partnership to Another Entity

Tax Forms referenced in this chapter

Form 1040	U.S. Individual Income Tax Return
Form 1040, Schedule C	Profit or Loss from Business
Form 1040, Schedule E	Supplemental Income and Loss
Form 1041	U.S. Income Tax Return for Estates and Trusts
Form 1065	U.S. Return of Partnership Income
Form 1120	U.S. Corporation Income Tax Return
Form 1120-S	U.S. Income Tax Return for an S Corporation
Form 8832	Entity Classification Election

9.1 Business Structures

LEARNING OBJECTIVE 1

Identify the legal forms available to business owners.

VIDEO CONTENT

In this section, we first review the legal forms available to business owners such as Aletta, and then describe how each legal form is classified for tax reporting. The simplest form is the sole proprietorship. There are several reasons why business owners may want to form a separate business entity rather than use a sole proprietorship, however, such as the following:

- **Limited liability** A sole proprietorship does not provide limited liability to the owner, whereas some business entities do.
- **Multiple owners** A sole proprietorship has only one owner. If a business needs more than one owner, then the owners must form a business entity. On the other hand, business entities such as corporations, S corporations, and single-member LLCs may have only one owner.
- **Separation of ownership and management** Some business owners do not want to manage the business. Rather, they want to invest in the business and hire managers to run the day-to-day business affairs. A business entity is required for this separation. Business forms that permit separation of ownership and management are corporations, limited partnerships, and limited liability companies.
- **Raising capital** An owner needs to be able to raise sufficient capital to meet the needs of the business. A business entity provides the structure that defines the roles of different types of owners and of management in this regard. C corporations have the greatest ability to raise large amounts of capital because the stock of the corporation can be publicly traded, which provides the flexibility to easily buy and sell the stock that many investors desire.
- **Benefit from a tax law** Forming a business entity may permit an owner to take advantage of certain tax laws that benefit the taxpayer. While transactions must have a valid business purpose, the IRS has approved certain arrangements where the primary reason to form the business entity is to benefit from a tax law, as shown in the following Example.

EXAMPLE 9.1.1
Using a Business Entity to Implement a Tax Strategy

Amber lived in Chattanooga, Tennessee, for five years before her employer transferred her to a new location in Charlotte, North Carolina. She bought a new house in Charlotte and rented her house in Chattanooga until she decided whether she was happy with her job in Charlotte. After renting her Chattanooga home for 30 months, she decided to sell the home. Amber estimates that she will have a realized gain on the sale of the house of $190,000. She is aware that she can exclude from income up to $250,000 of gain if she has owned the house and used it as a principal residence for at least two of the last five years.[2] It has been four months since Amber listed her Chattanooga house for sale, so she has not used her Chattanooga house as a principal residence for 34 months. She realizes that if she does not sell her home in the next two months, then when it is sold, she will not meet the two-year out of five-year rule. Therefore, she will not be able to exclude her $190,000 gain from the sale. How would you advise Amber in this situation?

[2] IRC §121.

SOLUTION

Amber should form a business entity and then sell her house to the business entity. She can form a C corporation, an S corporation, or a single-member LLC. This may seem unusual, because she will own 100% of the business, but recall that under the entity theory, business entities are treated as legal entities distinct from their owners.[3] She needs to do this quickly so she can sell the house before the 36-month period expires. Then she will have owned and used the Chattanooga house as a principal residence in at least two of the previous five years, and she can exclude her $190,000 gain from income. The business entity that she forms will then attempt to sell the house. Amber will need a business purpose for forming the new business, so she should seek advice from a tax professional on how to do that.

Potential Pitfall

A CPA should never draft the legal forms necessary for a business entity to be created. Creating these documents is considered the practice of law and must be done by a licensed attorney. However, the CPA should review the documents after legal counsel has prepared them to ensure that the attorney and business owner carefully considered the relevant accounting and tax issues.

Legal Forms of Business

A business owner has several different legal entities to choose from when forming an entity. Remember that a sole proprietorship is not a separate business entity. The most common legal forms include:

- **Corporations** A business that has met a state's requirements to organize as a legal entity that is distinct from its owners. In most states, the owners file articles of incorporation with the state and elect a board of directors.
- **General partnerships** A business for which two or more owners agree to assume the responsibility for managing the business, and to share profits, losses, and liquidation proceeds. All partners in a general partnership are general partners. General partners have unlimited liability, meaning that their personal assets are at risk to creditors of the partnership. Unlimited liability includes malpractice judgment against the partnership even though the partner may not have been personally involved in the malpractice.
- **Limited partnerships** A business in which two or more taxpayers agree to own and operate the business, and to share profits, losses, and liquidation proceeds. The partnership must have at least one general partner and at least one limited partner. A limited partner's personal assets are not at risk with respect to debts of the partnership. A limited partner's losses from the partnership are limited to the amount the partner has invested and promised to invest in the partnership. A limited partner cannot participate in the active management of the partnership.
- **Limited liability companies (LLCs)** An LLC is a formal business relationship for which articles of organization must be filed with the state in which the LLC is legally organized. Owners of an LLC are known as members. All members have limited liability. Many states do not allow professional service providers such as accountants and attorneys to organize as an LLC.
- **Limited liability partnerships (LLPs)** A **limited liability partnership** differs from general partnerships in that with an LLP, a partner is not liable for damages resulting from the negligence, malpractice, or fraud committed by other partners. However, each partner is personally liable for other debts of the partnership, as well as debts arising from their own negligence, malpractice, or fraud. LLPs are often used by service providers that may not be permitted to form LLCs, such as architects, accountants, attorneys, and physicians.
- **Business trust** A **business trust** is a legal entity that holds the rights to an individual's stake or interest in a business. The trust technically owns the business interest, and the trustee controls the interest. The trust can have multiple beneficiaries.

Related exercises: Discussion Questions 1, 2
Multiple Choice Questions 1, 2

[3] The IRS has approved transactions similar to this one in Private Letter Rulings 8350084 and 9625035.

Tax Planning Tip

A specialized type of partnership is the *electing large partnership*. An electing large partnership is a partnership that has elected to be taxed under a simplified reporting system that does not require as much separate reporting to partners as a regular partnership does. For example, charitable contributions are deductible by the partnership (subject to a 10% of taxable income limitation), and the Section 179 expense election is deducted in computing partnership ordinary income and not separately passed through to partners. To qualify, the partnership must not be a service partnership or engaged in commodity trading, must have at least 100 partners, and must file an election to be taxed as an electing large partnership. A partnership will cease to be an electing large partnership if it has fewer than 100 partners for a taxable year.

Tax Classifications for Businesses

Now that you know the various legal forms from which a business owner can choose, let's turn our attention to how these entities report for tax purposes. Businesses will generally report for federal income tax purposes as one of the business forms shown in Illustration 9.1.

The word *corporation* in this text always references a C corporation. An S corporation referenced in this text will always have an S designation

ILLUSTRATION 9.1 Tax Classifications for Businesses

Tax classification	Description	Federal tax forms used
C corporation	C corporation that has *not* made an election to be taxed as an S corporation.	**Form 1120** (U.S. Corporation Income Tax Return)
S corporation	Incorporated entity that *has* made an election to be taxed as an S corporation.	**Form 1120-S** (U.S. Income Tax Return for an S Corporation)
Partnership*	General partnerships, limited partnerships, LLCs, and LLPs are all generally taxed as a partnership.	**Form 1065** (U.S. Return of Partnership Income)
Trust	Legal entity that holds the rights to an individual's stake or interest in a business.	**Form 1041** (U.S. Income Tax Return for Estates and Trusts)
Sole proprietorship	If an owner does not create a separate business entity, then the owner will report as a sole proprietor.	**Schedule C**** (Profit or Loss from Business)
Tax-exempt organization***	A tax-exempt organization must pay tax on its unrelated business taxable income.	**Form 990-T** (Exempt Organization Business Income Tax Return)

*If there is more than one owner, and no separate entity is formally created, the business defaults to a partnership.
**As part of Form 1040, U.S. Individual Income Tax Return.
***These will be discussed in more detail in Chapter 15, Tax-Exempt Organizations.

To determine which of these tax reporting forms to use for a particular business, you must use the *check-the-box regulations*.

Check-the-Box Regulations

The check-the-box regulations determine how a business entity is taxed for federal income tax purposes,[4] and we show these rules in a flowchart in Illustration 9.2. The main premise

[4]Treas. Reg. §§301.7701-1, 301.7701-2, and 301.77-1-3.

of the check-the-box regulations is that an unincorporated entity may choose to be taxed as a corporation or a partnership. The regulations apply to all businesses other than sole proprietorships.

ILLUSTRATION 9.2 Check-the-Box Regulations Flowchart

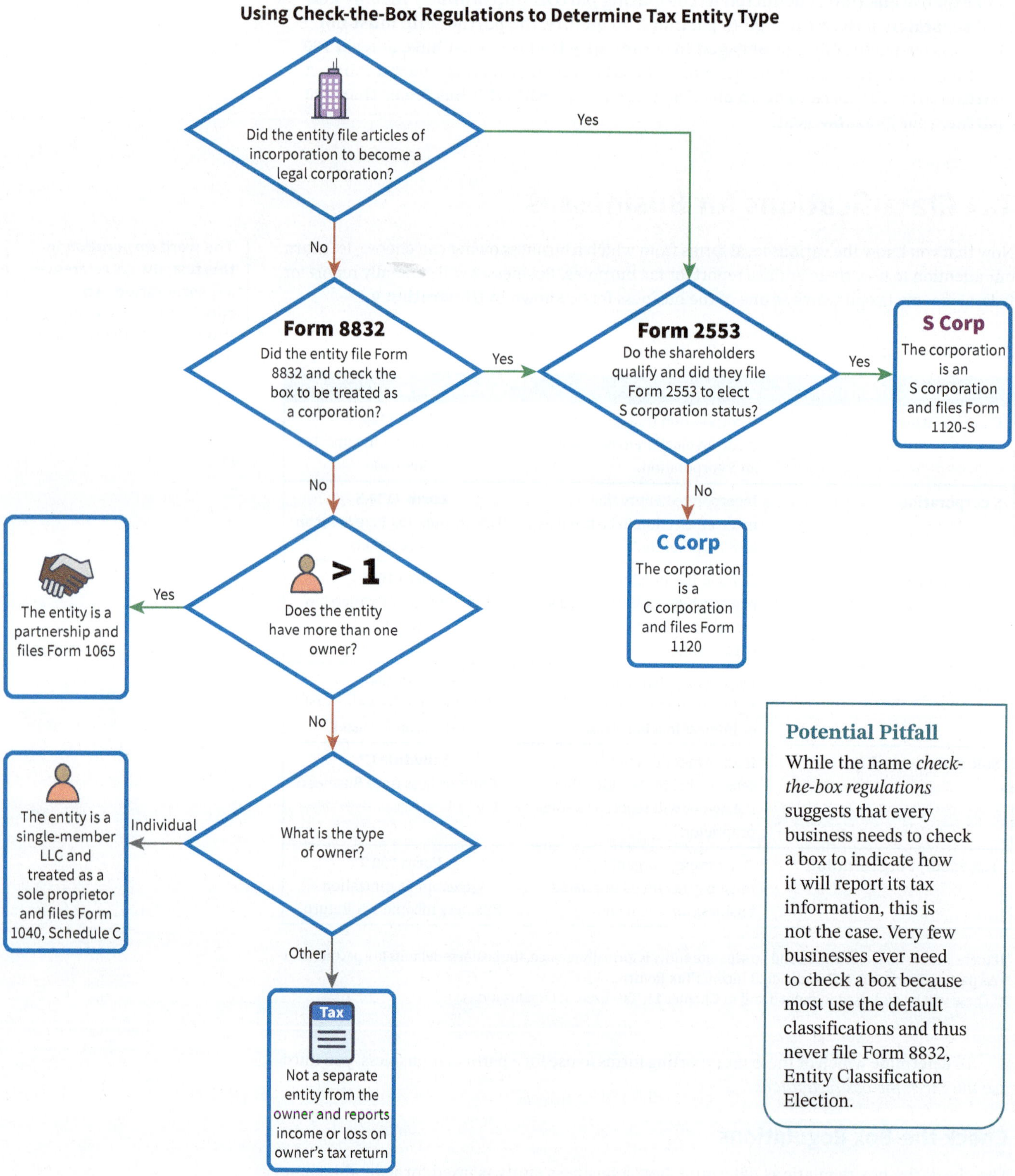

Potential Pitfall

While the name *check-the-box regulations* suggests that every business needs to check a box to indicate how it will report its tax information, this is not the case. Very few businesses ever need to check a box because most use the default classifications and thus never file Form 8832, Entity Classification Election.

Per Se Corporations

Per se corporations are not eligible to make an election as to how they want to be taxed. ***Per se* corporations** include business entities formed under statutes that refer to the entities as incorporated. These entities are taxed as either S corporations or C corporations and include the following:

- Entities incorporated under state law
- Insurance companies
- State-chartered banks (if deposits are insured by FDIC)
- Publicly traded partnerships[5]
- Specified foreign entities
- Certain other entities (such as real estate investment trusts [REITs],[6] tax-exempt organizations, etc.)

Other Entities

For entities not listed as *per se* corporations, the default option depends on whether the entity has one owner or more than one owner.

If the business has *two or more owners,* the rules are as follows:

- ***Default classification*: Partnership.** This default classification typically applies to partnerships, limited liability companies, and limited liability partnerships.
- ***Election option*: Corporation.** If an entity does not prefer the default classification, it can elect to be taxed as a corporation.

If an entity has only *one owner,* the rules are as follows:

- ***Default classification*: Disregarded.** If an entity is not incorporated and has only one owner, then by default the entity is disregarded for federal income tax purposes. The entity is known as a single-member limited liability company (SMLLC). A disregarded SMLLC that is owned by an individual reports its tax items on Schedule C as part of the individual's Form 1040. If the SMLLC has rental activity, then the tax results are reported on Schedule E. A disregarded entity that is owned by a corporation reports its tax items on the corporation's Form 1120.
- ***Election option*: Corporation.** If a SMLLC does not prefer the default classification, it can elect to be taxed as a corporation.

Illustration 9.3 summarizes these rules.

ILLUSTRATION 9.3 Determining Tax Entity Types for Businesses That Are Not *Per Se* Corporations

Ownership	Default classification	Election option
Two or more owners > 1	**Partnership** Typically applies to partnerships, limited liability companies, and limited liability partnerships.	**Corporation** If an entity does not prefer the default classification, it can elect to be taxed as a corporation.
One owner	**Disregarded** If an entity is not incorporated and has only one owner, then the default classification is that the entity is disregarded for federal income tax purposes.	**Corporation** If a SMLLC does not prefer the default classification, it can elect to be taxed as a corporation.

[5]IRC §7704. Publicly traded eligible entities are taxable as corporations, unless at least 90% of their gross income is from certain passive sources. Publicly traded partnerships, such as *master limited partnerships* (MLPs), often qualify for the gross income exception. Further discussion is beyond the scope of this book.

[6]*Real estate investment trusts* (REITs) are companies that own, operate, or finance income-producing real estate across a wide range of property sectors. These investments allow the owners to earn income from real estate without having to buy, manage, or finance properties themselves.

Other Check-the-Box Rules

- An election under the check-the-box regulations is effective for the current tax year if filed within the first 75 days of the business's tax year. Otherwise, the election is effective for the next tax year.
- An election can be changed after five years or with IRS permission. The five-year rule does not apply to a new corporation that uses the default classification.
- A business trust is taxed as a trust on Form 1041, U.S. Income Tax Return for Estates and Trusts.
- A check-the-box election is made on Form 8832, Entity Classification Election. The first two pages of Form 8832 are shown in **Illustration 9.4**, and the entire form is shown in Appendix B.[7]

The next Example illustrates the application of the check-the-box-regulations.

EXAMPLE 9.1.2
Check-the-Box Regulations

Which of the following statements is true regarding the check-the-box regulations?

a. C corporations can elect to be taxed as disregarded.

b. The default classification for a single-member LLC is to be disregarded, but it can elect to be taxed as a corporation.

c. For a change of tax form to be effective for the current tax year, Form 8832 must be completed and filed before the tax year begins.

d. It is possible for a partnership to elect to be disregarded.

SOLUTION

The correct answer is **b**. The default classification for a SMLLC is to be disregarded, but it can elect to be taxed as a corporation. Response **a** is incorrect because incorporated businesses must be taxed as either a C corporation or an S corporation. They cannot elect to be taxed as a partnership. Response **c** is incorrect because the form can be filed within 75 days of the business's tax year. Response **d** is incorrect because a partnership's default classification is to be taxed as a partnership, or it can elect to be taxed as a corporation; disregarded status is not an option.

Related exercises: Multiple Choice Questions 3, 4
Brief Exercise 1
Application Problem 1

[7]These rules are for U.S.-based entities. Different rules apply for foreign entities.

ILLUSTRATION 9.4 Form 8832, Entity Classification Election

DOWNLOAD DOCUMENTS & TEMPLATES

Form **8832**
(Rev. December 2013)
Department of the Treasury
Internal Revenue Service

Entity Classification Election

OMB No. 1545-1516

▶ **Information about Form 8832 and its instructions is at *www.irs.gov/form8832*.**

Type or Print	Name of eligible entity making election	Employer identification number
	Number, street, and room or suite no. If a P.O. box, see instructions.	
	City or town, state, and ZIP code. If a foreign address, enter city, province or state, postal code and country. Follow the country's practice for entering the postal code.	

▶ Check if: ☐ Address change ☐ Late classification relief sought under Revenue Procedure 2009-41
☐ Relief for a late change of entity classification election sought under Revenue Procedure 2010-32

Part I **Election Information**

1 **Type of election** (see instructions):

a ☐ Initial classification by a newly-formed entity. Skip lines 2a and 2b and go to line 3.
b ☐ Change in current classification. Go to line 2a.

2a Has the eligible entity previously filed an entity election that had an effective date within the last 60 months?

☐ **Yes.** Go to line 2b.
☐ **No.** Skip line 2b and go to line 3.

2b Was the eligible entity's prior election an initial classification election by a newly formed entity that was effective on the date of formation?

☐ **Yes.** Go to line 3.
☐ **No.** Stop here. You generally are not currently eligible to make the election (see instructions).

3 Does the eligible entity have more than one owner?

☐ **Yes.** You can elect to be classified as a partnership or an association taxable as a corporation. Skip line 4 and go to line 5.
☐ **No.** You can elect to be classified as an association taxable as a corporation or to be disregarded as a separate entity. Go to line 4.

4 If the eligible entity has only one owner, provide the following information:

a Name of owner ▶ ....
b Identifying number of owner ▶ ....

5 If the eligible entity is owned by one or more affiliated corporations that file a consolidated return, provide the name and employer identification number of the parent corporation:

a Name of parent corporation ▶ ....
b Employer identification number ▶ ....

For Paperwork Reduction Act Notice, see instructions. Cat. No. 22598R Form **8832** (Rev. 12-2013)

Department of the Treasury Internal Revenue Service/Public domain

DOWNLOAD DOCUMENTS & TEMPLATES

Form 8832 (Rev. 12-2013) Page 2

Part I Election Information (Continued)

6 Type of entity (see instructions):

- a ☐ A domestic eligible entity electing to be classified as an association taxable as a corporation.
- b ☐ A domestic eligible entity electing to be classified as a partnership.
- c ☐ A domestic eligible entity with a single owner electing to be disregarded as a separate entity.
- d ☐ A foreign eligible entity electing to be classified as an association taxable as a corporation.
- e ☐ A foreign eligible entity electing to be classified as a partnership.
- f ☐ A foreign eligible entity with a single owner electing to be disregarded as a separate entity.

7 If the eligible entity is created or organized in a foreign jurisdiction, provide the foreign country of organization ▶ ______________________

8 Election is to be effective beginning (month, day, year) (see instructions) . . . . ▶ __________

9 Name and title of contact person whom the IRS may call for more information	**10** Contact person's telephone number

Consent Statement and Signature(s) (see instructions)

Under penalties of perjury, I (we) declare that I (we) consent to the election of the above-named entity to be classified as indicated above, and that I (we) have examined this election and consent statement, and to the best of my (our) knowledge and belief, this election and consent statement are true, correct, and complete. If I am an officer, manager, or member signing for the entity, I further declare under penalties of perjury that I am authorized to make the election on its behalf.

Signature(s)	Date	Title

Form **8832** (Rev. 12-2013)

PRACTICE PROBLEM 9.1.1
Sole Proprietorship

Identify three disadvantages of being a sole proprietor.

SOLUTION

A sole proprietor has unlimited liability, is subject to self-employment tax, and cannot raise capital from other investors.

PRACTICE PROBLEM 9.1.2
Sole Owner

If a taxpayer would like to remain sole owner of their business, what choices are available?

SOLUTION

If an owner does not create a separate business entity, then the owner will report as a sole proprietorship and file Schedule C, Profit or Loss from Business, as part of Form 1040, U.S. Individual Income Tax Return. A sole owner can also choose to be a business entity and operate as a C corporation, an S corporation, or a single-member LLC (SMLLC).

INTERACTIVE SELF-SCORING QUIZZES

9.2 Characteristics of Tax Entities

LEARNING OBJECTIVE 2

Understand the tax and non-tax characteristics for each business entity.

VIDEO CONTENT

The owners of a business, such as Aletta from the introduction, should consider both tax and non-tax characteristics of a business entity when determining the most appropriate choice for tax reporting purposes. In this section, we review these characteristics and describe how they relate to each tax reporting form. For each business type, we indicate whether this is a **positive**, **negative**, or **mixed** characteristic for the business owners. These characteristics are summarized in Illustration 9.5.

Our discussion is limited to the federal income taxation factors that influence business entity choice. However, state income tax laws must also be considered before a final decision is made. State income tax laws do not always follow the federal income tax laws. For example, the states of New Hampshire, Tennessee, and Texas do not recognize S corporations as such and treat them as regular corporations.

We do not discuss the characteristics of business trusts in this section. We discuss trusts in detail in Chapter 11, Income Taxation of Estates and Trusts. Trusts are very costly to set up and maintain, so trusts are used for businesses in only specialized situations.

ILLUSTRATION 9.5 Characteristics of Tax Entities

Comparison of the Characteristics of Tax Entities

Characteristic	C corporation	S corporation	Partnership/LLP	Multi-member LLC	Sole proprietorship
Ability to raise capital?	Strong (Positive)	Weak (Negative)	Moderate (Mixed)	Moderate (Mixed)	Weak (Negative)
Limited liability?	Yes (Positive)	Yes (Positive)	General*—No (Negative) Limited—Yes (Mixed)	Yes (Positive)	No (Negative)
Double taxation of income?	Yes (Negative)	No (Positive)	No (Positive)	No (Positive)	No (Positive)
Able to retain income at lower tax cost?	Depends on relative tax rates (Positive)	No (Negative)	No (Negative)	No (Negative)	N/A
Tax-deferred entity formation?	Possibly—subject to control test (Mixed)	Possibly—subject to control test (Mixed)	Yes (Positive)	Yes (Positive)	N/A
Distributions taxable to owner?	Yes (Negative)	Possibly** (Mixed)	Rarely*** (Positive)	Rarely*** (Positive)	N/A
Distribution of appreciated property taxable to entity?	Yes (Negative)	Yes (Negative)	No (Positive)	No (Positive)	N/A
Owner's basis increased for entity-level debt?	No (Negative)	No (Negative)	Yes (Positive)	Yes (Positive)	N/A
Tax-free fringe benefits for owners?	Yes (Positive)	No for most benefits, if own more than 2% (Negative)	No for most benefits (Negative)	No for most benefits (Negative)	N/A
Passive loss rules apply?	No**** (Positive)	Yes (Negative)	Yes (Negative)	Yes (Negative)	Yes (Negative)
Alternative minimum tax available?	Rarely (Mixed)	Indirectly (Negative)	Indirectly (Negative)	Indirectly (Negative)	Directly (Negative)
Eligible for QBI deduction?	No (Negative)	Yes (Positive)	Yes (Positive)	Yes (Positive)	Yes (Positive)

* An LLP partner is not liable for damages resulting from the negligence, malpractice, or fraud committed by other partners. However, each partner is personally liable for other debts of the partnership, as well as debts arising from their own negligence, malpractice, or fraud.
** If FMV of distributions exceeds shareholder's basis in stock.
*** If cash distributed exceeds partner's basis in partnership interest.
**** The passive loss rules do apply to personal service corporations and closely held corporations.

Ability to Raise Capital

The ability to raise capital is an important characteristic for certain business owners, such as businesses that are growing rapidly or are capital-intensive. C corporations are the best entity for raising capital because:

- the shareholders have limited liability,
- the corporation can issue various types of stock to meet different needs of shareholders, such as common, preferred, and convertible stock,
- the stock can be publicly traded, *and*
- shareholders can freely transfer their ownership interest.

Multimember LLCs are also useful for raising capital because all the members can have limited liability and the number of owners is unlimited. S corporations are the weakest entity form for raising capital because they can have only one class of stock, and the number of shareholders is limited.

Positive characteristic: C corporations are the best entity for raising capital.

✓ C corporations

Negative characteristic: Difficult to meet the demands of potential investors with varying incentives.

✗ S corporations
✗ Sole proprietorship

Mixed characteristic: Multiple owners facilitate raising capital.

○ General partnerships
○ Limited liability partnerships (LLPs)
○ Limited liability companies (LLCs)

Limited Liability

Limited liability means that the owner is only at risk of losing what the owner has invested and promised to invest in the business. The owner is not responsible for the debts of the business.

Positive characteristic: All owners have limited liability.

✓ C corporations
✓ S corporations
✓ Limited liability partnerships (LLPs)
✓ Limited liability companies (LLCs)

Negative characteristic: All owners have unlimited liability.

✗ General partnerships
✗ Sole proprietorship

Mixed characteristic: Limited partners have limited liability, but the partnership must have at least one general partner who will have unlimited liability.

○ Limited partnerships

Tax Planning Tip

Even though a limited partnership must have at least one general partner, the general partner can be a corporation, and the shareholders of a corporation have limited liability. That means that the only amount that is at risk of being lost by a corporate general partner is their equity in the corporation. For example, if the corporation has $200,000 of net equity, then the maximum amount that can be lost by the corporation is $200,000. However, a corporation cannot take this rule to an extreme level of inadequate funding, because the corporation must have an appropriate amount of equity as a partner in the limited partnership. For example, if a corporation had equity of only $2,000, the structure would likely be considered a sham, and the courts would ignore the existence of the corporation. Therefore, the owners of the *so-called* corporation would have unlimited liability with respect to the debts of the general partnership.

In the following Example, we illustrate the entities that provide limited liability for a one-owner business.

EXAMPLE 9.2.1
A One-Owner Business

Stefano is planning to open a wine store, and he will be the only owner. He plans to take 60% of the profits each year to pay his personal living expenses. Stefano will reinvest the other 40% of the profits back in the business. What viable options does Stefano have for his form of business if he is concerned about liability?

SOLUTION

Because there will be only one owner and Stefano wants limited liability, the business forms available to him are:

- C corporation
- S corporation
- Single-Member LLC

A sole proprietorship will not provide him with limited liability.

Related exercises: Multiple Choice Question 5
Application Problem 2
Tax Planning Problem 1

Double Taxation of Income

Double taxation means that the income of the business is taxed at both the entity level and the owner level before it can be controlled and used by the owners. Thus, the income is taxed twice before it ends up in the hands of an owner. C corporations are the only entity that double-taxes income. The income is taxed once on Form 1120 when earned by the C corporation, and then taxed a second time when it is distributed to a shareholder.

Positive characteristic: The following business forms have single taxation. The business income flows through to the owners, so it is not taxed to the business. A sole proprietor reports the business income directly on Schedule C.

✓ S corporations
✓ General partnerships
✓ Limited partnerships
✓ Limited liability partnerships (LLPs)
✓ Limited liability companies (LLCs)
✓ Sole proprietorship

Negative characteristic: C corporations are subject to double taxation.

✗ C corporations

Tax Planning Tip

C corporations can temporarily delay the second level of taxation by not paying dividends to shareholders. However, if a C corporation accumulates income without a valid business purpose, then it may be subject to the accumulated earnings tax (Chapter 3, LO5, Penalty Taxes). The second level of taxation occurs if the corporation pays a dividend in the future, buys a shareholder's stock in a redemption, or liquidates. If a shareholder holds the stock until death, the beneficiaries' basis in the stock is its fair market value at the date of death. Therefore, the appreciation in the stock during the shareholder's life is never taxed, so the second level of taxation is permanently avoided.

There are three methods by which a C corporation can get profits into the hands of shareholders without the funds being taxed as dividends.

1. **Payments of salaries to a shareholder who is also employed by the corporation.**
2. **Payments of rent or royalties to a shareholder who allows the corporation to use their property.**
3. **Payments of interest to a shareholder who loans money to the corporation.**

While the shareholder recognizes income for each of these situations, the corporation is able to deduct the payments so that double taxation is avoided. The single taxation occurs at the shareholder level, and the corporation is not taxed because of the deduction. For the corporation to deduct the expenditures, they must be reasonable. Unreasonable amounts will be reclassified by the IRS.

Related exercises: Discussion Question 3
Multiple Choice Question 6

Retaining Income at Lower Current Tax Cost

The entity that may be able to retain income at a lower tax cost is the C corporation. Whether this is a benefit for the C corporation depends on the level of current tax rates for corporations and individuals. The highest marginal tax rate for corporations is currently 21%, which is less than the highest marginal tax rate for individuals at 37%. Flow-through entities do not have this advantage because income flows to the owners even if not distributed and will be taxed to the owner at the owner's marginal tax rate. An advantage of flow-through entities is that the income is taxed only once, but if the owner's marginal tax bracket is very high, this can be a disadvantage. For example, the highest marginal tax rate in 1981 was 70%, and in 1963, it was 91%. It is not hard to understand why partnerships and S corporations were not popular business entities in the 1960s and 1970s.

Positive characteristic:

✓ C corporations

Negative characteristic:

✗ S corporations

✗ General partnerships

✗ Limited partnerships

✗ Limited liability partnerships (LLPs)

✗ Limited liability companies (LLCs)

Not applicable

N/A Sole proprietorship

We illustrate the benefits of retaining income at a lower tax cost in the next Example.

EXAMPLE 9.2.2
Retaining Income at a Lower Tax Cost

Assume that the corporate tax rate is a flat rate of 21% and the highest individual tax rate is a flat rate of 37% (we use these rates as flat rates in this problem for simplicity). A restaurant owner expects to have $200,000 of taxable income for each of the next five years. The owner will reinvest the earnings in the business by opening new restaurant locations. Would it be better for the owner to be a C corporation or a partnership during this five-year period?

SOLUTION

If the business is a C corporation, it will pay tax at a 21% rate and retain the remaining income of $158,000 ($200,000 × [100% – 21%]), which will be reinvested in new restaurants. The second level of tax is avoided if dividends are not paid. The accumulated earnings tax is not of concern because the earnings are used to expand the business.

If the business is a partnership, the $200,000 of income will flow through to the owner and be taxed at 37% (ignoring any possible qualified business income deduction). The owner will have only $126,000 to reinvest in new restaurants ($200,000 × [100% – 37%]). Thus, if the business is a corporation, for each year during the five-year period, it will have an additional $32,000 ($158,000 – $126,000) to invest in new restaurants, adding up to $160,000 over the five-year period ($32,000 × 5).

Entity Formation

While both corporations and partnerships can be formed in such a manner that realized gains/losses are deferred, the rules are much more favorable for partnerships (and LLCs) because no 80% control test (see Chapter 3, LO1, Taxation of Corporate Formations) is required for deferral of gains and losses for partnerships.

Positive characteristic:

✓ General partnerships
✓ Limited partnerships
✓ Limited liability partnerships (LLPs)
✓ Limited liability companies (LLCs)

Mixed characteristic:

O C corporations (generally positive, but subject to the 80% control test)
O S corporations (generally positive, but subject to the 80% control test)

Not applicable:

N/A Sole proprietorship

In the following Example, we demonstrate the differences in the tax-deferred entity formation rules for corporations and partnerships.

EXAMPLE 9.2.3
Tax-Deferred Entity Formation

Oak Company has been in existence for five years and needs additional capital. Amber plans to contribute a building to Oak that has a FMV of $500,000 and an adjusted basis of $310,000. She will receive 25% of the ownership of Oak. What are the tax consequences to Amber if Oak is a corporation? A partnership?

SOLUTION

Amber has a realized gain of $190,000 on the contribution of the building to Oak.

Fair market value	$500,000
Less: Adjusted basis	(310,000)
Realized gain	$190,000

If Oak Company is a corporation, Amber will recognize the gain of $190,000. Amber does not meet the 80% control test required for a contribution of property to a corporation to be tax-deferred. If Oak Company is a partnership, then her recognized gain is $0. All contributions of property to a partnership in return for a partnership interest are tax-deferred because no control test needs to be met.

The 80% control requirement for corporations presents additional challenges when one or more of the shareholders is receiving stock in return for services rendered. The service shareholder has wage income regardless of whether the formation is tax-deferred or not. Therefore, the 80% control test is of relevance only to the shareholders who contribute property, because if they contribute appreciated assets and the 80% control is not met, then they must recognize gain. The 80% control requirement can also create problems when new shareholders contribute property to the corporation after the initial formation.

The next Example illustrates the complexity that a shareholder who contributes services can present for meeting the control test.

EXAMPLE 9.2.4
80% Control Test with Service Shareholder

Ren, Draymond, and Daniel are creating a corporation to begin a dock-building business in Florida. Ren is contributing a warehouse that has an adjusted basis of $130,000 and a fair market value of $200,000. Draymond is rendering services with a value of $160,000, and Daniel is contributing cash of $140,000. What are the tax consequences of the formation to Ren, Draymond, and Daniel? Are there alternatives that could lead to a better tax result?

SOLUTION

We begin by determining if the 80% control is met. The shareholders received stock as follows:

	FMV	% Ownership
Ren	$200,000	40%
Draymond	160,000	32%
Daniel	140,000	28%
Total	$500,000	100%

Ren and Daniel contributed property, and they own 68% of the corporation. Therefore, the 80% control test is not met, and gains will be recognized as follows:

Ren	$ 70,000 ($200,000 stock received – $130,000 basis in warehouse)
Draymond	$160,000 (wage income)
Daniel	$ 0 (contributed cash)

Draymond's and Daniel's tax consequences are the same whether or not the 80% control test is met. Ren is the only shareholder negatively impacted by the failure of the 80% control test. Therefore, Ren has a vested interest in seeking alternatives that would allow the 80% control test to be met.

There are two alternatives that could produce a better tax result. The first is for Draymond to receive stock ownership of 20% or less for his services, and perhaps receive additional compensation in the future after the corporation is formed so that the total cash he receives is the same. In that case, Ren and Daniel would own at least 80% of the corporation at initial formation, and the control test would be met.

The second alternative is for Draymond to contribute both services and property to the corporation. As long as the value of the property contributed is meaningful, then Draymond would be a contributor of property as well as services, and his 32% ownership would be included in the control test. The control test would be met because those contributing property would own 100% of the corporation, and Ren's $70,000 gain would be deferred. The IRS has ruled that the value of the property must be equal to *at least* 10% of the value of the services for the shareholder's stock ownership to be included in the control test. If this benchmark is met, then all the shareholder's stock is included in the control test, not just the stock received for property.[8]

Related exercise: Application Problem 3

Taxation of Distributions: Gain to Owner and Entity

Recall that partnerships, LLCs, and S corporations are flow-through entities. Thus, the income for the entity is taxed only once. The income flows through to the owners at the end of the tax year. The owners increase their bases in their ownership interests by the amount of the income, so that when they receive a distribution of the previously taxed income, it will not be taxed again. (Note that the double taxation for C corporations was discussed previously.)

However, if the distribution exceeds the basis in the ownership interest, then gain could be recognized. The rules for this situation vary across partnerships and S corporations, with the partnership rules being more taxpayer friendly.

[8]Treas. Reg. §1.351-1(a).

Tax Planning Tip

Partnerships can distribute property to partners, and the partners will not have to recognize gain.[9] The unrecognized gain or loss in the partnership asset transfers to the partner.

Partnerships also have preferential taxation over S corporations if appreciated assets are distributed. S corporations must recognize the appreciation in the year the asset is distributed, the gain is reported on Form 1120-S, and it flows to the shareholders and is taxed to them. The gain also increases the shareholders' bases in their stock. On the other hand, partnerships are not taxed on the appreciation if they distribute appreciated assets to a partner. The advantages that partnerships have for distributions of appreciated assets as compared to S corporations are shown in **Illustration 9.6**.

ILLUSTRATION 9.6 Distributions of Appreciated Assets for Partnerships vs. S Corporations

Favorable Distribution Rules for Partnerships Compared to S Corporations

- **Partnerships/LLCs:** Gain is recognized by the partner only if the *cash* distributed exceeds the partner's basis in the partnership interest.
- **S Corporations:** Gain is recognized by the shareholder if the FMV of the *cash and property* distributed exceeds the shareholder's basis in the stock.

Positive characteristic: Single taxation of earnings; gain to partner only if cash distributed exceeds partner's basis in interest.

✓ General partnerships
✓ Limited partnerships
✓ Limited liability partnerships (LLPs)
✓ Limited liability companies (LLCs)

Negative characteristic: Double taxation of earnings

✗ C corporations

Mixed characteristic: Single taxation of earnings; gain to shareholder if FMV of cash and property exceeds shareholder's basis in stock.

O S corporations

Not applicable: Owner cannot receive distributions because a sole proprietorship is not a separate business entity.

N/A Sole proprietorships

Related exercise: Application Problem 4

EXAMPLE 9.2.5
Distribution Rules for Partnerships vs. S Corporations

Assume a business entity owns land with an adjusted basis of $10,000 and FMV of $25,000. The land is distributed to a 10% business owner when the owner's basis in their ownership interest is $18,000. What are the tax consequences to the entity and to the owner assuming that the entity is a partnership/LLC, and alternatively an S corporation?

[9] Exceptions to this rule exist if the partnership has built-in gain property. See Chapter 7, LO7, Advanced Topic (Drilling Down)—Distributions of Built-In Gain Property.

SOLUTION:

The solution is summarized below:

Characteristic	Partnerships/LLCs	S corporations
Gain to entity for appreciation	**$0** No gain to partnership when appreciated property is distributed.	**$15,000** S corporation must recognize gain ($25,000 FMV – $10,000 adjusted basis).
Gain to owner	**$0** No gain to partner when partner receives a property distribution.	**$5,500** Basis increased to $19,500 for 10% of gain ($15,000 × 10%) or $1,500. Gain to shareholder if FMV exceeds stock basis ($25,000 FMV of land – $19,500 basis in stock).
Basis in land for owner	**$10,000** Partner has a basis in the land of $10,000, the same basis the partnership had.	**$25,000** Basis in land is FMV.

Owner's Basis for Entity-Level Debt

Only partners and LLC members can increase their basis in their ownership interest for entity-level debt. This benefits the partner/member because losses can be deducted on the owner's tax return only to the extent of basis in the ownership interest. This is the reason that partnerships are often used for tax shelters.

Positive characteristic: Basis of ownership interest may be increased for entity-level debt. (See Chapter 6, LO3, Impact of Partnership Debt on Partner's Basis in Partnership Interest for more detail.)

✓ General partnerships
✓ Limited partnerships
✓ Limited liability partnerships (LLPs)
✓ Limited liability companies (LLCs)

Negative characteristic: Basis of ownership interest is not increased for entity-level debt.

✗ C corporations
✗ S corporations

Not applicable: Owner's basis is in business assets; does not have a separate ownership interest.

N/A Sole proprietorship

Temporary Benefit of Debt Basis

While increasing an owner's basis for entity-level debt is a beneficial characteristic, for planning purposes it is important to realize that this is a temporary benefit. For example, let's compare the tax consequences involving entity-level debt for a general partner (Helen) and an S corporation shareholder (Jose). Helen and Jose each contribute $15,000 to their entity, so each has an initial basis of $15,000. The partnership and the S corporation each secure long-term debt. Assume that Helen's share of the debt is $35,000. Helen can increase her basis for her share of the $35,000 debt. However, Jose cannot increase the basis of his stock because he is not liable for the debt. Helen's total basis is now $50,000 while Jose's remains at $15,000.

In Year 1, assume that their share of the loss from the partnership and the S corporation is $18,000 and in Year 2, their share of the loss is $32,000. These losses reduce their bases to $0 as shown below:

	Helen (Partnership)	Jose (S corporation)
Beginning basis	$15,000	$15,000
Debt basis	35,000	0
Total basis before losses	$50,000	$15,000
Year 1 loss	(18,000)	(15,000) ($3,000 suspended loss)
Year 2 loss	(32,000)	0 ($32,000 suspended loss)
Basis at end of Year 2	$ 0	$ 0

Helen was able to use all her losses to reduce her basis to $0, but Jose was able to use only $15,000 of his losses. Jose must suspend the remaining $3,000 loss in Year 1 and $32,000 loss in Year 2 and then carry it forward. He can deduct the loss in future years if he has sufficient basis.

Although Helen has received tax benefits from $50,000 of losses, she invested only $15,000 in the partnership. Therefore, only $15,000 of her tax benefits are permanent. The tax benefits from the $35,000 of losses that Helen deducted because of the debt basis are temporary, meaning that Helen will recognize $35,000 of gain in the future to offset these losses. Helen could recognize the additional $35,000 of gain in several ways, including the following:

- Helen could sell her partnership interest for no consideration except the buyer's assumption of her $35,000 partnership debt. The debt relief would result in an amount realized of $35,000. Because Helen now would have no basis in her partnership interest, her recognized gain would be $35,000.
- The partnership could pay the debt back to the creditor. This would be treated as a $35,000 cash distribution to Helen. It would create a $35,000 gain for Helen because the cash distributed would exceed her basis by $35,000.

Jose has received tax benefits from $15,000 of losses, and those tax benefits are permanent. He was not allowed to deduct losses because of debt basis. Therefore, he has no gain to recognize in the future to offset any of the loss deductions. For example, if Jose sells his S corporation stock for no consideration, he will have no gain or loss. His amount realized is not increased for debt relief because he was never liable for the $35,000 debt. Thus, his amount realized due to the debt is $0.

The total gain or loss recognized over the life of the investment for both Helen and Jose after each sell their ownership interest for no consideration is ($15,000), as shown below:

	Helen (Partnership)	Jose (S corporation)
Year 1 loss	($18,000)	($15,000)
Year 2 loss	(32,000)	0
Gain on sale	35,000	0
Net gain or loss	($15,000)	($15,000)

Why **Why is the net loss the same?** The net loss over the life of the investment ($15,000) is the same, regardless of whether the investment is a partnership or an S corporation. This is because the owners both invested $15,000 in their business. ***Over the life of the investment, a business owner cannot lose more than they invested, which makes it clear that the benefits of the debt basis to Helen are temporary, not permanent.***

The temporary nature of the tax benefit from debt basis does not necessarily mean that debt basis is not an advantage for partnerships. The magnitude of the advantage depends on how much time passes before the additional $35,000 gain is recognized. If debt basis allows an additional $35,000 loss to be recognized now but the $35,000 gain does not materialize for many years, then this is a significant benefit. However, if the $35,000 gain is recognized within a couple of years of the loss, then there is not much of an advantage. The main point for you to remember from this discussion is that the tax benefits from debt basis are *temporary*, even though many taxpayers believe that they are *permanent*.

Related exercises: Multiple Choice Question 7
Tax Planning Problem 2

Taxation of Fringe Benefits

Certain fringe benefits (for example, group-term life insurance, health insurance, and dependent care benefits) are tax-free to employees if the business ensures that specified rules are met. Business owners who work in the business may or may not be able to treat fringe benefits as tax-free, as the rules vary across business entities. C corporations are definitely the winner for this characteristic, as shareholders of C corporations are eligible for tax-free fringe benefits, the same as other employees.

Because partners are not considered to be employees, the value of most fringe benefits that are tax-free to employees is taxable to partners. The cost of a partner's fringe benefits paid by the partnership are deductible by the partnership as guaranteed payments and must be included as ordinary income to the partner on Schedule K-1 (Form 1065). For example, the following common fringe benefits are taxable if a partnership pays for this benefit for a partner:

- Premium for $50,000 of group-term life insurance
- Premiums or benefits under an employer accident or health plan[10]
- Value of meals and lodging provided for the convenience of the employer
- Qualified transportation and parking benefits
- Adoption assistance

There are a few fringe benefits that partners *can* exclude from income, including:

- Educational assistance plans[11]
- Dependent care assistance plans[12]
- Qualified employee discounts
- Working-condition fringe benefits
- No-additional-cost services
- Employee length of service or safety achievement awards
- *De minimis* benefits

The same rules apply to S corporation shareholders who own more than 2% of the S corporation. S corporation shareholders who own 2% or less can benefit from tax-free fringe benefits.

Positive characteristic: Shareholders of C corporations who are employees can qualify for the same tax-free benefits as other employees.

✓ C corporations

---

[10]The partner can deduct the cost of premiums paid for health insurance by the partnership as a deduction for adjusted gross income (AGI) if the other requirements for this deduction are satisfied (such as when the partner and partner's spouse are not eligible to participate in an employer-subsidized health insurance plan).

[11]IRC §127(c)(3).

[12]IRC §1279(e)(4).

Negative characteristic: Partners and LLC members who work in their businesses are not treated as employees; therefore, they do not qualify for tax-free treatment of most fringe benefits.

- ✕ General partnerships
- ✕ Limited partnerships
- ✕ Limited liability partnerships (LLPs)
- ✕ Limited liability companies (LLCs)

Mixed characteristic: Shareholders who own 2% or more of an S corporation are treated the same as partners for purposes of the fringe-benefit rules.

- O S corporations

Not applicable: Sole proprietors do not qualify as employees, so they do not receive fringe benefits.

- **N/A** Sole proprietorship

The differences in the taxation of fringe benefits across different tax entities are shown in the next Example.

EXAMPLE 9.2.6 Taxation of Fringe Benefits

Shania, age 43, is a 30% owner of a business and also serves as the chief operating officer. As such, she receives the following nondiscriminatory fringe benefits for the year:

Benefit	Fair market value of benefit
Group-term life insurance coverage of $200,000	$ 1,100
Dependent care assistance plan	$ 5,000
Health insurance coverage for self and family	$18,000
Parking in a garage near the office ($300 monthly)	$ 3,600
Lunch provided in the office for her convenience	$ 1,200
Qualified employee discounts	$ 2,400

The $1,100 for the life-insurance coverage is the cost of the premiums. If the benefit qualifies for exclusion for up to $50,000 of employer-provided group-term life insurance, the value of the additional $150,000 of coverage per the IRS premium table (see Appendix A) is $180 (150 × $1.20).

How much of these benefits would be included in her taxable income if the business she works for is a regular corporation, an S corporation, or a partnership?

SOLUTION

Depending on the type of entity Shania worked for, the amount of each benefit included in her taxable income would be as follows:

	Amount of each benefit included in taxable income		
Benefit	**C corporation**	**S corporation**	**Partnership**
Group-term life insurance coverage of $200,000	$ 180	$ 1,100	$ 1,100
Dependent care assistance plan	$ 0	$ 0	$ 0
Health insurance coverage for self and family	$ 0	$18,000	$18,000
Parking in a garage near the office ($300 monthly)	$ 0	$ 3,600	$ 3,600
Lunch provided in office for her convenience	$1,200	$ 1,200	$ 1,200
Qualified employee discounts	$ 0	$ 0	$ 0

If Shania works for a corporation, she is eligible to exclude the first $50,000 of coverage for group-term life insurance, and the remaining coverage is taxed per the IRS premium table. If she works for an S corporation or a partnership, the fair market value of the life insurance premiums paid is included in income. The lunch benefit is taxable to her because it is provided for her convenience rather than the employer's convenience.

Her taxable benefits for a corporation or an S corporation are treated as wages and are also subject to social security and Medicare withholding. The taxable benefits received from a partnership are treated as guaranteed payments.

Related exercise: Brief Exercise 2

Application of Passive Loss Rules

The passive loss rules provide that passive losses can be offset only by passive income. Passive losses cannot offset active income such as wages, income from a business, or portfolio income. The passive loss rules do not apply the same across all business entities. These rules are summarized in **Illustration 9.7**. (See Chapter 6, LO5, Use of Partnership Losses for a discussion of the passive loss rules.)

ILLUSTRATION 9.7 Treatment of Passive Losses

What Type of Income Can Be Offset by Passive Losses?

	Active income	Passive income	Portfolio income
Individual	No	Yes	No
Corporation	Yes	Yes	Yes
Personal service corporation	No	Yes	No
Closely held corporation	Yes	Yes	No

The passive loss rules generally do not apply to C corporations. The passive loss rules *do* apply to personal service corporations and closely held corporations. A **personal service corporation** is a corporation whose principal activity is the performance of personal services by employees who own 95% or more of the corporation's stock, such as a medical corporation whose owners are also the doctors providing the medical services. For purposes of the passive loss rules, personal service corporations are treated just like individuals. That is, their passive losses cannot offset active income or portfolio income.

A **closely held corporation** exists if at any time during the last half of the taxable year more than 50 percent of the value of the corporation's outstanding stock is owned, directly or indirectly, by not more than five individuals. Closely held corporations can use passive losses to offset active corporate income but not portfolio income.

If a flow-through entity has a passive loss, then the owner can offset income with that loss as shown in Illustration 9.7.

Positive characteristic: Most corporations are not subject to the passive loss rules.

✓ C corporations

Negative characteristic: Other types of business owners are subject to the passive loss rules.

✗ S corporations

✗ General partnerships

✗ Limited partnerships

✗ Limited liability partnerships (LLPs)

✗ Limited liability companies (LLCs)

✗ Sole proprietorships

Alternative Minimum Tax

The application of the alternative minimum tax (AMT) varies across different tax entities.

Corporations

Congress created a corporate alternative minimum tax (AMT) beginning in 1987. The *Tax Cuts and Jobs Act of 2017* repealed the corporate AMT, so it was not in effect from 2018 to 2022. *The Inflation Reduction Act of 2022* reinstated the corporate AMT, but it is a much different type of tax than in the past and applies to a very small number of corporations.[13] The Joint Committee on Taxation has estimated that the new corporate AMT will apply to no more than 150 of the Fortune 500 companies. The new corporate AMT is effective for tax years beginning after 2022 and includes a 15% tax on the *adjusted financial statement income of applicable corporations* (see Chapter 3, LO4, Other Corporate Tax Issues). The minimum tax applies only to the extent that it exceeds the taxpayer's regular income tax, including its base erosion tax and anti-abuse tax for the tax year.[14]

S Corporations, Limited Liability Companies, Partnerships, and Sole Proprietorships

S corporations, LLCs, and partnerships do not pay taxes, so they do not pay the AMT. However, AMT adjustment items and preference items flow from the entity to the owner and can potentially cause individual owners to pay the AMT at the individual level, so there is an indirect relationship between these entities and the AMT. Tax items from a sole proprietorship can directly cause an individual to be subject to the AMT.

Positive characteristic: The AMT is never a positive characteristic for the taxpayer.

Negative characteristic: Adjustment items and preference items at the entity level can cause individual owners to be subject to the individual AMT.

- ✕ S corporations
- ✕ General partnerships
- ✕ Limited partnerships
- ✕ Limited liability partnerships (LLPs)
- ✕ Limited liability companies (LLCs)
- ✕ Sole proprietorship

Mixed characteristic: This is a mixed characteristic for C corporations because even though there is a corporate AMT, it applies to a small percentage of publicly traded companies, so most C corporations will never be affected by it.

- O C corporations

Related exercise: Multiple Choice Problem 8

Eligibility for QBI Deduction

Taxpayers can take advantage of the qualified business income (QBI) deduction, which is computed as 20% of the taxpayer's income from pass-through entities (partnerships, limited liability companies, and S corporations) and sole proprietorships. C corporation shareholders are not eligible for a QBI deduction on dividends received. To qualify for the QBI deduction, the taxpayer must generally conduct business activity in the United States.[15]

[13]IRC §55.

[14]Congress created the Base Erosion and Anti-Abuse Tax (BEAT) in 2017 to prevent foreign and domestic corporations operating in the United States from avoiding domestic tax liability by shifting profits outside the United States. See Chapter 13, LO6, U.S. Taxation of Foreign Corporations and Foreign Persons, for more detail.

[15]IRC §199A.

Positive characteristic:

- ✓ S corporations
- ✓ General partnerships
- ✓ Limited partnerships
- ✓ Limited liability partnerships (LLPs)
- ✓ Limited liability companies (LLCs)
- ✓ Sole proprietorship

Negative characteristic:

- ✗ C corporations

Related exercises: Discussion Question 4
Multiple Choice Problem 9
Brief Exercise 3

PRACTICE PROBLEM 9.2.1
Ability to Raise Capital

Describe which entity has the greatest ability to raise capital.

SOLUTION

C corporations are the best entity for raising capital because:

- the shareholders have limited liability,
- the corporation can issue various types of stock to meet different needs of shareholders, such as common, preferred, and convertible stock,
- the stock can be publicly traded, *and*
- shareholders can freely transfer their ownership interest.

PRACTICE PROBLEM 9.2.2
Tax Consequences from Contribution of Property

Party Company has been in existence for eight years and needs additional capital. Moses plans to contribute land to Party that has a FMV of $167,000 and an adjusted basis of $98,000. He will receive 45% of the ownership of Party. What are the tax consequences to Moses if Party is a corporation? A partnership?

SOLUTION

Moses has a realized gain of $69,000 on the contribution of the land to Party.

Fair market value	$167,000
Less: Adjusted basis	(98,000)
Realized gain	$ 69,000

If Party Company is a corporation, Moses will recognize the gain of $69,000. Moses does not meet the 80% control test required for a contribution of property to a corporation in return for stock to be tax-deferred. If Party Company is a partnership, then his recognized gain is $0. All contributions of property to a partnership in return for a partnership interest are tax-deferred because there is no control test that needs to be met.

PRACTICE PROBLEM 9.2.3
Tax Consequences from Distribution of Property

A business entity owns property with an adjusted basis of $22,000 and FMV of $47,000. The property is distributed to a 20% business owner when the owner's basis in their ownership interest is $35,000. What is the tax effect to the owner if the entity is a partnership? An S Corporation?

SOLUTION

The solution is summarized below:

Characteristic	Partnerships/LLCs	S corporations
Gain to entity for appreciation	**$0** No gain to partnership when appreciated property is distributed.	**$25,000** S corporation must recognize gain ($47,000 FMV − $22,000 adjusted basis).
Gain to owner	**$0** No gain to partner when partner receives a property distribution.	**$7,000** Basis increased to $40,000 for 20% of gain ($25,000 × 20%), or $5,000. Gain to shareholder if FMV exceeds stock basis ($47,000 FMV of land − $40,000 basis in stock).
Basis in land for owner	**$22,000** Partner has a basis in the land of $22,000, the same basis the partnership had.	**$47,000** Basis in land is FMV.

INTERACTIVE SELF-SCORING QUIZZES

9.3 Comparison of Partnerships/Limited Liability Companies and S Corporations

LEARNING OBJECTIVE 3

Compare the tax characteristics of partnerships/LLCs and S corporations.

VIDEO CONTENT

For many business owners, such as Aletta from the introduction, the choice of the proper business entity form will narrow to either a partnership/limited liability company or an S corporation. In this section, we directly compare the characteristics of these entities.

Similarities between Tax Laws for Partnerships/LLCs and S Corporations

There are several important similarities between the tax laws for partnerships/LLCs and S corporations. Recall that LLCs are taxed the same as partnerships (unless we have noted a difference).

- Both are flow-through entities with single taxation.
- LLC members, limited partners, and S corporation shareholders have limited liability, although general partners do not.
- Both partnerships/LLCs and S corporations have restrictions on what year-end must be used for the entity. Partnerships generally use the required year-end that minimizes the aggregate deferral of income for the partners as a group. S corporations typically use a calendar year-end.

Differences between Tax Laws for Partnerships/LLCs and S Corporations

There are also critical differences between the tax laws for partnerships/LLCs and S corporations. We summarize these characteristics in Illustration 9.8 and indicate whether each characteristic is an advantage for a partnership/LLC or an S corporation.

ILLUSTRATION 9.8 Differences between Tax Laws for Partnerships/LLCs and S Corporations

Comparison of Partnerships/LLCs and S Corporations

Characteristic	Advantage
Allocation of profits and losses	Partnerships/LLCs
Formation of entity	Partnerships/LLCs
Limited liability	S Corporations
Payroll taxes and self-employment tax	S Corporations
Basis increase for entity debt	Partnerships/LLCs
Preferential distributions	Partnerships/LLCs
Distributions taxable to owners	Partnerships/LLCs
Distribution of appreciated property taxable to entity	Partnerships/LLCs
Section 704(c) gains	Neutral*
Hot asset rules	S Corporations

*The rule is simpler for S corporations but more equitable for partnerships/LLCs.

Allocation of Profits and Losses

Partners have flexibility in determining profit- and loss-sharing ratios.[16] In contrast, S corporations must allocate all tax items according to the percentage of stock owned by each shareholder, so the shareholders have no flexibility with regard to sharing profits and losses.

We demonstrate how the flexibility for sharing profits and losses differs between partnerships and S corporations in the next Example.

EXAMPLE 9.3.1
Profit- and Loss-Sharing Ratios

Nia and Joakim create a new business. Nia provides cash of $1,000,000 and does not plan to work for the business. Joakim does not contribute any cash or property, but he will provide services using his expertise in software development and innovation. Each will own 50% of the business. What would be reasonable profit- and loss-sharing ratios for Nia and Joakim assuming the business is a partnership? What if the business is an S corporation?

[16]The only limitation on this flexibility is that the allocation must have substantial economic effect.

SOLUTION

It can be challenging for the owners to agree to a fair profit- and loss-sharing ratio when one owner contributes all the property, and the other partner contributes the expertise and services. Nia may believe that she should be allocated at least 75% of the profits because she contributed all the property. On the other hand, it is not likely that Joakim would be interested in a profit share of less than 50% when he is bringing all the expertise to the business.

A partnership provides the flexibility needed to satisfy the needs of both Nia and Joakim, as follows:

- Nia will receive 100% of the profits until she recoups her $1,000,000. Then, profits will be shared 50%/50%.
- Joakim will receive a guaranteed payment to compensate him for the services he provides to the partnership.

An S corporation cannot provide Nia and Joakim with this level of flexibility. If each owns 50% of the partnership, then their profit- and loss-sharing ratios must be 50%/50% every year. Additionally, the S corporation cannot provide the first $1,000,000 of profits to Nia because that would be a preferred distribution and would create a second class of stock, which would terminate the S election.

Formation of Entity

As discussed in LO2, the formation rules for partnerships/LLCs are better than for S corporations because partnerships/LLCs do not have to meet the 80% control test for gains and losses to be deferred.

Limited Liability

All shareholders of an S corporation and all members of an LLC have limited liability. However, for partnerships, only limited partners have limited liability. General partners have unlimited liability.

Payroll Taxes and Self-Employment Tax

Recall that the payroll tax rate for Social Security is 6.2% (on the first $176,100 of earnings in 2025) and the Medicare tax rate is 1.45%. These taxes apply to salaries earned by S corporation shareholders.

The self-employment tax rate is 15.3% on the first $176,100 of earnings and 2.9% on earnings above $176,100. Allocations of business income from partnerships to general partners and LLC members[17] are subject to the self-employment tax.[18] A limited partner's distributive share of earnings is usually not subject to the self-employment tax. Guaranteed payments received by both general and limited partners are subject to the self-employment tax. S corporations have an advantage over partnerships with regard to this characteristic because income allocations from S corporations are *not* subject to the self-employment tax.

The differences in the application of payroll taxes between shareholders and partners/LLC members are shown in the next Example.

[17]A full discussion of the application of the self-employment tax to LLC members is beyond the scope of this book. The primary guidance from the IRS on this issue is Prop. Reg. Section 1.1402(a)-2. This proposed regulation suggests that an LLC member who is more similar to a general partner is subject to the self-employment tax, and an LLC member who is more similar to a limited partner is not subject to the tax.

[18]Allocation of investment income to the partner or LLC member are not subject to the self-employment tax.

EXAMPLE 9.3.2 Self-Employment Tax and Payroll Tax

Kell and his sister operate an interior design business. He decides to transfer the business to an entity for liability protection and so that he can later transfer some of the ownership interest to other family members. Kell is uncertain whether he wants to create a partnership or an S corporation. He has been told that his liability for Social Security and Medicare taxes will be the same regardless of which entity he chooses. Is this correct? Assume that the business's ordinary income, after all deductions, is $100,000 and that Kell's compensation for his work is $70,000. Kell will own 90% of the business, and his sister will own 10%.

SOLUTION

If the business is an S corporation, Kell will have the combined Social Security and Medicare rate of 7.65% withheld from his wages. The corporation will have to match the 7.65%. However, his distributive share of $90,000 ($100,000 × 90%) is not subject to the self-employment tax. If the business is a partnership, Kell is not treated as an employee, and his $70,000 of compensation is classified as a guaranteed payment, which is subject to the self-employment tax rate of 15.3%. Additionally, his $90,000 distributive share is subject to the self-employment tax. These results are summarized as follows:

	S corporation	Partnership
Payroll tax		
Wages	$70,000	N/A
Payroll tax rate	× 7.65%	
Payroll taxes	$ 5,355	
Employer match	5,355	
Total payroll tax	$10,710	
Self-employment tax		
Guaranteed payment	N/A	$ 70,000
Distributive share		90,000
		$160,000
Self-employment tax rate		× 15.3%
Self-employment tax		$ 24,480

The liability for payroll taxes and self-employment tax is significantly higher if the entity is a partnership/LLC than if it is an S corporation. This increased liability for the partnership is offset by the deduction for AGI of 50% of the self-employment taxes paid. For a taxpayer in the 24% tax bracket, this deduction will result in tax savings of $2,938 ($24,480 × 50% × 24%). Additionally, if Kell has already met the ceiling for wages/earnings subject to the self-employment Social Security tax rate of 12.4% (the ceiling is $176,100 for 2025). from other sources of income, then Kell will be subject to only the self-employment Medicare tax of 2.9%.

Related exercise: Brief Exercise 4

Spotlight on the Law

S Corporations and Self-Employment Tax

Joshua has run his business, Jericho Demolition Company, as a sole proprietorship since its origination. Jericho Demolition is very profitable, and Joshua no longer wants to pay income tax and self-employment tax on the same earnings. Joshua filed articles of incorporation on behalf of Jericho Demolition on January 1 of the current year and properly filed Form 2553 to elect S corporation status. Joshua believes that if he doesn't pay himself a salary, he will only have to pay income tax on the ordinary business income generated by Jericho. Joshua will have Jericho pay him distributions instead of salary so he will have money for his living expenses. Joshua considers this strategy clever because for an S corporation, there is no self-employment tax on ordinary business income. What is Joshua not considering in his thought process?

While it is true that shareholders in S corporations do not pay self-employment tax on their earnings and that a distribution that is not in excess of Joshua's outside basis is not taxable, the IRS can assess tax and penalties on distributions that should be classified as salary. An unreasonably low salary is unacceptable. The IRS will look to see what factors are used to determine a reasonable salary in Joshua's line of work and his location based on the number of hours committed to Jericho. Also, by not paying employment taxes on his earnings, Joshua is leaving himself vulnerable to having no Social Security income in the future.

Basis Increase for Entity Debt

Partners receive a basis increase for partnership debt, whereas S corporation shareholders do not. This difference was discussed in detail in the previous section, where we explained that the advantage partnerships have with basis for entity debt is a temporary advantage.

Preferential Distributions

Partnerships can make preferential distributions to partners. For example, a partnership could make a $10,000 distribution to one partner while the other partners did not receive a distribution. This is not the case with S corporations, which cannot make preferential distributions. Each shareholder must receive a proportionate share of each distribution based on their stock ownership percentage. If an S corporation makes a preferential distribution, it has created a second class of stock, and the S election is terminated.

Related exercise: Discussion Question 5

Distributions Taxable to Owners

Gain is recognized by a partner only if the cash distributed exceeds the partner's basis in the partnership interest. Gain is recognized by an S corporation shareholder if the FMV of the cash and property distributed exceeds the shareholder's basis in the stock. Therefore, it is less likely that partners will recognize gains from a distribution.

Distribution of Appreciated Property: Taxable to Entity

Partnerships have preferential taxation over S corporations if appreciated assets are distributed. S corporations must recognize the appreciation in the year the asset is distributed, the gain is reported on Form 1120-S, and the gain flows to the shareholders and is taxed to them. On the other hand, partnerships are not taxed on the appreciation if they distribute appreciated assets to a partner.

Section 704(c) Gains

The built-in gain (BIG) rules that apply to partnerships under Section 704(c) do not apply to S corporations. (For more on the Section 704(c) rule, see Chapter 7, LO1, Built-In Gains and Losses.) The Section 704(c) rule is one of the most complicated provisions of the partnership tax law. The S corporation tax law is considered to be basic compared to many of the complex issues that can arise with partnership taxation. However, the simplicity of the S corporation tax law does not mean that it is more equitable. In fact, the S corporation law often provides less equitable results to the shareholders than would be the case for partners.

The following Example illustrates this inequity.

EXAMPLE 9.3.3. The Effects of the Absence of a Section 704(c) Rule for S Corporations

Mary Beth and Frank form a new business entity, of which each will own 50%. Mary Beth contributes cash of $50,000, and Frank contributes land with a FMV of $50,000 and adjusted basis of $30,000. Six months later, when the land still has a FMV of $50,000, the business sells the land. How is the gain on the sale of the land allocated to Mary Beth and Frank if the business is:

a. a partnership, or

b. an S corporation?

SOLUTION

The land that Frank contributes has a built-in gain of $20,000 ($50,000 FMV − $30,000 adjusted basis).

a. Partnership

When the partnership sells the land, the recognized gain will be allocated as follows, applying the Section 704(c) rule:

Amount realized	$50,000
Adjusted basis	(30,000)
Recognized gain	$20,000

Frank's Section 704(c) allocation is $20,000, the *lower* of:

1. the recognized gain from the sale of the disposition of the asset ($20,000), *or*
2. the Section 704(c) gain ($20,000).

The total gain is allocated as:

Frank	$20,000
Mary Beth	$ 0

b. S Corporation

S corporations do not have a rule similar to Section 704(c). Therefore, the $20,000 gain recognized from the sale of the land is allocated $10,000 to Frank and $10,000 to Mary Beth.

Analysis

Clearly, the S corporation solution is much simpler than the partnership solution. However, is the S corporation solution equitable? It definitely is *not*! Consider the tax and economic consequences to Mary Beth.

	FMV of 50% ownership interest for Mary Beth
Before the land sale ([$50,000 cash + $50,000 land] × 50%)	$50,000
After the land sale ($100,000 cash × 50%)	$50,000

Mary Beth's economic interest in the S corporation is $50,000 before and after the land sale. However, her K-1 will show a $10,000 gain from the land sale that she will have to report on her Form 1040 and pay tax on. In other words, Mary Beth has a *tax* gain of $10,000, but no *economic* gain. This is unfair to Mary Beth. No one wants to be taxed on a gain that is not real.

The Section 704(c) rule avoids this inequitable result by allocating the entire $20,000 gain to Frank and $0 to Mary Beth. Frank should be allocated all the gain because the $20,000 of gain accrued while he owned the property. The gain that accrued while the partnership owned the property is $0, which is why Mary Beth should not be allocated any gain.

Thus, you can see that while the S corporation tax law is less complex than the partnership tax law, this does not mean it is better, and in some situations, it creates inequitable results for the shareholders. You may wonder whether this inequitable result for Mary Beth is permanent. It is not, because she will receive a basis increase for the $10,000 gain, as shown below:

	Mary Beth's basis
Cash contribution	$50,000
Gain recognized	10,000
Basis	$60,000

The FMV of Mary Beth's stock is $50,000 and her outside basis is $60,000, so when she sells the stock, she will have a $10,000 loss. This will offset the $10,000 of gain she recognized when the S corporation sold the land. However, she may sell her stock in six weeks, six months, or sixty years or more. So the timing of when this inequitable result will be corrected is uncertain.

Why **Why is the S corporation tax law inherently simpler than the partnership tax law?** While any experienced tax professional will confirm that the partnership tax law is much more complex than the S corporation law, you may wonder why this is the case. The cause for this complexity is the flexibility afforded by the partnership tax law, combined with the inflexibility of the S corporation law. Innovative tax planners have found many ways to use the flexibility of the partnership tax law to devise strategies that provide tax benefits that were not intended by Congress, even though they are legal. To prevent these from continuing, Congress has created new tax laws and the U.S. Department of the Treasury has written new regulations to disallow the benefits from these strategies in the future. Over time, this has created a very complex set of partnership tax laws. On the other hand, Congress has not been concerned about tax planners using the S corporation laws in a similar manner, because the inflexibility of the laws does not provide opportunities for such innovative strategies. Therefore, the S corporation tax laws have remained stable and relatively simple.

Hot Asset Rules

The hot asset rules that apply to sales of partnership interests (see Chapter 7, LO 4, Sale of a Partnership Interest) and to disproportionate partnership distributions (see Chapter 7, LO5 Advanced Topic (Drilling Down)—Disproportionate Distributions) do not apply to S corporations. This is a clear advantage for S corporation shareholders, because all gains from the sale of S corporation stock are capital gains, whereas partners can have ordinary income from the sale of a partnership interest. This issue is discussed in more detail in the next section.

Related exercises: Discussion Question 6
Multiple Choice Question 10, 11
Application Problem 5

PRACTICE PROBLEM 9.3.1
Advantage of an S Corporation over a Partnership

What are two advantages that an S corporation has over a partnership?

SOLUTION

S corporation owners have limited liability and are not subject to the self-employment tax.

PRACTICE PROBLEM 9.3.2
Partnership vs. S Corporation—Flexibility

Describe why a partnership is considered more flexible than an S corporation.

SOLUTION

Partners have flexibility in determining profit- and loss-sharing ratios. S corporations must allocate all tax items according to the percentage of stock owned by each shareholder, so the shareholders have no flexibility with regard to sharing profits and losses. Also, the formation rules for partnerships are more favorable than those for S corporations, because partnerships do not have to meet the 80% control test for gains and losses to be deferred. S corporations must recognize the appreciation in the year an appreciated asset is distributed, which flows to the shareholders and is taxed to them. Partnerships are not taxed on the appreciation when they distribute appreciated assets to a partner. Perhaps most importantly, S corporations cannot make preferred distributions to owners, while partnerships can.

PRACTICE PROBLEM 9.3.3
Application of 704(c) Rule

Jason and Taylor form a new business entity, of which each will own 50%. Jason contributes cash of $24,000, and Taylor contributes Chiefs Inc. stock with a FMV of $24,000 and an adjusted basis of $15,000. Seven months later, when the stock still has a FMV of $24,000, the business sells the stock. How is the gain on the sale of the stock allocated to Jason and Taylor if the business is:

a. a partnership, or
b. an S corporation?

SOLUTION

The Chiefs Inc. stock that Taylor contributes has a built-in gain of $9,000 ($24,000 FMV – $15,000 adjusted basis).

a. **Partnership**

When the partnership sells the Chiefs Inc. stock, the recognized gain will be allocated as follows, applying the Section 704(c) rule:

Amount realized	$24,000
Adjusted basis	(15,000)
Recognized gain	$ 9,000

Taylor's Section 704(c) allocation is $9,000, the *lower* of:

1. the recognized gain from the sale of the disposition of the asset ($9,000), *or*
2. the Section 704(c) gain ($9,000).

The total gain recognized is allocated as:

Taylor	$ 9,000
Jason	$ 0

b. **S Corporation**

S corporations do not have a rule similar to Section 704(c); therefore, the $9,000 gain recognized from the sale of the Chiefs Inc. stock is allocated $4,500 to Jason and $4,500 to Taylor.

INTERACTIVE SELF-SCORING QUIZZES

9.4 Dispositions of Ownership Interests and Conversions to Other Entity Types

LEARNING OBJECTIVE 4

Distinguish the tax consequences from disposing of partnership interests, C corporation stock, or S corporation stock.

In this chapter, you have already learned the different tax rules involved in forming various entities. In this section, we compare the rules for disposing of ownership interests, focusing on C corporations, S corporations, and partnerships. (LLC rules are similar to those for partnerships; any reference to partnership rules also applies to LLCs.)

VIDEO CONTENT

Sale of an Ownership Interest

The tax consequences of selling stock in a regular corporation or an S corporation are the same. The shareholder recognizes a capital gain or loss. However, the tax consequences of selling an interest in a partnership or LLC are vastly different. The general rule indicates that a sale of a partnership interest is a sale of a capital asset, which means that the result would be a capital gain or loss, just as for corporate shareholders.[19] This reflects the entity theory, which treats the partnership as a separate entity from the partner.

However, the aggregate theory also applies to the sale of a partnership interest. If a partner sold a one-third interest in a partnership, under the aggregate theory, then the partner would have in effect sold one-third of each asset on the balance sheet, with the partner's gain or loss reflecting the character of each asset sold. This is how the sale of a partnership interest is treated.[20]

There are four types of assets on the balance sheet that can change the character of gain or loss from capital for the sale of a partnership interest. **Illustration 9.9** summarizes these rules for each asset and shows that the residual gain or loss is capital. For a detailed discussion on how the character of gain or loss is determined, see Chapter 7, LO4, Sale of a Partnership Interest.

ILLUSTRATION 9.9 Sale of a Partnership Interest

Types of Gain from Sale of a Partnership Interest

Asset type	Rule
Hot asset: Unrealized receivables and depreciation recapture	Treat as ordinary income.
Hot asset: Inventory	Treat as ordinary income.
Collectible gain	Taxed at a maximum rate of 28%.
Unrecaptured Section 1250 gain	Taxed at a maximum 25% rate.
Residual is capital gain/loss	Include in capital gain/loss netting process.

Related exercises: Discussion Questions 7, 8
Brief Exercise 5

EXAMPLE 9.4.1
Comparing the Tax Consequences of the Sale of Ownership Interests

RED Company had three owners. Raul owned 40% of RED, Ed owned 35%, and Denise owned 25%. Raul sold his ownership interest to Ramone for $116,000. Raul had originally paid $70,000 for his ownership interest and had owned the interest for seven years. RED uses the cash basis of accounting. What was Raul's gain or loss from this sale assuming that the business is a corporation? An S corporation? A partnership?

The company has the following balance sheet on the date of the sale if it is a corporation:

Corporation Balance Sheet

Assets	Adjusted basis	FMV	Debt and owners' equity	Adjusted basis	FMV
Cash	$ 50,000	$ 50,000	Debt	$ 80,000	$ 80,000
Inventory	75,000	115,000	Owners' Equity	140,000	290,000
Accounts receivable	0	60,000			
Collectibles	15,000	5,000			
Building*	80,000	140,000			
Total	$220,000	$370,000		$220,000	$370,000

*Original cost was $120,000. All depreciation was straight-line.

[19]IRC §742.
[20]IRC §751(a).

The company has the following balance sheet on the date of the sale if it is an S corporation:

S Corporation Balance Sheet

Assets	Adjusted basis	FMV	Debt and shareholders' equity	Adjusted basis	FMV
Cash	$ 50,000	$ 50,000	Debt	$ 80,000	$ 80,000
Inventory	75,000	115,000	Raul	56,000	116,000
Accounts receivable	0	60,000	Ed	49,000	101,500
			Denise	35,000	72,500
Collectibles	15,000	5,000			
Building*	80,000	140,000			
Total	$220,000	$370,000		$220,000	$370,000

*Original cost was $120,000. All depreciation was straight-line.

The company has the following balance sheet on the date of the sale if it is a partnership:

Partnership Balance Sheet

Assets	Adjusted basis	FMV	Debt and partners' capital	Adjusted basis	FMV
Cash	$ 50,000	$ 50,000	Debt	$ 0	$ 80,000
Inventory	75,000	115,000	Raul	88,000	116,000
Accounts receivable	0	60,000	Ed	77,000	101,500
			Denise	55,000	72,500
Collectibles	15,000	5,000			
Building*	80,000	140,000			
Total	$220,000	$370,000		$220,000	$370,000

*Original cost was $120,000. All depreciation was straight-line.

SOLUTION

We now compare the tax results for selling an interest in a corporation, an S corporation, and a partnership.

Corporation

Raul's gain from the sale of his corporate stock is computed as follows:

Cash received	$116,000
Adjusted basis	(70,000)
Recognized gain	$ 46,000

The gain is a long-term capital gain because Raul had owned the stock for seven years. Raul's amount realized is not increased for debt relief because corporate shareholders have limited liability and are not responsible for the debt of the corporation. Raul's basis is his original cost of $70,000 because the stock of a regular corporate shareholder is not adjusted each year for a proportionate share of the corporation's earnings.

S Corporation

Raul's gain from the sale of his S corporation stock is computed as follows:

Cash received	$116,000
Adjusted basis	(56,000) (from balance sheet)
Recognized gain	$ 60,000

The gain is a long-term capital gain because Raul had owned the stock for seven years. Raul's amount realized is not increased for debt relief because corporate shareholders have limited liability and are not responsible for the debt of the corporation. Raul's basis is taken from the equity section of the balance sheet. It is not the original cost of $70,000 because it has been adjusted each of the last seven years for Raul's share of the corporation's profits and losses, as well as for distributions.

Partnership

Raul's gain from the sale of his partnership interest is computed as follows:

Cash	$116,000	
Debt relief	32,000	
Amount realized	$148,000	
Adjusted basis	(88,000)	(from balance sheet)
Recognized gain	$ 60,000	

Raul's share of the partnership's debt is $32,000 ($80,000 × 40%). His basis of $88,000 already includes his share of the debt, because the basis of the debt on the balance sheet is $0. That means it has already been allocated to the partners' bases.

We next determine the character of the $60,000 gain by determining whether there are any assets on the balance sheet that can change the character, as follows:

Unrealized receivables: If the unrealized receivables had been collected by the partnership before Raul sold his interest, $24,000 of ordinary income would have been allocated to Raul ([$60,000 – $0 basis] × 40%) . Therefore, $24,000 of the gain is ordinary income.

Inventory: If the inventory had been sold by the partnership before Raul sold his interest, $16,000 of ordinary income would have been allocated to Raul (($115,000 – $75,000 basis) × 40%)). Therefore, $16,000 of the gain is ordinary income.

Collectibles: If the collectibles had been sold by the partnership before Raul sold his interest, a $4,000 loss would have been allocated to Raul (($5,000 – $15,000 basis) × 40%)). Therefore, there is no 28% collectible gain from the sale of the partnership interEst.

Unrecaptured Section 1250 gain: If the building had been sold by the partnership before Raul sold his interest, there would have been $40,000 of unrecaptured Section 1250 gain, computed as follows:

Amount realized	$140,000
Adjusted basis	(80,000)
Recognized gain	$ 60,000
Section 1250 recapture	0
Unrecaptured Section 1250 gain	(40,000)
Section 1231 gain	$ 20,000

There is no Section 1250 recapture because straight-line depreciation was used for the building. The gain is classified as unrecaptured Section 1250 gain to the extent of the straight-line depreciation claimed, which is $40,000 ($120,000 cost – $80,000 basis). The remaining $20,000 of gain is Section 1231 gain. Therefore, $16,000 of unrecaptured Section 1250 25% gain would have been allocated to Raul ($40,000 × 40%) if the building has been sold before Raul sold his interest. Therefore, $16,000 of the gain is unrecaptured Section 1250 25% gain.

Summary of Partnership Solution: Raul's recognized gain of $60,000 is taxed as follows:

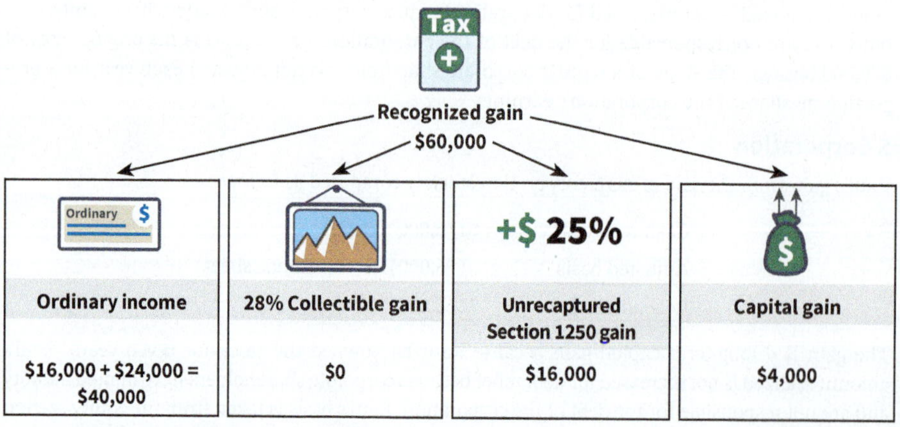

The residual is a capital gain of $4,000.

Related exercises: Application Problems 6, 7, 8

Liquidation of an Ownership Interest

The tax consequences for liquidating an ownership interest also vary significantly across C corporations, S corporations, and partnerships. These rules are summarized in **Illustration 9.10**.

ILLUSTRATION 9.10 Tax Consequences of Liquidations

Tax Consequences of Liquidations for C Corporations, S Corporations, and Partnerships

	C corporation	S corporation	Partnership
Gain to entity if assets with unrealized gains are distributed?	Yes	Yes	No
Loss to entity if assets with unrealized losses are distributed?	Yes* (with exceptions)	No	No
Gain to owner possible?	Yes	Yes	Yes (in limited circumstances)
Loss to owner possible?	Yes	Yes	Yes (in limited circumstances)
Basis to owner of asset received?	**FMV**	**FMV**	**Generally, the basis of property to the partnership**

*Exceptions to the loss disallowance rules are discussed in Chapter 4, LO5, Corporate Liquidations

Related exercise: Multiple Choice Question 12

Corporate Liquidations

Consistent with the general framework of the corporate tax law, corporate liquidations are subject to double taxation: taxation at both the corporate level and the shareholder level.

Shareholders The general rule for shareholders who surrender their shares in a complete liquidation is that gains and losses are recognized.[21] The gain or loss is computed as follows:

FMV of assets received from the corporation
Less: Adjusted basis of stock
Shareholder's gain or loss

Other important tax effects to the shareholder include the following:

- The shareholder's gain or loss is capital if the shareholder holds the stock as an investment.
- The shareholder's basis in the assets received by the corporation is the FMV of the assets on the date distributed.

Corporation Corporations recognize gains and losses on a distribution in complete liquidation as if they had sold each distributed asset for its fair market value.[22] The FMV is reduced by the adjusted basis of each asset to determine the corporate gain or loss on the distribution. The nature of the gain or loss depends on whether the asset is capital, Section 1231, or ordinary.

When a corporation has a realized loss from a complete liquidation, there are three situations for which loss recognition may be not allowed, or may at least be limited. (For more information on these limitations, see Chapter 4, LO5, Corporate Liquidations.)

[21]IRC §331.
[22]IRC §336(a). Exceptions are provided for liquidation of a subsidiary into a parent. See Chapter 4, LO5, Corporation Liquidations.

- The loss property was distributed to a *related party*, and the property distributed in complete liquidation is disqualified property, meaning that the property was contributed to the corporation in a tax-deferred corporate formation under IRC §351, or a contribution to capital, during the five-year period ending when the property was distributed. The loss that would be recognized if the asset had been sold for its FMV on the date it was distributed to the related party is disallowed.
- The loss property was distributed to a *related party*, and the property was *not* distributed pro rata to each shareholder (meaning that, e.g., a 60% shareholder would not have received exactly 60% of the loss property. The loss that would be recognized if the asset had been sold for its FMV on the date it was distributed to the related party is disallowed.
- Corporations can also have losses disallowed if the property distributed to shareholders who are *not related parties* in a complete liquidation is disqualified property, meaning that the property had been contributed to the corporation in a tax-deferred corporate formation under IRC §351, or a contribution to capital during the two-year period ending when the property was distributed. In such situations, only the built-in loss is disallowed. The built-in loss is the loss that would have been recognized had the asset been sold for its FMV on the date it was *contributed to the corporation*.

S Corporation Liquidations

Like C corporations, S corporations can recognize gain or loss at the entity level and the shareholder level due to a liquidation. However, any gain or loss recognized at the S corporation level flows through to the shareholder. For this discussion, we assume that the S corporation is not subject to the built-in gains tax that can potentially apply when an S corporation disposes of assets (see Chapter 8, LO6, S Corporation Taxes).

Shareholders The tax consequences for liquidations of a shareholder's interest in an S corporation are the same as for any S corporation distribution. Distributions to shareholders of previously taxed earnings are not taxable to the shareholders. The amount of the distribution is equal to the cash plus the FMV of property distributed (less any debt on the property assumed by the shareholder). The accumulated adjustments account (AAA) determines the amount of previously taxed earnings that have not been distributed, so if the distribution is from AAA, it is not taxable.

The steps to determine the tax consequences for the shareholder depend on whether the corporation has earnings and profits. (For a more detailed discussion, see Chapter 8, LO5, Taxation of S Corporation Distributions.)

Earnings and Profits Assuming the corporation does have E&P, the steps for determining the tax consequences are as follows:

Step 1. Evaluate: Distributions are tax-free to the extent of AAA (distributions from AAA also reduce stock basis).

Step 2. Verify: Dividend income is taxable to the extent of E&P.

Step 3. Ascertain: Distributions are tax-free to the extent of stock basis (reduced for distributions from AAA in Step 1).

Step 4. Assess: Any remaining distribution is a capital gain.

No Earnings and Profits If there is no E&P, then only steps 3 and 4 from above are needed to determine the tax consequences of a distribution:

Step 1. Ascertain: Distributions are tax-free to the extent of stock basis.

Step 2. Assess: The remaining distribution is a capital gain.

The shareholder's basis in the property received is the property's FMV.

S Corporation S corporations recognize gains and losses on a distribution in a complete liquidation as if they had sold each distributed asset for its fair market value.[23] The FMV is reduced by the adjusted basis of each asset to determine the corporate gain or loss on the distribution. The nature of the gain or loss depends on whether the asset is capital, Section 1231, or ordinary.

Related exercise: Brief Exercise 6

Partnership Liquidations

The tax consequences of liquidating distributions for partnerships are quite different than the consequences for corporations and S corporations. These rules apply when the partnership is liquidating, meaning that none of the partners will remain partners after the distribution. The partnership rules for when one partner liquidates their interest are provided in Chapter 7, LO3, Retirement Distributions.

Partners If a partner receives a liquidating distribution, the tax consequences are as follows:

- A partner recognizes gain only to the extent that the sum of the *cash* and *deemed cash* distributed to the partner exceeds the partner's basis in the partnership interest.
- If the partner receives a distribution of only property, the partner will never recognize a gain.[24]
- A partner recognizes a loss on the receipt of a distribution if the following three conditions are satisfied:[25]

    1. the distribution is liquidating,
    2. the distribution must consist only of cash, unrealized receivables, and inventory, *and*
    3. the outside basis of the partner's interest exceeds the sum of cash plus the basis of the receivables and inventory. In other words, the partner has some basis left in their partnership interest after subtracting the basis of the cash, inventory, and unrealized receivables.

Related exercise: Multiple Choice Question 13

Keep the following three guidelines in mind when computing basis for liquidating distributions:

- The general rule for the effect of partnership distributions on the partner's basis is that the basis is reduced by the amount of cash distributed and/or the basis of the property distributed.
- The ending basis in the partnership interest after the liquidation distribution must be zero. To meet this rule, in some situations the partner's basis in an asset distributed is *greater* than the partnership's basis in the asset.
- The basis in the partnership interest can never be reduced below zero. Therefore, if the total basis of all the assets distributed is greater than the partner's basis in the partnership interest, the reduction in basis is limited to the partner's basis. If that is the case, the partner's basis in the asset received is less than the partnership's basis in that asset before the distribution.

Partnership Partnerships do not recognize gain or losses for distributions to partners.[26] This rule applies for both current and liquidating distributions. This is the case whether the distribution is cash or property. **Recall** that corporations must recognize a gain when they distribute appreciated property to shareholders. The fact that partnerships do not recognize gains of appreciated property in making distributions is a major advantage of partnerships.

The following Example explores the effects of a liquidation on a corporation, S corporation, and partnership.

[23]IRC §336(a).
[24]There are some distributions involving Section 704(c) built-in gain property that are exceptions to this general rule, see Ch. 7, LO6, Advanced Topic (Drilling Down)—Optional Adjusted to Basis of Partnership Assets (Section 754 Elections).
[25]IRC §731(a)(2).
[26]IRC §731(b).

EXAMPLE 9.4.2 Comparing the Tax Consequences of Liquidating Distributions

RED Company has three owners. Raul owns 40% of RED, Ed owns 35%, and Denise owns 25%. Raul originally paid $70,000 for his ownership interest. Raul has owned the interest for seven years. RED uses the cash basis of accounting. Raul receives a liquidating distribution at the end of the year of the following assets:

	Adjusted basis	FMV
Cash	$20,000	$ 20,000
Inventory	30,000	46,000
Accounts receivable	0	24,000
Collectibles	6,000	2,000
Building	32,000	56,000
Total	$88,000	$148,000

What are the tax consequences to RED Company and Raul, assuming that the business is a corporation? An S corporation? A partnership?

The company has the following balance sheet on the date of the Raul's liquidating distribution if it is a corporation:

Corporation Balance Sheet

Assets	Adjusted basis	FMV	Debt and owners' equity	Adjusted basis	FMV
Cash	$ 50,000	$ 50,000	Debt	$ 80,000	$ 80,000
Inventory	75,000	115,000	Owners' equity	140,000	290,000
Accounts receivable	0	60,000			
Collectibles	15,000	5,000			
Building*	80,000	140,000			
Total	$220,000	$370,000		$220,000	$370,000

*Original cost was $120,000. All depreciation was straight-line.

The company has the following balance sheet on the date of the Raul's liquidating distribution if it is an S corporation:

S Corporation Balance Sheet

Assets	Adjusted basis	FMV	Debt and shareholders' equity	Adjusted basis	FMV
Cash	$ 50,000	$ 50,000	Debt	$ 80,000	$ 80,000
Inventory	75,000	115,000	Raul	56,000	116,000
Accounts receivable	0	60,000	Ed	49,000	101,500
			Denise	35,000	72,500
Collectibles	15,000	5,000			
Building*	80,000	140,000			
Total	$220,000	$370,000		$220,000	$370,000

*Original cost was $120,000. All depreciation was straight-line.

The company has the following balance sheet on the date of the Raul's liquidating distribution if it is a partnership:

Partnership Balance Sheet

Assets	Adjusted basis	FMV	Debt and partners' capital	Adjusted basis	FMV
Cash	$ 50,000	$ 50,000	Debt	$ 0	$ 80,000
Inventory	75,000	115,000	Raul	88,000	116,000
Accounts receivable	0	60,000	Ed	77,000	101,500
			Denise	55,000	72,500
Collectibles	15,000	5,000			
Building*	80,000	140,000			
Total	$220,000	$370,000		$220,000	$370,000

*Original cost was $120,000. All depreciation was straight-line.

SOLUTION

Corporation

RED Company: RED Company has distributed assets to Raul with unrealized gains and losses. The collectible has a realized loss. The other non-cash assets have unrealized gains, and RED must recognize the appreciation as gain, as follows:

	Adjusted basis	FMV	Gain/loss	Character
Cash	$ 20,000	$ 20,000	$ 0	
Inventory	30,000	46,000	16,000	Ordinary
Accounts receivable	0	24,000	24,000	Ordinary
Collectibles	6,000	2,000	0*	
Building	32,000	56,000	24,000**	Section 1231
Total	$88,000	$148,000	$ 64,000	

*Corporations cannot recognize losses generated by the distribution of property to a shareholder in a redemption.

**Corporations do have to recognize Section 291 recapture (See Chapter 1, LO3, Section 1231 Assets) as ordinary income when a building is sold, computed as follows:

Recapture if the building had been a Section 1245 asset	$40,000
Section 1250 recapture	0
Excess	$40,000
	× 20%
Section 291 recapture	$ 8,000

Therefore, $8,000 of the gain is ordinary income, and the remaining $16,000 ($24,000 − $8,000) is Section 1231 gain. If the building had been sold, the gain would be $60,000 ($140,000 amount realized − $80,000 basis). The depreciation claimed on the building is $40,000 ($120,000 cost − $80,000 basis), so the Section 1245 recapture is $40,000.

Raul: Raul's stock ownership has gone from 40% to 0%, so this liquidating distribution is treated as a redemption.

FMV of assets received from the corporation	$148,000
Less: Adjusted basis of stock	(70,000)
Long-term capital gain	$ 78,000

Raul's basis in the assets received is each asset's FMV.

S Corporation

RED Company: RED Company has distributed assets to Raul with unrealized gains and losses. The collectible has a realized loss. The other non-cash assets have unrealized gains, and RED must recognize the appreciation as gain, as follows:

	Adjusted basis	FMV	Gain/loss	Character
Cash	$20,000	$ 20,000	$ 0	
Inventory	30,000	46,000	16,000	Ordinary
Accounts receivable	0	24,000	24,000	Ordinary
Collectibles	6,000	2,000	0*	
Building	32,000	56,000	24,000**	$8,000 Section 1231 $16,000 25% gain
Total	$88,000	$148,000	$64,000	

*Corporations cannot recognize losses generated by the distribution of property to a shareholder in a redemption.

**If the building had been sold by the S corporation rather than distributed, there would have been $40,000 of 25% unrecaptured Section 1250 gain. Because 40% of the building was distributed, we show the computation for 40% of the building as follows:

	100% of building	40% of building
Amount realized	$140,000	$56,000
Adjusted basis	(80,000)	(32,000)
Recognized gain	$ 60,000	$24,000
Section 1250 recapture	0	0
Section 1250 unrecaptured gain	(40,000)	(16,000)
Section 1231 gain	$ 20,000	$ 8,000

There is no Section 1250 recapture, because straight-line depreciation was used for the building. The gain is classified as 25% unrecaptured Section 1250 gain to the extent of the straight-line depreciation claimed, which is $40,000 ($120,000 cost − $80,000 basis). The remaining $20,000 of gain is Section 1231 gain.

Raul: Raul's stock ownership has gone from 40% to 0%, so this liquidating distribution is treated as a redemption.

FMV of assets received from the corporation	$148,000
Less: Adjusted basis of stock	(56,000)
Long-term capital gain	$ 92,000

Raul's basis in the assets received is each asset's FMV.

Partnership

RED Company: Partnerships do not recognize gains or losses when assets are distributed to partners, so RED Company has no gain or loss for the liquidating distribution.

Raul: The tax consequences of the liquidation distributing are determined as follows:

	Raul's basis in partnership interest
Adjusted basis of assets received	$88,000
Cash	(20,000)
Remaining basis	$68,000
Inventory	(30,000)
Accounts receivable	(0)
Remaining basis	$38,000
Collectibles	(6,000)
Building	(32,000)
Ending basis	$ 0

The ordering rules must be followed. Cash is considered first, then the inventory and accounts receivable, and then the Section 1231 assets and capital assets, which are the collectibles and the building. Raul reduces his basis in his partnership interest by the basis of each of the assets to the partnership. Raul recognizes no gain or loss on the distribution, and his basis in each of the assets is the same basis that the partnership had in each of the assets.

Summary of Tax Consequences for RED Company and Raul

	C corporation	S corporation	Partnership
Gain for RED Company	$40,000 ordinary income; $24,000 Section 1231 gain	$40,000 ordinary income; $8,000 Section 1231 gain; $16,000 25% capital gain	N/A
Loss for RED Company	None	None	N/A
Gain to Raul	$78,000 capital gain	$92,000 capital gain	None
Loss to owner possible	None	None	None
Basis to Raul			
Cash	$20,000	$20,000	$20,000
Inventory	$46,000	$46,000	$30,000
A/R	$24,000	$24,000	$ 0
Collectibles	$ 2,000	$ 2,000	$ 6,000
Building	$56,000	$56,000	$32,000

Related exercises: Application Problems 9, 10, 11

Converting from One Entity Form to Another Entity Form

The tax consequences of converting from one entity form to another can vary tremendously. In this section, we review these consequences for sole proprietorships, C corporations, S corporations, and partnerships. The rules discussed below for partnerships also apply to LLCs.

Sole Proprietorships

The owner of a sole proprietorship could convert the business to a partnership or a corporation.

Partnership To form a partnership, at least two owners are needed. If an owner contributes assets to a partnership, no gain or loss is recognized, and the basis of the assets to the partnership remains the same. An owner's basis in the partnership interest is the same as the total basis of the adjusted basis of all the assets contributed.

Corporation If the owner contributes the assets to a corporation, no gain or loss is recognized as long as the 80% control test is met. The control test is always met if there is only one owner. The basis of the assets to the corporation remains the same. The owner's basis in their stock is the same as the total basis of the adjusted basis of all the assets contributed.

C Corporations

The shareholders of a C corporation could convert the corporation to a sole proprietor (if only one owner), a partnership (if at least two owners), or an S corporation.

Sole Proprietorship or Partnership It is very unlikely that the shareholders of a corporation would want to become a sole proprietorship. However, if they did, the tax consequences would be the same as if the owners wanted to operate their business as a partnership or an LLC. The corporation must first liquidate, with the following tax consequences:

- Gain or loss recognition to the corporation
- Gain or loss recognition to the shareholders
- FMV basis for the assets received by shareholders

If the former shareholders then want to operate as a partnership, the formation of the partnership should be tax-free.

S Corporation If the shareholders of a C corporation wish to operate as an S corporation, they need to make a timely S corporation election. The corporation does not need to liquidate, so there will be no recognized gain or loss, and the basis of the corporation's assets and the shareholders' stock remains the same. The shareholders need to keep the following criteria in mind when making the election:

- All eligibility criteria must be met at the time of the election (and for the entire tax year if made retroactively).
- The S corporation may have to pay the built-in gains tax if it has net unrealized gains on the date of the election and these assets are disposed of in the next five years. It could also be subject to the LIFO recapture tax (see Chapter 8, LO6, S Corporation Taxes).

S Corporations

The shareholders of an S corporation could convert the corporation to a sole proprietor (if only one owner), a partnership (if at least two owners), or a C corporation.

Sole Proprietorship or Partnership It is very unlikely that the shareholders of an S corporation would want to become a sole proprietorship. However, if they did, the tax consequences would be the same as if the owners wanted to operate their business as a partnership or LLC. The corporation must first liquidate, with the following tax consequences:

- Gain or loss recognition to the corporation
- Gain or loss recognition to the shareholders
- FMV basis for the assets received by shareholders

If the former shareholders then want to operate as a partnership, the formation of the partnership should be tax-free.

C Corporation The shareholders of an S corporation could revoke the S corporation election and begin operating as a C corporation. To terminate the S election, more than 50% of the shareholders (voting and non-voting) must agree to the termination. The corporation does not need to liquidate, so there will be no recognized gain or loss, and the basis of the corporation's assets and the shareholder's stock remains the same. Once the S election is terminated, the corporation cannot reelect S corporation status for five years.

Partnerships

The partners in a partnership could decide to operate their business as a sole proprietorship, a C corporation, or an S corporation. For all these alternatives, the partnership would have to liquidate, with the following tax consequences:

- There is no gain or loss to the partnership.
- A partner recognizes a gain only if the cash distributed to the partner exceeds their basis in their partnership interest.
- A partner recognizes a loss only if the partner receives no Section 1231 or capital assets, and the basis of the assets received is less than the partner's basis in their partnership interest.
- In general, the partner has the same basis in the assets received as the partnership had in the assets.

If the former partners then wish to operate as a corporation, the formation of the corporation will be tax-free as long as the 80% control test is met. If the former partners want to operate as an S corporation, a valid S corporation election will have to be filed.

Related exercise: Tax Planning Problem 3

PRACTICE PROBLEM 9.4.1
Unrealized Receivable

Golf Partnership owns machinery with an adjusted basis of $48,000 and a FMV of $63,000. Accumulated depreciation of $12,000 was taken on the machinery. If the partnership sold the asset for its FMV, what would be the tax consequences to Golf?

SOLUTION

Amount realized	$63,000
Adjusted basis	(48,000)
Gain	$15,000

$12,000 Section 1245 recapture Ordinary income ← Gain → $3,000 Section 1231 gain

Because $12,000 of Section 1245 recapture is imbedded in the machinery, then for hot asset purposes, the asset is treated as follows:

	Total	**Unrealized receivable**	**Section 1231 asset**
Fair market value	$63,000	$12,000	$51,000
Adjusted basis	$48,000	$ 0	$48,000

PRACTICE PROBLEM 9.4.2
S Corporation Liquidation

Jackson is a 100% shareholder of Heart Inc., an S corporation. On December 31, Heart distributes $18,000 cash to Jackson. On December 31, Jackson has an outside basis of $13,000 in Heart. Heart has always been an S corporation. What is the tax result of the distribution to Jackson and Heart?

SOLUTION

If there is no E&P from a previous C corporation year, then the distribution is tax-free to the extent of Jackson's outside basis in Heart. Any remaining distribution is a capital gain.

Jackson's outside basis	$13,000
Distribution	(13,000)
Ending outside basis	$ 0

The excess distribution is a $5,000 ($18,000 – $13,000) capital gain. S corporations recognize gains and losses on a distribution in a complete liquidation as if they had sold each distributed asset for its fair market value. Heart would have zero gain, because cash was distributed.

PRACTICE PROBLEM 9.4.3
Converting from a Partnership to Another Entity

What are the tax consequences of converting from a partnership to another entity?

SOLUTION

The partners in a partnership could decide to operate their business as a sole proprietorship, a C corporation, or an S corporation. For all these alternatives, the partnership would have to liquidate, with the following tax consequences:

- There is no gain or loss to the partnership.
- A partner recognizes a gain only if the cash distributed to the partner exceeds their basis in their partnership interest.
- A partner recognizes a loss only if the partner receives no Section 1231 or capital assets and the basis of the assets received is less than the partner's basis in their partnership interest.
- In general, the partner has the same basis in the assets received as the partnership had in the assets.

INTERACTIVE SELF-SCORING QUIZZES

Review and Practice

Chapter Summary

In this chapter, we build on what you have already learned so far in this book and summarize the factors that should be considered by business owners when choosing the best entity form for their business.

1 Identify the legal forms available to business owners.

The most common legal forms include:

- Corporations
- General partnerships
- Limited partnerships
- **Limited liability partnerships (LLP)**
- Limited liability companies (LLC)
- **Business trust**

Businesses will generally report for federal income tax purposes as one of the following:

Tax classification	Description	Federal tax forms used
C corporation	C corporation that has *not* made an election to be taxed as an S corporation.	**Form 1120** (U.S. Corporation Income Tax Return)
S corporation	Incorporated entity that *has* made an election to be taxed as an S corporation.	**Form 1120-S** (U.S. Income Tax Return for an S Corporation)
Partnership	General partnerships, limited partnerships, LLCs, and LLPs are all generally taxed as a partnership.	**Form 1065** (U.S. Return of Partnership Income)

Tax classification	Description	Federal tax forms used
Trust	Legal entity that holds the rights to an individual's stake or interest in a business.	**Form 1041** (U.S. Income Tax Return for Estates and Trusts)
Sole proprietorship	If an owner does not create a separate business entity, then the owner will report as a sole proprietorship.	**Schedule C** (Profit or Loss from Business)
Tax-exempt organization	A tax-exempt organization must pay tax on its unrelated business taxable income.	**Form 990-T** (Exempt Organization Business Income Tax Return)

2 Understand the tax and non-tax characteristics for each business entity.

In this section, we review the tax and non-tax characteristics for each business form. These characteristics are summarized as follows:

Comparison of the Characteristics of Tax Entities

Characteristic	C corporation	S corporation	Partnership/LLP	Multi-member LLC	Sole proprietorship
Ability to raise capital?	**Strong** (Positive)	**Weak** (Negative)	**Moderate** (Mixed)	**Moderate** (Mixed)	**Weak** (Negative)
Limited liability?	**Yes** (Positive)	**Yes** (Positive)	General—**No** (Negative) Limited—**Yes** (Mixed)	**Yes** (Positive)	**No** (Negative)
Double taxation of income?	**Yes** (Negative)	**No** (Positive)	**No** (Positive)	**No** (Positive)	**No** (Positive)
Able to retain income at lower tax cost?	**Depends on relative tax rates** (Positive)	**No** (Negative)	**No** (Negative)	**No** (Negative)	**N/A**
Tax-deferred entity formation?	**Possibly—subject to control test** (Mixed)	**Possibly—subject to control test** (Mixed)	**Yes** (Positive)	**Yes** (Positive)	**N/A**
Distributions taxable to owner?	**Yes** (Negative)	**Possibly** (Mixed)	**Rarely** (Positive)	**Rarely** (Positive)	**N/A**
Distribution of appreciated property taxable to entity?	**Yes** (Negative)	**Yes** (Negative)	**No** (Positive)	**No** (Positive)	**N/A**
Owner's basis increased for entity-level debt?	**No** (Negative)	**No** (Negative)	**Yes** (Positive)	**Yes** (Positive)	**N/A**
Tax-free fringe benefits for owners?	**Yes** (Positive)	**No** for most benefits, if own more than 2% (Negative)	**No** for most benefits (Negative)	**No** for most benefits (Negative)	**N/A**
Passive loss rules apply?	**No** (Positive)	**Yes** (Negative)	**Yes** (Negative)	**Yes** (Negative)	**Yes** (Negative)
Alternative Minimum Tax available?	**Rarely** (Mixed)	**Indirectly** (Negative)	**Indirectly** (Negative)	**Indirectly** (Negative)	**Directly** (Negative)
Eligible for QBI deduction?	**No** (Negative)	**Yes** (Positive)	**Yes** (Positive)	**Yes** (Positive)	**Yes** (Positive)

3 Compare the tax characteristics of partnerships/LLCs and S corporations.

There are several differences between the tax laws for partnerships/LLCs and S corporations. We summarize these characteristics below and indicate whether each is an advantage for a partnership/LLC or an S corporation.

Comparison of Partnerships/LLCs and S Corporations

Characteristic	Advantage
Allocation of profits and losses	Partnerships/LLCs
Formation of entity	Partnerships/LLCs
Limited liability	S Corporations
Payroll taxes and self-employment tax	S Corporations
Basis increase for entity debt	Partnerships/LLCs
Preferential distributions	Partnerships/LLCs
Distributions taxable to owners	Partnerships/LLCs
Distribution of appreciated property taxable to entity	Partnerships/LLCs
Section 704(c) gains	Neutral
Hot asset rules	S Corporations

4 Distinguish the tax consequences from disposing of partnership interests, corporate stock, or S corporation stock.

- The tax consequences of selling stock in a regular corporation or an S corporation are the same. The shareholder recognizes capital gain or loss. However, the tax consequences of selling an interest in a partnership or LLC are vastly different. There are four types of assets on the balance sheet that can influence the character of gain or loss from the sale of a partnership interest, as shown below. The residual gain or loss from the sale of the partnership interest is capital gain or loss.

Types of Gain from Sale of a Partnership Interest

Asset type	Rule
Hot asset: Unrealized receivables and depreciation recapture	Treat as ordinary income.
Hot asset: Inventory	Treat as ordinary income.
Collectible gain	Taxed at a maximum rate of 28%.
Unrecaptured Section 1250 gain	Taxed at a maximum 25% rate.
Residual is capital gain/loss	Include in capital gain/loss netting process.

- The tax consequences for liquidating an ownership interest also vary significantly across corporations, S corporations, and partnerships, as shown below.

Tax Consequences of Liquidations for C Corporations, S Corporations and Partnerships

	C corporation	S corporation	Partnership
Gain to entity if assets with unrealized gains are distributed?	Yes	Yes	No
Loss to entity if assets with unrealized losses are distributed?	Yes (with exceptions)	No	No
Gain to owner possible?	Yes	Yes	Yes (in limited circumstances)
Loss to owner possible?	Yes	Yes	Yes (in limited circumstances)
Basis to owner of asset received?	**FMV**	**FMV**	**Generally, the basis of property to the partnership**

Communication Application

Communication

Choice of Entity with Future Property Distributions

(LO2) Desiree and Olga are planning to start a business selling healthcare products and need advice on selecting the appropriate form of entity. They anticipate losses in the first three years, and both would like to participate in management decisions. Their long-term business plan contemplates receiving future in-kind property distributions. Desiree and Olga do not want the distributions to be taxable to the business entity or to them. Prepare a memo to Desiree and Olga indicating the best choice(s) for entity structure.

Solution

Memo to Client

Hello Desiree and Olga,

Thank you for allowing me to answer your question about entity choice for your new business. Your choices include a C corporation, an S corporation, a general partnership, a limited partnership, and a limited liability company (LLC). Because you anticipate losses in the first three years, I would recommend a flow-through entity (S corporation, LLC, partnership). This will allow you both to utilize the losses on your individual tax returns to the extent that you have basis in this entity. All the flow-through entity choices will allow both of you to participate in management decisions except for a limited partnership. A limited partnership must have at least one limited partner, and limited partners cannot participate in the management of the business, or they will lose their limited liability protection.

When appreciated property is distributed to a partner, no gain is recognized by a partnership or an LLC. However, if a C corporation or an S corporation distributes appreciated property, gain must be recognized by the corporation. At the owner level, property distributions never create gain for a partner. Gain is recognized by the partner only if cash distributed exceeds the basis in the partnership interest. C corporation and S corporation shareholders may have to recognize income when receiving property distributions.

Therefore, we recommend that you choose either a general partnership or a limited liability company. Both choices provide you with the opportunity to participate in management, utilize losses, and not create gains to the entity or yourself when a property distribution occurs. While you did not mention limited liability as a factor, it is an important consideration. A general partnership would not provide liability protection for either of you, as you would have unlimited liability.

Please let us know how we can service you further or if you have any questions.

Sincerely,
Carnes & Youngberg, CPAs

Ethics and Professional Responsibility Application

Ethics

Allocation of Losses

(LO3) Aaron and Caleb are shareholders in an S corporation, Chip Inc., owning 60% and 40% respectively. Chip Inc. has hired your accounting firm to prepare the S corporation tax return as well as Aaron's and Caleb's individual tax returns. While reviewing last year's return for Chip, you notice that the allocation of loss to Aaron and Caleb was not 60% and 40%. During a conversation with the two shareholders, it was revealed that Aaron was not able to deduct the loss on his tax return due to basis issues. So more than 40% of the losses were allocated to Caleb, because he had more outside basis to absorb the loss and deduct it on his individual tax return. What is your advice to Aaron and Caleb?

In addition to the chapter content, see *Statements on Standards for Tax Services* at www.aicpacima.com/resources/landing/statements-on-standards-for-tax-services, *Circular 230* at www.irs.gov/tax-professionals/office-of-professional-responsibility-and-circular-230, and Chapter 2, LO4, Tax Professional Responsibilities.

Solution

Partners have flexibility in determining profit- and loss-sharing ratios. S corporations must allocate all tax items according to the percentage of stock owned by each shareholder, so the shareholders have no flexibility with regard to sharing profits and losses. Aaron was supposed to report 60% of the loss, even if he is unable to deduct the loss. Caleb must report only 40% of the loss.

Under *SSTS* 1.2.6: Knowledge of Errors, a member should promptly inform a taxpayer upon becoming aware of the taxpayer's failure to file a required return, an error in a previously filed return, an error in a return that is the subject of an administrative proceeding, an error in an administrative filing, an error in a tax representation engagement, or an error in advice provided if discovered by the member while providing services for the taxpayer. A member should also advise the taxpayer of the potential consequences of the error and advise on corrective measures to be taken.

Also, under *Circular 230* §10.22, Diligence as to Accuracy, "a practitioner must exercise due diligence—(1) In preparing or assisting in the preparation of, approving, and filing tax returns, documents, affidavits, and other papers relating to Internal Revenue Service matters."

It is your responsibility as the tax practitioner to report all items of income and loss correctly on the current tax return. You must advise Aaron and Caleb of the corrections and of the consequences if they do not comply and correct the returns.

Key Terms

Business Trust 9-6
Closely Held Corporation 9-25
Double Taxation 9-16
Electing Large Partnership 9-7
Limited Liability Partnership 9-6
Per Se Corporation 9-9
Personal Service Corporation 9-25

End-of-Chapter Assessment

Discussion Questions

1. **(LO1)** What are some legal considerations in choosing an entity structure?

2. **(LO1)** Briefly describe the difference between a general partnership, a limited partnership, and a limited liability partnership.

3. **(LO2)** Why is a C corporation subject to double taxation?

4. **(LO2)** When determining entity choice, why is it important to consider how the entity is taxed and how the owner is taxed?

5. **(LO3)** If a business entity makes a distribution of $60,000 to its two owners, how is the distribution allocated if it is an S corporation? A partnership?

6. **(LO3)** Briefly describe the similarities and differences between a partnership and an S corporation.

7. **(LO4)** What is a hot asset?

8. **(LO4)** Explain the look-through rule and the transaction(s) to which it applies.

Multiple Choice Questions

1. **(LO1)** Which of the following business types is considered the simplest from a tax perspective?
   - **a.** Sole proprietor
   - **b.** Partnership
   - **c.** C corporation
   - **d.** S corporation

2. **(LO1)** Which of the following is not a separate legal business entity?
   - **a.** Limited liability company (LLC)
   - **b.** Partnership
   - **c.** Sole proprietorship
   - **d.** C corporation

3. **(LO1)** Which of the following statements is false regarding the check-the-box regulations?
   - **a.** The check-the-box regulations do not apply to sole proprietorships.
   - **b.** Under the check-the-box regulations, limited liability companies generally are "disregarded" if they have one owner.
   - **c.** Under the check-the-box regulations, entities that are incorporated may elect to be taxed as a partnership.
   - **d.** *Per se* corporations are not eligible to make an election as to how they want to be taxed.

4. (LO1) Which of the following statements is false regarding check-the-box regulations?

a. A regular C corporation can be taxed as a partnership.

b. A single-member LLC has a default classification to be disregarded.

c. An LLC with two members has a default classification of partnership.

d. An S corporation cannot be disregarded under the check-the-box regulations.

5. (LO2) Which of the following business owners has unlimited liability?

a. General partner

b. S corporation shareholder

c. Limited liability company member

d. Limited partner

6. (LO2) Which of the following entities is subject to double taxation?

a. S corporation

b. C corporation

c. Limited liability company

d. General partnership

7. (LO2) Which of the following entities will never permit the owner to receive an increase in their basis for the debt of the entity?

a. General partnership

b. Limited partnership

c. Limited liability company

d. S corporation

8. (LO2) Which of the following entities is subject to the AMT?

a. General partnership

b. Limited liability company

c. C corporation

d. S corporation

9. (LO2) Which of the following is not eligible for the QBI deduction?

a. General partner in a partnership

b. Member in a limited liability company

c. Shareholder in a C corporation

d. Shareholder in an S corporation

10. (LO3) Which of the following is a difference between a general partnership and an S corporation?

a. S corporation owners have limited liability, but general partners do not.

b. Ordinary business income (OBI) flowing from an S corporation is not subject to self-employment tax, but OBI flowing from a partnership is subject to self-employment tax for a general partner.

c. Distributions of property to partners are never taxable to the partner, but distributions of property to S corporation shareholders may be taxable to the shareholder.

d. All of the above are correct differences.

11. (LO3) Which of the following can be an advantage of a limited liability company over an S corporation?

a. Double taxation of profits is avoided.

b. Owners receive limited liability protection.

c. Appreciated property can be distributed tax-free to an owner.

d. Incentive stock options can be used to compensate owners.

12. (LO4) Which of the following entities would not have a recognized gain if an appreciated asset was distributed in a complete liquidation?

a. C corporations, S corporations, and partnerships

b. C corporations only

c. S corporations only

d. Partnerships only

13. (LO4) A loss might be recognized by a partner on a liquidating distribution for a partnership in which of the following circumstances?

a. A loss can never be recognized

b. If only cash and capital assets are distributed

c. If only Section 1231 assets are distributed

d. If only cash, unrealized receivables, and inventory are distributed

Brief Exercises

1. (LO1) Herman, who is a personal trainer operating as a sole proprietor, has noticed that some of his customers also take kickboxing classes in town from Francis, also a sole proprietor. Herman and Francis decide to combine their class offerings and split the profits equally. If Herman and Francis take no formal legal action to organize as another business form, what entity choice is appropriate?

2. (LO2) Demarcus is a 10% general partner in a partnership. He received $5,000 in educational assistance, a $350 watch for a qualified length of service award, and $10,000 in adoption assistance from the partnership. What is the tax effect to Demarcus?

3. (LO2) Describe three positive characteristics of being a C corporation, an S corporation, and a partnership.

4. (LO3) Thadeus is considering creating a partnership or an S corporation in which he is an 80% owner. Thadeus projects ordinary business income of $140,000 after all business deductions, including compensation for himself. He is planning on compensation for himself of $50,000. What will Thadeus's employment taxes be (Social Security and Medicare tax) if the entity operates as a partnership? An S corporation?

5. (LO4) Champion Partnership owns machinery with an adjusted basis of $62,000 and a FMV of $88,000. Accumulated depreciation of $22,000 was taken on the machinery. If the partnership sold the asset for its FMV, what would be the tax consequences to Champion? If a partner sold their partnership interest, would the partner have any ordinary income due to hot assets related to the machinery?

6. (LO4) Javier is a 100% shareholder of King Inc., an S corporation. On December 31, King distributes $35,000 cash to Javier. On December 31, Javier has an outside basis in King of $28,000. King has always been an S corporation. What is the tax result of the liquidating distribution to Javier and King?

Application Problems

1. **(LO1)** Moe, Larry, and Curly are three individuals who agree to merge their competing consulting service businesses. Each business has been operating as a sole proprietorship. Moe, Larry, and Curly sign an agreement to equally share profits, management rights, and co-ownership. No filing is made with any state. What is the appropriate entity status of the merged businesses?

2. **(LO2)** Christian forms a business in Year 10 that will develop training materials for computer programming companies. Christian is deciding what the best entity choice is for his business. He is considering the following alternatives. For each alternative, indicate the type of liability exposure Christian would have, using the following table:

Entity type	Unlimited liability	Limited liability
Sole proprietorship		
C corporation		
S corporation		
Single-member LLC		
General partnership		

3. **(LO2)** Spartan Company has been in existence for six years and needs additional capital. Avery plans to contribute land to Spartan that has a FMV of $330,000 and an adjusted basis of $280,000. He will receive 40% of the ownership of Spartan. What are the tax consequences to Avery if Spartan is a corporation? A partnership?

4. **(LO2)** A business entity owns property with an adjusted basis of $55,000 and a FMV of $85,000. The property is distributed to a 25% business owner when the owner's basis in their ownership interest is $72,000. What is the tax effect to the owner if the entity is an S corporation? A partnership?

5. **(LO3)** Tom and Jerry are forming a new business entity, of which each will own 50%. Tom contributes cash of $48,000, and Jerry contributes Walmart stock with a FMV of $48,000 and adjusted basis of $35,000. Nine months later, when the stock still has a FMV of $48,000, the business sells the stock. How is the gain on the sale of the stock allocated to Tom and Jerry if the business is

a. a partnership, or

b. an S corporation?

Which result is more equitable to the shareholders?

6. **(LO4)** Noah Company has three owners. Shem owns 45% of Noah, Ham owns 30%, and Japheth owns 25%. Shem sold his ownership interest to Lamech for $195,750. Shem had originally paid $105,000 for his ownership interest. Shem had owned the interest for six years. Noah Company uses the cash basis of accounting.

The company has the following balance sheet on the date of the sale if it is a corporation:

Assets	Adjusted basis	FMV	Debt and owners' equity	Adjusted basis	FMV
Cash	$ 75,000	$ 75,000	Debt	$120,000	$120,000
Inventory	112,500	172,500	Owners' equity	210,000	435,000
Accounts receivable	0	90,000			
Collectibles	22,500	7,500			
Building*	120,000	210,000			
Total	$330,000	$555,000		$330,000	$555,000

*Original cost was $180,000. All depreciation was straight-line.

What was Shem's gain or loss from this sale assuming that the business is a corporation?

7. **(LO4)** Noah Company has three owners. Shem owns 45% of Noah, Ham owns 30%, and Japheth owns 25%. Shem sold his ownership interest to Lamech for $195,750. Shem had originally paid $105,000 for his ownership interest. Shem had owned the interest for six years. Noah Company uses the cash basis of accounting.

The company has the following balance sheet on the date of the sale if it is an S corporation:

Assets	Adjusted basis	FMV	Debt and shareholders' equity	Adjusted basis	FMV
Cash	$ 75,000	$75,000	Debt	$120,000	$120,000
Inventory	112,500	172,500	Shem	94,500	195,750
Accounts receivable	0	90,000	Ham	63,000	130,500
Collectibles	22,500	7,500	Japheth	52,500	108,750
Building*	120,000	210,000			
Total	$330,000	$555,000		$330,000	$555,000

*Original cost was $180,000. All depreciation was straight-line.

What was Shem's gain or loss from this sale assuming that the business is an S corporation?

8. **(LO4)** Noah Company has three owners. Shem owns 45% of Noah, Ham owns 30%, and Japheth owns 25%. Shem sold his ownership interest to Lamech for $195,750. Shem had originally paid $105,000 for his ownership interest. Shem had owned the interest for six years. Noah Company uses the cash basis of accounting.

The company has the following balance sheet on the date of the sale if it is a partnership:

Assets	Adjusted basis	FMV	Debt and partners' capital	Adjusted basis	FMV
Cash	$ 75,000	$75,000	Debt	$ 0	$120,000
Inventory	112,500	172,500	Shem	148,500	195,750
Accounts receivable	0	90,000	Ham	99,000	130,500
Collectibles	22,500	7,500	Japheth	82,500	108,750
Building*	120,000	210,000			
Total	$330,000	$555,000		$330,000	$555,000

*Original cost was $180,000. All depreciation was straight-line.

What was Shem's gain or loss from this sale assuming that the business is a partnership?

9. **(LO4)** Noah Company has three owners. Shem owns 45% of Noah, Ham owns 30%, and Japheth owns 25%. Shem had originally paid $105,000 for his ownership interest. Shem had owned the interest for six years. Noah uses the cash basis of accounting. Shem receives a liquidating distribution at the end of the year of the following assets:

	Adjusted basis	FMV
Cash	$ 33,750	$ 33,750
Inventory	50,625	77,625
Accounts receivable	0	40,500
Collectibles	10,125	3,375
Building	54,000	94,500
Total	$148,500	$249,750

The company has the following balance sheet on the date of the distribution if it is a corporation:

Assets	Adjusted basis	FMV	Debt and owners' equity	Adjusted basis	FMV
Cash	$ 75,000	$ 75,000	Debt	$120,000	$120,000
Inventory	112,500	172,500	Owners' equity	210,000	435,000
Accounts receivable	0	90,000			
Collectibles	22,500	7,500			
Building*	120,000	210,000			
Total	$330,000	$555,000		$330,000	$555,000

*Original cost was $180,000. All depreciation was straight-line.

What are the tax consequences to Noah Company and Shem assuming that the business is a corporation?

10. **(LO4)** Noah Company has three owners. Shem owns 45% of Noah, Ham owns 30%, and Japheth owns 25%. Shem had originally paid $105,000 for his ownership interest. Shem had owned the interest for six years. Noah uses the cash basis of accounting. Shem receives a liquidating distribution at the end of the year of the following assets:

	Adjusted basis	FMV
Cash	$ 33,750	$ 33,750
Inventory	50,625	77,625
Accounts receivable	0	40,500
Collectibles	10,125	3,375
Building	54,000	94,500
Total	$148,500	$249,750

The company has the following balance sheet on the date of the distribution if it is an S corporation:

Assets	Adjusted basis	FMV	Debt and shareholders' equity	Adjusted basis	FMV
Cash	$75,000	$75,000	Debt	$120,000	$120,000
Inventory	112,500	172,500	Shem	94,500	195,750
Accounts receivable	0	90,000	Ham	63,000	130,500
Collectibles	22,500	7,500	Japheth	52,500	108,750
Building*	120,000	210,000			
Total	$330,000	$555,000		$330,000	$555,000

*Original cost was $180,000. All depreciation was straight-line.

What are the tax consequences to Noah Company and Shem assuming that the business is an S corporation?

11. **(LO4)** Noah Company has three owners. Shem owns 45% of Noah, Ham owns 30%, and Japheth owns 25%. Shem had originally paid $105,000 for his ownership interest. Shem had owned the interest for six years. Noah uses the cash basis of accounting. Shem receives a liquidating distribution at the end of the year of the following assets:

	Adjusted basis	FMV
Cash	$ 33,750	$ 33,750
Inventory	50,625	77,625
Accounts receivable	0	40,500
Collectibles	10,125	3,375
Building	54,000	94,500
Total	$148,500	$249,750

The company has the following balance sheet on the date of the distribution if it is a partnership:

Assets	Adjusted basis	FMV	Debt and partners' capital	Adjusted basis	FMV
Cash	$ 75,000	$75,000	Debt	$ 0	$120,000
Inventory	112,500	172,500	Shem	148,500	195,750
Accounts receivable	0	90,000	Ham	99,000	130,500
Collectibles	22,500	7,500	Japheth	82,500	108,750
Building*	120,000	210,000			
Total	$330,000	$555,000		$330,000	$555,000

*Original cost was $180,000. All depreciation was straight-line.

What are the tax consequences to Noah Company and Shem assuming that the business is a partnership?

Tax Planning Problems

Planning

1. **(LO2)** Manuel and Juan are surgeons who practice as general partners. Juan is concerned about his potential liability for lawsuits filed against Manuel and the general partnership. What entity type would be best for this partnership?

2. **(LO2)** Tristan owns a 25% interest as a general partner in Bear Partnership and has a beginning basis of $2,000, not including any debt basis. Recourse debt of $8,500 has been allocated to him based on his ownership percentage. The partnership anticipates losses of $20,000 in Year 1 and $22,000 in Year 2. If Tristan is in a 15% tax bracket for LTCGs and plans to sell his interest on January 1 of Year 3 for no consideration, would this sale be advantageous to Tristan? He is in the 35% marginal tax bracket for other income. Discuss the consequences of the debt allocation, the loss deductibility, and the sale of the partnership interest. Assume Bear Partnership does not have any hot assets on its balance sheet.

3. **(LO4)** Tracie, a U.S. citizen, and Hugo, a resident and citizen of Australia, want to form a business association to sell computer chips in the United States. Both Tracie and Hugo want to have limited liability to the extent of their investments, to have single taxation, and to actively participate in management. Which type (or types) of business organization best fits their needs?

Professional Development Skills

Communication Problems

Communication

1. **(LO2, 4) Single-Member LLC** Reuben, an individual, decides to open an escape room amusement facility. For legal purposes, he created an LLC. However, for tax purposes, he asks his CPA for advice on choice of taxation status. If you were Reuben's CPA, what answer would you give him? What other options could you provide to Reuben? Write a letter to Reuben explaining his possible choices.

2. **(LO1) Malpractice Liability: Who Is Responsible?** Simon, Ursula, and Rhashad are cosmetic surgeons in California and are equal partners in the SUR general partnership. Simon botched a facelift, and SUR is being sued for $1,000,000 by the patient. Ursula and Rhashad feel that Simon should be responsible for the liability from the lawsuit because Simon made the error. What is your response to Simon, Ursula, and Rhashad? Write a memo to the client.

Ethics and Professional Responsibilities Problem

Ethics

1. **(LO2) Deductibility of Losses** Chen and Yun formed CY Inc., an S corporation, five years ago as equal shareholders. Due to a recession, CY had a loss for the first time in Year 6. Your firm has been hired to prepare Year 7's tax return for CY and Chen and Yun. While reviewing Year 6, you notice that a loss in excess of basis was deducted on Yun's individual tax return. It appears that 50% of the debt of the S corporation was added to Yun's basis in Year 6. When discussing the Year 6 tax return, Chen and Yun ask that you leave Year 6 alone and prepare Year 7's tax returns based on Year 7 information. They say that because Year 7 is profitable, the loss would have been deducted anyway in Year 7 when Yun had increased basis again. What is your response to Chen and Yun?

In addition to the chapter content, see *Statements on Standards for Tax Services* at www.aicpacima.com/resources/landing/statements-on-standards-for-tax-services, *Circular 230* at www.irs.gov/taxprofessionals/office-of-professional-responsibility-and-circular-230, and Chapter 2, LO4, Tax Professional Responsibilities.

Research Problem

Research

1. (LO1, 2, 3) **Choosing a Business Entity Type** Marvin is starting his own business in Park City, Utah, operating a bed and breakfast, Mooselodge Inn. Mooselodge will also offer wedding venues and packages. Marvin will be active in the management of Mooselodge. He has developed a business plan and believes he will have losses for the first four years until his business and reputation are established. Marvin is currently in the 37% marginal tax bracket as an individual. He thinks forming a corporation is a smart move because a corporation's tax rate is only 21%. And he would like to protect himself from any potential liability. What advice can you provide Marvin? Review the chapter content and see www.irs.gov/businesses/small-businesses-self-employed/business-structures for more information.

CPA Exam Preparation: Task-Based Simulations

1. (LO1, 2, 3, 4) **Entity Choice** Maverick and Goose are brothers who would like to start a business training pilots in their new business venture, Top Flight Aviation Company. Maverick and Goose would each own 50% and would contribute equal cash and assets to the business. They are concerned about how to structure the entity and need your help answering a few questions.

In the boxes below, indicate if the situation or question applies to a partnership, S corporation, and/or C corporation by answering YES or NO.

A	Partnership	S corporation	C corporation
1. Is there a maximum number of owners for this entity type?			
2. Generally, is the entity subject to tax?			
3. Is the income generated subject to self-employment tax?			
4. Is the formation of the entity typically a taxable event?			
5. If an operating loss is not deductible at the entity or owner level, can it be carried forward?			
6. Do the passive loss rules apply to the deductibility of losses?			
7. Can organizational expenses of up to $5,000 be deducted immediately in some circumstances?			
8. Is the entity or owner possibly subject to the alternative minimum tax?			
9. Is there a restriction on choice of tax year?			
10. Is the tax rate on operating income a flat 21%?			

Go to Wiley's book companion site to complete the Task-Based Simulation.

2. (LO1, 2, 3, 4) **Deductibility of Losses** Archibald owns 30% of Star Kaleidoscope (SK). SK, a business entity, reported $200,000 of business loss for the tax year under consideration. Determine Archibald's allowable loss in each of the following independent situations. Enter Archibald's deductible loss in the associated area using positive whole numbers. If a value is zero, enter 0.

Description of independent situations	Deductible loss
a. SK is organized as a C corporation. Archibald has $40,000 basis in the entity.	
b. SK is organized as an LLC. Archibald has $40,000 tax and at-risk basis in SK. He materially participates in SK operations and management.	
c. SK is organized as an LLC. Archibald has $30,000 tax and at-risk basis in SK. He is not a material participant in SK's management. Archibald reports a salary of $65,000 from his job and has no other investment activity with income or loss.	
d. SK is organized as a partnership. Archibald contributed $40,000 cash to the partnership. He is a general partner. SK Partnership had $70,000 outstanding debt before Archibald's investment in it. He works full time for the partnership.	
e. SK is organized as an LLC. Archibald has $20,000 tax and at-risk basis in SK. Archibald does not work for SK. Archibald reports $15,000 of income from another business activity in which he is a passive investor.	

Go to Wiley's book companion site to complete the Task-Based Simulation.

CHAPTER 10

Taxes on the Financial Statements

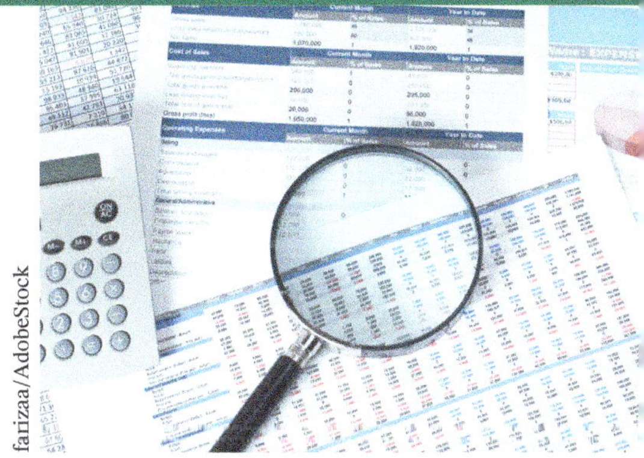

Before studying this chapter, you should know or, if necessary, review:

3.3 Corporate Taxable Income

3.4 Other Corporate Tax Issues (Accounting Methods and Periods)

Chapter Introduction

VIDEO CONTENT

As a new member of the tax department, Kay was assigned to the client service team for Hawkeye Corporation (Hawkeye). Her responsibilities included preparation of the client's tax return and preparation of the *income tax provision* for the audited financial statements under Generally Accepted Accounting Principles (GAAP). Getting started was overwhelming—the process seemed like a jigsaw puzzle. Then, taking the work one piece at a time, Kay completed the challenging task. It was so rewarding to see how all the pieces of the reporting requirements for the financial statements and the tax return fit together. Stepping back to see the big picture, Kay realized it was critical for a tax specialist to master the financial statement reporting requirements for income taxes.

In this chapter, you will learn the GAAP reporting requirements of the Financial Accounting Standards Board's ASC Topic 740, Income Taxes. The tax return for business entities requires disclosure of the difference between net income reported on the financial statements and taxable income reported on the tax return. In addition to disclosure on the tax return, these *book-tax differences* must be accounted for on the GAAP balance sheet and income statement and require disclosure in the footnotes of the financial statements. This work requires an understanding of both tax accounting principles and financial accounting principles. A tax professional must understand why and when book-tax differences occur and perform detailed tracking and measuring of the differences each year to accumulate the information necessary for the required disclosures. You will also learn how deferred tax assets and deferred tax liabilities are determined, and understand that these are real assets and liabilities like other items on the balance sheet.

The following illustration provides the framework for the computations and reporting that you will learn to perform in this chapter. We begin by explaining why identification of book-tax differences is the starting point for calculating taxes on the financial statements. You will learn how to calculate income tax assets and liabilities on the balance sheet and income tax expense on the income statement. We cover the required tax disclosures in the footnotes to the financial statements. Then, you will learn how the reporting requirements for the financial statements translate into required reporting on the tax return. Finally, we discuss issues that emphasize the need for you to develop professional skills and judgment beyond number crunching and simply balancing the debits and credits.

As you progress through the chapter, you will see financial statements, examples, and illustrations. It is important that you do not get ahead of yourself. You must work out each step in the income tax provision process one at a time, like pieces of a puzzle, and in the specified order. You cannot complete this process by trying to fast forward to the end.

The starting point for computing the income tax provision is *pre-tax book income*. The seven steps that we cover in this chapter to determine the income tax provision and its disclosure are summarized below and shown in the following illustration (LO = Learning Objective).

LO2 Step 1. Identify: Permanent and temporary differences and carryovers.

- Temporary differences
- Permanent differences
- Carryovers

LO2 Step 2. Calculate: The current income tax expense or benefit.

- Current income tax asset
- Current income tax liability

LO2 Step 3. Determine: The deferred income tax expense or benefit.

- Deferred income tax asset
- Deferred income tax liability

Income tax provision	=	Current income tax expense (benefit)	+	Deferred income tax expense (benefit)

LO2 Step 4. Evaluate: The need for a valuation allowance.

LO2 Step 5. Assess: The need of a reserve for uncertain tax positions.

LO3 Step 6. Create: Tax disclosures in the financial statements.

- Balance sheet
- Income statement
- Footnotes
    - Provision for income taxes
    - Deferred income tax assets and liabilities
    - Effective tax rate

LO4 Step 7: Prepare: Disclosures in the tax return

- Schedules M-1 and M-3

Determining the Income Tax Provision and Disclosures

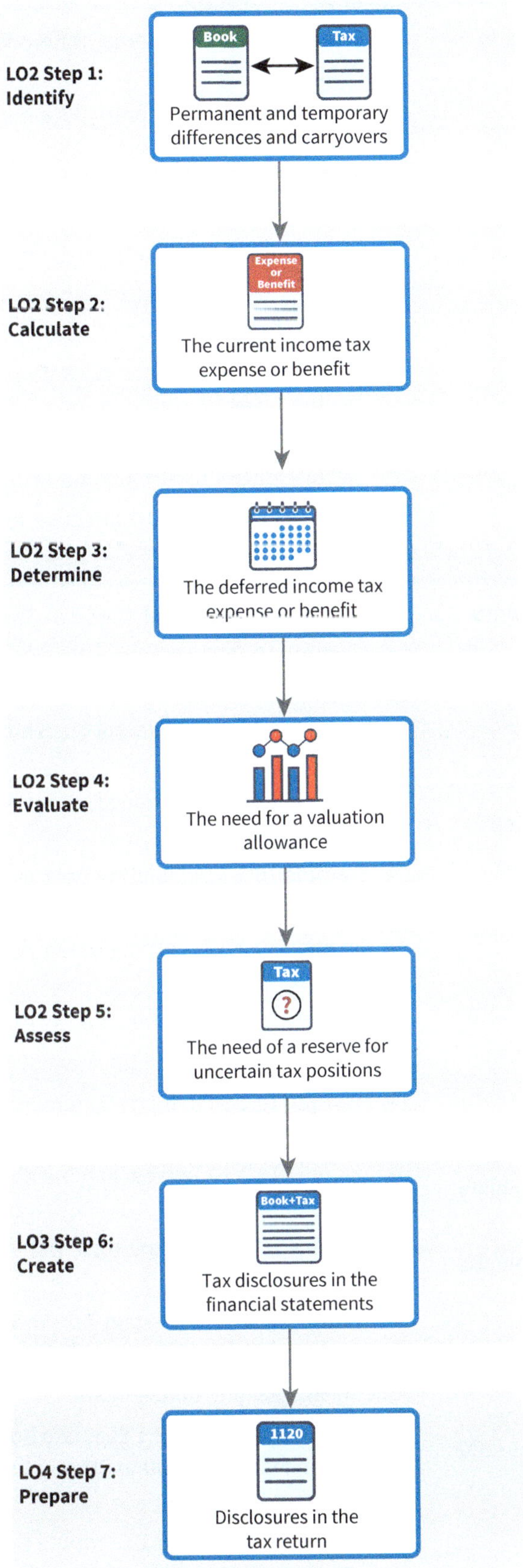

LEARNING OBJECTIVES	TOPICS	PRACTICE OPPORTUNITIES

1. Understand GAAP accounting for income taxes.	**10.1 Basics of Accounting for Income Taxes**
	• Book-Tax Differences
	  • Temporary Differences
	  • Permanent Differences
	  • Carryovers
	• GAAP Rules (ASC 740)
	  • Objectives
	  • Income Tax Provision
	  • Effective Tax Rate
		• Example 10.1.1 Temporary Difference—Prepaid Rental Income
		• Example 10.1.2 Temporary Difference—Accrued Charitable Contributions
		• Example 10.1.3 Temporary vs. Permanent Differences
		• Example 10.1.4 Carryovers
		• Example 10.1.5 Effective Tax Rate without Deferred Income Taxes
		• Example 10.1.6 Effective Tax Rate with Deferred Income Taxes
		• Practice Problem 10.1.1 Book-Tax Difference and the Calculation of Current Income Tax Expense
		• Practice Problem 10.1.2 Effective Tax Rate Comparison

2. Compute the current and deferred income tax expense, and evaluate the need for a valuation allowance and a reserve for uncertain tax positions.	**10.2 Determining the Income Tax Provision**
	• Identify Permanent and Temporary Differences and Carryovers (LO2 Step 1)
	• Calculate the Current Income Tax Expense or Benefit (LO2 Step 2)
	  • Current Income Tax Asset (Refund)
	  • Current Income Tax Liability (Payable)
	• Determine the Deferred Income Tax Expense or Benefit (LO2 Step 3)
	  • Deferred Income Tax Asset (DTA)
	  • Deferred Income Tax Liability (DTL)
	• Evaluate the Need for a Valuation Allowance (LO2 Step 4)
	  • Positive Evidence
	  • Negative Evidence
	• Assess the Need of a Reserve for Uncertain Tax Positions (LO2 Step 5)
		• Example 10.2.1 Identifying Book-Tax Differences
		• Example 10.2.2 Temporary Differences: Created This Year or in a Prior Year?
		• Example 10.2.3 Calculating Current Income Tax Expense (Benefit)
		• Example 10.2.4 Recording Current Income Tax Expense (Benefit)
		• Example 10.2.5 Calculating Deferred Income Tax Expense (Benefit)
		• Example 10.2.6 Recording Deferred Income Tax Expense (Benefit)
		• Example 10.2.7 Total Income Tax Provision
		• Example 10.2.8 Book Equivalent of Taxable Income
		• Example 10.2.9 Financial Statements Adjusted for Deferred Taxes
		• Example 10.2.10 Taxable Income after the Tax Provision
		• Example 10.2.11 Evaluation to Determine Need for a Valuation Allowance
		• Example 10.2.12 Uncertain Tax Positions
		• Example 10.2.13 Impact of Uncertain Tax Position on Current Year and Future Years
		• Practice Problem 10.2.1 Evaluate Book-Tax Differences and Calculate Current Income Tax Expense
		• Practice Problem 10.2.2 Compute the Deferred Tax Expense and Journal Entry

LEARNING OBJECTIVES	TOPICS	PRACTICE OPPORTUNITIES

3. Describe the required financial statement disclosures for income taxes.	**10.3 Tax Disclosures in the Financial Statements**
	• Balance Sheet
	• Income Statement
	• Footnotes
	  • Provision for Income Taxes
	  • Deferred Income Tax Assets and Liabilities
	  • Effective Tax Rate
		• Example 10.3.1 Income Taxes on the Balance Sheet
		• Example 10.3.2 Income Taxes on the Income Statement
		• Example 10.3.3 Footnote: Provision for Income Taxes
		• Example 10.3.4 Footnote: Deferred Income Tax Assets and Liabilities
		• Example 10.3.5 Footnote: Effective Tax Rate
		• Practice Problem 10.3.1 Calculation and Interpretation of the Effective Tax Rate

4. Understand the tax reporting and filing requirements for Form 1120.	**10.4 Disclosures in the Tax Return** • Schedule M-1 Items • Schedule M-3	• Example 10.4.1 Schedule M-1 Reconciliation • Practice Problem 10.4.1 Calculation of Taxable Income
5. Identify other special issues that impact accounting for income taxes.	**10.5 Special Issues** • Different Taxes and Taxing Jurisdictions • Different Timing for Income Tax Provision vs. Tax Return Preparation	• Example 10.5.1 Income Tax Provision for Different Taxes • Example 10.5.2 Income Tax Provision Adjustment for Estimates • Practice Problem 10.5.1 Taxes to Include in the Income Tax Provision • Practice Problem 10.5.2 IRS Audit Adjustment

Tax Forms referenced in this chapter

Form 1120	U.S. Corporation Income Tax Return
Form 1120, Schedule M-1	Reconciliation of Income (Loss) per Books With Income per Return
Form 1120, Schedule M-3	Net Income (Loss) Reconciliation for Corporations With Total Assets of $10 Million or More

10.1 Basics of Accounting for Income Taxes

LEARNING OBJECTIVE 1

Understand GAAP accounting for income taxes.

VIDEO CONTENT

Most items of income (revenue) and deductions (expenses) are included in both net income on the financial statements and taxable income on the tax return. **Book income** is defined as net income reported on the entity's financial statements. However, significant differences exist between book income and taxable income. **Book-tax differences** occur when the amount of an item of income or deduction recognized in book income is different for taxable income. Taxable income is computed by starting with net income on the financial statements and then adjusting to account for the differences between book income and taxable income.

Related exercise: Discussion Question 1

Book-Tax Differences

The differences between book income and taxable income are grouped into the following categories:

- Temporary differences
- Permanent differences
- Carryovers

Temporary Differences

In Chapter 3, LO4, Other Corporate Tax Issues, you learned there are exceptions to the accrual method for income tax purposes. For example, taxpayers must recognize certain types of prepaid income when received, while the income will be recognized on the financial statements when earned. On the expense side, an accrual-basis taxpayer cannot deduct charitable contributions accrued on the financial statements until they are actually paid (unless they make an election).[1]

Throughout this chapter, the word *book* refers to the financial statements of the entity prepared in accordance with GAAP.

These are examples of temporary differences. **Temporary differences** occur when items of income and deduction are recognized in book income in one year but are recognized in taxable income in a different year. Over time, the same amount of income or deduction is recognized in book income and taxable income because these temporary differences reverse. Temporary differences can increase or decrease book income compared to taxable income.

The following Examples illustrate temporary differences for prepaid rental income and the deduction for charitable contributions.

EXAMPLE 10.1.1
Temporary Difference—Prepaid Rental Income

Hawkeye is the landlord of commercial office space. Rent income is $1,000 per month. The tenant paid rent for Year 1 throughout Year 1, and paid rent for January through June of Year 2 in December, Year 1. Hawkeye is a calendar-year, accrual-basis taxpayer for book and tax purposes. How much rental income will Hawkeye recognize for Years 1 and 2 on the financial statements compared to the tax returns?

SOLUTION

There is a book-tax difference in the treatment of the prepaid rental income. Under the accrual method, Hawkeye recognizes prepaid income in the year earned. Hawkeye will recognize $12,000 of income in both Years 1 and 2 on the financial statements. On the tax returns, Hawkeye must recognize prepaid income when received. Hawkeye will recognize income of $18,000 in Year 1 ($12,000 for Year 1 plus $6,000 for Year 2) and $6,000 in Year 2. The book-tax difference is temporary because the difference reverses. The same amount of income totaling $24,000 is recognized on the financial statements and the tax returns over the two-year period.

[1]IRC §170(a)(2) provides that a calendar-year corporation may elect to treat as paid during the tax year any contribution that is actually paid by the 15th day of the fourth month after the close of the tax year if it was authorized by the board of directors during the year. If the election is not made, a deduction is only allowed for contributions paid during the year.

EXAMPLE 10.1.2 Temporary Difference—Accrued Charitable Contributions

Hawkeye is a calendar-year, accrual-basis taxpayer for book and tax purposes. On December 21 of Year 1, Hawkeye's board authorized a donation of $100,000 to the local city symphony orchestra. Hawkeye paid the contribution on May 1, Year 2. Assume there are no limitations on the charitable contribution based on taxable income. How much of the charitable contribution will Hawkeye deduct in Years 1 and 2 on the financial statements compared to the tax returns?

SOLUTION

There is a book-tax difference in the treatment of the charitable contribution. Under the accrual method, Hawkeye's financial statements will reflect the expense in Year 1, the year the board authorized the contribution. On the tax return, Hawkeye can deduct charitable contributions only when paid, with an exception if the board authorized the contribution before December 31 and it is paid by April 15,Year 2. Hawkeye did not pay the charitable contribution by April 15, Year 2, so it cannot make the election to deduct it in Year 1. Hawkeye will deduct the charitable contribution in Year 2. The book-tax difference is temporary because the difference reverses. The same amount of expense totaling $100,000 is recognized on the financial statements and the tax returns over the two-year period.

Permanent Differences

Permanent differences are items that create a permanent difference between book income and taxable income. These differences do not net over time.

The following Example distinguishes temporary differences versus permanent differences.

EXAMPLE 10.1.3 Temporary vs. Permanent Differences

Hawkeye has the following book-tax differences for the current tax year:

- Bad debt expense
- Charitable contributions
- Municipal bond interest income
- Fines and penalties
- Tax depreciation greater than book depreciation

Indicate which of these items are temporary differences and which are permanent differences.

SOLUTION

- Bad debt expense—Temporary difference
- Charitable contributions—Temporary difference
- Municipal bond interest income—Permanent difference
- Fines and penalties—Permanent difference
- Depreciation—Temporary difference

Bad debt expense, charitable contributions, and depreciation expense may create temporary differences. The financial statements use the allowance method of accounting for bad debts, while the direct write-off method must be used for tax purposes. The book-tax difference that may result from charitable contributions was explained in Example 10.1.2. Different depreciation methods are used for financial reporting and tax reporting, which creates temporary differences between book income and taxable income. Municipal bond interest income and fines and penalties are permanent differences. Municipal bond interest income is never taxed, and fines and penalties are never deductible for tax purposes. These differences do not reverse, so book income and taxable income will never be the same for these items.

Related exercises: Discussion Question 2
Multiple Choice Questions 1, 2
Brief Exercise 1

Carryovers

Carryovers occur when tax deductions and tax credits cannot be utilized on the tax return for the year in which they are created and are either carried back or carried forward to reduce the tax liability in prior or future years. Carryovers of *deductions* reduce *taxable income* in a year different from the year in which they were created. Carryovers of *tax credits* reduce the *tax liability* in a year different from the year in which they were created.

Tax deductions that create carryovers can be thought of as another type of temporary difference. However, this type of temporary difference occurs because tax laws limit the amount of certain deductions allowed for the current year, not because a deduction is recognized in book income for one year and in taxable income for a different year.

Tax credits are amounts that taxpayers can subtract from their income tax liability dollar for dollar. Certain tax credits may not be fully utilized on the tax return for the tax year in which they are created due to limitations. Tax credits that are subject to limitation can be carried back or forward to reduce the tax liability in a different year. Unlike carryovers for deductions, tax credit carryovers are not temporary book-tax differences. They impact the tax liability, not taxable income, so they are considered permanent differences.

The following Example illustrates possible carryover items.

EXAMPLE 10.1.4
Carryovers

Hawkeye's tax return reflects the following for the current tax year:

- Capital gains of $4,000
- Capital losses of $12,000
- Charitable contributions of $5,000 in excess of the allowable deduction for the current year
- Research tax credits of $10,000 in excess of the allowable amount for the current year

Which of these items create a carryover, and why?

SOLUTION

Corporations may deduct capital losses only to the extent of capital gains. The excess capital loss of $8,000 ($12,000 – $4,000) carries back to the prior three tax years or carries forward to the next five tax years. The excess charitable contributions of $5,000 may be carried forward to the next five tax years. Both the capital losses and the charitable contributions create carryovers that are temporary differences because they will be deducted on the tax return in one year and recognized on the financial statements in a different year. The research tax credit may be carried back two years or carried forward twenty years. A tax credit carryover is a permanent difference because it reduces the tax liability rather than taxable income.

Related exercise: Discussion Question 3

We summarize some of the more common temporary differences and carryovers in **Illustration 10.1** below and compare the GAAP treatment to the tax treatment.

ILLUSTRATION 10.1 Common Temporary Differences and Carryovers

Common Temporary Differences and Carryovers			
Income or expense	**GAAP treatment: Is this included in book income?**	**Tax treatment: Is this included in taxable income?**	**Adjustment to book income**
Unearned income received in advance (prepaid income) • **Rental income** • **Interest income**	NO Recognized when earned	YES Taxable upon receipt	↑INCREASE book income in the year of receipt ↓DECREASE book income in the year earned
Gain or loss on disposition of depreciable assets	YES Book gain or loss	YES Tax gain or loss	↑INCREASE if tax gain > book gain or if tax loss < book loss ↓DECREASE if tax gain < book gain or if tax loss > book loss
Net capital losses	YES Expensed in year of sale or disposition	NO Disallowed loss creates carryover	↑INCREASE book income for excess capital loss
Capital loss carryforward	**N/A**	YES (if utilized) May offset capital gains	↓DECREASE book income for carryforward used
Installment sales	YES Recognized upon sale	NO (for deferral) Realized gain is deferred until proceeds are received	↑INCREASE book income as payments are received ↓DECREASE book income for deferred gain
Bad debt expense	YES Allowance method	YES Direct write-off method	↑INCREASE book income for increase in allowance account ↓DECREASE book income for decrease in allowance account
Uniform capitalization (UNICAP)	NO Specific expenses are not capitalized in inventory	YES Specific expenses are capitalized in inventory	↑INCREASE book income for UNICAP adjustment when inventory on hand or capitalized costs increase ↓DECREASE book income when inventory on hand decreases
Depreciation expense	YES GAAP depreciation using book basis of asset	YES MACRS depreciation using tax basis of asset	↑INCREASE book income if tax depreciation < book depreciation ↓DECREASE book income if tax depreciation > book depreciation
Amortization: Goodwill	NO ASC 350 tests for annual impairment	YES Straight-line over 15 years	↑INCREASE book income for impairment expense ↓DECREASE book income for tax amortization

(*continued*)

ILLUSTRATION 10.1 Common Temporary Differences and Carryovers (cont.)

Common Temporary Differences and Carryovers			
Income or expense	**GAAP treatment: Is this included in book income?**	**Tax treatment: Is this included in taxable income?**	**Adjustment to book income**
Amortization: Organization & start-up costs	NO See AICPA SOP 98-5[2]	YES Straight-line over 180 months	↓DECREASE book income for tax amortization
Charitable contributions	YES Expensed when paid or accrued	YES Deducted when paid or election is made to pay by 15th day of fourth month after year end subject to 10% taxable income limitation	↑INCREASE book income for excess charitable contributions
Charitable contributions carryover	N/A	YES Deduction subject to 10% taxable income limitation	↓DECREASE book income for carryforward used
Deferred (accrued) compensation: bonuses, vacation pay, pension benefits	YES Expensed when accrued	YES Deducted when paid or if paid within 2-1/2 months after year-end	↑INCREASE book income for increase in accrued expense ↓DECREASE book income for decrease in accrued expense
Interest expense	YES Expensed when accrued	YES Deduction may be limited; excess creates a carryover	↑INCREASE book income for excess expense
Interest expense carryover	N/A	YES Subject to limitations on deduction	↓DECREASE book income for carryover used
Warranty expense	YES Expense based on estimates	YES Deducted based on actual expense	↑INCREASE book income for estimated deduction ↓DECREASE book income for actual expense when paid
Net operating losses	YES Expensed in year incurred	NO Not deductible; excess creates a carryover	↑INCREASE book income for net operating loss in year created
Net operating loss carryforward	N/A	YES (if utilized) May offset 80% of taxable income	↓DECREASE book income for net operating loss used

We list some of the more common permanent differences and carryovers in **Illustration 10.2** below and compare the GAAP treatment to the tax treatment.

[2]American Institute of Certified Public Accountants (AICPA) issued Statement of Position (SOP) No. 98-5, Reporting on the Costs of Start-Up Activities, in April 1998 to provide organizations with guidance on how to report start-up and organization costs. Discussion regarding this reporting is beyond the scope of this textbook.

ILLUSTRATION 10.2 Common Permanent Differences and Carryovers

Common Permanent Differences and Carryovers			
Income or expense	**GAAP treatment: Is this included in book income?**	**Tax treatment: Is this included in taxable income?**	**Adjustment to book income**
Municipal bond interest income	YES Included in book income	NO Excluded from taxable income	↓DECREASE book income for interest income
Proceeds from life insurance on key employees	YES Included in book income	NO Excluded from taxable income	↓DECREASE book income for proceeds received
Interest expense on loans to purchase municipal bonds	YES Expensed when accrued	NO Not deductible for tax purposes	↑INCREASE book income for interest expense
Premiums paid to purchase life insurance on key employees	YES Expensed when accrued	NO Not deductible for tax purposes	↑INCREASE book income for premiums paid
Meals expense	YES Expensed when accrued	YES Only 50% deductible for tax purposes	↑INCREASE book income for 50% of meals expense
Non-deductible expenses: fines, penalties, political contributions, lobbying expenses	YES Expensed when accrued	NO Not deductible for tax purposes	↑INCREASE book income for expenses
Entertainment expenses	YES Expensed when accrued	NO Not deductible for tax purposes	↑INCREASE book income for expenses
Federal income tax expense	YES Expensed when accrued	NO Not deductible for tax purposes	↑INCREASE book income for expense
Dividends received deduction (DRD)	N/A	YES Dividend income from another corporation either fully or partially excluded from taxable income	↓DECREASE book income for DRD
Tax credits	N/A	NO No deduction for tax purposes; reduces tax liability	No impact on book or taxable income

Why **Why are there differences between income and deductions recognized on the financial statements and the tax return?** Many businesses must issue financial statements to stakeholders, such as creditors and investors, to secure debt and equity financing. For these purposes, a business would like its financial statements to reflect the most profitable results. Financial statements are based on Generally Accepted Accounting Principles (GAAP), which require businesses to adhere to certain principles. The **matching principle** requires a business to record expenses incurred in the same period it recognizes the related revenues earned. The **conservatism principle** requires a business to recognize expenses and liabilities as soon as possible, even when there is some uncertainty about their existence, but to recognize revenues and assets only when they are assured of being received. Together, these principles are biased against overstating income and assets and against understating expenses and liabilities. In this way, financial statements avoid misleading creditors and investors.

On the other hand, the overall goal of tax law is to raise revenue to fund the government and collect taxes when taxpayers have the wherewithal (money) to pay the tax. This is best achieved by maximizing or accelerating revenues and limiting or deferring deductions. Congress also uses tax laws to achieve certain social, economic, and political objectives. Therefore, it is not surprising that book income and taxable income are calculated differently. For tax planning purposes, a business is highly motivated to find ways to report the least taxable income given its book income. As a result, there is natural tension between a business's goals for financial reporting and its goals for tax accounting. As a CPA, you will be responsible for accounting for the book-tax differences, and this chapter gives you the tools you will need to meet this responsibility.

Related exercises: Discussion Question 4
Brief Exercises 1, 2

Tax Planning Tip

As a tax professional, you must consider both the financial reporting and the tax implications of your recommendations to a business. A strategy that reduces taxes may also decrease financial income and cause financial reporting costs for the business.

GAAP Rules (ASC 740)

The Financial Accounting Standards Board's Accounting Standards Codification (ASC) 740, *Income Taxes*[3] (hereafter, ASC 740) governs the accounting and reporting requirements related to income taxes. ASC 740 implements the matching principle so that income tax expense incurred is recorded in the same period as the related income is recognized. The purpose of the reporting requirements is to provide additional information and transparency regarding financial position, cash flows, and operations to the users of financial statements.

Objectives

Potential Pitfall

ASC 740 does not directly address permanent differences, because permanent differences do not create deferred income tax assets and liabilities on the balance sheet. Only temporary differences and carryovers create deferred income tax assets and liabilities. Permanent differences are taken into account in calculating taxable income and thus the current income tax expense or benefit for the year.

The two primary objectives of ASC 740 are to recognize:

1. **Current income tax liability** or **current income tax asset**—the amount of taxes payable or refundable on the tax return for the current year.
2. **Deferred income tax liability** or **deferred income tax asset**—the expected future tax cost or the expected future tax savings attributable to temporary book-tax differences and carryforwards.

A deferred income tax liability is recognized when cumulative taxable income is less than book income and occurs when *either*:

- An expense is deducted on the tax return in the current year, but not deductible on the financial statements until a future year, *or*
- Income is recognized on the financial statements in the current year but not recognized on the tax return until a future year.

A deferred income tax asset is recognized when cumulative taxable income is greater than book income and occurs when *either*:

- Income is recognized on the tax return in the current year, but not recognized on the financial statements until a future year, *or*
- An expense is deducted on the financial statements in the current year, but not deductible on the tax return until a future year.

Related exercises: Discussion Question 5
Multiple Choice Question 3

Income Tax Provision

The **income tax provision** is the income tax expense (benefit) on the income statement. It is the *sum* of the following:

- The **current income tax expense (benefit)**, which is the amount of taxes payable (or refundable) on the tax return for the current year, *and*
- The **deferred income tax expense (benefit)**, which is the amount of the future tax cost (or savings) attributable to temporary book-tax differences and carryovers.

Related exercise: Discussion Question 6

[3]For more information, see https://www.fasb.org/page/ShowPdf?path=Prop_ASU-Income_Taxes_(Topic_740)-Simplifying_the_Accounting_for_Income_Taxes.pdf

In equation form, this is:

$$\text{Income tax provision/expense} = \text{Current income tax expense (benefit)} + \text{Deferred income tax expense (benefit)}$$

Illustration 10.3 shows where the current and deferred income tax expense is reported on the income statement for a hypothetical company.

ILLUSTRATION 10.3 Income Statement

Tottenham, Inc. **Income Statement** **For the Year Ending December 31, 2025**		
Revenues		$140,000
Expenses		70,000
Income before income taxes		70,000
Income tax expense		
Current	$9,000	
Deferred	7,000	16,000
Net income		$ 54,000

Effective Tax Rate

The **effective tax rate** is computed as:

$$\text{Effective tax rate} = \frac{\text{Income tax expense}}{\text{Pre-tax net income}}$$

Permanent differences impact the effective tax rate. A company must disclose its effective tax rate and reconcile it with the company's statutory U.S. tax rate (currently 21%). We discuss the financial statement disclosure requirements below in LO3, Tax Disclosures in the Financial Statements.

Why **Why do deferred income taxes matter?** Temporary differences impact the timing of recognition of income and deductions over more than one year. If a temporary difference increases taxable income and the related income tax expense in the current year, the temporary difference will decrease taxable income and the related income tax expense in a future year. The matching principle requires the financial statements to include the future tax cost or tax savings in the period the temporary difference occurs. A deferred tax asset results when book income is less than taxable income; more taxes have been paid than are recorded on the financial statements. Similarly, a deferred tax liability results when taxable income is less than book income; less taxes have been paid than are recorded on the financial statements. If the future savings or expense is not reported in the current year, users of the financial statements will not be fully informed about the financial position, cash flows, and operations of the company.

The following Examples revisit the scenario presented in Example 10.1.1. The facts are repeated here and used to demonstrate the importance of recording deferred income taxes to provide better information to users of financial statements. The first Example computes the effective tax rate without considering deferred income taxes.

EXAMPLE 10.1.5 Effective Tax Rate without Deferred Income Taxes

Hawkeye is the landlord of commercial office space. Rent income is $1,000 per month. The tenant paid rent for Year 1 throughout Year 1, and paid rent for January through June of Year 2 in December, Year 1. Hawkeye is a calendar-year, accrual-basis taxpayer for book and tax purposes. How much rental income will Hawkeye recognize for Years 1 and 2 on the financial statements compared to the tax returns? What is Hawkeye's effective tax rate for Years 1 and 2 if it reports income tax expense on the financial statements without recording deferred income taxes pursuant to ASC 740?

SOLUTION

We use the following steps to solve this problem.

Step 1. Prepaid rental income is a temporary book-tax difference. Under the accrual method, the rental income for book purposes is reported when the income is earned. For tax purposes, prepaid rental income is reported when it is received.

Step 2. Next, we prepare a workpaper comparing the amount of rental income recognized in book income and in taxable income for Years 1 and 2, as shown below (see rows highlighted in blue).

Step 3. We then calculate the income tax expense (benefit) on pre-tax income using the 21% tax rate (see row highlighted in yellow below).

Step 4. Finally, we determine the effective tax rate (see calculation highlighted in pink below).

$$\text{Effective tax rate} = \frac{\text{Income tax expense}}{\text{Book pre-tax income}}$$

	Book Year 1	Book Year 2	Tax Year 1	Tax Year 2
Rental income				
Year 1 January–December	$12,000	$ 0	$12,000	$ 0
Year 2 January–June	0	6,000	6,000	0
July–December	0	6,000	0	6,000
Pre-tax income	$12,000	$12,000	$18,000	$6,000
Income tax expense (benefit) @ 21% federal rate	$ 3,780	$ 1,260	$ 3,780	$1,260
Effective tax rate	31.5% ($3,780/$12,000)	10.5% ($1,260/$12,000)		

There is a book-tax difference in the treatment of the prepaid rental income. For book income, Hawkeye recognizes prepaid income in the year earned. Hawkeye will recognize $12,000 of income in both Year 1 and Year 2 on the financial statements. On the tax returns, Hawkeye must recognize prepaid income when received. Hawkeye will recognize income of $18,000 in Year 1 ($12,000 for Year 1 plus $6,000 for Year 2) and $6,000 in Year 2. The book-tax difference is temporary because the difference reverses. The same amount of income, totaling $24,000, is recognized on the financial statements and the tax returns over the two-year period. The effective tax rate is 31.5% for Year 1 and 10.5% for Year 2. In the effective tax rate equation, the numerator uses the tax payable on the tax return, whereas the denominator uses the book pre-tax income.

The next Example shows how the inclusion of deferred income taxes impacts the effective tax rate.

EXAMPLE 10.1.6 Effective Tax Rate with Deferred Income Taxes

Assume the same facts as in Example 10.1.5. What is Hawkeye's effective tax rate for Years 1 and 2 if it reports income tax expense on the financial statements with deferred income taxes pursuant to ASC 740?

SOLUTION

We use the following steps to solve this problem:

Step 1. Prepaid rental income is a temporary book-tax difference. Under the accrual method, the rental income for book purposes is reported when the income is earned. For tax purposes, prepaid rental income is reported when it is received.

Step 2. Next, we prepare a workpaper comparing the amount of rental income recognized in book income and in taxable income for Year 1 and Year 2, as shown below (see rows highlighted in blue).

Step 3. We then calculate the income tax expense (benefit) on pre-tax income using the 21% tax rate (see row highlighted in yellow below).

Step 4. Finally, we determine the effective tax rate (see calculation in pink below):

$$\text{Effective tax rate} = \frac{\text{Income tax expense}}{\text{Book pre-tax income}}$$

	Book Year 1	Book Year 2	Tax Year 1	Tax Year 2
Rental income:				
Year 1 January–December	$12,000	$ 0	$12,000	$ 0
Year 2 January–June	0	6,000	6,000	0
July–December	0	6,000	0	6,000
Pre-tax income	$12,000	$12,000	$18,000	$6,000
Income tax expense (benefit) @ 21% federal rate:				
Current income tax expense (benefit)	$ 3,780	$ 1,260	$ N/A	$ N/A
Deferred income tax expense (benefit)	(1,260)	1,260	N/A	N/A
Income tax expense (benefit)	$ 2,520	$ 2,520	$ 3,780	$1,260
Net income	$ 9,480	$ 9,480		
Effective tax rate	21% ($2,520/$12,000)	21% ($2,520/$12,000)		

ASC 740 applies the matching principle. For Years 1 and 2, Hawkeye is required to report the income tax expense associated with the income reported on the financial statements rather than the tax liability reported on the tax returns. The income tax expense for the prepaid rental income is deferred from Year 1 to Year 2, creating a deferred tax savings of $1,260 on the financial statements for Year 1. The savings reflect the future income tax expense, which will be recorded on the financial statements in Year 2. ASC 740 eliminates the wide swing in the effective tax rate between years shown in Example 10.1.5, which distorts the reporting of the company's operations. Users of the financial statements receive better information regarding financial position, cash flows, and company performance when ASC 740 is used.

Related exercises: Multiple Choice Question 4
Brief Exercise 3
Application Problems 1, 2

Now that you have a basic overview of GAAP reporting for income taxes, you are ready for the next section of the chapter. We explain how to implement the GAAP rules of accounting for income taxes and work toward the discussion of the tax return reporting required by the Internal Revenue Service.

PRACTICE PROBLEM 10.1.1
Book-Tax Difference and the Calculation of Current Income Tax Expense

Booker Inc. is an accrual-basis C corporation that manufactures and sells tennis and pickleball equipment on credit. The current year is Booker's first year of operations, and it has pre-tax book income of $85,000. Booker has estimated its bad debt expense to be $8,500. Booker did not have any accounts receivable writeoffs in the current year. What is Booker's book-tax difference and its current and deferred income tax expense?

SOLUTION

There is a book-tax difference in the treatment of the bad debt. Booker is allowed to estimate its bad debt for book purposes, but it must use the direct write-off method for tax purposes. Booker has a temporary book-tax difference of $8,500. The company's current income tax expense is $19,635.

Pre-tax book income	$85,000
Nondeductible bad debt	8,500
Taxable income	$93,500
Tax rate	× 21%
Current income tax expense	$19,635
Deferred tax benefit	$1,785 ($8,500 × 21%)

PRACTICE PROBLEM 10.1.2
Effective Tax Rate Comparison

Assume that Havel Inc. has pre-tax net income of $18,000, taxable income of $27,000, current income tax expense of $5,670, and deferred income tax expense of $1,890. What is the effective tax rate with ASC 740 and without ASC 740?

SOLUTION

	Without ASC 740	With ASC 740
Pre-tax net income	$18,000	$18,000
Current income tax expense	$ 5,670	$ 5,670
Deferred income tax expense	N/A	(1,890)
Total tax expense	$ 5,670	$ 3,780
Effective tax rate	31.5% ($5,670/$18,000)	21% ($3,780/$18,000)

INTERACTIVE SELF-SCORING QUIZZES

10.2 Determining the Income Tax Provision

LEARNING OBJECTIVE 2

Compute the current and deferred income tax expense, and evaluate the need for a valuation allowance and a reserve for uncertain tax positions.

VIDEO CONTENT

In this section, we provide a framework to compute the income tax provision. The framework consists of five steps that will guide you systematically through the calculations and analysis so you can accumulate the information necessary to meet the reporting requirements of ASC 740. As you have already seen, the chapter opening material includes these five steps. The two remaining steps, steps 6 and 7, are discussed in LO3 and LO4.

LO2 Step 1. **Identify:** Permanent and temporary differences and carryovers.
LO2 Step 2. **Calculate:** The current income tax expense or benefit.
LO2 Step 3. **Determine:** The deferred income tax expense or benefit.
LO2 Step 4. **Evaluate:** The need for a valuation allowance.
LO2 Step 5. **Assess:** The need of a reserve for uncertain tax positions.

Illustration 10.4 summarizes the steps to calculate the income tax provision. We demonstrate each of the steps by preparing the income tax provision for Hawkeye.

As you build your knowledge of ASC 740, keep the following big-picture concepts in mind:

- ASC 740 adopts a *balance sheet approach* to measuring deferred income taxes which focuses on assets and liabilities, not the income statement. The deferred income tax expense or benefit equals the change in the deferred income tax assets or liabilities from the beginning of the year to the end of the year.
- ASC 740 is applicable only to federal, state, local, and foreign income taxes. An **income tax** is defined as a tax based on income. The definition excludes property taxes, excise taxes, sales taxes, and value-added taxes. Taxes that have a tax base other than income are reported as expenses in the computation of net income before income taxes.

ILLUSTRATION 10.4 The Five Steps to Calculate the Income Tax Provision

Determining the Income Tax Provision

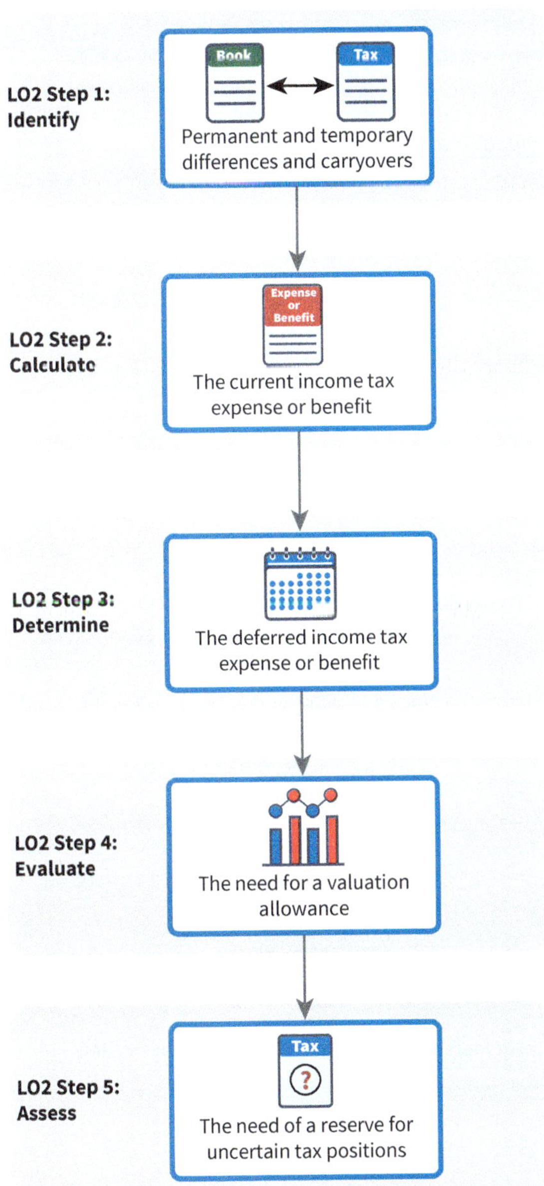

- Finally, the term **income tax provision process** refers to the entire process of determining the current and deferred income tax liability or asset, as well as the current and deferred income tax expense or benefit. The process also includes preparation of the financial statement footnote disclosures required by ASC 740.

In the chapter introduction, you learned that the tax members of the client service team have primary responsibility for preparing the *income tax provision* for the financial statements. Once the audit team has determined *pre-tax book income*, the tax team begins their work. **Pre-tax book income** is financial statement income before income tax expense.

To begin, you will need workpapers from the audit team as shown in **Illustration 10.5**, including:

1. Balance sheet for current year and prior year *and*
2. Income statement for pre-tax book income for current year.

You will prepare the workpapers shown later in Illustration 10.6 and Illustration 10.13 to calculate the income tax provision, which includes:

1. Book-tax reconciliation *and*
2. Deferred income tax provision roll forward.

ILLUSTRATION 10.5 Hawkeye Balance Sheet and Income Statement

Hawkeye pre-tax balance sheet	12-31-Y2		12-31-Y1	
Cash		$ 921,000		$ 750,000
Accounts receivable	$1,750,000		$1,250,000	
Less: Allowance for doubtful accounts	(87,500)		(62,500)	
Accounts receivable (net)		1,662,500		1,187,500
Inventory		450,000		275,000
Total current assets		3,033,500		2,212,500
Land		250,000		250,000
Fixed assets	$5,029,000		$5,000,000	
Less: Accumulated depreciation	(975,000)		(500,000)	
Fixed assets (net)		4,054,000		4,500,000
Investments		750,000		625,000
Total noncurrent assets		5,054,000		5,375,000
Total assets		$8,087,500		$7,587,500
Accounts payable	$1,600,000		$1,525,000	
Prepaid rental income (unearned revenue)	0		6,000	
Warranty reserve	87,000		27,000	
Income taxes payable*	0		0	
Total current liabilities		1,687,000		1,558,000
Notes payable	$3,600,000		$3,800,000	
Deferred income liability*	21,945		21,945	
Total noncurrent liabilities		3,621,945		3,821,945
Total liabilities		$5,308,945		$5,379,945
Capital stock	$ 100,000		$ 100,000	
Retained earnings	2,678,555		2,107,555	
Total shareholders' equity		2,778,555		2,207,555
Total liabilities and shareholders' equity		$8,087,500		$7,587,500

(continued)

ILLUSTRATION 10.5 Hawkeye Balance Sheet and Income Statement (cont.)

Hawkeye pre-tax income statement	Pre-tax book income
Sales revenue	$ 4,650,000
Cost of goods sold	(2,600,000)
Gross profit	2,050,000
Dividend income	35,000
Interest income	21,000
Municipal interest income	7,000
Capital gains (losses)	(8,000)
Gain (loss) on dispositions of fixed assets**	25,000
Rental income	12,000
Gross income	2,142,000
Expenses:	
Compensation	(550,000)
Repairs and maintenance	(50,000)
Bad debt expense	(33,000)
Rent expense	(75,000)
Interest expense	(80,000)
Charitable contributions	(65,000)
Depreciation expense***	(500,000)
Warranty expense	(70,000)
Meals expense	(30,000)
Officers' life insurance premiums	(20,000)
Fines and penalties	(5,000)
Other expenses	(93,000)
Total expenses	(1,571,000)
Pre-tax book income	$ 571,000

*The balance sheet and income statement do not reflect the income tax provision and ignore estimated tax payments for the current year.
**Gain on dispositions of fixed assets for tax is $41,000.
***Depreciation expense for tax is $650,000.

Identify Permanent and Temporary Differences and Carryovers (LO2 Step 1)

In LO1, Basics of Accounting for Income Taxes, you learned about book-tax differences. Pre-tax book income is adjusted to account for the differences between book income and taxable income. **Favorable book-tax differences** are subtracted from book income, resulting in lower taxable income. **Unfavorable book-tax differences** are added to book income, resulting in higher taxable income. Although only temporary book-tax differences and carryovers of deductions create deferred income tax assets or liabilities, permanent differences must also be identified to calculate taxable income. Identification of the book-tax differences requires you to think about each line on the balance sheet and income statement to identify items that are treated differently under tax accounting principles and financial accounting principles. Recall that we list some of the more common temporary differences and carryovers in Illustration 10.1 and some of the more common permanent differences and carryovers in Illustration 10.2. The illustrations compare the GAAP treatment to the tax treatment. An experienced tax professional can recall these book-tax differences without relying on charts. However, an inexperienced tax professional will need to depend on resources that provide the information shown in these illustrations until they no longer need them.

Related exercise: Discussion Question 7
Multiple Choice Questions 5, 6

Potential Pitfall

It may seem counterintuitive that favorable differences decrease taxable income for the current year, because you normally think of higher income as a good thing. Higher income is associated with profitability. In this case, the classification as favorable means that taxable income for the current year will be lower. Lower taxable income results in lower tax liability and less cash outflow, so that is favorable.

Whether a *temporary* difference is categorized as favorable or unfavorable depends on the effect it will have on taxable income for the current year and the future year(s). In the year a favorable temporary difference is created (the current year), the difference causes taxable income to be lower. The reversal of the temporary difference will increase taxable income in the future. Higher taxable income results in higher tax liability and more cash outflow, so in the future year the difference is unfavorable. This can be confusing if you do not apply the definition consistently. In summary, a *favorable* temporary difference for the current year becomes an *unfavorable* temporary difference in the future year(s) when it reverses. An *unfavorable* temporary difference for the current year becomes a *favorable* temporary difference in the future year(s) when it reverses.

A *permanent* difference is categorized as favorable if it decreases taxable income in the year it originates, and as unfavorable if it increases taxable income in the year it originates. A permanent difference does not reverse, so it does not impact future years. The following Example demonstrates how to identify book-tax differences and classify them as favorable or unfavorable.

EXAMPLE 10.2.1 Identifying Book-Tax Differences

Review the financial statements for Hawkeye (Illustration 10.5) to identify the temporary and permanent book-tax differences and indicate whether they are favorable or unfavorable, then calculate taxable income. Refer to Illustration 10.1 and Illustration 10.2 for the lists of possible adjustments.

SOLUTION

		(Favorable) Unfavorable
Temporary differences:		
Capital losses		$ 8,000
Gain on dispositions of fixed assets	($41,000 – $25,000)	16,000
Prepaid rental income	Change in balance sheet liability	(6,000)
Bad debt expense	Change in balance sheet allowance account	25,000
Charitable contributions*	($65,000 – $62,200)	2,800
Depreciation expense	($500,000 – $650,000)	(150,000)
Warranty expense	Change in balance sheet liability	60,000
Total temporary differences		($ 44,200)
Permanent differences:		
Municipal bond interest income		($ 7,000)
Meals expense	($30,000 × 50%)	15,000
Officers' life insurance premiums		20,000
Fines and penalties		5,000
Dividends received deduction	($35,000 × 50%)	(17,500)
Total permanent differences		$ 15,500

***Charitable contributions calculation:**

Taxable income (see Illustration 10.6)	$542,300
Plus: dividends received deduction	17,500
Plus: charitable contributions deduction	62,200
Modified taxable income	$622,000
Limitation	10%
Charitable contribution deduction allowed	$ 62,200

The temporary differences total to a favorable difference of $44,200 which will decrease book income, resulting in lower taxable income. The permanent differences total to an unfavorable difference of $15,500 which will increase book income, resulting in higher taxable income. The favorable and unfavorable differences net to a favorable difference of $28,700. Pre-tax book income of $571,000 is reduced by $28,700, resulting in taxable income of $542,300.

We have prepared Hawkeye's Book-Tax Reconciliation workpaper in **Illustration 10.6**. This workpaper summarizes the analysis identifying book-tax differences and the calculations to compute taxable income. An entry is made for each temporary and permanent book-tax difference that were identified in Example 10.2.1 to reflect its impact on pre-tax book income.

ILLUSTRATION 10.6 Hawkeye Book-Tax Reconciliation Workpaper

Hawkeye book-tax reconciliation	Pre-tax book income	Book-tax differences (DR)	CR	Taxable income
Sales revenue	$4,650,000			$4,650,000
Cost of goods sold	(2,600,000)			(2,600,000)
Gross profit	2,050,000			2,050,000
Dividend income	35,000			35,000
Interest income	21,000			21,000
Municipal bond interest income	7,000	(7,000)		0
Capital gains (losses)	(8,000)		8,000	0
Gain (loss) on dispositions of fixed assets	25,000		16,000	41,000
Prepaid rental income	12,000	(6,000)		6,000
Gross income	$2,142,000			$2,153,000
Expenses:				
Compensation	($ 550,000)			($ 550,000)
Repairs and maintenance	(50,000)			(50,000)
Bad debt expense	(33,000)		25,000	(8,000)
Rent expense	(75,000)			(75,000)
Interest expense	(80,000)			(80,000)
Charitable contributions	(65,000)		2,800	(62,200)
Depreciation expense	(500,000)	(150,000)		(650,000)
Warranty expense	(70,000)		60,000	(10,000)
Meals expense	(30,000)		15,000	(15,000)
Officers' life insurance premiums	(20,000)		20,000	0
Fines and penalties	(5,000)		5,000	0
Other expenses	(93,000)			(93,000)
Total expenses	(1,571,000)			(1,593,200)
Dividends received deduction	N/A	(17,500)		(17,500)
Pre-tax book income/taxable income	$ 571,000	($180,500)	$151,800	$ 542,300

Next, we discuss each of the book-tax differences to illustrate how you use this workpaper.

- *Municipal bond interest income* is a favorable permanent difference because this income is never taxed. The workpaper reflects a debit of $7,000, which reduces book income, resulting in lower taxable income.
- *Capital losses* are only deductible to the extent of capital gains. The excess capital loss is an unfavorable difference in the current year, and it is temporary because the loss may be carried back or forward, reducing taxable income in a different year. The workpaper reflects a credit for the difference of $8,000, which increases book income, resulting in higher taxable income.
- The *gain on sale of fixed assets* is $25,000 on the books and $41,000 on the tax return due to the differences between the book basis and tax basis of fixed assets. The workpaper reflects a credit of $16,000 for the unfavorable temporary difference, which increases book income, resulting in higher taxable income. The difference is temporary because it represents the reversal of favorable temporary differences in prior years for MACRS depreciation in excess of depreciation on the books.
- There is a book-tax difference in the treatment of the *prepaid rental income*, as we discussed in Examples 10.1.1, 10.1.5, and 10.1.6. For book income, prepaid income is recognized in the year earned. On the financial statements, $12,000 of income will be recognized in both Years 1 and 2. On the tax returns, prepaid income must be recognized when received. The tax returns will include income of $18,000 in Year 1 and $6,000 in Year 2. The workpaper reflects a debit of $6,000 reducing book income resulting in lower taxable income. The book-tax difference is a favorable temporary difference because it is the reversal of rental income taxed in the prior year.
- *Bad debts* are accounted for using the allowance method under GAAP. The direct write-off method must be used on the tax return. The bad debt expense totals $33,000, but only $25,000 is due to the increase in the allowance account. The remaining $8,000 is due to the write-off of accounts receivable. The direct write-off of accounts receivable is deductible, so the book-tax difference is the increase in the allowance account. The workpaper reflects a credit of $25,000, which is added back to book income to arrive at taxable income. This is an unfavorable difference, and it is temporary because accounts receivable currently reserved will be deductible for tax purposes if they are written off in the future.
- *Charitable contributions* are limited to 10% of taxable income before the dividends received deduction and the deduction for charitable contributions. Example 10.2.1 details the calculation resulting in $2,800 of charitable contributions, which cannot be deducted in the current year. This is an unfavorable difference, and it is temporary because the charitable contributions disallowed in the current year are carried forward and may reduce taxable income in the next five tax years. The workpaper reflects a credit of $2,800, which increases book income, resulting in higher taxable income.
- *Tax depreciation* is greater than *book depreciation* because MACRS accelerates tax depreciation in the early years. The workpaper reflects a debit of $150,000, which reduces book income, resulting in lower taxable income. The difference is a favorable difference, and it is temporary because in later years, book depreciation will exceed tax depreciation and create an unfavorable difference.
- The *warranty expense* of $70,000 on the books includes estimates of amounts to be paid in the future. The deduction for warranty expense on the tax return is based on amounts actually paid. The workpaper reflects a credit of $60,000 for the increase in the accrued liability on the balance sheet, which increases book income, resulting in higher taxable income. This is an unfavorable difference, and it is temporary because the estimated expense will be deducted on the tax return in future years when paid.
- *Meals expense* is an unfavorable permanent difference because 50% of the expense will never be deductible. The workpaper reflects a credit of $15,000, which increases book income, resulting in higher taxable income.

- *Officers' life insurance premiums* and *fines and penalties* are never deductible. The workpaper reflects a credit of $25,000 ($20,000 + $5,000) for the unfavorable permanent differences, which increase book income, resulting in higher taxable income.
- The *dividends received deduction* (DRD) allows dividend income from another corporation to be either fully or partially excluded from taxable income. This is a favorable permanent difference because the dividends will never be taxed. The workpaper reflects a debit of $17,500, which reduces book income, resulting in lower taxable income. This item appears at the end of the workpaper to facilitate calculations of other deductions that ignore the DRD. Charitable contributions are an example of a deduction computed before the DRD is taken.

You may have realized that identification of book-tax differences for the income tax provision is the same analysis you do for the tax return. In Chapter 3, LO4, Other Corporate Tax Issues, you were introduced to Schedule M-1, Reconciliation of Income (Loss) per Books With Income per Return. We discuss Schedule M-1 in more detail later in this chapter. Recall the Chapter 3 steps used to identify book-tax differences to complete Schedule M-1:

Step 1. Ask: Is the item treated differently for book purposes and tax purposes?

- If the answer is **NO**, then this is not a Schedule M-1 item.
- If the answer is **YES**, then proceed to step 2.

Step 2. Determine: Whether the adjustment increases or decreases book income.

This step is sometimes confusing to students. To avoid mistakes, ask two questions (refer to Illustration 3.14 in Chapter 3):

- Question 1: Is this included in the book income computation?
- Question 2: Should it be included in the taxable income computation?

The answers to these questions will determine whether the difference is favorable or unfavorable. In Chapter 3, a favorable difference was also given the name *negative adjustment* to book income and an unfavorable difference was given the name *positive adjustment* to book income. The book-tax reconciliation workpaper in Exhibit 10.6 uses debits for decreases and credits for increases.

The following Example provides illustrations of both favorable and unfavorable differences.

EXAMPLE 10.2.2 Temporary Differences: Created This Year or in a Prior Year?

For each of the temporary book-tax differences in Example 10.2.1, indicate whether it was created in the current year or represents a reversal of a difference created in a prior year.

	(Favorable) Unfavorable	Created in the current year or reversal?
Temporary differences:		
Capital losses	$ 8,000	
Gain on dispositions of fixed assets	16,000	
Prepaid rental income	(6,000)	
Bad debt expense	25,000	
Charitable contributions	2,800	
Depreciation expense	(150,000)	
Warranty expense	60,000	
Total	($ 44,200)	

SOLUTION

	(Favorable) Unfavorable	Created in the current year or reversal?
Temporary differences:		
Capital losses	$ 8,000	Current year
Gain on dispositions of fixed assets	16,000	Reversal
Prepaid rental income	(6,000)	Reversal
Bad debt expense	25,000	Current year
Charitable contributions	2,800	Current year
Depreciation expense	(150,000)	Current year
Warranty expense	60,000	Current year
Total	($ 44,200)	

The book-tax difference for the gain on the dispositions of fixed assets is a reversal of MACRS depreciation exceeding book depreciation in prior years. The tax basis in the fixed assets was less than the book basis because tax depreciation exceeded book depreciation, and this results in a larger gain for tax purposes. The prepaid rental income is a reversal of rental income included in taxable income in Year 1 but not included in book income until Year 2 under GAAP.

Calculate the Current Income Tax Expense or Benefit (LO2 Step 2)

Once you have identified both the temporary and permanent book-tax differences, you use the formula in **Illustration 10.7** to calculate the current income tax expense or benefit.

ILLUSTRATION 10.7 Current Income Tax Expense (Benefit) Formula

Calculate Current Income Tax Expense (Benefit)
GAAP financial statement pre-tax book income or (loss)
Plus or *Less:* Temporary book-tax differences
Plus or *Less:* Permanent book-tax differences
Taxable income
× Tax rate
Current income tax expense (benefit)

The following Example demonstrates the application of this formula.

EXAMPLE 10.2.3 Calculating Current Income Tax Expense (Benefit)

Use the temporary and permanent book-tax differences identified in Example 10.2.1 and the formula in Illustration 10.7 to calculate current income tax expense for Hawkeye.

SOLUTION

GAAP financial statement pre-tax book income	$571,000
Less: Temporary book-tax differences: (Favorable)*	(44,200)
Plus: Permanent book-tax differences: Unfavorable**	15,500
Taxable income	$542,300
× Tax rate	21%
Current income tax expense	$113,883

*See total from Example 10.2.2.

**Municipal bond interest income	($ 7,000)
Meals expense	15,000
Officers' life insurance premiums	20,000
Fines and penalties	5,000
Dividends received deduction	(17,500)
Total	$ 15,500

Notice that the book-tax reconciliation workpaper (Illustration 10.6) proves the calculation of taxable income of $542,300.

Current Income Tax Asset (Refund)

If the current income tax formula results in a benefit, there is a current income tax asset recorded as a receivable. The journal entry that records a current income tax asset is as follows:

Income taxes receivable	XX	
Current income tax expense		XX

Current Income Tax Liability (Payable)

If the current income tax formula results in an expense, there is a current income tax liability recorded as a payable. The journal entry that records a current income tax liability is as follows:

Current income tax expense	XX	
Income taxes payable		XX

In the next Example, we show the journal entry for Hawkeye.

EXAMPLE 10.2.4
Recording Current Income Tax Expense (Benefit)

What journal entry is required to record the current income tax expense or benefit for Hawkeye?

SOLUTION

Current income tax expense	$113,883	
Income taxes payable		$113,883

Hawkeye has taxable income of $542,300 for the current year, resulting in a tax balance due on the tax return of $113,883.

Related exercises: Discussion Question 8
Multiple Choice Question 7
Brief Exercises 4, 5
Application Problem 3

You have completed LO2 steps 1 and 2 for determining the income tax provision! You can now move on to LO2 step 3.

Determine the Deferred Income Tax Expense or Benefit (LO2 Step 3)

ASC 740 adopts a *balance sheet approach* to measuring deferred income taxes based on assets and liabilities, not an income statement approach. An income statement approach would focus on income items and expense items rather than on assets and liabilities. The deferred income tax expense or benefit is equal to the change in deferred income tax assets and deferred income tax liabilities from the beginning of the year to the end of the year. Accordingly, the calculation of the deferred income tax provision begins with the measurement of deferred income tax assets and liabilities.

Deferred Income Tax Asset (DTA)

A deferred income tax asset is the expected future tax benefit created by a deductible temporary book-tax difference or carryforward. A **deductible temporary book-tax difference** causes future taxable income to be less than book income due to reversal of an unfavorable book-tax temporary difference in the current year.

Deferred Income Tax Liability (DTL)

A deferred income tax liability is the expected future tax cost created by a taxable temporary book-tax difference. A **taxable temporary book-tax difference** causes future taxable income to be greater than book income due to reversal of a favorable temporary book-tax difference in the current year.

Related exercise: Discussion Question 9

When you were using LO2 step 1 (identify permanent and temporary differences and carryovers for the current year) to determine the income tax provision, you considered each line on the balance sheet *and* income statement to identify items that are treated differently under tax accounting principles and financial accounting principles. Identifying the impact of current-year book-tax differences on *future years* requires you to consider *only balance sheet items*—comparing the book basis with the tax basis and taking carryovers into account. Note that carryovers are not tracked on the balance sheet. The **book basis** of an asset is a taxpayer's investment in property that determines the amount of cost recovery and gain or loss upon disposition under GAAP. The **tax basis** of an asset is a taxpayer's investment in property that determines the amount of cost recovery and gain or loss upon disposition under tax accounting principles. The table in **Illustration 10.8** compares the events that create deferred income tax assets and deferred income tax liabilities. The levels build on each other. For example, Event 2 occurs because Event 1 has already happened.

ILLUSTRATION 10.8 Determining Deferred Income Tax Assets/Liabilities

Events Creating Deferred Income Tax Assets or Liabilities		
Events	**Deferred income tax assets**	**Deferred income tax liabilities**
Event 1	• The tax basis of an asset is greater than the book basis because the amount of investment in the asset that has been recovered on the tax return is less than the amount on the books. • The tax basis of a liability is less than the book basis because the amount of an expense that has been deducted on the tax return is less than the amount on the books *or* the amount of income that has been recognized on the tax return is greater than the amount on the books.	• The tax basis of an asset is less than the book basis because the amount of investment in the asset that has been recovered on the tax return is greater than the amount on the books. • The tax basis of a liability is greater than the book basis because the amount of an expense that has been deducted on the tax return is greater than the amount on the books *or* the amount of income that has been recognized on the tax return is less than the amount on the books.
Event 2	• More income taxes have been paid than have been recorded as income tax expense on the books; cash has been used to *prepay* income taxes.	• Less income taxes have been paid than have been recorded as income tax expense on the books; cash is available for other purposes until the taxes are paid in the future.
Event 3	• The cumulative unfavorable book-tax difference will reverse in the future, reducing taxable income compared to book income.	• The cumulative favorable book-tax difference will reverse in the future, increasing taxable income compared to book income.
Event 4	• The income tax savings resulting from future tax deductions have been deferred and represent an asset to be used in the future.	• The income tax liability resulting from future taxable income has been deferred and represents a liability to be paid in the future.

Let's look at the following three situations illustrating identification of temporary book-tax differences and carryovers to calculate the deferred income tax liability.

1. Depreciation
2. Prepaid rental income
3. Charitable contributions carryover

Depreciation Consider the difference between book basis and tax basis for equipment. The beginning book basis and tax basis are the same for equipment with an original cost of $100,000. The equipment will be depreciated straight-line using a 10-year life for book purposes. The equipment is 7-year property for MACRS. **Illustration 10.9** tracks the temporary book-tax difference and the impact on book basis and tax basis for the depreciation expense. In the early years, tax depreciation is greater than book depreciation (MACRS accelerates tax depreciation in early years). During these years, tax depreciation is a taxable temporary book-tax difference, which will cause future taxable income to be greater than book income due to reversal of a favorable book-tax difference created in the current year. Taxable temporary book-tax differences create a deferred income tax liability; less taxes have been paid in the current year, but these taxes will be paid in future years. The deferred income tax expense is computed as follows:

$$\text{Deferred income tax expense} = \text{Deferred income tax liability at beginning of the year (BOY)} - \text{Deferred income tax liability at the end of the year (EOY)}$$

The cumulative depreciation expense book-tax temporary differences equal the difference between the book basis and the tax basis. This means deferred income tax expense can be calculated by tracking the difference between the book basis and tax basis of items on the balance sheet.

ILLUSTRATION 10.9 Tracking Taxable Temporary Book-Tax Difference for Depreciation

Deferred Income Tax Computation for Depreciation Book-Tax Difference

	Depreciation expense		Temporary book-tax difference (favorable) unfavorable	Cumulative expense book-tax difference (favorable) unfavorable	End of year basis		Cumulative basis book-tax difference (favorable) unfavorable	Deferred income tax (liability) asset @ 21%	Deferred income tax expense (benefit) cumulative*
Year	Book	Tax			Book	Tax			
1	$ 10,000	$ 14,290	($ 4,290)	($4,290)	$90,000	$85,710	($4,290)	($901)	$901
2	10,000	24,490	(14,490)	(18,780)	80,000	61,220	(18,780)	(3,944)	3,043
3	10,000	17,490	(7,490)	(26,270)	70,000	43,730	(26,270)	(5,517)	1,573
4	10,000	12,490	(2,490)	(28,760)	60,000	31,240	(28,760)	(6,040)	523
5	10,000	8,930	1,070	(27,690)	50,000	22,310	(27,690)	(5,815)	(225)
6	10,000	8,920	1,080	(26,610)	40,000	13,390	(26,610)	(5,588)	(227)
7	10,000	8,930	1,070	(25,540)	30,000	4,470	(25,540)	(5,363)	(225)
8	10,000	4,460	5,540	(20,000)	20,000	0	(20,000)	(4,200)	(1,163)
9	10,000	0	10,000	(10,000)	10,000	0	(10,000)	(2,100)	(2,100)
10	10,000	0	10,000	0	0	0	0	0	0
Total	$100,000	$100,000	$ 0						

*The cumulative deferred income tax is calculated as the change in the deferred income tax liability/asset from the beginning of the year to the end of the year. Over time, as the temporary book-tax difference reverses, the deferred income tax expense/(benefit) also reverses to zero.

Prepaid Rental Income **Recall** the facts for prepaid income in Example 10.1.1. Hawkeye's beginning balance sheet reflected a $6,000 liability for prepaid rental income which will not be recognized until Year 2 for book. The book and tax journal entries in Year 1 to record the cash received for Year 2 are as follows:

	Book		Tax	
	DR	CR	DR	CR
Cash	$6,000		$6,000	
Prepaid rental income (liability)		$6,000		n/a
Rental income		n/a		$6,000

The prepaid rental income must be recognized in Year 1 for tax purposes. The book-tax difference for Year 1 is unfavorable because taxable income is greater than book income. In Year 2, the book-tax difference will reverse and become favorable. The financial statements for Year 2 will include $6,000 of Year 2 prepaid rental income, but the tax return will not. The book-tax difference will be favorable because taxable income will be less than book income.

In Year 1, the book basis of the prepaid rental liability is $6,000. There is no liability for tax purposes because the income has been recognized; for tax purposes, the liability is zero—it has no basis. The prepaid rental income liability represents a *deductible temporary book-tax difference*, which will cause future taxable income to be less than book income due to reversal of an unfavorable book-tax difference created in the current year. Deductible temporary book-tax differences create a deferred income tax asset; more taxes have been paid in the current year than are recorded as income tax expense on the financial statements. A deferred income tax asset of $1,260 ($6,000 × 21%) is recorded on the financial statements at the end of Year 1; more taxes have been paid than are recorded as income tax expense on the financial statements. You will see more detailed calculations of this deferred income tax asset in LO3.

Charitable Contributions Carryover Illustration 10.10 details the calculation of the deferred income tax asset and benefit for charitable contributions for a hypothetical corporation. In Year 1, the corporation's charitable contributions of $50,000 are deducted on the

ILLUSTRATION 10.10 Tracking Deductible Temporary Book-Tax Difference for Charitable Contributions Carryover

Deferred Income Tax Computation for Charitable Contributions Carryover						
Year	Book expense	Tax deduction	Temporary book-tax difference (favorable) unfavorable	Cumulative book-tax difference (favorable) unfavorable	Deferred income tax (liability) asset @21%	Deferred income tax expense (benefit) cumulative
1	$50,000	$ 5,000	$45,000	$45,000	$9,450	($ 9,450)
2	0	9,000	(9,000)	36,000	7,560	1,890
3	0	9,000	(9,000)	27,000	5,670	1,890
4	0	9,000	(9,000)	18,000	3,780	1,890
5	0	9,000	(9,000)	9,000	1,890	1,890
6	0	9,000	(9,000)	0	0	1,890
Total	$50,000	$50,000	$ 0			$ 0

financial statements. Assume that the tax deduction for the contributions is $5,000 because it is limited to 10% of taxable income. Recall that excess charitable contributions carry forward to the next five tax years. Also assume that the contribution carryover of $45,000 can be deducted evenly for each of the next five tax years. The charitable contribution carryover represents a deductible temporary book-tax difference because future taxable income will be less than book income. A deferred income tax asset of $9,450 ($45,000 × 21%) is recorded on the financial statements at the end of Year 1; more taxes have been paid than are recorded as income tax expense on the financial statements. The deferred income tax expense equals the change in the deferred income tax asset from the beginning of the year to the end of the year.

> **Potential Pitfall**
>
> Carryovers are a type of temporary difference. However, this type of temporary difference occurs because tax laws limit the amount of certain deductions allowed for the current year, not because a deduction is recognized in book income for one year and in taxable income for a different year. Identification of the book-tax differences for future years requires you to review balance sheet items comparing the book basis with the tax basis. However, carryovers are not recorded as assets on the balance sheet, so they must be tracked separately. Therefore, carryovers create a book-tax difference, which is accounted for on the book-tax reconciliation workpaper (Illustration 10.6), but they are not reflected on the balance sheet.

> **Tax Planning Tip**
>
> **Like carryovers for deductions, tax credit carryovers are not recorded as assets on the balance sheet and must be tracked separately. Unlike carryovers for deductions, tax credits are not temporary book-tax differences. Tax credits are permanent differences that do not impact book income or taxable income; rather, they impact the tax liability dollar for dollar. So, for ASC 740 purposes, tax credits reduce the current tax expense.**

Calculating Deferred Income Tax Expense You can now begin the calculations to determine the deferred income tax expense or benefit for Hawkeye. There are six steps in calculating the deferred income tax expense. They are substeps of LO2 step 3 in determining the income tax provision and are designated as 3.1, 3.2, and so forth, as shown in the following and Illustration 10.11.

LO2 Step 3.1. **Analyze:** The balance sheet to identify items accounted for differently for book and tax purposes.

LO2 Step 3.2. **Determine:** The book basis and the tax basis at the beginning of the year and the end of the year for each item identified. (Note: The end-of-year balances from the prior year workpapers *roll forward* as the beginning of the year balances for the current year.)

LO2 Step 3.3. **Determine:** Carryovers from prior years and carryovers created in the current year.

LO2 Step 3.4. **Calculate:** The cumulative temporary book-tax differences at the beginning of the year and the end of the year for each item identified.

LO2 Step 3.5. **Calculate:** The deferred income tax asset or liability for each item using the 21% corporate income tax rate.

LO2 Step 3.6. **Calculate:** The deferred income tax expense, which is the change in the deferred income tax assets or liabilities.

ILLUSTRATION 10.11 Determining Deferred Income Tax Expense or Benefit

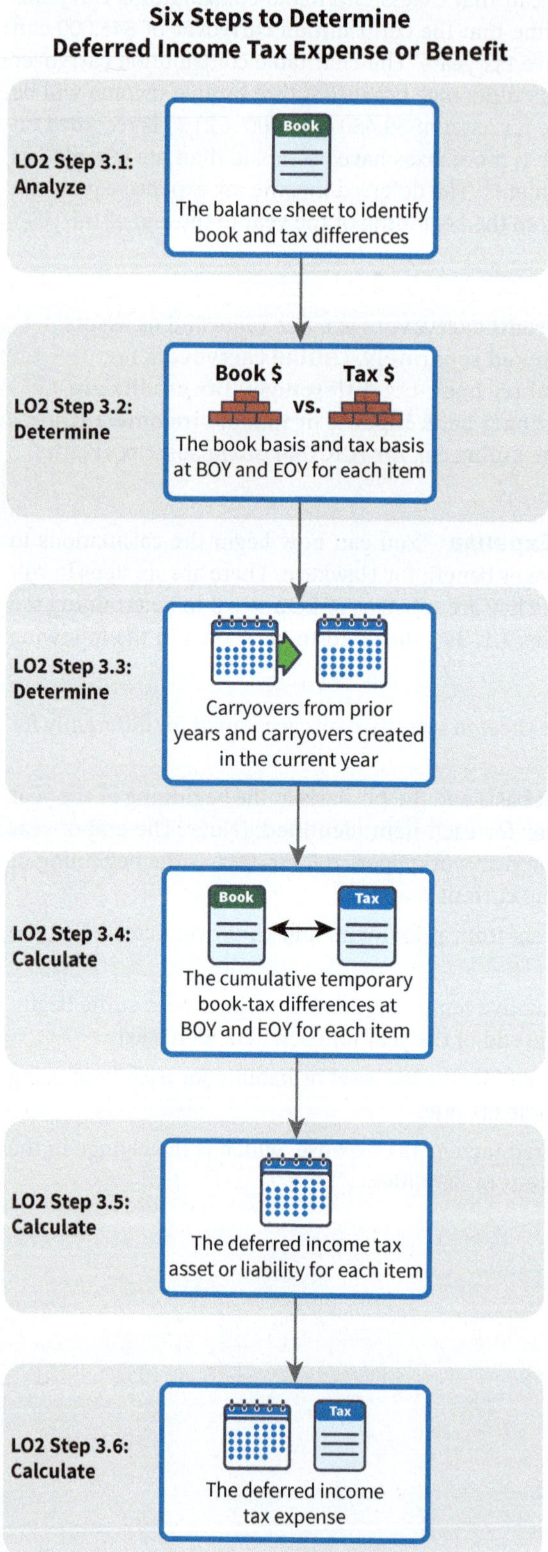

The next Example calculates the deferred income tax expense (benefit) for Hawkeye.

EXAMPLE 10.2.5 Calculating Deferred Income Tax Expense (Benefit)

Calculate the deferred income tax expense by following LO2 steps 3.1–3.6 for Hawkeye, using the information in Illustration 10.5 and that already learned previously in this chapter.

SOLUTION:

LO2 Step 3.1. Each of these balance sheet items has a book-tax difference because all are treated differently under tax accounting principles and financial accounting principles.

	Accounting treatment	
Balance sheet item:	**Book basis**	**Tax basis***
Accounts receivable (net)	Allowance method	Direct write-off method
Fixed assets (net)	GAAP depreciation (book basis)	MACRS depreciation (tax basis)
Prepaid rental income	Recognized when earned	Taxable on receipt
Warranty reserve	Deduction is estimated	Deduction based on actual

LO2 Step 3.2. The ending book-basis and tax-basis numbers are from the balance sheet in Illustration 10.5. You can find the beginning book-basis and tax-basis numbers on the prior year's income tax provision workpapers.

Balance sheet item:	**Book basis**		**Tax basis***	
	EOY	**BOY**	**EOY**	**BOY**
Accounts receivable (net)	$1,662,500	$1,187,500	$1,750,000	$1,250,000
Fixed assets (net)	4,054,000	4,500,000	3,720,000	4,300,000
Prepaid rental income	0	(6,000)	0	0
Warranty reserve	(87,000)	(27,000)	0	0

**Accounts receivable* tax basis is not reduced by the allowance for doubtful accounts. The allowance method is not allowed for tax purposes. *Fixed assets* tax basis is obtained from tax depreciation schedules. *Prepaid rental income* has been recognized for tax purposes, so there is no tax basis liability for income that is deferred. *Warranty reserve* is zero because the expense is not recognized until paid.

LO2 Step 3.3. In steps 1 and 2, temporary differences were identified on the balance sheet. The temporary differences for the capital loss carryover and charitable contributions carryover are not on the balance sheet. Carryovers are not recorded as assets on the balance sheet, so they must be tracked separately. Step 3.3 adds the timing difference for the capital loss and charitable contributions carryovers created in the current year. There were no additional carryovers noted on the prior year workpapers that carried over to the current year, so there is nothing to include in this analysis for prior year carryovers.

Balance sheet item and carryovers:	**Book basis**		**Tax basis**	
	EOY	**BOY**	**EOY**	**BOY**
Account receivable (net)	$1,662,500	$1,187,500	$1,750,000	$1,250,000
Fixed assets (net)	4,054,000	4,500,000	3,720,000	4,300,000
Prepaid rental income	0	(6,000)	0	0
Warranty reserve	(87,000)	(27,000)	0	0
Capital loss carryover	0	0	8,000	0
Charitable contributions carryover	0	0	2,800	0

LO2 Step 3.4: We next calculate the cumulative temporary book-tax differences as of the beginning of the year and the end of the year for each item identified by comparing the difference in the tax basis and book basis at the end of the year to the difference at the beginning of the year.

Balance sheet item and carryovers:	Tax basis *less* book basis		Cumulative change
	EOY	BOY	
Account receivable (net)	$ 87,500	$ 62,500	$ 25,000
Fixed assets (net)	(334,000)	(200,000)	(134,000)
Prepaid rental income	0	6,000	(6,000)
Warranty reserve	87,000	27,000	60,000
Capital loss carryover	8,000	0	8,000
Charitable contributions carryover	2,800	0	2,800
Total temporary differences	($148,700)	($104,500)	($ 44,200)

Notice that the cumulative change of ($44,200) equals the total temporary differences identified in Example 10.2.1 Also note that the cumulative change in fixed assets (net) of ($134,000) equals the sum of the favorable book-tax difference for depreciation of ($150,000) plus the $16,000 unfavorable book-tax difference for gain on dispositions of fixed assets. The unfavorable difference for the gain represents the reversal of depreciation taken in prior years for the assets disposed of in the current year.

LO2 Step 3.5: Remember that ASC 740 adopts a balance sheet approach to measuring deferred income taxes which focuses on assets and liabilities. The deferred income tax expense equals the change in the deferred income tax assets and liabilities from the beginning of the year to the end of the year. This is computed by multiplying the cumulative change from step 3.4 by the tax rate of 21%. For example, the accounts receivable line is computed as: $87,500 × 25% = $18,375; $62,500 × 21% = $13,125; and $25,000 × 21% = $5,250.

Balance sheet item and carryovers:	Deferred income tax asset (liability) @ 21%		Deferred income tax expense
	Ending	Beginning	
Account receivable (net)	$ 18,375	$ 13,125	$ 5,250
Fixed assets (net)	(70,140)	(42,000)	(28,140)
Prepaid rental income	0	1,260	(1,260)
Warranty reserve	18,270	5,670	12,600
Capital loss carryover	1,680	0	1,680
Charitable contributions carryover	588	0	588
Total	($31,227)	($21,945)	($ 9,282)

LO2 Step 3.6: The change in the deferred income tax assets and liabilities equals deferred income tax expense for the current year of $9,282.

If the calculation of deferred income taxes results in a benefit, there is a deferred income tax asset. The journal entry that records the deferred income tax asset is as follows:

Deferred income tax asset	XX	
Deferred income tax expense		XX

As you see with the journal entry, if the deferred tax asset increases, then the deferred income tax expense is reduced by the same amount.

If the calculation of deferred income taxes results in an expense, there is a deferred income tax liability. The journal entry that records the deferred income tax liability is as follows:

Deferred income tax expense	XX	
Deferred income tax liability		XX

The next Example shows the deferred income tax expense journal entry for Hawkeye.

EXAMPLE 10.2.6
Recording Deferred Income Tax Expense (Benefit)

What journal entry is required to record the deferred income tax expense or benefit for Hawkeye?

SOLUTION

Deferred income tax expense	$ 9,282	
Deferred income tax liability		$ 9,282

Deferred income tax expense equals the change in the deferred income tax liability from the beginning of the year to the end of the year. Step 3.5 calculated the change to be $9,282, an increase from $21,945 at the beginning of the year to $31,227 at the end of the year.

Related exercises: Multiple Choice Question 8
Brief Exercise 6
Application Problems 4, 5

Congratulations! You have completed steps 1, 2, and 3 of the income tax provision jigsaw puzzle (referred to in the chapter introduction). You have accomplished the two primary objectives of ASC 740 to recognize:

1. The current income tax liability or asset, *and*
2. The deferred income tax liability or asset.

Together, they determine the total income tax provision:

Total income tax provision = Current income tax provision + Deferred income tax provision

In the next Example, we compute the income tax provision for Hawkeye.

EXAMPLE 10.2.7
Total Income Tax Provision

What is the total income tax provision for Hawkeye for Year 2? What is the journal entry to record the total tax provision?

SOLUTION

We compute the total income tax expense by combining the current and deferred income tax expense.

Current income tax expense	$113,883	(Example 10.2.3)
Deferred income tax expense	9,282	(Example 10.2.5, step 3.6)
Total income tax expense	$123,165	

The journal entry is recorded as follows:

Current income tax expense	$113,883	
Deferred income tax expense	9,282	
Income taxes payable		$113,883
Deferred income tax liability		9,282

Related exercise: Application Problem 6

Tax Planning Tip

You can prove the calculation of the total income tax provision. Temporary differences impact taxable income in either the current year or a future year. However, because permanent differences never reverse, their adjustment to book income determines the income tax expense that will be paid without regard to deferred income taxes. Pre-tax book income adjusted for only permanent differences is the book equivalent of taxable income, as shown in the next three Examples.

EXAMPLE 10.2.8
Book Equivalent of Taxable Income

Show how Hawkeye's book equivalent of taxable income proves total income tax expense.

SOLUTION

GAAP financial statement pre-tax book income	$571,000	
Plus: Permanent book-tax differences: Unfavorable	15,500	(Example 10.2.1)
Book equivalent of taxable income	$586,500	
Tax rate	21%	
Total income tax expense	$123,165	(Example 10.2.7)

EXAMPLE 10.2.9
Financial Statements Adjusted for Deferred Taxes

What is Hawkeye's book income after recording the total tax provision?

SOLUTION

Pre-tax book income	$571,000	
Less: Income tax expense	(123,165)	($113,883 + $9,282)
Book income	$447,835	

EXAMPLE 10.2.10
Taxable Income after the Tax Provision

What is Hawkeye's taxable income after recording the total tax provision?

SOLUTION

Hawkeye's taxable income does not change for the federal income tax provision. Federal income taxes are a permanent book-tax difference, so the expense of $123,165 is an unfavorable difference between book income and taxable income.

Book income adjusted for income tax provision	$447,835	(Example 10.2.9)
Less: Temporary book-tax differences: (Favorable)	(44,200)	(Example 10.2.1)
Plus: Permanent book-tax differences: Unfavorable	15,500	(Example 10.2.1)
Plus: Permanent book-tax difference for federal income tax expense: Unfavorable	123,165	(Example 10.2.7)
Taxable income	$542,300	

Illustration 10.12 shows Hawkeye's balance sheet and income statement adjusted for the income tax provision. Income Taxes Payable and Federal Income Tax Expense now reflect the current income tax expense of $113,883, which equals the balance due on Hawkeye's Year 2 federal income tax return. The Deferred Income Tax Liability has increased from the Year 1 ending balance of $21,945 to reflect Hawkeye's Year 2 deferred income tax expense of $9,282. The ending balance for Year 2 is $31,227. Both financial statement income and retained earnings have been adjusted accordingly.

ILLUSTRATION 10.12 Hawkeye Year 2 Financial Statements

Hawkeye GAAP Balance Sheet and Income Statement for Year 2

Hawkeye Balance Sheet		12-31-Y2
Cash		$ 921,000
Accounts receivable	$1,750,000	
Less: Allowance for doubtful accounts	(87,500)	
Accounts receivable (net)		1,662,500
Inventory		450,000
Total current assets		3,033,500
Land		250,000
Fixed assets	$5,029,000	
Less: Accumulated depreciation	(975,000)	
Fixed assets (net)		4,054,000
Investments		750,000
Total noncurrent assets		5,054,000
Total assets		$8,087,500
Accounts payable		$1,600,000
Prepaid rental income		0
Warranty reserve		87,000
Income taxes payable*		113,883
Total current liabilities		1,800,883
Notes payable	$3,600,000	
Deferred income liability*	31,227	
Total noncurrent liabilities		3,631,227
Total liabilities		5,432,110
Capital stock	$ 100,000	
Retained earnings*	2,555,390	
Total shareholders' equity		2,655,390
Total liabilities and shareholders' equity		$8,087,500

*Adjusted by journal entry to record income tax provision

Hawkeye Income Statement	12-31-Y2
Sales revenue	$ 4,650,000
Cost of goods sold	(2,600,000)
Gross profit	2,050,000
Dividend income	35,000
Interest income	21,000
Municipal bond interest income	7,000
Capital gains (losses)	(8,000)
Gain (loss) on dispositions of fixed assets	25,000
Rental income	12,000
Gross income	2,142,000

(continued)

Hawkeye Income Statement	12-31-Y2
Expenses:	
Compensation	(550,000)
Repairs and maintenance	(50,000)
Bad debt expense	(33,000)
Rent expense	(75,000)
Interest expense	(80,000)
Charitable contributions	(65,000)
Depreciation expense	(500,000)
Warranty expense	(70,000)
Meals expense	(30,000)
Officers' life insurance premiums	(20,000)
Fines and penalties	(5,000)
Other expenses	(93,000)
Federal income tax expense*	(123,165)
Total expenses	(1,694,165)
Financial statement income*	$ 447,835

*Adjusted by journal entry to record income tax provision

In this section (LO2 step 3), we have provided a framework for determining the deferred income tax expense or benefit. The framework consists of six steps guiding you through the calculations and analysis in detail. With experience, practitioners can take some shortcuts in the process. **Illustration 10.13** shows an example of a workpaper commonly used in the real world using data for Hawkeye Corporation.

ILLUSTRATION 10.13 Deferred Income Tax Provision Roll Forward

Balance sheet item:	Book basis		Tax basis		Cumulative change	DTA/DTL* @ 21%		
	EOY	BOY	EOY	BOY		EOY	BOY	Change
Account receivable (net)	$1,662,500	$1,187,500	$1,750,000	$1,250,000	$25,000	$18,375	$13,125	$ 5,250
Fixed assets (net)	4,054,000	4,500,000	3,720,000	4,300,000	(134,000)	(70,140)	(42,000)	(28,140)
Prepaid rental income	0	(6,000)	0	0	(6,000)	0	1,260	(1,260)
Warranty reserve	(87,000)	(27,000)	0	0	60,000	18,270	5,670	12,600
Capital loss	0	0	8,000	0	8,000	1,680	0	1,680
Charitable contributions	0	0	2,800	0	2,800	588	0	588
Total	$5,629,500	$5,654,500	$5,480,800	$5,550,000	($44,200)	$31,227	$21,945	$ 9,282

*DTA is deferred income tax asset; DTL is deferred income tax liability.

Evaluate the Need for a Valuation Allowance (LO2 Step 4)

GAAP is based on the conservatism principle, which is biased against overstating assets and understating liabilities. A deferred income tax asset represents tax savings that will be realized on a tax return in the future. Consistent with the conservatism principle, ASC 740 requires a company to evaluate the risk that some portion of deferred income tax assets will not be realized. If management determines it is *more likely than not* that future tax benefits will not be realized, a valuation allowance is required. A **valuation allowance** is a contra-asset account that offsets a deferred income tax asset for the amount not expected to be realized in the future. The valuation allowance operates like the allowance for doubtful accounts, which is an estimate of accounts receivable that will not be collected.

Under the *more likely than not* standard, the probability that a deferred income tax asset will not be realized is greater than 50%. While the standard is clear, the evaluation of the risk is subjective and requires judgment by management. To determine if a valuation allowance is needed, management must consider all available evidence, both positive and negative, over an appropriate time horizon that would permit a tax planning strategy to be implemented.

Positive Evidence

Positive evidence suggests that an allowance may not be necessary because sufficient taxable income will exist in the future to utilize the deferred income tax asset. Positive evidence includes:

- Taxable income in prior carryback years:
  - Capital losses will offset prior capital gains.
  - Tax credits will offset prior tax liabilities.
- Taxable temporary differences that will reverse in the future:
  - Reversals of taxable temporary differences must offset reversals of deductible temporary differences.
- Expectation of future taxable income (not counting reversals of taxable temporary differences) because:
  - The company has a strong earnings history.
  - Losses experienced in recent years were unusual and should not repeat.
  - The company has a backlog of sales or existing contracts.
  - Appreciated assets would generate gains if sold.
- Tax planning strategies to generate future taxable income (*all* criteria must be met):
  - the strategy must be prudent and feasible,
  - management must have the ability to implement and control the strategy, *and*
  - implementation of a strategy is taken only to prevent expiration of carryforwards.

  This final type of positive evidence does not require actual implementation of the strategy.

Negative Evidence

Negative evidence suggests that an allowance may be necessary because the deferred income tax asset may not be fully utilized. Negative evidence includes:

- The company has a history of operating losses in recent years.
- There is a history of net operating loss, capital loss, or tax credit carryforwards that have expired unused.
- Future losses are expected, despite a history of operating profits.
- Future losses would occur if existing contingencies were not resolved favorably.
- The carryforward period for a tax benefit is brief.

The next Example demonstrates the computation of a valuation allowance.

EXAMPLE 10.2.11 Evaluation to Determine Need for a Valuation Allowance

You have calculated Hawkeye's deferred income tax assets and liabilities:

Deferred income tax assets:	
Accounts receivable (net)	$ 18,375
Warranty reserve	18,270
Capital loss carryover	1,680
Charitable contributions carryover	588
Total	$ 38,913
Deferred income tax (liabilities)	
Fixed assets (net)	($ 70,140)
Total	($ 70,140)

As you consider the need for a valuation allowance, indicate which of the following is positive evidence and which is negative evidence. Which are tax planning strategies?

SOLUTION

• There are capital gains in the prior three tax years to absorb a capital loss carryback.	Positive
• Expectations of future taxable income are supported by a strong earnings history and forecasts.	Positive
• There will be sufficient income in the next five tax years to absorb the charitable contributions carryover plus additional contributions that are anticipated so the carryover does not expire.	Positive
• The carryover period for capital losses and charitable contributions is only five years. There is a history of capital loss and charitable contributions carryforwards that have expired unused.	Negative
• Deferred income tax liabilities exceed deferred income tax assets; reversals of taxable temporary differences for depreciation are adequate to absorb the reversals of deductible temporary differences for accounts receivable and warranty expense.	Positive
• The company does not have appreciated capital assets that will generate capital gains within the next five tax years to offset a capital loss carryforward.	Negative
• Management is considering the sale of a small lot not used or needed in the business. The real estate has appreciated in value and will generate a gain of $200,000 if sold.	Positive/ Tax planning strategy
• The board of directors has voted to refrain from making charitable contributions until the existing carryover is utilized.	Positive/ Tax planning strategy
• Forecasts indicate future losses from operation or a negative outcome for an existing contingency.	Negative

Suppose that in Example 10.2.11, the capital loss cannot be carried back to offset capital gains in prior years, and the company does not own appreciated capital assets that could be sold to generate capital gains in the next five years. Management should conclude that, more likely than not, the capital loss carryover of $1,680 will expire unused and should record a valuation allowance. The journal entry to record the valuation allowance is as follows:

Deferred income tax expense	$1,680	
Valuation allowance		$1,680

If the capital loss carryforward expires before it can be used, the deferred income tax asset should be written off, and the valuation allowance should be reduced. The expiration of the carryforward does not impact deferred income tax expense on the income statement, because the impact occurred when the allowance was set up. The following journal entry would be made to adjust the asset and allowance on the balance sheet:

Account	Debit	Credit
Valuation allowance	$1,680	
Deferred income tax asset		$1,680

Suppose that circumstances change, and the company can generate a capital gain sufficient to utilize the capital loss carryover. The valuation allowance is no longer needed, and the impact to deferred income tax expense should be reversed. The journal entry to adjust the valuation allowance is as follows:

Account	Debit	Credit
Valuation allowance	$1,680	
Deferred income tax expense		$1,680

Related exercises: Discussion Question 10
Multiple Choice Question 9
Brief Exercise 7
Application Problem 7
Tax Planning Problem 1

Assess the Need of a Reserve for Uncertain Tax Positions (LO2 Step 5)

One of the founding fathers, Benjamin Franklin, famously said, "In this world, nothing is certain but death and taxes." Tax professionals know that the income tax law is anything but certain. The IRS often disagrees with a *tax position* taken on a tax return. A **tax position** is the way a set of facts are treated for tax purposes. Is income taxable, excluded, or deferred? Is an expense deductible, not deductible, or required to be capitalized? Some tax positions are crystal clear; they are black and white. Others are in a gray area. In LO2 step 2, the current income tax expense is calculated assuming that every tax position taken on the tax return will be allowed. An **uncertain tax position (UTP)** is a tax position that is highly subject to interpretation of tax law. ASC 740 requires a company to determine the liability for potential tax increases resulting from uncertain tax positions that may be challenged by the IRS.

ASC 740 applies to all tax positions for income taxes. Examples of tax positions include the following:

- Characterization of income
- A decision to omit income
- Timing of income or deductions
- A decision to not file a tax return

The identification of an uncertain tax position is shown in the next Example.

EXAMPLE 10.2.12
Uncertain Tax Positions

Hawkeye receives proceeds in exchange for property. Hawkeye consults with its tax advisor regarding the tax treatment of the exchange. The tax advisor concludes that based on the facts, the transaction could be treated in a variety of ways. The tax advisor tells Hawkeye, "It depends." Which of the following is a tax position for this situation?

- The proceeds are taxable.
- A portion of the proceeds are not taxable.
- A portion of the proceeds are not taxable this year.
- The taxable income is ordinary income.
- A portion of the proceeds are capital gain.

SOLUTION:

All of these are tax positions because they determine the way a transaction is treated for tax purposes. In addition, because treatment of the transaction is subject to interpretation, the tax positions are uncertain.

ASC 740 applies to positions taken on tax returns for:

- The current tax year,
- Prior tax years,
- Future years, if the tax position is reflected as a deferred income tax asset or liability (temporary differences), *and*
- Permanent differences.

The following Example shows how the impact of an uncertain tax position is determined.

EXAMPLE 10.2.13 Impact of Uncertain Tax Position on Current Year and Future Years

Hawkeye deducts an expense on its tax return for Year 1. The deduction creates a net operating loss that will be carried forward to future years. The deduction is likely to be challenged by the IRS. What is the impact of the tax position in Year 1?

SOLUTION

Deduction of the expense is an uncertain tax position. The deduction results in zero current income tax expense and a deferred income tax asset in Year 1. ASC 740 requires Hawkeye to determine if a liability for uncertain tax positions should be recorded to increase Year 1 income tax expense and a valuation allowance should be recorded for the NOL carryforward.

Why **Why are both a valuation allowance and an uncertain tax position liability required?** Recall that GAAP is based on the conservatism principle, which is biased against overstating income and assets and against understating expenses and liabilities. The purpose of a valuation allowance is to protect against overstating deferred income tax assets (balance sheet). The purpose of a liability for uncertain tax positions is to protect against understating income tax expense (income statement).

The process of calculating and recording the amount of the liability for uncertain tax positions uses a *more likely than not* standard like the one used for analyzing the need for a valuation allowance. The process is beyond the scope of this textbook. The take-away for you is that significant judgment by management, the tax team, and the audit team is necessary for LO2 steps 4 and 5 of the income tax provision process. Because of the expertise needed, it is not unusual for the national office of a public accounting firm to determine if either a valuation allowance or a liability for uncertain tax positions is required.

PRACTICE PROBLEM 10.2.1

Evaluate Book-Tax Differences and Compute Current Tax Expense

Chief, Inc. earns pre-tax book income of $285,000 in the current year. Chief has entertainment expense of $1,800, net capital gains of $6,000, and municipal interest income of $1,200. Chief reported no other book-tax differences. Compute Chief's current income tax expense.

SOLUTION

Chief's current income tax expense is $59,976, as follows:

Pre-tax book income	$285,000
Entertainment expense	1,800
Municipal bond interest income	(1,200)
Taxable income	$285,600
Tax rate	× 21%
Current income tax expense	$ 59,976

Capital gains are included in both book income and taxable income, so no adjustment is necessary.

PRACTICE PROBLEM 10.2.2

Compute the Deferred Tax Expense and Journal Entry

Assume that Pirate Corporation reported the following items on its balance sheet for the beginning of the year (BOY) and the end of the year (EOY):

Balance sheet items and carryover:	Book basis		Tax basis	
	EOY	BOY	EOY	BOY
Machinery	$3,300	$4,800	$2,800	$4,800
Charitable contributions carryover	$ 0	$ 0	$ 300	$ 0

Compute the deferred income tax expense and journal entry needed.

SOLUTION

We calculate the cumulative change in the temporary differences as follows:

Balance sheet items and carryover:	Tax basis *less* book basis		Cumulative change
	EOY	BOY	
Fixed assets (net)	($500)	($0)	($500)
Charitable contributions carryover	300	0	300
Total temporary differences	($200)	($0)	($200)

We calculate the deferred income tax expense as follows:

	Deferred income tax asset (liability)@ 21%		Deferred income tax (expense)
Balance sheet items and carryover:	Ending	Beginning	
Fixed assets (net)	($105)	($0)	($105)
Charitable contributions carryover	63	0	63
Total	($ 42)	($0)	($ 42)

The change in the deferred income tax assets and liabilities equals deferred income tax expense for the current year: $42.

Deferred income tax expense	$42	
Deferred income tax liability		$42

INTERACTIVE SELF-SCORING QUIZZES

10.3 Tax Disclosures in the Financial Statements

LEARNING OBJECTIVE 3

Describe the required financial statement disclosures for income taxes.

VIDEO CONTENT

The term *income tax provision process* refers to the entire process of determining the current and deferred income tax liability or asset, as well as the current and deferred income tax expense or benefit. In addition, the process includes preparation of the financial statement footnote disclosures required by ASC 740.

You have learned a step-by-step process to perform the calculations and analysis necessary to accumulate the information required to meet the reporting requirements of ASC 740. In this section, you will examine step 6, which explains how to report this information in the financial statements. The reporting is designed to provide additional information and transparency regarding financial position, cash flows, and operations of a company to the users of financial statements.

Balance Sheet

The balance sheet includes the following items related to tax disclosures:

- A line item for current income taxes receivable or payable
- A line item for deferred income tax assets or liabilities
- Deferred income taxes are shown net of any valuation allowance

The next Example reviews the appropriate disclosures on the balance sheet.

EXAMPLE 10.3.1 Income Taxes on the Balance Sheet

In Example 10.2.3., you calculated Hawkeye's current income tax liability of $113,883. In Example 10.2.11, you calculated Hawkeye's deferred income tax assets and liabilities as follows:

Deferred income tax assets:	
Accounts receivable (net)	$18,375
Warranty reserve	18,270
Capital loss carryover	1,680
Charitable contributions carryover	588
Total	$38,913
Deferred income tax (liabilities):	
Fixed assets (net)	($70,140)
Total	($70,140)

You subsequently calculated a valuation allowance of $1,680 for the capital loss carryforward. There are no uncertain tax positions. How should income taxes be reflected on Hawkeye's balance sheet?

SOLUTION

The current year income tax expense of $113,883 is shown as a separate line item, *current income taxes payable*. The deferred income tax assets are netted against the valuation allowance and the deferred income tax liabilities. The combined total of ($32,907) [(70,140) + 38,913 + (1,680)] is shown as one line item, *deferred income tax liability*.

Current income taxes payable	$113,833
Deferred income tax liability	($ 32,907)

Income Statement

On the income statement, there is one line item for the *provision for income taxes*, and this includes both current income tax expense and deferred income tax expense. In the next Example, we show the appropriate disclosure for the income statement.

EXAMPLE 10.3.2
Income Taxes on the Income Statement

In Example 10.2.3, you calculated Hawkeye's current income tax expense of $113,883. In Example 10.2.6, you calculated Hawkeye's deferred income tax expense of $9,282. How should income taxes be reflected on Hawkeye's income statement?

SOLUTION

The current and deferred income tax expense are combined and shown as follows:

Provision for income taxes	$123,165

Footnotes

ASC 740 requires additional information regarding income taxes, which is provided in the footnotes to the financial statements. The footnotes for income taxes include three components:

1. Provision for income taxes
2. Deferred income tax assets and liabilities
3. Effective tax rate

We discuss each of these components separately.

Provision for Income Taxes

The income tax footnote begins with a statement of the company's income (loss) before the income tax provision. The footnote then details the current income tax expense, the deferred income tax expense, and the total income tax provision. In this chapter, we have discussed the income tax provision only for federal income taxes. The income tax footnote should detail the income tax provision for each taxing jurisdiction—for example, state and foreign as well as federal. In the next Example, we demonstrate how the provision is disclosed for federal income taxes.

EXAMPLE 10.3.3 Footnote: Provision for Income Taxes

Complete the *provision for income taxes* section of the footnote for Hawkeye.

The company's income (loss) before income taxes is: $________

The provision (benefit) for income taxes is as follows:

Current tax provision (benefit)	$________
Deferred tax provision (benefit)	________
Income tax provision	$________

SOLUTION

Income before income taxes	$571,000 (Example 10.2.9)
Current tax provision	$113,883 (Example 10.2.3)
Deferred tax provision	9,282 (Example 10.2.5, LO2 step 3.6)
Income tax provision	$123,165

Deferred Income Tax Assets and Liabilities

This section of the income tax footnote individually details the deferred income tax assets, including the valuation allowance, the deferred income tax assets net of the valuation allowance, the deferred income tax liabilities, and finally the net deferred income tax assets or liabilities. This section also includes two separate statements detailing:

1. Each carryforward and its expiration date
2. The carryovers and/or deferred income tax assets included in the valuation allowance

In the next Example, we demonstrate how the deferred income tax assets and liabilities are disclosed in a footnote.

EXAMPLE 10.3.4 Footnote: Deferred Income Tax Assets and Liabilities

Complete this section of the footnote for Hawkeye. Assume a valuation allowance has been recorded for the capital loss carryover of $1,680 because it will expire unused.

The components of the deferred tax assets and liabilities as of December 31, Year 2, are as follows:

Deferred tax assets

Asset	$________
Asset	________
Total deferred tax assets	$________
Valuation allowance	________
Deferred tax assets net of valuation allowance	$________
Deferred tax liabilities	________
Liability	________
Liability	________
Total deferred tax liabilities	$________
Net deferred tax assets/liabilities	$________

The ________ carryover of $________ and ________ carryover of $________ expire ________. A valuation allowance has been recorded for the ________.

SOLUTION

Accounts receivable (net)	$ 18,375
Warranty reserve	18,270
Capital loss carryover	1,680
Charitable contributions carryover	588
Total deferred tax assets	$ 38,913
Valuation allowance	(1,680)
Deferred tax assets net of valuation allowance	$ 37,233
Fixed assets (net)	($70,140)
Total deferred tax liabilities	($70,140)
Net deferred tax liabilities	$ 32,907

The capital loss carryover of $1,680 and charitable contributions carryover of $588 expire December 31, Year 7. A valuation allowance has been recorded for the capital loss carryover.

Effective Tax Rate

The last section of the income tax footnote is a reconciliation of the company's expected tax rate and the effective tax rate. This section is often called the *effective tax rate footnote.* Recall the formula for the effective tax rate:

$$\text{Effective tax rate} = \frac{\text{Income tax expense}}{\text{Pre-tax net income}}$$

The footnote begins with income taxes computed at the statutory rate (currently 21%). You must detail the items accounting for the difference between income taxes computed at the statutory rate and the effective rate. These adjusting items generally include permanent book-tax differences. The following Example shows the effective tax rate footnote disclosure.

EXAMPLE 10.3.5
Footnote: Effective Tax Rate

Following is the effective tax rate footnote for Hawkeye. Show how each number in the footnote is calculated. As a reader of the financial statement footnotes, what do you conclude about the company's effective tax rate?

A reconciliation of the company's income taxes computed at the statutory federal tax rate (21%) on income before income taxes to the income tax provision is as follows:

Expected tax	$119,910
Tax-exempt interest income	(1,470)
Non-deductible expenses	
Meals	3,150
Officers' life insurance premiums	4,200
Fines and penalties	1,050
Dividends received deduction	(3,675)
Income tax provision	$123,165
Effective tax rate	21.6%

SOLUTION

Each of the following is multiplied by 21%:

		Statutory rate	Effective tax rate footnote
Income before taxes	$571,000	21%	$119,110
Tax-exempt interest income	(7,000)	21%	($ 1,470)
Non-deductible expenses			
Meals	15,000	21%	$ 3,150
Officers' life insurance premiums	20,000	21%	$ 4,200
Fines and penalties	5,000	21%	$ 1,050
Dividends received deduction	(17,500)	21%	($ 3,675)

Effective tax rate = $123,165 ÷ 571,000 = 21.6%. Hawkeye has an effective rate of 21.6%, which is higher than the statutory rate due to the magnitude of book expenses that are not deductible for tax purposes.

Related exercises: Discussion Question 11
Multiple Choice Question 10
Application Problems 8, 9

Spotlight on the Law

Are Investors Concerned about Transparency in Tax Footnotes?

Investors usually are in favor of as much transparency as possible in financial statements. Investors and other users of financial statements do not like surprises, and the best way to prevent surprises is for the financial statements to disclose all relevant information about the company. However, when it comes to tax footnotes in financial statements, some investors seem to have a different perspective on transparency.

The reason? The IRS is also keenly interested in the information that companies report in tax footnotes, as it may signal that the company is engaged in certain tax strategies that the IRS wishes to investigate. While investors may prefer transparency in tax footnotes for their own purposes, they may not favor it where the IRS is concerned. Research has indicated that investors prefer that firms with relatively high levels of tax avoidance have less straightforward tax footnotes. An article published in the *Journal of the American Taxation Association* investigated this issue.[4] One of the authors, Kerry Inger, commented on their results:

> IRS downloading of company annual reports becomes more likely as tax avoidance increases.... Presumably that reflects a heightened interest in the tax footnotes of those reports, so it is not surprising that managers who are adept at tax avoidance would be reluctant to make those notes models of clarity.[5]

The results are consistent with the idea that investors prefer firms with relatively high tax avoidance to have less straightforward tax footnotes. Apparently, investors believe that less transparent tax footnotes reflect more aggressive tax planning, which they assume leads to higher profits and higher future stock prices.

[4]Inger, Kerry K.; Meckfessel, Michael D.; Zhou, Mi; Weiquo, Fan. An Examination of the Impact of Tax Avoidance on the Readability of Tax Footnotes. *Journal of the American Tax Association* (2018) 40 (1): 1–29, doi.org/10.2308/atax-51812.

[5]McCann, David. "How Unclear Tax Footnotes Can Create Value." *CFO.com.* 17 Apr. 2018, www.cfo.com/news/how-unclear-tax-footnotes-can-create-value/659147/.

PRACTICE PROBLEM 10.3.1
Calculation and Interpretation of the Effective Tax Rate

Jude Inc. has income before taxes of $777,000. A reconciliation of Jude Inc.'s income taxes computed on income before income taxes at the statutory federal tax rate (21%) to the income tax provision is as follows:

Expected tax	$163,170
Tax-exempt interest income	(2,220)
Non-deductible expenses	
Entertainment	12,400
Meals	4,800
Officers' life insurance premiums	6,600
Dividends received deduction	(3,700)
Income tax provision	$181,050

a. Calculate Jude Inc.'s effective tax rate.

b. As a reader of the financial statement footnotes, what do you conclude about Jude's effective tax rate?

SOLUTION

a. Effective tax rate = $181,050 ÷ $777,000 = 23.30%.

b. Jude Inc. has an effective rate of 23.30%, which is higher than the statutory rate due to the magnitude of book expenses that are not deductible for tax purposes.

INTERACTIVE SELF-SCORING QUIZZES

10.4 Disclosures in the Tax Return

LEARNING OBJECTIVE 4

Understand the tax reporting and filing requirements of Form 1120.

VIDEO CONTENT

In Chapter 3, LO4, Other Tax Issues, you first learned about book-tax differences and Form 1120, Schedules M-1 and M-3. In this chapter, you have learned more about these concepts in the context of the income tax provision process and financial statement disclosures required by ASC 740. In this section, we review step 7 of the income tax provision process, the reporting and filing requirements of Form 1120, using the work we have done for Hawkeye Corporation.

Corporations must comply with different reporting rules for tax purposes and for GAAP. On Schedule M-1 of Form 1120 (shown in **Illustration 10.14**), corporations must reconcile their book income and taxable income by showing the temporary and permanent differences that account for the different measures of income. Schedule M-1 reconciles to taxable income before the dividends received and net operating loss deductions. Corporations with total assets of $10 million or more are required to file Schedule M-3 (see Appendix B), rather than Schedule M-1. Schedule M-3 requires significantly more detail than Schedule M-1.

Schedule M-1 Items

Differences between book income and taxable income fall into four distinct categories on Schedule M-1. We list the differences that apply to Hawkeye for each category.

1. Income included in taxable income that is not included in book income:
   - Prepaid rental income
   - Gains on dispositions of fixed assets
2. Expenses deducted for book income that are not deductible for taxable income:
   - Federal income tax expense
   - Net capital losses
   - Charitable contributions that exceed the limit of 10% of taxable income
   - 50% of meals
   - Fines, penalties, and other expenses in violation of public policy
   - Life insurance premiums on lives of key employees (corporation is beneficiary)
   - Bad debt expense
   - Warranty expense
3. Income included in book income that is not included in taxable income:
   - Municipal interest income
4. Expenses not deducted for book income that are deducted for taxable income:
   - Tax depreciation in excess of book depreciation

ILLUSTRATION 10.14 Schedule M-1 (Form 1120)

DOWNLOAD DOCUMENTS & TEMPLATES

Schedule M-1 Reconciliation of Income (Loss) per Books With Income per Return

Note: The corporation may be required to file Schedule M-3. See instructions.

1	Net income (loss) per books		7	Income recorded on books this year not included on this return (itemize): Tax-exempt interest $	
2	Federal income tax per books				
3	Excess of capital losses over capital gains				
4	Income subject to tax not recorded on books this year (itemize):		8	Deductions on this return not charged against book income this year (itemize):	
5	Expenses recorded on books this year not deducted on this return (itemize):		a	Depreciation $	
a	Depreciation $		b	Charitable contributions $	
b	Charitable contributions $				
c	Travel and entertainment $				
			9	Add lines 7 and 8	
6	Add lines 1 through 5		10	Income (page 1, line 28)—line 6 less line 9	

The following Example illustrates how book income is reconciled to taxable income.

EXAMPLE 10.4.1 Schedule M-1 Reconciliation

In Example 10.2.9, we calculated Hawkeye's book income of $447,835 after federal income tax expense of $123,165. We list Hawkeye's book-tax differences below. Compute Hawkeye's taxable income using the format for Schedule M-1.

Municipal bond interest income	$ 7,000
Net capital loss	$ 8,000
Book gain on dispositions of fixed assets	$ 25,000
Tax gain on dispositions of fixed assets	$ 41,000
Rental income per books	$ 12,000
Rental income per tax	$ 6,000
Increase in allowance for doubtful accounts	$ 25,000
Charitable contributions in excess of 10% limit	$ 2,800
Federal income tax	$123,165

Book depreciation	$500,000
Tax depreciation	$650,000
Increase in warranty reserve	$ 60,000
Meals expense	$ 15,000
Officers' life insurance premiums	$ 20,000
Fines and penalties	$ 5,000
Dividends received deduction	$ 17,500

SOLUTION

We compute taxable income as follows:

Book income after taxes	$447,835
Plus: Income included in taxable income that is not included in book income:	
Tax gain on dispositions of fixed assets ($41,000 – $25,000)	16,000
Plus: Expenses deducted for book income that are not deductible for taxable income:	
Federal income tax expense	123,165
Net capital loss	8,000
Bad debts	25,000
Charitable contributions in excess of 10% limit	2,800
Warranty expense	60,000
Meals expense	15,000
Officers' life insurance premiums	20,000
Fines and penalties	5,000
Less: Income included in book income that is not included in taxable income:	
Municipal interest income	(7,000)
Rental income ($6,000 – $12,000)	(6,000)
Less: Expenses not deducted for book income that are deducted for taxable income:	
Tax depreciation in excess of book depreciation ($650,000– $500,000)	(150,000)
Taxable income before dividends received deduction	$559,800

Note that the dividends received deduction is not reflected on Schedule M-1.

Schedule M-1 **Reconciliation of Income (Loss) per Books With Income per Return**

Note: The corporation may be required to file Schedule M-3. See instructions.

1	Net income (loss) per books	447,835	7	Income recorded on books this year not included on this return (itemize): Tax-exempt interest $ 7,000; Rental income $6,000	13,000
2	Federal income tax per books	123,165			
3	Excess of capital losses over capital gains	8,000			
4	Income subject to tax not recorded on books this year (itemize): Tax gain on dispositions of fixed assets	16,000	8	Deductions on this return not charged against book income this year (itemize):	
5	Expenses recorded on books this year not deducted on this return (itemize):		a	Depreciation $ 150,000	
a	Depreciation $		b	Charitable contributions $	
b	Charitable contributions $ 2,800				150,000
c	Travel and entertainment $ $25,000+$60,000+$15,000+$20,000+$5,000	127,800	9	Add lines 7 and 8	163,000
6	Add lines 1 through 5	722,800	10	Income (page 1, line 28)—line 6 less line 9	559,800

Schedule M-3

A corporation with total assets of at least $10 million must file Schedule M-3 instead of Schedule M-1. Certain large S corporations and partnerships must also file Schedule M-3. Schedule M-3 is divided into three sections:[6]

- Part I provides certain financial information and reconciles worldwide consolidated net income on the book financial statements to book income for the entities included on the corporate tax return.
- Part II reconciles the book income computed in Part I to the taxable income shown on the Form 1120. For each reconciling item, the effect due to permanent differences and timing differences must be shown.
- Part III provides a breakdown of the expense/deduction items that affect the reconciliation of book income to taxable income in Part II. This total is carried to Part II and combined with the income items listed in Part II.

Related exercises: Discussion Question 12
Multiple Choice Question 11
Brief Exercise 8
Application Problems 10, 11, 12

PRACTICE PROBLEM 10.4.1 Calculation of Taxable Income

Rose Inc.'s book income of $177,000 included municipal interest income of $1,100, fines paid of $500, and business meal expense of $1,800. Charitable contributions of $2,800 were carried forward from a prior year into the current year. What is Rose's taxable income based on this information?

SOLUTION

Book income	$177,000
Less: Municipal bond interest income	(1,100)
Plus: Fines paid	500
Plus: 50% business meals	900
Less: Charitable carryforward	(2,800)
Taxable income	$174,500

The charitable contribution carryforward does not exceed the 10% of income limitation, so the full amount can be deducted.

INTERACTIVE SELF-SCORING QUIZZES

10.5 Special Issues

LEARNING OBJECTIVE 5

Identify other special issues that impact accounting for income taxes.

VIDEO CONTENT

In LO2 step 4 (valuation allowance) and LO2 step 5 (uncertain tax positions reserve) of determining the income tax provision, you were introduced to concepts beyond number crunching and simply balancing debits and credits. You now understand that the income tax provision involves evaluating risk and making subjective judgments by management and tax professionals. In this section, we discuss special issues that create additional complexity in accounting for income taxes.

[6]Rev. Proc. 2004-45, §2004-31 IRB 140.

Different Taxes and Taxing Jurisdictions

In LO1, Basics of Accounting for Income Taxes, you learned that ASC 740 is applicable only to federal, state, local, and foreign income taxes. Because an income tax is defined as a tax based on income, other taxes, such as property taxes, excise taxes, sales taxes, and value-added taxes, are not part of the income tax provision. These taxes are reported as expenses, which are deducted when computing pre-tax book income. However, because ASC 740 is applicable to state, local, and foreign income taxes, it is necessary to compute the income tax provision for *each taxing jurisdiction*. The process you have learned in this chapter is done separately for each income tax jurisdiction and then combined in computing the corporation's total income tax provision.

The next Example contrasts the difference in the federal income tax liability on the tax return and the income tax provision on the financial statements.

Potential Pitfall

It is important to remember the term *income tax provision process* refers to the entire process of determining the current and deferred income tax liability or asset, as well as the current and deferred income tax expense or benefit. The process includes preparation of the financial statement footnote disclosures. The term *income tax provision* is also used to refer to the sum of the current income tax expense plus the deferred income tax expense. Either of these uses of the term refers to financial statements, not tax returns. The income tax liability (taxable income × tax rate) on the tax returns must be calculated to determine the current income tax liability and current income expense recorded on the financial statements.

EXAMPLE 10.5.1 Income Tax Provision for Different Taxes

Spartans has pre-tax book income of $1,000,000 and has the following expenses for various taxes:

$200,000 federal income tax
$ 50,000 state 1 income tax
$ 30,000 state 2 income tax
$ 5,000 city income tax
$ 40,000 real estate tax
$ 10,000 excise tax
$ 15,000 sales tax

Which of these taxes requires calculation of the income tax provision under ASC 740? What is the total income tax provision? Calculate Spartans' federal taxable income and tax liability (ignore any book-tax differences). Why is there a difference between the federal income tax provision and the federal tax liability? Assume that deferred income tax expense is $7,850.

SOLUTION

The income tax provision is calculated for federal, state 1, state 2, and city income taxes because these taxes are based on income. The income tax provision is calculated for each tax separately, and the results are combined to determine the total income tax expense or benefit. Real estate, excise, and sales taxes are not based on income, so it is not necessary to calculate the income tax provision for these taxes. These taxes are deducted in computing pre-tax book income.

The total income tax provision is $285,000 ($200,000 federal + $50,000 state 1 + $30,000 state 2 + $5,000 city).

Pre-tax book income	$1,000,000
Less: State 1 income tax	(50,000)
State 2 income tax	(30,000)
City income tax	(5,000)
Federal taxable income	$ 915,000
Federal income tax at 21%	$ 192,150

Real estate, excise, and sales taxes have been deducted in calculating pre-tax book income of $1,000,000. The income tax provision (expense) for state 1, state 2, and city income tax must be deducted in calculating federal taxable income. Federal income taxes are not deductible on the federal income tax return. The federal income tax provision includes the current income tax expense of $192,150 (current tax liability equal to the tax liability on the tax return) plus deferred income tax expense of $7,850 ($200,000– $192,150). The deferred income tax expense is the change in the deferred income tax liability on the balance sheet.

Different Timing for Income Tax Provision vs. Tax Return Preparation

There are multiple reasons that a corporation may not know all the facts necessary to determine the income tax provision at the time it is prepared. This chapter presumes the tax return is completed before or at approximately the same time as the income tax provision. However, corporations with a December year end usually prepare the income tax provision in February or March when the audit of the financial statements occurs. Corporate income tax returns are due on April 15 (for a December year-end), but the return may be automatically extended for six months and not filed until October 15.

Even after timely filing of the income tax return, a corporation may be examined by the IRS, with a resulting adjustment to its income tax liability. The statute of limitations for a timely filed return is three years, but due to the complexity of tax laws, the corporation may agree to extend the statute to allow the IRS additional time to complete its examination. At the time the income tax provision for the current tax year is in process, a corporation may have an examination of a prior tax year in process, while also anticipating a possible challenge in the future for a filing position taken for the current tax year. Additionally, carryback claims and amended returns may generate income tax refunds, while amended returns may result in additional tax liabilities.

All these timing issues may exist while the corporation is preparing the income tax provision for the current tax year. As a result, the income tax provision may require the use of estimates. Most likely, estimates used to calculate the current income tax expense will differ from tax return amounts upon filing. These differences become adjustments to the current income tax expense for the year in which they are identified. All of these require a corporation's management team and its public accounting audit and tax teams to exercise a high degree of judgment and foresight in preparing the income tax provision, specifically the valuation allowance and uncertain tax positions reserve.

The following Example illustrates how judgment is required when calculating the income tax provision.

EXAMPLE 10.5.2
Income Tax Provision Adjustment for Estimates

In March, Year 3, Hawkeye's audit of its financial statements was underway. At that time, Hawkeye determined the income tax provision of $123,165 for Year 2, as shown in Example 10.2.7. In September, Year 3, the IRS examination of Year 1 was completed. Hawkeye agreed to pay an additional $10,000 in federal income taxes. How should Hawkeye account for the additional assessment for financial statements purposes?

SOLUTION

The IRS examination adjustment for Year 1 is identified in Year 3. Hawkeye will include the additional $10,000 of tax paid for Year 1 in the current income tax expense for Year 3.

Related exercises: Discussion Question 13
Multiple Choice Question 12
Brief Exercise 9
Application Problem 13

PRACTICE PROBLEM 10.5.1

Taxes to Include in the Income Tax Provision

Rufas Inc. has pre-tax book income of $282,000. Rufas has the following expenses for various taxes:

Federal income tax	$58,000
State 1 income tax	$13,750
City income tax	$ 5,500
Real estate tax	$12,000
Sales tax	$10,000

a. Which of these taxes requires calculation of the income tax provision under ASC 740?

b. What is the total income tax provision?

SOLUTION

a. The income tax provision is calculated for federal, state 1, and city income taxes because these taxes are based on income. The income tax provision is calculated for each tax separately, and the results are combined to determine the total income tax expense or benefit. Real estate, excise, and sales taxes are not based on income, so it is not necessary to calculate the income tax provision for these taxes. These taxes are deducted in computing pre-tax book income.

b. The total income tax provision is $77,250 ($58,000 federal + $13,750 state 1 + 5,500 city).

Pre-tax book income	$282,000
Less: State 1 income tax	(13,750)
City income tax	(5,500)
Federal taxable income	$262,750
Federal income tax at 21%	$ 55,178

Real estate and sales taxes are not based on income. They have been deducted in calculating pre-tax book income of $282,000. The income tax provision (expense) for state 1 and city income tax must be deducted in calculating federal taxable income.

PRACTICE PROBLEM 10.5.2

IRS Audit Adjustment

In January, Year 6, Coral Corporation's audit of its financial statements was underway. At that time, Coral determined the income tax provision of $66,000 for Year 5. In June, Year 6, the IRS examination of Year 4 was completed. Coral agreed to pay an additional $8,000 in federal income taxes. How should Coral account for the additional assessment for financial statements purposes?

SOLUTION

The IRS examination adjustment for Year 4 is identified in Year 6. Coral will include the additional $8,000 of tax paid for Year 4 in the current income tax expense for Year 6.

INTERACTIVE SELF-SCORING QUIZZES

Featured Professional: Kay L. Hegarty, CPA

Kay has worked as a tax specialist for 35 years as a former partner at RSM US LLP. She is currently a Professor of Practice at the University of Iowa, teaching tax law to accounting majors.

From Classroom to Career Tax professionals must have technical competence in their understanding of the law. In my experience, the most difficult part of being a tax practitioner is competence in understanding how to deal with people, whether it be the client or coworkers. In today's complex world, one person cannot complete work alone; teamwork is essential. The most talented tax specialist is nothing if she cannot explain the issues and their resolution to the client who has hired her to be member of their team. The true test of success is the satisfaction of the client, not the tax professional.

Professional Skills Before providing answers to the client, a tax professional must first listen to identify the issues, whether they be matters of fact, law, or emotion. The best tax advice is worthless if the client disagrees with the facts or cannot process application of the law because their emotions or biases cloud their perceptions or judgment.

Future Tax Landscape In my lifetime, the most profound change to the profession will be the impact of artificial intelligence. AI must be embraced, or the tax professional will be left behind. AI should be viewed as a powerful tool to be used by the professional but it will not replace human judgment.

Review and Practice

Chapter Summary

In this chapter, you learned the GAAP reporting requirements of FASB ASC Topic 740, Income Taxes. This reporting is required to disclose the impact of the difference between book income reported on the financial statements and taxable income reported on the tax return. These book-tax differences must be accounted for on the GAAP balance sheet and income statement and require disclosure in the footnotes of the financial statements.

1 Understand GAAP accounting for income taxes.

- The difference in the purposes of financial statements based on Generally Accepted Accounting principles (GAAP) and tax laws written by Congress result in different computations of book income and taxable income.
- **Book-tax differences,** which may be temporary, permanent, or carryovers, occur when the amount of an item of income or deduction recognized in book income is different for taxable income.
- Accounting Standards Codification (ASC) 740, Income Taxes, governs the accounting and reporting requirements related to income taxes for the financial statements.
- The **income tax provision process** is the process of determining the **current and deferred income tax liability or asset**, the **current and deferred income tax expense or benefit,** and the preparation of the financial statement footnote disclosures.

2 Compute the current and deferred income tax expense, and evaluate the need for a valuation allowance and a reserve for uncertain tax positions.

- The framework for calculating the income tax provision is a five-step process:
  - **LO2 Step 1. Identify:** Permanent and temporary differences and carryovers.
  - **LO2 Step 2. Calculate:** The current income tax expense or benefit.
  - **LO2 Step 3. Determine:** The deferred income tax expense or benefit.
  - **LO2 Step 4. Evaluate:** The need for a valuation allowance.
  - **LO2 Step 5. Assess:** The need of a reserve for uncertain tax positions.

- The current income tax expense (benefit) is computed as:

  GAAP financial statement pre-tax book income or (loss)
  Plus or *Less:* Temporary book-tax differences
  Plus or *Less:* Permanent book-tax differences
  Taxable income
  × Tax rate
  Current income tax expense (benefit)

- ASC 740 adopts a *balance sheet approach* to measuring deferred income taxes, which focuses on assets and liabilities, not the income statement. The **deferred income tax expense or benefit** equals the change in the deferred tax assets or liabilities from the beginning of the year to the end of the year. Deferred income tax expense is computed as:

Deferred income tax expense	=	Deferred income tax liability at beginning of the year (BOY)	−	Deferred income tax liability at end of the year (EOY)

- If management determines it is *more likely than not* (probability greater than 50%) that future tax benefits will not be realized, a **valuation allowance** is required. The valuation allowance is a contra-asset account that offsets a deferred income tax asset for the amount not expected to be realized in the future.
- A liability for uncertain tax positions may be required for potential tax increases resulting from uncertain tax positions that may be challenged by the IRS.

3 Describe the required financial statement disclosures for income taxes.

- On the balance sheet, there is one line item for current income taxes receivable or payable and one line item for deferred income tax assets or liabilities. Deferred income taxes are shown net of any valuation allowance.
- On the income statement, there is one line item for the "provision for income taxes," and this includes both current income tax expense and deferred income tax expense.
- There are three components to the footnote for income taxes:
  1. Provision for income taxes
  2. Deferred income tax assets and liabilities
  3. Effective tax rate

4 Understand the tax reporting and filing requirements of Form 1120.

- On Schedule M-1 of Form 1120, corporations must reconcile their book income and taxable income by showing the timing and permanent differences that account for the different measures of income. Schedule M-1 reconciles to taxable income before the dividends received and net operating loss deductions.
- Corporations with total assets of $10 million or more are required to file Schedule M-3 rather than Schedule M-1.

5 Identify other special issues that impact accounting for income taxes.

- ASC 740 is only applicable to federal, state, local, and foreign income taxes.
- The computations and financial statement disclosures required by ASC 740 must be performed separately for each taxing jurisdiction.
- The income tax provision and the preparation of the tax returns are not usually completed at the same time. This requires the use of estimates that must be accounted for when the actual numbers are available.

Communication Application

Communication

Calculation of Book Income and Taxable Income

(LO1,2) Juwan is the sole shareholder of Tiger Corporation. Juwan is reviewing the tax return that you prepared and notices that the taxable income and tax liability reported on Form 1120 is greater than the book income and tax expense reported on the financial statements. He's asked you to explain why he's paying more in taxes than he's reporting on his financial statement. Prepare a memo to Juwan explaining why the two numbers are different.

Solution

Hello Juwan,

Thank you for providing me with an opportunity to explain why the federal income tax liability reported on the tax return is different from the federal income tax expense reported on the financial statements.

Form 1120 and taxable income are prepared according to the tax law set forth in the Internal Revenue Code. The financial statements and book income are prepared in accordance with Generally Accepted Accounting Principles (GAAP). There could be multiple reasons for the difference between book income and taxable income, which creates the difference in the federal tax liability and the federal income tax expense. The differences are primarily caused by the different definitions of taxes included in the income tax expense amount and different accounting methods allowed for calculating book income versus taxable income.

The income tax liability reported on Form 1120 is the current-year federal income tax liability calculated based on taxable income. The income tax expense reported on the financial statements includes federal income tax and possibly state, local, and foreign income taxes as well. Additional differences between book income and taxable income occur when the amount of an item of income or deduction recognized in book income is different from the amount used for taxable income. Taxable income is computed by starting with net income on the financial statements and then making adjustments to account for the differences between book income and taxable income.

Differences between book income and taxable income fall into the following four distinct categories:

- Income included in taxable income that is not included in book income
- Expenses deducted for book income that are not deductible for taxable income
- Income included in book income that is not included in taxable income
- Expenses not deducted for book income that are deducted for taxable income

Because of the differences explained above, Tiger Corporation has a different number for taxable income and the federal income tax liability than for book income and the federal income tax expense.

Please let me know if you have any further questions. I am happy to help!

Sincerely,
Carnes & Youngberg, CPAs

Ethics and Professional Responsibilities Application

Ethics

Importance of the Valuation Allowance

(LO2) Acre Inc. is a calendar year-end, accrual-based corporation that began its business three years ago. Acre has accumulated earnings and profits of $125,000. In the current year, Acre sold assets that created a net capital loss of $20,000. Acre also donated cash of $10,000 to a local charity. Because of lower taxable income in the current year, Acre's charitable contribution deduction was limited, and it has a carryforward of $5,000. Acre believes that its sales will pick up in future years and the charitable contribution carryforward will be utilized. Acre does not have appreciated capital assets that will generate capital gains within the next five tax years to offset a capital loss carryforward and does not have any capital gains to offset in its carryback years. Acre is looking for future investors and does not want to mention a valuation allowance for these items in its financial statements. If you are the company's CPA, what advice would you give Acre and its management?

In addition to the chapter content, see *Statements on Standards for Tax Services* at www.aicpa-cima.com/resources/landing/statements-on-standards-for-tax-services, *Circular 230* at www.irs.gov/tax-professionals/office-of-professional-responsibility-and-circular-230, and Chapter 2, LO4, Tax Professional Responsibilities.

Solution

ASC 740 requires a company to evaluate the risk that some portion of deferred income tax assets will not be realized. If management determines that it is more likely than not that future tax benefits will not be realized, a valuation allowance is required. A valuation allowance is a contra-asset account that offsets a deferred income tax asset for the amount not expected to be realized in the future. Under the more likely than not standard, the probability that a deferred income tax asset will not be realized is greater than 50%. To determine if a valuation allowance is needed, management must consider all available evidence, both positive and negative. Positive evidence suggests that an allowance may not be necessary because sufficient taxable income exists to utilize the deferred income tax asset. Negative evidence suggests that an allowance may be necessary because the deferred income tax asset may not be fully utilized.

As Acre's CPA, you have a responsibility to inform management that a valuation allowance is needed. Because Acre does not have foreseeable capital gains in the next five years, the capital loss carryforward will expire. Because Acre has generated profits in the past and believes it will have profits again in the near future, the charitable contribution carryforward will be used in the next five years, and a valuation allowance is not needed for this item.

Key Terms

End-of-Chapter Assessment

Discussion Questions

1. **(LO1)** Describe a book to tax difference.
2. **(LO1)** Compare and contrast a temporary difference and a permanent difference.
3. **(LO1)** What is the comparative usefulness of a loss carryover versus a tax credit?
4. **(LO1)** Briefly explain why book income and taxable income are calculated differently.
5. **(LO1)** Discuss the two primary objectives of ASC 740.
6. **(LO1)** What is the income tax provision?
7. **(LO2)** Describe a favorable and unfavorable book-tax difference.
8. **(LO2)** How is the current income tax expense calculated?
9. **(LO2)** Describe and compare a deferred tax asset and a deferred tax liability.
10. **(LO2)** What is a valuation allowance, and why is it created?
11. **(LO3)** Describe the required financial statement disclosures for income taxes.
12. **(LO4)** Explain when a Schedule M-3 is required.
13. **(LO5)** Provide three reasons why the income tax provision might initially be calculated using estimates.

Multiple Choice Questions

1. **(LO1)** Which of the following is a temporary difference?
   - **a.** Entertainment expense
   - **b.** Fine paid
   - **c.** Charitable contributions in excess of taxable income limitation
   - **d.** Municipal bond interest income
2. **(LO1)** Which of the following is a permanent difference?
   - **a.** Net operating loss
   - **b.** Bad debt expense
   - **c.** Goodwill
   - **d.** Federal income tax expense
3. **(LO1)** A deferred income tax asset is recognized when:
   - **a.** Cumulative taxable income is greater than book income.
   - **b.** Cumulative book income is greater than taxable income.
   - **c.** c. An expense is deducted on the tax return in the current year, but is not deductible on the financial statements until a future year.
   - **d.** d. Income is recognized on the financial statements in the current year, but is not recognized on the tax return until a future year.
4. **(LO1)** If Giant Inc.'s income tax expense is $2,900 and its pre-tax net income is $16,000, what is Giant's effective tax rate?
   - **a.** 15%
   - **b.** 18.13%
   - **c.** 20%
   - **d.** 21%
5. **(LO2)** Which of the following is a favorable book-tax difference?
   - **a.** Tax depreciation greater than book depreciation in the current year
   - **b.** Estimated bad debt expense greater than actual bad debt writeoffs
   - **c.** Fines and penalties
   - **d.** Entertainment expense
6. **(LO2)** Which of the following is an unfavorable book-tax difference?
   - **a.** Municipal bond interest income
   - **b.** Net capital losses
   - **c.** Dividends received deduction
   - **d.** Charitable contribution deducted in carryover year

7. **(LO2)** Saints, Inc. earns pre-tax book income of $120,000 in the current year. Saints has reported municipal interest income of $12,000. Saints has reported no other book-tax differences. What is Saint's current income tax expense?

a. $27,720 **c.** $22,680

b. $25,200 **d.** $2,520

8. **(LO2)** Timber Inc. sells products subject to a two-year warranty. Timber estimates that it will spend $15,000 to satisfy the repairs under warranty on products sold in the current year. The estimated warranty expense is not currently deductible on the tax return. Which of the following is correct?

a. Timber has a $3,150 deferred tax asset.

b. Timber has a $3,150 deferred tax liability.

c. Timber has a $3,150 current tax asset.

d. Timber has a $3,150 current tax liability.

9. **(LO2)** Which of the following is an example of negative evidence in determining whether the valuation allowance is needed?

a. The carryforward period for a tax benefit is extensive.

b. Appreciated assets would generate gains if sold.

c. The company has a backlog of sales or existing contracts.

d. The company has a history of operating losses in recent years.

10. **(LO3)** Which of the following should be included in the footnote for income taxes?

a. Provision for income taxes

b. Deferred income tax assets and liabilities

c. Effective tax rate

d. All of the above

11. **(LO4)** Which of the following is a deduction in calculating taxable income but is not a deduction in calculating book income?

a. Federal taxes paid

b. Entertainment expenses

c. Tax depreciation in excess of book depreciation

d. Fines and penalties

12. **(LO5)** King Corporation is an accrual-based corporation that operates domestically and internationally. King has pre-tax book income of $500,000. Which of the following taxes requires calculation of the income tax provision under ASC 740?

a. Sales tax

b. Foreign income tax

c. Excise tax

d. Property tax

Brief Exercises

1. **(LO1)** Identify whether each of the following is a temporary difference (T), a permanent difference (P), or not a difference (N) between book income and taxable income.

- Goodwill amortization
- Municipal interest income
- Advertising
- Federal income tax expense
- Prepaid income
- Business travel
- Excess capital losses
- Bad debt expense
- Warranty expense
- Salaries paid

2. **(LO1)** Huskie Inc.'s tax return reflects the following for the current tax year:

- Capital gains of $8,000
- Capital losses of $11,000
- Charitable contributions of $3,000 in excess of the allowable deduction for the current year
- General business tax credits of $15,000 in excess of the allowable amount for the current year

Which of these items will create a carryover, and why?

3. **(LO1)** Huskie Inc. is a calendar-year, accrual-based corporation that uses the allowance method for bad debts. The beginning balance in the allowance for uncollectible accounts was $35,000, and the ending balance was $45,000. The actual amount of accounts receivable written off was $8,000. Determine the book-tax difference.

4. **(LO2)** Fuschia, Inc. earns pre-tax book income of $650,000 in the current year. Fuschia acquires machinery in the current year and reports book depreciation of $45,000 and tax depreciation of $60,000. Fuschia reports no other book-tax differences. Compute Fuschia's current income tax expense.

5. **(LO2)** Lombardi, Inc. earns pre-tax book income of $128,000 in the current year. Lombardi has entertainment expense of $2,400, net capital gains of $5,000, and municipal bond interest income of $1,000. Lombardi reports no other book-tax differences. Compute Lombardi's current income tax expense.

6. **(LO2)** Fuschia, Inc. earns pre-tax book income of $650,000 in the current year. Fuschia acquires machinery in the current year and reports book depreciation of $45,000 and tax depreciation of $60,000. Fuschia reported no other book-tax differences. Compute Fuschia's deferred income tax expense. What journal entry is required to record the deferred income tax expense or benefit for Fuschia?

7. **(LO2)** Does the effective tax rate increase or decrease in each of the following situations?

a. A valuation allowance is created against the deferred tax asset for a net operating loss.

b. A valuation allowance is released against a deferred tax asset for a net operating loss.

8. **(LO4)** Dolphin Inc. has book income of $132,000. Included in book income is a fine paid of $1,300 and municipal interest income of $1,500. Calculate taxable income.

9. **(LO5)** In February, Year 5, Bull Corporation's audit of its financial statements was underway. At that time, Bull determined an income tax provision of $90,000 for Year 4. In June, Year 5, the IRS examination of Year 2 was completed. Bull agreed to pay an additional $18,000 in federal income taxes. How should Bull account for the additional assessment for financial statements purposes?

Application Problems

1. **(LO1)** Tortoise Inc. is a calendar-year, accrual-basis taxpayer for book and tax purposes. Tortoise owns a warehouse with an adjusted basis of $100,000 and FMV of $160,000. Tortoise sells the warehouse for $175,000 and receives $100,000 in Year 1 and $75,000 in Year 2. How much income will Tortoise recognize for Years 1 and 2 on the financial statements compared to the tax returns? What is Tortoise's effective tax rate for Years 1 and 2 if it reports income tax expense on the financial statements *and does not record* deferred income taxes?

2. **(LO1)** Tortoise Inc. is a calendar-year, accrual-basis taxpayer for book and tax purposes. Tortoise owns a warehouse with an adjusted basis of $100,000 and FMV of $160,000. Tortoise sells the warehouse for $175,000 and receives $100,000 in Year 1 and $75,000 in Year 2. How much income will Tortoise recognize for Years 1 and 2 on the financial statements compared to the tax returns? What is Tortoise's effective tax rate for Years 1 and 2 if it reports income tax expense on the financial statements *and does record* deferred income taxes pursuant to ASC 740?

3. **(LO2)** Cramer, Inc., an accrual-basis C corporation, reports the following amounts for the year:

Pre-tax book income	$500,000
Penalty paid to city	$ 1,200
Interest earned on a City of DeKalb bond	$ 2,300
Liability for estimated warranty expenses	$ 78,000
Actual warranty expenses paid	$ 72,000
Entertainment expenses	$ 6,400

Compute Cramer's current income tax expense. Identify which book-tax differences are temporary and which are permanent.

4. **(LO2)** Cramer, Inc., an accrual-basis C corporation, reports the following amounts for the year:

Pre-tax book income	$500,000
Penalty paid to city	$ 1,200
Interest earned on a City of DeKalb bond	$ 2,300
Liability for estimated warranty expenses	$ 78,000
Actual warranty expenses paid	$ 72,000
Entertainment expenses	$ 6,400

Compute Cramer's deferred income tax expense.

5. **(LO2)** Assume that Axel Corporation has the following items reported on its balance sheet for the beginning of the year (BOY) and the end of the year (EOY):

Balance sheet item and carryover:	**Book basis**		**Tax basis**	
	EOY	**BOY**	**EOY**	**BOY**
Equipment	$4,500	$5,000	$4,000	$5,000
Charitable contribution carryover	$ 0	$ 0	$ 400	$ 0

Compute the deferred income tax expense.

6. **(LO2)** Lynch, Inc., an accrual-basis C corporation, reports the following amounts for the year:

Pre-tax book income	$625,000
Fine paid	$ 1,000
Net capital loss	$ 2,200
Straight line depreciation	$ 44,000
MACRS depreciation	$ 60,000
Business meals expenses	$ 1,400

Also included in pre-tax book income is an installment sale gain of $45,000. No gain was reported for tax purposes. Compute the current income tax expense, deferred income tax expense, and total income tax provision for Lynch in the current year. What is the journal entry to record the total tax provision?

7. **(LO2)** Weeble Corporation reported pre-tax book income of $1,200,000. There are no temporary or permanent differences. Weeble reported a current federal income tax liability of $252,000 before tax credits. During the year, Weeble earned $75,000 in general business tax credits that it is not able to use on its current tax return. Weeble's management believes it is more likely than not that Weeble will be able to use the tax credits within the next 20 years.

a. Calculate the deferred tax expense (benefit), the total tax expense, and the journal entry needed to record these amounts.

b. Assume that Weeble's management believes that it is more likely than not that Weeble will be able to use only $35,000 of the $75,000 credit in any carryforward year, with the remaining $40,000 expiring unused. In addition to the entry in part a, what journal entry is needed to reflect this change?

8. **(LO3)** Badger Inc.'s current income tax liability is $170,825. Badger's deferred income tax assets and liabilities are as follows:

Deferred income tax assets:	
Accounts receivable (net)	$27,563
Warranty reserve	27,405
Capital loss carryover	2,520
Charitable contributions carryover	882
Total	$58,370
Deferred income tax (liabilities):	
Fixed assets (net)	($105,210)
Total	($105,210)

Badger subsequently calculated a valuation allowance of $2,520 for the capital loss carryforward. There are no uncertain tax positions. How should income taxes be reflected on Badger's balance sheet?

9. **(LO3)** Illini Inc. has income before taxes of $690,000. A reconciliation of Illini's income taxes computed on income before income taxes at the statutory federal tax rate (21%) to the income tax provision is as follows:

Expected tax	$144,900
Tax-exempt interest income	(1,550)
Non-deductible expenses:	
Entertainment	10,200
Meals	3,600
Fines and penalties	1,280
Dividends received deduction	(2,100)
Income tax provision	$156,330

a. Calculate Illini Inc.'s effective tax rate.

b. As a reader of the financial statement footnotes, what do you conclude about Illini's effective tax rate?

10. **(LO4)** Fox Corporation is an accrual-basis, calendar year-end C corporation with book income before federal taxes of $225,000. Fox's tax return reflects the following for the current tax year:

- Capital gains of $2,600
- Capital losses of $5,000

- Charitable contributions of $3,000 in excess of the allowable limit
- Business meals of $4,400

Calculate Fox's taxable income.

11. **(LO4)** Booker Corporation has total assets of $8 million. It reported book income of $320,000. In addition, the following information is available:

Federal income taxes per books	$70,000
Book depreciation in excess of tax depreciation	$16,000
Charitable contributions per books	$55,000

On the M-1 reconciliation, what amount is reported as taxable income?

12. **(LO4)** Peach Inc. is an accrual-basis, calendar-year C corporation that uses the allowance method for bad debts. In the current year, it reported book income before federal income taxes of $280,000. In addition, Peach reported the following:

Municipal bond interest income	$11,000
Corporate bond interest income	$22,000
Interest incurred on debt used to buy the municipal bonds	$ 1,500
Entertainment expense	$ 3,300
Excess tax deprecation over book depreciation	$ 6,000
Actual account receivables written off	$ 3,000

The beginning balance in the allowance for uncollectible account was $18,000, and the ending balance was $28,000. On the M-1 reconciliation, what amount is reported as taxable income?

13. **(LO5)** Raven Inc. has pre-tax book income of $450,000. Raven has the following expenses for various taxes:

Federal income tax	$84,000
State 1 income tax	$45,000
State 2 income tax	$27,000
City income tax	$ 1,350
Real estate tax	$18,000
Excise tax	$ 9,000
Sales tax	$12,000

a. Which of these taxes requires calculation of the income tax provision under ASC 740?

b. What is the total income tax provision?

c. Calculate Raven's federal taxable income and tax liability (ignore any book-tax differences).

d. Why is there a difference between the federal income tax provision and the federal tax liability?

Tax Planning Problems

Planning

1. **(LO2)** Sunny Inc. currently has a valuation allowance of $60,000. While listening to Fox News, you heard that Sunny Inc. has released 20% of its valuation allowance because of a positive forecast for harvesting oranges over the next nine months. What effect does this news release likely have on Sunny's current-year effective tax rate?

Professional Development Skills

Communication Problem

Communication

1. **(LO4)** **Determination of the Valuation Allowance** Kareem owns and operates a corporation that specializes in the production of lithium batteries for automobiles. The corporation currently has deferred income tax assets of $80,000. Kareem has read that deferred income tax assets can be reduced by an allowance account if certain conditions apply. He would like you to explain why and when an allowance account would be generated and recorded. Write a memo to Kareem explaining the allowance account and when it is needed.

Ethics and Professional Responsibilities Problem

Ethics

1. (LO2) **Reporting of Uncertain Tax Position** Clover, Inc owns 100% of three corporations, Iris, Inc., Rose, Inc., and Daisy, Inc. Iris claimed a tax deduction of $1,000,000 on its tax return and in its financial statements related to head-office royalty charges allocated to Iris by Clover. The likelihood that the deduction will be questioned by the IRS is slim. In addition, it is probable that, if the deduction is challenged, the tax authorities will ultimately give Iris a deduction for these charges. However, the amount of the deduction is uncertain. Stan Shady owns 80% of Iris and does not want to report an uncertain tax position (UTP) as it relates to the royalty charge. Explain to Stan the importance of reporting the UTP.

In addition to the chapter content, see *Statements on Standards for Tax Services* at www.aicpa-cima.com/resources/landing/statements-on-standards-for-tax-services, *Circular 230* at www.irs.gov/tax-professionals/office-of-professional-responsibility-and-circular-230, and Chapter 2, LO4, Tax Professional Responsibilities.

CPA Exam Preparation: Task-Based Simulation

1. (LO2) **Schedule M-1** MaidsRUs, Inc. was created in Year 18 to provide cleaning services in its surrounding community. It also offers rental of carpet cleaning equipment. MaidsRUs has net income from books of $40,000 in Year 32. The in-house accountant, Sara, has created an adjusted trial balance and Schedule M-1 for Year 32. She would like you to review the Schedule M-1 for accuracy. Review the adjusted trial balance, the accountant's Schedule M-1, and the exhibits provided. Provide the correct entries in the Excel spreadsheet provided.

Comprehensive Companion Income Tax Provision Problem

1. (LO1,2,3,4) **Determining the Income Tax Provision and its Presentation on the Financial Statements** Huskie Inc. is a calendar-year, accrual-basis corporation. Huskie's balance sheet and income statement for Year 1 and Year 2 will be provided. You will be asked to identify book-tax differences, prepare a book-tax reconciliation, calculate current income tax expense, prepare a journal entry to record the current income tax expense or benefit, calculate the deferred income tax computation for book-tax differences, calculate the deferred income tax expense, prepare the journal entry required to record the deferred income tax expense or benefit, and compute and present Huskie's balance sheet and income statement after tax.

Go to Wiley's book companion site for the complete Comprehensive Companion Income Tax Provision Problem.

CHAPTER 11

Income Taxation of Trusts and Estates

i_frontier/Getty Images

Chapter Introduction

VIDEO CONTENT

The income taxation of trusts and estates is a specialized area of the tax law that taxes the income earned by these entities each year. When an individual dies, their estate comes into existence, and the estate must pay income tax on income earned from the decedent's assets after the date of death. Trusts are created for a variety of reasons that are discussed in more detail below, and income earned by a trust will be taxed either to the trust or to the beneficiaries of the trust. Income is reported by trusts and estates on Form 1041, U.S. Income Tax Return for Estates and Trusts.

Based on the most recent data released by the IRS, approximately 3,200,000 Form 1041s are filed each year, with an aggregate tax liability of approximately $24 billion.[1] While these numbers may seem large, they represent a very small fraction of the revenue raised by the individual income tax (approximately $2 trillion).

Successful tax practitioners need to understand the basic income tax rules for trusts and estates to be able to properly advise their clients on wealth management (ensuring that the financial needs of family members are secured) and estate planning. Our goal in this chapter is not to make you an expert in the income taxation of trusts and estates, but to expose you to the foundational rules so that you understand the basic rules and the tax implications of certain planning tools.

In our immediate context, the term **fiduciary relationship** applies to both trusts and estates because a trustee or administrator has a legal duty to manage assets on behalf of someone else. Trusts and estates can be taxed on the income that accrues during their administration. The trust/estate is taxed on income retained by the fiduciary and not distributed currently to beneficiaries. Income distributed to beneficiaries is reported by the beneficiary as income during the beneficiary's tax year in which the estate year ends. Therefore, the income is taxed only once—either to the trust/estate or to a beneficiary.

[1]U.S. Department of the Treasury. *Fiduciary returns—Sources of income, deductions, and tax liability—Tax status and size of gross income.* Table 1, Statistics of Income Division, Oct. 2015, Internal Revenue Service. www.irs.gov/pub/irs-soi/14fd01.xls.

We begin the chapter by providing the definitions you need to know to understand the structure of trusts and estates. Next, we describe how to compute *fiduciary accounting income* which is used to determine how receipts and disbursements are allocated to the income interest or the remainder interest of a trust. We then review how to compute taxable income for a trust and an estate, including the distribution deduction that determines the amount of income taxed to the trust or estate versus the beneficiaries. We close the chapter by explaining how income from the trust or estate is taxed to the beneficiaries, including determining the character of the income.

LEARNING OBJECTIVES	TOPICS	PRACTICE OPPORTUNITIES

1 Define a trust and an estate, and understand how they are used for planning.	**11.1 Overview of Income Taxation of Trusts and Estates**
	• Trust
	• Components of a Trust
	  • Grantor
	  • Corpus
	  • Trustee
	  • Beneficiaries
	  • Terms
	• Probate Estate vs. Gross Estate
	• Operating Rules for Trusts
	• Estates
	• Probate Estate vs. Gross Estate
		• Example 11.1.1 Trust Creation
		• Example 11.1.2 Parts of a Trust
		• Example 11.1.3 Gross Estate vs. Probate Estate
		• Practice Problem 11.1.1 Gross Estate vs. Probate Estate

2 Compute fiduciary accounting income.	**11.2 Fiduciary Accounting**
	• Structure of a Trust
	  • Differing Interests of Beneficiaries
	• UPAIA Provisions
	  • General UPAIA Provisions for Trusts
	  • Income Provisions for Trusts
	  • Disbursement Provisions for Trusts
	  • General UPAIA Provisions for Estates
		• Example 11.2.1 Governing Authority for Trust
		• Example 11.2.2 Terms of Trust vs. UPAIA
		• Example 11.2.3 Allocations of Trust Income
		• Example 11.2.4 Allocations of Trust Disbursements
		• Example 11.2.5 Computing Fiduciary Accounting Income
		• Practice Problem 11.2.1 Allocations of Trust Income and Disbursements
		• Practice Problem 11.2.2 Calculating Fiduciary Income

3 Compute taxable income for trusts and estates.

11.3 Taxable Income for Trusts and Estates

- Key Concepts for Computing Taxable Income
- Income
    - Income in Respect of a Decedent
    - Distributions of Appreciated Property
- Deduction Rules Similar to Those for Individuals
    - Interest
    - Taxes
    - Losses
    - Capital Gains and Losses
    - Depreciation
    - Expenses Not Deducted by Decedent
    - Credits
- Deduction Rules That Differ from Those for Individuals
    - Exemption
    - Itemized Deductions
    - Miscellaneous Itemized Deductions
    - Charitable Contributions
    - Administration Expenses and Casualty Losses
    - Unused Capital Losses and NOLs
    - Section 179
- Other Issues for Fiduciary Income Taxation
    - Accounting Period for Estates
    - Accounting Period for Trusts
    - Accounting Methods
    - Due Dates
    - Ordinary Income Tax Rates
    - Capital Gain Tax Rate
    - Net Investment Income Tax
    - Estimated Tax Payments
    - Special Rules for Grantor Trusts

- Example 11.3.1 Income in Respect of a Decedent
- Example 11.3.2 Distributions of Appreciated Property
- Example 11.3.3 Tax Year-End for an Estate
- Example 11.3.4 Cash vs. Accrual Method of Accounting
- Example 11.3.5 Computing Tax Liability for a Trust or Estate
- Example 11.3.6 Net Investment Income Tax
- Example 11.3.7 Grantor Trusts
- Practice Problem 11.3.1 Income in Respect of a Decedent
- Practice Problem 11.3.2 Distribution of Appreciated Property
- Practice Problem 11.3.3 Computing Tax Liability for a Trust or Estate

4 Compute the income distribution deduction for trusts and estates.	**11.4 Income Distribution Deduction**
	• Distributable Net Income
	  • Computation of DNI
	  • Simple Trust vs. Complex Trust
	  • Amount of Income Distribution Deduction
	  • Character of Deduction
		• Example 11.4.1 Distribution Deduction Limited to DNI
		• Example 11.4.2 DNI Computation
		• Example 11.4.3 Simple vs. Complex Trust
		• Example 11.4.4 Income Distribution Deduction
		• Practice Problem 11.4.1 Use of DNI
		• Practice Problem 11.4.2 DNI Computation
		• Practice Problem 11.4.3 Income Distribution Deduction

5 Determine how beneficiaries of an estate or trust are taxed.	**11.5 Taxation of Beneficiaries**
	• Simple Trusts
	  • Amount of Income
	  • Character of Income
	  • Allocation of Deductions
	  • Timing of Flow-Through to Beneficiaries
	• Complex Trusts
	  • Allocation of Income
	  • Charitable Contributions
	• Summary
		• Example 11.5.1 Allocation of DNI for a Simple Trust
		• Example 11.5.2 Character of Income to Beneficiaries
		• Example 11.5.3 Character of Income to Beneficiaries—Specific Allocations
		• Example 11.5.4 Allocation of Excess Deductions to Tax-Exempt Income.
		• Example 11.5.5 Timing of Income to Beneficiaries
		• Example 11.5.6 Distributions from a Complex Trust
		• Example 11.5.7 Distributions from a Complex Trust Limited to DNI
		• Example 11.5.8 Discretionary Distributions from a Complex Trust
		• Example 11.5.9 Allocation of Charitable Contributions
		• Example 11.5.10 Comprehensive Problem
		• Practice Problem 11.5.1 Allocation of DNI for a Simple Trust
		• Practice Problem 11.5.2 Timing of Flow-Through to Beneficiaries for Simple Trust
		• Practice Problem 11.5.3 Distributions from a Complex Trust

Tax Forms referenced in this chapter

Form 706	United States Estate Tax Return
Form 1041	U.S. Income Tax Return for Estates and Trusts
Form 1041-T	Allocation of Estimated Tax Payments to Individuals
Form 7004	Application for Automatic Extension of Time
Schedule K (Form 1041)	Beneficiary's Share of Income, Deductions, Credits, etc.

11.1 Overview of Income Taxation of Trusts and Estates

LEARNING OBJECTIVE 1

Define a trust and an estate, and understand how they are used for planning.

VIDEO CONTENT

In this chapter, you will learn the income taxation rules for trusts and estates. The starting point for this analysis is understanding the definition of a trust and an estate. Let's begin by making sure you understand the reasons that trusts and estates exist. Remember, you should never determine the tax consequences of a transaction until you understand the economics of the transaction, so we begin with basic definitions.

Trust

A **trust** is a legal entity created by the transfer of property from a *grantor*. The purpose of the trust is to hold and administer property for *beneficiaries* according to the terms of the trust instrument. The trust exists for the period determined by the trust instrument and state law.[2]

Trusts can be set up for many reasons, such as:

- Protecting assets from creditors
- Transferring assets to others after one's death without having to go through the probate process. **Probate** is the legal process of distributing a decedent's assets according to the decedent's will, or as determined by state law if there is no will. Probate also includes the payment of any debts that the decedent owes at the time of death.
- Protecting assets for one's family to ensure that the assets are handled according to one's desires.
- Transferring assets to children or others to meet their needs without giving full control to them.

Related exercises: Discussion Questions 1, 2

The following Example describes a common situation for which a trust may be created.

EXAMPLE 11.1.1
Trust Creation

Lori was married for 15 years to Cory, and they have three children ages 8, 10, and 13. Lori is a successful CEO of a Fortune 500 company and has accumulated a net worth of $15,000,000. In the current year, Lori was diagnosed with cancer which led her to consider what would happen to her assets if she should pass away. While she would want Cory's financial needs to be met, she would like to ensure that her children receive most of the financial benefit from her wealth. However, she is concerned that if her children receive substantial assets at a young age, they may not have the maturity to use the assets wisely. What would you advise Lori to do?

[2]The regulations define a trust for tax purposes "as an arrangement created either by a will or by an *inter vivos* (lifetime) declaration whereby trustees take title to property for the purpose of protecting or conserving it for the beneficiaries under the ordinary rules applied in chancery or probate courts." Treas. Reg. §301.7701-4(a).

SOLUTION

Lori wants to ensure that she has control of her assets even after her death. Therefore, Lori should establish a trust that her assets will be transferred into at the time of her death. She also has the option to transfer some assets directly to Cory at the time of her death. For the assets transferred into the trust, Lori should include terms such as these in the trust document:

- Provide guidance on the financial strategies that the trustee should use to manage the trust's assets.
- Designate the trust department of a bank to serve as trustee (see definition below).
- Provide that the income from the trust will be distributed to her husband each year to be used for the financial needs of the family.
- Specify that trust's assets can be distributed to pay for medical, education, and housing needs of Cory and her children.
- Provide that at the time of Cory's death, the assets in the trust will be distributed to the children.

If Lori dies and Cory remarries, he cannot change how Lori's assets are managed. The trust ensures that the assets will ultimately be used to benefit her children.

Components of a Trust

There are five distinct components of a trust: *grantor*, *corpus*, *trustee*, *beneficiaries*, and *terms*.

Grantor

The **grantor** is the creator of the trust who transfers assets into the trust and determines the terms of the trust.

Corpus

The **corpus** is the assets transferred to the trust by the grantor, which can include stocks, bonds, homes, land, automobiles, and business assets.

Trustee

The **trustee** has the fiduciary responsibility to manage the assets in the trust according to the terms of the trust. The trustee must protect the interests of the beneficiaries and act in a prudent manner to protect the interests of the beneficiaries.[3]

Beneficiaries

The **beneficiaries** benefit economically from the assets in the trust. **Income beneficiaries** (sometimes referred to as **current beneficiaries**) receive distributions of the income earned by the trust assets each year based on the terms of the trust. **Remainder beneficiaries** receive distributions of the assets in the trust when the trust terminates.

Terms

The **terms** of a trust express the grantor's wishes for how the trust will be managed and the income and assets distributed.

[3]Restatement (Second) of Trusts Section 174.

The following Example illustrates the different components of a trust.

EXAMPLE 11.1.2
Parts of a Trust

Using the facts of Example 11.1.1, identify the grantor, corpus, trustee, beneficiaries, and terms.

SOLUTION

The components of this trust are as follows:

- The grantor is Lori.
- The corpus is the assets owned by Lori at her death, which her will indicates should be put into the trust.
- The trustee is the bank.
- The income beneficiary is Cory. The remainder beneficiaries are the children.
- The terms are the five terms of the trust included as bullet points in the solution to Example 11.1.1.

Related exercises: Discussion Question 3
Multiple Choice Question 1
Brief Exercise 1

The *income interest* in the trust and the *remainder interest* in the trust are separate assets with separate rights. The **income interest** consists of income that is earned each year such as investment income that is available to the income beneficiaries. The **remainder interest** consists of the assets in the trust that will pass to the remainder beneficiaries when the trust is terminated based on the conditions set up by the grantor. To help you understand this, consider the apple tree shown in **Illustration 11.1**. The apple tree is like the corpus of the trust, and the apples are like the income from the trust. The apples and the apple tree are two separate property interests. For example, assume that Mateo owns the tree, while Nia owns the rights to the apples from the tree. Nia can harvest the apples each year and sell them, and this will not impact Mateo's ownership interest in the tree. Similarly, Nia could be the income beneficiary of a trust, and she would receive the trust income each year. However, the corpus of the trust would still be intact, and Mateo could be the remainder beneficiary who receives the corpus when the trust terminates.

Potential Pitfall

Do not confuse the income interest and the remainder interest for a trust. These are separate assets with separate rights assigned to each.

ILLUSTRATION 11.1 Income Interest vs. Remainder Interest

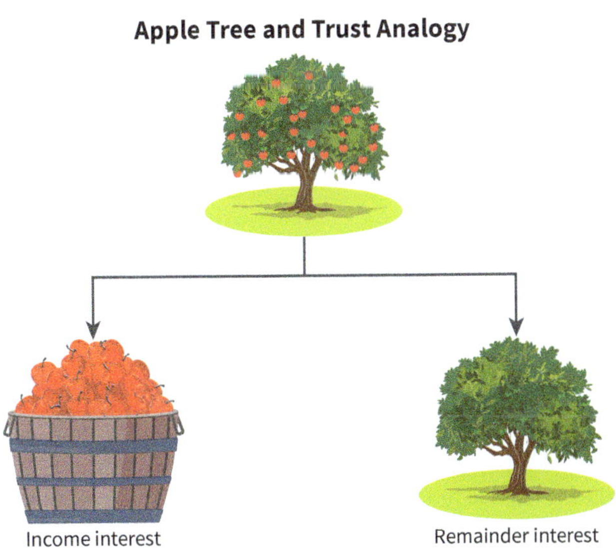

Operating Rules for Trusts

Generally, state law provides the rules that govern the administration of a trust, so theoretically, there could be 50 distinct sets of laws for trusts. However, there have been three efforts to provide uniformity across states with respect to these rules:

- In 2000, the **Uniform Trust Code (UTC)** was created by the Uniform Law Commission with the goal of making trust laws the same or similar across states. Approximately two-thirds of states have adopted a version of the UTC.[4]
- The American Law Institute completed the **Restatement of the Law Third, Trusts**, in 2015 which summarizes the principles of the field of trusts. It offers guidance to trustees, lawyers, and judges by explaining and illustrating the governing rules and discussing relevant cases, statutes, and secondary sources.[5]
- The **Uniform Principal and Income Act (UPAIA)** provides guidance to fiduciaries for administering both trusts and estates in the allocation or apportionment of receipts and payments to principal and income. This process is known as **fiduciary accounting**. *Computing fiduciary accounting income is a precursor to computing taxable income.* Guidance also addresses how fiduciaries can meet their investment responsibility by allowing them to use modern portfolio theory to guide investment decisions. The UPAIA has been adopted by 44 states and the District of Columbia.[6]

Estates

An **estate** for an individual is created on the date of the individual's death, and includes all assets comprising the net worth of the individual, including all real estate, possessions, financial investments, cash, and other assets that the individual owns or has a controlling interest in. The estate exists for as long as is needed to settle the legal and financial affairs for the deceased individual. For some individuals, the estate will be closed after a few months, whereas for others the estate could be open for many years.

For example, Elvis Presley died in 1977, but his estate is still open. Why would his estate still be open after approximately 50 years? It is open because he still has legal and/or financial affairs that continue. For example, the estate of Elvis Presley continues to receive royalties from the sales of Elvis's music; profits from those visiting his home, Graceland, in Memphis; and royalties from other products that use his image.

Forbes magazine ranks the estates that earned the most money for a given year, and in 2023 Elvis Presley was #2 on this list at $100 million, while Michael Jackson was #1 at $115 million.[7] Every year since Elvis's death, his estate has filed an income tax return on Form 1041, U.S. Income Tax Return for Estates and Trusts, to report the estate's income, deductions, tax liability, and tax payments. For example, the estate of Elvis Presley reported approximately $100 million of income on its 2023 Form 1041. In this chapter, you will learn the tax laws for filing such returns for trusts and for estates.

[4]Uniform Law Commission. Trust Code. As of 25 Mar. 2025. www.uniformlaws.org/committees/community-home?CommunityKey=193ff839-7955-4846-8f3c-ce74ac23938d.

[5]American Law Institute. "The American Law Institute Completes the Restatement Third of Trusts." 13 Apr. 2015. www.ali.org/news/articles/american-law-institute-completes-restatement-third-trusts.

[6]National Conference of Commissioners on Uniform State Laws. *Uniform Principal and Income Act.* 9 Feb. 2009. www.uniformlaws.org/HigherLogic/System/DownloadDocumentFile.ashx?DocumentFileKey=1a1c3076-4ac7-03fe-c432-129e4b9dbb3e&forceDialog=0.

[7]Dellatto, Marisa. "The Highest-Paid Dead Celebrities of 2023." *Forbes*. 31 Oct. 2023. www.forbes.com/sites/marisadellatto/2023/10/30/highest-paid-dead-celebrities-2023-michael-jackson-elvis-presley-whitney-houston/.

Spotlight on the Law

What Happens if You Die without a Will?

With the millions of dollars that entertainers, athletes, and the super-rich earn, you would think that each would have a will in place. Without a will, the surviving family members do not know the deceased's intent for distribution of their assets, which can lead to long legal battles. Prince's death is an example of this. The rock star's lack of a will left his family in emotional turmoil.

At the time of Prince's death, his estate was valued at approximately $200 million. It consisted of property and monetary assets as well as his master recordings and his unreleased music. Because Prince died unexpectedly and did not have a will, he died *intestate*. Typically, when a person dies intestate, the courts will award the assets of the estate to the immediate family. In Prince's case, he was survived by six family members.

The battle over Prince's estate went on for more than five years, involved multiple law firms, and cost millions in legal fees. Problems arose regarding the proper fair market value of the estate, taxes that were owed to the IRS, and managing the release of Prince's unreleased music. The estate, valued at approximately $156.4 million after IRS adjustments, was divided among Prince's siblings. A professional music company was awarded the job of managing the release of Prince's music.*

Having a will in place is important for everyone, not just the rich. The will indicates the deceased's last wishes regarding assets, distributions, and allocations to family and charities. While Prince did not have children, a will should also make clear who has custody of minor children if both parents are deceased. The probate process can be very long and time-consuming even with a will, and without a will, time and legal fees are even higher. Protect your family from the emotional anguish and legal strife of intestacy and create a will today!

*Trust & Will. "Prince's Infamous Estate Battle Finally Settled." https://trustandwill.com/learn/prince-estate?srsltid=AfmBOoo4h9xzrZjF4dzgmOI6BtyQWsECDgXUKkUM5Lx4MektOG40xq-e.

Probate Estate vs. Gross Estate

It is important to know the difference between the probate estate and the gross estate. The **probate estate**, in general, includes assets that are held solely by the decedent and does not include assets that pass to others outside of the will, such as:

- Life insurance and annuities,
- Retirement plans such as IRAs, Section 401(k) plans, and qualified retirement plans, *and*
- Property owned as **joint tenants with right of survivorship**, meaning that the property passes at death to the other owner(s).

Property owned jointly as a tenant in common is included in the probate estate. A **tenancy in common** is a type of co-ownership in which the owners do not have to be equal owners and each owner can transfer their ownership interest to others, meaning there is no right of survivorship.

The **gross estate** refers to the assets that must be included in computing the estate tax at the time of one's death. Property could be included in the gross estate but not in the probate estate. For example, property gifted by the decedent to another shortly before death would not be in the probate estate, but the estate tax laws could require that the property to be included in the gross estate.

Potential Pitfall

Do not confuse the estate tax with the income taxation of an estate. We discuss the estate tax in Chapter 12. If it is owed, it is paid one time on the value of an individual's estate at the time of death. The estate tax is reported on Form 706, United States Estate Tax Return. Alternatively, the income earned from an estate, after the date of death, is subject to income tax each year and reported on Form 1041.

Tax Planning Tip

It is the income from the assets in the probate estate that must be reported on the fiduciary income tax return (Form 1041) each year that the estate is in existence.

EXAMPLE 11.1.3 Gross Estate vs. Probate Estate

Joakim is a U.S. citizen who died in the current tax year. At the date of his death, he owned the assets shown below. Which assets would be included in Joakim's probate estate?

Asset	Fair market value
Personal residence	$450,000
Personal assets	$ 28,000
Stocks	$600,000
Checking account	$ 13,000
Corporate bonds	$120,000
Tax-exempt bonds	$ 45,000
Roth IRA (beneficiary is son)	$530,000
Section 401(k) plan (beneficiary is daughter)	$380,000
Rental property (co-owned with right of survivorship with his brother)	$175,000
Life insurance policy—term (beneficiary is wife)	$500,000
LLC interest (owned 60% as a tenancy in common with sister; full FMV is shown)	$ 80,000

SOLUTION

The assets that are *not* included in the probate estate are as follows:

Roth IRA	Passes directly to his son
Section 401(k) plan	Passes directly to his daughter
Rental property	100% passes directly to his brother because it was owned with right of survivorship
Life insurance	$500,000 proceeds pass directly to his wife

Therefore, the probate estate consists of the following assets:

	FMV
Personal residence	$ 450,000
Personal assets	28,000
Stocks	600,000
Checking account	13,000
Corporate bonds	120,000
Tax-exempt bonds	45,000
LLC interest	48,000*
Total probate estate	$1,304,000

*Only 60% of the LLC interest is included in the probate estate because Joakim's sister continues to own the other 40%, as this was held as a tenancy in common.

Related exercises: Discussion Question 5
Multiple Choice Question 2
Application Problem 1

PRACTICE PROBLEM 11.1.1
Gross Estate vs. Probate Estate

Cornell is a U.S. citizen who died in the current tax year. At the date of his death, he owned the assets shown below. Which assets would be included in Cornell's probate estate?

Asset	Fair market value
Houseboat	$280,000
Artwork	$ 22,000
Stocks	$135,000
Checking account	$ 3,000
Vintage car collection	$144,000
Section 401(k) plan (beneficiary is cousin)	$325,000
Life insurance policy—term (beneficiary is his spouse)	$500,000
Partnership interest (owned 75% as a tenancy in common with brother; full FMV is shown)	$220,000

SOLUTION

The assets that are *not* included in the probate estate are as follows:

Section 401(k) plan	$325,000 passes directly to his cousin
Life insurance	$500,000 proceeds pass directly to his spouse

Therefore, the probate estate consists of the following assets:

Assets	FMV
Houseboat	$280,000
Artwork	22,000
Stocks	135,000
Checking account	3,000
Vintage car collection	144,000
Partnership interest	165,000*
Total probate estate	$749,000

*Only 75% of the Partnership interest is included in the probate estate because Cornell's brother continues to own the other 25%, as this was held as a tenancy in common.

INTERACTIVE SELF-SCORING QUIZZES

11.2 Fiduciary Accounting

LEARNING OBJECTIVE 2

Compute fiduciary accounting income.

VIDEO CONTENT

Now that you understand what a trust is and what an estate is, we next show you how to compute fiduciary accounting income. The first step in computing taxable income for an estate or trust is to determine the financial accounting income, which is often referred to as *fiduciary accounting*. **Fiduciary accounting** determines how the receipts and disbursements of a trust or an estate are allocated to principal (the terms *principal* and *corpus* are interchangeable in this chapter) or income. You can think of fiduciary accounting as determining the economic consequences of the estate or trust for the year, and how the economics affect the income and corpus of the trust.

Related exercise: Discussion Question 6

Structure of a Trust

Let's look at a hypothetical trust to better understand the purpose of fiduciary accounting. A diagram of this trust in **Illustration 11.2**. Milton, a resident of Montana, has a 21-year-old daughter, Jana, and a sister, Melba, who has a serious medical condition and is 45 years old. Melba is not expected to live more than 10 years. Milton creates a trust and funds it with $1,000,000 of stocks and bonds. He appoints the trust department of Main Street Bank to be the trustee. The income from the trust is to be used to care for Melba until her death. At the time of Melba's death, the assets of the trust will be distributed to Jana. During the first year of the trust, administration fees of $3,000 are paid. Additionally, the trust has net capital gains of $45,000 from the sale of investments during the year. The gains are reinvested in United States Treasury bonds. The trust also receives qualified dividend income of $30,000 during Year 1.

The income that must be used to support Melba during Year 1 is the *fiduciary accounting* income, not the taxable income. To properly determine the fiduciary income, the trustee needs the answer to the following questions:

- How much of the $3,000 administrative fee should be allocated to income and to corpus?
- Should the net capital gain of $45,000 be distributed for the benefit of Melba, or should it be added to corpus?
- Should the $30,000 of dividend income be allocated to income or to corpus?

The answers to these questions are provided by the fiduciary accounting rules. Melba is the *income beneficiary* and Jana is the *remainder beneficiary*. Let's think about how the allocation of the administrative fee affects Melba and Jana. If the administrative fees are allocated 100% to the income interest, then this will reduce the amount of income that will be distributed for Melba's benefit by $3,000. In that case, there will be $3,000 of additional cash in the trust which can be distributed to Jana in the future. It would be better for Jana if the administrative fees were allocated to Melba. Conversely, it would be better for Melba if the $3,000 of administrative fees were allocated to corpus so that her income distribution will be $3,000 higher.

ILLUSTRATION 11.2 Diagram of a Trust

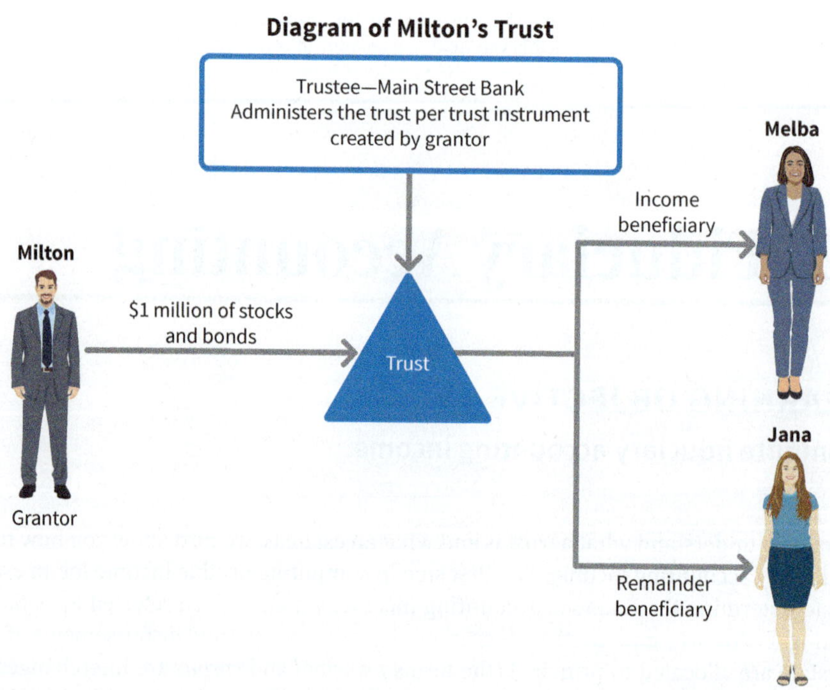

Differing Interests of Beneficiaries

The differing interests of the income and remainder beneficiaries are the reason that the trustee's role is so significant and emphasize the importance of the fiduciary accounting rules that will determine how the administrative fees are allocated. This conflict of interest means that the income beneficiary, Melba, would prefer that the trust assets be invested in investments that pay out income each year, whereas the remainder beneficiary, Jana, would prefer investments that appreciate over time. The *Uniform Prudent Investor Act*[8] provides protection to trustees by providing that:

> A trustee's investment and management decisions respecting individual assets must be evaluated not in isolation but in the context of the trust portfolio as a whole and as a part of an overall investment strategy having risk and return objectives reasonably suited to the trust.

The trustee has several sources of information to use in determining fiduciary accounting income:

- The first document is the trust instrument which was created by the grantor of the trust.
- If the trust instrument does not address the situation, then state law will determine the accounting treatment.
- Many states have adopted the Uniform Principal and Income Act (UPAIA), which was developed by the Commissioners on Uniform State Laws in 1997 to promote uniformity across states.

EXAMPLE 11.2.1 Governing Authority for Trust

Returning to the trust created by Milton, assume that the trust instrument stipulates that no more than 10% of the trust's assets can be invested in partnerships or limited liability companies. However, state law and the UPAIA provide the trustee with broader authority to invest in a manner consistent with that of a prudent investor. The trustee is aware of a great opportunity to invest in a new real estate limited partnership, but the minimum investment required would represent 18% of the trust's assets. The trustee believes she has the authority to make the investment because both state law and the UPAIA permit it. Is she correct?

SOLUTION

The trust instrument takes priority over state law and the UPAIA regarding investment policy. Therefore, the wishes of Milton, the grantor of the trust, must be followed, and no more than 10% of the trust's assets can be invested in the partnership. The trustee must follow the terms of the trust instrument and not exceed the 10% cap on partnership investments.

Related exercise: Multiple Choice Question 3

UPAIA Provisions

Because more than 40 states have adopted the UPAIA, we will use those guidelines to explain fiduciary accounting. We divide this discuss into four parts:

- General UPAIA provisions for trusts
- Income provisions for trusts
- Disbursement provisions for trusts
- General UPAIA provisions for estates

[8]The Uniform Prudent Investor Act (UPIA) was prepared by the Uniform Law Commission (ULC) in 1994 and was approved by the American Bar Association in 1995. More than 40 states have adopted this act. www.uniformlaws.org/committees/community-home?CommunityKey=58f87d0a-3617-4635-a2af-9a4d02d119c9.

General UPAIA Provisions for Trusts

Section 102 Definitions

- *Income* is defined as money or property that a fiduciary receives as a current return from a principal asset.
- *Principal* is defined as the property held in trust for distribution to a remainder beneficiary when the trust terminates.

Section 103 Allocation of Receipts and Disbursements Receipts and disbursements are allocated in the following order:

1. According to the terms of the trust or will, even if the UPAIA provides for a different allocation
2. Per the provisions of the UPAIA
3. To principal, if neither the terms of the trust or will nor the UPAIA provides specific guidance

EXAMPLE 11.2.2
Terms of Trust vs. UPAIA

The terms of a trust indicate that interest income received from bonds issued by LMN Corporation should be allocated to corpus. However, the UPAIA provides (see Section 406 below) that interest income should be allocated to the income interest. How should the trustee resolve this inconsistency?

SOLUTION

If the terms of a trust are different from the guidelines provided by the UPAIA, the terms of the trust control because that was the intent of the grantor when the trust was established. Therefore, the interest income from LMN Corporation should be allocated to corpus.

Section 104 Trustee's Power to Adjust A trustee may adjust between principal and income to the extent the trustee considers necessary, provided that:

- the trustee invests and manages trust assets as a prudent investor;
- the terms of the trust describe the amount that may or must be distributed to a beneficiary by referring to the trust's income; *and*
- the trustee determines that they are unable to administer the trust fairly and impartially without such adjustment.

Income Provisions for Trusts

Section 401 Receipts from Business Entities Other Than Estates or Trusts

- Receipts from business entities, including corporations, partnerships, and LLCs, are allocated to principal if the receipt is:
  - Property other than money
  - Money in exchange for part or all the trust's interest in the entity
  - Money received as part of a partial or complete liquidation
  - Money distributed as capital gains if it is from a regulated investment company or a real estate investment trust
- Otherwise, money received is allocated to income. Examples include cash dividends from a corporation and distributions of ordinary income from a partnership.

Section 402 Distribution from Other Estates or Trusts

- Distributions of income are allocated to income
- Distributions of principal are allocated to principal

Section 403 Income from Business Activities

- Income from a business operating as a sole proprietorship or single-member LLC can be allocated to income or principal at the trustee's discretion. Income from the sale of business assets must be allocated to principal.

Section 404 Principal Receipts The following items are always allocated to principal:

- Assets received from the transferor or from a decedent's estate
- Money or property received from the sale or disposition of a principal asset

Section 405 Rental Property

- Amounts received as rent from personal or real property, including amounts for lease cancellations or renewals, are allocated to income.
- Amounts received for nonrefundable deposits and prepaid rent are allocated to principal.

Section 406 Income from Interest-Bearing Assets

- Income received as interest from interest-bearing assets, such as bonds, is allocated to income.
- If the interest bearing asset matures or is sold within one year of acquisition at a gain, the gain is allocated to income.
- If the interest-bearing asset matures or is sold more than one year after acquisition at a gain, or within one year of acquisition at a loss, the amount is allocated to principal.

Section 407 Insurance Policies

- Proceeds from insurance policies that cover loss of income or profits are allocated to income.
- Proceeds from life insurance policies or policies covering losses of trust assets are allocated to principal.

Section 408 Insubstantial Allocations A trustee may allocate insubstantial amounts to principal. An allocation is presumed to be insubstantial if:

- the amount of the allocation would increase or decrease net income in an accounting period, as determined before the allocation, by less than 10%, *or*
- the value of the asset producing the receipt for which the allocation would be made is less than 10% of the total value of the trust's assets at the beginning of the accounting period.

Section 409 Deferred Compensation and Annuities

- Interest or dividends from deferred compensation or annuities is allocated to income. The remaining amount of the payment is generally allocated to principal.

In the next Example, we apply these UPAIA provisions to specific tax transactions.

EXAMPLE 11.2.3 Allocations of Trust Income

Are the following items allocated to the trust income or the trust principal? Also provide the relevant UPAIA section.

Transaction	UPAIA section	Income/principal
Land received as a property dividend from a corporation		
Interest income from a savings account		
Sale of a building used by a business trust for four years		
Capital gains distribution from a mutual fund		
Ordinary income from a single-member LLC owned by a trust		
Cash dividend from a corporation		
Cash received from rental of a house		
Cash distribution of ordinary income from a partnership		
Distribution of land from an S corporation		
Cash received from a tenant for a nonrefundable deposit		
Sale of a corporate bond held for two years at a gain		
Proceeds from an insurance policy to cover losses from a fire in a building used as rental property		

SOLUTION

Transaction	UPAIA section	Income/principal
Land received as a property dividend from a corporation	401	Principal
Interest income from a savings account	406	Income
Sale of a building used in a business operated by a trust that had been owned for four years	403	Principal
Capital gains distribution from a mutual fund	401	Principal
Ordinary income from a single-member LLC owned by a trust	403	Discretion of trustee
Cash dividend from a corporation	401	Income
Cash received from rental of a house	405	Income
Cash distribution of ordinary income from a partnership	401	Income
Distribution of land from an S corporation	401	Principal
Cash received from a tenant for a nonrefundable deposit	405	Principal
Sale of a corporate bond held for two years at a gain	406	Principal
Proceeds from an insurance policy to cover losses from a fire in a building used as rental property	407	Principal

Disbursement Provisions for Trusts

Section 501 Disbursements from Income The following disbursements are made from income:

- 50% of the recurring portion of the trustee's compensation
- 50% of fees for investment advisory services or other custodial services
- 50% of costs related to accounting services or judicial proceedings
- Recurring insurance premiums that cover the loss of a principal asset or income from an asset
- Ordinary expenses related to the administration, management, or preservation of trust property and the distribution of income, including:
  - Interest
  - Taxes assessed against principal assets
  - Ordinary repairs

Section 502 Disbursements from Principal The following disbursements are made from principal:

- 100% of the trustee's compensation for services related to distributions of assets, acceptance of assets, terminating interests, or preparing property for sale
- 50% of the recurring portion of the trustee's compensation
- 50% of fees for investment advisory services or other custodial services
- 50% of costs related to accounting services or judicial proceedings
- Principal portion of debt payments
- Expenses related to protecting trust property, including associated judicial proceedings
- Insurance premiums not included in Section 501
- Estate taxes and inheritance taxes
- Disbursements related to environmental issues

Section 503 Depreciation

- Trustees, at their discretion, may transfer income to principal to cover the depreciation of fixed assets (but not for estates).

Section 504 Transfers from Income to Principal

- The trustee can transfer money from income to reimburse principal for certain expenses paid from principal, such as:
  - Extraordinary repairs
  - Capital improvements to an asset
  - Expenses to prepare property for rental, including brokers' commissions

Section 505 Income Taxes

- A tax paid on receipts allocated to income must be paid from income.
- A tax paid on receipts allocated to principal must be paid from principal.

In the following Example, we apply these UPAIA provisions to specific disbursements.

EXAMPLE 11.2.4
Allocations of Trust Disbursements

Are the following items allocated to the trust income or the trust principal? Also provide the relevant UPAIA section.

Transaction	UPAIA section	Income/principal
Trustee's compensation for regular services		
Principal portion of payments on debt		
Depreciation		
Investment advisory fees		
Estate taxes		
Property taxes		
Property insurance premium		
Capital improvement to rental property		
Repairs of rental property		
State income taxes		

SOLUTION:

Transaction	UPAIA section	Income/principal
Trustee's compensation for regular services	501	50% to each
Principal portion of payments on debt	502	Principal
Depreciation	503	Income (trustee's discretion)
Investment advisory fees	501	50% to each
Estate taxes	502	Principal
Property taxes	501	Income
Property insurance premium	501	Income
Capital improvement to rental property	504	Income (trustee's discretion)
Repairs of rental property	501	Income
State income taxes	505	Income

Related exercises: Discussion Question 7
Multiple Choice Question 4
Brief Exercises 2, 3

General UPAIA Provisions for Estates

Estates operate much differently than trusts. Typically, income earned during the administration of an estate is not distributed to the beneficiaries. Rather, it is accumulated and then paid once the administration of the estate is complete. In that case, the computation of fiduciary accounting income is not needed because income and expenses are not divided between income and principal. On the other hand, some estates are open for many years, as we mentioned previously with respect to Elvis Presley's estate. When estates are open for longer than just the period needed for administrative purposes, the computation of fiduciary accounting income takes on increased importance.

Sections 201 and 202 Determination and Distribution of Net Income for an Estate The following expenses may be paid from income or principal at the discretion of the executor of the estate:

- Professional fees
- Court costs
- Interest on death taxes

The following expenses are paid from principal:

- Debts
- Funeral expenses
- Disposition of remains
- Estate taxes

Other guidelines regarding distributions for an estate include the following:

- If the will provides that a specific property is to be distributed to a beneficiary, then the income earned from that property is also distributed to the beneficiary.
- A gift of a specific amount of value is a **pecuniary gift**. In most states, the recipient of a pecuniary gift is entitled to a statutory amount of interest based on the amount of the gift.
- Other beneficiaries are allocated income based on their proportional interest in the assets of the estate.

The next Example is a comprehensive problem on computing fiduciary accounting income.

EXAMPLE 11.2.5 Computing Fiduciary Accounting Income

Recall the facts of the trust created by Milton. Milton, a resident of Montana, has a 21-year-old daughter, Jana, and a sister, Melba, who is 45 years old, has a serious medical condition, and is not expected to live more than 10 years. Milton creates a trust and funds it with $1,000,000 of stocks and bonds. He appoints the trust department of Main Street Bank to be the trustee. The income from the trust is to be used to care for his sister until her death. At the time of her sister's death, the assets of the trust will be distributed to his daughter. During the first year of the trust, administration fees of $3,000 are paid. Additionally, the trust has net capital gains of $45,000 from the sale of investments during the year. The gains are reinvested in United States Treasury bonds. The trust also receives qualified dividend income of $30,000 during Year 1.

In addition to the original facts, also consider the following:

- $7,000 paid for accounting services
- $12,000 of state income taxes paid
- Land valued at $40,000 received as a dividend from a corporation

Compute the trust's income for the current year and its principal balance at the end of the year.

SOLUTION

The best starting point is to summarize the items that must be allocated to income or principal:

Tax item	UPAIA section	Allocation
$1,000,000 contribution to trust	404	Principal
Administration fees paid of $3,000	501; 502	$1,500 to income; $1,500 to principal
Net capital gains of $45,000 from sale of investments	406	Income, because not held by trust for more than one year
Qualified dividend income received of $30,000	401	Income
Accounting services paid of $7,000	501; 502	$3,500 to income; $3,500 to principal
State income taxes paid of $12,000	505	Income
Property dividend received of $40,000	401	Principal

Principal and income are computed as follows:

Principal:

Contribution	$1,000,000
Property dividend	40,000
Administrative fees	(1,500)
Accounting services	(3,500)
Principal, end of year	$1,035,000

Income:

Net capital gains from assets not held more than one year	$ 45,000
Qualified dividend income	30,000
Administrative fees	(1,500)
Accounting services	(3,500)
State income taxes	(12,000)
Fiduciary income	$ 58,000

Related exercise: Application Problem 2

PRACTICE PROBLEM 11.2.1

Allocations of Trust Income and Disbursements

Are the following items allocated to the trust income or the trust principal? Also provide the relevant UPAIA section.

Transaction	UPAIA section	Income/principal
Sale of a mutual fund held for three years at a gain		
Cash received from rental of a house		
Dividends received from an annuity		
Disbursements related to environmental issues		
Ordinary repairs		
50% of the recurring portion of the trustee's compensation		

SOLUTION

Transaction	UPAIA section	Income/principal
Sale of a mutual fund held for three years at a gain	406	Principal
Cash received from rental of a house	405	Income
Dividends received from an annuity	409	Income
Disbursements related to environmental issues	502	Principal
Ordinary repairs	501	Income
50% of the recurring portion of the trustee's compensation	502	Income or principal (trustee's discretion)

PRACTICE PROBLEM 11.2.2
Calculating Fiduciary Income

Dante Dream is the sole beneficiary of the Dream Trust, which was created in November of the previous year when Datwon Dream died. In the current year, the trust had a $2,300 short-term capital gain, trustee fees of $3,400, funeral expenses of $4,000, qualified dividend income of $6,300, and tax-exempt interest income of $2,000. The trust agreement indicates that trustee fees are to be allocated to principal.

a. What is the Dream Trust's fiduciary income?

b. Assume the same facts as in part **a.** except that the trust agreement does not indicate the allocation of the trustee fees. What is the Dream Trust's fiduciary income?

SOLUTION

a.

Net capital gains from assets not held more than one year	$ 2,300
Tax-exempt interest income	2,000
Qualified dividend income	6,300
Fiduciary income	$10,600

The funeral expenses are allocated to principal according to UPAIA Sections 501 and 502. Trustee fees are allocated to principal according to the trust document.

b.

Net capital gains from assets not held more than one year	$2,300
Tax-exempt interest income	2,000
Qualified dividend income	6,300
Trustee fees	(1,700)
Fiduciary income	$8,900

The funeral expenses are allocated to principal according to UPAIA Sections 501 and 502. The trustee fee is reported 50% in calculating the fiduciary income per UPAIA Section 501.

INTERACTIVE SELF-SCORING QUIZZES

11.3 Taxable Income for Trusts and Estates

LEARNING OBJECTIVE 3

Compute taxable income for trusts and estates.

VIDEO CONTENT

The trust created by Milton, described earlier in the chapter, will earn income each year, and federal income tax must be paid on this income. The same is true for estates. In this section, you will learn how to compute taxable income for a trust and an estate. While you will learn many new rules for the income taxation of trusts and estates, you will be pleased to see that many of the rules are similar to the income tax rules for individuals!

Trusts and estates report taxable income on Form 1041, U.S. Income Tax Return for Estates and Trusts. Page 1 of the most current Form 1041 is shown in **Illustration 11.3**. We will refer to Form 1041 throughout this discussion.

ILLUSTRATION 11.3 Page 1 of Form 1041, U.S. Income Tax Return for Estates and Trusts (2024)

DOWNLOAD DOCUMENTS & TEMPLATES

Form **1041** Department of the Treasury—Internal Revenue Service
U.S. Income Tax Return for Estates and Trusts
Go to *www.irs.gov/Form1041* for instructions and the latest information.
2024 OMB No. 1545-0092

A Check all that apply:
- ☐ Decedent's estate
- ☐ Simple trust
- ☐ Complex trust
- ☐ Qualified disability trust
- ☐ ESBT (S portion only)
- ☐ Grantor type trust
- ☐ Bankruptcy estate—Ch. 7
- ☐ Bankruptcy estate—Ch. 11
- ☐ Pooled income fund

For calendar year 2024 or fiscal year beginning , 2024, and ending , 20

Name of estate or trust (If a grantor type trust, see the instructions.)

C Employer identification number

Name and title of fiduciary

D Date entity created

Number, street, and room or suite no. (If a P.O. box, see the instructions.)

E Nonexempt charitable and split-interest trusts, check applicable box(es). See instructions.
- ☐ Described in sec. 4947(a)(1). Check here if not a private foundation . . ☐
- ☐ Described in sec. 4947(a)(2)

City or town, state or province, country, and ZIP or foreign postal code

B Number of Schedules K-1 attached (see instructions)

F Check applicable boxes: ☐ Initial return ☐ Final return ☐ Amended return ☐ Net operating loss carryback ☐ Change in trust's name ☐ Change in fiduciary ☐ Change in fiduciary's name ☐ Change in fiduciary's address

G Check here if the estate or filing trust made a section 645 election . . . . ☐ Trust TIN

Income	1	Interest income	**1**	
	2a	Total ordinary dividends	**2a**	
	b	Qualified dividends allocable to: **(1)** Beneficiaries ______ **(2)** Estate or trust ______		
	3	Business income or (loss). Attach Schedule C (Form 1040)	**3**	
	4	Capital gain or (loss). Attach Schedule D (Form 1041)	**4**	
	5	Rents, royalties, partnerships, other estates and trusts, etc. Attach Schedule E (Form 1040) . .	**5**	
	6	Farm income or (loss). Attach Schedule F (Form 1040)	**6**	
	7	Ordinary gain or (loss). Attach Form 4797	**7**	
	8	Other income. List type and amount ______	**8**	
	9	**Total income.** Combine lines 1, 2a, and 3 through 8	**9**	
Deductions	10	Interest. Check if Form 4952 is attached ☐	**10**	
	11	Taxes	**11**	
	12	Fiduciary fees. If only a portion is deductible under section 67(e), see instructions	**12**	
	13	Charitable deduction (from Schedule A, line 7)	**13**	
	14	Attorney, accountant, and return preparer fees. If only a portion is deductible under section 67(e), see instructions	**14**	
	15a	Other deductions (attach schedule). See instructions for deductions allowable under section 67(e)	**15a**	
	b	Net operating loss deduction. See instructions	**15b**	
	16	Add lines 10 through 15b	**16**	
	17	Adjusted total income or (loss). Subtract line 16 from line 9 . . . . . **17**		
	18	Income distribution deduction (from Schedule B, line 15). Attach Schedules K-1 (Form 1041) . .	**18**	
	19	Estate tax deduction including certain generation-skipping taxes (attach computation)	**19**	
	20	Qualified business income deduction. Attach Form 8995 or 8995-A	**20**	
	21	Exemption	**21**	
	22	Add lines 18 through 21	**22**	
Tax and Payments	23	Taxable income. Subtract line 22 from line 17. If a loss, see instructions	**23**	
	24	**Total tax** (from Schedule G, Part I, line 9)	**24**	
	25	Current year net 965 tax liability paid from Form 965-A, Part II, column (k) (see instructions) . .	**25**	
	26	**Total payments** (from Schedule G, Part II, line 19)	**26**	
	27	Estimated tax penalty. See instructions	**27**	
	28	**Tax due.** If line 26 is smaller than the total of lines 24, 25, and 27, enter amount owed	**28**	
	29	**Overpayment.** If line 26 is larger than the total of lines 24, 25, and 27, enter amount overpaid . .	**29**	
	30	Amount of line 29 to be: **a Credited to 2025** ; **b Refunded**	**30**	

Sign Here

Under penalties of perjury, I declare that I have examined this return, including accompanying schedules and statements, and to the best of my knowledge and belief, it is true, correct, and complete. Declaration of preparer (other than taxpayer) is based on all information of which preparer has any knowledge.

Signature of fiduciary or officer representing fiduciary | Date | EIN of fiduciary if a financial institution

May the IRS discuss this return with the preparer shown below? See instructions. ☐ **Yes** ☐ **No**

Paid Preparer Use Only

Preparer's name	Preparer's signature	Date	Check ☐ if self-employed	PTIN
Firm's name			Firm's EIN	
Firm's address			Phone no.	

For Paperwork Reduction Act Notice, see the separate instructions. Cat. No. 11370H Form **1041** (2024)

Key Concepts for Computing Taxable Income

Let's begin by focusing on a few key concepts that underlie the computation of fiduciary taxable income.

Concept 1. Income is taxed only once to either the fiduciary or the beneficiary. This is also shown in **Illustration 11.4**.

Concept 2. You should assume that the tax rules for determining the taxable income for fiduciaries are the same as the rules for individuals unless you are provided a different rule.[9]

Concept 3. The fiduciary receives a distribution deduction for the current year's income that is distributed to beneficiaries. This deduction is the mechanism that prevents double taxation.

Concept 4. In general, the income that is distributed to the beneficiaries is taxed to the beneficiaries.

Concept 5. Income that is taxed to the beneficiaries retains the character it had to the fiduciary, such as ordinary, capital, or Section 1231.

Related exercise: Multiple Choice Question 5

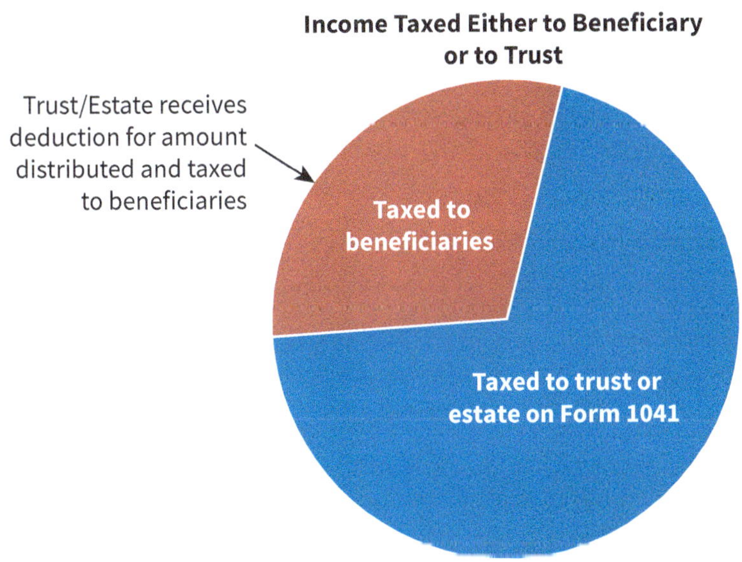

ILLUSTRATION 11.4 Single Taxation of Income to Trust or Estate

Income

The most common types of income that a trust or an estate will have are as follows:

- Interest
- Dividends
- Business income or loss
- Rent and royalty income
- Income from partnerships and S corporations
- Farm income
- Capital gain or loss
- Income in respect of a decedent

[9] IRC §641(b).

Illustration 11.5 shows, for the most recent year that the IRS has data, how many Form 1041s reported each type of income out of the 3,170,667 Form 1041s filed.[10] The three most common types of income are capital gains and losses, dividends, and interest income. Business income was reported on less than 1% of the returns filed, which indicates that trusts and estates are not preferred choices for business operations.

ILLUSTRATION 11.5 Most Common Types of Income Reported on Form 1041

Types of Income (Reporting out of 3,170,667 Form 1041s filed)		
Types of income	**Number of returns**	**Percentage of returns**
Capital gain or loss	1,792,088	56.5%
Dividends	1,740,514	54.9%
Interest	1,448,058	45.7%
Rent and royalty income; and income from partnerships and S corporations	547,048	17.3%
Farm income	27,706	0.9%
Business income or loss	17,868	0/6%
Income in respect of a decedent	Not reported	N/A

Income in Respect of a Decedent

Income in respect of a decedent (IRD) is income the decedent had earned before death but had not yet recognized as income because they were a cash-basis taxpayer. Examples of IRD include:

- Accrued bond interest at the time of death
- Earned wages that had not been received at time of death
- Rental income earned but not yet received at time of death

There are two important tax rules for IRD. First, IRD is taxed to the taxpayer who receives the funds, which is usually the estate of the decedent or a beneficiary. Second, the character of the income to the recipient is the same character that the income would have had if received by the decedent before death.[11]

When determining which income is IRD, if any, and which tax return should report the income, use the following three classifications:

- Income earned and received *before* death is reported on the decedent's final Form 1040.
- Income earned *before* death but received *after* death is IRD. This income is taxed to its recipient, which is often the decedent's estate. In that case, the income is taxed on the estate's Form 1041 for the current year.
- Income earned and received *after* death is taxed on the Form 1041 for the current year.

The following Example illustrates the difference between IRD and income received before death.

[10]U.S. Department of the Treasury. *Fiduciary Income Tax Returns Study*. Table 1. Internal Revenue Service, Statistics of Income Division, Oct. 2015. www.irs.gov/pub/irs-soi/14fd01.xls.

[11]Treas. Reg. §1.691(a)-3.

EXAMPLE 11.3.1
Income in Respect of a Decedent

Willie died on May 31 of the current tax year. Willie lived in one side of a duplex that he owned, and he rented the other side. The tenant's rent was $1,200 per month, and it was paid on the following dates during the current year. Willie reported his rental income on the cash basis.

Month	Date paid
January	January 31
February	March 20
March	June 3
April	June 28
May	July 15
June	July 31
July	August 27
August	September 15
September	October 5
October	October 31
November	November 30
December	December 30

How much rental income is reported on Willie's final Form 1040? How much income in respect of a decedent exists for Willie's estate? How much is reported on his first estate income tax return (Form 1041)?

SOLUTION

To determine the tax consequences of the rental income for the year of death, we divide the income into three groups:

- Income earned and received *before* death: Willie earned and received $2,400 of rental income before death (January and February). This income is reported on Willie's final Form 1040.
- Income earned *before* death but received *after* death: Willie earned $3,600 of income before death that was not received before death (March, April, and May). Therefore, the IRD is $3,600. This income is taxed to its recipient, which is Willie's estate, so the income is taxed on the Form 1041 for the current year.
- Income earned and received *after* death: Willie's estate earned and received $8,400 of income after Willie's death (June–December). This income is taxed on the Form 1041 for the current year.

Related exercises: Discussion Question 8
Multiple Choice Question 6
Brief Exercise 4

Distributions of Appreciated Property

Recall that when a corporation or an S corporation distributes appreciated property, they must recognize the appreciation as gain (but a loss would not be recognized). However, a partnership does not recognize gains or losses when property is distributed. What are the tax consequences to trusts and estates when they distribute appreciated property? It depends. The general rule is that fiduciaries are like partnerships, meaning that neither gains nor losses are recognized when property is distributed to a beneficiary. However, gain *is* recognized if the distribution is in satisfaction of the right to receive:

- a specific dollar amount,
- property other than the distributed property, *or*
- income, assuming that income is required to be distributed currently.[12]

[12]Treas. Reg. §1.661-1(a)-(2)(f).

If a trust or estate qualifies to not recognize the appreciation as gain for a distribution, the fiduciary can elect for the gain to be recognized.[13] If the election is made, it applies to all distributions made for that tax year. The beneficiary's basis in the property distributed from the trust or estate is the basis the trust or estate had in the property plus any gain recognized by the trust or estate.

The following Example demonstrates when gain could be recognized if property is distributed rather than cash.

EXAMPLE 11.3.2
Distributions of Appreciated Property

Shanice created a trust five years ago and, in addition to other assets, contributed stock in SY corporation that had a basis of $30,000 and a FMV of $45,000. The trust document provided that after five years, the stock would be distributed to her daughter. The stock was distributed this year when the FMV of the stock was $68,000.

a. How much gain or loss is recognized to the trust because of the distribution? What is the daughter's basis in the stock?

b. How would the answer change if the trust document required a distribution of $80,000 to Shanice's daughter, and the trustee chose to distribute the SY stock and $12,000 of cash?

SOLUTION

a. If the trust document requires a distribution of a specific asset to a beneficiary, then when that asset is distributed no gain or loss is recognized to the trust. The daughter's basis in the stock is $30,000, the same basis that the trust had.

b. If the trust document requires the distribution of a specific dollar amount, and the trustee uses appreciated property to satisfy all or part of the requirement, the trust must recognize the appreciation as gain. Therefore, the trust will recognize a long-term capital gain of $38,000 ($68,000 FMV – $30,000 adjusted basis). The daughter's basis in the stock will be its FMV of $68,000, which is the adjusted basis of $30,000 plus the gain recognized by the trust of $38,000.

Related exercises: Multiple Choice Question 7
Application Problem 3

Why **Why is the rule for income recognition when appreciated property is distributed by a trust or estate not always the same?** Example 11.3.2 illustrates that sometimes appreciation in a distributed asset by a trust is recognized, and sometimes it is not. The logic underlying the difference is based on the discretion that the trustee has with regard to the property. If the trust document requires that a specific asset be distributed, the trustee must abide by that term. In that case, the appreciation in the distributed asset is not recognized as gain, and it transfers to the beneficiary. However, if the trust document requires that a specified dollar amount be distributed, the trustee has discretion as to which assets will be used to satisfy the requirement. The trustee could sell the appreciated asset and distribute cash to the beneficiary, and the trust would recognize the gain from the sale of the asset on the Form 1041. Alternatively, the trustee could choose to not sell the asset but distribute the appreciated asset to satisfy the requirement. If that choice is made, the tax law assumes that the asset was sold for its FMV, so that the gain would be recognized just like if the asset had been sold.

Deductions and Credits Similar to Individuals

In general, the deduction rules for trusts and estates are the same as the rules for individuals. In this section, we emphasize a few of these similarities to ensure you know these rules apply to fiduciaries. These rules are summarized in **Illustration 11.6**.

[13]IRC §643(e).

ILLUSTRATION 11.6 Deduction Rules for Individuals vs. Trusts and Estates

Deductions: Comparing Individuals with Trusts and Estates		
Deduction	**Individuals**	**Trusts and estates**
Interest	Mortgage interest and investment interest are deductible subject to limitations	Same as for individuals
State and local taxes	Deductible but limited to $10,000	Same as for individuals
Losses	At-risk rules and passive loss rules apply	Same as for individuals
Long-term capital gains	0%/15%/20% rates apply	Same as for individuals
Capital losses	Net capital losses limited to $3,000	Same as for individuals
Depreciation	MACRS rules apply	Same as for individuals; there are special rules for how the depreciation is allocated between income and remainder interests
Exemption	Standard deduction allowed based on filing status	No standard deduction; exemption of $100, $300, or $600 allowed
Itemized deductions	Deduct the greater of itemized deductions or standard deduction	Itemized deductions are allowed regardless of their amount because there is no standard deduction
Charitable contributions	Limitations based on AGI apply	Deducted in full; no limitations apply
2% miscellaneous deductions	Not deductible	Deductible in certain circumstances
Administrative expenses	Not deductible if related to one's personal life	Trusts can deduct. Estates can deduct on Form 1041 or Form 706
Casualty losses	Deductible subject to limitations	Trusts can deduct. Estates can deduct on Form 1041 or Form 706
Section 179	Allowed	Not allowed

Interest

The same types of interest that are deductible for individuals are also deductible for trusts and estates. Acquisition indebtedness in a residence is deductible by a trust or estate if the home would be a qualified residence if owned by a beneficiary of the trust or estate. Additionally, investment interest is deductible only to the extent of net investment income.

Taxes

Only $10,000 of state and local taxes are deductible.

Losses

The at-risk rules and passive loss rules limit the ability to deduct losses for trusts and estates.

Capital Gains and Losses

Long-term capital gains are taxed at 0%/15%/28%. Capital losses offset capital gains, and a net capital loss of up to $3,000 can be deducted with the remainder carried forward indefinitely. (Reported on line 4 of Form 1041.)

Depreciation

The computation of the amount of depreciation uses the same MACRS rules as for individuals. The rules for the deduction of depreciation vary somewhat between trusts and estates. For estates, the depreciation is allocated between the estate and the beneficiaries based on the amount of income allocated to each. For a trust, depreciation is allocated between the remainder and the income beneficiaries based on the income allocated to each, unless the trust instrument or local law allows the trustee to maintain a reserve for depreciation.[14] Recall that

[14] Treas. Reg. §1.167(h)-1.

Section 503 of UPAIA allows the trustee to transfer a reasonable amount of income to principal to account for depreciation of corpus assets. If the trustee does so, then any remaining depreciation is allocated between income and corpus based on the income allocated to each.

The rules for amortization and depletion are similar to the rules for depreciation. If the trust instrument does not require a reserve for depreciation, and all taxable income is distributed to the beneficiaries, then no depreciation is deducted when calculating fiduciary accounting income, distributable net income, and taxable income.

Expenses Not Deducted by Decedent

If the following expenses were not deducted on the decedent's final income tax return (Form 1040), they can be deducted on the estate income tax return (Form 1041): interest, taxes, depletion, and other business expenses.[15]

Credits

In general, credits that are allowed for individuals are also allowed for trusts and estates, such as the foreign tax credit and the general business credit.

Deduction Rules That Differ from Those for Individuals

The following are some of the more common deductions for trusts and estates for which the tax rules vary from the rules for individuals.

Exemption

(Reported on line 21 of Form 1041.) Fiduciaries do not receive a standard deduction like individuals do. Rather, fiduciaries get an exemption depending on the type of fiduciary:

- $600 for estates,
- $300 for simple trusts, *and*
- $100 for complex trusts.

A **simple trust** is one that:

- must distribute all income currently,
- made no distributions of corpus in the current year, *and*
- made no charitable contributions in the current year.

Any trust that does not qualify as simple trust is a **complex trust**. A trust's status as simple or complex can vary from year to year.

Itemized Deductions

Because fiduciaries do not have a standard deduction, you do not have to compare the itemized deductions to the standard deduction to determine the greater of the two. Rather, all itemized deductions, such as interest, taxes, charitable contributions, and trustee fees are deductible regardless of their amount. If a trust or estate has tax-exempt income, then the deductible trustee fees must be reduced by the percentage of the tax-exempt income to total income.

Miscellaneous Itemized Deductions

Before 2019 individuals could deduct investment expenses, unreimbursed employee business expenses, and certain other expenditures to the extent that the total exceeded 2% of AGI. These itemized deductions have not been allowed for individuals since 2018. However, trusts

[15]IRC §691(b).

and estates are still allowed to deduct certain types of miscellaneous expenses. Miscellaneous expenses are deductible if the expense would not have been incurred if the property was not held by a trust or estate.[16] Deductible expenses include:

- the costs of preparing the estate- and generation-skipping transfer tax returns (line 14 of Form 1041),
- the costs of preparing fiduciary income tax returns (line 14 of Form 1041),
- appraisal fees to determine the FMV of the decedent's assets as of the date of death (or alternate valuation date), to determine the value for purposes of making distributions, or as otherwise required to properly prepare the estate or trust's tax returns (line 15a of Form 1041), *and*
- certain fiduciary expenses including probate costs, fiduciary bond premiums, legal publication costs of notices to creditors or heirs, and the cost of certified copies of the decedent's death certificate (line 21 of Form 1041).

Investment advisory fees are typically not deductible, because these fees are commonly incurred by individuals, and they are not currently deductible for individuals.

Charitable Contributions

Trusts and estates have an unlimited deduction for charitable contributions (these are reported on line 13 of Form 1041). They are not limited to a certain percentage of AGI, as is the case with individuals.[17] Trusts and estates can deduct contributions to foreign charities even though individuals and other business entities cannot.[18] The charitable contribution deduction is reduced proportionally for tax-exempt income that was earned by the trust or estate.

Administrative Expenses and Casualty Losses

Examples of administrative expenses include fiduciary fees, legal fees, accounting fees, and court costs. Legal expenses related to one's personal life are generally not deductible. The executor has the option of deducting administration expenses on the estate tax return (Form 706) or the estate's income tax return (Form 1041). If deducting on the income tax return, the executor must irrevocably waive the right to take the deduction on the federal estate tax return. Trusts can deduct administrative expenses. The same option applies to casualty losses for estates.

Unused Capital Losses and NOLs

Unused capital loss and net operating loss (NOL) carryovers from the decedent's final Form 1040 are not allowed as deductions on the fiduciary income tax return.

Section 179

Section 179 cannot be used by trusts or estates.

Related exercise: Multiple Choice Question 8

Other Issues for Fiduciary Income Taxation

In this section, we discuss several other rules that are important issues for fiduciary income taxation.

Accounting Period for Estates

On the date of death, the decedent's tax year ends for purposes of filing their final Form 1040, and the tax year begins on the following day for the estate of the decedent. The executor of the estate chooses the year-end for the estate. The tax year has to be 12 months or less for the

[16]IRC §67(e)(3).

[17]IRC §642(c).

[18]Treas. Reg. §1.642-(c)-2.

first year, and it must end on the last day of a month. In fact, the first tax year for the estate is almost always less than 12 months.

The next Example demonstrates the restrictions on choosing a tax year-end for an estate.

EXAMPLE 11.3.3 Tax Year-End for an Estate

Fredricka died on August 23 of Year 1.

a. Can the executor choose August 31, Year 2, as the first year-end for Fredricka's estate?

b. What are the possible year-ends that the executor can choose for Fredricka's estate?

c. Assuming that the executor chooses June 30 as the year-end for Fredricka's estate, what time periods will be covered by the first two income tax returns filed for the estate?

SOLUTION

a. No, August 31, Year 2, cannot be the end of the first tax year because that would result in a tax period that is longer than 12 months (August 24, Year 1, to August 31, Year 2).

b. The executor can choose the following year-ends for Fredricka's estate:

August 31, Year 1	February 28, Year 2
September 30, Year 1	March 31, Year 2
October 31, Year 1	April 30, Year 2
November 30, Year 1	May 31, Year 2
December 31, Year 1	June 30, Year 2
January 31, Year 2	July 31, Year 2

c. If the executor chooses June 30 for the year-end, the first two tax returns will be for the following periods:

First return:	August 24, Year 1, to June 30, Year 2
Second return:	July 1, Year 2, to June 30, Year 3

Tax Planning Tip

If the executor of an estate is aware that a significant amount of income will be earned in a future month, the executor could defer reporting the income from the trust by choosing a year-end that ends before the income is earned or received.

Accounting Period for Trusts

In general, trusts must adopt a calendar-year tax year. There are exceptions to this requirement for certain charitable, tax-exempt, and grantor trusts.[19]

Related exercise: Brief Exercise 5

Accounting Methods

A trust or estate can use the cash or accrual method of accounting. The method chosen for tax purposes needs to be the same as that used for keeping books and records.[20] Once the method is established, it can be changed only with the consent of the IRS.

Tax Planning Tip

It is common for trusts and estates to use the cash method of accounting, but if the payment of expenses comes later than the receipt of income, the accrual method may be preferable.

[19] IRC §644.

[20] IRC §446.

EXAMPLE 11.3.4
Cash vs. Accrual Method of Accounting

Continuing with the facts of Example 11.3.3 for Fredricka, assume that the executor chooses March 31 as the year-end for the estate. The first taxable year of the estate runs from August 24, Year 1, to March 31, Year 2. The executor finishes settling the legal and financial obligations of Fredricka by January 31, Year 3. The estate is officially closed on January 31, Year 3. The estate had the following income and expenses:

	Year-ended 3/31/Year 2	Year-ended 3/31/Year 3
Cash income	$29,000	$27,000
Cash expenses	$18,000	$22,000
Accrued expenses	$13,000	

a. If the estate reports on the cash basis, what is the taxable income (based just on this information) for Year 2 and Year 3?

b. If the estate reports on the accrual basis, what is the taxable income (based just on this information) for Year 2 and Year 3?

c. Is the cash method or the accrual method preferable in this situation?

SOLUTION

a. Under the cash method of accounting, the taxable income for Year 2 is $11,000 ($29,000 income – $18,000 expenses) and for Year 3 is $5,000 ($27,000 – $22,000).

b. Under the accrual method of accounting, the taxable loss for Year 2 is $2,000 ($29,000 income – $31,000 expenses) which creates an NOL that can be carried forward. The taxable income for Year 3 is $3,000 ($27,000 income – $22,000 expenses– $2,000 NOL carryforward).

c. When the receipt of income precedes the payment of expenses for a trust or estate, the accrual method may be preferable. Under the cash method, there is $11,000 of income for Year 2, but there is a ($2,000) loss under the accrual method. The NOL of $2,000 can be carried forward and used to reduce income in Year 3.

Due Dates

Form 1041 is due on the 15th day of the fourth month after the end of the tax year. For calendar-year trusts and estates, this is April 15. An extension of 5½ months can be requested by filing Form 7004, Application for Automatic Extension of Time. For calendar-year trusts and estates, this extends the due date to October 1.

Related exercise: Discussion Question 9

Ordinary Income Tax Rates

The tax rate structure for trusts and estates is very different from that for individuals. There are four tax brackets for trusts and estates—10%, 24%, 35%, and 37%—compared with seven brackets for individuals. The lowest rate and the highest rate are the same for both groups. However, trusts and estates are subject to the higher tax rates at much lower levels of income. For example, a trust is subject to the 37% tax rate for income over $15,650 (2025), but a single individual is not subject to the 37% rate until taxable income exceeds $626,350 (2025). The tax rate table for trusts and estates is shown in **Illustration 11.7**.

ILLUSTRATION 11.7 Tax Rate Schedule for Form 1041 (2025)

Tax Rate Schedule for Trusts and Estates			
If taxable income is:			
Over	**But not over**	**The tax is:**	**Of the amount over**
$ 0	$ 3,150	10%	$ 0
$ 3,150	$11,450	$ 315.00 + 24%	$ 3,150
$11,450	$15,650	$2,307.00 + 35%	$11,450
$15,650	—	$3,777.00 + 37%	$15,650

Why **Why are the income tax rate schedules for trusts and estates so much more compressed than those for individuals?** The income level where the 37% tax bracket begins for a trust or estate equals just 2.5% of the level where that bracket begins for an individual. On first realizing this fact, a person is often frustrated at a minimum and perhaps very angry. It is not unusual to hear the individual say, "These rates are not fair for trusts and estates." However, there is a good reason for the difference. What if trusts and estates did not reach the 37% tax rate until taxable income reached $50,000, and a wealthy taxpayer had investment income of $400,000 each year? The taxpayer could create eight trusts and put enough investments in each trust to generate approximately $50,000 of income, so that none of the income would be taxed at 37%. This incentive is minimized when the tax brackets are structured as they are currently for a trust. Also note that the tax rate schedule encourages trusts and estates to distribute their income to the beneficiaries, so that the income is not subject to these compressed rates.

The next Example shows the computation of the tax liability for a trust.

EXAMPLE 11.3.5 Computing Tax Liability for a Trust or Estate

A trust has taxable income of $14,000. What is the trust's tax liability before reduction for estimated tax payments made, and what is the trust's marginal tax rate?

SOLUTION

The tax liability is computed as follows:

Taxable income	$ 14,000
Less: Threshold	(11,450)
	$ 2,550
Tax rate	× 35%
	$ 892.50
Plus:	2,307.00
Tax liability	$3,199.50

The estate's marginal tax rate is 35%.

Related exercise: Brief Exercise 6

Capital Gain Tax Rates

The long-term capital gain tax rates for trusts and estates are also much more compressed than the capital gain rates for individuals, as shown in **Illustration 11.8**.

ILLUSTRATION 11.8 Tax Rate Schedule for Form 1041—Long-Term Capital Gains (2025)

Tax Rate Schedule for Trusts and Estates—LTCG			
If taxable income is:			
Over	**But not over**	**The tax is:**	**Of the amount over**
$ 0	$ 3,250	0%	$ 0
$ 3,250	$15,900	$ 0.00 + 15%	$ 3,250
$15,900	—	$ 1,897.50 + 20%	$15,900

Net Investment Income Tax

Trusts and estates are subject to the net investment income tax, just as are individuals. The tax is 3.8% times the *lower* of:

- the excess of the trust's or estate's AGI over $15,650 (the 37% rate income tax bracket threshold for 2025), *or*
- the trust's or estate's undistributed net investment income.

The AGI for a fiduciary is computed in the same manner as for an individual, with the following changes for deductions:

- All charitable contributions are deductible
- An exemption of $100, $300, or $600 is allowed
- A deduction of distributions to beneficiaries is allowed
- Some miscellaneous itemized deductions are allowed (as explained above in Deduction Rules That Differ from Those for Individuals).

In general, trusts set up to benefit only a qualified charity or tax-exempt organization are not subject to the net investment income tax.

Potential Pitfall

Remember that trusts and estates do not have a standard deduction, so there is no need to segment deductions into the two categories that individuals use: deductions *for* AGI and itemized deductions.

Tax Planning Tip

A trust can avoid the net investment income tax by distributing all its net investment income to the beneficiaries. In that case, the undistributed investment income is $0. However, it is possible that the investment income could be subject to the net investment income tax on the beneficiary's tax return.

EXAMPLE 11.3.6
Net Investment Income Tax

Trust ME is a complex trust that has the following income in the current year:

Interest income	$12,000
Qualified dividend income	$11,000
Long-term capital gain	$14,000

The trust distributes $15,000 to the beneficiary. How much net investment income tax does the trust owe for this year?

SOLUTION

The net investment income tax is 3.8% times the *lower* of:

- the excess of the trust's or estate's AGI over $15,650 *or*
- the trust's or estate's undistributed net investment income.

AGI is computed as:

Interest income	$12,000
Qualified dividend income	11,000
Long-term capital gain	14,000
Total income	$37,000
Less: Exemption—Complex trust	(100)
Distribution deduction	(15,000)
Adjusted gross income	$21,900

Undistributed net investment income is computed as:

Interest income	$12,000
Qualified dividend income	11,000
Long-term capital gain	14,000
Total income	$37,000
Less: Distribution	(15,000)
Undistributed net investment income	$22,000

The net investment income tax is $238, 3.8% times the *lower* of:

- $6,250 ($21,900 – $15,650), *or*
- $22,000

Related exercise: Application Problem 4

Estimated Tax Payments

Like individuals, a trust or estate will incur a penalty for underpayment of estimated tax if it owes $1,000 or more on the due date of the return. One major exception to this rule is that trusts and estates do not have to pay estimated income taxes for the first two years after the decedent's death. The underpayment penalty is waived if the estate or trust has paid:

- At least 90% of the current year's tax liability, *or*
- 100% of the prior year's tax liability (110% if the AGI on the prior year return is more than $150,000).

The penalty can also be reduced or avoided by using the annualization method.

Fiduciaries of trusts can make an election that will allow the beneficiaries of the trust to use the estimated taxes that were paid by the trust. The election is made by filing Form 1041-T, Allocation of Estimated Tax Payments to Individuals, by the 65th day after the close of the trust year.[21]

Related exercise: Discussion Question 10

Special Rules for Grantor Trusts

Special rules apply to the income taxation of a grantor trust. A **grantor trust** is a trust controlled by the grantor through retained powers or the possibility the property in the trust will revert to the grantor. At times, the grantor may want to fund a trust that provides economic benefits to the beneficiaries but also wants to retain the power to change their decision in the future, and perhaps even terminate the trust and take back the assets of the trust. This is known as a **revocable trust**—a trust that the grantor can revoke in the future.

Because the grantor has retained these powers, the income ordinarily taxable to a grantor trust is taxed directly to the grantor. In other words, the existence of a grantor trust is ignored for income tax purposes and the income is treated as if earned by the grantor.

EXAMPLE 11.3.7
Grantor Trusts

Grandpa establishes a trust for his four grandchildren to assist in paying for their college tuition, room, and board. He funds the trust this year with $1,000,000 of investments and provides that all income from the trust will be retained by the trust. The grandchildren range in age from four to ten this year. The corpus of the trust, plus 25% of the cumulative earnings of the trust, can be used by the trustee to pay for up to $250,000 of college expenses for each grandchild. Grandpa retains the right to revoke the terms of the trust for any or all of the grandchildren. He informed the grandchildren of this to encourage them to behave in the manner he desired. For the current year, the trust had taxable income of $63,000. How is this income taxed?

SOLUTION

Grandpa has established a revocable trust because he can take the funds in the trust back at any time he chooses. Therefore, this is a grantor trust, and the existence of the trust is ignored for income tax purposes. The $63,000 of income is taxed to Grandpa on his Form 1040. The income is not taxed to the trust or the beneficiaries, and a Form 1041 does not need to be filed for the trust.

[21] IRC §643(g).

PRACTICE PROBLEM 11.3.1
Income in Respect of a Decedent

Ying died on October 31 of the current year and was a cash-basis taxpayer. On November 15, her estate executor received a check from Ying's employer of $4,500 representing her wages earned through October 31. On November 30, her estate executor received a payment of $100,000 representing Ying's balance in her 401(k). Is this income reported on Ying's Form 1040 or the trust's Form 1041?

SOLUTION

Income in respect of a decedent (IRD) is income that was earned before the taxpayer died but not received before death. IRD is taxed to the taxpayer who receives the funds, which is usually the estate of the decedent or a beneficiary. Because the final wage payment was earned while Ying was living but not received until after Ying's death, it is IRD and is reported on Form 1041. The 401(k) distribution was received after Ying's death, so it is considered IRD and reported on Form 1041. The estate reports gross income of $104,500.

PRACTICE PROBLEM 11.3.2
Distribution of Appreciated Property

The Mario Trust was created ten years ago and holds a painting that had a basis of $13,000 and a FMV of $27,000 at the time the trust was created. The trust document provided that after ten years, the painting would be distributed to Mario's son. The painting was distributed in the current year when the FMV of the painting was $45,000.

a. How much gain or loss is recognized to the trust because of the distribution? What is the son's basis in the painting?

b. How would the answer change if the trust document required a distribution of $50,000 to Mario's son, and the trustee chose to distribute the painting and $5,000 of cash?

SOLUTION

a. If the trust document requires a distribution of a specific asset to a beneficiary, when that asset is distributed, no gain or loss is recognized to the trust. The son's basis in the painting is $13,000, the same basis that the trust had.

b. If the trust document requires the distribution of a specific dollar amount, and the trustee uses appreciated property to satisfy all or part of the requirement, the trust must recognize the appreciation as gain. Therefore, the trust will recognize a long-term capital gain of $32,000 ($45,000 FMV – $13,000 adjusted basis). The son's basis in the painting will be its FMV of $45,000, which is the adjusted basis of $13,000 plus the gain recognized by the trust of $32,000.

PRACTICE PROBLEM 11.3.3
Computing Tax Liability for a Trust or Estate

A trust has taxable income of $13,500. What is the trust's tax liability before reduction for estimated tax payments made, and what is the trust's marginal tax rate?

SOLUTION

The tax liability is computed as follows:

Taxable income	$ 13,500
Less: Threshold	(11,450)
	$ 2,050
Tax rate	× 35%
	$ 717.50
Plus:	2,307.00
Tax liability	$3,024.50

The estate's marginal tax rate is 35%.

INTERACTIVE SELF-SCORING QUIZZES

11.4 Income Distribution Deduction

LEARNING OBJECTIVE 4

Compute the income distribution deduction for trusts and estates.

VIDEO CONTENT

One unique aspect of the income taxation of trusts and estates is that the entity receives a deduction for distributions of income to the beneficiaries. Corporations cannot deduct dividend payments to shareholders, nor can partnerships or corporations reduce taxable income for distributions. Whether the trust or estate distributes income to the beneficiaries determines who is taxed on the income. Undistributed income is generally taxed to the trust or estate (unless the entity is a simple trust and the income required to be distributed was not distributed), and distributed income is taxed to the beneficiaries. The income distribution deduction means that the trust or estate is not taxed on the distributed income, ensuring single taxation for trust or estate income.

Illustration 11.9 visually depicts how the income distribution deduction affects the income taxation of trusts and estates. Income and deductions are earned or incurred by the trust or estate. The income is taxed to the trust, unless it is distributed through the bottom of the funnel to the beneficiaries. Distributed income, limited to *distributable net income (DNI)*, is taxed to the beneficiaries.

ILLUSTRATION 11.9 Income Distribution Deduction

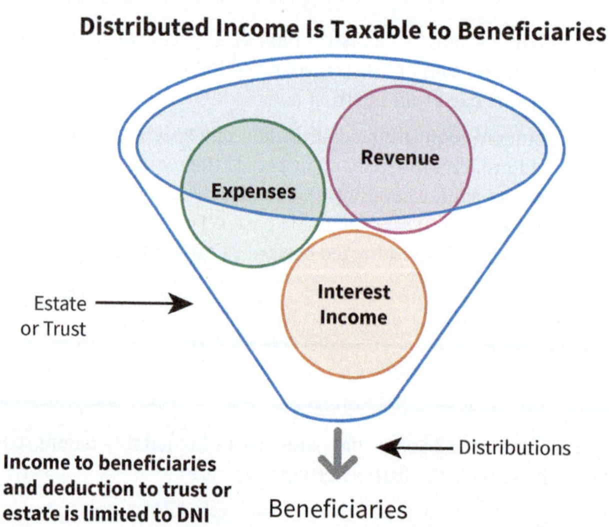

Distributable Net Income

Distributable net income (DNI) is the maximum amount of the income distribution deduction for a trust or estate, and it is also the maximum amount of income that the beneficiaries must recognize. The deduction or the income can be less than DNI, but not more than DNI.

EXAMPLE 11.4.1
Distribution Deduction Limited to DNI

Apple Trust is a simple trust that has $35,000 of fiduciary accounting income this year, all of which must be distributed to the beneficiaries.

a. If the trust has DNI of $38,500, what is the income distribution deduction for Apple?

b. If the trust has DNI of $33,500, what is the income distribution deduction for Apple?

SOLUTION

a. The income distribution deduction is $35,000 because this amount does not exceed DNI.

b. Even though the distribution is $35,000, the income distribution deduction is limited to the DNI of $33,500.

Computation of DNI

DNI does *not* include the following items:

- Income distribution deduction
- Exemption
- Capital gains allocated to corpus if not required to be distributed to a beneficiary or qualified charity
- Capital losses, unless the losses offset capital gains that are distributed to a beneficiary
- Extraordinary dividends or taxable stock dividends that are allocated to corpus

Tax-exempt interest *is included* in DNI, but it must be reduced by any nonbusiness-related expenses that were not deducted because they are related to tax-exempt income.[22]

The following Example illustrates how to compute DNI.

EXAMPLE 11.4.2
DNI Computation

Pear Trust has the following information for the current tax year:

Income:	
Interest	$10,000
Rental income	$25,000
Long-term capital gain	$12,000
Tax-exempt interest	$ 5,000
Deductions:	
Rental expenses	$15,000
Trustee's fees	$ 3,000
State income taxes	$ 2,000
Business interest expense	$ 4,000
Principal payment on debt	$ 1,000

Compute the trust's distributable net income.

[22] IRC §643(a).

SOLUTION

The computation of DNI includes the following items:

Income:		
Plus: Interest		$10,000
Plus: Rental income		25,000
Plus: Tax-exempt interest	$ 5,000	
Less: Expenses attributable to tax-exempt income	(375)	4,625
Total		$39,625
Deductions:		
Less: Rental expenses	($15,000)	
Less: Trustee's fees ($3,000 – $375)	(2,625)	
Less: State income taxes	(2,000)	
Less: Interest expense	(4,000)	
Total		(23,625)
Distributable net income		$16,000

- The $12,000 LTCG is not included in DNI because it is allocated to corpus.
- The $1,000 principal payment on the debt is not included in DNI because it is allocated to corpus.
- The $5,000 of tax-exempt interest was reduced for the trustee expenses allocable to it, as follows:

  Trustee's fees: $3,000 × (5,000/[$10,000 + $25,000 + $5,000]) = $375
- The rental expenses, state income taxes, and interest expense are business expenses, so they do not reduce the tax-exempt interest.
- The deduction for the exemption was not included because it is not included in DNI.

In some situations, DNI is computed after taxable income has been computed by making adjustments to taxable income. **Illustration 11.10** shows how to compute DNI when the starting point is taxable income.

ILLUSTRATION 11.10 DNI Computation

Adjusting Taxable Income to Compute DNI
Taxable income of the trust or estate
Plus: Income distribution deduction
Plus: Capital gains allocated to corpus, as long as not required to be distributed to a beneficiary or qualified charity
Less: Capital losses, unless the losses offset capital gains that are distributed to a beneficiary
Less: Extraordinary dividends or taxable stock dividends that are allocated to corpus
Plus: Tax-exempt interest, reduced by any nonbusiness-related expenses that were not deducted because they are related to tax-exempt income
Distributable net income

Related exercises: Discussion Question 11
Multiple Choice Question 9
Brief Exercise 7
Application Problem 5

Simple Trust vs. Complex Trust

The income distribution deduction is computed differently for simple trusts and complex trusts. Recall that a simple trust is one that:

- must distribute all income currently,
- made no distributions of corpus in the current year, *and*
- made no charitable contributions in the current year.

Any trust that does not qualify as a simple trust is a complex trust. A trust's status as simple or complex can vary from year to year. If distributions of corpus are required for a trust, but not made, then the trust is a simple trust for that year.

The next Example demonstrates the difference in a simple trust and complex trust.

EXAMPLE 11.4.3 Simple vs. Complex Trust

Wendy is the beneficiary of a trust that was set up by her grandmother when Wendy was 21 years old. Wendy is to receive all the income from the trust every year. Additionally, when she turns 25, she will receive 50% of the corpus of the trust, and when she turns 35, she will receive the remaining corpus. Is this trust a simple trust or a complex trust?

SOLUTION

The classification of a trust as simple or complex is made each year. A simple trust must distribute all its income each year, and it cannot make distributions from corpus. This trust is a simple trust for the years that Wendy is age 21, 22, 23, 24, 26, 27, 28, 29, 30, 31, 32, 33, and 34. In the years that she is 25 and 35, she will receive distributions of corpus, so for those years, the trust will be a complex trust.

The following are special rules that apply to determining whether a trust is simple or complex:

- If the trust allows income to be set aside for depreciation and transferred to corpus, the income set aside will not disqualify the trust from being a simple trust, even though not all of the income was distributed to the income beneficiary.[23]
- If income is distributed shortly after the end of the tax year because of the time needed to compute fiduciary accounting income and have the distribution made, this will not disqualify the trust from being a simple trust, even though technically not all the income was distributed during the tax year.
- While for a simple trust all income must be currently distributed, it is not a requirement that the trust instrument specify which beneficiary will receive the income distributions. The trust instrument can give the trustee discretion to determine which beneficiary of beneficiaries will receive the income distribution, if the trust clearly specifies the eligible beneficiary or beneficiaries.
- If the trust satisfies all or a portion of its requirement to distribute the current income by distributing property to the beneficiary, that is acceptable if the FMV of the property does not exceed the amount of income for the year. In that situation the law assumes that the trust sold the property for its FMV, and any resulting gain or loss must be recognized by the trust.

Potential Pitfall

One requirement of a simple trust is that it must distribute all its income each year. Remember that the income referred to for this rule is the fiduciary accounting income, *not* the taxable income. Thus, if capital gain income is allocated to corpus by the trustee, then the capital gain could not be distributed to the beneficiary and the trust would still be a simple trust.

Related exercise: Discussion Question 12

[23]Treas. Reg. §1.651(a)-2(a).

Amount of Income Distribution Deduction

For a *simple trust*, the income distribution deduction consists of the amount of the income that is required to be distributed currently.[24] For a *complex trust*, the income distribution deduction is equal to the sum of:

- any amount of income required to be distributed currently, *and*
- any other amounts properly paid or required to be distributed to the extent that they do not exceed the DNI of the trust or estate.[25] This would include property distributed in-kind to a beneficiary. It does not include amounts that qualify for the charitable contribution deduction.

Character of Deduction

What is the character of the income distribution deduction? That is, is it treated as an ordinary deduction, a capital loss, or a Section 1231 loss? The character is determined on a proportionate basis based on the character of the items that are included in computing the DNI of the trust (explained in LO5, Taxation of Beneficiaries).[26] Another implication of the character rule is that a distribution deduction is not allowed to the extent that the trust or estate has tax-exempt income. Similarly, any amount set aside for a charitable contribution deduction cannot also be deducted as part of the income distribution deduction.

EXAMPLE 11.4.4
Income Distribution Deduction

Continuing with the facts of Example 11.4.2, assume that Pear Trust is a complex trust and distributes $13,000 of income to its beneficiary, Lincoln. What would the income distribution deduction be for Pear?

SOLUTION

The distribution of $13,000 must be reduced on a proportional basis for the tax-exempt income in relation to the total income. Therefore, the deduction is reduced as follows:

$$\$13{,}000 \times \frac{\text{Net tax-exempt income (\$5,000)}}{\text{DNI (\$16,000)}} = \$4{,}063$$

The income distribution deduction is $8,937 ($13,000 − $4,063), which is less than the DNI of $16,000, so the deduction is $8,937.

Related exercises: Multiple Choice Questions 10, 11
Brief Exercise 8

PRACTICE PROBLEM 11.4.1
Use of DNI

Beneficiary Rhys is to receive 40% of the trust income, beneficiary Fynn is to receive 60%, and the income required to be distributed currently is $110,000. DNI is $118,000.

a. How much income will Rhys and Fynn recognize?

b. If the DNI is only $98,000, how much income will Rhys and Fynn recognize?

SOLUTION

a. Rhys will receive $44,000 ($110,000 × 40%) and Fynn will receive $66,000 ($110,000 × 60%). This will also be the income recognized by each because DNI is greater than $110,000.

b. The amounts distributed are still $44,000 and $66,000, respectively. However, income recognized by the beneficiaries is limited to DNI of $98,000 because it is less than the amounts distributed. Rhys will include $39,200 (40% × $98,000) of that sum in his gross income on his tax return, and Fynn will include $58,800 (60% × $98,000) in his gross income.

[24] IRC §651(a).

[25] IRC §661(a).

[26] Treas. Reg. §1.661(b)-1.

PRACTICE PROBLEM 11.4.2
DNI Computation

During the taxable year, the trust had the following items of income and expense.

Income	**Amount**
Dividend income	$38,000
Tax-exempt interest income	$12,000
Rental income	$24,000
Long-term capital gain	$10,000
Expenses	
Expenses attributable directly to rent	$ 5,000
Trustee commission	$ 4,000

The trust document indicates that the trustee commission is to be allocated 75% to income and 25% to corpus. Determine the DNI of the trust for the year.

SOLUTION

The distributable net income of the trust is $65,000, determined as follows:

Income	**Amount**	
Dividend income		$38,000
Tax-exempt interest income	$12,000	
**Less*: Expenses allocable to income: ($4,000 × $12,000/$74,000 = $649)	(649)	11,351
Rental income		24,000
Total income		$73,351
Less: Deductions		
Expenses directly attributable to rental income	($5,000)	
Trustee commission ($4,000 less $649 allocable to tax-exempt interest)	($3,351)	($8,351)
Distributable net income		$65,000

*$74,000 is the sum of dividend income, tax-exempt interest income, and rental income ($38,000 + $12,000 + $24,000). The LTCG is not included because it is allocated to principal.

No reductions were taken for distributions to the beneficiaries or the trust exemption because these are not deductions for DNI. Capital gains were excluded because it was allocated to corpus. The tax-exempt interest as adjusted for expenses was included.

PRACTICE PROBLEM 11.4.3
Income Distribution Deduction

Strawberry Trust is a complex trust and distributes $28,000 of income to its beneficiary, Selma. The trust has DNI of $32,000 and tax-exempt interest income included in DNI of $13,500. What would the income distribution deduction be?

SOLUTION

The distribution of $28,000 must be reduced on a proportional basis for the tax-exempt income in relation to the total income. Therefore, the deduction is reduced as follows:

$$\$28{,}000 \times \frac{\text{Net tax-exempt income } (\$13{,}500)}{\text{DNI } (\$32{,}000)} = \$7{,}188$$

The income distribution deduction is $20,812 ($28,000 − $7,188), which is less than the DNI of $32,000, so the deduction is $20,812.

INTERACTIVE SELF-SCORING QUIZZES

11.5 Taxation of Beneficiaries

LEARNING OBJECTIVE 5

Determine how beneficiaries of an estate or trust are taxed.

VIDEO CONTENT

In general, income that is distributed to a beneficiary is taxed to the beneficiary. In this section, we discuss how to determine the amount of income that the beneficiary will be taxed on, and the character of that income. Each beneficiary receives a Schedule K-1 (Form 1041) Beneficiary's Share of Income, Deductions, Credits, etc. (see **Illustration 11.11**) that shows the beneficiary's share of the income and deductions of the trust or estate. We close this chapter with a comprehensive problem that includes the most important computations you have learned.

ILLUSTRATION 11.11 Schedule K-1 (Form 1041)

DOWNLOAD DOCUMENTS & TEMPLATES

661117

☐ Final K-1 ☐ Amended K-1 OMB No. 1545-0092

Schedule K-1 (Form 1041) **2024**

Department of the Treasury
Internal Revenue Service

For calendar year 2024, or tax year

beginning / / 2024 ending / /

Beneficiary's Share of Income, Deductions, Credits, etc. **See back of form and instructions.**

Part I Information About the Estate or Trust

A Estate's or trust's employer identification number

B Estate's or trust's name

C Fiduciary's name, address, city, state, and ZIP code

D ☐ Check if Form 1041-T was filed and enter the date it was filed

E ☐ Check if this is the final Form 1041 for the estate or trust

Part II Information About the Beneficiary

F Beneficiary's identifying number

G Beneficiary's name, address, city, state, and ZIP code

H ☐ Domestic beneficiary ☐ Foreign beneficiary

Part III Beneficiary's Share of Current Year Income, Deductions, Credits, and Other Items

1	Interest income	11	Final year deductions
2a	Ordinary dividends		
2b	Qualified dividends		
3	Net short-term capital gain		
4a	Net long-term capital gain		
4b	28% rate gain	12	Alternative minimum tax adjustment
4c	Unrecaptured section 1250 gain		
5	Other portfolio and nonbusiness income		
6	Ordinary business income		
7	Net rental real estate income		
8	Other rental income	13	Credits and credit recapture
9	Directly apportioned deductions		
		14	Other information
10	Estate tax deduction		

* See attached statement for additional information.

Note: A statement must be attached showing the beneficiary's share of income and directly apportioned deductions from each business, rental real estate, and other rental activity.

For IRS Use Only

For Paperwork Reduction Act Notice, see the Instructions for Form 1041. www.irs.gov/Form1041 Cat. No. 11380D **Schedule K-1 (Form 1041) 2024**

Simple Trusts

Recall that a simple trust is required to distribute its income every year to the beneficiaries. Therefore, even if for some reason the income is not distributed, the beneficiaries are still taxed on the income.[27]

Amount of Income

The total amount of income recognized by the beneficiaries is limited to DNI. If the income exceeds the DNI, each beneficiary of the trust recognizes income equal to the DNI times a ratio, which is the income required to be distributed to that beneficiary divided by the total income:

$$\text{DNI} \times \frac{\text{Income required to be distributed to beneficiary}}{\text{Total income}} = \text{Total amount of income recognized}$$

The next Example illustrates the allocation of the DNI to the beneficiaries.

EXAMPLE 11.5.1
Allocation of DNI for a Simple Trust

The LN Trust is a simple trust for the current tax year with two beneficiaries, Lincoln and Maria, who are to receive 60% and 40% of the income, respectively. The fiduciary accounting income for the year is $70,000, and DNI is $62,000. How much income must Lincoln and Maria recognize for the current year?

SOLUTION

Lincoln is to receive a distribution of $42,000 of income ($70,000 × 60%) and Maria a distribution of $28,000 ($70,000 × 40%). However, the income recognized by the beneficiaries cannot exceed DNI which is $62,000. Therefore, the beneficiaries will recognize the following amounts of income:

Lincoln	$62,000 × 60% = $37,200
Maria	$62,000 × 40% = $24,800

Character of Income

The character of the income recognized by the beneficiaries is the same character that the income had in the hands of the trust or estate. Therefore, if the income was long-term capital gain to the trust, then it is also LTCG to the beneficiary. If the distributed income was tax-exempt income to the trust, then the income is not taxable to the beneficiaries.[28]

You also must know how to determine the amount of each type of income that has been distributed to the beneficiaries. For example, a trust may have dividend income, interest income, and LTCG, and a total distribution of $80,000. However, if DNI is $65,000, then the amount of income is limited to $65,000. In that case, how much of the $65,000 is dividend income, interest income, and LTCG? These amounts are determined based on the following formula:

$$\text{Amount of tax item} \times \frac{\text{Amount of item included in DNI}}{\text{Total DNI}}$$

Exceptions to this allocation formula are made if the trust instrument allocates certain types of income to specific beneficiaries, or if local law requires a different allocation. The next two Examples show how income is allocated to the beneficiaries of a trust or estate.

[27] Treas. Reg. §1.652(a)-1.

[28] Treas. Reg. §1.652(b)-1.

EXAMPLE 11.5.2
Character of Income to Beneficiaries

A simple trust allocates income to the beneficiaries as follows:

Denzel	40%
Antonio	35%
Marsha	25%

The trust has the following income for the current year:

Interest income	$50,000
Dividend income	$30,000
LTCG	$20,000
Tax-exempt income	$40,000

Assume that the DNI of the trust is $150,000. How much income is allocated to the beneficiaries for the current tax year?

SOLUTION

The fiduciary accounting income for the trust is $140,000 ($50,000 + $30,000 + $20,000 + $40,000). DNI does not limit the amount of income to the beneficiaries, because the DNI exceeds the trust income. The allocation of the income to each beneficiary is determined as follows:

Beneficiary	a. Income percentage	b. Total allocation of income	c. Interest	d. Dividend	e. LTCG	f. Tax-exempt
Formula		($140,000 × a)	($50,000 × a)	($30,000 × a)	($20,000 × a)	($40,000 × a)
Denzel	40%	$56,000	$20,000	$12,000	$8,000	$16,000
Antonio	35%	$49,000	$17,500	$10,500	$7,000	$14,000
Marsha	25%	$35,000	$12,500	$ 7,500	$5,000	$10,000

EXAMPLE 11.5.3
Character of Income to Beneficiaries—Specific Allocations

Assume the same facts as in Example 11.5.2 except that the trust document specifies the following:

- Interest income will be allocated to Denzel
- Dividend income and LTCG will be allocated to Antonio
- Tax-exempt interest income will be allocated to Marshall

How does this change the allocation of income to the beneficiaries?

SOLUTION

The allocation of income is determined as follows:

Beneficiary	Income percentage	Total allocation of income	Interest	Dividend	LTCG	Tax-exempt
Denzel	N/A	$50,000	$50,000	N/A	N/A	N/A
Antonio	N/A	$50,000	N/A	$30,000	$20,000	N/A
Marsha	N/A	$40,000	N/A	N/A	N/A	$40,000

Related exercises: Multiple Choice Question 12
Brief Exercise 9
Application Problem 6

Allocation of Deductions

Deductions are allocated to sources of income based on the following three steps:[29]

Step 1. Deductions directly attributable to an income source are allocated to that income source up to the amount of revenue. If the expenses exceed the revenue, then the excess is handled as in step 2 below. For example, rental expenses such as depreciation, utilities, and repairs are allocated to rental income. Business expenses are allocated directly to business income.

Step 2. Deductions directly attributable to an income source that exceed the revenue may be allocated to other sources of income at the discretion of the trustee, with one caveat. Excess deductions that are allocated to the production of tax-exempt income, based on the percentage of DNI that is tax-exempt income, are not allowed to reduce that source of income.

Step 3. Deductions not attributable to a specific income source may be allocated to income at the trustee's discretion. However, just as in step 2, a portion of these expenses, based on the percentage of DNI that is tax-exempt income, must be allocated to tax-exempt income and are not deductible. Step 3 expenses include trustee's commissions, state income taxes, and safe deposit box rental fees.

The following Example shows how excess deductions must be reduced for a portion of tax-exempt income.

EXAMPLE 11.5.4
Allocation of Excess Deductions to Tax-Exempt Income

A trust has the following sources of income for the current year after reduction for direct expenses in step 1:

Rental income	$40,000
Dividend income	$15,000
Tax-exempt income	$25,000

The trust has $4,000 of trustee's commissions that are not directly related to these income sources. How is the $4,000 expense allocated to the income sources?

SOLUTION

The trustee has discretion as to the allocation of the $4,000 commissions to the income sources, except that a pro rata amount must be allocated to the tax-exempt income, as follows:

$$\text{Amount of expense in step 3(\$4,000)} \times \frac{\text{Tax exempt income (\$25,000)}}{\text{Total DNI (\$40,000 + \$15,000 + \$25,00)}} = \$1,250$$

Therefore, $1,250 of the expense is not deductible. The remaining $2,750 ($4,000 − $1,250) of the expense may be allocated to the rental income and/or the dividend income at the trustee's discretion.

Related exercise: Application Problem 7

Timing of Flow-Through to Beneficiaries

For a simple trust, income is deemed to flow through to the beneficiaries on the last day of the trust's tax year. If the trust reports on a calendar-year basis, then this occurs on December 31, which would also be the last day of the tax year for an individual beneficiary. If the trust has

[29]Treas. Reg. §1.652(b)-3(a).

a year-end different from December 31, then the beneficiary will include the income distribution in the individual tax year that includes the year-end of the trust.[30]

EXAMPLE 11.5.5
Timing of Income to Beneficiaries

Mariana is the income beneficiary of a simple trust that has a year-end of May 31. The trust has fiduciary accounting income of $34,000 for the year ended May 31, Year 4, and $42,000 of income for the year ended May 31, Year 5. How much income must Mariana report from the trust for her Year 4 tax year?

SOLUTION

Mariana's tax year runs from January 1, Year 4, to December 31, Year 4. The trust year that ends during this period is the year ended May 31, Year 4, which has $34,000 of income. This income flows to Marianna on May 31, Year 4, as shown in **Illustration 11.12**. Therefore, Mariana must report $34,000 of trust income in Year 4.

ILLUSTRATION 11.12 Timing of Flow-Through to Beneficiaries for a Simple Trust

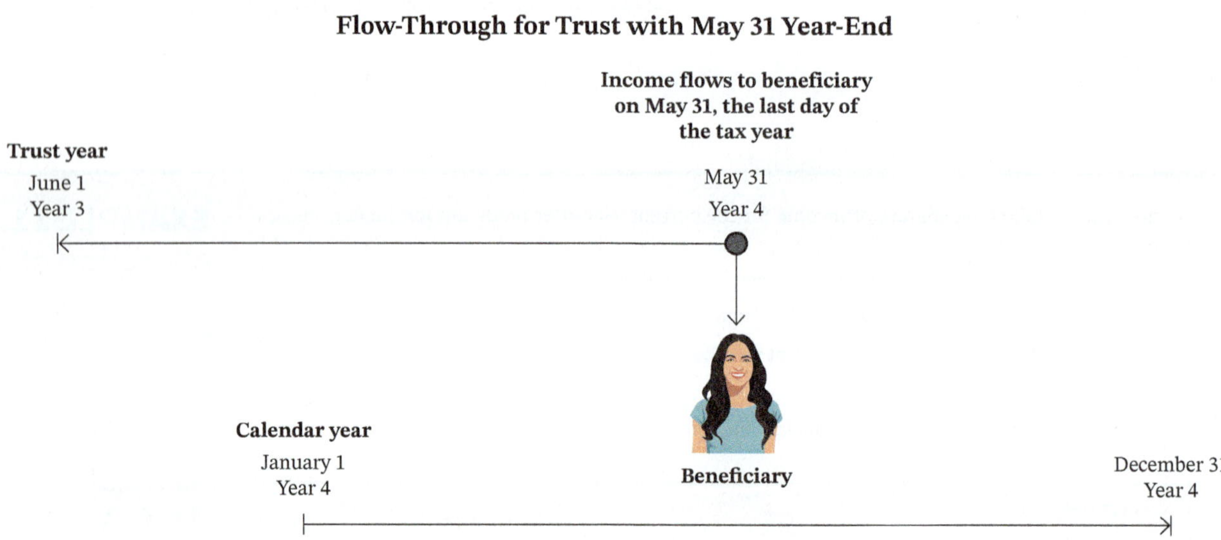

If an income beneficiary dies, then income distributed to the beneficiary before death is included in the beneficiary's final income tax return (Form 1040). Income distributed from the trust after the date of death is included in the income tax return of the estate (Form 1041). The income on Form 1041 would be income in respect of a decedent, because it was earned before death but paid after death.

Related exercise: Brief Exercise 10

Complex Trusts

Most of the general rules explained for simple trusts also apply when determining the tax consequences for beneficiaries of complex trusts. In this section, we discuss the rules for complex trusts that differ from what you learned for simple trusts.

[30]Treas. Reg. 1.652(c)-1.

Allocation of Income

Beneficiaries of complex trusts must include the following in income:[31]

Step 1. Income required to be distributed currently to beneficiaries is included in the beneficiaries' income, whether distributed or not, up to the amount of DNI.

Step 2. Other amounts distributed from income to a beneficiary are also included in the beneficiary's income, such as in-kind distributions of property or distributions on the occurrence of a certain event (for example, the beneficiary reaching a certain age), up to the amount of DNI remaining after step 1.

Step 3. Distributions from corpus are included in the beneficiaries' income only to the extent of any DNI remaining after steps 1 and 2.

If necessary, DNI is allocated to beneficiaries proportionally based on the value distributed to each. The following three Examples illustrate the distribution process for complex trusts.

EXAMPLE 11.5.6 Distributions from a Complex Trust

A trust instrument provides for the following to be made this year:

- $10,000 to be paid to a qualified charity
- $40,000 of income to Rudd, a beneficiary
- $18,000 to June from either income or corpus

The trust had fiduciary accounting income this year of $60,000. What are the tax consequences of these distributions?

SOLUTION

The trust is a complex trust because it has a charitable beneficiary. We apply the three steps discussed above to determine the tax consequences.

Step 1. Distributions that total $50,000 are required to be made from income this year: $10,000 to the charity and $40,000 to Rudd. Rudd is taxed on the $40,000 distribution.

Step 2. This leaves $10,000 of income ($60,000 – $10,000 – $40,000) to be used for the distribution to June. Therefore, $10,000 of the $18,000 distribution to June comes from income and is taxable to June.

Step 3. The remaining $8,000 distributed to June is from corpus and is not taxable to June.

Related exercise: Application Problem 8

EXAMPLE 11.5.7 Distributions from a Complex Trust Limited to DNI

Assume the same facts as in Example 11.5.6, except that the trust also has trustee expenses of $15,000 that are allocated to corpus. What are the tax consequences of these distributions?

SOLUTION

The fiduciary accounting income is still $60,000, because the additional expenses of $15,000 were allocated to corpus. Therefore, the $60,000 of income is first allocated to the $10,000 charitable contribution, which leaves $50,000 to be allocated to Rudd and June. As in the previous example, Rudd has income of $40,000, and June has income of $10,000.

[31]Treas. Reg. 1.662(a)-3.

However, DNI is reduced by the $15,000 expense to $45,000 ($60,000 − $15,000). Therefore, $50,000 is distributed to Rudd and June, but the income recognized by Rudd and June is limited to the DNI of $45,000. The DNI is allocated to Rudd and June as follows:

$$\text{Rudd: DNI (\$45,000)} \times \frac{\text{Distribution to Rudd (\$40,000)}}{\text{Total distributions from income to beneficiaries (\$50,000)}} = \$36,000$$

$$\text{June: DNI (\$45,000)} \times \frac{\text{Distribution to June (\$10,000)}}{\text{Total distributions from income to beneficiaries (\$50,000)}} = \$9,000$$

Rudd and June will recognize income of $36,000 and $9,000, respectively.

Related exercise: Application Problem 9

EXAMPLE 11.5.8 Discretionary Distributions from a Complex Trust

Huey, Dewey, and Louie are the beneficiaries of a trust. The trust instrument requires that $12,000 of income be distributed to Huey each year. Any remaining income can be distributed to the three beneficiaries at the trustee's discretion. The trustee also has discretion to make distributions from corpus. In the current year, fiduciary accounting income is $30,000, as is DNI. In addition to the required distribution of $12,000, the trustee distributes $8,000 of income each to Dewey and Louie, and $4,000 to Huey. How are these distributions taxed to the beneficiaries?

SOLUTION

Because the required distributions exceed fiduciary accounting income, distributions will be made from corpus. So this is a complex trust. We use the three steps described above to determine the tax consequences of the distributions to the beneficiaries. There is $30,000 of income that can be distributed.

Step 1. Income is first allocated to distributions that are required to be made. Here, that is the $12,000 to Huey. This leaves $18,000 ($30,000 − $12,000) of income and DNI that is available for distribution at the trustee's discretion.

Step 2. This step addresses the remaining distributions of $20,000 ($8,000 + $8,000 + $4,000). The DNI remaining after step 1 is $18,000, so it must be allocated to the beneficiaries based on the amount of their distributions, and this is the amount of income that must be reported:

$$\text{Huey: DNI (\$18,000)} \times \frac{\text{Distribution to Huey (\$4,000)}}{\text{Total distributions in step 2 to beneficiaries (\$20,000)}} = \$3,600$$

$$\text{Dewey: DNI (\$18,000)} \times \frac{\text{Distribution to Dewey (\$8,000)}}{\text{Total distributions in step 2 to beneficiaries (\$20,000)}} = \$7,200$$

$$\text{Louie: DNI (\$18,000)} \times \frac{\text{Distribution to Louie (\$8,000)}}{\text{Total distributions in step 2 to beneficiaries (\$20,000)}} = \$7,200$$

Step 3. The distributions that did not come from income had to come from corpus, and that amount is $2,000 ($20,000 − $18,000 from step 2). The DNI was exhausted in step 2, so none of the distributions from step 3 are taxable to the beneficiaries.

Summary The total income reported to the beneficiaries is as follows:

Huey: $12,000 + $3,600 = $15,600

Dewey: $7,200

Louie: $7,200

Related exercise: Application Problem 10

Charitable Contributions

Special rules apply if a trust makes a charitable contribution. **Recall** that any trust that has a charitable organization as its beneficiary is a complex trust. The charitable contribution deduction must be allocated among the classes of income before other deductions are allocated. For allocations of income and deductions to beneficiaries to whom income must be distributed currently, the charitable deduction is disregarded to the extent that it exceeds the income of the trust or estate reduced by amounts required to be currently distributed.[32]

In the next Example, we show how charitable contributions affect the allocations of income to the beneficiaries.

EXAMPLE 11.5.9 Allocation of Charitable Contributions

A trust has two beneficiaries, Richard and Jean. The trust instrument provides that the first $40,000 of income must be distributed each year to Richard. Any additional income can be distributed to Jean or to United Way, or can be accumulated. Accumulated income can be distributed to Jean or United Way at any time. For the current year, the trust has the following income:

Taxable interest income	$50,000
Tax-exempt income	$12,500

The trustee plans to distribute $15,000 to United Way and $12,000 to Jean this year. What are the tax consequences for this trust in the current year?

SOLUTION

This is a complex trust because not all income is required to be distributed currently, and there is a charitable beneficiary. We use the three steps described above to determine the tax consequences of the distributions to the beneficiaries. The trust has fiduciary accounting income of $62,500 ($50,000 + $12,500).

Step 1. Income is first allocated to distributions that are required to be made. The required distribution here is the $40,000 to Richard. DNI is computed as follows:

Taxable interest income	$50,000
Tax-exempt income	12,500
Less: Charitable contribution	(15,000)
DNI	$47,500

The charitable contribution deduction of $15,000 is taken into account for DNI only to the extent that the income of $62,500 exceeds the income required to be distributed currently ($40,000). These amounts differ by $22,500. The $15,000 of contributions taken into account is allocated proportionately to the income:

Taxable interest income $\$15,000 \times \dfrac{\$50,000}{\$62,500} = \$12,000$

Tax-exempt income $\$15,000 \times \dfrac{\$12,500}{\$62,500} = \$3,000$

The amount of income distributed to Richard comes from the following income amounts, netted for the charitable contribution:

Taxable interest income ($50,000 − $12,000)	$38,000
Tax-exempt income ($12,500 − $3,000)	$ 9,500
Income distributed to Richard	$47,500

Richard has taxable income of $38,000.

Steps 2 and 3. Due to the charitable contribution, all the DNI was used in step 1. Therefore, the distribution of $12,000 to Jean is not taxable to her. This $12,000 distribution is made from corpus because the income not distributed to Richard of $15,000 ($62,500 − $47,500) was allocated to United Way.

Related exercise: Application Problem 11

[32]Treas. Reg. 1.662(b)-2.

Summary

In this chapter, you have learned the major steps involved in the taxation of trust and estates, notably:

- LO2 Computing fiduciary accounting income
- LO3 Computing taxable income
- LO4 Computing distributable net income (DNI)
- LO5 Determining tax consequences to beneficiaries

Let's wrap up the chapter by completing a comprehensive problem that addresses all these areas.

EXAMPLE 11.5.10 Comprehensive Problem

During the current year, Dove Trust had the following tax items:

Income:	
Dividend income	$14,000
Rental income	$40,000
Long-term capital gain	$22,000
Tax-exempt interest	$24,000
Deductions:	
Rental expenses	$20,000
Trustee's fees	$ 5,000
Depreciation	$ 4,000

The trust has two beneficiaries, Priscilla and Garth, who will each receive 50% of the trust's income each year. The trust is a simple trust this year. The rental income does not qualify for the QBI deduction.

a. Compute the trust's fiduciary accounting income.

b. Compute the trust's DNI.

c. Compute the taxable income.

d. Determine the tax consequences to the beneficiaries. Assume that the trustee elects to allocate to the rental income the expenses not directly attributable to a specific item of income (other than the portion of such expenses allocated to tax-exempt interest).

SOLUTION

a. We begin by computing the fiduciary accounting income for the trust. The starting point is to summarize the items that must be allocated to income or principal:

Tax item	UPAIA section	Allocation
Dividend income received of $14,000	401	Income
Rental income of $40,000	405	Income
Net LTCG of $22,000 from sale of investments	404	Principal
Tax-exempt interest income of $24,000	406	Income
Rental expenses of $20,000	501	Income
Trustee's fees of $5,000	501; 502	$2,500 to income; $2,500 to principal
Depreciation of $4,000	504	Principal

Principal and income are computed as follows:

Principal:	
Net LTCG	$22,000
Trustee fees	(2,500)
Depreciation	(4,000)
Principal, end of year	$15,500

Income:	
Dividend income	$14,000
Rental income	40,000
Tax-exempt interest income	24,000
Rental expenses	(20,000)
Trustee fees	(2,500)
Fiduciary income	$55,500

The trust's fiduciary accounting income is $55,500.

b. The computation of DNI includes the following items:

Income:		
Dividend income		$14,000
Rental income		40,000
Tax-exempt interest income	$24,000	
Less: Expenses attributable to	(769)	23,231
Total		$77,231
Deductions:		
Less: Rental expenses	($20,000)	
Less: Trustee's fees ($2,500 – $769)	(1,731)	
Total		(21,731)
Distributable net income		$55,500

- The $22,000 LTCG is not included in DNI, because it is allocated to corpus.
- The $24,000 of tax-exempt interest is reduced for the trustee expenses allocable to it, as follows:

  Trustee's fees: $2,500 × (24,000/[$14,000 + $40,000 + $24,000]) = $769
- No deduction is allowed for depreciation unless the trust instrument provides for transferring income to principal to keep the trust corpus intact.

c. Before computing taxable income, we must first compute the distribution deduction. The fiduciary accounting income is $55,500. Priscilla and Garth will each receive a distribution of $27,750 ($55,500 × 50%). However, the distribution deduction for the trust is limited to the DNI of $55,500.

The distribution deduction needs to be further reduced to take into account the tax-exempt interest that was included in fiduciary accounting income. The tax-exempt interest is not included in taxable income, so a deduction cannot be allowed for distributing it.

Distributable net income		$55,500
Less: Tax-exempt interest income	$24,000	
Less: Expenses attributable to	(769)	23,231
Distribution deduction		$32,269

Taxable income for the trust is computed as follows:

Income:		
Dividend income		$14,000
Rental income		40,000
Net long-term capital gain		19,500*
Total		$73,500
Deductions:		
Less: Rental expenses	($20,000)	
Less: Trustee's fees ($2,500 – $769)	(1,731)	
Less: Exemption	(300)	
Less: Distribution deduction	($32,269)	($54,300)
Taxable income		$19,200

*Net LTCG is $19,500 ($22,000 LTCG – $2,500 trustee fees allocated to principal).

- The tax-exempt interest of $24,000 is not included in taxable income.
- No deduction is allowed for depreciation unless the trust instrument provides for transferring income to principal to keep the trust corpus intact.

d. To determine the tax consequences of the distributions to Priscilla and Garth, we must first determine the character of the amounts distributed, as shown below:

	Dividend income	Rental income	Tax-exempt interest	Total
Gross Fiduciary accounting income	$14,000	$40,000	$24,000	$78,000
Less:				
Rental expenses		(20,000)		(20,000)
Trustee fees		(1,731)	(769)	(2,500)
Character of distributions	$14,000	$18,269	$23,231	$55,500

As mentioned in part **c**, the fiduciary accounting income is $55,500. Priscilla and Garth will each receive a distribution deduction of $27,750 ($55,500 × 50%). However, the distribution deduction for the trust is limited to $32,269 ($55,500 DNI – $23,231 net tax-exempt income), so the trust has taxable income of $19,200. Priscilla and Garth will have taxable income of $27,750 each that has the following tax character:

Dividend income	$ 7,000	($14,000 × 50%)
Rental income	$ 9,135	($18,269 × 50%)
Tax-exempt interest	$11,615	($23,231 × 50%)
Total	$27,750	

Each beneficiary also receives a deduction for $2,000 (50% of the depreciation of $4,000) because it is related to the rental income distributed to them.

Summary The total income reported to the trust and the beneficiaries is:

Dove Trust	$19,200	
Priscilla	25,750	($27,750 – $2,000 depreciation)
Garth	25,750	($27,750 – $2,000 depreciation)
Total	$70,700	($74,700 – $4,000 depreciation)

PRACTICE PROBLEM 11.5.1
Allocation of DNI for a Simple Trust

The Kiwi Trust is a simple trust for the current tax year with two beneficiaries, Isabella and Juan, who are to receive 70% and 30% of the income, respectively. The fiduciary accounting income for the year is $110,000, and DNI is $95,000. How much income must Isabella and Juan recognize for the current year?

SOLUTION

Isabella is to receive a distribution of $77,000 of income ($110,000 × 70%) and Juan a distribution of $33,000 ($110,000 × 30%). However, the income recognized by the beneficiaries cannot exceed DNI, which is $95,000. Therefore, the beneficiaries will recognize the following amounts of income:

Isabella	$95,000 × 70% = $66,500
Juan	$95,000 × 30% = $28,500

PRACTICE PROBLEM 11.5.2 Timing of Flow-Through to Beneficiaries for a Simple Trust

Sven is the income beneficiary of a simple trust that has a year-end of March 31. The trust has fiduciary accounting income of $52,000 for the year ended March 31, Year 12, and $44,000 of income for the year ended March, Year 13. How much income must Sven report from the trust for his Year 12 tax year?

SOLUTION

Sven's tax year runs from January 1, Year 12, to December 31, Year 12. The trust year that ends during this period is the year ended March 31, Year 12, which has $52,000 of income. This income flows to Sven on March 31, Year 12. Therefore, Sven must report $52,000 of trust income in Year 12.

PRACTICE PROBLEM 11.5.3 Distributions from a Complex Trust

A trust instrument provides for the following to be made this year:

- $3,500 to be paid for estate taxes
- $18,000 of income to Mei, a beneficiary
- $10,000 to Beneo from either income or corpus

The trust had fiduciary accounting income this year of $30,000. What are the tax consequences of these distributions?

SOLUTION

Distributions that total $21,500 are required to be made from income this year: $3,500 for estate taxes and $18,000 to Mei. Mei is taxed on the $18,000 distribution. This leaves $8,500 of income ($30,000 – $3,500– $18,000) to be used for the distribution to Beneo. Therefore, $8,500 of the $10,000 distribution to Beneo comes from income and is taxable to Beneo. The remaining $1,500 distributed to Beneo is from corpus and is not taxable to Beneo.

INTERACTIVE SELF-SCORING QUIZZES

Review and Practice

Chapter Summary

The income taxation of trusts and estates is a specialized area of the tax law. When an individual dies, the individual's estate comes into existence, and the estate must pay income tax on income earned from the decedent's assets after the date of death. Trusts are created for a variety of reasons; income earned by a trust will be taxed either to the trust or to the beneficiaries of the trust. Income is reported by trusts and estates on Form 1041, U.S. Income Tax Return for Estates and Trusts.

1 Define a trust and an estate, and understand how they are used for planning.

- A **trust** is a legal entity created by the transfer of property from a *grantor*. The purpose of the trust is to hold and administer property for *beneficiaries* according to the terms of the trust instrument. The trust exists for the period determined by the trust instrument and state law. Trusts can be set up for many reasons, such as:
  - Protecting assets from creditors
  - Transferring assets to others after one's death without having to go through the probate process
  - Protecting assets for one's family to ensure that the assets are handled according to one's desires

- Transferring assets to children or others to meet their needs without giving full control to them
- There are five distinct components of a trust: *grantor*, *corpus*, *trustee*, *beneficiaries*, and *terms*.
  - The **grantor** is the creator of the trust, who transfers assets into the trust and determines the terms of the trust.
  - The **corpus** is the assets transferred to the trust by the grantor, which can include stocks, bonds, homes, land, automobiles, and business assets.
  - The **trustee** has the fiduciary responsibility to manage the assets in the trust according to the terms of the trust. The trustee must protect the interests of the beneficiaries and act in a prudent manner to protect the interests of the beneficiaries.
  - The **beneficiaries** benefit economically from the assets in the trust. **Income beneficiaries** receive distributions of the income earned by the trust assets each year based on the terms of the trust. **Remainder beneficiaries** receive distributions of the assets in the trust when the trust terminates.
  - The **terms** of a trust express the desires of the grantor for how the trust will be managed and the income and assets distributed.
- An **estate** for an individual is created on the date of the individual's death, and includes all assets comprising the net worth of the individual, including all real estate, possessions, financial investments, cash, and other assets that the individual owns or has a controlling interest in. The estate exists for as long as is needed to settle the legal and financial affairs for the deceased individual. For some individuals, the estate will be closed after a few months, whereas for others the estate could be open for many years.

2 Compute fiduciary accounting income.

- The first step in computing taxable income for an estate or trust is to determine the financial accounting income, which is often referred to as **fiduciary accounting**. Fiduciary accounting determines how the receipts and disbursements of a trust or an estate are allocated to principal (corpus) or income.
- The differing interest of the income and remainder beneficiaries is the reason that the trustee's role is so important.
- The trustee has several sources of information to use in determining fiduciary accounting income:
  - The first document is the trust instrument, which was created by the grantor of the trust.
  - If the trust instrument does not address the situation, then state law will determine the accounting treatment.
  - Many states have adopted the Uniform Principal and Income Act (UPAIA), which was developed by the Commissioners on Uniform State Laws in 1997 to promote uniformity across states.

3 Compute taxable income for trusts and estates.

- In general, the income and deduction rules for trusts and estates are the same as the rules for individuals.
- A few key concepts underlie the computation of fiduciary taxable income.

Concept 1.	Income is taxed only once, to either the fiduciary or the beneficiary.
Concept 2.	You should assume that the tax rules for determining the taxable income for fiduciaries are the same as the rules for individuals unless you are provided a different rule.
Concept 3.	The fiduciary receives a distribution deduction for the current year's income that is distributed to beneficiaries. This deduction is the mechanism that prevents double taxation.
Concept 4.	In general, the income that is distributed to the beneficiaries is taxed to the beneficiaries.
Concept 5.	Income that is taxed to the beneficiaries retains the character it had to the fiduciary, such as ordinary, capital, or Section 1231.

- **Income in respect of a decedent (IRD)** is income the decedent had earned before death but had not yet recognized as income because they were a cash-basis taxpayer. Examples of IRD include:
  - Accrued bond interest at the time of death
  - Earned wages that had not been received at time of death
  - Rental income earned but not yet received at time of death

  There are two important tax rules for IRD. First, IRD is taxed to the taxpayer who receives the funds, which is usually the estate of the decedent or a beneficiary. Second, the character of the income to the recipient is the same character that the income would have had if received by the decedent before death.
- A **simple trust** is one that:
  - must distribute all income currently,
  - made no distributions of corpus in the current year, *and*
  - made no charitable contributions in the current year.
- Any trust that does not qualify as simple trust is a **complex trust**. A trust's status as simple or complex can vary from year to year.
- Form 1041 is due on the 15th day of the fourth month after the end of the tax year. For calendar-year trusts and estates, this is April 15. An extension of 5½ months can be requested by filing Form 7004, Application for Automatic Extension of Time. For calendar-year trusts and estates, this extends the due date to October 1.

4 Compute the income distribution deduction for trusts and estates.

- One unique aspect of the income taxation of trusts and estates is that the entity receives a deduction for distributions of income to the beneficiaries. Whether the trust or estate distributes income to the beneficiaries determines who is taxed on the income. Undistributed income is generally taxed to the trust or estate (unless the entity is a simple trust and the income required to be distributed was not distributed), and distributed income is taxed to the beneficiaries. The income distribution deduction means that the trust or estate is not taxed on the distributed income, ensuring single taxation for trust or estate income.

- **Distributable net income (DNI)** is the maximum amount of the income distribution deduction for a trust or estate, and it is also the maximum amount of income that the beneficiaries must recognize. The deduction or the income can be less than DNI, but not more than DNI.
- The character of the income distribution deduction is determined on a proportionate basis based on the character of the items that are included in computing the DNI of the trust.

5 Determine how beneficiaries of an estate or trust are taxed.

- For a simple trust, the total amount of income recognized by the beneficiaries is limited to DNI. If the income exceeds DNI, each beneficiary of the trust recognizes income equal to DNI times a ratio, which is the income required to be distributed to that beneficiary divided by the total income.
- The character of the income recognized by the beneficiaries is the same character that the income had in the hands of the trust or estate. Therefore, if the income was long-term capital gain to the trust, then it is also LTCG to the beneficiary. If the distributed income was tax-exempt income to the trust, then the income is not taxable to the beneficiaries.
- For a simple trust, income is deemed to flow through to the beneficiaries on the last day of the trust's tax year. If the trust reports on a calendar-year basis, then this occurs on December 31, which would also be the last day of the tax year for an individual beneficiary. If the trust has a year-end different from December 31, then the beneficiary will include the income distribution in the individual tax year that includes the year-end of the trust.
- Most of the general rules explained for simple trusts also apply when determining the tax consequence for beneficiaries of complex trusts. Beneficiaries of complex trusts must include the following in income:

Step 1. Income required to be distributed currently to beneficiaries is included in the beneficiaries' income, whether distributed or not, up to the amount of DNI.

Step 2. Other amounts that are distributed from income to a beneficiary are also included in the beneficiary's income, such as in-kind distributions of property or distributions on the occurrence of a certain event (for example, the beneficiary reaching a certain age), up to the amount of DNI remaining after step 1.

Step 3. Distributions from corpus are included in the beneficiaries' income only to the extent of any DNI remaining after steps 1 and 2.

- Special rules apply if a trust makes a charitable contribution. Recall that any trust that has a charitable organization as its beneficiary is a complex trust. The charitable contribution deduction must be allocated among the classes of income before other deductions are allocated. For allocations of income and deductions to beneficiaries to whom income must be distributed currently, the charitable deduction is disregarded to the extent that it exceeds the income of the trust or estate reduced by amounts required to be currently distributed.

Communication Application

Probate vs. Gross Estate

(LO1) Mike and Carol Brady have a close relationship with their children, Greg, Marcia, Peter, Jan, Bobby, and Cindy. Unfortunately, Mike was diagnosed with terminal colorectal cancer in the current year. His death is imminent. Mike would like to arrange his affairs for the benefit of his family. Mike has asked you to review his assets and provide him with a list of which assets are included in his probate estate and which assets are included in his gross estate. Write a memo to Mike discussing this issue.

Asset	Fair market value
Primary residence	$475,000
Secondary residence	$380,000
SUV	$ 52,000
Mutual fund	$180,000
Checking account	$ 11,000
Corporate bonds	$100,000
Municipal bonds	$ 60,000
Traditional IRA (beneficiary is Greg)	$225,000
Section 401(k) plan (beneficiary is Marcia)	$200,000
Rental property (owned with right of survivorship with Alice, the maid)	$280,000
Boat received as a gift nine months before Mike's death	$ 75,000
Life insurance policy—Term (beneficiary is wife)	$750,000
Annuity (beneficiaries are Peter, Jan, Bobby, and Cindy)	$800,000
Partnership interest (owned 70% as a tenancy in common with Mike's father; full FMV is shown)	$ 90,000

Solution

Hello Mike and Carol,

Thank you for the opportunity to provide advice concerning your assets and your estate. I am so sorry to learn about Mike's diagnosis.

The probate estate, in general, includes assets that are held solely by the decedent and does not include assets that pass to others outside of the will. The gross estate refers to the assets that must be included in computing the estate tax at the time of death. Property could be included in the gross estate but not in the probate estate. Here is a breakdown of the assets that are *not* included in Mike's probate estate.

Traditional IRA, $225,000:	Passes directly to Greg
Section 401(k) plan, $200,000:	Passes directly to Marcia
Rental property, $280,000:	100% passes directly to Alice because it was owned with right of survivorship
Life insurance, $750,000:	Proceeds pass directly to Carol
Annuity, $800,000:	Passes directly to Peter, Jan, Bobby, and Cindy

Therefore, the probate estate consists of the following assets:

	FMV
Primary residence	$ 475,000
Secondary residence	380,000
SUV	52,000
Mutual fund	180,000
Checking account	11,000
Corporate bonds	100,000
Municipal bonds	60,000
Boat	75,000
Partnership interest	63,000*
Total probate estate	$1,396,000

*Only 70% of the partnership interest is included in the probate estate. Mike's father continues to own the other 30% because this interest was held as a tenancy in common.

Your overall estate is under the threshold of having to pay any estate tax at your death. Please let me know if we can be of further assistance.

Sincerely,
Carnes & Youngberg, CPAs

Ethics and Professional Responsibilities Application

Trustee Responsibilities

(LO2) The Salazar family had considerable wealth and created a will and trust with their sons, Marcus (age 26), Juan (age 23), and Pablo (age 19), as the beneficiaries. In April of the current year, both Mr. and Mrs. Salazar died in an auto accident. Mr. Salazar's brother, Antonio, has been appointed the trustee of the estate. Each son wants his "fair" share now. Marcus wants $100,000 to open a restaurant, Juan wants $100,000 as a down payment on rental property, and Pablo wants $100,000 to help pay for his education at Harvard. The trust document indicates that funds may not be distributed to a beneficiary until he reaches age 30. The trust document also indicates that a public education at any age can be paid for with estate asset funds. What is Antonio's ethical responsibility regarding his appointment as trustee?

Solution

The trustee has the fiduciary responsibility to manage the assets in the trust according to the terms of the trust. The trustee must protect the interests of the beneficiaries and act in a prudent manner to protect those interests. The trustee has several sources of information to use in managing the trust and in determining fiduciary accounting income:

- The first document is the trust agreement, which was created by the grantor of the trust.
- If the trust agreement does not address the situation, then state law will determine the accounting treatment.
- Many states have adopted the Uniform Principal and Income Act (UPAIA), which has increased uniformity across states.

It is Antonio's ethical responsibility to adhere to the trust agreement, which states that the beneficiaries are not to receive funds until age 30. If Pablo attends a public university, then funds may be distributed to pay for the public education. However, Harvard University is a private university and does not meet the terms of the trust instrument. Marcus, Juan, and Pablo will not be happy with this result, but Antonio has a fiduciary responsibility to abide by the wishes of his late brother and sister-in-law.

Key Terms

Beneficiaries 11-6
Complex Trust 11-28
Corpus 11-6
Current Beneficiaries 11-6
Distributable Net Income (DNI) 11-36
Estate 11-8
Fiduciary Relationship 11-1
Fiduciary Accounting 11-8
Grantor 11-6
Grantor Trust 11-34
Gross Estate 11-9
Income Beneficiaries 11-6
Income in Respect of a Decedent (IRD) 11-24
Income Interest 11-7
Joint Tenants with Right of Survivorship 11-9
Pecuniary Gift 11-19
Probate 11-5
Probate Estate 11-9
Remainder Beneficiaries 11-6
Remainder Interest 11-7
Restatement of the Law Third, Trusts 11-8
Revocable Trust 11-34
Simple Trust 11-28
Tenancy in Common 11-9
Terms 11-6
Trust 11-5
Trustee 11-6
Uniform Principal and Income Act (UPAIA) 11-8
Uniform Trust Code (UTC) 11-8

End-of-Chapter Assessment

Discussion Questions

1. **(LO1)** Provide the definition of a trust.
2. **(LO1)** Why would a trust be created? Give at least two reasons.
3. **(LO1)** Who is a beneficiary?
4. **(LO1)** Provide the definition of an estate.
5. **(LO1)** Distinguish between a probate estate and a gross estate.
6. **(LO2)** What is fiduciary accounting?
7. **(LO2)** Provide the definition of income and principal.
8. **(LO3)** Define income in respect of a decedent.
9. **(LO3)** What is the due date and extended due date of Form 1041?
10. **(LO3)** When can a trust avoid the underpayment of estimated tax penalty?
11. **(LO4)** Briefly describe distributable net income.
12. **(LO4)** Describe a simple trust and a complex trust.

Multiple Choice Questions

1. **(LO1)** Which *best* describes the trustee's fiduciary duty to the beneficiaries of the trust?
   - **a.** The fiduciary must act in a prudent manner to protect the interests of the beneficiaries.
   - **b.** The fiduciary cannot receive compensation for their services.
   - **c.** The fiduciary duty requires the trustee to have transparent and impartial communication with all beneficiaries.
   - **d.** The fiduciary duty requires that the trustee provide all information requested by the beneficiaries.
2. **(LO1)** The income taxation of an estate is reported on which tax form?
   - **a.** Form 1040
   - **b.** Form 1041
   - **c.** Form 706
   - **d.** None; the income is not subject to tax.
3. **(LO2)** Which person should decide the proper allocation of income and expenses for a trust?
   - **a.** Income beneficiary
   - **b.** Remainder beneficiary
   - **c.** Trustee
   - **d.** Any of the above
4. **(LO2)** Under Section 103 Allocation of Receipts and Disbursements, receipts and disbursements are allocated first:
   - **a.** According to the provisions of the UPAIA
   - **b.** According to the terms of the trust or will
   - **c.** According to the income beneficiary
   - **d.** To principal

5. **(LO3)** Which of the following is a false statement in regard to calculating taxable income for a trust or estate?

   a. The same item of income can be taxed to both the fiduciary and the beneficiary.

   b. The fiduciary receives a distribution deduction for the current year's income that is distributed to beneficiaries.

   c. Income that is taxed to the beneficiaries retains the character it had to the fiduciary, such as ordinary, capital, or Section 1231.

   d. All of the statements above are true.

6. **(LO3)** Which of the following is an example of income in respect of a decedent (IRD) if the taxpayer died on April 8?

   a. Wages earned through March 31 but paid on April 15

   b. Dividend declared on March 31, with a record date of April 6, but paid on April 30

   c. Rental income earned through March 31 but paid on April 25

   d. All examples are considered IRD.

7. **(LO3)** Which of the following statements is true regarding when an estate would recognize income on the distribution of appreciated property?

   a. Gain is recognized if the distribution is in satisfaction of the right to receive a specific dollar amount.

   b. Gain is recognized if the distribution is in satisfaction of the right to receive property other than the distributed property.

   c. Gain is recognized if the distribution is in satisfaction of the right to receive income, assuming that income is required to be distributed currently.

   d. All of the statements above are true.

8. **(LO3)** As a general rule, estates and trusts are taxed as individuals. Which of the following is a false statement?

   a. Only $10,000 of state and local taxes are deductible.

   b. Credits are allowed for both estates and trusts and individuals.

   c. Estates and trusts are permitted a Section 179 deduction.

   d. A net capital loss of $3,000 is allowed.

9. **(LO4)** Which statement is correct regarding DNI?

   a. DNI is the maximum amount of the income distribution deduction for a trust or estate.

   b. DNI is the maximum amount of income that the beneficiaries must recognize.

   c. The income distribution deduction or the income can be less than DNI, but not more than DNI.

   d. All of the above are correct.

10. **(LO4)** Which of the following is a correct statement when describing the income distribution deduction?

    a. The amount of deduction is unlimited.

    b. Estates and trusts are allowed a deduction against taxable income for distributions of income made to beneficiaries.

    c. The deduction is allowable only to estates and complex trusts.

    d. The deduction is allowable only to simple trusts.

11. **(LO4)** Which of the following is a false statement regarding simple trusts and complex trusts?

    a. It is a requirement that the trust instrument specify which beneficiary will receive the income distributions.

    b. If income is distributed shortly after the end of the tax year, this will not disqualify the trust from being a simple trust.

    c. For a simple trust, the income distribution deduction consists of the amount of the income that is required to be distributed currently.

    d. All of the statements are true.

12. **(LO5)** Which of the following is a false statement?

    a. A simple trust is required to distribute its income every year to the beneficiaries.

    b. Income recognized by the beneficiaries cannot exceed DNI.

    c. If the income was long-term capital gain to a trust, then it is also LTCG to the beneficiary.

    d. A trust document cannot allocate certain types of income to specific beneficiaries.

Brief Exercises

1. **(LO1)** Define the following terms.

   a. Grantor

   b. Corpus

   c. Trustee

   d. Beneficiary

   e. Terms

2. **(LO2)** Are the following items allocated to the trust income, to the trust principal, or at the trustee's discretion? Also provide the relevant UPAIA section.

Transaction	UPAIA section	Income/principal
Income from business operating as a sole proprietorship or single-member LLC		
Assets received from the transferor or from a decedent's estate		
Money received as part of a partial or complete liquidation		
Money or property received from the sale or disposition of a principal asset		
Interest or dividends from deferred compensation or annuities		

3. **(LO2)** Are the following items allocated to the trust income, to the trust principal, or at the trustee's discretion? Also provide the relevant UPAIA section.

Transaction	UPAIA section	Income/ principal
Disbursements related to environmental issues		
Expenses to prepare property for rental, including brokers' commissions		
Costs related to accounting services or judicial proceedings		
Ordinary repairs		
Recurring portion of the trustee's compensation		

4. **(LO3)** Bernice died on May 31 of the current year. Bernice worked as an administrative assistant and received $4,800 per month in wages. If wages are typically paid on the 15th day after month end, how much income will be reported on Bernice's Form 1040 and on her estate return?

5. **(LO3)** Mr. Franklin dies on March 23, Year 4. His estate elects its tax period when filing its first tax return. What is the earliest tax year that can be chosen? What are the possible year-ends that the executor can choose for Mr. Franklin's estate?

6. **(LO3)** A trust has taxable income of $150,000. What is the trust's tax liability before reduction for estimated tax payments made, and what is the trust's marginal tax rate?

7. **(LO4)** Beneficiary Cayton is to receive two-thirds of the trust income, beneficiary Maverick is to receive one-third, and the income required to be distributed currently is $99,000.

   a. What amount will be taxable to Cayton and Maverick?

   b. If the DNI is only $90,000, what amount will be taxable to Cayton and Maverick?

8. **(LO4)** Plum Trust is a complex trust and distributes $18,000 of income to its beneficiary, Peter. The trust has DNI of $22,000, with tax-exempt interest income of $3,500 included in DNI. What would the income distribution deduction be for Plum?

9. **(LO5)** The Redrock Trust is a simple trust for the current tax year with two beneficiaries, Greg and Suzanne, who are to receive 55% and 45% of the income, respectively. The fiduciary accounting income for the year is $98,000, and DNI is $80,000. How much income must Greg and Suzanne recognize for the current year?

10. **(LO5)** Olga is the income beneficiary of a simple trust that has a year-end of October 31. The trust has fiduciary accounting income of $77,000 for the year ended October 31, Year 10, and $66,000 of income for the year ended October, Year 11. How much income must Olga report from the trust for her Year 10 tax year?

Application Problems

1. **(LO1)** Tiara was a U.S. citizen who died in the current tax year. At the date of her death, she owned the assets shown with the corresponding market value. Which assets would be included in Tiara's probate estate?

Asset	Fair market value
Personal residence	$360,000
Personal assets	$ 42,000
Stocks	$325,000
Checking account	$ 8,000
Coin collection	$ 24,000
Tax-exempt bonds	$ 12,000
Traditional IRA (beneficiary is daughter)	$410,000
Section 401(k) plan (beneficiary is son)	$200,000
Vacation home (owned with right of survivorship with her sister)	$225,000
Life insurance policy—Term (beneficiary is her husband)	$500,000
Partnership interest (owned 80% as a tenancy in common with brother; full FMV is shown)	$180,000

2. **(LO2)** Herb Huskie is the sole beneficiary of the Huskie Trust, which was created in December of the previous year upon the death of Victor Huskie, Herb's father. In the current year, the trust had a $1,800 short-term capital gain, trustee fees of $2,500, funeral expenses of $5,000, qualified dividend income of $4,300, and tax-exempt interest income of $1,000. The trust agreement indicates that fees are to be allocated to principal.

   a. What is the Huskie Trust fiduciary income?

   b. Assume the same facts as in part **a** except that the trust agreement does not indicate the allocation of the trustee fees. What is the Huskie Trust fiduciary income?

3. **(LO3)** Jermaine created a trust seven years ago and contributed land that had a basis of $65,000 and a FMV of $110,000. The trust document provided that after seven years, the land would be distributed to Jermaine's son. The land was distributed in the current year when the FMV of the land was $145,000.

   a. How much gain or loss is recognized to the trust because of the distribution? What is the son's basis in the land?

   b. How would the answer change if the trust document required a distribution of $150,000 to Jermaine's son, and the trustee chose to distribute the land and $5,000 of cash?

4. **(LO3)** Trust ME is a complex trust that has the following income in the current year:

Interest income	$10,000
Qualified dividend income	$ 8,000
Royalty income	$25,000

The trust distributes $25,000 to the beneficiary. How much net investment income tax does the trust owe for this year?

5. **(LO3, 4)** During the taxable year, a trust had the following items of income and expense.

Income	Amount
Dividend income	$42,000
Tax-exempt interest income	$18,000
Rental income	$36,000
Long-term capital gain	$13,000
Expenses	
Expenses attributable directly to rent	$ 8,000
Trustee commission	$ 3,900

The trust document indicates that the trustee commission is to be allocated two-thirds to income and one-third to principal.

a. Determine the net fiduciary income of the trust for the year.

b. Determine the DNI of the trust for the year.

6. **(LO5)** A simple trust allocates income to the beneficiaries as follows:

Maverick	45%
Cayton	30%
Autumn	25%

The trust has the following income for the current year:

Dividend income	$12,000
STCG	$10,000
Tax-exempt income	$ 9,000

a. Assume that the DNI of the trust is $35,000. How much income is allocated to the beneficiaries for the current tax year?

b. Assume the same facts as in part **a** except that the trust document specifies the following:

- Dividend income will be allocated to Maverick.
- STCG will be allocated to Cayton.
- Tax-exempt interest income will be allocated to Autumn.

How does this change the allocations of income to the beneficiaries?

7. **(LO5)** A trust has the following sources of income for the current year after reduction for direct expenses allocated to an income source (step 1 of allocation process):

Interest income	$14,000
Rental income	$11,000
Tax-exempt income	$13,000

The trust has $3,800 of trustee's commissions that are not directly related to these income sources. How is the $3,800 expense allocated to the income sources?

8. **(LO5)** A trust instrument provides for the following to be made this year:

- $6,500 to be paid for estate taxes
- $22,000 of income to Amara, a beneficiary
- $13,000 to Alfred from either income or corpus

The trust had fiduciary accounting income this year of $40,000. What are the tax consequences of these distributions?

9. **(LO5)** A trust instrument provides for the following to be made this year:

- $6,500 to be paid for estate taxes
- $22,000 of income to Amara, a beneficiary
- $13,000 to Alfred from either income or corpus

The trust had fiduciary accounting income this year of $40,000. The trust also has trustee expenses of $8,000 that are allocated to corpus. What are the tax consequences of these distributions?

10. **(LO5)** Shadrach, Meshach, and Abednego are the beneficiaries of a trust. The trust instrument requires that $18,000 of income be distributed to Shadrach each year. Any remaining income can be distributed to the three beneficiaries at the trustee's discretion. The trustee also has discretion to make distributions from corpus. In the current year, fiduciary accounting income is $42,000, as is DNI. In addition to the required distribution of $18,000, the trustee distributes $10,000 of income each to Meshach and Abednego, and $6,000 to Shadrach. How are these distributions taxed to the beneficiaries?

11. **(LO5)** A trust has two beneficiaries, Abraham and Sarah. The trust instrument provides that the first $30,000 of income must be distributed each year to Abraham. Any additional income can be distributed to Sarah or to Habitat for Humanity, or can be accumulated. Accumulated income can be distributed to Sarah or Habitat for Humanity at any time. For the current year, the trust has the following income:

Taxable interest income	$40,000
Tax-exempt income	$ 2,500

The trustee plans to distribute $50,000 to Habitat for Humanity and $2,000 to Sarah this year. What are the tax consequences for this trust in the current year?

Tax Planning Problems

1. **(LO3)** Spartan Trust is a complex trust that has the following income in the current year:

Interest income	$4,000
Ordinary dividend income	$6,000
Short-term capital gain	$3,000

How much should the trust distribute to avoid the net investment income tax?

2. **(LO3)** If Volunteer Trust had a tax liability of $20,000 in the previous year and predicts a current tax liability of $22,000, what amount of estimated tax payments should be made for the current year to avoid an underpayment penalty?

Professional Development Skills

Communication Problem

Communication

1. **(LO2) Trustee Responsibilities** Anna and Elsa, two young sisters, have always been very close. Both of their parents recently passed. The passing was unexpected, and the parents had substantial wealth. A will and trust had been created, and Elsa, the older sister, had been named the executor/trustee of the estate. However, Elsa is only 15 years old and cannot manage the estate. Anna and Elsa have contacted you to help them understand their parents' estate and to select a trustee. Please provide guidance to Anna and Elsa.

Ethics and Professional Responsibilities Problem

Ethics

1. **(LO1, 3, 5) Income in Respect of a Decedent** Cassandra, a wealthy individual, owned several rental properties on the east coast with her daughter, Beatrice. Cassandra and Beatrice were owners with right of survivorship. For the last five years, the properties have generated rental income of over $2 million. Unfortunately, Cassandra died unexpectedly on April 30 of the current year in a skydiving accident. Beatrice is the only heir to her estate. According to Cassandra's will, Beatrice is to receive all assets and income in the event of her death. In the current year, rental income of $650,000 was earned and received by Cassandra through March 31. In April, rental income of $216,668 was earned but not received by Cassandra. In May through December, rental income of $1,733,332 was earned and received by the estate. Beatrice wants the executor of her mother's estate to report all income earned after her date of death on the estate trust tax return and not her individual tax return. If you are the staff accountant for Cassandra, the estate, and Beatrice, how do you respond to Beatrice's request?

   In addition to the chapter content, see *Statements on Standards for Tax Services* at www.aicpacima.com/resources/landing/statements-on-standards-for-tax-services, *Circular 230* at www.irs.gov/tax-professionals/office-of-professional-responsibility-and-circular-230, and Chapter 2, LO4, Tax Professional Responsibilities.

Research Problem

Research

1. **(LO3) Charitable Contribution Deduction** Julien died on November 18 of the current year. His estate income tax return has a December 31 year-end and does not have any tax-exempt income. Julien's will specifically requests that a charitable contribution of $100,0000 be made to Habitat for Humanity, a qualified 501(c)(3) charitable organization. If the $100,000 payment is made on February 14 of the following year, when is the charitable contribution deduction allowed? Hint: See IRC §642.

Excel Problem

Excel

1. **(LO4) Distribution Deduction Limited to DNI** Crane Trust is a simple trust that has $78,000 of fiduciary accounting income this year, all of which must be distributed to the beneficiaries.

   a. If the trust has DNI of $85,000, what is the income distribution deduction for Crane?

   b. If the trust has DNI of $70,000, what is the income distribution deduction for Crane?

Create an Excel spreadsheet to develop your solution.

Tax Compliance and Reporting Problem

Compliance

1. **(LO5) Form 1041** During the taxable year, the Dolphin Trust (a complex trust) had the following items of income and expense. The trust instrument requires that $10,000 a year be paid from income to a designated charity. All expenses are allocable against rental income, and the trust document requires no reserve for depreciation. The rental income does not qualify for the QBI deduction. During the taxable year, the trustee contributes $10,000 to a qualified charity. In addition, at the trustee's discretion, the trustee distributes $75,000 of income to Flip, the trust's sole beneficiary.

Income	
Rents	$44,000
Dividends	$15,000
Interest income	$12,000
Tax-exempt interest	$11,000
Expenses	
Taxes and expenses directly attributable to rent	$ 4,000
Trustee's commission	$ 3,000
Depreciation	$ 6,000

a. Compute the trust's fiduciary accounting income.
b. Compute the trust's DNI.
c. Determine the character of the amounts distributed.
d. Compute the taxable income.
e. Determine the tax consequences to the beneficiary.
f. Complete Form 1041.

CHAPTER 12

Gift and Estate Taxes

FG Trade/Getty Images

Before studying this chapter, you should know or, if necessary, review:

11.1 Overview of Income Taxation of Trusts and Estates

Chapter Introduction

VIDEO CONTENT

Benjamin and Casey are wealthy entrepreneurs who have been married for 35 years. Both are chemical engineers, and early in their careers they patented some new processes and products that make the use of car batteries more efficient and cost-effective. They have amassed a net worth of approximately $50 million. They have three adult children, Ella, Fynn, and Rhys, all of whom are married. They also have seven grandchildren. They are 60 years old and have done no estate planning yet, but realize they need to if they want to pass along their wealth to their family members in the most tax-efficient manner.

In this chapter, you will learn about two different taxes, the gift tax and the estate tax. Here are a few key points to keep in mind with these taxes:

- These taxes are *not* income taxes. The first 11 chapters of this text focused on the income tax rules for various types of taxpayers. This chapter introduces you to two new taxes.
- The **gift tax** is a wealth tax that is levied on the fair market value of property owned by an individual when it is gifted to another individual.
- The **estate tax** is a wealth tax that is levied on the fair market value of an individual's gross estate at the time of the individual's death.
- The gift tax and the estate tax fall under the overarching umbrella of *unified transfer taxes*. These taxes are unified in that the same tax rate schedule applies to the sum of the cumulative taxable gifts made during a person's life and the FMV of the person's estate at the time of death.
- Gift and estate taxes are paid by only the very wealthiest taxpayers. Single individuals should not be subject to these taxes unless their net worth exceeds approximately $14 million, and for married couples, these taxes are not applicable until their net worth exceeds approximately $28 million.

In 2021, there were only 250,827 gift tax returns filed, compared to approximately 161 million individual income tax returns (Form 1040). Of the 250,827 returns filed, only 1,813 had a tax liability, with a total tax liability of approximately $2,800,000.[1] In 2022, there were 8,130 estate tax returns filed, with a total estate tax liability of approximately $22,500,000,000.[2] It is clear that only a small percentage of the wealthiest Americans pay the gift and/or estate tax.

In this chapter, we begin by explaining why the gift and estate taxes are unified. Then we cover the details of the gift tax and conclude by discussing the laws for the estate tax. Tax professionals can provide appropriate advice to their wealthiest clients like Benjamin and Casey only if they have a broad understanding of how the gift tax and estate tax are structured.

Related exercise: Multiple Choice Question 1

LEARNING OBJECTIVES	TOPICS	PRACTICE OPPORTUNITIES
1 Understand the application of the unified transfer tax to gifts and estates.	**12.1 Unified Transfer Tax** • Unified Tax Rate Schedule • Applicable Credit Exclusion	• Example 12.1.1 Unified Tax Rate Schedule • Example 12.1.2 Applicable Credit • Practice Problem 12.1.1 Calculation of Estate Tax Liability • Practice Problem 12.1.2 Marginal Tax Bracket

2 Identify the items that are included in the gift tax calculation.	**12.2 Transfers Subject to the Gift Tax**
	• General Rules
	• Completed Gifts
	• Transfers to a Trust
	• Joint Ownership of Property
	• Annual Exclusion
	  • Present Interest
	  • Section 529 Plans
	• Gift-Splitting
		• Example 12.2.1 Gift Tax
		• Example 12.2.2 Incomplete Gift
		• Example 12.2.3 Transfers to a Trust
		• Example 12.2.4 Revocable Trust
		• Example 12.2.5 Jointly-Owned Property
		• Example 12.2.6 Jointly-Owned Checking Account
		• Example 12.2.7 Annual Exclusion
		• Example 12.2.8 Gift Tax
		• Example 12.2.9 Annual Exclusion for a Minor
		• Example 12.2.10 Section 529 Plans
		• Example 12.2.11 Gift-Splitting
		• Practice Problem 12.2.1 Gift Tax
		• Practice Problem 12.2.2 Annual Exclusion
		• Practice Problem 12.2.3 Gift-Splitting

[1] U.S. Department of the Treasury. *SOI tax stats – Gift tax statistics.* Table 1: Total gifts of donor, Total gifts, Deductions, Credits, and Net gift tax. Internal Revenue Service, Research and Applied Analytics, Statistics of Income Division, Gift Tax Study, July 2023. www.irs.gov/statistics/soi-tax-stats-gift-tax-statistics.

[2] U.S. Department of the Treasury. *Statistics of Income – Estate Tax Returns Filed for Wealthy Decedents, Filing Years 2013–2022.* Publication 5332 (Rev. 10–2024). Catalog Number 72106H. Internal Revenue Service, Oct. 2024. www.irs.gov/pub/irs-pdf/p5332.pdf.

3 Compute the gift tax liability using the gift tax formula.	**12.3 Gift Tax Formula**
	• Deductions Allowed for the Gift Tax
	  • Marriage Deduction
	  • Charitable Contribution Deduction
	• Gift Tax Formula
	  • Step 2: Add Previous Years' Taxable Gifts to Current Year's Taxable Gifts and Step 3: Calculate the Total Gift Tax Liability
	  • Step 4: Reduce the Total Gift Tax Liability by the Gift Tax Computed on Taxable Gifts from Previous Periods Using the Current Rates for the Unified Tax
	  • Step 5: Reduce Any Remaining Gift Tax by the Unused Portion of the Applicable Credit
	• Filing Requirements for Form 709
		• Example 12.3.1 Engagement Gift
		• Example 12.3.2 Charitable Contributions
		• Example 12.3.3 Marginal Tax Rate for Gifts
		• Example 12.3.4 Tax on Prior Year's Gifts
		• Example 12.3.5 Applicable Credit to Reduce Gift Tax
		• Example 12.3.6 Filing Requirements
		• Practice Problem 12.3.1 Calculation of Taxable Gifts
		• Practice Problem 12.3.2 Calculation of Transfer Tax for Current Year

4 Determine the value of the assets that are included in the gross estate.	**12.4 Estate Tax—General Rules**
	• Key Definitions
	  • Probate Estate vs. Gross Estate
	• Valuation Rules
	  • Alternate Valuation Date (AVD)
	  • Special Valuation for Certain Realty
		• Example 12.4.1 Gross Estate vs. Probate Estate
		• Example 12.4.2 Use of the Alternate Valuation Date
		• Example 12.4.3 Distribution before the AVD Date
		• Example 12.4.4 Restriction on Election of AVD
		• Example 12.4.5 Special Use Valuation
		• Practice Problem 12.4.1 Gross Estate vs. Probate Estate
		• Practice Problem 12.4.2 Use of the Alternate Valuation Date

5 Identify the property that is included in the gross estate.	**12.5 Inclusions in the Gross Estate**
	• Life Insurance
	• Jointly-Owned Property
	  • Right of Survivorship
	  • Tenancy in Common
	  • Tenancy by the Entirety
	• Retained Interests
	  • Life Interest
	  • Power to Designate
	  • Revocations
	• Transfers within Three Years of Death
		• Example 12.5.1 Life Insurance—Ownership
		• Example 12.5.2 Life Insurance—Beneficiary
		• Example 12.5.3 Joint Ownership of Property
		• Example 12.5.4 Life Interest
		• Example 12.5.5 Powers of Appointment
		• Example 12.5.6 Gift Tax Paid within Three Years of Death
		• Example 12.5.7 Transfers before Death
		• Practice Problem 12.5.1 Joint Ownership of Property
		• Practice Problem 12.5.2 Transfer within Three Years of Death

LEARNING OBJECTIVES	TOPICS	PRACTICE OPPORTUNITIES
6 Determine the deductions that can reduce the gross estate.	**12.6 Deductions from the Gross Estate** • Marital Deduction • Qualified Terminable Interest Property (QTIP) • Debts and Claims against the Estate • Charitable Contributions • Final Expenses • Casualty and Theft Losses	• Example 12.6.1 Transfers to a Spouse • Example 12.6.2 Final Expenses • Practice Problem 12.6.1 Marital Deduction • Practice Problem 12.6.2 Final Expenses

7 Compute the estate tax using the estate tax formula.	**12.7 Estate Tax Formula**
	• Estate Tax Formula
	• Computing the Net Estate Tax Liability
	  • Step 1. Gross-Up for Post-1976 Taxable Gifts
	  • Step 2. Apply Current Rates to Total Transfers
	  • Step 3. Reduce the Transfer Tax Paid for Prior Gift Taxes
	  • Step 4. Reduce Tax for Credits
	• Other Requirements
	  • Filing Requirements
	  • The Generation-Skipping Tax
		• Example 12.7.1 Adjusted Taxable Gifts
		• Example 12.7.2 Apply Current Rates to Total Transfers
		• Example 12.7.3 Reduce the Transfer Tax for Prior Gift Taxes
		• Example 12.7.4 Reduce Tax for Credits
		• Example 12.7.5 Portability of Applicable Credit
		• Practice Problem 12.7.1 Calculating the Net Estate Tax Liability

Tax Forms referenced in this chapter

Form 709	United States Gift (and Generation-Skipping Transfer) Tax Return
Form 8892	Application for Automatic Extension of Time To File Form 709 and/or Payment of Gift/Generation-Skipping Transfer Tax

12.1 Unified Transfer Tax

LEARNING OBJECTIVE 1

Understand the application of the unified transfer tax to gifts and estates.

VIDEO CONTENT

The **unified transfer tax** applies to the transfer of an individual's wealth to another either during the individual's life or at the time of the individual's death. There are two types of unified transfer taxes. The *gift tax* is paid by the donor, and the *estate tax* is paid from the assets of the decedent.

Why **Why is the gift tax paid by the donor rather than the donee?** Students and taxpayers are always surprised when they learn that the gift tax is paid by the donor. For example, assume that Morio gifts $100,000 to a friend to pay off his friend's debt, and that the transaction is subject to the gift tax. One would expect that the friend would pay any required gift taxes because the friend has the $100,000. However, Morio must pay the tax. This seems illogical, until you consider why the gift tax exists.

The only reason that there is a gift tax is because the United States has an estate tax. If there was no gift tax, and someone worth $40 million knew that death was imminent in the next few months because of a disease, they could gift most of their wealth to others and avoid the estate tax because they would no longer own these funds or assets at death. To prevent such a simple tax avoidance scheme, there must be a gift tax. In that case, if the funds are gifted before death, then the gift tax is paid by the donor. If the property had *not* been gifted, it would have been subject to the estate tax at death, which would also be paid from the donor's assets.

The logical linkage of the gift tax and the estate tax is the reason these taxes are the two parts of the unified transfer tax. The taxes are unified in two key ways: the unified tax rate schedule, and the *applicable credit*.

Related exercise: Discussion Question 1

The gift tax and estate tax may be levied on anyone who is a citizen or resident of the United States, even if the property transferred is not located in the United States. Further, an individual who is neither a citizen nor resident of the United States is subject to these taxes if the property they transfer is located in the United States.[3]

Unified Tax Rate Schedule

The unified transfer tax rate schedule applies to both the gift tax and the estate tax, as shown in Illustration 12.1.[4] This is a progressive tax system with rates ranging from 18% to 40%. The

ILLUSTRATION 12.1 Unified Tax Rate Schedule

Tax Year 2025 Unified Tax Rate Schedule					
Column A Taxable amount (dollars) in excess of amount below	Column B But not exceeding amount below	Column C Maximum taxable amount for given tax rate (Column B minus Column A)	Column D Tax rate on amount in Column C	Column E Maximum amount of tax at this rate (Column C × Column D)	Column F Cumulative tax on amount shown in Column A
$ 0	$ 10,000	$ 10,000	18%	$ 1,800	$ 0
$ 10,000	$ 20,000	$ 10,000	20%	$ 2,000	$ 1,800
$ 20,000	$ 40,000	$ 20,000	22%	$ 4,400	$ 3,800
$ 40,000	$ 60,000	$ 20,000	24%	$ 4,800	$ 8,200
$ 60,000	$ 80,000	$ 20,000	26%	$ 5,200	$ 13,000
$ 80,000	$ 100,000	$ 20,000	28%	$ 5,600	$ 18,200
$ 100,000	$ 150,000	$ 50,000	30%	$15,000	$ 23,800
$ 150,000	$ 250,000	$100,000	32%	$32,000	$ 38,800
$ 250,000	$ 500,000	$250,000	34%	$85,000	$ 70,800
$ 500,000	$ 750,000	$250,000	37%	$92,500	$155,800
$ 750,000	$1,000,000	$250,000	39%	$97,500	$248,300
$1,000,000	—	No maximum	40%	No maximum	$345,800

[3]IRC §§2001(a), 2511(a), and 2801.

[4]Department of the Treasury. *Instructions for Form 706 - United States Estate (and Generation-Skipping Transfer) Tax Return*. Table A. (Rev. 10–2024). Catalog Number 16779E. Internal Revenue Service, Oct. 2024. www.irs.gov/pub/irs-pdf/i706.pdf.

marginal tax rate is determined based on the sum of the gifts made during a taxpayer's life and the taxpayer's taxable estate at death. Thus, the tax rate schedule *unifies* the transfers made during a taxpayer's life and those made at the taxpayer's death when determining the marginal tax rate for the current year's gifts.

EXAMPLE 12.1.1 Unified Tax Rate Schedule

Assume that all the gifts in this problem are subject to the gift tax. Betty has made the following gifts in prior years:

2010	$ 20,000
2014	$ 50,000
2019	$115,000
2023	$ 30,000

In 2025, she made $60,000 of gifts. What marginal gift tax rate(s) applies for each of these years?

SOLUTION

To determine the marginal tax rate(s), we must look at the cumulative taxable gifts each year, as follows:

Year	Cumulative Taxable Gifts	Marginal Tax Rate
2010	$20,000	18% ($10,000); 20% ($10,000)
2014	$70,000 ($20,000 + $50,000)	22% ($20,000); 24% ($20,000); 26% ($10,000)
2019	$185,000 ($70,000 + $115,000)	26% ($10,000); 28% ($20,000); 30% ($50,000); 32% (35,000)
2023	$215,000 ($185,000 + $30,000)	32% ($30,000)
2025	$275,000 ($215,000 + $60,000)	32% ($35,000); 34% ($25,000)

You can see that as the lifetime gifts increase over time, the marginal tax rate increases also.

Related exercise: Brief Exercise 1

Potential Pitfall

The applicable credit exclusion is not actually a credit. Credits reduce the tax liability dollar for dollar, but the applicable credit exclusion here functions as a deduction. The $13,990,000 represents the fair market value of transfers that will not be subject to the gift or estate tax. Thus, a wealthy individual can cumulatively gift or bequeath a total of $13,990,000 (as of 2025) to others and not be subject to the unified transfer tax.

Applicable Credit Exclusion

The **applicable credit exclusion** is an inflation-adjusted statutory amount that provides the total amount of transfers that an individual can make to others during the individual's life and at death without being subject to the unified transfer tax. The applicable credit exclusion for 2025 is $13,990,000.[5] The gift and estate taxes are also unified because the applicable credit exclusion applies to the total lifetime gifts plus the value of the estate at death. The applicable credit exclusion is per individual, so each spouse in a married couple has a separate exclusion of $13,990,000 to use.[6] The applicable credit exclusion of $13,990,000 offsets up to $5,541,800 of unified tax for 2025. The $5,541,800 is the **applicable credit**, which is sometimes referred to as the *unified credit*.

[5]§2510.
[6]IRC §2505.

EXAMPLE 12.1.2
Applicable Credit

Assume that Mary Margaret dies in 2025 and that she never made any gifts during her life that were subject to the gift tax. What is the value of her assets that can be excluded from the estate tax, and what is the maximum value of the credit that Mary Margaret's estate could have for the applicable credit?

SOLUTION

The applicable credit exclusion is $13,990,000 in 2025, and this is the value of Mary Margaret's assets that can be excluded from the estate tax. To determine the actual value of the credit, we must compute what the estate tax liability would be for a taxable estate of $13,990,000. Such an estate would be taxed as follows:

Tax bracket	Estate value		Estate tax
18%	$ 10,000		$ 1,800
20%	$ 10,000		$ 2,000
22%	$ 20,000		$ 4,400
24%	$ 20,000		$ 4,800
26%	$ 20,000		$ 5,200
28%	$ 20,000		$ 5,600
30%	$ 50,000		$ 15,000
32%	$ 100,000		$ 32,000
34%	$ 250,000		$ 85,000
37%	$ 250,000		$ 92,500
39%	$ 250,000		$ 97,500
40%	$12,990,000		$5,196,000
Total estate value	$13,990,000	Total credit amount	$5,541,800

The actual credit generated by the applicable credit is $5,541,800. If an individual had a taxable estate of $13,990,000, their tax liability before the applicable credit would be $5,541,800, and the credit of $5,541,800 would reduce the tax liability to $0.

Tax Planning Tip

The applicable credit exclusion was increased significantly by the *Tax Cuts and Jobs Act of 2017*. In 2017, the exclusion could offset $5,490,000 of value, and the applicable credit was $2,141,800. For 2018, the exclusion doubled in value to $11,180,000 from the inflation-adjusted amount it would have been. While this is great for wealthy taxpayers, the problem is that most of the individual tax provisions changed by the 2017 Act expire at the end of 2025 unless Congress votes to extend them. If Congress did not extend this, then the applicable credit exclusion would have been reduced by 50% from 2025 to 2026. In that case, wealthy taxpayers should have considered making sizable gifts in 2025 to make use of the larger applicable credit before it expired. However, in 2025 Congress did make the increased applicable credit exclusion permanent.

Related exercise: Tax Planning Problem 1

PRACTICE PROBLEM 12.1.1
Calculation of Estate Tax Liability

The Jane Doe Estate has a taxable estate value of $22,000. What is the estate tax liability?

SOLUTION

The estate tax liability is $4,240 [($10,000 × 18%) + ($10,000 × 20%) + ($2,000 × 22%)]

PRACTICE PROBLEM 12.1.2
Marginal Tax Bracket

Assume that Lazarus died in June 2025, leaving a taxable estate value of $900,000. Lazarus had made no prior taxable gifts. What is the estate's marginal tax bracket?

SOLUTION

The estate's marginal tax bracket is 39%.

INTERACTIVE SELF-SCORING QUIZZES

12.2 Transfers Subject to the Gift Tax

LEARNING OBJECTIVE 2

Identify the items that are included in the gift tax calculation.

VIDEO CONTENT

The next two sections of this chapter focus on the gift tax. In this section, you will learn how to determine which gifts are subject to the gift tax, and in the next section, you will learn the formula used to compute the gift tax. Returning to the facts of Benjamin and Casey in the Introduction, they need a long-term gifting plan if they want to transfer their wealth to future generations in the most tax-efficient manner.

General Rules

A **gift** is a voluntary transfer of property from one person (the donor) to another (the donee) without full valuable consideration received by donor.[7] That is, the recipient of the gift, the donee, does not return consideration to the donor equal to the value of what the donee received. Let's look at some common transactions that are subject to the gift tax:

- Transfers made for love and affection
- Transfers made as a marriage proposal
- Cash and property transfers
- Debt forgiveness to family members and friends
- Sales at bargain prices to family members and friends
- Loans to family members at below-market interest rates
- Transfers of property into trust for the benefit of others
- Purchases of jointly-owned real estate or securities if one co-owner contributes more than their proportionate share

The following gifts are *not* subject to the gift tax:[8]

- Payment of another individual's medical or educational expenses (tuition and fees only). These payments must be made directly to the medical provider or the educational institution to qualify for the exclusion.

[7]IRC §2501.
[8]IRC §2503.

- Political contributions
- Transfers to a spouse
- The satisfaction of an obligation, such as the payment of debt
- Transfers to civic leagues (for example, Rotary, Kiwanis) and social welfare organizations; labor, agricultural, and horticultural organizations; and business leagues are not gifts.
- Donations of personal services
- Transfers that can be revoked, such as placing assets in revocable trusts
- Payments to minor family members for food, shelter, clothing, and other reasonable support needs. This also includes providing assets and services to a minor family member so they can maintain the lifestyle to which they are accustomed (even if that lifestyle is lavish).
- Payments to an employee that in substance are compensation for personal services
- Property settlements incident to divorce

The following Example demonstrates whether transfers are subject to the gift tax.

EXAMPLE 12.2.1
Gift Tax

Wes made the following transfers during the current year. Indicate whether each transfer is subject to the gift tax.

a. An engagement ring to his fiancé
b. Tuition and fees for his niece paid to The Ohio State University
c. A new car for his father
d. Cash transfer to the national Republican party
e. Cash transfer to his local Rotary Club
f. Forgave a loan he had made to a friend who had lost a job
g. Volunteered at an animal shelter for 20 Saturday mornings
h. A new car for his 17-year-old daughter for her birthday
i. Sold a boat valued at $50,000 to his brother for $20,000
j. Cash given to a friend to pay medical bills

SOLUTION

a. Subject to the gift tax because the transfer is not to a spouse
b. Not subject to the gift tax because it is for tuition and fees and paid directly to the educational institution
c. Subject to the gift tax because made for love or affection
d. Not subject to the gift tax because made to a political organization
e. Not subject to the gift tax because made to a civic league
f. Subject to the gift tax because made for love or affection
g. Not subject to the gift tax because it is personal services
h. Not subject to the gift tax because it is support for a dependent child
i. Subject to the gift tax because this is a bargain sale made for love or affection
j. Subject to the gift tax; if the payment had been made directly to the medical provider, it would not subject to the gift tax

Related exercise: Brief Exercise 2

Potential Pitfall

Do not confuse the income tax effects of gifts with the gift tax effects. Gifts and inheritances are not income to the donee. The gift tax is also never levied on the donee. However, the donor may have to pay gift tax.

Completed Gifts

For a gift to occur, the gift must be completed. A gift is completed once the following has occurred:

- The gift must be delivered to the donee.
- The donor must give up control of the property, which includes giving up the use of or enjoyment of the property.
- The donee must accept the gift; the donee cannot disclaim or refuse the gift, or it will be incomplete.

If a potential gift is incomplete, then it is not subject to the gift tax. We explore an incomplete gift in the following Example.

EXAMPLE 12.2.2 Incomplete Gift

Hala is 72 years old and owns a home that is valued at $830,000. She has lived in the home for the last 35 years. She has decided that she wants her daughter to live in the house after her death. Her daughter is concerned that her mother may change her mind later, so she asks her to transfer ownership of the house to her now. The daughter agrees in writing that Hala can continue to live alone in the house until she passes away. What are the gift tax implications of this transaction?

SOLUTION

The transfer of the house to Hala's daughter is not subject to the gift tax. Hala has reserved the right to live in the house until her death, which means that she can enjoy the benefits of ownership of the property. Therefore, this is an incomplete gift. Hala will be treated as the owner of the property at her death for estate tax purposes, and the house will then be bequeathed to her daughter.

Related exercise: Discussion Question 2

Potential Pitfall

In a situation like that in Example 12.2.2, once Hala transfers ownership of the house to her daughter, then her daughter is the owner of the property for non-tax purposes. For example, her daughter will be legally responsible for paying the property taxes, even though this transfer is ignored for gift tax and estate tax purposes because it is incomplete.

Transfers to a Trust

When a taxpayer transfers property to a trust, the taxpayer has made two gifts, the income interest and the remainder interest (unless the donor retains one of these interests). (See Chapter 11, LO1, Overview of Income Taxation of Trusts and Estates).

The beneficiary of the income interest receives the income from the trust each year. The beneficiary of the remainder interest receives the property (corpus) of the trust when the trust terminates. The present value of the income and remainder interests are valued using actuarial tables provided by the IRS. The rate used in the valuation is 120% of the applicable federal midterm rate (published by the IRS) for the month in which the transfer is made. The sum of the present value of the income and remainder interests will be equal to the FMV of the property transferred to the trust.

The next Example illustrates how transfers to a trust are treated for gift tax purposes.

EXAMPLE 12.2.3
Transfers to a Trust

Pranav has decided to set up a trust for the benefit of his granddaughter, who is six years old. He transfers $500,000 of stock to the trust. Each year, 50% of the income from the trust will be paid to his daughter, and the other 50% will be accumulated. The principal of the trust can be used by the trustee to support the granddaughter's medical or educational needs. When the granddaughter reaches the age of 30, the trust will terminate, and the principal will be distributed to her. What are the gift tax implications of this trust if the value of the income interest is $60,000 and the value of the remainder interest is $440,000? Will any gifts be made in years after the trust was created?

SOLUTION

When Pranav creates this trust, he makes a gift to both his daughter, the income beneficiary, and his granddaughter, the remainder beneficiary. Both gifts are subject to the gift tax and are valued using the IRS actuarial tables based on the ages of the daughter and granddaughter and the expected life of the trust. The gift to his daughter is $60,000, and the gift to his granddaughter is $440,000.

There are no gifts in the years after the trust is created. The future distributions to Pranav's daughter and granddaughter are not considered additional gifts.

A revocable transfer to a trust is an incomplete gift, as shown in the following Example.

EXAMPLE 12.2.4
Revocable Trust

Assume the same facts as in Example 12.2.3, except that Pranav includes a stipulation in the trust agreement that he has the right to have all the accumulated income and the $500,000 returned to him any time before his granddaughter reaches the age of 25. He tells his granddaughter that he will likely only exercise this right if she does not graduate from college. What are the gift tax implications of this trust for the current year? Will any gifts be made in years after the trust was created?

SOLUTION

Pranav has not made a gift to his granddaughter because the transfer is an incomplete gift. Pranav has the right to revoke the transfer until his granddaughter turns 25, so for gift tax purposes this is treated as if the transfer was never made. He has also not made a gift to his daughter in the current year because the creation of the trust could be revoked.

There will be gift tax implications for years after the trust is created. When 50% of the income is distributed to his daughter in future years, that will be considered a gift. When his granddaughter has her 25th birthday, the gift to her will be complete and the $500,000 and accumulated income will be subject to the gift tax.

Related exercises: Multiple Choice Question 2
Application Problem 1

Joint Ownership of Property

Several gift tax implications arise related to property that is owned by more than one individual. The creation of a joint ownership interest without equal consideration from each co-owner is considered a gift of the excess contribution to the owner making the smaller contribution. The following gift tax rules apply to jointly-owned property:

- Transfers of cash to a joint bank account do not constitute completed gifts until the donee withdraws the cash.
- A purchase of a savings bond held jointly in the name of the donee and the donor is not a completed gift. No gift occurs until the donee receives cash proceeds from the bond.

- The creation of a joint interest with a spouse is not subject to the gift tax because of the marital deduction (discussed in the next section).
- The termination of joint ownership may also trigger a tax, if the proceeds are not divided according to each owner's interest.

The next two Examples demonstrate the gift tax implications of jointly-owned property.

EXAMPLE 12.2.5
Jointly-Owned Property

Bindu purchases real estate for $500,000 and titles the property as owned by him and his son as tenants in common (one-half interest each).

a. Are there any gift tax implications for this purchase?

b. Would the answer change if Bindu transferred 50% ownership of the real estate to his spouse?

SOLUTION

a. Bindu has made a gift of $250,000 to his son that is subject to the gift tax. His son now owns a $250,000 interest in the real estate, for which he paid no consideration.

b. Gifts to a spouse do not create any gift tax liability because a spousal deduction is allowed for the value of the transfer.

EXAMPLE 12.2.6
Jointly-Owned Checking Account

Meredith and her friend Katie have lived together for the last four years. This year, they decide to open a joint checking account. In December, Meredith deposits $5,000 into the account and tells Katie that she can use $2,000 of the funds as her Christmas gift from Meredith. Katie uses $800 of the funds in December and the remaining $1,200 in the following year. What are the gift tax implications of these transactions?

SOLUTION

The deposit of the $5,000 into the joint checking account is not subject to the gift tax. A gift does not occur until Katie withdraws or spends the cash. Meredith makes a gift of $800 in December of the current year and a gift of $1,200 in the next year.

Related exercise: Application Problem 2

Annual Exclusion

The annual exclusion is a great tax planning tool that Benjamin and Casey from the chapter opener can use to transfer wealth to their family members without having to pay the unified transfer tax. The **annual exclusion** is the amount that an individual can transfer to another individual during a tax year without having the transfer be subject to the gift tax. The annual exclusion is $19,000 (2025) per donee and is indexed for inflation.[9] The purpose of the annual exclusion is to eliminate modest gifts from being subject to the gift tax. For example, birthday gifts to family members could potentially be subject to the gift tax if there were no annual exclusion.

[9] IRC §2503(b).

Using the annual exclusion is a very simple tax strategy that can result in significant tax savings if used over a long time period, as shown in the next Example.

EXAMPLE 12.2.7
Annual Exclusion

Return to the facts of Benjamin and Casey in the introduction—specifically, recall that they have three married children and seven grandchildren.

a. Using just the annual exclusion, how much can they transfer to their family members this year without being subject to the gift tax?

b. How much could they transfer over 10 years without being subject to the gift tax? Assume that the annual exclusion remains at $19,000 for the next 10 years. How much gift tax would they avoid over the 10 years assuming that all gifts would have been taxable at the 40% rate?

SOLUTION

a. Benjamin can transfer $19,000 to each family member this year without having any gifts subject to the gift tax. He has 13 family members that he can transfer $19,000 to:

- Fynn and spouse
- Rhys and spouse
- Ella and spouse
- Grandchildren (7)

Therefore, he can transfer $247,000 this year ($19,000 × 13).

Casey can also transfer $19,000 to each of the family members for a total of $247,000. Combined, Benjamin and Case can transfer $494,000 to their family members with none being subject to the gift tax.

b. Over 10 years, they can transfer $4,940,000 ($494,000 × 10 years). The gift tax that would be avoided is $1,976,000 ($4,940,000 × 40%).

Tax Planning Tip

As shown in Example 12.2.7, an annual gifting plan is essential for wealthy taxpayers who want to transfer their wealth to future generations so that the annual exclusion can be used for each donee each year. The applicable credit can also be used to transfer wealth and avoid the gift tax. Both tools can be used because they are independent of each other. Using the annual exclusion does not reduce the amount of the applicable credit.

We show how the annual exclusion is applied in the next Example.

EXAMPLE 12.2.8
Gift Tax

Here, we return to the facts of Example 12.2.1 for the items subject to the gift tax but we have added the value of the property transferred. Wes made the following transfers during the current year. What is the net taxable gift after reduction for the annual exclusion, if any? Assume that these are the only gifts given to each individual by Wes this year.

a. A $40,000 engagement ring to his fiancé

b. A new car for his father valued at $35,000

c. Forgave a $10,000 loan he had made to a friend who had lost a job

d. Sold a boat valued at $50,000 to his brother for $20,000

e. $26,000 given to a friend to pay medical bills

SOLUTION

a. Subject to the gift tax because the transfer is not to a spouse. Net taxable gift is $21,000 ($40,000 – $19,000).

b. Subject to the gift tax because made for love or affection. Net taxable gift is $16,000 ($35,000 – $19,000).

c. Subject to the gift tax because made for love or affection. The annual exclusion is limited to $10,000, the value of the gift, and the net taxable gift is $0.

d. Subject to the gift tax because this is a bargain sale made for love or affection. The value of the gift is $30,000 ($50,000 – $20,000). The net taxable gift is $11,000 ($30,000 – $19,000).

e. Subject to the gift tax; if the payment had been made directly to the medical provider it would not be subject to the gift tax. Net taxable gift is $7,000 ($26,000 – $19,000).

Related exercises: Discussion Question 3
Brief Exercise 3
Tax Planning Problem 1

Present Interest/Future Interest

The annual exclusion applies only to a gift of a present interest.[10] A **present interest** is a recipient's right to receive income or enjoy property currently. Thus, if a gift is made in trust and will not benefit the recipient currently, no annual exclusion is allowed. This recipient has a **future interest** and so will not benefit from the income or property until a future date. For example, if a trust instrument provides that a beneficiary can receive a distribution of $50,000 in 2030 that was transferred to the trust this year, that is a gift of a future interest.

A gift to a minor in a trust is considered a present interest if the trustee has the ability to use the funds for the benefit of the minor before the age of 21 (such as for education, medical, or similar purposes), and any remaining funds will be distributed to the minor upon reaching age 21.[11]

We show the different gift tax consequences of a present interest and a future interest in the next Example.

EXAMPLE 12.2.9
Annual Exclusion for a Minor

Returning to the facts of Example 12.2.3, Pranav has decided to set up a trust for the benefit of his granddaughter, who is six years old. He transfers $500,000 of stock to the trust. Each year, 50% of the income from the trust will be paid to his daughter, and the other 50% will be accumulated. The principal of the trust can be used by the trustee to support medical or educational needs of his granddaughter. When his granddaughter reaches the age of 30, the trust will terminate, and the principal will be distributed to her. The value of the income interest is $60,000, and the value of the remainder interest is $440,000. Will Pravad receive an annual exclusion for the gifts to his daughter and granddaughter?

SOLUTION

Pranav made of gift of $60,000 to his daughter and $440,000 to his granddaughter. The gift to his daughter is a present interest because she will receive 50% of the income earned by the trust each year. Therefore, Pranav will receive an exclusion of $19,000 for the gift to his daughter, and the net taxable gift will be $41,000 ($60,000 – $19,000). Pranav does not receive an annual exclusion for the gift to his granddaughter because this is a gift of a future interest. His granddaughter will not receive any benefit from the trust until she is 30 years old.

Related exercise: Application Problem 3

[10]IRC §2503(c)§2503(b)(1).
[11]IRC §2503(c).

Section 529 Plans

The use of the annual exclusion has a special rule for gifts made to Section 529 plans. Section 529 plans can be created by the donor to help pay for future education costs of the plan's beneficiary. From a tax perspective, contributions to the plan are not deductible for income tax purposes. However, the earnings inside the plan are not taxed in the year earned. Further, when the funds are distributed from the plan, as long as they are used to pay for education costs for the beneficiary, the earnings are never taxed.

There are also gift tax advantages for Section 529 plans. A donor can use five years of annual exclusions (per donee) in one year for contributions to these plans. Thus, for 2025, \$95,000 (\$19,000 × 5 years) can be contributed to the plan for the future benefit of the beneficiary, and none of the transfers would be subject to the gift tax. However, any additional gifts to the beneficiary during the five-year period would be subject to the gift tax because the annual exclusions for those years have been used.[12]

EXAMPLE 12.2.10
Section 529 Plans

Jaylen would like to set up a Section 529 plan for his grandson to begin saving to pay his college expenses when he is older. In 2025, Jaylen contributed \$125,000 to the Section 529 plan and his grandson is designated as the beneficiary. What are the gift tax implications of this transfer?

SOLUTION

Jaylen can use the annual exclusion of \$19,000 for his grandson for this year and the next four years. Therefore, \$95,000 of the transfer is not subject to the gift tax. The remaining value of \$30,000 (\$125,000 – \$95,000) is subject to the gift tax in 2025.

Related exercise: Multiple Choice Question 3

Gift-Splitting

Gift-splitting is an election that applies only to married individuals. However, the gift tax form is filed by an individual (not jointly). In order to elect gift-splitting, a spouse must file Form 709, United States Gift (and Generation-Skipping Transfer) Tax Return, and make the election on Line 19, as shown in **Illustration 12.2**. If both spouses want to elect gift-splitting, each must file a gift tax return.

If elected, then it is deemed that every gift made by either spouse was made 50% by each spouse. This allows each spouse to use their annual exclusion of \$19,000 (2025) for their portion of the gift if the gift is of a present interest.[13] There are two key timing rules:

- The election is an annual election.
- The donor must be married at the time of the transfer.

Why **Why is the gift-splitting election permitted by Congress?** The gift-splitting election came into being because nine states use community property laws (Arizona, California, Idaho, Louisiana, Nevada, New Mexico, Texas, Washington, and Wisconsin). In community property states, one-half of all property generally belongs to each spouse. Hence, a gift of community property is automatically split between the spouses. To equalize this effect for married couples in the other 41 states, gift-splitting can be elected.

[12] IRC §529.

[13] IRC §2513.

ILLUSTRATION 12.2 Form 709, Gift-Splitting Election

DOWNLOAD DOCUMENTS & TEMPLATES

Gift-Splitting Election (Line 19)

Form **709**

Department of the Treasury
Internal Revenue Service

United States Gift (and Generation-Skipping Transfer) Tax Return

Go to *www.irs.gov/Form709* for instructions and the latest information.

(For gifts made during calendar year 2024)

OMB No. 1545-0020

2024

Part I General Information

1 Donor's first name and middle initial	2 Donor's last name	3 Donor's social security number
4 Address (number and street). If you have a P.O. box, see instructions.		5 Apt. no.

6 City, town, or post office. If you have a foreign address, also complete spaces below.	7 State	8 ZIP code
9 Foreign country name	10 Foreign province/state/county	11 Foreign postal code
12 Legal residence (domicile)	13 Citizenship (see instructions)	

		Yes	No
14	If the donor died during the year, check here ☐ and enter date of death ____________, ______.		
15	If an amended return, check here ☐		
16	If you extended the time to file this Form 709, check here ☐		
17	Enter the total number of donees listed on Schedule A. Count each person only once ____________		
18a	Have you (the donor) previously filed a Form 709 (or 709-A) for any other year? If "No," skip line 18b		
b	Has your address changed since you last filed Form 709 (or 709-A)?		
19	**Gifts by spouses to third parties.** Did you and your spouse make gifts to third parties? See instructions. (If the answer is "Yes," complete Part III on page 2.)		
20	Have you applied a deceased spousal unused exclusion (DSUE) amount received from a predeceased spouse to a gift or gifts reported on this or a previous Form 709? If "Yes," complete Schedule C		
21	Does any gift or other transfer reported on this Form 709 include a digital asset (or a financial interest in a digital asset)? See instructions		

EXAMPLE 12.2.11
Gift-Splitting

Terri and Samuel were married for the entire year in 2025. During 2025, Terri gave a $50,000 cash gift to her sister. They made no other gifts in 2025.

a. What amount of the 2025 gift is taxable to Terri if gift-splitting is not elected?

b. If Terri files a Form 709 and elects gift-splitting, how much of the gift is taxable?

SOLUTION

a. If gift-splitting is not elected, then Terri made a $50,000 gift and can use a $19,000 annual exclusion for her sister, so the taxable gift is $31,000 ($50,000 – $19,000).

b. If gift-splitting is elected by Terri and Samuel, then the gift is deemed to be made $25,000 by Terri and $25,000 by Samuel. Each spouse can use an annual exclusion of $19,000 for Terri's sister, so each made a taxable gift as follows:

Terri: $25,000 – $19,000 exclusion = $6,000

Samuel: $25,000 – $19,000 exclusion = $6,000

The total taxable gift is $12,000, contrasted with $31,000 if gift-splitting is not elected.

Related exercises: Discussion Question 4
Application Problem 4

PRACTICE PROBLEM 12.2.1
Gift Tax

The following transfers were made during the current year. Indicate whether each transfer is subject to the gift tax.

a. Julio gave a purse worth $1,000 to his daughter.
b. Sabrina received a vacation home from Julio due to their divorce.
c. Julio received a car as the company's top salesperson.
d. Julio made a payment of $1,000 to the Florence Kiwanis Club.
e. Julio forgave a $12,000 loan to his brother.

SOLUTION

a. Subject to the gift tax because made for love or affection
b. Not subject to the gift tax because this transfer is a property settlement incident to divorce
c. Not subject to the gift tax because it is a payment to an employee that is compensation for personal services
d. Not subject to the gift tax because it is a transfer to a civic league
e. Subject to the gift tax because it is debt forgiveness to a family member

PRACTICE PROBLEM 12.2.2
Annual Exclusion

Timothy, single, transferred the following in 2025.

- Cash of $22,000 to his friend
- Car worth $45,000 to his grandfather
- Stock worth $15,000 to his niece

What are his total taxable gifts in 2025?

SOLUTION

Timothy can transfer $19,000 (2025) to each person this year without having any gifts subject to the gift tax.

Cash of $22,000 to his friend—$19,000 annual exclusion	$ 3,000
Car worth $45,000 to his grandfather—$19,000 annual exclusion	26,000
Stock worth $15,000 to his niece—$15,000 annual exclusion*	0
Total taxable gifts	$29,000

*Limited to the value of the gift if less than $19,000.

PRACTICE PROBLEM 12.2.3
Gift-Splitting

Elijah and Taryn, U.S. citizens, were married for the entire year in 2025. During 2025, Elijah gave a $25,000 cash gift to his father. They made no other gifts in 2025.

a. What amount of the 2025 gift is taxable to Elijah if gift-splitting is not elected?
b. If Elijah and Taryn elect gift-splitting, how much of the gift is taxable?

SOLUTION

a. If gift-splitting is not elected, then Elijah made a $25,000 gift and can use an $19,000 annual exclusion for his father, so the taxable gift is $6,000 ($25,000 – $19,000).

b. If gift-splitting is elected by Elijah and Taryn, then the gift is deemed to be made $12,500 by Elijah and $12,500 by Taryn. Each spouse can use an annual exclusion of up to $19,000 for Elijah's father, so each made a taxable gift as follows:

Elijah: $12,500 – $12,500 exclusion = $0

Taryn: $12,500 – $12,500 exclusion = $0

The annual exclusion of $19,000 is limited to the actual gift made of $12,500. The total taxable gift is $0, contrasted with $6,000 if gift-splitting is not elected.

INTERACTIVE SELF-SCORING QUIZZES

12.3 Gift Tax Formula

LEARNING OBJECTIVE 3

Compute the gift tax liability using the gift tax formula.

VIDEO CONTENT

Potential Pitfall

Do not confuse a deduction with an exclusion. Many gifts are excluded from the gift tax, so they are never included in the gift tax formula. For example, gifts to political organizations are excluded from the gift tax, as are gifts for university tuition and fees if paid directly to the educational organization. On the other hand, gifts to charities and to spouses *are* included in the potentially taxable gifts on Form 709, and then either the marital deduction or the charitable deduction reduces the taxable gifts.

In this section, you will learn how to compute an individual's gift tax liability using the gift tax formula as shown on Form 709, United States Gift (and Generation-Skipping Transfer) Tax Return. The section has three main parts. First, we review the deductions that are allowed in computing the taxable gifts. Second, we explain the gift tax formula, including how to use the unified transfer tax rate schedule to compute the gift tax liability. Third, we summarize the filing requirements for Form 709.

Deductions Allowed for the Gift Tax

Only two deductions are allowed on Form 709: the marital deduction and the charitable contribution deduction.

Marriage Deduction

A marital deduction is allowed for most gifts to a spouse.[14] One major exception to this rule is that gifts of terminable interests generally do not qualify for the deduction. A **terminable interest** is an interest in property that terminates upon the occurrence of a future event, such as the death of the recipient. For example, a taxpayer who receives the right to occupy property for the duration of their life has received a terminable interest because the taxpayer's rights terminate upon death. The following rules apply for the marital deduction:

- The deduction is unlimited in amount.
- The amount of the deduction is the FMV of the gift less the annual exclusion (if the gift is a present interest).
- The marital deduction does not apply for gifts to a spouse who is not a U.S. citizen. In such a situation, an annual exclusion of $190,000 (2025) is permitted.

[14] IRC §2523(a).

We delve into the application of the marriage deduction in the next Example.

EXAMPLE 12.3.1
Engagement Gift

Juan and April became engaged in April of the current year, when Juan gave April a ring with a value of $50,000. In December of this year, they married, and after the wedding, April gave Juan a car worth $75,000. What are the gift tax implications of these transactions, if any?

SOLUTION

For the gift of the ring, Juan can claim an annual exclusion of $19,000 (2025). However, he does not receive a marital deduction for this gift because he was not married to April at the time of the gift. So $31,000 ($50,000 – $19,000) is subject to the gift tax.

For the gift of the car, April will receive deductions equal to the $75,000 value of the car, so none of the gift is subject to the gift tax. She receives an annual exclusion of $19,000 and a marital deduction of $56,000 ($75,000 – $19,000).

Related exercises: Multiple Choice Question 4
Brief Exercise 4

Charitable Contribution Deduction

A charitable contribution deduction is allowed for gifts to qualified charitable organizations. A qualified charity is defined similarly to the way it is defined for income tax purposes, broadly including organizations whose mission is educational, scientific, or religious.[15] The charitable deduction is the amount that exceeds the annual exclusion of $19,000. Three major differences from the income tax definition are that qualified charities for gift tax purposes:

- Include foreign charities,
- Exclude cemeteries, *and*
- Are unlimited.

The next Example highlights the rules regarding the charitable contribution deduction.

EXAMPLE 12.3.2
Charitable Contributions

Belina is a technology entrepreneur who founded a successful artificial intelligence company several years ago. Her net worth is estimated to be $125 million. During the current year, Belina gifts $25 million to her alma mater to name the Department of Accountancy in honor of her parents.

a. How much of the $25 million is subject to the gift tax?

b. Would your answer change if her alma mater was in the United Kingdom?

c. How does this vary from the treatment of charitable contribution deductions for income tax purposes?

SOLUTION

a. None of the $25 million gift is subject to the gift tax, because Belina will receive a $25 million deduction on her gift tax return for the annual exclusion and charitable contribution combined.

[15]IRC §2501(a)(6); IRC §2522.

b. The answer would be the same if her alma mater was in the UK, because foreign charities qualify for the charitable contribution deduction for gift tax purposes.

c. For income tax purposes, her $25 million deduction would be limited to 60% of her adjusted gross income for the year, and any excess amount could be carried over for five years. If the university was in the UK, no income deduction would be allowed because the university is a foreign charity.

Related exercises: Discussion Question 5
Application Problem 5

Gift Tax Formula

You know what is considered a gift from LO2, and what exclusions and deductions are allowed from LO2 and the beginning of LO3. Now, let's look at the gift tax formula.[16]

Cash gifts
Plus: FMV of property given away
Less: 50% of gifts made if gift-splitting elected
Plus: 50% of spouse's gifts if gift-splitting elected
Less: Annual exclusion ($19,000 × eligible donees)
Less: Charitable gifts (remainder of charitable gifts after annual exclusion)
Less: Marital deduction (remainder of gifts to spouse after annual exclusion)
Taxable gifts for current year (**Step 1 below**)
Plus: Taxable gifts for prior years (**Step 2 below**)
Total taxable gifts

Gift tax on total taxable gifts (**Step 3 below**)
Less: Gift tax on taxable gifts made prior to current year (**Step 4 below**)
Gift tax for current year
Applicable tax credit not used in prior years (**Step 5 below**)
Net gift tax liability

The most complex part of the gift tax formula is reconciling two items:

- Gift tax should be paid only on gifts made during the current tax year.
- To determine the tax rate to apply to this year's gifts, you must look at total cumulative giving from the current year and all prior years.

Using the following five steps to calculate the gift tax liability will help you understand how these two items impact the calculation:

Step 1. **Determine:** The current year's taxable gifts (the amount of gifts reduced by exclusions and deductions, discussed previously)

Step 2. **Add:** All previous years' taxable gifts to current year's taxable gifts

Step 3: **Calculate:** The total gift tax liability

Step 4. **Reduce:** The total gift tax liability by the gift tax computed on taxable gifts from previous periods using the current rates for the unified tax.

Step 5. **Reduce:** Any remaining gift tax by the unused portion of the applicable credit.

Illustration 12.3 provides a flowchart for this process.

[16]IRC §2502.

ILLUSTRATION 12.3 The Five Steps of the Gift Tax Liability Calculation

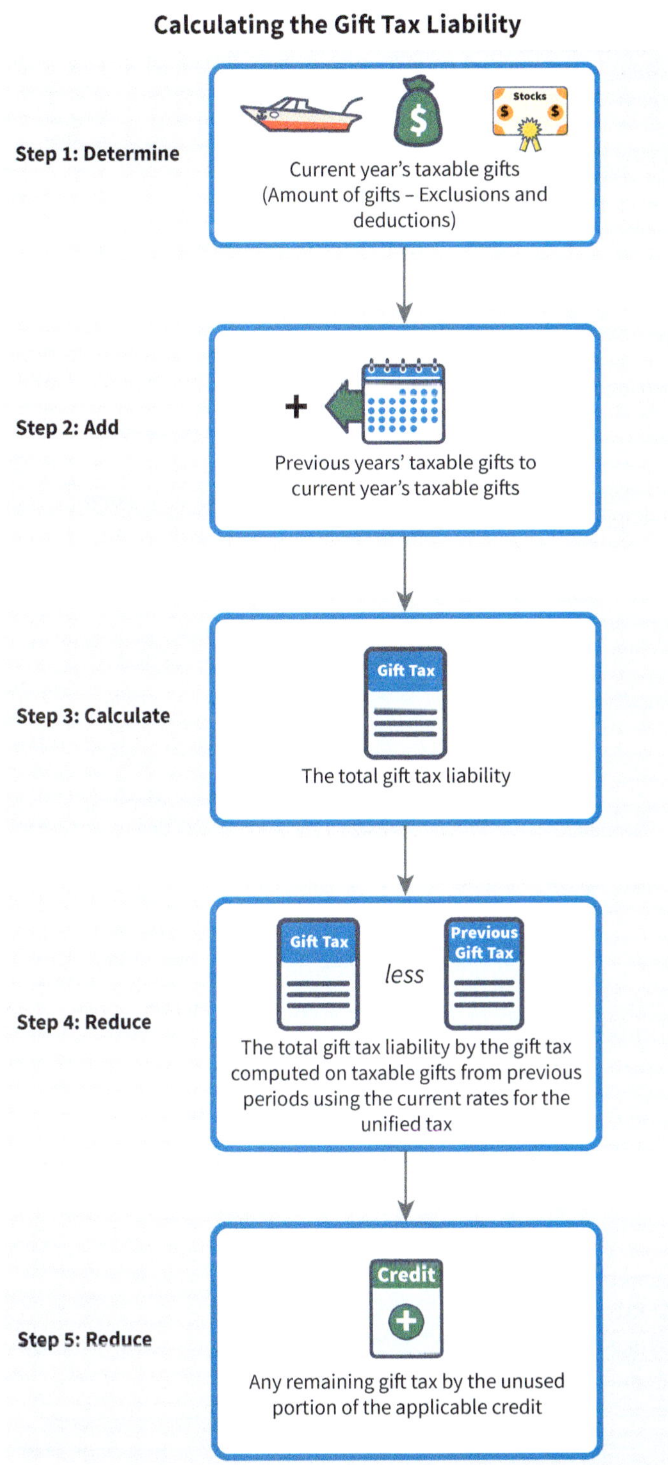

Step 2: Add Previous Years' Taxable Gifts to Current Year's Taxable Gifts and Step 3: Calculate the Total Gift Tax Liability

The total for taxable gifts in the formula includes the taxable gifts from all prior years (known as the **gross-up**). This is done so that the marginal tax rate for this year's taxable gifts is determined by the cumulative lifetime taxable gifts, as shown in Example 12.3.3.

Calculating the gross-up for prior-year gifts, using steps 2 and 3, is demonstrated in the following Example.

EXAMPLE 12.3.3 Marginal Tax Rate for Gifts

Sophia made $440,000 of taxable gifts in the current year. What is the marginal gift tax rate for these gifts if she had taxable gifts in prior years as follows?

2015	$ 50,000
2018	$ 75,000
2020	$134,000
2022	$215,000

Assume that the total gift taxes paid on the gifts in the prior years is $142,000.

SOLUTION

The unified tax rate table shown earlier in Illustration 12.1 is as follows:

Tax Year 2025 Unified Tax Rate Schedule

Column A Taxable amount (dollars) in excess of amount below	Column B But not exceeding amount below	Column C Maximum taxable amount for given tax rate (Column B minus Column A)	Column D Tax rate on amount in Column C	Column E Maximum amount of tax at this rate (Column C × Column D)	Column F Cumulative tax on amount shown in Column A
$ 0	$ 10,000	$ 10,000	18%	$ 1,800	$ 0
$ 10,000	$ 20,000	$ 10,000	20%	$ 2,000	$ 1,800
$ 20,000	$ 40,000	$ 20,000	22%	$ 4,400	$ 3,800
$ 40,000	$ 60,000	$ 20,000	24%	$ 4,800	$ 8,200
$ 60,000	$ 80,000	$ 20,000	26%	$ 5,200	$ 13,000
$ 80,000	$ 100,000	$ 20,000	28%	$ 5,600	$ 18,200
$ 100,000	$ 150,000	$ 50,000	30%	$15,000	$ 23,800
$ 150,000	$ 250,000	$100,000	32%	$32,000	$ 38,800
$ 250,000	$ 500,000	$250,000	34%	$85,000	$ 70,800
$ 500,000	$ 750,000	$250,000	37%	$92,500	$155,800
$ 750,000	$1,000,000	$250,000	39%	$97,500	$248,300
$1,000,000	—	No maximum	40%	No maximum	$345,800

Step 2 from Illustration 12.3: Sophia's cumulative taxable gifts before the current year are $474,000 ($50,000 + $75,000 + $134,000 + $215,000). Her total taxable gifts include the gross-up discussed above:

Taxable gifts for current year	$440,000
Plus: Taxable gifts for prior years	474,000
Total taxable gifts	$914,000

Step 3 from Illustration 12.3: The $474,000 of prior years' gifts places Sophia in the 34% tax bracket. The $440,000 of gifts this year are taxed as follows:

	Tax Liability
34% bracket: $ 26,000 ($500,000 top of bracket – $474,000)	$ 8,840
37% bracket: 250,000 (from $500,000 to $750,000)	92,500
39% bracket: 164,000 (from $750,000 to $914,000)	63,960
$440,000	$165,300

Potential Pitfall

The gift tax on previous gifts is computed using the current tax rate schedule and ignores the use of the applicable credit. This amount does not represent the amount of gift tax paid in previous years.

Step 4: Reduce the Total Gift Tax Liability by the Gift Tax Computed on Taxable Gifts from Previous Periods Using the Current Rates for the Unified Tax

To prevent double taxation of the gifts from prior years, the gift tax on prior taxable gifts is next subtracted from the transfer tax computed on the total taxable gifts. The gift tax on prior taxable gifts is *not* the gift tax paid, but the amount of tax computed using the *current year's rates*, ignoring any prior payments.

Computing the transfer tax on prior years' gifts is shown in the next Example.

EXAMPLE 12.3.4
Tax on Prior Year's Gifts

Continue with the facts from Example 12.3.3. Compute the transfer tax for the current year, before the applicable credit.

SOLUTION

Sophia's total taxable gifts for this year are:

Taxable gifts for current year	$440,000
Plus: Taxable gifts for prior years	474,000
Total taxable gifts	$914,000

The transfer tax on the total taxable gifts of $914,000, using the transfer tax rate schedule, is computed as:

$$\$248,300 + [(\$914,000 - \$750,000) \times 39\%] = \$312,260$$

Step 4 from Illustration 12.3: The transfer tax on the taxable gifts for prior years of $474,000, using the transfer tax rate schedule, is computed as:

$$\$70,800 + [(\$474,000 - \$250,000) \times 34\%] = \$146,960$$

Sophia's transfer tax for the current year is:

Transfer tax on total taxable gifts	$312,260
Less: Transfer tax on taxable gifts made prior to current year	(146,960)
Transfer tax for current year	$165,300

Based on the original facts, the actual gift taxes paid in prior years was $142,000, but that is not the amount used to reduce the transfer tax for the current year. Rather, the reduction amount is based on the gift tax rates in effect for the current year.

Related exercise: Brief Exercise 5

Step 5: Reduce Any Remaining Gift Tax by the Unused Portion of the Applicable Credit.

If a taxpayer has a current gift tax liability, it can be reduced by the applicable credit. Recall that the applicable credit exclusion is an inflation-adjusted statutory amount that specifies the total amount of transfers that an individual can make to others during the individual's life and at death without being subject to the unified transfer tax ($13,990,000 for 2025). The actual amount of the applicable credit in 2025 is $5,541,800.

A taxpayer can only use the value of the applicable credit to offset lifetime gifts and the value of the estate at death *in total*. Most taxpayers choose to use a portion of the applicable credit to offset any gift tax liability during their lifetime, with the remainder available to offset any estate tax liability. However, some taxpayers choose not to use any of the applicable credit to reduce their gift tax liability and use the entire credit to reduce their estate tax liability. One reason to do this would be that the taxpayer believes that the unified tax rates will be higher in the future.

EXAMPLE 12.3.5
Applicable Credit to Reduce Gift Tax

Continuing with the facts of Example 12.3.2 and 12.3.4, Sophia has paid gift taxes in the past on the prior years' gifts. However, she does not want to pay any gift tax this year, so she uses her applicable credit. How much of the applicable credit will she use in 2025?

SOLUTION

Her transfer tax is $165,300 this year. So she can use $165,300 of the applicable credit to reduce her gift tax liability to $0.

Filing Requirements for Form 709

An individual must file a gift tax return only if they made taxable gifts during the year. Note that a gift tax return does not have to be filed for gifts in the following categories:[17]

- A gift that does not exceed the annual exclusion per donee ($19,000 for 2025)
- A gift to a charity that exceeds the annual exclusion, as long as the entire value of the transfer qualifies as a charitable contribution
- A gift to a spouse, as long as the gift is not a terminable interest[18]
- A gift to a noncitizen spouse that does not exceed the annual exclusion for a noncitizen spouse ($190,000 for 2025)
- A gift that is excludable because it is for medical or educational expenses.

Tax Planning Tip

Even if a taxpayer is not required to file a gift tax return, it may be advisable to do so. If a return is filed, then the three-year statute of limitations begins to run. If a gift is not appropriately disclosed on a gift tax return, then the IRS can assess tax at any time in the future.

The due date of the gift tax return is April 15 for gifts made in the previous year. The date for filing the return can be extended for six months to October 15. If a taxpayer extends their income tax return, then the gift tax return is automatically extended also. Alternatively, the taxpayer can file Form 8892, Application for Automatic Extension of Time To File Form 709 and/or Payment of Gift/Generation-Skipping Transfer Tax, to extend the return.

For the year of death of the donor, the gift tax return for the year of death is due not later than the due date for filing the decedent's federal estate tax return (generally nine months after the date of death).

Potential Pitfall

Extending the gift tax return only extends the time to file the return. The gift tax liability must be paid by April 15.

Tax Planning Tip

Because the gift tax return is due at the same time a taxpayer's income tax return is due, a tax professional who is gathering information to complete the income tax return should also inquire about gifts made during the previous year.

The next Example emphasizes the filing requirements for the gift tax return.

EXAMPLE 12.3.6 Filing Requirements

Frank is a wealthy investor who made the following gifts in 2025:

- $18,000 to his mother
- $40,000 paid to Baptist Hospital to cover the medical costs of a colleague
- $100,000 to a trust for which his sister is the income beneficiary (value is $34,000) and his three children are the remainder beneficiaries (value is $66,000)

Does Frank need to file a gift tax return this year?

SOLUTION

Yes, Frank is required to file a gift tax return for 2025 because of the gift he made to the trust. All the other gifts are excluded from the gift tax. The $34,000 gift to his sister exceeds the $19,000 annual exclusion, so Frank has made a taxable gift of $15,000. The $22,000 gift to each child from the trust is not eligible for the annual exclusion because it is a future interest, so these are taxable gifts as well. When he files his gift tax return, he can choose to offset his gift tax liability with some of his applicable credit if he prefers.

Related exercises: Multiple Choice Question 5
Application Problem 6

---

[17]IRC §6019(a).

[18]A gift of a terminable interest means that the gift will terminate upon the occurrence of a future event. Treas. Reg. §25.6019-1(a).

PRACTICE PROBLEM 12.3.1
Calculation of Taxable Gifts

Shalin, married, has made the following gifts in 2025:

- $22,000 cash to his cousin
- $450,000 home to his father
- $50,000 stock to his wife
- $75,000 to the Salvation Army

Assume that Shalin has made no prior taxable gifts. What are Shalin's taxable gifts?

SOLUTION

$22,000 cash – $19,000 annual exclusion	$ 3,000
$450,000 home to his father – $19,000 annual exclusion	431,000
$50,000 stock to his wife – $19,000 annual exclusion	31,000
$75,000 to the Salvation Army – $19,000 annual exclusion	56,000
Total gifts	$521,000
Less: Marital deduction	(31,000)
Less: Charitable contribution deduction	(56,000)
Taxable gifts	$434,000

PRACTICE PROBLEM 12.3.2
Calculation of Transfer Tax for Current Year

Kevin has made prior taxable gifts of $600,000. His 2025 taxable gifts are $850,000. Compute the transfer tax for the current year, before the applicable credit.

SOLUTION

Kevin's total taxable gifts for this year are:

Taxable gifts for current year	$ 850,000
Plus: Taxable gifts for prior years	600,000
Total taxable gifts	$1,450,000

The transfer tax on the total taxable gifts of $1,450,000, using the transfer tax rate schedule, is computed as:

$$\$345,800 + [(\$1,450,000 - \$1,000,000) \times 40\%] = \$525,800$$

The transfer tax on the taxable gifts for prior years of $600,000, using the transfer tax rate schedule, is computed as:

$$\$155,800 + [(\$600,000 - \$500,000) \times 37\%] = \$192,800$$

His transfer tax for the current year is:

Transfer tax on total taxable gifts	$525,800
Less: Transfer tax on taxable gifts made prior to current year	(192,800)
Transfer tax for current year	$333,000

INTERACTIVE SELF-SCORING QUIZZES

12.4 Estate Tax—General Rules

LEARNING OBJECTIVE 4

Determine the value of the assets that are included in the gross estate.

VIDEO CONTENT

The estate tax is potentially triggered when an individual passes away. The estate tax applies only to very wealthy individuals such as Ben and Casey whose estates are valued above the applicable credit exclusion. While in this chapter we focus on the economic consequences of the estate tax, when advising your clients, you need to ensure that they have planned appropriately for other consequences of death, such as the following:

- Having an appropriate amount of life insurance to benefit surviving family members
- Having a will in place to ensure that assets are bequeathed as desired (When a person dies without a will, state law determines who will receive the person's assets.)
- For a person who has dependent children, having a will that specifies who will have guardianship of the children
- A living will that specifies preferred medical care in the event that the person is unable to communicate these preferences
- Taking appropriate action to minimize the assets that are part of the gross estate and the probate estate

In this section, you will learn how the *probate estate* differs from the *gross estate* and how property is valued for the gross estate.

Spotlight on the Tax Law

No Estate Tax in 2010—Is This True?

It's true! In 2010, a very unusual thing happened with the estate tax law due to tax changes made in 2001. In 2001, Congress passed the *Economic Growth and Tax Relief Reconciliation Act*. This legislation gradually reduced the estate tax rates until the estate tax was eliminated in 2010. However, the law did not make these changes permanent, so the estate tax was scheduled to return in 2011 with a top tax rate of 55%.

When the 2001 legislation was originally passed, no one thought that Congress would let the estate tax disappear for one year. Perhaps Congress would eliminate the estate tax permanently, but having the estate tax disappear for just one year created unusual, and some might say improper, incentives. In 2011, the estate tax returned for estates with an overall value greater than $1 million and with a top tax rate of 55%. So a decedent dying with a $5 million estate on December 31, 2010, would incur no estate tax liability. If that same decedent instead died one day later on January 1, 2011, $4 million would be subject to estate tax. At a rate of 55%, the estate tax liability would be $2.2 million.

Did any wealthy U.S. citizens die in 2010? Yes, one of those being George Steinbrenner, the business tycoon and long-time owner of the New York Yankees. Steinbrenner died in 2010 at the age of 80 after an extended illness. His estate is estimated to have been over $1 billion. Therefore, his family saved over $500,000,000 in estate taxes from what would have been owed had he died in 2011.* While likely not planned, the timing of his death was the best tax planning strategy Steinbrenner ever executed. Because he died in 2010, his estate escaped any estate tax liability!

*Leahey, Andrew. "Steinbrenner's Legacy Shows Importance of Federal Estate Tax." Bloomberg Tax. 7 Nov. 2023. https://news.bloombergtax.com/tax-insights-and-commentary/steinbrenners-legacy-shows-importance-of-federal-estate-tax.

Key Definitions

We begin by defining an *estate*, the *probate estate*, and the *gross estate*. An **estate** is created at the time of a person's death, and includes all assets comprising the net worth of that person, including all cash, possessions, financial investments, real estate, and any other assets that the person either owns or has a controlling interest in. The estate exists for as long as is needed to settle the legal and financial affairs of the deceased person. For some individuals, the estate will be closed after a few months, whereas for others the estate could be open for many years.

Discussion Question 6

Probate Estate vs. Gross Estate

It is important to know the difference between the probate estate and the gross estate. The **probate estate**, in general, includes assets that are held solely by the decedent and does not include assets that pass to others outside of the will, such as:

- Life insurance and annuities
- Retirement plans such as IRAs, Section 401(k) plans, and qualified retirement plans
- Property owned with **right of survivorship**, meaning that the property passes at death to the other owner(s)

The probate estate includes cash, stocks, and assets such as a residence, clothing, and jewelry. Property owned jointly as tenants by the entirety is included in the probate estate. The **executor** of the estate is appointed by the decedent's will or the court, and collects the assets of the decedent, pays the decedent's debts, and distributes the remaining assets to the beneficiaries according to the decedent's will or according to the state law governing inheritances.

The **gross estate** refers to the assets that must be included in computing the estate tax at the time of death. Property could be included in the gross estate but not in the probate estate. For example, property that was gifted shortly before death would not be in the probate estate, but the estate tax laws could require that the property be included in the gross estate.

Potential Pitfall

Do not confuse the probate estate with the gross estate. The probate estate is a collection of the decedent's possessions for legal purposes, whereas the gross estate is a measure of the value of these possessions for estate tax purposes.

EXAMPLE 12.4.1
Gross Estate vs. Probate Estate

Lillian is a U.S. citizen who died in the current tax year. At the date of her death, she owned the assets shown below with the corresponding market value. Which assets would be included in Lillian's probate estate?

Asset	Fair market value
Personal residence	$450,000
Personal assets	$ 28,000
Stocks	$600,000
Checking account	$ 13,000
Corporate bonds	$120,000
Tax-exempt bonds	$ 45,000
Roth IRA (beneficiary is son)	$530,000
Section 401(k) plan (beneficiary is daughter)	$380,000
Rental property (owned with right of survivorship with her brother)	$175,000
Life insurance policy—term (beneficiary is husband)	$500,000
LLC interest (owned 60% as a tenancy in common with sister; full FMV is shown)	$ 80,000

SOLUTION

The assets that are not included in the probate estate are as follows:

Roth IRA	Passes directly to her son
Section 401(k) plan	Passes directly to her daughter
Rental property	100% passes directly to her brother because it was owned with right of survivorship
Life insurance	$500,000 proceeds pass directly to her husband

Therefore, the probate estate consists of the following assets:

	FMV
Personal residence	$ 450,000
Personal assets	28,000
Stocks	600,000
Checking account	13,000
Corporate bonds	120,000
Tax-exempt bonds	45,000
LLC interest	48,000*
Total probate estate	$1,304,000

*Only 60% of the LLC interest is included in the probate estate because Lillian's sister continues to own the other 40%, as the LLC interest was held as a tenancy in common.

Related exercises: Discussion Question 7
Application Problem 7

Valuation Rules

Two special valuation rules apply to the estate tax: the *alternate valuation date (AVD)* and the *special valuation rule for certain realty.*

Alternate Valuation Date (AVD)

In general, property is included in the gross estate at its fair market value on the date of death. However, the executor can sometimes elect to have the property valued on the **alternate valuation date (AVD),** which is the date six months after the decedent's date of death. If the property is distributed before the AVD, then the basis on the date the property is distributed is the beneficiary's basis. The election to use the alternate valuation date is only available if two conditions are met:

- The gross estate is lower on the AVD than on the date of death, *and*
- The estate tax payable is lower if using the AVD than if using the date of death.[19]

The AVD option was created by Congress to benefit estates where the value of the estate declines in the months following the date of death, so the estate tax is not based on values that no longer exist when the estate tax is paid. The next example illustrates the use of the alternate valuation date.

[19]IRC §2032.

EXAMPLE 12.4.2 Use of the Alternate Valuation Date

Mario died on October 17 of Year 10. The fair market value of his gross estate on the date of death was $19,000,000. In January of Year 11, the stock market underwent a significant correction and lost 22% of its value. On April 17, Year 11, the FMV of Mario's gross estate is $16,800,000. If the AVD is elected, the estate tax payable will be $880,000 less than if the date of death value is used. Can the executor elect the AVD for Mario's estate?

SOLUTION

Mario's executor can elect the AVD because both required conditions are satisfied:

- The gross estate is less on the AVD ($16,800,000) than on the date of death ($19,000,000), and
- The estate tax is $880,000 lower on the AVD than on the date of death.

In the following Example, we demonstrate how distributions are handled when the AVD is elected and the property is distributed before the AVD.

EXAMPLE 12.4.3 Distribution before the AVD Date

Assume the same facts as in Example 12.4.2. One of the assets owned by Mario was stock in Target, which was distributed by the estate to Mario's son on February 21, Year 11. The stock had the following fair market values:

October 17, Year 10	$470,000
February 21, Year 11	$410,000
April 17, Year 11	$390,000

a. What is the son's basis in the Target stock?

b. What would be the son's basis if the FMV of the stock in April 17, Year 11, was $500,000?

SOLUTION

a. The AVD is six months after the date of death. If the AVD is elected and the property is distributed before the AVD, then the basis on the date the property is distributed is the beneficiary's basis. Therefore, the son's basis in the property is $410,000, the fair market value on the date of distribution.

b. The solution would be the same, even though the value of the stock is higher on the AVD ($500,000) than on the date of death ($470,000). The criteria that must be met to elect the AVD apply to the total gross estate, not each asset.

Why **Why is the use of the alternate valuation date limited to estates where the gross estate and estate tax payable are lower if using the AVD than if using the date of death?** An important basis rule for property transactions is that the basis of property that is inherited by the beneficiary of an estate is the property's FMV. This creates tax planning opportunities because there is a tax-free step up in basis to FMV for the property. For example, assume that on the date of death, a decedent owns stock with an adjusted basis of $12,000 and a FMV of $20,000. The beneficiary who inherits the stock will have a basis in the stock of $20,000. The $8,000 of unrealized appreciation in the stock is not recognized on the final income tax return of the decedent, the estate income tax return, or the beneficiary's income tax return. Thus, for income tax purposes, one should not sell appreciated property shortly before death. On the other hand, there is a step-down in basis to FMV for loss property at the date of death, so property with an unrealized loss should be disposed of before death.

The tax-free step up in basis at death is the reason for restrictions on the use of the AVD. Remember that most individuals are not subject to the estate tax, whether property is valued at the date of death or the AVD. Therefore, if the gross estate had a higher value on the AVD than the date of death, but the estate tax was $0 in either case, then the executor would elect the AVD so the beneficiaries would have a higher basis in the inherited property. The restrictions on the use of the AVD prevents the executor from doing this.

The next Example shows some situations in which the election of the AVD is not allowed.

EXAMPLE 12.4.4
Restriction on Election of AVD

Ross died on May 12 of the current tax year with the following estate tax characteristics:

	May 12	November 12
Gross estate	$2,000,000	$2,300,000
Estate tax	$ 0	$ 0

a. Can the executor elect the AVD for Ross's estate?

b. Would the answer change if the value of the gross estate on November 12 was $1,900,000?

SOLUTION

a. The executor cannot elect the AVD because the value of the gross estate is not lower on the AVD than it is on the date of death. While that is sufficient to disallow the AVD, note that the estate tax is also not lower on the AVD ($0) than on the date of death ($0).

b. The gross estate is lower on the AVD than on the date of death, so the first condition to elect the AVD is satisfied. However, the second condition is not met because the estate tax is not lower on the AVD ($0) than on the date of death ($0).

Related exercises: Discussion Question 8
Multiple Choice Question 6
Application Problems 8, 9

Special Valuation for Certain Realty

An executor can elect to value certain realty used in farming or in connection with a closely held business at a **special use valuation**. This special rule permits the realty to be valued based on its current use rather than its true FMV, which would be based on its best and higher use. The decrease in value based on this rule cannot exceed $1,420,000 (2025). To qualify for the valuation reduction, all of the following conditions must be met:[20]

- The decedent must be a citizen or resident of the United States.
- The realty must be located in the United States.
- The realty must be used in an active farming operation or in an active business by the decedent or a family member on the date of death.
- The decedent or a family member materially participated in the farm or business that uses the real estate for at least five years during the eight-year period before the date of death.
- The value of the realty (less any mortgages) for which special use valuation was elected was 25% or more of the value of the gross estate (less mortgages on the realty).
- The value of the realty and personalty (less any mortgages) used in an active farming or business operation must constitute a substantial portion of the gross estate, measured as 50% or more of the value of the gross estate (less mortgages on the realty).
- The family member must continue to use the realty in a qualified use (that is, active farm or business) for 10 years after the decedent's death. If not, then a recapture tax must be paid.

Family Member A qualifying family member includes the following:

- Ancestors of the decedent
- Spouse of the decedent

[20] IRC §2032A.

- Any lineal descendants (and their spouses) of the decedent, such as children, grandchildren, and great-grandchildren, as well as lineal descendants (and their spouses) of the decedent's spouse
- Any lineal descendants (and their spouses) of the decedent's parents, which would include brothers and sisters, aunts and uncles, nieces and nephews, and cousins

Recapture Tax The executor must sign a recapture agreement when the special use valuation is elected. The **recapture agreement** requires that if the qualified heir disposes of the realty or ceases using the realty for a qualified purpose in the 10 years after the death of the decedent, then additional tax will be due. The recapture tax does not apply if the family member dies before the 10-year period ends, or the family member transfers the realty to another qualified family member. The amount of tax that must be recaptured is the amount of estate tax that was saved because of the reduced valuation of the realty.

Why **Why does Congress permit special use valuation of real estate used in farming or business activities?** Assume that a family has operated a farm for over 70 years, and the farm is currently owned by Martina. The farm includes 150 acres of real estate, all of which is used in the farming business. The land is located 25 miles from the downtown area of Nashville, Tennessee, one of the fastest growing cities in the United States. As Nashville has grown and developers have built more office buildings and subdivisions in the suburbs, the value of real estate has increased significantly. Developers have offered Martina $50,000 per acre, or $7,500,000. Assume that Martina dies this year, and her family is committed to continuing the farming business rather than selling the land. While the land's true FMV may be $7,500,000, it is not worth that much if it continues to be used as a farm. This is the situation for which Congress allows a valuation discount. Otherwise, the family may have to sell the land in order to have enough cash to pay the estate tax on the true FMV.

EXAMPLE 12.4.5
Special Use Valuation

Samuel owns a closely held business that manufactures engine parts for Ford automobiles. He has managed the business for the last 20 years. During the current year, Samuel dies, and his three children are committed to continue operating the business. The business is located on 25 acres of property that has appreciated significantly in value over the last 20 years and is now valued at $10,000,000. Land used in similar businesses would be valued at $7,500,000. Assume that the 50% and 25% valuation tests are met for the 25 acres. If the executor of Samuel's estate elects special use valuation, how would this asset be valued in the gross estate?

SOLUTION

The realty qualifies for special use valuation because Samuel materially participated in the manufacturing on the date of death and for at least five of the eight years before death. Additionally, the property continues to be used by a qualified family member, the children, in a qualified use. While the executor would like to value the property at its current use value of $7,500,000, this would be a valuation discount of $2,500,000 ($10,000,000 – $7,500,000), and the maximum discount permitted in 2025 is $1,420,000. Therefore, the property will be valued at $8,580,000 ($10,000,000 – $1,420,000).

Related exercises: Discussion Question 9
Brief Exercise 7

PRACTICE PROBLEM 12.4.1

Gross Estate vs. Probate Estate

Devon, a U.S. citizen, died in the current tax year. At the date of his death, he owned the assets shown with the corresponding market values. Which assets would be included in Devon's probate estate?

Asset	FMV
Personal residence	$395,000
Bank accounts	$ 22,000
Pension plan (beneficiary is daughter)	$325,000
Partnership interest (owned 55% as a tenancy in common with brother; full FMV is shown)	$100,000

SOLUTION

The probate estate consists of the following assets:

Personal residence	$395,000
Bank accounts	22,000
Partnership interest	55,000*
Total probate estate	$472,000

The pension plan will pass directly to his daughter.

*Only 55% of the partnership interest is included in the probate estate because his brother continues to own the other 45%, as this interest was held as a tenancy in common.

PRACTICE PROBLEM 12.4.2

Use of the Alternate Valuation Date

Manuel died on April 8, Year 6, and bequeathed his entire $14,500,000 estate to his daughter, Maria. His estate included investment real estate that had a tax basis to Manuel of $480,000. This property was distributed to Maria four months after Manuel's death. The executor of Manuel's estate validly elected the alternate valuation date. Fair market values for the real estate were:

At the date of Manuel's death	$600,000
Four months after Manuel's death	$610,000
Six months after Manuel's death	$605,000

What is Maria's basis in the real estate?

SOLUTION

The alternate valuation date (AVD) is six months after the date of death. This date is used if the AVD is properly elected by the executor and the property is distributed after the AVD. Because the AVD was elected and the property was distributed after the date of death but before the AVD, the date of distribution value of $610,000 is Maria's basis in the real estate.

INTERACTIVE SELF-SCORING QUIZZES

12.5 Inclusions in the Gross Estate

LEARNING OBJECTIVE 5

Identify the property that is included in the gross estate.

VIDEO CONTENT

In this section, we discuss the assets that must be included in the gross estate, and in the following section, we discuss deductions allowed against the gross estate. From a big-picture perspective, it is simple to determine what is included in the gross estate: all assets owned by the decedent at their death. This includes investments such as stocks and bonds, ownership in businesses such as partnerships and S corporations, land, and other real estate. It also includes more basic assets, such as clothes, cars, boats, furniture, and other items owned and used in one's personal life.[21]

In spite of this simple perspective, there are certain assets for which the laws governing inclusion in the gross estate are more complex, and those are the items discussed in this section. They include as life insurance, jointly-owned property, retained interests, and transfers within three years of death.

Life Insurance

Returning to Ben from the chapter introduction, assume that at the time of his death, he owns an insurance policy on his life for $1,000,000. Is the $1,000,000 included in Ben's gross estate? It is if Ben has an incident of ownership in the policy at the time of his death. An incident of ownership includes the right to:[22]

- Change the beneficiary
- Borrow against the policy's cash value
- Assign the policy to a new owner
- Surrender the policy for cash
- Cancel the policy

If Ben has any one or more of these rights, then the $1,000,000 is included in his gross estate.

Tax Planning Tip

Many wealthy individuals have a dilemma with life insurance planning for estate purposes. On the one hand, they do not want the life insurance proceeds included in their gross estates. On the other hand, to achieve that, they must relinquish control of the policies, and they do not want to give up that control. For example, suppose that several wealthy individuals make a university the beneficiary of their life insurance policies, but they want the power to change the beneficiary in the future if the university does something they disagree with it. Unfortunately, they cannot keep the control and also keep the proceeds out of their gross estates. Life insurance trusts can be used to do some planning in this area, but even there, the individual cannot control the life insurance trust.[23]

In addition to incident of ownership, a second reason that life insurance proceeds could be included in the gross estate is that the decedent's estate is the beneficiary of the policy.

The next two Examples illustrate how life insurance is treated for estate planning purposes.

[21] IRC §2033.

[22] IRC §2042.

[23] Life insurance trusts can be useful for estate planning, but the complexity is beyond the scope of our coverage.

EXAMPLE 12.5.1
Life Insurance—Ownership

Fynn, who is 40 years old, owns a $2,000,000 life insurance policy on his life, and he names his spouse as the beneficiary. Fynn has given up certain ownership rights in the policy, but he has retained the right to change the beneficiary. He wants to keep this right in case his spouse ever decides to divorce him, in which case he would change the beneficiary. Once Fynn reaches the age of 70, he plans to give up all incidents of ownership to keep the proceeds out of his gross estate. Fynn unexpectedly dies in a plane crash this year. Is the $2,000,000 included in his gross estate?

SOLUTION

The $2,000,000 is included in his gross estate because Fynn had at least one incident of ownership in the policy, the right to change the beneficiary.

EXAMPLE 12.5.2
Life Insurance—Beneficiary

Assume the same facts as in Example 12.5.1, except that Fynn has placed the insurance into a life insurance trust and has no incidents of ownership in the policy. His spouse is still his primary beneficiary, and his contingent beneficiary is his estate. The contingent beneficiary receives the proceeds if the primary beneficiary is also deceased. Fynn and his wife have two young children, and they want the insurance proceeds passing directly to the children. Unfortunately, his wife was also on the plane that crashed. Will the insurance proceeds be included in Fynn's gross estate?

SOLUTION

Yes, the $2,000,000 will be included in his gross estate because these funds were paid directly to his estate by the insurance company.

Related exercises: Multiple Choice Question 5
Brief Exercise 8

Potential Pitfall

Wealthy individuals may use an attorney to set up a life insurance trust for them to assist with estate planning. For the trust to be effective, the beneficiary of the life insurance policy must be the life insurance trust. Sometimes, the individual forgets to change their beneficiary on the policy to the trust, which defeats the whole purpose of the trust. Make sure your clients don't fall into this trap.

Jointly-Owned Property

We discussed jointly-owned property in relation to the gift tax earlier in this chapter. Now we follow up that discussion to explain the estate tax consequences of jointly-owned property. Property can be jointly owned in three main ways: *joint tenants with right of survivorship*, *tenancy in common*, and *tenancy by the entirety*.[24] See **Illustration 12.4** for a summary of the differences in these forms of ownership.

ILLUSTRATION 12.4 Summary of Ownership and Inclusion

Type of ownership	Married/ unmarried	Amount included in gross estate	Included in probate estate?
Joint tenants with right of survivorship	Married	50% of the FMV	No
Joint tenants with right of survivorship	Unmarried	Percent of FMV of decedent's contribution to total cost of the property	No
Tenancy in common	Married or unmarried	FMV of property × % of property owned by the decedent	Yes
Tenancy by the entirety	Married	50% of the FMV in estate of first spouse to die	No

[24]IRC §2040.

Right of Survivorship

If property is owned by **joint tenants with right of survivorship**, the property passes directly to the other owner when one owner passes away. Therefore, the property does not have to be included in the probate estate. For married owners, 50% of the FMV of the property is included in the estate of the first spouse to die. For unmarried owners, the estate tax consequences provide that 100% of the value of the property is included in the gross estate of the first owner to die, unless the executor can establish that the decedent did not pay the entire cost of the property. In that case, the estate includes the following amount in the gross estate:

$$\text{FMV of property} \times \frac{\text{Original cost paid by decedent}}{\text{Total cost of the property}}$$

Tenancy in Common

With a **tenancy in common,** the property does not pass to the other owner at death. Rather, the percentage of the property owned by the decedent passes into the probate estate, and the decedent's will determines who receives the property. For estate tax purposes, the rule is the same for the gross estate, and the estate includes the following amount:

$$\text{FMV of property} \times \text{\% of property owned by the decedent}$$

Tenancy by the Entirety

A **tenancy by the entirety** is a tenancy in which property is jointly owned by a married couple. When one spouse dies, the property immediately passes to the other spouse and need not go through the probate process. For estate tax purposes, 50% of the value goes into the estate of the first spouse to die.

The following Example explores situations with jointly-owned property.

EXAMPLE 12.5.3
Joint Ownership of Property

Camila and Michael owned land jointly. Camila died this year, and on her date of death, the property was valued at $700,000. When the property was originally purchased eight years ago, Camila paid $200,000 of the total cost of $500,000. How much of the land will be included in Camila's gross estate in the following situations?

a. Camila and Michael are work colleagues, and they owned the property with right of survivorship.

b. Camila and Michael are work colleagues, and they owned the property as joint tenants in common.

c. Camila and Michael are married, and they owned the property in a tenancy by the entirety.

SOLUTION

We begin by computing the percentage that Camila paid for the property, which is 40% ($200,000/$500,000).

a. The general rule for right of survivorship is that 100% of the value of the property ($700,000) would be included in Camila's estate. However, because Camila paid for 40% of the property, only 40% of the value, or $280,000 (40% × $700,000), is included in her gross estate.

b. With a joint tenancy in common, 40% of the value, or $280,000 (40% × $700,000), would be included in Camila's gross estate.

c. With a tenancy by the entirety, 50% of the value, or $350,000 (50% × $700,000), would be included in Camila's gross estate.

Related exercises: Discussion Question 10
Multiple Choice Question 8
Application Problem 10

Potential Pitfall

For jointly-owned property, some portion of the property is almost always included in the estate of the first owner to die. Does that mean that only the remaining percentage of the property will be included in the remaining owner's estate? For example, if 40% of the property in Example 12.5.3 is included in Camila's estate, does this mean that only the other 60% will be included in Michael's estate when he dies? No, that is not case. Michael now owns 100% of the property, so the entire value of the property will be included in his gross estate on his death.

Retained Interests

Special estate tax rules apply to retained interests. With a **retained interest,** an individual has transferred property to another person but has retained some aspect of ownership in the property or the right to use the property. Because the individual has retained this interest, at death, the property may be included in the individual's gross estate even though legally the property is titled in another person's name.[25] There are three types of retained interests:

1. Retained life interest
2. Retained power to designate who enjoys a benefit from the property
3. Retained right to revoke the transfer of the property

Life Interest

A **life interest** is an interest in property that is retained for the life of the transferor. For example, a life interest in a residence means that the transferor can occupy the residence for life even though the property itself has already been transferred to another individual. Congress believes that retaining the right to use property is significant enough to deem that appropriate ownership has not been transferred.

The following Example explores the life interest in property.

EXAMPLE 12.5.4
Life Interest

Colton is 80 years old and lives in Hawaii in a home with a value of $4,000,000. He planned to bequeath this home to his two daughters at his death, but decided this year that he would rather gift the property to them now. He has lived in the home for 35 years and wants to continue to live in the home until death. Therefore, he retains the right to live in his home, even though his daughters now own the home. What are the gift and estate tax consequences of this transfer?

SOLUTION

Colton has a retained life interest in the property. As such, for gift and estate tax purposes, the transfer to his daughters is ignored. There is no gift tax on the transfer because it was not a completed gift. When Colton dies, the FMV of the property at the date of his death will be included in his gross estate.

Related exercise: Discussion Question 11

Power to Designate

The power to designate possession or enjoyment of property or income can also cause the property to be included in the gross estate. This also includes a power created by someone else that could have been exercised in the decedent's favor before death. There are two types of powers of appointment:

[25]IRC §2036.

- A **general power of appointment** allows an individual to designate property owned by the creator of the power to the recipient of the power, to the recipient's creditors, or to other individuals. If the recipient of the power dies while retaining the general power, the property subject to the appointment is included in the decedent's gross estate.[26]
- A **special power of appointment** does not allow the recipient of the power to designate property to the recipient of the power or the recipient's creditors. The property can be appointed only to other individuals. Therefore, if the recipient of the power dies while retaining the special power, the property subject to the appointment is not included in the recipient's gross estate.[27]

The following Example shows how powers of appointment determine which assets are included in the gross estate.

EXAMPLE 12.5.5
Powers of Appointment

Juliana owns 100 acres of land with a fair market value of $500,000. Juliana gave Paulo a general power of appointment that permitted Paulo to transfer ownership to himself or to one of his three children. Paulo died during the current year, and at his death, he had not exercised his power of appointment.

a. What are the estate tax consequences to Paulo?

b. How would your answer change if Paulo held a special power of appointment and could only transfer ownership to one of his three children?

c. Same as **a**, but instead of Paulo dying, Juliana dies before Paulo appoints the property. What are the tax consequences to Juliana and to Paulo?

SOLUTION

a. At any time up to the moment of Paulo's death, he had the power to transfer ownership of the land to himself and fully control it. Therefore, it is treated as if Paulo did own the property at his death, and the $500,000 value of the land would be included in his gross estate.

b. In this situation, Paulo never had the opportunity to transfer ownership to himself. Therefore, the value of the land is not included in his gross estate.

c. Juliana retained ownership of the property at her date of death, so the land would be included in her gross estate at $500,000. There are no tax consequences to Paulo because he lost the power to appoint the property once Juliana died.

Related exercise: Brief Exercise 9

Revocations

Some individuals who transfer property to others retain the right to revoke the transfer; this is often done through a revocable trust. Revocable trusts may be set up to provide more privacy than wills or to avoid probate for the assets in the trust. If the transfer is still revocable on the date of the transferor's death, the assets are included in the decedent's assets. Similar to life insurance and powers of appointment, if a revocable transfer is made irrevocable within three years of death, the property is still included in the decedent's estate (see next section).

[26]IRC §2041(b).

[27]Treas. Reg §20.2041-1(c)(1)(a).

Transfers within Three Years of Death

If the retained element on any of the following gifts is released within three years of death, then the value of the gift is included in the gross estate:

- Removing the retained interest on a transfer
- Making a revocable transfer irrevocable
- Removing all incidents of ownership on a life insurance policy

The property is included at the date of death at FMV. Additionally, the **gross-up provision** states that the gift tax paid on a gift is included in the estate for any gifts made within three years of death.

Why **Why are certain gifts made within three years of death pulled back into the gross estate even though they were not legally owned by the decedent on the date of death?** We explained previously that individuals often want to transfer property to others but maintain some level of control over the transfer so that the individual can cancel the transfer and take the property back should they choose to do so. Returning to Example 12.5.4, Colton retained the right to live in his home until death even though he transferred ownership of the property to his children. Assume that Colton later is diagnosed with an incurable disease, and he knows he is not likely to live more than a year. Knowing the negative estate tax consequences of keeping a retained interest in the house, Colton could release the retained interest a few months before his death, and then on the date of his death, he would not hold a retained interest. However, because he released it just a short time before death (up to three years), then the estate tax law includes it in his gross estate anyway. Individuals could take similar actions shortly before death by making an irrevocable transfer revocable or by transferring ownership of a life insurance policy to someone else.

Why **Why is the gift tax paid on all gifts within three years of death pulled back into the gross estate?** With regard to the **Why** just discussed, one may wonder why it matters that a transfer is subject to the gift tax or the estate tax. Because this is a unified tax, aren't the overall tax consequences the same regardless of whether the property is transferred as a gift or at death? The tax consequences may be better if gifts are made during one's life, as shown in the following Example.

EXAMPLE 12.5.6 Gift Tax Paid within Three Years of Death

Return to the facts of Benjamin and Casey from the chapter introduction. Assume that in 2021, Benjamin was 88 years old and had a net worth of $50 million. Based on several health conditions, he did not think it was likely he would live for more than five years. Therefore, he made the following gifts over the next four years before he passed away on October 7, 2025:

Date of gift	FMV of gift	Gift tax paid
December 31, 2021	$5,000,000	$2,000,000
December 31, 2022	$4,000,000	$1,600,000
December 31, 2023	$6,000,000	$2,400,000
December 31, 2024	$5,000,000	$2,000,000
September 30, 2025	$8,000,000	$3,200,000

a. How much of the total gift amount is included in Benjamin's gross estate?

b. How much of the gift tax paid is included in Benjamin's gross estate?

c. Did Benjamin reduce his overall gift and estate tax liability from what it would have been if he had not made the gifts?

SOLUTION

a. None of the gifts made are included in Benjamin's gross estate. None of these gifts involved a retained interest that had been changed or canceled within three years of death.

b. Benjamin must include any gift tax paid on gifts made within three years of death in his gross estate, which would be the gifts made in 2022, 2023, 2024, and 2025. The total gift tax included in his gross estate is $9,200,000 ($1,600,000 + $2,400,000 + $2,000,000 + $3,200,000).

c. Benjamin did receive an overall tax savings for the gifts made, but only for the gift made in 2021. The $2,000,000 of gift taxes paid in 2021 were never subject to the gift tax. These funds were paid to the IRS for his 2021 gift taxes, and they were not pulled into his gross estate by the three-year rule because they were made more than three years before the date of death. Assuming his marginal unified tax rate is 40%, his tax savings are $800,000 ($2,000,000 × 40%).

If Benjamin had not made the $5,000,000 gift in 2021, the $5,000,000 would have been include in his gross estate when he died. Additionally, the $2,000,000 of gift taxes paid in 2021 would have been in his gross estate and subject to the estate tax.

Tax Planning Tip

As Example 12.5.6 demonstrates, an individual who is subject to the gift tax can reduce their overall unified tax liability by making gifts more than three years before the date of death, because the gift tax paid escapes taxation under both the gift tax and the estate tax.

Potential Pitfall

While making gifts more than three years before death may reduce the overall unified taxes paid, if the property gift is highly appreciated, the unified tax savings may be offset by increased income taxes that will be paid later by the beneficiary. If the property is gifted, the donee's basis in the property will be the donor's basis. However, if the property is bequeathed at death, the beneficiary's basis is the donor's FMV at death. Return to the facts of Example 12.5.6. Assume that Benjamin's basis in the property contributed in 2021 was $400,000, and its FMV was still $5,000,000. If Benjamin held this property until death and its FMV was still $5,000,000, then the beneficiary's basis in the property would be its FMV of $5,000,000. However, if the property was gifted in 2021, the donee's basis would be $400,000. If the donee's LTCG rate is 20%, then when the property is sold, the donee will pay an additional $920,000 in income tax ([$5,000,000 FMV − $400,000 donee's basis] × 20%) compared to that due if the property had been bequeathed ($0).

The next Example reviews the rules for what type of prior transfers must be included in the gross estate.

EXAMPLE 12.5.7 Transfers before Death

In Year 23, Iris transferred ownership of a life insurance policy on her life to her daughter. She also transferred Google stock with a FMV of $2,000,000 to her daughter. Iris paid gift tax of $820,000 on these transfers. Iris died in Year 25, and the daughter received life insurance proceeds of $1,000,000. What are the estate tax consequences of these transfers, if any?

SOLUTION

Iris transferred ownership in the life insurance policy to her daughter within three years of death, so the $1,000,000 of life insurance proceeds is included in Iris's estate. The gift tax paid of $820,000 was also paid within three years of death, so it is also included in Iris's gross estate. However, the Google stock is not included in her estate because Iris did not retain any interest in the ownership of that property.

Related exercises: Brief Exercise 10
Application Problem 11
Tax Planning Problem 3

PRACTICE PROBLEM 12.5.1
Joint Ownership of Property

Cayton and Rhys, who file as married filing jointly, own land jointly with a fair market value of $160,000. Cayton contributed $75,000 and Rhys contributed $25,000 to the purchase price two years ago.

a. If Cayton dies in the current year, what is included in her gross estate?

b. If Rhys dies two years later, when the land has a fair market value of $180,000, what is included in his gross estate?

SOLUTION

a. In a tenancy by the entirety, property is jointly owned by a married couple. When one spouse dies, the property immediately passes to the other spouse and need not go through the probate process. For estate tax purposes, 50% of the value goes into the estate of the first spouse to die. Therefore, $80,000 ($160,000 × 50%) is included in Cayton's estate.

b. When Rhys dies, Rhys owns 100% of the property, so the entire value of the property will be included in his gross estate at $180,000.

PRACTICE PROBLEM 12.5.2
Transfer within Three Years of Death

Krishna owned his principal residence and transferred all incidents of ownership in the home to Mounica, his daughter, two years before he died. Krishna reserved the right to continue to live in this home until his death. At the time of the gift, Krishna paid $28,000 in gift taxes. When Krishna died, the FMV of the home was $650,000. What amount was included in Krishna's gross estate?

SOLUTION

Krishna's estate included the $650,000 value of the home and the gift taxes paid of $28,000 because the gift was made within three years of Krishna's death. Krishna had a retained interest in the home because he retained the right to live in the home until his death.

INTERACTIVE SELF-SCORING QUIZZES

12.6 Deductions from the Gross Estate

LEARNING OBJECTIVE 6

Determine the deductions that can reduce the gross estate.

VIDEO CONTENT

In the previous section, you learned about the items that must be included in the gross estate. In this section, we review the expenditures that can be deducted from the gross estate. Make sure you have the proper mindset for understanding these deductions—that is, the estate tax is not an income tax, but a wealth tax. The deductions are expenditures that reduce net worth.

Marital Deduction

In order to avoid taxing a married couple's estate twice, a deduction is provided for a bequest to a surviving spouse. To qualify for the marital deduction, the spouse must receive property outright and be able to control its ultimate destination. Most of the marital deduction rules are straightforward, but keep the following in mind:[28]

[28] IRC §2056.

- Property that passes to the surviving spouse because it is owned jointly with the decedent qualifies for the marital deduction.
- The net value of property subject to a mortgage that is transferred to the surviving spouse qualifies for the marital deduction.
- Property must be included in the gross estate for a marital deduction to be allowed.
- The deduction is unlimited in amount and is equal to the FMV of the property transferred to the spouse less the annual exclusion amount.
- No marital deduction is allowed for noncitizen spouses. An exception to this rule is a transfer to a qualified domestic trust, which assures estate tax imposition upon a noncitizen spouse's death. Additionally, an annual exclusion for estate transfers to noncitizen spouses of $190,000 (2025) is permitted.
- Property rights that are terminable do not qualify. A terminable interest is an interest that will terminate or fail in the future due to a contingency or to the passage of time—as, for example, when a decedent has granted the spouse the right to occupy a residence until such time as the spouse remarries.

Qualified Terminable Interest Property (QTIP)

Qualified terminable interest property (QTIP) *will* qualify for the marital deduction. For a terminable interest to be QTIP, some or all of the deceased spouse's property is transferred after death into a trust and the following conditions must be met:[29]

- An election is made by the executor of the estate to use the marital deduction for a transfer to a surviving spouse of less than a complete interest in the trust.
- The surviving spouse must receive all the trust income at least annually for the spouse's life.
- No individual has power to appoint any of the property in the trust to any person other than the surviving spouse (during the spouse's life).
- The decedent's will determines how the corpus of the trust will be distributed when the surviving spouse dies.
- The executor agrees in the QTIP election that the property must be included in the surviving spouse's estate at its FMV on the date of death of the surviving spouse.[30]

The following Example shows which items can be used in computing the marital deduction.

EXAMPLE 12.6.1
Transfers to a Spouse

Marquis dies during 2025, and his will provides the following:

- $500,000 of Treasury Bonds to his spouse
- His spouse can continue to live in their residence, valued at $1,400,000, until she remarries. If she remarries, then ownership of the property will transfer to his children.
- $1,000,000 donation to United Way, a qualified charity
- The remainder of his assets consist of $20,000,000 of stock in Meta. This stock is placed in a trust, with the income from the trust paid to his surviving spouse each year. At her death, the remainder of the trust will be transferred to his children and grandchildren.

Marquis also owned land in joint tenancy with his spouse that had a value of $400,000. How much will the marital deduction be for Marquis's estate assuming the executor makes an election to maximize the use of his applicable credit?

[29]IRC §2044.

[30]IRC §2056(b)(7).

SOLUTION

Marquis will receive a marital deduction of $20,681,000, determined as follows:

- Treasury Bonds — $481,000 ($500,000 – $19,000 annual exclusion)
- Meta stock — $20,000,000
- Land (joint tenancy) — $200,000 ($400,000 × 50%)

The estate does not receive a marital deduction for the value of the residence because the interest of Marquis's spouse in the property will terminate if she remarries. The estate does receive a marital deduction for the Meta stock of $20,000,000 because the trust qualifies as a QTIP:

- An election is made by the executor of the estate to qualify the trust as a QTIP.
- The surviving spouse will receive all the trust income at least annually for the spouse's life (even if she remarries).
- The decedent's will indicates that the corpus will be paid to Marquis's children and grandchildren after the death of the spouse.
- The executor agrees with the QTIP election that the Meta stock must be included in the surviving spouse's estate at its FMV on the date of the spouse's death.

Related exercises: Discussion Question 12
Multiple Choice Question 9
Brief Exercise 11

Debts and Claims against the Estate

Debts of the estate, such as mortgages, credit card debt, automobile loans, and accrued property and income taxes, are allowed as deductions against the gross estate.

Charitable Contributions

Deductions for charitable contributions are allowed without limitation. Just as for the gift tax, deductions for charitable contributions to foreign charities are permitted. No deduction is allowed for contributions to nongovernment or non-church-owned cemeteries.[31] The deduction is not allowed unless the contribution was required by the decedent's will. However, the will can direct the executor or another person to select the charity that receives the donation.[32]

Final Expenses

Expenses incurred to wrap up the final legal and administration expenses of the decedent's life are deductible against the gross estate. Examples include: [33]

- Funeral expenses, but not the cost of the burial lot
- Estate and inheritance taxes paid to state and local governments[34]
- Administration expenses, including attorneys' and accountants' fees, executor fees, and court costs. The executor has the option of deducting administration expenses on the

[31]Rev. Rul. 67-170, 1967-1 CB 272.

[32]IRC §2055.

[33]IRC §2053.

[34]IRC §2508.

estate tax return (Form 706, United States Estate (and Generation-Skipping Transfer) Tax Return) or the estate's income tax return (Form 1041, U.S. Income Tax Return for Estates and Trusts), but not on both. If deducting on the income tax return, the executor must indicate on that return that the deduction will not also be taken on the estate tax return.

- Medical expenses. The executor has a similar option for medical expenses that were incurred before the date of death and paid after the date of death; the executor can elect to deduct these on the estate tax return (Form 706) or the decedent's final income tax return (Form 1040), but not on both.

Related exercise: Multiple Choice Question 10

Casualty and Theft Losses

Casualty and theft losses are deductible without any floor limitation, meaning that the reductions for the $100 floor and 10% of AGI do not apply. The executor has the option of deducting casualty and theft losses on the estate tax return (Form 706) or the estate's income tax return (Form 1041), but not on both. Two conditions must be met for a loss to be deductible:

- The loss must be incurred during the administration of the estate. If the casualty loss was incurred before the date of death, then if it is deductible, it is on the decedent's final tax return (Form 1040).
- The casualty must be attributable to a federally declared disaster area.

See Illustration 12.5 for a table that summarizes the elections that the executor has with respect to deductions.

ILLUSTRATION 12.5 Executor Elections

Executor Elections with Respect to Deductions		
Deduction type	**Option 1**	**Option 2**
Administration expenses	Form 706, Estate Tax Return	Form 1041, Estate Income Tax Return
Medical expenses incurred before death, paid after death	Form 706, Estate Tax Return	Form 1040, Decedent's Final Income Tax Return
Casualty losses	Form 706, Estate Tax Return	Form 1041, Estate Income Tax Return

In the following Example, we apply the rules for computing the deductions against the gross estate.

EXAMPLE 12.6.2
Final Expenses

Ellis died during the current year on April 19, and the following expenses were incurred during the administration of his estate:

Funeral expenses	$8,500
Burial lot	$7,200
Inheritance tax paid to the state of Kentucky	$9,300
Medical expenses	$6,900
Attorney's fees	$2,300
Court costs	$ 600
Casualty loss	$4,100

- The medical expenses were incurred in March and April of this year but were not paid until June. The executor elected to claim these expenses on the estate tax return.
- The executor elected to claim the attorney's fees and the court costs on the estate income tax return.

- The casualty was incurred in February of the current year and was part of a federally declared disaster area.

What deductions are allowed on Ellis's estate tax return?

SOLUTION

The total deductions on Ellis's estate tax return are $24,700 ($8,500 + $9,300 + $6,900).

- The funeral expenses ($8,500) are deducted on the estate tax return, but the burial lot is not allowed.
- The inheritance tax ($9,300) is deductible.
- The medical expenses ($6,900) are deductible. The executor elected to deduct them on the estate tax return, which prohibits them from being deducted on Ellis's final income tax return (Form 1040).
- The attorney's fees and court costs are not deductible on the estate tax return because the executor elected to deduct them on the estate income tax return (Form 1041).
- The casualty loss is not deductible in the estate tax return because it was incurred before the date of death. It may be deductible on Ellis's final income tax return (Form 1040).

Related exercise: Application Problem 12

PRACTICE PROBLEM 12.6.1
Marital Deduction

Franklin gifts his spouse the following assets during the year: $150,000 cash, stock with a fair market value of $45,000, and a new car with a fair market value of $65,000. Both spouses are U.S. citizens.

a. What is the amount of the marital deduction?

b. Assume the spouse receiving the gifts is not a U.S. citizen. What is the amount of the marital deduction? Is an annual exclusion allowed?

SOLUTION

a. Because both spouses are U.S. citizens, the marital deduction for gifts is unlimited. The gross gifts of $241,000 ($150,000 cash – $19,000 annual exclusion + $45,000 FMV of stock + $65,000 FMV of car) are offset by an equivalent $241,000 marital deduction.

b. No marital deduction is allowed for noncitizen spouses. An annual exclusion for estate transfers to noncitizen spouses of $190,000 (2025) is permitted.

PRACTICE PROBLEM 12.6.2
Final Expenses

Dominique died during the current year on October 31, and the following expenses were incurred during the administration of her estate:

Funeral expenses	$ 5,600
Auto loan	$18,000
Credit card debt	$ 3,500
Accountant's fees	$ 1,500
Casualty loss (occurred on November 15)	$11,000

- The executor elected to claim the accountant's fees on the estate income tax return.
- The casualty was part of a federally declared disaster area.

What deductions are allowed on Dominique's estate tax return?

SOLUTION

The total deductions on Dominique's estate tax return are $38,100 ($5,600 + $18,000 + $3,500 + $11,000).

- The funeral expenses ($5,600) are deducted on the estate tax return.
- Debts of the estate, such as mortgages, credit card debt, automobile loans, and accrued property and income taxes, are allowed as deductions against the gross estate. The $18,000 auto loan liability and the credit card debt of $3,500 are deductible.
- The accountant's fees are not deductible on the estate tax return because the executor elected to deduct them on the estate income tax return (Form 1041).
- The casualty loss ($11,000) is deductible on the estate tax return because:
  - The loss must be incurred during the administration of the estate. If the casualty loss was incurred before the date of death, then if it is deductible, it is on the decedent's final tax return (Form 1040). Dominique's loss was incurred after the date of death.
  - The casualty is attributable to a federally declared disaster area.

INTERACTIVE SELF-SCORING QUIZZES

12.7 Estate Tax Formula

LEARNING OBJECTIVE 7

Compute the estate tax using the estate tax formula.

Now that we have discussed the income and deductions that are included in computing the estate tax, in this section, we explain the formula that is used to compute the estate tax liability.

VIDEO CONTENT

Estate Tax Formula

This estate tax formula is consistent with that shown on page 1 of Form 706, United States Estate (and Generation-Skipping Transfer) Tax Return, which is shown in Illustration 12.6.

ILLUSTRATION 12.6 Form 706, United States Estate (and Generation-Skipping Transfer) Tax Return (page 1)

DOWNLOAD DOCUMENTS & TEMPLATES

Form 706 (page 1)

Form **706** (Rev. August 2019) Department of the Treasury Internal Revenue Service

United States Estate (and Generation-Skipping Transfer) Tax Return

▶ Estate of a citizen or resident of the United States (see instructions). To be filed for decedents dying after December 31, 2018.
▶ Go to *www.irs.gov/Form706* for instructions and the latest information.

OMB No. 1545-0015

Part 1—Decedent and Executor

1a Decedent's first name and middle initial (and maiden name, if any)	1b Decedent's last name			2 Decedent's social security no.
3a City, town, or post office; county; state or province; country; and ZIP or foreign postal code	3b Year domicile established	4 Date of birth		5 Date of death
6a Name of executor (see instructions)	6b Executor's address (number and street including apartment or suite no.; city, town, or post office; state or province; country; and ZIP or foreign postal code) and phone no.			
6c Executor's social security number (see instructions)	Phone no.			

6d If there are multiple executors, check here ☐ and attach a list showing the names, addresses, telephone numbers, and SSNs of the additional executors.

7a Name and location of court where will was probated or estate administered | 7b Case number

8 If decedent died testate, check here ▶ ☐ and attach a certified copy of the will. 9 If you extended the time to file this Form 706, check here ▶ ☐

10 If Schedule R-1 is attached, check here ▶ ☐ 11 If you are estimating the value of assets included in the gross estate on line 1 pursuant to the special rule of Reg. section 20.2010-2(a)(7)(ii), check here ▶ ☐

Part 2—Tax Computation

1	Total gross estate less exclusion (from Part 5—Recapitulation, item 13)			1	
2	Tentative total allowable deductions (from Part 5—Recapitulation, item 24)			2	
3a	Tentative taxable estate (subtract line 2 from line 1)			3a	
b	State death tax deduction			3b	
c	Taxable estate (subtract line 3b from line 3a)			3c	
4	Adjusted taxable gifts (see instructions)			4	
5	Add lines 3c and 4			5	
6	Tentative tax on the amount on line 5 from Table A in the instructions			6	
7	Total gift tax paid or payable (see instructions)			7	
8	Gross estate tax (subtract line 7 from line 6)			8	
9a	Basic exclusion amount	9a			
b	Deceased spousal unused exclusion (DSUE) amount from predeceased spouse(s), if any (from Section D, Part 6—Portability of Deceased Spousal Unused Exclusion)	9b			
c	Restored exclusion amount (see instructions)	9c			
d	Applicable exclusion amount (add lines 9a, 9b, and 9c)	9d			
e	Applicable credit amount (tentative tax on the amount in line 9d from Table A in the instructions)	9e			
10	Adjustment to applicable credit amount (May not exceed $6,000. See instructions.)	10			
11	Allowable applicable credit amount (subtract line 10 from line 9e)			11	
12	Subtract line 11 from line 8 (but do not enter less than zero)			12	
13	Credit for foreign death taxes (from Schedule P). (Attach Form(s) 706-CE.)	13			
14	Credit for tax on prior transfers (from Schedule Q)	14			
15	Total credits (add lines 13 and 14)			15	
16	Net estate tax (subtract line 15 from line 12)			16	
17	Generation-skipping transfer (GST) taxes payable (from Schedule R, Part 2, line 10)			17	
18	Total transfer taxes (add lines 16 and 17)			18	
19	Prior payments (explain in an attached statement)			19	
20	Balance due (or overpayment) (subtract line 19 from line 18)			20	

Under penalties of perjury, I declare that I have examined this return, including accompanying schedules and statements, and to the best of my knowledge and belief, it is true, correct, and complete. Declaration of preparer (other than the executor) is based on all information of which preparer has any knowledge.

Sign Here

▶ Signature of executor ▶ Date

▶ Signature of executor ▶ Date

Paid Preparer Use Only

Print/Type preparer's name	Preparer's signature	Date	Check ☐ if self-employed	PTIN
Firm's name ▶			Firm's EIN ▶	
Firm's address ▶			Phone no.	

For Privacy Act and Paperwork Reduction Act Notice, see instructions. Cat. No. 20548R Form **706** (Rev. 8-2019)

The formula is as follows:

Gross estate (assets owned at the date of death) (Line 1)
Less: Deductions (Line 2)
Less: Funeral expenses
Less: Administrative expenses
Less: Debts and mortgages
Less: Casualty losses
Less: Charitable bequests (unlimited)
Less: Marital deduction (unlimited)
Tentative taxable estate (Line 3a)
Less: State death taxes (Line 3b)
Taxable estate (Line 3c)
Plus: Post-1976 adjusted taxable gifts (Line 4)
Total taxable life and death transfers (Line 5)

Transfer tax on total transfers (Line 6)
Less: Post-1976 gift taxes paid (computed at unified tax rates in effect at time of death) (Line 7)
Less: Gross estate tax (Line 8)
Less: Applicable credit ($5,541,800 for 2025 (Line 10)
Less: Credit for foreign death taxes (Line 13)
Less: Credit for tax on prior transfers (Line 14)
Net estate tax liability (Line 16)

We described the computation of the gross estate in Learning Objectives 4 and 5 and the allowable deductions in Learning Objective 6. Thus, you know how to compute the taxable estate, which is shown on Line 3. The next section picks up the estate tax formula at Line 4.

Related exercise: Multiple Choice Question 11

Computing the Net Estate Tax Liability

In this section, we explain the remaining parts of the estate tax formula, which computes the net estate tax liability. This computation can be divided into four steps, as shown in **Illustration 12.7**:

Step 1. **Gross-up:** For post-1976 taxable gifts

Step 2. **Apply:** Current rates to total transfers

Step 3. **Reduce:** The transfer tax paid for prior gift taxes

Step 4. **Reduce:** Tax for credits

Step 1. Gross-Up for Post-1976 Taxable Gifts

The estate tax calculation uses the taxable estate increased by adjusted taxable gifts made after 1976. **Adjusted taxable gifts** are post-1976 taxable gifts other than gifts already included in the gross estate. Adjusted taxable gifts are included at their date-of-gift values. This is done so the marginal tax rate is determined by the cumulative lifetime taxable gifts plus the value of the taxable estate. However, these gifts are not double-taxed, because the unified tax attributable to the post-1976 gifts is allowed as a credit. The taxable estate is increased for gifts made only after 1976 because 1976 is the year that the gift tax and the estate tax were unified. Before 1977, the gift tax had different tax rates than the estate tax.

The gross-up for prior-year gifts is shown in the following Example.

ILLUSTRATION 12.7 Computing the Net Estate Tax Liability

Four Steps for Computing Net Estate Tax

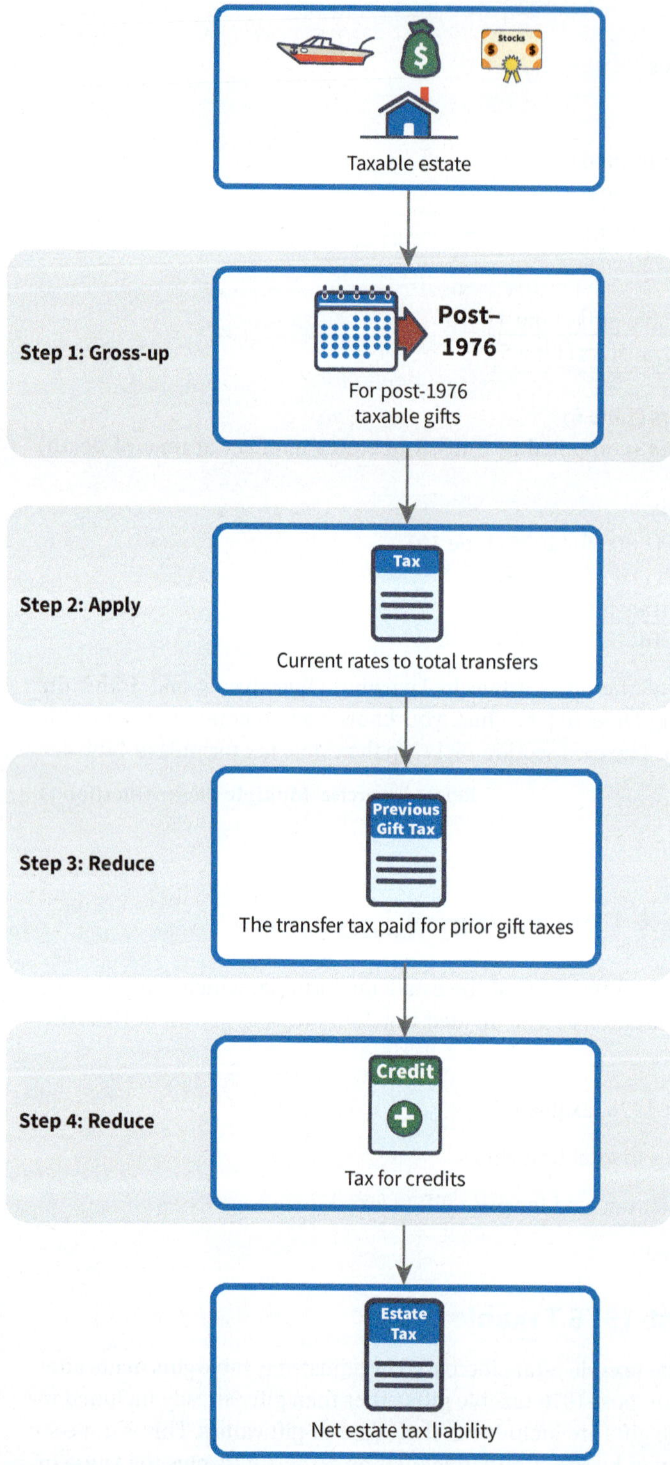

EXAMPLE 12.7.1 Adjusted Taxable Gifts

Juliana had a taxable estate of $17,200,000 and made adjusted taxable gifts after 1976 of $1,300,000. Juliana did not pay gift tax on the prior gifts because she had used her applicable credit to offset the gift tax in previous years. How much of Juliana's estate will be subject to the unified tax, if the applicable credit exclusion can shelter $13,990,000 from the unified tax?

SOLUTION

Juliana's estate will owe tax on $4,510,000, computed as follows:

Taxable estate	$17,200,000
Plus: Post-1976 adjusted taxable gifts	1,300,000
Total taxable life and death transfers	$18,500,000
Less: Value sheltered by the applicable credit	(13,990,000)
Value that is subject to the unified tax	$ 4,510,000

Related exercises: Discussion Question 13
Brief Exercise 12

Step 2. Apply Current Rates to Total Transfers

Once the post-1976 adjusted taxable gifts are added, you next compute the unified tax on the total taxable life and death transfers. This is illustrated in the next Example.

EXAMPLE 12.7.2
Apply Current Rates to Total Transfers

Continuing with the facts of Example 12.7.1, compute the transfer tax on the total transfers.

SOLUTION

The total taxable life and death transfers are $18,500,000. Using the 2025 Unified Tax Rate Schedule from Illustration 12.1, the transfer tax is computed as:

($18,500,000 − $1,000,000) × 40% + $345,800 = $7,345,800.

Step 3. Reduce the Transfer Tax Paid for Prior Gift Taxes

You next reduce the transfer tax on total transfers by the gift taxes paid or payable on post-1976 gifts to compute the gross estate tax. The unified rates from the year of death are used, as shown in the next Example.

Potential Pitfall

Do not use the tax rates that were in effect when the post-1976 gifts were originally made. The tax rates for the year of death must be used.

EXAMPLE 12.7.3
Reduce the Transfer Tax for Prior Gift Taxes

Continuing with the facts of Examples 12.7.1 and 12.7.2, compute the gross estate tax.

SOLUTION

We begin with the transfer tax on the total transfers of $7,345,800 from Example 12.7.2. If gift taxes had been paid in the past, we would reduce the gross estate tax by the gift taxes paid on post-1976 gifts, using the current unified transfer tax rates. However, Juliana did not pay gift taxes in the past, so her gross estate tax is the same as her transfer tax on total transfers.

The gross estate tax is computed as:

Transfer tax on total transfers	$7,345,800
Less: Post-1976 gift taxes paid	(0)
Gross estate tax	$7,345,800

Related exercise: Brief Exercise 13

Step 4. Reduce Tax for Credits

The last step is to reduce the gross estate tax by the allowed tax credits, beginning with the applicable credit.

Applicable Credit As discussed with gift taxes, the applicable credit is an inflation-adjusted statutory amount that provides the total amount of transfers that an individual can make to others during their life and at death without being subject to the unified transfer tax. The applicable credit exclusion for 2025 is $13,990,000. The applicable credit exclusion applies to the total lifetime gifts plus the value of the estate at death. The applicable credit exclusion is per individual, so each spouse in a married couple has a separate exclusion of $13,990,000 to use. The actual credit generated by the applicable credit exclusion is $5,541,800. The use of the actual applicable credit is illustrated by the following Example.

EXAMPLE 12.7.4
Reduce Tax for Credits

Continuing with the facts of the last three Examples, compute the net estate tax liability.

SOLUTION

Juliana can use her applicable credit of $5,541,800 to reduce her estate tax liability, as follows:

Gross estate tax	$7,345,800
Applicable credit	(5,541,800)
Net estate tax liability	$1,804,000

Related exercise: Applicable Problem 13

Portability of Applicable Credit **Portability** in the context of estate taxes means that any unused credit from a spouse dying after 2010 may be used in the future by the surviving spouse. An election to use the remaining credit must be made by filing Form 706 even if the estate of the decedent would otherwise not require a return to be filed. This portability feature has greatly simplified estate planning for married couples.

EXAMPLE 12.7.5
Portability of Applicable Credit

Lavern died in 2020 with a taxable estate of $7 million when the applicable credit exclusion was $11,580,000. An election was made on Lavern's estate tax return to permit his wife, Eva, to access his unused applicable credit, which could shelter assets of $4,580,000 ($11,580,000 − $7,000,000). Eva, who had not made any lifetime taxable gifts, died in 2025 with a taxable estate of $20 million. What is the total applicable exclusion amount available to Eva's estate?

SOLUTION

The amount of assets that Eva can shelter from the unified tax is her applicable credit exclusion amount of $13,990,000 million (2025) plus the $4,580,000 from Lavern's unused exclusion amount, for a total exclusion of $18,570,000.

Related exercise: Tax Planning Problem 4

Credit for Foreign Death Taxes Property located outside the United States could be subject to foreign death taxes in addition to the U.S. estate tax. To prevent double taxation, a foreign death tax credit is allowed for foreign death taxes paid by the decedent's estate. The credit is permitted for estate, inheritance, legacy, or succession taxes paid to a foreign country.[35]

Credit for Tax on Prior Transfers Some policymakers believe that the estate tax is a significant burden on accumulated wealth, given that the highest marginal tax rate is 40%. Others believe that the estate tax is an appropriate way to prevent large concentrations of wealth from accumulating in the hands of a very small percentage of the population. Regardless of one's opinion on the need for the estate tax, almost everyone agrees that it would be unfair to subject the same assets to the estate tax twice if two individuals died within a short time of one another.

For example, assume that a father dies in 2023 and bequeaths $25 million to his daughter, and then, in 2025, his daughter dies. Would it be appropriate for the $25 million to be taxed a second time within two years of the father's death? Congress has determined that this would not be fair, and it created a credit for tax on prior transfers to adjust for taxes on deaths within ten years before or two years after the decedent's death. A detailed discussion of this credit is beyond the scope of this book.[36]

Other Requirements

Before closing this chapter, we need to discuss two other important rules for the estate tax: filing requirements and the related generation-skipping tax.

Filing Requirements

The estate tax return (Form 706) is due nine months after the date of death. An automatic six-month extension is available, but the tax due must be paid by the original due date. The requirement for filing a return is based on whether the gross estate plus post-1976 gifts exceeds the applicable credit exclusion.

The Generation-Skipping Tax

The **generation-skipping tax (GST)** is a supplemental tax that prevents taxpayers from avoiding the unified transfer taxes by skipping one generation of recipients. The tax is in addition to the gift or estate tax.

Usually, wealth is passed to the next generation. For example, grandparents may bequeath their wealth to their children, and then later, when the children die, they bequeath their assets to their children, who are the grandchildren of the grandparents. Estate tax would be due twice, at the deaths of the grandparents and of the parents. Without the GST, wealthy families might decide to skip one generation to avoid the 40% estate tax for that generation. Thus, the grandparents could skip their children's generation and bequeath their wealth directly to their grandchildren.

To prevent this tax avoidance, the GST is imposed on the donor or the decedent if the transfer skips a generation. The donor or the estate of the decedent pays two taxes on the transfer. First, either the gift tax or the estate tax is paid. Second, the GST is paid because a generation was skipped.[37] The applicable credit applies to the GST in the same manner as it applies to the estate tax.

The tax rate used for the GST is the highest rate imposed by the unified transfer tax, which is 40%.

Related exercises: Discussion Question 14
Multiple Choice Question 12

[35]IRC §2014.

[36]IRC §2013.

[37]IRC §2631.

PRACTICE PROBLEM 12.7.1
Calculating the Net Estate Tax Liability

Trevion had a taxable estate of $35,000,000 and had made adjusted taxable gifts after 1976 of $8,800,000. Trevion did not pay gift tax on the prior gifts because he used his applicable credit to offset the gift tax in a previous year. Calculate the net estate tax liability.

SOLUTION

To solve this problem, we use the steps show in Illustration 12.7:

Step 1:

Taxable estate	$35,000,000
Add: Post-1976 adjusted taxable gifts	8,800,000
Total taxable life and death transfers	$43,800,000

Step 2: The transfer tax on total transfers is $17,465,800 [($43,800,000 – $1,000,000) × 40% + $345,800]

Step 3: The gross estate tax is computed as:

Transfer tax on total transfers	$17,465,800
Less: Post-1976 gift taxes paid	(0)
Gross estate tax	$17,465,800

Step 4: Trevion can use his applicable credit of $5,541,800 to reduce his estate tax liability, as follows:

Gross estate tax	$17,465,800
Applicable credit	(5,541,800)
Net estate tax liability	$11,924,000

Trevion's estate will owe a net tax liability of $11,924,000.

Featured Professional: Alan Spigelman, CPA, JD

Alan has worked as a tax accountant for 41 years and before he retired was a partner at RSM US. He specialized in individual and fiduciary income tax planning and compliance, estate tax, and gift and generation-skipping taxation planning and compliance.

From Classroom to Career Solving challenging issues confronting a client can enhance the relationship with the client and bring much personal satisfaction. One day, a charitably-inclined client was advised that they would be taxed on a significant amount of phantom income caused by recapture of negative capital in a real estate partnership. The client was illiquid, with much of their wealth tied up in hard assets including vacation homes. The planning challenge was to reduce their income tax while not reducing their cash or assets. Ultimately, the client implemented our recommendation to gift a remainder interest in one of their vacation homes to charity. Done properly, under Internal Revenue Code §170(f)(3)(B)(i), a taxpayer can gift title in their home at their death while retaining use of the home during life and obtaining a current-year income tax deduction for the present value of the remainder interest. The solution solved the problem.

Professional Skills The ability to communicate verbally and in writing are extremely important. Communication skills can differentiate a good performer from a great performer as the ability to distill complicated information into words that are understandable to a specific audience is critical for success. Intellectual curiosity coupled with analytical and technology skills are imperative when working as a tax accountant. Intellectual curiosity drives professionals to grow professionally and personally, and the profession has always required analytical skills to do even the most basic functions. Today, the ability to adapt and work efficiently in an ever-changing world of technology is critical for success.

Future Tax Landscape I suspect that technology and artificial intelligence will cause much of the record keeping and tax compliance work to be done without human interaction. Understanding technical rules and applying data to develop unique consulting skills will likely be a driving force for tax professionals in the years to come.

Review and Practice

Chapter Summary

In this chapter, we begin by explaining why the gift and estate taxes are unified. Then we cover the details of the gift tax and conclude by discussing the laws for the estate tax. Tax professionals can provide appropriate advice to their wealthiest clients only if they have a broad understanding of how the gift tax and estate tax are structured.

1 Understand the application of the unified transfer tax to gifts and estates.

- The **unified transfer tax** applies to the transfer of an individual's wealth to another during the individual's life or at the time of the individual's death. The gift tax is paid by the donor, and the estate tax is paid from the assets of the decedent.
- The unified transfer tax rate schedule applies to both the gift tax and the estate tax. This is a progressive tax system with rates ranging from 18% to 40%. The marginal tax rate is generally determined based on the sum of the gifts made during a taxpayer's life and the taxpayer's taxable estate at death. Thus, the tax rate schedule *unifies* the transfers made during a taxpayer's life and those made at the taxpayer's death when determining the marginal tax rate for the current year's gifts.
- The applicable credit is an inflation-adjusted statutory amount that provides the total amount of transfers that an individual can make to others during the individual's life and at death without being subject to the unified transfer tax. The **applicable credit exclusion** for 2025 is $13,990,000. The gift and estate taxes are also unified because the applicable credit exclusion applies to the total lifetime gifts plus the value of the estate at death. The applicable credit is per individual, so each spouse in a married couple has a separate exclusion of $13,990,000 to use.

2 Identify the items that are included in the gift tax calculation.

- A **gift** is a voluntary transfer of property from one person (the donor) to another (the donee) for less than full consideration. Several exclusions from the gift tax are listed in the chapter.
- When a taxpayer transfers property to a trust, the taxpayer has made two gifts, the income interest and the remainder interest (unless the donor retains one of these interests). The beneficiary of the income interest receives the income from the trust each year. The beneficiary of the remainder interest receives the property (corpus) of the trust when the trust terminates. The present value of the income and remainder interests are valued using actuarial tables provided by the IRS.
- Several gift tax implications arise related to property that is owned by more than one individual. The creation of a joint ownership interest without equal consideration from each co-owner is considered a gift of the excess contribution to the owner making the smaller contribution.
- The **annual exclusion** is the amount that an individual can transfer to another individual during a tax year without having the transfer be subject to the gift tax. The annual exclusion is $19,000 (2025) and is indexed for inflation. The annual exclusion applies only to a gift of a present interest. A **present interest** is a gift recipient's right to receive income or enjoy property currently.
- **Gift-splitting** is an election that applies only to married individuals. If gift-splitting is elected, then it is deemed that every gift made by either spouse was made 50% by each spouse. This allows each spouse to use the annual exclusion of $19,000 (2025) for their portion of the gift if the gift involves a present interest.

3 Compute the gift tax liability using the gift tax formula.

- A marital deduction is allowed for most gifts to a spouse. The following rules apply for the marital deduction:
  - The deduction is unlimited in amount.
  - The amount of the deduction is the FMV of the gift less the annual exclusion (if the gift is a present interest).
  - The marital deduction does not apply for gifts to a spouse who is not a U.S. citizen. In such a situation, an annual exclusion of $190,000 (2025) is permitted.
- A charitable contribution deduction is allowed for gifts to qualified charitable organizations. Three major differences from the income tax definition are that qualified charities for gift tax purposes:
  - Includes foreign charities,
  - Excludes cemeteries, *and*
  - Are unlimited.
- There are five main steps to computing the gift tax liability:

  Step 1. Determine: The current year's taxable gifts (the amount of gifts reduced by exclusions and deductions).
  Step 2. Add: All previous years' taxable gifts to the current year's taxable gifts.

  Step 3. Calculate: The total gift tax liability.

  Step 4. Reduce: The total gift tax liability by the gift tax computed on taxable gifts from previous periods using the current rates for the unified tax.

  Step 5. Reduce: Any remaining gift tax by the unused portion of the applicable credit.

- The due date of the gift tax return is April 15 for gifts made in the previous year. The date for filing the return can be extended for six months to October 15. If a taxpayer extends their income tax return, then the gift tax return is automatically extended also.

4 Determine the value of the assets that are included in the gross estate.

- It is important to know the difference between the probate estate and the gross estate. The **probate estate,** in general, includes assets that are held solely by the decedent and does not include assets that pass to others outside of the will. The **gross estate** refers to the assets that must be included in computing the estate tax at the time of death.
- In general, property is included in the gross estate at its fair market value on the date of death. However, the executor can sometimes elect to have the property valued on the **alternate valuation date (AVD)**, which is six months after the date of death. If the property is distributed before the AVD, then the basis on the date the property is distributed is the beneficiary's basis. The election to use the alternate valuation date (AVD) is only available if two conditions are met:
  - The gross estate is lower on the AVD than on the date of death, *and*
  - The estate tax payable is lower if using the AVD than if using the date of death.
- An executor can elect to value certain realty used in farming or in connection with a closely held business at a special use valuation. This special rule permits the realty to be valued based on its current use rather than its true FMV, which would be based on its best and higher use. The decrease in value based on this rule cannot exceed $1,420,000 (2025).

5 Identify the property that is included in the gross estate.

- In general, all assets owned on the date of death must be included in the gross estate. This includes investments such as stocks and bonds, ownership in businesses such as partnerships and S corporations, land, and other real estate. It also includes more basic assets such as clothes, cars, boats, furniture, and other items owned and used in one's personal life.
- Life insurance proceeds are included in the gross estate if the decedent has an incident of ownership in the policy at the time of his death. An incident of ownership includes the right to:
  - Change the beneficiary
  - Borrow against the policy's cash value
  - Assign the policy to a new owner
  - Surrender the policy for cash
  - Cancel the policy
- Property can be jointly owned in three main ways: **joint tenants with right of survivorship**, **tenancy in common**, and **tenancy by the entirety**). See Illustration 12.4 for a summary of the differences in these forms of ownership.
- Special estate tax rules apply to retained interests. With a **retained interest**, an individual has transferred property to another person but has retained some aspect of ownership in the property or the right to use the property. Because the individual has retained this interest, at death, the property may be included in the individual's gross estate even though legally the property is titled in another person's name. There are three types of retained interests:
  - Retained life estate
  - Retained power to designate who enjoys a benefit from the property
  - Retained right to revoke the transfer of the property
- If the retained element on any of the following gifts is released within three years of death, then the value of the gift is included in the gross estate:
  - Removing the retained interest on a transfer
  - Making a revocable transfer irrevocable
  - Removing all incidents of ownership on a life insurance policy

The property is included at the date of death at FMV. Additionally, the **gross-up provision** states that the gift tax paid on a gift is included in the estate for any gifts made within three years of death.

6 Determine the deductions that can reduce the gross estate.

- In order to avoid taxing a married couple's estate twice, a deduction is provided for a bequest to a surviving spouse. To qualify for the marital deduction, the spouse must receive property outright and be able to control its ultimate destination. Property rights that are terminable do not qualify. A **terminable interest** is an interest that will terminate or fail in the future due to a contingency or to the passage of time. A **qualified terminable interest property (QTIP)** *will* qualify for the marital deduction.
- Debts of the estate, such as mortgages, credit card debt, automobile loans, and accrued property and income taxes, are allowed as deductions against the gross estate.
- Deductions for charitable contributions are allowed without limitation. Just as for the gift tax, deductions for charitable contributions to foreign charities are permitted. No deduction is allowed for contributions to nongovernment or non-church-owned cemeteries. The deduction is not allowed unless the contribution was required by the decedent's will.
- Expenses incurred to wrap up the final legal and administration expenses of the decedent's life are deductible against the gross estate.
- Casualty and theft losses are deductible without any floor limitation, meaning that the reductions for the $100 floor and 10% of AGI do not apply. The executor has the option of deducting casualty and theft losses on the estate tax return (Form 706) or the estate's income tax return (Form 1041), but not on both.

7 Compute the estate tax using the estate tax formula.

- The estate tax formula is consistent with that shown on page 1 of Form 706, United States Estate (and Generation-Skipping Transfer) Tax Return.
- The net estate tax liability computation can be divided into four steps:

Step 1. Gross-up: For post-1976 taxable gifts

Step 2. Apply: Current rates to total transfers

Step 3. Reduce: The transfer tax paid for prior gift taxes

Step 4. Reduce: Tax for credits

- The applicable credit exclusion for 2025 is $13,990,000. The applicable credit exclusion applies to the total lifetime gifts plus the value of the estate at death. The applicable credit exclusion is per individual, so each spouse in a married couple has a separate exclusion of $13,990,000 to use. The actual credit generated by the applicable credit exclusion is $5,541,800.
- To prevent double taxation, a foreign death tax credit is allowed for foreign death taxes paid by the decedent's estate. The credit is permitted for estate, inheritance, legacy, or succession taxes paid to a foreign county.
- The estate tax return (Form 706) is due nine months after the date of death. An automatic six-month extension is available, but the tax due must be paid by the original due date. The requirement for filing a return is based on whether the gross estate plus post-1976 gifts exceeds the applicable credit exclusion.
- The **generation-skipping tax (GST)** is a supplemental tax that prevents taxpayers from avoiding the unified transfer taxes by skipping one generation of recipients. The tax is in addition to the gift or estate tax.

Communication Application

Communication

Sale of an Asset Received as Inheritance

(LO4) Dee is a very good friend of yours and your tax client. She was wearing an expensive necklace when you were out for dinner recently. She mentioned that she had received some stock from her late aunt, who passed away earlier in the year. The fair market value of the stock at the time of her aunt's death was $17,000. Dee sold the stock for $25,000 and purchased the necklace and some other jewelry. She tells you that an inheritance is not taxable income. Dee is surprised when you state otherwise and asks you to explain the tax consequences of these events.

Solution

Hello Dee,

I enjoyed our dinner a few days ago and am writing to continue our discussion regarding the stock inheritance you received from your late aunt. You are correct that you can exclude the value of an inheritance from your taxable income. However, the sale of the stock is a property transaction, and you must compute your gain or loss from the sale. Your basis in the stock is $17,000, the fair market value as of your aunt's date of death. Your gain is $8,000 ($25,000 amount realized − $17,000 adjusted basis). Stock is an investment, so the gain is a capital gain.

The good news is that the tax law treats inherited property as if held long term, so the $8,000 is a long-term capital gain and thus is taxed at preferential rates.

Please let me know if you have any further questions.

Thank you,
Carnes & Youngberg, CPAs

Ethics and Professional Responsibilities Application

Ethics

Error on Previously Filed Estate Tax Return

(LO7) You are the tax accountant for your college friend, who has asked you to prepare his mom's estate tax return. While gathering information for the return, you notice his dad's estate tax return from three years ago and review it. The family is quite wealthy, and you know firsthand that his family has been very generous and has previously gifted your friend cash, an expensive car, and a home in Beverly Hills, but none of these previous gifts were properly reported on the dad's estate tax return. What is your responsibility, and what do you tell your college friend?

In addition to the chapter content, see *Statements on Standards for Tax Services* at www.aicpacima.com/resources/landing/statements-on-standards-for-tax-services; *Circular 230* at www.irs.gov/tax-professionals/office-of-professional-responsibility-and-circular-230; and Chapter 2, LO4, Tax Professional Responsibilities.

Solution

You must tell your college friend that his dad's estate tax return was incorrectly filed. These previous gifts should have been reported and will affect the completion of his mom's estate tax return as well. *Circular 230,* §10.22, Diligence as to accuracy states that: "(a) In general. A practitioner must exercise due diligence (1) In preparing or assisting in the preparation of, approving, and filing tax returns, documents, affidavits, and other papers relating to Internal Revenue Service matters."

Statement on Standards for Tax Services No. 1.2.6, Knowledge of Error, sets forth standards for a member who becomes aware of an error in a taxpayer's previously filed tax return. "A member should inform the taxpayer promptly upon becoming aware of an error in a previously filed return, an error in a return that is the subject of an administrative proceeding, or a taxpayer's failure to file a required return. A member also should advise the taxpayer of the potential consequences of the error and recommend the corrective measures to be taken."

You should inform your friend of these issues and offer to file a corrected Form 706 for his dad's estate.

Key Terms

Adjusted Taxable Gifts (Estate Tax) 12-47
Alternate Valuation Date (AVD) 12-54
Annual Exclusion 12-12
Applicable Credit 12-6
Applicable Credit Exclusion 12-6
Estate 12-27
Estate Tax 12-1
Executor 12-27
Future Interest 12-14
General Power of Appointment 12-37
Generation-Skipping Tax (GST) 12-51
Gift 12-8
Gift Tax 12-1
Gift-Splitting 12-15
Gross Estate 12-27
Gross-Up 12-21
Gross-Up Provision 12-38
Joint Tenants with Right of Survivorship 12-35
Life Interest 12-36
Portability 12-50
Present Interest 12-14
Probate Estate 12-27
Qualified Terminable Interest Property (QTIP) 12-41
Recapture Agreement (Estate Tax) 12-31
Retained Interest 12-36
Right of Survivorship 12-27
Special Power of Appointment 12-37
Special Use Valuation 12-30
Tenancy by the Entirety 12-35
Tenancy in Common 12-35
Terminable Interest 12-18
Unified Transfer Tax 12-4

End-of-Chapter Assessment

Discussion Questions

1. **(LO1)** Describe the unified transfer tax.

2. **(LO2)** When is a gift considered to be completed?

3. **(LO2)** What is the annual exclusion, and why does it exist?

4. **(LO2)** Why is the gift-splitting election an important tool for gift tax planning?

5. **(LO3)** Discuss three major differences in how the income tax and the gift tax define qualified charities.

6. **(LO4)** Provide a definition for estate.

7. **(LO4)** Distinguish between a probate estate and a gross estate.

8. **(LO4)** Which dates are typically used to value an asset when an asset is received through inheritance?

9. **(LO4)** What is the recapture tax as it pertains to the special use valuation election?

10. **(LO5)** Briefly describe and contrast joint tenants with right of survivorship, tenancy in common, and tenancy by the entirety.

11. **(LO5)** Discuss the three types of retained interests.

12. **(LO6)** Describe the marital deduction.

13. **(LO7)** Define adjusted taxable gifts in terms of computing the estate tax.

14. **(LO7)** Discuss the generation-skipping tax.

Multiple Choice Questions

1. (LO1) Which of the following is a true statement?
   a. The gift tax and the estate tax are other types of income tax.
   b. The estate tax is a wealth tax that is levied on the adjusted basis of an individual's gross estate at the time of their death.
   c. Gift and estate taxes are paid by only the very wealthiest taxpayers.
   d. The gift tax is a wealth tax that is levied on the adjusted basis of property when it is gifted to another individual.
2. (LO2) Which of the following is a false statement?
   a. The beneficiary of an income interest receives the income from the trust each year.
   b. The beneficiary of a remainder interest receives the property (corpus) of the trust when the trust terminates.
   c. If a potential gift is incomplete, then it is not subject to the gift tax.
   d. A revocable transfer to a trust is a completed gift.
3. (LO2) What is the maximum amount per donee that a donor can contribute to a Section 529 plan in 2025 and not be subject to gift tax?
   a. $0
   b. $19,000
   c. $50,000
   d. $95,000
4. (LO3) The annual exclusion for a marital deduction when the spouse is not a U.S. citizen is:
   a. $0
   b. $10,000
   c. $19,000
   d. $190,000
5. (LO3) The due date for a gift tax return is:
   a. Six months after the date of the gift
   b. March 15 for gifts made in the previous year
   c. April 15 for gifts made in the previous year
   d. Nine months after the date of the gift
6. (LO4) Carlos Anderson died on March 13, Year 9, and bequeathed his entire $4,000,000 estate to his daughter, Derna. His estate included investment real estate that had a tax basis to Carlos of $230,000. This property was distributed to Derna seven months after Carlos's death. The executor of Carlos's estate validly elected the alternate valuation date. Fair market values for the real estate were:

At the date of Carlos's death	$500,000
Six months after Carlos's death	$460,000
Seven months after Carlos's death	$470,000

   What is Derna's basis in the real estate?
   a. $0
   b. $460,000
   c. $470,000
   d. $500,000
7. (LO5) Regarding life insurance, an incident of ownership does not include the right to:
   a. Cancel the policy
   b. Recommend to a family member who the beneficiary should be
   c. Surrender the policy for cash
   d. Change the beneficiary
8. (LO5) Which of the following types of ownership includes a portion of the FMV of the property in the probate estate?
   a. Tenancy by the entirety
   b. Joint tenants with right of survivorship
   c. Tenancy in common
   d. None of the above
9. (LO6) Which of the following is a false statement concerning the marital deduction?
   a. Property rights that are terminable do not qualify for the deduction unless a QTIP election is made.
   b. Property must be included in the gross estate for a marital deduction to be allowed.
   c. Property that passes to the surviving spouse as a result of being owned jointly with the decedent qualifies for the marital deduction.
   d. A marital deduction is allowed for non-citizen spouses.
10. (LO6) Ordinary and necessary administrative expenses paid by an estate are deductible:
    a. Only on the fiduciary income tax return (Form 1041) and never on the federal estate tax return (Form 706)
    b. Only on the federal estate tax return (Form 706) and never on the fiduciary income tax return (Form 1041)
    c. On the fiduciary income tax return (Form 1041) only if the estate tax deduction is waived for these expenses
    d. On both the fiduciary income tax return (Form 1041) and the estate tax return (Form 706) by adding a tax computed on the proportionate rates attributable to both returns
11. (LO7) An estate tax return is filed on which tax form?
    a. Form 1040
    b. Form 1041
    c. Form 709
    d. Form 706
12. The tax rate used for the generation-skipping tax is:
    a. Undeterminable without knowing the amount of the gift
    b. 20%
    c. 30%
    d. 40%

Brief Exercises

1. **(LO1)** Ayo has made the following taxable gifts in prior years:

2014	$35,000
2018	$40,000
2021	$75,000

In 2025, he made $80,000 of taxable gifts. What marginal gift tax rate(s) applies for each of these years?

2. **(LO2)** The following transfers were made during the current year. Indicate whether each transfer is subject to the gift tax.

   a. Javier gives 100 shares of stock to his daughter.

   b. Desmond received a principal residence due to his divorce.

   c. Janelle receives a bonus as the company's top salesperson.

   d. Mark makes a payment of $5,000 to the St. Charles Rotary Club.

   e. Destiny loans her daughter $50,000 interest-free.

3. **(LO2)** A single taxpayer wants to gift his five children $250,000 each to help start their businesses. How much are the taxable gifts before considering use of any lifetime unified transfer tax applicable credit exclusion?

4. **(LO3)** Calvin and Penny were engaged in January of the current year. Calvin gave Penny a car with a value of $60,000. In October of this year, they married, and after the wedding, Penny gave Calvin a motorcycle worth $30,000. What are the gift tax implications of these transactions, if any?

5. **(LO3)** Christian is very generous and has made taxable gifts of $350,000 in prior years. In 2025, Christian plans on making taxable gifts of $600,000. Compute the transfer tax for the current year, before the applicable credit.

6. **(LO4)** Shelby inherited land worth $82,000 from her grandmother as of August 15, her grandmother's date of death. Her grandmother had purchased the land for $44,000 twenty years ago. The value of the land as of December 31 is $80,000. What is Shelby's basis in the land inherited?

7. **(LO4)** Betty owns a cattle ranch in Ciudad Juárez, Mexico, that she has managed for the last 25 years. During the current year, Betty dies, and her sons are committed to continuing to operate the ranch. The ranch is located on 125 acres of property that has appreciated significantly in value over the last 25 years and is valued at $8,500,000. Land used in similar businesses would be valued at $5,000,000. Assume that the 50% and 25% valuation tests are met for the 125 acres. If the executor of Betty's estate wishes to elect the special use valuation, how would this asset be valued in the gross estate?

8. **(LO5)** Beatrice is 68 years old and owns a life insurance policy with a fair market value of $500,000. Beatrice has named her daughter the beneficiary of her policy. She has given up certain ownership rights in the policy, but she has retained the right to surrender the policy for cash just in case she needs to as she ages. If Beatrice were to die this year, would the $500,000 be included in her estate?

9. **(LO5)** Kwame owns vacation property with a fair market value of $350,000. Kwame provided Abeba with a general power of appointment that permitted Abeba to transfer ownership to himself or his sister, Amari. Abeba died during the current year, and at his death, he had not exercised his power of appointment.

   a. What are the estate tax consequences to Abeba?

   b. How would your answer change if Abeba held a special power of appointment and could only transfer ownership to Amari?

   c. Same as **a**, but instead of Abeba dying, Kwame dies before Abeba appoints the property. What are the tax consequences to Kwame and to Abeba?

10. **(LO5)** Zenith created a revocable trust with his daughter, Zelda, as the beneficiary, two years before Zenith died. At the time of the transfer, no gift taxes were paid because the trust was revocable and not a completed gift. Zenith died in the current year, and the trust had a FMV of $1,350,000 What amount is included in Zenith's gross estate?

11. **(LO6)** Francois gifts his spouse the following assets during the year: $200,000 cash and a new car with a FMV of $55,000. Both spouses are U.S. citizens.

    a. What is the amount of the marital deduction?

    b. Assume the spouse receiving the gifts is not a U.S. citizen. What is the amount of the marital deduction? Is an annual exclusion allowed?

12. **(LO7)** Olayinka had a taxable estate of $22,500,000 and made adjusted taxable gifts before 1977 of $1,500,000 and after 1976 of $2,800,000. Olayinka did not pay gift tax on the prior gifts because he used his applicable credit to offset the gift tax in a previous year. How much of Olayinka's estate will be subject to the unified tax, if the applicable credit equivalent can shelter $13,990,000 from the unified tax?

13. **(LO7)** Desmond had a taxable estate of $18,700,000 and made adjusted taxable gifts after 1976 of $3,300,000. Desmond did not pay gift tax on the prior gifts because he used his applicable credit to offset the gift tax in a previous year. Calculate the transfer tax on total transfers and the gross estate tax.

Application Problems

1. **(LO2)** Fredrick transfers $750,000 to a trust. The trust purchases an annuity for $500,000. The annuity income is paid to Fredrick's son each year. Fredrick's grandson will receive the principal and other earnings of the trust when he reaches the age of 25.

   a. What are the gift tax implications of this trust creation?

   b. Will there be any gifts made in years after the trust was created?

2. **(LO2)** Terrell and Gizelle were married on February 14, Year 5. On December 25, Year 4, Gizelle deposited $100,000 in a joint checking account for Terrell and Gizelle. Terrell withdrew $45,000 on December 28, Year 4, and purchased an Audi. On March 1, Year 5, Terrell withdrew $5,000 and purchased a new watch. What are the gift tax implications of these transactions?

3. **(LO2)** Ricardo irrevocably transfers money to a trust for the benefit of his grandson, Juan, who is 10 years old. The present value of this

transfer is $200,000. The trustee cannot use the income or the corpus for the benefit of Juan until Juan is 18 years old. What is Ricardo's taxable gift, if any?

4. **(LO2)** Sarai and Ying, U.S. citizens, were married for the entire year in 2025. During 2025, Sarai gave a $32,000 cash gift to her mother. They made no other gifts in 2025.

a. What amount of the 2025 gift is taxable to Sarai if gift-splitting is not elected?

b. If Sarai and Ying elect gift-splitting, how much of the gift is taxable?

5. **(LO3)** Kramer successfully trades in bitcoin, and his net worth is estimated to be $300 million. During the current year, Kramer gifts $15 million to Habitat for Humanity.

a. How much of the $15 million is subject to the gift tax?

b. How does this vary from the treatment of charitable contribution deductions for income tax purposes?

6. **(LO3)** Lance has made the following gifts in 2025:

- $20,000 cash to his sister
- $350,000 home to his mother
- $50,000 stock to his brother
- $100,000 to the American Cancer Society

Assume that Lance has made no prior taxable gifts. What is Lance's gift tax liability before and after the applicable tax credit?

7. **(LO4)** Tiara is a U.S. citizen who died in the current tax year. At the date of her death, she owned the assets shown with the corresponding market value. Which assets would be included in Tiara's probate estate? Which assets would be included in the gross estate?

Asset	Fair market value
Personal residence	$390,000
Personal assets	$ 63,000
Stocks	$372,000
Checking account	$ 7,000
Coin collection	$ 27,000
Tax-exempt bonds	$ 11,000
Traditional IRA (beneficiary is daughter)	$435,000
Section 401(k) plan (beneficiary is son)	$225,000
Vacation home (owned with right of survivorship with her sister; Tiara contributed 40% to the cost of the home)	$280,000
Life insurance policy—term (beneficiary is her husband)	$500,000
Partnership interest (owned 75% as a tenancy in common with brother; full FMV is shown)	$190,000

8. **(LO4)** Arjun died on April 3, Year 4, with a gross estate of $11,500,000. In his will, he left his personal residence to his grandson. Arjun had originally purchased the home for $172,000. Fair market values for the home were as follows:

April 3, Year 4	$400,000
May 28, Year 4	$410,000
October 3, Year 4	$430,000
April 3, Year 5	$450,000

The executor of the estate did not elect the alternate valuation date. The home was distributed to the grandson on May 28. What is the grandson's basis in the home? What is the grandson's holding period?

9. **(LO4)** Hazel died on February 22, Year 7, with a gross estate of $5.6 million. In her will, she left her vacation home in Florida to her daughter and her vacation home in South Carolina to her son. Hazel had purchased the Florida home for $250,000 and the South Carolina home for $365,000. Fair market values for the homes were as follows:

	Florida home	South Carolina home
February 22, Year 7	$400,000	$500,000
July 29, Year 7	$420,000	$510,000
August 22, Year 7	$425,000	$515,000
October 31, Year 7	$430,000	$530,000
February 22, Year 8	$450,000	$550,000

The executor of the estate properly elected the alternate valuation date. The Florida home was distributed on July 29, and the South Carolina home was distributed on October 31. What is the daughter's basis in the Florida home? What is the son's basis in the South Carolina home? What is the holding period for the daughter and for the son?

10. **(LO5)** In each of the following independent situations, determine the amount that must be included in the gross estate.

a. Brad and his son, Andrew, own land as tenants in common that is valued at $78,000, with Brad owning a two-thirds interest and Andrew owning a one-third interest. If Brad dies in the current year, what amount is included in Brad's gross estate?

b. Nate and his friend, Melissa, own a vacation property in Sedona with right of survivorship. Nate paid $40,000 and Melissa paid $60,000 to purchase the vacation property six years ago. It currently has a FMV of $220,000. If Nate dies in the current year, what amount is included in Nate's gross estate?

c. Nate and his wife, Melissa, own a vacation property in Sedona with right of survivorship. Nate paid $40,000 and Melissa paid $60,000 to purchase the vacation property six years ago. It currently has a FMV of $220,000. If Nate dies in the current year, what amount is included in Nate's gross estate?

11. **(LO5)** Malik made the following transfers and gift tax payments in previous years:

Transfer	Date	FMV of gift	Gift tax paid
ABC Stock	12/31/20	$ 100,000	$ 40,000
Cash	12/31/21	$1,000,000	$ 400,000
XYZ Stock	12/31/22	$2,500,000	$1,000,000
Antique collection	12/31/23	$3,800,000	$1,520,000
*Revocable trust	12/31/24	$3,200,000	$1,280,000
Vacation home	10/31/25	$4,000,000	$1,600,000

*Malik created the revocable trust in Year 18, and in Year 24, he converted it to an irrevocable trust.

Malik died on November 30, 2025.

a. How much of the total gift amount is included in Malik's gross estate?

b. How much of the gift tax paid is included in Malik's gross estate?

12. **(LO6)** Francesca died during the current year on June 27, and the following expenses were incurred during the administration of her estate:

Funeral expenses	$ 7,800
Auto loan	$22,000
Credit card debt	$ 5,500
Inheritance tax paid to the state of New Jersey	$ 8,900
Attorney's fees	$ 2,500
Accountant's fees	$ 1,000
Court costs	$ 750
Casualty loss (occurred on July 15)	$10,200

- The executor elected to claim the attorney's fees, accountant's fees, and court costs on the estate income tax return.
- The casualty was part of a federally declared disaster area.

What deductions are allowed on Francesca's estate tax return?

13. **(LO7)** Maryam had a taxable estate of $21,600,000 and made adjusted taxable gifts after 1976 of $1,750,000. Maryam did not pay gift tax on the prior gifts because she used her applicable credit to offset the gift tax in a previous year. Calculate the net estate tax liability.

Tax Planning Problems

Planning

1. **(LO1)** Jenny Russ is a wealthy taxpayer who is considering making a $1.1 million gift to each of her five children and nine grandchildren. Assume that Jenny has not made any previous gifts. Should Jenny make these gifts in 2025, 2026, or 2027?

2. **(LO2)** In December of the current year, an aunt wants to give her niece $35,000 for a car she is planning to purchase. The money is needed by January of next year. The aunt does not want the gift to be taxable. How can the aunt structure the gift to avoid paying gift tax?

3. **(LO5)** Shirley is very wealthy, but her health is failing. She does not know how much longer she will live and would like to provide for her family. She is considering gifting her home to her daughter (who is in the highest income tax bracket). The home has a current fair market value of $6,500,000, and her basis in the home is $1,200,000. What tax considerations should Shirley consider? When would be the best time to make the transfer, at her death or now?

4. **(LO7)** Beatrice and Bernie have been married for 65 years! Both Beatrice and Bernie are well off financially. Beatrice has a gross estate of $15 million, and Bernie has a gross estate of $9.5 million at the beginning of the current year. Unfortunately, Bernie's health has been failing, and he passes away in 2025 with a net estate value of $9.25 million.

   a. Is there any estate tax liability due in 2025 upon Bernie's death?

   b. What proper family wealth planning could be used to help offset Beatrice's possible estate tax in the future when she passes?

Professional Development Skills

Communication Problem

Communication

1. **(LO4) Basis in Inherited Property** Pasquel informs you that he has received a large inheritance from his late grandmother. In particular, he received her vacation home in Hawaii, and he needs your help in determining his basis in the home. Pasquel thinks that he has no basis because he did not pay anything for the house. The executor of the estate has told Pasquel that he elected the alternate valuation date, but Pasquel does not understand what this means. How would you respond given the following information?

FMV at date of death	$325,000
FMV at date of distribution 3 months after date of death	$335,000
FMV 6 months after date of death	$345,000

Ethics and Professional Responsibilities Problem

Ethics

1. **(LO2) Gifting to a Special Friend** Gary and Jenny have been married for 35 years. Gary has a mistress and would like to give her jewelry worth $25,000. You are his tax accountant, and he let this information slip when you had lunch to discuss his income tax return and gift tax return. Gary does not want to report this gift on his gift tax return. What is your response to Gary?

In addition to the chapter content, see *Statements on Standards for Tax Services* at www.aicpacima.com/resources/landing/statements-on-standards-for-tax-services, *Circular 230* at www.irs.gov/tax-professionals/office-of-professional-responsibility-and-circular-230, and Chapter 2, LO4, Tax Professional Responsibilities.

Research Problem

Research

1. **(LO4) Gifting of Assets to Terminally Ill Relative.** For as long as there has been an estate tax, people have been trying to avoid it by making gifts. Initially, it made sense to give one's assets away before death to avoid having any estate tax liability. The IRS caught on to this planning quickly and enacted the gift tax. The gift tax is paid when the donor exceeds their lifetime applicable credit exclusion and annual exclusion (both adjusted for inflation annually). If you are the fortunate recipient of a gift, the gift itself is excludable from your income for income tax purposes. Also, if you receive an asset through inheritance, the value of the asset is not taxable to you on your income tax return. In most situations, the recipient receives a FMV basis in the asset received. You are familiar with this basis rule and decide to gift your home, stock, and other valuable assets to your terminally ill grandfather. Your grandfather includes in his will a provision to bequeath these assets back to you when he dies. What is the result if your grandfather dies 13 months after you make your gift? What is the result if your grandfather dies 11 months after you make your gift? Hint: See IRC §1014(c).

Excel Problem

1. **(LO4) Basis of Property Received through Inheritance.** Magdalena was very close to her grandpa, Willie Makit, and was devastated when he died. Willie left Magdalena his New England cottage in his will. He had paid $85,000 for the cottage in 1975. When Willie died on January 14 of the current year, the cottage had a fair market value of $535,000. The cottage had a fair market value of $515,000 on the alternate valuation date of July 14. The cottage was distributed to Magdalena on March 31, when its fair market value was $522,000.

   a. What is Magdalena's basis in the cottage if the executor does not elect the alternate valuation date?

   b. What is Magdalena's basis in the cottage if the executor does elect the alternate valuation date?

Create an Excel spreadsheet using a Lookup table to solve for your answer.

Tax Compliance and Reporting Problems

1. **(LO1, 2, 3) Form 709** Jasper and Melanie Tervor are a married couple. Jasper is 58, and Melanie is 55. The following transfers were made in 2025:

   1. Jasper gave cash of $50,000 to his son, River, and cash of $50,000 to his daughter, Rose.
   2. Jasper gave Melanie jewelry valued at $25,000.
   3. Jasper purchased a home for his son, Ranier, valued at $250,000. The title named Jasper and Ranier as joint tenants with the right of survivorship.
   4. Jasper transferred $100,000 of cash to the Denny Trust for the benefit of Denny, who is currently eight years old. The trustee of the Denny Trust may use the income or corpus for Denny's benefit and is required to distribute all the trust assets to Denny upon Denny's 25th birthday.

5. Jasper transferred stock worth $300,000 to the Cloud Trust. The trustee must pay income to brother James for his life, and upon James's death, must pay the remainder to Junior, James's son. At the time of the transfer, James is 35 years old, and the remainder interest rate is 5%.
6. Jasper donated $125,000 to Northern Illinois University.
7. Jasper paid $22,000 to Good Shepherd Hospital on behalf of his mother's medical expenses.

What is the value of Jasper's current taxable gifts in 2025? Assuming that Jasper has made $1,500,000 in prior taxable gifts, complete Form 709 for 2025. We use the 2024 Form 709 because the 2025 version was not available at the time of publication.

2. **(LO4, 5, 6, 7) Form 706** Hedon Makeit died on August 31, 2025. Hedon filed jointly with his wife, Athena. Hedon's son, Giannis, is the executor of Hedon's estate. Giannis took an inventory of his father's assets. Hedon's property includes the following:

Asset	FMV
Corvette	$ 65,000
Clothing	$ 4,000
Furniture	$ 20,000
Personal home	$800,000
Vacation home	$650,000
Vacant land	$530,000
Bank accounts	$ 75,000
Investments	$125,000

Additional information was provided at the time of his death:

1. Hedon owned and paid annual premiums on a life insurance policy worth $750,000. Hedon's daughter, Sophia, is named as the beneficiary.
2. Hedon owns the vacation home jointly with his brother, Christos. The title is held in joint ownership with the right of survivorship. At the time of purchase, Hedon paid $250,000 of the $400,000 purchase price.
3. Hedon owns the personal home jointly with his wife, Athena. The title is held in joint ownership with the right of survivorship.
4. Hedon owns the vacant land with his brother, Dimitrios, as tenants in common with Hedon owning a 25% interest and Dimitrios owning the remaining 75%.
5. Hedon made a revocable transfer of $950,000 to his son in 2016, and twenty-six months ago he converted this to an irrevocable transfer.
6. Hedon's will bequeaths $100,000 to his church.
7. Hedon made prior taxable gifts of $2,500,000 in 2024, the tax on which was entirely offset by the applicable credit.
8. All property not mentioned previously is bequeathed to his wife, Athena.

The following expenses were incurred by the estate and approved for payment by Giannis:

Mortgage on personal home	$140,000
Credit card debt	$ 12,000
Funeral expenses	$ 10,000
Executor fees	$ 5,000
Attorney fees	$ 8,000

The state that Hedon lived in has no state death or inheritance tax.

Giannis elects to deduct the executor fees and attorney fees on the estate tax return (Form 706).

Calculate Hedon's gross estate, adjusted gross estate, and taxable estate. Complete page 1 of Form 706.

CHAPTER 13

Taxation of Multinational Transactions

Sergey Nivens/AdobeStock

Before studying this chapter, you should know or, if necessary, review

6.1 Definitions Related to Partnerships (specifically, check-the-box regulations)

Chapter Introduction

VIDEO CONTENT

Robbins Flooring, Inc. has manufactured flooring in the United States for over 60 years. All of the company's sales have been in the United States. Robbins is considering building a manufacturing plant in India so that it can expand its sales to Asia. This would be a major investment of capital and the most aggressive strategy that the company had ever pursued. Robbins has no knowledge of how the United States would tax its operations in India. Fortunately, the CEO of Robbins has a neighbor who is a tax partner in an international public accounting firm. When the CEO discussed this potential decision with the partner, the partner advised him to hire a tax professional who could bring tax strategy into this decision-making process.

Our focus in this book has been on the taxation of income that was earned in the United States by U.S. citizens, residents, or businesses. However, businesses operate in a global economy today, so tax professionals need to understand how the United States taxes international transactions so they can advise companies such as Robbins Flooring. For example, in 2020, total services supplied by U.S.-based firms to foreign persons through both trade and sales by foreign affiliates of U.S. multinational enterprises was $2.25 trillion (*outbound transactions*, discussed below). Further, total services supplied to the United States by foreign-based firms through both trade and sales by U.S. affiliates of foreign multinational enterprises was $1.33 trillion (*inbound transactions*, discussed below).[1]

When considering international taxation, there are two important questions that must be answered.

- Which taxpayers are subject to the United States tax law?
- What income is subject to taxation under the United States tax laws?

We answer these questions throughout this chapter. We can separate the international transactions that are subject to the U.S. tax laws into two groups: outbound transactions and inbound transactions.

> **Outbound transactions** are foreign activities by a United States taxpayer, meaning that a U.S. taxpayer is conducting business outside the United States. The general notion for outbound transactions is that U.S. taxpayers are taxed on their income earned anywhere in the

[1]Allen, Shari A., and Fatima, Maryam. "U.S. International Services: Trade in Services in 2021 and Services Supplied Through Affiliates in 2020." *Survey of Current Business*, Vol. 102, No. 10, Oct. 2022. https://apps.bea.gov/scb/issues/2022/10-october/pdf/1022-international-services.pdf.

world. If the income is also taxed in a foreign country, then the United States allows a foreign tax credit for some, or all, the foreign taxes paid. If Robbins Flooring began selling its products in Asia, these would be outbound transactions.

Inbound transactions are activities in the United States conducted by a non-U.S. taxpayer. If a flooring company based in India began manufacturing its products in the United States, that would an inbound transaction.

Most of this chapter relates to outbound transactions. We begin the chapter by discussing the worldwide taxation policy used by the United States and explain the sourcing of income and deductions as either U.S. or foreign. We then discuss several tax laws that apply to outbound transactions. One goal of United States tax policy over the last few years has been to encourage U.S. companies that do business offshore to invest their offshore earnings back in the United States. There are two taxes that corporations may have to pay on their offshore earnings, and these taxes can be minimized if these earnings are repatriated to the United States. We close the chapter by discussing the tax laws related to inbound transactions by foreign persons earning income in the United States.

Related exercise: Discussion Question 1

LEARNING OBJECTIVES	TOPICS	PRACTICE OPPORTUNITIES

1 Identify U.S. taxpayers and foreign taxpayers.	**13.1 General Rules for International Taxation**
	• U.S. Tax Residents
	  • U.S. Tax Residents—Individuals
	  • U.S. Tax Residents—Business Entities
	  • Foreign Entities: Check-the-Box Regulations
	• Worldwide Taxation vs. Territorial Taxation
	• Tax Treaties
		• Example 13.1.1 U.S. Citizens
		• Example 13.1.2 Substantial Presence Test
		• Example 13.1.3 Foreign Entity Classification
		• Example 13.1.4 Sole Owner Foreign Entity
		• Example 13.1.5 Treaties
		• Practice Problem 13.1.1 Treaties

2 Determine the sourcing of income and the foreign tax credit.	**13.2 Sourcing of Income and Expenses**
	• Sourcing of Income
	  • Interest Income
	  • Dividend Income
	  • Rental and Royalty Income
	  • Personal Service Income
	  • Income from the Sale or Disposition of Property
	  • Distributive Share of Partnership Income
	  • Social Security Income
	  • Income from Software and Computer Programming
		• Example 13.2.1 Interest Income
		• Example 13.2.2 Sourcing of Partnership Income
		• Example 13.2.3 Royalty Income or Service Income
		• Example 13.2.4 Research and Experimental Expenses
		• Example 13.2.5 Allocation of Income and Expenses
		• Example 13.2.6 Foreign Tax Credit
		• Practice Problem 13.2.1 R&E Expenses
		• Practice Problem 13.2.2 Foreign Tax Credit

	• Sourcing of Deductions
	  • General Rules
	  • Interest Expense
	  • Research and Experimental Expenses
	• Foreign Tax Credit
	• Transfer Pricing	

3 Determine how U.S. taxpayers are taxed on outbound investments in foreign corporations.	**13.3 U.S. Taxpayers with Outbound Investment through Corporations**
	• Controlled Foreign Corporations
	• Subpart F Income Anti-Deferral Regime
	  • Foreign Personal Holding Company Income (FPHCI)
	  • Foreign Base Company Sales Income (FBC Sales Income)
	  • Foreign Base Company Services Income (FBC Services Income)
	  • Other Rules for Subpart F Income
	  • 100% Dividends Received Deduction
	• Global Intangible Low-Tax Income (GILTI) Anti-Deferral Regime
	  • CFC Tested Income
	  • Net Deemed Tangible Income Return
	• Passive Foreign Investment Company Anti-Deferral Regime
	• Base Erosion and Anti-Abuse Tax (BEAT)
		• Example 13.3.1 Application of Anti-Deferral Regimes
		• Example 13.3.2 Definition of a Controlled Foreign Corporation
		• Example 13.3.3 Foreign Personal Holding Company Income
		• Example 13.3.4 Foreign Base Company Sales Income
		• Example 13.3.5 Foreign Base Company Services Income
		• Example 13.3.6 Computation of Foreign Base Company Income
		• Example 13.3.7 100% Dividends Received Deduction
		• Example 13.3.8 GILTI Computation
		• Practice Problem 13.3.1 Subpart F
		• Practice Problem 13.3.2 GILTI Tax

4 Determine the U.S. income tax on foreign persons.	**13.4 Inbound Taxation on Foreign Persons**
	• FDAP Income
	  • Withholding Requirements
	  • Exceptions to Withholding
	• Business Income
	  • Definition of Effectively Connected Income
	  • Income from Provision of Services by Individuals
		• Example 13.4.1 Athletic Prizes Won by Foreign Athletes
		• Example 13.4.2 FDAP Income
		• Example 13.4.3 Business Activity for Foreign Persons from Treaty Countries
		• Example 13.4.4 Business Activity for Foreign Persons from Non-Treaty Countries
		• Practice Problem 13.4.1 FDAP
		• Practice Problem 13.4.2 Provision of Services by Individuals from a Non-Treaty Country

Tax forms referenced in this chapter:

Form 1040	U.S. Individual Income Tax Return
Form 1116	Foreign Tax Credit
Form 1120	U.S. Corporation Income Tax Return
Form 8832	Entity Classification Election

13.1 General Rules for International Taxation

LEARNING OBJECTIVE 1

Identify U.S. taxpayers and foreign taxpayers.

VIDEO CONTENT

Because most tax professionals do not deal with multinational transactions, the U.S. laws for international taxation can seem complex. Therefore, to understand the rules clearly and apply them appropriately, it is critical that you understand the concepts that are the foundation of how the United States approaches international taxation. In this section, we:

- Define U.S. tax residents and non-U.S. tax residents
- Explain how the check-the-box regulations apply to foreign business entities
- Distinguish between worldwide taxation and territorial taxation
- Discuss the importance of tax treaties

U.S. Tax Residents

In defining U.S. tax residents and non-U.S. tax residents, we first discuss the residency rules for individuals, and then for business entities. U.S. tax residents are subject to **worldwide taxation**, meaning that they are taxed on their income earned anywhere in the world.

U.S. Tax Residents—Individuals

There are four groups of individuals who are U.S. tax residents (sometimes referred to as **U.S. tax persons**).[2]

- **U.S. citizens** The **U.S. citizen** group includes both individuals born in the United States and naturalized U.S. citizens.
- **U.S. green card holders** A **U.S. green card holder** is a permanent resident who has been granted authorization to live and work in the United States on a permanent basis.
- **Resident aliens** A **resident alien** is someone who meets the **substantial presence test**. The substantial presence test is met if a person is in the United States for 183 days or more in a calendar year.
- **Election** A U.S. taxpayer whose spouse is a *nonresident alien* can make an election for the spouse to also be treated as a U.S. taxpayer.[3] (We further discuss nonresident aliens later in the chapter.)

The substantial presence test can also be met by considering an individual's presence in the United States in previous years. For this lookback rule to apply, the individual must have been in the United States for at least 31 days in the current year. In that case, the individual's presence in the United States for the previous two years must also be considered, as shown in the following formula:

100% of days in current year
Plus: 1/3 of the days in U.S. in prior year
Plus: 1/6 of the days in U.S. in second preceding year
Total days for alternate substantial presence test

[2]IRC §7701(b).

[3]IRC §6013.

If the sum of the days over this three-year period is greater than or equal to 183 days, the substantial presence test is met, and the individual is treated as a U.S. taxpayer.

The two following Examples illustrate the rules for determining when an individual is a U.S. taxpayer.

EXAMPLE 13.1.1
U.S. Citizens

Benjamin has been a U.S. citizen since birth and has lived in Germany for the last four years. During this time, he has not returned to the United States, and he has worked for an employer in Germany. How is Benjamin classified for U.S. tax purposes?

SOLUTION

Even though Benjamin has not been in the United States for the last four years, he is classified as a U.S. tax resident because he is a citizen of the United States.

EXAMPLE 13.1.2
Substantial Presence Test

Assume that Year 10 is the current tax year. Ying is a citizen of Taiwan who has been in the United States for the following number of days per year over the last three years:

Year 10:	140
Year 9:	120
Year 8:	48

Does Ying meet the substantial presence test for Year 10?

SOLUTION

To determine if Ying meets the substantial presence test, we must apply the formula for the three-year rule as follows:

100% of days in current year	140
Plus: 1/3 of the days in U.S. in prior year (120)	40
Plus: 1/6 of the days in U.S. in second preceding year (48)	8
Total days for alternate substantial presence test	188

Because the total days are at least 183, Ying is considered to have met the substantial presence test for Year 10. She is a U.S. tax resident for Year 10.

Related exercises: Discussion Question 2
Multiple Choice Questions 1, 2
Brief Exercise 1
Application Problems 1, 2
Tax Planning Problem 1

U.S. Tax Residents—Business Entities

Corporations and partnerships are considered to be U.S. tax residents and subject to worldwide taxation if they are organized under the laws of one of the 50 states or of Washington DC. The rules are different for trusts. A trust is considered to be a U.S. tax resident if it is under the supervision of a United States court and a majority of its trustees are U.S. citizens or residents. Corporations and partnerships that are formed in possessions of the United States are not considered to be U.S. tax residents.[4] For example, Guam is a United States possession, but businesses formed in Guam are not considered to be U.S. tax residents. Any business that does not qualify as a U.S. tax resident under one of the above guidelines is considered a foreign entity, as we'll discuss next.

[4]IRC §7701(b)(3)(B).

Foreign Entities: Check-the-Box Regulations

We discussed how the check-the-box (CTB) regulations apply to domestic businesses in Chapter 6, LO1, Definitions Related to Partnerships (see Illustration 6.1). We now explain how the check-the-box regulations apply to foreign entities.[5] There are three *default* classification rules for foreign entities, as follows:

- A foreign entity that has one owner and that owner has unlimited liability is treated as a *disregarded entity*.
- A foreign entity that has two or more owners and at least one owner has unlimited liability is considered a *partnership*.
- A foreign entity that has one or more owners and all the owners have limited liability is treated as a *corporation*.

If a foreign entity does not want to use its default classification, it may be able to elect a different tax status. There are two possible entity elections: corporation and partnership.

- A foreign flow-through entity may be able to elect to be taxed as a corporation for U.S. federal income tax purposes.
- Only foreign eligible entities can elect to be taxed as a partnership. A foreign eligible entity is one that is not a *per se* corporation. The regulations provide a list of foreign entities that are *per se* corporations. In general, ***per se* corporations** are entities for which at least some of the owners have limited liability.

Foreign business entities wishing to have a tax status different from their default classification can file Form 8832, Entity Classification Election. The form must be filed no later than 75 days after the effective date of the election.

Related exercises: Discussion Question 3
Multiple Choice Question 3

> **Potential Pitfall**
>
> **Recall** that foreign entities cannot elect to be taxed as an S corporation. Thus, all foreign entities taxed as corporations are C corporations.

The following steps are used to determine the proper U.S. tax classification for a foreign entity. These steps are also outlined in **Illustration 13.1**.

Step 1. **Determine:** If the entity is a U.S. tax resident. If the answer is YES, then the domestic check-the-box rules in Chapter 6 apply. If the answer is NO, then the entity is a foreign entity, and you proceed to step 2.

Step 2. **Assess:** If all the owners have limited liability, even if there is only one owner. If the answer is YES, then the default classification is a corporation, and you proceed to step 5. If the answer is NO, then go to step 3.

Step 3. **Determine:** If there is only one owner and that owner has unlimited liability. If the answer is YES, the entity is a disregarded entity, and you proceed to step 6. If the answer is NO, then go to step 4.

Step 4. **Ascertain:** If there are two or more owners and at least one owner has unlimited liability. If so, the entity is considered a partnership, and you proceed to step 6.

Step 5. **Elect:** If the entity has more than one owner, is not a *per* se corporation, and does not want to use the default classification of corporation from step 2, then it can elect to be taxed as a partnership. If the entity has one owner with limited liability, is not a *per se* corporation, and does not want to use the default classification of corporation from step 2, then it can elect to be a disregarded entity.

[5]Treas. Reg. §§301.7701-2(b) and 301.7701-3(a).

Step 6. **Elect:** If the entity does not want to use the default classification from step 3 or from step 4, the entity can elect to be taxed as a corporation.

ILLUSTRATION 13.1 Check-the-Box Regulations for Foreign Entities

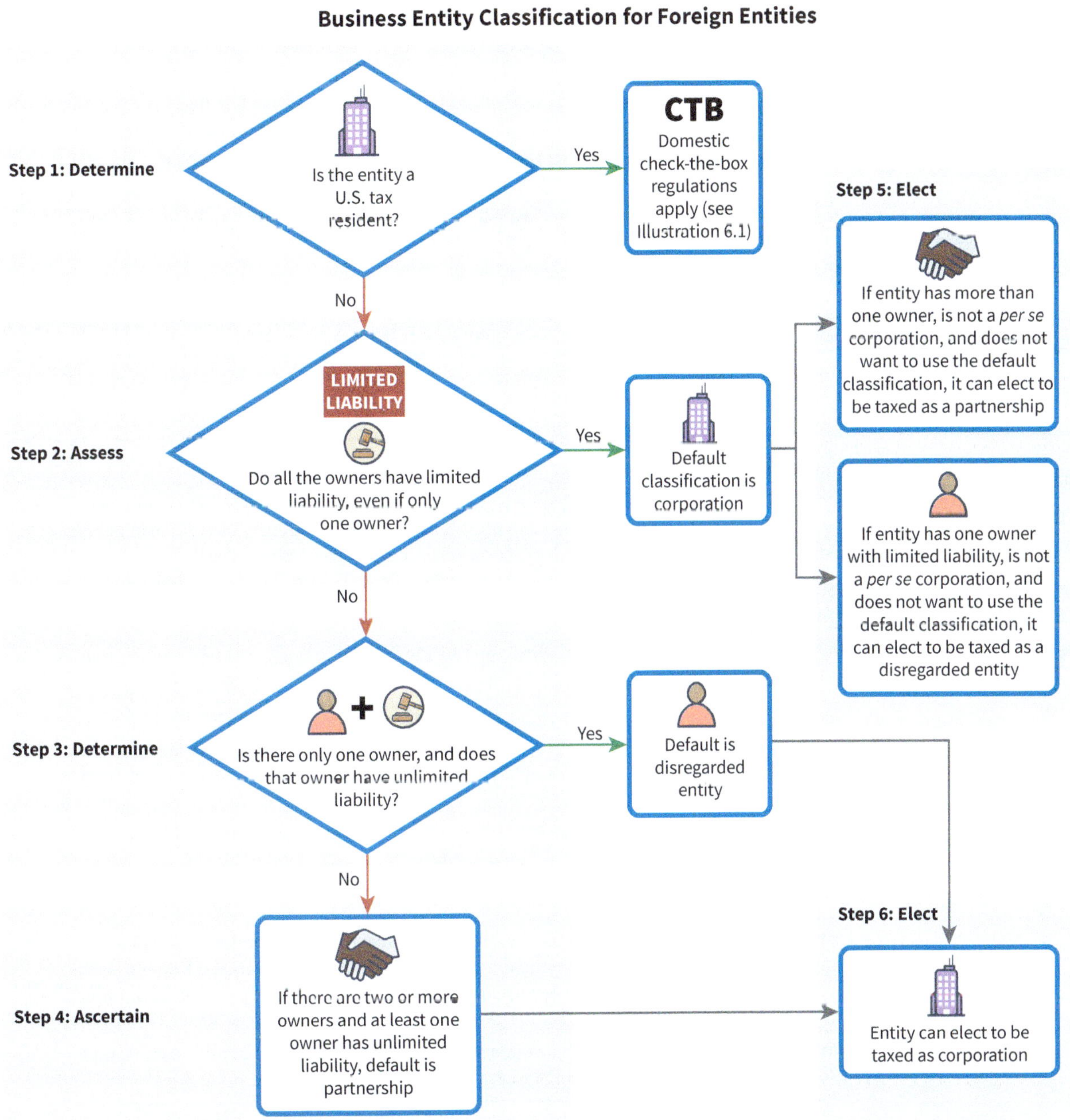

A foreign entity's tax status for U.S. tax purposes may be different from its tax status under foreign law. A **hybrid entity** is one that is treated as a partnership in the United States but as a corporation under foreign law. A **reverse hybrid entity** is a foreign entity that is treated as a corporation for U.S. tax purposes but as a partnership under foreign law.

Related exercise: Discussion Question 4

In the two following Examples, we demonstrate how the check-the-box regulations apply to foreign entities.

EXAMPLE 13.1.3
Foreign Entity Classification

Red Company is a partnership that was formed in India. All the partners in Red Company have limited liability. What is the default entity classification for Red? Do the owners of Red have any other options for the entity's tax classification in the United States?

SOLUTION

We use the steps outlined in Illustration 13.1 to determine Red's appropriate U.S. tax classification.

Step 1. **Determine**: If the entity is a U.S. tax resident. If the answer is YES, then the domestic check-the-box rules in Chapter 6 apply. If the answer is NO, then the entity is a foreign entity, and we proceed to step 2. Red is a foreign entity, so you proceed to step 2.

Step 2. **Assess**: If all the owners have limited liability, even if there is only one owner. If the answer is YES, then the default classification is corporation, and we proceed to step 5. If the answer is NO, we go to step 3. All of Red's owners have limited liability, so Red's default classification is corporation, and we proceed to step 5.

Step 5. **Elect**: Red has more than one owner. Thus, if it does not want to use the default classification of corporation, it can elect to be taxed as a partnership.

EXAMPLE 13.1.4
Sole Owner Foreign Entity

Amber owns 100% of a small business entity in Canada named Northern Lights. Her company does a significant amount of business in the northeastern United States. Based on her ownership structure in Canada, Amber does not have limited liability. What is the default entity classification of her business under the United States tax law, and what other classification can it elect to be?

SOLUTION

We again use the steps outlined in Illustration 13.1 to determine Northern Light's appropriate U.S. tax classification.

Step 1. **Determine**: If the entity is a U.S. tax resident. If the answer is YES, then the domestic check-the-box rules in Chapter 6 apply. If the answer is NO, then the entity is a foreign entity, and we proceed to step 2. Northern Lights is a foreign entity, so we proceed to step 2.

Step 2. **Assess**: If all the owners have limited liability, even if there is only one owner. If the answer is YES, then the default classification is corporation, and we proceed to step 5. If the answer is NO, we go to step 3. Amber does not have limited liability, so we proceed to step 3.

Step 3. **Determine**: If there is only one owner and that owner has unlimited liability. If the answer is YES, the entity is a disregarded entity, and we proceed to step 6. If the answer is NO, we go to step 4. Northern Lights does have one owner with unlimited liability, so its default classification is disregarded entity, and we proceed to step 6.

Step 6. **Elect**: If Northern Lights does not want to use the disregarded entity classification from step 3, it can elect to be taxed as a corporation.

Related exercises: Brief Exercise 2
Application Problem 3

Worldwide Taxation vs. Territorial Taxation

Historically, U.S. taxpayers, whether individuals or business entities, have been subject to tax on **worldwide income**, not just income earned in the United States. This meant that, in the U.S. in the past, foreign-earned income was always taxed by the United States. Many other countries also used a worldwide taxation approach; but over the last 30 years, most of them realized that this approach was a barrier to international trade and switched to a territorial system. **Territorial taxation** does not include foreign-earned income in the domestic country's income tax base. Today, the only three developed countries that still use a fully worldwide taxation system are Chile, South Korea, and Mexico. The *Tax Cuts and Jobs Act of 2017* made a significant change to the worldwide taxation system for certain U.S. corporations.

Let's first consider how U.S. corporations were taxed on their foreign-earned income before 2018. The highest corporate income tax rate in the United States in 2017 was 35%. Assume that a U.S.-based corporation had a foreign subsidiary operating in a European country and that it paid a 15% tax rate in the foreign country on its profits. The United States would also tax this income, but it would delay the taxation until the U.S. corporation repatriated the money back to the United States. At that time, it would be included in the worldwide income of the U.S. corporation and potentially taxed at a rate of 35%. The corporation would receive a foreign tax credit for the 15% tax rate paid in the foreign country, so the net tax rate in the United States would be 20%.

Many policymakers felt that U.S. companies were at a competitive disadvantage compared to their global counterparts under this worldwide taxation approach. The 35% corporate tax rate in the United States was the highest corporate tax rate in the world. Therefore, it was very likely that anytime a U.S. corporation repatriated money back to the United States, additional tax would be due. As a result, many U.S.-based corporations would never repatriate the funds to the United States, which in turn meant that those profits were being reinvested in the economies of other countries rather than the U.S. economy. Some economists estimated that unrepatriated earnings amounted to more than $2.5 trillion in 2017.[6]

In response to these concerns, the *Tax Cuts and Jobs Act of 2017* moved to a territorial tax system for income from foreign subsidiaries controlled by U.S. corporations. We discuss the current law in more detail later in the chapter. Your key insight for now is to understand the difference between a worldwide versus a territorial system, and to know that the United States still has a worldwide tax system for all foreign income except that earned by controlled foreign subsidiaries.

Tax Treaties

The United States has tax treaties with approximately 70 countries, as shown in **Illustration 13.2**.[7] Generally, in such a treaty, the United States agrees that it will treat taxpayers from the other country similarly to the way it treats U.S. taxpayers; and the other nation agrees to do the same for U.S. taxpayers. U.S. tax treaties only deal with federal income taxation, and do not apply to the income taxation of state or local governments. In some situations, the treaty will provide for a different tax outcome than the regular income tax law. When a treaty conflicts with other general income tax laws, the authority that was passed most recently will be the applicable authority. For example, dividend income is treated as qualified and therefore taxed at long-term capital gain rates only if paid by a domestic corporation. But many tax treaties provide that dividends paid by corporations from that foreign country will be treated as qualified dividends for purposes of the federal income tax law.

Most treaties address the issue of which country can tax particular income by separating income into two parts. First, investment income, such as interest, dividends, and royalties, is taxed to the country of residence of the taxpayer. Second, income earned by an active business is taxed by the country in which the business has a fixed business location. Addressing these issues in the treaty prevents double taxation of this income by providing certainty as to which country has the right to tax. While the country of residence can also tax the business income that was earned in the other country, it must provide a credit that the business can use to offset the taxes paid in the other country.

[6]Lautz, Andrew. "The 2025 Tax Debate: Mandatory Repatriation and the Dividends Received Deduction Under the Tax Cuts and Jobs Act. Bipartisan Policy Center. 26 Aug. 2024. https://bipartisanpolicy.org/explainer/the-2025-tax-debate-mandatory-repatriation-and-the-dividends-received-deduction-under-the-tax-cuts-and-jobs-act/.

[7]U.S. Department of the Treasury. "United States Income Tax Treaties - A to Z." Internal Revenue Service, Updated 19 Nov. 2024. www.irs.gov/businesses/international-businesses/united-states-income-tax-treaties-a-to-z.

ILLUSTRATION 13.2 U.S. Income Tax Treaties

U.S. Income Tax Treaties—2024					
Armenia	Cyprus	Indonesia	Malta	Russia*	Turkey
Australia	Czech Republic	Ireland	Mexico	Slovak Republic	Turkmenistan
Austria	Denmark	Israel	Moldova	Slovenia	Ukraine
Azerbaijan	Egypt	Italy	Morocco	South Africa	United Kingdom
Bangladesh	Estonia	Jamaica	Netherlands	Spain	Uzbekistan
Barbados	Finland	Japan	New Zealand	Sri Lanka	Venezuela
Belarus*	France	Kazakhstan	Norway	Sweden	
Belgium	Georgia	Korea	Pakistan	Switzerland	
Bulgaria	Germany	Kyrgyzstan	Philippines	Tajikistan	
Canada	Greece	Latvia	Poland	Thailand	
Chile	Iceland	Lithuania	Portugal	Trinidad	
China	India	Luxembourg	Romania	Tunisia	

*Partially suspended.[8]

EXAMPLE 13.1.5
Treaties

Green Company, Ltd. is a company created under the laws of Ireland. Ireland has a tax treaty that is in force with the United States. For the current tax year, Green Company has a fixed business location in Florida. The business activity from the Florida location generated income this year of $2,000,000. Green Company also earned investment income this year of $18,000. Is this income taxed by the United States or by Ireland?

SOLUTION

The business income of $2,000,000 is taxed by the United States because Green has a permanent place of business in the United States. However, the investment income is taxed to Ireland because it is the country of residence for Green Company. If Ireland chooses to also tax the business income of $2,000,000, it must provide Green with a credit or offset for the taxes paid in the United States.

Related exercises: Discussion Question 5
Multiple Choice Question 4
Brief Exercise 3

PRACTICE PROBLEM 13.1.1
Treaties

Holiday Company, S.A. is a company created under the laws of Venezuela. Venezuela has a tax treaty that is in force with the United States. For the current tax year, Holiday Company had a fixed business location in Vermont. The business activity generated the following income:

Vermont net operating income	$888,000
Venezuelan net operating income	$999,000
Interest income	$ 1,600
Dividend income	$ 4,400

Is this income taxed by the United States or by Venezuela?

[8]On December 17, 2024, the U.S. Department of the Treasury provided formal notice to the Republic of Belarus to confirm the suspension of the operation of paragraph 1, subparagraph (g), of Article III of the Convention, as it relates to Belarus, by mutual agreement. The suspension takes effect both for taxes withheld at source and in respect of other taxes as of December 17, 2024, and will continue until December 31, 2026, or earlier if mutually determined by the two governments. On June 17, 2024, the U.S. Department of the Treasury provided formal notice to the Russian Federation to confirm the suspension of the operation of Paragraph 4 of Article 1 and Articles 5–21 and 23 of the Convention and its accompanying Protocol. The suspension takes effect both for taxes withheld at source and in respect of other taxes as of August 16, 2024, and will continue until otherwise decided by the two governments.

SOLUTION

The Vermont business income of $888,000 is taxed by the United States because Holiday has a permanent place of business in the United States. However, the interest income and dividend income are investment income and taxed to Venezuela because it is the country of residence for Holiday Company. If Venezuela chooses to also tax the Vermont business income of $888,000, it must provide Holiday with a credit or offset for the taxes paid in the United States. The income generated in Venezuela of $999,000 is taxed in Venezuela.

INTERACTIVE SELF-SCORING QUIZZES

13.2 Sourcing of Income and Expenses

LEARNING OBJECTIVE 2

Determine the sourcing of income and the foreign tax credit.

VIDEO CONTENT

Now that you understand who is a U.S. tax person, the next step in understanding international taxation is to distinguish between income that is U.S.-sourced and income that is foreign-sourced. The sourcing rules will be used later in the section to compute the foreign tax credit and to determine the income of a foreign person that is taxed by the United States. Non U.S. taxpayers are usually taxed only on their U.S.-sourced income.

While we will discuss this in more detail in LO4, Inbound Taxation on Foreign Persons, it's important for this section that you understand who is characterized for tax purposes as a *foreign person* and as a *nonresident alien*. **Foreign persons** are individuals who are nonresident aliens, foreign corporations, foreign partnerships, or foreign estates and trusts. **Nonresident aliens** are individuals who are not citizens or residents of the United States.

Sourcing of Income

The first step in determining the sourcing of income is to know the category that the income falls into. The sourcing rules vary by the type of income. For example, the sourcing of service income is different from the sourcing of interest income.

Interest Income

Interest income is usually sourced to the residence of the payor. If the interest is paid by a resident of the United States, including domestic corporations and domestic partnerships, the interest is U.S.-sourced. If the interest is paid by a non-U.S. resident, then it is foreign-sourced.[9] Interest paid by a foreign corporation or partnership is treated as U.S.-sourced income if it is paid from earnings of a U.S. trade or business owned by the foreign corporation.

There are two major exceptions to these general rules:

- Interest income received from a U.S. corporation that earned at least 80% of its active business income over the last three years from foreign sources is treated as foreign-sourced income.
- Interest income received from deposits in a foreign branch of a U.S. corporation that is engaged in commercial banking is foreign-sourced income.

[9] IRC §861(a)(1).

EXAMPLE 13.2.1
Interest Income

Emma is a citizen and resident of the United States. She has a vacation home in Jamaica and earned $1,200 of interest income from funds deposited with a bank in Jamaica. How is the interest income sourced to Emma?

SOLUTION

The $1,200 of interest income is foreign-sourced income for Emma because the payor is a Jamaican bank, which is a non-U.S. resident.

Related exercises: Discussion Question 6
Multiple Choice 5
Brief Exercise 4

Dividend Income

The sourcing rules for dividend income are relatively simple. Dividends paid by a U.S. corporation are U.S.-sourced income, and dividends paid by a foreign corporation are foreign-sourced income. If the dividends from the foreign corporation are from a U.S. trade or business owned by the foreign corporation, the dividends are U.S.-sourced income.[10]

Rental and Royalty Income

If rental or royalty income is from property located in the United States, it is U.S.-sourced income. If the asset is located outside the United States, then the rental or royalty income from the property is foreign-sourced income.[11]

Personal Service Income

If services are provided in the United States, then the income is U.S.-sourced income. If the services are provided outside the United States, then the income is foreign-sourced.[12]

Income from the Sale or Disposition of Property

The sourcing rules for income from the sale or disposition of property vary depending on the type of property.

- Inventory purchased for resale is sourced based on the location where title transfers, so if the inventory is sold in the United States, then it is U.S.-sourced income, and if it is sold outside the United States, it is foreign-sourced income.
- Inventory that is manufactured or produced within the United States is U.S.-sourced income, while inventory manufactured or produced outside the United States is foreign-sourced income.[13]
- For other personalty, income from the sale or disposition of property is sourced based on the residence of the seller. Sales by residents of the United States are U.S.-sourced, and sales by non-U.S. taxpayers are foreign-sourced.[14]
- For realty, the location of the property determines the sourcing. If the property is located in the United States, the income is U.S.-sourced, and if the property is located outside the United States, it is foreign-sourced.[15]

Related exercise: Brief Exercise 5

[10]IRC §861(a)(2).
[11]IRC §862(a)(4).
[12]IRC §861(a)(3).
[13]IRC §863(b).
[14]IRC §865(a).
[15]IRC §861(a)(5).

Distributive Share of Partnership Income

The distributive share of partnership income is sourced based on the type of income, as described previously, that flows to the partner. If property is sourced based on the residence of the seller, then the income allocated to a partner is sourced based on the residence of the partner.[16]

EXAMPLE 13.2.2
Sourcing of Partnership Income

Partnership ABC is organized in Costa Rica and has two equal partners, Stefano and Manuel. Stefano is a resident of the United States, and Manuel is a resident of Costa Rica. During the current tax year, ABC sells land in Costa Rica and recognizes a gain of $120,000. ABC also sells a large truck used in its business and recognizes a gain of $16,000. How are these gains sourced to Stefano and Manuel?

SOLUTION

The distributive share of partnership income is sourced based on the type of income. Therefore, the gain from the land, which is realty, is sourced based on the location of the property. The property is located in Costa Rica, so the $120,000 gain is foreign-sourced. Therefore, both Stefano and Manuel have foreign-sourced income of $60,000 ($120,000 × 50%) because the land is located in Costa Rica. The gain from the truck, which is personalty, is sourced based on the residence of the seller, which is determined by the residence of the partner. The $8,000 gain ($16,000 × 50%) allocated to Stefano is U.S.-sourced income, and the $8,000 allocated to Manuel is foreign-sourced income. However, based just on these facts, Manuel is not a U.S. tax person and is not required to file a U.S. tax return. If Manuel had to file a U.S. return for other reasons, then the classification of this income as foreign-sourced would be relevant.

Related exercise: Application Problem 4

Social Security Income

United States Social Security benefits are always treated as U.S.-sourced income.

Income from Software and Computer Programming

Income from software, computer programming, and technology accounts for an ever-increasing percentage of the income generated by businesses. Therefore, the proper sourcing of this income is very important. Regulations categorize this type of income broadly as computer program income. A **computer program** is any software application or set of statements or instructions used by a computer to bring about a certain result.[17] Income from computer programs is divided into four categories, with the *company* being the developer of the program:

- **Transfer of a copyright by the *company***, such as selling the right to another business to sell the computer program in a certain region of the United States or in the world. This could result in income from the sale of property if the rights and risks are transferred to the purchasers; otherwise, it would be a licensing agreement that generates royalty income.
- **Sale of a copyrighted article by the *company***, meaning that the user purchases the right to use the computer program on the user's computer. Again, this could result in income from the sale of property or royalty income. The income would be from the sale of property if the rights and risks are transferred to the purchaser; otherwise, this would be a licensing agreement that generates royalty income.
- **Provision of customized services by the *company*** related to the development of a computer program that will function precisely as the user needs it to. This would be sourced as income from services.

[16]IRC §1366(b).

[17]Treas. Reg. §1.861-18(a)(3).

- **Provision of advice as a consultant by the *company*** related to a computer program developed by the user, such as assistance with implementing, troubleshooting, and integrating with other software. This would be sourced as income from services.

EXAMPLE 13.2.3
Royalty Income or Service Income

Taylor is a filmmaker who is a resident and citizen of France. While visiting the United States, she met an investor, Ella, who hired her to make a documentary on the growth of cryptocurrency over recent years. Taylor accepted the job for a fee of $75,000 but had to lengthen her visit to the United States to six months to complete the assignment.

a. Assume that Ella will retain full ownership of the film after it is produced. How would Taylor's income of $75,000 be sourced?

b. Assume that Taylor will own all rights to the film, and that Ella has the right to distribute the film in the United States. Taylor has the right to distribute the film anywhere else in the world. How would Taylor's income be sourced?

SOLUTION

To determine the proper sourcing of the $75,000 to Ella, we must determine the type of income that she received: service income or royalty income.

a. Because Taylor will have no ownership rights in the film, she has received $75,000 of service income. Taylor performed the services in the United States, so the $75,000 will be U.S.-sourced income.

b. Taylor owns the film and has licensed to Ella the right to distribute the film in the United States. Therefore, the $75,000 is royalty income to Taylor. It will be U.S.-sourced income because the fee is for the licensing of the film in the United States.

Related exercises: Multiple Choice Question 6
Application Problem 5

Sourcing of Deductions

U.S. taxpayers also need to know the sourcing rules for deductions, particularly for the computation of the foreign tax credit. Deductions are first allocated to a specific class of income and then, based on that class, apportioned as U.S.-sourced income or foreign-sourced income.[18]

Related exercise: Discussion Question 7

General Rules

Certain deductions have specific sourcing rules, and these are discussed below. For all other deductions, each should first be allocated to the class of gross income that it is associated with, such as:

- Interest income
- Dividend income
- Service income
- Income from sale of property
- Royalty income
- Rental income

Deductions that are not associated with a specific class of gross income are allocated proportionally across all classes of income. Once the class of income is determined, then the

[18]Treas. Reg. §1.861-8(a).

deduction is apportioned between U.S.-sourced and foreign-sourced, based on either gross income, gross receipts, units sold, or cost of goods sold.

Interest Expense

Interest expense is allocated based on the ratio of U.S. assets and foreign assets, determined based on the type of income generated by the asset.

Research and Experimental Expenses

The apportionment of research and experimental (R&E) expenses is a three-step process.

Step 1: First, if the expenses are incurred because of the legal requirements of a particular jurisdiction or government, then the expenses are sourced to that location.

Step 2: Other R&E expenses are apportioned 50% to the location where the research occurs.

Step 3: The other 50% remaining after step 2 is apportioned based on either gross income or gross sales.

Illustration 13.3 summarizes the steps for this computation, and Example 13.2.4 demonstrates how to complete it.

ILLUSTRATION 13.3 Allocation of Research and Experimental Expenses

Steps in Allocating Research and Experimental Expenses (Shaded cells should be filled in; see Example 13.2.3)				
R&E categories	**Incurred in foreign country**	**Incurred in U.S.**	**Sourced to foreign country**	**Sourced to U.S.**
Total R&E				
Step 1. Based on legal requirements				
Remaining R&E				
Step 2. 50% to location where incurred				
Remaining R&E				
Total R&E left to allocate				
Step 3. Based on gross income or gross sales				
Total allocation				

EXAMPLE 13.2.4 Research and Experimental Expenses

Brown Inc. incurred $2,000,000 of R&E expenditures this year. Brown has research facilities in the United States and in Germany. The expenditures are classified as follows:

- Incurred to meet legal requirements in Germany $ 300,000
- Other R&E expenses incurred in Germany $ 300,000
- R&E expenses incurred in the United States $1,400,000

Gross sales for the year are apportioned 70% to the United States and 30% to Germany.

How are the R&E expenses sourced?

SOLUTION

The first step is to allocate the $300,000 incurred in Germany to meet legal requirements to Germany. The remaining R&E expenses are $300,000 in Germany and $1,400,000 in the United States. Of these, 50% is allocated to the location where incurred—$150,000 to Germany and $700,000 to the United States. The remaining R&E expenses are allocated based on gross income or gross sales, and Brown uses gross sales. Thus, $255,000 is allocated to Germany ($850,000 × 30%), and $595,000 is allocated to the United States ($850,000 × 70%). The allocation is summarized as follows:

R&E categories	Incurred in Germany	Incurred in U.S.	Sourced to Germany	Sourced to U.S.
Total R&E	$600,000	$1,400,000		
Step 1. Based on legal requirements	$300,000	$ 0	**$ 300,000**	**$ 0**
Remaining R&E	$300,000	$1,400,000		
Step 2. 50% to location where incurred			**$ 150,000** ($300,000 × 50%)	**$ 700,000** ($1,400,000 × 50%)
Remaining R&E	$150,000	$ 700,000	$ 150,000	$ 700,000
Total R&E left to allocate	$850,000			
Step 3. Based on gross income or gross sales			**$ 255,000** ($ 850,000 × 30%)	**$ 595,000** ($ 850,000 × 70%)
Total allocation			**$ 705,000**	**$ 1,295,000**

Now let's review an Example that includes several of the expenses discussed in this section.

EXAMPLE 13.2.5
Allocation of Income and Expenses

Purple Inc. has the following items of income and expense for the current year:

- Service income of $150,000, all of which is generated by employees who work in the United States
- Royalty income of $225,000, which is 75% U.S.-sourced and 25% foreign-sourced
- Expenses of $70,000 related to the service income
- Interest expense of $10,000
- General and administrative (G&A) expenses of $100,000

Purple also has the following income-producing assets:

- $1,000,000 of intangible property that generates royalty income
- $250,000 of property that is used in the service business

How should Purple allocate its expenses?

SOLUTION

We begin by determining the process needed for each type of expense:

- Service-related expenses ($70,000): allocated to the service income. 100% is U.S.-sourced income because the services are 100% U.S.-sourced.
- Interest expense ($10,000): allocated based on the ratio of U.S. assets and foreign assets, which is determined as follows:
    - $1,000,000 of intangible property that generates royalty income. These assets are 75% U.S. assets ($1,000,000 × $75% = $750,000) and 25% foreign assets ($1,000,000 × 25% = $250,000).

- $250,000 of property that is used in the service business. These assets are all U.S. assets because the service income is 100% U.S.-sourced.

To summarize, interest expense is apportioned based on the following allocations:

- U.S. assets: $250,000 (service related) + $750,000 (royalty related) = $1,000,000
- Foreign assets: $250,000 (royalty related)

Thus, 80% ($1,000,000/$1,250,000) of the interest expense is U.S.-sourced, totaling $8,000 ($10,000 × 80%); and 20% ($250,000/$1,250,000) is foreign-sourced, totaling $2,000 ($10,000 × 20%).

- G&A expenses ($100,000): allocated pro rata across all sources of income. Purple's income is 40% service income ($150,000/[$150,000 + $225,000]) and 60% royalty income ($225,000/[$150,000 + $225,000]). Therefore, the G&A expenses are allocated as follows:
    - To service income: $100,000 × 40% = $40,000
    - To royalty income: $100,000 × 60% = $60,000

  We next apportion the G&A expenses as U.S.-sourced or foreign-sourced. The $40,000 of expenses allocated to service income are all U.S.-sourced. The $60,000 allocated to royalty income is 75% U.S.-sourced ($60,000 × 75% = $45,000) and 25% foreign-sourced ($60,000 × 25% = $15,000). To summarize, the G&A expenses are apportioned as follows:
    - U.S.-sourced: $40,000 (service related) + $45,000 (royalty related) = $85,000
    - Foreign-sourced: $15,000 (royalty related)

Related exercises: Application Problems 6 & 7

Illustration 13.4 summarizes the sourcing rules for income and deduction.

ILLUSTRATION 13.4 Summary of Sourcing Rules

General Sourcing Rules for Income and Deductions	
Income	**Source rule**
Interest income	Based on residence of the payor
Dividend income	If paid by U.S. corporations, U.S.-sourced; if paid by foreign corporations, foreign-sourced
Rental income	Based on location of property
Royalty income	Based on location of property
Sale of purchased inventory	Based on where title transfers
Sale of manufactured inventory	Based on where manufactured
Sale of other personalty	Based on residence of the seller
Sale of realty	Based on location of the property
Share of partnership income	Based on the sourcing rules for the type of income; income that is sourced based on the residence of seller is based on the residence of each partner
U.S. Social Security	U.S.-sourced
Income from computer programs	See four categories in LO2
Deductions	**Source rule**
General rule	Sourced same as income it is associated with, unless a specific sourcing rule exists; otherwise, allocated proportionally across all classes of income
Interest expense	Based on ratio of U.S. assets and foreign assets
Research and experimental expenses	See Illustration 13.3

Foreign Tax Credit

Now that you can distinguish between U.S.-sourced income and foreign-sourced income, you need to understand how to apply the sourcing rules when computing the foreign tax credit. The **foreign tax credit** is necessary because the United States taxes worldwide income, and any foreign-sourced income was likely also taxed in the country where it was earned. The foreign tax credit reduces the U.S. tax on the foreign income to the extent of the foreign taxes paid. Note that foreign taxes that are creditable include taxes imposed *in lieu* of an income tax.

The foreign tax credit is limited to the *lower* of:[19]

1. foreign income tax paid, *or*
2. U.S. tax on worldwide income $\times \dfrac{\text{Foreign-sourced taxable income}}{\text{Worldwide taxable income}}$

The second part of this formula is referred to as the **foreign tax credit limitation**. The limitation is applied separately for each country. The foreign taxes paid in excess of the foreign tax credit limitation can be carried back one year and carried forward ten years. The foreign tax credit is claimed on Form 1116, Foreign Tax Credit. We show how the foreign tax credit limitation is applied in the next Example.

EXAMPLE 13.2.6
Foreign Tax Credit

Gray, Inc. has $830,000 of U.S.-sourced income and $210,000 of foreign-sourced income, and Gray paid foreign taxes of $43,500. Assume that the U.S. income tax liability before the foreign tax credit is $205,000. How much is Gray's foreign tax credit? How much is Gray's foreign tax credit carryback/carryforward, if any?

SOLUTION

Gray's foreign tax credit is limited to the *lower* of:

1. foreign tax paid ($43,500), *or*
2. U.S. tax on worldwide income $\times \dfrac{\text{Foreign source taxable income}}{\text{Worldwide taxable income}}$

$$\$205{,}000 \times \frac{\$210{,}000}{(\$830{,}000 + \$210{,}000)} = \$41{,}394$$

Therefore, Gray's foreign tax credit is limited to $41,394. Gray has a foreign tax credit carryback/carryforward of $2,106 ($43,500 − $41,394).

Why **Why is the foreign tax credit limited by the foreign tax credit limitation?** The foreign tax credit limitation is based on the proportion of worldwide income that is foreign-sourced. In other words, the foreign tax credit cannot exceed what the U.S. tax liability would be on the same income. That proportion is multiplied by the U.S. tax liability on worldwide income. For example, if 24% of the worldwide income is foreign-sourced, then the foreign tax credit cannot exceed 24% of the U.S. tax liability on worldwide income. The foreign tax credit limitation limits the credit when the effective foreign tax rate on foreign-sourced income exceeds the U.S. statutory rate of 21%.

Related exercises: Discussion Question 8
Brief Exercise 6
Application Problem 8

The foreign tax credit limitation must be computed for ten separate categories of income, because different categories of income are taxed at different rates.[20] We will not explain all ten

[19]IRC §901.

[20]IRC §904(d).

categories because that is beyond the scope of this book. Two of the most common categories used are:[21]

- General category, which includes active business income
- Passive category, which includes investment income

Transfer Pricing

When goods or services are being bought and sold between related parties, the parties have an opportunity to set the transfer price of the items at the optimal level to minimize taxes. For example, an automobile manufacturer in the United States may own a subsidiary in Canada that manufacturers headlights. The parent company purchases all headlights made by the Canadian subsidiary. Clearly, the parent company has the ability to determine how much it will pay for these headlights. If it sets a higher price, then the Canadian subsidiary will have higher profits, and the U.S. parent will have lower profits. If it sets a lower price, then the Canadian subsidiary will have lower profits, and the U.S. parent will have higher profits.

One factor that will influence the transfer price is the tax rates in the two countries. For example, if the United States has a higher corporate income tax than Canada, then the transfer price may be set higher to maximize profits in Canada, the lower-tax country. Many years ago, Congress realized that tax laws were needed that would result in related companies setting reasonable transfer prices that were not manipulated to minimize taxes, so IRC §482 was created. This law requires that the accounting methods used *clearly reflect income*. If the IRS does not agree that income is clearly stated, it can reallocate gross income, deductions, credits, and other allocations to ensure that the taxable income reported is appropriate.

Because of the power given to the IRS by IRC §482, corporations that are selling products or services to related corporations have a significant burden to justify that the transfer price they used is appropriate. As you might imagine, the IRS and taxpayers often disagree on the appropriate transfer price, so significant litigation occurs in this area. To minimize these disputes, the IRS created the Advance Pricing Agreement program, which allows a taxpayer to submit the transfer pricing policy it used to determine prices for cross-border transactions. If the IRS accepts the justification for the transfer price, then the IRS cannot challenge the price later.

PRACTICE PROBLEM 13.2.1
R&E Expenses

Spartan Inc. incurred $750,000 of R&E expenditures this year. Spartan has research facilities in the United States and in Pakistan. The expenditures are classified as follows:

- Incurred to meet legal requirements in Pakistan $105,000
- Other R&E expenses incurred in Pakistan $185,000
- R&E expenses incurred in the United States $460,000

Gross sales for the year are apportioned 60% to the United States and 40% to Pakistan. How are the R&E expenses sourced?

SOLUTION

The first step is to allocate the $105,000 incurred in Pakistan to meet legal requirements to Pakistan. The remaining R&E expenses are $185,000 in Pakistan and $460,000 in the United States. Of these, 50% is allocated to the location where incurred—$92,500 to Pakistan and

[21]The definitions of the terms used for these categories are often different than the definitions used for other areas of the federal income tax law.

$230,000 to the United States. The remaining R&E expenses are allocated based on gross income or gross sales, and Spartan uses gross sales. Thus, $129,000 is allocated to Pakistan ($322,500 × 40%), and $193,500 is allocated to the United States ($322,500 × 60%). The allocation is summarized below:

R&E categories	Incurred in Pakistan	Incurred in U.S.	Sourced to Pakistan	Sourced to U.S.
Total R&E	$290,000	$460,000		
Step 1. Based on legal requirements	$105,000	$ 0	**$ 105,000**	**$ 0**
Remaining R&E	$185,000	$460,000		
Step 2. 50% to location where incurred			**$ 92,500** ($185,000 × 50%)	**$ 230,000** ($460,000 × 50%)
Remaining R&E	$ 92,500	$230,000	$ 92,500	$ 230,000
Total R&E left to allocate	$322,500			
Step 3. Based on gross income or gross sales			**$ 129,000** ($322,500 × 40%)	**$ 193,500** ($322,500 × 60%)
Total allocation			**$ 326,500**	**$ 423,500**

PRACTICE PROBLEM 13.2.2
Foreign Tax Credit

Volunteer Corporation has $428,000 of U.S.-sourced income and $113,000 of foreign-sourced income, and it paid foreign taxes of $24,860. Assume that the U.S. income tax liability before the foreign tax credit is $105,000.

a. How much is Volunteer's foreign tax credit?

b. How much is Volunteer's foreign tax credit carryback/carryforward, if any?

SOLUTION

a. Volunteer's foreign tax credit is limited to the *lower* of:

1. foreign tax paid ($24,860), *or*
2. U.S. tax on worldwide income $\times \dfrac{\text{Foreign source taxable income}}{\text{Worldwide taxable income}}$

$$\$105{,}000 \times \frac{\$113{,}000}{(\$428{,}000 + \$113{,}000)} = \$21{,}931$$

Therefore, Volunteer's foreign tax credit is limited to $21,931.

b. Volunteer has a foreign tax credit carryback/carryforward of $2,929 ($24,860 – $21,931).

INTERACTIVE SELF-SCORING QUIZZES

13.3 U.S. Taxpayers with Outbound Investment through Corporations

LEARNING OBJECTIVE 3

Determine how U.S. taxpayers are taxed on outbound investments in foreign corporations.

VIDEO CONTENT

Outbound transactions are foreign activities by a U.S. taxpayer, meaning that a U.S. taxpayer is conducting business outside of the United States. As mentioned previously, income earned from foreign corporations is typically not taxed in the United States until it is repatriated. This provides an incentive for U.S. shareholders to delay bringing the earnings back to the United States, because the delay defers taxation of the earnings. You will learn in this section that certain *anti-deferral regimes*, or rules, result in taxation to the U.S. shareholders when the income is earned by the foreign corporation rather than when it is distributed. **Anti-deferral regimes** prevent the deferral by U.S. corporations of income earned in foreign countries. There are three anti-deferral regimes for income earned from foreign corporations:

- Subpart F
- Global intangible low-tax income (GILTI)
- Passive foreign investment company (PFIC)

A fourth anti-deferral regime, known as the *base erosion and anti-abuse tax (BEAT)*, exists to prevent companies from shifting income earned in the United States to foreign countries.

See **Illustration 13.5** for a summary of the acronyms used in this chapter.

ILLUSTRATION 13.5 Summary of Chapter 13 Acronyms

Acronyms Related to International Taxation	
BEAT	Base erosion and anti-abuse tax (BEAT)
CFC	Controlled foreign corporation
DTIR	Deemed tangible income return
ECI	Effectively connected income
FBCI	Foreign-based company income
FBC sales income	Foreign base company sales income
FBC services income	Foreign base company services income
FDAP income	Fixed, determinable, annual, or periodic income
FPHCI	Foreign personal holding company income
GILTI	Global intangible low-tax income
PFIC	Passive foreign investment company
QBAI	Qualified business asset investment

Two questions must be answered YES for an anti-deferral regime to apply to a foreign corporation:

- Was the income earned by a foreign corporation? A **foreign corporation** is one not formed in one of the states or the District of Columbia.
- Is the foreign entity taxed as a corporation for U.S. tax purposes? Entities classified as flow-through for U.S. taxation are not subject to these regimes.

Related exercise: Discussion Question 9

In the next Example, we apply these two questions to determine if the anti-deferral regimes apply.

EXAMPLE 13.3.1
Application of Anti-Deferral Regimes

Is each of the following entities subject to the U.S. anti-deferral regimes? Reference the check-the-box regulations for foreign entities in LO1 (see Illustration 13.1) as needed.

- Crimson SC is located in Portugal, where it is treated as a partnership but as a corporation for U.S. tax purposes.
- Peach, SNC, is a partnership in France that has some owners with limited liability, so its default classification is corporation. However, it checked the box to elect to be a flow-through entity for U.S. tax purposes.
- Orange, Inc. is a U.S. corporation that does not have any foreign investments.

SOLUTION

Crimson SC: Crimson is a foreign corporation. Crimson is subject to the anti-deferral regimes because it is treated as a corporation for U.S. tax purposes. Its tax classification in Portugal does not matter for this decision.

Peach, SNC: Peach is a foreign corporation. Peach is not subject to the anti-deferral regimes because it is taxed as a partnership for U.S. tax purposes. Its default classification of corporation in the United States is not relevant because Peach chose to be taxed as a partnership.

Orange, Inc.: Orange is a U.S. taxpayer, so it is not subject to the anti-deferral regimes. Also, it has no investments in foreign corporations that might be subject to the anti-deferral regimes.

Related exercise: Brief Exercise 7

Two of the anti-deferral regimes, Subpart F and GILTI, apply only to *controlled foreign corporations (CFCs)*, so we define CFCs in the next section.

Controlled Foreign Corporations

A foreign corporation is treated as a **controlled foreign corporation (CFC)** if on any day during the year, more than 50% of the voting stock or value is owned by U.S. shareholders.[22] U.S. shareholders are limited to U.S. taxpayers that own at least 10% of the voting stock or value of the foreign corporation.[23] When determining stock ownership, stocks owned directly and indirectly through related parties are included.

The next Example illustrates the determination of whether a foreign corporation is a CFC.

EXAMPLE 13.3.2
Definition of a Controlled Foreign Corporation

Aqua Corporation is a foreign corporation that is owned as follows:

Emma, a U.S. taxpayer	15%
Kathleen, a U.S. taxpayer	25%
Antonio, a foreign taxpayer	40%
Zhang, a U.S. taxpayer	13%
Fredericka, a foreign taxpayer	7%

Is Aqua a CFC?

[22] IRC §957(a).
[23] IRC §951(b).

SOLUTION

To determine if Aqua is a CFC, we first need to identify the U.S. shareholders, defined as U.S. taxpayers who own at least 10% of the stock of Aqua: Emma, Kathleen, and Zhang. Next, we determine if the U.S. shareholders own more than 50% of the stock of Aqua, as follows:

Emma, a U.S. taxpayer	15%
Kathleen, a U.S. taxpayer	25%
Zhang, a U.S. taxpayer	13%
Total	53%

The U.S. shareholders own more than 50% of Aqua, so Aqua is a CFC.

Related exercises: Discussion Question 10
Multiple Choice Question 7
Brief Exercise 8

Subpart F Income Anti-Deferral Regime

The Subpart F anti-deferral regime applies only to CFCs. Subpart F income is deemed to be distributed to U.S. shareholders when it is earned by the CFC. It does not matter whether the income has been distributed to the shareholders. This prevents U.S. shareholders from deferring the taxation of the income by delaying its distribution, or repatriation, to the U.S. shareholders.

Subpart F income is taxed as ordinary income to the U.S. shareholders. Individual shareholders are not eligible to treat Subpart F income as qualified dividends, which they would have preferred because qualified dividends are taxed at LTCG rates.

Potential Pitfall

The Subpart F and GILTI anti-deferral regimes apply only to CFCs. Do not apply these regimes to foreign corporations that are not CFCs.

Tax Planning Tip

The taxation of Subpart F income is analogous to how partnership income is taxed to partners, in that such income flows to the partners on the last day of the partnership tax year, regardless of whether it has been distributed.

Subpart F income consists of the following categories:[24]

- Foreign-based company income (FBCI)
- Insurance income
- A portion of international boycott income
- Illegal bribes and kickbacks
- Income earned in certain disfavored countries

The Subpart F rules apply to all income in these categories even if the U.S. shareholders did not have an intent to defer income.

We will discuss only FBCI income further. FBCI consists of the following categories:

- Foreign personal holding company income (FPHCI)
- Foreign base company sales income (FBC sales income)
- Foreign base company services income (FBC services income)

Foreign Personal Holding Company Income (FPHCI)

FPHCI generally consists of investment income earned in the foreign country, including:[25]

- Dividends, interest, rents, royalties, and annuities

[24]IRC §952(a).

[25]Treas. Reg. §1.954-2(a)(1).

- Net gain from the sale or exchange of assets that produce FPHCI (such as stocks and bonds)
- Excess of foreign currency gains over foreign currency losses

Rents and royalties that are earned from an active trade or business are not included in FPHCI.

Why **Why is FPHCI treated as Subpart F income?** FPHCI is treated as Subpart F income because the U.S. shareholders could have invested these funds in the United States rather than the foreign country without significant inconvenience or cost.

EXAMPLE 13.3.3
Foreign Personal Holding Company Income

Black Company is a CFC located in Sweden that has the following income:

Interest income from a bank branch in Sweden	$ 6,800
Dividend income from a Swedish corporation whose stock is held in Sweden	$14,000
Royalty income from intangible property created as part of Black's business operations	$80,000
Gain from the sale of foreign-held stock	$23,000

How much of this income is FPHCI?

SOLUTION:

The royalty income is not FPHCI because it was earned as part of Black's business activities. The interest, dividends, and gain from the stock sale are included in FPHCI, so the total is $43,800 ($6,800 + $14,000 + $23,000).

Related exercises: Discussion Question 11
Multiple Choice Question 8
Brief Exercise 9

Foreign Base Company Sales Income (FBC Sales Income)

FBCSI includes income from the sale of personalty that meets the following two criteria:

- The personalty was either purchased from or sold to a related party, *and*
- The product was manufactured outside the CFC's country of incorporation and sold to customers outside the CFC's country of incorporation.[26]

If the personalty was either manufactured in the CFC's country of incorporation or sold to customers in the CFC's country of incorporation, the income is not FBC sales income.

Why **Why is FBC sales income treated as Subpart F Income?** Assume that a foreign corporation, Q, is a CFC incorporated in Country R. Company Q sells equipment that is manufactured in Country F to customers located in Country W. Because the equipment is not manufactured in Country R or sold to customers in Country R, there appears to be little reason for the sales transactions to flow through Company Q rather than through a U.S. corporation. Thus, the structure appears to be arranged to produce deferral of income to U.S. shareholders.

In the next Example, we show how FBC sales income is computed.

[26]IRC §954(d).

EXAMPLE 13.3.4
Foreign Base Company Sales Income

Azure Company owns 100% of the stock of Foreign Company, a CFC that is organized in Japan. Azure manufactures clothes in Vietnam that are sold to Foreign Company. Foreign Company then sells the clothes to customers in Japan and in Europe. Foreign Company's income from these sales in the current tax year is $1,000,000, with 70% of the sales in Japan and 30% of the sales in Europe. How much of the income is FBC sales income?

SOLUTION

The income must meet the two criteria above to be FBC sales income.

- The clothing was purchased by Foreign Company from Azure, which is a related party, *and*
- The clothing was manufactured in Vietnam and 30% was sold in Europe, outside of Japan.

Therefore, $300,000 ($1,000,000 × 30%) of the income is FBC sales income. The $700,000 ($1,000,000 × 70%) of income generated from the sale of clothing in Japan is not FBC sales income.

Related exercises: Discussion Question 12
Application Problem 9

Foreign Base Company Services Income (FBC Services Income)

FBC services income is income that a CFC performs on behalf of or for a related party if the services are performed outside the CFC's country of incorporation. Thus, if the services are performed by the CFC in its country of incorporation, then the service income is not Subpart F income.[27]

EXAMPLE 13.3.5
Foreign Base Company Services Income

Continue with the facts from Example 13.3.4. Azure also provides sales training to customers if requested. The services provided are paid for separately by the customers. The services are provided by Foreign Company. Foreign Company earned $150,000 of service income from customers in Japan and $45,000 of service income from customers in Europe. How much of the income is FBC services income?

SOLUTION

Foreign Company is providing services on behalf of Azure Company, which is a related party. Therefore, the $45,000 of service income earned from customers in Europe is FBC services income. The $150,000 of service income earned from customers in Japan is not FBC services income.

Related exercise: Brief Exercise 10

Other Rules for Subpart F Income

Once the total Subpart F income is computed, four additional rules must be used to determine the final amount reported on the return, as follows:

- Subpart F income is limited to the CFC's current earnings and profits (E&P). Subpart F income in excess of current E&P is carried forward and treated as Subpart F income when there is sufficient current E&P in the future.[28]
- If the Subpart F income is more than 70% of the CFC's total income, then all of the CFC's income is treated as Subpart F income.[29]

[27]IRC §954(e).

[28]IRC §952(c)(1)(A).

[29]IRC §954(b)(3)(B).

- If the Subpart F income does not exceed the *lower* of \$1,000,000 *or* 5% of gross income, then the CFC is treated as having no Subpart F income.[30]
- If the CFC's Subpart F income is taxed at an effective rate of more than 90% of the highest U.S. corporate income tax rate (currently 21%), then the CFC can elect to exclude that income from Subpart F.[31]

We demonstrate the first two limitations on Subpart F income in the next Example.

EXAMPLE 13.3.6
Computation of Foreign Base Company Income

Assume the same facts as in Example 13.3.4. What would the Subpart F income be in the following independent situations?

a. Foreign Company's current E&P is \$200,000.

b. Foreign Company's sales were 80% in Europe and 20% in Japan.

SOLUTION

a. In Example 13.3.4, the Subpart F income was \$300,000. If Foreign Company's current E&P is \$200,000, then the Subpart F income is limited to \$200,000. The excess \$100,000 of Subpart F income is carried forward to future years.

b. Foreign Company's Subpart F income would be \$800,000 (\$1,000,000 × 80%) because 80% of the sales were in Europe. However, because the Subpart F income is more than 70% of the CFC's total income, then all (\$1,000,000) of Foreign Company's income is considered Subpart F income.

Related exercise: Application Problem 10

100% Dividends Received Deduction

Since 2018, the U.S. income tax law has allowed U.S. corporations to benefit from a 100% dividends received deduction for distributions made from the earnings and profits of a 10%-owned foreign subsidiary.[32] The purpose of this DRD is to encourage U.S. corporations to bring their foreign earned income back to the United States. The following requirements apply to this deduction:

- The U.S. parent corporation must have owned the stock in the foreign subsidiary for at least one year to qualify for the DRD.
- The DRD is allowed regardless of whether the foreign subsidiary is a CFC.
- Subpart F income is not eligible for the DRD because, as you have already learned, it is deemed distributed and taxed to the U.S. shareholders in the year it is earned.
- If a U.S. parent sells stock in a 10%-owned foreign subsidiary that is a CFC, the gain from the sale is treated as dividend income and the parent receives a 100% DRD, so that the gain is not taxed. The DRD is limited to the parent's share of the unrepatriated earnings and profits of the subsidiary.

[30]IRC §954(b)(3)(A).

[31]IRC §954(b)(4).

[32]IRC §245A.

EXAMPLE 13.3.7
100% Dividends Received Deduction

Return to the facts of Example 13.3.4. Azure Company owns 100% of the stock of Foreign Company, a CFC that is organized in Japan. Foreign Company has $4,600,000 of income for the current year that is not Subpart F income, and this amount is transferred to Azure before the end of the tax year. How is this income taxed to Azure Company?

SOLUTION

Azure Company has dividend income of $4,600,000 and an offsetting DRD of $4,600,000, so the increase in taxable income is $0.

Related exercise: Brief Exercise 11

Global Intangible Low-Tax Income (GILTI) Anti-Deferral Regime

The global intangible low-tax income (GILTI) anti-deferral regime has been in effect since 2018 and applies only to CFCs. Congress believed that GILTI was needed in addition to Subpart F because Subpart F does not address income earned from intangible assets. As technology became an ever-increasing part of the value of many corporations, Congress was concerned that U.S. taxpayers were moving intangible property offshore so that the income derived from those assets could be deferred until repatriated to the United States. For example, many technology companies, such as Google, have established headquarters in Ireland that own the company's intangible property. One reason for this is that Ireland's corporate income tax rate on income generated from the intangible property is 12.5%, much lower than the U.S. corporate income tax rate of 21%.[33]

The GILTI anti-deferral regime provides a global minimum tax on income generated by intangible assets. GILTI is implemented by allowing CFCs a 10% return on their tangible assets; any additional return is assumed to be from intangible assets and subject to GILTI. GILTI is computed at the shareholder level.

Potential Pitfall

Subpart F and GILTI are similar in that both are anti-deferral schemes that apply only to CFCs. However, they differ in that while Subpart F is computed at the entity level, GILTI is computed and paid at the shareholder level. Also, Subpart F income is not included in the GILTI inclusion computation, so the same income is never subject to both Subpart F and GILTI.

GILTI is based on the following formula. Every CFC must apply this formula to determine if it is liable for GILTI.

$$\text{GILTI} = \text{CFC tested income} - (\text{Net deemed tangible income return} \times 10\%)^{34}$$

CFC Tested Income

CFC tested income is a CFC's taxable income computed as if the CFC were a U.S. taxpayer, except that the following items are not included.

- Subpart F income
- Income effectively connected with a U.S. trade or business
- Dividends received from a related person
- Certain oil and gas income

Net Deemed Tangible Income Return

Net deemed tangible income return (DTIR) is computed as follows:

$$\text{Net deemed tangible income return} = \text{QBAI} - \text{Net specified interest expense of the CFC}$$

[33]Ghosh, Sucharita. "Why Is Google Headquartered in Ireland." *Pleaders.* 8 Aug. 2016. https://blog.ipleaders.in/google-headquartered-ireland/.

[34]IRC §951A.

> **Potential Pitfall**
>
> The QBAI of a CFC with a tested loss is not included in the computation of GILTI.

QBAI is qualified business asset investment, which includes the fixed assets of the CFC and any tangible depreciable property, measured as the adjusted tax basis of the assets.

The computation of GILTI includes the following factors:

- GILTI is treated as ordinary income.
- U.S. shareholders in a CFC receive a 50% deduction for the CFC's GILTI. This deduction cannot exceed the CFC's taxable income.[35] An individual U.S. shareholder can elect to be taxed as a C corporation for purposes of the GILTI inclusion.
- The foreign tax credit is allowed against the GILTI tax to the extent of 80% of the foreign taxes paid. No carryback or carryover is allowed for any unused foreign tax credit.

We show the computation of GILTI in the following Example.

EXAMPLE 13.3.8
GILTI Computation

Gadin is a U.S. taxpayer who owns 100% of Turquoise Corporation, a Dutch BV. Turquoise has the following information for the current tax year:

Taxable income	$4,200,000
Adjusted tax basis of depreciable tangible assets	$6,500,000
Net specific interest expenses	$ 125,000
Subpart F income	$1,700,000

Compute Gadin's GILTI inclusion amount. How much tax is due, assuming Gadin has elected to be taxed as a C corporation?

SOLUTION

We use the following formulas and definitions to compute the GILTI inclusion amount for Gadin:

- QBAI is $6,500,000.
- Net DTIR = QBAI ($6,500,00) – Net specified interest expense of the CFC ($125,000) = $6,375,000
- CFC tested income is taxable income ($4,200,000) less Subpart F income ($1,700,000) = $2,500,000
- GILTI = CFC tested income ($2,500,000) – [Net DTIR ($6,375,000 × 10%)] = $1,862,500.

Gadin has elected to be taxed as a corporation, so he receives a 50% deduction for the GILTI inclusion and is taxed at a 21% rate. His tax due is $195,563 ($1,862,500 × 50% × 21%).

Related exercises: Discussion Question 13
Multiple Choice Questions 9, 10
Application Problem 11
Tax Planning Problem 2

Spotlight on the Law

Google—Brilliant Tax Minds Save Billions in Taxes

Who hasn't heard of Google and the phrase "Just Google it"? No one! Everyday life for most individuals and businesses includes using Google to perform searches, as well as using Google services such as Chrome, Gmail, YouTube, and Google Docs. Google is an American multinational company founded in 1996 by two Ph.D. students from Stanford University, Sergey Brin

[35] IRC §250(a).

and Larry Page. Their goal was to organize the world's information. They have accomplished that goal, as a simple Google search will immediately retrieve almost any information you are looking for.

Google's main headquarters are located in California. What most people do not know is that Google's European headquarters are located in Dublin, Ireland. The main reason that Google chose Ireland is because of its low corporate tax rate of 12.5%, compared with the current U.S. corporate tax rate of 21%. Google has adopted several different tax strategies to reduce its overall tax liability. One technique is to transfer its profits on patent royalties to Ireland. If a Google product is sold in the United States, it is subject to the 21% tax rate. However, if the money is paid to an Irish subsidiary as royalties on patents the Irish subsidiary owns, then it can be taxed at the lower 12.5% rate.* Also, if the Irish subsidiary is controlled by managers elsewhere, in a lower-tax or no-tax country, then the profits might escape tax entirely!

Typically, income earned from foreign corporations is not taxed in the United States until it is repatriated. However, certain anti-deferral regimes result in taxation to U.S. shareholders when the income is earned by the foreign corporation rather than when it is distributed. Global intangible low-tax income (GILTI) is an example of an anti-deferral regime for income earned from foreign corporations. The GILTI anti-deferral regime applies to controlled foreign corporations and provides a global minimum tax on income generated by intangible assets. As we've seen, determining the GILTI tax is a complicated calculation, but it does prevent income earned from intangible assets in a foreign country from escaping current taxation. Google and other tech companies doing business overseas will continue to have European headquarters for a variety of other reasons, but some of their undistributed earnings will likely be taxed in the United States due to the GILTI tax provision.

*Ghosh, Sucharita. "Why Is Google Headquartered in Ireland." *Pleaders*. 8 Aug. 2016. https://blog.ipleaders.in/google-headquartered-ireland/.

Passive Foreign Investment Company (PFIC) Anti-Deferral Regime

A passive foreign investment company (PFIC) is a corporation that meets *one* of the following conditions:

- More than 75% of its gross income is passive-type income, *or*
- More than 50% of its assets are investments that generate passive income.[36]

The PFIC regime was added by Congress as part of the Tax Reform Act of 1986 because, as with Subpart F income related to FPHCI, U.S. taxpayers may transfer investment assets to foreign corporations to defer taxation of the investment income. In general, passive income for purposes of the PFIC anti-deferral rules is defined the same as it is for the FPHCI rules.

The application of the PFIC regime must be tested if a U.S. taxpayer is a shareholder in a foreign corporation that has passive-type income. This means that the PFIC rules apply to more than just CFCs. Rather, these rules have much broader coverage than the Subpart F and GILTI regimes. The tax consequences for PFICs fall into one of three treatments, the discussion of which is beyond the scope of this text.

Related exercise: Discussion Question 14

Base Erosion and Anti-Abuse Tax Regime (BEAT)

The first three anti-deferral regimes we discussed target income earned abroad by U.S. corporations. The **base erosion and anti-abuse tax (BEAT)** differs in that its goal is to prevent companies from shifting income earned in the United States to foreign countries. The BEAT is

[36]IRC §1297(a).

a 10% minimum tax aimed at keeping both foreign and domestic corporations doing business in the United States from shifting profits out of the United States. The BEAT applies only to large multinational corporations with gross receipts of $500 million or more. In addition, the BEAT does not apply unless payments made by a U.S.-based corporation to related foreign corporations exceed 3% of total deductions taken by that corporation. Further discussion of the BEAT is beyond the scope of this textbook.

Illustration 13.6 summarizes the most important aspects of the anti-deferral regimes discussed in this section.

ILLUSTRATION 13.6 Anti-Deferral Regimes

Comparing Anti-Deferral Regimes for Multinational Corporations			
Anti-deferral regime	**Corporations targeted**	**Tax consequence**	**Who pays tax?**
Subpart F	Controlled foreign corporations	Subpart F income taxed to U.S. shareholders when earned rather than when distributed	Parent corporation
GILTI	Controlled foreign corporations	Global minimum tax on income from intangible assets	Shareholder
PFIC	Corporations for which more than 75% of gross income is passive, or more than 50% of assets generate passive income	Taxes can be levied on passive income not distributed in prior years, plus interest	Shareholder
BEAT	Multinational companies (U.S. and foreign) with gross receipts of $500 million or more	Prevents shifting income earned in U.S. to foreign countries by denying deductions for payments to foreign entities	Corporation

PRACTICE PROBLEM 13.3.1
Subpart F

Lion Company owns 100% of the stock of International Company, a CFC that is organized in Norway. Lion manufactures equipment in Denmark that is sold to International Company. International Company then sells the equipment to customers in Norway and throughout Europe. International Company's income from these sales in the current tax year is $580,000, with 60% of the sales in Norway and 40% of the sales in the rest of Europe. What is the Subpart F income in the following independent situations?

a. International Company's current E&P is $168,000.

b. International Company's sales were 72% in the rest of Europe and 28% in Norway.

SOLUTION

a. The Subpart F income is $232,000 ($580,000 × 40%). If International Company's current E&P is $168,000, then the Subpart F income is limited to $168,000. The remaining Subpart F income of $64,000 ($232,000 − $168,000) can be carried forward.

b. International Company's Subpart F income is $417,600 ($580,000 × 72%) because 72% of the sales were in the rest of Europe. However, because the Subpart F income is more than 70% of the CFC's total income, then all ($580,000) of International Company's income is considered to be Subpart F income.

INTERACTIVE SELF-SCORING QUIZZES

PRACTICE PROBLEM 13.3.2
GILTI Tax

Artem is a U.S. taxpayer who owns 100% of Browser LLC, located in Ukraine. Browser has the following information for the current tax year:

Taxable income	$3,220,000
Adjusted tax basis of depreciable tangible assets	$5,100,000
Net specific interest expenses	$ 110,000
Subpart F income	$1,460,000

Determine Artem's GILTI inclusion amount. How much tax is due, assuming Artem has elected to be taxed as a C corporation?

SOLUTION

We use the following formulas and definitions to determine the GILTI inclusion amount for Artem:

- QBAI is $5,100,000
- Net DTIR = QBAI ($5,100,00) – Net specified interest expense of the CFC ($110,000) = $4,990,000
- CFC tested income is taxable income ($3,220,000) – Subpart F income ($1,460,000) = $1,760,000
- GILTI = CFC tested income ($1,760,000) – [Net DTIR ($4,990,000 × 10%)] = $1,261,000.

Artem has elected to be taxed as a corporation, so he receives a 50% deduction for the GILTI inclusion and is taxed at a 21% rate. His tax due is $132,405 ($1,261,000 × 50% × 21%)

INTERACTIVE SELF-SCORING QUIZZES

13.4 Inbound Taxation on Foreign Persons

LEARNING OBJECTIVE 4

Determine the U.S. income tax on foreign persons.

VIDEO CONTENT

Inbound transactions are activities conducted in the United States by non-U.S. taxpayers, also known as foreign persons. As defined in LO2, Determine the Sourcing of Income and the Foreign Tax Credit, *foreign persons* include nonresident aliens, foreign corporations, foreign partnerships, and foreign estates and trusts. *Nonresident aliens* are individuals who are not citizens or residents of the United States. As discussed in LO1, General Rules for Individual Taxation, an individual can be a resident of the United States by having a green card or by meeting the substantial presence test.

Foreign persons may be subject to U.S. income taxation for two different reasons:

- The foreign person has U.S.-sourced income that is fixed, determinable, annual, or periodic income (FDAP income), *or*
- The foreign person has earned business income from an active trade or business in the United States.

Related exercise: Multiple Choice Question 11

In this section, we review how income is taxed in each of these situations.

FDAP Income

Fixed, determinable, annual, or periodic income (FDAP income) includes certain types of U.S.-sourced income received by a foreign person that is subject to a 30% withholding tax requirement.[37] Income is *fixed* when the amount can be pre-determined. Income is *determinable* when there is a basis of calculation for determining the amount to be paid in the future. Income is *annual* if it is distributed on at least a yearly basis. Income is *periodic* if it is paid from time to time, but it does not have to be paid annually or at regular intervals. Income can be determinable or periodic even if the length of time during which the payments are made is increased or decreased.[38] FDAP income received by a foreign person includes the following:

- Investment income such as interest, dividends, royalties, and rents (other than gains from the sale of real property)
- Compensation for personal services (unless it is *effectively connected income*, as described below)
- Pensions and annuities
- Alimony
- Prizes and awards
- 85% of Social Security benefits

The following types of income are not FDAP income:

- Gains and losses from the sale of realty or personalty
- Tax-exempt income, such as municipal interest income and qualified scholarship income

EXAMPLE 13.4.1
Athletic Prizes Won by Foreign Athletes

Gustavo is a professional boxer from Cuba. During the current tax year, he was invited to participate in a boxing match in Las Vegas, with the winner earning $250,000. Gustavo won the match. He spent three weeks in the United States before returning to Cuba. How is the award taxed to Gustavo in the United States?

SOLUTION

The $250,000 award to Gustavo is treated as FDAP income. It is an award and will be taxed by the United States.

Related exercises: Multiple Choice Question 12
Brief Exercise 12

Withholding Requirements

Congress had concerns that collecting the income tax on FDAP income from foreign persons would be difficult. Therefore, the tax law imposes a 30% withholding tax on the gross FDAP income of foreign persons.[39] The payor of the FDAP income must remit the withheld tax to the IRS. A payor that does not withhold the FDAP tax and remit it to the IRS is liable for the tax, plus interest and penalties.[40] The foreign person who receives the FDAP income is required to file a tax return and will receive a credit for the 30% tax withheld.[41]

[37] IRC §871.

[38] Treas. Reg. 1.441-2(b).

[39] IRC §§1441(a) and 1442(a).

[40] IRC §1461.

[41] IRC §1462.

The following rules are used to determine if FDAP income is U.S.-sourced:

Interest: Paid by a U.S tax resident
Dividends: Paid by a U.S. corporation or a foreign corporation with *effectively connected income*
Royalties: Connected to intangible assets being used in the United States
Rents: From U.S. real property or from the rental of property in the United States
Wages: Based on location where services are performed

The next Example explains the application of the FDAP rules.

EXAMPLE 13.4.2
FDAP Income

Felipe is a citizen of Costa Rica who is considered a foreign person for U.S. income tax purposes. Felipe has the following U.S.-sourced income this year:

- Dividends received from Johnson & Johnson, a U.S.-based corporation $ 22,000
- Rental income $300,000

The rental income is from a warehouse in Arizona that is being rented by Amazon. How much FDAP income does Felipe have, and how will the income be taxed?

SOLUTION

Felipe is a foreign person with FDAP income, so the payor of this income is required to withhold 30% of the income and remit the withholding to the IRS. Johnson & Johnson must withhold $6,600 ($22,000 × 30%), and Amazon must withhold $90,000 ($300,000 × 30%). Felipe must file a U.S. income tax return, Form 1040, and will receive a credit for total withholdings of $96,600.

Exceptions to Withholding

There are two major exceptions to the 30% withholding rule:

- Exceptions based on treaties
- Portfolio interest exception

Treaties Many U.S. income tax treaties provide for a reduced rate of withholding on certain types of FDAP income, especially interest, dividends, and royalties. Additionally, withholding is often not required on compensation received if *all* the following requirements are met:[42]

- The individual is present in the United States for 183 days or less for the tax year,
- The employee's compensation is paid by an employer that is not a U.S. resident, *and*
- The cost of the compensation is not borne by a U.S. corporation.

Portfolio Interest Exception Portfolio interest is not subject to withholding. Portfolio interest is U.S.-sourced interest on certain debt obligations.[43] Interest on bank deposits is also exempt from withholding if it is not effectively connected income (discussed below). This exception does not apply if the interest is paid to a shareholder that owns at least 10% of the corporation.[44] The portfolio interest exception allows foreign persons to invest in U.S. Treasury bonds without being subject to the 30% withholding.

Related exercise: Application Problem 12

[42]Article 14(2) of the 2016 U.S. Model Treaty.

[43]The description of the debt obligations that qualify for portfolio interest is beyond the scope of this book.

[44]IRC §871(h).

Business Income

The second category of income on which foreign persons may have to pay U.S. income tax is **effectively connected income (ECI)**—income earned by a foreign taxpayer that is connected with active U.S. trades or businesses. Individuals with ECI report it on Form 1040, and corporations with ECI report it on Form 1120.

Definition of Effectively Connected Income

The method used to determine ECI differs depending on whether the foreign person is from a country that has a treaty with the United States. Foreign corporations may operate in the United States through a U.S. subsidiary or a branch of the foreign corporation. Income earned in the United States by either subsidiaries or branches owned by foreign corporations are subject to U.S. income taxation.

Non-Treaty Country If the foreign person is from a country that does not have a treaty with the United States, then the definition of *trade or business* is determined by the U.S. tax law. Unfortunately, the Internal Revenue Code and the Treasury Regulations do not provide a clear definition of a *trade or business*, so most of the relevant tax authority for this definition is from judicial law, which has held that a foreign person's involvement with a business must be considerable, continuous, and regular for the foreign person to be effectively connected to a U.S. business.[45]

Treaty Country If the foreign person is from a country that does have a treaty with the United States, then the definition of *trade or business* is based on how the treaty defines a **permanent establishment (PE)**. A PE generally exists in *one* of the following situations:

- The foreign person has a fixed place of business in the United States, unless that place is not central to the ongoing business operations, *or*
- The foreign party has dependent agents in the United States who can exercise sales contracts for the foreign party.[46]

Self-employed foreign individuals are not subject to U.S. income taxation if they do not have a fixed place of business in the United States from which they regularly engage with clients or customers.

Income from Provision of Services by Individuals

An individual's performance of personal services is often considered to be the person's trade or business. The method used to determine if income from the provision of personal services is ECI differs depending on whether the foreign person is from a country that has a treaty with the United States.

Non-Treaty Country Congress has provided that income earned for personal services by a foreign individual is not ECI if *all* of the following requirements are met:

- The individual is in the United States for 90 days or less for a given tax year,
- The individual is paid no more than $3,000 for the U.S. services, *and*
- The individual works for a foreign person that is not engaged in a trade or business in the United States.[47]

Treaty Country Foreign individuals may be exempt from U.S. income taxation for income earned as employees if they are from a treaty country and are in the United States for no more than 183 days for a given year. To qualify for the exclusion, the compensation must be paid by

[45] *United States v. Balanovski*, 236 F. 2d 298 (1956).

[46] Article 5 of the 2016 U.S. Model Treaty.

[47] IRC §864(b).

a non-U.S. employer, and it cannot be paid by or earned in a permanent establishment in the U.S. of the foreign employer.

In the next two Examples, we show how U.S. income received for personal services by foreign persons is taxed.

EXAMPLE 13.4.3
Business Activity for Foreign Persons from Treaty Countries

Plum Company is a Belgium SA corporation that sells appliances throughout the world, including the United States. Belgium has an income tax treaty with the United States. Plum has sales agents who travel throughout the world to promote its products with potential retailers. Six of these agents visit the United States once per quarter. Each agent is in the United States for 15 days each quarter. Retailers who express an interest in learning more about the appliances are connected with a manager in Belgium for further discussions. Is Plum subject to United States income tax for the income earned from U.S. customers?

SOLUTION

We begin this analysis by determining if Belgium has an income treaty with the United States. Because it does, then the criteria for analyzing whether Plum has an active business in the United States is based on whether:

- Plum has a fixed place of business in the United States, unless that place is not central to the ongoing business operations, *or*
- Plum has dependent agents in the United States who can exercise sales contracts for Plum.

Plum does not have a fixed place of business in the United States, and its sales agents cannot finalize sales contracts with U.S. customers. Therefore, Plum does not have a permanent establishment in the United States and is not subject to U.S. income taxes.

EXAMPLE 13.4.4
Business Activity for Foreign Persons from Non-Treaty Countries

Assume the same facts as in Example 13.4.2 except that Plum is based in Singapore. Therefore, the managers finalizing the sales contracts are in Singapore. Singapore does not have an income tax treaty with the United States. Is Plum subject to U.S. income tax for the income earned from U.S. customers?

SOLUTION

Because Singapore does not have a treaty with the United States, Plum cannot rely on the permanent establishment rules. Rather, it must determine if it has an *active trade or business* in the United States. Most of the relevant tax authority for this definition is in the judicial law, which has held that a foreign person's involvement with a business must be considerable, continuous, and regular for the foreign person to be effectively connected to the business. Based on the case law history, it is likely that Plum would be considered to have an active trade or business in the United States and would be subject to the U.S. income tax based on its net income from U.S. operations.

Related exercises: Discussion Question 15
Multiple Choice Question 13
Application Problems 13, 14

PRACTICE PROBLEM 13.4.1
FDAP

Agata is a citizen of Poland who is considered a foreign person for U.S. income tax purposes. Agata has the following U.S.-sourced income this year:

- Dividends received from Chevron, a U.S.-based corporation — $ 1,100
- Pension received from XYZ company, located in United States — $80,000
- Wages earned in United States — $18,000
- Interest income from U.S. Treasury Bonds — $ 1,200

How much FDAP income does Agata have, and how will the income be taxed?

SOLUTION

Agata is a foreign person with FDAP income, so the payor of this income is required to withhold 30% of the income and remit the withholding to the IRS. Chevron must withhold $330 ($1,100 × 30%), XYZ Company must withhold $24,000 ($80,000 × 30%), and Agata's employer must withhold $5,400 ($18,000 × 30%). Portfolio interest is FDAP but is not subject to withholding. The portfolio interest exception allows foreign persons to invest in U.S. Treasury bonds without being subject to the 30% withholding. Agata must file a U.S. income tax return, Form 1040, and will receive a credit for the total withholdings of $29,730.

PRACTICE PROBLEM 13.4.2

Provision of Services by Individuals from a Non-Treaty Country

Anne works for Salmon A/S, a Greenland company that sells fish in Greenland and the United States. Salmon does not have a physical location in the United States, but Anne visits the U.S. to conduct business on behalf of Salmon. Anne spent 13 days in the U.S. and earned $2,750. Is the income earned while working in the U.S. subject to U.S. taxation?

SOLUTION

The United States and Greenland do not have an existing treaty. Salmon A/S does not have a fixed U.S. business location, but Anne has worked in the United States. Anne's compensation was paid by a non-U.S. employer. Congress has provided that income earned for personal services by a foreign individual is not effectively connected income if *all* of the following requirements are met:

- The individual is in the United States for 90 days or less for a tax year,
- The individual is paid no more than $3,000 for the U.S. services, *and*
- The individual works for a foreign person not engaged in a trade or business in the United States.

Anne was in the United States for less than 90 days, and her compensation related to U.S. activities was less than $3,000. Salmon is not engaged in a trade or business in the United States because it does not have a physical location in the country. Therefore, Anne's $2,750 will not be taxed by the United States.

INTERACTIVE SELF-SCORING QUIZZES

Featured Professional: Jessica Bieneman

Jessica has worked for 18 years for the Internal Revenue Service, where she is currently a manager in the Advance Pricing Mutual Agreement Program (part of the U.S. Competent Authority Office). Her areas of specialty include transfer pricing, tax controversy/tax dispute resolution, and audit risk assessment.

From Classroom to Career I was part of the IRS team negotiating with Mexico's *Servicio de Administración Tributaria* on the second renewal of the *Qualified Maquiladora Approach Agreement* (QMA). The QMA is a coordination arrangement between the U.S. and Mexican competent authorities that allows a U.S. taxpayer to avoid double taxation on the contract manufacturing and assembly functions performed by its maquiladora (a foreign-owned factory in Mexico) if the Mexican taxpayer enters into a unilateral advance pricing agreement (APA) with Mexico's *Servicio de Administración Tributaria* under terms negotiated in advance between the competent authorities. The renewal agreement was reached in November 2020.

Professional Skills I believe analytical skills are critical for a successful career in tax accounting. All areas of tax accounting require you to research and solve problems, but the ability to communicate your thinking and the analysis you perform to support a proposed solution to a tax problem is key.

Future Tax Landscape In the international area, in 2025 the Organisation for Economic Co-operation and Development (OECD) plans to finalize guidance to address the challenge of taxing global digital companies (Pillar 1 and Pillar 2). On the domestic front, there may be additional major tax law changes with the possible modification or repeal of certain international areas of the 2017 *Tax Cut and Jobs Act*. There are always new international tax law changes on the horizon as business changes and tax administrations need to adapt to the changes. The rapidly changing environment keeps the work interesting and the need for tax professionals high.

Review and Practice

Chapter Summary

When considering international taxation, there are two important questions that must be answered.

- Which taxpayers are subject to the United States tax law?
- What income is subject to taxation under the United States tax laws?

1 Identify U.S. taxpayers and foreign taxpayers.

- **U.S. tax residents** are subject to **worldwide taxation**, meaning that they are taxed on their income earned anywhere in the world.
- There are four groups of individuals who are U.S. tax residents.
  - **U.S. citizens** The **U.S. citizen** group includes both individuals born in the United States and naturalized U.S. citizens.
  - **U.S. green card holders** A **U.S. green card holder** is a permanent resident who has been granted authorization to live and work in the United States on a permanent basis.
  - **Resident aliens** A **resident alien** is someone who meets the **substantial presence test**. The substantial presence test is met if a person is in the United States for 183 days or more in a calendar year.
  - **Election** A U.S. taxpayer whose spouse is a nonresident alien can make an election for the spouse to also be treated as a U.S. taxpayer.

Corporations and partnerships are considered to be U.S. tax residents if they are organized under the laws of one of the 50 states or of Washington DC.

- There are three *default* classification rules for foreign entities, as follows:
  - A foreign entity that has one owner and that owner has unlimited liability is treated as a *disregarded entity*.
  - A foreign entity that has two or more owners and at least one owner has unlimited liability is considered a *partnership*.
  - A foreign entity that has one or more owners and all the owners have limited liability is treated as a *corporation*.
- Historically, U.S. taxpayers have been subject to tax on **worldwide income**, not just income earned in the United States. **Territorial taxation** does not include foreign-earned income in the domestic country's income tax base. The *Tax Cuts and Jobs Act of 2017* moved to a territorial tax system for income from foreign subsidiaries that are controlled by U.S. corporations.
- The United States has tax treaties with approximately 70 countries, as shown in Illustration 13.2. Generally, in such a treaty, the United States agrees that it will treat taxpayers from the other country similarly to the way it treats U.S. taxpayers; and the other nation agrees to do the same for U.S. taxpayers. U.S. tax treaties only deal with federal income taxation, and do not apply to the income taxation of state or local governments.

2 Determine the sourcing of income and the foreign tax credit.

- The first step in determining the sourcing of income is to know the category that the income falls into. The sourcing rules vary by the type of income. For example, the sourcing of service income is different from the sourcing of interest income.
- Deductions are first allocated to a specific class of income and then, based on that class, apportioned as U.S.-sourced income or foreign-sourced income. Certain deductions have specific sourcing rules. For all other deductions, each should first be allocated to the class of gross income that it is associated with, such as:
  - Interest income
  - Dividend income
  - Service income
  - Income from sale of property
  - Royalty income
  - Rental income

Deductions that are not associated with a specific class of gross income are allocated proportionally across all classes of income.

- The **foreign tax credit** is necessary because the United States taxes worldwide income, and any foreign-sourced income was likely also taxed in the country where it was earned. This credit reduces the U.S. tax on the foreign income to the extent of the foreign taxes paid. Foreign income taxes that are creditable include taxes imposed *in lieu* of an income tax.

  The foreign tax credit is limited to the *lower* of:

  1. foreign income tax paid, or

  2. U.S. tax on worldwide income × $\frac{\text{Foreign-sourced taxable income}}{\text{Worldwide taxable income}}$

3 Determine how U.S. taxpayers are taxed on outbound investments in foreign corporations.

- **Outbound transactions** are foreign activities by a U.S. taxpayer, meaning that a U.S. taxpayer is conducting business outside of the United States. Income earned from foreign corporations is typically not taxed in the United States until it is repatriated. This provides an incentive for U.S. shareholders to delay bringing the earnings back to the United States, because the delay defers taxation of the earnings. Certain anti-deferral regimes, or rules, result in taxation to the U.S. shareholders when the income is earned by the foreign corporation rather than when it is distributed. There are three anti-deferral regimes for income earned from foreign corporations:

- Subpart F
- Global intangible low-tax income (GILTI)
- Passive foreign investment company (PFIC)

- Two questions must be answered YES for an anti-deferral regime to apply to a foreign corporation:
    - Was the income earned by a foreign corporation? A foreign corporation is one not formed in one of the states or the District of Columbia.
    - Is the foreign entity taxed as a corporation for U.S. tax purposes? Entities classified as flow-through for U.S. taxation are not subject to these regimes.
- A foreign corporation is treated as a **controlled foreign corporation (CFC)** if on any day during the year, more than 50% of the voting stock or value is owned by U.S. shareholders. U.S. shareholders are limited to U.S. taxpayers that own at least 10% of the voting stock or value of the foreign corporation.
- The Subpart F anti-deferral regime applies only to CFCs. Subpart F income is deemed to be distributed to U.S. shareholders when it is earned by the CFC, whether or not it has been distributed to the shareholders. This prevents U.S. shareholders from deferring the taxation of the income by delaying its distribution, or repatriation, to the U.S. shareholders. Subpart F income is taxed as ordinary income to the U.S. shareholders.
- The global intangible low-tax income (GILTI) anti-deferral regime has been in effect since 2018 and applies only to CFCs. Congress believed that GILTI was needed in addition to Subpart F because Subpart F does not address income earned from intangible assets. The GILTI anti-deferral regime provides a global minimum tax on income generated by intangible assets. GILTI allows CFCs a 10% return on tangible assets; any additional return earned by the CFC is assumed to be from intangible assets and subject to GILTI. GILTI is computed at the shareholder level.
- A passive foreign investment company (PFIC) is a corporation that meets *one* of the following conditions:
    - More than 75% of its gross income is passive-type income, *or*
    - More than 50% of its assets are investments that generate passive income.

The PFIC regime was added by Congress because, as with Subpart F income related to FPHCI, U.S. taxpayers may transfer investment assets to foreign corporations to defer the taxation of the investment income.

4 Determine the U.S. income tax on foreign persons.

- Inbound transactions are activities conducted in the United States by non-U.S. taxpayers, also known as foreign persons. **Foreign persons** include nonresident aliens, foreign corporations, foreign partnerships, and foreign estates and trusts. Foreign persons may be subject to U.S. income taxation for two different reasons:
    - The foreign person has U.S.-sourced income that is fixed, determinable, annual, or periodic income (FDAP income), *or*
    - The foreign person has earned business income from an active trade or business in the United States.
- **Fixed, determinable, annual, or periodic income (FDAP income)** includes certain types of U.S.-sourced income received by a foreign person that is subject to a 30% withholding tax requirement. Income is *fixed* when the amount can be predetermined, *determinable* when there is a basis for determining the amount to be paid in the future, *annual* if distributed on at least a yearly basis, and *periodic* if paid from time to time.
- The second category of income on which foreign persons may have to pay U.S. income tax is **effectively connected income (ECI)**—income earned by a foreign taxpayer that is connected with active U.S. trades or businesses. Individuals with ECI report it on Form 1040, and corporations with ECI report it on Form 1120.

Communication Application

Communication

Foreign Tax Credit Application

(LO2) Chocolate Corporation specializes in cocoa and chocolate production in the United States. In previous years, all of its sales were domestic. In the current year, Chocolate Corporation has sales in the United States of $980,000 and sales in Belgium of $330,000. Michael is the sole shareholder of Chocolate and would like to learn more about worldwide taxation and any available tax credits his corporation can utilize. Michael had his accountant in Belgium file Chocolate Corporation's Belgian tax return, which resulted in $75,000 in Belgian taxes. Assume that Chocolate has $310,000 of operating expenses and the U.S. income tax liability before the foreign tax credit is $210,000. How do the Belgian sales and taxes affect Chocolate Corporation's U.S. tax return? As Chocolate Corporation's tax advisor, prepare a memo to Michael.

Solution

Memo to the client

Hello Michael,

Thank you for asking about Chocolate Corporation's tax return and how your U.S. income tax liability will be calculated. Chocolate Corporation will pay tax on its domestic income and foreign-earned income.

Because income earned in a foreign country may also be taxed in that country, the purpose of the foreign tax credit is to mitigate the double taxation of foreign income. Foreign income taxes that are creditable include taxes imposed *in lieu* of an income tax. The credit is limited to the *lower* of:

1. foreign income tax paid, *or*
2. U.S. tax on worldwide income $\times \frac{\text{Foreign-sourced taxable income}}{\text{Worldwide taxable income}}$

Chocolate Corporation would have a foreign tax credit of $52,901, which is the lower of:

1. $75,000 or
2. $\$210{,}000 \times \frac{\$330{,}000}{\$1{,}310{,}000} = \$52{,}901$

The foreign tax credit limitation is based on the proportion of worldwide income that is foreign-sourced. In other words, the foreign tax credit cannot exceed what the U.S. tax liability would be on the same income. The foreign tax credit limitation limits the credit when the effective foreign tax rate on foreign-sourced income exceeds the U.S. statutory rate of 21%. The foreign taxes paid in excess of the foreign tax credit limitation can be carried back one year and carried forward ten years. Chocolate Corporation will be able to carry back $22,099 ($75,000 – $52,901) one year and then any remainder for ten years. The foreign tax credit is claimed on Form 1116, Foreign Tax Credit.

I look forward to preparing your tax return this year. Please do not hesitate to contact me for further information.

Sincerely,
Carnes & Youngberg, CPAs

Ethics and Professional Responsibility Application

Ethics

Withholding Requirements on FDAP Income

(LO4) Delectable SA is a foreign corporation located in Chile that sells coconuts, pineapples, and mangos across the globe. Delectable hires salespeople to work in the United States, and the salespeople are in the country for 200 days on average. The CEO for Delectable has hired your accounting firm to prepare the company's U.S. income tax return. When reviewing prior years' tax returns, you notice that Delectable did not withhold income tax on the compensation paid to the salespeople who worked in the United States. The CEO said that this is not required because the U.S. and Chile have a treaty. What is your response to the CEO? Does Delectable have to withhold income tax?

In addition to the chapter content, see *Statements on Standards for Tax Services* at www.aicpa-cima.com/resources/landing/statements-on-standards-for-tax-services; *Circular 230* at www.irs.gov/tax-professionals/office-of-professional-responsibility-and-circular-230; and Chapter 2, LO4, Tax Professional Responsibilities.

Solution

Congress had concerns that collecting the income tax on FDAP income from foreign persons would be difficult. Therefore, the tax law imposes a 30% withholding tax on the gross FDAP income of foreign persons. The payor of the FDAP income must remit the withheld tax to the IRS. A payor that does not withhold the FDAP tax and remit it to the IRS is liable for the tax, plus interest and penalties. If a treaty exists, then withholding is often not required on compensation received if the following requirements are met:

- The individual is present in the United States for 183 days or less for the tax year,
- The employee's compensation is paid by an employer that is not a U.S. resident, and
- The cost of the compensation is not borne by a U.S. corporation.

Because Delectable has employees in the United States for more than 183 days, the company must withhold 30% for U.S. income taxes. The foreign persons who receive the FDAP income are required to file a U.S. income tax return and will receive a credit for the 30% tax withheld.

Under *Circular 230* §10.21, Knowledge of Client's Omission, "A practitioner who, having been retained by a client with respect to a matter administered by the Internal Revenue Service, knows that the client has not complied with the revenue laws of the United States or has made an error in or omission from any return, document, affidavit, or other paper which the client submitted or executed under the revenue laws of the United States, must advise the client promptly of the fact of such noncompliance, error, or omission. The practitioner must advise the client of the consequences as provided under the Code and regulations of such noncompliance, error, or omission."

As the tax advisor for Delectable SA, you must inform the company's management of the error and advise them of the actions they should take to correct this.

Key Terms

End-of-Chapter Assessment

Discussion Questions

1. **(LO1)** Describe an outbound transaction and an inbound transaction.

2. **(LO1)** Describe the four groups of individuals who are considered to be U.S. tax residents.

3. **(LO1)** What is a *per se* corporation in the context of foreign businesses?

4. **(LO1)** Discuss the difference between a hybrid entity and a reverse hybrid entity.

5. **(LO1)** Distinguish between worldwide taxation and territorial taxation.

6. **(LO2)** Interest income is usually sourced to the residence of the taxpayer. Discuss two exceptions to this rule.

7. **(LO2)** Briefly describe how deductions are sourced.

8. **(LO2)** Briefly explain the concept of taxing worldwide income and the foreign tax credit.

9. **(LO3)** List the three anti-deferral regimes for income earned by U.S. taxpayers from foreign corporations, and what two questions must be answered YES for an anti-deferral regime to apply to a foreign corporation.

10. **(LO3)** Describe a controlled foreign corporation.

11. **(LO3)** What types of income are generally included as foreign personal holding company income (FPHCI)?

12. **(LO3)** What two criteria must be met for income to be classified as FBC sales income?

13. **(LO3)** What is the global intangible low-tax income anti-deferral regime, and why did Congress feel it was needed in addition to Subpart F?

14. **(LO3)** Describe a passive foreign investment company.

15. **(LO4)** Explain how income earned by a foreign person for services performed in the United States differs depending on whether or not a treaty exists between the foreign person's country and the United States.

Multiple Choice Questions

1. **(LO1)** Which of the following is not considered to be a U.S. tax resident?
   - **a.** U.S. citizen
   - **b.** U.S. green card holder
   - **c.** Nonresident alien
   - **d.** Resident alien

2. **(LO1)** For a person to meet the substantial presence test, how many days must the person reside in the United States?
   - **a.** 100 days
   - **b.** 150 days
   - **c.** 175 days
   - **d.** 183 days

3. **(LO1)** Which of the following is a false statement?
   - **a.** A foreign entity that has one owner, and that owner has unlimited liability, is treated as a disregarded entity.
   - **b.** A trust is considered a U.S. tax resident if it is under the supervision of a U.S. court and a majority of its trustees are U.S. persons.
   - **c.** Corporations and partnerships that are formed in possessions of the United States are not considered to be U.S. tax residents.
   - **d.** All of the statements are true.

4. **(LO1)** Which of the following statements is true?
   - **a.** Territorial taxation includes foreign-earned income in the domestic country's income tax base.

b. When a treaty conflicts with other general income tax laws, the authority that was passed most recently will be the applicable authority.

c. When a treaty conflicts with other general income tax laws, the treaty will be the applicable authority.

d. When a treaty conflicts with other general income tax laws, the other general income tax laws will be the applicable authority.

5. **(LO2)** Which of the following statements is incorrect regarding the allocation of interest income?

a. Interest income is usually sourced to the residence of the taxpayer.

b. If the interest is paid by a resident of the United States, including domestic corporations and domestic partnerships, the interest is U.S.-sourced.

c. If the interest is paid by a non-U.S. resident, then it is foreign-sourced.

d. Interest income received from a U.S. corporation that earned at least 50% of its active business income over the last three years from foreign sources is treated as foreign-sourced income.

6. **(LO2)** Which of the following types of income is not U.S.-source income?

a. Salary earned in the United States

b. Interest income on U.S. Treasury Bonds

c. Income from the sale of land located in South Korea by a South Korean resident to a taxpayer who is a U.S. resident

d. Rents received from property located in the United States

7. **(LO3)** Which of the following is incorrect regarding controlled foreign corporations?

a. U.S. shareholders are limited to U.S. taxpayers that own at least 50% of the voting stock or value of the foreign corporation.

b. More than 50% of the voting stock or value is owned by U.S. shareholders.

c. When determining stock ownership, stock owned directly and indirectly through related parties is included.

d. The Subpart F and GILTI anti-deferral regimes apply only to CFCs.

8. **(LO3)** Foreign personal holding company income (FPHCI) includes investment income earned in the foreign country except which of the following?

a. Interest income

b. Net gain from the sale or exchange of assets that produces FPHCI (such as stocks and bonds)

c. Rents and royalties earned from an active trade or business

d. Excess of foreign currency gains over foreign currency losses

9. **(LO3)** Which of the following is not included in calculating a controlled foreign corporation's tested income?

a. Subpart F income

b. Income effectively connected with a U.S. trade or business

c. Dividends received from a related person

d. All of these are included in calculating a CFC's tested income.

10. **(LO3)** Which of the following is a false statement regarding global intangible low-tax income (GILTI)?

a. GILTI is treated as ordinary income.

b. U.S. shareholders in a CFC receive a 50% deduction for its GILTI.

c. The foreign tax credit is allowed against the GILTI tax to the extent of 80% of the foreign taxes paid.

d. All of the above are true statements.

11. **(LO4)** Foreign persons include all the following except:

a. Individuals who are nonresident aliens

b. Individuals who are resident aliens

c. Foreign corporations

d. Foreign partnerships

12. **(LO4)** Fixed, determinable, annual, or periodic income (FDAP income) includes which of the following?

a. Pensions and annuities

b. Prizes and awards

c. Interest income

d. All of the income items are FDAP income.

13. **(LO4)** Which of the following is an incorrect statement in regard to effectively connected income (ECI)?

a. Self-employed foreign individuals from a treaty country are not subject to U.S. income taxation if they do not have a fixed U.S. place of business from which they regularly engage with clients or customers.

b. With a nontreaty country, income earned for personal services by a foreign individual is not ECI if the individual is in the United States for 90 days or less for a tax year.

c. If an employee is from a treaty country and is in the United States for no more than 183 days, then the employee is usually exempt from U.S. income taxation.

d. All of the statements are correct.

Brief Exercises

1. **(LO1)** Determine which of the following is considered a U.S. tax resident.

a. Krishna is a permanent resident and has been granted authorization to work in the United States.

b. Jasper, a citizen of the Netherlands, has lived and worked in the United States for 285 days.

c. Brenda is a U.S. citizen who has lived and worked in Hong Kong for the past six years.

d. Javier, a nonresident alien, is the spouse of Sandra, a U.S. citizen, and lives with Sandra in the United States.

2. **(LO1)** Venkata, a U.S. resident taxpayer, is the sole owner of an LLC that is organized in Illinois. The LLC is a computer manufacturing

company located in Chicago, Illinois. The company sells computers worldwide. What is the default entity classification of this business under U.S. tax law?

3. **(LO1)** Turtle Company, Ltd. is a company created under the laws of Barbados. Barbados has a tax treaty that is in force with the United States. For the current tax year, Turtle Company had a fixed business location in Texas. The business activity generated the following income:

Texas net operating income	$220,000
Barbados net operating income	$950,000
Interest income	$ 2,800
Dividend income	$ 6,500

Is this income taxed by the United States or by Barbados?

4. **(LO2)** Jakari is a citizen and resident of the United States living in Skokie, IL. He has a vacation home in Israel. Jakari has the following interest income:

Skokie savings and loan	$1,200
Tel-Aviv bank	$1,000
Dreidel Corporation	$1,250

Dreidel Corporation is a U.S. corporation that earned 85% of its active business earnings in Israel over the last five years. How is the interest income sourced to Jakari?

5. **(LO2)** Indicate if the following property produces U.S.-sourced income or foreign-sourced income.

a. Inventory purchased for resale sold in Florence, Alabama

b. Inventory manufactured in Paris, France, and sold to U.S. corporations

c. Equipment sold by a corporation located in Buffalo, New York, to businesses in London, England

d. A building in Destin, Florida, owned and sold by a U.S. corporation

e. A warehouse in Munich, Germany, owned and sold by a U.S. corporation

6. **(LO2)** Tanisha Inc. had $127,000 of U.S.-sourced income and $86,000 of foreign-sourced income, and it paid foreign taxes of $38,000. Assume that the U.S. income tax liability before the foreign tax credit is $105,000. How much is Tanisha Inc.'s foreign tax credit? How much is its foreign tax credit carryback/carryforward, if any?

7. **(LO3)** Indicate whether each of the following entities subject to the U.S. anti-deferral regimes. Reference the check-the-box regulations for foreign entities in LO1 as needed.

- Danny Boy owns Irish Specialties, a sole proprietorship that sells Irish novelties around the globe. Danny did not elect to be treated as a different entity from its default status.
- Tanker GmbH is located in Germany and operates as a partnership in Germany. All partners have limited liability.
- Dunkin Partnership SNC is a general partnership located in Belgium. All partners have unlimited liability.
- Morton, Inc. is a U.S. corporation that does not have any foreign investments.

8. **(LO3)** Storm Corporation is a foreign corporation that is owned as follows:

Stefanie, a U.S. taxpayer	10%
Eric, a U.S. taxpayer	15%
Jamie, a U.S. taxpayer	20%
Jasper, a foreign taxpayer	43%
Kaitlyn, a U.S. taxpayer	6%
Cheng, a foreign taxpayer	6%

Is Storm a CFC?

9. **(LO3)** Desert Company is a CFC located in Iraq that has the following income:

Gain from the sale of foreign-held stock	$18,000
Excess of foreign currency gains over foreign currency losses	$10,000
Dividend income from an Iraqi corporation whose stock is held in Iraq	$11,000
Royalty income from intangible property that was not part of business operations	$65,000

How much of this income is FPHCI?

10. **(LO3)** Plainfield Company owns 100% of the stock of Foreign Company, a CFC that is organized in Scotland. Plainfield manufactures equipment in Wales that is sold to Foreign Company. Foreign Company then sells the equipment to customers in Scotland and throughout Europe. Plainfield also provides services to customers who purchase the equipment. The services provided are paid for separately by the customers and include installation and testing of the equipment. The services are provided by Foreign Company. Foreign Company earned $175,000 of service income from customers in Scotland and $58,000 of service income from customers elsewhere in Europe. How much of the income is FBC services income?

11. **(LO3)** Astro Inc. owns 20% of Saare Inc., a foreign company. Saare pays Astro a $15,000 dividend. How is this income taxed to Astro Inc.?

12. **(LO4)** Annemijn is a citizen of the Netherlands and has the following income:

Interest income from First National Bank of New York	$ 2,600
Lottery winnings from scratch-off ticket bought while visiting New York	$250,000

How is the income taxed to Annemijn in the United States?

Application Problems

1. **(LO1)** Assume that Year 6 is the current tax year. Shalin is a citizen of India who has been in the United States the following number of days over the last three years:

Year 6:	90
Year 5:	240
Year 4:	120

Does Shalin meet the substantial presence test for Year 6?

2. **(LO1)** Assume that Year 6 is the current tax year. Shalin is a citizen of India who has been in the United States the following number of days over the last three years:

Year 6:	30
Year 5:	360
Year 4:	240

Does Shalin meet the substantial presence test for Year 6?

3. **(LO1)** Olayinka owns 100% of a small business entity in Nigeria named Chinara Company Ltd. His company does a significant amount of business in the United States. Based on his ownership structure in Nigeria, Olayinka has limited liability. What is the default entity classification of his business under U.S. tax law?

4. **(LO2)** Sunshine Corporation AG is organized in Lucerne, Switzerland, and has two equal shareholders, Anders and Lars. Anders is a resident of the United States, and Lars is a resident of Switzerland. During the current tax year, Sunshine has the following income sources:

Rental income from a skiing business located in Grindelwald, Switzerland	$120,000
Dividend income from Zurich Corporation, a Swiss corporation	$ 8,000
Gain from the sale of land located in Bern, Switzerland	$245,000
Inventory manufactured in the United States and sold in Thun, Switzerland	$375,000

How is this income sourced to Anders and Lars?

5. **(LO2)** WeSeeYou, Inc. (WSY) is a computer programming company that manufactures, sells, repairs, and provides guidance on computer software and applications. WSY is located in San Francisco, California, and has the following transactions:

- WSY sells the rights to its popular DIY home remodeling software to a company located in Belgium for $1,500,000.
- WSY has a licensing agreement with a company in Rome, Italy, to use its spreadsheet application, generating income of $500,000.
- WSY receives $80,000 to provide tech services to its customers in Italy. The tech reps are located in Italy.

Indicate how the income received should be sourced to WSY.

6. **(LO2)** Cross Inc. incurred $1,000,000 of R&E expenditures this year. Cross has research facilities in the United States and in Italy. The expenditures are classified as follows:

• Incurred to meet legal requirements in Italy	$150,000
• Other R&E expenses in Italy	$200,000
• R&E expenses incurred in United States	$650,000

Gross sales for the year are apportioned 60% to the U.S. and 40% to Italy. How are the R&E expenses sourced?

7. **(LO2)** Churn Inc. has the following items of income and expense for the current year:

- Service income of $280,000, all of which is generated by employees who work in the United States
- Royalty income of $325,000, which is 65% U.S.-sourced and 35% foreign-sourced
- Income of $500,000 from sale of property located in a foreign country
- Expenses of $80,000 related to the service income
- Commissions paid of $5,000 to sell the property
- Interest expense of $12,000
- General and administrative (G&A) expenses of $125,000

Churn also has the following income-producing assets:

- $1,200,000 of intangible property that generates royalty income
- $350,000 of property that is used in the service business

How should Churn allocate its expenses as U.S.-sourced or foreign-sourced?

8. **(LO2)** Blizzard Corporation has $445,000 of U.S.-sourced income and $108,000 of foreign-sourced income, and it paid foreign taxes of $31,000. Assume that the U.S. income tax liability before the foreign tax credit is $116,130.

   a. How much is Blizzard's foreign tax credit?

   b. How much is Blizzard's foreign tax credit carryback/carryforward, if any?

9. **(LO3)** Plainfield Company owns 100% of the stock of Foreign Company, a CFC that is organized in Scotland. Plainfield manufactures equipment in Wales that is sold to Foreign Company. Foreign Company then sells the equipment to customers in Scotland and throughout Europe. Foreign Company's income from these sales in the current tax year is $800,000, with 65% of the sales in Scotland and 35% of the sales from the rest of Europe. How much of the income is FBC sales income?

10. **(LO3)** Plainfield Company owns 100% of the stock of Global Company, a CFC that is organized in Scotland. Plainfield manufactures equipment in Wales that is sold to Global Company. Global Company then sells the equipment to customers in Scotland and in Europe. Global Company's income from these sales in the current tax year is $800,000, with 65% of the sales in Scotland and 35% of the sales in Europe. What would the Subpart F income be in the following independent situations?

    a. Global Company's current E&P is $250,000.

    b. Global Company's sales were 75% in Europe and 25% in Scotland.

11. **(LO3)** Ivy is a U.S. taxpayer who owns 100% of Leaf Corporation, located in Finland. Leaf has the following information for the current tax year:

Taxable income	$3,800,000
Adjusted tax basis of depreciable tangible assets	$5,900,000
Net specific interest expenses	$ 105,000
Subpart F income	$1,550,000

Compute Ivy's GILTI inclusion amount. How much tax is due assuming Ivy has elected to be taxed as a C corporation?

12. **(LO4)** Ashma is a citizen of India who is considered a foreign person for U.S. income tax purposes. Ashma has the following U.S.-sourced income this year:

- Dividends received from Amazon, a U.S.-based corporation — $ 4,000
- Alimony received from ex-spouse located in the United States — $36,000
- Wages for work performed in United States — $25,000
- Interest income from U.S. Treasury Bonds — $ 2,200

How much FDAP income does Ashma have, and how will the income be taxed?

13. **(LO4)** Enrique works for GoGreen Inc., a Mexican company that sells organic soil in Mexico and the United States. GoGreen does not have a physical location in the United States, but Enrique visits the country frequently and has spent 200 days in the United States in the past year. Is the income he earned while working in the United States subject to U.S. taxation?

14. **(LO4)** Juan works for Soil Inc., a Guatemalan company that sells organic soil in Guatemala and the United States. Soil does not have a physical location in the United States, but Juan visits the country to conduct business on behalf of Soil. Juan spent 32 days in the United States in the past year and earned $2,500. Is the income earned while working in the United States subject to U.S. taxation?

Tax Planning Problems

Planning

1. **(LO1)** Mateo is an Italian citizen who worked part-time in the United States in Year 1 and Year 2. During December of Year 2, Mateo became concerned that he would become a resident alien in Year 3 and be considered a U.S. tax resident. Mateo has worked the following number of days in the United States:

Year 1	100 days
Year 2	65 days

What is your advice to Mateo if he would like to avoid being considered a U.S. tax resident?

2. **(LO3)** Drainer Corporation is a foreign corporation concerned about how it will be taxed on its earnings in the United States. Drainer does not want to fall under the Subpart F and/or GILTI tax provisions. Currently, Drainer's voting stock and value are partially owned by a 35% U.S. shareholder. Drainer has been approached by a new investor who is a U.S. citizen. If Drainer's objective is to avoid the Subpart F and/or GILTI tax provisions, what advice should you provide to Drainer?

Professional Development Skills

Communication Problem

Communication

1. **(LO1) Income Taxed in U.S.?** Maverick is a U.S. citizen hired as an employee by a consulting company to provide consulting services in the United States, the United Kingdom, France, and Germany. In the current year, Maverick has spent 290 days outside and 75 days inside the United States. Maverick has hired you as his tax accountant. He believes he should not have to pay tax on his income earned outside of United States because he has to pay tax to the United Kingdom, France, and Germany for income earned in the other countries. What is your advice to Maverick?

Ethics and Professional Responsibilities Problem

Ethics

1. **(LO3) Subpart F Income** Chandler Inc. is a controlled foreign corporation located in Italy. Chandler has hired your accounting firm to prepare its current-year tax return. While reviewing the previous three years' tax returns, you notice in Chandler's workpapers that some income generated in Italy was not included in the U.S. tax returns. Chandler had the following unreported income:

Interest income from a bank branch in Italy	$ 3,300
Dividend income from an Italian corporation whose stock is held in Italy	$13,000
Gain from the sale of foreign-held stock	$22,000

This income was not distributed to Chandler shareholders, so Chandler did not report it on its U.S. tax returns for the last three years. What should you say to Chandler and its shareholders?

In addition to the chapter content, see *Statements on Standards for Tax Services* at www.aicpa-cima.com/resources/landing/statements-on-standards-for-tax-services; *Circular 230* at www.irs.gov/tax-professionals/office-of-professional-responsibility-and-circular-230; and Chapter 2, LO4, Tax Professional Responsibilities.

Research Problem

Research

1. **(LO1) Substantial Presence Test** Miguel is employed by Blanco Manufacturing Company. Both Miguel and Blanco are located in Mexico. Miguel frequently travels to the United States for business purposes but does not want to meet the substantial presence test and be taxed as a resident alien. Determine what days count as resident days for this test. Hint: See IRS Publication 519, U.S. Tax Guide for Aliens.

Excel Problem

1. **(LO2) Foreign Tax Credit** Juniper Corporation has U.S.-sourced income and foreign-sourced income, and it paid foreign taxes. How much is Juniper's foreign tax credit in each of the following independent situations, and what is its potential carryback/carryforward?

	a.	b.	c.
U.S.-sourced income	$500,000	$250,000	$680,000
Foreign-sourced income	$180,000	$400,000	$520,000
Foreign taxes paid	$ 18,000	$ 60,000	$130,000
U.S. income tax liability before the FTC	$115,500	$105,000	$210,000

State and Local Taxation

Klodien/AdobeStock

Before studying this chapter, you should know or, if necessary, review

5.2 Affiliated Groups and Consolidated Returns

Chapter Introduction

VIDEO CONTENT

Eagle Corporation is incorporated in the state of Delaware, and its headquarters are in New York City. Eagle manufactures computer chips at a plant in Ohio. This year, it sold $10,000,000 of chips to Flamingo Corporation, an artificial intelligence company based in Texas. Eagle's sales representative for the Flamingo account lives in Oklahoma. All sales orders are reviewed and approved at Eagle's facility in Oregon. In a situation such as this, it is often not clear which state or states can legally tax the $10,000,000 of revenue that Flamingo paid Eagle. All the states have a vested interest in the answer, as each state would like to maximize its revenue. On the other hand, Eagle does not want to have the income taxed by more than one state. Eagle's main competitor is based in Taiwan, and if Eagle's tax burden increases any more, it will not be able to compete on price.

While the primary focus of this book has been on federal income taxes, there are many more taxes levied at the state and local levels than at the federal level. Managing a business's state and local tax liability is an essential part of a tax-efficient strategic plan. In fact, certain consulting firms focus significantly on helping businesses manage their state and local tax liabilities. For example, Ryan is an accounting firm founded in 1991 with a focus on state and local tax planning. The firm grew rapidly because of the need for this service. It later began to expand into other tax services, and recent data shows that the firm has over 3,600 employees and more than $700 million in annual revenue.[1] It is common for international and national CPA firms to have divisions that focus on state and local taxation (SALT). Tax professionals must be equipped to help businesses manage their state and local taxes.

[1] "Dallas tax services firm Ryan soars to $2.5 billion valuation with new investment." *Dallas Morning News.* 26 May 2022. https://www.dallasnews.com/business/local-companies/2022/05/26/dallas-tax-services-firm-ryan-soars-to-25-billion-valuation-with-new-investment/. Todd, Samantha. "America's Best Midsize Employers." *Forbes.* 10 Feb. 2022. www.forbes.com/companies/ryan/?list=best-midsize-employers&sh=32425c60772e.

In the first section of this chapter, we discuss the wide range of taxes levied by state and local governments. Next, we explain *nexus*, which measures the degree of the relationship that must exist between a state and a business for the state to have the right to impose a tax. We then summarize the rules for computing state taxable income for corporations. In the final section, we compare three different filing methods that states can use for corporate income taxation.

LEARNING OBJECTIVES	TOPICS	PRACTICE OPPORTUNITIES

1 Identify the types of taxes levied by state and local governments.	**14.1 Types of State and Local Taxes (SALT)**
	• Corporate Income Taxes
	  • State Highlights
	• Individual Income Taxes
	  • State Highlights
	• Sales and Use Taxes
	  • State Highlights
	• Property Taxes
	  • State Highlights
	• Franchise Taxes
	• Excise Taxes
	  • State Highlights
	• Unemployment Tax
		• Example 14.1.1 State and Local Taxes
		• Practice Problem 14.1.1 State Income Taxation
		• Practice Problem 14.1.2 Various Types of State and Local Taxes

2 Determine which state has the authority to tax a business.	**14.2 Jurisdiction to Tax**
	• Primary Authority for Nexus
	  • Constitution—Due Process Clause
	  • Constitution—Commerce Clause
	• Sales Tax Nexus
	  • *National Bellas Hess, Inc. v. Department of Revenue*
	  • *Quill Corp. v. North Dakota*
	  • *South Dakota v. Wayfair, Inc.*
	  • Multistate Tax Commission
	• Income Tax Nexus
	  • Public Law 86-272
	  • Remote Workers
	  • Soliciting
		• Example 14.2.1 Domestic and Foreign Corporations
		• Example 14.2.2 Due Process
		• Example 14.2.3 Provision of Services
		• Example 14.2.4 Nexus—Out-of-State Sales
		• Example 14.2.5 Nexus—Services for Out-of-State Sales
		• Example 14.2.6 Nexus—Delivery for Out-of-State Sales
		• Example 14.2.7 Nexus—Outside Salesperson
		• Example 14.2.8 Nexus—In-State Salesperson
		• Practice Problem 14.2.1 Creating Income Tax Nexus
		• Practice Problem 14.2.2 Public Law 86-272

3 Compute state income tax for corporations.	**14.3 State Income Tax Computation**
	• Computing Taxable Income
	  • Dividends Received Deduction
	  • Interest Income and Related Expenses
	  • State Income Taxes
	  • Depreciation and Gain/Loss on Sale of Depreciable Assets
	  • Net Operating Losses
	  • Refunds of State Income Taxes
	• Apportionment and Allocation
	  • Uniform Division of Income for Tax Purposes Act (UDITPA)
	  • Business Income vs. Nonbusiness Income
	  • Apportionment
		• Example 14.3.1 Depreciation Adjustments for State Taxable Income
		• Example 14.3.2 State Income Tax Refunds
		• Example 14.3.3 Computation of State Taxable Income
		• Example 14.3.4 Transactional and Functional Tests
		• Example 14.3.5 Rental Income
		• Example 14.3.6 Income from Intangible Assets
		• Example 14.3.7 Interest Income
		• Example 14.3.8 Dividend Income
		• Example 14.3.9 Apportionment Factors
		• Practice Problem 14.3.1 Computation of State Taxable Income
		• Practice Problem 14.3.2 Allocated Nonbusiness Income
		• Practice Problem 14.3.3 Apportionment

4 Distinguish among separate, consolidated, and combined filing.	**14.4 Filing Methods and Other Topics** • Separate Filing • Consolidated Filing • Combined Reporting • Other Entities	• Example 14.4.1 Separate, Consolidated, and Combined Filing • Example 14.4.2 State Taxes and Planning • Practice Problem 14.4.1 Affiliated Group • Practice Problem 14.4.2 Consolidated Tax Return

Tax forms referenced in this chapter

Form 1120 U.S. Corporation Income Tax Return

14.1 Types of State and Local Taxes (SALT)

LEARNING OBJECTIVE 1

Identify the types of taxes levied by state and local governments.

VIDEO CONTENT

State and local governments collect revenue from a wide variety of taxes. In this section, we discuss the nature of these taxes. No two states have identical tax structures, as each state has developed its tax structure over many years and for many distinct reasons. In this chapter, we discuss state and local taxes (SALT) from a general perspective, although at times we do mention specific states.

Ernst & Young has reported that businesses paid $951.4 billion in state and local taxes for fiscal years ending in 2021 (FY21), which was 43.6% of all tax revenue at the state and local level. Businesses paid $493.7 billion in state taxes in FY21, which was 17.0% higher than in the prior fiscal year, and $457.6 billion in local taxes, which was 10.2% higher, for a combined year-over-year growth rate of 13.6% over FY20.[2]

While businesses pay a significant amount of state and local income taxes, corporate income taxes are a relatively small percentage of the overall state and local government revenues, as shown in **Illustration 14.1**.[3] The largest source of revenue is transfers from the federal government, while revenue from corporate income taxes is the smallest revenue source at approximately 2%.

ILLUSTRATION 14.1 Sources of State and Local Government Revenue (2021)

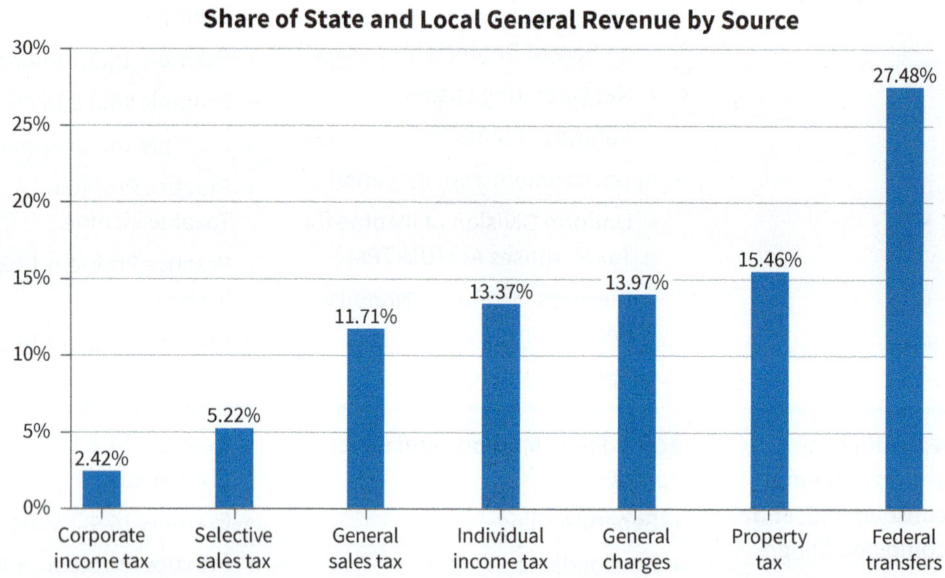

Source: Tax Policy Center

Related exercise: Multiple Choice Question 1

Corporate Income Taxes

Corporate income taxes account for less than 3% of the revenue raised by state and local governments, representing approximately $99 billion in revenue. While these numbers may seem shockingly low, remember that over 95% of business income is taxed at individual tax rates because the business is a sole proprietorship, a partnership/LLC, or an S corporation.[4] The manner in which states compute taxable income for corporations is discussed in detail in LO3, State Income Tax Computation.

State Highlights

Approximately 90% of state and local corporate income taxes are collected by state governments, leaving only 10% for local governments. Interestingly, over 77% of the corporate income taxes collected by local governments were for New York City, showing that very few cities rely on corporate income taxes. The states that rely on corporate income taxes the most are New Hampshire (7.3% of state and local revenue), Connecticut (4.9%), New Jersey (4.9%),

[2]Phillips, Andrew. "Total State and Local Business Taxes for FY21." Ernst & Young. 8 Dec. 2022. www.ey.com/en_us/insights/tax/total-state-and-local-business-taxes-for-fy21.

[3]Unless stated otherwise in the text or in a footnote, state and local tax information comes from "U.S. Census Bureau Annual Survey of State and Local Government Finances, 1977–2021" (compiled by the Urban Institute, "State and Local Finance Data: Exploring the Census of Governments," accessed 3 Aug. 2023 at https://state-local-finance-data.taxpolicycenter.org), as summarized by the Tax Policy Center Briefing Book.

[4]Krupkin, Aaron, and Looney, Adam. "9 Facts about pass-through businesses." Brookings Institute. 15 May 2017. www.brookings.edu/articles/9-facts-about-pass-through-businesses/.

Tennessee (4.1%), California (4.1%), and Wisconsin (4.0%). Nevada, Texas, Washington, and Wyoming do not have a corporate income tax.

Individual Income Taxes

In 2021, state and local governments collected $545 billion in individual income taxes. This represented approximately 13% of overall revenue for state and local governments.

State Highlights

Forty-three states levy individual income taxes. Seven states do not have an individual state income tax: Alaska, Florida, Nevada, South Dakota, Tennessee, Texas, and Wyoming. Nevada's individual income tax will be phased out in 2027. The states that rely on state income taxes the most for revenue are California (23% of revenue), Maryland (22%), Minnesota (20%), and New York (20%). In 2023, the top state individual income tax rates range from 2.5% in Arizona and North Dakota to 13.3% in California. Only 17 states and the District of Columbia allow local governments to levy income taxes, so the vast majority of income taxes an individual pays on the state and local level benefit state governments.[5]

Sales and Use Taxes

Sales taxes are levied by both state and local governments on the value of tangible personal property and some services sold. Exemptions vary by state but usually include items bought for resale by wholesalers and/or used in manufacturing. Many states also exempt groceries from sales tax, or tax them at a rate lower than the general sales tax rate. **Use taxes** are levied on the use of property within a state. States impose use taxes to prevent losing revenue from their residents who travel to another state with lower sales tax rates to purchase property. Most states have a destination-based sales tax, which means that sales are taxed at the location where title passes to the buyer. However, a few states have an origin-based sales tax, which means that sales are taxed at the location of the seller.

Sales taxes are collected from the seller, so the compliance rate is extremely high, but it is very hard for states to collect use taxes, as many residents do not know they exist. The chart in Illustration 14.1 shows that approximately 12% of state and local government revenue comes from general sales taxes, representing $477 billion in 2021.

State Highlights

Approximately 25% of Nevada's and Washington's revenue comes from general sales tax revenues, while the percentage is more than 20% in South Dakota and Washington. New Hampshire, Delaware, Montana, and Oregon do not have a state sales tax. States rely on general sales tax revenue more than local governments. State governments collected $370 billion (14% of state general revenue) from general sales taxes in 2021, while local governments collected $107 billion (5% of local general revenue).

Property Taxes

Property taxes are *ad valorem* taxes based on the value of realty and certain personalty. Property taxes are levied on the owner of a property as of a specific date. There are usually exemptions for certain types of property, including inventory. A few states also tax intangible property.

Illustration 14.1 shows that more than 15% of state and local government revenue comes from property taxes ($630 billion), and property taxes provide more revenue to state and local

[5]Walczak, Jared. "Local Income Taxes in 2019." Tax Foundation. 30 Jul. 2019. https://taxfoundation.org/research/all/state/local-income-taxes-2019/.

governments than any other tax. Property taxes on realty primarily benefit local governments. In 2021, 99% of property taxes went to local governments and only 1% to state governments.

State Highlights

New Hampshire collected 33% of its state and local revenue from property taxes, making it the state most reliant on property taxes. This is not surprising, as New Hampshire does not have an individual income tax or a general sales tax. The next states most reliant on property taxes were New Jersey, Connecticut, and Maine—all at 23% or more. The states that were least reliant on property taxes were Alabama, Arkansas, Delaware, Kentucky, Louisiana, New Mexico, Oklahoma, and West Virginia—all at below 10%.

Franchise Taxes

A **franchise tax** is levied on the privilege of doing business in a state. It is based on the value of the capital used in the jurisdiction as measured by common stock, paid-in-capital, and retained earnings. Franchise taxes are levied by state governments and do not raise a significant amount of revenue for state and local governments. The states with a franchise tax are Alabama, Arkansas, Delaware, Georgia, Illinois, Louisiana, Massachusetts, Mississippi, Nebraska, New York, North Carolina, Oklahoma, South Carolina, Tennessee, West Virginia, and Wyoming.[6]

Excise Taxes

Excise taxes are usually levied on the quantity of an item rather than the sales price. Excise taxes are often called *sin taxes* because they are levied on items like cigarettes, alcohol, marijuana, and more recently sugar-sweetened soda to discourage purchase of these items. States also levy an excise tax on gasoline. The federal government adds its own excise tax to many items subject to a state excise tax.

State Highlights

- As of 2021, Missouri, Georgia, North Dakota, and North Carolina had the lowest cigarette taxes, while the District of Columbia, Connecticut, New York, and Rhode Island had the highest. Taxes ranged from a low of just $0.17 per pack to over $4.00 per pack, with over $19 billion collected in total.
- State and local governments collected $53 billion in gasoline taxes in 2021. Gasoline taxes ranged from 8.95 cents in Alaska to 62.9 cents in California.
- Over $8 billion was collected by state and local governments for alcohol taxes. As of January 2023, the per-gallon tax rates on beer ranged from $0.02 in Wyoming to $1.29 in Tennessee.
- No states tax sugared sodas, but 10 cities do, including 4 in California.
- As of August 2024, 25 states allow the sale of cannabis, and 21 of those states tax these sales. Interestingly, the sale of cannabis is still illegal under federal law.

Unemployment Tax

Unemployment taxes are levied on employers by state government based on taxable wages. The taxes are typically levied on the first $7,000 in wages paid per employee per year. The rate that each employer pays varies based on the unemployment experience of the employer. These taxes are used to pay unemployment benefits to qualified individuals.

[6]Fritts, Janelle. "Does Your State Levy a Capital Stock Tax?" Tax Foundation. 21 Mar. 2023. https://taxfoundation.org/data/all/state/state-capital-stock-taxes-franchise-taxes-2023.

EXAMPLE 14.1.1
State and Local Taxes

Indicate which of the following taxes are *primarily* a revenue raiser for state governments, and which are *primarily* a revenue raiser for local governments.

- Corporate income tax
- Individual income tax
- Sales and use tax
- Property tax
- Franchise tax
- Excise tax
- Unemployment tax

SOLUTION:

Tax	State government	Local government
Corporate income tax	✓	
Individual income tax	✓	
Sales and use tax	✓	
Property tax		✓
Franchise tax	✓	
Excise tax	✓	
Unemployment tax	✓	

Related exercises: Discussion Question 1
Multiple Choice Question 2

PRACTICE PROBLEM 14.1.1
State Income Taxation

Which of the following states is not subject to a state income tax?

a. Illinois
b. California
c. Tennessee
d. Iowa

SOLUTION

The correct answer is **c**, Tennessee. Seven states do not have an individual state income tax: Alaska, Florida, Nevada, South Dakota, Tennessee, Texas, and Wyoming.

PRACTICE PROBLEM 14.1.2
Various Types of State and Local Taxes

Which of the following is a false statement?

a. Unemployment taxes are levied on employers by state governments based on the taxable wages of its employees.
b. Excise taxes are often called sin taxes because they are levied on items like cigarettes, alcohol, and marijuana.
c. Property taxes are primarily a revenue raiser for local governments.
d. All the above statements are true.

SOLUTION

The correct answer is **d**. All the statements are true.

INTERACTIVE SELF-SCORING QUIZZES

14.2 Jurisdiction to Tax

LEARNING OBJECTIVE 2

Determine which state has the authority to tax a business.

VIDEO CONTENT

As demonstrated with Eagle Corporation in the chapter introduction, many businesses conduct operations in more than one state, so a significant issue is determining which states have the authority to levy a tax on a particular business. If more than one state taxes a transaction, then the business will have double (or worse) taxation. Therefore, a complex set of rules has been developed over time to determine which state has nexus for a particular transaction. **Nexus** measures the degree of the relationship that must exist between a state and a *foreign corporation* for the state to have the right to impose a tax. Nexus is determined on a year-by-year basis.

Tax Planning Tip

If a business has no nexus with a state, then the state cannot tax the company. So, for planning purposes, the key is to minimize nexus.

From the state law perspective, there are domestic corporations and foreign corporations. A **domestic corporation** is a corporation doing business in the state in which it was incorporated. A **foreign corporation** is a corporation doing business in a state other than the state in which it was incorporated, as shown in the following Example.

EXAMPLE 14.2.1
Domestic and Foreign Corporations

Robin Corporation is incorporated under the laws of the state of Minnesota. Robin does business in Minnesota, Michigan, and Wisconsin. Wren Corporation is incorporated in the state of Wisconsin and has business operations in Wisconsin, Michigan, and Illinois. Identify the domestic and foreign corporations based on these facts.

SOLUTION

Domestic and foreign corporations are defined with respect to a particular state, as follows.

Illinois

Foreign corporation:	Wren Corporation

Minnesota

Domestic corporation:	Robin Corporation

Michigan

Foreign corporations:	Robin Corporation, Wren Corporation

Wisconsin

Domestic corporation:	Wren Corporation
Foreign corporation:	Robin Corporation

The purpose of nexus is to determine the degree of power a state possesses to tax foreign corporations. Clearly, Minnesota can tax Robin Corporation and Wisconsin can tax Wren Corporation because these are domestic corporations. But can Wisconsin tax Robin? Further, can Illinois tax Wren, and can Michigan tax Robin and Wren? The nexus rules vary for different types of taxes. Our focus is on the nexus rules for state sales taxes and for state income taxes.

Related exercises: Discussion Questions 2, 3

Primary Authority for Nexus

In this section, we summarize the historical developments that have created the set of laws that exist today for nexus. We begin by describing two clauses in the U.S. Constitution that relate to nexus. We then focus on the specific laws for sales tax nexus and conclude with the laws for income tax nexus.

Constitution—Due Process Clause

Two clauses in the U.S. Constitution relate to nexus. The first is the 14th Amendment, or the Due Process Clause, which prohibits states from denying any person "life, liberty, or property, without due process of law." States cannot take property through taxation without due process of law. Based on the Supreme Court's decision in *Quill v. North Dakota*, the 14th Amendment provides two requirements a state must meet before it can impose a tax:

- There must be a minimum connection between the taxpayer and the state, *and*
- There must be "some definite link, some minimum connection, between a state and the person, property, or transaction it seeks to tax."[7]

The Due Process Clause has not been a difficult standard for states to meet because the Supreme Court in *Quill* indicated that due process is met if a company only solicits business from the state's residents, even if the business has no physical presence in the state.

EXAMPLE 14.2.2
Due Process

Before large quantities of retail sales were moved to the internet, it was common for larger retailers such as Sears and J.C. Penney to mail out special catalogs for the Christmas season that focused primarily on children's toys. The creative marketing idea was to put the catalog in the hands of children, who would then make their wish lists from the company's merchandise. Assume that Sears's only connection with a particular state—say, New Mexico—was mailing the catalog to residents of the state, and these residents called a store in a different state to order merchandise. Would Sears have met the due process standard for creating nexus with New Mexico?

SOLUTION

Yes, the due process standard would have been met. That does not mean nexus would be created, however. Other tests must be met, as discussed below.

Constitution—Commerce Clause

The second constitutional provision that has relevance for nexus is the Commerce Clause, which regulates interstate commerce. The Commerce Clause states that "Congress shall have the power to regulate Commerce with foreign Nations, and among the several states, and with the Indian tribes."[8] This clause can be used to question the constitutionality of a tax if the tax:

- Provides an advantage to local businesses over other businesses, *or*
- Creates double taxation on interstate commerce.

[7]*Quill v. North Dakota*, citing *Miller Brothers v. Maryland*, 347 U.S. 340, 344-345 [1954].
[8]*U.S. Constitution*, Art. I, Section 8, Cl. 3.

The U.S. Supreme Court in *Complete Auto Transit, Inc. v. Brady* developed a four-part test in applying the Commerce Clause to determine if a tax was constitutional:[9]

1. Business activity must have substantial nexus with state.
2. The tax must be fairly apportioned.
3. The tax cannot discriminate against interstate commerce.
4. The tax must be fairly related to services that the state provides.

To be fairly apportioned, the tax must have internal and external consistency. **Internal consistency** means that if every state imposed the same tax, the overall income tax rate would not exceed 100%. **External consistency** means that the tax is in proportion to the business's activity in the state.

Related exercise: Discussion Question 4

Sales Tax Nexus

The tax laws providing the guidance for sales tax nexus are grounded in three landmark Supreme Court cases.

National Bellas Hess, Inc. v. Department of Revenue

In *National Bellas Hess* (NBH), the Supreme Court ruled in 1967 that NBH did not have nexus with the state of Illinois. NBH was a mail order house based in Missouri.

- NBH's only activity in Illinois was mailing catalogs twice per year, *and*
- NBH's products were delivered by independent trucking companies.[10]

The state of Illinois assessed sales tax on NBH because NBH was regularly engaged in substantial solicitation of business from residents of Illinois. The Supreme Court disagreed and ruled that because NBH did not have a *physical presence* in Illinois, there was no nexus with the state. **Physical presence** means that the business has property, employees, or perhaps independent contractors in the state. The state of Illinois was in violation of both the Due Process Clause and the Commerce Clause. The Supreme Court commented that an undue burden would be placed on NBH and other interstate retailers if they had to remit sales tax to hundreds of state and local jurisdictions across the United States.

Quill Corp. v. North Dakota

Quill sold business equipment and supplies, and it had no physical presence or employees in North Dakota. It solicited sales in North Dakota by telephone and through the mailing of catalogs and flyers. All sales to businesses in North Dakota were delivered by the U.S. Postal Service. North Dakota believed that Quill had an *economic presence* in the state and assessed sales tax on Quill's sales. Even though the facts were very similar to *National Bellas Hess*, the Supreme Court agreed to hear the case because:

- The lower courts were split on ruling in favor of Quill or North Dakota, *and*
- New technology, such as mobile phones, fax machines, and the introduction of the internet, had significantly changed how business was conducted from 1967 to 1992.[11]

The U.S. Supreme Court ruled in favor of Quill, but its reasoning was somewhat different than in *National Bellas Hess*. The Court ruled that North Dakota had not violated the Due Process Clause because changes in technology since *National Bellas Hess* had changed how due process should be evaluated. However, the Court determined that North Dakota had violated the Commerce Clause for reasons similar to those given in *National Bellas Hess*.

[9] *Complete Auto Transit, Inc. v. Brady* 430 U.S. 274 [1977].

[10] National Bellas Hess, Inc. v. Department of Revenue, 386 U.S. 753 (1967).

[11] *Quill Corp. v. North Dakota*, 504 U.S. 298 (1992).

The Court also affirmed that the four-part test for evaluating the Commerce Clause from the *Complete Auto Transit* case remained valid.

The *Quill* decision was a small step forward for states that were looking to maintain their sales tax base, because the Supreme Court did recognize that the economic presence had validity for applying the Due Process Clause. However, states were disappointed that the Court determined that the physical presence test still applied for the Commerce Clause. After *Quill*, the Commerce Clause made it very difficult for states to tax sales from out-of-state vendors that did not have a physical presence in the state.

South Dakota v. Wayfair, Inc.

After *Quill*, advances in technology led to a significant increase in consumers' ability to use the internet, and thus an enormous shift in the percentage of purchases made in brick-and-mortar stores versus through the internet. States began to see their sales tax base erode, leading to a significant decline in state revenue. These advances in technology also led states to speculate that perhaps the Commerce Clause should no longer prohibit their ability to tax sales from out-of-state vendors that did not have a physical presence in their state. Even though there are thousands of different jurisdictions in the United States that levy a sales tax, technology could efficiently manage this data and allow for the collection of tax on these sales without, in the states' opinion, placing an undue burden on interstate commerce.

South Dakota was one of the first states to use this approach to tax out-of-state companies for sales tax purposes. South Dakota passed a two-pronged test in 2016 providing that any out-of-state seller without a physical presence would have nexus if it either had more than $100,000 in gross sales or 200 or more sales transactions per year in the state. Wayfair is an e-commerce company based in Massachusetts that had significant sales in South Dakota, and it refused to comply with this new nexus definition. South Dakota sued Wayfair, and the case eventually made it to the U.S. Supreme Court.[12]

South Dakota based its arguments on the significant loss of sales tax revenue as more consumer sales moved to the internet, and how technology could allow sales tax to be collected from out-of-state businesses without an undue burden. The Court was sympathetic to this reasoning and voted 5-4 to overturn *National Bellas Hess* and *Quill*. This was a monumental change for the sales tax landscape, as states could now collect sales tax from out-of-state vendors that did not have a physical presence in the state, but did have an economic presence. The Court agreed that with changes in technology, South Dakota had not violated the Due Process Clause or the Commerce Clause.

Of course, each state now had to define what economic nexus meant, and all states with a state sales tax have done so. The most common definition is the same as South Dakota's—more than $100,000 in gross sales or 200 or more sales transactions. This definition allows businesses with a nonsignificant presence in the state to remain exempt from sales tax.[13]

Illustration 14.2 delineates the different opinions of the Supreme Court in the three cases discussed above.

ILLUSTRATION 14.2 Landmark Supreme Court Cases

Supreme Court Cases for Sales Tax Nexus			
Case	***National Belle Haas***	***Quill***	***Wayfair***
Year	**1967**	**1992**	**2018**
Due Process Clause	Requires physical presence	Does not require physical presence; economic presence is sufficient	Does not require physical presence; economic presence is sufficient
Commerce Clause	Requires physical presence	Requires physical presence	Does not require physical presence; economic presence is sufficient

[12] *South Dakota v. Wayfair, Inc.*, 138 S. Ct. 2080 (2018).

[13] Cole, Gail. "Sales Tax Disputes Continue as Wayfair Ruling Turns 6." Alavara. 20 Jun. 2024. www.avalara.com/blog/en/north-america/2024/06/sales-tax-disputes-continue-six-years-after-wayfair.html.

Multistate Tax Commission

Seven states formed the Multistate Tax Commission (MTC) and developed the Multistate Tax Compact in 1967 to increase the uniformity of state laws regarding nexus. The MTC proposed a single standard for determining nexus between a state and a foreign corporation. Under this standard, substantial nexus is established if any of the following thresholds is exceeded during a given tax period:

- $50,000 of property,
- $50,000 of payroll,
- $500,000 of sales, *or*
- 25% of total property, total payroll, or total sales.

Currently, 16 states use the Multistate Compact as their state law for nexus. Some states use a similar framework as the MTC but use different amounts for the thresholds. All other states are either sovereign members or associate members.[14]

Related exercise: Multiple Choice Question 3

Income Tax Nexus

Let's now turn our attention to the nexus rules for income taxes. Given the Supreme Court's attention to sales tax nexus, it may seem surprising that the Court has never addressed nexus for income tax purposes. The application of nexus to state income taxation is governed by Public Law 86-272.

Public Law 86-272

Public Law 86-272 provides guidance for nexus for income tax purposes, not for sales tax. This law applies to sales of *tangible personal property* and does not apply to the sale of services or to the leasing or renting of property. Nexus for taxing a corporation's income does not exist if activity in the state is limited to:

1. Soliciting sales of tangible personal property that are approved, and shipped from, outside the state
2. Advertising
3. Determining reorder needs of customers
4. Furnishing autos to sales staff

Some implications of these rules are as follows:

- The sale of services is not protected from income tax nexus by Public Law 86-272.
- If a business has an office in the state where its salespersons work, then a physical presence has been established. An independent contractor that works with the business can have an office without creating nexus.
- The licensing of intangible assets is not protected by Public Law 86-272.

Related exercise: Discussion Question 5

Remote Workers

Remote workers who live in one state and work for a company based in a different state can create nexus problems for the employer. Before COVID-19, this was an uncommon, though not rare, situation. During the COVID-19 pandemic, many states issued temporary guidance providing that remote workers in this situation would not create new nexus issues for the employer. However, these temporary provisions have expired in most states.

[14]See this website for descriptions of these membership types: www.mtc.gov/the-commission/member-states/.

Many businesses have never returned to a 100% face-to-face work environment. Many employees, particularly those who provide professional services, continue to work remotely on at least a part-time basis. Therefore, the risk that these situations could create nexus issues is high. Working from home in a state other than the residence for the business may not cause nexus issues if it occurs only occasionally, but this is a subjective test that may not be protected by Public Law 86-272.

Related exercise: Discussion Question 6

EXAMPLE 14.2.3
Provision of Services

Jackson, who lives in State A, is a cybersecurity analyst for Bluejay Corporation. Jackson's spouse is transferred to State B, and Jackson plans to move to State B with his spouse. Due to a shortage of cybersecurity experts, Bluejay wants to retain Jackson's services and tells him he can work remotely from State B. However, Jackson must maintain a structured work schedule just as if he was working in the home office in State A. Jackson communicates with his manager and his team through email, text, and web meetings. Does Bluejay Corporation have income tax nexus with State B?

SOLUTION

Bluejay Corporation does have income tax nexus with State B. Bluejay has a non-salesperson employee who resides and works in State B. This activity is not a protected activity under Public Law 86-272.[15]

Soliciting

The definition of *soliciting* is critical to determining what activities are protected from creating income tax nexus. The MTC provides that **soliciting** includes:

- Actions that explicitly or implicitly invite an order, *and*
- Other actions that are ancillary to an order. Ancillary activities have no independent business function for the seller other than being connected to a solicitation of an order.

Soliciting does *not* include *de minimis* activities that have only a trivial connection with the state. Illustration 14.3 summarizes the transactions that Public Law 86-272 indicates are unprotected (that is, will create nexus) and are protected (that is, will not create nexus).

ILLUSTRATION 14.3
Unprotected and Protected Activities under Public Law 86-272

Unprotected activities that can create nexus for income tax purposes include:

- Collecting receivables
- Installing purchased property
- Providing repairs
- Approving orders
- Providing training other than to salespersons
- Maintaining a sample or display room for more than 14 days at any one location within the state during the tax year
- Carrying samples for sale
- Performing credit checks
- Securing deposits
- Hiring, training, or supervising employees other than salespersons
- Owning or leasing property for repairs, parts, warehousing, or meetings for employees or agents; an in-home office within an employee's residence is not included in this definition
- Selling franchises or licenses

(continued)

[15] *TeleBright Corp. v. New Jersey*, No. A-5096-09T2, N. J. Super. Ct. [March 2, 2012].

ILLUSTRATION 14.3
Unprotected and Protected Activities under Public Law 86-272 (cont.)

Protected activities that will *not* create nexus include:

- Soliciting orders by a state resident employee as long as an office is not maintained, unless it is a qualifying home office
- Sending orders or complaints to home office
- Setting up display racks without charge
- Recruiting and training salespersons
- Carrying samples and promotional materials only for display
- Providing automobiles for salespersons to use for protected activities
- Checking customers' inventories for reordering if there is no additional charge
- Maintaining a sample or display room for 14 days or less at any one location within the state during the tax year
- Owning or leasing personalty for a qualifying in-home office or a car, if property is used in a protected activity

The MTC added the following activities to reflect *Wayfair*'s impact on internet-based activities that are unprotected and can therefore create nexus. States are still in the process of determining if they will implement these activities:

- Providing post-sale assistance using electronic chat or emails on a regular basis
- Maintaining a business website where applicants can apply for non-salesperson positions
- Selling extended warranties on the business's website

Tax Planning Tip

A business can have physical activity in a state and not have income tax nexus if the activity is protected by Public Law 86-272.

The next five Examples demonstrate when nexus is created for different levels of activity.

EXAMPLE 14.2.4
Nexus—Out-of-State Sales

Barrett Furniture Company is a retailer that sells furniture in Kansas City, Missouri. It also has a strong internet sales business, with 80% of its sales from the internet and the remaining 20% from the store in Kansas City. All employees work from the Kansas City location. The furniture must be assembled after it is shipped to the consumer. Camila lives in State X and orders bedroom furniture from Barrett through the internet. Barrett uses a third-party trucking company to transport the bedroom furniture to Camila. Camila assembles the furniture. Does Barrett have to remit sales tax to State X for this sale? Must Barrett file a State X income tax return for this sale?

SOLUTION

Barrett has not created economic nexus with State X. It has no employees in State X and does not provide any services to residents of State X. Therefore, nexus has not been created for sales tax or income tax in State X.

EXAMPLE 14.2.5
Nexus—Services for Out-of-State Sales

Assume the same facts as in Example 14.2.4, except that Barrett has agreements with an individual in State X who will assemble the furniture for the consumer and repair the furniture during a two-year warranty period. Does Barrett have to remit sales tax to State X for this sale? Must Barrett file a State X income tax return for this sale?

SOLUTION

It is very likely that Barrett now has physical nexus with State X. By contracting with others in State X to assemble and repair the furniture, there is sufficient activity in the state to create nexus for both sales tax and income tax.

EXAMPLE 14.2.6
Nexus—Delivery for Out-of-State Sales

Assume the same facts as in Example 14.2.4, except that Barrett uses its employees and trucks to deliver the furniture to Camila in State X. Does Barrett have to remit sales tax to State X for this sale? Must Barrett file a State X income tax return for this sale?

SOLUTION

In this situation, the answer likely depends on how often Barrett delivers furniture to State X. The answer may also vary for sales tax and income tax. If the deliveries are infrequent, then there is likely no nexus for either sales tax or income tax. If the deliveries are routine and frequent, then nexus is likely created for sales tax purposes, but not for income tax purposes.

EXAMPLE 14.2.7
Nexus—Outside Salesperson

Assume the same facts as in Example 14.2.4, except that Barrett has a salesperson who makes three trips a year to State X. Does Barrett have to remit sales tax to State X for this sale? Must Barrett file a State X income tax return for this sale? Would the answer change if the salesperson made twelve trips a year to State X?

SOLUTION

The solution varies depending on the state. Some states have determined that as few as two visits by an outside salesperson can create nexus,[16] while most states require more activity than that. Other states base the nexus decision on the total amount of sales from the state rather than the number of visits by a salesperson.

EXAMPLE 14.2.8
Nexus—In-State Salesperson

Assume the same facts as in Example 14.2.4. All employees of Barrett work from the Kansas City, Missouri, location, except for one salesperson who lives in State X and works full-time soliciting orders from State X. Orders are fulfilled in Kansas City and are shipped from Kansas City to State X. The furniture must be assembled after it is shipped to the consumer. Camila lives in State X and orders bedroom furniture from Barrett through the internet. Barrett uses a third-party trucking company to transport the bedroom furniture to Camila. Camila assembles the furniture.

a. Does Barrett have physical presence with State X, and must it remit sales tax to State X for sales to State X residents?

b. Must Barrett file a State X income tax return for sales to State X residents?

SOLUTION

a. Because there is a full-time salesperson who resides in State X and solicits orders from State X, Barrett does have a physical presence in State X, and nexus has been created for sales tax purposes. Barrett must collect sales tax and remit it to State X for all sales made to residents of State X.

b. Barrett has not created nexus with State X for income tax purposes. Per Public Law 86-272, if activity is limited to soliciting sales of tangible personal property that are approved, and shipped from, outside the state, then nexus has not been created for income tax purposes.

Related exercises: Multiple Choice Questions 4, 5
Brief Exercise 1
Application Problems 1, 2, 3

[16]For example, the state of Washington, see *Lamtec Corp. v. Washington*, 246 P.3d 788 [Wash. 2011].

PRACTICE PROBLEM 14.2.1
Creating Income Tax Nexus

Turtle Corporation, located in Alabama, engages in the following activities:

- Sells $775,000 of supplies in Alabama
- Maintains an office in Tennessee
- Advertises in Arkansas
- Recruits and trains salespersons to operate in Texas

Does Turtle Corporation have income tax nexus for these four states?

SOLUTION

- **Alabama:** Yes, Turtle is located in Alabama and has Alabama sales
- **Tennessee:** Yes, Turtle has a physical presence in Tennessee because it maintains an office there
- **Arkansas:** No, advertising alone will not create nexus
- **Texas:** No, recruiting and training only sales personnel does not create nexus

PRACTICE PROBLEM 14.2.2
Public Law 86-272

Which of the following activities are protected under Public Law 86-272, and therefore do not create nexus with the foreign state?

- Checking customer inventory level for reorder
- Sale of services
- Furnishing autos to sales staff
- Maintaining an office (other than an in-home office)

SOLUTION

- Checking customer inventory level for reorder—Protected
- Sale of services—Unprotected
- Furnishing autos to sales staff—Protected
- Maintaining an office (other than an in-home office)—Unprotected

INTERACTIVE SELF-SCORING QUIZZES

14.3 State Income Tax Computation

LEARNING OBJECTIVE 3

Compute state income tax for corporations.

VIDEO CONTENT

In this section, we explain how to determine the state income tax liability for a corporation. Our discussion is general in nature because every state has its own definition of taxable income. However, the starting point for most states when determining taxable income is usually federal taxable income. There are resources available that summarize the income tax laws for every state, such as Commerce Clearing House's *State Tax Handbook*.

Computing Taxable Income

Most states begin computing state income taxes using federal taxable income, increased or decreased for certain tax items. Some states do not start with federal taxable income because they do not want decisions of federally elected officials to impact their state income tax law. However, those states must evaluate changes made in the federal tax law to determine if they want to make a similar change at the state level. For states that do start with federal taxable income, the adjustments depend on each state's income tax laws.

Federal taxable income as reported in line 28 (taxable income before NOLs and special deductions) of Form 1120, U.S. Corporation Income Tax Return, is usually the starting point for states. Special deductions include the dividends received deduction. Some states, such as Illinois and Florida, use line 30 (taxable income) as the starting point. See **Illustration 14.4** to understand how these amounts are computed.

ILLUSTRATION 14.4 U.S. Corporation Income Tax Return

Starting Point for Computing State Taxable Income

Form **1120** — Department of the Treasury, Internal Revenue Service

U.S. Corporation Income Tax Return

For calendar year 2024 or tax year beginning ________, 2024, ending ________, 20 ____

Go to *www.irs.gov/Form1120* for instructions and the latest information.

OMB No. 1545-0123 — **2024**

A Check if:	**TYPE OR PRINT**		
1a Consolidated return (attach Form 851) ☐		Name	**B Employer identification number**
b Life/nonlife consolidated return ☐		Number, street, and room or suite no. If a P.O. box, see instructions.	**C** Date incorporated
2 Personal holding co. (attach Sch. PH) ☐		City or town, state or province, country, and ZIP or foreign postal code	**D** Total assets (see instructions) $
3 Personal service corp. (see instructions) ☐			
4 Schedule M-3 attached ☐	**E** Check if: (1) ☐ Initial return (2) ☐ Final return (3) ☐ Name change (4) ☐ Address change		

Income	1a	Gross receipts or sales	1a
	b	Returns and allowances	1b
	c	Balance. Subtract line 1b from line 1a	1c
	2	Cost of goods sold (attach Form 1125-A)	2
	3	Gross profit. Subtract line 2 from line 1c	3
	4	Dividends and inclusions (Schedule C, line 23)	4
	5	Interest	5
	6	Gross rents	6
	7	Gross royalties	7
	8	Capital gain net income (attach Schedule D (Form 1120))	8
	9	Net gain or (loss) from Form 4797, Part II, line 17 (attach Form 4797)	9
	10	Other income (see instructions—attach statement)	10
	11	**Total income.** Add lines 3 through 10	11
Deductions (See instructions for limitations on deductions.)	12	Compensation of officers (see instructions—attach Form 1125-E)	12
	13	Salaries and wages (less employment credits)	13
	14	Repairs and maintenance	14
	15	Bad debts	15
	16	Rents	16
	17	Taxes and licenses	17
	18	Interest (see instructions)	18
	19	Charitable contributions	19
	20	Depreciation from Form 4562 not claimed on Form 1125-A or elsewhere on return (attach Form 4562)	20
	21	Depletion	21
	22	Advertising	22
	23	Pension, profit-sharing, etc., plans	23
	24	Employee benefit programs	24
	25	Energy efficient commercial buildings deduction (attach Form 7205)	25
	26	Other deductions (attach statement)	26
	27	**Total deductions.** Add lines 12 through 26	27
	28	Taxable income before net operating loss deduction and special deductions. Subtract line 27 from line 11	28
	29a	Net operating loss deduction (see instructions)	29a
	b	Special deductions (Schedule C, line 24)	29b
	c	Add lines 29a and 29b	29c
Tax, Refundable Credits, and Payments	30	**Taxable income.** Subtract line 29c from line 28. See instructions	30
	31	Total tax (Schedule J, line 12)	31
	32	Reserved for future use	32
	33	Total payments and credits (Schedule J, line 23)	33
	34	Estimated tax penalty. See instructions. Check if Form 2220 is attached ☐	34
	35	**Amount owed.** If line 33 is smaller than the total of lines 31 and 34, enter amount owed	35
	36	**Overpayment.** If line 33 is larger than the total of lines 31 and 34, enter amount overpaid	36
	37	Enter amount from line 36 you want: **Credited to 2025 estimated tax** — **Refunded**	37

Starting point for computing state taxable income in most states (→ line 28)

Starting point for computing state taxable income in some states (→ line 30)

Sign Here — Under penalties of perjury, I declare that I have examined this return, including accompanying schedules and statements, and to the best of my knowledge and belief, it is true, correct, and complete. Declaration of preparer (other than taxpayer) is based on all information of which preparer has any knowledge.

Signature of officer | Date | Title

May the IRS discuss this return with the preparer shown below? See instructions. ☐ Yes ☐ No

Paid Preparer Use Only	Print/Type preparer's name	Preparer's signature	Date	Check ☐ if self-employed	PTIN
	Firm's name			Firm's EIN	
	Firm's address			Phone no.	

For Paperwork Reduction Act Notice, see separate instructions. Cat. No. 11450Q Form **1120** (2024)

Some of the more common adjustments that *increase* federal taxable income include:

- Dividends received deduction (if beginning with line 30 of Form 1120, page 1)
- Expenses related to interest earned on U.S. bonds
- State income taxes
- Depreciation in excess of that allowed for state (most states do not allow bonus depreciation)
- Municipal interest taxed for state purposes
- Federal net operating losses
- Additional gain on the sale or disposition of assets

Some of the adjustments that *decrease* federal taxable income include:

- Federal income taxes paid
- Expenses related to municipal interest income
- Interest on U.S. bonds
- Depreciation in addition to that allowed for federal purposes
- State net operating losses
- Refunds of state income taxes if included in federal taxable income

Related exercise: Multiple Choice Question 6

Let's discuss a few of these adjustments in more detail.

Dividends Received Deduction

If the state taxable income computation begins with line 30 of Form 1120, then the federal dividends received deduction (DRD) has reduced taxable income. If the state does not permit a DRD, or if the DRD is computed differently for state purposes, then the DRD will need to be partially or completely added back to federal taxable income.

Interest Income and Related Expenses

Municipal interest income is excluded from federal income taxation, and the expenses related to earning the income are not deductible. On the other hand, interest earned on U.S. bonds is taxable for federal income tax.

Most states treat these items in the opposite fashion. That is, municipal interest income is included in state taxable income, although most states do not tax interest from bonds issued by their own state or their local governments. That also means that expenses related to earning income on municipal bonds are deductible. However, most states do not tax interest earned on U.S. bonds, so expenses incurred to earn that interest are not deductible. **Illustration 14.5** summarizes the rules for interest income.

ILLUSTRATION 14.5 Taxability of Interest on Government Bonds

Income and Deductions Related to Government Bonds		
	U.S. federal income tax	State income tax (State X)
Interest received for U.S. bonds	Taxable	Not taxable
Deductions related to U.S. bonds	Deductible	Not deductible
Interest received for state and local bonds (other than State X)	Not taxable	Taxable
Deductions related to state and local bonds (other than State X)	Not deductible	Deductible
Interest received for state and local bonds (State X)	Not taxable	Not taxable
Deductions related to state and local bonds (State X)	Not deductible	Not deductible

State Income Taxes

The federal income tax law allows businesses to deduct state and local income taxes, but it does not allow a deduction for federal income taxes. Three states allow a full or partial deduction for federal income taxes paid: Alabama, Missouri, and Oregon. Most states do not allow businesses to deduct federal income taxes, and they usually do not allow a deduction for state income taxes, as shown in **Illustration 14.6**. If a business has nexus in more than one state, then it may pay income taxes in more than one state. A few states allow a deduction for state income taxes paid to other states, but most do not.

ILLUSTRATION 14.6 Deduction for Income Taxes

Income Tax Deduction on Federal and State Income Tax Returns		
	U.S. federal income tax	**State income tax (State X)**
Federal income taxes	Not deductible	Usually not deductible
State income taxes	Deductible	Usually not deductible

Depreciation and Gain/Loss on Sale of Depreciable Assets

The depreciation allowed for computing state income taxes is usually less than the federal depreciation allowed. This is primarily because most states do not allow a deduction for bonus depreciation, and some do not allow Section 179 expense. The federal depreciation in excess of the state depreciation must be added back to federal taxable income.

The basis of the depreciable assets will differ for federal and state purposes because the depreciation differs. Therefore, when depreciable assets are sold, there will usually be less gain for state purposes than for federal, resulting in an adjustment to decrease federal taxable income for this difference.

EXAMPLE 14.3.1 Depreciation Adjustments for State Taxable Income

For the current tax year, Owl Corporation reported federal taxable income after the DRD of $234,000. Included in this income was $61,000 of bonus depreciation that is not allowed for state income tax purposes. Owl also sold a building this year for $480,000. Owl's federal tax basis in the building was $320,000, and its state tax basis was $395,000. Compute Owl's state taxable income for this year.

SOLUTION

Owl needs to make two adjustments to federal taxable income in computing state taxable income:

- Current year's bonus depreciation ($61,000)
- Different gain from the sale of the building; the gain included in federal taxable income is $160,000 (Amount realized $480,000 – Adjusted basis $320,000), while the gain for state taxable income is $85,000 (Amount realized $480,000 – Adjusted basis $395,000)

State taxable income is computed as follows:

Federal taxable income	$234,000
Add: Bonus depreciation now allowed for state	61,000
Less: Excess federal gain from sale of building ($160,000 – $85,000)	(75,000)
State taxable income	$220,000

Related exercise: Brief Exercise 2

Net Operating Losses

While some states do allow a deduction for federal net operating losses, most states require the NOL to be computed using state income tax laws. Federal NOLs incurred after 2020 cannot be carried back but can be carried forward indefinitely. States often have different carryback and carryforward rules, so these must be checked carefully for corporations that have NOLs.

Refunds of State Income Taxes

Under the tax benefit rule, if state income taxes reduced federal taxable income in a previous year, and the taxpayer receives a refund of a portion of these taxes in the current year, the taxpayer will have federal taxable income for the amount of the refund only to the extent that the taxpayer received a tax benefit from the taxes in the past. Individual taxpayers receive a tax benefit from the state income taxes only if they itemized their deductions, and even then, only if the state income taxes are not limited by the $10,000 federal cap on state and local income tax deductions. Corporations can always deduct state income taxes for computing federal taxable income.

State income taxes are usually not allowed as a deduction for state taxable income. Therefore, no benefit is received for state income taxes on the state income tax return, and a refund of state income taxes would never be taxable to the taxpayer for computing state income taxes. Thus, if the state income tax refund was included in federal taxable income, a negative adjustment is required to properly compute state taxable income.

The following Example demonstrates the varying treatment of state income tax refunds across federal and state income taxes.

EXAMPLE 14.3.2
State Income Tax Refunds

Parrot Corporation paid $27,000 of state income taxes in Year 7 related to its Year 7 tax liability. In Year 8, Parrot received a refund of Year 7 state income taxes of $3,600. What are the tax consequences of the refund for federal and state income tax purposes?

SOLUTION

Parrot's state income taxes of $27,000 reduced federal taxable income in Year 7. Parrot received a refund of $3,600 of these taxes in Year 8. Under the tax benefit rule, the taxpayer will have to report income of $3,600 because Parrot received a tax benefit from the taxes in Year 7. However, Parrot has no income from the refund for Year 8 for state income taxes, because the $27,000 taxes paid was not deductible on the Year 7 state income tax return.

The next Example applies the computation of state taxable income rules for several adjustment items:

EXAMPLE 14.3.3
Computation of State Taxable Income

Flamingo Corporation's business activities are in State M, and its income and expenses are as follows for the current tax year:

Federal taxable income	$230,000
Interest earned on U.S. bonds	$ 12,000
Interest earned on State M government bonds	$ 17,000
Interest earned on State N government bonds	$ 4,000
Dividend income received from Stork Corporation*	$ 11,000
Federal income taxes paid	$ 49,000
State income taxes paid	$ 21,000
Federal net operating loss carried forward to current year	$ 52,000
State M net operating loss carried forward to current year	$ 47,000

*Flamingo owns 25% of Stork Corporation.

State M has the following corporate state income tax laws:

- Corporation taxable income is based on federal taxable income, Line 30 of Form 1120.
- Interest earned on U.S. bonds and State M bonds is not taxable.
- Interest earned on bonds issued by other states is taxable.
- The dividends received deduction is not allowed.
- No deduction is allowed for federal income taxes paid and state income taxes paid.

Calculate Flamingo's state taxable income.

SOLUTION

We begin by comparing how the tax items listed are treated for federal income tax and for State M income tax.

	Federal tax treatment	State tax treatment
Interest earned on U.S. bonds	Taxable	Not taxable
Interest earned on State M government bonds	Not taxable	Not taxable
Interest earned on State N government bonds	Not taxable	Taxable
Dividends received deduction	Deductible	Not deductible
Federal income taxes paid	Not deductible	Not deductible
State income taxes paid	Deductible	Not deductible
Federal net operating loss carried forward to current year	Deductible	Not deductible
State M net operating loss carried forward to current year	Not deductible	Deductible

Adjustments are required for items that are treated differently for federal tax and state tax.

Federal taxable income	$230,000
Interest earned on U.S. bonds	(12,000)
Interest earned on State N government bonds	4,000
Dividends received deduction*	7,150
State income taxes paid	21,000
Federal net operating loss carried forward to current year	52,000
State M net operating loss carried forward to current year	(47,000)
State M taxable income	$255,150

*The dividends received deduction on the federal return is $7,150 ($11,000 × 65%) because Flamingo owns more than 20% of Stork but less than 80%.

Related exercise: Application Problem 4

Spotlight on the Law

Worldwide Combined Reporting

Just as the federal government wants to make sure that it is collecting all tax revenue owed to it by corporations, state and local governments are aiming to do the same. Differing apportionment methods across states can muddy the water on how to apportion business income effectively. Because many states use federal taxable income as the beginning tax base for state taxable income, there is the potential that billions of tax dollars may be lost when corporations operate internationally and the federal income tax base does not properly include all international revenue.

If states choose to do so, they can help correct this situation. States could drastically reduce the omission of international revenue by implementing a policy called *worldwide combined reporting* (*WWCR*). This method treats the parent corporation and all its subsidiaries, including foreign subsidiaries, as a single unit and combines all the income as the first step in calculating state tax liability.

States can receive two primary benefits by using WWCR:

- Abusive international profit shifting will be reduced, allowing states to collect sorely needed tax revenue.
- Large multinational corporations will have less incentive to set up operations in tax havens—operations that give them a competitive advantage over smaller, purely domestic corporations.

State governments have discovered that corporations are able to reduce their income tax payments by manipulating the sales price of transactions among the various members of the corporate groups. Using WWCR can decrease this manipulation, allowing states to use their own apportionment method to assess and collect taxes. WWCR calculates tax liability based on income earned domestically and in foreign countries, limiting interstate and international profit shifting.

Any underreporting of U.S. profits for federal tax purposes due to international profit shifting automatically results in underreporting for state tax purposes for states not using WWCR. According to Michael Mazerov in "States Can Fight Corporate Tax Avoidance by Requiring Worldwide Combined Reporting," in 2017, international profit shifting just by multinational corporations with U.S. parents cost the federal government at least $60 billion in corporate income tax revenue and possibly as much as $94 billion.* Research indicates that states could recover as much as $10–$15 billion in tax revenue by adopting WWCR.

International profit shifting is prevalent in many industry types, including technology and drug manufacturing. The U.S. Supreme Court has twice upheld the constitutionality of WWCR, so it is already a legal method of reporting income. If they pooled their efforts, states could generate the revenue they so desperately need.

*Mazerov, Michael. "States Can Fight Corporate Tax Avoidance by Requiring Worldwide Combined Reporting." Center on Budget and Policy Priorities. 27 Jun. 2024. www.cbpp.org/research/state-budget-and-tax/states-can-fight-corporate-tax-avoidance-by-requiring-worldwide-0.

Apportionment and Allocation

A corporation that has nexus with more than one state for income tax purposes must determine how much of its income should be taxed in each state. The separation of income among the various states is done by either apportionment or allocation. **Allocation** is the assignment of *nonbusiness income* to a specific state based on the nature of the income. **Apportionment** is the assignment of *business income* to states based on a formula that uses a combination of the company's payroll, property, and sales.

Uniform Division of Income for Tax Purposes Act (UDITPA)

A model law known as the Uniform Division of Income for Tax Purposes Act (UDITPA) helps to minimize some differences among state tax laws. UDITPA is a model act adopted in 1957 by the Uniform Law Commission, and it is now included as Article IV of the Multistate Tax Compact. Its purpose is to promote uniformity in state allocation and apportionment rules. Thirty states have adopted UDITPA, and many states that have not adopted it still used many of its provisions when developing their own laws.[17] Income can be allocated or apportioned to states that do not have a state income tax if the business had activity in that state.

Related exercise: Discussion Question 7

The definitions of *business income* and *nonbusiness income* are very important because business income is apportioned, while nonbusiness income is allocated. UDITPA defines **business income** as:

> Income arising from transactions and activity in the regular course of the taxpayer's trade or business and includes income from tangible and intangible property if the acquisition, management and disposition of the property constitute integral parts of the taxpayer's regular trade or business operations.

If more than one state has nexus to tax the income of a business entity, then the income must be apportioned among the states. Business income is apportioned among all the states in which the corporation does business. **Nonbusiness income** is defined as income that is not business income. Business income is sometimes referred to as **apportionable income**, and nonbusiness income as **nonapportionable income**.

Related exercises: Discussion Questions 8, 9

[17]Uniform Law Commission. "Division of Income for Tax Purposes Act." https://www.uniformlaws.org/committees/community-home?CommunityKey=f2ef73d2-2e5b-488e-a525-51be29fbee47.

Business income is commonly generated:

- From a business's regular operations, known as the **transactional test**, *or*
- From the sale of property that is an integral part of the business, known as the **functional test**.

Most states use both the transactional test and the functional test to identify business income.

Nonbusiness income generally includes investment income and income from transactions that are not part of regular operations. Nonbusiness income is generally allocated to the state of incorporation. However, if investment income is generated by regular business operations, it is classified as business income.

The classification of income as business income or nonbusiness income is shown in the following Example.

Potential Pitfall

A company's income is allocated or apportioned only to states for which the company has nexus. If a company has business activity in a state but does not have nexus, then no income tax is due to that state.

EXAMPLE 14.3.4
Transactional and Functional Tests

Falcon Corporation manufactures paper and has four plants across the United States, in States A, B, C, and D. During the year, its income from paper sales was $32,000,000. It sold the plant in State D at a gain of $5,000,000 and sold some land in State A that had been held as an investment for eight years at a gain of $2,000,000.

a. How is this income classified for state nexus purposes?

b. How is it allocated or apportioned to the states?

SOLUTION

a. The income of $32,000,000 from paper sales is business income under the transactional test because it is from the business's regular operations. The gain of $5,000,000 from the sale of the plant is business income under the functional test because the plant was an integral part of Falcon's business. The $2,000,000 gain for the sale of the land is nonbusiness income because the land was not being used as an integral part of the business.

b. The $37,000,000 business income ($32,000,000 + $5,000,000) will be apportioned to the four states based on the states' apportionment formulas. The $2,000,000 of nonbusiness income is allocated to State A.

Business Income vs. Nonbusiness Income

We next explain when certain types of income are classified as business income or nonbusiness income. State tax laws are not uniform for some of these classifications, so our discussion is based on the Multistate Tax Compact's regulations.

Rental and Royalty Income If rental property or royalty property is integral to the operation of a business, or incidental to the business, the income is business income. Otherwise, it is nonbusiness income.

EXAMPLE 14.3.5
Rental Income

Blue Jay Corporation rents tools and equipment to individuals and businesses. Blue Jay also owns a building that it rents to other businesses. Blue Jay used to occupy the building, but it moved into a new facility four years ago. Is Blue Jay's rental income classified as business income or nonbusiness income?

SOLUTION

The income from renting tools and equipment is business income because Blue Jay's ordinary business is renting tools and equipment. The rental income from the building is nonbusiness income because that property is not used in Blue Jay's business operations.

Income from Intangible Assets Income from intangible assets, such as copyrights, trademarks, or patents, is treated as business income if the intangible asset is used in the company's core business operations. If the intangible asset is not used in the company's core business, then the income is nonbusiness income.

EXAMPLE 14.3.6 Income from Intangible Assets

Toucan Corporation manufactures batteries, and it has a patent on a process that extends a battery's life by 50%. Toucan sells batteries in the northeastern United States. It has licensed the use of its patent to a manufacturer in California, and it receives a fee for every battery sold by the California company. How is the licensing fee income classified?

SOLUTION

The patent is used in Toucan's core business operations. Therefore, the licensing fee revenue received from the California company is classified as business income.

Interest Income Interest income is another source of income that can be classified as either business or nonbusiness income, depending on how it is generated. If interest income is generated from business operations, such as interest charged to customers who are paying for their purchases over several months, then it is business interest. However, if it is from investments, then it is nonbusiness income.

EXAMPLE 14.3.7 Interest Income

Redbird Corporation has the following sources of interest income this year:

$ 800 received with a federal income tax refund

$4,600 from funds it keeps on reserve to repurchase inventory when needed

$8,900 from one-year U.S. Treasury Bonds received on funds held as an investment

How are these sources of interest income classified?

SOLUTION

The income is classified as follows:

$ 800 **business income**, because the payment of federal income taxes is part of ordinary business operations

$4,600 **business income**, because the replenishment of inventory is part of ordinary business operations

$8,900 **nonbusiness income**, because this is investment income and not part of ordinary business operations

Dividend Income Dividends are classified as business income if the stock for which the dividends are paid is acquired in the regular course of the taxpayer's business operations.

EXAMPLE 14.3.8 Dividend Income

Crow Corporation owns 70% of the stock of a corporation that manufactures aluminum Crow uses in producing soft drink and beer cans. This year, the corporation paid Crow dividends of $53,000. Crow also invested excess profits in an investment account and received dividends from that account of $39,000 this year. Crow does not use the investment account funds as part of its manufacturing business. How are these dividends classified?

SOLUTION

The $53,000 of dividends from the aluminum company is business income because the stock is owned as an important part of the supply chain for Crow's business. However, the dividends of $39,000 are nonbusiness income because the stock ownership is not part of Crow's manufacturing business operations.

Related exercise: Multiple Choice Question 7

Apportionment

Business income is apportioned among the states in which it is earned based on apportionment factors such as sales, property, and payroll. In general, states have discretion to apply different tax rules to different types of income. The U.S. Supreme Court has allowed states great flexibility to choose an apportioning formula and to tax income of an interstate business.[18]

Some states use only one apportionment factor. Others vary in how they weight the factors. Some states also use different types of factors for financial institutions and service businesses than for other businesses.

Sales Factor The sales factor for State X is computed as:

$$\frac{\text{Total sales in State X}}{\text{Total sales}} = \text{Sales factor}$$

The determination of the sales in State X is determined based on the **point of delivery**—that is, the location at which property or a product is delivered or service rendered. If the business does not have nexus in the state of delivery, then the sale is apportioned to the state where the sale originated.

Property Factor The property factor for State X is computed as:

$$\frac{\text{Average value of property in State X}}{\text{Value of all property}} = \text{Property factor}$$

The definition of property is limited to realty and tangible personalty, and does not include cash or intangible property. Property is valued at cost or book value depending on the state. Property also includes leased property, which is usually valued at the annual lease times eight. Property is included only if used in the production of business income.

Payroll Factor The payroll factor for State X is computed as:

$$\frac{\text{Compensation paid or accrued in State X}}{\text{Total compensation paid or accrued}} = \text{Payroll factor}$$

Compensation is included only for employees who are involved in the production of business income. Compensation includes fringe benefits if taxable under federal law. Payments to independent contractors and amounts contributed to Section 401(k) plans are usually not included in the payroll factor.

Formulas States have flexibility in determining the formula used to apportion income. At one time, states tended to use an average of the sales, property, and payroll factors, as follows:

$$\frac{\text{Sales factor} + \text{Property factor} + \text{Payroll factor}}{3} = \text{Apportionment factor}$$

Some states have decided to double the weight of the sales factor, as follows:

$$\frac{\text{Sales factor} + \text{Sales factor} + \text{Property factor} + \text{Payroll factor}}{4} = \text{Apportionment factor}$$

More recently, states have begun to shift to a single factor based only on sales. In fact, today more than 60% of states use only the sales factor as the apportionment factor.

The next Example illustrates the computation of several apportionment factors.

EXAMPLE 14.3.9
Apportionment Factors

Heron Corporation has nexus with two states for income tax purposes. For the current year, it has the following data for sales, property, and payroll. Heron's federal income after adjustments for state income tax differences is $700,000.

	State A	State B	Total
Sales	$ 4,000,000	$1,600,000	$ 5,600,000
Property	$10,000,000	$7,000,000	$17,000,000
Payroll	$ 1,000,000	$ 800,000	$ 1,800,000

[18]*Moorman Mfg. Co. v. Bair*, 437 U. S. 267 (1978).

a. Compute Heron's apportioned income to each state if the apportionment formula equally weights the three factors.

b. Compute Heron's apportioned income to each state if the apportionment formula equally weights property and payroll but double-weights sales.

c. Compute Heron's apportioned income to each state if the apportionment formula is based solely on sales.

SOLUTION

a. The apportionment formula is computed as follows if the three factors are weighted equally.

	State A	%	State B	%	Total
Sales	$4,000,000/$5,600,000	71.4%	$1,600,000/$5,600,000	28.6%	$ 5,600,000
Property	$10,000,000/$17,000,000	58.8%	$7,000,000/$17,000,000	41.2%	$17,000,000
Payroll	$1,000,000/$1,800,000	55.6%	$ 800,000/$1,800,000	44.4%	$ 1,800,000
Average		61.9%		38.1%	

The income allocated to State A is $433,300 ($700,000 × 61.9%).

The income allocated to State B is $266,700 ($700,000 × 38.1%).

b. The apportionment formula is computed as follows if it equally weights property and payroll but double-weights sales.

	State A	%	State B	%	Total
Sales	$4,000,000/$5,600,000	71.4%	$1,600,000/$5,600,000	28.6%	$ 5,600,000
Sales		71.4%		28.6%	
Property	$10,000,000/$17,000,000	58.8%	$7,000,000/$17,000,000	41.2%	$17,000,000
Payroll	$1,000,000/$1,800,000	55.6%	$ 800,000/$1,800,000	44.4%	$ 1,800,000
Average		64.3%		35.7%	

The income allocated to State A is $450,100 ($700,000 × 64.3%).

The income allocated to State B is $249,900 ($700,000 × 35.7%).

c. The apportionment formula is computed as follows if it is based solely on sales.

	State A	%	State B	%	Total
Sales	$4,000,000/$5,600,000	71.4%	$1,600,000/$5,600,000	28.6%	$ 5,600,000

The income allocated to State A is $499,800 ($700,000 × 71.4%).

The income allocated to State B is $200,200 ($700,000 × 28.6%).

Companies rarely pay tax on exactly 100% of their income for state income taxes, because the states often differ in how they weight their factors and the composition of the factors. Thus, some companies may pay tax on more (or less) than 100% of their taxable income. For example, in Example 14.3.9, what if State A used only a single sales factor but State B used the average of the three factors? State A's apportionment percentage would be 71.4% and State B's would be 38.1%, which totals 109.5%.

Related exercises: Multiple Choice Question 8
Brief Exercises 3, 4
Application Problems 5, 6, 7
Tax Planning Problem 1

PRACTICE PROBLEM 14.3.1
Computation of State Taxable Income

Timber Corporation, located in State M, provided the following information.

Revenue from operations	$1,440,000
Interest earned on U.S. federal bonds	$ 11,000
Interest earned on State M government bonds	$ 2,000
Interest earned on State N government bonds	$ 4,000
Operating expenses	$ 420,000
Bonus depreciation	$ 55,000
State income taxes paid	$ 13,000
Federal net operating loss carried forward to current year	$ 100,000
State M net operating loss carried forward to current year	$ 58,000

Calculate state taxable income, assuming that Timber taxes only interest earned on state government bonds issued by other states, bonus depreciation is not allowed, and state income taxes paid are not deductible.

SOLUTION

Timber's state taxable income is $966,000, as follows:

Revenue from operations	$1,440,000
Interest earned on State N government bonds	4,000
Operating expenses	(420,000)
State M net operating loss carried forward to current year	(58,000)
Timber state taxable income	$ 966,000

Interest earned from U.S. federal bonds is excluded from state income, as well as interest income earned from State M government bonds. The federal net operating loss is not included in the computation, but the State M net operating loss is included. Bonus depreciation and state taxes paid are not allowed for computing State M taxable income.

PRACTICE PROBLEM 14.3.2
Allocated Nonbusiness Income

During the year, Pepper Corporation, a North Carolina corporation, had $1,500,000 of taxable income, comprising $1,000,000 business income and $500,000 nonbusiness income. The $500,000 of nonbusiness income consisted of:

Rental income from real property located in South Carolina	$275,000
Dividend income	$100,000
Interest income	$ 25,000

What is Pepper Corporation's allocated nonbusiness income to North Carolina and to South Carolina?

SOLUTION

North Carolina is allocated the $100,000 of dividend income and the $25,000 of interest income because Pepper Corporation is domiciled in North Carolina. South Carolina is allocated the $275,000 of rental income because the real property generating the rental income is located in South Carolina.

PRACTICE PROBLEM 14.3.3
Apportionment

Assume Chipper Corp. conducts business in two states and has provided relevant information as follows:

	State Y	State Z	Total
Sales	$2,000,000	$3,800,000	$5,800,000
Property	$3,000,000	$4,000,000	$7,000,000
Payroll	$ 500,000	$ 300,000	$ 800,000

Chipper has business income before apportionment of $1,200,000 and interest income of $12,000. Chipper is located in State Z. State Y and State Z use the UDITPA apportionment formula to compute state taxable income for Chipper Corp.'s business income. What are the apportionment factors for State Y and State Z? Calculate the income apportioned and allocated to each state.

SOLUTION

The apportionment formula is computed as follows if the three factors are weighted equally as required by UDITPA.

	State Y	%	State Z	%	Total
Sales	$2,000,000/$5,800,000	34.5%	$3,800,000/$5,800,000	65.5%	$ 5,800,000
Property	$3,000,000/$7,000,000	42.9%	$4,000,000/$7,000,000	57.1%	$ 7,000,000
Payroll	$ 500,000/$800,000	62.5%	$ 300,000/$800,000	37.5%	$ 800,000
Average		46.6%		53.4%	

The income apportioned to State Y is $559,200 ($1,200,000 × 46.6%).
The income apportioned to State Z is $640,800 ($1,200,000 × 53.4%).
The interest income is nonbusiness income, so it is allocated to State Z, where Chipper is headquartered.

INTERACTIVE SELF-SCORING QUIZZES

14.4 Filing Methods and Other Topics

LEARNING OBJECTIVE 4

Distinguish among separate, consolidated, and combined filing.

VIDEO CONTENT

In this final section of the chapter, we discuss the general filing requirements that states have for corporate income tax. The filing approaches vary across states and include the following:

- Each entity reports separately.
- Affiliated corporations file a consolidated return.
- Members of a *unitary group* combine their transactions on one return.

Before describing these three filing methods, let's review the definition of affiliated groups for federal income tax returns from Chapter 5, LO2, Affiliated Groups and Consolidated Returns. An affiliated group can elect to file a consolidated return. An affiliated group exists if *both* conditions below are met:

- **80% Test** One or more of the other corporations in the group possesses stock with at least 80% of the voting power of all classes of stock entitled to vote, *and* at least 80% of the total value of shares of all classes of stock of each of the corporations (except the common parent), *and*

- **Common Parent Test** The common parent owns stock possessing at least 80% of the total combined voting power of all classes of stock entitled to vote, *and* at least 80% of the total value of shares of all classes of stock of at least one of the other corporations in the group.

Related exercises: Discussion Question 10
Multiple Choice Question 9
Brief Exercise 5
Application Problem 8

Separate Filing

In separate-filing states, every corporation that has nexus with the state files its own state income tax return, even if the corporation is part of an affiliated group. The advantage of separate filing is that a corporation can structure its operations so that high-income activities tend to be in low-tax states. The disadvantage is the same as for a corporation that cannot consolidate more than one corporation on a single return: losses from one corporation cannot offset gains from another corporation.

Consolidated Filing

Most states that allow separate filing also allow corporations to file a consolidated return, as allowed for federal income taxes, although the requirements for consolidating can vary from state to state. Some states only allow corporations that have nexus with the state to join in a consolidated return. The advantages of electing to consolidate are discussed in Chapter 5 and include:

- Netting capital gains and losses across corporations
- Netting income and losses across corporations
- Deferring gains from sales until sold outside the controlled group
- Avoiding limitations on deductions based on taxable income, such as the 10% limit on charitable contributions

The disadvantages of filing a consolidated return include:

- The election is binding for future years
- Creation of short-tax years
- Deferral of losses from sales until sold outside the controlled group
- Complexity of a consolidated tax return

These advantages and disadvantages are summarized in Illustration 14.7.

ILLUSTRATION 14.7 The Decision to Consolidate

Advantages and Disadvantages of Electing to Consolidate	
Advantages	**Disadvantages**
Netting capital gains and losses across group members	Election is binding for future tax years
Netting income and losses against income of other group members	Creation of short-tax years
Deferral of gains from sale of assets to other group members	Deferral of losses from sale of assets to other group members
Avoiding limitations on deductions based on taxable income by using income from all group members	Complexity of tax return

Related exercise: Multiple Choice Question 10

Combined Reporting

States that have combined reporting require corporations that are part of a *unitary group* to compute state taxable income on a combined worksheet. The term *unitary* refers to the rules that define the tax base to which a state can apply its apportionment formulas. It can be described as an accounting method for businesses that operate in more than one state. The Multistate Tax Commission defines a **unitary group** as:

> [A] single economic enterprise that is made up either of separate parts of a single business entity or of a commonly controlled group of business entities that are sufficiently interdependent, integrated and interrelated through their activities so as to provide a synergy and mutual benefit that produces a sharing or exchange of value among them and a significant flow of value to the separate parts.

Potential Pitfall

Unitary reporting is not a tax return. Rather, the combined report combines the income from all corporations that form an integrated economic unit and assigns the income to the appropriate states based on a common apportionment factor. The combined income can be reported on separate returns or a consolidated return.

Approximately 30 states require at least some form of combined reporting.[19] Combined reporting focuses on the similarity of the economic substance of corporations rather than on their legal status. Unitary groups are formed to meet the definitional requirements of a specific state. Generally, the three following requirements are evaluated to determine if entities should be combined:

- Common ownership of more than 50%
- Common operations
- Centralized management across the businesses

Several general guidelines apply to combined reporting, such as the following:

- If an affiliated group elects to file a consolidated return for federal income taxes, then it likely will be required to file a unitary return for state income taxes. However, the composition of the corporations could be different for state purposes.
- The federal consolidated group is based on ownership, while the state combined group will be based on economic factors such as functional integration or economies of scale.
- Businesses may be included in a unitary group even if there is no nexus with a state.

EXAMPLE 14.4.1 Separate, Consolidated, and Combined Filing

Blackbird Corporation has two subsidiaries, and all three corporations file a consolidated federal income tax return. The corporations have nexus with State M as follows:

	State M
Blackbird	Yes
Subsidiary One	Yes
Subsidiary Two	No

- Subsidiary Two had no business activity in State M.
- Subsidiary Two is included in a unitary group with Blackbird and Subsidiary One because economically they are similar.
- State M apportions income based just on sales.

Each company's relevant tax data is as follows. Compute the group's taxable income in State M under separate filing, consolidated filing, and combined filing.

[19] "State Corporate Income Taxation: Trends in Combined Reporting." Marcum LLP. 29 Nov. 2022. www.marcumllp.com/insights/state-corporate-income-taxation-trends-in-combined-reporting.

Corporation	Nexus— State M	Taxable Income	Corp. Sales in M	Total Sales	Apportionment Factor	Separate Filing	Consolidated Filing	Combined Filing
Blackbird	Yes	$250	$60	$ 500	12.0%			
Sub One	Yes	$200	$30	$ 400	7.5%			
Consolidated Total		$450	$90	$ 900	10.0%			
Sub Two	No	$150	$ 0	$ 200	0.0%			
Combined Total		$600	$90	$1,100	8.2%			

SOLUTION

- For separate filing, only Blackbird and Subsidiary One report income for State M, and each reports separately.
- For consolidated filing, income from only Blackbird and Subsidiary One is included in the consolidated return, and the apportionment factor is computed based on consolidated sales.
- For combined filing, the apportionment factor includes only sales of Blackbird and Subsidiary One in the numerator ($90), but the denominator includes sales of Blackbird, Subsidiary One, and Subsidiary Two ($1,100). The apportionment factor is then multiplied by the total taxable income for all three corporations ($1,100) since they are part of a unitary group. State M is taxing only the income of Blackbird and Subsidiary One, but the tax base and apportionment factors is being measured by including Subsidiary Two.

Corporation	Nexus— State M	Taxable Income	Corp. Sales in M	Total Sales	Apportionment Factor	Separate Filing	Consolidated Filing	Combined Filing
Blackbird	Yes	$250	$60	$ 500	12.0%	$250 × 12% = $30		
Sub One	Yes	$200	$30	$ 400	7.5%	$200 × 7.5% = $15		
Consolidated Total		$450	$90	$ 900	10.0%		$450 × 10% = $45	
Sub Two	No	$150	$ 0	$ 200	0.0%			
Combined Total		$600	$90	$1,100	8.2%			$600 × 8.2% = $49.20

Admittedly, combined reporting is a difficult concept to grasp. An example of this valuation method from a historic Supreme Court case (*State Railroad Tax Cases*) is useful to understand the unitary principle that underlies combined reporting.[20] The case involved determining the value of a railroad track in Kansas for property tax purposes. The rail line began in Missouri and ended in Colorado. Can the value of the railroad track in Kansas be determined by ignoring the segments of the railroad track that are not in Kansas? Clearly not, because the value of the railroad track is that it can transport people and products a very long distance, a portion of which passes through Kansas. Once the value of the entire railroad track is determined, then the value can be pro-rated to determine what percentage of the value is in Kansas. Similarly (see **Illustration 14.8**), combined reporting uses the data from the entire corporation to determine the value of the business, but then the apportionment percentage used for one state is based just on that state's data.

Related exercises: Discussion Questions 11, 12
Application Problem 9

[20]*In re State Railroad Tax Cases*, 92 U.S. 575, 608 [1875].

ILLUSTRATION 14.8 Example of Unitary Valuation

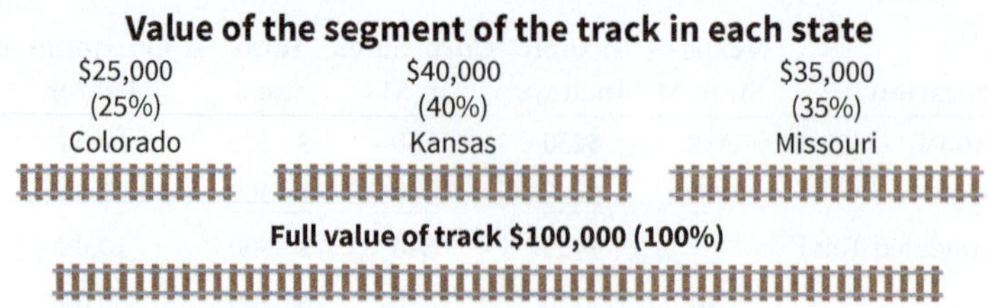

Analogy to Combined Reporting:
Assume Toucan Corporation has nexus with Colorado and Missouri but not with Kansas and apportionment is based on sales. First, the taxable income of the entire corporation (equivalent of full value of track) is determined, including data from Colorado, Kansas, and Missouri. Second, the taxable income is apportioned to Toucan as follows:

$$\text{Taxable income (all three states)} \times \frac{\text{Sales (Colorado and Missouri)}}{\text{Sales (all three states)}}$$

Other Entities

Most states recognize partnerships, LLCs, and federal S corporations at the state level. In those states, income from these entities flows to the shareholder's state income tax return and is taxed to the shareholder. Many of these states require the entity to withhold taxes for owners who are not residents of that state or to make estimated tax payments on the nonresident owners' behalf.

Some states treat flow-through entities differently than they are treated for federal income tax purposes, such as Tennessee. Tennessee has an excise tax and a franchise tax that are levied on corporations. The excise tax is a tax on earnings, and the franchise tax is a tax on the net worth of a business. The way Tennessee taxes certain entities that would be treated as flow-throughs at the federal level affects their liability for the excise tax and the franchise tax, as described in the following.

- **S Corporations** Tennessee does not recognize the S corporation election and taxes S corporations the same as other corporations. S corporations must pay the excise tax and the franchise tax. The S corporation income and losses do not flow to the shareholders. Tennessee chooses to tax the S corporation income at the entity level because it does not have a personal income tax, so if the income flows to the shareholders, it would never be taxed in Tennessee.
- **Limited Liability Companies** Tennessee taxes LLCs the same as S corporations. They are not treated as pass-through entities. Rather, the LLC is subject to the corporate excise tax and franchise tax.
- **General Partnerships** Tennessee treats general partnerships as flow-through entities, so the partnership income flows to the partners. If the partner is an individual, then the income is not taxed in Tennessee because Tennessee does not have a personal income tax.
- **Limited Partnerships and Limited Liability Partnerships** Tennessee taxes partnerships that have one or more partners with limited liability as corporations. These partnerships are subject to the corporate excise tax and franchise tax.

Tax Planning Tip

The income tax laws in Tennessee remind us that states often do not follow the federal income tax laws. Therefore, when developing tax planning strategies for businesses, it is essential that state taxes are considered. All state taxes are relevant in the planning process, with the most substantive being the income tax, property tax, and sales and use tax.

EXAMPLE 14.4.2
State Taxes and Planning

Crane Company is incorporated in State R and has made an election to be taxed as an S corporation for federal income tax purposes. State R treats Crane as a flow-through entity at the state level. Crane is considering building a new plant in State T and opening several retail outlets in State T. Crane's CFO is assuming that State T taxes income in the same manner as State R. What advice would you give Crane?

SOLUTION

Crane should not assume that State T taxes income the same as State R. Every state has its own unique set of laws. Further, a final decision on expanding operations into State T should not be made until Crane thoroughly understands the taxes that Crane would pay in State T, including income, property, and sales and use taxes, among others.

PRACTICE PROBLEM 14.4.1
Affiliated Group

Sad Corporation owns stock in the following corporations:

- 69% (voting and value) of the stock of Frown Corporation
- 80% of the voting and 85% of the value of the stock of Scared Corporation
- 70% (voting and value) of the stock of Desperate Corporation

Determine the largest group of corporations that qualify as an affiliated group, assuming that these ownership percentages are for every day of the tax year.

SOLUTION

We begin by determining which corporations meet the 80% test. Frown does not, because only 69% of its stock is owned by the other corporations. Scared does not, because Sad owns 85% of Scared's value but only 80% of the voting stock, so it does not own more than 80% of both Scared's voting stock and its value. Desperate does not meet the test because only 70% of its stock is owned by Sad. Therefore, none of the corporations qualify as an affiliated group, and the group cannot elect to file a consolidated tax return.

PRACTICE PROBLEM 14.4.2
Consolidated Tax Return

Price Corporation plans to contribute $55,000 per year for the next four years to qualified charitable organizations that support Price Corporation's mission to improve its impact on ESG (Environmental, Social, and Corporate Governance). Price expects to have taxable income of approximately $400,000 per year during this period. Dollar Corporation should generate at least $750,000 of taxable income over the next four years, and it does not plan to make any charitable contributions. Based on just the information given, and assuming that Price and Dollar are part of an affiliated group, would it be advantageous for the corporations to elect to file a consolidated tax return?

SOLUTION

Price and Dollar will make a smart tax decision if they elect to file a consolidated tax return. Price's charitable contribution deduction will be limited to $40,000 each year ($400,000 of taxable income × 10%), so $15,000 ($55,000 contribution − $40,000) of the contribution each year will be carried forward. However, contributions can be carried forward for only five years. Consolidated taxable income would be $1,150,000 ($400,000 + $750,000), and charitable contributions of up to $115,000 ($1,150,000 × 10%) could be deducted each year.

INTERACTIVE SELF-SCORING QUIZZES

Review and Practice

Chapter Summary

While the primary focus of this book has been on federal income taxes, there are many more taxes levied at the state and local levels than at the federal level. Managing a business's state and local tax liability is an essential part of an efficient tax strategic plan.

1 Identify the types of taxes levied by state and local governments.

State and local governments collect revenue from a wide variety of taxes. No two states have identical tax structures, as each state has developed its tax structure over many years and for many distinct reasons. The taxes that raise the most revenue for state and local governments are property taxes, individual income taxes, sales taxes, and the corporate income tax.

2 Determine which state has the authority to tax a business.

- **Nexus** measures the degree of the relationship that must exist between a state and a foreign corporation for the state to have the right to impose a tax. Nexus is determined on a year-by-year basis. From the state law perspective, there are domestic corporations and foreign corporations. A **domestic corporation** is a corporation doing business in the state in which it was incorporated. A **foreign corporation** is a corporation doing business in a state other than the state in which it was incorporated.
- Two clauses in the U.S. Constitution relate to nexus: the Due Process Clause, which prohibits states from denying any person "life, liberty, or property," and the Commerce Clause, which regulates interstate commerce.
- The tax laws providing the guidance for sales tax nexus are grounded in three landmark Supreme Court cases. In *National Bellas Hess* (*NBH*), the Supreme Court ruled that if a business did not have a physical presence in a state, then there was no nexus. **Physical presence** means that the business has property, employees, or perhaps independent contractors in the state.

  In *Quill*, the Supreme Court recognized that a business's economic presence has validity for applying the Due Process Clause. However, the Court determined that the physical presence test still applied for the Commerce Clause. After *Quill*, the Commerce Clause made it very difficult for states to tax sales from out-of-state vendors that did not have a physical presence in the state.

  In *Wayfair*, the Supreme Court ruled that states could collect sales tax from out-of-state vendors that did not have a physical presence in the state, but did have an economic presence. The Court justified the departure from *Quill* by pointing to changes in technology.
- Public Law 86-272 provides guidance for nexus for income tax purposes. This law applies to sales of tangible personal property and does not apply to the sale of services or to the leasing or renting of property. Nexus for taxing a corporation's income does not exist if activity in the state is limited to:
  - **Soliciting** sales of tangible personal property that are approved, and shipped from, outside the state
  - Advertising
  - Determining reorder needs of customers
  - Furnishing autos to sales staff

3 Compute state income tax for corporations.

- The starting point in most states for computing state income taxes is federal taxable income, increased or decreased for certain tax items. Some of the more common adjustments that *increase* federal taxable income include:
  - Dividends received deduction (if beginning with line 30)
  - Expenses related to interest earned on U.S. bonds
  - State income taxes
  - Depreciation in excess of that allowed for state (most states do not allow bonus depreciation)
  - Municipal interest taxed for state purposes
  - Federal net operating losses
  - Additional gain on the sale or disposition of assets
- Some of the adjustments that *decrease* federal taxable income include:
  - Federal income taxes paid
  - Expenses related to municipal interest income
  - Interest on U.S. bonds
  - Depreciation in addition to that allowed for federal purposes
  - State net operating losses
  - Refunds of state income taxes if included in federal taxable income
- A corporation that has nexus with more than one state for income tax purposes must determine how much of its income should be taxed in each state. The separation of income among the various states is done by either apportionment or allocation. **Allocation** is the assignment of **nonbusiness income** to a specific state based on the nature of the income.

Apportionment is the assignment of **business income** to states based on a formula that uses a combination of the company's payroll, property, and sales.

4 Distinguish among separate, consolidated, and combined filing.

- The general filing requirements that states have for corporate income tax vary. State filing approaches include the following:
  - Each entity reports separately.
  - Affiliated corporations file a consolidated return.
  - Members of a unitary group combine their transactions on one return.
- In separate-filing states, every corporation that has nexus with the state files its own state income tax return, even if the corporation is part of an affiliated group.
- Most states that allow separate filing also allow corporations to file a consolidated return, as allowed for federal income taxes, although the requirements for consolidating can vary from state to state. Some states only allow corporations that have nexus with the state to join in a consolidated return.
- States that have combined reporting require corporations that are part of a **unitary group** to compute state taxable income on a combined worksheet. The term *unitary* refers to the rules that define the tax base to which a state can apply its apportionment formulas. It can be described as an accounting method for businesses that operate in more than one state.

Communication Application

Communication

Has Nexus Been Created?

(LO2) Roberto owns an appliance distribution warehouse in State X. Currently, the sales of his appliances have been in State X only, but Roberto would like to expand to State Y. He wonders whether he will owe income tax on sales and distribution of appliances in State Y. Currently, the business uses an outside transportation company to deliver the goods. Roberto's customers would like him to provide installation and repair services as well. Roberto would like to know the implications of selling and distributing appliances in State Y and the implications of providing installation and repair services in State Y. Write a memo to Roberto explaining your findings.

Solution

Hello Roberto,

It was good to see you last week. I have researched your question regarding potential tax liability in State Y from selling and distributing appliances in State Y and the implications of providing installation and repair services in State Y. Many businesses conduct operations in more than one state, so a significant issue is determining which states have the authority to levy a tax on a particular business. Nexus measures the degree of the relationship that must exist between a state and a foreign corporation for the state to have the right to impose a tax. Nexus is determined on a year-by-year basis.

First, we must address sales taxes. Typically, if your business has more than $100,000 in gross sales or 200 or more sales transactions in State Y in a given year, you will need to collect sales tax on those sales. This definition allows businesses with a nonsignificant presence in the state to still be exempt from collecting sales tax.

Next, we need to discuss potential income tax in State Y. Public Law 86-272 allows a business to go, or send a representative, into a state to solicit orders for goods without being subject to a net income tax. The law applies exclusively to orders for tangible personal property and *either*:

- Orders solicited by employees that are approved, and shipped from, outside the state; *or*
- Orders solicited by independent contractors that are shipped from outside the state.

A state may impose an income tax on an entity that is doing business in that state if the entity establishes nexus in a state, indicating that it has a presence in that state. The sales of services are not protected from income tax nexus by Public Law 86-272.

Therefore, the sale of appliances alone will not create nexus in State Y if the orders are approved in State X and shipped from outside of State Y. However, if you provide services such as installation and repairs, then your business will have created nexus with State Y, and State Y can assess income tax liability.

If you would like to discuss this topic further, I would be happy to. I look forward to seeing you again.

Sincerely,
Carnes & Youngberg, CPAs

Ethics and Professional Responsibility Application

Ethics

Incorrect Apportionment

(LO3) Shady Sam owns his own sporting goods supply business, which operates stores in multiple states. His state of domicile has a low, 2% tax rate on business income. The other states he operates in have an average tax rate of 5%. Sam became a new client of your firm after firing his last accountant. He has asked you, a new staff accountant at your firm, to prepare this year's federal and state income tax returns. When reviewing previous state returns, you notice that the apportionment factors were not determined correctly, with most sales apportioned to Sam's state of domicile. What is your responsibility, and how do you respond to Shady Sam?

In addition to the chapter content, see Statements on Standards for Tax Services at www.aicpa-cima.com/resources/landing/statements-on-standards-for-tax-services, Circular 230 at www.irs.gov/tax-professionals/office-of-professional-responsibility-and-circular-230, and Chapter 2, LO4, Tax Professional Responsibilities.

Solution

Business income is apportioned among the states in which it is earned based on apportionment factors such as sales, property, and payroll. In general, states have discretion to apply different tax rules to different types of income. The U.S. Supreme Court has allowed states great flexibility to choose an apportioning formula and to tax income of an interstate business. But this apportionment must use an accurate apportioning formula.

Under *Circular 230,* §10.22 Diligence as to accuracy: "A practitioner must exercise due diligence ... [i]n preparing or assisting in the preparation of, approving, and filing tax returns, documents, affidavits, and other papers relating to Internal Revenue Service matters."

Statement on Standards for Tax Services No. 1.2.6, Knowledge of Error, sets forth applicable standards for a member who becomes aware of an error in a taxpayer's previously filed tax return: "A member should inform the taxpayer promptly upon becoming aware of an error in a previously filed return, an error in a return that is the subject of an administrative proceeding, or a taxpayer's failure to file a required return. A member also should advise the taxpayer of the potential consequences of the error and recommend the corrective measures to be taken."

As a staff accountant, you should recommend to your senior manager or partner that they discuss these issues with Sam and determine the need for amended returns to be filed promptly.

Key Terms

Allocation 14-22
Apportionable Income 14-22
Apportionment 14-22
Business Income 14-22
Domestic Corporation (for State Taxes) 14-8
Excise Taxes 14-6
External Consistency 14-10
Foreign Corporation (for State Taxes) 14-8
Franchise Tax 14-6
Functional Test 14-23
Internal Consistency 14-10
Nexus 14-8
Nonapportionable Income 14-22
Nonbusiness Income 14-22
Physical Presence 14-10
Point of Delivery 14-25
Property Taxes 14-5
Sales Taxes 14-5
Soliciting (State and Local Tax Nexus) 14-13
Transactional Test 14-23
Unitary Group 14-30
Use Taxes 14-5

End-of-Chapter Assessment

Discussion Questions

1. **(LO1)** List and describe the seven most common taxes that state and local governments collect.

2. **(LO2)** Distinguish between a domestic corporation and a foreign corporation as they relate to state income and sales tax.

3. **(LO2)** Provide a definition for nexus.

4. **(LO2)** Discuss the four-part test that was developed by the Supreme Court in applying the Commerce Clause to determine if a tax is constitutional.

5. **(LO2)** Briefly describe Public Law 86-272.

6. **(LO2)** Discuss how remote workers can affect whether a corporation has nexus with a state.

7. **(LO3)** Describe UDITPA.

8. **(LO3)** Define and discuss allocation and apportionment.

9. **(LO3)** Define and discuss business income and nonbusiness income.

10. **(LO4)** What two tests must be met for two corporations to be considered an affiliated group?

11. **(LO4)** Provide a definition for a unitary group.

12. **(LO4)** What three requirements are evaluated to determine if entities should be combined as a unitary group?

Multiple Choice Questions

1. **(LO1)** Which of the following generates the least amount of revenue for state and local governments?
   - **a.** Corporate income tax
   - **b.** General sales tax
   - **c.** Individual income tax
   - **d.** Property tax

2. **(LO1)** Taxes collected by state governments include which of the following?
   - **a.** Franchise tax
   - **b.** Use tax
   - **c.** Excise tax
   - **d.** All of the above

3. **(LO2)** Which of the following is a false statement?
   - **a.** Nexus is determined on a year-by-year basis.
   - **b.** Under current law, physical presence is needed to create nexus and impose sales tax.
   - **c.** Physical presence means that the business has property, employees, or perhaps independent contractors in the state.
   - **d.** The Multistate Tax Compact was created to increase the uniformity of state laws with regard to nexus.

4. **(LO2)** Which of the following is a true statement?
   - **a.** Nexus is created if the corporation solicits sales of tangible personal property that are approved, and shipped from, outside the state.
   - **b.** Furnishing autos to sales staff creates nexus.
   - **c.** An independent contractor that works with the business can have an office without creating nexus.
   - **d.** The sales of services are protected from income tax nexus by Public Law 86-272.

5. **(LO2)** Activities that can create nexus for income tax purposes include which of the following?
   - **a.** Collecting receivables in the state
   - **b.** Approving orders in the state
   - **c.** Carrying samples for sale in the state
   - **d.** All of the above

6. **(LO3)** Which of the following is a common adjustment that increases federal taxable income to arrive at state taxable income?
   - **a.** Interest on U.S. federal bonds
   - **b.** State net operating losses
   - **c.** Federal net operating losses
   - **d.** Federal income taxes paid

7. **(LO3)** Which of the following types of income would likely be considered business income for state income tax purposes?
   - **a.** Interest income earned on a certificate of deposit
   - **b.** Gain from the sale of property that is not used in the taxpayer's regular business operations
   - **c.** Royalties generated from the creation of a textbook by the original author
   - **d.** Dividend income from stock held for four years

8. **(LO3)** Business income is apportioned among the states using which of the following apportionment methods?
   - **a.** Using the sales factor only
   - **b.** Using an average of the sales, property, and payroll factors
   - **c.** Using double the sales factor, single property factor, and single payroll factor
   - **d.** All of the above are acceptable methods for apportioning business income.

9. **(LO4)** Franz, an individual, owns 85% and 90% of the total value and voting power of A and B Corps., which in turn own the following (both value and voting power):

	Ownership	
Property	**A Corp**	**B Corp**
C Corp	90%	–
D Corp	–	80%

All companies are C corporations except B Corp., which elected S status at inception. Which of the following statements is correct with respect to the companies' ability to file a consolidated return?
   - **a.** A, C, and D may file as a group.
   - **b.** A and C may not file as a group, and B and D may not file as a group.
   - **c.** A and C may file as a group, and B and D may file as a group.
   - **d.** A and C may file as a group, and B and D may not file as a group.

10. **(LO4)** Which of the following is an advantage of filing a consolidated tax return?
   - **a.** Complexity of a consolidated tax return
   - **b.** Election is binding for future years
   - **c.** Netting income and losses across corporations
   - **d.** Deferral of losses from sales until sold outside the controlled group

Brief Exercises

1. **(LO2)** Identify which of the following will create nexus for income tax purposes.
   - **a.** Installing purchased property
   - **b.** Setting up display racks without charge
   - **c.** Recruiting and training salespersons
   - **d.** Selling franchises or licenses
   - **e.** Hiring, training, or supervising employees other than salespersons
   - **f.** Checking customers' inventories for reordering if there is no additional charge
   - **g.** Collecting receivables

2. **(LO3)** For the current tax year, Oregano Corporation reported federal taxable income after the DRD of $335,000. Included in this income was $58,000 of Section 179 depreciation that is not allowed for state income tax purposes. Oregano also sold land this year for $230,000. Oregano's federal tax basis in the land was $180,000, and its state's tax basis was $200,000. Compute Oregano's state taxable income for this year.

3. **(LO3)** Basil Inc. is incorporated in Alabama. Basil owns and operates two companies, one in Alabama and the other in Florida. Basil rents 20% of its operating facility in Alabama to another company and receives $230,000 in rental income. Basil has $1,800,000 of income from manufacturing. Assume that rental income is considered allocable income. If Basil has determined that its apportionment factors are 60% for Alabama and 40% for Florida, what amount of income is attributable to Alabama and Florida?

4. **(LO3)** Paprika Corporation manufactures products in Florida and sells the products in Florida and Georgia. Paprika's sales are as follows for the current year:

Sales shipped from Florida to customers in Florida	$20,000
Sales shipped from Florida to customers in Georgia	$80,000

   - **a.** Assume that Paprika has nexus in both Florida and Georgia. What is Paprika's sales factor in Florida for the current year?
   - **b.** Assume that Paprika has nexus in Florida only. What is Paprika's sales factor in Florida for the current year?

5. **(LO4)** Happy Corporation owns stock in the following corporations:
   - 79% (voting and value) of the stock of Mad Corporation
   - 75% of the voting and 85% of the value of the stock of Fear Corporation
   - 60% (voting and value) of the stock of Excited Corporation

   Determine the largest group of corporations that qualify as an affiliated group, assuming that these ownership percentages are for every day of the tax year.

Application Problems

1. **(LO2)** Spice Corporation has the following data for State L:
   - Owns land, a warehouse building, and other assets with a value of $480,000
   - Pays $45,000 in payroll
   - Has $900,000 of sales

   Has Spice Corporation created nexus with State L using the Multistate Tax Compact?

2. **(LO2)** Evergreen Corporation manufactures construction tools and is located in Illinois. Evergreen sends a sales representative to Wisconsin to maintain a showroom for one week displaying the company's construction tools. As a result, Wisconsin residents order $170,000 of tools. The tool orders are approved in Illinois and shipped from Illinois to Wisconsin. Is Evergreen Corporation subject to Wisconsin income tax?

3. **(LO2)** Pine Corporation paints residential and commercial buildings and has a home office in Indiana. Pine has contracted with several businesses in Ohio to paint the businesses' office buildings, generating $225,000 in revenue. Pine sends a team of five painters to Ohio to complete the work, and they are in Ohio for ten days. Is Pine Corporation subject to Ohio income tax?

4. **(LO3)** Oak Corporation, located in State I, provided the following information.

Revenue from operations	$1,320,000
Interest earned on U.S. federal bonds	$ 15,000
Dividend income from Jasmine Corporation (Oak owns 2% of Jasmine)	$ 10,000
Interest earned on State I government bonds	$ 2,000
Interest earned on State T government bonds	$ 3,000
Operating expenses	$ 680,000
Federal net operating loss carried forward to current year	$ 100,000
State I net operating loss carried forward to current year	$ 65,000

   Calculate state taxable income, assuming that Oak does not allow a dividends received deduction and only includes interest earned on state government bonds from other states.

5. **(LO3)** During the year, Salt Corporation, a Vermont corporation, had $5,500,000 of taxable income, comprising $3,500,000 business income and $2,000,000 nonbusiness income. The $2,000,000 of nonbusiness income consisted of:

Rental income from real property located in Massachusetts	$1,800,000
Dividend income	$ 125,000
Interest income	$ 75,000

   What is Salt Corporation's allocated nonbusiness income to Vermont and to Massachusetts?

6. **(LO3)** Maple Corp. has total business income of $2 million and is located in Wisconsin. Wisconsin has a sales factor of 55%, a payroll factor of 40%, and a property factor of 45%. What is Maple's Wisconsin apportionment factor if Wisconsin uses an apportionment formula in which the property factor is double-weighted?

7. **(LO3)** Walnut Corporation has nexus with two states for income tax purposes. For the current year, it has the following data for sales, property, and payroll. Walnut's federal income after adjustments for state income tax differences is $500,000.

	State X	State Y	Total
Sales	$2,200,000	$1,100,000	$ 3,300,000
Property	$8,000,000	$4,500,000	$12,500,000
Payroll	$1,500,000	$ 900,000	$ 2,400,000

a. Compute Walnut's apportioned income to each state if the apportionment formula equally weights the three factors.

b. Compute Walnut's apportioned income to each state if the apportionment formula equally weights sales and payroll but double-weights property.

c. Compute Walnut's apportioned income to each state if the apportionment formula is based solely on sales.

8. **(LO4)** Gold Corporation owns 85% (voting and value) of the stock of Silver Corporation, 55% (voting and value) of the stock of Platinum Corporation, and 35% (voting and value) of the stock of Copper Corporation. Silver Corporation owns 45% (voting and value) of the stock of Copper Corporation. Determine the largest group of corporations that qualify as an affiliated group, assuming that these ownership percentages are for every day of the tax year.

9. **(LO4)** Palm Corporation has two subsidiaries, and all three corporations file a consolidated federal income tax return. The corporations have nexus with State P as follows:

	State P
Palm	Yes
Subsidiary One	Yes
Subsidiary Two	No

- Subsidiary Two had no business activity in State P.
- Subsidiary Two is included in a unitary group with Palm and Subsidiary One because economically they are similar.
- State P apportions income based just on sales.

Each company's relevant tax data is as follows. Compute the group's taxable income in State P under separate filing, consolidated filing, and combined filing.

Corporation	Nexus—State P	Taxable Income	Corp. Sales in P	Total Sales	Apportionment Factor	Separate Filing	Consolidated Filing	Combined Filing
Palm	Yes	$620	$ 90	$ 900	10.0%			
Sub One	Yes	$240	$ 45	$ 500	9.0%			
Consolidated Total		$860	$135	$1,400	9.6%			
Sub Two	No	$125	$ 0	$ 300	0.0%			
Combined Total		$985	$135	$1,700	7.9%			

Tax Planning Problems

Planning

1. **(LO3)** Bean Inc. operates in multiple states. Assume State D has an income tax rate of 5% and State E has an income tax rate of 8%. State E uses a double weight for its property factor. The current apportionment factors are as follows:

	State D	State E	Total	Factor D	Factor E
Sales	$500,000	$750,000	$1,250,000	40.0%	60.0%
Property	$900,000	$250,000	$1,150,000	78.3%	21.7%
Payroll	$150,000	$175,000	$ 325,000	46.2%	53.8%
Average				54.83%	39.3%*

*Using double weight for property factor.

Assume that Bean's business income is $900,000. If Bean would like to purchase property with a fair market value of $300,000, in which state should Bean purchase the property if the company wants to minimize its state taxes?

Professional Development Skills

Communication Problem

Communication

1. **(LO1) Types of Taxes That a State and Local Government Can Assess** Shauna is interested in opening a gas station/convenience store as a corporation in her hometown of Austin, Texas. Shauna is aware that the corporation will be assessed a federal income tax liability on its net earnings. She has asked you, her tax accountant, what types of taxes she could expect the state and local government to assess. Write a memo to Shauna explaining your findings.

Ethics and Professional Responsibilities Problem

Ethics

1. **(LO3) Incorrect Sales Apportionment** It is busy season, and you are a staff tax accountant for a regional CPA firm. Because the filing deadline for corporate tax returns is approaching quickly, you rely on information furnished from your client in a summary statement and do not review the client's sales invoices or QuickBooks. Your client has been forthcoming and reliable in previous years, so you have no reason to think that the summary statement is inaccurate. After the return is filed, you realize that the client's sales apportionment was incorrect, resulting in less overall tax liability on the filed return. Can you rely on information provided by a client? What is your responsibility and advice to your client?

In addition to the chapter content, see Statements on Standards for Tax Services at www.aicpa-cima.com/resources/landing/statements-on-standards-for-tax-services, Circular 230 at www.irs.gov/tax-professionals/office-of-professional-responsibility-and-circular-230, and Chapter 2, LO4, Tax Professional Responsibilities.

Research Problem

Research

1. **(LO1) Have All States Adopted the Standards Set by Wayfair?** As discussed in this chapter, in 2018, the Supreme Court ruled in favor of South Dakota in *South Dakota v. Wayfair, Inc.*, to allow the imposition of sales tax collection on remote sellers who meet certain thresholds. This landmark case overturned the physical presence test requirement for sales tax nexus in *National Bellas Hess, Inc. v. Department of Revenue* in 1967 and subsequently affirmed in *Quill Corp. v. North Dakota* in 1992. So, what has happened since 2018? Research state apportionment since the *Wayfair* decision in 2018 and summarize your findings.

Excel Problem

Technology

1. **(LO3) Apportionment** Chestnut Inc. is incorporated in State A but also has offices in States B and C. Chestnut's federal income after adjustments for state income tax differences is $900,000.

	State A	State B	State C	Total
Sales	$ 450,000	$ 700,000	$ 380,000	$1,530,000
Property	$3,000,000	$2,000,000	$1,000,000	$6,000,000
Payroll	$ 200,000	$ 300,000	$ 125,000	$ 625,000

a. Compute Chestnut's apportioned income to each state if the apportionment formula equally weights the three factors. Create an Excel spreadsheet using the rounding function to one tenth percent (three decimal places; for example: 0.241 = 24.1%).

b. Compute Chestnut's apportioned income to each state if the apportionment formula equally weights property and payroll but double weights sales. Create an Excel spreadsheet using the rounding function to one tenth percent (three decimal places; for example: 0.241 = 24.1%).

CHAPTER 15

Tax-Exempt Organizations

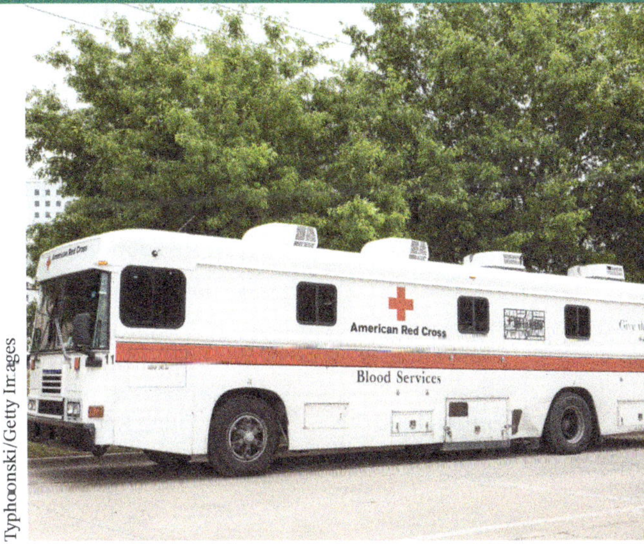

Typhoonski/Getty Images

Chapter Introduction

VIDEO CONTENT

Certain types of organizations do not have a profit motive. Rather, they are created for reasons such as educational, religious, improving healthcare, or meeting the needs of certain groups of people. **Not-for-profit organizations** may or may not be exempt from paying income taxes. Most tax-exempt entities must request tax-exempt status formally from the IRS.

When most individuals think of tax-exempt organizations (also known as exempt organizations), they focus on churches or other religious organizations, or large charities such as the American Red Cross and Goodwill. However, many tax-exempt organizations have activities that are like those of for-profit businesses. For example, credit unions are tax-exempt while banks are taxable businesses. Some hospitals are tax-exempt while other hospitals are for-profit businesses who have owners seeking to maximize profits. Other non-profit businesses include utilities, insurance companies, and universities. Surprisingly, charitable contributions comprise only 12% of the revenue of all nonprofits combined, while over 70% of their revenue comes from activities like those of for-profit businesses.[1]

It would be a mistake to presume that nonprofit organizations play only a minor role in the United States economy. To the contrary, tax-exempt organizations comprise approximately 15% of gross domestic product. There are more than 1.8 million tax-exempt organizations in the United States that account for more than $238 billion in net income. The largest nonprofit in America is Kaiser Permanente. Kaiser's health plan, hospitals, and state health plans generated over $110 billion in revenues in 2019.[2]

Now that you have a better understanding of the significance of tax-exempt organizations in the United States, you are ready to learn the tax laws surrounding them. We begin by describing the different types of tax-exempt organizations. Next, we describe the filing requirements for these organizations, followed by a summary of certain taxes that they may have to pay. We end the chapter with a discussion of the most significant tax for exempt organizations, the tax on *unrelated business taxable income*.

[1] Hodge, Scott. "Reining in America's $3.3 Trillion Tax-Exempt Economy." Tax Foundation. 18 Jun. 2024. https://taxfoundation.org/research/all/federal/501c3-nonprofit-organization-tax-exempt/.

[2] Ibid.

LEARNING OBJECTIVES	TOPICS	PRACTICE OPPORTUNITIES

1 Identify the different types of tax-exempt organizations, including private foundations.	**15.1 Types of Tax-Exempt Organizations**
	• Types of §501(c) Organizations
	• Number of Tax-Exempt Entities Filing Form 990
	• Private Foundations
	  • Definition of a Private Foundation
	  • Tax Consequences for Private Foundations
		• Practice Problem 15.1.1 Tax-Exempt Entity Type

2 Understand the initial and annual filing requirements for tax-exempt organizations.	**15.2 Filing Requirements**
	• Request for Tax-Exempt Status
	• Annual Information Returns
	  • Form 990-N (e-Postcard)
	  • Filing Deadlines
	  • Publicity
	  • Religious Organizations
		• Example 15.2.1 Applying for Tax-Exempt Status
		• Example 15.2.2 Annual Information Return
		• Example 15.2.3 Late-Filing Penalty
		• Example 15.2.4 Late-Filing Penalty—Large Gross Receipts
		• Practice Problem 15.2.1 Requesting Tax-Exempt Status

3 Compute certain taxes applicable to tax-exempt entities.	**15.3 Taxation of Tax-Exempt Entities**
	• Lobbying Tax
	  • Computation of Tax
	  • Implication of Tax
	• Excess Benefits Tax
	• Private Foundations
	  • Self-Dealing Tax
	  • Undistributed Income Tax
	• Private Universities Investment Income Tax
	• Excessive Compensation Tax
		• Example 15.3.1 Determining the Lobbying Tax
		• Example 15.3.2 Implication of Lobbying Expenditures
		• Example 15.3.3 Excess Benefit Tax
		• Example 15.3.4 Additional Excess Benefit Tax
		• Example 15.3.5 Self-Dealing Tax
		• Example 15.3.6 Undistributed Income Tax
		• Practice Problem 15.3.1 Computing the Lobbying Nontaxable Amount and the Grass Roots Nontaxable Amount
		• Practice Problem 15.3.2 Compute the Excess Lobbying Expenditures and Liability
		• Practice Problem 15.3.3 Excess Benefits Tax
		• Practice Problem 15.3.4 Undistributed Income Tax

4 Compute the tax on unrelated business taxable income for a tax-exempt organization.	**15.4 Unrelated Business Income**
	• Definition of Unrelated Business Income
	  • Trade of Business Activity
	  • Regularly Carried On
	  • Not Substantially Related to the Tax-Exempt Purpose
	• Computation of Unrelated Business Taxable Income Tax
	  • Adjustments to Net Unrelated Business Income
	  • Unrelated Debt-Financed Income Adjustment
		• Example 15.4.1 Unrelated Business Income
		• Example 15.4.2 University Rental of Property
		• Example 15.4.3 Selling of Merchandise
		• Example 15.4.4 Low-Cost Items
		• Example 15.4.5 Adjustment for Charitable Contributions
		• Example 15.4.6 Computation of Unrelated Business Taxable Income Tax
		• Example 15.4.7 Unrelated Debt-Financed Income
		• Practice Problem 15.4.1 Income Subject to Unrelated Business Income Tax?
		• Practice Problem 15.4.2 Calculation of Unrelated Business Income

Tax forms referenced in this chapter:

Form 990	Return of Organization Exempt from Income Tax
Form 990-N	Electronic Notice (e-Postcard) for Tax-Exempt Organizations not Required To File Form 990 or 990-EZ
Form 990-PF	Return of Private Foundation
Form 990-T	Exempt Organization Business Income Tax Return
Form 1023	Application for Recognition of Exemption Under Section 501(c)(3) of the Internal Revenue Code
Form 1023-EZ	Streamlined Application for Recognition of Exemption Under Section 501(c)(3) of the Internal Revenue Code
Form 1024	Application for Recognition of Exemption Under Section 501(a) or Section 521 of the Internal Revenue Code
Form 8868	Application for Automatic Extension of Time To File an Exempt Organization Return.

15.1 Types of Tax-Exempt Organizations

LEARNING OBJECTIVE 1

Identify the different types of tax-exempt organizations, including private foundations.

VIDEO CONTENT

Tax-exempt organizations include charities, labor organizations, social clubs, pension and profit-sharing trusts, and private foundations. A tax-exempt organization may be in the form of a corporation, trust, or limited liability company. The tax law defines 20 different types of tax-exempt organizations under Internal Revenue Code (IRC) §501(c). The general characteristics of a tax-exempt organization include:

- The purpose of the organization is to meet some common good as opposed to creating wealth for its owners.
- The organization can earn a profit even though it is a nonprofit organization. That is, revenues can exceed cash expenses.
- The organization generally does not pay income taxes. As discussed below, income tax may be owed if the organization has *unrelated business income*.
- Tax-exempt organizations are generally subject to taxes other than income tax, such as payroll taxes, excise taxes, property taxes, and sales taxes. Some states exempt tax-exempt organizations from certain state and local taxes such as property taxes and sales taxes.
- The organization cannot influence legislation or support political candidates or parties.

Related exercise: Discussion Question 1

Types of §501(c) Organizations

The most common types of tax-exempt organizations are:

- **§501(c)(3)** Religious, charitable, scientific, literary, educational, literary, promoting amateur sports, prevention of cruelty to children and animals, etc.

  Examples: United Way, Red Cross, churches, universities,

  - §501(c)(3) entities are sometimes referred to as charitable tax-exempt organizations because donors can deduct contributions to these entities as charitable contribution deductions.

- §501(c)(3) organizations cannot be involved in activities to influence legislation or to support political candidates.

- **§501(c)(4)** Civic leagues, social welfare organizations, and local associations of employees
  Examples: Concerned Veterans for Americans, Rotary clubs, Kiwanis clubs
- **§501(c)(5)** Labor, agriculture, and horticultural organizations
  Examples: Farm bureaus, rodeos, garden clubs, American Postal Workers Union
- **§501(c)(6)** Business leagues, chambers of commerce, and real estate boards
  Examples: Major League Baseball, National Basketball Association, Better Business Association, United States Chamber of Commerce
- **§501(c)(7)** Social and recreational clubs
  Examples: College fraternities and sororities, Augusta National Golf Club, Beta Alpha Psi, homeowners associations
- **§501(c)(8)** Fraternal beneficiary societies and associations
  Examples: Knights of Columbus, Modern Woodmen of America
- **§501(c)(9)** Voluntary employee beneficiary associations
  Examples: AT&T Welfare Benefit Trust, Wal-Mart Stores Inc. Associate Health & Welfare Trust
- **§501(c)(14)** Credit unions
  Examples: Alliant Credit Union (Chicago, IL), Listerhill Credit Union (Florence, AL)
- **§501(c)(15)** Mutual insurance companies
  Examples: Kenosha County Mutual Insurance Company (Kenosha, WI)

Potential Pitfall

Many individuals believe that contributions to all tax-exempt organizations are deductible as charitable contributions. However, only contributions to §501(c)(3) organizations are deductible as charitable contributions. Payments to other tax-exempt entities may be deductible under other tax laws, such as if they are for advertising or membership dues.

Related exercise: Multiple Choice Question 1

Number of Tax-Exempt Entities Filing Form 990

The IRS has released information for certain tax-exempt organization that filed a Form 990. Form 990, Return of Organization Exempt from Income Tax, must be filed by most tax-exempt organizations. **Illustration 15.1** provides the number of Form 990 returns filed for 2021 for different types of tax-exempt organizations. There were 317,151 charitable organizations that filed a tax return for 2021.

ILLUSTRATION 15.1 Number of Form 990 Returns Filed

Form 990s Filed for 2021			
Type of Tax-Exempt Organization	Number of Returns—Form 990[3]	Number of Returns—Form 990-EZ[4]	Total
§501(c)(3)	232,329	84,822	317,151
§501(c)(4)	12,271	6,232	18,503
§501(c)(5)	10,290	5,863	34.656
§501(c)(6)	17,931	6,438	24,369
§501(c)(7)	9,261	5,669	14,930
§501(c)(8)	4,941	1,907	6,848
§501(c)(9)	4,660	95	4,755

[3]U.S. Department of the Treasury. "Form 990 Returns of 501(c)(3)-(9) Organizations: Balance Sheet and Income Statement Items, by Internal Revenue Code Section, Tax Year 2021." Table 3, Internal Revenue Service, Statistics of Income Division, Exempt Organizations (Except Private Foundations), Sept. 2024. www.irs.gov/pub/irs-soi/21eo03.xlsx.

[4]U.S. Department of the Treasury. "Form 990-EZ Returns of 501(c)(3)-(9) Organizations: Balance Sheet and Income Statement Items, by Internal Revenue Code Section, Tax Year 2021." Table 4, Internal Revenue Service, Statistics of Income Division, Exempt Organizations (Except Private Foundations), Sept. 2024. www.irs.gov/pub/irs-soi/21eo04.xlsx.

Private Foundations

Private foundations are §501(c)(3) organizations that are independent legal entities set up solely for charitable purposes whose funding comes primarily from an individual, a family, or a corporation. For 2020, 103,968 private foundations filed Form 990-PF, Return of Private Foundation or Section 4947(a)(1) Nonexempt Charitable Trust Treated as a Private Foundation.[5] Some of the largest private foundations in the United States are listed in **Illustration 15.2**, and they have significant impact around the world. For example, the Gates Foundation has assets of over $60 billion. Part of its mission is spurring innovation that improves the human condition by stepping in where governments and businesses leave gaps.

ILLUSTRATION 15.2 Well-Known Private Foundations

Largest Private Foundations in the United States[6]	
Name	**Value**
Gates Foundation	$60,023,136,000
Lilly Endowment	$40,801,432,198
Howard Hughes Medical Institute	$24,177,090,000
Ford Foundation	$16,383,378,000
Robert Wood Johnson Foundation	$13,837,817,000
Silicon Valley Community Foundation	$13,822,021,000
J. Paul Getty Trust	$12,545,917,000
William and Flora Hewlett Foundation	$12,455,788,000
Kamehameha Schools	$11,621,172,512
Foundation to Promote Open Society	$10,600,000,000

Definition of a Private Foundation

The tax law defines **private foundations** by describing what they are *not*. Broadly, private foundations are §501(c)(3) organizations *other than*

- churches,
- educational organizations,
- hospitals or medical research organizations operated in conjunction with hospitals,
- endowment funds operated for the benefit of certain state and municipal colleges and universities,
- governmental units, *and*
- publicly supported organizations.[7]

A §501(c)(3) organization must meet one of the following three requirements to *not* be classified as a private foundation:

1. It is classified as a **favored activity** meaning it is a church, educational institution, hospital, medical research organization, or governmental unit.
2. It is broadly supported by the general public, a governmental unit, or by organizations listed in #1 above. Specifically, private foundations receive less than one-third of their

[5]U.S. Department of the Treasury. "Historical Table 16 (expanded version) Nonprofit Charitable Organization and Domestic Private Foundation Information Returns, and Exempt Organization Business Income Tax Returns: Selected Financial Data, 1985-2020." Internal Revenue Service, Statistics of Income Division, Exempt Organizations (Forms 990/990-EZ, 990-PF, and 990-T) Studies, Sept. 2024, www.irs.gov/pub/irs-soi/histab16e.xlsx.

[6]Arco. "World's 100 Largest Philanthropic Foundations." Updated Mar. 2024. www.arcolab.org/en/worlds-100-largest-philanthropic-foundations-list/. Values are as of 2022.

[7]IRC §509.

annual support from their members and the general public. Support can be received in the form of gifts, grants, contributions, membership fees, gross receipts from admissions, sales of merchandise, etc.

Amounts received from disqualified persons cannot count toward meeting the one-third support test. **Disqualified persons** include donors:

- whose contributions exceeded 2% of total contributions and $5,000, *and*
- officers, directors, trustees, and their family members.

Additionally, investment income and *unrelated business taxable income* cannot exceed one-third of total support.

3. It is classified as a supporting organization, meaning it exists to exclusively benefit an organization in #1 or #2 above. For example, an organization may exist to manage the endowment funds for a hospital.

Tax Consequences for Private Foundations

There are two negative consequences of being classified as a private foundation. First, more stringent requirements apply to donors of private foundations when determining how much of their contribution is deductible. Specifically, the deduction for contributions to private foundations by an individual cannot exceed 30% of the donor's adjusted gross income.[8] Second, the private foundation may have to pay additional taxes, as discussed in more detail later in the chapter.

Related exercises: Discussion Questions 2, 3
Brief Exercises 1, 2
Multiple Choice Question 2

Spotlight on the Law

College Athletes Working with Tax-Exempt Organizations

College sports have changed drastically in recent years. One major change that began in 2021 is allowing players to receive large sums of money for the use of their name, image, and likeness (NIL) while still enrolled at the university. Previously, this was not allowed and the athlete and university suffered severe consequences if athletes accepted benefits other than for tuition, fees, and room and board.

Donor-backed organizations are organizations that heavily rely on donations from individuals, foundations, and corporations to support their mission, often called collectives. Many of these organizations have requested nonprofit status from the IRS and have been approved. These donor-backed organizations are paying college athletes to promote charities that have partnered with the collective. The athletes are paid for these promotional activities from donated funds, and the donors receive a tax-deductible donation. These collectives have become very large for the universities that have well-known athletic teams, and some athletes now receive more than $1 million per year from them.

However, many of these collectives could lose their tax-exempt status if their main purpose is paying athletes instead of supporting charitable works. If the organizations are not tax-exempt, then the donations they collect that are used to pay quarterbacks, point guards, and pitchers would not be deductible by the donors. The IRS has addressed this issue in a memo dated June 9, 2023, indicating that the collectives must meet certain guidelines to maintain their tax-exempt charitable status.[9] Congress has also been involved in this arena. A bipartisan bill introduced in the Senate in 2023 would limit tax deductions for funding nonprofit NIL collectives, but it has yet to pass.[10] This could change the landscape of college athletics if donors' contributions to collectives are no longer tax deductible.

---

[8]IRC §170(e)(1)(B).

[9]Legal Advice Issued by Associate Chief Counsel 2023-004 Electronic Miscellaneous Document AM 2023-004.

[10]Athlete Opportunity and Taxpayer Integrity Act, introduced May 4, 2023.

PRACTICE PROBLEM 15.1.1
Tax-Exempt Entity Type

Identify the correct type of tax-exempt entity for the following organizations:

a. DeKalb Farm Bureau
b. United Way
c. Omaha Mutual Insurance Company
d. Rockford Kiwanis Club
e. National Basketball Association
f. Medinah Country Club
g. Good Samaritan Hospital

SOLUTION

a. DeKalb Farm Bureau—§501(c)(5)
b. United Way—§501(c)(3)
c. Omaha Mutual Insurance Company—§501(c)(15)
d. Rockford Kiwanis Club—§501(c)(4)
e. National Basketball Association—§501(c)(6)
f. Medinah Country Club—§501(c)(7)
g. Good Samaritan Hospital—§501(c)(3)

INTERACTIVE SELF-SCORING QUIZZES

15.2 Filing Requirements

LEARNING OBJECTIVE 2

Understand the initial and annual filing requirements for tax-exempt organizations.

VIDEO CONTENT

There are two main federal filing requirements that exempt organizations have. First, most exempt organizations must request that the IRS approve their tax-exempt status. Second, once the tax-exempt status is approved, then most exempt organizations must file an annual information return. We discuss both filing requirements in this section.

Request for Tax-Exempt Status

Most tax-exempt organizations must apply for and receive an exemption from taxation on either Form 1023/Form 1023-EZ or Form 1024. Form 1023 is used by organizations seeking tax-exempt status as charitable organizations (which means they qualify under IRC §501(c)(3)). Form 1024 is used by organizations seeking tax-exempt status under other sections of the Internal Revenue Code, as discussed in the previous section. Religious organizations do not have to file Form 1023 to be a qualified charitable organization. The following forms are used to request tax-exempt status:

- Form 1023, Application for Recognition of Exemption Under §501(c)(3) of the IRC. This is used by charitable organizations applying under §501(c)(3). To be eligible for tax-exempt status under this section, an organization must meet certain requirements, such as having a charitable purpose, operating exclusively for that purpose, and not engaging in prohibited activities, such as political campaigning.

- Form 1023-EZ, Streamlined Application for Recognition of Exemption Under §501(c)(3) of the IRC, can be used by charitable organizations with assets of $250,000 or less and annual gross receipts of $50,000 or less (measured as the average over the three preceding tax years) Form 1023-EZ cannot be used by foreign organizations, churches, schools, hospitals, and private foundations.
- Form 1024, Application for Recognition of Exemption Under §501(a) or §521 of the Internal Revenue Code. Form 1024 is used by non-charitable organizations seeking tax-exempt status. IRC §521 is for a farmer's cooperative that is requesting tax-exempt status.

An organization utilizing any of these forms must submit the form and applicable user fee online at pay.gov.

The following Example applies these rules to determine the proper form to use to request tax-exempt status.

EXAMPLE 15.2.1
Applying for Tax-Exempt Status

Which form should an organization use to request tax-exempt status from the IRS?

- Cat Rescue, a charitable organization with assets of $350,000 and average gross receipts of $40,000
- Dog Savers, a charitable organization with assets of $110,000 and average gross receipts of $40,000
- Elephant Watch, a charitable organization with assets of $90,000 and average gross receipts of $75,000
- Fox Run Park, a non-charitable organization with assets of $350,000 and average gross receipts of $40,000
- Giraffe Habitat, a non-charitable organization with assets of $110,000 and average gross receipts of $40,000

SOLUTION

Cat Rescue—Form 1023; assets are too high to use Form 1023-EZ

Dog Savers—Form 1023-EZ; assets do not exceed $250,000 and average gross receipts do not exceed $50,000

Elephant Watch—Form 1023; average gross receipts exceed $50,000 so cannot use Form 1023-EZ

Fox Run Park—Form 1024; all non-charitable organizations must use Form 1024

Giraffe Habitat—Form 1024; all non-charitable organizations must use Form 1024

Related exercises: Multiple Choice Question 3
Brief Exercise 3

Annual Information Returns

Most tax-exempt organizations must file an annual information return, Form 990, Return of Organization Exempt from Income Tax. This form reports income, expenses, and substantial contributors.[11] It also must include total lobbying and political expenditures. Other key points regarding annual information returns are as follows:

- A tax-exempt organization does not have to file an information return if gross receipts are $50,000 or less.
- Churches, state institutions, and governmental units do not have to file Form 990.

[11]IRC §6033(a).

- Form 990-EZ, Short Form Return of Organization Exempt From Income Tax, can be used unless gross receipts exceed $200,000 or total assets exceed $500,000.
- Private foundations must file Form 990-PF, Return of Private Foundation.
- Political organizations that have gross receipts more than $25,000 must file Form 990 or Form 990-EZ.[12]

Form 990-N (e-Postcard)

Most tax-exempt organizations that are not required to file an information return must file an annual electronic notice with the IRS (Form 990-N, Electronic Notice (e-Postcard) for Tax-Exempt Organizations not Required To File Form 990 or 990-EZ). This form includes demographic information and justifies the continuing basis for tax-exempt status. The tax-exempt organization must also confirm that annual gross receipts are $50,000 or less. Other key points are as follows:

- The groups that are exempt from the electronic notice requirement include churches, state institutions, and governmental units.
- The form must be filed by the 15th day of the fifth month after the end of the tax year, and the due date *cannot* be extended.
- There is no monetary penalty for organizations required to file the Form 990-N that do not. However, if it does not meet these filing requirements for three consecutive years, it will lose its tax-exempt status.

The next Example applies these rules to determine the proper annual information return to file.

EXAMPLE 15.2.2 Annual Information Return

Which form should the following organizations use to meet their annual information filing requirements? If the organization is excluded from filing, please state as such.

- Lady of Hope, a church with annual gross receipts of $800,000
- Mayfair Foundation, a charitable organization (not a church) with annual gross receipts of $320,000
- Nashville Library Foundation, a charitable organization (not a church) with annual gross receipts of $40,000
- Orville Foundation, a charitable organization (not a church) with annual gross receipts of $187,000
- Pennsylvania Infrastructure Trust, a nonprofit corporation formed to finance the restoration of a state's utility infrastructure that was damaged by natural disasters

SOLUTION

Lady of Hope—No filing; Churches are not required to file Form 990 or Form 990-N (e-postcard).

Mayfair Foundation—Form 990; gross receipts exceed $200,000 so Form 990-EZ is not permitted.

Nashville Library Foundation—Form 990-N (e-postcard); the Form 990 is not required because gross receipts do not exceed $50,000, but the Form 990-N is required.

Orville Foundation—Form 990-EZ; gross receipts do not exceed $200,000 so the Form 990-EZ can be used.

Pennsylvania Infrastructure Trust—No filing; State organizations are not required to file Form 990 or Form 990-N (e-postcard).

Related exercises: Discussion Question 4
Application Problem 1

[12] IRC §6033(g)(1).

Filing Deadlines

Form 990, 990-EZ, and 990-PF must be filed on or before the 15th day of the fifth month after the close of the tax year, which is May 15th for a calendar-year organization. An automatic six-month extension is available, which would extend the due date to November 15th for calendar-year organizations. The due date is extended by filing Form 8868, Application for Automatic Extension of Time To File a Tax-Exempt Organization Return.

Tax-exempt organizations can incur significant penalties if the Form 990 is not filed on time. The penalty is $25 for each day that the return is filed late. For 2025 returns, the maximum penalty cannot exceed the *lower* of:

- $13,000, *or*
- 5% of the gross receipts of the organization for the year.

The late filing penalty is significantly larger for tax-exempt organizations that have gross receipts of more than $1,309,500 for 2025 returns. For these larger tax-exempt organizations, the penalty is the *lower* of:

- $130 per day, *or*
- $65,000.[13]

The two following Examples show the computation of the late-filing penalty for a tax-exempt organization.

EXAMPLE 15.2.3 Late-Filing Penalty

African Transformational Leadership (ATL) is a calendar-year tax-exempt corporation that builds water wells and schools in Africa. ATL filed Form 990 for 2025 on June 14, 2026. ATL did not request for its return to be extended. ATL's gross receipts for 2025 are $300,000.

a. How much is ATL's late-filing penalty for its 2025 return?

b. How much is the late-filing penalty if the return was validly extended to November 15, 2026, and was filed on June 30, 2027, and the gross receipts are $100,000?

SOLUTION

a. ATL's tax return was due on May 15, 2026, because it did not request an extension of time to file. The late-filing penalty is $25 for each day that the return is filed late. For 2025 returns, the maximum penalty cannot exceed the *lower* of:

- $13,000, *or*
- 5% × the gross receipts of the organization for the year.
- The return was filed on June 14, 2026, which is 30 days late (16 days in May and 14 days in June), so the penalty is $750 (30 days × $25). This does not exceed the lower of $13,000 or $15,000 ($300,000 × 5%).

b. Now the return was not due until November 15, 2026, because it was validly extended. The late-filing penalty begins on November 16, 2026, and runs for 227 days determined as follows:

	Days late
November 2025	15
December 2025	31
January 2026	31
February 2026	28
March 2026	31
April 2026	30
May 2026	31
June 2026	30
Total	227

The initial penalty is $5,675 (227 days × $25), but this cannot exceed the lower of $13,000 or $5,000 ($100,000 × 5%). Therefore, the penalty is limited to $5,000.

13 IRC §6652(1)(c)(A).

EXAMPLE 15.2.4
Late-Filing Penalty—Large Gross Receipts

Assume the same facts for African Transformational Leadership (ATL) as in Example 15.2.3 (part a), except that ATL's gross receipts for 2025 are $1,500,000. How much is ATL's late-filing penalty for its 2025 return?

SOLUTION

ATL's tax return was due on May 15, 2026, because it did not request an extension of time to file. The late-filing penalty is $130 for each day that the return is filed late because ATL's gross receipts exceed $1,309,500, but it cannot exceed $65,000.

The return was filed on June 14, 2026, which is 30 days late (16 days in May and 14 days in June), so the penalty is $3,900 (30 days × $130). This does not exceed the ceiling of $65,000.

Related exercises: Discussion Question 5
Application Problems 2, 3

Publicity

Most exempt organizations must make their last three years' tax returns and their tax-exempt application available to interested parties. The three-year period runs from the extended due date of the tax return.[14] An exact copy of a return must be made available that includes all information furnished to the IRS on the return, as well as schedules, attachments and supporting documents. Information about donors does not have to be disclosed unless the organization is a private foundation. In addition to requesting a copy of a Form 990 from the exempt organization, an individual can request a copy from the IRS.[15] Organizations such as GuideStar also make Form 990s available to the public through a free database that allows names of exempt organization to be searched.[16]

Religious Organizations

Religious organizations are exempt from the following filing requirements summarized in this section, such as:

- Religious organizations do not have to file Form 1023 to be recognized as a §501(c)(3) charitable organization.
- Religious organizations do not have to file the Form 990 annual information return.
- Religious organizations do not have to file the Form 990-e-postcard.

Many taxpayers make tax-deductible contributions to religious organizations every year. Therefore, it is important to know how a *religious organization* is defined for purposes of these exemptions. A **religious organization** must meet the following requirements to be tax-exempt and qualify as a charitable organization:

- Be organized and operated exclusively for a religious purpose to be exempt.[17]
- Not be involved in political activities.
- The revenue of the organization cannot be used to benefit private individuals or shareholders.
- The organization's activities cannot be illegal or a violation of public policy.

[14] IRC §6104(d)(2).

[15] Taxpayers must use IRS's Tax Exempt Organization Search tool (TEOS) to request copies of tax-exempt organization documents. https://apps.irs.gov/app/eos/.

[16] GuideStar also has subscription-based services that provide additional data on exempt organizations that are compiled from their Form 990s.

[17] Treas. Reg. § 1.501(c)(3)-1(d)(1)(i)(a).

Religious organizations include the following:

- Temples, churches, mosques, and other places of worship
- Church conventions
- Auxiliaries of churches
- Church associations
- All other organizations associated with churches

Some individuals have labeled their organization as *religious,* but their primary purpose was tax avoidance, and the IRS and the courts have consistently determined that these were not tax-exempt. Some activities that suggest an organization is not primarily organized for religious purposes include:

- Being engaged in commercial activities with the intent to make a profit
- Publishing religious literature for profit
- Handling personal financial transactions related to the personal life of its members
- Engages in legislative activities
- Provides tax advice related to tax avoidance

Example of organizations that claimed religious status whose tax-exempt status was reviewed by a court are listed in **Illustration 15.3**.

ILLUSTRATION 15.3 Judicial Rulings on Religious Organizations

The following organizations were determined to *not* meet the definition of a religious organization.

- A church had only two members, no scheduled services, no location for services, and no bank account. *American Guidance Foundation Inc. v. U.S.* (1980, DC Dist Col) 46 AFTR 2d 80-5006, 490 F Supp 304.
- A church was supposedly formed by a chiropractor, and the church's sacrament of spinology was very similar to the practice of other chiropractors who charge a fee for their services. Triune of Life Church, Inc. (1985) 85 TC 45, affd without op (1986, CA3) 791 F2d 922.
- A resort was advertised as a religious retreat, but it had no regular minister. Participation in religious services and activities by guests was optional. Schoger Foundation (1981) 76 TC 380.
- An organization held supper club meetings and published a newsletter for members, but the activities were politically related rather than religious. First Libertarian Church (1980) 74 TC 396.
- An organization that used marijuana as its sacrament but was an illegal commercial drug-smuggling business. King Shipping Consum, Inc. (1989) TC Memo 1989-593.

The following organizations were determined to meet the definition of a religious organization.

- An organization where the members practiced miraculous healing. Allen, A. A. Revivals Inc. (1963) TC Memo 1963-281.
- An organization that puts college-age individuals together with church leaders, educators, and business professionals to discuss religion and current events and to provide vocational counseling. Rev. Rul. 68-72, 1968-1 CB 25.
- A small organization that was generally a street church that had a creed, a formal code of doctrine, and regular religious services. While several members were children of the founder, there were also other members. Purnell, Deborah A. (1992) TC Memo 1992-289.
- An organization providing temporary low-cost housing to families who are on furlough from the mission field. Rev. Rul. 75-434, 1975-2 CB 205.

Related exercises: Multiple Choice Question 4, 5

PRACTICE PROBLEM 15.2.1
Requesting Tax-Exempt Status

Which form should each of the following organizations use to request tax-exempt status from the IRS?

- Snapdragon, a non-charitable organization with assets of $520,000 and average gross receipts of $80,000
- Zinnia, a non-charitable organization with assets of $198,000 and average gross receipts of $44,000
- Azalea, a charitable organization with assets of $220,000 and average gross receipts of $64,000
- Aster, a charitable organization with assets of $292,000 and average gross receipts of $33,000
- Lavender, a charitable organization with assets of $78,000 and average gross receipts of $42,000

SOLUTION

- Snapdragon—Form 1024; all non-charitable organizations must use Form 1024
- Zinnia—Form 1024; all non-charitable organizations must use Form 1024
- Azalea—Form 1023; average gross receipts exceed $50,000 so cannot use Form 1023-EZ
- Aster—Form 1023; assets are too high to use Form 1023-EZ
- Lavender—Form 1023-EZ; assets do not exceed $250,000, and average gross receipts do not exceed $50,000

PRACTICE PROBLEM 15.2.2
Late-Filing Penalty

Chrysanthemum (CH) is a calendar-year tax-exempt corporation that provides inner cities with the tools to create their own sustainable gardens. CH filed Form 990 for 2025 on June 28, 2026. CH did not request that its return be extended. CH's gross receipts for 2025 are $625,000.

a. How much is CH's late-filing penalty for its 2025 return?

b. How much is the late-filing penalty if the return was validly extended to November 15, 2026, it was filed on June 15, 2027, and the gross receipts are $95,000?

SOLUTION

a. CH's tax return was due on May 15, 2026, because it did not request an extension of time to file. The late-filing penalty is $25 for each day that the return is filed late. For 2025 returns, the maximum penalty cannot exceed the *lower* of:

- $13,000, *or*
- 5% × the gross receipts of the organization for the year.

The return was filed on June 28, 2026, which is 44 days late (16 days in May and 28 days in June), so the penalty is $1,100 (44 days × $25). This penalty does not exceed the lower of $13,000 or $31,250 ($625,000 × 5%).

b. Here, the return was not due until November 15, 2026, because it was validly extended. The late-filing penalty begins on November 16, 2026, and runs for 227 days, determined as follows:

	Days late
November 2025	15
December 2025	31
January 2026	31
February 2026	28
March 2026	31
April 2026	30
May 2026	31
June 2026	15
Total	212

The initial penalty is $5,300 (212 days × $25), but the penalty cannot exceed the lower of $13,000 or $4,750 ($95,000 × 5%). Therefore, the penalty is limited to $4,750.

INTERACTIVE SELF-SCORING QUIZZES

15.3 Taxation of Tax-Exempt Entities

LEARNING OBJECTIVE 3

Compute certain taxes applicable to tax-exempt entities.

VIDEO CONTENT

While most tax-exempt entities do not pay any federal income tax, there are several situations that will result in a tax-exempt entity paying taxes. In this section, we classify these taxes as follows:

- Lobbying tax
- Excess benefits tax
- Taxes on private foundations
- Tax on private universities' investment income
- Tax on excess compensation

In the following section, we discuss *unrelated business taxable income,* which is an additional situation that can result in tax liabilities for an exempt organization.

Some of the taxes listed above arise because officers of tax-exempt organizations engaged in prohibited transactions. **Prohibited transactions** are not consistent with the tax-exempt purpose of the organization and may make it more difficult for the organization to meet its mission.

Lobbying Tax

The first prohibited transaction tax relates to being too involved in lobbying activities. Charitable exempt organizations (IRC §501(c)(3)) are divided into two broad classes: public charities and private foundations. Public charities are prohibited from having a *substantial* part of their activities related to lobbying or influencing legislation. Such involvement can result in the entity losing its exempt status. Churches are prohibited from engaging in any lobbying activity.

Public charities involved in lobbying have two options. First, they can pay a tax of 5% on the expenses involved in lobbying activities, although they could still potentially lose their tax-exempt status.[18] Second, they can make a §501(h) election. In that case, the exempt status is not at risk unless the organization repeatedly exceeds a ceiling amount of lobbying expenditures (defined below). Once the election is made, it is effective for all years ending after the election is made and continues to apply until the organization revokes the election.[19]

Computation of Tax

Lobbying expenditures are expenditures for the purpose of influencing legislation by communicating with any member or employee of a legislative body, or with any government official or employee who may participate in the formulation of the legislation. **Grass roots expenditures** are attempts to influence legislation by affecting the opinions of the general public or any segment of it.[20]

A pattern of substantial lobbying expenditures will cause an organization to lose its tax-exempt status even if the §501(h) election is made. Churches cannot be involved in any lobbying activities and maintain their tax-exempt status.

Private foundations are not subject to this tax. However, they may be subject to a 20% tax on the amount of their expenditures that attempt to influence legislation or public elections. A separate tax can be imposed on foundation managers who allow the expenditures to occur. If these expenditures are corrected, then the taxes can be abated by the IRS.[21]

Related exercise: Discussion Question 6

[18]IRC §4912.

[19]IRC §501(h)(6).

[20]IRC §4911(d)(1)(B).

[21]IRC §4945.

If the §501(h) election is made, the lobbying tax is computed as follows. An accompanying flowchart for the computation is shown in Illustration 15.4:

ILLUSTRATION 15.4 Lobbying Tax

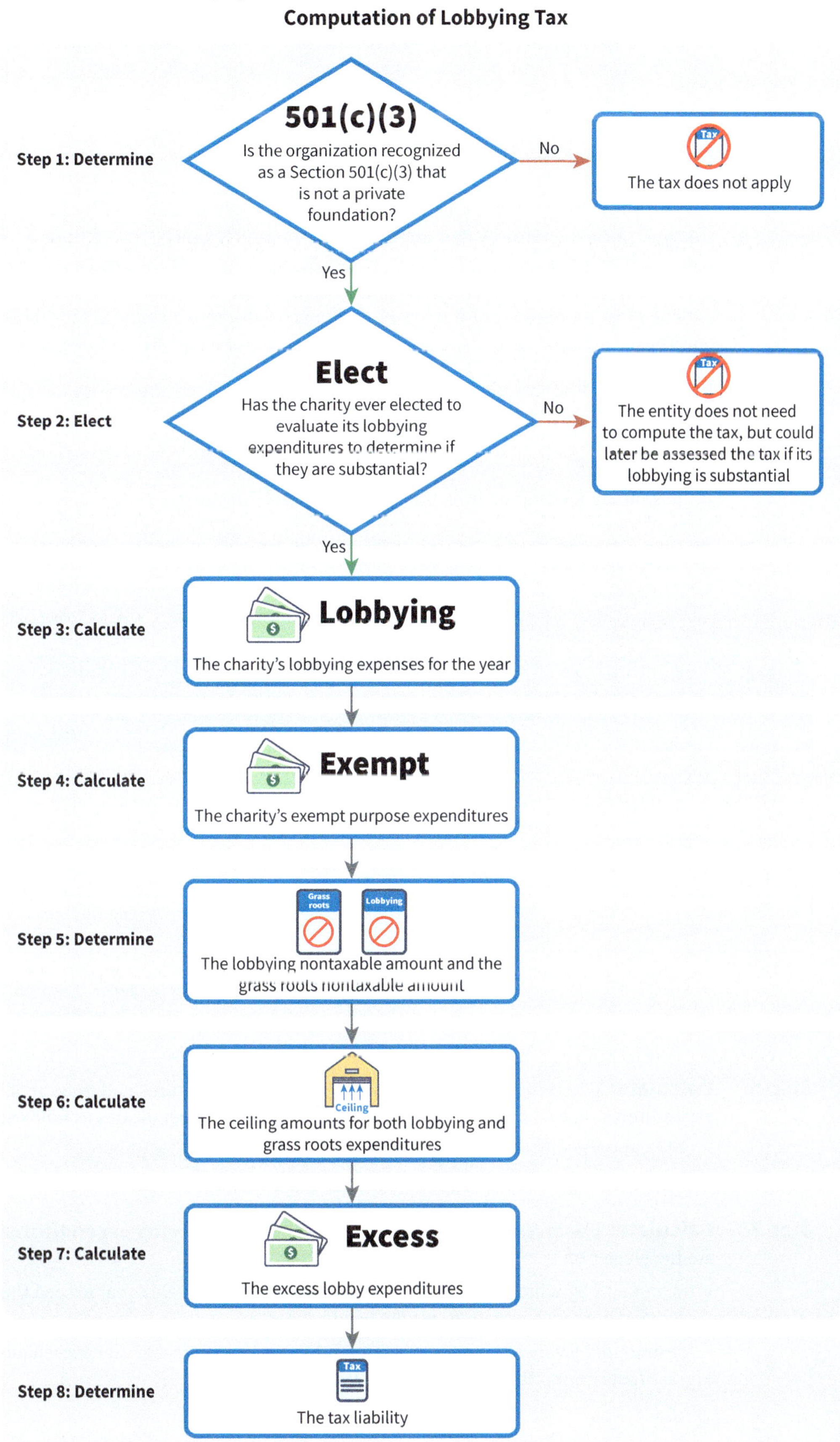

Step 1. **Determine:** If the organization is a public charity. Is the organization recognized as a §501(c)(3) organization that is not a private foundation? If YES, go to step 2. If NO, then the tax does not apply.

Step 2. **Elect:** Has the charity elected to evaluate its lobbying expenditures to determine if they are substantial? If YES, go to step 3. If NO, the entity does not need to compute the tax but could later be assessed the tax if its lobbying is substantial.

Step 3. **Calculate:** The charity's lobbying expenses for the year.

Step 4. **Calculate:** The charity's exempt purpose expenditures.

Exempt purpose expenditures are amounts paid or incurred for the taxable year for expenditures that are related to the organization's tax-exempt purpose, such as for religious, charitable, scientific, literary, or educational purposes, amateur sports, or the prevention of cruelty to children or animals. They also include all amounts paid or incurred to influence legislation even if not for those purposes.[22]

Step 5. **Determine:** The lobbying nontaxable amount and the grass roots nontaxable amount. The **lobbying nontaxable amount** is the *lower* of:

- $1 million, *or*
- the amount determined from the table shown in **Illustration 15.5**.

The **grass roots nontaxable amount** is 25% of the lobbying nontaxable amount.

ILLUSTRATION 15.5 Lobbying Nontaxable Activities

Table for Computing Lobbying Nontaxable Activities	
If the exempt purpose expenditures are—	**The lobbying nontaxable amount is—**
≤ $500,000	20% of the exempt purpose expenditures
> $500,000 but ≤ $1,000,000	$100,000 + 15% of the excess of the exempt purpose expenditures > $500,000
> $1,000,000 but ≤ $1,500,000	$175,000 + 10% of the excess of the exempt purpose expenditures > $1,000,000
> $1,500,000	$225,000 + 5% of the excess of the exempt purpose expenditures > $1,500,000

Related exercises: Multiple Choice Question 6
Brief Exercise 4

Step 6. **Calculate:** The ceiling amounts for both lobbying expenditures and grass roots expenditures. The ceiling amount is determined for these expenditures as follows:

- Lobbying expenditures ceiling = 150% × Lobbying nontaxable amount
- Grass roots expenditures ceiling = 150% × Grass roots nontaxable amount

Step 7. **Calculate:** The excess lobbying expenditures. **Excess lobbying expenditures** are the *greater* of:

- the amount by which the lobbying expenditures for the taxable year exceed the lobbying nontaxable amount for the taxable year, *or*
- the amount by which the grass roots expenditures for the taxable year exceed the grass roots nontaxable amount for the taxable year.

[22]IRC §4911(e)(1).

Step 8. Determine: The tax liability. The tax levied is 25% of the excess lobbying expenses.

The following Example demonstrates the computation of the lobbying tax.

EXAMPLE 15.3.1
Determining the Lobbying Tax

Circle, Inc. is a qualifying §501(c)(3) organization and is not a private foundation. It focuses on providing job training for individuals with disabilities. It has the following information for the current tax year:

Exempt purpose expenditures	$8,000,000
Lobbying expenditures	$ 400,000
Grass roots expenditures	$ 300,000

Assuming that Circle makes a §501(h) election, what is its lobbying tax for the year, if any?

SOLUTION

We use the steps described In Illustration 15.4 to determine the lobbying tax.

Step 1. Determine: Is the organization a public charity? Yes, Circle is a public charity because it is an exempt charitable organization and is not a private foundation.

Step 2. Elect: Has the charity elected to evaluate its lobbying expenditures to determine if they are substantial? Yes, Circle has made the §501(h) election.

Step 3. Calculate: The charity's lobbying expenses for the year total $400,000.

Step 4. Calculate: The charity's exempt purpose expenditures total $8,000,000.

Step 5. Determine: The lobbying nontaxable amount and the grass roots nontaxable amount. The lobbying nontaxable amount is the *lower* of:

- $1 million, *or*
- the amount determined from the table in Illustration 15.5.

The exempt purpose expenditures are $8,000,000, so the lobbying nontaxable amount is:

$$\$225,000 + 5\% \ (\$8,000,000 - \$1,500,000) = \$550,000$$

The grass roots nontaxable amount is 25% of the lobbying nontaxable amount, or

$$25\% \times \$550,000 = \$137,500$$

Step 6. Calculate: The ceiling amounts for both lobbying expenditures and grass roots expenditures. The ceiling amount is determined for these expenditures as follows:

- Lobbying expenditures ceiling = 150% × Lobbying nontaxable amount ($550,000) = $825,000
- Grass roots expenditures ceiling = 150% × Grass roots nontaxable amount ($137,500) = $206,250

Step 7. Calculate: The excess lobbying expenditures. Excess lobbying expenditures are the *greater* of:

- the amount by which the lobbying expenditures ($400,000) for the taxable year exceed the lobbying nontaxable amount ($550,000) for the taxable year (which is $0), *or*
- the amount by which the grass roots expenditures ($300,000) for the taxable year exceed the grass roots nontaxable amount ($137,500) for the taxable year (which is $162,500).

The greater of these two amounts is $162,500.

Step 8. Determine: The tax liability. The tax levied is 25% of the excess lobbying expenses ($162,500), which is $40,625.

Related exercise: Application Problem 4

Implication of Tax

If the §501(h) election is made, once the computation above is completed, the broader implications to the exempt organization are as follows:

- **Lobbying expenditures below the lobbying/grass roots nontaxable amount:** No tax is due.
- **Lobbying expenditures above the lobbying/grass roots nontaxable amount and below the ceiling amount:** 25% tax is due, but the tax-exempt status is not at risk.
- **Lobbying expenditures above the lobbying/grass roots ceiling amount:** 25% tax is due, and the tax-exempt status is at risk.

In the next Example, we demonstrate the various implications if incurring lobbying expenditures.

EXAMPLE 15.3.2
Implication of Lobbying Expenditures

Rectangle, Inc. is a public charity that has incurred lobbying expenditures this year of $250,000. None of the expenditures are grass roots expenditures.

a. Assume that the lobbying nontaxable amount is $320,000 and the lobbying expenditures ceiling is $480,000 ($320,000 × 150%). What are the tax implications to Rectangle, Inc., if it does not make a §501(h) election?

b. Assume the same facts as in **a** except that Rectangle does make a §501(h) election.

c. Assume the same facts as in **b** except that the lobbying expenditures are $340,000.

d. Assume the same facts as in **b** except that the lobbying expenditures are $500,000.

SOLUTION

a. Because the §501(h) election was not made, the lobbying tax is $12,500 ($250,000 × 5%) and the tax-exempt status for Rectangle is at risk.

b. The lobbying expenditures of $250,000 are less than the lobbying nontaxable amount of $320,000, so no tax is due.

c. The lobbying expenditures of $340,000 are above the lobbying nontaxable amount of $320,000 and below the ceiling amount of $480,000. Therefore, the 25% tax is due, but the tax-exempt status is not at risk. The tax is $5,000 ([$340,000– $320,000] × 25%).

d. The lobbying expenditures of $500,000 are above the lobbying ceiling amount of $480,000, so the 25% tax is due, and the tax-exempt status is at risk if the ceiling amount is exceeded repeatedly. The tax is $45,000 ([$500,000 – $320,000] × 25%).

Related exercises: Brief Exercise 5
Application Problem 5

Excess Benefits Tax

The second prohibited transaction is levied on a disqualified person who receives excess benefits from the exempt organization. In that case, the tax-exempt status is not revoked, but the disqualified person pays an excise tax equal to 25% of the excess benefit.[23] A **disqualified person** is one who could exercise substantial influence over the affairs of an exempt organization during the five-year period ending on the date of the excess benefit transaction. Family members of a disqualified person are also disqualified, defined as the disqualified person's spouse, siblings and siblings' spouses, ancestors, children, grandchildren, great grandchildren, and spouses of these descendants.[24] If the disqualified person owns more than 35% of a corporation, partnership, or trust or estate, the entity is also a disqualified person.

[23]IRC §4958(a)(1).

[24]Treas. Reg. §53.4958-3(b).

An **excess benefit transaction** is a transaction in which the economic benefit provided by an exempt organization to a disqualified person exceeds the value of the consideration or services received by the exempt organization.[25] Examples of excess benefit transactions include:

- Purchasing property from the exempt organization at a significant discount
- Paying compensation above a reasonable amount to a disqualified individual
- Repaying loans to the exempt organization's president when the loans were not substantiated
- Renting property from a disqualified person at an amount substantially greater than fair market value.

If the excess benefit is not paid back to the exempt organization by the disqualified person before the 25% tax is due, then an additional tax of 200% of the excess benefit is levied against the disqualified person.[26] If a manager of a tax-exempt organization willfully participates in an excess benefit transaction, the manager is subject to an excise tax equal to 10% of the excess benefit, with a maximum of $20,000.[27]

The computation of the excess benefit tax is shown in the next two Examples.

EXAMPLE 15.3.3
Excess Benefit Tax

Alice is president of Square, Inc., a public charity. Square sells land to Alice for $120,000 that has a fair market value of $330,000. Robert, who is a manager at Square but not a part of the executive team, was aware that the land was being sold at a significant discount. What are the tax consequences of this transaction to Alice, Square, and Robert?

SOLUTION

Alice is a disqualified person because as president she could exercise substantial influence over Square. She received an excess benefit of $210,000 ($330,000 FMV − $120,000 amount paid). Therefore, her excise tax is $52,500 ($210,000 × 25%). There are no tax consequences to Square. Because Robert was aware of the transaction, Robert is assessed a tax of $21,000 ($210,000 × 10%), limited to the maximum of $20,000.

EXAMPLE 15.3.4
Additional Excess Benefit Tax

Assume the same facts as in Example 15.3.3. Alice is told by the IRS to return the excess benefit of $210,000 to Square. However, she refuses to do so. Are there any additional tax consequences to Alice?

SOLUTION

Yes, if the excess benefit is not paid back to the exempt organization by the disqualified person before the 25% tax is due, then an additional tax of 200% of the excess benefit is levied against the disqualified person. Therefore, Alice must pay an additional tax of $420,000 ($210,000 × 200%).

Related exercises: Discussion Question 7
Brief Exercise 6
Application Problem 6

[25]IRC §4958(c)(1)(A).

[26]IRC §4958(b).

[27]IRC 4958(a)(2).

Private Foundations

Private foundations were defined previously in this chapter. Generally, private foundations are §501(c)(3) organizations that are independent legal entities set up solely for charitable purposes. The funding for a private foundation usually comes from an individual, a family, or a corporation. Private foundations may be subject to taxes based on investment income, self-dealing, failure to distribute income, excess business holdings, investments that jeopardize charitable purposes, and taxable expenditures. We cover two of the most common of these taxes in this section.

Self-Dealing Tax

A tax is assessed if a private foundation engages in self-dealing with a disqualified person.[28] Disqualified persons include:

- donors whose contributions exceeded 2% of total contributions and $5,000, *and*
- officers, directors, trustees, and their family members.

Examples of self-dealing between a private foundation and disqualified persons include:

- A sale, exchange, or lease of property
- Lending of money
- Furnishing of goods or services

The tax assessed to the disqualified person is 10% of the amount involved, and if the transaction is not corrected in a timely manner once assessed by the IRS, an additional tax of 200% of the amount involved is due. A manager who willingly participates in the transaction is taxed at 5% of the amount involved (capped at $20,000). If that tax is not paid on time, an additional tax of 50% of the amount involved is due (capped at $20,000).

The computation of the self-dealing is shown in the next Example.

EXAMPLE 15.3.5
Self-Dealing Tax

Darwin is a disqualified person for Hexagon, Inc. During the current tax year, Hexagon loaned Darwin $60,000. What are the potential tax consequences to Darwin?

SOLUTION

The lending of money from a private foundation to Darwin is a self-dealing transaction. Darwin will be assessed a tax of $6,000 ($60,000 × 10%). If Darwin does not correct the transaction by returning the $60,000 to Hexagon within an appropriate time period, he will be assessed an additional tax of $120,000 (200% × $60,000).

Related exercises: Discussion Question 8
Brief Exercise 7

Undistributed Income Tax

The **undistributed income tax** is levied if the private foundation does not distribute at least 5% of the fair market value of its assets each year by the end of the following tax year. The 5% represents a reasonable return that the private foundation should be expected to earn each year. The tax is 30% of the undistributed income.[29] **Undistributed income** is equal to the required distributions less the actual distributions. The undistributed income can be reduced by salaries and administrative expenses.

[28]IRC §4941(a).

[29]IRC §4942.

If the undistributed income is not distributed within 90 days after the IRS issues a notice of deficiency for the undistributed income tax, then an additional tax of 100% of the undistributed income is assessed.

The computation of the undistributed income tax is demonstrated in the following Example.

EXAMPLE 15.3.6
Undistributed Income Tax

Polygon, Inc. is a private foundation that has investment assets of $10,000,000 for 2024. Distributions made by the end of 2025 related to 2024 income amounted to $200,000. Polygon has salaries and administrative expenses in 2024 of $80,000. How much tax is owed by Polygon, if any?

SOLUTION

Polygon's assumed minimum investment return for 2024 is $500,000 (5% × $10,000,000). Undistributed income is computed as follows:

Minimum investment return	$500,000
Salaries and administrative expenses	(80,000)
Actual distributions made by end of 2025	(200,000)
Undistributed income	$220,000

The undistributed income tax for 2025 is $66,000 ($220,000 × 30%).

Related exercises: Discussion Question 9
Application Problem 7

Private Universities Investment Income Tax

Certain private universities and colleges must pay a **private universities investment income tax**, a 1.4% excise tax on net investment income.[30] This tax applies to private universities and colleges with the following characteristics:

- They had at least 500 tuition-paying students during the preceding tax year.
- More than 50% of their students were located in the United States.
- The aggregate fair market value of their assets (excluding those used directly in carrying out their exempt purposes, see below) was at least $500,000 per student at the end of the preceding tax year.

In 2023, 56 universities were subject to this tax, and paid around $380 million.[31] For example, in 2025, Harvard's average endowment per student was approximately $2.2 million (total endowment was over $53.2 billion),[32] and it paid close to $40 million in investment income tax for the year.[33]

[30]IRC §4968(a).

[31]Watson, Garrett and Bunn, Daniel. "New Efforts on Taxing Endowments Raise Questions on Neutrality and Revenue Collection." *Tax Foundation*. 28 Jan. 2025. taxfoundation.org/blog/taxing-endowments-revenue-analysis/.

[32]Wood, Sarah. "20 Colleges with the Biggest Endowments." *U.S. News & World Report*. 12 Mar. 2025. www.usnews.com/education/best-colleges/the-short-list-college/articles/universities-with-the-biggest-endowments.

[33]Binkley, Collin. "A tax on college endowments began in Trump's first administration. It could soon rise." *Associated Press*. 6 May 2025. apnews.com/article/college-endowment-tax-congress-harvard-republicans-f2d67dca253b65aa21ba3e2363b076fa.

Excessive Compensation Tax

The **excessive compensation tax** is an excise tax levied on the compensation of highly paid employees of tax-exempt organizations. The tax potentially applies to the five highest-paid employees of the organization. The excise tax is 21% of the compensation in excess of $1,000,000 for the year.[34]

Related exercise: Multiple Choice Question 7

PRACTICE PROBLEM 15.3.1
Computing the Lobbying Nontaxable Amount and the Grass Roots Nontaxable Amount

Orchid, Inc. is a qualifying §501(c)(3) organization and is not a private foundation. It focuses on providing discharged service members with service dogs. It has the following information for the current tax year:

Exempt purpose expenditures	$980,000
Lobbying expenditures	$140,000
Grass roots expenditures	$113,000

Compute the lobbying nontaxable amount and the grass roots taxable amount.

SOLUTION

From step 5 in Illustration 15.4, the lobbying nontaxable amount is the *lower* of:

- $1 million, *or*
- the amount determined from the table in Illustration 15.5.

The exempt purpose expenditures are $980,000, so the lobbying nontaxable amount is:

$$\$100,000 + 15\% \ (\$980,000 - \$500,000) = \$172,000$$

The grass roots nontaxable amount is 25% of the lobbying nontaxable amount, or

$$25\% \times \$172,000 = \$43,000.$$

PRACTICE PROBLEM 15.3.2
Compute the Excess Lobbying Expenditures and Liability

Assuming the same facts as in Practice Problem 15.3.1, compute the excess lobbying expenditures and potential lobbying tax.

SOLUTION

From step 6 in Illustration 15.4, the ceiling amount is determined for these expenditures as follows:

- Lobbying expenditures ceiling = 150% × Lobbying nontaxable amount ($172,000) = $258,000
- Grass roots expenditures ceiling = 150% × Grass roots nontaxable amount ($43,000) = $64,500

From step 7 in Illustration 15.4, the excess lobbying expenditures are the greater of:

- the amount by which the lobbying expenditures ($140,000) for the taxable year exceed the lobbying nontaxable amount ($172,000) for the taxable year (which is $0), *or*
- the amount by which the grass roots expenditures ($113,000) for the taxable year exceed the grass roots nontaxable amount ($43,000) for the taxable year (which is $70,000).

  The greater of these two amounts is $70,000.

From step 8 in Illustration 15.4, the tax levied is 25% of the excess lobbying expenses ($70,000), which is $17,500.

[34] IRC §4960.

PRACTICE PROBLEM 15.3.3
Excess Benefits Tax

Asaka is a disqualified person and is told by the IRS to return an excess benefit of $95,000 to Marigold, Inc. However, she refuses to do so. Are there any additional tax consequences to Asaka?

SOLUTION

Yes, if the excess benefit is not paid back to the exempt organization by the disqualified person before the 25% tax is due, then an additional tax of 200% of the excess benefit is levied against the disqualified person. Therefore, Asaka must pay an additional tax of $190,000 ($95,000 × 200%).

PRACTICE PROBLEM 15.3.4
Undistributed Income Tax

Larkspur, Inc. is a private foundation that has investment assets of $4,200,000 for 2024. Distributions made by the end of 2025 related to 2024 income were $120,000. Larkspur has salaries and administrative expenses in 2024 of $58,000. How much tax is owed by Larkspur, Inc., if any?

SOLUTION

Larkspur Inc.'s assumed minimum investment return for 2024 is $210,000 (5% × $4,200,000). Undistributed income is computed as follows:

Minimum investment return	$210,000
Salaries and administrative expenses	(58,000)
Actual distributions made by end of 2025	(120,000)
Undistributed income	$ 32,000

The undistributed income tax is $9,600 ($32,000 × 30%).

INTERACTIVE SELF-SCORING QUIZZES

15.4 Unrelated Business Income (UBI)

LEARNING OBJECTIVE 4

Compute the tax on unrelated business taxable income for a tax-exempt organization.

VIDEO CONTENT

If an exempt organization is involved in activities that are not related to its tax-exempt purpose, then it must pay income tax on the *unrelated business income*. Such organizations must file Form 990-T, Exempt Organization Business Income Tax Return. The unrelated business income tax (UBIT) applies to all tax-exempt organizations under IRC §501(c) and to state colleges and universities.[35] The most recent IRS data shows that more than 80,000 exempt organizations file a Form 990-T, reporting a total of $15.4 billion in taxable income and generating $871.4 million in tax. Over half of all organizations that were required to file Form 990-T did not report unrelated business income tax liability after subtracting deductions from gross

[35]IRC §511(a)(2).

unrelated business income. Charitable organizations, exempt under Internal Revenue Code §501(c)(3), were the most common Form 990-T filers.[36]

If a tax-exempt organization consistently earns *substantially* unrelated business income, then it could eventually lose its tax-exempt status. Unfortunately, the term *substantially* is subjective, and it is based on facts-and-circumstances. While this makes it difficult for tax professionals to advise clients in this area, the good news is that the loss of tax-exempt status rarely occurs and has only happened with flagrant abuses.

Definition of Unrelated Business Income

Unrelated business income (UBI) is income from substantial commercial activities that are not related to the exempt purpose of the organization.[37] Specifically, the law defines income as unrelated business income if it meets the following criteria:[38]

- The organization has an activity that is a trade or business, meaning that it is engaged in the production of income from the sales of goods or the performance of services.
- The activity is regularly carried on in a similar manner to comparable commercial activities of businesses that are not exempt from taxation.
- The activity is not substantially related to the organization's exempt purpose. An activity may be deemed to generate unrelated business income even if the tax-exempt organization uses that income to support its mission.

EXAMPLE 15.4.1
Unrelated Business Income

Shelter Inc., an exempt organization, provides shelters for homeless individuals in 15 cities across the Midwest. To help support its operations, Shelter received a contribution of a 10% interest in a local restaurant that typically has net income of at least $1,000,000 each year. Shelter will use the income from the restaurant to support and expand its operations. Is Shelter's 10% share of the income from the restaurant exempt from federal income taxation?

SOLUTION

The income from the restaurant is treated as unrelated business income because the restaurant business is not an activity related to Shelter's tax-exempt mission. Therefore, the restaurant income will be taxed as unrelated business taxable income. This is the case even though Shelter uses the income to support its mission.

Related exercise: Discussion Question 10

Trade or Business Activity

The first criterion that must be satisfied is that the exempt organization has a trade or business activity. An activity does not need to produce a profit to qualify as a trade or business. If an exempt organization has more than one trade or business activity, a loss from one activity cannot offset income from a different activity. Investment activities of the exempt organization are treated as one business activity, which allows investment expenses to offset investment income.

[36]U.S. Department of the Treasury. *Tax-Exempt Organizations' Unrelated Business Income Tax, Tax Year 2017*. Publication 5812 (6–2023) Catalog Number 94103M, Internal Revenue Service. www.irs.gov/pub/irs-pdf/p5812.pdf.

[37]IRC §512(a)(1).

[38]IRC §513 and Treas. Reg. §1.513-1(d).

Tax Planning Tip

Tax professionals should not suggest to their tax-exempt clients that unrelated business income is something to be avoided. It is very difficult for tax-exempt organizations to generate the revenue they need to meet their missions. If they are fortunate enough to have a stream of revenue that helps them meet their mission, that is positive. It is true that the tax-exempt organization will pay a tax rate of 21% on the income, and possibly state income tax. But it will have the remaining after-tax income to help it meet its mission.

Regularly Carried On

The second criterion that must be satisfied is that the business activity must be regularly carried on. This criterion is assessed by considering the frequency and continuity of the activity.[39] If the activity is not regularly carried on, then the tax-exempt organization cannot be competing with nonexempt organizations (that is for-profit businesses) that are operating similar businesses.

Why **Why are tax-exempt entities taxed on unrelated business income?** Congress taxes unrelated business income of exempt organizations because not doing so creates an unfair playing field for exempt organizations. Consider the university coffee shop that is located at its downtown campus. Assume that a taxable business owner owned a coffee shop near the university campus for ten years before the university coffee shop opened. The business owner must pay income taxes on the shop's profits. If the university did not have to pay any taxes on its income, then the university could charge lower prices than the business owner and eventually cause the taxable coffee shop to close. The tax-exempt status of the university would create an unfair advantage compared to the business owner because most of the university's customers are not students, so they would buy coffee from other businesses if the university did not have the shop.

Not Substantially Related to the Tax-Exempt Purpose

The third criterion is that the activity is not substantially related to the tax-exempt purpose of the organization. Examples of unrelated business income include:

- A charity that sells its membership list to vendors
- An exempt organization that sells advertising in its newsletter or magazine
- An art museum that leases apartments and studio space to aspiring artists
- An animal shelter that also provides pet boarding and grooming services to the general public
- An exempt university that leases its football facilities to a professional football team for preseason training and practices

The next Example demonstrates a type of unrelated business income.

EXAMPLE 15.4.2 University Rental of Property

A public university sells the naming rights to its football stadium to a local company for $10,000,000. The naming right will last for 10 years, and the company's name will be featured prominently throughout the stadium. Is this $10,000,000 exempt from federal income tax?

SOLUTION

The income is unrelated business activity because advertising revenue is unrelated business income, and the unrelated business income will be taxed.

[39] Treas. Reg. §1.513-1(c).

Potential Pitfall

An important issue for determining whether an activity generates unrelated business income is the composition of the customers. If the customers are part of the exempt organization's tax-exempt mission, then the income is *not* unrelated. For example, an exempt university that sells snacks and soft drinks at a venue that is primarily used by students does not have unrelated business income. The educational institution's mission is to provide students with a conducive environment for learning. The revenue generated from selling food to the students is no different from the revenue from tuition and fees in that it helps the university cover its expenses. However, if the university has a coffee shop at its downtown location and a substantial percentage of the customers are not university students, then the activity would generate unrelated business income.

The Nuance of Identifying Unrelated Business Income While determining the activities that qualify as unrelated is not difficult in many situations, other circumstances can be challenging and may give an unexpected result. Consider the rulings related to art museums and unrelated business income:

- The sale by an art museum of greeting cards that show reproductions of works displayed at the museum was not an unrelated activity, even when the cards were sold through mail order catalogues.[40]
- The sale of reproductions of works from the collections of an American folk art museum was determined to be related to the museum's exempt purpose. However, the sale in the same museum of articles unrelated to art, such as scientific books and souvenirs relating to the area where the museum is located, was an unrelated business activity.[41]
- The sale of souvenirs that had no relationship with the museum's exempt purpose was determined to be an unrelated activity, even if the souvenirs carried the museum's logo.[42]

Other Guidance on Unrelated Activities Congress provided specific rules for certain activities that are commonly encountered by tax-exempt organizations.

- The solicitation and receipt of qualified sponsorship payments is not considered unrelated activity.
- Income from a bingo game is related income as long as the game is legal under local law and bingo games operated for a profit are not allowed in that jurisdiction.
- The awarding of low-cost items to donors who make charitable contributions to the exempt organization does not create unrelated business income. A low-cost item is one that has an inflation-adjusted value of less than $13.60 (2025).
- Selling or renting the organization's donor or membership lists does not produce unrelated business income if the lists are sold or rented to other tax-exempt organizations.
- If an exempt organization sells merchandise that was produced as part of its exempt purpose, the activity is considered related.

The next two Examples demonstrate income that is not unrelated business income.

EXAMPLE 15.4.3
Selling of Merchandise

An exempt organization provides job training skills for individuals with disabilities. One such activity is training the individuals to make pastries. The pastries are then sold to the general public, and the revenue is used to support the exempt organization. Is the pastry activity an unrelated business activity?

SOLUTION

The pastry activity is not an unrelated business activity because the production of the pastries is a training activity that is related to the organization's tax-exempt purpose.

[40]Rev. Rul. 73-104, 1973-1 CB 263.

[41]Rev. Rul. 73-105, 1973-1 CB 264.

[42]IRS Private Letter Ruling 8034022.

EXAMPLE 15.4.4
Low-Cost Items

Nico makes a donation of $100 to Easter Seals, and in return receives address labels with a value of $12. Is this transaction considered a sale of address labels, and therefore an unrelated business activity?

SOLUTION

The address labels are a low-cost item because the value is less than $13.60. Therefore, this activity is not considered unrelated for the exempt organization.

Related exercises: Discussion Question 11
Multiple Choice Question 8
Application Problem 8

Computation of Unrelated Business Taxable Income Tax

For an organization that has an unrelated trade or business activity, **unrelated business taxable income (UBTI)** is computed as follows, beginning with the revenue generated from the unrelated activity (including investment income, but note that investment expenses are deducted later):

Gross unrelated business income (including investment income)
Less: Deductions associated with the unrelated business income
Net unrelated business income
Plus/*Less*: Adjustments
Less: Specific deduction ($1,000)
Unrelated business taxable income
× 21%
UBTI tax

If the exempt organization is a trust rather than a corporation, then the trust income tax rates are used to compute the UBTI tax.

Adjustments to Net Unrelated Business Income

Some of the adjustments required for computing UBTI are positive and some are negative. The following positive adjustments are added to net unrelated business income:

- Charitable contributions to another §501(c)(3) charity that exceeded 10% of UBTI computed before the charitable contribution deduction (similar conceptually to the corporate limit on the charitable contribution deduction of 10% times taxable income).
- Unrelated debt-financed income net of unrelated debt-financed deductions (discussed in detail below).

In the following Example, we show how the adjustment for charitable contributions is computed.

EXAMPLE 15.4.5
Adjustment for Charitable Contributions

Agape, Inc., an exempt organization, has UBTI of $250,000 before charitable contributions. During the current year, Agape contributes $35,000 to the Salvation Army, a qualified charity. What is Agape's UBTI after the charitable contribution?

SOLUTION

To compute UBTI, we must reduce it for the charitable contribution of $35,000 and then add back the amount of the contribution that exceeds 10% of $250,000 (UBTI before the charitable contribution).

UBTI before the charitable contribution	$250,000
Less: Charitable contributions	(35,000)
Plus: Charitable contribution addback:	
$35,000 – ($250,000 × 10%)	10,000
UBTI before specific deduction	$225,000

Related exercise: Multiple Choice Question 9

The following negative adjustments are subtracted from net unrelated business income, which means that investment income is included in UBTI only to the extent that it exceeds investment expenses:

- Income from dividends, interest, and annuities, net of associated expenses
- Royalty income, net of associated expenses
- Rental income from real property, net of associated expenses
- Rental income from personal property if personal property is leased with real property. To be included in the negative adjustment, the personal property rental income cannot exceed 10% of the gross income under the lease. Additionally, if more than 50% of the gross rent income is from personal property, then none of the rents, including real property rents, are included in the negative adjustment.
- Gains and losses from the sale or disposition of property other than inventory
- A specific deduction of $1,000

EXAMPLE 15.4.6 Computation of Unrelated Business Taxable Income Tax

Food, Inc. is an exempt organization that delivers free bags of groceries to the needy. Food had the following information for the current tax year:

Gross unrelated business income (including investment income)	$2,800,000
Deductions associated with unrelated business income	$2,250,000
Dividend income (included above)	$ 21,000
Gain from the sale of land (included above)	$ 165,000

What is Food's unrelated business taxable income tax for the years?

SOLUTION

Unrelated business taxable income is computed as follows:

Gross unrelated business income	$2,800,000
Less: Deductions associated with business income	(2,250,000)
Net unrelated business income	$ 550,000
Less: Dividend income	(21,000)
Less: Gain from the sale of land	(165,000)
Less: Specific deduction	(1,000)
Unrelated business taxable income	$ 363,000
Corporate tax rate	× 21%
Unrelated business taxable income tax	$ 76,230

Related exercise: Multiple Choice Question 10

Unrelated Debt-Financed Income Adjustment

One of the positive adjustments to net unrelated business income is the **unrelated debt-financed income adjustment**, which is unrelated debt-financed income net of unrelated debt-financed deductions. A percentage of the income from debt-financed income and deductions is included in UBTI.[43] The purpose of this adjustment is to prevent an exempt organization from borrowing funds to purchase unrelated property and then using tax-exempt earnings to pay for the property. Income from debt-financed property includes rent income from realty and from tangible personal property.

Debt-financed property is property of an exempt organization that has acquisition indebtedness and is held for the production of income,[44] with the following exceptions:[45]

- Property for which at least 85% of the use is related to the organization's exempt purposed is not treated as debt-financed property, because if this is the case, then the financing of the property did not have a tax avoidance purpose. If this test is not met, then only the portion of the property that is not used for an exempt purpose is treated as debt-financed property.
- Property whose gross income is otherwise treated as unrelated business income, such as rents from personal property, is not treated as debt financed property.
- Property whose income is related to research activities and is not otherwise treated as unrelated business income is not treated as debt-financed property.
- Land acquired by an exempt organization that will not be used for an exempt purpose until a future date is not treated as debt-financed property if the exempt use begins within 10 years of the acquisition date (15 years for churches) and the property is in the same neighborhood as other property used in the exempt activities (no neighborhood requirement for churches). This allows organizations such as churches to buy property for future growth and not be concerned that it may cause unrelated business income tax issues.

The percentage of income from debt financed property included in computing unrelated business taxable income is computed as follows:

$$\text{Gross rental income} = \frac{\text{The average acquisition indebtedness for the nonexempt use of property}}{\text{The average adjusted basis of the debtfinanced property for the nonexempt use}}$$

The debt/basis percentage may not exceed 100%.

The next Example demonstrates the computation of unrelated debt financed income.

EXAMPLE 15.4.7 Unrelated Debt-Financed Income

Workforce Inc., a tax-exempt organization, provides job training in a 25,000-square-foot warehouse that it bought for $4,000,000 three years ago. Workforce borrowed $3,000,000 to purchase the building and has not paid off any of the debt. Workforce uses 15,000 square feet to provide training related to its exempt purpose. The other 10,000 square feet is leased to various professionals as commercial office space. Workforce has $150,000 of net rental income for the year. The average adjusted basis for the warehouse this year is $3,800,000. What will the adjustment be for unrelated debt financed income?

SOLUTION

We begin by computing the percentage of the property that is used for Workforce's exempt purpose, which is 60% (15,000/25,000). This is not at least 85%, so the rental income from the non-exempt use is included in income, as follows:

$$\text{Gross rental income} \times \frac{\text{The average acquisition indebtedness for the nonexempt use of property}}{\text{The average adjusted basis of the debtfinanced property for the nonexempt use}}$$

$$\$150,000 \times \frac{\$3,000,000 \times 10,000\text{ sq. ft.}/25,000\text{ sq. ft.}}{\$3,800,000 \times 10,000\text{ sq. ft.}/25,000\text{ sq. ft.}} = \$118,421$$

Related exercises: Discussion Question 12
Brief Exercise 9
Application Problems 9, 10

[43] IRC §514.

[44] Production of income includes investment activities and the maintenance or management of property from which income is being collected. See IRC §212.

[45] IRC §514(h).

PRACTICE PROBLEM 15.4.1
Income Subject to Unrelated Business Income Tax?

DeKalb County VFW, a tax-exempt organization, operates a video gaming parlor seven days a week and is open to the public. The total revenue of the VFW from all sources is $880,000. Dues generate $660,000 of revenue, and the gaming parlor generates $220,000 of net income. The gaming parlor operations are conducted by four full-time, paid employees and five part-time, paid employees. How much unrelated business income does the VFW have?

SOLUTION

DeKalb County VFW has unrelated business income of $220,000. Unrelated business income is income from substantial commercial activities that are not related to the exempt purpose of the organization. Although members of the VFW frequent the gaming parlor, it is also open to the public and has paid employees, making it a regularly carried on trade or business.

PRACTICE PROBLEM 15.4.2
Calculation of Unrelated Business Income

CarNow, Inc. is an exempt organization that provides transportation service for elderly and homeless persons to use for doctors' appointments and interviews. CarNow has the following information for the current tax year:

Gross unrelated business income (including interest income and rental income)	$635,000
Deductions associated with unrelated business income	$158,000
Interest income	$ 2,500
Rental income from rental of cars for personal use (100% personal property rental income)	$ 95,000

What is CarNow's unrelated business taxable income tax for the year?

SOLUTION

The tax on unrelated business taxable income is computed as follows:

Gross unrelated business income	$635,000
Less: Deductions associated with business income	(158,000)
Net unrelated business income	$477,000
Less: Interest income	(2,500)
Less: Specific deduction	(1,000)
Unrelated business taxable income	$473,500
Corporate tax rate	× 21%
Unrelated business taxable income tax	$ 99,435

Rental income that comes 100% from renting personal property is not included in the negative adjustment. If the rental income comes from both real and personal property and more than 50% of the gross rental income comes from personal property, then none of the rents are included in the negative adjustment.

INTERACTIVE SELF-SCORING QUIZZES

Review and Practice

Chapter Summary

1 Identify the different types of tax-exempt organizations, including private foundations.

- The tax law defines 20 different types of tax-exempt organizations under Internal Revenue Code (IRC) §501(c). The general characteristics of a **tax-exempt organization** include the following:
  - The purpose of the organization is to meet some common good as opposed to creating wealth for its owners.
  - The organization can earn a profit even though it is a non-profit organization. That is, cash receipts can exceed cash expenses.
  - The organization generally does not pay income taxes. However, income tax may be owed if the organization has **unrelated business income**.
  - Tax-exempt organizations are generally subject to taxes other than income tax, such as payroll taxes, property taxes, and sales taxes.
  - The organization cannot influence legislation or support political candidates or parties.
- **Private foundations** are §501(c)(3) organizations that are independent legal entities set up solely for charitable purposes. The funding for a private foundation usually comes from an individual, a family, or a corporation.
- Being classified as a private foundation has two negative consequences. First, more stringent requirements apply to donors of private foundations when determining how much of their contribution is deductible. Specifically, the deduction for contributions to private foundations by an individual cannot exceed 30% of the donor's adjusted gross income. Second, the private foundation may have to pay some federal income tax.

2 Understand the initial and annual filing requirements for tax-exempt organizations.

- Most tax-exempt organizations must apply for and receive an exemption from taxation on either Form 1023/Form 1023-EZ or Form 1024. Form 1023 is used by organizations seeking tax-exempt status as charitable organizations (which means they qualify under IRC §501(c)(3)). Form 1024 is used by organizations seeking tax-exempt status under other sections of the Internal Revenue Code. **Religious organizations** do not have to file Form 1023 to be qualified charitable organizations.
- Most exempt organizations must file an annual information return, Form 990, Return of Organization Exempt from Income Tax. This form reports income, expenses, and substantial contributors. It also must include total lobbying and political expenditures. Other key points are as follows:
  - An exempt organization does not have to file an information return if gross receipts are $50,000 or less.
  - Churches, state institutions, and governmental units do not have to file Form 990.
  - Form 990-EZ, Short Form Return of Organization Exempt From Income Tax, can be used unless gross receipts exceed $200,000 or total assets exceed $500,000.
  - Private foundations must file Form 990-PF, Return of Private Foundation.
  - Political organizations that have gross receipts more than $25,000 must file Form 990 or Form 990-EZ.
- Forms 990, 990-EZ, and 990-PF must be filed on or before the 15th day of the fifth month after the close of the tax year, which is May 15th for a calendar-year organization. An automatic six-month extension is available, which would extend the due date to November 15th for calendar-year organizations.
- Exempt organizations can incur significant penalties if Form 990 is not filed on time.
- Most exempt organizations must make their last three years' tax returns and their tax-exempt applications available to interested parties.
- Religious organizations are not required to file Form 1023, Form 990, or Form 990-N (e-postcard).

3 Compute certain taxes applicable to tax-exempt entities.

- While most tax-exempt entities do not pay any federal income tax, a tax-exempt entity may be subject to some taxes, including the following:
  - Lobbying tax
  - Excess benefits tax
  - Taxes on private foundations
  - Tax on private universities' investment income
  - Tax on excess compensation
- Public charities are prohibited from having a *substantial* part of their activities related to lobbying or influencing legislation. Such involvement can result in the entity losing its exempt status. Churches are prohibited from engaging in any lobbying activity.
- Private foundations may be subject to taxes based on investment income, self-dealing, failure to distribute income, excess business holdings, investments that jeopardize charitable purposes, and taxable expenditures.
- Certain private universities and colleges must pay a 1.4% excise tax on their net investment income.

4 Compute the tax on unrelated business taxable income for a tax-exempt organization.

- If an exempt organization is involved in activities that are not related to its tax-exempt purpose, then it must pay income tax on the unrelated business income. Such organizations must file Form 990-T, Exempt Organization Business Income Tax Return. The unrelated business income tax (UBIT) applies to all tax-exempt organizations under IRC §501(c) and to state colleges and universities. If an exempt organization consistently earns substantially unrelated business income, then it could eventually lose its tax-exempt status.
- **Unrelated business income** is income from substantial commercial activities that are not related to the exempt purpose of the organization.

Communication Application

Are Contributions to All Tax-Exempt Organizations Deductible by an Individual?

(LO1) You have recently been hired by new clients, Ashma and Shalin Patel, to review their current contributions in preparation for filing their Form 1040. The Patels have provided you with the following list of contributions:

Hindu Temple of Greater Chicago	$12,000
Mayoral campaign in Chicago	$10,000
Oak Brook Country Club	$ 5,000
American Red Cross	$ 2,500
Chicago Chamber of Commerce	$ 7,500
Northwestern University	$15,000

Are all these contributions deductible on the Patels' Form 1040? Write a memo to the Patels discussing your findings.

Solution

Hello Ashma and Shalin,

Thank you for allowing me to assist you in preparing your Form 1040. You have asked for advice concerning your contributions to various organizations in the current year and whether those contributions are deductible as itemized deductions on your Form 1040.

The tax law defines 20 different types of tax-exempt organizations under IRC §501(c). Many individuals believe that contributions to all tax-exempt organizations are deductible as charitable contributions. However, only contributions to §501(c)(3) organizations are deductible as charitable contributions, although payments to other tax-exempt entities may be deductible under other tax laws. Following is a list of your deductible contributions on Form 1040, Schedule A:

Hindu Temple of Greater Chicago	$12,000
American Red Cross	$ 2,500
Northwestern University	$15,000

The tax-exempt organizations listed above are §501(c)(3) organizations. Political contributions like your contribution to the Chicago mayoral campaign are not deductible. The Oak Brook Country Club is a §501(c)(7) organization and the Chicago Chamber of Commerce is a §501(c)(6) organization, so neither of these contributions is deductible.

Please let me know if I can be of further assistance. Thank you.

Sincerely,
Carnes and Youngberg, CPAs

Ethics and Professional Responsibilities Application

Ethics

Unrelated Business Income or Not?

(LO2, 4) Durant Drummond is the lead pastor for a church in Chicago, IL. His church has several sources of revenue to fund its operations and its outreach programs. Gross revenue from all sources is $13,225,000. Included in this amount is net revenue of $550,000 from food trucks allowed to use the church parking lot on Tuesdays and Wednesdays throughout the year. Any members of the community can purchase food from the trucks. In the past, a member of the church was its bookkeeper. Because the revenue has continued to grow, Drummond has asked you to review the church's books. He does not believe the church should owe any taxes on its revenue because it is a religious organization. What is your advice to Drummond as the tax staff accountant?

In addition to the chapter content, see *Statements on Standards for Tax Services* at www.aicpa-cima.com/resources/landing/statements-on-standards-for-tax-services; *Circular 230* at www.irs.gov/tax-professionals/office-of-professional-responsibility-and-circular-230; and Chapter 2, LO4, Tax Professional Responsibilities.

Solution

A religious organization must meet certain requirements to be tax-exempt and qualify as a charitable organization, including being organized and operated exclusively for a religious purpose. Most of the revenue generated by Drummond's church is from offerings and interest income, which is considered tax-exempt income and is used for carrying out the church's religious purpose.

Unrelated business income is considered taxable income. Three requirements must be met for the income to be classified as UBI:

- The activity generating UBI must be an active trade or business.
- The activity must be conducted with frequency and continuity.
- The activity is not substantially related to the tax-exempt purpose.

The $550,000 net revenue generated from the food trucks operating in the church parking lot is ongoing income unrelated to the church's tax-exempt purpose. Tax will be due on the unrelated business income at a tax rate of 21%, but the church will not lose its tax-exempt status.

Under *Circular 230* §10.22 Diligence as to accuracy: "A practitioner must exercise due diligence ... [i]n preparing or assisting in the preparation of, approving, and filing tax returns, documents, affidavits, and other papers relating to Internal Revenue Service matters"

Statement on Standards for Tax Services No. 1.2.6, Knowledge of Error, sets forth applicable standards for a member who becomes aware of an error in a taxpayer's previously filed tax return: "A member should inform the taxpayer promptly upon becoming aware of an error in a previously filed return, an error in a return that is the subject of an administrative proceeding, or a taxpayer's failure to file a required return. A member also should advise the taxpayer of the potential consequences of the error and recommend the corrective measures to be taken."

As the tax staff accountant, you should recommend that your senior manager or partner discuss these issues with Drummond and discuss the need for Form 990 to be filed promptly.

Key Terms

End-of-Chapter Assessment

Discussion Questions

1. **(LO1)** Discuss the general characteristics of a tax-exempt organization.
2. **(LO1)** Provide a definition of a private foundation.
3. **(LO1)** Discuss two negative consequences of being classified as a private foundation.
4. **(LO2)** What is the purpose of Form 990-N, and when should it be filed?
5. **(LO2)** Describe what penalties might be incurred if Form 990 is not filed in a timely manner.
6. **(LO3)** Explain lobbying expenditures and why they are important for a tax-exempt entity.
7. **(LO3)** What is an excess benefit transaction, and why is it important?
8. **(LO3)** Describe three examples of self-dealing between a private foundation and disqualified persons.
9. **(LO3)** Describe the undistributed income tax.
10. **(LO4)** Define unrelated business income.
11. **(LO4)** Expand on the three criteria used to determine if an activity is an unrelated business income activity.
12. **(LO4)** How is unrelated business taxable income (UBTI) computed?

Multiple Choice Questions

1. **(LO1)** The correct Internal Revenue Code section number for a charitable organization is:
   a. §501(c)(3)
   b. §501(c)(4)
   c. §501(c)(5)
   d. §501(c)(6)

2. **(LO1)** Which of the following is a private foundation?
   a. Christ Community Church
   b. Northwestern Hospital
   c. The Ford Foundation
   d. City of St. Charles

3. **(LO2)** Which of the following tax-exempt organizations has to file Form 1023/Form 1023-EZ or Form 1024 to be a qualified charitable organization?
   a. Temple Beth Israel
   b. Bethlehem Lutheran Church
   c. Al-Sadiq Mosque
   d. None of the above

4. **(LO2)** Which of the following is not a religious organization?
   a. United Methodist Church Women's Retreat
   b. Mosque Maryam
   c. Freedom Press, which specializes in publishing religious pamphlets for profit
   d. Chicago Loop Synagogue

5. **(LO2)** Oak Avenue Assembly, a tax-exempt religious organization, operates an outreach program for poor residents in its community. A candidate for the local city council has endorsed Oak's antipoverty program. Which of the following activities is inconsistent with Oak's tax-exempt status?
   a. Collecting contributions for the candidate from members
   b. Endorsing the candidate to members
   c. Hosting a meal for members and people who are homeless at which the candidate is a speaker
   d. All of these activities are inconsistent with Oak's tax-exempt status.

6. **(LO3)** If an entity is a qualifying §501(c)(3) organization and is not a private foundation, and its exempt purpose expenditures are $18 million, what is the correct lobbying nontaxable amount?
   a. $0
   b. $225,000
   c. $1,000,000
   d. $1,050,000

7. **(LO3)** An excise tax is levied on the compensation of highly paid employees of tax-exempt organizations. Which of the following is true?
   a. The excise tax is 21% of the compensation in excess of $1,000,000 for the year.
   b. The excise tax is 20% of the compensation in excess of $1,500,000 for the year.
   c. The excise tax is 25% of the compensation in excess of $2,000,000 for the year.
   d. There is no excise tax owed on highly paid employees of tax-exempt organizations.

8. **(LO4)** Which of the following is not an example of an unrelated business income activity?
   a. Advertising in a synagogue newsletter
   b. A hospital pharmacy that is available to the general public and that has employees paid by the hospital
   c. Tax-exempt art gallery merchandise with the art gallery logo sold to gallery members only
   d. Church garage sale held twice a year

9. **(LO4)** Northern Illinois Food Drive, Inc. (NIFD), an exempt organization, has UBTI of $180,000 before charitable contributions. During the current year, NIFD contributes $22,000 to Goodwill, a qualified charity. What is NIFD's UBTI after the charitable contribution?
   a. $180,000
   b. $162,000
   c. $158,000
   d. $157,000

10. **(LO4)** Homes for the Elderly is a tax-exempt organization with the following:
    - Gross unrelated business income (including investment income) $123,000
    - Deductions associated with unrelated business income $120,000

    What is the organization's unrelated business income tax?
    a. $0
    b. $420
    c. $630
    d. $1,000

Brief Exercises

1. **(LO1)** A §501(c)(3) organization must meet which requirements to not be classified as a private foundation?

2. **(LO1)** Identify the correct type of tax-exempt entity for the following organizations:

    a. Delnor Community Hospital

    b. St. Paul Catholic Church

    c. Beta Alpha Psi

    d. Florence Rotary Club

    e. Major League Baseball

    f. DeKalb Credit Union

    g. St. Charles Garden Club

3. **(LO2)** Which form should each of the following organizations use to request tax-exempt status from the IRS?

    - Coconut, a non-charitable organization with assets of $425,000 and average gross receipts of $35,000
    - Orange, a non-charitable organization with assets of $220,000 and average gross receipts of $45,000
    - Pear, a charitable organization with assets of $145,000 and average gross receipts of $55,000
    - Plum, a charitable organization with assets of $265,000 and average gross receipts of $30,000
    - Kiwi, a charitable organization with assets of $180,000 and average gross receipts of $48,000

4. **(LO3)** Daffodil, Inc. is a qualifying §501(c)(3) organization and is not a private foundation. It focuses on providing counseling for pregnant women. It has the following information for the current tax year:

Exempt purpose expenditures	$860,000
Lobbying expenditures	$125,000
Grass roots expenditures	$110,000

Compute the lobbying nontaxable amount and the grass roots taxable amount.

5. **(LO3)** Lily, Inc. is a public charity that has incurred lobbying expenditures this year of $460,000. None of the expenditures are grass roots expenditures.

    a. Assume that the lobbying nontaxable amount is $590,000, and the lobbying expenditures ceiling is $885,000. What are the tax implications to Lily, Inc. if it does not make a §501(h) election?

    b. Assume the same facts as in **a** except that Lily, Inc. does make a §501(h) election.

6. **(LO3)** Dashawn is a disqualified person and is told by the IRS to return an excess benefit of $88,000 to Daisy, Inc. However, he refuses to do so. Are there any additional tax consequences to Dashawn?

7. **(LO3)** Mounica is a disqualified person for Begonia, Inc. During the current tax year, Begonia furnished Mounica with the use of a car valued at $45,000. What are the potential tax consequences to Mounica?

8. **(LO4)** Christ Community Church (CCC) operates a café seven days a week that is open to the public. The total revenue of the church from all sources is $850,000. Offerings generate $650,000 of revenue, and the café generates $200,000 of net income. The café operations are conducted by three full-time, paid employees and seven part-time, paid employees. How much unrelated business income does CCC have?

9. **(LO4)** Hydrangea, Inc., an exempt organization, has UBTI of $97,000 before charitable contributions. During the current year, Hydrangea contributes $10,000 to the United Way, a qualified charity. What is Hydrangea's UBTI after the charitable contribution and before the specific deduction?

Application Problems

1. **(LO2)** Which form should the following organizations use to meet their annual information filing requirements? If the organization is excluded from filing, please state as such.

    a. ABC, a charitable organization (not a church) with annual gross receipts of $195,000

    b. DEF, a nonprofit corporation formed to finance people's needs after a tornado

    c. GHI, a charitable organization (not a church) with annual gross receipts of $48,000

    d. JKL, a church with annual gross receipts of $1,200,000

    e. MNO, a charitable organization (not a church) with annual gross receipts of $480,000

2. **(LO2)** Help Today (HT) is a calendar-year tax-exempt corporation that provides relief for towns that have experienced a natural disaster. HT filed Form 990 for 2025 on July 10, 2026. HT did not request that its return be extended. HT's gross receipts for 2025 are $460,000.

    a. How much is HT's late-filing penalty for its 2025 return?

    b. How much is the late-filing penalty if the return was validly extended to November 15, 2026, it was filed on March 31, 2027, and the gross receipts are $90,000?

3. **(LO2)** Helpful Elderly Care (HEC) is a calendar-year tax-exempt corporation that provides services to persons who are elderly. HEC filed Form 990 for 2025 on August 14, 2026. HEC did not request that its return be extended. HEC's gross receipts for 2025 are $1,350,000. How much is HEC's late-filing penalty for its 2025 return?

4. **(LO3)** Rose, Inc. is a qualifying §501(c)(3) organization and is not a private foundation. It focuses on providing grief counseling. It has the following information for the current tax year:

Exempt purpose expenditures	$1,300,000
Lobbying expenditures	$ 210,000
Grass roots expenditures	$ 185,000

Assuming that Rose makes a §501(h) election, what is its lobbying tax for the year, if any?

5. **(LO3)** Carnation, Inc. is a public charity that has incurred lobbying expenditures this year of $770,000. None of the expenditures are grass roots expenditures.

   a. Assume that the lobbying nontaxable amount is $980,000, and the lobbying expenditures ceiling is $1,470,000. What are the tax implications to Carnation, Inc. if it does not make a §501(h) election?

   b. Assume the same facts as in **a** except that Carnation does make a §501(h) election.

   c. Assume the same facts as in **b** except that the lobbying expenditures are $1,100,000.

   d. Assume the same facts as in **b** except that the lobbying expenditures are $1,500,000.

6. **(LO3)** Amarah is president of Sunflower, Inc., a public charity. Sunflower pays Amarah's personal credit card debt of $42,000. Krishna, who is a manager at Sunflower but not a part of the executive team, was aware that Sunflower had paid Amarah's loans when the loans were not substantiated. What are the tax consequences of this transaction to Sunflower, Amarah, and Krishna?

7. **(LO3)** Iris, Inc. is a private foundation that has investment assets of $7,800,000 for 2024. Distributions made by the end of 2025 related to 2024 income was $175,000. Iris has salaries and administrative expenses in 2024 of $65,000. How much tax is owed by Iris, Inc., if any?

8. **(LO4)** A tax-exempt animal sanctuary sells stuffed animals similar to the animals that it houses and generates $355,000 in net revenue. Is the sale of stuffed animals an unrelated business activity?

9. **(LO4)** Poppies, Inc. is an exempt organization that grows vegetables and delivers them to people in need in the neighborhood. Poppies has the following information for the current tax year:

Gross unrelated business income (including investment income)	$135,000
Deductions associated with unrelated business income	$ 42,000
Interest income (included above)	$ 1,500
Dividend income (included above)	$ 8,000
Rental income from electric gardening equipment (included above) (100% personal property rental income)	$ 60,000

What is Poppies' unrelated business taxable income tax for the year?

10. **(LO4)** Amaryllis Church, an exempt organization, is a religious organization that conducts three services every weekend and children's religious education on Wednesday nights. Amaryllis occupies a building that it bought for $2,300,000 two years ago. Amaryllis borrowed $1,800,000 to purchase the building and still owes the full amount. Assume that the average adjusted basis of the building is $2,000,000 in the current year. Amaryllis uses 10,000 square feet for its exempt purpose. The other 5,000 square feet is leased as commercial office space. Amaryllis has $100,000 of net rental income for the year. What will be the adjustment for unrelated debt-financed income when computing unrelated business taxable income?

Professional Development Skills

Communication Problem

Communication

1. **(LO2, 4) Is a Church Bookstore an Unrelated Business Income Activity?** James Nico operates a megachurch in Naperville, IL. His church generates millions of dollars in revenue from various sources, and he wants to make sure that the church maintains its tax-exempt status. While reviewing the accounting records maintained by a church member, you notice that the church operates a bookstore that generates over a million dollars in net revenue. During your conversation with James, you mention the bookstore and tell him that its revenue could potentially be taxed as unrelated business income. James would like to know how to prevent this from happening. Write a memo to James explaining how this can be accomplished.

Ethics and Professional Responsibilities Problem

Ethics

1. **(LO2) Late Filing of Form 990** Addiction Free Services (AFS) is a tax-exempt organization providing counseling and housing to individuals who suffer from drug and alcohol addiction. In its first few years, AFS received small donations and sponsorships. The director of AFS believes that his organization does not have to file any tax returns because it qualifies as tax exempt. For the current year, the director has hired your CPA firm to assist with the bookkeeping for the organization, as it is now quite large and receives donations and sponsorships from across the country. Upon reviewing the books, you notice that the gross receipts for each of the first three years were under $50,000, and therefore no Form 990 was needed. For the last three years, gross receipts exceeded $250,000. What is your advice to the director of AFS?

In addition to the chapter content, see *Statements on Standards for Tax Services* at www.aicpa-cima.com/resources/landing/statements-on-standards-for-tax-services; *Circular 230* at www.irs.gov/tax-professionals/office-of-professional-responsibility-and-circular-230; and Chapter 2, LO4, Tax Professional Responsibilities.

CHAPTER 16

Tax Research and Professional Issues

viperagp/AdobeStock

Chapter Introduction

VIDEO CONTENT

Roxana is a CPA who is licensed to practice in South Carolina. Nicolás recently contacted her to help with a tax dispute with the Internal Revenue Service (IRS). Two years ago, an S corporation owned by Nicolás donated a famous painting by Alan Shuptrine to the National Gallery of Art in Washington, D.C. The S corporation bought the painting in 2004 for $25,000. An art dealer told Nicolás at the time of the contribution that the painting had a value between $150,000 and $350,000. Nicolás claimed a charitable contribution on the S corporation tax return for the fair market value of the painting, which Nicolás stated to be $400,000. Nicolás then deducted the flow-through contribution on his individual tax return. The IRS has begun an audit of the tax returns because the IRS believes the value of the painting is no more than $125,000.

In this chapter, you will learn how Roxana should proceed in working with Nicolás. Roxana needs to:

- Know how to research the tax law, including court decisions, to determine how valuations for contributions should be determined.
- Understand the IRS audit process, including her responsibilities to Nicolás and his rights as a taxpayer.
- Determine whether to use the appeals process within the IRS if she and Nicolás are not satisfied with the findings of the IRS agent.
- Advise Nicolás on whether he should incur the cost of challenging the IRS decision in court, if necessary.

Tax law in the United States comes from many different sources, which is one of the reasons learning and applying it can be challenging. In this chapter, we cover the sources of tax authority from the legislative, administrative, and judicial branches of government. We also review the importance of each source of authority, which accountants must consider when making a recommendation for a specific tax situation. We next describe the compliance rules for tax preparers who do not comply with the rules. We close by providing a high-level summary of the audit and appeals processes within the IRS. The better you and your client understand these, the better prepared you will be to work with the IRS to determine your client's proper tax liability.

After researching the law, the taxpayer takes a position on the tax return, and the return is filed. The IRS checks the return for accuracy and decides whether to examine it. If the audit reveals that the taxpayer did not file properly, the IRS assesses the additional tax due, often including penalties and interest. The taxpayer can pay the assessment or appeal it with the IRS. If the taxpayer is not satisfied with the outcome of the appeals process, the taxpayer can litigate the matter in court.

LEARNING OBJECTIVES	TOPICS	PRACTICE OPPORTUNITIES

1 Classify sources of tax authority as legislative, administrative, or judicial.	**16.1 Sources of Tax Authority**
	• Legislative Sources of Tax Authority
	  • U.S. Constitution
	  • Internal Revenue Code
	  • Treaties
	  • Congressional Committee Reports
	• Administrative Sources of Tax Authority
	  • Treasury Regulations
	  • Revenue Rulings
	  • Revenue Procedures
	  • Private Letter Rulings
	  • Other Sources of Tax Authority
	• Judicial Sources of Tax Authority
	  • Courts of Original Jurisdiction
	    • U.S. Tax Court
	    • U.S. District Courts
	    • U.S. Court of Federal Claims
	  • Appellate Courts
	    • U.S. Courts of Appeals
	    • U.S. Court of Appeals for the Federal Circuit
	  • U.S. Supreme Court
	  • Evaluating Judicial Sources of Tax Authority
	• Secondary Sources of Tax Authority
		• Example 16.1.1 Primary vs. Secondary Authority
		• Example 16.1.2 Precedents
		• Example 16.1.3 *Golsen* Rule
		• Practice Problem 16.1.1 Determining Primary Authority
		• Practice Problem 16.1.2 Evaluating a Treasury Regulation
		• Practice Problem 16.1.3 Which Court Venue Should Your Client Choose?

2 Properly evaluate sources of tax authority when making a tax recommendation.	**16.2 Locating and Evaluating Authority**
	• Weighting of Tax Authority
	• The Research Process
	  • Step 1. Identify: All relevant facts.
	  • Step 2. State clearly: The problem to be solved.
	  • Step 3. Locate: The applicable tax authority.
	  • Step 4. Evaluate: The relevance and weight of the authorities.
	  • Step 5. Identify: Possible solutions.
	  • Step 6. Identify: The recommended solutions.
	  • Step 7. Communicate: Your results to your client.
		• Example 16.2.1 Locating Authority
		• Practice Problem 16.2.1 Conducting Research

LEARNING OBJECTIVES	TOPICS	PRACTICE OPPORTUNITIES
3 Apply the rules for tax preparer penalties.	**16.3 Tax Preparer Penalties**	• Example 16.3.1 Tax Preparer Penalty • Practice Problem 16.3.1 Determining a Tax Preparer Penalty
4 Identify the steps in the audit and appeals process within the Internal Revenue Service.	**16.4 Tax Practice and Procedure** • Audit Process • Appeals Process • Other Audit Issues • Signing a Return	• Example 16.4.1 Signing a Tax Return • Practice Problem 16.4.1 The Audit Process

Tax forms referenced in this chapter

Form 870-AD	Offer to Waive Restrictions on Assessment and Collection of Tax Deficiency and to Accept Overassessment
Form 2848	Power of Attorney and Declaration of Representative
Form 4549	Income Tax Examination Changes

16.1 Sources of Tax Authority

LEARNING OBJECTIVE 1

Classify sources of tax authority as legislative, administrative, or judicial.

VIDEO CONTENT

Tax professionals rely on two types of authority when researching the tax consequences of a proposed or completed transaction: *primary authority* and *secondary authority*. You must know the difference between these types of authority and understand when to use each.

Primary authority comes from actions taken by the three branches of the federal government. The original sources of the tax law are:

1. Legislative authority (Congress)
2. Administrative authority (the executive branch)
3. Judicial authority (the courts)

Secondary authority consists of commentary on the tax law, found in treatises, journals, and publications provided by editorial services. You can use a secondary authority to help you locate the relevant primary authority, but *not* as the basis for a tax decision.

We first review the primary sources of the tax law, and then we describe the most common types of secondary authority. These are the authorities that Roxana, from the chapter introduction, will search to find relevant authority for the valuation of property given as a charitable contribution.

Potential Pitfall

Do not confuse *treatise* with *treaty*. A *treatise* is a written, systematic, detailed analysis of a topic. A *treaty* is a written agreement between two or more countries that has been approved by the appropriate lawmaking authorities.

EXAMPLE 16.1.1
Primary vs. Secondary Authority

A corporate client has contacted you to find out whether it can deduct a large fine it had to pay for violation of safety regulations. You do an online search and find an article on this topic published in the *Journal of Accountancy*. You send the client a memo in which you provide the citation for the article and explain that, based on details in the article, it cannot deduct the fine. Have you provided appropriate advice to your client?

SOLUTION

No, you have not provided appropriate advice. You based your conclusion on an article in a professional journal, which is a secondary source of authority. When providing tax advice to clients, you must find primary sources of authority on which to base your recommendation.

Related exercises: Discussion Question 1
Multiple Choice Questions 1, 2, 3

Legislative Sources of Tax Authority

As the legislative branch of government, Congress creates all tax laws through the legislative process. The executive branch and the courts, as the other primary sources of the tax law, interpret and apply the laws that Congress has created. The sources of legislative authority, listed in order of highest to lowest authority, are:

- U.S. Constitution
- Internal Revenue Code and certain treaties
- Congressional committee reports

U.S. Constitution

Only one source of tax authority outranks the laws promulgated by Congress, and that is the U.S. Constitution. All laws passed by Congress must be permissible under the Constitution. The 16th Amendment established the right of Congress to impose a federal income tax. Congress passed the 16th Amendment in 1909, and the states ratified it in 1913. It reads as follows:

> The Congress shall have power to lay and collect taxes on incomes, from whatever source derived, without apportionment among the several States, and without regard to any census or enumeration.

Internal Revenue Code

Once Congress has approved a new law and it is signed by the president, it is codified in the **Internal Revenue Code (IRC)**. The IRC is the most often cited source of tax authority because it organizes all the tax laws passed by Congress. If Congress repeals a tax law, that law is removed from the IRC.

Congress has organized the IRC in a very logical fashion, beginning with chapters and subchapters. Most of the tax laws we include in this book are in Chapter 1 of the IRC (Normal Taxes and Surtaxes). There are currently 23 subchapters in Chapter 1. The subchapters that are most relevant to our material are:

- Subchapter A—Determination of Tax Liability (§§1–59B)
- Subchapter B—Computation of Taxable Income (§§61–291)
- Subchapter C—Corporate Distributions and Adjustments (§§301–385)
- Subchapter E—Accounting Periods and Methods of Accounting (§§441–483)
- Subchapter K—Partners and Partnerships (§§701–777)
- Subchapter O—Gain or Loss on Disposition of Property (§§1001–1111)
- Subchapter P—Capital Gains and Losses (§§1201–1298)
- Subchapter S—Tax Treatment of S Corporations and Their Shareholders (§§1361–1379)

Each subchapter has code sections that provide the law for specific economic transactions. The code sections in each subchapter relevant to this book are shown in parentheses in the list above. You learned about Section 351 formations in Chapter 3 (LO1, Taxation of Corporate Formations), for instance, and the S corporation eligibility rules are in Subchapter S. Experienced tax professionals can often refer to a specific tax law based on its code section, just as you can now refer to a "Section 1231 Asset." (Tax professionals rarely refer to subchapters.)

You will often encounter citations to the Internal Revenue Code. **Illustration 16.1** provides a guide for how to read such citations.

ILLUSTRATION 16.1 The Meaning of Each Part of an IRC Citation

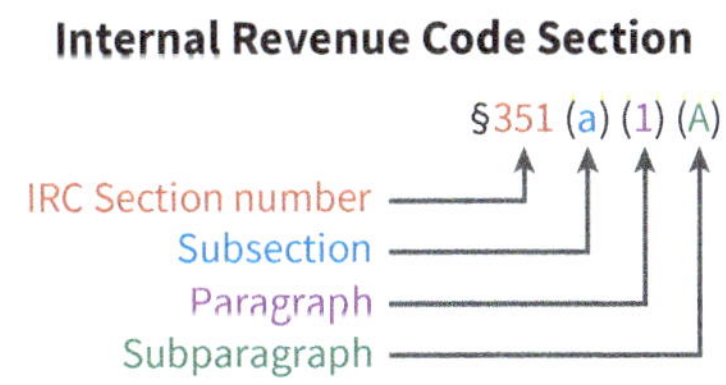

Related exercises: Discussion Question 3
Multiple Choice Question 4

Illustration 16.2 shows the process Congress must use to create a tax law. All bills require a majority vote to pass. The steps in the process are as follows:

Step 1. All tax bills must originate and be approved in the House of Representatives Ways and Means Committee.

Step 2. The full House of Representatives debates and votes on the bill, which must pass by a majority vote.

Step 3. Once approved by the House, the House sends the bill to the Senate Finance Committee. This committee is free to do as it wants with the House bill (even striking the entire bill and starting anew). However, the Senate Finance Committee can take no action without receiving a bill from the House. If the Senate Finance Committee approves a bill, it then goes to the full Senate.

Step 4. The Senate debates its own version of the bill and votes. The bill passes if it wins a majority.

Step 5. The House and Senate versions of the bill that pass usually differ, so Congress creates a Joint Conference Committee, with members from both chambers, to draft a compromise bill, which is then voted on by the Committee.

Step 6. Once the Joint Conference Committee has approved its version of the bill, that version must return to the House and Senate for another vote (assuming the new compromise bill differs from the original bills). If both the House and Senate approve it (via majority vote), the bill goes to the president.

Step 7. The president either signs the bill into law or vetoes it.

Step 8. If the president vetoes a bill, Congress can override the veto with a two-thirds vote in each chamber.

ILLUSTRATION 16.2 The Steps in the Legislative Process for Passing a Tax Bill

Legislative Process for a Tax Bill

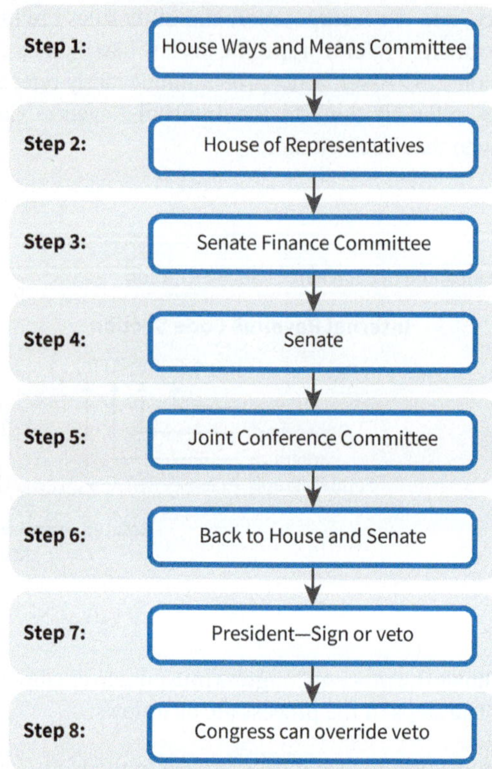

Treaties

The next source of primary legislative authority is treaties. A **treaty** is a formal written agreement between two countries that specifies legal and economic rights for each, often including provisions related to income taxation of the citizens of the countries. For example, residents or citizens of a foreign country who earn income in the United States may be taxed at a reduced rate or be exempt from U.S. taxes on some of this income. Similarly, certain items of income earned within foreign countries by residents or citizens of the United States may be taxed at a reduced rate or be exempt from foreign taxes. The United States currently has income tax treaties with approximately 65 countries.

Which has greater authority if they are in conflict, the IRC or a treaty? In general, courts have treated these as having equal authority, and if they are in conflict with each other, the one passed "last in date" will have precedence over the earlier provision. A very old Supreme Court case held that "a treaty may supersede a prior act of Congress, and an act of Congress may supersede a prior treaty."[1] Congress codified this principle in 1998.[2]

Related exercises: Discussion Questions 2, 3
Multiple Choice Question 5

Congressional Committee Reports

As a bill moves through the legislative process, Committee Reports are developed by the House Ways and Means Committee, Senate Finance Committee, and Joint Conference Committee. These reports are considered to be primary sources of the law by most legal scholars, and they are often useful to discover what Congress intended to achieve with a specific law.

[1]The Cherokee Tobacco, 78 U.S. 616 (1870).
[2]IRC §7852(d).

Administrative Sources of Tax Authority

The president of the United States ultimately has the responsibility to administer the tax laws Congress has passed but delegates this to the secretary of the Department of the Treasury. Day-to-day responsibility for administering the tax law falls to the commissioner of the IRS, who reports directly to the Treasury secretary.

The IRS issues numerous sources of the tax law. Here, we discuss the following sources of administrative authority, listed in order of authority, and show how to cite each:

- Treasury regulations
  - Legislative regulations
  - Interpretive regulations
  - Procedural regulations
- Revenue rulings
- Revenue procedures
- Private letter rulings

Related exercise: Discussion Question 4

Treasury Regulations

Regulations are the highest authority issued by the Treasury Department and are published in the Federal Register and later in the Internal Revenue Bulletin. Regulations are numbered sequentially, with numerals preceding and following a decimal point. The numbers preceding the decimal point, the prefix, indicate the type of regulation or applicable area of tax law to which they pertain, while the numbers following the decimal point indicate the Internal Revenue code section being interpreted by the regulation. Some of the more common prefixes are shown in **Illustration 16.3**.

ILLUSTRATION 16.3 Common Treasury Regulation Prefixes

Regulation Topics

Number	Type
1	Income Tax
20	Estate Tax
25	Gift Tax
301	Procedure and Administration
601	Procedural Rules

As was the case with citations to the Internal Revenue Code, you will often encounter citations to Treasury regulations. **Illustration 16.4** provides a guide for how to read such citations. The number after the hyphen shows which regulation is referenced in a particular code section (for example, Treas. Reg. §1.351-1).

ILLUSTRATION 16.4 What Each Number Means in a Treasury Regulation Citation

Treasury Regulation

Treas. Reg. §1.351-1

Prefix showing this is an income tax regulation

This regulation is for IRC §351

This is the first regulation for IRC §351

Treasury regulations can be classified as *legislative*, *interpretive*, or *procedural*, based on the nature of the law under consideration.[3]

- **Legislative regulations** have almost as much weight as the IRC, because Congress has authorized the Treasury to develop regulations dealing with a specific issue. If Congress specified a desired result in the statute but did not offer guidance on how it is to be achieved, the regulations written to achieve that result are legislative regulations.

[3] U.S. Department of the Treasury. *Internal Revenue Manual*. 32.1.1.2.8. Internal Revenue Service. 2 Aug. 2018, www.irs.gov/irm.

- **Interpretive regulations** are written under the general mandate given to the Treasury to interpret the tax laws enacted by Congress. Most regulations are interpretive. If Congress provided specific rules in the statute and left gaps for the Treasury secretary to complete, then the regulation is interpretive.
- **Procedural regulations** apply to procedural issues, such as the information that must be submitted with a tax return and the process for making tax elections.

Regulations can also be classified based on when they take effect.[4] These regulation types and their relative weight of authority are summarized in **Illustration 16.5**.

- **Proposed regulations** must be issued at least 30 days before becoming final, although they may exist in a proposed form for many years. Proposed regulations do not have the effect of law, but they do provide an indication of the IRS's view on a tax issue.
- **Temporary regulations** have the effect of law, but only for three years. They are usually issued when taxpayers need immediate guidance on a substantive matter of the law.
- **Final regulations** have the effect of law until revoked. Proposed and temporary regulations can later be issued as final regulations.

Related exercise: Discussion Question 5

ILLUSTRATION 16.5 Development of Treasury Regulations

Regulation Types and Authority

Type of regulation	Description	Weight of authority
Proposed	Provides information about how the IRS is considering interpreting a law and offers opportunity for feedback from taxpayers.	Cannot be relied on for authority unless the regulation states otherwise.
Temporary	Issued when taxpayers need immediate guidance on a tax issue; valid for three years from the date issued.	Same authority as final regulations.
Final	Proposed and temporary regulations may later be issued as final regulations.	Highest authority issued by Treasury Department.

Revenue Rulings

Revenue rulings do not have as much weight as regulations, but they are the second highest authority issued by the IRS. While regulations address many issues related to a tax law, the IRS limits the scope of revenue rulings to a specific set of facts. Perhaps, for example, you have had an employer who reimbursed you for some of your commuting expenses. What if instead of reimbursing you with cash, the employer gave you a debit card for your expenses? A relatively recent revenue ruling dealt with this situation, indicating that its purpose was to:

> ... provide updated guidance on employer use of smartcards, debit cards or other electronic media to provide employees with qualified transportation fringes.[5]

In general, if the employer gives cash directly to the employee to purchase transportation passes, it is taxable to the employee. This ruling explains that if the employee can use the debit card for purchases other than mass transit, the tax law treats it the same as cash. This illustrates the type of detail addressed by revenue rulings.

Revenue Procedures

Revenue procedures are official statements of procedures that affect the rights or duties of taxpayers or other members of the public.[6] Whereas revenue rulings explain the "why" of a tax

---

[4]IRC §7805.

[5]Rev. Rul. 2014-32.

[6]Rev. Proc. 89-14, 1989-8.

ruling, revenue procedures explain "how" a taxpayer is to apply a law and/or carry out the filing process. Assume that your employer reimburses you for the cost of your meals while traveling away from home on business. Can you exclude the reimbursement from your income? A revenue procedure addressed a method of using IRS-issued per diem rates for reimbursement so that it would not be taxable.

> IRS has issued revised guidance on using per diem rates to substantiate the amount of ordinary and necessary business expense paid or incurred while traveling away from home.[7]

Private Letter Rulings

Private letter rulings (PLR) are issued only when requested by a taxpayer for a proposed transaction. The taxpayer must thoroughly describe the specific set of facts for which they are requesting a ruling. The IRS does not have to respond to the request. If it does, and if it indicates that it agrees with the taxpayer's proposed result, the ruling applies *only* for the taxpayer who requested the ruling. Other taxpayers cannot use that PLR as a primary authority to support a position they take on their own tax returns. Taxpayers can use PLRs, however, to establish "substantial authority" so that the IRS cannot penalize them if they take the same position. We will discuss substantial authority later, in LO3, Tax Preparer Penalties.

Related exercise: Discussion Question 7

Illustration 16.6 provides examples of how citations to Treasury rulings and procedures are formatted.

ILLUSTRATION 16.6 Examples of Citations for IRS Rulings and Procedures

Rulings/Procedures Citations

Type of ruling or procedure	Citation example
Revenue ruling	Rev. Rul. 2014-32
Revenue procedure	Rev. Proc. 2008-2
Private letter ruling (PLR)	PLR 200948009

Other Sources of Tax Authority

Other sources of authority issued by the IRS include technical advice memoranda, notices, announcements, and general counsel memoranda.

Judicial Sources of Tax Authority

If the IRS challenges a position your client has taken on a tax return, is the IRS always correct? No, which is why taxpayers have the option of using the IRS appeals process (described later, in LO4, Tax Practice and Procedure) or spending the time and money to take the issue to court and have a judge or jury decide the outcome. Judicial authority is the third source of primary authority.

Taxpayers who opt not to appeal their case to the IRS first, or who appeal and are not satisfied with the IRS's response, have several different options for the type of court in which to begin the judicial proceeding. You should know the advantages and disadvantages of each. Illustration 16.7 shows the hierarchy of the judicial system discussed in this section.

[7]Rev. Proc. 2019-48, 2019-51 IRB.

ILLUSTRATION 16.7 Judicial Sources of Tax Authority

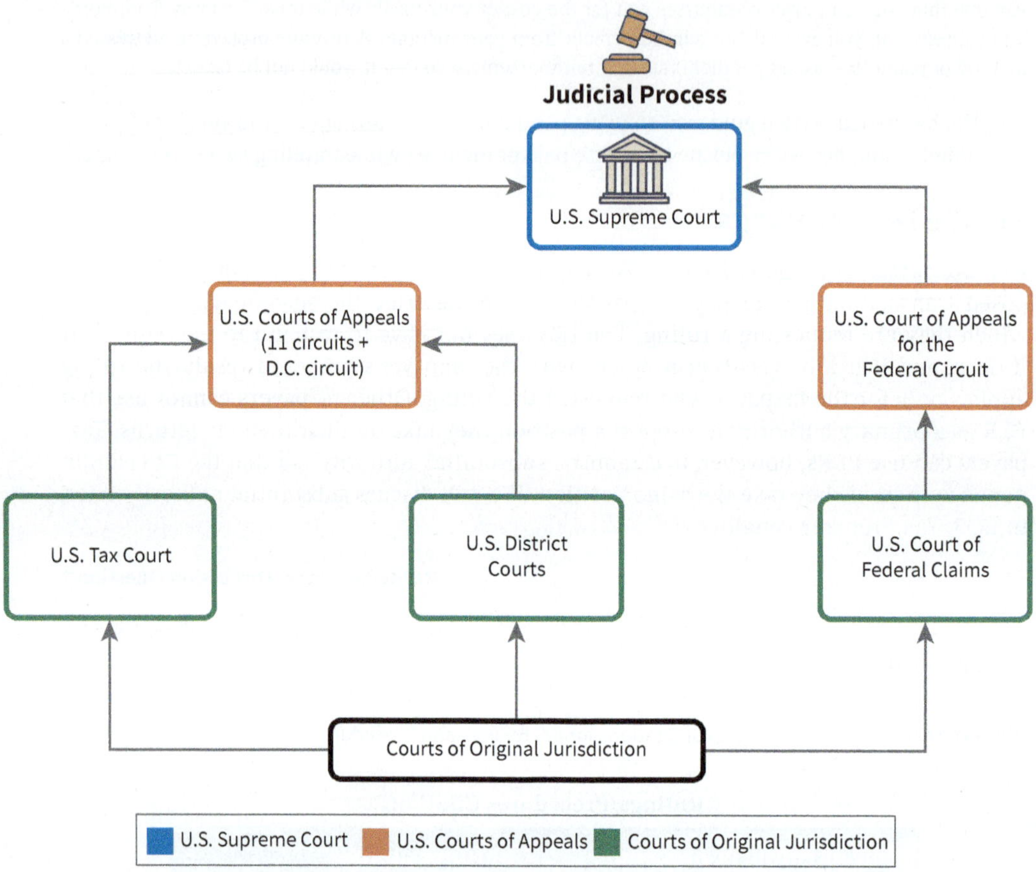

There are three levels of the judicial process for tax disputes, just as there are for any other legal matter in the United States:

- The *court of original jurisdiction*, which hears the facts and renders a decision.
- An *appellate court*, for when either party believes the judge or jury made a material error (for example, applied the law incorrectly) during the original trial. Parties cannot appeal just because they do not agree with the decision of the original court.
- The *United States Supreme Court*, for when either party is not satisfied with the decision made at the appellate level. The Supreme Court hears relatively few tax cases.

Courts of Original Jurisdiction

Any tax dispute between the taxpayer and the IRS that goes to court must begin in a court of original jurisdiction. There are three options: the U.S. Tax Court, a district court, and the U.S. Court of Federal Claims. The court of original jurisdiction must respect the precedents set by other courts to which the IRS or taxpayer could appeal its decision. A **precedent** is a decision in a previous legal case that is binding on a court when it is hearing subsequent cases that have similar facts and issues. We'll look at the three options next.

Related exercise: Discussion Question 8

U.S. Tax Court If the IRS still asserts that the taxpayer has a deficiency at the end of the IRS audit/appeals process (discussed later), it will mail the taxpayer a **Statutory Notice of Deficiency (90-day letter)**. The taxpayer has 90 calendar days from the date of the letter to file a petition with the U.S. Tax Court to hear the matter. The taxpayer *does not* have to pay the deficiency before trial if the petition is filed in a timely manner. This is a major advantage of taking the case to the Tax Court.

The Tax Court hears only tax cases and conducts only non-jury trials. It is one national court, but the 19 judges that comprise it travel in smaller groups throughout the country to hear cases. If a case has broad implications, all judges may hear it. If you believe your client would benefit from a detailed analysis of the law, the Tax Court may be your preferred option, because the judges are tax experts.

The IRS has adopted an acquiescence policy for regular Tax Court decisions (as well as other civil tax cases) that it loses. **Acquiescence** indicates that the IRS will follow the decision in future situations that have similar facts and issues. **Nonacquiescence** indicates that, even though the IRS lost the current case, the IRS will not follow the decision, and taxpayers can expect the IRS to challenge similar facts and issues in the future.

Related exercise: Discussion Question 9

Decisions of the Tax Court are appealed to a U.S. Court of Appeals. As a matter of policy known as the ***Golsen* Rule**,[8] the Tax Court will follow the law of the U.S. circuit courts of appeals to which a case is appealable. For example, if Nicolás (from the chapter introduction) challenged the IRS in Tax Court and lost, Nicolás would appeal to the Fourth Circuit Court of Appeals (see **Illustration 16.8**) because he lives in South Carolina. However, if Nicolás lived in California, he would appeal to the Ninth Circuit Court of Appeals. The Tax Court will follow precedent from the Fourth Circuit if Nicolás lives in South Carolina, and the Ninth Circuit if he lives in California.

Related exercise: Multiple Choice Question 6

The Small Case Division of the U.S. Tax Court is another option for taxpayers, but they should consider it cautiously because there is no appeal from this court. The amount of the deficiency must be $50,000 or less, and taxpayers can represent themselves. Taxpayers cannot use decisions from the Small Case Division as precedent.

Related exercises: Discussion Question 10
Application Problem 1

Spotlight on the Law

Impact of Filing a Petition Late

Mary Jane Toker owns and operates several marijuana dispensaries in Colorado and reports the activity on her Schedule C as a sole proprietor. The IRS audited Mary Jane's tax return, resulting in an additional tax liability of $28,250 plus penalty and interest. She received a Statutory Notice of Deficiency. Mary Jane and her tax attorney disagreed with the IRS's conclusion and pursued filing a petition for redetermination of her tax liability. The petition was due to the Tax Court on April 15, 2019, as required under the 90-day time limit set forth in IRC §6213(a). The tax attorney used FedEx Overnight to send the petitions for filing in the Tax Court. Unfortunately, the petitions were delivered to the Tax Court on the morning of April 16, 2019, one day beyond the petition's due date. Is Mary Jane responsible for filing her petition late?

Yes, the Tax Court can dismiss the petition for redetermination of federal income tax deficiencies due to the fact that the petition was not timely, which was the outcome in *Organic Cannabis Foundation (OCF), LLC vs Commissioner*. The tax attorney for OCF argued that the petition was timely because of the "mailbox" rule set forth in IRC §7502. This rule allows that a document will be deemed filed when dispatched—but only if the taxpayer uses one of the delivery services that the IRS has specifically designated for that purpose in a published notice. However, the Tax Court said that because the particular FedEx service used was not on the IRS's formal list of designated delivery services to which the mailbox rule applies, the petition was deemed late.

The Ninth Circuit declined to reconsider its earlier decision that two California-based cannabis companies (including OCF) could not challenge a $2 million tax bill from the IRS because they filed their U.S. Tax Court petitions one day late. The Supreme Court also denied the companies' petition for a *writ of certiorari* and would not hear the case.

It is imperative to understand how important procedural matters are in tax work. In this unhappy result, Mary Jane has no recourse and must pay the deficiency.

[8] *Golsen v. Commissioner of Internal Revenue*, 54 T.C. 742 (1970), aff'd on other grounds, 445 F.2d 985 (Tenth Cir. 1971), cert. denied, 404 U.S. 940 (1971).

U.S. District Courts There are 94 U.S. district courts, with at least one in each state. If you choose one of these district courts for your tax dispute, you must file the case based on the taxpayer's principal place of business. District courts hear all types of legal matters, so the judges are not tax specialists. As opposed to U.S. Tax Court, jury trials are possible in district courts. If you believe your client would benefit from having a jury of peers render the verdict as opposed to a judge, then this may be the best option.

One significant weakness of district courts is that the taxpayer must first pay the tax deficiency and then request a refund from the IRS. If the IRS denies the refund request, the taxpayer then has legal standing to pursue the matter in district court. If the taxpayer does not have the funds to pay the deficiency, district court is not a viable option.

U.S. Court of Federal Claims The U.S. Court of Federal Claims (also known as the U.S. Claims Court) is a national court in Washington, D.C., that has 16 judges. Cases are tried only at this location. Like a district court, the Claims Court hears all types of legal matters, not just tax issues. As is the case in the U.S. Tax Court, jury trials are not available at the U.S. Claims Court. Claims Court has the same weakness as district court in that the taxpayer must pay the deficiency to the IRS and request a refund before gaining the legal standing to take the matter to court.

One significant advantage of Claims Court, however, is that it follows the precedents set only by the U.S. Court of Appeals for the Federal Circuit and the Supreme Court (see **Illustration 16.7**). It is not bound by precedents set by other circuit courts of appeals. Thus, if a taxpayer lives in the Ninth Circuit and the Ninth Circuit has ruled against another taxpayer in a similar situation, and if the U.S. Court of Appeals for the Federal Circuit has *not* ruled against a taxpayer in a similar situation, the taxpayer may prefer to begin their case in the U.S. Court of Federal Claims.

Related exercise: Brief Exercise 1

Tax Planning Tip

A tax professional has the responsibility to work with the client and the client's attorney to advise the client on the most appropriate court of original jurisdiction for the case. Specifically, taxpayers should be advised on three important issues:

- **The taxpayer must file a timely petition with the U.S. Tax Court if they do not want to pay the tax deficiency before having a court hear their case.**
- **If the taxpayer wants a jury trial, they must have the case heard by the appropriate U.S. district court.**
- **If the taxpayer believes having a judge who is an expert in tax law is to their advantage, they should choose the Tax Court for their case.**

EXAMPLE 16.1.2 Precedents

The IRS has audited Robbins Corporation and sent it a Statutory Notice of Deficiency for $40,000. Robbins is not convinced that it owes this. Robbins is organized in California, which is in the Ninth Circuit. In a similar case three years ago, the Ninth Circuit Court of Appeals ruled against the taxpayer. Robbins has asked you how it should proceed with the dispute in the courts.

SOLUTION

The Ninth Circuit Court's earlier ruling is a major problem for Robbins. If it files the case with the Tax Court or a district court within the Ninth Circuit, these courts are bound to follow the precedent set by the Ninth Circuit. You should inform Robbins that if it files with the Federal Court of Claims, this court will not be obligated to follow the precedent from the Ninth Circuit, because appeals from the Claims Court go to the Court of Appeals for the Federal Circuit. The Ninth Circuit would not have jurisdiction over the case. You also need to remind Robbins that to go to the Claims Court, it will first have to pay the $40,000 deficiency and then request a refund from the IRS.

Appellate Courts

The appellate level includes eleven U.S. courts of appeals, as well as the U.S. Court of Appeals for the Federal Circuit. There is no jury at the appeals level, and the appellate courts do not retry cases or hear new evidence. They review the procedures and the decisions in the court of original jurisdiction to ensure that the law was applied correctly.

U.S. Courts of Appeals U.S. courts of appeals hear appeals from the U.S. Tax Court and from district courts located in their region. Illustration 16.8 shows the geographic region represented by each court. A district court must follow precedents set by the U.S. court of appeals for the circuit in which the district court is located. The Tax Court will follow precedents established in the circuit that would have jurisdiction on appeal (*Golsen* rule).

EXAMPLE 16.1.3
Golsen Rule

Assume the Seventh Circuit Court of Appeals has ruled that income earned from Activity A is not taxable, whereas the Fifth Circuit Court of Appeals has ruled that this type of income is taxable. Corporation I, which is organized in Illinois, and Corporation T, which is organized in Texas, have both filed petitions with the Tax Court related to the taxability of income earned from Activity A. Because the Tax Court is a national court, does it have to provide the same ruling to Corporation I and Corporation T?

SOLUTION

No. In fact the Tax Court cannot render the same opinion to Corporation I and Corporation T due to the *Golsen* Rule. The Tax Court must follow the precedent set by the court to which a decision is appealable. Illinois is in the Seventh Circuit, so the Tax Court must rule that Corporation I's income from Activity A is not taxable. Texas is in the Fifth Circuit, so it must rule that Corporation T's income from Activity A is taxable. Because the Fifth Circuit has already decided that Corporation T's income is taxable, it would be advisable for it to use the Court of Federal Claims as the court of original jurisdiction.

ILLUSTRATION 16.8 Map of the Boundaries for United States Courts of Appeals

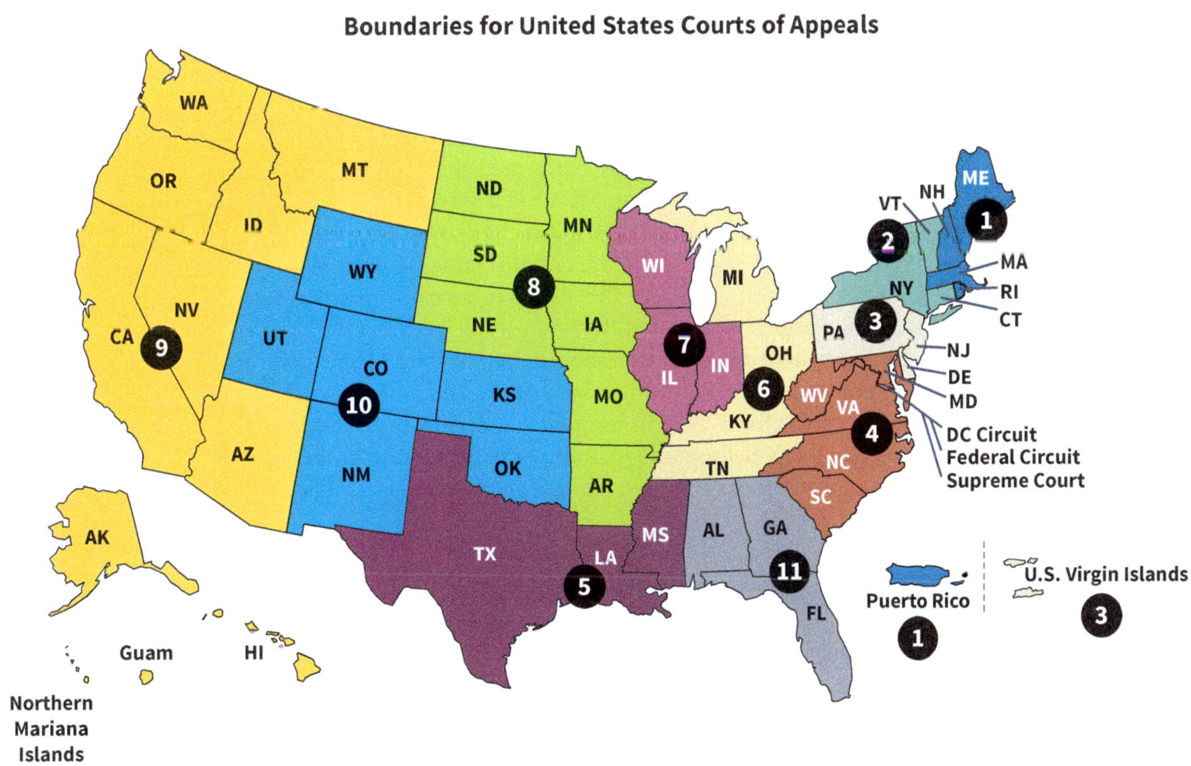

Source: https://www.uscourts.gov/sites/default/files/u.s._federal_courts_circuit_map_1.pdf/Public Domain

U.S. Court of Appeals for the Federal Circuit The U.S. Court of Appeals for the Federal Circuit hears appeals *only* from the U.S. Court of Federal Claims. This court hears cases for a wide range of topics, including the tax law.

U.S. Supreme Court

The U.S. Supreme Court hears appeals from the U.S. courts of appeals, including the Court of Appeals for the Federal Circuit. This is the highest court in the United States, and its nine justices are appointed for life. The Supreme Court agrees to hear very few tax cases, and they are usually cases that have resulted in conflicting opinions in different courts of appeals. In Example 16.1.3, for instance, because the Fifth and Seventh Circuits have made opposite rulings on the same issue, the Supreme Court might agree to hear an appeal to provide a consistent precedent for the entire country.

Related exercises: Discussion Question 11
Application Problems 2, 3

Evaluating Judicial Sources of Tax Authority

When weighting judicial authority, consider the factors below:

- Level of court, with Supreme Court being the highest
- Legal residence of the taxpayer
- Whether the IRS has acquiesced in the court's decision
- The date of the decision (everything else being the same, more recent cases have greater weight)
- Whether later court decisions have concurred with the opinion

Related exercises: Discussion Question 12
Tax Planning Problem 1

Secondary Sources of Tax Authority

Secondary sources of the tax law are commentaries on the law. IRS publications, legal journals, treatises, and tax articles (to name just a few) all provide commentary on the tax law. We have already established that secondary sources of authority should not be cited as the legal support for a tax opinion. The support should always come from primary sources of authority. What, then, is the benefit of secondary sources?

Secondary sources are very useful for finding the primary sources that relate to a specific research question. For example, we performed the following search on the internet: Can a CPA deduct expenses of getting an MBA? The search found several articles that discuss this issue, one being an article from *CPA Practice Advisor*.[9] The article cites and summarizes two recent U.S. Tax Court cases that addressed this issue (*Santos*, TC Memo 2016-100; *Kopaigora*, TC Summary Opinion 2016-35). This demonstrates how a secondary source of the law can lead to finding primary sources of the law.

Another benefit of secondary sources is that they help explain the law. Some tax laws are quite complicated, and having a tax expert explain the law with commentary and examples is often very helpful. Certain commercial services provide commentary on all the income tax laws. Access to at least one of these services is a necessity for tax professionals when conducting tax research. The most popular commercial tax services are:

- Bloomberg Tax
- CCH's AnswerConnect
- Checkpoint Edge's Federal Tax Coordinator

[9]CPA Practice Advisor. "Accountant Wins Case to Deduct MBA Expenses." *CPA Practice Advisor*, 29 Aug. 2016, www.cpapracticeadvisor.com/tax-compliance/news/12250987/accountant-wins-case-to-deduct-mba-expenses.

PRACTICE PROBLEM 16.1.1
Determining Primary Authority

Your tax textbook is very informative and useful in your development of an understanding of tax law. If you took a position on your tax return based on your textbook, would it be a primary authority in a court of law? Why or why not?

SOLUTION

No, your tax textbook is a secondary authority. Although detailed enough to provide information about business income inclusion and expense deduction, it is not a primary authority, and you cannot use it as such.

PRACTICE PROBLEM 16.1.2
Evaluating a Treasury Regulation

When researching the deductibility of an expense, you came across a proposed regulation supporting the client's ability to deduct the expense. Can you rely on a proposed regulation? Why or why not?

SOLUTION

No, you may not rely on a proposed regulation. Proposed regulations do not have the effect of law—though they do provide an indication of the IRS's view on a tax issue.

PRACTICE PROBLEM 16.1.3
Which Court Venue Should Your Client Choose?

Your corporate client underreported income in Year 24, and the IRS has audited the corporation's return, resulting in a deficiency of $12,800 plus penalty and interest. You are helping the corporation's tax attorney decide in which court to file a claim for refund. The underreported income came from a court decision in a lawsuit concerning gain recognized after the corporation's manufacturing plant was destroyed by a tornado, which resulted in a shutdown of nine months. What court might be best if you would like a jury to hear the case?

SOLUTION

To have a jury hear your case, you must file in a U.S. district court. Your client may be willing to pay the assessed taxes before going to court to have a jury decide the case. A jury, rather than a judge, is more likely to side with the taxpayer in a highly emotional situation such as this.

INTERACTIVE SELF-SCORING QUIZZES

16.2 Locating and Evaluating Authority

LEARNING OBJECTIVE 2

Properly evaluate sources of tax authority when making a tax recommendation.

VIDEO CONTENT

When researching a tax issue for a client, you will often find multiple primary tax authorities that address that issue or a similar one. Sometimes, these sources will vary in whether they support the position that favors the client. In evaluating these sources of authority to come to a proper conclusion, you must weigh the importance of each authority.

Weighting of Tax Authority

Illustration 16.9 shows the weight of each authority from highest to lowest within each branch of government.

ILLUSTRATION 16.9 Weighting of Tax Authority within Each Branch of Government

	Tax Authority		
	Legislative	**Administrative**	**Judicial**
Highest Authority	U.S. Constitution	Treasury Regulations: Legislative	U.S. Supreme Court
↓	Internal Revenue Code and Treaties	Treasury Regulations: Interpretative	U.S. Circuit Courts of Appeals (including Federal Circuit)
		Treasury Regulations: Procedural	U.S. Tax Court
		Revenue Rulings	U.S. District Courts/U.S. Court of Federal Claims
		Revenue Procedures	
Lowest Authority		Private Letter Rulings (for taxpayer who requested)	

The greatest challenge comes in weighting authority across the different sources of legislative, administrative, and judicial. Here are a few general guidelines:

- The Internal Revenue Code is generally considered the highest authority. Although a Supreme Court opinion might find a tax law unconstitutional, if Congress disagrees with the decision, it can pass a new law that overturns the decision for taxpayers in similar circumstances in the future.
- Judicial decisions often have more weight than Treasury regulations, because the courts can rule that a Treasury regulation is invalid because it is not consistent with the intent of Congress. While the courts have found some Treasury regulations to be invalid, this happens very infrequently.
- Similarly, judicial decisions usually have more weight than IRS revenue rulings.

Related exercises: Application Problem 4
Brief Exercise 2

The Research Process

There are several steps to follow when researching a tax issue, as shown in **Illustration 16.10**. We'll take a closer look at each one in this section.

ILLUSTRATION 16.10 The Research Process

Steps for Successful Research

Step 1. Identify: All relevant facts.

Step 2. State clearly: The problem to be solved.

Step 3. Locate: The applicable tax authority.

Step 4. Evaluate: The relevance and weight of the authorities.

Step 5. Identify: Possible solutions.

Step 6. Identify: The recommended solution.

Step 7. Communicate: Your results to your client.

Related exercise: Discussion Question 13

Step 1. Identify: All relevant facts.

Identifying all the relevant facts may seem like the simplest part of the research process. However, the experienced researcher knows that this is often the most difficult part, and a step where mistakes can be costly. Any fact that may affect the outcome of the case is relevant. You will need strong communication skills to listen carefully to the client and ask the appropriate questions to secure all relevant facts. When tax professionals make mistakes in the tax research process, it is often because they were researching the wrong question. No one does this intentionally, but if you are missing some key facts about the client's issue, you may not properly understand the underlying economics of the transaction. This can lead you to research a different transaction from the one that occurred or is being planned.

Step 2. State clearly: The problem to be solved.

Clearly state the problem back to the client. Doing so at this point in the process allows the client to alert you if you have misunderstood their transaction. You need to state the problem narrowly enough so that it is possible to find a clear and concise answer. Broad statements of issues lead to ambiguity in the later stages of the tax research process.

Step 3. Locate: The applicable tax authority.

This is the step for which you will use secondary sources of the tax law to lead you to the appropriate primary sources. For example, this textbook is a secondary source of the law. Some of the footnotes in the chapters provide citations that refer you to the appropriate primary sources of the tax law. You should be skilled in using at least one of the commercial tax services mentioned earlier to ensure that if primary authority sources related to your tax issue exist, you will locate them. When you do not find any primary authority, it creates an interesting dilemma for you, as shown in the next Example.

EXAMPLE 16.2.1
Locating Authority

Your client has asked you whether her distributive share from her LLC interest is subject to the 3.8% net investment income tax. You research the issue for an hour using a commercial tax service and do not find any primary authority related to the issue. What should you do?

SOLUTION

The dilemma you face is that there are two possible reasons you did not find a relevant authority: either there is no relevant authority, or there is a relevant authority, but you have not found it yet. If you decide to research the issue for a few more hours and you still find no relevant authority, you have wasted valuable time you could have used on other projects. If you stop searching, and some authority does exist, without it your firm may provide incorrect tax advice to your client, and this could expose you and your firm to legal liability. This is a difficult dilemma, particularly for an inexperienced researcher. You need to invest the time to become a skilled researcher so that if you do not find any authority, you can be highly confident it does not exist. But everyone begins as an inexperienced researcher. In this situation, you should consult with a manager or partner in your firm to seek advice before you continue to invest time in the research process.

Step 4. Evaluate: The relevance and weight of the authorities.

There are two steps in evaluating the relevance of the authorities. First, decide how closely the facts in each authority line up with your client's facts. If the facts are identical or extremely similar, the authority is said to be "**on all fours**," meaning that the facts are very relevant to your client's facts that you are researching. As the facts in a source of authority become more dissimilar to your client's facts, the relevance of the authority declines. The second step is to weigh the authority of each item, as discussed in the preceding section, "Weighting of Tax Authority."

Step 5. Identify: Possible solutions.

Based on the law you find, list the possible solutions to the problem to make sure you consider all of them. For more complex issues, you should discuss the issue with other tax professionals to gather their input as well.

Step 6. Identify: The recommended solution.

You now need to formulate a recommendation to your client. However, never forget that your client makes the final decision about how to report the tax issue. LO4 discusses your professional responsibilities if you do not agree with how your client wants to report the issue.

Step 7. Communicate: Your results to your client.

The last step in the process is to notify your client of the results of your research. Even if you speak to the client in person or on the phone, your communication should always include a written memorandum that summarizes the steps you have taken as outlined above. An example of a research memo is provided in the Communication Application at the end of this chapter.

PRACTICE PROBLEM 16.2.1
Conducting Research

When performing research for your client, you have found two cases with fact patterns similar to your client's. In one case, the U.S. Tax Court ruled for a business in Colorado. In the other case, the Tax Court ruled against a business in California. If your client's business is in Oregon, can you rely on the decision for the business in Colorado?

SOLUTION

Your client's business is in the Ninth Circuit, and the favorable opinion from Colorado was issued in the Tenth Circuit (see Illustration 16.8). The Ninth Circuit Court of Appeals has not yet ruled on this issue, so you must evaluate the two Tax Court decisions. Because California and Oregon are both in the Ninth Circuit, if you want to rely on the Tax Court case from the Tenth Circuit, you must distinguish the fact patterns in the two cases. The Tax Court ruled against the California business, so you must show that your client's fact pattern is different, and that the California decision shouldn't apply to your client. You will need to argue that the case for the Colorado business is more similar to your Oregon client's fact pattern.

INTERACTIVE SELF-SCORING QUIZZES

16.3 Tax Preparer Penalties

LEARNING OBJECTIVE 3

Apply the rules for tax preparer penalties.

VIDEO CONTENT

Tax preparers are subject to penalties if they sign a tax return that includes an inaccurate position. These penalties apply to tax return preparers, including preparers for estate, gift, employment, excise, and exempt organization returns. A tax preparer should sign a tax return only if the taxpayer paid them to prepare the return.

A tax return preparer who prepares a return or refund claim that includes an **unreasonable position** must pay a penalty equal to the *greater* of $1,000 *or* 50% of the income they derived for preparing the return. A position is unreasonable if it does not have substantial authority. **Substantial authority** is based on the likelihood that a taxpayer's position would be supported if the matter were taken to court. While the law does not identify a specific percentage of success that represents substantial authority, it is well accepted that the likelihood does not need to exceed 40%. There is an exception to this rule if the taxpayer disclosed the position on the tax return and there is a *reasonable basis* for it.[10] The *reasonable cause* exception (see Chapter 1, LO2, Tax Compliance for Business Entities) applies to tax preparers as well.

If the understated tax liability is due to an unreasonable position and the preparer willfully attempts to understate the tax liability—or recklessly or intentionally disregards rules or regulations—the penalty is the *greater* of $5,000 *or* 75% of the income earned by the tax preparer for preparing the return or claim. The IRS can also file criminal charges against a tax preparer who engages in fraudulent activity.

Additional penalties may be imposed on tax preparers, as shown in **Illustration 16.11**.

ILLUSTRATION 16.11 Additional Tax Preparer Penalties (2025)

Tax Preparer Penalties

Scenario	Penalty per return	Maximum penalty
Not exercising due diligence in establishing whether a taxpayer is eligible for the Earned Income Tax Credit (EITC), Child Tax Credit (CTC), or American Opportunity Tax Credit (AOTC)	$650	No limit
Failing to provide the taxpayer's identifying number on the return	$ 65	$32,500
Not signing returns done for compensation	$ 65	$32,500
Failure to include PTIN (Preparer Tax Identification Number) on a tax return	$ 65	$32,500
Not providing a copy of the return for the taxpayer	$ 65	$32,500
Endorsing or negotiating a client's refund check	$650	No limit
Not keeping a list of returns filed	$ 65	$32,500
Not keeping a list of tax return preparers hired to prepare returns, including employees and independent contractors	$ 65	$32,500

Tax preparers are also subject to penalties for knowingly or recklessly disclosing tax return information. A tax preparer who uses or discloses tax return information without the client's explicit written consent can be fined up to $1,000, imprisoned for one year, or both for each violation. Exceptions are provided for disclosures related to quality or peer reviews. If the disclosure results in taxpayer identity theft, the penalty is $1,000 for each disclosure with an annual maximum of $50,000.

EXAMPLE 16.3.1

Tax Preparer Penalty

Taxes-R-Us prepared ABC partnership's tax return for 2025 and charged $3,000 for the work. The preparer signed the return but did not properly follow the law related to valuation of property for tax purposes. What penalty will the IRS assess for the preparer in this situation?

SOLUTION

Taxes-R-Us will be assessed a penalty of $5,000, the greater of $5,000 or $2,250 (75% of $3,000).

Related exercises: Discussion Questions 14, 15
Multiple Choice Question 7
Application Problem 5

[10] This exception applies to reportable transactions and tax shelters only if the position has a more-likely-than-not chance of being sustained.

PRACTICE PROBLEM 16.3.1
Determining a Tax Preparer Penalty

Benny, a local CPA, prepared tax returns for 285 clients for compensation in 2025 and failed to sign any of the returns. What penalty is Benny subject to, and what will be the amount?

SOLUTION

Benny owes the failure to sign a tax return penalty of $65 per return, not to exceed $32,500. His total penalty is $18,525 ($65 × 285).

16.4 Tax Practice and Procedure

LEARNING OBJECTIVE 4

Identify the steps in the audit and appeals processes within the Internal Revenue Service.

VIDEO CONTENT

The final section of this chapter deals with the IRS's audit and appeals process, as well as the important implications of signing a tax return. It is important that tax practitioners, such as Roxana from the chapter introduction, understand the audit and appeals process, so they can properly advise their clients.

Audit Process

The IRS audits a very small percentage of tax returns each year. Sometimes an audit can be handled in just a few hours, but, in many cases, it can require significant time and resources from the taxpayer. Illustration 16.12 shows the percentage of returns that were audited for tax year 2021.[11]Overall audit rates are very small, with the highest rate of 0.49% being for estate tax returns.

ILLUSTRATION 16.12 IRS Audits of Tax Returns

IRS Audit Statistics for 2021

Business form	All returns filed	Returns examined	% of returns examined
Individual (Form 1040)	161,206,833	341,276	0.21%
Corporations (Form 1120)	1,556,982	4,168	0.27%
Partnerships (Form 1065)	4,467,584	4,434	0.10%
S corporations (Form 1120-S)	5,120,552	4,819	0.09%
Estate and trust (Form 1041)	3,033,133	*	*
Estate tax return (Form 706)	32,374	158	0.49%

*Not disclosed by IRS because numbers are too small.

The audit process is quite complicated. We present the following facts and rules to give you a basic understanding of the process. Refer to Illustration 16.13 to understand the most important steps in the process.

[11]U.S. Department of the Treasury. *Data Book, 2023*. Publication 55-B. Internal Revenue Service, Washington, DC, April 2024. Table 17, p. 36, www.irs.gov/pub/irs-pdf/p55b.pdf. This is the most recent year for which completed audit data is available.

ILLUSTRATION 16.13 IRS Audit/Appeals/Litigation Process

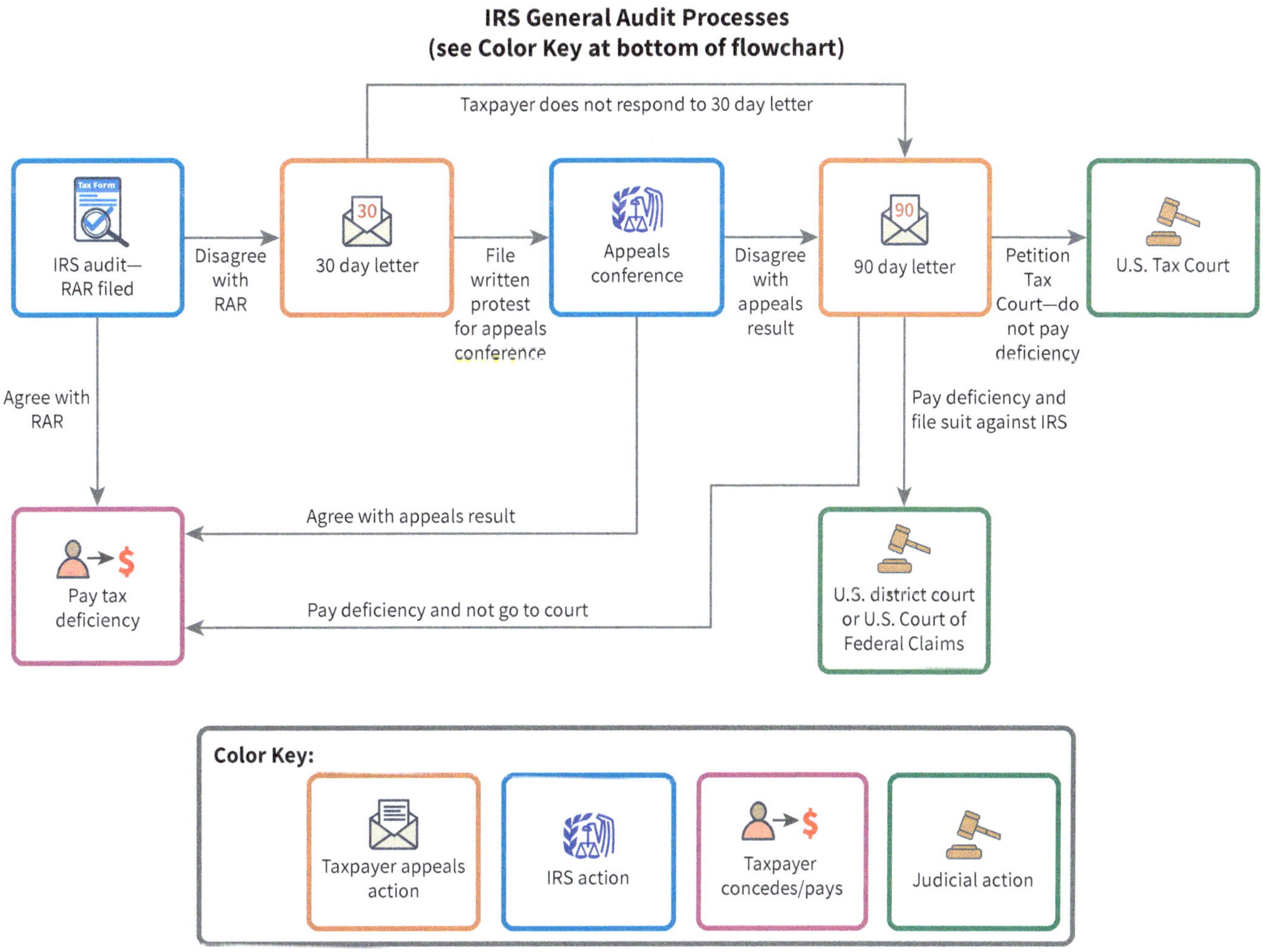

The process begins with an automated review of returns for mathematical errors and to match information from W-2 forms, 1099 forms, and similar documents. This review is applied to all tax returns. Each return is given a score, using formulas that are part of the IRS's Discriminate Function System (DIF). The DIF score is used to select returns to review for possible audit.

If the IRS decides to conduct an audit, it chooses from several types of examinations. Simple audits are often handled through written correspondence, referred to as a **correspondence examination**. The IRS initiates a correspondence examination by notifying the taxpayer that a return has been selected and listing the items to be verified. The IRS may also have proposed adjustments based on information documents issued by third parties, such as Form W-2, Wage and Tax Statement; Form 1099-DIV, Dividends and Distributions; and Form 1098, Mortgage Interest Statement. The IRS usually handles correspondence examinations at an IRS Service Center.

The IRS can also conduct audits in its offices (called *office examinations*) or in the field (called *field examinations*). An **office examination** occurs at the local district office of the IRS. The IRS notifies the taxpayer by letter of the date and time of exam, as well as the items being questioned. Taxpayers can represent themselves at an office examination. A **field examination** is conducted at the taxpayer's place of business and is more complex and extensive than an office examination. The taxpayer may appoint a qualified individual to represent them before the IRS, usually a CPA, attorney, or enrolled agent, by completing Form 2848, Power of Attorney and Declaration of Representative. The IRS has the power to summon the taxpayer's records and witnesses to testify.

Related exercise: Discussion Question 16

The IRS reports its findings from the audit on Form 4549, Income Tax Examination Changes, which is sent to the taxpayer. The **Revenue Agent Report (RAR)** that accompanies Form 4549 should provide the information necessary to explain the adjustments and demonstrate how the IRS computed the tax liability. The IRS will take positions consistent with its administrative sources of the tax law. The RAR is a proposed agreement that the IRS offers the taxpayer. If the taxpayer agrees to the audit changes proposed in the RAR, they cannot pursue tax relief through the appeals process or through the Tax Court (but can do so through other courts). The signed agreement binds the IRS and taxpayer only with regard to items in the agreement. Even if the taxpayer agrees to the changes and pays the deficiency, they can later pursue a claim for refund through a U.S. district court or U.S. Claims Court. If the IRS issues a no change report in the RAR after an audit, it generally cannot reopen the examination unless fraud or other similar misrepresentation is involved.

Related exercise: Brief Exercise 3

If the IRS and the taxpayer do not reach agreement through the audit process, the taxpayer will receive a copy of the RAR and a *30-day letter*. The **30-day letter** explains the assessments the IRS has made and gives the taxpayer 30 days to agree to them before the IRS takes further action. The IRS encourages the taxpayer to agree to the RAR or request an appellate conference. However, the taxpayer is not required to respond to this letter.

Appeals Process

A taxpayer who receives the 30-day letter and disagrees with the RAR can request an appellate conference with the IRS Independent Office of Appeals. The steps of the appeals process are as follows:

Step 1. A written protest must be filed with the request for an appellate conference. The protest must explain the taxpayer's position for each issue and provide the support on which the taxpayer is relying for questions of law. The IRS is not required to grant an appeal in all cases. In general, the IRS may not raise new issues during the appeal.

Step 2. The appellate conference is held. The conference is informal compared with a judicial proceeding.

Step 3. If the case is settled, a Form 870-AD, Offer to Waive Restrictions on Assessment and Collection of Tax Deficiency and to Accept Overassessment, is signed by the taxpayer, which means the case will not be reopened unless there is a significant mathematical error or fraud.

Step 4. If a taxpayer does not respond to the 30-day letter, or does not reach agreement in the appeals process, a Statutory Notice of Deficiency (90-day letter) is issued. The 90-day letter is significant in that this is the time the taxpayer has to file a petition with the Tax Court. If the taxpayer does not file the petition in a timely manner, the taxpayer's only judicial recourse is through a U.S. district court or the U.S. Claims Court, both of which require the deficiency to be paid before the judicial process can begin.

Related exercise: Multiple Choice Question 8

Step 5. Once a petition has been filed with the Tax Court, the IRS cannot issue a Statutory Notice of Deficiency until the court's decision in the matter has been finalized.

Other Audit Issues

There are a few other issues related to the audit process of which you need to be aware:

- In some situations, the IRS will agree to an **offer in compromise**, which is a program that allows a taxpayer to settle a tax liability for less than the actual amount owed.

- The IRS may request the taxpayer to extend the statute of limitations period. While the taxpayer is not required to agree, a refusal to extend will usually lead the IRS to assess a tax deficiency before the statute expires.
- Any communication that would be privileged between a taxpayer and an attorney is also privileged between a taxpayer and any person who is authorized to practice before the IRS. This privilege does *not* apply to criminal tax matters or to corporate tax shelters.

Related exercise: Application Problem 6

Signing a Return

Anyone who signs a tax return does so under the penalty of perjury; the tax return is not complete without a signature. Both spouses must sign a Form 1040 that is jointly filed; this creates *joint and several liability* for each spouse, which means that the IRS can collect the entire tax liability from either spouse. Corporate tax returns (Form 1120 and Form 1120-S) must be signed by an authorized corporate officer. Partnership tax returns (Form 1065) must be signed by a partner or an LLC member. You should always review your tax return carefully before you sign it. A taxpayer who knowingly signs a false tax return can be subject to civil and/or criminal penalties.

A taxpayer can use an electronic signature to sign a return that is e-filed. To file electronically, an individual needs a personal identification number (PIN) (both parties in a married couple filing a joint return need PINs). A taxpayer can self-select a PIN or have the tax practitioner randomly generate a PIN for him. Note that if a return is filed electronically, no forms or paper need to be mailed to the IRS. Any corporation that is required to file 10 or more tax returns, or that has $10 million or more in total assets, must file electronically. A corporation failing to meet this requirement is treated as if it failed to file its return, and any elections made on the return will be considered to not be made in a timely manner. Partnerships with more than 100 partners are also required to file electronically.

Related exercise: Application Problem 7

EXAMPLE 16.4.1 Signing a Tax Return

Lauren has been married to Kyle for seven years. Kyle has always handled the financial affairs for their household, including filing the tax return. When he brings her the tax return to sign this year, Lauren notices that their AGI is only $60,000, which is significantly lower than previous years. She has not noticed any change in their lifestyle, which includes expensive vacations, and Kyle just bought a new sports car last month for $70,000. Lauren believes their AGI last year was over $300,000 and asks Kyle why the AGI on the return is so much lower. Kyle tells her not to worry about it and just sign the return. Lauren is surprised by Kyle's defensiveness. You are her sibling, so she calls you to ask your advice about signing the tax return. What advice should you give Lauren?

SOLUTION

You need to tell Lauren that she is very wise to make sure she is comfortable with the information on the tax return, because she is signing it under penalty of perjury. She needs to ask Kyle to explain what has happened in the last year for their income to have dropped so dramatically. In the best case, Kyle will be able to give her a reasonable explanation. If he refuses to do so, Lauren should not sign the return. If Kyle refuses to discuss the issue with her, Lauren may have to use the option to file as married filing separately so that she does not have to sign a tax return with Kyle's information on it.

Related exercise: Tax Planning Problem 2

PRACTICE PROBLEM 16.4.1
The Audit Process

Your client, a corporation, has received an audit notification from the IRS concerning its travel expenses. Will the IRS have to conduct the audit at the IRS office?

SOLUTION

The letter from the IRS will indicate how to respond. Typically, the tax professional can handle basic questions of this nature by mail or electronically with the tax compliance officer assigned to the audit.

INTERACTIVE SELF-SCORING QUIZZES

Review and Practice

Chapter Summary

In this chapter, we reviewed the sources of tax authority in the legislative, administrative, and judicial branches of government. We also discussed how accountants determine the importance of each source when making a reporting recommendation to a client for a specific tax situation. We then described the penalties the IRS can levy against tax preparers who do not comply with the rules. Finally, we provided a high-level summary of the audit and appeals processes within the IRS.

1 Classify sources of tax authority as legislative, administrative, or judicial.

- **Primary authority** consists of the original sources of the tax law. Tax conclusions must be supported by primary authority. Primary authority comes from each of the three branches of the federal government:
  1. Legislative authority (Congress)
  2. Administrative authority (the executive branch)
  3. Judicial authority (the courts)
- **Secondary authority** is commentary on tax law, which is found in sources such as treatises, journals, and commentaries provided by editorial services. Secondary authorities cannot be used as the sole basis for a tax decision.
  - The sources of legislative authority, listed in order of importance, are:
    - U.S. Constitution
    - Internal Revenue Code and certain **treaties**
    - Congressional committee reports (secondary authority)
- The sources of administrative authority, listed in order of importance, are:
  - Treasury regulations
    - **Legislative regulations**
    - **Interpretive regulations**
    - **Procedural regulations**
  - **Revenue rulings**
  - **Revenue procedures**
  - **Private letter rulings (PLRs)**
- When weighting judicial authority, the factors below must be considered when comparing different court opinions.
  - Level of court, with Supreme Court being the highest
  - Legal residence of the taxpayer
  - Whether the IRS has acquiesced in the court's decision
  - The date of the decision (everything else being the same, more recent cases have greater weight)
  - Whether later court decisions have concurred with the opinion

2 Properly evaluate sources of tax authority when making a tax recommendation.

- There are several steps to follow when researching a tax issue:
  - Step 1. Identify: All relevant facts.
  - Step 2. State clearly: The problem to be solved.
  - Step 3. Locate: The applicable tax authority.
  - Step 4. Evaluate: The relevance and weight of the authorities.
  - Step 5. Identify: Possible solutions.
  - Step 6. Identify: The recommended solution.
  - Step 7. Communicate: Your results to your client.

3 Apply the rules for tax preparer penalties

- A tax return preparer who prepares a return or refund claim that includes an **unreasonable position** must pay a penalty of the *greater* of $1,000 *or* 50% of the income derived by the preparer for preparing the return. A position is unreasonable if it does not have **substantial authority**. There is an exception to this rule if the position was disclosed and there is a reasonable basis for it.

- If the understated tax liability is due to an unreasonable position and the preparer willfully attempts to understate the tax liability or recklessly or intentionally disregards rules or regulations, the penalty is the *greater* of $5,000 *or* 75% of the income earned by the tax preparer for preparing the return or claim.

4 Identify the steps in the audit and appeals processes within the Internal Revenue Service.

- Simple audits may be handled through written correspondence (**correspondence examination**). Other audits may be conducted in an IRS office (**office examination**) or in the taxpayer's place of business (**field examination**). A taxpayer may appoint qualified individuals to represent them before the IRS, usually a CPA, an attorney, or an enrolled agent. The IRS has the power to summon the taxpayer's records and witnesses to testify.
- A tax return is signed under the penalty of perjury. Corporate tax returns (Form 1120 and Form 1120-S) must be signed by an authorized corporate officer. Partnership tax returns (Form 1065) must be signed by a partner or an LLC member. You should always review your tax return carefully before you sign it. If a taxpayer knowingly signs a false tax return, the taxpayer can be subject to civil and/or criminal penalties.
- A taxpayer can use an electronic signature to sign a return that is e-filed. Note that if a return is filed electronically, no forms or paper need to be mailed to the IRS. Any corporation that is required to file 10 or more tax returns, or that has $10 million or more in total assets, must file electronically. A corporation failing to meet this requirement is treated as if it failed to file its return, and any elections made on the return will be considered to not be made in a timely manner. Partnerships with more than 100 partners are also required to file electronically.

Communication Application

Communication

Preparer Responsibility

(LO1) Sly and Suzy own a bar and restaurant that specializes in serving local breweries' beverages. They frequently visit their vendors and pay for the meals and entertainment. Sly and Suzy have hired you as their new accountant because the previous accountant was too conservative for them. They feel they are missing out on deducting legitimate business expenses on their tax return. In 2025, their QuickBooks account reflects $8,000 in entertainment expenses and $12,000 for business meals served in a restaurant. They would like to deduct all of these expenses because they are all business related. Prepare a memo to Sly and Suzy and an internal research memo for their file explaining your findings.

Solution

Memo to Client

Hello Sly and Suzy,

I have visited your bar and restaurant several times and have always enjoyed the experience. I will definitely recommend it to friends and family. I know that you would like to deduct all your meals and entertainment expenses because they relate to your business, but the Internal Revenue Code (IRC) is very clear that there are limitations on their deductibility.

In order for an expense to be deductible, it must be ordinary and necessary as it relates to the business. I believe that your meals and entertainment expenses fit this criterion. However, the IRC states that 50% of business meals are deductible in 2025 and none of the business entertainment expenses are deductible. The government does not want to subsidize the pleasure element of these activities, and therefore curbs the entertainment deduction.

I am sorry that I did not have better news for you. I hope to see you soon at your restaurant!

Sincerely,
Carnes & Youngberg, CPAs

Tax memo to the file

Facts: Sly and Suzy own a bar and restaurant in town that specializes in serving local breweries' beverages. They frequently visit their vendors and pay for the meals and entertainment. For the current year, their QuickBooks account reflects $8,000 in entertainment expenses and $12,000 for meals. Sly and Suzy would like to deduct all of these expenses because they are all business related.

Issue: Can Sly and Suzy deduct all their business meals and entertainment expenses?

Conclusion: No, they may deduct 50% of their business meals and 0% of the entertainment expenses.

Analysis: §162(a) of the Internal Revenue Code defines business expenses as the ordinary and necessary expenses of carrying on a trade or business. Generally, business expenses are tax deductible. It would be expected that a bar and restaurant owner would incur business meals and entertainment expenses in the ordinary course of running their business. §274(a)(1)(A) generally disallows a deduction for any item with respect to an activity of a type considered to constitute entertainment, amusement, or recreation (entertainment expenditures). §274(n)(1) generally limits the deduction of food or beverage expenditures to 50 percent of the amount that otherwise would have been allowable. The expenditures must not be lavish or extravagant. Substantiation is needed for the food and beverages expense under §162.

Ethics and Professional Responsibilities Application

Ethics

Tax Preparer Penalty

(LO3) Shan Shady, CPA, is a tax accountant and prepares hundreds of tax returns for individuals and businesses each year. She promises large refunds and has been aggressively advising clients to take large deductions on their tax returns due to the low chance that they will be audited. It has been discovered that Shan has been selling her clients' contact information. Also, to attract new clients, she has disclosed names and income levels of her prominent, well-known current clients to the potential new clients to encourage them to hire her. What is Shan Shady's ethical exposure in this situation?

In addition to the chapter content, see *Statements on Standards for Tax Services* at www.aicpa-cima.com/resources/landing/statements-on-standards-for-tax-services, and *Circular 230* at www.irs.gov/tax-professionals/office-of-professional-responsibility-and-circular-230.

Solution

Tax professionals need to ensure that their clients meet all compliance requirements. Tax preparers are subject to penalties for knowingly or recklessly disclosing tax return information. A tax preparer who uses or discloses tax return information without the client's explicit written consent can be fined up to $1,000, imprisoned for one year, or both for each violation. Exceptions are provided for disclosures related to quality or peer reviews. If the disclosure results in taxpayer identity theft, the penalty is $1,000 for each disclosure with an annual maximum of $50,000.

Circular 230 contains the IRS's rules of practice governing CPAs, attorneys, enrolled agents, and others authorized to practice before the IRS. The government may censure, fine, suspend, or disbar tax advisors from practice before the IRS if they violate *Circular 230*'s standards of conduct.

The *Statements on Standards for Tax Services (SSTS)* are issued by the AICPA and provide a summary of the professional responsibilities to which CPAs must adhere in performing tax services. No. 1.3.4: Data Protection states that a member should make reasonable efforts to safeguard taxpayer data, including data transmitted or stored electronically.

Shan Shady did not follow the proper protocol and willfully disclosed confidential information on her current clients without their consent. Shan could be assessed penalties and possibly imprisoned.

Key Terms

30-Day Letter 16-22
90-Day Letter 16-10
Acquiescence 16-11
Correspondence Examination 16-21
Field Examination 16-21
Final Regulations 16-8
Golsen Rule 16-11
Internal Revenue Code (IRC) 16-4
Interpretive Regulations 16-8
Legislative Regulations 16-7
Nonacquiescence 16-11
Offer in Compromise 16-22
Office Examination 16-21
On All Fours 16-17
Precedent 16-10
Primary Authority 16-3
Private Letter Rulings (PLR) 16-9
Procedural Regulations 16-8
Proposed Regulations 16-8
Revenue Agent Report (RAR) 16-22
Revenue Procedures 16-8
Revenue Rulings 16-8
Secondary Authority 16-3
Statutory Notice of Deficiency (90-Day Letter) 16-10
Substantial Authority 16-18
Temporary Regulations 16-8
Treaty 16-6
Unreasonable Position 16-18

End-of-Chapter Assessment

Discussion Questions

1. **(LO1)** Distinguish between a *primary authority* and a *secondary authority*.
2. **(LO1)** Describe the legislative process, indicating where the bill begins and how the bill finally becomes law.
3. **(LO1)** If a tax treaty and the Internal Revenue Code are in direct conflict with one another, which must a taxpayer rely on?
4. **(LO1)** In IRC §280A(c)(1)(A), what labels are used for the subparts?
5. **(LO1)** What is included in the administrative sources of tax law?
6. **(LO1)** Distinguish between a *proposed regulation*, a *temporary regulation*, and a *final regulation*.
7. **(LO1)** What is the difference between a revenue ruling and a private letter ruling?
8. **(LO1)** Name the three courts of original jurisdiction that hear federal tax issues.
9. **(LO1)** Define the terms *acquiescence* and *nonacquiescence*.
10. **(LO1)** What is the Small Case Division of the U.S. Tax Court?
11. **(LO1)** When will the Supreme Court hear a tax case?
12. **(LO1)** What variables might you consider when assessing the validity of sources of tax law?
13. **(LO2)** Briefly describe the steps in the tax research process.
14. **(LO3)** Provide two examples of a tax preparer penalty.
15. **(LO3)** What is meant by the term *substantial authority*?
16. **(LO4)** Name three types of IRS audits.

Multiple Choice Questions

1. **(LO1)** Which of the following is a primary authority?
   - **a.** *Journal of Taxation* article
   - **b.** Wiley tax textbook
   - **c.** Tax Court decision
   - **d.** IRS publication
2. **(LO1)** Which of the following is a secondary authority?
   - **a.** Revenue ruling
   - **b.** Supreme Court decision
   - **c.** Internal Revenue Code section
   - **d.** Wiley tax textbook
3. **(LO1)** Which of the following is a not a primary source of tax authority?
   - **a.** The *Wall Street Journal*
   - **b.** Legislative source
   - **c.** Administrative source
   - **d.** Judicial source
4. **(LO1)** In IRC §179(b)(3)(A), what subpart is (3)?
   - **a.** Section
   - **b.** Subsection
   - **c.** Paragraph
   - **d.** Subparagraph
5. **(LO1)** Which of the following carries the higher weight of authority?
   - **a.** Internal Revenue Code section
   - **b.** Treaty
   - **c.** Both are equal, and weighting depends on which is more recent
   - **d.** None of these
6. **(LO1)** What rule states that the Tax Court will follow previous decisions in the circuit that will have jurisdiction on appeal?
   - **a.** *Goldberg* Rule
   - **b.** *Golden* Rule
   - **c.** *Molsen* Rule
   - **d.** *Golsen* Rule
7. **(LO3)** What is the penalty per tax return for a tax practitioner's failure to sign a tax return?
   - **a.** $0
   - **b.** $65
   - **c.** $105
   - **d.** $1,000
8. **(LO4)** What is another common name for the Statutory Notice of Deficiency?
   - **a.** 10-day letter
   - **b.** 30-day letter
   - **c.** 90-day letter
   - **d.** 120-day letter

Brief Exercises

1. **(LO1)** List two unique distinctions for each of the following: the U.S. district courts, the U.S. Tax Court, and the U.S. Court of Federal Claims.
2. **(LO2)** List the administrative sources of authority from highest to lowest.
3. **(LO4)** Describe a no change report and identify whether or not it is advantageous for the taxpayer.

Application Problems

1. **(LO1)** Classify the following tax sources as primary, secondary, both, or neither.
   - **a.** Tax treaty between the United States and Canada
   - **b.** Senate Finance Committee Report
   - **c.** Revenue ruling
   - **d.** U.S. Tax Court decision
   - **e.** *Journal of Accountancy* article
   - **f.** Tax Court Small Case Division decision
   - **g.** Revenue procedure
2. **(LO1)** For each of the following citations, identify the type of authority (legislative, administrative, or judicial)
   - **a.** IRC §1031(a) (Internal Revenue Code section)
   - **b.** Rev. Proc. 2004-34, 2004-1 C.B. 911 (revenue procedure)
   - **c.** *U.S. vs Jones*, 2010-2 USTC (Supreme Court decision)
   - **d.** PLR 201701001 (private letter ruling)
   - **e.** H. Rep No. 242, 82nd Cong. (House Ways and Means Committee Report)
   - **f.** BF Davis, 76 TC 418 (2013) (Tax Court decision)
3. **(LO1)** A taxpayer living in the following places would appeal a U.S. district court decision to which U.S. court of appeals?
   - **a.** Illinois
   - **b.** Alabama
   - **c.** California
   - **d.** Massachusetts
   - **e.** Washington D.C.
   - **f.** Hawaii
4. **(LO2)** Rank the weight of the authorities below, beginning with the highest authority.
   - **a.** Internal Revenue Code section
   - **b.** Private letter ruling
   - **c.** Article in the *Journal of Taxation*
   - **d.** Tax Court decision
   - **e.** Temporary regulation
5. **(LO3)** Dale is a CPA and prepares many tax returns during the year. When one of his client's returns was audited, it was discovered that Dale had taken an unreasonable position that the IRS disagreed with. Dale had charged $1,750 for the preparation of the client's tax return. What tax preparer penalty will Dale be subject to?
6. **(LO4)** CPA Sanjay has been representing his client, Dee Inc., before the IRS regarding an audit of Dee's 2023 corporate tax return. Most issues have been resolved, but one major issue is still in disagreement. What options do Sanjay and Dee Inc. have with regard to this matter?
7. **(LO4)** Holly, age 17, models and has a single-member LLC (SMLLC). The SMLLC makes over $100,000 in the current year. Holly's mom prepares Holly's tax return, which includes Schedule C for the SMLLC, and signs the return for Holly. If you were Holly's tax accountant, what advice might you give Holly?

Tax Planning Problems

Planning

1. **(LO1)** Butch Inc. has been working with the IRS to resolve issues pertaining to its 2024 corporate income tax return. The tax liability being disputed is $24,000. The company has received a 90-day letter (Statutory Notice of Deficiency) from the IRS and is considering filing suit in either Tax Court or district court. Discuss the advantages and disadvantages of each for Butch Inc.
2. **(LO4)** Bob and Sherry have been married for 26 years, and Bob has been responsible for paying all the bills and handling the preparation of their tax return. He has not hired a CPA to review his work. Sherry has always allowed Bob to sign their return for her, trusting that the return had been prepared accurately. Bob and Sherry are filing for divorce in the current year, and Sherry has hired you to help her with the tax return. What exposure does Sherry have for previous tax return filings and tax liability?

Professional Development Skills

Communication Problem

Communication

1. (LO4) **The Appeals Process** Ian and Ima Taxpayer prepared and filed their own tax return for 2023 and were audited. To save money, they did not hire a CPA and represented themselves in front of the IRS during the office examination. The examination resulted in the Taxpayers' owing $8,200 in tax liability and penalties. They have hired you to review the Revenue Agent Report and resulting liability because they feel they do not owe this money. Ian and Ima would like you to explain the appeals process to them and discuss what their next course of action should be.

Ethics and Professional Responsibilities Problem

Ethics

1. (LO1, 3) **Inappropriate Tax Authority** Sly Specious, CPA, operates as a sole proprietor and prepares individual and business tax returns. He is very busy and sometimes cuts corners and does not exercise due diligence when preparing tax returns for his clients. Sly filed a tax return for a client in which he took a questionable position that is now being audited. It is discovered that Sly relied on an article in the *Journal of Taxation* to substantiate the position taken. What has Sly done wrong, and what could be the result?

In addition to the chapter content, see *Statements on Standards for Tax Services* at www.aicpa-cima.com/resources/landing/statements-on-standards-for-tax-services, and *Circular 230* at www.irs.gov/tax-professionals/office-of-professional-responsibility-and-circular-230.

Research Problem

Research

1. (LO3) **Incorrect Tax Preparer Advice** Flora and Diego Martinez own several rental properties and frequently sell the properties for other like-kind property. The Martinezes were considering selling a specific piece of property, but they were told by their adviser that they could sell it in a transaction that would be treated as tax-free. The Martinezes sold the property and omitted the gain from their return. The Martinezes' tax return was audited by the IRS. On reviewing the return, the IRS required the Martinezes to recognize the gain and pay the additional tax. The Martinezes were not happy with the result, and the tax preparer reimbursed the Martinezes for the additional tax liability from this transaction.

Is the indemnity payment received by the Martinezes from the tax preparer considered taxable income to the Martinezes? Research this issue and provide a conclusion. Hint: See Cosentino, T.C. Memo. 2014-186.

Appendix A

Tax Formula Items

Table of Contents

Tax Formula for Corporations

Corporate Income Tax Computation	
(Line references are for Form 1120, U.S. Corporation Income Tax Return page 1, unless noted otherwise.)	
Gross receipts or sales	(Line 1a)
Less: Returns and allowances	(Line 1b)
Net receipts or sales	(Line 1c)
Less: Cost of goods sold	(Line 2)
Gross profit	(Line 3)
Plus: Other income	(Lines 4–10)
Total income	(Line 11)
Less: Other business deductions	(Lines 12–27)
Taxable income before net operating loss (NOL) and special deduction	(Line 28)
Less: NOL	(Line 29a)
Less: Special deductions	(Line 29b)
Taxable income	(Line 30)
× Tax rate (21%)	
Gross tax	
Plus: Other taxes	
Less: Tax credits	
Total tax	(From Schedule J and Line 31)
Less: Estimated tax payments	(Line 33)
Tax due/overpayment	(Lines 35 and 36)

Income Tax Rates, Estates and Trusts (2025)

If taxable income is:

Over	But not over	The tax is:	Of the amount over
$ 0	$ 3,150	10%	$ 0
$ 3,150	$11,450	$ 315.00 + 24%	$ 3,150
$11,450	$15,650	$2,307.00 + 35%	$11,450
$15,650	—	$3,777.00 + 37%	$15,650

Unified Transfer Tax Rates (2025)

Tax Year 2025 Unified Tax Rate Schedule					
Column A Taxable amount (dollars) in excess of amount below	Column B But not exceeding amount below	Column C Maximum taxable amount for given tax rate (Column B minus Column A)	Column D Tax rate on amount in Column C	Column E Maximum amount of tax at this rate (Column C × Column D)	Column F Cumulative tax on amount shown in Column A
$ 0	$ 10,000	$ 10,000	18%	$ 1,800	$ 0
$ 10,000	$ 20,000	$ 10,000	20%	$ 2,000	$ 1,800
$ 20,000	$ 40,000	$ 20,000	22%	$ 4,400	$ 3,800
$ 40,000	$ 60,000	$ 20,000	24%	$ 4,800	$ 8,200
$ 60,000	$ 80,000	$ 20,000	26%	$ 5,200	$ 13,000
$ 80,000	$ 100,000	$ 20,000	28%	$ 5,600	$ 18,200
$ 100,000	$ 150,000	$ 50,000	30%	$15,000	$ 23,800
$ 150,000	$ 250,000	$100,000	32%	$32,000	$ 38,800
$ 250,000	$ 500,000	$250,000	34%	$85,000	$ 70,800
$ 500,000	$ 750,000	$250,000	37%	$92,500	$155,800
$ 750,000	$1,000,000	$250,000	39%	$97,500	$248,300
$1,000,000	—	No maximum	40%	No maximum	$345,800

Appendix B

Tax Forms

All tax forms can be obtained from the IRS website: www.irs.gov/forms-instructions. The IRS will begin releasing 2025 tax forms a few months before the filing season begins in January 2026.

Forms listed here are available to download at Wiley's book companion site.

Form **706**

(Rev. August 2019)

Department of the Treasury
Internal Revenue Service

United States Estate (and Generation-Skipping Transfer) Tax Return

▶ Estate of a citizen or resident of the United States (see instructions). To be filed for decedents dying after December 31, 2018.

▶ Go to *www.irs.gov/Form706* for instructions and the latest information.

OMB No. 1545-0015

Part 1—Decedent and Executor

1a	Decedent's first name and middle initial (and maiden name, if any)	**1b** Decedent's last name		**2** Decedent's social security no.
3a	City, town, or post office; county; state or province; country; and ZIP or foreign postal code	**3b** Year domicile established	**4** Date of birth	**5** Date of death
		6b Executor's address (number and street including apartment or suite no.; city, town, or post office; state or province; country; and ZIP or foreign postal code) and phone no.		
6a	Name of executor (see instructions)			
6c	Executor's social security number (see instructions)	Phone no.		
6d	If there are multiple executors, check here ☐ and attach a list showing the names, addresses, telephone numbers, and SSNs of the additional executors.			
7a	Name and location of court where will was probated or estate administered			**7b** Case number
8	If decedent died testate, check here ▶ ☐ and attach a certified copy of the will.	**9** If you extended the time to file this Form 706, check here ▶ ☐		
10	If Schedule R-1 is attached, check here ▶ ☐	**11** If you are estimating the value of assets included in the gross estate on line 1 pursuant to the special rule of Reg. section 20.2010-2(a)(7)(ii), check here ▶ ☐		

Part 2—Tax Computation

1	Total gross estate less exclusion (from Part 5—Recapitulation, item 13)			1	
2	Tentative total allowable deductions (from Part 5—Recapitulation, item 24)			2	
3a	Tentative taxable estate (subtract line 2 from line 1)			3a	
b	State death tax deduction			3b	
c	Taxable estate (subtract line 3b from line 3a)			3c	
4	Adjusted taxable gifts (see instructions)			4	
5	Add lines 3c and 4			5	
6	Tentative tax on the amount on line 5 from Table A in the instructions			6	
7	Total gift tax paid or payable (see instructions)			7	
8	Gross estate tax (subtract line 7 from line 6)			8	
9a	Basic exclusion amount	9a			
b	Deceased spousal unused exclusion (DSUE) amount from predeceased spouse(s), if any (from Section D, Part 6—Portability of Deceased Spousal Unused Exclusion)	9b			
c	Restored exclusion amount (see instructions)	9c			
d	Applicable exclusion amount (add lines 9a, 9b, and 9c)	9d			
e	Applicable credit amount (tentative tax on the amount in line 9d from Table A in the instructions)	9e			
10	Adjustment to applicable credit amount (May not exceed $6,000. See instructions.)	10			
11	Allowable applicable credit amount (subtract line 10 from line 9e)			11	
12	Subtract line 11 from line 8 (but do not enter less than zero)			12	
13	Credit for foreign death taxes (from Schedule P). (Attach Form(s) 706-CE.)	13			
14	Credit for tax on prior transfers (from Schedule Q)	14			
15	Total credits (add lines 13 and 14)			15	
16	Net estate tax (subtract line 15 from line 12)			16	
17	Generation-skipping transfer (GST) taxes payable (from Schedule R, Part 2, line 10)			17	
18	Total transfer taxes (add lines 16 and 17)			18	
19	Prior payments (explain in an attached statement)			19	
20	Balance due (or overpayment) (subtract line 19 from line 18)			20	

Under penalties of perjury, I declare that I have examined this return, including accompanying schedules and statements, and to the best of my knowledge and belief, it is true, correct, and complete. Declaration of preparer (other than the executor) is based on all information of which preparer has any knowledge.

Sign Here	▶ Signature of executor		▶ Date		
	▶ Signature of executor		▶ Date		
Paid Preparer Use Only	Print/Type preparer's name	Preparer's signature	Date	Check ☐ if self-employed	PTIN
	Firm's name ▶			Firm's EIN ▶	
	Firm's address ▶			Phone no.	

Form 706 (Rev. 8-2019)

Estate of:	**Decedent's social security number**

Part 3—Elections by the Executor

Note: For information on electing portability of the decedent's DSUE amount, including how to opt out of the election, see Part 6—Portability of Deceased Spousal Unused Exclusion.

Note: Some of the following elections may require the posting of bonds or liens.

	Please check "Yes" or "No" for each question. See instructions.		Yes	No
1	Do you elect alternate valuation?	1		
2	Do you elect special-use valuation? If "Yes," you must complete and attach Schedule A-1	2		
3	Do you elect to pay the taxes in installments as described in section 6166? If "Yes," you must attach the additional information described in the instructions. **Note: By electing section 6166 installment payments, you may be required to provide security for estate tax deferred under section 6166 and interest in the form of a surety bond or a section 6324A lien.**	3		
4	Do you elect to postpone the part of the taxes due to a reversionary or remainder interest as described in section 6163?	4		

Part 4—General Information

Note: Please attach the necessary supplemental documents. **You must attach the death certificate.** See instructions.

Authorization to receive confidential tax information under Reg. section 601.504(b)(2)(i); to act as the estate's representative before the IRS; and to make written or oral presentations on behalf of the estate:

Name of representative (print or type)	State	Address (number, street, and room or suite no., city, state, and ZIP code)

I declare that I am the ☐ attorney/ ☐ certified public accountant/ ☐ enrolled agent (check the applicable box) for the executor. I am not under suspension or disbarment from practice before the Internal Revenue Service and am qualified to practice in the state shown above.

Signature	CAF number	Date	Telephone number

1 Death certificate number and issuing authority (attach a copy of the death certificate to this return).

2 Decedent's business or occupation. If retired, check here ▶ ☐ and state decedent's former business or occupation.

3a Marital status of the decedent at time of death:

☐ Married ☐ Widow/widower ☐ Single ☐ Legally separated ☐ Divorced

3b For all prior marriages, list the name and SSN of the former spouse, the date the marriage ended, and whether the marriage ended by annulment, divorce, or death. Attach additional statements of the same size if necessary.

4a Surviving spouse's name	4b Social security number	4c Amount received (see instructions)

5 Individuals (other than the surviving spouse), trusts, or other estates who receive benefits from the estate (do not include charitable beneficiaries shown in Schedule O) (see instructions).

Name of individual, trust, or estate receiving $5,000 or more	Identifying number	Relationship to decedent	Amount (see instructions)
All unascertainable beneficiaries and those who receive less than $5,000 ▶			
Total			

	If you answer "Yes" to any of the following questions, you must attach additional information as described.		**Yes**	**No**
6	Is the estate filing a protective claim for refund? If "Yes," complete and attach two copies of Schedule PC for each claim.			
7	Does the gross estate contain any section 2044 property (qualified terminable interest property (QTIP) from a prior gift or estate)? See instructions			
8a	Have federal gift tax returns ever been filed? If "Yes," attach copies of the returns, if available, and furnish the following information.			
b	Period(s) covered	c Internal Revenue office(s) where filed		
9a	Was there any insurance on the decedent's life that is not included on the return as part of the gross estate?			
b	Did the decedent own any insurance on the life of another that is not included in the gross estate?			

Page 2

Form 706 (Rev. 8-2019)

Estate of: | **Decedent's social security number**

Part 4—General Information *(continued)*

If you answer "Yes" to any of the following questions, you must attach additional information as described.		**Yes**	**No**
10	Did the decedent at the time of death own any property as a joint tenant with right of survivorship in which **(a)** one or more of the other joint tenants was someone other than the decedent's spouse, and **(b)** less than the full value of the property is included on the return as part of the gross estate? If "Yes," you must complete and attach Schedule E		
11a	Did the decedent, at the time of death, own any interest in a partnership (for example, a family limited partnership), an unincorporated business, or a limited liability company; or own any stock in an inactive or closely held corporation?		
b	If "Yes," was the value of **any** interest owned (from above) discounted on this estate tax return? If "Yes," see the instructions on reporting the total accumulated or effective discounts taken on Schedule F or G		
12	Did the decedent make any transfer described in sections 2035, 2036, 2037, or 2038? See instructions. If "Yes," you must complete and attach Schedule G		
13a	Were there in existence at the time of the decedent's death any trusts created by the decedent during his or her lifetime?		
b	Were there in existence at the time of the decedent's death any trusts not created by the decedent under which the decedent possessed any power, beneficial interest, or trusteeship?		
c	Was the decedent receiving income from a trust created after October 22, 1986, by a parent or grandparent?		
	If "Yes," was there a GST taxable termination (under section 2612) on the death of the decedent?		
d	If there was a GST taxable termination (under section 2612), attach a statement to explain. Provide a copy of the trust or will creating the trust, and give the name, address, and phone number of the current trustee(s).		
e	Did the decedent at any time during his or her lifetime transfer or sell an interest in a partnership, limited liability company, or closely held corporation to a trust described in line 13a or 13b?		
	If "Yes," provide the EIN for this transferred/sold item. ▶		
14	Did the decedent ever possess, exercise, or release any general power of appointment? If "Yes," you must complete and attach Schedule H		
15	Did the decedent have an interest in or a signature or other authority over a financial account in a foreign country, such as a bank account, securities account, or other financial account?		
16	Was the decedent, immediately before death, receiving an annuity described in the "General" paragraph of the instructions for Schedule I or a private annuity? If "Yes," you must complete and attach Schedule I		
17	Was the decedent ever the beneficiary of a trust for which a deduction was claimed by the estate of a predeceased spouse under section 2056(b)(7) and which is not reported on this return? If "Yes," attach an explanation		

Part 5—Recapitulation.

Note: If estimating the value of one or more assets pursuant to the special rule of Reg. section 20.2010-2(a)(7)(ii), enter on both lines 10 and 23 the amount noted in the instructions for the corresponding range of values. See instructions for details.

Item no.	Gross estate		Alternate value	Value at date of death
1	Schedule A—Real Estate	1		
2	Schedule B—Stocks and Bonds	2		
3	Schedule C—Mortgages, Notes, and Cash	3		
4	Schedule D—Insurance on the Decedent's Life (attach Form(s) 712)	4		
5	Schedule E—Jointly Owned Property (attach Form(s) 712 for life insurance)	5		
6	Schedule F—Other Miscellaneous Property (attach Form(s) 712 for life insurance)	6		
7	Schedule G—Transfers During Decedent's Life (att. Form(s) 712 for life insurance)	7		
8	Schedule H—Powers of Appointment	8		
9	Schedule I—Annuities	9		
10	Estimated value of assets subject to the special rule of Reg. section 20.2010-2(a)(7)(ii)	10		
11	Total gross estate (add items 1 through 10)	11		
12	Schedule U—Qualified Conservation Easement Exclusion	12		
13	Total gross estate less exclusion (subtract item 12 from item 11). Enter here and on line 1 of Part 2—Tax Computation	13		

Item no.	Deductions		Amount
14	Schedule J—Funeral Expenses and Expenses Incurred in Administering Property Subject to Claims	14	
15	Schedule K—Debts of the Decedent	15	
16	Schedule K—Mortgages and Liens	16	
17	Total of items 14 through 16	17	
18	Allowable amount of deductions from item 17 (see the instructions for item 18 of the Recapitulation)	18	
19	Schedule L—Net Losses During Administration	19	
20	Schedule L—Expenses Incurred in Administering Property Not Subject to Claims	20	
21	Schedule M—Bequests, etc., to Surviving Spouse	21	
22	Schedule O—Charitable, Public, and Similar Gifts and Bequests	22	
23	Estimated value of deductible assets subject to the special rule of Reg. section 20.2010-2(a)(7)(ii)	23	
24	Tentative total allowable deductions (add items 18 through 23). Enter here and on line 2 of the Tax Computation	24	

Form 706 (Rev. 8-2019)

Estate of:	Decedent's social security number

Part 6—Portability of Deceased Spousal Unused Exclusion (DSUE)

Portability Election

A decedent with a surviving spouse elects portability of the DSUE amount, if any, by completing and timely filing this return. No further action is required to elect portability of the DSUE amount to allow the surviving spouse to use the decedent's DSUE amount.

Section A. Opting Out of Portability

The estate of a decedent with a surviving spouse may opt out of electing portability of the DSUE amount. Check here and do not complete Sections B and C of Part 6 only if the estate opts **NOT** to elect portability of the DSUE amount. ☐

Section B. Qualified Domestic Trust (QDOT)

	Yes	No
Are any assets of the estate being transferred to a QDOT?		

If "Yes," the DSUE amount portable to a surviving spouse (calculated in Section C, below) is preliminary and shall be redetermined at the time of the final distribution or other taxable event imposing estate tax under section 2056A. See instructions for more details.

Section C. DSUE Amount Portable to the Surviving Spouse (To be completed by the estate of a decedent making a portability election.)

Complete the following calculation to determine the DSUE amount that can be transferred to the surviving spouse.

1	Enter the amount from line 9d, Part 2—Tax Computation	1	
2	Reserved	2	
3	Enter the value of the cumulative lifetime gifts on which tax was paid or payable. See instructions	3	
4	Add lines 1 and 3	4	
5	Enter amount from line 10, Part 2—Tax Computation	5	
6	Divide amount on line 5 by 40% (0.40) (do not enter less than zero)	6	
7	Subtract line 6 from line 4	7	
8	Enter the amount from line 5, Part 2—Tax Computation	8	
9	Subtract line 8 from line 7 (do not enter less than zero)	9	
10	DSUE amount portable to surviving spouse (Enter lesser of line 9 or line 9a, Part 2—Tax Computation)	10	

Section D. DSUE Amount Received From Predeceased Spouse(s) (To be completed by the estate of a deceased surviving spouse with DSUE amount from predeceased spouse(s))

Provide the following information to determine the DSUE amount received from deceased spouses.

A Name of Deceased Spouse (dates of death after December 31, 2010, only)	B Date of Death (enter as mm/dd/yy)	C Portability Election Made? Yes	C No	D If "Yes," DSUE Amount Received From Spouse	E DSUE Amount Applied by Decedent to Lifetime Gifts	F Year of Form 709 Reporting Use of DSUE Amount Listed in col. E	G Remaining DSUE Amount, if any (subtract col. E from col. D)
Part 1 — DSUE RECEIVED FROM LAST DECEASED SPOUSE							
Part 2 — DSUE RECEIVED FROM OTHER PREDECEASED SPOUSE(S) AND USED BY DECEDENT							
Total (for all DSUE amounts from predeceased spouse(s) applied)							

Add the amount from Part 1, column D, and the total from Part 2, column E. Enter the result on line 9b, Part 2—Tax Computation ▶

Form **709**

Department of the Treasury
Internal Revenue Service

United States Gift (and Generation-Skipping Transfer) Tax Return

Go to *www.irs.gov/Form709* for instructions and the latest information.
(For gifts made during calendar year 2024)

OMB No. 1545-0020

2024

Part I General Information

1 Donor's first name and middle initial	2 Donor's last name	3 Donor's social security number
4 Address (number and street). If you have a P.O. box, see instructions.		5 Apt. no.
6 City, town, or post office. If you have a foreign address, also complete spaces below.	7 State	8 ZIP code
9 Foreign country name	10 Foreign province/state/county	11 Foreign postal code
12 Legal residence (domicile)	13 Citizenship (see instructions)	

		Yes	No
14	If the donor died during the year, check here ☐ and enter date of death ____________, ______		
15	If an amended return, check here ☐		
16	If you extended the time to file this Form 709, check here ☐		
17	Enter the total number of donees listed on Schedule A. Count each person only once ____________		
18a	Have you (the donor) previously filed a Form 709 (or 709-A) for any other year? If "No," skip line 18b		
b	Has your address changed since you last filed Form 709 (or 709-A)?		
19	**Gifts by spouses to third parties.** Did you and your spouse make gifts to third parties? See instructions. (If the answer is "Yes," complete Part III on page 2.)		
20	Have you applied a deceased spousal unused exclusion (DSUE) amount received from a predeceased spouse to a gift or gifts reported on this or a previous Form 709? If "Yes," complete Schedule C		
21	Does any gift or other transfer reported on this Form 709 include a digital asset (or a financial interest in a digital asset)? See instructions		

Part II Tax Computation

1	Enter the amount from Schedule A, Part 4, line 11	1	
2	Enter the amount from Schedule B, line 3	2	
3	Total taxable gifts. Add lines 1 and 2	3	
4	Tax computed on amount on line 3 (see *Table for Computing Gift Tax* in instructions)	4	
5	Tax computed on amount on line 2 (see *Table for Computing Gift Tax* in instructions)	5	
6	Balance. Subtract line 5 from line 4	6	
7	Applicable credit amount. If donor has DSUE amount from predeceased spouse(s) or Restored Exclusion Amount, enter amount from Schedule C, line 5; otherwise, see instructions	7	
8	Enter the applicable credit against tax allowable for all prior periods from Schedule B, line 1, col. (c)	8	
9	Balance. Subtract line 8 from line 7. Do not enter less than zero	9	
10	Enter 20% (0.20) of the amount allowed as a specific exemption for gifts made after September 8, 1976, and before January 1, 1977. See instructions	10	
11	Balance. Subtract line 10 from line 9. Do not enter less than zero	11	
12	Applicable credit. Enter the smaller of line 6 or line 11	12	
13	Credit for foreign gift taxes. See instructions	13	
14	Total credits. Add lines 12 and 13	14	
15	Balance. Subtract line 14 from line 6. Do not enter less than zero	15	
16	Generation-skipping transfer taxes from Schedule D, Part 3, col. (g), total	16	
17	**Total tax.** Add lines 15 and 16	17	
18	Gift and generation-skipping transfer taxes prepaid with extension of time to file	18	
19	If line 18 is less than line 17, enter **balance due**. See instructions	19	
20	If line 18 is greater than line 17, enter **amount to be refunded**	20	

Sign Here

Under penalties of perjury, I declare that I have examined this return, including any accompanying schedules and statements, and to the best of my knowledge and belief, it is true, correct, and complete. Declaration of preparer (other than donor) is based on all information of which preparer has any knowledge.

May the IRS discuss this return with the preparer shown below? See instructions. ☐ **Yes** ☐ **No**

Signature of donor | Date

Paid Preparer Use Only

Preparer's name	Preparer's signature	Date	Check ☐ if self-employed	PTIN
Firm's name			Firm's EIN	
Firm's address			Phone no.	

For Disclosure, Privacy Act, and Paperwork Reduction Act Notice, see the instructions for this form. Cat. No. 16783M Form **709** (2024)

Form 709 (2024) Page **2**

Part III Spouse's Consent on Gifts to Third Parties

		Yes	No
1	**Gifts by spouses to third parties.** Do you consent to have the gifts (including generation-skipping transfers) made by you and by your spouse to third parties during the calendar year considered as made one-half by each of you? See instructions. (If the answer is "Yes," the following information must be furnished. **If the answer is "No," skip lines 2–7.**)		
2	Name of consenting spouse		
3	SSN of consenting spouse		
4	Were you married to one another during the entire calendar year? See instructions		
5	If line 4 is "No," check whether ☐ married ☐ divorced or ☐ widowed/deceased, and give date. See instructions		
6	Will a gift tax return for this year be filed by your spouse? If "Yes," mail both returns in the same envelope		
7	**Consent of Spouse.** Have you obtained required spousal consent for gifts made to third parties to be considered as made one-half by each spouse? If "Yes," **you must attach a Notice of Consent**. See instructions		

Form **709** (2024)

Click on the question-mark icons to display help windows.
The information provided will enable you to file a more complete return and reduce the chances the IRS will need to contact you.

Form **990-EZ**

Department of the Treasury
Internal Revenue Service

Short Form
Return of Organization Exempt From Income Tax

Under section 501(c), 527, or 4947(a)(1) of the Internal Revenue Code (except private foundations)
Do not enter social security numbers on this form, as it may be made public.
Go to *www.irs.gov/Form990EZ* for instructions and the latest information.

OMB No. 1545-0047
2024
Open to Public Inspection

A For the 2024 calendar year, or tax year beginning ______, 2024, and ending ______, 20__

B Check if applicable:	C Name of organization		D Employer identification number
☐ Address change ☐ Name change	Number and street (or P.O. box if mail is not delivered to street address)	Room/suite	E Telephone number
☐ Initial return ☐ Final return/terminated ☐ Amended return ☐ Application pending	City or town, state or province, country, and ZIP or foreign postal code		F Group Exemption Number

G Accounting Method: ☐ Cash ☐ Accrual Other (specify): ______

I Website: ______

J Tax-exempt status (check only one) – ☐ 501(c)(3) ☐ 501(c) ( ) (insert no.) ☐ 4947(a)(1) or ☐ 527

H Check ☐ if the organization is **not** required to attach Schedule B (Form 990).

K Form of organization: ☐ Corporation ☐ Trust ☐ Association ☐ Other: ______

L Add lines 5b, 6c, and 7b to line 9 to determine gross receipts. If gross receipts are $200,000 or more, or if total assets (Part II, column (B)) are $500,000 or more, file Form 990 instead of Form 990-EZ . . . . $

Part I Revenue, Expenses, and Changes in Net Assets or Fund Balances (see the instructions for Part I)

Check if the organization used Schedule O to respond to any question in this Part I . . . . ☐

Section	Line	Description	Sub-line	Sub-amount	Line	Amount
Revenue	1	Contributions, gifts, grants, and similar amounts received			1	
	2	Program service revenue including government fees and contracts			2	
	3	Membership dues and assessments			3	
	4	Investment income			4	
	5a	Gross amount from sale of assets other than inventory	5a			
	b	Less: cost or other basis and sales expenses	5b			
	c	Gain or (loss) from sale of assets other than inventory (subtract line 5b from line 5a)			5c	
	6	Gaming and fundraising events:				
	a	Gross income from gaming (attach Schedule G if greater than $15,000)	6a			
	b	Gross income from fundraising events (not including $ ______ of contributions from fundraising events reported on line 1) (attach Schedule G if the sum of such gross income and contributions exceeds $15,000) . .	6b			
	c	Less: direct expenses from gaming and fundraising events . . .	6c			
	d	Net income or (loss) from gaming and fundraising events (add lines 6a and 6b and subtract line 6c)			6d	
	7a	Gross sales of inventory, less returns and allowances	7a			
	b	Less: cost of goods sold	7b			
	c	Gross profit or (loss) from sales of inventory (subtract line 7b from line 7a)			7c	
	8	Other revenue (describe in Schedule O)			8	
	9	**Total revenue.** Add lines 1, 2, 3, 4, 5c, 6d, 7c, and 8			9	
Expenses	10	Grants and similar amounts paid (list in Schedule O)			10	
	11	Benefits paid to or for members			11	
	12	Salaries, other compensation, and employee benefits			12	
	13	Professional fees and other payments to independent contractors			13	
	14	Occupancy, rent, utilities, and maintenance			14	
	15	Printing, publications, postage, and shipping			15	
	16	Other expenses (describe in Schedule O)			16	
	17	**Total expenses.** Add lines 10 through 16			17	
Net Assets	18	Excess or (deficit) for the year (subtract line 17 from line 9)			18	
	19	Net assets or fund balances at beginning of year (from line 27, column (A)) (must agree with end-of-year figure reported on prior year's return)			19	
	20	Other changes in net assets or fund balances (explain in Schedule O)			20	
	21	Net assets or fund balances at end of year. Combine lines 18 through 20			21	

For Paperwork Reduction Act Notice, see the separate instructions. Cat. No. 10642I Form **990-EZ** (2024)

Form 990-EZ (2024) Page 2

Part II **Balance Sheets** (see the instructions for Part II)

Check if the organization used Schedule O to respond to any question in this Part II . . . . ☐

		(A) Beginning of year		(B) End of year
22	Cash, savings, and investments		22	
23	Land and buildings		23	
24	Other assets (describe in Schedule O)		24	
25	**Total assets**		25	
26	**Total liabilities** (describe in Schedule O)		26	
27	**Net assets or fund balances** (line 27 of column (B) **must** agree with line 21)		27	

Part III **Statement of Program Service Accomplishments** (see the instructions for Part III)

Check if the organization used Schedule O to respond to any question in this Part III . . ☐

What is the organization's primary exempt purpose?

Describe the organization's program service accomplishments for each of its three largest program services, as measured by expenses. In a clear and concise manner, describe the services provided, the number of persons benefited, and other relevant information for each program title.

			Expenses (Required for section 501(c)(3) and 501(c)(4) organizations; optional for others.)
28	(Grants $) If this amount includes foreign grants, check here . . . . . ☐	28a	
29	(Grants $) If this amount includes foreign grants, check here . . . . . ☐	29a	
30	(Grants $) If this amount includes foreign grants, check here . . . . . ☐	30a	
31	Other program services (describe in Schedule O) (Grants $) If this amount includes foreign grants, check here . . . . . ☐	31a	
32	**Total program service expenses** (add lines 28a through 31a)	32	

Part IV **List of Officers, Directors, Trustees, and Key Employees** (list each one even if not compensated—see the instructions for Part IV)

Check if the organization used Schedule O to respond to any question in this Part IV . . . . ☐

(a) Name and title	(b) Average hours per week devoted to position	(c) Reportable compensation (Forms W-2/1099-MISC/ 1099-NEC) (if not paid, enter -0-)	(d) Health benefits, contributions to employee benefit plans, and deferred compensation	(e) Estimated amount of other compensation

Form **990-EZ** (2024)

Form 990-EZ (2024) Page 3

Part V **Other Information** (Note the Schedule A and personal benefit contract statement requirements in the instructions for Part V.) Check if the organization used Schedule O to respond to any question in this Part V . ☐

		Line	Yes	No
33	Did the organization engage in any significant activity not previously reported to the IRS? If "Yes," provide a detailed description of each activity in Schedule O	33		
34	Were any significant changes made to the organizing or governing documents? If "Yes," attach a conformed copy of the amended documents if they reflect a change to the organization's name. Otherwise, explain the change on Schedule O. See instructions	34		
35a	Did the organization have unrelated business gross income of $1,000 or more during the year from business activities (such as those reported on lines 2, 6a, and 7a, among others)?	35a		
b	If "Yes" to line 35a, has the organization filed a Form 990-T for the year? If "No," provide an explanation in Schedule O	35b		
c	Was the organization a section 501(c)(4), 501(c)(5), or 501(c)(6) organization subject to section 6033(e) notice, reporting, and proxy tax requirements during the year? If "Yes," complete Schedule C, Part III	35c		
36	Did the organization undergo a liquidation, dissolution, termination, or significant disposition of net assets during the year? If "Yes," complete applicable parts of Schedule N	36		
37a	Enter amount of political expenditures, direct or indirect, as described in the instructions **37a**			
b	Did the organization file **Form 1120-POL** for this year?	37b		
38a	Did the organization borrow from, or make any loans to, any officer, director, trustee, or key employee; **or** were any such loans made in a prior year and still outstanding at the end of the tax year covered by this return?	38a		
b	If "Yes," complete Schedule L, Part II, and enter the total amount involved **38b**			
39	Section 501(c)(7) organizations. Enter:			
a	Initiation fees and capital contributions included on line 9 **39a**			
b	Gross receipts, included on line 9, for public use of club facilities **39b**			
40a	Section 501(c)(3) organizations. Enter amount of tax imposed on the organization during the year under: section 4911: ________; section 4912: ________; section 4955: ________			
b	Section 501(c)(3), 501(c)(4), and 501(c)(29) organizations. Did the organization engage in any section 4958 excess benefit transaction during the year, or did it engage in an excess benefit transaction in a prior year that has not been reported on any of its prior Forms 990 or 990-EZ? If "Yes," complete Schedule L, Part I	40b		
c	Section 501(c)(3), 501(c)(4), and 501(c)(29) organizations. Enter amount of tax imposed on organization managers or disqualified persons during the year under sections 4912, 4955, and 4958 ________			
d	Section 501(c)(3), 501(c)(4), and 501(c)(29) organizations. Enter amount of tax on line 40c reimbursed by the organization ________			
e	All organizations. At any time during the tax year, was the organization a party to a prohibited tax shelter transaction? If "Yes," complete Form 8886-T	40e		

41 List the states with which a copy of this return is filed: ________

42a The organization's books are in care of: ________ Telephone no. ________
Located at: ________ ZIP + 4 ________

		Line	Yes	No
b	At any time during the calendar year, did the organization have an interest in or a signature or other authority over a financial account in a foreign country (such as a bank account, securities account, or other financial account)? If "Yes," enter the name of the foreign country: ________ See the instructions for exceptions and filing requirements for FinCEN Form 114, Report of Foreign Bank and Financial Accounts (FBAR).	42b		
c	At any time during the calendar year, did the organization maintain an office outside the United States? If "Yes," enter the name of the foreign country: ________	42c		

43 Section 4947(a)(1) nonexempt charitable trusts filing Form 990-EZ in lieu of **Form 1041**—Check here ☐
and enter the amount of tax-exempt interest received or accrued during the tax year **43**

		Line	Yes	No
44a	Did the organization maintain any donor advised funds during the year? If "Yes," Form 990 must be completed instead of Form 990-EZ	44a		
b	Did the organization operate one or more hospital facilities during the year? If "Yes," Form 990 must be completed instead of Form 990-EZ	44b		
c	Did the organization receive any payments for indoor tanning services during the year?	44c		
d	If "Yes" to line 44c, has the organization filed a Form 720 to report these payments? If "No," provide an explanation in Schedule O	44d		
45a	Did the organization have a controlled entity within the meaning of section 512(b)(13)?	45a		
b	Did the organization receive any payment from or engage in any transaction with a controlled entity within the meaning of section 512(b)(13)? If "Yes," Form 990 and Schedule R may need to be completed instead of Form 990-EZ. See instructions	45b		

Form **990-EZ** (2024)

			Yes	No
46	Did the organization engage, directly or indirectly, in political campaign activities on behalf of or in opposition to candidates for public office? If "Yes," complete Schedule C, Part I	**46**		

Part VI **Section 501(c)(3) Organizations Only**

All section 501(c)(3) organizations must answer questions 47–49b and 52, and complete the tables for lines 50 and 51.

Check if the organization used Schedule O to respond to any question in this Part VI ☐

			Yes	No
47	Did the organization engage in lobbying activities or have a section 501(h) election in effect during the tax year? If "Yes," complete Schedule C, Part II	**47**		
48	Is the organization a school as described in section 170(b)(1)(A)(ii)? If "Yes," complete Schedule E	**48**		
49a	Did the organization make any transfers to an exempt non-charitable related organization?	**49a**		
b	If "Yes," was the related organization a section 527 organization?	**49b**		

50 Complete this table for the organization's five highest compensated employees (other than officers, directors, trustees, and key employees) who each received more than $100,000 of compensation from the organization. If there is none, enter "None."

(a) Name and title of each employee	**(b)** Average hours per week devoted to position	**(c)** Reportable compensation (Forms W-2/1099-MISC/ 1099-NEC)	**(d)** Health benefits, contributions to employee benefit plans, and deferred compensation	**(e)** Estimated amount of other compensation

f Total number of other employees paid over $100,000 ______

51 Complete this table for the organization's five highest compensated independent contractors who each received more than $100,000 of compensation from the organization. If there is none, enter "None."

(a) Name and business address of each independent contractor	**(b)** Type of service	**(c)** Compensation

d Total number of other independent contractors each receiving over $100,000 ______

52 Did the organization complete Schedule A? **Note:** All section 501(c)(3) organizations must attach a completed Schedule A ☐ **Yes** ☐ **No**

Under penalties of perjury, I declare that I have examined this return, including accompanying schedules and statements, and to the best of my knowledge and belief, it is true, correct, and complete. Declaration of preparer (other than officer) is based on all information of which preparer has any knowledge.

Sign Here	Signature of officer	Date
	Type or print name and title	

Paid Preparer Use Only	Print/Type preparer's name	Preparer's signature	Date	Check ☐ if self-employed	PTIN
	Firm's name			Firm's EIN	
	Firm's address			Phone no.	

May the IRS discuss this return with the preparer shown above? See instructions ☐ **Yes** ☐ **No**

Form **990-T**

Department of the Treasury
Internal Revenue Service

Exempt Organization Business Income Tax Return
(and proxy tax under section 6033(e))

For calendar year 2024 or other tax year beginning __________, 2024, and ending __________, 20 ____

Go to *www.irs.gov/Form990T* for instructions and the latest information.
Do not enter SSN numbers on this form as it may be made public if your organization is an 501(c)(3).

OMB No. 1545-0047

2024

Open to Public Inspection for 501(c)(3) Organizations Only

A ☐ Check box if address changed.

B Exempt under section
☐ 501( )( )
☐ 408(e) ☐ 220(e)
☐ 408A ☐ 530(a)
☐ 529(a) ☐ 529A

Print or Type

Name of organization (☐ Check box if name changed and see instructions.)

Number, street, and room or suite no. If a P.O. box, see instructions.

City or town, state or province, country, and ZIP or foreign postal code

C Book value of all assets at end of year . . . .

D Employer identification number

E Group exemption number (see instructions)

F ☐ Check box if an amended return.

G Check organization type ☐ 501(c) corporation ☐ 501(c) trust ☐ 401(a) trust ☐ Other trust ☐ State college/university
☐ 6417(d)(1)(A) Applicable entity

H Check if filing only to claim ☐ Credit from Form 8941 ☐ Refund shown on Form 2439 ☐ Elective payment amount from Form 3800

I Check if a 501(c)(3) organization filing a consolidated return with a 501(c)(2) titleholding corporation . . . . ☐

J Enter the number of attached Schedules A (Form 990-T) . . . .

K During the tax year, was the corporation a subsidiary in an affiliated group or a parent-subsidiary controlled group? ☐ **Yes** ☐ **No**
If "Yes," enter the name and identifying number of the parent corporation

L The books are in care of Telephone number

Part I Total Unrelated Business Taxable Income

1	Total of unrelated business taxable income computed from all unrelated trades or businesses (see instructions)	1	
2	Reserved	2	
3	Add lines 1 and 2	3	
4	Charitable contributions (see instructions for limitation rules)	4	
5	Total unrelated business taxable income before net operating losses. Subtract line 4 from line 3 . .	5	
6	Deduction for net operating loss. See instructions	6	
7	Total of unrelated business taxable income before specific deduction and section 199A deduction. Subtract line 6 from line 5	7	
8	Specific deduction (generally $1,000, but see instructions for exceptions)	8	
9	**Trusts.** Section 199A deduction. See instructions	9	
10	**Total deductions.** Add lines 8 and 9	10	
11	**Unrelated business taxable income.** Subtract line 10 from line 7. If line 10 is greater than line 7, enter zero	11	

Part II Tax Computation

1	**Organizations taxable as corporations.** Multiply Part I, line 11, by 21% (0.21)	1	
2	**Trusts taxable at trust rates.** See instructions for tax computation. Income tax on the amount on Part I, line 11, from: ☐ Tax rate schedule or ☐ Schedule D (Form 1041)	2	
3	**Proxy tax.** See instructions	3	
4a	Amount from Form 4255, Part I , line 3, column (q)	4a	
b	Other tax amounts. See instructions	4b	
5	Alternative minimum tax	5	
6	**Tax on noncompliant facility income.** See instructions	6	
7	**Total.** Add lines 3 through 6 to line 1 or 2, whichever applies	7	

Part III Tax and Payments

1a	Foreign tax credit (corporations attach Form 1118; trusts attach Form 1116) .	1a			
b	Other credits (see instructions)	1b			
c	General business credit. Attach Form 3800 (see instructions)	1c			
d	Credit for prior-year minimum tax (attach Form 8801 or 8827)	1d			
e	**Total credits.** Add lines 1a through 1d			1e	
2	Subtract line 1e from Part II, line 7			2	
3a	Amount from Form 4255, Part I, line 3, column (r) (see instructions)	3a			
b	Amount due from Form 8611	3b			
c	Amount due from Form 8697	3c			
d	Amount due from Form 8866	3d			
e	Other amounts due (see instructions)	3e			
f	Total amounts due. Add lines 3a through 3e			3f	
4	**Total tax.** Add lines 2 and 3f (see instructions). ☐ Check if includes tax previously deferred under section 1294. Enter tax amount here			4	

Form 990-T (2024) Page **2**

Part III Tax and Payments *(continued)*

5	Current net 965 tax liability paid from Form 965-A, Part II, column (k)			5	
6a	Payments: Preceding year's overpayment credited to the current year	6a			
b	Current year's estimated tax payments. Check if section 643(g) election applies ☐	6b			
c	Tax deposited with Form 8868	6c			
d	Foreign organizations: Tax paid or withheld at source (see instructions)	6d			
e	Backup withholding (see instructions)	6e			
f	Credit for small employer health insurance premiums (attach Form 8941)	6f			
g	Elective payment election amount from Form 3800	6g			
h	Payment from Form 2439	6h			
i	Credit from Form 4136	6i			
j	Other (see instructions)	6j			
7	**Total payments.** Add lines 6a through 6j			7	
8	Estimated tax penalty (see instructions). Check if Form 2220 is attached ☐			8	
9	**Tax due.** If line 7 is smaller than the total of lines 4, 5, and 8, enter amount owed			9	
10	**Overpayment.** If line 7 is larger than the total of lines 4, 5, and 8, enter amount overpaid			10	
11	Enter the amount of line 10 you want: **Credited to 2025 estimated tax** **Refunded**			11	

Part IV Statements Regarding Certain Activities and Other Information (see instructions)

		Yes	No
1	At any time during the 2024 calendar year, did the organization have an interest in or a signature or other authority over a financial account (bank, securities, or other) in a foreign country? If "Yes," the organization may have to file FinCEN Form 114, Report of Foreign Bank and Financial Accounts. If "Yes," enter the name of the foreign country here ________		
2	During the tax year, did the organization receive a distribution from, or was it the grantor of, or transferor to, a foreign trust? If "Yes," see instructions for other forms the organization may have to file.		
3	Enter the amount of tax-exempt interest received or accrued during the tax year $________		
4	Enter available pre-2018 NOL carryovers here $________. Do not include any post-2017 NOL carryover shown on Schedule A (Form 990-T). Don't reduce the NOL carryover shown here by any deduction reported on Part I, line 6.		
5	Post-2017 NOL carryovers. Enter the Business Activity Code and available post-2017 NOL carryovers. Don't reduce the amounts shown below by any NOL claimed on any Schedule A, Part II, line 17, for the tax year. See instructions.		

Business Activity Code	Available post-2017 NOL carryover
	$
	$
	$
	$

		Yes	No
6a	Reserved for future use		
b	Reserved for future use		

Part V Supplemental Information

Provide any additional information. See instructions.

____

Sign Here

Under penalties of perjury, I declare that I have examined this return, including accompanying schedules and statements, and to the best of my knowledge and belief, it is true, correct, and complete. Declaration of preparer (other than taxpayer) is based on all information of which preparer has any knowledge.

Signature of officer	Date	Title	May the IRS discuss this return with the preparer shown below (see instructions)? ☐ **Yes** ☐ **No**

Paid Preparer Use Only

Print/Type preparer's name	Preparer's signature	Date	Check ☐ if self-employed	PTIN
Firm's name			Firm's EIN	
Firm's address			Phone no.	

SCHEDULE A (Form 990-T)

Department of the Treasury
Internal Revenue Service

Unrelated Business Taxable Income From an Unrelated Trade or Business

Go to *www.irs.gov/Form990T* for instructions and the latest information.

Do not enter SSN numbers on this form as it may be made public if your organization is a 501(c)(3).

OMB No. 1545-0047

2024

Open to Public Inspection for 501(c)(3) Organizations Only

A Name of the organization

B Employer identification number

C Unrelated business activity code (see instructions) . . . .

D Sequence: of

E Describe the unrelated trade or business

Part I Unrelated Trade or Business Income		(A) Income	(B) Expenses	(C) Net
1a Gross receipts or sales				
b Less returns and allowances ____ c Balance	1c			
2 Cost of goods sold (Part III, line 8)	2			
3 Gross profit. Subtract line 2 from line 1c	3			
4a Capital gain net income (attach Schedule D (Form 1041 or Form 1120)). See instructions	4a			
b Net gain (loss) (Form 4797) (attach Form 4797). See instructions	4b			
c Capital loss deduction for trusts	4c			
5 Income (loss) from a partnership or an S corporation (attach statement)	5			
6 Rent income (Part IV)	6			
7 Unrelated debt-financed income (Part V)	7			
8 Interest, annuities, royalties, and rents from a controlled organization (Part VI)	8			
9 Investment income of section 501(c)(7), (9), or (17) organizations (Part VII)	9			
10 Exploited exempt activity income (Part VIII)	10			
11 Advertising income (Part IX)	11			
12 Other income (see instructions; attach statement)	12			
13 **Total.** Combine lines 3 through 12	13			

Part II Deductions Not Taken Elsewhere. See instructions for limitations on deductions. Deductions must be directly connected with the unrelated business income.

1 Compensation of officers, directors, and trustees (Part X)			1	
2 Salaries and wages			2	
3 Repairs and maintenance			3	
4 Bad debts			4	
5 Interest (attach statement). See instructions			5	
6 Taxes and licenses			6	
7 Depreciation (attach Form 4562). See instructions	7			
8 Less depreciation claimed in Part III and elsewhere on return	8a		8b	
9 Depletion			9	
10 Contributions to deferred compensation plans			10	
11 Employee benefit programs			11	
12 Excess exempt expenses (Part VIII)			12	
13 Excess readership costs (Part IX)			13	
14 Other deductions (attach statement)			14	
15 **Total deductions.** Add lines 1 through 14			15	
16 Unrelated business income before net operating loss deduction. Subtract line 15 from Part I, line 13, column (C)			16	
17 Deduction for net operating loss. See instructions			17	
18 **Unrelated business taxable income.** Subtract line 17 from line 16			18	

For Paperwork Reduction Act Notice, see instructions. Cat. No. 74036O **Schedule A (Form 990-T) 2024**

Schedule A (Form 990-T) 2024 Page 2

Part III Cost of Goods Sold

Enter method of inventory valuation

1	Inventory at beginning of year	1	
2	Purchases	2	
3	Cost of labor	3	
4	Additional section 263A costs (attach statement)	4	
5	Other costs (attach statement)	5	
6	**Total.** Add lines 1 through 5	6	
7	Inventory at end of year	7	
8	**Cost of goods sold.** Subtract line 7 from line 6. Enter here and in Part I, line 2	8	

9 Do the rules of section 263A (with respect to property produced or acquired for resale) apply to the organization? ☐ **Yes** ☐ **No**

Part IV Rent Income (From Real Property and Personal Property Leased With Real Property)

1 Description of property (property street address, city, state, ZIP code). Check if a dual-use. See instructions.

A ☐

B ☐

C ☐

D ☐

		A	B	C	D
2	Rent received or accrued				
a	From personal property (if the percentage of rent for personal property is more than 10% but not more than 50%)				
b	From real and personal property (if the percentage of rent for personal property exceeds 50% or if the rent is based on profit or income)				
c	Total rents received or accrued by property. Add lines 2a and 2b, columns A through D				

3 Total rents received or accrued. Add line 2c, columns A through D. Enter here and on Part I, line 6, column (A)

		A	B	C	D
4	Deductions directly connected with the income in lines 2a and 2b (attach statement)				

5 **Total deductions.** Add line 4, columns A through D. Enter here and on Part I, line 6, column (B)

Part V Unrelated Debt-Financed Income (see instructions)

1 Description of debt-financed property (street address, city, state, ZIP code). Check if a dual-use. See instructions.

A ☐

B ☐

C ☐

D ☐

		A	B	C	D
2	Gross income from or allocable to debt-financed property				
3	Deductions directly connected with or allocable to debt-financed property				
a	Straight line depreciation (attach statement)				
b	Other deductions (attach statement)				
c	Total deductions (add lines 3a and 3b, columns A through D)				
4	Amount of average acquisition debt on or allocable to debt-financed property (attach statement)				
5	Average adjusted basis of or allocable to debt-financed property (attach statement)				
6	Divide line 4 by line 5	%	%	%	%
7	Gross income reportable. Multiply line 2 by line 6				

8 **Total gross income** (add line 7, columns A through D). Enter here and on Part I, line 7, column (A)

		A	B	C	D
9	Allocable deductions. Multiply line 3c by line 6				

10 **Total allocable deductions.** Add line 9, columns A through D. Enter here and on Part I, line 7, column (B)

11 **Total dividends — received deductions** included in line 10

Part VI Interest, Annuities, Royalties, and Rents From Controlled Organizations (see instructions)

		Exempt Controlled Organizations			
1. Name of controlled organization	**2.** Employer identification number	**3.** Net unrelated income (loss) (see instructions)	**4.** Total of specified payments made	**5.** Part of column 4 that is included in the controlling organization's gross income	**6.** Deductions directly connected with income in column 5
(1)					
(2)					
(3)					
(4)					

Nonexempt Controlled Organizations				
7. Taxable income	**8.** Net unrelated income (loss) (see instructions)	**9.** Total of specified payments made	**10.** Part of column 9 that is included in the controlling organization's gross income	**11.** Deductions directly connected with income in column 10
(1)				
(2)				
(3)				
(4)				
Totals			Add columns 5 and 10. Enter here and on Part I, line 8, column (A).	Add columns 6 and 11. Enter here and on Part I, line 8, column (B).

Part VII Investment Income of a Section 501(c)(7), (9), or (17) Organization (see instructions)

1. Description of income	**2.** Amount of income	**3.** Deductions directly connected (attach statement)	**4.** Set-asides (attach statement)	**5. Total deductions and set-asides** (add columns 3 and 4)
(1)				
(2)				
(3)				
(4)				
Totals	Add amounts in column 2. Enter here and on Part I, line 9, column (A).			Add amounts in column 5. Enter here and on Part I, line 9, column (B).

Part VIII Exploited Exempt Activity Income, Other Than Advertising Income (see instructions)

1	Description of exploited activity:		
2	Gross unrelated business income from trade or business. Enter here and on Part I, line 10, column (A)	2	
3	Expenses directly connected with production of unrelated business income. Enter here and on Part I, line 10, column (B)	3	
4	Net income (loss) from unrelated trade or business. Subtract line 3 from line 2. If a gain, complete lines 5 through 7	4	
5	Gross income from activity that is not unrelated business income	5	
6	Expenses attributable to income entered on line 5	6	
7	Excess exempt expenses. Subtract line 5 from line 6, but do not enter more than the amount on line 4. Enter here and on Part II, line 12	7	

Schedule A (Form 990-T) 2024 Page **4**

Part IX Advertising Income

1 Name(s) of periodical(s). Check box if reporting two or more periodicals on a consolidated basis.

A ☐
B ☐
C ☐
D ☐

Enter amounts for each periodical listed above in the corresponding column.

		A	B	C	D
2	Gross advertising income				
a	Add columns A through D. Enter here and on Part I, line 11, column (A)				
3	Direct advertising costs by periodical				
a	Add columns A through D. Enter here and on Part I, line 11, column (B)				
4	Advertising gain (loss). Subtract line 3 from line 2. For any column in line 4 showing a gain, complete lines 5 through 8. For any column in line 4 showing a loss or zero, do not complete lines 5 through 7, and enter -0- on line 8				
5	Readership costs				
6	Circulation income				
7	Excess readership costs. If line 6 is less than line 5, subtract line 6 from line 5. If line 5 is less than line 6, enter -0-				
8	Excess readership costs allowed as a deduction. For each column showing a gain on line 4, enter the lesser of line 4 or line 7				
a	Add line 8, columns A through D. Enter the greater of the line 8a columns total or -0- here and on Part II, line 13				

Part X Compensation of Officers, Directors, and Trustees (see instructions)

	1. Name	**2.** Title	**3.** Percentage of time devoted to business	**4.** Compensation attributable to unrelated business
(1)			%	
(2)			%	
(3)			%	
(4)			%	
Total. Enter here and on Part II, line 1				

Part XI Supplemental Information (see instructions)

Schedule A (Form 990-T) 2024

Form **1041** Department of the Treasury—Internal Revenue Service
U.S. Income Tax Return for Estates and Trusts
Go to *www.irs.gov/Form1041* for instructions and the latest information.
2024 OMB No. 1545-0092

A Check all that apply:
- ☐ Decedent's estate
- ☐ Simple trust
- ☐ Complex trust
- ☐ Qualified disability trust
- ☐ ESBT (S portion only)
- ☐ Grantor type trust
- ☐ Bankruptcy estate—Ch. 7
- ☐ Bankruptcy estate—Ch. 11
- ☐ Pooled income fund

For calendar year 2024 or fiscal year beginning , 2024, and ending , 20

Name of estate or trust (If a grantor type trust, see the instructions.)

Name and title of fiduciary

Number, street, and room or suite no. (If a P.O. box, see the instructions.)

City or town, state or province, country, and ZIP or foreign postal code

C Employer identification number

D Date entity created

E Nonexempt charitable and split-interest trusts, check applicable box(es). See instructions.
- ☐ Described in sec. 4947(a)(1). Check here if not a private foundation . . ☐
- ☐ Described in sec. 4947(a)(2)

B Number of Schedules K-1 attached (see instructions)

F Check applicable boxes: ☐ Initial return ☐ Final return ☐ Amended return ☐ Net operating loss carryback ☐ Change in trust's name ☐ Change in fiduciary ☐ Change in fiduciary's name ☐ Change in fiduciary's address

G Check here if the estate or filing trust made a section 645 election . . . . ☐ Trust TIN

Income	1	Interest income	1	
	2a	Total ordinary dividends	2a	
	b	Qualified dividends allocable to: (1) Beneficiaries ______ (2) Estate or trust ______		
	3	Business income or (loss). Attach Schedule C (Form 1040)	3	
	4	Capital gain or (loss). Attach Schedule D (Form 1041)	4	
	5	Rents, royalties, partnerships, other estates and trusts, etc. Attach Schedule E (Form 1040)	5	
	6	Farm income or (loss). Attach Schedule F (Form 1040)	6	
	7	Ordinary gain or (loss). Attach Form 4797	7	
	8	Other income. List type and amount	8	
	9	**Total income.** Combine lines 1, 2a, and 3 through 8	9	
Deductions	10	Interest. Check if Form 4952 is attached ☐	10	
	11	Taxes	11	
	12	Fiduciary fees. If only a portion is deductible under section 67(e), see instructions	12	
	13	Charitable deduction (from Schedule A, line 7)	13	
	14	Attorney, accountant, and return preparer fees. If only a portion is deductible under section 67(e), see instructions	14	
	15a	Other deductions (attach schedule). See instructions for deductions allowable under section 67(e)	15a	
	b	Net operating loss deduction. See instructions	15b	
	16	Add lines 10 through 15b	16	
	17	Adjusted total income or (loss). Subtract line 16 from line 9 17		
	18	Income distribution deduction (from Schedule B, line 15). Attach Schedules K-1 (Form 1041)	18	
	19	Estate tax deduction including certain generation-skipping taxes (attach computation)	19	
	20	Qualified business income deduction. Attach Form 8995 or 8995-A	20	
	21	Exemption	21	
	22	Add lines 18 through 21	22	
Tax and Payments	23	Taxable income. Subtract line 22 from line 17. If a loss, see instructions	23	
	24	**Total tax** (from Schedule G, Part I, line 9)	24	
	25	Current year net 965 tax liability paid from Form 965-A, Part II, column (k) (see instructions)	25	
	26	**Total payments** (from Schedule G, Part II, line 19)	26	
	27	Estimated tax penalty. See instructions	27	
	28	**Tax due.** If line 26 is smaller than the total of lines 24, 25, and 27, enter amount owed	28	
	29	**Overpayment.** If line 26 is larger than the total of lines 24, 25, and 27, enter amount overpaid	29	
	30	Amount of line 29 to be: **a Credited to 2025** ; **b Refunded**	30	

Sign Here

Under penalties of perjury, I declare that I have examined this return, including accompanying schedules and statements, and to the best of my knowledge and belief, it is true, correct, and complete. Declaration of preparer (other than taxpayer) is based on all information of which preparer has any knowledge.

Signature of fiduciary or officer representing fiduciary | Date | EIN of fiduciary if a financial institution

May the IRS discuss this return with the preparer shown below? See instructions. ☐ **Yes** ☐ **No**

Paid Preparer Use Only

Preparer's name	Preparer's signature	Date	Check ☐ if self-employed	PTIN
Firm's name			Firm's EIN	
Firm's address			Phone no.	

For Paperwork Reduction Act Notice, see the separate instructions. Cat. No. 11370H Form **1041** (2024)

Form 1041 (2024) Page **2**

Schedule A Charitable Deduction. Don't complete for a simple trust or a pooled income fund.

1	Amounts paid or permanently set aside for charitable purposes from gross income. See instructions	1	
2	Tax-exempt income allocable to charitable contributions. See instructions	2	
3	Subtract line 2 from line 1	3	
4	Capital gains for the tax year allocated to corpus and paid or permanently set aside for charitable purposes	4	
5	Add lines 3 and 4	5	
6	Section 1202 exclusion allocable to capital gains paid or permanently set aside for charitable purposes. See instructions	6	
7	**Charitable deduction.** Subtract line 6 from line 5. Enter here and on page 1, line 13	7	

Schedule B Income Distribution Deduction

1	Adjusted total income. See instructions			1	
2	Adjusted tax-exempt interest			2	
3	Total net gain from Schedule D (Form 1041), line 19, column (1). See instructions			3	
4	Enter amount from Schedule A, line 4 (minus any allocable section 1202 exclusion)			4	
5	Capital gains for the tax year included on Schedule A, line 1. See instructions			5	
6	Enter any gain from page 1, line 4, as a negative number. If page 1, line 4, is a loss, enter the loss as a positive number			6	
7	**Distributable net income.** Combine lines 1 through 6. If zero or less, enter -0-			7	
8	If a complex trust, enter accounting income for the tax year as determined under the governing instrument and applicable local law	8			
9	Income required to be distributed currently			9	
10	Other amounts paid, credited, or otherwise required to be distributed			10	
11	Total distributions. Add lines 9 and 10. If greater than line 8, see instructions			11	
12	Enter the amount of tax-exempt income included on line 11			12	
13	Tentative income distribution deduction. Subtract line 12 from line 11			13	
14	Tentative income distribution deduction. Subtract line 2 from line 7. If zero or less, enter -0-			14	
15	**Income distribution deduction.** Enter the smaller of line 13 or line 14 here and on page 1, line 18			15	

Schedule G Tax Computation and Payments (see instructions)

Part I — Tax Computation

1		**Tax:**				
	a	Tax on taxable income. See instructions	1a			
	b	Tax on lump-sum distributions. Attach Form 4972	1b			
	c	Alternative minimum tax (from Schedule I (Form 1041), line 54)	1c			
	d	Amount from Form 4255, Part I, line 3, column (q)	1d			
	e	**Total.** Add lines 1a through 1d			1e	
2a		Foreign tax credit. Attach Form 1116	2a			
	b	General business credit. Attach Form 3800	2b			
	c	Credit for prior year minimum tax. Attach Form 8801	2c			
	d	Bond credits. Attach Form 8912	2d			
	e	**Total credits.** Add lines 2a through 2d			2e	
3		Subtract line 2e from line 1e. If zero or less, enter -0-			3	
4		Tax on the ESBT portion of the trust (from ESBT Tax Worksheet, line 17). See instructions			4	
5		Net investment income tax from Form 8960, line 21			5	
6a		Amount from Form 4255, Part I, line 3, column (r)			6a	
	b	Recapture tax from Form 8611			6b	
	c	Other recapture taxes:			6c	
7		Household employment taxes. Attach Schedule H (Form 1040)			7	
8		Other taxes and amounts due			8	
9		**Total tax.** Add lines 3 through 8. Enter here and on page 1, line 24			9	

Form **1041** (2024)

Form 1041 (2024) Page **3**

Schedule G **Tax Computation and Payments** (see instructions) *(continued)*

Part II — Payments

10	Current year's estimated tax payments and amount applied from preceding year's return	10	
11	Estimated tax payments allocated to beneficiaries (from Form 1041-T)	11	
12	Subtract line 11 from line 10	12	
13	Tax paid with Form 7004. See instructions	13	
14	Federal income tax withheld. If any is from Form(s) 1099, check here ☐	14	
15	Current year net 965 tax liability from Form 965-A, Part I, column (f) (see instructions)	15	
16	Payments from Form 2439	16	
17	Payments from Form 4136	17	
18a	Elective payment election amount from Form 3800	18a	
b	Other credits or payments (see instructions)	18b	
19	**Total payments.** Add lines 12 through 18b. Enter here and on page 1, line 26	19	

Other Information

		Yes	No
1	Did the estate or trust receive tax-exempt income? If "Yes," attach a computation of the allocation of expenses. Enter the amount of tax-exempt interest income and exempt-interest dividends . . . $		
2	Did the estate or trust receive all or any part of the earnings (salary, wages, and other compensation) of any individual by reason of a contract assignment or similar arrangement?		
3	At any time during calendar year 2024, did the estate or trust have an interest in or a signature or other authority over a bank, securities, or other financial account in a foreign country? See the instructions for exceptions and filing requirements for FinCEN Form 114. If "Yes," enter the name of the foreign country		
4	During the tax year, did the estate or trust receive a distribution from, or was it the grantor of, or transferor to, a foreign trust? If "Yes," the estate or trust may have to file Form 3520. See instructions		
5	Did the estate or trust receive, or pay, any qualified residence interest on seller-provided financing? If "Yes," see the instructions for the required attachment		
6	If this is an estate or a complex trust making the section 663(b) election, check here. See instructions ☐		
7	To make a section 643(e)(3) election, attach Schedule D (Form 1041), and check here. See instructions ☐		
8	If the decedent's estate has been open for more than 2 years, attach an explanation for the delay in closing the estate, and check here ☐		
9	Are any present or future trust beneficiaries skip persons? See instructions		
10	Was the trust a specified domestic entity required to file Form 8938 for the tax year? See the Instructions for Form 8938		
11a	Did the estate or trust distribute S corporation stock for which it made a section 965(i) election?		
b	If "Yes," did each beneficiary enter into an agreement to be liable for the net tax liability? See instructions		
12	Did the estate or trust either make a section 965(i) election or enter into a transfer agreement as an eligible section 965(i) transferee for S corporation stock held on the last day of the tax year? See instructions		
13	At any time during the tax year, did the estate or trust (a) receive (as a reward, award, or payment for property or services); or (b) sell, exchange, or otherwise dispose of a digital asset (or a financial interest in a digital asset)? See instructions		
14	**ESBTs only.** Does the ESBT have a nonresident alien grantor? If "Yes," see instructions		
15	**ESBTs only.** Did the S portion of the trust claim a qualified business income deduction? If "Yes," see instructions		

Form **1041** (2024)

661117

☐ Final K-1 ☐ Amended K-1 OMB No. 1545-0092

Schedule K-1 (Form 1041) **2024**

Department of the Treasury
Internal Revenue Service

For calendar year 2024, or tax year

beginning / / 2024 ending / /

Beneficiary's Share of Income, Deductions, Credits, etc.

See back of form and instructions.

Part I Information About the Estate or Trust

A Estate's or trust's employer identification number

B Estate's or trust's name

C Fiduciary's name, address, city, state, and ZIP code

D ☐ Check if Form 1041-T was filed and enter the date it was filed

E ☐ Check if this is the final Form 1041 for the estate or trust

Part II Information About the Beneficiary

F Beneficiary's identifying number

G Beneficiary's name, address, city, state, and ZIP code

H ☐ Domestic beneficiary ☐ Foreign beneficiary

Part III Beneficiary's Share of Current Year Income, Deductions, Credits, and Other Items

1	Interest income	11	Final year deductions
2a	Ordinary dividends		
2b	Qualified dividends		
3	Net short-term capital gain		
4a	Net long-term capital gain		
4b	28% rate gain	12	Alternative minimum tax adjustment
4c	Unrecaptured section 1250 gain		
5	Other portfolio and nonbusiness income		
6	Ordinary business income		
7	Net rental real estate income		
		13	Credits and credit recapture
8	Other rental income		
9	Directly apportioned deductions		
		14	Other information
10	Estate tax deduction		

* See attached statement for additional information.

Note: A statement must be attached showing the beneficiary's share of income and directly apportioned deductions from each business, rental real estate, and other rental activity.

For IRS Use Only

Form **1065**

Department of the Treasury
Internal Revenue Service

U.S. Return of Partnership Income

For calendar year 2024, or tax year beginning ______, 2024, ending ______, 20 ___.

Go to *www.irs.gov/Form1065* for instructions and the latest information.

OMB No. 1545-0123

2024

	Type or Print		
A Principal business activity		Name of partnership	D Employer identification number
B Principal product or service		Number, street, and room or suite no. If a P.O. box, see instructions.	E Date business started
C Business code number		City or town, state or province, country, and ZIP or foreign postal code	F Total assets (see instructions) $

G Check applicable boxes: **(1)** ☐ Initial return **(2)** ☐ Final return **(3)** ☐ Name change **(4)** ☐ Address change **(5)** ☐ Amended return

H Check accounting method: **(1)** ☐ Cash **(2)** ☐ Accrual **(3)** ☐ Other (specify): ______

I Number of Schedules K-1. Attach one for each person who was a partner at any time during the tax year: ______

J Check if Schedules C and M-3 are attached . . . ☐

K Check if partnership: **(1)** ☐ Aggregated activities for section 465 at-risk purposes **(2)** ☐ Grouped activities for section 469 passive activity purposes

Caution: Include **only** trade or business income and expenses on lines 1a through 23 below. See instructions for more information.

Income	1a	Gross receipts or sales ______ **b** Less returns and allowances ______ **c** Balance		1c	
	2	Cost of goods sold (attach Form 1125-A)		2	
	3	Gross profit. Subtract line 2 from line 1c		3	
	4	Ordinary income (loss) from other partnerships, estates, and trusts (attach statement)		4	
	5	Net farm profit (loss) (attach Schedule F (Form 1040))		5	
	6	Net gain (loss) from Form 4797, Part II, line 17 (attach Form 4797)		6	
	7	Other income (loss) (attach statement)		7	
	8	**Total income (loss).** Combine lines 3 through 7		8	
Deductions (see instructions for limitations)	9	Salaries and wages (other than to partners) (less employment credits)		9	
	10	Guaranteed payments to partners		10	
	11	Repairs and maintenance		11	
	12	Bad debts		12	
	13	Rent		13	
	14	Taxes and licenses		14	
	15	Interest (see instructions)		15	
	16a	Depreciation (if required, attach Form 4562)	16a		
	b	Less depreciation reported on Form 1125-A and elsewhere on return	16b	16c	
	17	Depletion **(Do not deduct oil and gas depletion.)**		17	
	18	Retirement plans, etc.		18	
	19	Employee benefit programs		19	
	20	Energy efficient commercial buildings deduction (attach Form 7205)		20	
	21	Other deductions (attach statement)		21	
	22	**Total deductions.** Add the amounts shown in the far right column for lines 9 through 21		22	
	23	**Ordinary business income (loss).** Subtract line 22 from line 8		23	
Tax and Payment	24	Interest due under the look-back method—completed long-term contracts (attach Form 8697)		24	
	25	Interest due under the look-back method—income forecast method (attach Form 8866)		25	
	26	BBA AAR imputed underpayment (see instructions)		26	
	27	Other taxes (see instructions)		27	
	28	**Total balance due.** Add lines 24 through 27		28	
	29	Elective payment election amount from Form 3800		29	
	30	Payment (see instructions)		30	
	31	**Amount owed.** If the sum of line 29 and line 30 is smaller than line 28, enter amount owed		31	
	32	**Overpayment.** If the sum of line 29 and line 30 is larger than line 28, enter overpayment		32	

Sign Here

Under penalties of perjury, I declare that I have examined this return, including accompanying schedules and statements, and to the best of my knowledge and belief, it is true, correct, and complete. Declaration of preparer (other than partner or limited liability company member) is based on all information of which preparer has any knowledge.

Signature of partner or limited liability company member ______ Date ______

May the IRS discuss this return with the preparer shown below? See instructions. ☐ **Yes** ☐ **No**

Paid Preparer Use Only

Print/Type preparer's name	Preparer's signature	Date	Check ☐ if self-employed	PTIN
Firm's name			Firm's EIN	
Firm's address			Phone no.	

For Paperwork Reduction Act Notice, see separate instructions. Cat. No. 11390Z Form **1065** (2024)

Form 1065 (2024) Page 2

Schedule B Other Information

		Yes	No
1	What type of entity is filing this return? Check the applicable box: a ☐ Domestic general partnership b ☐ Domestic limited partnership c ☐ Domestic limited liability company d ☐ Domestic limited liability partnership e ☐ Foreign partnership f ☐ Other:		
2	At the end of the tax year:		
a	Did any foreign or domestic corporation, partnership (including any entity treated as a partnership), trust, or tax-exempt organization, or any foreign government own, directly or indirectly, an interest of 50% or more in the profit, loss, or capital of the partnership? For rules of constructive ownership, see instructions. If "Yes," attach Schedule B-1, Information on Partners Owning 50% or More of the Partnership		
b	Did any individual or estate own, directly or indirectly, an interest of 50% or more in the profit, loss, or capital of the partnership? For rules of constructive ownership, see instructions. If "Yes," attach Schedule B-1, Information on Partners Owning 50% or More of the Partnership		
3	At the end of the tax year, did the partnership:		
a	Own directly 20% or more, or own, directly or indirectly, 50% or more, of the total voting power of all classes of stock entitled to vote of any foreign or domestic corporation? For rules of constructive ownership, see instructions. If "Yes," complete (i) through (iv) below		

(i) Name of corporation	(ii) Employer identification number (if any)	(iii) Country of incorporation	(iv) Percentage owned in voting stock

		Yes	No
b	Own directly an interest of 20% or more, or own, directly or indirectly, an interest of 50% or more in the profit, loss, or capital in any foreign or domestic partnership (including an entity treated as a partnership) or in the beneficial interest of a trust? For rules of constructive ownership, see instructions. If "Yes," complete (i) through (v) below		

(i) Name of entity	(ii) Employer identification number (if any)	(iii) Type of entity	(iv) Country of organization	(v) Maximum percentage owned in profit, loss, or capital

		Yes	No
4	Does the partnership satisfy **all four** of the following conditions?		
a	The partnership's total receipts for the tax year were less than $250,000.		
b	The partnership's total assets at the end of the tax year were less than $1 million.		
c	Schedules K-1 are filed with the return and furnished to the partners on or before the due date (including extensions) for the partnership return.		
d	The partnership is not filing and is not required to file Schedule M-3 If "Yes," the partnership is not required to complete Schedules L, M-1, and M-2; item F on page 1 of Form 1065; or item L on Schedule K-1.		
5	Is this partnership a publicly traded partnership, as defined in section 469(k)(2)?		
6	During the tax year, did the partnership have any debt that was canceled, was forgiven, or had the terms modified so as to reduce the principal amount of the debt?		
7	Has this partnership filed, or is it required to file, Form 8918, Material Advisor Disclosure Statement, to provide information on any reportable transaction?		
8	At any time during calendar year 2024, did the partnership have an interest in or a signature or other authority over a financial account in a foreign country (such as a bank account, securities account, or other financial account)? See instructions for exceptions and filing requirements for FinCEN Form 114, Report of Foreign Bank and Financial Accounts (FBAR). If "Yes," enter the name of the foreign country		
9	At any time during the tax year, did the partnership receive a distribution from, or was it the grantor of, or transferor to, a foreign trust? If "Yes," the partnership may have to file Form 3520, Annual Return To Report Transactions With Foreign Trusts and Receipt of Certain Foreign Gifts. See instructions		
10a	Is the partnership making, or had it previously made (and not revoked), a section 754 election? If "Yes," enter the effective date of the election See instructions for details regarding a section 754 election.		
b	For this tax year, did the partnership make an optional basis adjustment under section 743(b)? If "Yes," enter the total aggregate net positive amount $ ________ and the total aggregate net negative amount $ (________) of such section 743(b) adjustments for all partners made in the tax year. The partnership must also attach a statement showing the computation and allocation of each basis adjustment. See instructions		

Form 1065 (2024) Page **3**

Schedule B	**Other Information** *(continued)*	**Yes**	**No**
c	For this tax year, did the partnership make an optional basis adjustment under section 734(b)? If "Yes," enter the total aggregate net positive amount $ ________ and the total aggregate net negative amount $(________) of such section 734(b) adjustments for all partnership property made in the tax year. The partnership must also attach a statement showing the computation and allocation of each basis adjustment. See instructions		
d	For this tax year, is the partnership required to adjust the basis of partnership property under section 743(b) or 734(b) because of a substantial built-in loss (as defined under section 743(d)) or substantial basis reduction (as defined under section 734(d))? If "Yes," enter the total aggregate amount of such section 743(b) adjustments and/or section 734(b) adjustments for all partners and/or partnership property made in the tax year $ ________. The partnership must also attach a statement showing the computation and allocation of the basis adjustment. See instructions		
11	Check this box if, during the current or prior tax year, the partnership distributed any property received in a like-kind exchange or contributed such property to another entity (other than disregarded entities wholly owned by the partnership throughout the tax year) ☐		
12	At any time during the tax year, did the partnership distribute to any partner a tenancy-in-common or other undivided interest in partnership property?		
13	If the partnership is required to file Form 8858, Information Return of U.S. Persons With Respect to Foreign Disregarded Entities (FDEs) and Foreign Branches (FBs), enter the number of Forms 8858 attached. See instructions ________		
14	Does the partnership have any foreign partners? If "Yes," enter the number of Forms 8805, Foreign Partner's Information Statement of Section 1446 Withholding Tax, filed for this partnership ________		
15	Enter the number of Forms 8865, Return of U.S. Persons With Respect to Certain Foreign Partnerships, attached to this return ________		
16a	Did you make any payments in 2024 that would require you to file Form(s) 1099? See instructions		
b	If "Yes," did you or will you file required Form(s) 1099?		
17	Enter the number of Forms 5471, Information Return of U.S. Persons With Respect to Certain Foreign Corporations, attached to this return ________		
18	Enter the number of partners that are foreign governments under section 892 ________		
19	During the partnership's tax year, did the partnership make any payments that would require it to file Forms 1042 and 1042-S under chapter 3 (sections 1441 through 1464) or chapter 4 (sections 1471 through 1474)?		
20	Was the partnership a specified domestic entity required to file Form 8938 for the tax year? See the Instructions for Form 8938		
21	Is the partnership a section 721(c) partnership, as defined in Regulations section 1.721(c)-1(b)(14)?		
22	During the tax year, did the partnership pay or accrue any interest or royalty for which one or more partners are not allowed a deduction under section 267A? See instructions If "Yes," enter the total amount of the disallowed deductions $ ________		
23	Did the partnership have an election under section 163(j) for any real property trade or business or any farming business in effect during the tax year? See instructions		
24	Does the partnership satisfy one or more of the following? See instructions		
a	The partnership owns a pass-through entity with current, or prior year carryover, excess business interest expense.		
b	The partnership's aggregate average annual gross receipts (determined under section 448(c)) for the 3 tax years preceding the current tax year are more than $30 million and the partnership has business interest expense.		
c	The partnership is a tax shelter (see instructions) and the partnership has business interest expense. If "Yes" to any, complete and attach Form 8990.		
25	Is the partnership attaching Form 8996 to certify as a Qualified Opportunity Fund? If "Yes," enter the amount from Form 8996, line 15 $ ________		
26	Enter the number of foreign partners subject to section 864(c)(8) as a result of transferring all or a portion of an interest in the partnership or of receiving a distribution from the partnership ________ Complete Schedule K-3 (Form 1065), Part XIII, for each foreign partner subject to section 864(c)(8) on a transfer or distribution.		
27	At any time during the tax year, were there any transfers between the partnership and its partners subject to the disclosure requirements of Regulations section 1.707-8?		
28	Since December 22, 2017, did a foreign corporation directly or indirectly acquire substantially all of the properties constituting a trade or business of your partnership, and was the ownership percentage (by vote or value) for purposes of section 7874 greater than 50% (for example, the partners held more than 50% of the stock of the foreign corporation)? If "Yes," list the ownership percentage by vote and by value. See instructions. Percentage: By vote: ________ By value: ________		
29	Is the partnership required to file Form 7208, Excise Tax on Repurchase of Corporate Stock (see instructions):		
a	Under the applicable foreign corporation rules?		

Form **1065** (2024)

Form 1065 (2024) Page 4

Schedule B	**Other Information** *(continued)*	**Yes**	**No**
b	Under the covered surrogate foreign corporation rules?		
	If "Yes" to either (a) or (b), complete Form 7208. See the Instructions for Form 7208.		
30	At any time during this tax year, did the partnership (a) receive (as a reward, award, or payment for property or services); or (b) sell, exchange, or otherwise dispose of a digital asset (or financial interest in a digital asset)? See instructions		
31	Reserved for future use		
32	Check this box if an election out of subchapter K under section 761 is being made. See instructions . . . . . ☐		
33	Is the partnership electing out of the centralized partnership audit regime under section 6221(b)? See instructions		
	If "Yes," the partnership must complete Schedule B-2 (Form 1065). Enter the total from Schedule B-2, Part III, line 3 . . . . ________		
	If "No," complete Designation of Partnership Representative below.		

Designation of Partnership Representative (see instructions)

Enter below the information for the partnership representative (PR) for the tax year covered by this return.

Name of PR	
U.S. address of PR	U.S. phone number of PR
If the PR is an entity, name of the designated individual for the PR	
U.S. address of designated individual	U.S. phone number of designated individual

Form **1065** (2024)

Form 1065 (2024) Page **5**

Section	Line	Schedule K — Partners' Distributive Share Items		Line	Total amount
Income (Loss)	1	Ordinary business income (loss) (page 1, line 23)		1	
	2	Net rental real estate income (loss) (attach Form 8825)		2	
	3a	Other gross rental income (loss)	3a		
	b	Expenses from other rental activities (attach statement)	3b		
	c	Other net rental income (loss). Subtract line 3b from line 3a		3c	
	4	Guaranteed payments: **a** Services 4a ____ **b** Capital	4b		
		c Total. Add lines 4a and 4b		4c	
	5	Interest income		5	
	6	Dividends and dividend equivalents: **a** Ordinary dividends		6a	
		b Qualified dividends 6b ____ **c** Dividend equivalents	6c		
	7	Royalties		7	
	8	Net short-term capital gain (loss) (attach Schedule D (Form 1065))		8	
	9a	Net long-term capital gain (loss) (attach Schedule D (Form 1065))		9a	
	b	Collectibles (28%) gain (loss)	9b		
	c	Unrecaptured section 1250 gain (attach statement)	9c		
	10	Net section 1231 gain (loss) (attach Form 4797)		10	
	11	Other income (loss) (see instructions) Type:		11	
Deductions	12	Section 179 deduction (attach Form 4562)		12	
	13a	Cash contributions		13a	
	b	Noncash contributions		13b	
	c	Investment interest expense		13c	
	d	Section 59(e)(2) expenditures: **(1)** Type: ____ **(2)** Amount:		13d(2)	
	e	Other deductions (see instructions) Type:		13e	
Self-Employment	14a	Net earnings (loss) from self-employment		14a	
	b	Gross farming or fishing income		14b	
	c	Gross nonfarm income		14c	
Credits	15a	Low-income housing credit (section 42(j)(5))		15a	
	b	Low-income housing credit (other)		15b	
	c	Qualified rehabilitation expenditures (rental real estate) (attach Form 3468, if applicable)		15c	
	d	Other rental real estate credits (see instructions) Type:		15d	
	e	Other rental credits (see instructions) Type:		15e	
	f	Other credits (see instructions) Type:		15f	
International	16	Attach Schedule K-2 (Form 1065), Partners' Distributive Share Items—International, and check this box to indicate that you are reporting items of international tax relevance ☐			
Alternative Minimum Tax (AMT) Items	17a	Post-1986 depreciation adjustment		17a	
	b	Adjusted gain or loss		17b	
	c	Depletion (other than oil and gas)		17c	
	d	Oil, gas, and geothermal properties—gross income		17d	
	e	Oil, gas, and geothermal properties—deductions		17e	
	f	Other AMT items (attach statement)		17f	
Other Information	18a	Tax-exempt interest income		18a	
	b	Other tax-exempt income		18b	
	c	Nondeductible expenses		18c	
	19a	Distributions of cash and marketable securities		19a	
	b	Distributions of other property		19b	
	20a	Investment income		20a	
	b	Investment expenses		20b	
	c	Other items and amounts (attach statement)			
	21	Total foreign taxes paid or accrued		21	

Form **1065** (2024)

Form 1065 (2024) Page **6**

Analysis of Net Income (Loss) per Return

1	Net income (loss). Combine Schedule K, lines 1 through 11. From the result, subtract the sum of Schedule K, lines 12 through 13e, and 21					1	
2	Analysis by partner type:	**(i)** Corporate	**(ii)** Individual (active)	**(iii)** Individual (passive)	**(iv)** Partnership	**(v)** Exempt organization	**(vi)** Nominee/Other
a	General partners						
b	Limited partners						

Schedule L Balance Sheets per Books

		Beginning of tax year		End of tax year	
	Assets	**(a)**	**(b)**	**(c)**	**(d)**
1	Cash				
2a	Trade notes and accounts receivable				
b	Less allowance for bad debts				
3	Inventories				
4	U.S. Government obligations				
5	Tax-exempt securities				
6	Other current assets (attach statement)				
7a	Loans to partners (or persons related to partners)				
b	Mortgage and real estate loans				
8	Other investments (attach statement)				
9a	Buildings and other depreciable assets				
b	Less accumulated depreciation				
10a	Depletable assets				
b	Less accumulated depletion				
11	Land (net of any amortization)				
12a	Intangible assets (amortizable only)				
b	Less accumulated amortization				
13	Other assets (attach statement)				
14	Total assets				
	Liabilities and Capital				
15	Accounts payable				
16	Mortgages, notes, bonds payable in less than 1 year				
17	Other current liabilities (attach statement)				
18	All nonrecourse loans				
19a	Loans from partners (or persons related to partners)				
b	Mortgages, notes, bonds payable in 1 year or more				
20	Other liabilities (attach statement)				
21	Partners' capital accounts				
22	Total liabilities and capital				

Schedule M-1 Reconciliation of Income (Loss) per Books With Analysis of Net Income (Loss) per Return

Note: The partnership may be required to file Schedule M-3. See instructions.

1	Net income (loss) per books		**6**	Income recorded on books this year not included on Schedule K, lines 1 through 11 (itemize):	
2	Income included on Schedule K, lines 1, 2, 3c, 5, 6a, 7, 8, 9a, 10, and 11, not recorded on books this year (itemize):		**a**	Tax-exempt interest $	
3	Guaranteed payments (other than health insurance)		**7**	Deductions included on Schedule K, lines 1 through 13e, and 21, not charged against book income this year (itemize):	
4	Expenses recorded on books this year not included on Schedule K, lines 1 through 13e, and 21 (itemize):		**a**	Depreciation $	
a	Depreciation $		**8**	Add lines 6 and 7	
b	Travel and entertainment $		**9**	Income (loss) (*Analysis of Net Income (Loss) per Return*, line 1). Subtract line 8 from line 5	
5	Add lines 1 through 4				

Schedule M-2 Analysis of Partners' Capital Accounts

1	Balance at beginning of year		**6**	Distributions: **a** Cash	
2	Capital contributed: **a** Cash			**b** Property	
	b Property		**7**	Other decreases (itemize):	
3	Net income (loss) (see instructions)				
4	Other increases (itemize):		**8**	Add lines 6 and 7	
5	Add lines 1 through 4		**9**	Balance at end of year. Subtract line 8 from line 5	

Form **1065** (2024)

651123

☐ Final K-1 ☐ Amended K-1 OMB No. 1545-0123

Schedule K-1 (Form 1065) **2024**

Department of the Treasury
Internal Revenue Service

For calendar year 2024, or tax year

beginning / / 2024 ending / /

Partner's Share of Income, Deductions, Credits, etc.

See separate instructions.

Part I Information About the Partnership

A Partnership's employer identification number

B Partnership's name, address, city, state, and ZIP code

C IRS center where partnership filed return:

D ☐ Check if this is a publicly traded partnership (PTP)

Part II Information About the Partner

E Partner's SSN or TIN (Do not use TIN of a disregarded entity. See instructions.)

F Name, address, city, state, and ZIP code for partner entered in E. See instructions.

G ☐ General partner or LLC member-manager ☐ Limited partner or other LLC member

H1 ☐ Domestic partner ☐ Foreign partner

H2 ☐ If the partner is a disregarded entity (DE), enter the partner's:

TIN ____ Name ____

I1 What type of entity is this partner? ____

I2 If this partner is a retirement plan (IRA/SEP/Keogh/etc.), check here . ☐

J Partner's share of profit, loss, and capital (see instructions):

	Beginning	Ending
Profit	%	%
Loss	%	%
Capital	%	%

Check if decrease is due to:

☐ Sale or ☐ Exchange of partnership interest. See instructions.

K1 Partner's share of liabilities:

	Beginning	Ending
Nonrecourse . . .	$	$
Qualified nonrecourse financing . . .	$	$
Recourse . . .	$	$

K2 Check this box if item K1 includes liability amounts from lower-tier partnerships ☐

K3 Check if any of the above liability is subject to guarantees or other payment obligations by the partner. See instructions . . . . . ☐

L **Partner's Capital Account Analysis**

Beginning capital account . . . $

Capital contributed during the year . . $

Current year net income (loss) . . . $

Other increase (decrease) (attach explanation) $

Withdrawals and distributions . . . $( )

Ending capital account . . . . $

M Did the partner contribute property with a built-in gain (loss)?

☐ **Yes** ☐ **No** If "Yes," attach statement. See instructions.

N **Partner's Share of Net Unrecognized Section 704(c) Gain or (Loss)**

Beginning . . . . $

Ending . . . . $

Part III Partner's Share of Current Year Income, Deductions, Credits, and Other Items

1	Ordinary business income (loss)	14	Self-employment earnings (loss)
2	Net rental real estate income (loss)		
3	Other net rental income (loss)	15	Credits
4a	Guaranteed payments for services		
4b	Guaranteed payments for capital	16	Schedule K-3 is attached if checked . . . . . ☐
4c	Total guaranteed payments	17	Alternative minimum tax (AMT) items
5	Interest income		
6a	Ordinary dividends		
6b	Qualified dividends	18	Tax-exempt income and nondeductible expenses
6c	Dividend equivalents		
7	Royalties		
8	Net short-term capital gain (loss)	19	Distributions
9a	Net long-term capital gain (loss)		
9b	Collectibles (28%) gain (loss)	20	Other information
9c	Unrecaptured section 1250 gain		
10	Net section 1231 gain (loss)		
11	Other income (loss)		
12	Section 179 deduction	21	Foreign taxes paid or accrued
13	Other deductions		

22 ☐ More than one activity for at-risk purposes*

23 ☐ More than one activity for passive activity purposes*

*See attached statement for additional information.

For IRS Use Only

For Paperwork Reduction Act Notice, see the Instructions for Form 1065. www.irs.gov/Form1065 Cat. No. 11394R **Schedule K-1 (Form 1065) 2024**

Form **1120** | Department of the Treasury | Internal Revenue Service

U.S. Corporation Income Tax Return

For calendar year 2024 or tax year beginning ________, 2024, ending ________, 20 ____

Go to *www.irs.gov/Form1120* for instructions and the latest information.

OMB No. 1545-0123 | **2024**

A Check if:	TYPE OR PRINT		
1a Consolidated return (attach Form 851) ☐		Name	B Employer identification number
b Life/nonlife consolidated return ☐		Number, street, and room or suite no. If a P.O. box, see instructions.	C Date incorporated
2 Personal holding co. (attach Sch. PH) ☐		City or town, state or province, country, and ZIP or foreign postal code	D Total assets (see instructions) $
3 Personal service corp. (see instructions) ☐			
4 Schedule M-3 attached ☐	E Check if: (1) ☐ Initial return (2) ☐ Final return (3) ☐ Name change (4) ☐ Address change		

Income	1a	Gross receipts or sales	1a	
	b	Returns and allowances	1b	
	c	Balance. Subtract line 1b from line 1a	1c	
	2	Cost of goods sold (attach Form 1125-A)	2	
	3	Gross profit. Subtract line 2 from line 1c	3	
	4	Dividends and inclusions (Schedule C, line 23)	4	
	5	Interest	5	
	6	Gross rents	6	
	7	Gross royalties	7	
	8	Capital gain net income (attach Schedule D (Form 1120))	8	
	9	Net gain or (loss) from Form 4797, Part II, line 17 (attach Form 4797)	9	
	10	Other income (see instructions—attach statement)	10	
	11	**Total income.** Add lines 3 through 10	11	
Deductions (See instructions for limitations on deductions.)	12	Compensation of officers (see instructions—attach Form 1125-E)	12	
	13	Salaries and wages (less employment credits)	13	
	14	Repairs and maintenance	14	
	15	Bad debts	15	
	16	Rents	16	
	17	Taxes and licenses	17	
	18	Interest (see instructions)	18	
	19	Charitable contributions	19	
	20	Depreciation from Form 4562 not claimed on Form 1125-A or elsewhere on return (attach Form 4562)	20	
	21	Depletion	21	
	22	Advertising	22	
	23	Pension, profit-sharing, etc., plans	23	
	24	Employee benefit programs	24	
	25	Energy efficient commercial buildings deduction (attach Form 7205)	25	
	26	Other deductions (attach statement)	26	
	27	**Total deductions.** Add lines 12 through 26	27	
	28	Taxable income before net operating loss deduction and special deductions. Subtract line 27 from line 11	28	
	29a	Net operating loss deduction (see instructions)	29a	
	b	Special deductions (Schedule C, line 24)	29b	
	c	Add lines 29a and 29b	29c	
Tax, Refundable Credits, and Payments	30	**Taxable income.** Subtract line 29c from line 28. See instructions	30	
	31	Total tax (Schedule J, line 12)	31	
	32	Reserved for future use	32	
	33	Total payments and credits (Schedule J, line 23)	33	
	34	Estimated tax penalty. See instructions. Check if Form 2220 is attached ☐	34	
	35	**Amount owed.** If line 33 is smaller than the total of lines 31 and 34, enter amount owed	35	
	36	**Overpayment.** If line 33 is larger than the total of lines 31 and 34, enter amount overpaid	36	
	37	Enter amount from line 36 you want: **Credited to 2025 estimated tax** ____ **Refunded**	37	

Sign Here

Under penalties of perjury, I declare that I have examined this return, including accompanying schedules and statements, and to the best of my knowledge and belief, it is true, correct, and complete. Declaration of preparer (other than taxpayer) is based on all information of which preparer has any knowledge.

Signature of officer | Date | Title

May the IRS discuss this return with the preparer shown below? See instructions. ☐ **Yes** ☐ **No**

Paid Preparer Use Only	Print/Type preparer's name	Preparer's signature	Date	Check ☐ if self-employed	PTIN
	Firm's name			Firm's EIN	
	Firm's address			Phone no.	

For Paperwork Reduction Act Notice, see separate instructions. Cat. No. 11450Q Form **1120** (2024)

Form 1120 (2024) Page **2**

Schedule C **Dividends, Inclusions, and Special Deductions** (see instructions)	**(a)** Dividends and inclusions	**(b)** %	**(c)** Special deductions **(a)** × **(b)**
1 Dividends from less-than-20%-owned domestic corporations (other than debt-financed stock)		50	
2 Dividends from 20%-or-more-owned domestic corporations (other than debt-financed stock)		65	
3 Dividends on certain debt-financed stock of domestic and foreign corporations		See instructions	
4 Dividends on certain preferred stock of less-than-20%-owned public utilities		23.3	
5 Dividends on certain preferred stock of 20%-or-more-owned public utilities		26.7	
6 Dividends from less-than-20%-owned foreign corporations and certain FSCs		50	
7 Dividends from 20%-or-more-owned foreign corporations and certain FSCs		65	
8 Dividends from wholly owned foreign subsidiaries		100	
9 **Subtotal.** Add lines 1 through 8. See instructions for limitations		See instructions	
10 Dividends from domestic corporations received by a small business investment company operating under the Small Business Investment Act of 1958		100	
11 Dividends from affiliated group members		100	
12 Dividends from certain FSCs		100	
13 Foreign-source portion of dividends received from a specified 10%-owned foreign corporation (excluding hybrid dividends) (see instructions)		100	
14 Dividends from foreign corporations not included on line 3, 6, 7, 8, 11, 12, or 13 (including any hybrid dividends)			
15 Reserved for future use			
16a Subpart F inclusions derived from the sale by a controlled foreign corporation (CFC) of the stock of a lower-tier foreign corporation treated as a dividend (attach Form(s) 5471) (see instructions)		100	
b Subpart F inclusions derived from hybrid dividends of tiered corporations (attach Form(s) 5471) (see instructions)			
c Other inclusions from CFCs under subpart F not included on line 16a, 16b, or 17 (attach Form(s) 5471) (see instructions)			
17 Global Intangible Low-Taxed Income (GILTI) (attach Form(s) 5471 and Form 8992)			
18 Gross-up for foreign taxes deemed paid			
19 IC-DISC and former DISC dividends not included on line 1, 2, or 3			
20 Other dividends			
21 Deduction for dividends paid on certain preferred stock of public utilities			
22 Section 250 deduction (attach Form 8993)			
23 **Total dividends and inclusions.** Add column (a), lines 9 through 20. Enter here and on page 1, line 4			
24 **Total special deductions.** Add column (c), lines 9 through 22. Enter here and on page 1, line 29b			

Form **1120** (2024)

Form 1120 (2024) Page **3**

Schedule J Tax Computation and Payment (see instructions)

1a	Income tax (see instructions)	1a			
b	Tax from Form 1120-L (see instructions)	1b			
c	Section 1291 tax from Form 8621	1c			
d	Tax adjustment from Form 8978	1d			
e	Additional tax under section 197(f)	1e			
f	Base erosion minimum tax from Form 8991	1f			
g	Amount from Form 4255, Part I, line 3, column (q)	1g			
z	Other chapter 1 tax	1z			
2	Total income tax. Add lines 1a through 1z			2	
3	Corporate alternative minimum tax from Form 4626, Part II, line 13 (attach Form 4626)			3	
4	Add lines 2 and 3			4	
5a	Foreign tax credit (attach Form 1118)	5a			
b	Credit from Form 8834 (see instructions)	5b			
c	General business credit (see instructions—attach Form 3800)	5c			
d	Credit for prior year minimum tax (attach Form 8827)	5d			
e	Bond credits from Form 8912	5e			
f	Adjustment from Form 8978	5f			
6	**Total credits.** Add lines 5a through 5f			6	
7	Subtract line 6 from line 4			7	
8	Personal holding company tax (attach Schedule PH (Form 1120))			8	
9a	Amount from Form 4255, Part I, line 3, column (r)	9a			
b	Recapture of low-income housing credit (attach Form 8611)	9b			
c	Completed long-term contract look-back interest due (attach Form 8697)	9c			
d	Interest due under the look-back method—income forecast method (attach Form 8866)	9d			
e	Alternative tax on qualifying shipping activities (attach Form 8902)	9e			
f	Interest/tax due under section 453A(c)	9f			
g	Interest/tax due under section 453(l)	9g			
z	Other (see instructions—attach statement)	9z			
10	**Total.** Add lines 9a through 9z			10	
11a	Total tax before deferred taxes. Add lines 7, 8, and 10	11a			
b	Deferred tax on the corporation's share of undistributed earnings of a qualified electing fund	11b			
c	Deferred LIFO recapture tax (section 1363(d))	11c			
12	Total tax. Subtract the sum of lines 11b and 11c from 11a. Enter here and on page 1, line 31			12	
13	Preceding year's overpayment credited to the current year			13	
14	Current year's estimated tax payments			14	
15	Current year's refund applied for on Form 4466			15	( )
16	Reserved for future use			16	
17	Tax deposited with Form 7004			17	
18	Withholding (see instructions)			18	
19	**Total payments.** Combine lines 13 through 18			19	
20	Refundable credits from:				
a	Form 2439	20a			
b	Form 4136	20b			
c	Credit for tax withheld under chapter 3 or 4 from Form 1042-S, Form 8805, or Form 8288 (attach the applicable form)	20c			
z	Other (attach statement—see instructions)	20z			
21	**Total credits.** Add lines 20a through 20z			21	
22	Elective payment election amount from Form 3800			22	
23	**Total payments and credits.** Add lines 19, 21, and 22. Enter here and on page 1, line 33			23	

Form **1120** (2024)

Schedule K Other Information (see instructions)

		Yes	No
1	Check accounting method: a ☐ Cash b ☐ Accrual c ☐ Other (specify) ________		
2	See the instructions and enter the:		
a	Business activity code no. ________		
b	Business activity ________		
c	Product or service ________		
3	Is the corporation a subsidiary in an affiliated group or a parent–subsidiary controlled group?		
	If "Yes," enter name and EIN of the parent corporation ________		
4	At the end of the tax year:		
a	Did any foreign or domestic corporation, partnership (including any entity treated as a partnership), trust, or tax-exempt organization own directly 20% or more, or own, directly or indirectly, 50% or more of the total voting power of all classes of the corporation's stock entitled to vote? If "Yes," complete Part I of Schedule G (Form 1120) (attach Schedule G)		
b	Did any individual or estate own directly 20% or more, or own, directly or indirectly, 50% or more of the total voting power of all classes of the corporation's stock entitled to vote? If "Yes," complete Part II of Schedule G (Form 1120) (attach Schedule G) .		
5	At the end of the tax year, did the corporation:		
a	Own directly 20% or more, or own, directly or indirectly, 50% or more of the total voting power of all classes of stock entitled to vote of any foreign or domestic corporation not included on **Form 851**, Affiliations Schedule? For rules of constructive ownership, see instructions		
	If "Yes," complete (i) through (iv) below.		

(i) Name of Corporation	(ii) Employer Identification Number (if any)	(iii) Country of Incorporation	(iv) Percentage Owned in Voting Stock

		Yes	No
b	Own directly an interest of 20% or more, or own, directly or indirectly, an interest of 50% or more in any foreign or domestic partnership (including an entity treated as a partnership) or in the beneficial interest of a trust? For rules of constructive ownership, see instructions		
	If "Yes," complete (i) through (iv) below.		

(i) Name of Entity	(ii) Employer Identification Number (if any)	(iii) Country of Organization	(iv) Maximum Percentage Owned in Profit, Loss, or Capital

		Yes	No
6	During this tax year, did the corporation pay dividends (other than stock dividends and distributions in exchange for stock) in excess of the corporation's current and accumulated earnings and profits? See sections 301 and 316		
	If "Yes," file **Form 5452**, Corporate Report of Nondividend Distributions. See the instructions for Form 5452.		
	If this is a consolidated return, answer here for the parent corporation and on Form 851 for each subsidiary.		
7	At any time during this tax year, did one foreign person own, directly or indirectly, at least 25% of the total voting power of all classes of the corporation's stock entitled to vote or at least 25% of the total value of all classes of the corporation's stock? .		
	For rules of attribution, see section 318. If "Yes," enter:		
	(a) Percentage owned ________ and (b) Owner's country ________		
	(c) The corporation may have to file **Form 5472**, Information Return of a 25% Foreign-Owned U.S. Corporation or a Foreign Corporation Engaged in a U.S. Trade or Business. Enter the number of Forms 5472 attached ________		
8	Check this box if the corporation issued publicly offered debt instruments with original issue discount . . . . ☐		
	If checked, the corporation may have to file **Form 8281**, Information Return for Publicly Offered Original Issue Discount Instruments.		
9	Enter the amount of tax-exempt interest received or accrued during this tax year $ ________		
10	Enter the number of shareholders at the end of the tax year (if 100 or fewer) ________		
11	If the corporation has an NOL for the tax year and is electing to forego the carryback period, check here (see instructions) . ☐		
	If the corporation is filing a consolidated return, the statement required by Regulations section 1.1502-21(b)(3) must be attached or the election will not be valid.		
12	Enter the available NOL carryover from prior tax years (do not reduce it by any deduction reported on page 1, line 29a) $		

Form 1120 (2024) Page **5**

Schedule K Other Information *(continued from page 4)*

		Yes	No
13	Are the corporation's total receipts (page 1, line 1a, plus lines 4 through 10) for the tax year **and** its total assets at the end of the tax year less than $250,000?		
	If "Yes," the corporation is not required to complete Schedules L, M-1, and M-2. Instead, enter the total amount of cash distributions and the book value of property distributions (other than cash) made during this tax year $ ________		
14	Is the corporation required to file Schedule UTP (Form 1120), Uncertain Tax Position Statement? See instructions		
	If "Yes," complete and attach Schedule UTP.		
15a	Did the corporation make any payments that would require it to file Form(s) 1099?		
b	If "Yes," did or will the corporation file required Form(s) 1099?		
16	During this tax year, did the corporation have an 80%-or-more change in ownership, including a change due to redemption of its own stock?		
17	During or subsequent to this tax year, but before the filing of this return, did the corporation dispose of more than 65% (by value) of its assets in a taxable, non-taxable, or tax deferred transaction?		
18	Did this corporation receive assets in a section 351 transfer in which any of the transferred assets had a fair market basis or fair market value of more than $1 million?		
19	During this corporation's tax year, did the corporation make any payments that would require it to file Forms 1042 and 1042-S under chapter 3 (sections 1441 through 1464) or chapter 4 (sections 1471 through 1474) of the Code?		
20	Is the corporation operating on a cooperative basis?		
21	During this tax year, did the corporation pay or accrue any interest or royalty for which the deduction is not allowed under section 267A? See instructions		
	If "Yes," enter the total amount of the disallowed deductions $ ________		
22	Does this corporation have gross receipts of at least $500 million in any of the 3 preceding tax years? (See sections 59A(e)(2) and (3).)		
	If "Yes," complete and attach Form 8991.		
23	Did the corporation have an election under section 163(j) for any real property trade or business or any farming business in effect during this tax year? See instructions		
24	Does the corporation satisfy one or more of the following? If "Yes," complete and attach Form 8990. See instructions		
a	The corporation owns a pass-through entity with current, or prior year carryover, excess business interest expense.		
b	The corporation's aggregate average annual gross receipts (determined under section 448(c)) for the 3 tax years preceding the current tax year are more than $30 million and the corporation has business interest expense.		
c	The corporation is a tax shelter and the corporation has business interest expense.		
25	Is the corporation attaching Form 8996 to certify as a Qualified Opportunity Fund?		
	If "Yes," enter amount from Form 8996, line 15 $ ________		
26	Since December 22, 2017, did a foreign corporation directly or indirectly acquire substantially all of the properties held directly or indirectly by the corporation, and was the ownership percentage (by vote or value) for purposes of section 7874 greater than 50% (for example, the shareholders held more than 50% of the stock of the foreign corporation)? If "Yes," list the ownership percentage by vote and by value. See instructions		
	Percentage: By Vote ________ By Value ________		
27	At any time during this tax year, did the corporation (a) receive a digital asset (as a reward, award, or payment for property or services); or (b) sell, exchange, or otherwise dispose of a digital asset (or a financial interest in a digital asset)? See instructions		
28	Is the corporation a member of a controlled group?		
	If "Yes," attach Schedule O (Form 1120). See instructions.		
29	Corporate Alternative Minimum Tax:		
a	Was the corporation an applicable corporation under section 59(k)(1) in any prior tax year?		
	If "Yes," go to question 29b. If "No," skip to question 29c.		
b	Is the corporation an applicable corporation under section 59(k)(1) in the current tax year because the corporation was an applicable corporation in the prior tax year?		
	If "Yes," complete and attach Form 4626. If "No," continue to question 29c.		
c	Does the corporation meet the requirements of the safe harbor method as provided under section 59(k)(3)(A) for the current tax year? See instructions		
	If "No," complete and attach Form 4626. If "Yes," the corporation is not required to file Form 4626.		
30	Is the corporation required to file Form 7208 relating to the excise tax on repurchase of corporate stock (see instructions):		
a	Under the rules for stock repurchased by a covered corporation (or stock acquired by its specified affiliate)?		
b	Under the applicable foreign corporation rules?		
c	Under the covered surrogate foreign corporation rules?		
	If "Yes" to either 30a, 30b, or 30c, complete Form 7208, Excise Tax on Repurchase of Corporate Stock. See the Instructions for Form 7208.		
31	Is this a consolidated return with gross receipts or sales of $1 billion or more and a subchapter K basis adjustment, as described in the instructions, of $10 million or more?		
	If "Yes," attach a statement. See instructions.		

Form **1120** (2024)

Form 1120 (2024) Page 6

Schedule L **Balance Sheets per Books**

	Assets	Beginning of tax year (a)	(b)	End of tax year (c)	(d)
1	Cash				
2a	Trade notes and accounts receivable				
b	Less allowance for bad debts	( )		( )	
3	Inventories				
4	U.S. government obligations				
5	Tax-exempt securities (see instructions)				
6	Other current assets (attach statement)				
7	Loans to shareholders				
8	Mortgage and real estate loans				
9	Other investments (attach statement)				
10a	Buildings and other depreciable assets				
b	Less accumulated depreciation	( )		( )	
11a	Depletable assets				
b	Less accumulated depletion	( )		( )	
12	Land (net of any amortization)				
13a	Intangible assets (amortizable only)				
b	Less accumulated amortization	( )		( )	
14	Other assets (attach statement)				
15	Total assets				
	Liabilities and Shareholders' Equity				
16	Accounts payable				
17	Mortgages, notes, bonds payable in less than 1 year				
18	Other current liabilities (attach statement)				
19	Loans from shareholders				
20	Mortgages, notes, bonds payable in 1 year or more				
21	Other liabilities (attach statement)				
22	Capital stock: **a** Preferred stock				
	b Common stock				
23	Additional paid-in capital				
24	Retained earnings—Appropriated (attach statement)				
25	Retained earnings—Unappropriated				
26	Adjustments to shareholders' equity (attach statement)				
27	Less cost of treasury stock		( )		( )
28	Total liabilities and shareholders' equity				

Schedule M-1 **Reconciliation of Income (Loss) per Books With Income per Return**

Note: The corporation may be required to file Schedule M-3. See instructions.

1	Net income (loss) per books		7	Income recorded on books this year not included on this return (itemize): Tax-exempt interest $	
2	Federal income tax per books				
3	Excess of capital losses over capital gains				
4	Income subject to tax not recorded on books this year (itemize):		8	Deductions on this return not charged against book income this year (itemize):	
5	Expenses recorded on books this year not deducted on this return (itemize):		a	Depreciation $	
a	Depreciation $		b	Charitable contributions $	
b	Charitable contributions $				
c	Travel and entertainment $				
			9	Add lines 7 and 8	
6	Add lines 1 through 5		10	Income (page 1, line 28)—line 6 less line 9	

Schedule M-2 **Analysis of Unappropriated Retained Earnings per Books (Schedule L, Line 25)**

1	Balance at beginning of year		5	Distributions: **a** Cash	
2	Net income (loss) per books			**b** Stock	
3	Other increases (itemize):			**c** Property	
			6	Other decreases (itemize):	
			7	Add lines 5 and 6	
4	Add lines 1, 2, and 3		8	Balance at end of year (line 4 less line 7)	

Form **1120** (2024)

SCHEDULE M-3 (Form 1120)
(Rev. December 2019)
Department of the Treasury
Internal Revenue Service

Net Income (Loss) Reconciliation for Corporations With Total Assets of $10 Million or More

▶ Attach to Form 1120 or 1120-C.
▶ Go to *www.irs.gov/Form1120* for instructions and the latest information.

OMB No. 1545-0123

Name of corporation (common parent, if consolidated return) | **Employer identification number**

Check applicable box(es): (1) ☐ Non-consolidated return (2) ☐ Consolidated return (Form 1120 only)
(3) ☐ Mixed 1120/L/PC group (4) ☐ Dormant subsidiaries schedule attached

Part I Financial Information and Net Income (Loss) Reconciliation (see instructions)

1a Did the corporation file SEC Form 10-K for its income statement period ending with or within this tax year?
☐ **Yes.** Skip lines 1b and 1c and complete lines 2a through 11 with respect to that SEC Form 10-K.
☐ **No.** Go to line 1b. See instructions if multiple non-tax-basis income statements are prepared.

b Did the corporation prepare a certified audited non-tax-basis income statement for that period?
☐ **Yes.** Skip line 1c and complete lines 2a through 11 with respect to that income statement.
☐ **No.** Go to line 1c.

c Did the corporation prepare a non-tax-basis income statement for that period?
☐ **Yes.** Complete lines 2a through 11 with respect to that income statement.
☐ **No.** Skip lines 2a through 3c and enter the corporation's net income (loss) per its books and records on line 4a.

2a Enter the income statement period: Beginning MM/DD/YYYY Ending MM/DD/YYYY

b Has the corporation's income statement been restated for the income statement period on line 2a?
☐ **Yes.** (If "Yes," attach an explanation and the amount of each item restated.)
☐ **No.**

c Has the corporation's income statement been restated for any of the five income statement periods immediately preceding the period on line 2a?
☐ **Yes.** (If "Yes," attach an explanation and the amount of each item restated.)
☐ **No.**

3a Is any of the corporation's voting common stock publicly traded?
☐ **Yes.**
☐ **No.** If "No," go to line 4a.

b Enter the symbol of the corporation's primary U.S. publicly traded voting common stock . . . ☐☐☐☐☐

c Enter the nine-digit CUSIP number of the corporation's primary publicly traded voting common stock . . . ☐☐☐☐☐☐☐☐☐

4a	Worldwide consolidated net income (loss) from income statement source identified in Part I, line 1 .	**4a**	
b	Indicate accounting standard used for line 4a (see instructions): (1) ☐ GAAP (2) ☐ IFRS (3) ☐ Statutory (4) ☐ Tax-basis (5) ☐ Other (specify)		
5a	Net income from nonincludible foreign entities (attach statement) . . .	**5a**	( )
b	Net loss from nonincludible foreign entities (attach statement and enter as a positive amount) . .	**5b**	
6a	Net income from nonincludible U.S. entities (attach statement) . . .	**6a**	( )
b	Net loss from nonincludible U.S. entities (attach statement and enter as a positive amount)	**6b**	
7a	Net income (loss) of other includible foreign disregarded entities (attach statement) . . .	**7a**	
b	Net income (loss) of other includible U.S. disregarded entities (attach statement) . . .	**7b**	
c	Net income (loss) of other includible entities (attach statement) . . .	**7c**	
8	Adjustment to eliminations of transactions between includible entities and nonincludible entities (attach statement) . . .	**8**	
9	Adjustment to reconcile income statement period to tax year (attach statement) . . .	**9**	
10a	Intercompany dividend adjustments to reconcile to line 11 (attach statement) . . .	**10a**	
b	Other statutory accounting adjustments to reconcile to line 11 (attach statement) . . .	**10b**	
c	Other adjustments to reconcile to amount on line 11 (attach statement) . . .	**10c**	
11	**Net income (loss) per income statement of includible corporations.** Combine lines 4 through 10 .	**11**	

Note: Part I, line 11, must equal Part II, line 30, column (a), or Schedule M-1, line 1 (see instructions).

12 Enter the total amount (not just the corporation's share) of the assets and liabilities of all entities included or removed on the following lines.

		Total Assets	Total Liabilities
a	Included on Part I, line 4 . . . ▶		
b	Removed on Part I, line 5 . . . ▶		
c	Removed on Part I, line 6 . . . ▶		
d	Included on Part I, line 7 . . . ▶		

Schedule M-3 (Form 1120) (Rev. 12-2019) Page 2

Name of corporation (common parent, if consolidated return)	Employer identification number

Check applicable box(es): (1) ☐ Consolidated group (2) ☐ Parent corp (3) ☐ Consolidated eliminations (4) ☐ Subsidiary corp (5) ☐ Mixed 1120/L/PC group

Check if a sub-consolidated: (6) ☐ 1120 group (7) ☐ 1120 eliminations

Name of subsidiary (if consolidated return)	Employer identification number

Part II Reconciliation of Net Income (Loss) per Income Statement of Includible Corporations With Taxable Income per Return (see instructions)

Income (Loss) Items (Attach statements for lines 1 through 12)	(a) Income (Loss) per Income Statement	(b) Temporary Difference	(c) Permanent Difference	(d) Income (Loss) per Tax Return
1 Income (loss) from equity method foreign corporations				
2 Gross foreign dividends not previously taxed				
3 Subpart F, QEF, and similar income inclusions				
4 Gross-up for foreign taxes deemed paid				
5 Gross foreign distributions previously taxed				
6 Income (loss) from equity method U.S. corporations				
7 U.S. dividends not eliminated in tax consolidation				
8 Minority interest for includible corporations				
9 Income (loss) from U.S. partnerships				
10 Income (loss) from foreign partnerships				
11 Income (loss) from other pass-through entities				
12 Items relating to reportable transactions				
13 Interest income (see instructions)				
14 Total accrual to cash adjustment				
15 Hedging transactions				
16 Mark-to-market income (loss)				
17 Cost of goods sold (see instructions)	( )			( )
18 Sale versus lease (for sellers and/or lessors)				
19 Section 481(a) adjustments				
20 Unearned/deferred revenue				
21 Income recognition from long-term contracts				
22 Original issue discount and other imputed interest				
23a Income statement gain/loss on sale, exchange, abandonment, worthlessness, or other disposition of assets other than inventory and pass-through entities				
b Gross capital gains from Schedule D, excluding amounts from pass-through entities				
c Gross capital losses from Schedule D, excluding amounts from pass-through entities, abandonment losses, and worthless stock losses				
d Net gain/loss reported on Form 4797, line 17, excluding amounts from pass-through entities, abandonment losses, and worthless stock losses				
e Abandonment losses				
f Worthless stock losses (attach statement)				
g Other gain/loss on disposition of assets other than inventory				
24 Capital loss limitation and carryforward used				
25 Other income (loss) items with differences (attach statement)				
26 **Total income (loss) items.** Combine lines 1 through 25				
27 **Total expense/deduction items** (from Part III, line 39)				
28 Other items with no differences				
29a Mixed groups, see instructions. All others, combine lines 26 through 28				
b PC insurance subgroup reconciliation totals				
c Life insurance subgroup reconciliation totals				
30 **Reconciliation totals.** Combine lines 29a through 29c				

Note: Line 30, column (a), must equal Part I, line 11, and column (d) must equal Form 1120, page 1, line 28.

Schedule M-3 (Form 1120) (Rev. 12-2019)

Schedule M-3 (Form 1120) (Rev. 12-2019) Page **3**

Name of corporation (common parent, if consolidated return)	**Employer identification number**

Check applicable box(es): **(1)** ☐ Consolidated group **(2)** ☐ Parent corp **(3)** ☐ Consolidated eliminations **(4)** ☐ Subsidiary corp **(5)** ☐ Mixed 1120/L/PC group

Check if a sub-consolidated: **(6)** ☐ 1120 group **(7)** ☐ 1120 eliminations

Name of subsidiary (if consolidated return)	**Employer identification number**

Part III Reconciliation of Net Income (Loss) per Income Statement of Includible Corporations With Taxable Income per Return—Expense/Deduction Items (see instructions)

	Expense/Deduction Items	(a) Expense per Income Statement	(b) Temporary Difference	(c) Permanent Difference	(d) Deduction per Tax Return
1	U.S. current income tax expense				
2	U.S. deferred income tax expense				
3	State and local current income tax expense				
4	State and local deferred income tax expense				
5	Foreign current income tax expense (other than foreign withholding taxes)				
6	Foreign deferred income tax expense				
7	Foreign withholding taxes				
8	Interest expense (see instructions)				
9	Stock option expense				
10	Other equity-based compensation				
11	Meals and entertainment				
12	Fines and penalties				
13	Judgments, damages, awards, and similar costs				
14	Parachute payments				
15	Compensation with section 162(m) limitation				
16	Pension and profit-sharing				
17	Other post-retirement benefits				
18	Deferred compensation				
19	Charitable contribution of cash and tangible property				
20	Charitable contribution of intangible property				
21	Charitable contribution limitation/carryforward				
22	Domestic production activities deduction (see instructions)				
23	Current year acquisition or reorganization investment banking fees				
24	Current year acquisition or reorganization legal and accounting fees				
25	Current year acquisition/reorganization other costs				
26	Amortization/impairment of goodwill				
27	Amortization of acquisition, reorganization, and start-up costs				
28	Other amortization or impairment write-offs				
29	Reserved				
30	Depletion				
31	Depreciation				
32	Bad debt expense				
33	Corporate owned life insurance premiums				
34	Purchase versus lease (for purchasers and/or lessees)				
35	Research and development costs				
36	Section 118 exclusion (attach statement)				
37	Section 162(r)—FDIC premiums paid by certain large financial institutions (see instructions)				
38	Other expense/deduction items with differences (attach statement)				
39	**Total expense/deduction items.** Combine lines 1 through 38. Enter here and on Part II, line 27, reporting positive amounts as negative and negative amounts as positive				

Form **1120-S** Department of the Treasury Internal Revenue Service

U.S. Income Tax Return for an S Corporation

Do not file this form unless the corporation has filed or is attaching Form 2553 to elect to be an S corporation.
Go to *www.irs.gov/Form1120S* for instructions and the latest information.

OMB No. 1545-0123

2024

For calendar year 2024 or tax year beginning , 2024, ending , 20

A S election effective date	TYPE OR PRINT	Name	D Employer identification number
B Business activity code number (see instructions)		Number, street, and room or suite no. If a P.O. box, see instructions.	E Date incorporated
C Check if Sch. M-3 attached ☐		City or town, state or province, country, and ZIP or foreign postal code	F Total assets (see instructions) $

G Is the corporation electing to be an S corporation beginning with this tax year? See instructions. ☐ Yes ☐ No

H Check if: **(1)** ☐ Final return **(2)** ☐ Name change **(3)** ☐ Address change **(4)** ☐ Amended return **(5)** ☐ S election termination

I Enter the number of shareholders who were shareholders during any part of the tax year . . . .

J Check if corporation: **(1)** ☐ Aggregated activities for section 465 at-risk purposes **(2)** ☐ Grouped activities for section 469 passive activity purposes

Caution: Include **only** trade or business income and expenses on lines 1a through 22. See the instructions for more information.

Income	1a	Gross receipts or sales ____ **b** Less returns and allowances ____ **c** Balance			1c	
	2	Cost of goods sold (attach Form 1125-A)			2	
	3	Gross profit. Subtract line 2 from line 1c			3	
	4	Net gain (loss) from Form 4797, Part II, line 17 (attach Form 4797)			4	
	5	Other income (loss) (see instructions—attach statement)			5	
	6	**Total income (loss).** Add lines 3 through 5			6	
Deductions (see instructions for limitations)	7	Compensation of officers (see instructions—attach Form 1125-E)			7	
	8	Salaries and wages (less employment credits)			8	
	9	Repairs and maintenance			9	
	10	Bad debts			10	
	11	Rents			11	
	12	Taxes and licenses			12	
	13	Interest (see instructions)			13	
	14	Depreciation from Form 4562 not claimed on Form 1125-A or elsewhere on return (attach Form 4562)			14	
	15	Depletion **(do not deduct oil and gas depletion)**			15	
	16	Advertising			16	
	17	Pension, profit-sharing, etc., plans			17	
	18	Employee benefit programs			18	
	19	Energy efficient commercial buildings deduction (attach Form 7205)			19	
	20	Other deductions (attach statement)			20	
	21	**Total deductions.** Add lines 7 through 20			21	
	22	**Ordinary business income (loss).** Subtract line 21 from line 6			22	
Tax and Payments	23a	Excess net passive income or LIFO recapture tax (see instructions)	23a			
	b	Tax from Schedule D (Form 1120-S)	23b			
	c	Add lines 23a and 23b (see instructions for additional taxes)			23c	
	24a	Current year's estimated tax payments and preceding year's overpayment credited to the current year	24a			
	b	Tax deposited with Form 7004	24b			
	c	Credit for federal tax paid on fuels (attach Form 4136)	24c			
	d	Elective payment election amount from Form 3800	24d			
	z	Add lines 24a through 24d			24z	
	25	Estimated tax penalty (see instructions). Check if Form 2220 is attached ☐			25	
	26	**Amount owed.** If line 24z is smaller than the total of lines 23c and 25, enter amount owed			26	
	27	**Overpayment.** If line 24z is larger than the total of lines 23c and 25, enter amount overpaid			27	
	28	Enter amount from line 27: **Credited to 2025 estimated tax** ____ **Refunded**			28	

Sign Here

Under penalties of perjury, I declare that I have examined this return, including accompanying schedules and statements, and to the best of my knowledge and belief, it is true, correct, and complete. Declaration of preparer (other than taxpayer) is based on all information of which preparer has any knowledge.

Signature of officer | Date | Title

May the IRS discuss this return with the preparer shown below? See instructions. ☐ **Yes** ☐ **No**

Paid Preparer Use Only				
Print/Type preparer's name	Preparer's signature	Date	Check ☐ if self-employed	PTIN
Firm's name			Firm's EIN	
Firm's address			Phone no.	

For Paperwork Reduction Act Notice, see separate instructions. Cat. No. 11510H Form **1120-S** (2024)

Form 1120-S (2024) Page **2**

Schedule B **Other Information** (see instructions)

		Yes	No
1	Check accounting method: **a** ☐ Cash **b** ☐ Accrual **c** ☐ Other (specify)		
2	See the instructions and enter the: **a** Business activity ________ **b** Product or service ________		
3	At any time during the tax year, was any shareholder of the corporation a disregarded entity, a trust, an estate, or a nominee or similar person? If "Yes," attach Schedule B-1, Information on Certain Shareholders of an S Corporation		
4	At the end of the tax year, did the corporation:		
a	Own directly 20% or more, or own, directly or indirectly, 50% or more of the total stock issued and outstanding of any foreign or domestic corporation? For rules of constructive ownership, see instructions. If "Yes," complete (i) through (v) below		

(i) Name of Corporation	**(ii)** Employer Identification Number (if any)	**(iii)** Country of Incorporation	**(iv)** Percentage of Stock Owned	**(v)** If Percentage in (iv) Is 100%, Enter the Date (if applicable) a Qualified Subchapter S Subsidiary Election Was Made

		Yes	No
b	Own directly an interest of 20% or more, or own, directly or indirectly, an interest of 50% or more in the profit, loss, or capital in any foreign or domestic partnership (including an entity treated as a partnership) or in the beneficial interest of a trust? For rules of constructive ownership, see instructions. If "Yes," complete (i) through (v) below		

(i) Name of Entity	**(ii)** Employer Identification Number (if any)	**(iii)** Type of Entity	**(iv)** Country of Organization	**(v)** Maximum Percentage Owned in Profit, Loss, or Capital

		Yes	No
5a	At the end of the tax year, did the corporation have any outstanding shares of restricted stock? If "Yes," complete lines (i) and (ii) below. **(i)** Total shares of restricted stock ________ **(ii)** Total shares of non-restricted stock ________		
b	At the end of the tax year, did the corporation have any outstanding stock options, warrants, or similar instruments? If "Yes," complete lines (i) and (ii) below. **(i)** Total shares of stock outstanding at the end of the tax year ________ **(ii)** Total shares of stock outstanding if all instruments were executed ________		
6	Has this corporation filed, or is it required to file, **Form 8918**, Material Advisor Disclosure Statement, to provide information on any reportable transaction?		
7	Check this box if the corporation issued publicly offered debt instruments with original issue discount ☐ If checked, the corporation may have to file **Form 8281**, Information Return for Publicly Offered Original Issue Discount Instruments.		
8	If the corporation (**a**) was a C corporation before it elected to be an S corporation **or** the corporation acquired an asset with a basis determined by reference to the basis of the asset (or the basis of any other property) in the hands of a C corporation, **and** (**b**) has net unrealized built-in gain in excess of the net recognized built-in gain from prior years, enter the net unrealized built-in gain reduced by net recognized built-in gain from prior years. See instructions $ ________		
9	Did the corporation have an election under section 163(j) for any real property trade or business or any farming business in effect during the tax year? See instructions		
10	Does the corporation satisfy one or more of the following? See instructions		
a	The corporation owns a pass-through entity with current, or prior year carryover, excess business interest expense.		
b	The corporation's aggregate average annual gross receipts (determined under section 448(c)) for the 3 tax years preceding the current tax year are more than $30 million and the corporation has business interest expense.		
c	The corporation is a tax shelter and the corporation has business interest expense. If "Yes," complete and attach **Form 8990**, Limitation on Business Interest Expense Under Section 163(j).		
11	Does the corporation satisfy **both** of the following conditions?		
a	The corporation's total receipts (see instructions) for the tax year were less than $250,000.		
b	The corporation's total assets at the end of the tax year were less than $250,000. If "Yes," the corporation is not required to complete Schedules L and M-1.		

Form **1120-S** (2024)

Form 1120-S (2024) Page 3

Schedule B Other Information (see instructions) *(continued)*

		Yes	No
12	During the tax year, did the corporation have any non-shareholder debt that was canceled, was forgiven, or had the terms modified so as to reduce the principal amount of the debt?		
	If "Yes," enter the amount of principal reduction . . . $		
13	During the tax year, was a qualified subchapter S subsidiary election terminated or revoked? If "Yes," see instructions		
14a	Did the corporation make any payments that would require it to file Form(s) 1099?		
b	If "Yes," did or will the corporation file required Form(s) 1099?		
15	Is the corporation attaching Form 8996 to certify as a Qualified Opportunity Fund?		
	If "Yes," enter the amount from Form 8996, line 15 . . . $		
16	At any time during the tax year, did the corporation: (a) receive (as a reward, award, or payment for property or services); or (b) sell, exchange, or otherwise dispose of a digital asset (or a financial interest in a digital asset)? See instructions		

Schedule K Shareholders' Pro Rata Share Items

Section	Line	Description			Line	Total amount
Income (Loss)	1	Ordinary business income (loss) (page 1, line 22)			1	
	2	Net rental real estate income (loss) (attach Form 8825)			2	
	3a	Other gross rental income (loss)	3a			
	b	Expenses from other rental activities (attach statement)	3b			
	c	Other net rental income (loss). Subtract line 3b from line 3a			3c	
	4	Interest income			4	
	5	Dividends: **a** Ordinary dividends			5a	
		b Qualified dividends	5b			
	6	Royalties			6	
	7	Net short-term capital gain (loss) (attach Schedule D (Form 1120-S))			7	
	8a	Net long-term capital gain (loss) (attach Schedule D (Form 1120-S))			8a	
	b	Collectibles (28%) gain (loss)	8b			
	c	Unrecaptured section 1250 gain (attach statement)	8c			
	9	Net section 1231 gain (loss) (attach Form 4797)			9	
	10	Other income (loss) (see instructions) Type:			10	
Deductions	11	Section 179 deduction (attach Form 4562)			11	
	12a	Cash charitable contributions			12a	
	b	Noncash charitable contributions			12b	
	c	Investment interest expense			12c	
	d	Section 59(e)(2) expenditures Type:			12d	
	e	Other deductions (see instructions) Type:			12e	
Credits	13a	Low-income housing credit (section 42(j)(5))			13a	
	b	Low-income housing credit (other)			13b	
	c	Qualified rehabilitation expenditures (rental real estate) (attach Form 3468, if applicable)			13c	
	d	Other rental real estate credits (see instructions) Type:			13d	
	e	Other rental credits (see instructions) Type:			13e	
	f	Biofuel producer credit (attach Form 6478)			13f	
	g	Other credits (see instructions) Type:			13g	
International	14	Attach Schedule K-2 (Form 1120-S), Shareholders' Pro Rata Share Items—International, and check this box to indicate you are reporting items of international tax relevance ☐				
Alternative Minimum Tax (AMT) Items	15a	Post-1986 depreciation adjustment			15a	
	b	Adjusted gain or loss			15b	
	c	Depletion (other than oil and gas)			15c	
	d	Oil, gas, and geothermal properties—gross income			15d	
	e	Oil, gas, and geothermal properties—deductions			15e	
	f	Other AMT items (attach statement)			15f	
Items Affecting Shareholder Basis	16a	Tax-exempt interest income			16a	
	b	Other tax-exempt income			16b	
	c	Nondeductible expenses			16c	
	d	Distributions (attach statement if required) (see instructions)			16d	
	e	Repayment of loans from shareholders			16e	
	f	Foreign taxes paid or accrued			16f	

Form **1120-S** (2024)

Form 1120-S (2024) Page 4

Schedule K **Shareholders' Pro Rata Share Items** *(continued)*

				Total amount
Other Information	17a	Investment income	17a	
	b	Investment expenses	17b	
	c	Dividend distributions paid from accumulated earnings and profits	17c	
	d	Other items and amounts (attach statement)		
Recon-ciliation	18	**Income (loss) reconciliation.** Combine the total amounts on lines 1 through 10. From the result, subtract the sum of the amounts on lines 11 through 12e and 16f	18	

Schedule L **Balance Sheets per Books**

	Assets	Beginning of tax year (a)	(b)	End of tax year (c)	(d)
1	Cash				
2a	Trade notes and accounts receivable				
b	Less allowance for bad debts	( )		( )	
3	Inventories				
4	U.S. government obligations				
5	Tax-exempt securities (see instructions)				
6	Other current assets (attach statement)				
7	Loans to shareholders				
8	Mortgage and real estate loans				
9	Other investments (attach statement)				
10a	Buildings and other depreciable assets				
b	Less accumulated depreciation	( )		( )	
11a	Depletable assets				
b	Less accumulated depletion	( )		( )	
12	Land (net of any amortization)				
13a	Intangible assets (amortizable only)				
b	Less accumulated amortization	( )		( )	
14	Other assets (attach statement)				
15	Total assets				
	Liabilities and Shareholders' Equity				
16	Accounts payable				
17	Mortgages, notes, bonds payable in less than 1 year				
18	Other current liabilities (attach statement)				
19	Loans from shareholders				
20	Mortgages, notes, bonds payable in 1 year or more				
21	Other liabilities (attach statement)				
22	Capital stock				
23	Additional paid-in capital				
24	Retained earnings				
25	Adjustments to shareholders' equity (attach statement)				
26	Less cost of treasury stock		( )		( )
27	Total liabilities and shareholders' equity				

Form **1120-S** (2024)

Schedule M-1 **Reconciliation of Income (Loss) per Books With Income (Loss) per Return**

Note: The corporation may be required to file Schedule M-3. See instructions.

1	Net income (loss) per books		5	Income recorded on books this year not included on Schedule K, lines 1 through 10 (itemize):	
2	Income included on Schedule K, lines 1, 2, 3c, 4, 5a, 6, 7, 8a, 9, and 10, not recorded on books this year (itemize):		a	Tax-exempt interest $	
3	Expenses recorded on books this year not included on Schedule K, lines 1 through 12e, and 16f (itemize):		6	Deductions included on Schedule K, lines 1 through 12e, and 16f, not charged against book income this year (itemize):	
a	Depreciation $		a	Depreciation $	
b	Travel and entertainment $		7	Add lines 5 and 6	
4	Add lines 1 through 3		8	Income (loss) (Schedule K, line 18). Subtract line 7 from line 4	

Schedule M-2 **Analysis of Accumulated Adjustments Account, Shareholders' Undistributed Taxable Income Previously Taxed, Accumulated Earnings and Profits, and Other Adjustments Account** (see instructions)

		(a) Accumulated adjustments account	**(b)** Shareholders' undistributed taxable income previously taxed	**(c)** Accumulated earnings and profits	**(d)** Other adjustments account
1	Balance at beginning of tax year				
2	Ordinary income from page 1, line 22				
3	Other additions				
4	Loss from page 1, line 22	( )			
5	Other reductions	( )			( )
6	Combine lines 1 through 5				
7	Distributions				
8	Balance at end of tax year. Subtract line 7 from line 6				

671124

☐ Final K-1 ☐ Amended K-1 OMB No. 1545-0123

Schedule K-1 (Form 1120-S) **2024**

Department of the Treasury
Internal Revenue Service

For calendar year 2024, or tax year

beginning / / 2024 ending / /

Shareholder's Share of Income, Deductions, Credits, etc.

See separate instructions.

Part I Information About the Corporation

A Corporation's employer identification number

B Corporation's name, address, city, state, and ZIP code

C IRS Center where corporation filed return

D Corporation's total number of shares
Beginning of tax year . . . . . . ____________
End of tax year . . . . ____________

Part II Information About the Shareholder

E Shareholder's identifying number

F1 Shareholder's name, address, city, state, and ZIP code

F2 If the shareholder is a disregarded entity, a trust, an estate, or a nominee or similar person, enter the individual or entity responsible for reporting:

TIN ____________ Name ____________

F3 What type of entity is this shareholder? ____________

G Current year allocation percentage . . . ____________ %

H Shareholder's number of shares
Beginning of tax year . . . . . . ____________
End of tax year . . . . ____________

I Loans from shareholder
Beginning of tax year . . . . . . $ ____________
End of tax year . . . . $ ____________

For IRS Use Only

Part III Shareholder's Share of Current Year Income, Deductions, Credits, and Other Items

1	Ordinary business income (loss)	13	Credits
2	Net rental real estate income (loss)		
3	Other net rental income (loss)		
4	Interest income		
5a	Ordinary dividends		
5b	Qualified dividends	14	Schedule K-3 is attached if checked . . . . . ☐
6	Royalties	15	Alternative minimum tax (AMT) items
7	Net short-term capital gain (loss)		
8a	Net long-term capital gain (loss)		
8b	Collectibles (28%) gain (loss)		
8c	Unrecaptured section 1250 gain		
9	Net section 1231 gain (loss)	16	Items affecting shareholder basis
10	Other income (loss)		
		17	Other information
11	Section 179 deduction		
12	Other deductions		

18 ☐ More than one activity for at-risk purposes*
19 ☐ More than one activity for passive activity purposes*

* See attached statement for additional information.

Form **2553**
(Rev. December 2017)
Department of the Treasury
Internal Revenue Service

Election by a Small Business Corporation

(Under section 1362 of the Internal Revenue Code)
(Including a late election filed pursuant to Rev. Proc. 2013-30)
▶ You can fax this form to the IRS. See separate instructions.
▶ Go to *www.irs.gov/Form2553* for instructions and the latest information.

OMB No. 1545-0123

Note: This election to be an S corporation can be accepted only if all the tests are met under *Who May Elect* in the instructions, all shareholders have signed the consent statement, an officer has signed below, and the exact name and address of the corporation (entity) and other required form information have been provided.

Part I Election Information

Type or Print	Name (see instructions)	**A** Employer identification number
	Number, street, and room or suite no. If a P.O. box, see instructions.	**B** Date incorporated
	City or town, state or province, country, and ZIP or foreign postal code	**C** State of incorporation

D Check the applicable box(es) if the corporation (entity), after applying for the EIN shown in **A** above, changed its ☐ name or ☐ address

E Election is to be effective for tax year beginning (month, day, year) (see instructions) . . . . ▶ ________

Caution: A corporation (entity) making the election for its first tax year in existence will usually enter the beginning date of a short tax year that begins on a date other than January 1.

F Selected tax year:
(1) ☐ Calendar year
(2) ☐ Fiscal year ending (month and day) ▶ ________
(3) ☐ 52-53-week year ending with reference to the month of December
(4) ☐ 52-53-week year ending with reference to the month of ▶ ________
If box (2) or (4) is checked, complete Part II.

G If more than 100 shareholders are listed for item J (see page 2), check this box if treating members of a family as one shareholder results in no more than 100 shareholders (see test 2 under *Who May Elect* in the instructions) ▶ ☐

H Name and title of officer or legal representative whom the IRS may call for more information	Telephone number of officer or legal representative

I If this S corporation election is being filed late, I declare I had reasonable cause for not filing Form 2553 timely. If this late election is being made by an entity eligible to elect to be treated as a corporation, I declare I also had reasonable cause for not filing an entity classification election timely and the representations listed in Part IV are true. See below for my explanation of the reasons the election or elections were not made on time and a description of my diligent actions to correct the mistake upon its discovery. See instructions.

Sign Here

Under penalties of perjury, I declare that I have examined this election, including accompanying documents, and, to the best of my knowledge and belief, the election contains all the relevant facts relating to the election, and such facts are true, correct, and complete.

▶ Signature of officer | Title | Date

Form 2553 (Rev. 12-2017) Page **2**

Name	Employer identification number

Part I **Election Information** *(continued)* **Note:** If you need more rows, use additional copies of page 2.

J Name and address of each shareholder or former shareholder required to consent to the election. (see instructions)	**K** **Shareholder's Consent Statement** Under penalties of perjury, I declare that I consent to the election of the above-named corporation (entity) to be an S corporation under section 1362(a) and that I have examined this consent statement, including accompanying documents, and, to the best of my knowledge and belief, the election contains all the relevant facts relating to the election, and such facts are true, correct, and complete. I understand my consent is binding and may not be withdrawn after the corporation (entity) has made a valid election. If seeking relief for a late filed election, I also declare under penalties of perjury that I have reported my income on all affected returns consistent with the S corporation election for the year for which the election should have been filed (see beginning date entered on line E) and for all subsequent years.		**L** Stock owned or percentage of ownership (see instructions)		**M** Social security number or employer identification number (see instructions)	**N** Shareholder's tax year ends (month and day)
	Signature	Date	Number of shares or percentage of ownership	Date(s) acquired		

Form **2553** (Rev. 12-2017)

Form 2553 (Rev. 12-2017) Page **3**

Name	**Employer identification number**

Part II **Selection of Fiscal Tax Year** (see instructions)

Note: All corporations using this part must complete item O and item P, Q, or R.

O Check the applicable box to indicate whether the corporation is:

1. ☐ A new corporation **adopting** the tax year entered in item F, Part I.

2. ☐ An existing corporation **retaining** the tax year entered in item F, Part I.

3. ☐ An existing corporation **changing** to the tax year entered in item F, Part I.

P Complete item P if the corporation is using the automatic approval provisions of Rev. Proc. 2006-46, 2006-45 I.R.B. 859, to request (1) a natural business year (as defined in section 5.07 of Rev. Proc. 2006-46) or (2) a year that satisfies the ownership tax year test (as defined in section 5.08 of Rev. Proc. 2006-46). Check the applicable box below to indicate the representation statement the corporation is making.

1. Natural Business Year ▶ ☐ I represent that the corporation is adopting, retaining, or changing to a tax year that qualifies as its natural business year (as defined in section 5.07 of Rev. Proc. 2006-46) and has attached a statement showing separately for each month the gross receipts for the most recent 47 months. See instructions. I also represent that the corporation is not precluded by section 4.02 of Rev. Proc. 2006-46 from obtaining automatic approval of such adoption, retention, or change in tax year.

2. Ownership Tax Year ▶ ☐ I represent that shareholders (as described in section 5.08 of Rev. Proc. 2006-46) holding more than half of the shares of the stock (as of the first day of the tax year to which the request relates) of the corporation have the same tax year or are concurrently changing to the tax year that the corporation adopts, retains, or changes to per item F, Part I, and that such tax year satisfies the requirement of section 4.01(3) of Rev. Proc. 2006-46. I also represent that the corporation is not precluded by section 4.02 of Rev. Proc. 2006-46 from obtaining automatic approval of such adoption, retention, or change in tax year.

Note: If you do not use item P and the corporation wants a fiscal tax year, complete either item Q or R below. Item Q is used to request a fiscal tax year based on a business purpose and to make a back-up section 444 election. Item R is used to make a regular section 444 election.

Q Business Purpose—To request a fiscal tax year based on a business purpose, check box Q1. See instructions for details including payment of a user fee. You may also check box Q2 and/or box Q3.

1. Check here ▶ ☐ if the fiscal year entered in item F, Part I, is requested under the prior approval provisions of Rev. Proc. 2002-39, 2002-22 I.R.B. 1046. Attach to Form 2553 a statement describing the relevant facts and circumstances and, if applicable, the gross receipts from sales and services necessary to establish a business purpose. See the instructions for details regarding the gross receipts from sales and services. If the IRS proposes to disapprove the requested fiscal year, do you want a conference with the IRS National Office?

☐ Yes ☐ No

2. Check here ▶ ☐ to show that the corporation intends to make a back-up section 444 election in the event the corporation's business purpose request is not approved by the IRS. See instructions for more information.

3. Check here ▶ ☐ to show that the corporation agrees to adopt or change to a tax year ending December 31 if necessary for the IRS to accept this election for S corporation status in the event (1) the corporation's business purpose request is not approved and the corporation makes a back-up section 444 election, but is ultimately not qualified to make a section 444 election, or (2) the corporation's business purpose request is not approved and the corporation did not make a back-up section 444 election.

R Section 444 Election—To make a section 444 election, check box R1. You may also check box R2.

1. Check here ▶ ☐ to show that the corporation will make, if qualified, a section 444 election to have the fiscal tax year shown in item F, Part I. To make the election, you must complete **Form 8716,** Election To Have a Tax Year Other Than a Required Tax Year, and either attach it to Form 2553 or file it separately.

2. Check here ▶ ☐ to show that the corporation agrees to adopt or change to a tax year ending December 31 if necessary for the IRS to accept this election for S corporation status in the event the corporation is ultimately not qualified to make a section 444 election.

Form 2553 (Rev. 12-2017) Page 4

Name	Employer identification number

Part III **Qualified Subchapter S Trust (QSST) Election Under Section 1361(d)(2)* Note:** If you are making more than one QSST election, use additional copies of page 4.

Income beneficiary's name and address	Social security number
Trust's name and address	Employer identification number

Date on which stock of the corporation was transferred to the trust (month, day, year) . . . . ▶

In order for the trust named above to be a QSST and thus a qualifying shareholder of the S corporation for which this Form 2553 is filed, I hereby make the election under section 1361(d)(2). Under penalties of perjury, I certify that the trust meets the definitional requirements of section 1361(d)(3) and that all other information provided in Part III is true, correct, and complete.

Signature of income beneficiary or signature and title of legal representative or other qualified person making the election Date

*Use Part III to make the QSST election only if stock of the corporation has been transferred to the trust on or before the date on which the corporation makes its election to be an S corporation. The QSST election must be made and filed separately if stock of the corporation is transferred to the trust **after** the date on which the corporation makes the S election.

Part IV **Late Corporate Classification Election Representations** (see instructions)

If a late entity classification election was intended to be effective on the same date that the S corporation election was intended to be effective, relief for a late S corporation election must also include the following representations.

1 The requesting entity is an eligible entity as defined in Regulations section 301.7701-3(a);

2 The requesting entity intended to be classified as a corporation as of the effective date of the S corporation status;

3 The requesting entity fails to qualify as a corporation solely because Form 8832, Entity Classification Election, was not timely filed under Regulations section 301.7701-3(c)(1)(i), or Form 8832 was not deemed to have been filed under Regulations section 301.7701-3(c)(1)(v)(C);

4 The requesting entity fails to qualify as an S corporation on the effective date of the S corporation status solely because the S corporation election was not timely filed pursuant to section 1362(b); **and**

5a The requesting entity timely filed all required federal tax returns and information returns consistent with its requested classification as an S corporation for all of the years the entity intended to be an S corporation and no inconsistent tax or information returns have been filed by or with respect to the entity during any of the tax years, **or**

b The requesting entity has not filed a federal tax or information return for the first year in which the election was intended to be effective because the due date has not passed for that year's federal tax or information return.

Form **8832** (Rev. December 2013) Department of the Treasury Internal Revenue Service

Entity Classification Election

▶ **Information about Form 8832 and its instructions is at *www.irs.gov/form8832*.**

OMB No. 1545-1516

Type or Print	Name of eligible entity making election	**Employer identification number**
	Number, street, and room or suite no. If a P.O. box, see instructions.	
	City or town, state, and ZIP code. If a foreign address, enter city, province or state, postal code and country. Follow the country's practice for entering the postal code.	

▶Check if: ☐ Address change ☐ Late classification relief sought under Revenue Procedure 2009-41
☐ Relief for a late change of entity classification election sought under Revenue Procedure 2010-32

Part I Election Information

1 **Type of election** (see instructions):

a ☐ Initial classification by a newly-formed entity. Skip lines 2a and 2b and go to line 3.
b ☐ Change in current classification. Go to line 2a.

2a Has the eligible entity previously filed an entity election that had an effective date within the last 60 months?

☐ **Yes.** Go to line 2b.
☐ **No.** Skip line 2b and go to line 3.

2b Was the eligible entity's prior election an initial classification election by a newly formed entity that was effective on the date of formation?

☐ **Yes.** Go to line 3.
☐ **No.** Stop here. You generally are not currently eligible to make the election (see instructions).

3 Does the eligible entity have more than one owner?

☐ **Yes.** You can elect to be classified as a partnership or an association taxable as a corporation. Skip line 4 and go to line 5.
☐ **No.** You can elect to be classified as an association taxable as a corporation or to be disregarded as a separate entity. Go to line 4.

4 If the eligible entity has only one owner, provide the following information:

a Name of owner ▶ ______________________
b Identifying number of owner ▶ ______________________

5 If the eligible entity is owned by one or more affiliated corporations that file a consolidated return, provide the name and employer identification number of the parent corporation:

a Name of parent corporation ▶ ______________________
b Employer identification number ▶ ______________________

For Paperwork Reduction Act Notice, see instructions. Cat. No. 22598R Form **8832** (Rev. 12-2013)

Form 8832 (Rev. 12-2013) Page **2**

Part I **Election Information** (Continued)

6 **Type of entity** (see instructions):

a ☐ A domestic eligible entity electing to be classified as an association taxable as a corporation.
b ☐ A domestic eligible entity electing to be classified as a partnership.
c ☐ A domestic eligible entity with a single owner electing to be disregarded as a separate entity.
d ☐ A foreign eligible entity electing to be classified as an association taxable as a corporation.
e ☐ A foreign eligible entity electing to be classified as a partnership.
f ☐ A foreign eligible entity with a single owner electing to be disregarded as a separate entity.

7 If the eligible entity is created or organized in a foreign jurisdiction, provide the foreign country of organization ▶ ______________________

8 Election is to be effective beginning (month, day, year) (see instructions) . . . . ▶ __________

9 Name and title of contact person whom the IRS may call for more information	10 Contact person's telephone number

Consent Statement and Signature(s) (see instructions)

Under penalties of perjury, I (we) declare that I (we) consent to the election of the above-named entity to be classified as indicated above, and that I (we) have examined this election and consent statement, and to the best of my (our) knowledge and belief, this election and consent statement are true, correct, and complete. If I am an officer, manager, or member signing for the entity, I further declare under penalties of perjury that I am authorized to make the election on its behalf.

Signature(s)	Date	Title

Form **8832** (Rev. 12-2013)

Form 8832 (Rev. 12-2013) Page 3

Part II Late Election Relief

11 Provide the explanation as to why the entity classification election was not filed on time (see instructions).

Under penalties of perjury, I (we) declare that I (we) have examined this election, including accompanying documents, and, to the best of my (our) knowledge and belief, the election contains all the relevant facts relating to the election, and such facts are true, correct, and complete. I (we) further declare that I (we) have personal knowledge of the facts and circumstances related to the election. I (we) further declare that the elements required for relief in Section 4.01 of Revenue Procedure 2009-41 have been satisfied.

Signature(s)	Date	Title

Form **8832** (Rev. 12-2013)

Glossary

12-Month Rule Taxpayers may take an immediate deduction for prepaid business expenses, as long as the benefits from those expenses do not extend beyond the *earlier* of:

- 12 months after benefits first begin, *or*
- The end of the year after the year in which the taxpayer made the payment.

30-Day Letter Letter explaining the assessments the IRS has made in an audit and giving the taxpayer 30 days to agree to them before the IRS takes further action.

50% Test (Brother-Sister Controlled Group) This test is met if the five or fewer shareholders have common ownership of more than 50% of the total combined voting powers of all classes of stock entitled to vote, *or* more than 50% of the total value of shares of all classes of stock of each corporation.

80% Test (Affiliated Group) One or more of the other corporations in the group possess stock with at least 80% of the voting power of all classes of stock entitled to vote, and at least 80% of the total value of shares of all classes of stock of each of the corporations (except the common parent).

80% Test (Brother-Sister Controlled Group) This test is met if five or fewer shareholders in the group possess at least 80% of the voting power of all classes of stock entitled to vote, *or* at least 80% of the total value of all classes of stock of each of the corporations.

80% Test (Controlled Group) This test is met if one or more of the other corporations in the group possess at least 80% of the voting power of all classes of stock entitled to vote, *or* at least 80% of the total value of all classes of stock of each of the corporations (except the common parent).

90-Day Letter *See* Statutory Notice of Deficiency.

A

AAA Bypass Election S corporation election to distribute its E&P before its AAA.

Accumulated Adjustments Account (AAA) Represents an S corporation's accumulated earnings that have never been distributed to shareholders for the years it has been an S corporation. All items of income, deductions, gains, and losses are included in AAA, *except* for tax-exempt income, expenses relating to production of tax-exempt income, and federal taxes relating to a C corporation year.

Accumulated E&P A corporation's earnings and profits as of the beginning of the tax year.

Accumulated Earnings Credit Permits corporations to accumulate at least a minimum amount of business income and not be subject to the accumulated earnings tax, even if there is no business purpose for the accumulation. The corporation also earns a credit for income accumulated for the reasonable needs of the business. The accumulated earnings credit is the *greater* of:

- $250,000 ($150,000 for service corporations) less the accumulated earnings and profits at the close of the preceding year, *or*
- The reasonable needs of the business.

Accumulated Earnings Tax (AET) A tax of 20% imposed on a corporation's undistributed accumulated taxable income (ATI). Congress designed the accumulated earnings tax to mitigate the use of the corporate form to shelter business earnings from the higher individual income tax rates by not paying dividends. Personal holding companies, tax-exempt corporations, and S corporations are not subject to the AET.

Accumulated Taxable Income (ATI) Measures the corporation's ability to pay a dividend for purposes of the accumulated earnings tax.

Acquiescence Indicates that the IRS will follow a particular judicial decision in future situations involving similar facts and issues.

Acquisitive Reorganizations Occurs when two or more corporations are merged or consolidated into one organization.

Active Income Any income that is not passive income or portfolio income.

Adjusted Basis The original cost of an asset plus capital improvements and less accumulated depreciation.

Adjusted Financial Statement Income (Corporate Minimum Tax) The net income or loss of the taxpayer as presented in the taxpayer's applicable financial statements. Various adjustments are made to determine adjusted financial statement income. Certain items are taken into account on a tax basis, rather than on a financial statement (book) income basis.

Adjusted Ordinary Gross Income (AOGI) For the purposes of the personal holding company tax, this amount is computed as follows:

Gross Income (after reduction for cost of goods sold)
Less: Net capital gains and net Section 1231 gains
Ordinary Gross Income
Less: Certain rental expenses
Adjusted ordinary gross income

Adjusted Taxable Gifts (Estate Tax) Post-1976 taxable gifts other than gifts already included in the gross estate. Adjusted taxable gifts are included at their date of gift values.

Affiliated Group Exists if the 80% test and the common parent test are met. An affiliated group can elect to file a consolidated tax return.

After-Tax Income Net income after reducing revenue for all expenses, including federal income taxes.

Aggregate Theory Holds that a partnership does not exist as a separate entity from the partners. That is, a partnership is simply an aggregation of the partners. To determine the tax result of a partnership transaction using the aggregate theory, you should ask what the result would be if the partnership did not exist.

Allocation The assignment of nonbusiness income to a specific state based on the nature of the income.

Alternate Valuation Date For an estate, the date six months after the decedent's date of death. In general, property is included in the gross estate at its fair market value on the date of death, but the alternate valuation date can sometimes be used.

Amount Realized The value that the owner of the property receives from a sale or disposition.

Annual Exclusion The amount that an individual can transfer to another individual during a tax year without having the transfer be subject to the gift tax. The annual exclusion is $19,000 (2025) per donee and is indexed for inflation.

Anti-Deferral Regimes Rules that prevent the deferral by U.S. corporations of income earned in foreign countries.

Applicable Corporation A corporation whose average annual adjusted financial statement income for a 3-tax-year period for one or more previous tax years, determined without regard to loss carryovers, exceeds $1 billion (for a tax year that ends after December 31, 2021). This rule does not apply to S corporations, regulated investment companies, or real estate investment trusts.

Applicable Credit The applicable credit exclusion of $13,990,000 offsets up to $5,541,800 of unified tax for 2025. The $5,541,800 is the applicable credit, which is sometimes referred to as the *unified credit*.

Applicable Credit Exclusion An inflation-adjusted statutory amount that provides the total amount of transfers that an individual can make to others during the individual's life and at death without being subject to the unified transfer tax. The applicable credit exclusion for 2025 is $13,990,000.

Applicable Financial Statement A statement generally prepared in accordance with either GAAP, IFRS, or prepared for use by creditors.

Apportionable Income Business income for state nexus purposes.

Apportionment The assignment of business income to states based on a formula that uses a combination of the company's payroll, property, and sales.

At-Risk Hurdle A limitation on deductions incurred in a trade or business or in the production of income to the amount a taxpayer has *at-risk*. The at-risk amount is calculated as the cash and adjusted basis of property contributed by the taxpayer, plus liabilities for which the taxpayer is personally liable.

B

Base Erosion and Anti-Abuse Tax (BEAT) A 10% minimum tax aimed at preventing both foreign and domestic corporations doing business in the United States from shifting profits out of the United States; applies only to large multinational corporations with gross receipts of $500 million or more.

Basis Hurdle A limitation on the amount of losses and deductions that a taxpayer can deduct related to a particular investment to the individual's tax basis. Losses in excess of basis can be carried forward and used in future years when the taxpayer has sufficient basis.

Beneficiaries Those who benefit economically from the assets in a trust. *Income beneficiaries* (sometimes referred to as *current beneficiaries*) receive distributions of the income earned by the trust assets each year based on the terms of the trust. *Remainder beneficiaries* receive distributions of the assets in the trust when the trust terminates.

Book Basis A taxpayer's investment in property that determines the amount of cost recovery and gain or loss upon disposition under GAAP.

Book Equivalent of Taxable Income Pretax book income adjusted for only permanent differences.

Book Income Net income reported on the entity's financial statements.

Book-Tax Differences Differences that arise when the amount of an item of income or deduction recognized in book income is different from the amount used for taxable income.

Boot Any property exchanged that is not qualifying like-kind property, including cash.

Boot (Corporate Formation) Cash or property transferred as part of a corporate formation to the shareholder from the corporation that is not common stock or preferred stock.

Boot (Corporate Reorganization) Any consideration in a qualified reorganization provided to a target corporation other than qualifying stock.

Boot (Partnerships) Any property received by a partner in a partnership formation other than a partnership interest.

Brother-Sister (B-S) Controlled Groups Common ownership by individuals for a group of corporations. A B-S controlled group exists if the shareholder test, 50% test, and 80% test are met. Certain tax attributes are limited for controlled groups.

Built-In Gain (BIG) (S Corporation) The excess of the fair market value over the adjusted basis of an asset on the effective date of the S corporation election.

Built-In Gain or Loss Occurs when a partner contributes an asset to a partnership that has a different fair market value from its adjusted basis in exchange for a partnership interest. Built-in gains and losses are also known as *precontribution gains and losses*, or *Section 704(c) gains and losses.*

Built-In Gains (BIG) Tax When a C corporation makes an S election, it must measure the built-in gains and losses on the election date for all its assets and liabilities. If there is a net built-in gain on the election date, and the S corporation recognizes some or all of this built-in gain over the next five years, the S corporation must pay tax at a 21% rate on the recognized built-in gain.

Built-In Loss (BIL) (Corporate Liquidations) A loss that would have been recognized had the asset been sold for its FMV on the date it was *contributed to the corporation* during the previous two years.

Built-In Loss (BIL) (S Corporation) The excess of the adjusted basis of an asset over its fair market value on the effective date of the S corporation election.

Business Income Income arising from transactions and activity in the regular course of the taxpayer's trade or business; includes income from tangible and intangible property if the acquisition, management, and disposition of the property constitute integral parts of the taxpayer's regular trade or business operations.

Business Purpose A judicial doctrine that must be met to have a qualified reorganization.

Business Trust A legal entity that holds the rights to an individual's stake or interest in a business. The trust technically owns the business interest, and the trustee controls the interest. The trust can have multiple beneficiaries.

C

Capital Account The liquidation proceeds that a partner should receive when the partnership liquidates. Therefore, the capital account should reflect the fair market value of the partner's interest in the partnership.

Capital Asset Any asset that is not an ordinary asset or Section 1231 asset. The most common types of capital assets are property held for investment use and property held for personal use.

Capital Improvements Expenditures that either restore an asset, resulting in an increase in value, extend the asset's life, or adapt the asset to a new use.

Carried Interest A profits interest that is received in return for services, and held in partnerships that have significant assets in investments or real estate.

Carryover Basis The partnership's basis in an asset received from the partner and is the same basis as the partner had in the asset.

Carryovers Amounts transferred from one period to another. Carryovers occur when tax deductions and tax credits cannot be utilized on the tax return for the year in which they are created and are carried back or carried forward to reduce the tax liability in prior or future years.

Check-the-Box Regulations Regulations that determine how a business entity is taxed for federal income tax purposes. The main premise of the check-the-box regulations is that unincorporated entities may choose to be taxed as a corporation or a partnership. Incorporated entities are taxed as either a C corporation or an S corporation.

Circular 230 The IRS's rules of practice governing CPAs, attorneys, enrolled agents, and others authorized to practice before the IRS.

Closed Year A year in which the statute of limitations has expired for the year.

Closely Held Corporation A corporation is considered closely held if at any time during the last half of the taxable year more than 50% of the value of its outstanding stock is owned, directly or indirectly, by not more than five individuals.

Collectible Tangible personal property such as coins, art, gold, silver, and antiques purchased for investment purposes.

Common Parent Test (Affiliated Group) The common parent owns stock possessing at least 80% of the total combined voting power of all classes of stock entitled to vote, *and* at least 80% of the total value of shares of all classes of stock of at least one of the other corporations in the group.

Common Parent Test (Controlled Group) The common parent owns stock possessing at least 80% of the total combined voting power of all classes of stock entitled to vote, *or* at least 80% of the total value of shares of all classes of stock of at least one of the other corporations in the group.

Complex Trust Any trust that does not qualify as a simple trust.

Computer Program Any software application or set of statements or instructions used by a computer to bring about a certain result.

Consent Dividends Hypothetical dividends that are treated as if they were paid to shareholders on the last day of the corporation's taxable year. A corporation can declare a consent dividend at any time if the corporation has a reasonable basis to believe that it may be subject to the accumulated earnings tax (AET).

Conservatism Principle For financial reporting, a principle requiring that a business recognize expenses and liabilities as soon as possible, even when there is some uncertainty about the existence of the liability, but recognize revenues and assets only when they are assured of being received.

Consolidated Return A tax return that includes the taxable income of more than one corporation. Even though the corporations are legally separate entities, for tax purposes, they file only one return.

Consolidation Occurs in a reorganization when both the acquired and acquiring corporations dissolve into a new (surviving) corporation.

Constructive Dividends Benefits paid to shareholders in a form other than cash, property, or stock with no expectation of repayment.

Constructive Ownership The constructive ownership rules provide that a shareholder is deemed to own stock owned by those related to the shareholder, in addition to the shares held directly by the shareholder. There are three sets of constructive ownership rules that apply:

- Family attribution
- Entity-to-owner attribution
- Owner-to-entity attribution

Continuity of Business Enterprise A judicial (now regulatory) doctrine that requires that the acquiring corporation must either continue the historic business of the target corporation, or use a significant portion of target corporation's assets in the continuing business of acquiring corporation.

Continuity of Interest A judicial (now regulatory) doctrine that requires that a substantial amount of the consideration that an acquiring corporation gives to a target corporation must be stock in the acquiring corporation.

Contraction of the Corporate Business (Partial Liquidation) Occurs when there is a significant reduction in the level of business activities, such as the number of employees, services, income, or assets.

Control Club Includes the shareholders who contributed property and received corporate stock. The *control club* must own 80% or more of the voting power and number of shares of the corporation immediately after the exchange for the Section 351 requirements to be met.

Control Test Met if 80% or more of the voting power and number of shares of the corporation is owned by the control club immediately after the exchange.

Controlled Foreign Corporation (CFC) A foreign corporation in which, on any day during the year, more than 50% of the voting stock or value is owned by U.S. shareholders.

Controlled Group Two or more corporations that have a certain level of common ownership between them. There are three types of controlled groups: parent-subsidiary groups, brother-sister groups, and certain insurance companies.

Corporate Liquidation Occurs when a corporation dissolves and distributes any remaining assets to the shareholders.

Corporation A business that has met a state's requirements to organize as a legal entity that is distinct from its owners. In most states, the owners file articles of incorporation with the state and elect a board of directors.

Corpus The assets transferred to a trust by the grantor, which can include stocks, bonds, homes, land, automobiles, and business assets.

Correspondence Examination A simple audit handled through written correspondence.

Current Beneficiaries Beneficiaries that receive distributions of the income earned by the trust assets each year based on the terms of the trust. Also known as *income beneficiaries*.

Current Distribution A distribution for which the partner continues to be a partner after the distribution.

Current E&P A corporation's earnings and profits generated during the current tax year.

Current Income Tax Asset The amount of taxes refundable on the tax return for the current year.

Current Income Tax Expense (Benefit) The amount of taxes payable (refundable) on the tax return for the current year

Current Income Tax Liability The amount of taxes payable on the tax return for the current year.

D

Debt Basis (S Corporation) S corporation shareholders have debt basis to the extent that the shareholder has loaned money directly to the S corporation. Guarantees of corporate debt are not sufficient to create debt basis.

Debt-Financed Property (Tax-Exempt Organizations) Property of an exempt organization that has acquisition indebtedness and is held for the production of income.

Declaration Date Date that a corporation announces it will pay a dividend, the amount, and other important details.

Deductible Temporary Book-Tax Difference Book-tax difference that causes future taxable income to be less than book income due to reversal of an unfavorable temporary book-tax difference in the current year.

Deemed Cash The amount of debt relief if the partner's share of partnership debt decreases, or if the partnership assumes the partner's debt. Treated as a cash distribution to the partner.

Deferral Rule Allows a taxpayer to elect to defer prepaid service income to the following tax year if the taxpayer treats it the same way for financial reporting purposes.

Deferred Gain or Loss A gain or loss that the tax law includes in taxable income in a later year. It equals the realized gain or loss less the recognized gain or loss.

Deferred Income Tax Asset The expected future tax benefit (savings) attributable to deductible temporary differences and carryovers.

Deferred Income Tax Expense (Benefit) The amount of the future tax cost (savings) attributable to temporary book-tax differences and carryovers.

Deferred Income Tax Liability The expected future tax cost attributable to taxable temporary differences.

Deficiency Dividend A dividend paid to avoid the personal holding company (PHC) tax. It must be paid within 90 days of the imposition of the tax by the IRS or a court decision.

Disabled Access Credit A tax credit available to eligible small businesses for expenditures incurred to make the business accessible to individuals with disabilities. The amount of this credit is equal to 50% of the amount of the eligible access expenditures for a year over a $10,000 range from greater than $250 but not greater than $10,250.

Discount Factor The taxpayer's rate of return to determine the present value of future income received or taxes owed.

Disproportionate (Distribution) The partner who receives the distribution does not have the same interest in the ordinary income potential in the hot assets before and after the distribution.

Disqualified Person (Excess Benefits Tax) A person who could exercise substantial influence over the affairs of an exempt organization during the five-year period ending on the date of the excess benefit transaction. Family members of a disqualified person are also disqualified, defined as the disqualified person's spouse, siblings and siblings' spouses, ancestors, children, grandchildren, great grandchildren, and spouses of these descendants.

Disqualified Persons (Private Foundations and Self-Dealing Tax) Donors whose contributions exceeded 2% of total contributions and $5,000, as well as officers, directors, trustees, and their family members.

Disqualified Property (Corporate Liquidation) Property that was contributed to the corporation recently (two-year period for nonrelated parties and five-year period for related parties) in a tax-deferred transaction or as a contribution to capital.

Distributable Net Income (DNI) The maximum amount of the income distribution deduction for a trust or estate; it is also the maximum amount of income that the beneficiaries must recognize. The deduction or the income can be less than DNI, but not more than DNI.

Dividend Any distribution of cash or property from a corporation to its shareholders, if the distribution is made from the corporation's earnings and profits.

Dividends Received Deduction (DRD) A corporate deduction allowed to offset some or all the dividend income a corporation receives from other corporations. The domestic DRD is either 50%, 65%, or 100% of the qualifying dividend received. The percentage used to compute the DRD depends on the percentage of stock owned in the dividend-paying corporation.

Divisive Reorganizations Occur when one corporation divides into two or more corporations.

Domestic Corporation (for State Taxes) A corporation doing business in the state in which it was incorporated.

Double Taxation Taxation of the income of a business at both the entity level and the owner level before it can be controlled and used by the owners.

E

Earnings and Profits (E&P) The cumulative earnings for a corporation that it has never distributed as a dividend or a redemption. Conceptually, it is very similar to retained earnings, but it is computed based on the tax law rather than financial reporting rules.

Economic Performance Occurs when the taxpayer receives services or property or uses property another party provided.

Effective Tax Rate (Business Entities) Total income tax expense divided by pre-tax net income.

Effectively Connected Income (ECI) Income earned by a foreign taxpayer that is connected with a U.S. trade or business. The method used to determine ECI differs depending on whether the foreign taxpayer is from a country that has a treaty with the United States.

Electing Large Partnership A partnership that has elected to be taxed under a simplified reporting system that does not require as much separate reporting to partners as a regular partnership does.

Employer-Paid Medical and Family Leave Credit A general business tax credit equal to 12.5% of wages paid to qualifying employees while on family and medical leave. The 12.5% is increased by 0.25 percentage points for each percentage point by which the wages paid exceed 50%. The maximum percentage is 25%.

Employer-Provided Childcare Credit A credit for expenses incurred to provide childcare facilities to their employees during normal working hours. The credit is equal to 25% of qualified childcare expenditures, and 10% of qualified childcare resource and referral expenditures.

Enrolled Agent A person who has passed a three-part comprehensive IRS test covering individual and business tax returns, or who has substantial experience as a former IRS employee.

Entity Theory A theory that holds that a business is a distinct entity from its owners. Thus, any time that cash or property passes between the entity and the owners, there are potential tax consequences. This is the theory used by C corporations and for most S corporation transactions.

Entity-to-Owner Attribution If an individual has an ownership interest in a business entity, then the individual may be deemed to own stock that the business entity owns.

Estate The total assets comprising the net worth of an individual at the time of death, including all real estate, possessions, financial investments, cash, and other assets that the individual owns or has a controlling interest in. The estate exists for as long as is needed to settle the legal and financial affairs for the deceased individual. For some individuals the estate will be closed after a few months, whereas for others the estate could be open for many years.

Estate Tax A wealth tax that is levied on the fair market value of an individual's gross estate at the time of their death.

Excess Benefit Transaction A transaction in which the economic benefit provided by an exempt organization to a disqualified person exceeds the value of the consideration or services received by the exempt organization.

Excess Depreciation Depreciation claimed in excess of the amount that would have been claimed under the straight-line depreciation method.

Excess Lobbying Expenditures The *greater* of:

- the amount by which the lobbying expenditures for the taxable year exceed the lobbying nontaxable amount for the taxable year, *or*
- the amount by which the grass roots expenditures for the taxable year exceed the grass roots nontaxable amount for the taxable year.

Excess Loss Account A parent corporation's share of its subsidiary's losses cannot reduce the parent's stock basis below zero, even though the entire loss can reduce the consolidated income. The parent must add any loss that cannot reduce the basis to the excess loss account. If the parent sells the subsidiary's stock, or the group is deconsolidated, while an excess loss exists, the parent must recognize the amount in the excess loss account as a capital gain.

Excess Net Passive Investment Income Net passive income in excess of 25% of gross receipts. Excess net PII cannot exceed the S corporation's taxable income for the year computed as if it were a C corporation.

Excessive Compensation Tax An excise tax levied on the compensation of highly paid employees of tax-exempt organizations.

Excise Taxes Taxes levied on the purchase of tangible personal property, like sales taxes, but based on the volume of the product sold rather than on the sales price.

Excluded Gain or Loss A gain or loss that the tax law never includes in taxable income.

Ex-dividend Date The day after the record date.

Executor The official representative of an estate, appointed by the decedent's will or by the court. The executor collects the assets of the decedent, pays the decedent's debts, and distributes the remaining assets to the beneficiaries according to the decedent's will or according to the state law governing inheritances.

Exempt Purpose Expenditures Amounts paid or incurred for the taxable year for expenditures that are related to the organization's tax-exempt purpose, such as for religious, charitable, scientific, literary, or educational purposes, amateur sports, or the prevention of cruelty to children or animals. They also include all amounts paid or incurred to influence legislation even if not for those purposes.

External Consistency A measure of whether a tax is fairly apportioned; exists if the tax is in proportion to the business's activity in the state.

F

Family Attribution An individual is deemed to indirectly own the stock owned by the individual's spouse, children, grandchildren, and parents. An individual is not attributed shares from former spouses.

Family Members (S Corporation) Defined as lineal descendants of a *common ancestor* and the spouses (or former spouses) of the common ancestor and lineal descendants. The family members cannot be more than six generations removed from the common ancestor.

Favorable Book-Tax Differences Book-tax differences that decrease book income, resulting in lower taxable income.

Favored Activity Activity that allows a tax-exempt organization to not be treated as a private foundation, commonly occurring with churches, educational institutions, hospitals, medical research organizations, or governmental units.

Fiduciary Accounting Accounting that determines how the receipts and disbursements of a trust or an estate are allocated to principal (corpus) or income. You can think of fiduciary accounting as determining the economic consequences of the estate or trust for the year. The Uniform Principal and Income Act (UPAIA) provides guidance to fiduciaries for administering both trusts and estates regarding the allocation or apportionment of receipts and payments to principal and income.

Fiduciary Relationship A relationship in which a trustee or administrator has a legal duty to manage assets in a trust or estate on behalf of someone else.

Field Examination An IRS examination conducted at the taxpayer's place of business; it is more complex and extensive than an office examination.

Final Regulations IRS regulations that have the effect of law until revoked.

Fixed, Determinable, Annual, or Periodic Income (FDAP Income) Certain types of U.S.-sourced income received by a foreign person that is subject to a 30% withholding tax requirement. Income is *fixed* when the amount can be pre-determined, *determinable* when there is a basis for determining the amount to be paid in the future, *annual* if distributed on at least a yearly basis, and *periodic* if paid from time to time.

Floor Plan Financing Interest Interest paid or accrued for the tax year on debt used to finance motor vehicles held for sale or lease, and which is secured by that same inventory.

Flow-Through Entities Tax entities where income flows through to the owners, who report the income on their tax returns, and is therefore taxed only once. Flow-through entities include S corporations, partnerships, and limited liability companies.

Foreign Corporation (for State Taxes) A corporation doing business in a state other than the state in which it was incorporated.

Foreign Corporation (Multinational) A corporation that is not formed in one of the states or the District of Columbia.

Foreign Persons Nonresident aliens, foreign corporations, foreign partnerships, and foreign estates and trusts.

Foreign Tax Credit Exists to mitigate the double taxation of income also taxed in a foreign country. The credit is limited to the *lower* of:

1. foreign tax paid, *or*
2. U.S. tax on worldwide income × $\frac{\text{Foreign-sourced taxable income}}{\text{Worldwide taxable income}}$

Foreign Tax Credit Limitation The credit for foreign taxes paid is limited to the foreign tax credit limitation, which is defined as:

$$\text{U.S. tax on worldwide income} \times \frac{\text{Foreign-sourced taxable income}}{\text{Worldwide taxable income}}$$

Franchise Tax A tax levied on the privilege of doing business in a state; based on the value of the capital used in the jurisdiction as measured by common stock, paid-in-capital, and retained earnings.

Fraud A deliberate action by a taxpayer to conceal information, misrepresent information, or deceive tax authorities about a tax deficiency.

Functional Test A test for whether income is classified as business income; under this test, income from the sale of property that is an integral part of the business is considered business income.

Future Interest A gift from which the recipient will not benefit until a future date.

G

General Business Credit A combination of credits designed to subsidize certain activities. While each credit is calculated independently, the combination of credits is subject to an overall limit. Unused credits are carried back one year and then forward 20 years.

General Partners Partners that can participate in management and have unlimited liability, so they are personally liable for partnership debt. All partnerships must have at least one general partner.

General Partnership A partnership in which all of the partners are general partners. General partners have unlimited liability, meaning that their personal assets are at risk to creditors of the partnership.

General Power of Appointment Allows and individual to designate property owned by the creator of the power to the recipient of the power, to the recipient's creditors, or to other individuals. If the recipient of the power dies while retaining the general power, the property subject to the appointment is included in the recipient's gross estate.

Generation-Skipping Tax (GST) A supplemental tax that prevents taxpayers from avoiding the unified transfer taxes by skipping one generation of recipients. The tax is in addition to the gift or estate tax.

Gift A voluntary transfer of property from one person (the donor) to another (the donee) without full valuable consideration.

Gift-Splitting An election that applies only to married individuals If elected, then it is deemed that every gift made by either spouse was made 50% by each spouse. This allows each spouse to use their annual exclusion of $19,000 (2025) for their portion of the gift if the gift is of a present interest.

Gift Tax A wealth tax that is levied on the fair market value of property when it is gifted to another individual.

***Golsen* Rule** Rule providing that the U.S. Tax Court will follow the law of the U.S. circuit courts of appeals to which a case is appealable.

Grantor The creator of a trust, who transfers assets into the trust and determines the terms of the trust.

Grantor Trust A trust controlled by a grantor through retained powers or the possibility the property in the trust will revert to the grantor.

Grass Roots Expenditures Attempts to influence legislation by affecting the opinions of the general public or any segment of it.

Grass Roots Nontaxable Amount Twenty-five percent of the lobbying nontaxable amount.

Gross Estate The assets that must be included in computing the estate tax at the time of someone's death. Property could be included in the gross estate but not in the probate estate. For example, property gifted shortly before death would not be in the probate estate, but the estate tax laws could require the property to be included in the gross estate.

Gross Misvaluation Misvaluation that occurs when property is valued on a tax return at 400% or more of the correct amount.

Gross Receipts (Net Passive Investment Income Tax) Includes receipts from active operations and investment income (including tax-exempt interest). Only the net gain from the disposition of capital assets (other than stock and securities) is included in gross receipts. For stocks and securities all capital gains are included in gross receipts.

Gross-Up The total for taxable gifts in the gift tax formula includes the taxable gifts from all prior years. This is done so that the marginal tax rate for this year's taxable gifts is determined by the cumulative lifetime taxable gifts.

Gross-Up Provision Provision stating that the gift tax paid on a gift is included in the estate for any gifts made within three years of death.

Guaranteed Payment Compensation paid to partners for services rendered or the use of capital that is not tied to the income of the partnership.

H

Holding Period The amount of time that a taxpayer has owned an asset. The holding period always begins the day after the taxpayer acquires the asset and ends on the day the asset is sold.

Hot Assets Assets on the balance sheet that have ordinary income potential; specifically, unrealized receivables and inventory.

Hybrid Entity An entity that is treated as a partnership in the United States but as a corporation under foreign law.

I

Inaccurate Position Occurs when a taxpayer disregards the tax rules without reasonable cause.

Inbound Transactions Activities in the United States conducted by non-U.S. taxpayers.

Income Beneficiaries Beneficiaries that receive distributions of the income earned by trust assets each year based on the terms of the trust. Also known as *current beneficiaries*.

Income in Respect of a Decedent (IRD) Income the decedent had earned before death but had not yet recognized as income because they were a cash-basis taxpayer.

Income Interest Consists of income that is earned each year, such as investment income, that is available to the income beneficiaries.

Income Tax A tax based on income. The definition excludes property taxes, excise taxes, sales taxes, and value-added taxes.

Income Tax Provision The income tax expense (benefit) on the income statement, calculated as follows:

$$\text{Income tax provision/ expense} = \text{Current income tax expense (benefit)} + \text{Deferred income tax expense (benefit)}$$

Income Tax Provision Process The entire process of determining the current and deferred income tax liability or asset, as well as the current and deferred income tax expense or benefit. The process also includes preparation of the financial statement footnote disclosures required by ASC 740.

Income Test (PHC Tax) A test for the personal holding company (PHC) tax that is met if personal holding company income constitutes 60% or more of adjusted ordinary gross income (AOGI).

Inside Basis The total basis of all assets on the partnership's balance sheet.

Intangible Property Property that does not have a physical form and is an abstraction in that it represents an ownership right.

Internal Consistency A measure of whether a tax is fairly apportioned; exists if the overall income tax rate would not exceed 100% if every state imposed the same tax.

Internal Revenue Code (IRC) Codifies all the tax laws passed by Congress in a logical order.

Interpretive Regulations Regulations written under the general mandate given to the Treasury Department to develop regulations to interpret the laws enacted by Congress.

Inventory (Partnerships) For purposes of partnership taxation, inventory includes all assets other than cash, capital assets, and Section 1231 assets.

J

Joint Tenants with Right of Survivorship Owners that have equal ownership rights in property; at death, the decedent owner's interest passes to the other owner(s).

L

Least Aggregate Deferral Method Method used to determine the partnership's required tax year if neither the majority interest test nor principal partner test is met.

Legislative Regulations Regulations that Congress has authorized the Treasury Department to develop dealing with a specific issue.

Life Interest An interest in property that is retained for the life of the transferor.

Limited Liability Company (LLC) A hybrid form of business that offers both limited liability and certain tax advantages. Articles of organization must be filed with the state in which the LLC is legally organized. Owners of an LLC are known as members, and all members have limited liability.

Limited Liability Partnership (LLP) A type of partnership that differs from a general partnership in that a partner is not liable for damages resulting from the negligence, malpractice, or fraud committed by other partners. Each partner is personally liable for other debts of the partnership, as well as debts arising from their own negligence, malpractice, or fraud.

Limited Partners Partners with limited liability and who can lose only what they have invested and promised to invest in the partnership. Limited partners cannot participate in the management of the partnership.

Limited Partnership A partnership that must have at least one general partner and at least one limited partner.

Liquidating Distribution A distribution of an owner's investment in a business after which the recipient is no longer an owner. The entity will remain in existence as long as it has other owners. If all owners receive liquidating distributions, then the entity is dissolved.

Liquidating Distribution (Partnerships) A distribution for which the partnership is dissolving, and the partner will no longer hold a partnership interest.

Lobbying Expenditures Expenditures for the purpose of influencing legislation by communicating with any member or employee of a legislative body, or with any government official or employee who may participate in the formulation of the legislation.

Lobbying Nontaxable Amount The *lower* of:

- $1 million, *or*
- the amount determined from the table for computing lobbying non-taxable activities (Illustration 15.5).

Long-Term Holding Period A holding period where a taxpayer has owned an asset for more than one year.

Lookback Rule A rule providing that the net Section 1231 gains must be offset by net Section 1231 losses from the five preceding tax years that have not already been recaptured. To the extent of these losses, the net Section 1231 gain is treated as ordinary income.

Look-Through Rules If a partnership has collectibles on the balance sheet, then some of the gain recognized by a partner who sells their partnership interest could be collectible gain taxed at maximum rate of 28%. If a partner has unrecaptured Section 1250 gain on the balance sheet, then some of the gain recognized by a partner who sells their partnership interest could be taxed at a maximum rate of 25% up to the partner's share of this gain.

Lower of Cost or Market An inventory valuation method for taxpayers not using LIFO which requires inventory to be reported at the lower of cost or market, defined as replacement cost or reproduction cost.

M

Majority Interest Test A test that determines a partnership's required year-end, if partners having the same tax year own more than 50% of partnership capital and profits.

Marginal Tax Rate The tax rate applied to the next additional dollar of income earned.

Matching Principle For financial reporting, a principle requiring that a business record expenses incurred in the same period it recognizes the related revenues as earned.

Material Participation The level of activity that must be achieved by a business owner for the business activity to not be classified as passive. The taxpayer must satisfy one of seven tests to be considered to materially participate in an activity.

Merger Occurs in a reorganization when the acquired corporation (target) dissolves into another corporation (the acquiring corporation).

Modified Taxable Income (MTI) Taxable income *before* the QBI deduction.

More Likely Than Not Standard A standard of evaluating a taxpayer's position; indicates that the taxpayer has a greater than 50% chance of succeeding if the taxpayer's position is ruled on in court.

N

Natural Business Year A year in which 25% or more of the gross receipts occur in the last two months of the year being tested for three consecutive years. Once this criterion is met, a partnership can switch to the natural business year for the following year.

Natural Resources A source of wealth that occurs in a natural state and has value, such as timber, mineral deposits, and water.

Negligence An intentional disregard of rules and regulations without intent to defraud. Congress imposes a penalty of 20% of the tax due to the inaccuracy if the taxpayer's position results from negligence.

Net Operating Loss (NOL) Occur when a corporation has a taxable loss for the year. Generally, NOLs can only be carried forward to reduce income in future tax years.

Net Passive Investment Income Passive investment income reduced by expenses incurred to produce the PII.

Net Passive Investment Income Tax For any year that passive investment income exceeds 25% of gross receipts, the excess net passive investment income is taxed at a 21% rate to the S corporation. This provision applies only if the S corporation was previously a C corporation and has earnings and profits from C corporation years on its balance sheet.

Net Unrealized Built-in Gain The excess of all BIGs over BILs on the effective date of the S corporation election.

Nexus A measure of the degree of the relationship that must exist between a state and a foreign corporation for the state to have the right to impose a tax.

Nonacquiescence Indicates that the IRS will not follow a particular judicial decision and can be expected to litigate in situations involving similar facts and issues.

Nonapportionable Income Nonbusiness income for state nexus purposes.

Nonbusiness Income Income that is not business income.

Nonqualified Preferred Stock Exists if the holder of such stock has the right to require the issuer or a related person to redeem or purchase the stock, or if the dividend rate on such stock varies in whole or in part with reference to interest rates, commodity prices, or other similar indices. Preferred stock is not treated as nonqualified preferred stock if the corporation has to wait at least 20 years from the date the stock was issued to redeem it.

Nonrecourse Debt Debt for which no partner, or a person related to a partner, has the potential for an economic risk of loss.

Nonresident Aliens Individuals who are not citizens or residents of the United States. They cannot be shareholders of an S corporation because it would be difficult for the government to collect taxes from them.

Nonseparately Stated Items Tax items for a partnership or S corporation that are not separately stated. These items are reported on page 1 of either Form 1065 or Form 1120-S.

Non-Tax Costs All expenses other than tax costs, as well as non-financial factors such as risk, location, brand reputation, and sustainability concerns.

Not Essentially Equivalent to a Dividend (NEED) The Supreme Court has ruled that the NEED standard can be satisfied only if there is a *meaningful reduction* in the redeemed shareholder's proportionate interest in the distributing corporation. A meaningful reduction occurs if there is an appropriate reduction in the shareholder's voting interest and right to share in profits.

Not-for-Profit Organizations Organizations that do not have a profit motive but are created for reasons such as pursuing educational or religious goals, improving healthcare, or meeting the needs of certain groups of people. They may or may not be exempt from paying income taxes.

O

Objective Test (Partial Liquidation) Provides that the corporation must have at least two qualifying trades or businesses before the partial liquidation, and at least one qualifying trade or business after the partial liquidation.

Offer in Compromise A program that allows a taxpayer to settle a tax liability for less than the actual amount owed.

Office Examination An IRS examination conducted at the local IRS district office.

On All Fours A research term describing the situation in which the facts for an item of tax authority are identical or extremely similar to your client's facts that you are researching.

Open Year A year in which the statute of limitations has not expired for the year.

Operating Distribution A distribution of income by a business after which the recipient continues to be an owner.

Ordinary Assets Assets that produce ordinary income and ordinary loss when disposed of or sold.

Ordinary Business Income or Loss The net of the nonseparately stated items, as reported on page 1 of Form 1065.

Ordinary Dividends Distributions from a corporation's earnings and profits that are taxed at ordinary income rates.

Ordinary Income Income taxed at the taxpayer's marginal tax rate, which currently ranges from 10% to 37%.

Ordinary Losses Losses that can reduce all types of income without limitation.

Organizational Expenses Expenditures incurred in connection with the organization of a corporation. Typical organizational expenses are legal services, accounting services, organizational meetings of directors and shareholders that are incident to organization, and fees paid to incorporate.

Other Adjustments Account (OAA) For an S corporation, an account consisting of tax-exempt income, expenses relating to production of tax-exempt income, and federal taxes relating to a C corporation year.

Outbound Transactions Foreign activities by a U.S. taxpayer, meaning that a U.S. taxpayer is conducting business outside of the United States.

Outside Basis A partner's basis in their partnership interest. Outside basis represents a partner's investment in the partnership for tax purposes, and is a culmination of their contributions, distributions, and their distributive share of partnership income and losses.

Ownership Test (PHC Tax) For the purposes of the personal holding company tax, a corporation meets the test if more than 50% of the value of the stock is owned directly or indirectly by five or fewer individuals at any time during the last half of the year.

Owner-to-Entity Attribution A business entity may be deemed to own a portion of the stock held by one of its owners.

P

Parent-Subsidiary (P-S) Controlled Group Exists if both the 80% test and the common parent test are both met.

Partial Liquidation Occurs when a corporation that has more than one distinct line of business terminates one of those lines. The corporation remains in existence and continues to operate the remaining lines of business. If the necessary requirements are met for this to be a qualified redemption, then noncorporate shareholders are treated as if they sold their stock and have capital gain or loss.

Partnership An association of two or more taxpayers to operate a business that has an objective to make a profit that is not taxed as a corporation. Additionally, there must be an intent to share profits among the partners. Just the co-ownership of property does not necessarily create a partnership, nor does the sharing of only expenses.

Passive Income Income earned by a profit-seeking activity in which the taxpayer does not materially participate in its management. Losses from passive activities can offset only passive income.

Passive Investment Income (PII) (Net Passive Investment Income Tax) Includes interest (including tax-exempt interest), dividends (except dividends from a subsidiary to the extent the subsidiary is conducting an active trade or business), royalties, rents (unless substantial extra services are provided to the tenants), and annuities.

Passive Loss Hurdle Losses from passive activities are limited to the amount of passive income a taxpayer has in a given tax year.

Payment Date The date that a corporation pays a dividend.

Pecuniary Gift A gift of a specific value. In most states, the recipient of a pecuniary gift is entitled to a statutory amount of interest based on the amount of the gift.

***Per Se* Corporation** A business entity formed under statutes that refer to the entities as incorporated. These entities are taxed as either S corporations or C corporations and include the following:

- Entities incorporated under state law
- Insurance companies
- State-chartered banks (if deposits are insured by FDIC)
- Publicly traded partnerships
- Specified foreign entities

- Certain other entities (such as real estate investment trusts [REITs], tax-exempt organizations, etc.)

***Per Se* Corporations (Foreign Businesses)** Foreign entities for which at least some of the owners have limited liability.

Permanent Differences Items that create a permanent difference between book income and taxable income. These differences do not net over time.

Permanent Establishment (PE) Used to define *trade or business* in determining effectively connected income for a foreign person whose country has a treaty with the United States. Generally exists if:

- The foreign person has a fixed place of business in the United States, unless that place is not central to the ongoing business operations, *or*
- The foreign party has dependent agents in the United States who can exercise sales contracts for the foreign party.

Personal Holding Company Income Includes taxable:

- dividends (before the dividends received deduction),
- interest,
- rental income, unless more than 50% of the corporation's gross income is from rents,
- amounts a corporation receives for providing personal services if the services are performed by a shareholder owning more than 25% of the stock, *and*
- certain royalties, including adjusted income from mineral, oil, and gas interests, and copyright royalties.

Personal Holding Company (PHC) tax A 20% tax imposed only on corporations qualifying as personal holding companies. Banks, insurance, and finance companies are exempt from the tax because their business purpose is to manage investments. The tax base for the PHC tax is taxable income adjusted to reflect retained economic income. Like the accumulated earnings tax, the PHC tax can be avoided by paying dividends.

Personal Service Corporation A corporation whose principal activity is the performance of personal services performed by employees who own 95% or more of the corporation's stock.

Personalty Any asset that is not realty.

Physical Presence Exists if a business has property, employees, or perhaps independent contractors in the state.

Point of Delivery The location at which property or a product is delivered or service rendered.

Portability In the context of estate taxes, a principle that allows any unused credit from a spouse dying after 2010 to be used in the future by the surviving spouse. An election to use the remaining credit must be made by filing Form 706 even if the estate of the decedent would otherwise not require a return to be filed.

Portfolio Income Investment income such as interest, dividends, annuities, and royalties that one does not derive from a trade or business, and capital gains from selling property that generates investment income.

Post-Termination Transition Period (PTTP) The one-year period following the termination of an S corporation. More specifically, the PTTP begins on the day the S election is terminated and ends as of the *later* of 1) one year later, 2) the date of the final S corporation return (including extensions), *or* 3) 120 days after it is determined that the S election was terminated.

Power of Attorney The legal right of one person to represent another person for specified purposes, which usually include financial and/or medical issues.

Practice before the IRS Practice that includes all matters related to a presentation to the IRS or any of its officers or employees about a taxpayer's rights, privileges, or liabilities under IRS laws or regulations.

Precedent A decision in a previous legal case that is binding on a court when it is hearing subsequent cases that have similar facts and issues.

Precontribution Gain or Loss *See* Built-In Gain or Loss.

Present Interest A gift recipient's right to receive income or enjoy property currently.

Pre-Tax Book Income Financial statement income before income tax expense.

Primary Authority Authority held by one of the three branches of the federal government and consisting of the original sources of the tax law.

Principal Partner A partner that owns at least a 5% interest in either partnership capital or profits.

Principal Partner Test Requires that a partnership must use the same year-end that all its principal partners have.

Private Foundations §501(c)(3) organizations that are independent legal entities set up solely for charitable purposes whose funding comes primarily from an individual, a family, or a corporation. They do *not* include:

- churches,
- educational organizations,
- hospitals or medical research organizations operated in conjunction with hospitals,
- endowment funds operated for the benefit of certain state and municipal colleges and universities,
- governmental units, *or*
- publicly supported organizations.

Private Letter Rulings (PLR) IRS rulings issued only when requested by a taxpayer for a proposed transaction. If the IRS agrees with the taxpayer's proposed result, the ruling applies only for the taxpayer who requested it. Other taxpayers can use PLRs to establish substantial authority, so that the IRS cannot penalize them for taking the same position.

Private Universities Investment Income Tax A 1.4% excise tax that certain private universities and colleges must pay on their net investment income.

Privileged Information Communications between a tax practitioner and a taxpayer to the extent that the communication would be privileged if it were between an attorney and a taxpayer. This privilege for a tax professional is limited to noncriminal matters and does not apply to communications regarding tax shelters.

Probate The legal process of distributing a decedent's assets according to the decedent's will, or as determined by state law if there is no will. Probate also includes the payment of any debts that the decedent owes at the time of death.

Probate Estate A measure of estate value that includes assets held solely by the decedent and that does not include assets that pass to others outside of the will, such as:

- Life insurance and annuities,
- Retirement plans such as IRAs, Section 401(k) plans, and qualified retirement plans, and
- Property owned with right of survivorship, meaning that the property passes at death to the other owner(s).

Procedural Regulations IRS regulations that apply to procedural issues, such as the information that must be submitted with a tax return and the process for making tax elections.

Prohibited Transactions Transactions that are not consistent with the tax-exempt purpose of an organization and may make it more difficult for the organization to meet its mission.

Property Taxes *Ad valorem* taxes based on the value of realty and certain personalty.

Proportionate (Distribution) The partner who receives the distribution has the same interest in the ordinary income potential in the hot assets before and after the distribution.

Proposed Regulations IRS regulations that do not have the effect of law but do provide an indication of the IRS's view on a tax issue.

Q

Qualified Business Income (QBI) Deduction A deduction allowed for 20% of the taxpayer's income from flow-through entities (partnerships, limited liability companies, and S corporations) and sole proprietorships.

Qualified Dividends Distributions from a corporation's earnings and profits that are taxed at long-term capital gain rates.

Qualified Nonrecourse Debt Debt used for real estate activities and secured by the real property used in the activity. Qualified nonrecourse debt is included in a taxpayer's at-risk amount.

Qualified Property for QBI Tangible property subject to depreciation that the taxpayer used in the production of qualified business income.

Qualified Property Property meeting the specific requirements for a particular deferral transaction.

Qualified Subchapter S Subsidiary (QSSS) A corporation that meets all eligibility requirements for an S corporation and is owned 100% by a parent S corporation.

Qualified Terminable Interest Property (QTIP) A type of terminable interest that qualifies for the marital deduction. For a terminable interest to be QTIP, some or all of the deceased spouse's property is transferred after death into a trust and certain conditions must be met. The executor agrees in the QTIP election that the property must be included in the surviving spouse's estate at its FMV on the date of death of the surviving spouse.

Qualifying Trade or Business (Partial Liquidation) A trade or business that the corporation has operated for at least five years. If the corporation acquired the business during the five-year period in a tax-free transaction, the business is still a qualifying business as long it had been active during the entire five-year period.

R

Realized Gain or Loss The amount realized from a sale or disposition reduced by the property's adjusted basis.

Realty Land and any structure permanently attached to the land.

Reasonable Basis A standard of evaluating a taxpayer's position; exists when at least one primary authority supports the taxpayer's position and has not been overruled.

Reasonable Cause A circumstance outside the control of the taxpayer and not due to neglect, such as irregularities in mail delivery, death or serious illness, unavoidable absence, or disaster.

Reasonable Needs of the Business While determining the reasonable needs of the business is a subjective determination that requires judgment, in the past, reasonable business needs have existed for amounts to:

- Finance business expansion (actual or planned)
- Provide working capital
- Retire liabilities
- Set aside funds required by creditors
- Build up appropriate working capital

For the purposes of the accumulated earnings credit, a reasonable business need must be approved by the corporation's board of directors. Thus, it is not sufficient just that the corporation has a need; the corporation must have specific plans to meet that need.

Reattribution Occurs when stock that is attributed from one taxpayer to a second taxpayer is then reattributed to a third taxpayer. However, stock constructively owned by a person under the family attribution rules cannot be reattributed to another individual. Additionally, stock that has been attributed to a corporation, partnership, estate or trust cannot be reattributed to another taxpayer.

Recapture Agreement (Estate Tax) An agreement requiring that if the qualified heir to realty that falls under the special use valuation ceases using the realty for a qualified purpose in the 10 years after the death of the decedent, then the tax saved from the special use valuation must be paid. See *Special Use Valuation*.

Recognized Gain or Loss A gain or loss that the taxpayer includes in the computation of taxable income.

Record Date The date that a corporation determines who owns the stock for purposes of paying the dividend later.

Recourse Debt (Partnership) Debt for which at least one of the partners, or a person related to a partner, has the potential for an economic risk of loss with respect to the debt.

Rehabilitation Credit A credit allowed for the rehabilitation of certified historic buildings.

Related Party For purposes of the loss disallowance rule, any of the following members of a family: spouse, children, grandchildren/other descendants, parents, grandparents/other ancestors, and brothers and sisters. The definition of related party includes relationships between individuals and business entities, and between certain business entities.

Religious Organization In the context of defining a tax-exempt charitable organization, an organization that meets the following requirements:

- It is organized and operated exclusively for a religious purpose.
- It is not involved in political activities.
- It does not use its revenue to benefit private individuals or shareholders.
- It does not engage in activities that are illegal or violations of public policy.

Religious organizations include temples, churches, mosques, and other places of worship; church conventions; auxiliaries of churches; church associations; and other organizations associated with churches.

Remainder Beneficiaries Beneficiaries that receive distributions of the assets in a trust when the trust terminates.

Remainder Interest Consists of the assets in a trust that will pass to the remainder beneficiaries when the trust is terminated based on the conditions set up by the grantor.

Reorganizations Occurs when one or more corporations rearrange their legal ownership structure to merge two or more corporations into one entity (acquisitive reorganizations), or to divide a corporation into two or more entities (divisive reorganizations).

Required Tax Year The year-end that a partnership must use unless it meets one of a few limited exceptions.

Research and Development Expenses Costs that are incident to the development or improvement of a product in the experimental or laboratory sense. Expenditures qualify as research and development costs in the experimental or laboratory sense if they are for activities intended to discover information that eliminates uncertainty as to the development or improvement of a product.

Research Credit To encourage businesses to invest in research and development, incremental research expenditures are eligible for a 20% credit. Research expenditures qualify for the credit if companies are developing new or improved business components, including products, processes, computer software, formulas or inventions, that result in new or improved functionality or quality.

Resident Alien Someone who is not a citizen of the United States and meets the substantial presence test.

Restatement of the Law Third, Trusts A publication created by the American Law Institute that summarizes the court decisions related to trusts.

Retained Interest A property interest wherein an individual has transferred property to another person but has retained some aspect of ownership in the property or the right to use the property. Because the individual has retained this interest, at death, the property may be included in the individual's gross the individual has retained this interest, at death, the property may be included in the individual's gross estate even though legally the property is titled in another person's name.

Retirement Distribution (Partnerships) Occurs when the interest of only one partner is liquidated, and the partnership continues in existence.

Revenue Agent Report (RAR) Report that accompanies and explains the IRS's findings.

Revenue Procedures IRS statements of procedures that affect the rights or duties of taxpayers or other members of the public.

Revenue Rulings IRS interpretations limited to a specific set of facts; a ruling does not have as much weight as an IRS regulation.

Reverse Hybrid Entity A foreign entity that is treated as a corporation for U.S. tax purposes but as a partnership under foreign law.

Revocable Trust A trust that the grantor can revoke in the future.

Right of Offset The disallowed loss from a related-party sale, which taxpayers can use to reduce a gain upon the ultimate sale of the property to an unrelated taxpayer. The right of offset cannot create a loss, nor can it make a loss greater.

Right of Survivorship Property passes at death to the other owner(s).

S

Sale or Disposition Includes sales, exchanges, trade-ins, casualties, condemnations, thefts, and retirements of an asset. When one of these events occurs, the taxpayer must compute the realized gain or loss.

Sales Taxes Taxes that are levied by both state and local governments on the value of tangible personal property and some services sold; exemptions usually include items bought for resale and/or used in manufacturing.

Secondary Authority Commentary on tax law such as treatises, journals, and commentaries provided by editorial services.

Section 162 Expenses Deductible business expenses if the expenses:

- are incurred while operating a trade or business, *and*
- are ordinary, necessary, and reasonable

Section 291 Depreciation Recapture Applies only to corporations. Additional depreciation recapture computed by assuming the property is actually Section 1245 property, as follows:

Section 1245 recapture IF the property had been Section 1245 property
Less: Actual Section 1250 recapture
Excess Amount
× 20%
Section 291 recapture

Section 351 Formation Shareholders must satisfy the following three requirements for gains and losses to be deferred on a corporate formation:

- Contribute property to the corporation (rather than services)
- Receive only stock in return from the corporation
- The *control club* must own at least 80% of the voting power and number of shares of the corporation immediately after the exchange

If these conditions are met, the transaction can be labeled as a Section 351 formation.

Section 704(c) Gain or Loss *See* Built-In Gain or Loss.

Section 734(b) Adjustment If a Section 754 election is in effect, the adjustment to the inside basis of assets due to the distribution of an asset.

Section 743(b) Adjustment If a Section 754 election is in effect, the adjustment to the inside basis of assets due to the sale of a partnership interest.

Section 754 Election If made, the partnership may be required to adjust the basis for its assets when a partnership interest is sold or when a partner receives a distribution of property. If the Section 754 election is not in effect, then the adjustments are not made. However, that can result in inequities to certain partners. Election is made by the partnership. Once made, the election is irrevocable without the permission of the IRS

Section 1231 Assets Depreciable assets and land used in a trade or business that have been owned for more than one year.

Section 1245 Assets Assets that include any tangible, depreciable, or amortizable property, other than land or buildings, that is used in a trade or business and that has been owned for more than one year.

Section 1250 Assets Depreciable buildings used in a trade or business and owned for more than one year.

Separately Stated Items Tax items for a partnership or an S corporation that could potentially impact a shareholder's or partner's tax liability differently. Separately stated items are reported on Schedule K. Each owner's share is reported on Schedule K-1.

Shareholder Test (Brother-Sister Controlled Group) Met if two or more corporations are owned by five or fewer persons (individuals, estates, or trusts) who meet the 80% test and 50% test.

Short Tax Year A tax year consisting of less than 12 months.

Short-Term Holding Period A holding period where a taxpayer has owned an asset for one year or less.

Significant Participation Activity Any trade or business activity in which the taxpayer participated for more than 100 hours during the year.

Simple Trust A trust that:

- must distribute all income currently,
- made no distributions of corpus in the current year, *and*
- made no charitable contributions in the current year.

Single-Member Limited Liability Company (SMLLC) An LLC with only one owner that generally reports all income and expenses on Schedule C if the owner is an individual.

Small Business Corporation A corporation whose average gross receipts over the last three tax years does not exceed $31 million (2025).

Small Employer Health Insurance Credit A credit equal to 50% of an eligible small employer's nonelective contributions for health insurance for its employees.

Soliciting (State and Local Tax Nexus) Actions that explicitly or implicitly invite an order, as well as other actions that are ancillary to an order.

Special Power of Appointment Does not allow the recipient of the power to designate property to the recipient of the power or the recipient's creditors. The property can be appointed only to other individuals. Therefore, if the taxpayer dies while retaining the special power, the property subject to the appointment is not included in the gross estate.

Special Use Valuation A special rule that permits realty to be valued for estate tax purposes based on its current use rather than its true FMV, which would be based on its best and higher use. The realty must be used in an active farming operation or in an active business by the decedent or a family member on the date of death.

Specified Service Trade or Business Trade or business engaged in the services of health, law, accounting, actuarial sciences, performing arts, consulting, athletics, financial services, brokerage services, or any business where the principal asset is the reputation of an employee or owner. These businesses are often not eligible for the QBI deduction.

Spin-Off A Type D reorganization in which the parent distributes the subsidiary shares to its shareholders.

Split-Off A Type D reorganization in which the parent uses the subsidiary to redeem shares of the parent.

Split-Up A Type D reorganization in which the parent is liquidated into two new corporations and the parent no longer exists.

Start-Up Costs Expenses that would be deductible as ordinary and necessary business expenses if a business had already begun, including investigation expenses, advertising, training employees, and rent paid before the business officially begins.

Stated Goodwill Goodwill that is provided for in the partnership agreement.

Statements on Standards for Tax Services (SSTS) Guidelines issued by the AICPA providing a summary of the professional responsibilities to which CPAs must adhere when performing tax services.

Statute of Limitations The period that a taxpayer has to file an amended return or that the IRS has to assess a tax deficiency.

Statutory Merger A merger or consolidation that complies with the laws of the applicable state.

Statutory Notice of Deficiency (90-Day Letter) Letter notifying a taxpayer, at the end of the audit/appeals process, that the IRS has determined that the taxpayer has a tax deficiency. The taxpayer has 90 days from the date of the letter to file a petition with the U.S. Tax Court to hear the matter.

Step Transaction A judicial doctrine that permits multiple steps to be collapsed into a single step when the steps are so interdependent on one another that one would not have occurred without the other(s). Collapsing these steps may lead to a tax result other than that desired by the taxpayer.

Stock Dividend A payment to shareholders made in the form of shares of stock rather than cash or property.

Stock Redemption Occurs when a corporation purchases stock from a shareholder. If the purchase qualifies as a redemption for tax purposes, the transaction is treated as a property transaction and the shareholder will have a capital gain or loss.

Straight Debt S corporation debt that must be evidenced by a written promise where the interest rate and interest payment dates are not contingent on profits. The debt cannot be convertible into stock. Straight debt will never be reclassified as equity by the IRS.

Subjective Test (Partial Liquidation) Provides that a transaction is a partial liquidation if it is not essentially equivalent to a dividend and there is a contraction of the corporate business.

Substantial Authority A standard of evaluating a taxpayer's position; describes the likelihood that a taxpayer's position would be supported if the matter were taken to court. While the law does not identify a specific percentage of success that represents substantial authority, it is well accepted that the likelihood does not need to exceed 40%.

Substantial Built-In Loss (Section 754) Exists if the partnership's adjusted basis in its property exceeds its fair market value by more than $250,000. Similarly, an adjustment is required if there would be a substantial basis reduction of more than $250,000 due to the distribution of partnership assets.

Substantial Economic Effect There must be economic consequences for the allocations of tax items to be respected for tax purposes.

Substantial Misvaluation Misvaluation that occurs if property is valued on a tax return at 150% or more of the correct amount.

Substantial Presence Test Residence requirement met if a foreign person is in the United States for 183 days or more in a calendar year.

Substantial Understatement Tax understatement that results when the additional tax due exceeds the *greater* of $5,000 *or* 10% of the total tax on the return.

Substantially All For a Type C reorganization, *substantially all* the assets is defined by the IRS as 90% of net asset value and 70% of gross asset value.

Substantially Appreciated Inventory Inventory is substantially appreciated if its FMV exceeds its adjusted basis by more than 20%. Inventory must be substantially appreciated to be a hot asset for purposes of distributions.

Substantially Disproportionate A stock sale is substantially disproportionate if:

- the shareholder owns less than 50% of the voting power of the stock after the sale, *and*
- the shareholder's ownership of the corporation's voting stock after the sale is less than 80% of their voting stock ownership before the sale.

Both of these conditions must be satisfied for the substantially disproportionate test to be met.

Substantially Rehabilitated A building has been substantially rehabilitated if qualified rehabilitation expenditures during a 24-month period exceed the *greater* of:

- The adjusted basis of the property before the rehabilitation expenditures, *or*
- $5,000.

Substituted Basis Basis determined by substituting the basis of the transferred asset for the basis of the asset received in a tax-deferred transaction.

Syndication Costs Expenses related to issuing and selling stock. Typical syndication costs include brokerage fees, stock registration fees, underwriter fees, and printing costs of the prospectus and other selling or promotional material.

T

Tangible Property Property that has physical qualities and can be touched and moved.

Taxable Temporary Book-Tax Difference Book-tax difference that causes future taxable income to be greater than book income due to reversal of a favorable temporary book-tax difference in the current year.

Tax Attributes (Corporation) The tax characteristics of the corporation. The most common attributes are as follows:

- adjusted basis of assets
- earnings and profits of the corporation
- carryforwards, including net operating losses, capital losses, and excess charitable contributions
- accounting methods, including depreciation methods, *and*
- tax credit carryforward.

Tax Avoidance Structuring a transaction or arranging financial affairs in a legal manner to maximize after-tax income.

Tax Basis A taxpayer's investment in property that determines the amount of cost recovery and gain or loss upon disposition under tax accounting principles.

Tax Costs Any type of tax paid to a local, state, federal, or foreign government.

Tax Evasion Reducing tax liability illegally.

Tax-Exempt Organizations Organizations recognized by the IRS as being exempt from paying income taxes. They include charities, labor organizations, social clubs, pension and profit-sharing trusts, and private foundations and may take the form of corporations, trusts, or limited liability companies. The tax law defines 20 different types of tax-exempt organizations under IRC §501(c). Also known as *exempt organizations*.

Tax Position The way a set of facts is treated for tax purposes.

Tax Practitioner An individual who is authorized to practice before the IRS. Generally, this right is limited to CPAs, attorneys, and enrolled agents.

Tax Preparer Anyone who prepares a tax return for compensation. All tax preparers are required to have a preparer tax identification number (PTIN).

Tax Shelter A plan, arrangement, or entity where a significant purpose is the avoidance or evasion of federal income tax.

Temporary Differences Differences created when items of income and deduction are recognized in book income in one year but are recognized in taxable income for a different year.

Temporary Regulations IRS regulations that have the effect of law, but only for three years.

Tenancy by the Entirety Tenancy in which property is jointly owned by a married couple.

Tenancy in Common A type of co-ownership in which the owners do not have to be equal owners and each owner can transfer their ownership interest to others, meaning there is no right of survivorship. Property does not pass to the other owner at death. Rather, the percentage of the property owned by the decedent passes into the probate estate and the decedent's will determines who receives the property.

Terminable Interest An interest in property that terminates upon the occurrence of a future event, such as the death of the recipient.

Terms The expressions in a trust of the grantor's wishes for how the trust will be managed and the income and assets distributed.

Territorial Taxation Taxation that does not include foreign earned income in the domestic country's income tax base.

Testamentary Trust A trust created when an individual dies based on the decedent's will.

Time Value of Money The concept that funds available today are worth more than the identical sum in the future due to their earnings potential if invested.

Transactional Test A test for whether income is classified as business income; under this test, income generated by a business's regular operations is business income.

Treaty A formal written agreement between two countries that specifies legal and economic rights between the countries.

Trust A legal entity created by the transfer of property from a grantor. The purpose of the trust is to hold and administer property for *beneficiaries* according to the terms of the trust instrument. The trust exists for a period determined by the trust instrument and state law.

Trustee One who has the fiduciary responsibility to manage the assets in a trust according to the terms of the trust. The trustee must protect the interests of the beneficiaries and act in a prudent manner to protect those interests.

Type A Reorganization An acquisitive reorganization that is a stock-for-asset reorganization, meaning that an acquiring corporation exchanges its stock for the target corporation's assets. It must qualify as a statutory merger under state law.

Type B Reorganization An acquisitive reorganization that is a stock-for-stock reorganization, meaning that an acquiring corporation exchanges its voting stock for the target corporation's stock.

Type C Reorganization An acquisitive reorganization that is a stock-for-asset reorganization, meaning that an acquiring corporation exchanges its voting stock for the target corporation's assets.

Type D Reorganization A divisive reorganization meaning that a parent corporation divides into two corporations by transferring assets to a subsidiary corporation in exchange for shares of the subsidiary in a spin-off, split-off, or split-up.

Type E Reorganization Involves only one corporation that is adjusting its capital structure.

Type F Reorganization A mere change in identity, form, or place of organization of one corporation.

Type G Reorganization Used as a part of a reorganization necessitated by a bankruptcy filing.

U

Uncertain Tax Position (UTP) A tax position that is highly subject to interpretation of tax law.

Undistributed Income (Tax-Exempt Organizations) An amount equal to the required distributions less the actual distributions. The undistributed income can be reduced by salaries and administrative expenses.

Undistributed Income Tax A tax levied if the private foundation does not distribute at least 5% of the fair market value of its assets each year by the end of the following tax year. The tax is 30% of the undistributed income.

Unfavorable Book-Tax Differences Book-tax differences that increase book income, resulting in higher taxable income.

Unified Transfer Tax A tax that applies to the transfer of an individual's wealth to another during the individual's life or at the time of the individual's death. The gift tax is paid by the donor, and the estate tax is paid from the assets of the decedent.

Uniform Capitalization Rules (UNICAP) The rules for valuing inventory including direct and indirect costs for property produced and property bought for resale. Manufacturers and certain retailers and wholesalers must use the uniform capitalization method to capitalize all the direct and indirect costs allocable to property they produce and for property bought for resale. These costs are then allocated to ending inventory and property sold during the year, which usually results in an increase in the basis of the inventory for tax purposes.

Uniform Principal and Income Act (UPAIA) Provides guidance to fiduciaries for administering trusts and estates in the allocation or apportionment of receipts and payments to principal and income, known as fiduciary accounting. The UPAIA has been adopted by 44 states and the District of Columbia.

Uniform Trust Code (UTC) Created in 2000 by the Uniform Law Commission with the goal of making trust laws the same or similar across states. Approximately two-thirds of states have adopted a version of the UTC.

Unitary Group A single economic enterprise that is made up either of separate parts of a single business entity or of a commonly controlled group of business entities that are sufficiently interdependent, integrated, and interrelated through their activities so as to provide a synergy and mutual benefit that produces a sharing or exchange of value among them and a significant flow of value to the separate parts.

Unrealized Receivable Account receivable of a cash-basis taxpayer.

Unreasonable Position A tax position that does not have substantial authority.

Unrecaptured Section 1250 Gain Capital gain taxed at a maximum rate of 25% to the extent of accumulated straight-line depreciation claimed on the real estate.

Unrelated Business Income (UBI) Income from substantial commercial activities that are not related to the exempt purpose of the organization.

Unrelated Business Taxable Income (UBTI) For tax-exempt organizations that have unrelated business income, the total revenue generated from unrelated business activities less related expenses.

Unrelated Debt-Financed Income Adjustment Unrelated debt-financed income net of unrelated debt-financed deductions; a positive adjustment made to net unrelated business income.

Unstated Goodwill Goodwill that is not provided for in the partnership agreement.

U.S. Citizen An individual born in the United States or a naturalized U.S. citizen.

U.S. Green Card Holder A permanent resident who has been granted authorization to live and work in the United States on a permanent basis.

U.S. Tax Persons U.S. residents that are subject to the U.S. income tax system.

Use Taxes State taxes that are levied on the use of tangible personal property that was not purchased in the state. States impose use taxes to prevent losing revenue from residents who travel to another state with lower sales tax rates to purchase property.

V

Valuation Allowance A contra-asset account that offsets a deferred income tax asset for the amount not expected to be realized in the future.

W

Work Opportunity Tax Credit (WOTC) A credit calculated on the amount of wages paid per eligible employee from certain targeted groups during the first year of employment. The credit is 40% of qualified wages with maximum wages of $6,000, so the maximum credit is $2,400.

Worldwide Income Foreign-earned income taxed by the United States.

Worldwide Taxation Taxation of income earned anywhere in the world.

Subject Index

U